Impact of Globalization on Healthcare

Impact of Globalization on Healthcare

Editors

Joachim G. Voss
Sandul Yasobant

MDPI

Basel • Beijing • Wuhan • Barcelona • Belgrade • Novi Sad • Cluj • Manchester

Editors
Joachim G. Voss
Frances Payne Bolton School of Nursing
Case Western Reserve University
Cleveland, USA

Sandul Yasobant
Indian Institute of Public Health Gandhinagar
Gujarat, India

Editorial Office
MDPI
St. Alban-Anlage 66
4052 Basel, Switzerland

This is a reprint of articles from the Topic published online in the open access journals *Healthcare* (ISSN 2227-9032), *International Journal of Environmental Research and Public Health* (ISSN 1660-4601), and *Medicina* (ISSN 1648-9144) (available at: https://www.mdpi.com/topics/healthcare).

For citation purposes, cite each article independently as indicated on the article page online and as indicated below:

Lastname, A.A.; Lastname, B.B. Article Title. *Journal Name* **Year**, *Volume Number*, Page Range.

ISBN 978-3-0365-9506-1 (Hbk)
ISBN 978-3-0365-9507-8 (PDF)
doi.org/10.3390/books978-3-0365-9507-8

Cover image courtesy of Sandul Yasobant

Contents

Preface

Globalization has a dramatic impact on healthcare systems and health outcomes. The effect of globalization on health systems and individuals is complex. The impact of globalization has dual effects, both positive and negative, and these impacts need to be explored further. Globalization has shown potential positive impacts by minimizing the gaps in health inequalities between rich and poor people and between the Global South and North and by improving healthcare for all. However, there are also downsides to global health, such as the spread of infectious diseases due to rapid mobility, which is emerging as the greatest threat to all. Nevertheless, globalization is neither inherently good nor bad but rather an inexorable force that needs to be understood and channeled for the ecosystem's well-being. As we have understood globalization beyond economic development, such as institutional, sociocultural, and environmental transitions, this would be the right time to value its understanding of healthcare impacts. The topic "Impacts of the Globalism of Healthcare" was established by the *International Journal of Environmental Research and Public Health*, *Healthcare*, and *Medicina*, and 37 manuscripts were published as a part of the topic. Thus, this book presents 37 innovative articles on diverse aspects of globalization and its impact on healthcare, which are grouped into the following thematic areas. The Global Quality of Healthcare section (articles 1–9) explores gender, workforce, political, and cultural influences related to quality of care, the Global Health Care and Determinants section (articles 10–16) explores determinants of care on four continents in a variety of populations, the Global Risk of Chronic Diseases section (articles 17–25) explores oral health, cancer risk, aging, and the risk of glaucoma and Parkinson's disease as well as chronic lung disease, the Global Digital Health section (articles 26–29) dives into the use of the Internet, smartphone addiction, and web-based and telehealth intervention, and finally, the Educational Programs and Measurement Tools section (articles 30–37) introduces educational programs related to health emergencies, school fruit and vegetable schemes, a stress assessment tool, and five new tools.

Thus, this book includes recent advances in the understanding and impacts of health outcomes and health systems of drivers and risks that impact system changes on a wide spectrum of topics. The manuscript collection process took place during the height of the COVID-19 pandemic, which is reflected in the content of several of the manuscripts.

Joachim G. Voss and Sandul Yasobant
Editors

healthcare

MDPI

Article

Exploring Healthcare Professionals' Practices and Attitudes towards Monitoring and Reporting of Severe Adverse Drug Reactions

Warisara Srisuriyachanchai [1], Anthony R. Cox [2] and Narumol Jarernsiripornkul [1,*]

[1] Division of Clinical Pharmacy, Faculty of Pharmaceutical Sciences, Khon Kaen University, Khon Kaen 40002, Thailand; warisara.sr@kkumail.com
[2] School of Pharmacy, Institute of Clinical Sciences, College of Medical and Dental Sciences, University of Birmingham, Birmingham B15 2TT, UK; a.r.cox@bham.ac.uk
* Correspondence: narumol@kku.ac.th

Abstract: Healthcare professionals (HCPs) play a key role in the monitoring of severe adverse drug reactions (ADRs). The present study aims to explore practices and barriers of HCPs in severe ADR monitoring and reporting, to evaluate their attitudes towards the monitoring and to assess the related factors. Self-administered questionnaires produced in hard copy and Google form were sent to 510 HCPs by stratified random sampling. Of the 350 HCPs that responded (68.6%), 44.9% had ever monitored ADRs. The most common practices were the observation of abnormal symptoms for ADR identification (88.5%), discontinuation of the suspected drug for ADR management (88.5%) and advice on recurrent drug allergy for ADR prevention (88.5%). Most HCPs (93.0%) obtained further patient history to identify severe ADRs. The uncertainty of the causal relationship was a major barrier to ADR reporting (60.0%). Pharmacists were more involved with practices in ADR monitoring and reporting (OR 20.405; $p < 0.001$), whereas longer work experience (>20 years) was negatively related to the practices (OR 0.271; $p = 0.024$). Over one-third (37.6%) of HCPs had a positive attitude towards severe ADR monitoring. In conclusion, the practices in severe ADR monitoring varied among different professions. However, the barriers to the reporting of ADRs still exist; hence, improving knowledge and cooperation among HCPs should be promoted.

Keywords: practice; attitude; severe adverse drug reaction; monitoring; healthcare professionals

Citation: Srisuriyachanchai, W.; Cox, A.R.; Jarernsiripornkul, N. Exploring Healthcare Professionals' Practices and Attitudes towards Monitoring and Reporting of Severe Adverse Drug Reactions. *Healthcare* **2022**, *10*, 1077. https://doi.org/10.3390/healthcare10061077

Academic Editors: Joachim G. Voss and Sandul Yasobant

Received: 10 May 2022
Accepted: 8 June 2022
Published: 10 June 2022

1. Introduction

Pharmacovigilance is a key part of monitoring ADRs around the world. The detection, assessment, management, prevention and reporting of suspected ADRs is the responsibility of HCPs in adverse drug reaction monitoring systems [1]. Physicians, pharmacists and nurses make up the majority of HCPs in Thailand and are the primary resource for reporting severe ADRs.

In Thailand, physicians and nurses are mainly responsible for direct patient care with pharmacists providing medication and dispensing and counseling services, during which pharmacists obtain additional information from the patients that could identify potential ADRs. Therefore, pharmacists play an important role in ADR monitoring systems and reporting ADRs to the Health Product Vigilance Center (HPVC) in Thailand. The spontaneous reporting system (SRS) that utilizes HCP reporting of ADRs is, globally, the most commonly employed method for pharmacovigilance. Such systems are a rapid and effective way to collate suspected ADRs, but they have a well-known limitation of under-reporting. One comprehensive systematic review found that only 6% of potential ADRs are reported in spontaneous reporting systems [2]. The success or failure of any SRS depends on the intrinsic and extrinsic factors [3]. The intrinsic factors are the knowledge, skill and attitudes of the reporters, while the extrinsic factors are related to the systems employed to identify and report ADRs [4–6]. The involvement of all of the HCPs that provide patient care in the ADR reporting process is one key to good post-marketing safety surveillance [7], but, in recent years, the increased involvement of patients in the ADR reporting process in many countries has led to an increased reporting of ADRs [8–11]. Differences exist in the types of ADRs reported by direct patient reports and by HCPs. HCPs report a higher proportion of serious ADRs that result in death, hospitalization and prolongation of hospital stay than patients [10]. This is because HCPs are more likely to become involved with patients when they experience more severe ADR.

While most studies show that physicians, pharmacists and nurses have a reasonable knowledge of, and attitudes towards, ADR reporting [12–23], the under-reporting of severe ADRs remains a serious concern. The aims of this study are to identify the practices methods concerning severe ADR monitoring, to explore the barriers to ADR reporting, the factors affecting practices in ADR monitoring and reporting, and attitudes towards severe ADR monitoring among physicians, pharmacists and nurses in Thailand.

2. Materials and Methods

This research is a cross-sectional study conducted at two university hospitals in northeast Thailand from June to September 2020. Eligible participants were physicians, pharmacists and nurses who worked at clinical departments in the two hospitals. The study excluded HCPs without Internet access. The sample-size calculation for the study was determined using Taro Yamane [24]. The minimum appropriate number of participants was 350, assuming a participation refusal rate of 45.2% from a previous study [25]. A total sample size of 510 enrolled participants was chosen, consisting of 134 physicians, 69 pharmacists and 307 nurses by stratified sampling.

The questionnaire for self-administration was developed by the research team following previous relevant studies [12,17,26,27]. Three HCPs with expertise in the field of pharmacovigilance and ADRs (one physician, one clinical pharmacist and one nurse) evaluated the developed questionnaire for content validity. The index of consistency (IOC) was calculated to assess the internal consistency [28–30]. All the questions in the draft questionnaire passed content validity testing with an IOC > 0.5 for each item. The questionnaire was adjusted and piloted using 15 HCPs from other hospitals. The 15 HCPs were asked to complete the questionnaire and they were then asked to comment on each question individually, in terms of ease of understanding and for any general recommendations for improving the questionnaire. The questionnaire was appropriately re-adjusted following the suggestions from the pilot study, and subjected to validation testing to obtain the final version. HCPs were asked about all ADRs from any types of drugs that the HCPs had ever monitored in all departments of the hospitals. The final questionnaire consisted of the three following sections:

Section 1: Closed questions were used with a checklist to obtain demographic data on gender, education level, profession, income, inpatient or outpatient department, number of patients per day and time spent per patient. Open questions were used to obtain data on age and time since professional qualification.

Section 2: Closed questions were used with checklists to explore the severe ADR monitoring methods and barriers towards ADR reporting experienced by HCPs.

Section 3: Attitudes towards severe ADR monitoring methods. This section contained 8 questions made up of 4 positive statements (1, 4, 7 and 8) and 4 negative statements (2, 3, 5 and 6). The agreement with each statement was measured on a 5-point Likert scale. The scores ranged from 1 to 5 for strongly disagree to strongly agree for positive statements and from 1 to 5 for strongly agree to strongly disagree for negative statements. The total score was calculated by summing the scores for all questions for a total score range from 8 to 40. The total score range was divided into three equal parts, categorized as poor (8–18), moderate (19–29) and good (30–40) attitudes.

The final questionnaire was constructed as both a hard copy and as Google Documents form that could be accessed via a QR code or a URL (both provided in the letter of invitation).

The online version of the self-administered questionnaire was also tested in the pilot study. Letters of invitation containing a hard copy of the questionnaire were directly distributed to the HCPs through the various Heads of Department by stratified sampling. After 2 weeks, non-responders were sent a reminder letter with a hard copy of the questionnaire. Two weeks later, non-responders were sent a second reminder letter and another hard copy of the questionnaire. The final collection of the responses was completed at sixteen weeks from the date of distribution of the first questionnaire. Questionnaires received after this date were excluded from the analysis. The survey was conducted from June to September 2020.

Questionnaire responses were entered into SPSS for Windows version 26.0 for analysis. Demographic data, frequency, types of severe ADR monitoring method and attitude scores were analyzed using descriptive statistics. Pearson's chi-squared and Fisher's exact test were used to compare subgroups for categorical data, and independent-sample *t*-tests or ANOVA were used for continuous variables with normal distributions. The Mann–Whitney U or Kruskal–Wallis tests were used to determine the distribution for the continuous data of non-parametric variables. Univariate analysis of the factors related to the variables was analyzed using the chi-squared test. The variables associated with the practices of HCPs in ADR monitoring and reporting with *p*-values < 0.25 in the univariate analyses were entered into a multivariate analysis. Multivariate analysis of the factors related to xpractices of HCPs in ADR monitoring and reporting was analyzed using logistic regression. The results with *p*-values less than 0.05 were considered statistically significant. The study was approved by the Ethics Committee of the Khon Kaen University Ethics Committee for Human Research (Number HE621444 on 16 December 2019).

3. Results

3.1. Response Rate

A total of 510 questionnaires were distributed by hand to HCPs at the two hospitals. Of the 350 valid questionnaires that were returned (68.6%), 314 were from Srinagarind Hospital (89.7%) and 36 were from the Queen Sirikit Heart Center of the Northeast (10.3%). The 350 respondents comprised 65 physicians (18.6%), 29 pharmacists (8.3%) and 256 nurses (73.1%).

3.2. Demographic Data

The majority of respondents were female (88.9%) aged 18–34 years (59.7%) and had a bachelor's degree (82.0%). Almost two-thirds of the respondents (60.3%) had less than 10 years' work experience (Table 1).

3.3. Methods of ADR Monitoring

A total of 191 (54.6%) respondents claimed that they knew about ADR monitoring methods in Thailand, and 157 (44.9%) respondents said that they had been involved in ADR monitoring. Among these 157 respondents, the most frequently known ADR identification method was the observation of abnormal symptoms following the administration of drugs (88.5%) (Table 2). The top three frequently used methods of ADR identification were the same, with the observation of abnormal symptoms after the administration of drugs reported by 126 respondents (80.3%), followed by reports from patients (56.7%) and high-alert drug lists (35.7%). For the physicians and nurses, the observation of abnormal symptoms following the administration of drugs was the most well-known ADR identification method (100.0% and 89.8%, respectively). For the pharmacists, a report from the patients was the most common known ADR identification method (85.2%). An awareness of the high-alert drug list ADR identification method was not significantly different between professions ($p = 0.441$), but an awareness of all the other methods of ADR identification were significantly different between professions ($p < 0.05$). The practice of these methods of severe ADR identification varied among the respondents, but the further patient history taking was used by nearly all the respondents (93.0%) with no statistical difference between professions

(p = 0.271). Other methods were less well-known using specific ADR criteria (18.5%), the next most common among all respondents, but there was a significant difference between professions (p = 0.001). There was also a significant difference between professions for drug-gene testing (p = 0.003) and confirmation by additional laboratory data (p < 0.001) (Table 2).

Approximately half of the respondents (49.0%) did not know about the causality assessment of ADRs. Of the 157 respondents who had been involved in ADR monitoring, 39.5% and 21.7% had known the WHO-UMC criteria and Naranjo's algorithm, respectively. The awareness of Naranjo's algorithm was significantly different between professions (p < 0.001) (Table 2), due to the very high rate of awareness among the pharmacists (96.3%). Only 24.8% of the respondents claimed that they used causality assessment methods, with Naranjo's algorithm (69.2%), and consulted with the HCP team (59.0%) in relation to the most frequently reported methods.

Table 1. Respondent demographic characteristics.

Characteristic	Profession of Respondents, N (%)			
	Physician (n = 65)	Pharmacist (n = 29)	Nurse (n = 256)	Total (n = 350)
Hospital				
Srinagarind Hospital	63 (96.9)	21 (72.4)	230 (89.8)	314 (89.7)
Queen Sirikit Heart Center	2 (3.1)	8 (27.6)	26 (10.2)	36 (10.3)
Gender				
Male	32 (49.2)	1 (3.4)	6 (2.3)	39 (11.1)
Female	33 (50.8)	28 (96.6)	250 (97.7)	311 (88.9)
Age (years)				
18–34	48 (73.8)	11 (37.9)	150 (58.6)	209 (59.7)
35–50	15 (23.1)	17 (58.6)	70 (27.3)	102 (29.1)
>50	1 (1.5)	1 (3.4)	36 (14.1)	38 (10.9)
Mean ± S.D.	29.8 ± 6.51	37.7 ± 7.50	36.2 ± 10.52	35.2 ± 10.00
Median (range)	27 (23–53)	39 (27–57)	33 (21–66)	32 (21–66)
Routine work				
OPD	56 (96.2)	28 (96.6)	82 (32.0)	166 (47.4)
IPD	60 (92.3)	23 (79.3)	211 (82.4)	294 (84.0)
Both	51 (78.5)	22 (75.9)	37 (14.5)	110 (31.4)
Highest education level				
Bachelor's degree	39 (60.0)	14 (48.3)	234 (91.4)	287 (82.0)
Master's degree or higher	26 (40.0)	15 (51.7)	22 (8.6)	63 (18.0)
Years of work experience (years)				
<10	56 (86.2)	13 (44.8)	142 (55.5)	211 (60.3)
10–20	8 (12.3)	11 (37.9)	50 (19.5)	69 (19.7)
>20	1 (1.5)	5 (17.2)	64 (25.0)	70 (20.0)
No. of patients per day (cases)				
<10	8 (12.3)	1 (3.4)	105 (41.0)	114 (32.6)
10–30	46 (70.8)	0 (0.0)	107 (41.8)	153 (43.7)
>30	11 (16.9)	28 (96.6)	44 (17.2)	83 (23.7)
Time spent on care per patient (min)				
<20	43 (66.2)	27 (96.4)	56 (21.9)	126 (36.1)
>20	22 (33.8)	1 (3.6)	200 (78.1)	223 (63.9)
Proportion of time spent in direct patient contact				
<50% of all working time	34 (52.3)	11 (37.9)	76 (29.7)	121 (34.6)
>50% of all working time	31 (47.7)	18 (62.1)	180 (70.3)	229 (65.4)
No. of ADRs identified in the previous year				
<20	18 (27.7)	5 (17.2)	96 (37.5)	119 (34.0)
>20	4 (6.2)	21 (72.4)	12 (4.7)	37 (10.6)

S.D.: standard deviation; OPD: outpatient department; IPD: inpatient department; No.: number.

Table 2. Methods of ADR monitoring by profession.

Method	Profession of Respondents, N (%)				p-Value [a]
	Physician (n = 22)	Pharmacist (n = 27)	Nurse (n = 108)	Total (n = 157)	
General ADR identification methods					
Observe abnormal symptoms	22 (100.0)	20 (74.1)	97 (89.8)	139 (88.5)	**0.015** [b,*]
High-alert drug list	11 (50.0)	12 (44.4)	62 (57.4)	85 (54.1)	0.441
Abnormal laboratory data	11 (50.0)	13 (48.1)	18 (16.7)	42 (26.8)	**<0.001** [*]
Alerting orders	10 (45.5)	14 (51.9)	24 (22.2)	48 (30.6)	**0.003** [*]
Trigger tools or antidotes	8 (36.4)	18 (66.7)	24 (22.2)	50 (31.8)	**<0.001** [*]
Report from patients	13 (59.1)	23 (85.2)	58 (53.7)	94 (59.9)	**0.012** [*]
HCP team ADR monitoring systems	10 (45.5)	19 (70.4)	32 (29.6)	61 (38.9)	**<0.001** [*]
Additional methods for identification of severe ADRs					
Drug-gene testing	5 (22.7)	8 (29.6)	8 (7.4)	21 (13.4)	**0.003** [b,*]
Skin test	3 (13.6)	6 (22.2)	12 (11.1)	21 (13.4)	0.279 [b]
Additional patient history taking	20 (90.9)	27 (100.0)	99 (91.7)	146 (93.0)	0.271 [b]
Additional laboratory data	5 (22.7)	8 (29.6)	3 (2.8)	16 (10.2)	**<0.001** [b,*]
Use specific ADR criteria [c]	4 (18.2)	12 (44.4)	13 (12.0)	29 (18.5)	**0.001** [b,*]
Recognize methods of ADR causality assessment					
WHO-UMC criteria	8 (36.4)	14 (51.9)	40 (37.0)	62 (39.5)	0.352
Naranjo's algorithm	8 (36.4)	26 (96.3)	0 (0.0)	34 (21.7)	**<0.001** [*]
ADR management methods					
Stop the suspected drug	22 (100.0)	27 (100.0)	90 (83.3)	139 (88.5)	**0.005** [b,*]
Change to alternative drug	17 (77.3)	19 (70.4)	20 (18.5)	56 (35.7)	**<0.001** [*]
Use additional drug to treat ADR symptoms	10 (45.5)	14 (51.9)	1 (0.9)	25 (15.9)	**<0.001** [b,*]
Decrease drug dose	6 (27.3)	9 (33.3)	6 (5.6)	21 (13.4)	**<0.001** [b,*]
Change drug administration time	4 (18.2)	4 (14.8)	4 (3.7)	12 (7.6)	**0.013** [b,*]
Change drug administration rate	5 (22.7)	15 (55.6)	8 (7.4)	28 (17.8)	**<0.001** [b,*]
Change drug dosage form	7 (31.8)	1 (3.7)	2 (1.9)	10 (6.4)	**<0.001** [b,*]
Advise patients about the drug	11 (50.0)	18 (66.7)	63 (58.3)	92 (58.6)	0.497
Monitor patient	5 (22.7)	8 (29.6)	18 (16.7)	31 (19.7)	0.296
ADR prevention methods					
Advise patients about recurrent drug allergy	20 (90.9)	26 (96.3)	93 (86.1)	139 (88.5)	0.370 [b]
Drug allergy card	15 (68.2)	27 (100.0)	41 (38.0)	83 (52.9)	**<0.001** [*]
Transfer drug allergy data to responsible agency	13 (59.1)	18 (66.7)	82 (75.9)	113 (72.0)	0.221
Adjust drug dose in special populations	10 (45.5)	9 (33.3)	9 (8.3)	28 (17.8)	**<0.001** [b,*]
Check drug interactions	12 (54.5)	11 (40.7)	23 (21.3)	46 (29.3)	**0.003** [*]
Search ADR reference books	4 (18.2)	8 (29.6)	16 (14.8)	28 (17.8)	0.213 [b]
Record ADR history in medical notes	16 (72.7)	24 (88.9)	44 (40.7)	84 (53.5)	**<0.001** [*]
Record ADR history in computer programs	12 (54.5)	25 (92.6)	37 (34.3)	74 (47.1)	**<0.001** [*]
Attach drug allergy sticker to medical notes	6 (27.3)	25 (92.6)	43 (39.8)	74 (47.1)	**<0.001** [*]
Attach drug allergy label to the patient's bed	5 (22.7)	5 (18.5)	24 (22.2)	34 (21.7)	0.908
Staff/organization to whom HCPs reported the ADRs					
Responsible physicians	12 (54.5)	19 (70.4)	97 (89.8)	128 (81.5)	**<0.001** [b,*]
Pharmacists on ADR duty	21 (95.5)	21 (77.8)	82 (75.9)	124 (79.0)	0.121
Responsible nurses	13 (59.1)	15 (55.6)	67 (62.0)	95 (60.5)	0.818
Pharmacy department	7 (31.8)	13 (48.1)	29 (26.9)	49 (31.2)	0.102
The Ministry of Public Health (MOPH)	0 (0.0)	5 (18.5)	0 (0.0)	5 (3.2)	**<0.001** [b,*]

[a] Pearson's chi-squared Test; [b] Fisher's exact test; [c] Specific ADR criteria: vancomycin evaluation criteria (n = 1), anaphylaxis evaluation criteria (n = 1), drug-use manual for hospital (n = 10), RegiSCAR (Registry of Severe Cutaneous Adverse Reactions) score for DRESS (n = 4), not identified (n = 13); * the level of significant different < 0.05.

The method for ADR management most frequently reported by the HCPs was stopping the suspected drug (88.5%). The used methods of ADR management were significantly different between professions, except for providing patient advice about drug use ($p = 0.497$) and monitoring patients ($p = 0.296$) (Table 2). The methods for ADR prevention most frequently reported by the HCPs was providing patient advice about recurrent drug allergies (88.5%). The common ADR prevention methods were different among the professions. There were significant differences between the professions in relation to the awareness of different ADR prevention methods, except for providing patient advice about recurrent drug allergies ($p = 0.370$), transferring drug allergy data to a responsible agency ($p = 0.221$), search data from ADR reference books (p = 0.213) and attaching drug allergy labels to the patient's bed (p = 0.908) (Table 2).

Of the 157 respondents who were involved in ADR monitoring, 81.5% claimed that they reported all suspected ADR cases. Table 2 shows that the respondents most commonly reported suspected ADR symptoms to the responsible physicians (81.5%), followed by the pharmacists on ADR duty (79.0%) and the responsible nurses (60.5%). Only pharmacists reported suspected ADRs to the Ministry of Public Health (18.5% of pharmacist respondents).

3.4. Barriers to ADR Reporting

Among 155 respondents, the top three barriers to ADR reporting were the uncertainty of a causal relationship between drug and reactions (60.0%) well-known ADRs (22.6%), not understanding the processes and steps of ADR monitoring and unavailability of ADR reporting forms (both 19.4%). The rates of not understanding the processes and steps of ADR monitoring (p = 0.017), inadequate time for ADR reporting (p = 0.001) and the shortage of staff (p = 0.022) were significantly different between professions (Table 3).

Table 3. Barriers to ADR reporting experienced by profession.

Reasons	Profession of Respondents, N (%)				p-Value [a]
	Physician (n = 22)	Pharmacist (n = 27)	Nurse (n = 106)	Total (n = 155)	
Well-known ADRs	6 (27.3)	6 (22.2)	23 (21.7)	35 (22.6)	0.849
Not serious ADRs	5 (22.7)	8 (29.6)	16 (15.1)	29 (18.7)	0.196
Uncertainty of the causal relationship between drug and reactions	17 (77.3)	18 (66.7)	58 (54.7)	93 (60.0)	0.107
Not understanding the ADR monitoring process	9 (40.9)	3 (11.1)	18 (17.0)	30 (19.4)	**0.017** *
ADR reporting forms unnavailable	4 (18.2)	2 (7.4)	24 (22.6)	30 (19.4)	0.200
ADR reporting forms too complicated	3 (13.6)	4 (14.8)	5 (4.7)	12 (7.7)	0.078 [b]
Inadequate time for ADR reporting	6 (27.3)	11 (40.7)	11 (10.4)	28 (18.1)	**0.001** [b,*]
Lack of cooperation between healthcare teams	2 (9.1)	3 (11.1)	7 (6.6)	12 (7.7)	0.581 [b]
Staff shortage	3 (13.6)	7 (25.9)	8 (7.5)	18 (11.6)	**0.022** [b,*]
Lack of support from leaders	2 (9.1)	0 (0.0)	4 (3.8)	6 (3.9)	0.195 [b]
Lack of technology to monitor ADRs	4 (18.2)	1 (3.7)	5 (4.7)	10 (6.5)	0.055 [b]

[a] Pearson's chi-squared test; [b] Fisher's exact test; * the level of significant different < 0.05.

3.5. Factors Related to Practices in ADR Monitoring and Reporting

The univariate analysis of the factors related to practices in ADR monitoring showed that hospital (p = 0.015), gender (p = 0.027), age (p = 0.025), profession ($p < 0.001$) and years of work experience (p = 0.030) were significantly associated with practices in the monitoring and reporting ADRs. Multiple logistic regression analysis identified pharmacists' professions (OR 20.405; 95% CI 4.098, 101.607; $p < 0.001$) and more than 20 years of work experience (OR 0.271; 95% CI 0.087, 0.845; p = 0.024) as the factors independently associated with reporting ADRs (Table 4).

3.6. Attitudes towards Severe ADR Monitoring

Attitudinal scores could be calculated for 157 respondents. The overall mean attitude score was 28.5 ± 3.27 (min-max = 8–40). Just under under two-thirds of respondents (62.4%) had a moderate attitude (mean = 26.5 ± 2.16); the remaining 59 respondents (37.6%) had a good attitude (mean = 31.8 ± 1.82). Physicians had the highest overall mean attitude score, followed by pharmacists and nurses (29.3 ± 2.53, 28.9 ± 2.32, and 28.2 ± 3.57, respectively), and the overall mean attitude scores were not significantly different between the three professions (p = 0.121).

A large majority of the respondents agreed with the following statements: severe ADRs are manageable and preventable (90.5%), the management of severe ADRs can improve patient compliance (89.1%) and an ADR monitoring tool can decrease the severity level of ADRs (87.3%). Conversely, approximately two-thirds of the respondents disagreed with the statement that the management of severe ADRs is a waste of time (63.0%), half of the respondents disagreed with the statement that the treatment of severe ADRs is the responsibility of HCPs only (49.1%) and one-third of some respondents disagreed with the statement that the monitoring of severe ADRs is difficult and complicated (32.5%) (Table 5).

Table 4. Multiple logistic regression analysis of the factors related to practices in ADR monitoring and reporting.

Variables	No. of Respondents; N (%)		Adjusted OR	95% CI		*p*-Value
	Monitor and Report ADRs (*n* = 157)	Not Monitor and Report ADRs (*n* = 193)		Lower	Upper	
Hospital						
Srinagarind Hospital	134 (85.4)	180 (93.3)	1			0.396
Queen Sirikit Heart Center	23 (14.6)	13 (6.7)	1.418	0.633	3.174	
Gender						
Male	11 (7.0)	28 (14.5)	1			0.152
Female	146 (93.0)	165 (85.5)	1.944	0.783	4.824	
Age (years)						
18–34	91 (58.0)	118 (61.1)	1			
35–50	55 (35.0)	47 (24.4)	2.145	0.929	4.954	0.074
>50	11(7.0)	27 (14.0)	1.728	0.470	6.351	0.410
Profession						
Physician	22 (14.0)	43 (22.3)	1			
Pharmacist	27 (17.2)	2 (1.0)	20.405	4.098	101.607	**<0.001** *
Nurse	108 (68.8)	148 (76.7)	1.289	0.626	2.656	0.491
Years of work experience (years)						
<10	96 (61.1)	115 (59.6)	1			
10–20	38 (24.2)	31 (16.1)	0.643	0.276	1.498	0.306
>20	23 (14.6)	47 (24.4)	0.271	0.087	0.845	**0.024** *

Variables included in the multiple logistic regression analysis are hospital, gender, age, profession and years of work experience. * The level of significant different < 0.05

Table 5. Attitudes of respondents towards severe ADR monitoring.

Statements	Attitudes (N, %)					Mean ± S.D.
	Absolutely Agree	Agree	Not Sure	Disagree	Absolutely Disagree	
1. Severe ADR monitoring is a direct role of HCPs.	48 (30.6)	85 (54.1)	13 (8.3)	6 (3.8)	5 (3.2)	4.05 ± 0.911
2. Treatment for severe ADRs is the responsibility of HCPs.	11 (7.0)	49 (31.2)	20 (12.7)	64 (40.8)	13 (8.3)	3.12 ± 1.151
3. Monitoring severe ADRs is difficult and complicated.	10 (6.4)	63 (93.6)	36 (53.5)	45 (30.6)	3 (1.9)	2.80 ± 0.992
4. Severe ADRs are manageable and preventable.	29 (18.5)	113 (72.0)	11 (7.0)	1 (0.6)	3 (1.9)	4.04 ± 0.673
5. It can be difficult to differentiate between severe ADRs and symptoms due to other causes.	9 (5.7)	69 (43.9)	48 (30.6)	28 (17.8)	3 (1.9)	2.66 ± 0.903
6. Severe ADR management is a waste of time.	4 (2.5)	27 (17.2)	27 (17.2)	69 (43.9)	30 (19.1)	3.60 ± 1.061
7. Severe ADR management can improve patient compliance.	36 (22.9)	104 (66.2)	17 (10.8)	0 (0.0)	0 (0.0)	4.12 ± 0.570
8. ADR monitoring tools can decrease the severity level of ADRs.	37 (23.6)	100 (63.7)	18 (11.5)	0 (0.0)	2 (1.3)	4.08 ± 0.679

S.D.: standard deviation; N: number of respondents.

4. Discussion

This cross-sectional study had a reasonable overall response rate of 68.6%, slightly lower than reported in comparable previous studies [17,26], but with a similar majority of female respondents [17]. The proportions of HCPs by profession in our study (physicians 18.6%, pharmacists 8.3% and nurses 73.1%) were broadly similar to those reported in the previous studies (physicians 13.8%, pharmacists 8.08% and nurses 77.4% and physicians 17.6%, pharmacists 20.5% and nurses 61.9%) [17,26]. The key element to identify a suspected ADR in the current study was the temporal relationship between the administration of a medicine and the observation of an adverse effect. Overall, the known general methods of ADR identification in the current study were similar to the previous studies [31,32]. Pharmacists most frequently used reports from patients to identify ADRs; physicians and nurses used the observation of abnormal symptoms after the drugs were administered. This could be because physicians and nurses are more able to directly observe patients' symptoms. Pharmacists also used ADR monitoring systems by HCP teams to identify ADRs much more frequently than physicians and nurses. Patient history taking was the most common way of identifying severe ADRs, in line with the previous studies [33], and using specific criteria for severe ADR identification was needed, as reported in the previous studies [34–36]. This suggests that the selection of methods for ADR identification by HCPs depends on their pattern of patient care.

Few respondents were aware of causality tools, such as the WHO-UMC criteria and Naranjo's algorithm, despite reports of the widespread use of these tools [37,38]. Therefore, the strategies to increase knowledge about the causality assessment methods of ADRs should be established for all HCPs. Pharmacists were the main profession to use these tools for causality assessments. The most frequently used method for causality assessment by physicians and pharmacists was the Naranjo's algorithm, although pharmacists predominated in this category. The most frequently selected methods for ADR management by all HCPs were to stop the suspected drugs, provide patient advice about drug use and changing new drugs, which is also in line with a previous study [12]. However, the study was conducted in a primary healthcare center that used referral to a tertiary health facility as ADR management. This result differs from our study conducted in tertiary care teaching hospitals, where referral was not used. The prevention of the suspected drug was suitable for severe ADR management. We found that physicians and pharmacists were, in general, far more involved in ADR management than nurses.

This study found that the most used methods of ADR prevention by all professions were providing patient advice about recurrent drug allergy and recording ADR history in medical notes, which is also in line with the previous studies [26,39]. This indicated that HCPs were aware of patient safety, especially concerning the information about recurrent drug allergies in patients. The individual professions used different methods of ADR prevention, which seemed to be aligned to their professional role. The physicians mainly focused on the methods that directly affected the patients and recorded safety data in medical notes rather than using systemic processes, such as recording the ADR history in computer database or attaching drug allergy stickers. The pharmacists usually started with drug allergy card provision to patients, followed by advice to patients, recording the ADR history and attaching allergy labels to the medical notes. The evidence from the previous studies suggests that hospital pharmacists can not only identify and report ADRs, but also help in the prevention of ADRs [40], and this is one of the main roles of pharmacists in Thailand [39]. It can be observed from our survey that the most frequently employed method of ADR prevention by nurses was transferring drug allergy data to a responsible agency or hospital management, presumably because of their close patient contact in nursing care. Responsible physicians were the most likely to receive ADR reports from other HCPs. This finding was comparable to other studies [41–45]. The nurses usually reported ADRs to the responsible physicians and pharmacists who were on ADR duty, rather than directly to the pharmacy department in the hospitals, as can be observed in the previous studies [41,45]. The pharmacists had the highest proportion of reporting ADRs to the regulatory authority. In Thailand, pharmacists have the responsibility of reporting ADRs to the Thai Health Product Vigilance Center, and our study confirmed that pharmacists understand this role.

The most common barrier to ADR reporting by all professions was the uncertainty about the causal relationship between drug and reactions. Similar results were found in the previous studies of pharmacists [19,23,27,46–48] and nurses [42]. This is regrettable, since regulatory authorities only require a suspicion that a drug was linked to an adverse effect. The knowledge of a causal relationship should be promoted among HCPs. The other barriers to ADR reporting found in this study were at rates similar to those found in the previous studies [4,12,16,19,23,42,44,46–50]. However, in our study, not understanding the ADR monitoring process was a frequent barrier to ADR reporting by physicians, in contrast to the previous studies that showed that the main barrier was unavailable ADR reporting forms [12,16,51]. Not only improving the knowledge of causal relationships, but also understanding the ADR monitoring process should be promoted. For nurses, the main barrier to ADR reporting was the unavailability of ADR reporting forms, which matched similar results obtained in the previous studies [4,44,50]. Therefore, providing adequate ADR reporting forms will support nurses to increase ADR reporting. However, in our study, it was only nurses that had a fear of legal complaints as a barrier to ADR reporting, in contrast to the previous studies that showed that physicians, pharmacists and nurses all had a fear of the legal issues [12,13,48]. The profession of the HCPs and the years of work experience were significantly associated with the practices in ADR monitoring and reporting. The pharmacists were more likely to monitor and report ADRs, which is in line with the pharmacists having the responsibility of monitoring and reporting ADRs to the national pharmacovigilance system in Thailand. A recent study found that senior pharmacists were more likely to report ADRs than general pharmacists [49], and that physicians with more than six years of work experience were 4.6 times more likely to report an ADR, compared to physicians with one to three years of work experience [52]. Our study shows that pharmacists in practice for less than 10 years are more likely to monitor ADRs than pharmacists practicing for more than 20 years, which is in agreement with a previous study [53]. Other studies also reported that having more than 10 years of work experience was associated with poor ADR reporting practice by HCPs [26], and that younger pharmacists and those who had received ADR training were significantly more likely to report ADRs [48].

The majority of respondents had a positive attitude towards ADR monitoring or reporting. Our study shows that around 40% of all HCPs have a positive attitude towards severe ADR monitoring, which is a lower proportion than the previous studies [12,17,26,27]. However, our study includes all the steps in the monitoring and reporting of severe ADRs, whereas the other studies only measure the attitudes towards ADR reporting. Our HCPs agreed that the management of severe ADRs could improve patient compliance, confirming a previous study that found that ADRs influence medication adherence [54]. In the current study, the HCP respondents agreed that it can be difficult to differentiate between severe ADRs and adverse events with other causes, as found in the previous studies [42,46].

The current study has some limitations. It was conducted only in the northeastern region of Thailand; hence, our findings may not be generalized to all HCPs in Thailand. Moreover, the gathered findings were obtained from self-administered questionnaire, which may be subject to recall and social desirability biases.

5. Conclusions

HCPs frequently used the further patient history taking as the main method of severe ADR identification. The uncertainty of the causal relationship between drugs and reactions was a major barrier to reporting ADRs. HCPs with less work experience and with a pharmacist profession were more likely to monitor and report ADRs. However, HCPs had a positive attitude towards severe ADR monitoring. Improving the knowledge of ADR monitoring should be promoted to all HCPs. This could enhance the awarness of HCPs to recognize the importance of ADR monitoring and reporting, which would lead to medication safety for patients.

Author Contributions: Conceptualization, N.J. and A.R.C.; methodology, N.J., A.R.C. and W.S.; software, W.S. and N.J.; validation, W.S. and N.J.; formal analysis, W.S. and N.J.; investigation, N.J. and A.R.C.; resources, N.J.; data curation, W.S.; writing—original draft preparation, W.S.; writing—review and editing, N.J. and A.R.C.; visualization, W.S. and N.J.; supervision, N.J. and A.R.C.; project administration, N.J.; funding acquisition, N.J. All authors have read and agreed to the published version of the manuscript.

Funding: This research was funded by the Royal Golden Jubilee Ph.D. Programme Scholarship (Grant No. PHD/0161/2561) of the Thailand Research Fund.

Institutional Review Board Statement: The study was conducted in accordance with the Declaration of Helsinki, and approved by the Ethics Committee of the Khon Kaen University Ethics Committee for Human Research (Number HE621444 on 16 December 2019).

Informed Consent Statement: Informed consent was obtained from all subjects involved in the study.

Data Availability Statement: Not applicable.

Acknowledgments: We thank the Royal Golden Jubilee Ph.D. Programme of the Thailand Research Fund for supporting this research (Grant No. PHD/0161/2561). We also thank the physicians, pharmacists and nurses from Srinagarind Hospital and Queen Sirikit Heart Centre of the Northeast who participated in the study, and to all the staff who provided help in the data collection. The authors would like to thank Sirinya Kampichit for her facilitation during the data collection periods.

Conflicts of Interest: The authors declare no conflict of interest. The funders had no role in the design of the study; in the collection, analyses, or interpretation of data; in the writing of the manuscript, or in the decision to publish the results.

References

1. Shewale, B.; Patil, P.; Agrawal, S.; Kosalge, S.; Fursule, R.; Sapkal, N. Adverse drug reporting: Role of health care professionals. *J. Pharm. Res.* **2009**, *2*, 327–330.
2. Hazell, L.; Shakir, S.A.W. Under-reporting of adverse drug reactions. *Drug Saf.* **2006**, *29*, 385–396. [CrossRef] [PubMed]
3. Agency, E.M. Guideline on Good Pharmacovigilance Practices (GVP) Module VI-Management and Reporting of Adverse Reactions to Medicinal Products. Available online: https://www.ema.europa.eu/en/documents/scientific-guideline/guideline-good-pharmacovigilance-practices-module-vi-management-reporting-adverse-reactions_en-1.pdf (accessed on 21 October 2020).
4. De Angelis, A.; Colaceci, S.; Giusti, A.; Vellone, E.; Alvaro, R. Factors that condition the spontaneous reporting of adverse drug reactions among nurses: An integrative review. *J. Nurs. Manag.* **2016**, *24*, 151–163. [CrossRef] [PubMed]
5. Kasliwal, R. Spontaneous reporting in pharmacovigilance: Strengths, weaknesses and recent methods of analysis. *J. Clin. Prev. Cardiol.* **2012**, *1*, 20–23.
6. World Health Organization. The Importance of Pharmacovigilance (Safety Monitoring of Medicinal Products). Available online: https://www.paho.org/hq/dmdocuments/2011/who-Pharmacovigilance-The-Importance-of.pdf (accessed on 5 April 2019).
7. Lopez-Gonzalez, E.; Herdeiro, M.T.; Figueiras, A. Determinants of under-reporting of adverse drug reactions. *Drug Saf.* **2009**, *32*, 19–31. [CrossRef]
8. Aagaard, L.; Nielsen, L.H.; Hansen, E.H. Consumer reporting of adverse drug reactions. *Drug Saf.* **2009**, *32*, 1067–1074. [CrossRef]
9. Avery, A.J.; Anderson, C.; Bond, C.; Fortnum, H.; Gifford, A.; Hannaford, P.; Hazell, L.; Krska, J.; Lee, A.; McLernon, D.; et al. Evaluation of patient reporting of adverse drug reactions to the UK 'Yellow Card Scheme': Literature review, descriptive and qualitative analyses, and questionnaire surveys. *Health Technol. Assess.* **2011**, *15*, 1–234. [CrossRef]
10. de Langen, J.; van Hunsel, F.; Passier, A.; den Berg, L.D.J.-V.; van Grootheest, K. Adverse drug reaction reporting by patients in the Netherlands three years of experience. *Drug Saf.* **2008**, *31*, 515–524. [CrossRef]
11. Inch, J.; Watson, M.C.; Anakwe-Umeh, S.; Collaboration, Y.C.S. Patient versus healthcare professional spontaneous adverse drug reaction reporting. *Drug Saf.* **2012**, *35*, 807–818. [CrossRef]
12. Adisa, R.; Omitogun, T.I. Awareness, knowledge, attitude and practice of adverse drug reaction reporting among health workers and patients in selected primary healthcare centres in Ibadan, southwestern Nigeria. *BMC Health Serv. Res.* **2019**, *19*, 926. [CrossRef]
13. Bahekar, S.; Patil, S. Evaluation of knowledge, attitude, and practice of adverse drug reactions reporting among doctors and nursing staff of a rural tertiary care teaching hospital of Maharashtra. *J. Med. Sci. Res.* **2018**, *1*, 145–150. [CrossRef]
14. Bateman, D.N.; Sanders, G.L.; Rawlins, M.D. Attitudes to adverse drug reaction reporting in the Northern Region. *Br. J. Clin. Pharmacol.* **1992**, *34*, 421–426. [PubMed]
15. Belton, K.J. Attitude survey of adverse drug-reaction reporting by health care professionals across the European Union. The European Pharmacovigilance Research Group. *Eur. J. Clin. Pharmacol.* **1997**, *52*, 423–427. [CrossRef] [PubMed]
16. Belton, K.J.; Lewis, S.C.; Payne, S.; Rawlins, M.D.; Wood, S.M. Attitudinal survey of adverse drug reaction reporting by medical practitioners in the United Kingdom. *Br. J. Clin. Pharmacol.* **1995**, *39*, 223–226. [CrossRef] [PubMed]

17. Gordhon, Y.; Padayachee, N. Evaluating the knowledge, attitudes and practices of healthcare workers towards adverse drug reaction reporting at a public tertiary hospital in Johannesburg. *Int. J. Afr. Nurs. Sci.* **2020**, *12*, 100191. [CrossRef]
18. Green, C.F.; Mottram, D.R.; Rowe, P.H.; Pirmohamed, M. Attitudes and knowledge of hospital pharmacists to adverse drug reaction reporting. *Br. J. Clin. Pharmacol.* **2001**, *51*, 81–86. [CrossRef] [PubMed]
19. Hadi, M.A.; Neoh, C.F.; Zin, R.M.; Elrggal, M.E.; Cheema, E. Pharmacovigilance: Pharmacists' perspective on spontaneous adverse drug reaction reporting. *Integr. Pharm. Res. Pract.* **2017**, *6*, 91–98. [CrossRef]
20. Morrison-Griffiths, S.; Walley, T.J.; Park, B.K.; Breckenridge, A.M.; Pirmohamed, M. Reporting of adverse drug reactions by nurses. *Lancet* **2003**, *361*, 1347–1348. [CrossRef]
21. Oshikoya, K.A.; Awobusuyi, J.O. Perceptions of doctors to adverse drug reaction reporting in a teaching hospital in Lagos, Nigeria. *BMC Clin. Pharm.* **2009**, *9*, 1–8. [CrossRef]
22. van Grootheest, K.; Olsson, S.; Couper, M.; de Jong-van den Berg, L. Pharmacists' role in reporting adverse drug reactions in an international perspective. *Pharmacoepidemiol. Drug Saf.* **2004**, *13*, 457–464. [CrossRef]
23. Vessal, G.; Mardani, Z.; Mollai, M. Knowledge, attitudes, and perceptions of pharmacists to adverse drug reaction reporting in Iran. *Pharm. World Sci.* **2009**, *31*, 183–187. [CrossRef] [PubMed]
24. Yamane, T. *Statistics: An Introductory Analysis*, 3rd ed.; Harper and Row Publications: New York, NY, USA, 1970.
25. Phueanpinit, P.; Jarernsiripornkul, N.; Pongwecharak, J.; Krska, J. Hospital pharmacists' roles and attitudes in providing information on the safety of non-steroidal anti-inflammatory drugs in Thailand. *Int. J. Clin. Pharm.* **2014**, *36*, 1205–1212. [CrossRef] [PubMed]
26. Gidey, K.; Seifu, M.; Hailu, B.Y.; Asgedom, S.W.; Niriayo, Y.L. Healthcare professionals knowledge, attitude and practice of adverse drug reactions reporting in Ethiopia: A cross-sectional study. *BMJ Open* **2020**, *10*, e034553. [CrossRef]
27. Al-Worafi, Y. Knowledge, attitude and practice of yemeni physicians toward pharmacovigilance: A mixed method study. *Int. J. Pharm. Pharm. Sci.* **2018**, *10*, 74–77. [CrossRef]
28. Turner, R.C.; Carlson, L. Indexes of item-objective congruence for multidimensional items. *Int. J. Test.* **2003**, *3*, 163–171. [CrossRef]
29. Kampichit, S.; Pratipanawatr, T.; Jarernsiripornkul, N. Confidence and accuracy in identification of adverse drug reactions reported by outpatients. *Int. J. Clin. Pharm.* **2018**, *40*, 1559–1567. [CrossRef]
30. Wongtaweepkij, K.; Krska, J.; Pongpunna, S.; Pongwecharak, J.; Jarernsiripornkul, N. Thai patients' Drug Safety knowledge and perceptions relating to different forms of written medicine information: A comparative study. *Patient Prefer. Adherence* **2022**, *16*, 1141–1152. [CrossRef]
31. Thürmann, P. Methods and systems to detect adverse drug reactions in hospitals. *Drug Saf.* **2001**, *24*, 961–968. [CrossRef]
32. Institute for Healthcare Improvement. Trigger Tool for Measuring Adverse Drug Events. Available online: http://www.ihi.org/resources/Pages/Tools/TriggerToolforMeasuringAdverseDrugEvents.aspx (accessed on 15 January 2019).
33. White, R.W.; Wang, S.; Pant, A.; Harpaz, R.; Shukla, P.; Sun, W.; DuMouchel, W.; Horvitz, E. Early identification of adverse drug reactions from search log data. *J. Biomed. Inform.* **2016**, *59*, 42–48. [CrossRef]
34. Cartotto, R.; Mayich, M.; Nickerson, D.; Gomez, M. SCORTEN accurately predicts mortality among Toxic Epidermal Necrolysis patients treated in a burn center. *J. Burn Care Res.* **2008**, *29*, 141–146. [CrossRef]
35. Castellazzi, M.; Esposito, S.; Claut, L.; Daccò, V.; Colombo, C. Drug reaction with eosinophilia and systemic symptoms (DRESS) syndrome in two young children: The importance of an early diagnosis. *Ital. J. Pediatr.* **2018**, *44*, 93. [CrossRef] [PubMed]
36. Thompson, D.; Sharp, R. Identification and reduction of adverse drug reactions. *J. Healthc. Leadersh.* **2010**, *2*, 43–48. [CrossRef]
37. Naranjo, C.A.; Busto, U.; Sellers, E.M.; Sandor, P.; Ruiz, I.; Roberts, E.A.; Janecek, E.; Domecq, C.; Dj, G. A method for estimating the probability of adverse drug reactions. *Clin. Pharmacol. Ther.* **1981**, *30*, 239–245. [CrossRef] [PubMed]
38. The Uppsala Monitoring Centre. The Use of the WHO-UMC System for Standardised Case Causality Assessment. Available online: https://www.who.int/medicines/areas/quality_safety/safety_efficacy/WHOcausality_assessment.pdf (accessed on 20 September 2019).
39. Chaikoolvatana, A.; Chanakit, T.; Juengrakpong, A. The evaluation of a recurrent Adverse Drug Reaction Prevention Program in the north-east region of Thailand. *J. Med. Assoc. Thail.* **2006**, *89*, 699–705.
40. Mawhibah, M.A.A.; Atiah, M.A.Q. The role of clinical pharmacists in reducing adverse drug reactions. *Int. J. Med. Dev. Ctries.* **2020**, *4*, 236–239.
41. Hanafi, S.; Torkamandi, H.; Hayatshahi, A.; Gholami, K.; Javadi, M. Knowledge, attitudes and practice of nurse regarding adverse drug reaction reporting. *Iran. J. Nurs. Midwifery Res.* **2012**, *17*, 21–25.
42. John, L.J.; Arifulla, M.; Cheriathu, J.J.; Sreedharan, J. Reporting of adverse drug reactions: An exploratory study among nurses in a teaching hospital, Ajman, United Arab Emirates. *Daru* **2012**, *20*, 44. [CrossRef]
43. Khalili, H.; Mohebbi, N.; Hendoiee, N.; Keshtkar, A.-A.; Dashti-Khavidaki, S. Improvement of knowledge, attitude and perception of healthcare workers about ADR, a pre- and post-clinical pharmacists' interventional study. *BMJ Open* **2012**, *2*, e000367. [CrossRef]
44. Li, Q.; Zhang, S.M.; Chen, H.T.; Fang, S.P.; Yu, X.; Liu, D.; Shi, L.Y.; Zeng, F.D. Awareness and attitudes of healthcare professionals in Wuhan, China to the reporting of adverse drug reactions. *Chin. Med. J.* **2004**, *117*, 856–861.
45. Salehifar, E.; Ala, S.H.; Gholami, K.H. Knowledge, attitude and performance of pharmacists and nurses in Mazandaran province, Iran regarding adverse drug reaction and its reporting, 2005. *J. Maz. Univ. Med. Sci.* **2007**, *16*, 115–125.

46. Duarte, M.; Ferreira, P.; Soares, M.; Cavaco, A.; Martins, A. Community pharmacists' attitudes towards adverse drug reaction reporting and their knowledge of the new pharmacovigilance legislation in the southern region of Portugal: A mixed methods study. *Drugs Ther. Perspect.* **2015**, *31*, 316–322. [CrossRef]
47. Mes, K.; den Berg, L.T.W.d.J.-V.; Van Grootheest, A.C. Attitudes of community pharmacists in the Netherlands towards adverse drug reaction reporting. *Int. J. Pharm. Pract.* **2002**, *10*, 267–272. [CrossRef]
48. Su, C.; Ji, H.; Su, Y. Hospital pharmacists' knowledge and opinions regarding adverse drug reaction reporting in Northern China. *Pharmacoepidemiol. Drug Saf.* **2010**, *19*, 217–222. [CrossRef] [PubMed]
49. Sweis, D.; Wong, I.C. A survey on factors that could affect adverse drug reaction reporting according to hospital pharmacists in Great Britain. *Drug Saf.* **2000**, *23*, 165–172. [CrossRef]
50. Ekman, E.; Petersson, G.; Tågerud, S.; Bäckström, M. Awareness among nurses about reporting of adverse drug reactions in Sweden. *Drug Healthc. Patient Saf.* **2012**, *4*, 61–66. [CrossRef]
51. Vallano, A.; Cereza, G.; Pedròs, C.; Agustí, A.; Danés, I.; Aguilera, C.; Arnau, J.M. Obstacles and solutions for spontaneous reporting of adverse drug reactions in the hospital. *Br. J. Clin. Pharmacol.* **2005**, *60*, 653–658. [CrossRef]
52. Nadew, S.S.; Beyene, K.G.M.; Beza, S.W. Adverse drug reaction reporting practice and associated factors among medical doctors in government hospitals in Addis Ababa, Ethiopia. *PLoS ONE* **2020**, *15*, e0227712. [CrossRef]
53. Generali, J.A.; Danish, M.A.; Rosenbaum, S.E. Knowledge of and attitudes about adverse drug reaction reporting among Rhode Island pharmacists. *Ann. Pharmacother.* **1995**, *29*, 365–369. [CrossRef]
54. Jimmy, B.; Jose, J. Patient medication adherence: Measures in daily practice. *Oman Med. J.* **2011**, *26*, 155–159. [CrossRef]

healthcare MDPI

Article

Satisfaction with the Care Received and the Childbirth and Puerperium Experience in Christian and Muslim Pregnant Women

Francisco Javier Fernández-Carrasco [1,2], Gustavo Adolfo Silva-Muñoz [1], Juana María Vázquez-Lara [1,2], Juan Gómez-Salgado [3,4,*], Juan Jesús García-Iglesias [3] and Luciano Rodríguez-Díaz [5]

1 Department of Obstetrics, Punta de Europa Hospital, 11207 Algeciras, Spain; fjavier.fernandez@uca.es (F.J.F.-C.); guslavosm@hotmail.com (G.A.S.-M.); juana.vazquez@uca.es (J.M.V.-L.)
2 Nursing and Physiotherapy Department, Faculty of Nursing, University of Cádiz, 11207 Algeciras, Spain
3 Department of Sociology, Social Work and Public Health, Faculty of Labour Sciences, University of Huelva, 21007 Huelva, Spain; juanjesus.garcia@dstso.uhu.es
4 Safety and Health Postgraduate Programme, University of Espíritu Santo, Guayaquil 092301, Ecuador
5 School of Health Sciences, University of Granada, 51003 Ceuta, Spain; lucianin000@gmail.com
* Correspondence: salgado@uhu.es; Tel.: +34-959-219-700

Abstract: Over the last three decades, there has been an increase in the population as a result of the migratory flow due to the arrival of migrants to Spain, including young women of childbearing age and with reproductive capacity. This phenomenon has made childbirth assistance an extremely important priority in recent years. The aim of this study was to assess the satisfaction and experience during childbirth and the postpartum period in pregnant women according to their religion after assistance in a tertiary hospital. A descriptive cross-sectional study was conducted on a sample of 242 women using the validated Spanish version of the Mackey Childbirth Satisfaction Rating Scale (MCSRS) to measure satisfaction with the childbirth experience during the months of January to April 2021. Statistically significant differences were found in the domains of birth satisfaction ($p < 0.01$), satisfaction with the obstetrician ($p < 0.01$), and perception of pain during labour ($p < 0.01$). The Christian group of women scored higher in these three domains as compared to the Muslim group. The rate of breastfeeding at birth was 5.26 times higher among the Muslim group compared to the Christian group ($p = 0.02$). The experience of childbirth and the puerperium significantly influenced the levels of satisfaction of pregnant women with the process of childbirth in a different way according to the religious culture of the patient.

Keywords: childbirth; childbirth experience; patient satisfaction; cultural diversity; Christianity; Islam; pregnant women; postpartum period

Citation: Fernández-Carrasco, F.J.; Silva-Muñoz, G.A.; Vázquez-Lara, J.M.; Gómez-Salgado, J.; García-Iglesias, J.J.; Rodríguez-Díaz, L. Satisfaction with the Care Received and the Childbirth and Puerperium Experience in Christian and Muslim Pregnant Women. *Healthcare* **2022**, *10*, 725. https://doi.org/10.3390/healthcare10040725

Academic Editors: Joachim G. Voss, Sandul Yasobant and Masafumi Koshiyama

Received: 10 March 2022
Accepted: 11 April 2022
Published: 13 April 2022

1. Introduction

Lived experiences during childbirth have the potential to impact women's lives. The quality of these experiences is specifically related to fragility, vulnerability, stress, and emotional alterations that mark the experience and constitute memories of various kinds in pregnant women [1]. Throughout the pregnancy process, the woman creates expectations related to childbirth, generally established by cultural and social influences such as the support of her family network or access to and knowledge of the health system. If a good relationship is established between the health professional and the patient, the patient can gain positive reinforcement regarding her subsequent labour. If this link is not established, the woman is more likely to have doubts, conflicts or fears due to previous poor experience, lack of knowledge, and low confidence in the system [1,2].

The approach provided by Leininger's nursing theory of diversity and universality of cultural nursing care [3] offers patients from different cultures the opportunity to express their wishes by guiding professionals to achieve culturally appropriate health care. Social life cannot be conceived without a religious dimension, since it is through it that the moral status that governs a society can be analysed, as well as the worldview around it, which gives a unique identity to the residing inhabitants. Culture and religion are not two distinct spheres of social life but part of a general construct that defines the creation of societies. This is why the study of their interrelationship helps us understand the dimensions of culture more precisely, insofar as religion is a human creation and activity that is conceivable only and thanks to society itself. Religion gains strength as a cultural phenomenon because it helps build personality in childhood and ensure social cohesion [4]. In this research, when referring to both Christian and Muslim culture, we do not refer to religion as person's relationship with a divinity but rather as the set of beliefs, behavioural norms, and morality that are associated with culture.

Likewise, over the last three decades, there has been an increase in the population as a result of the flow of migrants to Spain, including young women of childbearing age and with reproductive capacity. This phenomenon has made childbirth assistance an extremely important priority in recent years [5]. In this sense, the different cultural approaches that people from other cultures may take to pregnancy, childbirth, and puerperium depending on their country of origin must be considered, and this factor could have a significant influence on the perception and experience of childbirth [6]. Cultural aspects are fundamental factors in the perception and acceptance of health services by migrant women, as the literature shows that their reproductive behaviours are influenced by the socio-cultural and health conceptions of their country of origin [7,8]. According to the Spanish Statistical Office, immigrants living in Spain correspond to 11.5% of the population. In terms of religion, 97% of the Spanish population is Christian, 2% is Muslim, and the remaining 0.7% belongs to other minority religions [9].

In the field of obstetrics, maternal satisfaction after childbirth has consequences for the health of the mother and her newborn [10], so its measurement could provide a valuable result to improve the quality of care provided [11]. Some authors relate satisfaction to the fulfilment of women's expectations of care [10]. In this sense, Hodnett identifies the personal expectations of pregnant women, women's participation in decision-making, and the support and quality of the relationship with health professionals [11] as key elements for experience satisfaction. Additionally, a positive birth experience may have implications in the satisfaction of a subsequent pregnancy, as it has been observed that, in these cases, women are more likely to have positive expectations for their next birth [12].

The concept of satisfaction with the experience of childbirth and with the health care received during this process is currently an important indicator of the quality of maternity care [13]. Despite this, it is difficult to measure factors such as perceived quality and satisfaction with health care, since, as previously mentioned, women construct their experience of childbirth differently depending on multiple emotional, social, cultural, and psychological factors [14]. Self-esteem and autonomy can be affected by the support a mother receives, how she prepares for childbirth, and how she accepts her feelings before, during, and after birth [13]. Having a positive experience of motherhood can improve interaction with the child, which may lead to a strong foundation for long-term family health. However, satisfaction is a life-changing event, and positive birth satisfaction outcomes are subject to a variety of individual and environmental factors that must be considered in any assessment [13].

Therefore, the aim of this study was to assess the satisfaction and experience during childbirth and the postpartum period in pregnant women after being assisted in a tertiary hospital according to whether they are socialised in Christian or Muslim culture.

2. Materials and Methods

2.1. Design and Participants

A descriptive cross-sectional study was designed. The sample consisted of women who gave birth to full-term children at the Hospital Punta de Europa in Algeciras (Spain) from 1 January 2021 to 30 April 2021. This hospital is considered a Level 3 hospital. The Sample Size Calculator was used to calculate the sample size. A confidence level of 95% with a margin of error of 0.05 was established. The total population was estimated at 366, and for these data, the sample size should be at least 188 individuals. Eventually, a sample of $n = 242$ was obtained. The sample was obtained from a consecutive sampling of all women visiting the centre to give birth who met the inclusion criteria and wished to participate in the study on a voluntary basis. The two groups were configured as follows: 176 subjects represented the Christian culture group and 66 subjects represented the Muslim culture group.

The inclusion criteria were as follows: (1) women for whom the birth was normal, without any complications beyond the usual ones, be it normal birth, instrumental, or caesarean section; (2) women whose newborns were born healthy, without any complications and not requiring more time in hospital than usual; (3) women who were Christian or Muslim; and (4) women who were fluent in Spanish, both spoken and written.

In the study period, a total of 360 births were attended in the study hospital. Of these patients, 261 were Christian, 98 were Muslim, and only 1 declared a different religion. In total, there were 11 Muslim women who did not speak or understand Spanish. In terms of maternal complications during childbirth, there was only one case of severe postpartum haemorrhage, and in terms of neonatal complications, there were only 2 cases in which the newborns required more time in hospital than usual.

After informed consent was requested, the patient was asked to fill in the questionnaire before her discharge from hospital. Data collection was carried out by the research team.

2.2. Measuring Instrument

A self-administered questionnaire consisting of one part including socio-demographic data and a second part focused on a Spanish validated questionnaire of the Mackey Childbirth Satisfaction Rating Scale (MCSRS) [13] was used as the measuring instrument. The MCSRS was originally developed in English, and it was administered to the woman after delivery. In 2012, Mas-Pons et al. [14] validated the scale in Spanish to measure the satisfaction after the experience of childbirth, obtaining a Cronbach's alpha coefficient of 0.94 for the total scale. The scale consists of 34 items grouped into five domains referring to the woman (9 items), the partner (2 items), the newborn (3 items), the midwife (9 items), and the obstetrician (8 items). It also contains an overall experience rating subscale (3 items). Each item is evaluated on a 5-point Likert scale ranging from very dissatisfied (1) to very satisfied (5). The final score of the scale is obtained by adding the values assigned to each item, so the higher the score, the higher the satisfaction. In addition, the scale allows partial scores to be given for each subscale.

2.3. Statistical Analysis

Descriptive statistics were presented as percentages and frequencies. The Kolmogorov–Smirnov test was used to determine whether the data showed normal behaviour; the Kruskal–Wallis test was used to test whether there were differences in the analysed groups with respect to the assessment of the different dimensions; and the Mann–Whitney U test, with Bonferroni correction, was used to analyse which subgroups differed from each other.

Finally, a binary logistic regression analysis was performed on those factors that were considered most influential after the preliminary study (marital status, level of education, income, presence of a companion at birth, and breastfeeding after the first hour). To study the goodness of fit of the logistic regression model, the Nagelkerke R-squared test and the Hosmer and Lemeshow test were used.

SPSS software version 20.0 was used for the study, and a confidence level equal to or greater than 0.05 was established for the entire analysis as a criterion for considering that a statistically significant effect exists.

2.4. Ethical Considerations

Participants answered the questionnaire voluntarily and accepted the informed consent. Participants' responses were recorded anonymously and the information was treated confidentially in accordance with Organic Law 3/2018, of 5 December, on Personal Data Protection and guarantee of digital rights.

In addition, this study was approved by the Research Ethics Committee of Cadiz as a body attached to the Ministry of Health and Families of the Andalusian Regional Government (Spain) in April 2021.

3. Results

Table 1 presents the sociodemographic characteristics of the sample. A total of 242 patients were included, of whom 72.7% belonged to the Christian culture group (n = 176) and 27.3% belonged to the Muslim culture group (n = 66).

Table 1. Description of sociodemographic characteristics.

Quantitative Variables						
Variable	**Minimum**	**Maximum**	**M**		**SD** [1]	**N**
Age	19	44	30.59		5.38	242
Number of children	0	5	1.69		0.89	242
Qualitative Variables						
					N	**%**
Marital status		Single		104	103 Christians 1 Muslim	43%
		Married		130	65 Christians 65 Muslims	53.7%
		Separate/Divorced		6	6 Christians 0 Muslim	2.5%
		Widow		2	2 Christians 0 Muslims	0.8%
Educational level		No studies		15	5 Christians 10 Muslims	6%
		Primary education		70	40 Christians 30 Muslims	29%
		High School/Vocational		97	80 Christians 17 Muslims	40%
		University/Post-Graduate		60	51 Christians 9 Muslims	25%
Culture		Christian Muslim			176 66	72.7% 27.3%

[1] SD: Standard Deviation.

Table 2 shows the means of the different test domains as well as the total score.

According to Table 3, women of Christian culture obtained a higher mean score in the pain (M = 8.31, SD = 1.79), dilation phase (M = 21.05, SD = 5.04), expulsive phase (M = 18.63, SD = 4.55), and obstetrician (M = 27.09; SD = 6.05) domains; on the other hand, women of Muslim culture obtained a higher mean score in the midwife (M = 28.03; SD = 3.31) and newborn (M = 10.30; SD = 1.85) domains. Statistically significant differences were found in the pain, satisfaction with the delivery, and satisfaction with the obstetrician variables. In terms of overall satisfaction with the questionnaire, the Christian group (M = 6.96, SD = 1.44) scored slightly higher than the Muslim group (M = 6.82, SD = 1.20), but these differences were not statistically significant (p = 0.11).

Table 2. Test domains and total score.

Variables	N	Minimum	Maximum	M	SD [1]
Pain domain	242	2	10	8.13	1.87
Dilatation domain	242	4	28	20.99	4.88
Expulsive domain	242	6	24	18.31	4.44
Newborn domain	242	4	12	10.29	1.97
Midwife domain	242	6	32	27.64	5.05
Obstetrician domain	242	4	32	26.78	5.82
Overall experience domain	242	0	8	6.92	1.37
Final score	242	37	136	110.93	19.29

[1] SD: Standard Deviation.

Table 3. Comparison between means according to the culture.

Domains	Culture			*p*-Value [1]
Pain	Christian	M	8.31	0.01 *
		SD	1.79	
		N	176	
	Muslim	M	7.64	
		SD	2.03	
		N	66	
Dilatation	Christian	M	21.05	0.69
		SD	5.04	
		N	176	
	Muslim	M	20.85	
		SD	4.46	
		N	66	
Expulsive	Christian	M	18.63	0.01 *
		SD	4.55	
		N	176	
	Muslim	M	17.48	
		SD	4.05	
		N	66	
Newborn	Christian	M	10.28	0.7
		SD	2.03	
		N	176	
	Muslim	M	10.30	
		SD	1.85	
		N	66	
Midwife	Christian	M	27.49	0.46
		SD	5.57	
		N	176	
	Muslim	M	28.03	
		SD	3.31	
		N	66	
Obstetrician	Christian	M	27.09	0.01 *
		SD	6.05	
		N	176	
	Muslim	M	25.94	
		SD	5.09	
		N	66	

Table 3. *Cont.*

Domains	Culture			p-Value [1]
Overall experience	Christian	M	6.96	0.11
		SD	1.44	
		N	176	
	Muslim	M	6.82	
		SD	1.20	
		N	66	

[1] U de Mann–Whitney; * $p < 0.05$.

A binary logistic regression model was used for the multivariate analysis. Culture was taken as the dependent variable, and all variables that were statistically significant in the bivariate analysis were taken as independent variables. These variables were marital status, level of education, income, presence of a birth companion, initiation of breastfeeding after the first hour of labour, pain experienced during labour, methods of pain relief, satisfaction during the second stage of labour, and satisfaction with the obstetrician (Table 4).

Table 4. Binary logistic regression model for culture.

	Exp (B)	95% C.I. to EXP (B) [1]		Sig.
		Lower	Higher	
Marital status				
Single	Ref.			0.003
Married	0.24	0.06	0.87	0.03
Separate/Divorced	1.34	0.39	4.53	0.63
Widow	0.11	0.008	1.62	0.10
Educational level				
No studies	Ref.			0.006
Primary education	5.74	0.40	81.55	0.19
High School/Vocational	0.27	0.07	1.01	0.05
University/Post-Graduate	1.92	0.66	5.55	0.22
Incomes				
None	Ref			0.005
EUR <500	26.81	2.84	252.6	0.004
EUR 500–1000	3.13	0.20	48.28	0.41
EUR 1000–2000	13.46	2.85	63.58	0.001
EUR >2000	14.19	3.16	63.64	0.001
Presence of a birth companion	17.90	6.56	48.78	0.01
Breastfeeding after the first hour postpartum	0.19	0.06	0.54	0.002
Constant	0.02			0.01

[1] Hosmer–Lemeshow test (Chi squared = 11.71) $p = 0.16$ and Nagelkerke's R^2 (0.51).

According to this model, the following results were found as regards marital status:

Muslim women were 4.16 times more likely to be married than single, compared to Christian women.

With regard to educational level, Christian women were 1.92 times more likely to have university education than no studies, compared to Muslim women.

In terms of income, Christian women were 14.19 times more likely to have an income of more than EUR 2000 than no income, compared to Muslim women.

In relation to accompaniment during birth, the model indicates that Christian women were 17.9 times more likely to be accompanied than being alone, compared to Muslim women.

Finally, the model predicts that, in relation to the initiation of breastfeeding after the first hour postpartum, Muslim women were 5.26 times more likely to breastfeed their newborns than Christian women.

4. Discussion

The main findings of this study were that statistically significant differences were found in the domains of birth satisfaction, satisfaction with the obstetrician, and perception of pain during labour. The Christian group of women scored higher in these three domains compared to the Muslim group. The rate of breastfeeding at birth was 5.26 times higher among the Muslim group compared to the Christian group.

There are few studies in the literature that measure the satisfaction with the birth experience [11–15]. In this case, the experience was measured in women from different cultures, specifically Muslim women from the north of Morocco and Christian women from Spain.

Studies in the UK, Australia, Canada, and Sweden have found that continuous support from health care staff, a close relationship with them, and a warm atmosphere in birth centres may be factors that encourage women to obtain more information, participate in decision making, and have greater overall satisfaction [16,17].

Handelzalts et al. [18] conducted a study to assess the experience of childbirth in emergency situations in the second stage of labour. They concluded that, in instrumental deliveries and emergency caesarean sections, women were less satisfied than those who did not undergo an emergency intervention. In the present study, it was Christian women who had a higher number of caesarean sections and instrumental deliveries compared to Muslim women, and the latter had a higher level of satisfaction, although with no statistically significant differences. A recent study [19] compared the level of satisfaction with the birth experience when accompanied or unaccompanied. This study indicated that women who were accompanied during labour had higher levels of satisfaction with the birth experience than those who were not. In this study sample, the proportion of Christian women who were accompanied at birth was much higher than in the Muslim group. An odds ratio of 5.01 was identified; i.e., Christian women were five times more likely to be accompanied at birth than Muslim women. Although there was no significant difference, these data agree with the previous study that Christian women scored higher levels of satisfaction than Muslim women.

Many studies [18–22] have shown that the response to pain varies according to culture. As for the perception of the pain of labour contractions, both the perception and the expression of pain may be socio-culturally constructed [23,24]. In some cultures, women in labour pain are urged to remain silent, while in other cultures they are allowed to express their pain [25]. Although not generalisable to all women, those from North Africa tend to be less inhibited and more exaggerated in their expression of pain. Many Muslim women are reluctant to use epidural analgesia, often due to lack of knowledge [26]. In the present study, the percentage of Muslim women who received epidural analgesia was 33%. However, in women of Christian culture, about 60% made use of the different methods of pain relief. The perception of pain may be influenced by other issues such as pre-birth information, e.g., attendance of childbirth preparation classes, as well as different psychosocial conditions that women may have; e.g., increased fear of the birth process, loneliness, and lack of emotional support predisposes women to a lower pain tolerance [25]. Eighty-five per cent of the sample did not attend childbirth preparation classes, which could have caused a higher perception of pain, but there is little difference between women from Christian and Muslim cultures in this respect, as the proportion between the two groups was similar. In a study on Islamic women [26], it was shown that those who received pre-birth information had significantly reduced levels of pain during labour. Although Luque-Fernández and Oliver-Reche [25] stated that Muslim women are more vocal when it comes to expressing their pain in labour, in our case the opposite was true, with a greater verbalisation and expression of feelings about the perception of pain being higher for the group of Christian women than for the group of Muslim women, and statistically significant differences were found in this respect. Another recent study correlated accompaniment during the birth process with perceived pain during labour. The authors indicated that patients who were accompanied at birth reported less pain than those who were not accompanied [27].

On the other hand, the World Health Organisation recommends exclusive breastfeeding until the sixth month of life and mixed breastfeeding until 2 years or more. However, at least 85% of mothers in the world do not follow these recommendations, and only 35% of infants under 4 months of age are exclusively breastfed [28]. In the present study, Christian women breastfed less than Muslim women in the first hour of life. Muslim women were 5.26 times more likely to breastfeed their baby in the first hour of life than Christian women.

Regarding the possible limitations, the first difficulty encountered is the small number of studies available in the scientific literature that assess levels of satisfaction with the birth experience, and it is even more difficult to find those which relate the birth experience to other cultures. Secondly, another limitation may be that the proportion of women of Muslim culture is smaller than the proportion of women of Christian culture, so comparisons may be affected even though the sample was significant. In addition, the type of sampling used, i.e., non-probabilistic, allows for an orientation of the results, but not a representativeness of the sample. In this sense, it should be noted that the results point to associations, but do not allow us to establish cause-and-effect relationships, as it is a cross-sectional study. Finally, another possible limitation may lie in the fact that the sample was drawn from a single hospital. The results obtained should not be generalised to other different populations; however, due to the proximity to North Africa, the population may be representative of both cultures. Further research would be necessary to assess satisfaction with the birth experience in order to adapt and improve the health services offered to the population regardless of their culture.

5. Conclusions

Satisfaction in childbirth can be influenced by the woman's culture, as women of a Christian culture show greater satisfaction in general. Nevertheless, they perceive the birth experience as more painful given the use of epidural analgesia. In addition, they have more dystocic deliveries, leading to higher satisfaction with the obstetrician.

On the other hand, women of Muslim culture have a higher number of eutocic deliveries and score higher in terms of satisfaction with the midwife. They also show higher rates of breastfeeding and were less accompanied by a family member during the dilation and expulsive phases of labour.

Author Contributions: Conceptualization, J.M.V.-L., J.G.-S., J.J.G.-I. and L.R.-D.; methodology, G.A.S.-M., F.J.F.-C. and L.R.-D.; software, G.A.S.-M. and F.J.F.-C.; validation, G.A.S.-M., J.G.-S. and J.J.G.-I.; formal analysis, G.A.S.-M. and L.R.-D.; investigation, J.M.V.-L. and J.G.-S.; resources, G.A.S.-M.; data curation, F.J.F.-C.; writing—original draft preparation, J.M.V.-L.; writing—review and editing, F.J.F.-C.; visualization, J.M.V.-L.; supervision, L.R.-D.; project administration, G.A.S.-M.; funding acquisition, J.G.-S. and J.J.G.-I. All authors have read and agreed to the published version of the manuscript.

Funding: This research received no external funding.

Institutional Review Board Statement: The study was conducted according to the guidelines of the Declaration of Helsinki and was approved by the Research Ethics Committee of Cadiz as a body attached to the Ministry of Health and Families of the Andalusian Regional Government (Spain) in April 2021.

Informed Consent Statement: Informed consent was obtained from all subjects involved in the study.

Data Availability Statement: All data are available within this article.

Conflicts of Interest: The authors declare no conflict of interest.

References

1. Jafari, E.; Mohebbi, P.; Mazloomzadeh, S. Factors Related to Women's Childbirth Satisfaction in Physiologic and Routine Childbirth Groups. *Iran. J. Nurs. Midwifery Res.* **2017**, *22*, 219–224. [CrossRef] [PubMed]
2. Peñacoba-Puente, C.; Carmona-Monge, F.J.; Marín-Morales, D.; Écija Gallardo, C. Evolution of childbirth expectations in Spanish pregnant women. *Appl. Nurs. Res.* **2016**, *29*, 59–63. [CrossRef] [PubMed]

3. Leininger, M. Culture care theory: A major contribution to advance transcultural nursing knowledge and practices. *J. Transcult. Nurs.* **2002**, *13*, 189–192. [CrossRef] [PubMed]
4. Camarena-Adame, M.E.; Tunal-Santiago, G. La religión como una dimensión de la cultura. Nómadas. *Crit. J. Soc. Jurid. Sci.* **2009**, *22*, 1–15.
5. Stoll, K.; Hauck, Y.; Downe, S.; Edmonds, J.; Gross, M.M.; Malott, A.; McNiven, P.; Swift, E.; Thomson, G.; Hall, W.A. Cross-cultural development and psychometric evaluation of a measure to assess fear of childbirth prior to pregnancy. *Sex. Reprod. Healthc.* **2016**, *8*, 49–54. [CrossRef] [PubMed]
6. Giraldo-Montoya, D.; González-Mazuelo, E.; Henao-López, C. Experiencias de las mujeres durante el trabajo de parto y parto [Experiences of women during labor and delivery]. *Avances En Enfermería* **2015**, *33*, 271–281. [CrossRef]
7. Weis, J. Longitudinal Trends in Childbirth Practices in Ethiopia. *Matern. Child Health J.* **2017**, *21*, 1531–1536. [CrossRef]
8. Ohaja, M.; Murphy-Lawless, J. Unilateral collaboration: The practices and understanding traditional birth attendants in south-eastern Nigeria. *Women Birth* **2017**, *30*, e165–e171. [CrossRef]
9. Instituto Nacional de Estadística. Población Extranjera por Nacionalidad, Sexo y Año. 2021. Available online: www.ine.es (accessed on 28 March 2021).
10. Goodman, P.; Mackey, M.; Tavakoli, A. Factors related to childbirth satisfaction. *J. Adv. Nurs.* **2004**, *46*, 212–219. [CrossRef]
11. Hodnett, E. Pain and women's satisfaction with the experience of childbirth: A systematic review. *Am. J. Obs. Gynecol.* **2002**, *186*, S160–S172. [CrossRef]
12. Kringeland, T.; Daltveit, A.; Møller, A. What characterizes women who want to give birth as naturally as possible without painkillers or intervention? *Sex. Reprod. Healthc.* **2010**, *1*, 21–26. [CrossRef] [PubMed]
13. Hasenmiller, R. *Do Birth Plans Influence Childbirth Satisfaction?* Frontier School of Midwifery & Family Nursing: Philadelphia, PA, USA, 2001.
14. Caballero, P.; Delgado-García, B.; Orts-Cortes, I.; Moncho, J.; Pereyra-Zamora, P.; Nolasco, A. Validation of the Spanish version of Mackey childbirth satisfaction rating scale. *BMC Pregnancy Childbirth* **2016**, *16*, 78. [CrossRef] [PubMed]
15. Mas-Pons, R.; Barona-Vilar, C.; Carreguí-Vilar, S.; Ibáñez-Gil, N.; Margaix-Fontestad, L.; Escribà-Agüir, V. Satisfacción de las mujeres con la experiencia del parto: Validación de la Mackey Satisfaction Childbirth Rating Scale [Women's satisfaction with the experience of childbirth: Validation of the Mackey Childbirth Satisfaction Rating Scale]. *Gac. Sanit.* **2012**, *26*, 236–242. [CrossRef]
16. Waldenström, U.; Rudman, A.; Hildingsson, I. Intrapartum and postpartum care in Sweden: Women's opinions and risk factors for not being satisfied. *Acta Obstet. Gynecol. Scand.* **2006**, *85*, 551–560. [CrossRef]
17. Harvey, S.; Rach, D.; Stainton, M.C.; Jarrell, J.; Brant, R. Evaluation of satisfaction with midwifery care. *Midwifery* **2002**, *18*, 260–267. [CrossRef]
18. Handelzalts, J.E.; Waldman Peyser, A.; Krissi, H.; Levy, S.; Wiznitzer, A.; Peled, Y. Indications for Emergency Intervention, Mode of Delivery, and the Childbirth Experience. *PLoS ONE* **2017**, *12*, e0169132. [CrossRef]
19. Vlaar, A.P.; ten Klooster, P.M.; Taal, E.; Gheith, R.E.; El-Garf, A.K.; Rasker, J.J.; van de Laar, M.A. A cross-cultural study of pain intensity in Egyptian and Dutch women with rheumatoid arthritis. *J. Pain* **2007**, *8*, 730–736. [CrossRef]
20. Watson, P.J.; Latif, R.K.; Rowbotham, D.J. Ethnic differences in thermal pain responses: A comparison of South Asian and White British healthy males. *Pain* **2005**, *118*, 194–200. [CrossRef]
21. Portenoy, R.K.; Ugarte, C.; Fuller, I.; Haas, G. Population-based survey of pain in the United States: Differences among white, African American, and Hispanic subjects. *J. Pain* **2004**, *5*, 317–328. [CrossRef]
22. Riley, J.L., 3rd; Wade, J.B.; Myers, C.D.; Sheffield, D.; Papas, R.K.; Price, D.D. Racial/ethnic differences in the experience of chronic pain. *Pain* **2002**, *100*, 291–298. [CrossRef]
23. Le Breton, D. *Anthropologie de la Douleur*; Métailié: París, France, 1995.
24. Lipson, J. Cultura y cuidados de Enfermería [Culture and nursing care]. *Index Enferm.* **2000**, *28*, 19–25.
25. Luque-Fernández, M.; Oliver-Reche, M. Diferencias culturales en la percepción y vivencia del parto. El caso de las mujeres inmigradas [Culture differences on perceiving and living delivery: The case of inmigrant women]. *Index Enferm.* **2005**, *14*, 9–13. [CrossRef]
26. Desmawati, W.K.; Chatchawet, W. Effect of Nursing Intervention Integrating an Islamic Praying Program on Labor Pain and Pain Behaviors in Primiparous Muslim Women. *Iran. J. Nurs. Midwifery Res.* **2019**, *24*, 220–226. [CrossRef] [PubMed]
27. Machado, M.C.; Assis, K.F.; Oliveira Fde, C.; Ribeiro, A.Q.; Araújo, R.M.; Cury, A.F.; Priore, S.E.; Franceschini Sdo, C. Determinants of the exclusive breastfeeding abandonment: Psychosocial factors. *Rev. Saude Publica* **2014**, *48*, 985–994. [CrossRef]
28. Medeiros, R.M.K.; Teixeira, R.C.; Nicolini, A.B.; Alvares, A.S.; Corrêa, Á.C.D.P.; Martins, D.P. Humanized Care: Insertion of obstetric nurses in a teaching hospital. *Rev. Bras. Enferm.* **2016**, *69*, 1091–1098. [CrossRef] [PubMed]

International Journal of
Environmental Research and Public Health

MDPI

Article

From Health Campaign to Interpersonal Communication: Does Traditional Diet Culture Hinder the Communication of the Chinese *Gongkuai* Campaign?

Jing Yan [1], Jing Ji [1] and Lan Gao [2,*]

[1] School of Health Service Management, Anhui Medical University, No. 81, Meishan Road, Hefei 230032, China
[2] School of Management, University of Science and Technology of China, No. 96, Jinzhai Road, Hefei 230026, China
* Correspondence: glan2019@mail.ustc.edu.cn; Tel.: +86-18756074842

Abstract: Interpersonal communication is beneficial in promoting individuals' tendency to accept health-campaign-targeted behavior. Based on the protective action decision model, this study investigated the key factors underlying individual's interpersonal communication on the *Gongkuai* campaign, which was carried out during Coronavirus disease 2019 (COVID-19). The main goal of the *Gongkuai* campaign was to change traditional communal eating habits and reduce public health risks. An online questionnaire survey involving 618 respondents was conducted in China after the 2020 *Gongkuai* campaign propagated, and the data were analyzed by using the structural equation modeling technique. The results indicated that health campaign exposure is a critical determinant of perceived campaign-related knowledge and health risk perception, which are significant predictors of interpersonal communication. Meanwhile, campaign-related knowledge can elicit risk perception. Furthermore, campaign exposure influenced interpersonal communication in ways that traditional diet culture did not predict. Risk perception was also unaffected by traditional diet culture. It is worth noting that individuals' agreement with traditional diet culture does not hinder health campaign-generated interpersonal communication in the context of public health crisis. Based on the findings, theoretical and policy implications for motivating interpersonal communication were discussed, and research limitations were pointed out.

Keywords: health campaign; interpersonal communication; traditional diet culture; health risk perception; *Gongkuai* campaign

Citation: Yan, J.; Ji, J.; Gao, L. From Health Campaign to Interpersonal Communication: Does Traditional Diet Culture Hinder the Communication of the Chinese *Gongkuai* Campaign? *Int. J. Environ. Res. Public Health* **2022**, *19*, 9992. https://doi.org/10.3390/ijerph19169992

Academic Editors: Joachim G. Voss and Sandul Yasobant

Received: 18 June 2022
Accepted: 10 August 2022
Published: 13 August 2022

1. Introduction

The outbreak of COVID-19 in China in 2019 sparked anxiety worldwide, causing significant economic and psychological harm [1]. Fortunately, the spread of the virus can be slowed if the public takes appropriate precautions, such as wearing a face mask and not sharing food and drinks. Following the coronavirus outbreak, the Chinese government is pushing for a "dining table revolution" (a national campaign to persuade diners to use designated serving chopsticks known as public chopsticks, short for "*GongkKuai* Campaign") to change long-held traditions of communal eating habits, in which diners take from shared plates with their own chopsticks (https://uk.news.yahoo.com/chinas-dining-table-revolution-takes-104024594.html, accessed on 1 May 2020). Celebrities, public health experts, and propaganda officials have disseminated health information about the use of serving chopsticks through various information channels such as television, radio, newspaper and social media, etc. As a result, the *Gongkuai* campaign has become a hot sociopolitical issue that received extensive media coverage.

The use of serving chopsticks during meals has been emphasized in literature as an important factor in decreasing the transmission of bacteria among family members [2,3]. The *GongKuai* campaign, on the other hand, has raised concerns about whether the pandemic will change the country's time-honored communal eating tradition that has been a dominant part of social life (http://www.globaltimes.cn/content/1181261.shtml, accessed on 1 March 2020). A similar campaign was launched after the 2003 SARS epidemic, but it was not propagated effectively [4]. Culture has long been recognized as having a significant impact on shaping an individual's health behaviors [5]. Prior research explained why using serving chopsticks is a difficult feat to accomplish, given that the shared use of chopsticks has been a part of Chinese culture for many centuries [6,7].

However, the data on this topic are limited. A previous study showed that the lack of behavior change could result from the failure to adapt the intervention to the culture [8]. This fact was experimentally proven by [9] that social culture is an important barrier to the use of serving chopsticks. In health information research, [10] suggested that cultural values determine how immigrants seek health information in the United States. However, it has not been a priority to explore the role of cultural values on interpersonal communication in the context of large-scale health campaigns. Considering that interpersonal communication is critical in disseminating health information from mass media to the public, various studies have suggested that large-scale health campaigns can be extended through interpersonal communication [11]. Research further proposed that conversations stimulated by health campaign messages are more effective at delivering campaign-directed outcomes than simple exposure to the mass media messages [12]. That is to say, campaign-generated interpersonal communication is significant in bringing about desired health outcomes or health behavior change. As a result, it appears that whether and how people communicate information about the *Gongkuai* campaign is a critical factor in improving the public's willingness to use serving chopsticks.

To fill the research gap, current research aims to examine the effect of *Gongkuai* campaign exposure and traditional diet culture on campaign-generated interpersonal communication. To achieve this goal, the Protective Action Decision Model (PADM) was adopted as the basic theoretical framework, derived initially from the literature on public protective actions in response to impending disasters (Lindell & Perry, 2012) [13]. Later, this theory was extended to explain people's long-term risk adjustment. According to PADM, socially transmitted warnings initiate a series of preliminary decision-making processes, generating core perceptions of the external threat and alternative protective measures. In the following sections, firstly, we introduced PADM and then proposed the research hypotheses; later, the methodology of data collection was described before conducting the analysis. Finally, we discussed the results and implications and pointed out the limitations and future research directions.

2. Theory and Hypotheses

2.1. Interpersonal Communication and Protective Action Decision Model (PADM)

Since most health communication campaigns are based on media outlets such as television and social networking sites, expanding health information through interpersonal communication with the public is the first and important step in achieving public health objectives. Therefore, interpersonal communication can be seen as rational and protective behavior [14]. In contrast to other health campaigns (e.g., blood donation), which focus on personal health behavior, the *Gongkuai* campaign can only be successful if a wide range of people participate. People who effectively communicate health information are more receptive to suggestions from health campaigns and are more likely to change their unhealthy habits [15,16]. Thus, the communicative action of sharing and discussing health messages can stimulate outcomes such as obtaining personal goals [11]. Intuitively, *Gongkuai*-related conversations can be seen as a goal-oriented and protective action in which individuals discuss the health campaign with others (e.g., families, friends, and coworkers) to raise awareness regarding the importance of using serving chopsticks.

PADM is a crucial model for investigating people's protective actions [13]. According to this multistage model, psychological processes (Figure 1) are the main stages that illustrate people's response to environmental threats. Moreover, in the psychological processes of PADM, risk perception is a major determinant of protective measures relating to people's expectations of the personal impact of an extreme public event. These personal impacts include death, injury, health, and property damage [17]. PADM proposed that in the context of public emergencies, people's risk perception was influenced by a combination of event-related information from external sources and past knowledge of the individual. People will decide to take protective action if a risk is perceived to exist. In the past decades, several scholars have used PADM to illustrate people's protective action in response to social risks, such as water contamination emergencies [18], influenza outbreaks [19], and vaccine scandals [20]. This theory allows us to identify core variables (health campaign-related knowledge, information exposure, risk perception, etc.) to predict how *Gongkuai*-related information is shared and diffused. Thus, we tentatively adopted PADM to explain how information from external sources, risk perception, and campaign-related knowledge influenced information-sharing behavior in the context of the COVID-19 outbreak.

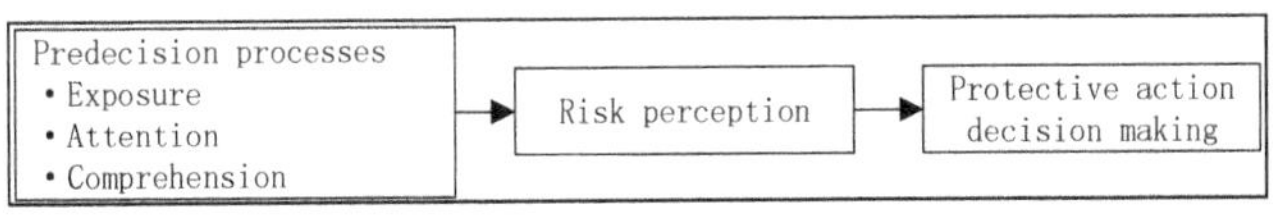

Figure 1. Psychological Processes of PADM.

2.2. *Campaign Exposure, Campaign-Related Knowledge, and Risk Perception*

Health campaign exposure refers to the frequency and duration of information delivered via mass and social media about the benefits of using serving chopsticks [21]. Additionally, campaign-related knowledge refers to an individual's tendency to use serving chopsticks as well as their familiarity with the *Gongkuai* campaign. Individuals' health knowledge increases because of media exposure which subsequently triggers positive health behavior [22,23]. For example, residents' perceptions about the benefits of waste separation are based on adequate exposure to information through a waste separation campaign [24]. Furthermore, [22] demonstrated that vaccine-related health campaigns are significant reasons for increasing awareness in parents regarding the vaccination of their children. However, a prior study suggested that exposure to a campaign does not improve people's recognition of campaign-related messages [25]. As a result, further studies are necessary to see if exposure to the *Gongkuai* campaign is an essential predictor of individuals' health knowledge about using serving chopsticks.

Furthermore, many health campaigns aim to raise public awareness and risk perceptions of unhealthy behaviors to render the behavior of interest more or less appealing [26]. Health risk perception is defined as an individual's response to the possibility of developing a disease or illness [27]. Repeated media exposure to a health crisis can lead to increased worry and vulnerability [28]. Seo and Matsaganis [29] found that exposure to media reports increases an individual's risk perceptions regarding breast cancer. Other research scholars [30] found that media exposure positively influences adolescents' smoking risk perception. Based on the evidence presented above, it appears that exposure to the *Gongkuai* campaign-related information will enhance risk perceptions of not using serving chopsticks.

In addition, the knowledge people have about health behavior is related to their risk perception. For example, Perettiwatel et al. [31] showed that highly educated people with greater knowledge of certain health behavior are more likely to perceive the risks associated with noncompliance. Similarly, other studies found that people who know more about diabetes are more likely to be aware of its negative consequences [32]. This argument is consistent with previous research showing that the provision of knowledge about the causes and consequences of unhealthy behavior (such as smoking) is significantly correlated with health risk concerns [33].

Based on the viewpoints mentioned above, the following hypotheses can be proposed:

Hypothesis 1: *Higher levels of Gongkuai campaign exposure will be associated with higher levels of individuals' knowledge of using serving chopsticks.*

Hypothesis 2: *Higher levels of Gongkuai campaign exposure will be positively associated with level of individuals' health risk perception of noncompliance with using serving chopsticks.*

Hypothesis 3: *Higher levels of health knowledge of using serving chopsticks will be positively associated with levels of individuals' risk perception of not using serving chopsticks.*

2.3. The Role of Traditional Diet Culture

Culture is widely accepted as a factor that plays an essential role in public health communication programs and interventions [5,34]. Traditional diet culture refers to engagement, respect, and acceptance of customs and norms of traditional diet values and practices [35]. Additionally, traditional diet culture can affect an individual's food intake and physical behavior [36,37]. The most popular reflection of traditional culture in most Chinese dining situations is communally shared dishes [7,38]. Communal eating habit is an integral part of Chinese traditional dietary culture. Using serving chopsticks and spoons to prevent COVID-19 infection is encouraged as a part of the *Gongkuai* campaign, even though it goes against Chinese tradition.

Most studies investigated how traditional diet culture influences health behaviors [39,40]. Zhang et al. [9] found that more than half of the participants did not use serving chopsticks despite being aware of COVID-19 infection risk because such behaviors contradict their traditional diet culture. Similarly, Arroyo and Harwood [41] observed that women are more likely to experience physical problems when culturally idealized body type norms are associated with slenderness and toned physique. That is to say, culture shapes health-related values and beliefs [5]. In this study, it can be speculated that health risk perception is negatively influenced by an individual's awareness of traditional dining culture. A related hypothesis can be proposed as follows:

Hypothesis 4: *Higher levels of health risk perception of not using serving chopsticks will be negatively associated with level of agreement with traditional diet culture.*

Given that open discussion of specific health campaign is inappropriate according to existing social norms in India, Frank et al. [42] found that risk perception of HIV through sexual transmission is less likely to form interpersonal communication of the condom normalization campaign. The research on immigrants' acculturation also showed that people with a strong desire to maintain their original health culture's traditions and values are more likely to seek and adopt health information from websites hosted in their original culture [15]. Individuals who have a strong attachment to their native culture, on the other hand, may be less likely to engage in health information behaviors such as seeking new healthcare knowledge or discussing a new healthcare culture with their friends [10,43]. Conversely, new health information is more likely to be passed on and adopted if people feel that it is compatible with their existing norms [15]. Due to the incompatibility of Chinese traditional dining culture and using *Gongkuai*, it can be hypothesized that:

Hypothesis 5: *Higher levels of agreement with traditional diet culture of dining will be negatively associated with campaign-generated interpersonal communication.*

2.4. Motivation for Campaign-Generated Interpersonal Communication

The risk perception in any specific context is an antecedent of information behaviors [13]. Emotions such as fear and sadness may particularly engender social communication [44]. Feelings of worry and anxiety about a risky situation may promote one's motivation to use and share more gathered health information [16,45]. For example, women with more risk perception associated with having unsafe sex in the context of exposure to safer sex media campaigns are more inclined to discuss this theme with their friends or significant others [46]. Moreover, under some circumstances, people who feel uncertain about themselves generally consider simple talk within their social networks as a useful and predominant means for self-verification [29]. Based on the above views, it can be concluded that perception of health risks will increase an individual's willingness to talk and discuss specific health campaigns. Hence, it is hypothesized that:

Hypothesis 6: *Higher levels of health risk perception will be positively associated with interpersonal communication about the Gongkuai campaign.*

Individuals may be unable to engage in related information behaviors due to a lack of knowledge about them [24]. Jepsen [47] found that people with a high level of knowledge are more confident in determining what information they require and obtaining it effectively. These people are more likely to participate in health communication. Similarly, according to [48], existing health knowledge can predict chronic patients' willingness to share information. Kim et al. [49] proposed that the objective component of prior knowledge can increase motivation to share information with others. On the other hand, people with a low level of health knowledge are less likely to engage in health information behaviors [50].

In addition, there is much empirical evidence suggesting that mass media health campaigns can promote interpersonal communication [14,51]. Like in early research [52], it was found that women who were more exposed to AIDS-related information through mass media were significantly more likely to discuss the disease within their social networks. Additionally, if individuals are fully informed about health campaign-targeted behaviors, they will be more likely to conduct conversations about the health campaign [53,54]. As a result, exposure to media health campaigns may encourage people to talk about specific health issues. Taking these perspectives into account, related hypotheses are stated as follows:

Hypothesis 7: *Higher levels of health knowledge will be positively associated with interpersonal communication about the Gongkuai campaign.*

Hypothesis 8: *Higher levels of health campaign exposure will be positively associated with interpersonal communication about the Gongkuai campaign.*

Based on the above analysis, the research framework and model are proposed in Figure 2.

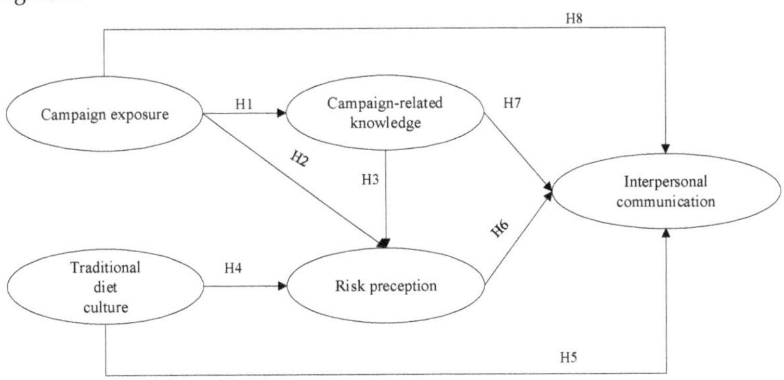

Figure 2. Research framework of interpersonal communication about *Gongkuai* campaign.

3. Research Method

3.1. Data Collection and Samples

Since the post-lockdown period of the COVID-19 pandemic in China, the *Gongkuai* campaign has aimed to raise awareness, inform about, and encourage the use of utensils.

This research was conducted in the form of a questionnaire survey after the *Gongkuai* campaign, which was officially propagated across the country in March 2020. The questionnaire was divided into four sections based on a review of previous studies. The first section briefly explained the study's purpose and expressed gratitude for the respondent's participation. The second part provided an overview of the *Gongkuai* campaign's progress to refresh respondents' memories of the campaign. The third part contained lists of items designed to identify scales of constructs. The final part included questions regarding demographics and eating habits.

Due to the prevailing COVID-19 pandemic, the online survey was conducted through a professional survey platform—Wenjuanxing (www.sojump.com (accessed on 2 April 2020), a website similar to SurveyMonkey), which is a widely accepted online questionnaire survey platform in china for data collection and has more than 28.7 million registered members [55]. A sample of 1000 people was randomly selected as potential participants from the registered members of Wenjuanxing. The survey link and a brief introduction were then distributed to these 1000 potential participants via email. To motivate respondents to participate in the survey and ensure data quality, two methods were adopted. First, to encourage the respondents to participate in the survey and increase the response rate, CNY 5 (equivalent to USD 0.7) were rewarded after the questionnaires were checked and approved by the research team. Second, some questionnaires were discarded based on the users' fill-in time (less than three minutes is assessed to be unqualified) and rules (those with the same answers on all different variables were eliminated; eligible participants had to be at least 18 years of age).

Since the *Gongkuai* campaign is a nationwide health campaign, the survey was conducted randomly and was not limited to a specific area. The online survey lasted six weeks (from 2 April to 19 May 2020). In the end, 659 participants completed the questionnaire; 41 questionnaires were deemed invalid by research teams, and 618 valid questionnaires were obtained. The sample distribution is shown in Figure 3, and the detailed profile information of the respondents is presented in Table 1. According to the results, 317 respondents were men, and 301 were women. Approximately 89.6% of respondents were between 20 and 50 years old, and 57.6% had an associate or bachelor's degree. Almost one-third of the respondents (33.6%) reported that their monthly household income is between CNY 10,000 and CNY 15,000. Overall, 41.6% of those surveyed live in urban areas. In general, the demographic characteristic of the participants, such as gender and residential location, were consistent with the demographic profile of actual Chinese residents. Additionally, age, educational level, and monthly household income were congruent with the demographic profile of Survey Star members, which registered members were relatively young, rich, and well educated [56].

3.2. Measures

Each variable was measured using multiple items derived from previous research and modified to fit the research context (see Table 2). Each item was scored on a 5-point scale ranging from strongly disagree (1) to strongly agree (5). Three measurement items for campaign exposure were referenced from the research of Shen et al. [57] and Karletsos et al. [58]. Three items of perceived traditional diet culture were developed based on the research of Zhang et al. [9] and Swierad et al. [5]. According to the studies of Gaspar et al. [59] and Yan et al. [20], three items were developed to measure campaign-related knowledge. Three items of health risk perception were referenced from the work of Lindell and Perry [13] and Yan et al. [20]. Three items of interpersonal communication were referenced from the works of Kim and Grunig [49] and Karletsos et al. [58]. The research teams conducted a pilot survey among several research scholars and commuters, and their feedback and suggestions were used to improve the questionnaire's quality.

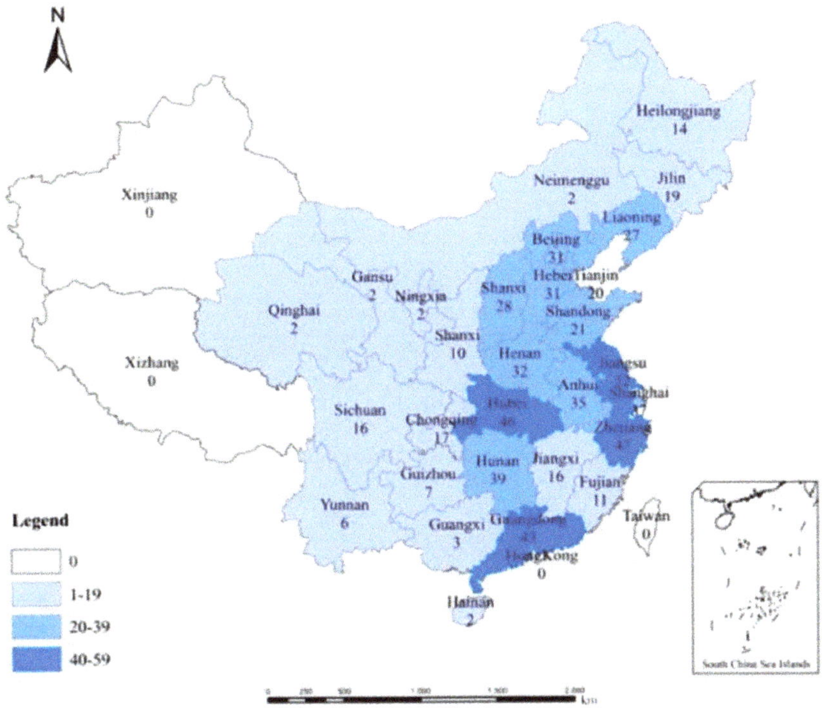

Figure 3. Sample distribution.

Table 1. Profile information of respondents (n = 618).

Demographic Characteristic		**Frequency**	**%**
Gender	Male	317	51.3
	Female	301	48.7
Age	Less than 20	59	9.6
	20–30	158	25.6
	31–40	188	30.4
	41–50	148	24.0
	More than 50	65	10.4
Education	Senior high school or below	109	17.6
	Associate or bachelor's degree	318	51.5
	Master's or higher degree	191	30.9
Monthly Household income	Less than CNY 10,000	133	21.5
	CNY 10,000–15,000	208	33.6
	CNY 15,001–20,000	161	26.1
	More than CNY 20,000	116	18.8
Residential location	Urban	257	41.6
	Suburban	242	39.2
	Rural	119	19.2

Table 2. Constructs and measurement items.

Construct	Item	Measurement	Reference
Campaign exposure (CE)	CE1	I often browsed or heard information about *Gongkuai* campaign in the past 2 months	[57,58]
	CE2	I often browse or hear information about *Gongkuai* campaign from traditional sources (e.g., television/radio/newspaper)	
	CE3	I often browse or hear information about *Gongkuai* campaign from social media sites (e.g., Wechat/Weibo/TikTok)	
Traditional diet culture (TDC)	TDC1	I believe the shared use of chopsticks is an important traditional diet culture	[5,9]
	TDC2	Using serving chopsticks is very different from traditional customs.	
	TDC3	I have a duty to uphold the traditional diet culture of dishes being shared communally	
Campaign-related knowledge (CK)	CK1	I know *Gongkuai* campaign policy	[20,59]
	CK2	I have knowledge of how to use serving chopsticks	
	CK3	I know many of the negative aspects of not using serving chopsticks	
Risk perception (RP)	RP1	I worry about the danger of not using serving chopsticks	[13,20]
	RP2	It will be dangerous to dine outside if not using serving chopsticks	
	RP3	Not using utensils will negatively influence my future health	
Interpersonal communication (IC)	IC1	In the past two months, I have had conversation with my family or friends about *Gongkuai* campaign	[49,58]
	IC2	In the past two months, I have had conversations with any relevant person about *Gongkuai* campaign	
	IC3	In the past two months, I have actively looked for chances to share my knowledge and thoughts about *Gongkuai* campaign	

3.3. Descriptive Statistics and Correlations

Before testing the research hypotheses, we performed a descriptive statistics analysis to obtain general information about the variables. The results of descriptive statistics and bivariate correlations are presented in Table 3. There are significant associations between each variable among the various constructs; thus, a deeper analysis is warranted. Meanwhile, the square root of the average variance extracted (AVEs) was greater than the correlations between each construct, indicating that the discriminant validity meets the criterion. In addition, it should be noted that some correlations between constructs were higher than the benchmark of 0.6, so a multicollinearity test was needed. The highest variance inflation factor (VIF) found in the analysis was 4.1, indicating that multicollinearity is not a significant problem in this dataset [60].

Table 3. Discriminant validity and descriptive statistics analysis.

	Mean	Standard Deviation	CE	TDC	CK	RP	IC	$\sqrt{AVE}$
CE	3.69	0.72	1					0.83
TDC	3.02	1.20	−0.03	1				0.92
CK	3.75	0.77	0.55 **	−0.04	1			0.77
RP	3.63	0.72	0.60 **	−0.04	0.44 **	1		0.81
IC	3.60	0.72	0.67 **	−0.03	0.51 **	0.69 **	1	0.79

Note: ** $p < 0.01$.

4. Results

Given that the variables were latent, the proposed model was evaluated using the structural equation modeling (SEM) technique. Data analysis was performed in two steps [61]. A confirmatory factor analysis (CFA) was performed to determine whether the questionnaire items accurately measured their intended constructs. After the measurement model was proven to fit well, the second step involved conducting a path analysis to test the hypothesized relationships in the proposed model.

4.1. Measurement Model

The measurement model's fit indicators were listed as follows: $\chi^2 = 22.405$, df = 80, $\chi^2/df = 2.505$; TLI = 0.973, CFI = 0.980; RMSEA = 0.049. These figures reveal a good fit between the measurement model and the dataset. Additionally, confirmatory factor analysis (CFA) was implemented to test the construct's reliability and validity. Cronbach's alpha value and the composite reliability value were used to evaluate the reliability of constructs. Table 4 shows that Cronbach's alphas ranged from 0.80 to 0.94, greater than the threshold condition. In addition to this, the composite reliability ranged from 0.84 to 0.94, higher than the benchmark value of 0.7 [62]. Moreover, factor loadings and average variance extracted (AVE) were used to test the convergent validity. The factor loadings ranged between 0.60 and 0.85. The AVEs of all five constructs exceed the criterion of 0.6. According to the above two findings, all constructs have good convergent validity.

Table 4. Confirmatory factor analysis results.

Construct	Items	Loadings	Cronbach's Alpha	Composite Reliability	AVE
Campaign exposure (CE)	CE1 CE2 CE3	0.876 0.837 0.778	0.87	0.87	0.69
Traditional diet culture (TDC)	MC1 MC2 MC3	0.855 0.971 0.914	0.94	0.94	0.85
Campaign-related knowledge (CK)	CK1 CK2 CK3	0.700 0.775 0.833	0.80	0.81	0.60
Risk perception (RP)	RP1 RP2 RP3	0.822 0.809 0.794	0.85	0.85	0.65
Interpersonal communication (IC)	IC1 IC2 IC3	0.771 0.807 0.804	0.83	0.84	0.63

4.2. Structural Equation Model Analysis

The structural model's fit indicators were acceptable as shown in the results ($\chi^2 = 150.817$, df = 79, $\chi^2/df = 1.909$; TLI = 0.984, CFI = 0.988; RMSEA = 0.038). t-values (t) and path coefficients (β) are used to test the verified relationships of all constructs in the proposed model, as shown in Figure 4. Campaign exposure significantly influences individuals' perceived campaign-related knowledge (H1: $\beta = 0.62$, t = 12.34) and health-risk perception (H2: $\beta = 0.60$, t = 10.42). Individuals who perceive more campaign-related knowledge tend to have a high level of risk perception of not using serving chopsticks (H3: $\beta = 0.14$, t = 2.03). However, traditional diet culture fails to significantly predict risk perception (H4 $\beta = -0.01$, t = −0.03) and interpersonal communication (H5: $\beta = 0.03$, t = 1.00). In addition, individuals who perceive more knowledge about the *Gongkuai* campaign (H6: $\beta = 0.16$, t = 2.21) and more risk perception (H7: $\beta = 0.47$, t = 9.62) tend to share and discuss information about the *Gongkuai* campaign actively. Finally, exposure to health campaigns positively influences interpersonal communication (H8: $\beta = 0.42$, t = 7.71). From these results, we concluded that all but two of the hypotheses (H4 and H5) were supported.

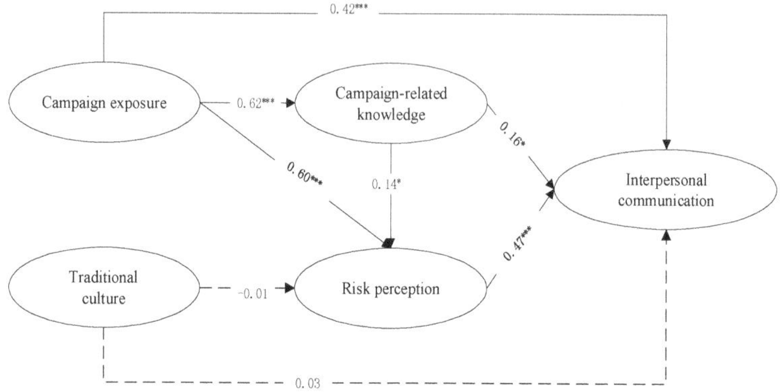

Figure 4. Results of hypothesis testing. Note: * $p < 0.05$ and *** $p < 0.001$.

5. Discussion and Implication

5.1. Discussion

Consistent with previous studies on interpersonal communication in healthcare [11,12], this study demonstrated the positive and significant effect of exposure to health campaigns on interpersonal communication. At the same time, higher levels of campaign exposure also positively improve levels of health awareness and risk perception. In addition, higher levels of campaign-related knowledge are a significant predictor of levels of health risk perception and interpersonal communication, as those who gain more knowledge about the campaign are more likely to perceive the risk of not using serving chopsticks. The previous studies suggest that gaining more knowledge from a mass media campaign in the context of public health crisis influences an individual's risk perception of unhealthy behaviors positively [18]. Perettiwatel et al. [31], on the other hand, emphasized that if parents do not understand basic human papillomavirus (HPV) and HPV vaccine information, they will not realize the efficacy and benefits of HPV vaccination. Meanwhile, campaign-related knowledge can encourage individuals to share and discuss health campaigns. This finding is consistent with previous studies that show that knowledge about specific health issues [63] and health behaviors [48] lead to more active sharing and discussion of information with others.

Furthermore, the findings indicate that higher levels of health risk perception directly affect individuals' communication of health campaign messages, implying that improving people's health risk perception of unhealthy behavior is valuable for motivating interpersonal communication. The finding is consistent with previous studies. For example, Arroyo and Harwood [41] demonstrated that people who perceive a high risk of eating disorders are more likely to discuss obesity actively. Furthermore, Kim and Grunig [49] observed that perception of a problem predicts information behaviors (e.g., information seeking and sharing).

Levels of agreement with traditional diet culture, on the other hand, do not directly predict levels of risk perception. According to a previous study (Zhang et al., 2020), Chinese dining culture has never stopped evolving and is at another critical crossroads as the country itself is undergoing a historic transformation. Extending this idea to the current study, it was seen that, while the media consensus reported that social culture is an impediment to the *Gongkuai* campaign, the changing features of dining culture contribute to the insignificant influence on an individual's risk perception. Moreover, PADM emphasized that in the context of a risk event, people will be more active in information seeking and processing and will use this information to evaluate the severity of the event to their safety and health [13]. Thus, based on PADM, the current study concluded that the level of agreements with the traditional social culture of sharing utensils would not negatively influence levels of individuals' perceptions of health risk in the context of a public health crisis (e.g., a devastating pandemic).

Finally, contrary to our expectations, levels of agreement with traditional diet culture did not negatively affect interpersonal communication. One possible reason is that the constantly evolving characteristics of traditional Chinese culture can lead to differentiated interpersonal communication between individuals (active, passive, and neutral). In China, there are two more possible subjective explanations. First, despite the perception that people's health behaviors are rooted in cultural relationships and interactions [5], their social activities are more powerful and can be explained by their perceived risks from external hazards and warning messages [13]. Second, interpersonal communication can be thought of as reasoned and problem-solving behavior that occurs when a person perceives a problem and its connections [49]. People in China are highly concerned about various aspects of the food chain because of the ongoing pandemic [9]. Meanwhile, the *Gongkuai* campaign has raised public awareness regarding the importance of changing the traditional communal dining style. These feelings of anxiety and awareness encourage people to pay attention to more information about the food chain during COVID-19, which leads to an increase in motivation to engage in communication behaviors.

5.2. Implications

This study has a wide range of theoretical implications. First, interpersonal communication is critical for achieving health campaign-targeted outcomes (Jeong & Bae, 2018). Although the *Gongkuai* campaign is vital for improving healthy eating habits, it has received little scholarly attention. The current study considers interpersonal communication as an explicit outcome of campaigns to conduct in-depth research. Meanwhile, the findings can help us better understand the communication processes that underpin the *Gongkuai* campaign's reactions. Second, using PADM, the current study investigated how health campaign affects individuals' perceptions of health risk and campaign-related interpersonal communication in the context of post-COVID-19. As a result of this research, the applied range of PADM can be expanded from natural hazards to public health emergencies. Third, this research focuses on the role of traditional diet culture. In contrast to the previous study [15,64], our findings suggest that the influence of traditional social culture on health behaviors is debatable. In the context of a health crisis, the primary factor influencing campaign-generated interpersonal communication is a perception of external health risks.

In addition, two practical implications of this study are proposed. For starters, communal dining is an essential component of Chinese cuisine, distinguished by intimate food sharing at the dinner table. During the COVID-19 epidemic, it is increasingly viewed as a public risk rather than a tradition or traditional diet culture to be treasured in China. However, such a shift is unlikely to occur quickly. Our results revealed that campaigns promoting individuals' risk perception and health knowledge effectively improve their interpersonal communication. Thus, health campaign designers should take more concrete measures to improve people's risk perception and health knowledge. Second, a previous study proved that campaigns aimed at changing an old habit are unlikely to have a large impact on outcomes [12]. This study tentatively proposed that an external public crisis serves as a catalyst for this type of health campaign, generating situational motivation to reconsider people's old behaviors. In the context of an external health crisis, a health campaign aimed at changing old habits is more likely to stimulate interpersonal communication and subsequently improve the campaign's success. Furthermore, while traditional diet culture is not an obstacle between campaign exposure and interpersonal communication; it is worth noting that if people talk negatively about the *Gongkuai* campaign in a way that reinforces traditional dining culture, new social norms for health behavior may weaken rather than strengthen [42]. Thus, public officials should carefully craft campaign-related information that is mixed with information that reminds people of the health hazard posed by COVID-19 before disseminating it through online websites or newspapers. These efforts could help raise people's risk perception of not using serving chopsticks and stimulate campaign-related interpersonal communication.

5.3. Conclusions

The main goal of *Gongkuai* campaign was to change traditional communal eating habits and reduce public health risks. The current study investigated the determinants of participants' interpersonal communication about *Gongkuai* campaign using PADM. The results support most hypotheses and provide a better understanding of how health campaigns intrigue interpersonal communication.

6. Limitations and Future Directions

There were several limitations to this research. This study focuses on the effects of health campaign exposure, traditional diet culture, perceived knowledge about the *Gongkuai* campaign, and perceived risk of not using serving chopsticks on individuals' interpersonal communication. Other possible factors such as health literacy and individuals' attitudes towards health campaigns may affect levels of health risk perception. In addition, given the complexity of communication behavior, many other factors such as conversation partners and situational facilitators may also influence it. Hence, future research should take these factors into account. Second, changes in behaviors—the level at which people used serving chopsticks before and after the *Gongkuai* campaign was not captured because this study was a cross-sectional survey. A longitudinal design should be considered in future research. Finally, the results are limited in generalizability due to the small sample size. Hence, data from more cities and sources should be considered in future studies.

Author Contributions: J.Y.: Participated in Conceptualization, methodology, software selection, validation, resources, data curation, formal analysis, writing-original draft preparation, supervision, project administration and funding acquisition. J.J.: Participated in validation, resources, data curation, writing-review and editing, visualization, visualization and supervision. L.G.: Participated in Conceptualization, methodology, validation, formal analysis, investigation, resources, data curation, writing-review and editing, visualization, supervision and project administration. All authors have read and agreed to the published version of the manuscript.

Funding: This research was funded by the National Social Science Foundation of China (Grant number 19CGL062).

Informed Consent Statement: Informed consent was obtained from all subjects involved in the study.

Data Availability Statement: The data set supporting the findings of this study are available in the form of tables and figures in the manuscript file. In case of further information needed it could be obtained from the corresponding author upon reasonable request.

Acknowledgments: We would like to express our deepest heartfelt thanks to Shanyong Wang, Xiaoli Xiang and Jing Cheng for their immense contribution on consulting and giving comments.

Conflicts of Interest: The authors declare no conflict of interest.

References

1. Cheng, Y.; Yu, J.; Shen, Y.; Huang, B. Coproducing Responses to COVID-19 with Community-Based Organizations: Lessons from Zhejiang Province, China. *Public Adm. Rev.* **2020**, *80*, 866–873. [CrossRef] [PubMed]
2. Lee, S.H. The SARS epidemic in Hong Kong: What lessons have we learned? *J. R. Soc. Med.* **2003**, *96*, 374.
3. Tang, M.Y.L.; Chung, P.H.Y.; Chan, H.Y.; Tam, P.K.H.; Wong, K.K. Recent trends in the prevalence of Helicobacter Pylori in symptomatic children: A 12-year retrospective study in a tertiary centre. *J. Pediatr. Surg.* **2019**, *54*, 255–257. [CrossRef] [PubMed]
4. Tam, K.-P.; Lau, I.Y.-M.; Chiu, C.-Y. Biases in the perceived prevalence and motives of severe acute respiratory syndrome prevention behaviors among Chinese high school students in Hong Kong. *Asian J. Soc. Psychol.* **2004**, *7*, 67–81. [CrossRef]
5. Swierad, E.; Vartanian, L.R.; King, M. The Influence of Ethnic and Mainstream Cultures on African Americans' Health Behaviors: A Qualitative Study. *Behav. Sci.* **2017**, *7*, 49. [CrossRef]
6. Delport, W.; Merwe, S.W.V.D. The transmission of Helicobacter pylori: The effects of analysis method and study population on inference. *Best Pract. Res. Clin. Gastroenterol.* **2007**, *21*, 215–236. [CrossRef]
7. Leung, W.; Sung, J.; Ling, T.; Siu, K.; Cheng, A. Does the use of chopsticks for eating transmit Helicobacter pylori? *Lancet* **1997**, *350*, 31. [CrossRef]
8. Bagozzi, R.P.; Lee, K.-H.; Van Loo, M.F. Decisions to donate bone marrow: The role of attitudes and subjective norms across cultures. *Psychol. Health* **2001**, *16*, 29–56. [CrossRef]

9. Zhang, J.; Zhao, A.; Ke, Y.; Huo, S.; Ma, Y.; Zhang, Y.; Ren, Z.; Li, Z.; Liu, K. Dietary Behaviors in the Post-Lockdown Period and Its Effects on Dietary Diversity: The Second Stage of a Nutrition Survey in a Longitudinal Chinese Study in the COVID-19 Era. *Nutrients* **2020**, *12*, 3269. [CrossRef]
10. Wang, W.; Yu, N. Coping with a New Health Culture: Acculturation and Online Health Information Seeking Among Chinese Immigrants in the United States. *J. Immigr. Minor. Health* **2015**, *17*, 1427–1435. [CrossRef]
11. Southwell, B.G.; Yzer, M.C. When (and Why) Interpersonal Talk Matters for Campaigns. *Commun. Theory* **2009**, *19*, 1–8. [CrossRef]
12. Jeong, M.; Bae, R.E. The Effect of Campaign-Generated Interpersonal Communication on Campaign-Targeted Health Outcomes: A Meta-Analysis. *Health Commun.* **2017**, *33*, 988–1003. [CrossRef] [PubMed]
13. Lindell, M.K.; Perry, R.W. The Protective Action Decision Model: Theoretical Modifications and Additional Evidence. *Risk Anal.* **2011**, *32*, 616–632. [CrossRef] [PubMed]
14. Southwell, B.; Yzer, M.C. The Roles of Interpersonal Communication in Mass Media Campaigns. *Ann. Int. Commun. Assoc.* **2007**, *31*, 420–462. [CrossRef]
15. Crook, B.; Stephens, K.K.; Pastorek, A.E.; Mackert, M.; Donovan, E.E. Sharing Health Information and Influencing Behavioral Intentions: The Role of Health Literacy, Information Overload, and the Internet in the Diffusion of Healthy Heart Information. *Health Commun.* **2015**, *31*, 60–71. [CrossRef]
16. Yan, J.; Wei, J.; Zhao, D.; Vinnikova, A.; Li, L.; Wang, S. Communicating Online Diet-Nutrition Information and Influencing Health Behavioral Intention: The Role of Risk Perceptions, Problem Recognition, and Situational Motivation. *J. Health Commun.* **2018**, *23*, 1–10. [CrossRef]
17. Lindell, M.K.; Hwang, S.N. Households' Perceived Personal Risk and Responses in a Multihazard Environment. *Risk Anal.* **2008**, *28*, 539–556. [CrossRef]
18. Lindell, M.K.; Mumpower, J.L.; Huang, S.-K.; Wu, H.-C.; Samuelson, C.D.; Wei, H.-L. Perceptions of protective actions for a water contamination emergency. *J. Risk Res.* **2016**, *20*, 887–908. [CrossRef]
19. Wang, F.; Wei, J.; Huang, S.-K.; Lindell, M.K.; Ge, Y.; Wei, H.-L. Public reactions to the 2013 Chinese H7N9 Influenza outbreak: Perceptions of risk, stakeholders, and protective actions. *J. Risk Res.* **2016**, *21*, 809–833. [CrossRef]
20. Yan, J.; Wei, J.; Ouyang, Z.; Vinnikova, A.; Zhao, D.; Zhang, H. The influence of parents' information processing on childhood vaccine acceptance after a vaccine crisis in China. *Health Risk Soc.* **2019**, *21*, 284–303. [CrossRef]
21. Tan, A.S.; Lee, C.-J.; Bigman, C. Public support for selected e-cigarette regulations and associations with overall information exposure and contradictory information exposure about e-cigarettes: Findings from a national survey of U.S. adults. *Prev. Med.* **2015**, *81*, 268–274. [CrossRef] [PubMed]
22. Jung, M.; Lin, L.; Viswanath, K. Associations between health communication behaviors, neighborhood social capital, vaccine knowledge, and parents' H1N1 vaccination of their children. *Vaccine* **2013**, *31*, 4860–4866. [CrossRef] [PubMed]
23. Jones, K.O.; Denham, B.E.; Springston, J.K. Effects of Mass and Interpersonal Communication on Breast Cancer Screening: Advancing Agenda-Setting Theory in Health Contexts. *J. Appl. Commun. Res.* **2006**, *34*, 94–113. [CrossRef]
24. Wang, S.; Wang, J.; Zhao, S.; Yang, S. Information publicity and resident's waste separation behavior: An empirical study based on the norm activation model. *Waste Manag.* **2019**, *87*, 33–42. [CrossRef] [PubMed]
25. Salmon, C.T. Message Discrimination and the Information Environment. *Commun. Res.* **1986**, *13*, 363–372. [CrossRef]
26. Murdock, M.R.; Rajagopal, P. The sting of social: How emphasizingsocial consequences in warning messages influences perception of risk. *J. Mark. A Q. Publ. Am. Mark. Assoc.* **2017**, *81*, 83–98. [CrossRef]
27. Ferrer, R.A.; Portnoy, D.; Klein, W.M.P. Worry and Risk Perceptions as Independent and Interacting Predictors of Health Protective Behaviors. *J. Health Commun.* **2013**, *18*, 397–409. [CrossRef]
28. Garfin, D.R.; Silver, R.C.; Holman, E.A. The novel coronavirus (COVID-2019) outbreak: Amplification of public health consequences by media exposure. *Health Psychol.* **2020**, *39*, 355–357. [CrossRef]
29. Seo, M.; Matsaganis, M.D. How Interpersonal Communication Mediates the Relationship of Multichannel Communication Connections to Health-Enhancing and Health-Threatening Behaviors. *J. Health Commun.* **2013**, *18*, 1002–1020. [CrossRef]
30. Sudo, A.; Kuroda, Y. Media exposure, interactive health literacy, and adolescents' susceptibility to future smoking. *Int. J. Adolesc. Med. Health* **2015**, *29*, 20150052. [CrossRef]
31. Perettiwatel, P.; Raude, J.; Sagaonteyssier, L.; Constant, A.; Verger, P.; Beck, F. Attitudes toward vaccination and the H1N1 vaccine: Poor people's unfounded fears or legitimate concerns of the elite? *Soc. Sci. Med.* **2014**, *109*, 10–18. [CrossRef] [PubMed]
32. Van Der Heide, I.; Uiters, E.; Rademakers, J.; Struijs, J.N.; Schuit, J.; Baan, C.A. Associations among Health Literacy, Diabetes Knowledge, and Self-Management Behavior in Adults with Diabetes: Results of a Dutch Cross-Sectional Study. *J. Health Commun.* **2014**, *19*, 115–131. [CrossRef] [PubMed]
33. Andrews, J.C.; Netemeyer, R.G.; Burton, S.; Moberg, D.P.; Christiansen, A. Understanding Adolescent Intentions to Smoke: An Examination of Relationships among Social Influence, Prior Trial Behavior, and Antitobacco Campaign Advertising. *J. Mark.* **2004**, *68*, 110–123. [CrossRef]
34. Kreuter, M.W.; McClure, S.M. The role of culture in health communication. *Annu. Rev. Public Health* **2004**, *25*, 439–455. [CrossRef]

35. Schwartz, S.H. Universals in the Content and Structure of Values: Theoretical Advances and Empirical Tests in 20 Countries. *Adv. Exp. Soc. Psychol.* **1992**, *25*, 1–65. [CrossRef]
36. Iwelunmor, J.; Newsome, V.; Airhihenbuwa, C.O. Framing the impact of culture on health: A systematic review of the PEN-3 cultural model and its application in public health research and interventions. *Ethn. Health* **2013**, *19*, 20–46. [CrossRef] [PubMed]
37. Kumanyika, S.; Taylor, W.C.; Grier, S.A.; Lassiter, V.; Lancaster, K.J.; Morssink, C.B.; Renzaho, A.M. Community energy balance: A framework for contextualizing cultural influences on high risk of obesity in ethnic minority populations. *Prev. Med.* **2012**, *55*, 371–381. [CrossRef]
38. Panicker, A.; Basu, K.; Chung, C.-F. Changing Roles and Contexts: Symbolic Interactionism in the Sharing of Food and Eating Practices between Remote, Intergenerational Family Members. *Proc. ACM Hum.-Comput. Interact.* **2020**, *4*, 1–19. [CrossRef]
39. E Chapman, G.; Ristovski-Slijepcevic, S.; Beagan, B.L. Meanings of food, eating and health in Punjabi families living in Vancouver, Canada. *Health Educ. J.* **2010**, *70*, 102–112. [CrossRef]
40. Rowe, J. Voices from the Inside: African American Women's Perspectives on Healthy Lifestyles. *Health Educ. Behav.* **2010**, *37*, 789–800. [CrossRef]
41. Arroyo, A.; Harwood, J. Exploring the Causes and Consequences of Engaging in Fat Talk. *J. Appl. Commun. Res.* **2012**, *40*, 167–187. [CrossRef]
42. Frank, L.B.; Chatterjee, J.S.; Chaudhuri, S.T.; Lapsansky, C.; Bhanot, A.; Murphy, S.T. Conversation and Compliance: Role of Interpersonal Discussion and Social Norms in Public Communication Campaigns. *J. Health Commun.* **2012**, *17*, 1050–1067. [CrossRef] [PubMed]
43. Basu, A.; Dutta, M.J. Sex Workers and HIV/AIDS: Analyzing Participatory Culture-Centered Health Communication Strategies. *Hum. Commun. Res.* **2009**, *35*, 86–114. [CrossRef]
44. Brennan, E.; Durkin, S.J.; Wakefield, M.; Kashima, Y. Why Do Smokers Talk About Antismoking Campaigns? Predictors of the Occurrence and Content of Campaign-Generated Conversations. *Health Commun.* **2016**, *32*, 1539–1556. [CrossRef] [PubMed]
45. Grasso, K.L.; Bell, R.A. Understanding Health Information Seeking: A Test of the Risk Perception Attitude Framework. *J. Health Commun.* **2015**, *20*, 1406–1414. [CrossRef]
46. Helme, D.W.; Noar, S.M.; Allard, S.; Zimmerman, R.S.; Palmgreen, P.; McClanahan, K.J. In-Depth Investigation of Interpersonal Discussions in Response to a Safer Sex Mass Media Campaign. *Health Commun.* **2011**, *26*, 366–378. [CrossRef]
47. Jepsen, A.L. Factors affecting consumer use of the Internet for information search. *J. Interact. Mark.* **2007**, *21*, 21–34. [CrossRef]
48. Fu, H.; Dong, N.; Feng, D.; He, Z.; Tang, S.; Fu, Q.; Feng, Z. To Share or Not to Share: A Cross-Sectional Study on Health Information Sharing and Its Determinants Among Chinese Rural Chronic Patients. *J. Health Commun.* **2017**, *22*, 1–8. [CrossRef]
49. Kim, J.-N.; Grunig, J.E. Problem Solving and Communicative Action: A Situational Theory of Problem Solving. *J. Commun.* **2011**, *61*, 120–149. [CrossRef]
50. Fransen, M.P.; von Wagner, C.; Essink-Bot, M.-L. Diabetes self-management in patients with low health literacy: Ordering findings from literature in a health literacy framework. *Patient Educ. Couns.* **2012**, *88*, 44–53. [CrossRef]
51. Dunlop, S.M.; Kashima, Y.; Wakefield, M. Predictors and Consequences of Conversations About Health Promoting Media Messages. *Commun. Monogr.* **2010**, *77*, 518–539. [CrossRef]
52. Chatterjee, N. AIDS-related information exposure in the mass media and discussion within social networks among married women in Bombay, India. *AIDS Care* **1999**, *11*, 443–446. [CrossRef] [PubMed]
53. Jeong, M.; Tan, A.; Brennan, E.; Gibson, L.; Hornik, R. Talking About Quitting: Interpersonal Communication as a Mediator of Campaign Effects on Smokers' Quit Behaviors. *J. Health Commun.* **2015**, *20*, 1196–1205. [CrossRef] [PubMed]
54. Parks, M.J.; Slater, J.S.; Rothman, A.J.; Nelson, C.L. Interpersonal Communication and Smoking Cessation in the Context of an Incentive-Based Program: Survey Evidence from a Telehealth Intervention in a Low-Income Population. *J. Health Commun.* **2015**, *21*, 125–133. [CrossRef]
55. Si, H.; Shen, L.; Liu, W.; Wu, G. Uncovering people's mask-saving intentions and behaviors in the post-COVID-19 period: Evidence from China. *Sustain. Cities Soc.* **2020**, *65*, 102626. [CrossRef]
56. Shi, H.; Wang, S.; Zhao, D. Exploring urban resident's vehicular PM2.5 reduction behavior intention: An application of the extended theory of planned behavior. *J. Clean. Prod.* **2017**, *147*, 603–613. [CrossRef]
57. Shen, C.; Wang, M.P.; Wan, A.; Viswanath, K.; Chan, S.S.C.; Lam, T.H. Health information exposure from information and communication technologies and its associations with health behaviors: Population-based survey. *Prev. Med.* **2018**, *113*, 140–146. [CrossRef]
58. Karletsos, D.; Hutchinson, P.; Leyton, A.; Meekers, D. The effect of interpersonal communication in tobacco control campaigns: A longitudinal mediation analysis of a Ghanaian adolescent population. *Prev. Med.* **2020**, *142*, 106373. [CrossRef]
59. Gaspar, R.; Luís, S.; Seibt, B.; Lima, M.L.; Marcu, A.; Rutsaert, P.; Fletcher, D.; Verbeke, W.; Barnett, J. Consumers' avoidance of information on red meat risks: Information exposure effects on attitudes and perceived knowledge. *J. Risk Res.* **2014**, *19*, 533–549. [CrossRef]
60. James, W.L.; Hatten, K.J. Further evidence on the validity of the self-typing paragraph approach: Miles and snow strategic archetypes in banking. *Strat. Manag. J.* **1995**, *16*, 161–168. [CrossRef]
61. Anderson, J.C.; Gerbing, D.W. Structural equation modeling in practice: A review and recommended two-step approach. *Psychol. Bull.* **1988**, *103*, 411–423. [CrossRef]
62. Nunnally, J.C.; Bernstein, I.H. Psychometric Theory. *Am. Educ. Res. J.* **1994**, *5*, 83.

63. Yan, J.; Ouyang, Z.; Vinnikova, A.; Chen, M. Avoidance of the Threats of Defective Vaccines: How a Vaccine Scandal Influences Parents' Protective Behavioral Response. *Health Commun.* **2020**, *36*, 962–971. [CrossRef] [PubMed]
64. Fadyl, J.K. How can societal culture and values influence health and rehabilitation outcomes? *Expert Rev. Pharm. Outcomes Res.* **2020**, *21*, 5–8. [CrossRef] [PubMed]

International Journal of
Environmental Research and Public Health

MDPI

Article

Tuberculosis among People Living on the Street and Using Alcohol, Tobacco, and Illegal Drugs: Analysis of Territories in Extreme Vulnerability and Trends in Southern Brazil

Alessandro Rolim Scholze [1,*], Josilene Dália Alves [2], Thaís Zamboni Berra [1], Antônio Carlos Vieira Ramos [1], Flávia Meneguetti Pieri [3], Sandra Cristina Pillon [4], Júlia Trevisan Martins [3], Maria José Quina Galdino [5], Emiliana Cristina Melo [5], Felipe Mendes Delpino [1], Ariela Fehr Tártaro [1], Inês Fronteira [6] and Ricardo Alexandre Arcêncio [1]

1 Department of Maternal-Infant and Public Health Nursing, Ribeirão Preto College of Nursing, University of São Paulo, Ribeirão Preto 14040-902, Brazil; thais.berra@usp.br (T.Z.B.); antonio.ramos@usp.br (A.C.V.R.); felipedelpino@usp.br (F.M.D.); ariela.fehr@gmail.com (A.F.T.); ricardo@eerp.usp.br (R.A.A.)
2 Institute of Biological Sciences and Health, Federal University of Mato Grosso, Barra do Garças 78605-091, Brazil; josilene.alves@ufmt.br
3 Department of Nursing, State University of Londrina, Londrina 86057-970, Brazil; fpieri@uel.br (F.M.P.); jtmartins@uel.br (J.T.M.)
4 Department of Psychiatric Nursing and Human Sciences, Ribeirão Preto College of Nursing, University of São Paulo, Ribeirão Preto 14040-902, Brazil; pillon@eerp.usp.br
5 Department of Nursing, State University of Northern Paraná, Bandeirantes 86360-000, Brazil; mariagaldino@uenp.edu.br (M.J.Q.G.); ecmelo@uenp.edu.br (E.C.M.)
6 Global Health and Tropical Medicine, Instituto de Higiene e Medicina Tropical, University Nova de Lisboa, 1349-008 Lisboa, Portugal; ifronteira@ihmt.unl.pt
* Correspondence: scholze@uenp.edu.br; Tel.: +55-(43)-99602-8846

Citation: Scholze, A.R.; Alves, J.D.; Berra, T.Z.; Ramos, A.C.V.; Pieri, F.M.; Pillon, S.C.; Martins, J.T.; Galdino, M.J.Q.; Melo, E.C.; Delpino, F.M.; et al. Tuberculosis among People Living on the Street and Using Alcohol, Tobacco, and Illegal Drugs: Analysis of Territories in Extreme Vulnerability and Trends in Southern Brazil. *Int. J. Environ. Res. Public Health* **2022**, *19*, 7721. https://doi.org/10.3390/ijerph19137721

Academic Editor: Paul B. Tchounwou

Received: 26 March 2022
Accepted: 21 June 2022
Published: 23 June 2022

Abstract: (1) Background: Tuberculosis presents an epidemiological trend toward inequality, especially among people in social exclusion and situations of vulnerability. This study aimed to analyze territories with a concentration of people diagnosed with tuberculosis in a street situation and who partake in chronic use of alcohol, tobacco, and illicit drugs. We also analyzed trends in this health condition in southern Brazil. (2) Methods: Ecological study, developed in the 399 municipalities of Paraná, southern Brazil, with all tuberculosis cases in the homeless population registered in the Information System of Notifiable Diseases between 2014 and 2018. For data analysis, we used descriptive statistics, the Prais–Winsten autoregression method for the time series, and the Getis-Ord Gi technique* for spatial analysis. (3) Results: in total, 560 cases were reported. We found a predominance of alcohol, smoking, and illicit drug users, with an increasing trend in the state and clusters of spatial risk in the East health macro-region. (4) Conclusions: We observed territories with critical levels of highly vulnerable people who use psychoactive substances and are in a street situation. The results highlight the importance of incorporating public policies of social protection for these individuals and resolutive health services that receive these cases and assist in eradicating TB.

Keywords: tuberculosis; vulnerable populations; homeless persons; substance-related disorders

1. Introduction

Tuberculosis (TB) is an infectious disease caused by *Mycobacterium tuberculosis*. Considered a serious public health problem, it is among the ten most common causes of preventable death in the world [1–3]. Historically, TB presents an epidemiological trend toward inequality, especially among people in social exclusion and situations of vulnerability [4]. Thus, the homeless population, the population deprived of liberty (PPL), people infected with human immunodeficiency virus (HIV), and users or addicts of psychoactive substances, alcohol, tobacco, and other drugs [5,6] are considered at high risk of contributing to the spread of this disease.

In this sense, the homeless population is defined as a heterogeneous population that has extreme poverty, interrupted or weakened family ties, and the absence of regular conventional housing in common. This population uses public spaces and degraded areas as a living and subsistence space, temporarily or permanently, as well as reception units for temporary accommodation or as temporary housing [7].

Being homeless is an aggravating factor for the spread of TB in social exclusion groups since TB infection is transmitted via the respiratory route by inhaling the sputum droplets expelled by an infected person [6]. Given the social situation of homeless people, there may be a considerable spread of the disease among them since they tend to congregate in groups. Especially among the homeless population, TB has a high prevalence due to close contact within a large contingent of homeless people and frequent movement between different shelters and territories [8].

In addition, most infected people do not present signs and symptoms of the disease and are classified as carriers of latent infection by TB. The absence of signs and symptoms prevents the search for treatment and intensifies the spread of the disease. It is estimated that approximately 2 to 3 billion people in the world are infected with TB, and of these, about 5% to 15% will evolve to active TB during their lifetime [9,10]. Studies point out that TB among the homeless population is the third-largest cause of illness and has a 10 to 85 times higher rate of developing into latent or active TB infection when compared with the general population [11]. In the United States, about 5% of TB cases have been homeless at some point in the 12 months prior to diagnosis [12].

Among individuals diagnosed with TB in the United States, the incidence rate is 36 to 47 cases per 100 inhabitants, compared to the incidence in the general population of 2.8 cases per 100 inhabitants [13]. In Germany, TB in the homeless has 30 cases per 100 inhabitants, compared to the general population of 18 cases per 100 inhabitants [8]. In western Europe, the prevalence of TB among homeless people ranges from 1% to 2% for active TB infection and up to 45% for latent infection [14].

TB among the homeless population is a challenge since even those countries with low endemicity show a high TB incidence among homeless people. This factor contributes to the maintenance of the TB burden in these countries, thus making it difficult to achieve the goals established by the End TB strategy.

This evidence indicates that vulnerable populations have become a major challenge for countries to develop strategies and achieve their TB elimination goals globally. In social epidemiology, there are several resources available that demonstrate the strength of the social determinants of territories in the TB progression chain, with a large number of studies using spatial analysis in the general population. However, this is not the reality for the homeless population since an address is an aspect required for geoprocessing/georeferencing; as such, many studies using these approaches exclude this population.

Another gap is that vulnerability is multifaceted. Within the same context, many vulnerabilities end up countering each other, causing cases to become overly complex, requiring equally complex approaches toward alleviating suffering and bringing solutions to the problem. Given the presented problems, the present study is of great importance. It brings together the question of territories and the homeless population with TB and the relationship with alcohol, tobacco, and illicit drugs; as a result, disease control is far from being achieved in some regions and territories. Therefore, this study aimed to analyze territories where there is a concentration of people diagnosed with tuberculosis, in a street situation, and who partake in chronic use of alcohol, tobacco, and illicit drugs. We also analyzed trends in this health condition in southern Brazil.

2. Materials and Methods

2.1. Study Design

Ecological study [15].

2.2. Study Location and Population

This study was carried out in the 399 municipalities of Paraná, located in the southern region of Brazil at the geographic coordinates 24°59′ S latitude and 53°56′ W longitude; the estimated population is 11.34 million inhabitants. It is the fifteenth state of Brazil with the largest national territory and the fifth-highest population [5].

In 2020, Paraná had 2190 TB cases, obtaining an incidence of 19 cases per 100,000 inhabitants; there were 157 deaths, with an incidence of 1.4 per 100,000 inhabitants. About 6.2% of patients abandon treatment [3].

According to the Inter-sector Committee for Monitoring and Monitoring the Population Policy in Street Situation (CIAMP Street/PR), which aims to enable and assist in the implementation and monitoring of public policies aimed at the population in a street situation, it is estimated that, in 2021, the state had about 8,659 people registered at CIAMP street/PR. It is noteworthy that this may be an under notification, indicating that the number should be higher, mainly due to the current situation in the country, as well as the high turnover of homeless people. Between 2015 and 2020, the state showed a 65% increase in TB cases in the homeless population, and in 2020, a 6.8% increase in the percentage of cases [16].

To develop the spatial distribution, we subdivided the 399 municipalities that make up the state of Paraná into four health macro-regions (East, North, Northwest, and West) and used these as a unit of geographical analysis. Figure 1 illustrates the location of the state and its health macro-regions.

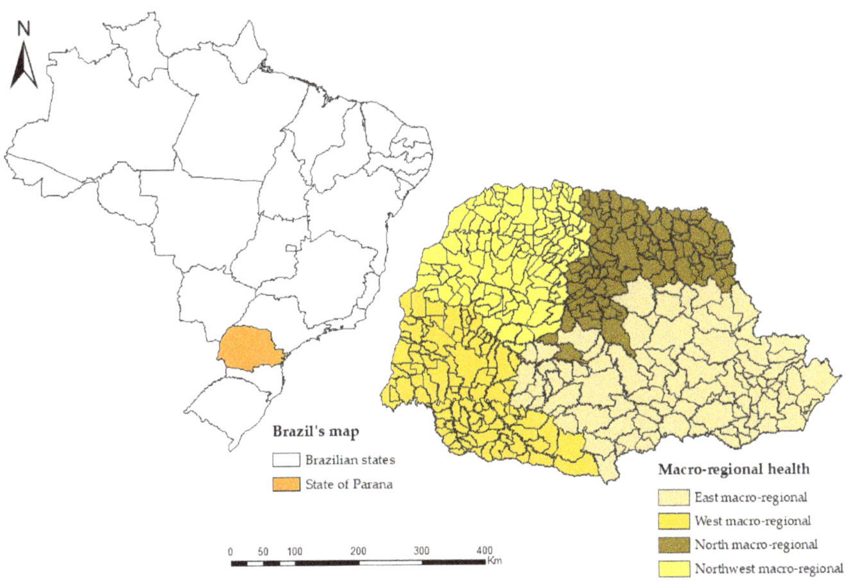

Figure 1. Geographical location of health macro-regions according to municipalities in the state of Paraná.

2.3. Inclusion Criteria

We considered all cases of TB in the homeless population obtained in the Information System of Notifiable Diseases (SINAN) from 2014 to 2018. These data were made available by the Health Department of the State of Paraná in an electronic spreadsheet in Excel.

The adopted inclusion criteria were people diagnosed with TB, included in the notification form as a person living on the street, alcohol, tobacco, or illicit drug user, and aged 18 years or older. To identify risk areas and time series, the population was subdivided into general TB, TB alcoholism, TB smoking, and TB users of illicit drugs. It is emphasized that an individual may belong simultaneously to one or more study groups.

2.4. Analysis Plan

First, the descriptive statistics of the data were performed utilizing absolute and relative frequency, which used the following variables: alcoholism, smoking, and illicit drugs, sex, age group, race/color and education, TB/HIV coinfection, diabetes mellitus, mental disorder, and data related to the clinical profile of TB, such as type of entry, form, radiography, sputum smear, histopathology, molecular test, and case closure. It should be noted that the terminologies described in the Sinan notification form were kept in full; it should be noted that this form is a structured document recommended by the Ministry of Health and applies throughout the national territory of Brazil.

The IBM SPSS software version 25 was used to analyze the data.

2.5. Time Series

Time series are characterized as observations taken sequentially over time [17]. It is worth noting that the temporal trend refers to the direction in which the time series develops according to a determined time interval, which may follow a growth, decrease, or stationary pattern [18,19]. The month and year of notification of TB cases were used to perform the analysis.

The Prais–Winsten autoregression method [18] was performed in STATA software, version 14, to classify the event's temporal trend as increasing, decreasing, or stationary in the study period. When the temporal trend was classified as increasing or decreasing, the percentage of monthly variation (MPC—monthly percent change) and their respective 95% confidence intervals (95 CI) were calculated [17].

Next, we used the robust time series decomposition method called seasonal trend by Loess (STL by Loess) [16]. This decomposition method is based on a locally weighted regression (Loess). It is the method used to estimate nonlinear relations, managing to separate the components that make up a time series: trend, seasonality, and noise [19,20]. For the analysis, RStudio software and the forecast package were used.

In contrast to the Prais–Winsten method, where the time trend assessment is global and a constant is generated by classifying the whole period under study, the STL method allows for the evaluation of the time trend over the whole period under analysis, notes variations over time, checks if the trend has always been increasing/decreasing/stationary, or if there have been periods of variations with peaks and/or decreases.

2.6. Spatial Analysis

The techniques called Getis-Ord General G and Getis-Ord Gi* were used to identify whether clusters were formed, using the number of cases per municipality. The Getis-Ord General G technique is based on the Moran Global Index, and, as in inferential statistics, the results are based on the null hypothesis that there is no spatial grouping. If p is significant, the null hypothesis can be rejected, and the z-score value becomes important, where its values of ± 3 represent a 99% confidence level [21,22]. If the z-score value is positive, the observed G-Index is higher than expected, indicating high event indices grouped in the area under study. A negative z-score value of the G-index is considered lower than the expected index, indicating that low values are grouped in the study area [23].

The Getis-Ord Gi* technique indicates a local association, considering the values for each census tract from a neighborhood matrix. In this analysis, a z-score was generated for statistically significant municipalities, and the higher the z-score, the more intense the grouping of high values is (hotspot). The logic is the same for the z-negative score, i.e., the lower the z-score, the more intense the grouping of low values (cold spot) [23].

In addition to the z-score, the *p*-value and significance level (Gi-Bin) are also provided, which identify statistically significant hot and cold spots. The values may vary between $+/-$ 3 and reflect statistical significance with a confidence level of 99%, $+/-$ 2 with a confidence level of 95%, and +/− 1 with a confidence level of 90%, with a zero-value corresponding to non-statistically significant areas [23].

2.7. Ethical Aspects

The study was approved by the Research Ethics Committee of the *Escola de Enfermagem de Ribeirão Preto da Universidade de São Paulo*, under CAAE (Process number: 24963319.1.0000.5393).

3. Results

Between 2014 and 2018, 560 cases of TB were reported among the homeless population. The analysis showed that the consumption of psychoactive substances was prevalent in homeless users (n = 420; 36.30%), as were smokers (n = 382; 33.02%), and users of other drugs (n = 355; 30.68%).

Table 1 shows the characterization of TB cases in the homeless population subdivided by type of psychoactive substance. The total sample showed a higher predominance of TB in males, in the age group above 40 years of white race/color, with education from the fifth to eighth grade of elementary school, and living in the urban perimeter. The sociodemographic characteristics of the homeless population of users of alcohol, tobacco, and illicit drugs are similar to that of the general homeless population. Some peculiarities were noted, such as one-third of alcohol and tobacco users had a poor education (first to fourth grade), 43.1% (n = 153) of other drug users were younger (30 to 39 years of age) when compared to alcohol users (50.2%; n = 211) and tobacco (47.1%; n = 180) users, who were in the age group of 40 years or older. Notably, 73.7% (n = 412) of the general street population who had TB did not receive government benefits. Regarding the presence of chronic diseases, it was observed that TB-AIDS coinfection was the most prevalent among all variables studied, followed by the categories "other diseases" and mental illness.

Table 1. Sociodemographic characterization of tuberculosis cases in the homeless population of the state of Paraná, Brazil (2014–2018).

Variables	Street Population Using Alcohol		Street Population Using Tobacco		Street Population Using Illicit Drugs		General Street Population	
	n	%	*n*	%	*n*	%	*n*	%
Gender								
Male	362	82.3	318	83.2	281	79.2	472	84.4
Female	58	13.2	64	16.8	74	20.8	87	15.6
Age group								
18 to 29 years	61	14.5	65	17.0	77	21.7	97	17.4
30 to 39 years	148	35.2	137	35.9	153	43.1	197	35.2
40 or more	211	50.2	180	47.1	125	35.2	265	47.4
Race								
White	217	51.7	197	51.6	180	50.7	292	52.2
Black	51	12.1	47	12.3	39	11.0	61	10.9
Yellow	2	0.5	1	0.3	4	1.1	4	0.7
Brown	143	34.0	125	32.7	122	34.4	183	32.7
Indigenous	1	0.2	1	0.3	1	0.3	2	0.4
Schooling								
Illiterate	11	2.6	11	2.9	11	3.1	17	3.0
First to fourth grade	126	30.0	111	29.1	84	23.7	149	26.7
Fifth to eighth grade	112	26.7	103	27.0	108	30.4	157	28.1
> Eight years of study	39	9.3	41	10.7	35	9.9	55	9.8
Housing perimeter								
Urban	367	87.4	334	87.4	323	91.0	485	86.8

Table 1. *Cont.*

Variables	Street Population Using Alcohol		Street Population Using Tobacco		Street Population Using Illicit Drugs		General Street Population	
	n	%	*n*	%	*n*	%	*n*	%
Rural	16	3.8	16	4.2	10	2.8	25	4.5
Periurban	1	0.2	-	-	-	-	2	0.4
Government benefit								
Yes	22	5.2	24	6.3	24	6.8	39	7.0
No	312	74.3	288	75.4	266	74.9	412	73.7
Alcoholism								
Yes	420	100.0	318	83.2	284	80.0	420	75.1
No	-	-	56	14.7	60	16.9	118	21.1
Smoking								
Yes	318	75.7	382	100.0	274	77.2	382	68.3
No	82	19.5	-	-	65	18.3	140	25.0
Other drugs								
Yes	284	67.6	274	71.7	355	100.0	355	63.5
No	110	26.2	94	24.6	-	-	163	29.2
HIV/AIDS								
Yes	110	26.2	106	27.7	117	33.0	153	27.4
No	291	69.3	258	67.5	224	63.1	378	67.6
Diabetes mellitus								
Yes	15	3.6	14	3.7	11	3.1	19	3.4
No	389	92.6	354	92.7	331	93.2	511	91.4
Mental illness								
Yes	28	6.7	28	7.3	26	7.3	36	6.4
No	371	88.3	338	88.5	310	87.3	487	87.1
Other diseases								
Yes	50	11.9	46	12.0	41	11.5	64	11.4
No	287	68.3	263	68.8	245	69.0	389	69.6

Regarding the clinical profile of TB cases in the homeless population (Table 2), in the general street population, there was a prevalence of new cases, pulmonary TB, with suspect chest radiography, positive sputum culture, histopathology not performed, HIV negative test, molecular tests not performed, sensitivity tests not reported, and curative TB treatment. When analyzing the clinical profile of cases associated with the type of drug, it was found that the same specificities of the total population occurred, noting that, regarding the closure situation, abandonment and death due to TB and other causes were more present among patients who used alcohol, tobacco, and other drugs.

Table 2. Clinical profile of tuberculosis cases in the homeless population of the state of Paraná, Brazil (2014–2018).

Variables	Street Population Using Alcohol		Street Population Using Tobacco		Street Population Using Illicit Drugs		General Street Population	
	n	%	*n*	%	*n*	%	*n*	%
Type of entry								
New case	256	61.0	232	60.7	217	61.1	351	62.8
Recurrence	37	8.8	33	8.6	31	8.7	46	8.2
Reentry after loss to follow-up	80	19.0	73	19.1	72	20.3	102	18.2
Do not know	2	0.5	-	-	2	0.6	3	0.5
Transfer	41	9.8	41	10.7	31	8.7	51	9.1
Clinical form								
Pulmonary	378	90.0	343	89.8	313	88.2	504	90.2

Table 2. *Cont.*

Variables	Street Population Using Alcohol		Street Population Using Tobacco		Street Population Using Illicit Drugs		General Street Population	
	n	%	*n*	%	*n*	%	*n*	%
Extrapulmonary	20	4.8	17	4.5	19	5.4	24	4.3
Pulmonary + extrapulmonary	22	5.2	22	5.8	23	6.5	31	5.5
Chest radiography								
Suspect	356	84.8	329	86.1	292	82.3	466	83.4
Normal	7	1.7	5	1.3	7	2.0	9	1.6
Other pathology	1	0.2	1	0.3	1	0.3	1	0.2
Not performed	52	12.4	43	11.3	52	14.6	78	14.0
Sputum smear microscopy								
Positive	265	63.1	247	64.7	222	62.5	359	64.2
Negative	63	15.0	62	16.2	52	14.6	85	15.2
Not performed	88	21.0	71	18.6	78	22.0	110	19.7
Sputum culture								
Positive	168	40.0	153	40.1	145	40.8	221	39.5
Negative	80	19.0	82	21.5	77	21.7	106	19.0
In progress	15	3.6	14	3.7	11	3.1	18	3.2
Not performed	157	37.4	133	34.8	122	34.4	214	38.3
Histopathology								
Baar positive	46	11.0	45	11.8	41	11.5	67	12.0
Suggestive of TB	12	2.9	10	2.6	9	2.5	14	2.5
Non-suggestive of TB	2	0.5	3	0.8	4	1.1	4	0.7
In progress	12	2.9	9	2.4	6	1.7	13	2.3
Not performed	343	81.7	311	81.4	291	82.0	454	81.2
HIV test								
Positive	113	26.9	107	28.0	120	33.8	156	27.9
Negative	270	64.3	247	64.7	208	58.6	352	63.0
Not performed	36	8.6	27	7.1	27	7.6	50	8.9
Final status								
Cure	152	36.2	149	39.0	114	32.1	200	35.8
Primary abandonment	13	3.1	10	2.6	10	2.8	14	2.5
Abandonment	91	21.7	85	22.3	85	23.9	137	24.5
Death by TB	31	7.4	26	6.8	23	6.5	39	7.0
Death from other causes	44	10.5	36	9.4	39	11.0	52	9.3
Transference	68	16.2	64	16.8	67	18.9	91	16.3
TB-DR	12	2.9	10	2.6	8	2.3	13	2.3
Molecular testing								
Detectable at rifampin	112	26.7	107	28.0	108	30.4	158	28.3
Detectable rifampin resistant	9	2.1	6	1.6	8	2.3	11	2.0
Undetectable	13	3.1	13	3.4	11	3.1	14	2.5
Inconclusive	6	1.4	5	1.3	4	1.1	6	1.1
Not performed	262	62.4	235	61.5	213	60.0	344	61.5
Not reported	18	4.3	16	4.2	11	3.1	26	4.7
Sensitivity test								
Resistant to isoniazid only	6	1.4	6	1.6	3	0.8	7	1.3
Resistance to rifampin only	2	0.5	1	0.3	2	0.6	3	0.5
Resistant to isoniazid and rifampin	4	1.0	4	1.0	2	0.6	5	0.9
Resistant to other first line drugs	3	0.7	4	1.0	4	1.1	4	0.7
Sensitive	74	17.6	66	17.3	62	17.5	98	17.5
In progress	6	1.4	7	1.8	4	1.1	8	1.4
Not performed	61	14.5	51	13.4	45	12.7	77	13.8
Not reported	264	62.9	243	63.6	233	65.6	357	63.9

The temporal trend of TB cases in the homeless population (Table 3) presented an increasing scenario for all categories analyzed. For the population using alcohol, the growth was 29.71% per month (95% CI 18.03–42.56), tobacco 27.93% per month (95% CI 16.68–39.95), other drugs 30.31% per month (95% CI 18.57–43.21), and general drugs 38.35% (95% CI 23.31–55.23).

Table 3. Temporal trend of tuberculosis incidence in the street population according to the consumption of psychoactive substances, Paraná, Brazil (2014–2018).

Variable	Coefficient (CI * 95%)	Temporal Trend	MPC ** (CI95%)
Street population using alcohol	2.47 (1.50–3.54)	Crescent	29.71 (18.03–42.56)
Street population using tobacco	3.32 (1.39–3.32)	Crescent	27.93 (16.68–39.95)
Street population of illicit drugs	2.52 (1.54–3.60)	Crescent	30.31 (18.57–43.21)
General street population	3.19 (1.94–4.60)	Crescent	38.35 (23.31–55.23)

* Confidence interval ** Monthly percent change.

Figure 2 shows the time series decomposition technique. We found an increase in the temporal trend of TB cases in the homeless population for alcohol, tobacco, and other drugs and in the general street population. We identified slight fluctuations of the temporal trend concerning the number of cases over the months, thus corroborating the findings presented in Table 1 referring to the Prais–Winsten analysis.

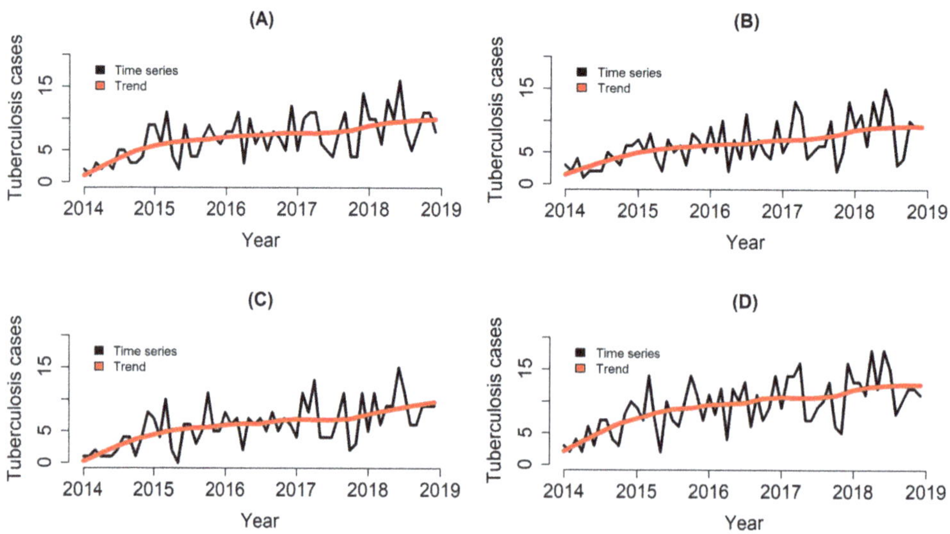

Figure 2. Time series of the homeless population diagnosed with tuberculosis in the state of Paraná, Brazil (2014–2018). (**A**) Alcohol; (**B**) Tobacco; (**C**) Illicit drugs; (**D**) General street population.

For the results of the global spatial association (G), we observed that the values of the z-score and the pseudo-significance test confirmed the non-randomness of TB cases in the population using alcohol (z-score of 3.00 and $p < 0.00$), tobacco (z-score 3.12 and $p < 0.00$), illicit drugs (z-score 2.79 and $p < 0.00$), and general drugs (total) (z-score 3.78 and $p < 0.00$). Figure 3 shows the local spatial association (Gi*) of TB cases, which shows hotspots in the Eastern macro-region in the metropolitan region of Curitiba for users of alcohol, tobacco, and illicit drugs and in the general street population.

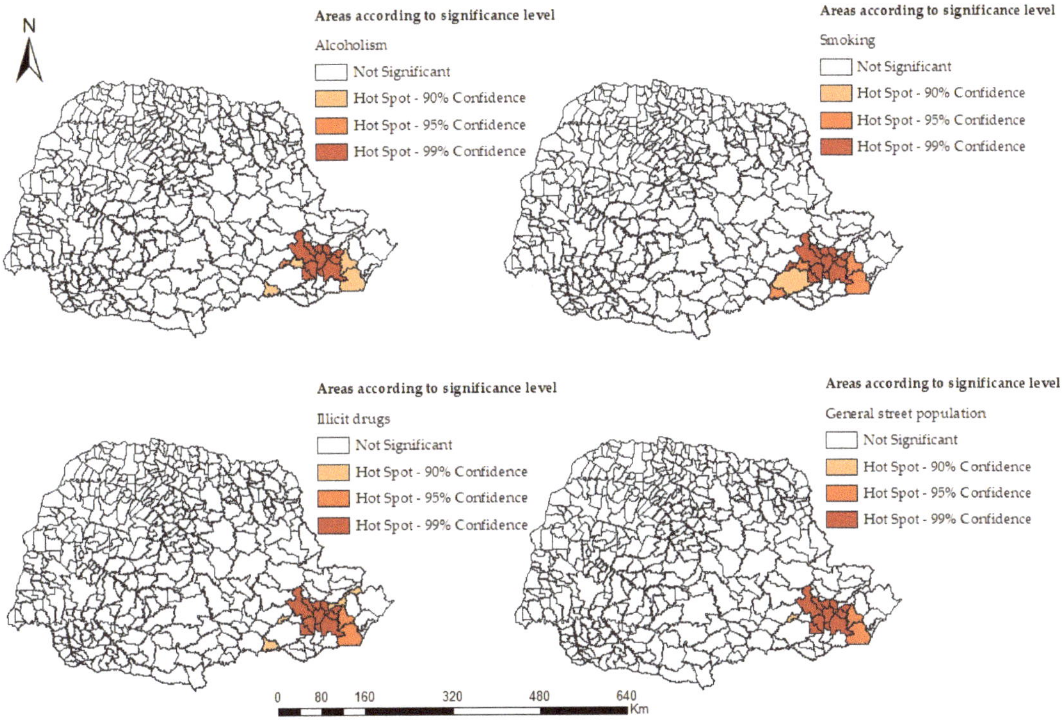

Figure 3. High clusters and low clusters of tuberculosis cases in the homeless population in the state of Paraná, Brazil (2014–2018).

4. Discussion

We analyzed territories with a concentration of people diagnosed with tuberculosis, in a homeless situation, and who partake in the chronic use of alcohol, tobacco, and illicit drugs; we also assessed the trends of this health condition in southern Brazil. We observed that, in the south of Brazil, despite being considered one of the most developed regions of the country, there were still clusters or areas of the population with extreme vulnerability, people diagnosed with TB, using psychoactive substances, and still on the street. There was also a growing increase in this situation in the East health macro-region (metropolitan region of Curitiba, the state capital).

International and national studies indicate that the homeless population has a high prevalence of TB associated with the use of alcohol, tobacco, and illicit drugs, which are risk factors that favor the development of new cases and the maintenance of the TB transmission cycle [4,8,24]. Thus, the homeless population has a 48 to 67 times greater chance of developing TB when compared to the general population [25].

A study conducted in the United States between 2006 and 2010 found that the annual incidence of TB among the homeless population ranged from 36 to 47 cases per 100,000 inhabitants [26]. In Germany, the incidence of TB is 30 cases per 100,00 inhabitants [8], whereas, in Brazil, there are no specific data that address this population.

It is worth noting that Brazil does not have official data on the size of the homeless population, considering that the demographic census does not include homeless residents in the investigation. Since these data are collected in fixed residences, it is impossible to correctly quantify these individuals, which makes them invisible [27].

The high prevalence of TB in this population is related to precarious urbanization, sanitary conditions (close contact with a contingent of people and movement between different shelters), social exclusion, and extreme poverty [28]. These individuals experience a highly vulnerable environment on a daily basis, which leads to health problems and infections, including TB [8]. This population also has high rates of avoidable death from all causes compared to the general population, which exemplifies the influence of inequalities and social determinants of health in the illness process of these individuals [29].

In addition, this population has specificities that favor the development of health problems, such as poor education, which consequently generates ignorance regarding primary health care and the health-disease process. Moreover, many have difficulties in accessing health services, experience stigma, prejudice, conflicting or nonexistent family ties, and the lack of a life project, among other factors [4,28].

The homeless population presents a deficit in self-care concerning hygiene and eating habits, which contributes to a precarious lifestyle and a high prevalence of complications due to chronic diseases, infectious conditions, and injuries related to violence [30]. Therefore, strategic actions should be implemented for the coverage and supply of health services, social assistance, and effective housing to these individuals so that basic human needs are guaranteed.

When evaluating the spatial determinants and the conformation of the clusters when applying the Getis-Ord Gi* technique, clusters of hotspots were identified in the East health macro-region. It is estimated that, in Brazil, there is a population of approximately 100,000 homeless and that 75% of this population lives in municipalities with more than 100,000 inhabitants [27].

Access to housing is understood as an important determinant of health, and homelessness is directly related to an increase in morbidity and mortality compared to the sheltered population. Mortality among the homeless population is 3 to 11 times higher [31].

In addition, it can be highlighted that mobility among homeless people, loss of follow-up, lack of attendance to follow-up appointments, unstable housing, incarceration, fear of invasive investigations and the side effects of TB treatment, transportation and location of health services, lack of flexible hours of care, and problems with remembering commitments and the correct use of medicines are some barriers that hinder a favorable outcome of TB treatment among the homeless population and users/addicts of psychoactive substances [32].

It is necessary to recognize the magnitude of the public health problem present in large cities among the street population and to implement public policies aimed at this heterogeneous group that is in extreme social vulnerability [33,34]. Thus, implementing policies in terms of social support and reintegration of the street population into society is extremely important, as are programs aimed at income distribution, such as the *Bolsa Família* Program. The Bolsa Família Program aims to provide income to families in poverty and extreme poverty. The aid seeks to overcome the situation of vulnerability and poverty, thus ensuring the right to food and access to education and health [35]. The implementation of the Bolsa Família Program provided an increase in the rate of adherence and cure of patients with TB, highlighting the need to implement policies aimed at social support [36].

Another behavior analyzed in this study was that TB is growing among alcohol, tobacco, and illicit drug users. This result is extremely important since the higher the consumption of psychoactive substances by the homeless population, the worse the prognosis of these individuals; other problems include maintenance, increased incidence, and the recurrence of new cases of TB and drug-resistant TB TB-DR. In addition, homeless people who use psychoactive substances move through spaces/territories with a high number of individuals, a characteristic that contributes to a greater spread of the disease.

Therefore, the use of psychoactive substances is considered an aggravating and complicating factor for the containment and eradication of TB in the world. It is noteworthy that the Sustainable Development Goals of the World Health Organization reinforce the importance of implementing prevention and treatment of disorders related to the use of alcohol and other drugs among vulnerable populations [37].

In this sense, investing in public policies, health services targeted at vulnerable populations, and skilled professionals can be an effective tool for early diagnosis, correct treatment, a decrease in the incidence of TB, guaranteed access to health services and social support, and a direction for the social reintegration of individuals who are on the street.

Moreover, the use of psychoactive substances among vulnerable populations promotes community transmission and TB contamination since these individuals live in an environment of extreme sanitary prevarication and share objects and materials such as pipes and needles to make use of psychoactive substances. This characteristic contributes to the spread and dissemination of latent and active TB in these territories [38].

It was also observed that the worst outcomes in treatment and death were present in vulnerable populations that used or were dependent on any substance. Therefore, the vulnerable population has a high TB infectivity rate and thus makes it a strategic population for actions aimed at eradicating TB in the world. Developing public policies aimed at vulnerable populations is a way to contain the spread of the disease in these territories [33,39] and thus achieve the goals established through the End TB strategy.

In order to reduce the infection rate and decrease the number of new cases of TB or relapses, countries need to develop specific strategies aimed at vulnerable populations, such as users of alcohol, tobacco, and other drugs, whereas by implementing health actions directed at these individuals, it is possible to ensure early detection and diagnosis of TB and, consequently, effective treatment [39]. It should be emphasized that countries need to act and invest in research to highlight the territories with the greatest risk of illness and thus identify why people get sick in different territorial regions [40].

Ensuring health services that are responsive and targeted to vulnerable populations is of utmost importance, as is ensuring reception and, consequently, providing the correct sequence during treatment. However, what is observed in health services is a barrier to access and health care for vulnerable populations, which makes these people invisible to the public health system and contributes to the maintenance of TB and other health problems [41].

Strategies that can enhance and provide more comprehensive health care to these populations are the incorporation of health services within vulnerable territories and the implementation of street offices and health care within prisons. The purpose of street offices is to expand the access of the homeless population to health services and to provide comprehensive health care to individuals who are in vulnerable conditions or with fragile family ties [41,42].

The street office has a work dynamic that allows for the active search for people living on the street in several places in the city, valuing welcoming and the creation of links in order to supply the needs of these individuals, without judgment or social standards, and guaranteeing them the right to health advocated in the constitution [43].

It is also relevant to consider the implementation in the country of networks that seek better social protection for vulnerable populations, considering that, when investing in measures that aid equity in health and poverty reduction, a reversal will occur in the context of morbidity and mortality of TB. This strategy is emphasized and recommended by the World Health Organization.

Another measure to be adopted is the incorporation of health policies aimed at reducing the consumption of psychoactive substances in vulnerable territories and throughout society. One aim is the development of prevention and promotion actions related to early consumption among children and adolescents, promoting actions in vulnerable populations, and, in general, a conscious consumption of the substance; by incorporating measures aimed at conscious consumption, this factor reduces exposure to risk, as well as health problems [16].

When analyzing the strategies used to control TB in other countries, it was found that, in the United States, actions such as monetary incentives and education programs are implemented to improve adherence to treatment since these measures help in adherence to treatment and contribute to a better level of treatment completion and thus interruption of the TB transmission cycle [44].

Another feature that helps to reduce the risk of infection and improves the chance of successful treatment is the implementation of programs focused on the health education of the homeless population. In other words, the development of early interventions aimed at preventing TB infection, promoting early diagnosis, and reducing treatment abandonment, drug-resistant TB, and death.

Finally, this study provides significant contributions and joins the global effort to control TB since it was possible to incorporate statistical methods that identified areas of spatial risk for TB among users dependent on alcohol, tobacco, and illicit drugs.

5. Conclusions

This study advances scientific knowledge since few studies have addressed the geoepidemiology of TB between the homeless population and the relation of chronic use of alcohol, tobacco, and illicit drugs. In this sense, it was possible to highlight territories at risk for the development of TB in the homeless population and their relationship with the territories that have a large number of people.

It is necessary to incorporate public policies of social protection for these individuals and resolutive, welcoming health services that will assist in eradicating TB.

Author Contributions: Conceptualization, A.R.S., J.D.A. and R.A.A.; methodology, A.R.S., J.D.A., T.Z.B., F.M.P. and R.A.A.; software, A.R.S. and A.C.V.R.; formal analysis, A.R.S., J.D.A., T.Z.B., A.C.V.R., I.F. and R.A.A.; investigation, A.R.S.; data curation, A.R.S., J.D.A., T.Z.B., A.C.V.R. and R.A.A.; writing—original draft preparation, A.R.S.; writing—review and editing, A.R.S., F.M.P., S.C.P., J.T.M., M.J.Q.G., E.C.M., F.M.D., F.M.P., A.F.T., I.F. and R.A.A.; supervision, R.A.A.; project administration, A.R.S. All authors have read and agreed to the published version of the manuscript.

Funding: This research received no external funding.

Institutional Review Board Statement: The study was approved by the Research Ethics Committee of the Escola de Enfermagem de Ribeirão Preto da Universidade de São Paulo, under CAAE (Process number: 24963319.1.0000.5393).

Informed Consent Statement: Consent was waived for all subjects involved in the study.

Data Availability Statement: The data presented in this study are available on request from the corresponding author on reasonable request.

Conflicts of Interest: The authors declare no conflict of interest.

References

1. Adjobimey, M.; Ade, S.; Wachinou, P.; Esse, M.; Yaha, L.; Bekou, W.; Campbell, J.R.; Toundoh, N.; Adjibode, O.; Attikpa, G.; et al. Prevalence, acceptability, and cost of routine screening for pulmonary tuberculosis among pregnant women in Cotonou, Benin. *PLoS ONE* **2022**, *17*, e0264206. [CrossRef]
2. Word Health Organization. *Global Tuberculosis Report 2020*; WHO: Geneva, Switzerland; p. 208. Available online: https://apps.who.int/iris/bitstream/handle/10665/336069/9789240013131-eng.pdf (accessed on 14 December 2021).
3. Ministry of Health. Health Surveillance Secretariat. In *Epidemiological Bulletin, Brasília. Special Issue. March 2021.*. Available online: https://www.gov.br/saude/pt-br/media/pdf/2021/marco/24/boletim-tuberculose-2021_24.03 (accessed on 14 December 2021).
4. Dos Santos, A.C.E.D.; Brunfentrinker, C.; Pena, L.D.S.; Saraiva, S.D.S.; Boing, A.F. Analysis and comparison of tuberculosis treatment outcomes in the homeless population and in the general population of Brazil. *J. Bras. Pneumol.* **2021**, *47*, e20200178. [CrossRef]
5. Pedro, A.S.; Gibson, G.; Santos, J.P.C.; Toledo, L.M.; Sabroza, P.C.; Oliveira, R.M. Tuberculosis as a marker of inequities in the context of socio-spatial transformation. *J. Public Health* **2017**, 51. [CrossRef] [PubMed]
6. Eddabra, R.; Neffa, M. Epidemiological profile among pulmonary and extrapulmonary tuberculosis patients in Laayoune, Morocco. *Pan Afr. Med J.* **2020**, *37*, 56. [CrossRef]
7. Presidency of the Republic. *Establishes the National Policy for the Homeless Population and Its Intersectoral Follow-Up and Monitoring Committee and Other Measures*; Decree No. 7053, of 23 December 2009; Official Federal Gazette: Brasilia, Brazil, 2009. Available online: http://www.planalto.gov.br/ccivil_03/_ato2007-2010/2009/decreto/d7053.htm (accessed on 14 December 2021).

8. Von Streit, F.; Bartels, C.; Kuczius, T.; Cassier, C.; Gardemann, J.; Schaumburg, F. Prevalence of latent tuberculosis in homeless persons: A single-centre cross-sectional study, Germany. *PLoS ONE* **2019**, *14*, e0214556. [CrossRef]
9. Anton, C.; Machado, F.D.; Ramirez, J.M.A.; Bernardi, R.M.; Palominos, P.E.; Brenol, C.V.; Mello, F.C.D.Q.; Silva, D.R. Latent tuberculosis infection in patients with rheumatic diseases. *J. Bras. Pneumol.* **2019**, *45*, e20190023. [CrossRef]
10. Sterling, T.R.; Njie, G.; Zenner, D.; Cohn, D.L.; Reves, R.; Ahmed, A.; Menzies, D.; Horsburgh, C.R.; Crane, C.M.; Burgos, M.; et al. Guidelines for the Treatment of Latent Tuberculosis Infection: Recommendations from the National Tuberculosis Controllers Association and CDC, 2020. *MMWR. Recomm. Rep.* **2020**, *69*, 1–11. [CrossRef]
11. Chekesa, B.; Gumi, B.; Chanyalew, M.; Zewude, A.; Ameni, G. Prevalence of latent tuberculosis infection and associated risk factors in prison in East Wollega Zone of western Ethiopia. *PLoS ONE* **2020**, *15*, e0233314. [CrossRef]
12. Schmit, K.M.; Wansaula, Z.; Pratt, R.; Price, S.F.; Langer, A.J. Tuberculosis—United States, 2016. *MMWR. Morb. Mortal. Wkly. Rep.* **2017**, *11*, 289–294. [CrossRef]
13. Nwana, N.; Marks, S.M.; Lan, E.; Chang, A.H.; Holcombe, M.; Morris, S.B. Treatment of latent Mycobacterium tuberculosis infection with 12 once weekly directly-observed doses of isoniazid and rifapentine among persons experiencing homelessness. *PLoS ONE* **2019**, *3*, e0213524. [CrossRef]
14. Janssens, J.-P.; Wuillemin, T.; Adler, D.; Jackson, Y. Screening for tuberculosis in an urban shelter for homeless in Switzerland: A prospective study. *BMC Infect. Dis.* **2017**, *17*, 347. [CrossRef]
15. Morgenstern, H. Ecologic Studies. In *Modern Epidemiology*, 3rd ed.; Rothman, K.J., Greenland, S., Lash, T.L., Eds.; Lippincott Williams & Wilkins: Philadelphia, PA, USA, 2008; pp. 512–531.
16. Secretary of Justice, Family and Labor. Intersectoral Committee for Follow-Up and Monitoring of Homeless Population Policy. In *Period from July 2021 to December 2021.*. Available online: https://www.justica.pr.gov.br/Pagina/CIAMP-Rua#:~{}:text=Atualmente%2C%20o%20Cadastro%20%C3%9Anico%20do,em%20situa%C3%A7%C3%A3o%20de%20rua%20cadastradas (accessed on 6 January 2022).
17. Antunes, J.L.F.; Cardoso, M.R.A. Using time series analysis in epidemiological studies. *Epidemiol. Serv. Saude* **2015**, *24*, 565–576. [CrossRef]
18. Prais, S.J.; Winsten, C.B. Trend estimators and serial correlation. In *Trend Estimates and Serial Correlation*; Cowles Commission Discussion Paper, Stat. No. 383; University of Chicago: Chicago, IL, USA, 1954.
19. Cleveland, R.B.; Cleveland, W.S.; McRae, J.E.; Terpenning, I. STL: A seasonal-trend decomposition procedure based on Loess. *J. Off. Stat.* **1990**, *6*, 3–73.
20. Brockwell, P.J.; Davis, R.A. *Introduction to Time Series and Forecasting*, 2nd ed.; Springer-Verlag: New York, NY, USA, 2002.
21. Caliari, J.S.; Figueiredo, R.M. Tuberculosis: Patient profile, service flowchart, and nurses opinions. *Acta Paul. Enferm.* **2012**, *25*, 43–47. [CrossRef]
22. Furlan, M.C.R.; Oliveira, S.P.; Marcon, S.S. Factors associated with nonadherence of tuberculosis treatment in the state of Paraná. *Acta Paul. Enferm.* **2012**, *25*, 108–114.
23. Getis, A.; Ord, J.K. The analysis of spatial association by use of distance statistics. *Geogr. Anal.* **1992**, *24*, 189–206.
24. Aldridge, R.W.; Hayward, A.C.; Hemming, S.; Yates, S.K.; Ferenando, G.; Possas, L.; Garber, E.; Watson, J.M.; Geretti, A.M.; McHugh, T.D.; et al. High prevalence of latent tuberculosis and bloodborne virus infection in a homeless population. *Thorax* **2018**, *73*, 557–564. [CrossRef]
25. Alecrim, T.F.; Mitano, F.; Reis, A.A.; Roos, C.M.; Palha, P.F.; Protti-Zanatta, S.T. Experience of health professionals in care of the homeless population with tuberculosis. *Rev. Esc. Enferm. USP* **2016**, *50*, 808–815. [CrossRef]
26. Agarwal, S.; Nguyen, D.T.; Graviss, E.A. Homelessness and Mortality Among Persons With Tuberculosis in Texas, 2010–2017. *Public Health Rep.* **2019**, *134*, 643–650. [CrossRef]
27. Hungaro, A.A.; Gavioli, A.; Christóphoro, R.; Marangoni, S.R.; Altrão, R.F.; Rodrigues, A.L.; De Oliveira, M.L.F. Homeless population: Characterization and contextualization by census research. *Rev. Bras. Enferm.* **2020**, *73*, e20190236. [CrossRef]
28. Hino, P.; Yamamoto, T.T.; Bastos, S.H.; Beraldo, A.A.; Figueiredo, T.M.R.M.; Bertolozzi, M.R. Tuberculosis in the street population: A systematic review. *Rev. Esc. Enferm. USP* **2021**, *55*, e03688. [CrossRef]
29. Hashmi, S.S.; Saad, A.; Leps, C.; Gillies-Podgorecki, J.; Feeney, B.; Hardy, C.; Falzone, N.; Archibald, D.; Hoang, T.; Bond, A.; et al. A student-led curriculum framework for homeless and vulnerably housed populations. *BMC Med. Educ.* **2020**, *20*, 232. [CrossRef]
30. Wiens, J.D.; Dugger, K.M.; Higley, J.M.; Lesmeister, D.B.; Franklin, A.B.; Hamm, K.A.; White, G.C.; Dilione, K.E.; Simon, D.C.; Bown, R.R.; et al. Invader removal triggers competitive release in a threatened avian predator. *Proc. Natl. Acad. Sci. USA* **2021**, *118*, e2102859118. [CrossRef]
31. Baxter, N.T.; Schmidt, A.W.; Venkataraman, A.; Kim, K.S.; Waldron, C.; Schmidt, T.M. Dynamics of Human Gut Microbiota and Short-Chain Fatty Acids in Response to Dietary Interventions with Three Fermentable Fibers. *mBio* **2019**, *10*, e02566-18. [CrossRef]
32. Johnson, L.; Lewer, D.; Aldridge, R.W.; Hayward, A.C.; Story, A. Protocol for a systematic review of treatment adherence for HIV, hepatitis C and tuberculosis among homeless populations. *Syst. Rev.* **2020**, *9*, 211. [CrossRef] [PubMed]
33. Omerov, P.; Craftman, Å.G.; Mattsson, E.; Klarare, A. Homeless persons' experiences of health- and social care: A systematic integrative review. *Health Soc. Care Community* **2020**, *28*, 1–11. [CrossRef]
34. Andrade, R.; Costa, A.A.S.; Sousa, E.T.; Rocon, P.C. Access to health services by the homeless population: An integrative review. *Health Debate* **2022**, *46*, 227–239. [CrossRef]

35. Baroni, L.; Alves, R.F.S.; Boccolini, C.S.; Salles, R.; Gritz, R.; Paixão, B.; Boccolini, P.D.M.M. Database on the coverage of the "Bolsa-Família" conditioning cash-transfer program: Brazil, 2005 to 2021. *BMC Res. Notes* **2021**, *14*, 435. [CrossRef]
36. Torrens, A.W.; Rasella, D.; Boccia, D.; Maciel, E.L.N.; Nery, J.S.; Olson, Z.D.; Barreira, D.C.N.; Sanchez, M.N. Effectiveness of a conditional cash transfer programme on TB cure rate: A retrospective cohort study in Brazil. *Trans. R. Soc. Trop. Med. Hyg.* **2016**, *110*, 199–206. [CrossRef]
37. Silva, D.R.; Muñoz-Torrico, M.; Duarte, R.; Galvão, T.; Bonini, E.H.; Arbex, F.F.; Arbex, M.A.; Augusto, V.M.; Rabahi, M.F.; Mello, F.C.D.Q. Risk factors for tuberculosis: Diabetes, smoking, alcohol use, and the use of other drugs. *J. Bras. Pneumol.* **2018**, *44*, 145–152. [CrossRef]
38. Cruz, V.D.; Harter, J.; Oliveira, M.M.; Gonzales, R.I.C.; Alves, P.F. Consumo de crack y la tisis: Una revisión integrativa. *Rev. Eletrônica Saúde Ment. Álcool Drog.* **2013**, *9*, 48–55. [CrossRef]
39. Heuvelings, C.C.; Greve, P.F.; De Vries, S.G.; Visser, B.J.; Bélard, S.; Janssen, S.; Cremers, A.L.; Spijker, R.; Shaw, E.; Hill, R.; et al. Effectiveness of service models and organisational structures supporting tuberculosis identification and management in hard-to-reach populations in countries of low and medium tuberculosis incidence: A systematic review. *BMJ Open* **2018**, *8*, e019642. [CrossRef] [PubMed]
40. Breilh, J. *Critical Epidemiology: Emancipatory Science and Interculturality*; FIOCRUZ: Rio de Janeiro, Brazil, 2006.
41. Viegas, S.M.F.; Nitschke, R.G.; Bernardo, L.A.; Tholl, A.D.; Borrego, M.A.R.; Soto, P.J.L. The routine of the street outreach office team: Weaving networks for health promotion. *Esc. Anna Nery Rev. Enferm.* **2021**, *25*, e20200222. [CrossRef]
42. Marques, L.S.; Costa, J.H.M.; Gomes, M.M.; Silva, M.M. Knowledge, territories, and drug use: Street ways of life and reinventing care. *Cien. Saude Colet.* **2022**, *27*, 123–132. [CrossRef]
43. Timóteo, A.V.G.; Silva, J.V.S.; Gomes, L.K.G.; Alves, A.S.S.; Barbosa, V.M.S.; Brendão, T.M. Characterization of the work and actions developed by the consultant's teams in the street of Maceió—AL. *Enferm. Foco* **2020**, *11*, 126–130.
44. Lutge, E.E.; Wiysonge, C.S.; Knight, S.E.; Sinclair, D.; Volmink, J. Incentives and enablers to improve adherence in tuberculosis. *Cochrane Database Syst. Rev.* **2015**, *9*, CD007952. [CrossRef]

International Journal of
Environmental Research and Public Health

MDPI

Article

Association of Hospital Characteristics and Previous Hospitalization-Related Experiences with Patients' Perceptions of Hospital Care in China

Yufan Wang [1], Beizhu Ye [1], Yimei Zhu [2], Xiaoyu Wang [1] and Yuan Liang [1,*]

[1] Department of Social Medicine and Health Management, School of Public Health, Tongji Medical College, Huazhong University of Science and Technology, Wuhan 430074, China; wyufan226@163.com (Y.W.); yebeizhu@163.com (B.Y.); wangxiaoyu361@163.com (X.W.)
[2] School of Media, Communication and Sociology, University of Leicester, Leicester LE1 7JA, UK; yz411@leicester.ac.uk
* Correspondence: liangyuan217@hust.edu.cn

Citation: Wang, Y.; Ye, B.; Zhu, Y.; Wang, X.; Liang, Y. Association of Hospital Characteristics and Previous Hospitalization-Related Experiences with Patients' Perceptions of Hospital Care in China. *Int. J. Environ. Res. Public Health* **2022**, *19*, 7856. https://doi.org/10.3390/ijerph19137856

Academic Editors: Alessandra Casuccio, Joachim G. Voss and Sandul Yasobant

Received: 28 March 2022
Accepted: 24 May 2022
Published: 27 June 2022

Abstract: Patients' perceptions of healthcare vary over time and by setting, and previous studies have rarely focused on these factors. We aimed to measure patients' perceptions of hospital care in China and to examine how patients' perceptions of hospital care vary by hospital characteristics (differences in setting) and previous hospitalization-related experiences (changes with time). We conducted a national cross-sectional survey of 7267 inpatients between July 2014 and April 2015 in China. Hospital characteristics measured were hospital technical level, hospital type, teaching status, and the ratio of doctors/nurses to ward beds. Previous hospitalization-related experiences measured were current admission length, number of previous admissions, and hospital selection (hospital advertisements or personal recommendations). Patients' perceptions of hospital care included perceptions of doctors, nurses, and hospital organization. Scores were highest for perceptions of nurses, followed by perceptions of doctors, and hospital organization. Of the five hospital characteristics rated, the technical level was most strongly associated with patient perceptions of healthcare. The effect of hospital admission length and frequency of hospitalization on patients' perceptions was represented by a $\surd$-shaped dose–response curve (scores were initially high, then decreased, then rebounded to higher than the initial scores). Patients who selected a hospital with hospital advertisements gave lower scores than those without hospital advertisements, and patients who selected a hospital with personal recommendations gave higher scores than those without If the observed $\surd$-shaped dose–response curves indicate a causal relationship between patients' perceptions and hospital admission length or frequency of hospitalization, this may help to guide the timing of patient satisfaction assessments. The negative association between patient perception and advertising, and the positive association with personal recommendations (word-of-mouth) and hospital technical level, could provide important information for clinicians and hospital administrators.

Keywords: patients' perceptions of healthcare; healthcare quality; patient satisfaction; hospital management

1. Introduction

Just as people need mirrors to clearly see themselves, healthcare providers require an external perspective on their services. As a measure of healthcare quality, patients' perceptions of healthcare (commonly referred to as patient satisfaction) may provide such a perspective [1,2]. Patients' perceptions of healthcare are a multi-dimensional construct encompassing numerous elements of healthcare, such as waiting time of pre-care, environment of wards, interactions with clinicians, availability of examination, and coordination of care. In addition, patients' perceptions of healthcare, as a type of patient-reported outcome, are important not only in identifying physical and mental discomfort, but also in examining the process by which patients report symptoms of physical and mental discomfort to clinicians, including emerging or previously forgotten symptoms. Therefore, patients' perceptions of healthcare reflect not only clinicians' interpersonal communication skills, but also clinicians' clinical interrogation ability [3,4]. With the advent of pay-per-performance and value-based reimbursement in the healthcare system, as well as the aging of the population and the chronicity of the disease, patients' perceptions of healthcare are becoming increasingly important for healthcare providers and administrators [5,6].

Nonetheless, controversy exists regarding the interpretation and use of measures of patients' perceptions of healthcare to improve the quality of healthcare and organizational management [7–10]. Differences in patients' perceptions according to region and setting mean that most studies have examined predictors at the hospital level, such as nonprofit status, higher surgical volume, low mortality index, and low readmission rates (which often positively correlate with more positive patient perceptions) [4,7,11]. Previous research findings are inconsistent regarding the relationship between patient perceptions and some predictors, such as teaching status, number of beds, and the staff-to-patient ratio [12,13]. Patient-level predictors include age, sex, ethnicity, socioeconomic status, and chronic conditions, and existing studies often demonstrate divergent findings [5,6]. It is commonly accepted that patient perceptions of healthcare are impacted by their socioeconomic status, namely a lower education level with a more positive satisfaction rating. However, such frequently explored patient attributes are unsuitable as references or strategies to improve the quality of hospital care and patient satisfaction (usually as a risk adjustment) [13–17]. Furthermore, consumer perception is not static and is shaped both by sensory inputs from the current environment and by expectations generated from past experience [18,19]. Therefore, patients' perceptions vary over time and are affected by factors such as previous hospitalization experiences and length of hospital stay. Previous studies have rarely focused on these factors. To our knowledge, only one survey of acute care general hospitals has investigated these aspects [20], and further empirical studies are needed on general care that use more rigorous methodologies to simultaneously incorporate hospital- and patient-level predictors to understand the complex nature of patients' perceptions of healthcare [2,3,11].

To address the above gap, this study aimed to determine the association of hospital characteristics (differences in setting) and previous hospitalization-related experiences (changes with time) with patients' perceptions of current hospital care, using data from a national sample of inpatients at general hospitals in China.

2. Methods

2.1. Study Design and Setting

We used stratified cluster sampling in 77 hospitals across seven provinces in China from July 2014 to April 2015. The details of this survey have been described in a previous report [21,22]. Briefly, we selected six provinces (Gansu, Yunnan, Jiangsu, Shandong, Hubei, and Guangdong) and Beijing, China's capital, which have a combined population of 427.15 million, accounting for 31.88% of the total population of China. There were 85 eligible hospitals in the selected regions, of which 8 refused to participate, leaving a total of 77 participating hospitals (90.59%). In each hospital, convenience sampling was used to select patients from three to four surgical departments of different specialties and another three to four internal medicine departments, excluding obstetrics and pediatrics. A total of 528 departments were involved and the inpatients in the 528 departments were eligible to complete the survey. There were 24,250 eligible participants, of whom 11,884 did not complete the survey (49.01%). We excluded 4128 (17.02%) invalid questionnaires that contained errors or erratic responses. We also excluded 674 (2.78%) questionnaires with missing key variables. Following previous study [18], we also excluded 297 (1.22%) participants whose current admission length (days) was less than 1 day or more than 30 days. Finally, the analysis used data from the 7267 (29.97%) remaining responses (Figure S1 in the Supplementary Materials). The three departments with the most participants were general surgery (1187), orthopedics (946), and cardiology (613) (Table 1). Participants provided oral informed consent for interviews. The institutional review board at the authors' institutes approved the study protocol (No. IORG0003571).

Table 1. Socio-demographic characteristics of participants.

	Unweighted Samples	Weighted Samples	X^2	p
Gender				
Male	3650 (50.23)	3653 (50.26)	0.003	0.959
Female	3333 (45.86)	3330 (45.83)		
missing	284 (3.91)	284 (3.91)		
Age (years old)				
15–44	2782 (38.28)	2408 (33.14)	109.372	<0.001
45–59	2075 (28.55)	1840 (25.32)		
≥60	2410 (33.16)	3019 (41.54)		
Education status				
Primary school and lower	1440 (19.82)	1602 (22.05)	12.803	0.005
Junior high school	2083 (28.66)	2083 (28.66)		
Senior high school	2123 (29.21)	2045 (28.14)		
Undergraduate and above	1535 (21.12)	1445 (19.88)		
missing	86 (1.18)	92 (1.27)		
Marital status				
Married	5793 (79.72)	5796 (79.76)	0.009	0.923
Single/divorced/widowed/other	1411 (19.42)	1406 (19.35)		
missing	63 (0.87)	65 (0.89)		
Self-reported economic status				
Good	1958 (26.94)	1988 (27.36)	0.984	0.611
Fair	3974 (54.69)	3986 (54.85)		
Bad	1274 (17.53)	1231 (16.94)		
missing	61 (0.84)	62 (0.85)		
Medical insurance				
Yes	6440 (88.62)	6464 (88.95)	0.634	0.426
No	631 (8.68)	604 (8.31)		
missing	196 (2.70)	199 (2.73)		
Special				
Internal medicine	3637 (50.05)	3737 (51.42)	2.753	0.097
Neurology	302 (4.16)	316 (4.35)		
Respiratory medicine	410 (5.64)	438 (6.03)		
Cardiology	613 (8.44)	672 (9.25)		
Gastroenterology	598 (8.23)	600 (8.26)		
Endocrinology	442 (6.08)	437 (6.01)		
Nephrology	223 (3.07)	225 (3.10)		
Hematology	129 (1.78)	123 (1.69)		
Oncology	141 (1.94)	142 (1.96)		
Rheumatology	115 (1.58)	109 (1.50)		
General internal medicine	195 (2.68)	201 (2.77)		
Others	469 (6.45)	472 (6.50)		
Surgery	3630 (49.95)	3530 (48.58)		
Brain surgery	204 (2.81)	199 (2.74)		
Thoracic/cardiac surgery	311 (4.28)	318 (4.37)		
General Surgery	1187 (16.31)	1168 (16.07)		
Urology	360 (4.95)	362 (4.99)		
Orthopedics	946 (13.02)	914 (12.58)		
Gynecology	278 (3.83)	249 (3.42)		
Otolaryngology	138 (1.90)	128 (1.77)		
Others	206 (2.83)	192 (2.64)		

2.2. Measures

Patients' perceptions of hospital care were measured using a scale (Cronbach's alpha, 0.844, Table S1 in the Supplementary Materials) comprising 11 items drawn mainly from the Consumer Assessment of Healthcare Providers and Systems (CAHPS) [8,9] and partly from the Picker Patient Experience Questionnaire [10]. The 11 items were categorized into three dimensions: care provided by doctors (4 items), by nurses (4 items), and by hospital organization (3 items: Clean environment, Quiet environment, and Convenience of medical exams). The doctor and nurse dimensions contained the same four items: (1) During your hospital stay, how often did doctors/nurses explain things in a way you could understand? (Communication); (2) When you had important questions to ask a doctor/nurse, was it difficult or easy to access your doctors/nurses? (Accessibility); (3) How much were you involved in medical/nursing services? (Involvement); (4) How much were doctors/nurses concerned about your mood? (Concern for patients' mood). The service provided by the hospital organization was measured using three questions: (1) In general, during your hospital stay, how often was your ward cleaned? (Clean environment); (2) In general, during your hospital stay, how often was the area around your ward quiet? (Quiet environment); (3) How convenient were your medical exams during your current admission? (Convenience of medical exams). For each statement, patients were asked to indicate their perceptions on a 5-point scale (range of scores for each factor, 1–5; higher scores indicated more positive perceptions) (Table S1 in the Supplementary Materials). The patient experience domains were highly correlated overall (Cronbach's alpha, 0.844); individual correlation coefficients ranged from 0.065 (correlation between communication with nurses and nurses' concern for patients' mood) to 0.647 (correlation between accessibility to doctors and doctors' concern for patients' mood) (Table S2 in the Supplementary Materials).

Although the CAHPS includes care provided by pharmacists [8,9], pharmacists in China have almost no direct contact with patients. As patients' medication is prescribed by physicians, pharmacists are responsible only for the delivery of medication (according to physicians' prescriptions) to the nurses' ward station, so we did not examine their services in this study.

Previous hospitalization-related experiences were assessed using four statements: [22–24] (1) How many days have you been hospitalized in your current admission? (length of the current admission in days, with a blank filling question and divided into five levels: 1–3, 4–7, 8–14, 15–21, 22–30 days); (2) Excluding the current admission, how many times have you been hospitalized in this hospital in the last 3 years? (number of previous admissions (frequency), with five response options: 0, 1, 2, 3, and 4 and above); (3) Did you choose this hospital for your current admission because you saw an advertisement for it? (hospital advertisement: yes or no); (4) Did you choose this hospital for your current admission because it was recommended by relatives, friends, colleagues, etc.? (personal recommendation: called word-of-mouth in China: yes or no).

Hospital characteristics were assessed using five items: technical level of the current admission hospital (secondary or tertiary public hospital certified by the Chinese Ministry of Health (MOH)), hospital type (Western medicine (WM), or traditional Chinese medicine (TCM)), teaching status (teaching or non-teaching), and the ratio of doctors/nurses to ward beds. Data on hospital characteristics come from hospital official sources. Following the Chinese MOH and previous study [17], we divided ratios into three categories for doctors ($\geq$0.3, 0.2–0.3, <0.2) and four for nurses ($\geq$0.6, 0.5–0.6, 0.4–0.5, <0.4).

We collected most study data using patient questionnaires. Trained survey interviewers sent copies of the questionnaire to each department, with an explanation of the survey purpose and method. It was explained that participation was voluntary and that contributions would be anonymous. The survey was a self-administered paper survey, and family members were allowed to help patients fill in questionnaires. After 1 or 2 days, the survey interviewers returned to the department to collect completed questionnaires. We collected the data for the number of doctors, nurses, and beds in the department from the dean of the department or the nursing station. The data for hospital teaching status were obtained from the official website of hospitals and their affiliated universities. As some teaching hospitals in China are only nominal teaching hospitals (a status adopted

to improve their social reputation), they were not included in the study. The status of teaching hospitals was verified by the administrative departments of hospitals and their affiliated universities.

Demographic characteristics measured included sex (male, female), age (15–29, 30–44, 45–59, ≥60 years), education level (middle school and below, high school, bachelor's degree and above), marital status (married, unmarried, or other), medical insurance (yes, no), and self-reported economic status (good, fair, poor). A coding system was used to anonymously link patient data with the correct hospital and department.

2.3. Statistical Analysis

Data were weighted to adjust for nonresponses and improve the representativeness of the sample so that participants responding to the initial questions matched the demographic characteristics of the total hospitalization population issued by the National General Hospital in 2015 [25]. Owing to the limited parameters of the 2015 data reported by the National General Hospital, the present data were only weighted by age. To create condition-specific summary scores [9], we used a common method, in which the summary score is a percentage derived from individual actual scores from three dimensions, and the total (numerator) is divided, respectively, by the corresponding theoretical score from three dimensions and the total scores for patients' perceptions of hospital care (denominator).

The key outcome variable in each analysis was patients' perceptions of hospital care, comprising total scores, scores on the three dimensions, and scores on each of the 11 items. For crude comparisons, we used *t*-tests for continuous variables and chi-square tests for categorical variables. We then used a linear regression model and a binary logistic regression model to examine the association of hospital characteristics and patients' previous hospitalization-related experiences with patients' perceptions of hospital care (comprising total scores, dimension scores, and item scores). Negative parameter estimates in the model indicate lower (worse) adjusted mean patients' perception percentiles, whereas positive estimates indicate higher (better) adjusted mean patients' perception percentiles.

Although total scores and dimension scores for patients' perceptions of hospital care are useful for general comparisons, and can provide operational guidance for reimbursement of Medicare rewards and penalties, these scores are too broad to provide detailed information for healthcare providers, especially clinicians. By contrast, an analysis of individual items can provide specific and targeted guidance for clinicians to evaluate their service behavior, so we further analyzed each of the 11 items in detail.

All models were adjusted for the following patient demographic characteristics, which have previously been associated with patients' perceptions of healthcare: demographic [26–30]. sex, age, educational level, marital status, medical insurance, and self-reported economic status. Two-sided tests were used for all the analyses, and *p*-values of 0.05 or less were considered statistically significant. All analyses were performed using SPSS, version 22.0 (SPSS Inc., Chicago, IL, USA).

3. Results

The demographic characteristics of participants are summarized in Table 1. In the unweighted sample, the ratios of sex (male vs. female) and department (internal vs. surgical medicine) were almost half to half (50.23% vs. 45.86%, 50.05% vs. 49.95%, respectively). Patients aged 60 years and over accounted for about 33% of respondents; those with undergraduate education and above and who were unmarried/widowed accounted for about 20%, and those with medical insurance accounted for about 90%. The difference between the weighted and unweighted samples for almost all demographic characteristics except age and education level were not statistically significant; the weighted samples contained more participants over 60 years and more with an educational level of primary school and below ($X^2 = 109.372$, $p < 0.001$; $X^2 = 12.803$, $p = 0.005$, respectively).

Overall, the highest scores (indicating more positive perceptions of hospital care) were for nurses (75.10%; 95%CI: 74.70% to 75.49%), followed by doctors (71.21%; 95%CI: 70.79%

to 71.64%), and hospital organizational management (69.42%: 95%CI: 69.01% to 69.84%). The distribution of scores for all 11 items showed that the lowest (worst) ratings were for convenience of medical exams (17.90%), followed by clean environment (20.62%), and involvement in medical service (24.46%). For both the perception of doctor and nurse dimensions, the lowest ratings were for involvement in clinical care (24.46% for doctors and 27.88% for nurses); the highest rating for doctors was for communication (39.09%), followed by accessibility (30.88%); the highest rating for nurses was for accessibility (48.30%), followed by communication (45.96%) (Figure 1).

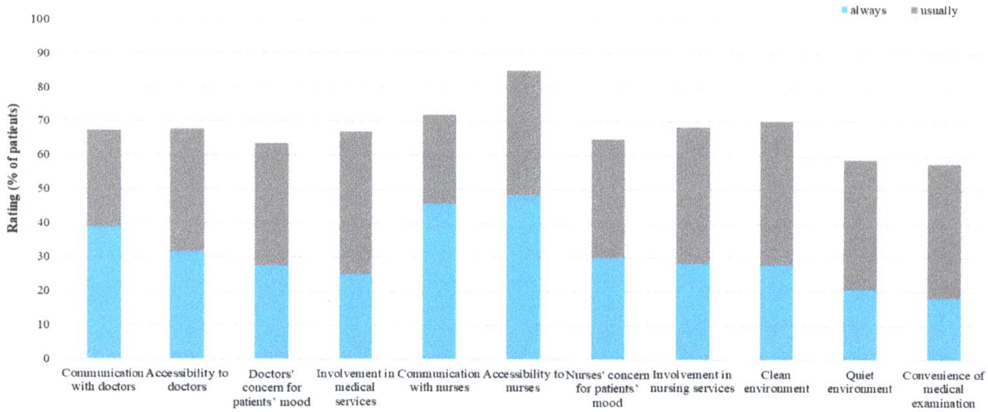

Figure 1. Percentage of patients' perceptions of hospital care.

The analysis of total and dimension scores for patients' perceptions by the five hospital characteristics indicated that the only statistically significant differences were for hospital technical level, with tertiary hospitals achieving higher scores ($t = -4.128$, $p < 0.001$; $t = -4.631$, $p < 0.001$; $t = -3.310$, $p = 0.001$; $t = -4.706$, $p < 0.001$, respectively). The differences by hospital type (WM vs. TCM) and doctor–bed ratio were not significant for any dimensions. The difference in hospital teaching status was statistically significant only for the doctor dimension, with non-teaching hospitals achieving higher scores ($t = 2.991$, $p = 0.003$). Additionally, scores on the nurse dimension ($t = 4.063$, $p = 0.017$) for the nurse–bed ratio $\geq$0.6 were significantly higher than scores for other nurse–bed ratio groups (Table 2).

We then examined each of the five hospital characteristics and the ratings on individual items in detail (Table S3). Owing to space constraints, we only present the highest ratings for the five response levels of the 11 patient perception items by hospital characteristics and previous hospitalization-related experiences. Generally, the differences between ratings on the 11 items by the five hospital characteristics were similar to the scoring differences for the three dimensions and total score, and provide further insight into patient perceptions. The scoring differences between all 11 items by hospital levels were statistically significant; accessibility to doctors, quiet environment, and convenience of medical exams achieved higher ratings in tertiary hospitals. Of the 11 items, only accessibility to doctors, communication with nurses, and quiet environment were significantly correlated with teaching status; non-teaching hospitals had higher ratings. The scoring differences between the 11 items by hospital type were not statistically significant; however, clean environment and convenience of medical exams were rated lower in TCM hospitals. Similarly, the scoring differences between the 11 items by the doctor–bed ratio were not statistically significant; however, a quieter environment was associated with a doctor–bed ratio ≥ 0.3, and greater convenience of medical exams was associated with a doctor–bed ratio < 0.2. The nurse–bed ratio was not significant for all items analyzed.

Table 2. Patients' perceptions of hospital care according to hospital characteristics and patients' previous hospitalization-related experiences.

	%	Provided by Doctors		Provided by Nurses		Provided by Hospital Organization		Total	
		Mean Score (95%CI)	*p* Value	Mean Score (95%CI)	*p* Value	Mean Score (95%CI)	*p* Value	Mean Score (95%CI)	*p* Value
Total		71.21 (70.79,71.64)		75.1 (74.7,75.49)		69.42 (69.01,69.84)		71.91 (71.56,72.26)	
Hospital characteristics									
Hospital technical level									
SH	11.76	68.84 (67.64, 70.03)	<0.001	72.53 (71.35, 73.71)	<0.001	67.51 (66.27, 68.75)	0.001	69.63 (68.63, 70.63)	<0.001
TH	88.24	71.53 (71.08, 71.98)		75.44 (75.02, 75.86)		69.68 (69.24, 70.12)		72.22 (71.85, 72.59)	
Hospital type									
WM	71.98	71.05 (70.55, 71.56)	0.238	75.10 (74.63, 75.57)	0.995	69.49 (69.01, 69.98)	0.593	71.88 (71.47, 72.30)	0.790
TCM	28.02	71.62 (70.84, 72.41)		75.10 (74.36, 75.83)		69.24 (68.46, 70.02)		71.99 (71.34, 72.63)	
Teaching status									
Non-teaching	77.99	71.56 (71.08, 72.04)	0.003	74.93 (74.48, 75.38)	0.125	69.34 (68.87, 69.81)	0.462	71.94 (71.55, 72.34)	0.731
Teaching	22.01	69.99 (69.07, 70.92)		75.68 (74.84, 76.52)		69.72 (68.84, 70.59)		71.80 (71.05, 72.54)	
Ratio of doctors to ward beds									
<0.20	32.86	71.43 (70.69, 72.17)	0.764			68.98 (68.24, 69.71)	0.187	70.2 (69.56, 70.84)	0.687
0.20–0.30	42.56	71.06 (70.40, 71.72)				69.43 (68.81, 70.06)		70.25 (69.69, 70.8)	
≥0.30	24.58	71.19 (70.35, 72.04)				70.01 (69.17, 70.85)		70.6 (69.86, 71.34)	
Ratio of nurses to ward beds									
<0.4	59.36			75.22 (74.70, 75.73)	0.017	69.63 (69.09, 70.17)	0.234	72.42 (71.96, 72.88)	0.396
0.4–0.6	34.76			74.56 (73.89, 75.24)		69.29 (68.6, 69.99)		71.93 (71.33, 72.53)	
≥0.6	5.88			77.06 (75.48, 78.63)		68.13 (66.45, 69.81)		72.59 (71.17, 74.01)	
Previous hospitalization-related experiences									
Number of previous admissions in the last three years									
No (0)	53.13	71.89 (71.31, 72.47)	0.001	75.47 (74.92, 76.02)	0.058	70.06 (69.49, 70.62)	0.001	72.47 (71.99, 72.95)	0.001
Yes (≥1)	45.41	70.37 (69.75, 71.00)		74.69 (74.11, 75.28)		68.68 (68.07, 69.3)		71.25 (70.74, 71.76)	
Hospital selection by personal recommendations									
No	53.13	71.02 (70.44, 71.60)	0.357	74.87 (74.33, 75.42)	0.133	68.91 (68.34, 69.47)	0.006	71.60 (71.13, 72.07)	0.041
Yes	45.36	71.43 (70.79, 72.06)		75.49 (74.90, 76.08)		70.09 (69.47, 70.7)		72.33 (71.81, 72.85)	
Hospital selection by advertisements									
No	86.16	71.47 (71.01, 71.92)	<0.001	75.34 (74.91, 75.76)	0.011	69.36 (68.92, 69.8)	0.566	72.05 (71.68, 72.42)	0.023
Yes	11.62	68.73 (67.43, 70.04)		73.63 (72.39, 74.87)		69.76 (68.45, 71.07)		70.71 (69.61, 71.80)	

Note: WM, Western Medicine. TCM, Traditional Chinese Medicine. TH, Tertiary Hospital. SH, Secondary Hospital.

Multivariate linear regression analysis showed significant differences between doctor dimension scores, nurse dimension scores, and total scores by hospital level ($ß$ = 1.53, 95%CI: 0.1 to 2.96; p = 0.036; $ß$ = 2.01, 95%CI: 0.65 to 3.38; p = 0.004; $ß$ = 1.46, 95%CI: 0.28 to 2.64; p = 0.015, respectively) (Table 3). Consistent with the results of the univariate analysis, there was no significant difference between the three dimensions and total score by hospital type. There were significant score differences by teaching status only for the doctor dimension ($ß$ = −2.36, 95%CI:−3.48 to −1.24; $p < 0.001$). The difference for the doctor dimension and the total score remained significant in the multivariate analysis ($ß$ = −2.34, 95%CI: −3.76 to −0.92; p = 0.001; $ß$ = −1.20, 95%CI: −2.37 to −0.04; p = 0.044, respectively). Contrary to patients whose hospital selection was not based on personal recommendation, those whose selection was based on personal recommendation reported higher scores ($ß_{\text{total scores}}$ = 1.02, 95%CI: 0.27 to 1.77; p = 0.008).

The data in Table 2 show that, compared with patients whose hospital selection for the current admission was based on hospital advertisements, those whose selection was not based on hospital advertisements gave higher (better) scores on the doctor dimension, the nurse dimension, and total scores (t = 4.035, $p < 0.001$; t = 2.561, p =0.011; t = 2.283, p = 0.023, respectively). Table 2 also shows that patients who had previous hospitalization experience provided lower ratings than those without previous hospitalization experience, which is consistent with previous findings [13]. The mean length of the current hospital admission was 8.35 ± 6.16 days, and the median was 7 days. Figure 2 shows the dose–response relationship between the care score reported by patients by length of hospital admission and number of previous hospitalizations. For length of hospital admission, in the first 3 days, the scores were relatively high. However, on the 4th to 7th days, there was a downward trend in scores. One week later, scores continued to increase and exceeded the score of the first 3 days, showing a √-shaped (not U-shaped) dose–response curve. The score differences on the doctor dimension and the total score were statistically significant.

For the number of previous hospitalizations, the √-shaped dose–response curve was more obvious, and the score differences for the doctor dimension, nurse dimension, hospital organization dimension, and the total score were statistically significant. In the multivariate analysis, this pattern of a drop in scores followed by an increase was generally consistent, and score differences on the doctor dimension by length of hospital admission and number of previous hospitalizations were statistically significant (Table 3).

Table 3. Multivariate linear regression model to examine the association of hospital characteristics and patients' previous hospitalization-related experiences with patients' perceptions of hospital care.

	Provided by Doctors		**Provided by Nurses**		**Provided by Hospital Organization**		**Total**	
	β (95%CI)	***p* Value**	**β (95%CI)**	***p* Value**	**β (95%CI)**	***p* Value**	**β (95%CI)**	***p* Value**
Hospital characteristics								
Hospital technical level (ref = Secondary hospital)								
Tertiary hospital	1.53 (0.10, 2.96)	0.036	2.01 (0.65, 3.38)	0.004	1.02 (−0.4, 2.44)	0.158	1.46 (0.28, 2.64)	0.015
Hospital type (ref= WM)								
TCM	0.44 (−0.58, 1.46)	0.396	−0.59 (−1.56, 0.38)	0.231	−0.99 (−2, 0.02)	0.054	−0.41 (−1.24, 0.43)	0.344
Teaching status (ref = Non-teaching)								
Teaching	−2.36 (−3.48, −1.24)	<0.001	0.38 (−0.70, 1.46)	0.491	0.17 (−0.95, 1.29)	0.768	−0.55 (−1.49, 0.38)	0.246
Ratio of doctors to ward beds (ref = <0.20)								
0.20–0.30	−0.48 (−1.53, 0.57)	0.369			0.44 (−0.61, 1.49)	0.415	0.17 (−0.70, 1.04)	0.704
≥0.30	0.12 (−1.08, 1.32)	0.844			1.52 (0.25, 2.78)	0.019	0.97 (−0.09, 2.02)	0.073
Ratio of nurses to ward beds (ref = <0.4)								
0.4–0.6			−0.57 (−1.49, 0.35)	0.225	−0.73 (−1.72, 0.27)	0.151	−0.92 (−1.75, −0.09)	0.029
≥0.6			1.95 (0.09, 3.80)	0.040	−2.2 (−4.22, −0.17)	0.033	−0.27 (−1.95, 1.42)	0.756
Previous hospitalization-related experiences								
Current admission length (days) (ref = 1–3 days)								
4–7	−0.85 (−2.08, 0.38)	0.174	−0.59 (−1.75, 0.57)	0.317	−1.02 (−2.23, 0.18)	0.096	−0.82 (−1.83, 0.18)	0.108
8–14	0.39 (−0.89, 1.67)	0.548	0.33 (−0.88, 1.55)	0.590	−0.62 (−1.88, 0.64)	0.334	0.04 (−1.01, 1.09)	0.936
15–21	1.09 (−0.62, 2.81)	0.212	0.20 (−1.42, 1.83)	0.805	−0.09 (−1.78, 1.60)	0.917	0.39 (−1.02, 1.80)	0.590
≥22 days	2.73 (0.49, 4.97)	0.017	1.28 (−0.84, 3.40)	0.237	0.66 (−1.55, 2.86)	0.559	1.56 (−0.27, 3.40)	0.095
Number of previous admissions in the last three years (ref = 0)								
1	−4.07 (−5.23, −2.91)	<0.001	−1.54 (−2.64, −0.45)	0.006	−3.07 (−4.21, −1.93)	<0.001	−2.89 (−3.84, −1.94)	<0.001
2	−1.71 (−3.17, −0.24)	0.022	−1.17 (−2.55, 0.22)	0.099	−1.25 (−2.70, 0.19)	0.088	−1.38 (−2.58, −0.17)	0.025
3	−1.27 (−3.34, 0.80)	0.230	0.55 (−1.40, 2.51)	0.580	−0.94 (−2.98, 1.1)	0.366	−0.53 (−2.23, 1.16)	0.538
≥4 times	2.67 (0.91, 4.43)	0.003	2.32 (0.65, 3.98)	0.007	0.4 (−1.34, 2.14)	0.650	1.78 (0.33, 3.22)	0.016
Hospital selection by personal recommendations (ref = No)								
Yes	1.08 (0.16, 1.99)	0.021	0.82 (−0.04, 1.69)	0.063	1.20 (0.30, 2.10)	0.009	1.02 (0.27, 1.77)	0.008
Hospital selection by advertisements (ref= No)								
Yes	−2.34 (−3.76, −0.92)	0.001	−1.34 (−2.68, 0.01)	0.051	0.12 (−1.28, 1.52)	0.863	−1.20 (−2.37, −0.04)	0.044

Note: All models were adjusted for the following patient demographic characteristics: sex, age, educational level, marital status, medical insurance, and self-reported economic status.

As described above, we then examined ratings on the four items assessing previous hospitalization-related experience and patients' perception ratings in detail (Table S3). Compared with patients whose hospital selection was based on hospital advertisements, those whose selection was not based on advertisements reported higher scores for communication and accessibility ($X^2 = 88.089$, $p < 0.001$; $X^2 = 25.992$, $p < 0.001$, respectively), but lower scores for concern and involvement ($X^2 = 26.405$, $p < 0.001$; $X^2 = 14.352$, $p = 0.006$, respectively) on the nurse dimension. These individuals gave similar scores on the doctor dimension (except for the concern item). Compared with patients whose hospital selection was based on hospital advertisements, those who had not selected based on advertisements reported lower scores on clean environment, quiet environment, and convenience of medical exams (the differences were significant for clean environment and quiet environment: $X^2 = 24.499$, $p < 0.001$; $X^2 = 9.785$, $p = 0.044$, respectively). Items that remained significant in the multivariate analysis were communication with doctors and nurses (OR = 0.75, 95%CI: 0.64 to 0.89; $p = 0.001$; OR = 0.78, 95%CI:0.67 to 0.92; $p = 0.003$, respectively: lower ratings for patients whose selection was based on advertisements), nurses' concern, and involvement in nursing services (OR = 1.30, 95%CI: 1.10 to 1.54; $p = 0.002$; OR = 1.22, 95%CI:1.03 to 1.45; $p = 0.022$, respectively: higher ratings for patients whose selection was based on advertisements). Patients whose selection was based on personal recommendation reported higher scores on all 11 items. Most of these differences were significant, except communication with doctors, accessibility to nurses, and convenience of medical exams. After adjustment in the multivariate analysis (Table S4), only the items doctors' concern for patients' mood, nurses' concern for patients' mood (OR = 1.21, 95%CI: 1.07 to 1.36; $p = 0.002$; OR = 1.16, 95%CI:1.04 to 1.30; $p = 0.009$, respectively), and involvement in nursing services (OR = 1.14, 95%CI: 1.02 to 1.28; $p = 0.024$) remained significant.

Differences on the 11 items by length of hospital admission were generally consistent with differences on the three dimensions and total score; that is, the scoring pattern was initially high, then decreased, then rebounded to a higher level than the initial scores. Additionally, doctors' and nurses' concern ($OR_{\geq 22days}$ = 1.60, 95%CI: 1.22 to 2.10; $p < 0.001$; OR = 1.35, 95%CI:1.03 to 1.76; $p = 0.028$; respectively) and involvement ($OR_{\geq 22days}$ = 1.50, 95%CI: 1.13 to 1.98; $p = 0.005$; OR = 1.50, 95%CI:1.14 to 1.96; $p = 0.003$, respectively), and convenience of medical exams ($OR_{\geq 22days}$ = 1.36, 95%CI: 1.10 to 1.85; $p = 0.047$) showed significant differences. Similarly, differences on the 11 items by number of previous hospitalizations were generally consistent with those on the three dimensions and total score (i.e., the scoring pattern was initially high, then decreased, then rebounded to a higher level than the initial scores, and doctors' and nurses' accessibility ($OR_{\geq 4times}$ = 1.29, 95%CI: 1.05 to 1.59; $p = 0.014$; OR = 1.25, 95%CI: 1.03 to 1.52; $p = 0.027$, respectively), concern ($OR_{\geq 4times}$ = 1.38, 95%CI: 1.12 to 1.71; $p = 0.002$; OR = 1.32, 95%CI: 1.07 to 1.62; $p = 0.009$, respectively), and involvement ($OR_{\geq 4times}$ = 1.51, 95%CI: 1.22 to 1.87; $p < 0.001$; OR = 1.42, 95%CI: 1.15 to 1.75; $p = 0.001$, respectively) showed significant differences (Table S4).

We also found significant cross-regional differences in patients' perceptions of hospital care (Tables S5 and S6). Regions in eastern China had the highest scores (total score 74.3%, 95% CI: 73.44% to 74.95%) and regions in central China had the lowest scores (total score 68.96%, 95% CI: 68.13% to 69.79%). There was a similar range in the percentage of patients who rated their care highly. For example, for doctors' concern for patients' mood, there was a more than 10 percentage point difference between the best (33.24%) and worst (20.70%) regions.

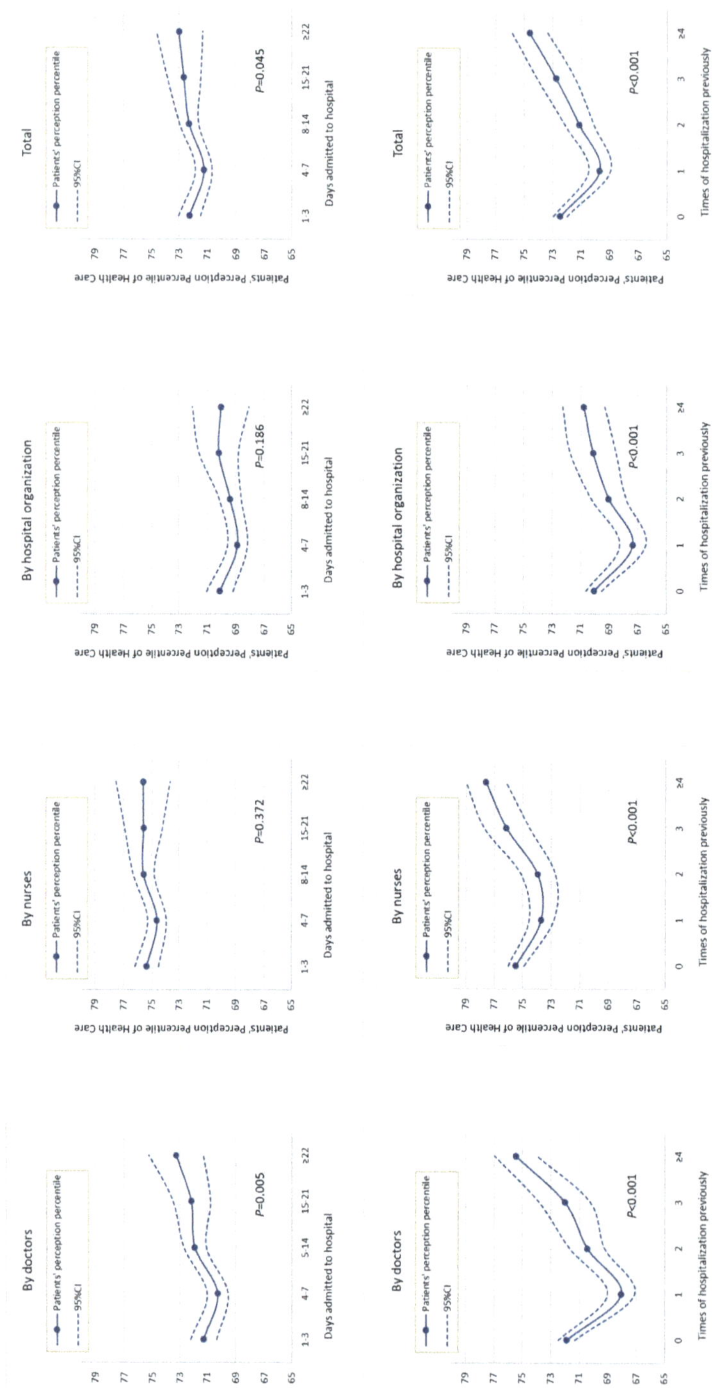

Figure 2. Dose–response curves of patients' perceptions with days admitted to hospital and times of hospitalization previously.

4. Discussion

To our knowledge, this study provides the first national data on patients' perceptions of healthcare in China. Overall, the highest (best) ratings of healthcare were found for nurse care, and the lowest (worst) ratings for hospital organization. For care by both doctors and nurses, the lowest ratings were for involvement in care (24.46% and 27.88%, respectively). Scores of patient perceptions of hospital care by length of hospital admission and number of previous hospitalizations showed a $\sqrt{}$-shaped dose–response curve. Of the five hospital characteristics rated, the technical level was most strongly associated with patient perceptions of healthcare. The association of patient perceptions with advertising was negative and that with personal recommendations was positive.

Patients' ratings of hospital care in China were relatively low compared with similar ratings in previous studies, particularly ratings in the US report [7,9,27,31]. There are two main possible explanations. First, as market-oriented reform of medical services in China began in 1985, most hospitals, including public hospitals, need to increase revenue and reduce expenditure. Therefore, hospitals often need to try to reduce the number of medical staff or persuade them to work full-time. Sometimes medical staff are overloaded and doctors in particular often must see as many patients as possible. Although the market-oriented reform of medical services stopped in 2005 [32], most hospitals need to generate their own income owing to lack of government investment. The so-called "three long, one short" conditions (i.e., long registration and queue times; long waiting times; long dispensary and payment queue times; and short physician visit times) and the corresponding deterioration in patient–provider relationships in China are testimony to the low opinion of healthcare by patients in China [22,33]. Second, unlike in the US, patients in China are completely free to visit hospitals, including outpatient clinics, and go directly to the hospital without seeing a primary care provider in the community. This not only increases the burden on hospital doctors, but also aggravates their job burnout, which may lead to a lower level of patient-oriented care of doctors in China than that in the US, especially in hospital settings. Third, the current practice in the US of publicly reporting data on the quality of healthcare, and incentivizing (or penalizing) clinicians based on patient satisfaction data, act as external motivations to improve the quality of healthcare, but these practices are not followed in China. Additionally, patient-centered care in the US is advanced compared with similar care in China; however, lessons are being learned from the US, and healthcare in China is slowly developing. In the three dimensions of patients' perceptions of hospital care, the service provided by hospital organizations is the lowest score; furthermore, the convenience of medical exams is the lowest score among the three items of the hospital organization dimension. This may further verify the above-mentioned "three long, one short", and more importantly, it also reveals the shortcomings of the service provided by the hospital organization dimension, compared to those by the doctor and nurse dimension [22,33]. Among the four items of the doctor/nurse dimension, the scores of nurses are higher than those of doctors, especially the accessibility, which may be related to a higher nurse-to-bed ratio and more emphasis on patient-oriented services by nursing policies.

The demographic characteristics of patients' perceptions with significant differences are consistent with most previous studies [5,6]. For example, patients with poor self-reported economic status reported lower perceptions of hospital care, which may be due to their physical distress combined with their psychosocial distress, and those may be the key target group of Medicaid policy.

The technical level of each hospital in China is certified by the government, and mainly comprises the quality of clinical care (i.e., the professional competence of clinicians, rather than medical equipment) and hospital organization (although clinical care quality is dominant) [20,22]. Information about hospital technical levels is in the public domain. The positive association between the hospital technical level and patients' perceptions of hospital care in this study may indicate a positive association between the quality of clinical care and patient reporting quality, which is consistent with previous study findings from different countries and regions [3,4]. As described above, patients' perceptions of healthcare reflect not only clinicians' interpersonal communication skills, but also on clinicians' clinical interrogation skills. Therefore, the quality of patient reports not only improves patient satisfaction and rewards for medical insurance (an external mechanism for quality improvement), but also informs the development of clinical interrogation and professional competence (an internal mechanism for quality improvement). Clinicians should be more concerned with internal mechanisms than with external mechanisms, as internal mechanisms are more relevant to the task of improving clinical quality.

Although TCM has been practiced for several thousand years in China, and the new Chinese National Health Guiding Principles emphasize the importance of both TCM and WM [34]; the development of WM has been rapid in the past decades; in contrast, the development of TCM has been very slow (even retrogressive) in some areas. TCM practice is currently learning from WM, and to a certain extent, even emulating WM practice. These factors may explain why we found no significant difference in patients' perceptions of TCM and WM healthcare. It is worrying that the current combination of TCM and WM seems to be evolving into an assimilation of TCM into WM. Understanding and developing the traditional wisdom of TCM to serve human health is the responsibility and mission of healthcare providers and managers, and TCM may play a special role in addressing the suffering of patients in the future.

Compared with predictors of hospital characteristics, predictors of previous hospitalization-related experiences had more impact on patient ratings, particularly length of hospital admission and number of previous hospitalizations. Patients' perceptions of healthcare related to these two factors showed a $\surd$-shaped dose–response curve, and the association largely remained significant after adjustment for other factors. The dose–response curves may indicate changes in consumer perceptions over time. The initial high score, regardless of whether it reflects the first hospitalization occurrence or the first 1–3 days of hospitalization, may be related to the novelty of the situation and a corresponding positive attitude in patients. Subsequently, this attitude may change; the patient may not experience immediate relief for their illness (they may be undergoing tests and awaiting the results of exams, but not receiving treatment) and may experience a sense of loss and anxiety, leading to a reduction in subsequent scores. As time passes and their treatment progresses, the patient may experience an improvement in their condition and develop a deeper understanding and trust in the clinicians, leading to higher scores. Specifically, regarding the length of hospital admission, patients' scores within 7 days of admission may be lowest; regarding the number of previous hospitalizations, the lowest scores may be from patients who have had one hospitalization. The average length of hospital stay in 2014 in China was 9.6 days [35]. Therefore, the above factors suggest that it may be more reasonable to measure the perception of healthcare in patients who have been hospitalized for more than 7 days or who have had one hospitalization experience, indicating the importance of timing in assessing patients' perceptions of healthcare, which may be worthy of further study in the future.

Patients in China are free to choose which doctor to consult. Therefore, many hospitals, including public hospitals, advertise for patients. Interestingly, only 11.5% of patients in this study selected the hospital for their current hospitalization based on advertisements, and 45.5% of patients selected their hospital based on personal recommendation (word-of-mouth). More interestingly, there was a negative association between patient perceptions and advertising, and a positive association between patient perceptions and personal recommendations. A possible explanation is that the advertisements issued by hospitals tend to highlight only the positive qualities of the hospital. This may mean that patients' expectations tend to be high before admission; after admission, they are more aware of both the positive and negative qualities of the hospital, so their ratings decrease. In contrast, personal recommendations (unlike advertising) may be more balanced, and may include both positive and negative qualities.

A low doctor–bed ratio or nurse–bed ratio avoids overstaffing but increases the workload (and may even lead to overload) of doctors and nurses in China [21]. We generally found no significant differences in patients' perceptions of healthcare according to the doctor–bed ratio or nurse–bed ratio. A possible explanation may be related to income allocation. As mentioned above, hospitals need to increase revenue and reduce expenditure; the more staff in a department, the less income can be allocated. Conversely, the fewer staff, the more income can be allocated. Therefore, the size of the doctor/nurse–bed ratio may not impact perceptions of healthcare quality.

5. Strengths and Limitations

This study had a number of strengths and limitations. First, our study extends this line of inquiry by focusing on a range of topics, especially hospital characteristics (differences in setting) and previous hospitalization-related experiences (changes with time). Second, to our knowledge, this study provides the first national data on patients' perceptions of healthcare in China. Third, private hospitals were not included in the study. Private hospitals in China are mainly specialized hospitals, such as beauty hospitals, eye hospitals, etc. The hospitalization services provided by private hospitals accounted for only 12.65% of the total inpatient services in China [26]. Fourth, the social network and information channel are not covered in this survey, and are the direction of future research [36,37]. Fifth, our study relied on cross-sectional data and therefore causality cannot be established.

6. Conclusions

Using a nationally representative sample, this study extends previous research that has described disparities in patients' perceptions of healthcare for both hospital characteristics and previous hospitalization-related experiences. The results suggest that the technical level of the hospital is the factor most strongly associated with patients' perceptions of healthcare, rather than any hospital characteristics, which indicates that the quality of patient reports is important not only to improve patient satisfaction and medical insurance reimbursement, but also to increase the quality of clinicians' professional competence.

Patients' perceptions of healthcare vary not only according to settings, but also across time, reflecting a $\sqrt{}$-shaped dose–response curve of patients' perceptions by length of hospital admission and number of previous hospitalizations. If it could be established that these associations were causal, this would help in determining the timing of patient satisfaction assessments. Additionally, the negative correlation between patient perception and advertising, and the positive correlation between patient perception and personal recommendations (word-of-mouth), could also provide important information for clinicians and hospital administrators.

Supplementary Materials: The following supporting information can be downloaded at: https://www.mdpi.com/article/10.3390/ijerph19137856/s1, Figure S1. Flowchart for recruitment and response rates of the participants. Table S1. Correlations among index of patients' perception of hospital care. Table S2. Patients' Perception of Hospital Care. Table S3. Difference of Patients' perception of hospital care in detail according to regional characteristics. Table S4. Patients' perception of hospital care according to hospital characteristics and patients' previous hospitalization-related experiences-Results of all independent variables. Table S5. Difference of Patients' perception of hospital care in detail according to regional characteristics. Table S6. Difference of three dimensions' and total score of patients' perception of hospital care according to regional characteristics.

Author Contributions: B.Y. and Y.W. had full access to all of the data in the study and takes responsibility for the integrity of the data and the accuracy of the data analysis. Concept and design: B.Y., Y.W. and Y.L. Acquisition, analysis, or interpretation of data: All authors. Drafting of the manuscript: All authors. Critical revision of the manuscript for important intellectual content: Y.W., B.Y., Y.Z. and Y.L. Statistical analysis: B.Y., Y.W., X.W. and Y.L. Obtained funding: Y.L. Administrative, technical, or material support: Y.W., B.Y., Y.Z. and Y.L. Supervision: Y.L. All authors have read and agreed to the published version of the manuscript.

Funding: This study was supported by grants from the National Natural Science Foundation of China (№: 71273098). The funders had no role in study design, data collection and analysis, decision to publish, or preparation of the manuscript.

Institutional Review Board Statement: The institutional review board at the Tongji Medical College, Huazhong University of Science and Technology (Wuhan, China) approved the study protocol [No. IORG0003571].

Informed Consent Statement: Informed consent was obtained from all subjects involved in the study.

Data Availability Statement: The study database is available via e-mail to the corresponding authors: Yuan Liang [liangyuan217@hust.edu.cn].

Acknowledgments: We would like to thank all the health staff and inpatients at 77 general hospitals who participated in the study.

Conflicts of Interest: The authors have declared that no competing interest exist.

References

1. Frosch, D.L. Patient-Reported Outcomes as a Measure of Healthcare Quality. *J. Gen. Intern. Med.* **2015**, *30*, 1383–1384. [CrossRef]
2. Fowler, F.J., Jr.; Gerstein, B.S.; Barry, M.J. How Patient Centered Are Medical Decisions? Results of a National Survey. *JAMA Intern. Med.* **2013**, *173*, 1215–1221. [CrossRef]
3. Schmocker, R.K.; Holden, S.E.; Vang, X.; Leverson, G.E.; Cherney Stafford, L.M.; Winslow, E.R. Association of Patient-Reported Readiness for Discharge and Hospital Consumer Assessment of Health Care Providers and Systems Patient Satisfaction Scores: A Retrospective Analysis. *J. Am. Coll. Surg.* **2015**, *221*, 1073–1082. [CrossRef]
4. Sacks, G.D.; Lawson, E.H.; Dawes, A.J.; Russell, M.M.; Maggard-Gibbons, M.; Zingmond, D.S.; Ko, C.Y. Relationship Between Hospital Performance on a Patient Satisfaction Survey and Surgical Quality. *JAMA Surg.* **2015**, *150*, 858–864. [CrossRef]
5. Roberto, N.S.; Maider, U.L.; Esther, L.; Sara, P.; Juan, F.O.; María, E.R. Inequalities in health care experience of patients with chronic conditions: Results from a population-based study. *Healthcare* **2021**, *9*, 1005.
6. Forestier, B.; Anthoine, E.; Reguiai, Z.; Fohrer, C.; Blanchin, M. A systematic review of dimensions evaluating patient experience in chronic illness. *Health Qual. Life Outcomes* **2019**, *17*, 19. [CrossRef]
7. Al-Amin, M.; Schiaffino, M.K.; Park, S.; Harman, J. Sustained Hospital Performance on Hospital Consumer Assessment of Healthcare Providers and Systems Survey Measures: What Are the Determinants? *J. Healthc. Manag.* **2018**, *63*, 15–28. [CrossRef]
8. Figueroa, J.F.; Feyman, Y.; Zhou, X.; Joynt Maddox, K. Hospital-level care coordination strategies associated with better patient experience. *BMJ Qual. Saf.* **2018**, *27*, 844–851. [CrossRef]
9. Jha, A.K.; Orav, E.J.; Zheng, J.; Epstein, A.M. Patients' perception of hospital care in the United States. *N. Engl. J. Med.* **2008**, *359*, 1921–1931. [CrossRef]
10. Jenkinson, C.; Coulter, A.; Bruster, S. The Picker Patient Experience Questionnaire: Development and validation using data from in-patient surveys in five countries. *Int. J. Qual. Health Care* **2002**, *14*, 353–358. [CrossRef]
11. Manary, M.; Staelin, R.; Kosel, K.; Schulman, K.A.; Glickman, S.W. Organizational Characteristics and Patient Experiences with Hospital Care: A Survey Study of Hospital Chief Patient Experience Officers. *Am. J. Med. Qual.* **2015**, *30*, 432–440. [CrossRef]
12. Groene, O.; Lombarts, M.J.; Klazinga, N.; Alonso, J.; Thompson, A.; Suñol, R. Is patient-centredness in European hospitals related to existing quality improvement strategies? Analysis of a cross-sectional survey (MARQuIS study). *Qual. Saf. Health Care* **2009**, *18*, i44–i50. [CrossRef]
13. Kraska, R.A.; Weigand, M.; Geraedts, M. Associations between hospital characteristics and patient satisfaction in Germany. *Health Expect.* **2017**, *20*, 593–600. [CrossRef]
14. Schoenfelder, T.; Klewer, J.; Kugler, J. Determinants of patient satisfaction: A study among 39 hospitals in an in-patient setting in Germany. *Int. J. Qual. Health Care* **2011**, *23*, 503–509. [CrossRef]
15. Al-Abri, R.; Al-Balushi, A. Patient satisfaction survey as a tool towards quality improvement. *Oman Med. J.* **2014**, *29*, 3. [CrossRef]
16. Ahmad, I.; Nawaz, A.; Khan, S.; Khan, H.; Rashid, M.A.; Khan, M.H. Predictors of patient satisfaction. *Gomal. J. Med. Sci.* **2012**, *9*, 183–188.
17. Gavurova, B.; Dvorsky, J.; Popesko, B. Patient Satisfaction Determinants of Inpatient Healthcare. *Int. J. Environ. Res. Public Health* **2021**, *18*, 11337. [CrossRef]
18. Rajagopal, P.; Montgomery, N.V. I Imagine I Experience, I Like: The False Experience Effect. *J. Consum. Res.* **2011**, *38*, 578–594. [CrossRef]
19. Joseph, P.S.; Leif, D.N.; Jeff, G.; Shane, F. Intuitive Biases in Choice versus Estimation: Implications for the Wisdom of Crowds. *J. Consum. Res.* **2011**, *38*, 1–15.
20. Elliott, M.N.; Lehrman, W.G.; Goldstein, E.; Hambarsoomian, K.; Beckett, M.K.; Giordano, L.A. Do Hospitals Rank Differently on HCAHPS for Different Patient Subgroups? *Med. Care Res. Rev.* **2010**, *67*, 56–73. [CrossRef]

21. Zhang, P.; Wang, F.; Cheng, Y.; Zhang, L.Y.; Ye, B.Z.; Jiang, H.W.; Sun, Y.; Zhu, X.; Liang, Y. Impact of organizational and individual factors on patient-provider relationships: A national survey of doctors, nurses and patients in China. *PLoS ONE* **2017**, *96*, 71–94. [CrossRef]
22. Liu, N.; Zhu, Y.; Wang, X.; Jiang, H.; Liang, Y. Association of organizational behavior with work engagement and work-home conflicts of physician in China. *Int. J. Environ. Res. Public Health* **2021**, *18*, 5405. [CrossRef]
23. Elliott, D.J.; Young, R.S.; Brice, J.; Aguiar, R.; Kolm, P. Effect of hospitalist workload on the quality and efficiency of care. *JAMA Intern. Med.* **2014**, *174*, 786–793. [CrossRef]
24. The Central People's Government of the People's Republic of China, 2011. China's Sixth National Census (2010) Main Data Bulletin № 2. Available online: http://www.gov.cn/gzdt/2011-04/29/content_1854891.htm (accessed on 12 September 2021).
25. Kahn, C.N.; Ault, T.; Isenstein, H.; Potetz, L.; Van Gelder, S. Snapshot of hospital quality reporting and pay-for-performance under Medicare. *Health Aff.* **2006**, *25*, 148–162. [CrossRef]
26. *China National Health and Family Planning Commission, Health and Family Planning Statistics Yearbook 2015*; China Union Medical University Press: Beijing, China, 2015.
27. Dyer, N.; Sorra, J.S.; Smith, S.A.; Cleary, P.D.; Hays, R.D. Psychometric properties of the Consumer Assessment of Healthcare Providers and Systems (CAHPS®) Clinician and Group Adult Visit Survey. *Med. Care* **2012**, *50*, S28–S34. [CrossRef]
28. Perneger, T.V. Adjustment for patient characteristics in satisfaction surveys. *Int. J. Qual. Health Care* **2004**, *16*, 433–435. [CrossRef]
29. McLeod, T.G.; Costello, B.A.; Colligan, R.C.; Dierkhising, R.A.; Beebe, T.J.; Offord, K.P.; Locke, G.R. Personality characteristics of health care satisfaction survey non-respondents. *Int. J. Health Care Qual. Assur.* **2009**, *22*, 145–156. [CrossRef]
30. Lyratzopoulos, G.; Elliott, M.; Barbiere, J.M.; Henderson, A.; Staetsky, L.; Paddison, C.; Campbell, J.; Roland, M. Understanding ethnic and other socio-demographic differences in patient experience of primary care: Evidence from the English General Practice Patient Survey. *BMJ Qual. Saf.* **2012**, *21*, 21–29. [CrossRef]
31. Warren, F.C.; Abel, G.; Lyratzopoulos, G.; Elliott, M.N.; Richards, S.; Barry, H.E.; Roland, M.; Campbell, J.L. Characteristics of service users and provider organisations associated with experience of out of hours general practitioner care in England: Population based cross sectional postal questionnaire survey. *BMJ* **2015**, *350*, h2040. [CrossRef]
32. Tang, C.; Xu, J.; Zhang, M. The choice and preference for public-private health care among urban residents in China: Evidence from a discrete choice experiment. *BMC Health Serv. Res.* **2016**, *16*, 580. [CrossRef]
33. Dai, J.; Wang, X.; Ayala, F.J. Medical Informatics and the "Three Long, One Short" Problem of Large Urban Hospitals in China. *JAMA* **2016**, *316*, 269–270. [CrossRef]
34. Zhang, P.; Liang, Y. China's National Health Guiding Principles: A perspective worthy of healthcare reform. *Prim. Health Care Res. Dev.* **2018**, *19*, 99–104. [CrossRef]
35. Xie, F.; Zhu, Z. Resources and utilizations of medical service in poverty-stricken areas in China. *Chin. J. Public Health* **2018**, *34*, 1013–1016.
36. Harris, J.; Atkinson, A.; Mink, M.; Porcellato, L. Young people's experiences and perceptions of YouTuber-produced health content: Implications for health promotion. *Health Educ. Behav.* **2020**, *48*, 199–207. [CrossRef]
37. Sampson, M.; Cumber, J.; Li, C.; Pound, C.M.; Fuller, A.; Harrison, D. A systematic review of methods for studying consumer health YouTube videos, with implications for systematic reviews. *Peer J.* **2013**, *1*, e147. [CrossRef]

International Journal of
Environmental Research and Public Health

MDPI

Article

Factors Affecting Delayed Hospital Arrival of Patients with Acute Myocardial Infarction in Kinmen

Yu-Han Huang [1], Chorng-Kuang How [2,3] and Ching-Sung Ho [4,*]

1 Cardiovascular Care Center, Kinmen Hospital, Ministry of Health and Welfare, Kinmen 89142, Taiwan; cindy7303067676@kmhp.mohw.gov.tw
2 Emergency Department, Taipei Veterans General Hospital, Taipei 11217, Taiwan; ckhow@vghtpe.gov.tw
3 Department of Emergency Medicine, School of Medicine, National Yang Ming Chiao Tung University, Taipei 11221, Taiwan
4 Department of Long Term Care, National Quemoy University, 1 University RD. Jinning Township, Kinmen 89250, Taiwan
* Correspondence: csho@nqu.edu.tw; Tel.: +886-8231-3909; Fax: +886-8231-3934

Abstract: This study explores factors related to delayed emergency medical treatment for acute myocardial infarction patients on Kinmen Island. A cross-sectional study was performed in the only hospital in Kinmen Island. The study group consisted of 116 patients diagnosed with acute myocardial infarction (AMI, ICD-10 codes: I21.9) from November 2015 to May 2019. The binary logistic regression analyses were performed for the inferential statistical analysis. The mean age of the study group was 63.0 $\pm$ 14.5 years, 39.7% of the patients arrived at the emergency medicine longer than 6 h after the onset of symptoms. The related factors for delayed arrival the hospital emergency medicine department were female sex, age over 65 years, less than nine years' education, and Killip Class, but only Killip Class reached the significant difference of statistics (OR = 3.616, 95% C.I. = 1.574 to 8.310, p = 0.002), and patients with delayed arrival times (>6 h) were found to have a higher percentage of Killip Class $\geq$ II. Therefore, it is essential to remind the physicians to proceed with risk stratification for acute coronary syndrome patients. In addition, health authorities should provide effective programs to increase awareness of the symptoms and timely treatment of acute myocardial infraction to the general public, especially the elderly.

Keywords: acute myocardial infarction; health visit delay; Killip Class; Kinmen

Citation: Huang, Y.-H.; How, C.-K.; Ho, C.-S. Factors Affecting Delayed Hospital Arrival of Patients with Acute Myocardial Infarction in Kinmen. *Int. J. Environ. Res. Public Health* **2022**, *19*, 1323. https://doi.org/10.3390/ijerph19031323

Academic Editor: Paul B. Tchounwou

Received: 24 December 2021
Accepted: 22 January 2022
Published: 25 January 2022

1. Introduction

Heart disease is a major health problem worldwide and is currently the leading cause of death in the USA [1]. There are more than 1000 deaths caused by cardiovascular diseases (CVD) daily, with 2.2 million hospitalizations and 415,480 deaths in 2016 [2]. In 2017, about 17.8 million deaths were attributed to CVD globally, an increase of 21.1% from 2007 [3]. Heart disease has been the second leading cause of death in Taiwan since 2007 [4]. There were 20,644 deaths due to heart disease in 2016 [5].

Myocardial infarction is the main contributor to the high incidence of heart failure [6,7]. Acute myocardial infarction (AMI) is defined as cardiomyocyte necrosis in a clinical setting consistent with acute myocardial ischemia, the detection of a rise and/or fall of cTn values with at least one value above the 99th percentile URL and at least one of the five indications: (1) symptoms of myocardial ischemia; (2) new ischemic electrocardiogram (ECG) changes; (3) development of pathological Q waves; (4) imaging evidence of new loss of viable myocardium or new regional wall motion abnormality in a pattern consistent with an ischemic etiology; (5) identification of a coronary thrombus by angiography or autopsy [8].

ST-elevation myocardial infarction (STEMI) is defined as ST elevation or left bundle branch block on the first or subsequent 12-lead electrocardiogram (ECG). In contrast, patients without ST-segment elevation at presentation are usually designated as having a non-ST-segment elevation myocardial infarction (NSTEMI) [9]. In the USA, there were six times as many patients with STEMI versus NSTEMI in 1990, but by 2000, the proportions had equalized, and subsequently, the proportion of NSTEMI exceeded that of STEMI [10]. Similarly, NSTEMI to STEMI incidence ratio increased from 1.93 in 2009 to 2.47 in 2015 in Taiwan [11]. This may be due to the increased use of troponin as a sensitive biomarker for diagnosing AMI, an aging population, the growing prevalence of antecedent coronary revascularization, the increased use of aspirin, and improved health system and medical therapy [10].

The Killip classification is a common clinical tool for cardiovascular assessment and risk stratification. According to Killip classification, patients are categorized into four classes during clinical examination. Patients in Class I have no evidence of heart failure (HF), patients in Class II had indications along with mild to moderate HF, patients in Class III had obvious pulmonary edema, and patients in Class IV were in cardiogenic shock [12]. Patients with higher Killip Class were found to have more severe angiographic coronary artery disease, higher occurrence of ventricular failure, and greater myocardial infarctions [13].

For patients who receive prompt care, reperfusion therapy including surgical or pharmacologic treatments can modify the progression of a heart attack and limit heart damage and subsequent morbidity and mortality [14,15]. The shorter the interval, the better the outcome, so patients should arrive at the hospital emergency room as soon as possible to maximize the chances of survival.

Delay in seeking medical treatment after symptoms begin may be due to misunderstanding the urgency of signs and symptoms, or psychological denial [16]. Numerous studies have found socio-demographic and clinical issues related to delayed treatment after the onset of a heart condition, and the elderly, females and those with a history of diabetes tend to have a longer delay in seeking medical treatment than the others [17–20]. Internationally, the median prehospital delay for AMI patients ranged from 2 to 6.5 h [21], and females had a longer delay in obtaining hospital treatment than males (median: 270 min versus 240 min) [22]. Therefore, it is important to clarify the gender difference between the onset of disease symptoms and the patient's arrival at a hospital emergency department.

Kinmen is a small island of 150 square kilometers, located near the major Chinese city of Xiamen, and administered as part of Taiwan. It has a permanent resident population of nearly 60,000 people and only one public district hospital (Kinmen Hospital of the Ministry of Health and Welfare), with 300 beds, which is the major center for medical care. The standardized mortality rate is 314.5 per 100,000 residents for all causes and heart disease is the second leading cause of death, as in Taiwan overall [23]. Although Kinmen Hospital is the only medical facility caring for HF patients and provides percutaneous coronary intervention (PCI) 24/7, patients diagnosed as too severe to be treated are transferred to major medical centers in Taiwan by plane or helicopter. Therefore, it is important to propose effective intervention strategies to help patients detect physiological signs of acute myocardial infarction and seek medical care promptly.

This study explored factors related to a delayed response to AMI in Kinmen and proposes suggestions for developing interventions to reduce the time from onset of symptoms to obtaining proper medical care.

2. Materials and Methods

A hospital-based cross-sectional study was conducted in Kinmen from January 2020 to June 2020 at the Kinmen hospital of the Ministry of Health and Welfare. The study sample consisted of 116 patients, aged 37 to 100 years, diagnosed with acute myocardial infarction (AMI, ICD-10 codes: I21.9) at the emergency department. This follows the definition of the European Society of Cardiology and the American College of Cardiology (ESC/ACC): The existence of at least two of the following three features: (1) Chest pain lasting more than 20 min, (2) ST-elevation of at least 2 mm in two or more contiguous leads with successive evolution of the electrocardiogram, and (3) elevated cardiac marker (CK-MB) or positive troponin I or T [24]. All patients in the study group were admitted between 20 November

2015, and 31 May 2019. According to ESC guidelines, two kinds of time intervals are mainly important: (1) the time delay between the onset of symptoms and the first medical contact (FMC) and (2) the time delay between FMC and the beginning of reperfusion [25]. Early ($\leq$6 h) treatment of PCI on the artery responsible for the myocardial infarction is a significant determinant factor of survival beyond the hospital phase of ST-elevation myocardial infarction [26]. The emergency medical service travel time is usually less than 30 min in Kinmen. Late arrival was defined as a time interval from the onset of symptoms to arrival at the hospital emergency room (ER) greater than six hours.

2.1. Statistical Analysis

Frequency analyses were conducted to assess AMI patients' late arrival distribution and classify the associated factors of late arrival. The distribution of late arrival was obtained for the arrival time from onset of symptoms to arrival at the ER. To assess significant issues related to patients' arrival levels, the Chi-Square test and binary logistic regressions were performed for inferential statistical analysis. The SPSS software package (version 18.0 was used for statistical analyses. The significance level for the Alpha value was set at 0.05).

2.2. Ethics Approval

The study protocol was approved by the Medical Ethics Committee of National Cheng Kung University (IRB no. 108-331). The institutional review board of the Medical Ethics Committee of National Cheng Kung University approved this study without requiring written informed consent from the patients under study.

3. Results

The study included 116 patients with a mean age of 63.0 $\pm$ 14.53 years, with 69 (59.5%) above 65 years of age. There were 64 (55.2%) with no more than nine years' education, most (94.8%) were married, and 101 (87.1%) were living with their family. Furthermore, 91.3% of the patients arrived at the ER by ambulance, 69 (59.5%) were diagnosed with ST-elevation myocardial infarction (STEMI), 60 (51.7%) were of Killip Class I, and only two were on IV. Comparing the chronic disease status, 60 (51.7%) had hypertension, 33.6% and 22.4% had diabetes mellitus and hyperlipidemia, respectively. 70 (60.3%) were found to have reached the ER equal to or less than 6 h after the onset of symptoms. The samples' basic sociodemographic and clinical characteristics are shown in Table 1.

Differences in the time to ER distribution among the AMI patients by the X^2 tests are shown in Table 2. There were various variables such as marital status, living with family status, and the means of travel to the ER, but most of the cases were concentrated in a single category. As such, inferential statistics analysis was not used Since there were only 27 patients with Killip scores three or higher, cases whose Killip Class was $\geq$II were combined as the high score group for the inferential analysis. Variables that reached significance included gender (p = 0.011), age (p = 0.004), educational level (p = 0.025), and Killip Class (p = 0.001). Comparing gender and time to ER, 65.0% of females showed > 6 h to ER, compared to 34.4% of males. A higher prevalence of time to ER > 6 h was related to higher age, with 53.3% of the patients older than 65 having time to ER longer than 6 h, while 29.0% of those 64 or younger were in this bracket. There was a higher prevalence of time to ER > 6 h in patients with less education. Among the patients with time to ER > 6 h, 57.0% had $\leq$ nine years of education, compared to 27.1% with 10 or more years of schooling. In the group of time to ER > 6 h, 57.1% had Killip Class of I, while 42.9% were equal or higher than II. The AMI patients diagnosed as STEMI were found to have a higher prevalence of time to ER > 6 h than NSTEMI (48.9% vs. 33.3%), but AMI type and chronic disease status, such as hypertension, diabetes mellitus, and hyperlipidemia, did not reach statistically significant difference (p > 0.05).

Table 1. The distribution of sociodemographic and clinical factors among the AMI patients in Kinmen.

	N		%
Gender			
Female	20		17.2
male	96		82.8
Age		Mean ± SD = 63.01 ± 14.53	
≤64	69		59.5
≥65	47		40.5
Marriage status			
Unmarried	6		5.2
Married	90		77.6
Divorced/Separated	11		9.5
Widow	9		7.8
Educational level (years)			
≤9	64		55.2
≥10	52		44.8
Living with family			
Yes	101		87.1
No	15		12.9
Way to ER Visit			
Self	10		8.7
By ambulance	106		91.3
AMI Type			
STEMI	69		59.5
NSTEMI	47		44.4
Killip Classification			
I	60		51.7
II	29		25.0
III	25		21.6
IV	2		1.7
With Hypertension			
Yes	60		51.7
No	56		48.3
With Diabetes Mellitus			
Yes	39		33.6
No	77		66.4
Hyperlipidemia			
Yes	26		22.4
No	90		77.6
Late Arrival			
Yes	46		39.7
No	70		60.3
Total	116		100.0

Table 3 shows results from the binary logistic regression analyses, indicating that the difference of time to ER among genders, age groups, and educational levels did not reach significance. This result illustrates that the Killip Class is a correlation factor for time to ER distribution. Patients with delayed arrival times (>6 h) were found to have a higher percentage of Killip Class ≥ II. (OR = 3.616, 95% C.I. = 1.574 to 8.310, p = 0.002).

The prevalence of time to ER > 6 h for female patients was higher than for males (OR = 1.084) However, the distribution of time to ER among gender, age group, and educational level did not significantly differ.

The limited case numbers may lead to underpowered results. Table 3a,b indicate the results of two independent variables analyzed in the binary logistic regression analyses. Killip Class reached a significant difference in both models (OR = 3.936, 95% C.I. = 1.736 to 8.823, p = 0.001 and OR = 4.214, 95% C.I. = 1.835 to 9.266, p = 0.001), respectively. Higher age (≥65) having time to ER longer than 6 h than those 64 or younger (OR = 2.602, 95% C.I. = 1.149 to 5.895, p = 0.022) and educational levels did not reach statistically significant difference.

Table 2. The distribution of different factors related to late arrival of AMI patients.

	Late Arrival N (%)			p Value
	No	Yes	Total	
Gender *				0.011
Female	7(35.0)	13(65.0)	20(100)	
Male	63(65.6)	33(34.4)	96(100)	
Age **				0.004
≤64	49(71.0)	20(29.0)	69(100)	
≥65	21(44.7)	26(53.3)	47(100)	
Educational level (years) *				0.025
≤9	33(51.6)	31(48.4)	64(100)	
≥10	70(72.9)	26(27.1)	96(100)	
AMI type				0.068
STEMI	24(51.1)	23(48.9)	47(100)	
NSTEMI	46(76.7)	23(33.3)	69(100)	
With Hypertension				0.394
Yes	35(58.3)	25(41.7)	60(100)	
No	35(62.5)	21(37.3)	56(100)	
With Diabetes Mellitus				0.331
Yes	25(64.1)	14(35.9)	39(100)	
No	44(57.9)	33(42.1)	77(100)	
With Hyperlipidemia				0.462
Yes	15(57.7)	11(42.3)	26(100)	
No	55(61.1)	35(38.9)	90(100)	
Killip Classification **				0.001
I	46(76.7)	14(23.3)	60(100)	
≥II	24(42.9)	32(57.1)	56(100)	

*: $p < 0.05$; **: $p < 0.01$.

Table 3. The logistic regression analysis of late arrival in different factors. (**a**) The logistic regression analysis of late arrival in age and Killip Classification. (**b**) The logistic regression analysis of late arrival in educational level and Killip Classification.

	OR	95% C.I.	p Value
Gender			
Male	Reference		
Female	1.804	0.576–5.648	0.311
Age			
≤64	Reference		
≥65	2.041	0.786–5.298	0.143
Educational Level			
≤9	1.172	0.485–3.338	0.625
≥10	Reference		
Killip Classification			
I	Reference		
≥II	3.616	1.574–8.310	0.002
			$R^2 = 0.224$

(**a**)

	OR	95% C.I.	p Value
Age			
≤64	Reference		
≥65	2.602	1.149–5.895	0.022
Killip Classification			
I	Reference		
≥II	3.936	1.736–8.823	0.001
			$R^2 = 0.209$

(**b**)

	OR	95% C.I.	p Value
Educational Level			
≤9	2.060	0.908–4.643	0.084
≥10	Reference		
Killip Classification			
I	Reference		
≥II	4.214	1.835–9.266	0.001
			$R^2 = 0.186$

4. Discussion

To the best of our knowledge, this is the first study to analyze the clinical and sociodemographic factors for the time to ER of AMI patients in Kinmen Island. This study finds that almost 40% of the AMI patients were late for arrival to the ER. This is higher than prior studies reported that 25% to 30% of AMI patients arrive at the hospital >6 h after symptom onset [27]. Since early treatment is crucial to reducing mortality, developing effective programs to help people respond quickly and obtain medical service is important.

Some studies indicated that age and gender (female) were associated with a delayed presentation for clinical service, and our findings agree with reports that the elderly experienced longer delays in looking for hospital treatment [28,29]. More than 50% of patients over 65 had a late arrival to ER, whereas only 29.0% of younger patients (<65 years) arrived late. This may be due to the elderly having restricted access to medical care or insufficient medical knowledge, particularly when living in rural areas or alone. Furthermore, the elderly may not identify the symptoms of acute coronary disease or recognize their severity. Designing intervention programs to help the elderly recognize symptoms of this disease and provide timely treatment in rural areas requires further research.

This study finds that 65% of female patients delayed more than six hours before being admitted to ER, compared to 34.4% of male patients, concurring with previous studies [28,29]. Females have delayed seeking medical care more than men due to a lower occurrence of acute coronary diseases. Hence, they are more likely to ignore the signs and symptoms. In addition, differences in biological, sociodemographic, and behavioral characteristics between females and males may contribute to the gender discrepancy in time delay. However, since age and gender are not significant predictors for delayed arrival in the multiple logistic model, the relationship between the influence of age, gender, and delayed presentation for clinical service needs further investigation. Therefore, public health authorities should design and propagate programs about early treatment of AMI for the elderly and females.

This study finds that people with more years of formal education have a lower prevalence of delayed presentation to the hospital than those with formal education less than 10 years. It is clear that people with higher educational levels have better knowledge about health status or disease symptoms and how to deal with medical problems. People in the United States with fewer years of education are inclined more have a higher prevalence of cardiovascular disease [30]. The elderly in Kinmen, as well as Taiwan generally, usually have less education than younger people. The actual effect between delayed presentation to the hospital and the education level combined with age needs further investigation.

According to the National Health Insurance Research Database (NHIRD) of the National Health Research Institute in Taiwan, the ratio of NSTEMI to STEMI incidence was 2.47 in 2015 [11]. Still, the prevalence of STEMI is higher than NSTEMI (59.5% vs. 44.5%) in Kinmen, and the reasons for this difference need further investigation. It was found that STEMI was associated with a higher risk of short-term mortality, but NSTEMI was associated with a higher risk of long-term mortality [31]. Early treatment or revascularization is important for better long-term outcomes for both STEMI and NSTEMI, but the late arrival rate to ER did not reach a significant difference of statistics in Kinmen.

We found that Killip Class is a significant issue relating to delayed arrival at ER for medical care of AMI patients in Kinmen. This result is consistent with previous findings from Middle Eastern countries that patients with higher Killip Class sought medical care later than 12 h and those with higher resting heart rate and irregular blood sugar barely showed chest pain at presentation [12]. This has been found to result in physician selection bias where patients with higher Killip Class tend to receive fewer coronary angiography- and evidence-based therapies than patients with Class I. Since high Killip Class was a significant indicator of mortality in STEMI and NSTEMI myocardial infarction and non–ST-elevation acute coronary syndrome, emergency medicine physicians should be attentive to clinical examination in the risk classification for patients with acute coronary conditions.

We performed the binary logistic regression with just two independent variables. The results reveal that age (elderly patients ≥65 years) and higher Killip Class (≥II) are significant factors related to delayed arrival at ER, but the educational level did not reach a significant difference of statistics. Therefore, the relationship between delayed arrival and Killip Class, age, educational level, gender in Kinmen should be investigated in future studies.

Strengths and Limitations

This study presents the empirical finding that patients' Killip Class, gender, age, and educational level are important factors related to delayed ER arrival for medical care of AMI patients in Kinmen. Killip Class was found to have the most significant correlation. This information could help provide a direction for future research in planning effective care regimes for AMI patients in areas with insufficient medical resources.

There are some limitations to this study. The sample was taken from the only hospital in Kinmen Island, and the case number was limited, which limited the application of more advanced inferential statistics. Since this is a cross-sectional study, the effects of factors relating to delayed arrival at the ER for medical care need further exploration.

5. Conclusions

The study determines that delayed arrival at ER is highly correlated to higher Killip Class. It is important to remind physicians to proceed with risk stratification for patients with acute coronary syndrome. Health authorities should propose effective education programs to the general public, and especially the elderly, for the symptoms and timely treatment of acute myocardial infarction.

Author Contributions: Conceptualization, Y.-H.H. and C.-S.H.; methodology, Y.-H.H. and C.-S.H.; formal analysis, Y.-H.H. and C.-S.H.; investigation, C.-K.H. and C.-S.H.; writing—original draft preparation, Y.-H.H. and C.-S.H.; writing—review and editing, Y.-H.H., C.-K.H., and C.-S.H.; project administration, Y.-H.H. and C.-S.H. All authors have read and agreed to the published version of the manuscript.

Funding: This research received no external funding.

Institutional Review Board Statement: The study protocol was approved by the Medical Ethics Committee of National Cheng Kung University (IRB no. 108-331). The institutional review board of the Medical Ethics Committee of National Cheng Kung University approved this study without requiring written informed consent from any study patients.

Informed Consent Statement: Patient consent was waived due to analysis of the clinical data having no connection with the personal data.

Acknowledgments: The authors thank John Baker, assistant professor of the Department of Business Administration, National Quemoy University, for editing.

Conflicts of Interest: The authors declare no conflict of interest.

References

1. National Center for Health Statistics. National Vital Statistics System: Public Use Data File Documentation: Mortality Multiple Cause-of-Death Micro-Data Files. Centers for Disease Control and Prevention website. 2017. Available online: https://www.cdc.gov/nchs/nvss/mortality_public_use_data.htm (accessed on 1 April 2019).
2. Wright, J.S.; Wall, H.K.; Ritchey, M.D. Million Hearts 2022: Small steps are needed for cardiovascular disease prevention. *JAMA* **2018**, *320*, 1857–1858. [CrossRef]
3. Virani, S.S.; Alonso, A.; Benjamin, E.J.; Bittencourt, M.S.; Callaway, C.W.; Carson, A.P.; Chamberlain, A.M.; Chang, A.R.; Cheng, S.; Delling, F.N. Heart disease and stroke statistics—2020 update: A report from the American Heart Association. *Circulation* **2020**, *141*, E139–E596. [CrossRef] [PubMed]
4. Department of Statistics, Ministry of Health and Welfare. Cause of Death Statistics. Available online: https://dep.mohw.gov.tw/DOS/lp-1828-113.html (accessed on 1 April 2019).
5. Department of Statistics, Ministry of Health and Welfare. Taipei Taiwan Cause of Death Statistics. Available online: https://www.mohw.gov.tw/cp-3795-41794-1.html (accessed on 1 April 2019).

6. Hellermann, J.P.; Jacobsen, S.J.; Redfield, M.M.; Reeder, G.S.; Weston, S.A.; Roger, V.L. Heart failure after myocardial infarction: Clinical presentation and survival. *Eur. J. Heart Fail.* **2005**, *7*, 119–125. [CrossRef] [PubMed]
7. Weir, R.A.; McMurray, J.J.; Velazquez, E.J. Epidemiology of heart failure and left ventricular systolic dysfunction after acute myocardial infarction: Prevalence, clinical characteristics, and prognostic importance. *Am. J. Cardiol.* **2006**, *97*, 13–25. [CrossRef]
8. Thygesen, K.; Alpert, J.S.; Jaffe, A.S.; Chaitman, B.R.; Bax, J.J.; Morrow, D.A.; White, H.D. ESC Scientific Document Group. Fourth universal definition of myocardial infarction (2018). *Eur. Heart J.* **2019**, *40*, 237–269. [CrossRef]
9. Collet, J.P.; Thiele, H.; Barbato, E.; Barthélémy, O.; Bauersachs, J.; Bhatt, D.L.; Dendale, P.; Dorobantu, M.; Edvardsen, T.; Folliguet, T.; et al. ESC Scientific Document Group. 2020 ESC Guidelines for the management of acute coronary syndromes in patients presenting without persistent ST-segment elevation. *Eur. Heart J.* **2021**, *42*, 1289–1367. [CrossRef] [PubMed]
10. Rogers, W.J.; Frederick, P.D.; Stoehr, E.; Canto, J.G.; Ornato, J.P.; Gibson, C.M.; Pollack, C.V., Jr.; Gore, J.M.; Chandra-Strobos, N.; Peterson, E.D. Trends in presenting characteristics and hospital mortality among patients with ST elevation and non-ST elevation myocardial infarction in the National Registry of Myocardial Infarction from 1990 to 2006. *Am. Heart J.* **2008**, *156*, 1026–1034. [CrossRef]
11. Lee, C.-H.; Fang, C.-C.; Tsai, L.-M.; Gan, S.-T.; Lin, S.-H.; Li, Y.-H. Patterns of acute myocardial infarction in Taiwan from 2009 to 2015. *Am. J. Cardiol.* **2018**, *122*, 1996–2004. [CrossRef]
12. DeGeare, V.S.; Boura, J.A.; Grines, L.L.; O'Neill, W.W.; Grines, C.L. Predictive value of the Killip classification in patients undergoing primary percutaneous coronary intervention for acute myocardial infarction. *Am. J. Cardiol.* **2001**, *87*, 1035–1038. [CrossRef]
13. El-Menyar, A.; Zubaid, M.; AlMahmeed, W.; Sulaiman, K.; AlNabti, A.; Singh, R.; Al Suwaidi, J. Killip classification in patients with acute coronary syndrome: Insight from a multicenter registry. *Am. J. Emerg. Med.* **2012**, *30*, 97–103. [CrossRef]
14. Finnegan, J.R., Jr.; Meischke, H.; Zapka, J.G.; Leviton, L.; Meshack, A.; Benjamin-Garner, R.; Estabrook, B.; Hall, N.J.; Schaeffer, S.; Smith, C. Patient delay in seeking care for heart attack symptoms: Findings from focus groups conducted in five US regions. *Prev. Med.* **2000**, *31*, 205–213. [CrossRef]
15. Khan, M.S.; Jafary, F.H.; Faruqui, A.M.; Rasool, S.I.; Hatcher, J.; Chaturvedi, N.; Jafar, T.H. High prevalence of lack of knowledge of symptoms of acute myocardial infarction inPakistan and its contribution to delayed presentationto the hospital. *BMC Public Health* **2007**, *7*, 284. [CrossRef] [PubMed]
16. O'Carroll, R.; Smith, K.; Grubb, N.; Fox, K.; Masterton, G. Psychological factors associated with delay in attending hospital following a myocardial infarction. *J. Psychosom. Res.* **2001**, *51*, 611–614. [CrossRef]
17. De Luca, G.; Suryapranata, H.; Ottervanger, J.P.; Antman, E.M. Time delay to treatment and mortality in primary angioplasty for acute myocardial infarction: Every minute of delay counts. *Circulation* **2004**, *109*, 1223–1225. [CrossRef] [PubMed]
18. Dracup, K.; Moser, D.K.; Eisenberg, M.; Meischke, H.; Alonzo, A.A.; Braslow, A. Causes of delay in seeking treatment for heart attack symptoms. *Soc. Sci. Med.* **1995**, *40*, 379–392. [CrossRef]
19. Moser, D.K.; McKinley, S.; Dracup, K.; Chung, M.L. Gender differences in reasons patients delay in seeking treatment for acute myocardial infarction symptoms. *Patient Educ. Couns.* **2005**, *56*, 45–54. [CrossRef]
20. Ottesen, M.M.; Dixen, U.; Torp-Pedersen, C.; Køber, L. Prehospital delay in acute coronary syndrome—an analysis of the components of delay. *Int. J. Cardiol.* **2004**, *96*, 97–103. [CrossRef]
21. Dracup, K.; Moser, D.K.; McKinley, S.; Ball, C.; Yamasaki, K.; Kim, C.J.; Doering, L.V.; Caldwell, M.A. An international perspective on the time to treatment for acute myocardial infarction. *J. Nurs. Scholarsh.* **2003**, *35*, 317–323. [CrossRef]
22. Bugiardini, R.; Ricci, B.; Cenko, E.; Vasiljevic, Z.; Kedev, S.; Davidovic, G.; Zdravkovic, M.; Miličić, D.; Dilic, M.; Manfrini, O. Delayed care and mortality among women and men with myocardial infarction. *J. Am. Heart Assoc.* **2017**, *6*, e005968. [CrossRef]
23. Department of Statistics, Ministry of Health and Welfare. Cause of Death Statistics. Available online: https://dep.mohw.gov.tw/DOS/lp-1861-113.html (accessed on 1 April 2019).
24. French, J.K.; White, H.D. Clinical implications of the new definition of myocardial infarction. *Heart* **2004**, *90*, 99–106. [CrossRef]
25. Silber, S. Evidence-based management of ST-segment elevation myocardial infarction (STEMI). Latest guidelines of the European Society of Cardiology (ESC) 2010. *Herz* **2010**, *35*, 558–564. [CrossRef]
26. Wierzbicka, M.; Kośmider, M.; Bielecka-Dąbrowa, A.; Goch, J.H. The meaning of early percutaneous coronary intervention in acute coronary syndrome with preserved ST elevation. *Cent. Eur. J. Med.* **2009**, *4*, 265–271. [CrossRef]
27. Sheifer, S.E.; Rathore, S.S.; Gersh, B.J.; Weinfurt, K.P.; Oetgen, W.J.; Breall, J.A.; Schulman, K.A. Time to presentation with acute myocardial infarction in the elderly: Associations with race, sex, and socioeconomic characteristics. *Circulation* **2000**, *102*, 1651–1656. [CrossRef]
28. McGinn, A.P.; Rosamond, W.D.; Goff, D.C., Jr.; Taylor, H.A.; Miles, J.S.; Chambless, L. Trends in prehospital delay time and use of emergency medical services for acute myocardial infarction: Experience in 4 US communities from 1987–2000. *Am. Heart J.* **2005**, *150*, 392–400. [CrossRef] [PubMed]
29. Moser, D.K.; Kimble, L.P.; Alberts, M.J.; Alonzo, A.; Croft, J.B.; Dracup, K.; Evenson, K.R.; Go, A.S.; Hand, M.M.; Kothari, R.U. Reducing delay in seeking treatment by patients with acute coronary syndrome and stroke: A scientific statement from the American Heart Association Council on cardiovascular nursing and stroke council. *Circulation* **2006**, *114*, 168–182. [CrossRef]
30. Steptoe, A.; Marmot, M. Socioeconomic status and coronary heart disease: A psychobiological perspective. *Popul. Dev. Rev.* **2004**, *30*, 133–150.
31. Puymirat, E.; Simon, T.; Cayla, G.; Cottin, Y.; Elbaz, M.; Coste, P.; Lemesle, G.; Motreff, P.; Popovic, B.; Khalife, K. Acute myocardial infarction: Changes in patient characteristics, management, and 6-month outcomes over a period of 20 years in the FAST-MI Program (French Registry of Acute ST-Elevation or Non-ST-Elevation Myocardial Infarction) 1995 to 2015. *Circulation* **2017**, *136*, 1908–1919. [CrossRef] [PubMed]

International Journal of
Environmental Research and Public Health

MDPI

Article

Political Populism, Institutional Distrust and Vaccination Uptake: A Mediation Analysis

Almudena Recio-Román *, Manuel Recio-Menéndez and María Victoria Román-González *

Department of Economics and Business, University of Almería, Carretera de Sacramento s/n, 04120 Almería, Spain; mrecio@ual.es
* Correspondence: arr306@inlumine.ual.es (A.R.-R.); mvroman@ual.es (M.V.R.-G.)

Abstract: Politics is ubiquitous in public health, but vaccines had never been weaponized to instill distrust to gain political advantage. In pandemic and post-pandemic scenarios, populist political parties could use vaccine-related issues to generate distrust in evidence-based knowledge. Therefore, some questions arise. What impact could populist political parties impinge on vaccination uptake rates through sowing political discontent? What could the medical institutions do to avoid the adverse effects that these political strategies could infringe? For answering these research questions, we first hypothesized that vaccine uptake was negatively associated with distrust in the institutions. Furthermore, we analyzed whether populism mediates this relationship. In doing so, we hypothesized a positive association between distrust and populism, because populists, mainly fueled by politically discontent citizens, offer hope of a better future, blaming their misfortune on the actions of the elite. Additionally, we hypothesized that those citizens with a higher level of political dissatisfaction, following the claims of the populist political parties, will have lower vaccine uptake results, because they will be discouraged from making the efforts to counter the pandemic. Based on a survey carried out by the European Commission that covered 27 E.U. + U.K. countries (totaling 27,524 respondents), this paper proves that an individual's political discontent fully mediates the relationship between distrust in institutions and vaccine uptake. Targeting the vaccine-hesitant population is quite convenient for populists because they only need to convince a minority of citizens not to be vaccinated to achieve their destabilizing goals. New outbreaks will appear if the minimum herd immunity coverage is not reached, reinforcing a vicious circle of distrust in elites, in consequence. For tackling this matter, recommendations are given to institutional managers from a social marketing standpoint.

Keywords: vaccine hesitancy; populism; consumer behavior; social marketing

Citation: Recio-Román, A.; Recio-Menéndez, M.; Román-González, M.V. Political Populism, Institutional Distrust and Vaccination Uptake: A Mediation Analysis. *Int. J. Environ. Res. Public Health* **2022**, *19*, 3265. https://doi.org/10.3390/ijerph19063265

Academic Editors: Joan Costa-Font and Paul B. Tchounwou

Received: 22 December 2021
Accepted: 8 March 2022
Published: 10 March 2022

1. Introduction

COVID-19 has brought forward a new role for politics, in the global vaccines scenario [1]. Governments buy vaccines and decide who will be jabbed, and when. Traditionally, the pharmaceutical industry and the health system's institutions (at national, regional, or local levels) took these decisions. In addition, politics played, and still plays nowadays, an essential role in several other vaccine-related dimensions: research and development, procurement, production, and marketing activities [2]. Hence, politics is ubiquitous in public health [3], but vaccines have never been weaponized to instill distrust to gain a political advantage [4].

An upward trend supporting populist parties is present in developed and developing countries, implying a significant challenge for universal healthcare [5]. Several studies showed that votes for populist parties are mainly based on dissatisfaction with the political establishment [6]. Political populism defends ordinary people in contrast with the real or perceived elite. The elite usually refers to mainstream political parties, the media, the upper classes, intellectuals, and, in the territorial scope of this work, the European Union [7]. When applied to healthcare issues, medical populism [8] is based on a distrust of evidence-based policy interventions and the condemnation of technocratic knowledge [3,9,10]. Worsening population health may cause more significant social discontent and the growth of populist sentiments [11]. Hence, populist leaders will exploit health crises for political gain [7,11].

Resistance to vaccination could be seen in disenchanted citizens as a way to express their discontent [12]. The populist approach appeals to groups of citizens that have been left behind for various reasons, including the consequences of the globalization process [3,13]. Populist leaders take advantage of their discontent, blaming their misfortune on the elite's actions. Populist politicians offer politically dissatisfied people the hope of a better future, attracting their votes [13,14]. Consequently, a worrisome circle occurs: populism fuels the spread of infectious diseases and infectious diseases fuel populism [13]. Several real examples illustrate that medical populism is not occasional but a frequent response to pandemic emergencies [8]. A common medical populism framework for action was shared in cases, such as the H.I.V. denialism in South Africa [15], the measles-rubella vaccine scare in Ukraine [16], the Nigerian boycott of the polio vaccine [17], the Dengue vaccine scandal in the Philippines and other countries of the global south [18], the West African Ebola virus epidemic scare [19], the anti-vaccination movement in Italy [20], and the more recent responses to the COVID-19 pandemic [13], in the U.S.A., Brazil, the Philippines, Poland, Russia, India, and the United Kingdom. Populist governments implemented soft policy measures and discouraged citizens' efforts to counter the pandemic in all these cases. As a result, populist-governed countries are hit worse by a pandemic than conventional ones [21].

The main goal of this paper is to measure how the relationship between distrust of institutions and vaccine uptake is mediated by political dissatisfaction. To the best of our knowledge, no one has ever studied it before.

2. Conceptual Background

2.1. Trust and Vaccine Uptake

Public trust in vaccination has declined in the last two decades [22]. Following Larson [22], trust is the "relationship that exists between individuals, as well as between individuals and a system, in which one party accepts a vulnerable position, assuming the best interests and competence of the other, in exchange for a reduction in decision complexity". Vaccine-related information and decision-making are technically complex enough to rely on people's confidence in the different health system components [23]. There are several levels of trust involved in the vaccine uptake process. The core of the vaccine's trust framework comprises three items [24]: the trust in the vaccine, the provider, and the political system. Quantitative studies that examined the relationship between trust in the health system and vaccine uptake found a positive association among them [25–28]. However, other studies showed that the variation in trust between vaccines and healthcare providers does not explain the variation in vaccination coverage [29,30]. Therefore, to study the variability in the influence of trust in vaccine uptake, we must mainly consider other social institutions that could influence the vaccination decision-making process. Among these social institutions, we thought it essential to analyze the information media, the political parties, the regional or local public authorities, the national government, the national Parliament, and, due to the territorial scope of this paper, the European Union [24,31]. These could explain how vaccine hesitancy increases worldwide, while having highly effective vaccines [32]. Building on Recio-Román et al. [32], we measured trust using a simplified scale that considers the social institutions mentioned earlier (from now on referred to as Distrust because it was reverse coded). Following the previous reasoning, we expected that the higher a person's distrust in the institutions, the lower the vaccine uptake will be.

Hypothesis 1 (H1). *The higher the Distrust in the institutions, the lower the Vaccine Uptake is.*

2.2. Political Dissatisfaction, Populism, Vaccine Hesitancy, and Vaccine Uptake

Vaccines have a differential characteristic from other medicines; to be effective, it is necessary to immunize a high percentage of the population. Also known as herd immunity—the level at which immunization coverage must be maintained to be effective—this percentage varies between 80% and 90% in most vaccines [23,33]. If this level is not reached and maintained, the risk of new outbreaks increases—also called the small pockets issue. Vaccine reluctance and refusal are not the same things. Vaccine hesitancy—the reluctance or refusal to vaccinate despite the availability of vaccines—lies between those who accept all vaccines without any doubt and those who reject all vaccines without any doubt [34]. It is an increasing trend all around the world [35].

The existing body of literature on the rising support of populist movements across the globe emphasizes the highly significant role of political discontent [36–38]. Therefore, political dissatisfaction is critical in developing definitions of populism [8,39,40]. Populism is a consequence of democratic dysfunction, caused by the feeling that democratic institutions are not working well [41,42]. Following Kitschelt [43], populism is an expression of dissatisfaction with existing modes of organized elite mass political intermediation and the desire to abandon the intermediaries that stand between citizens and rulers. Furthermore, political discontent increases the likelihood of stable voting for populist parties [44]. Vaccine hesitancy matches flawlessly in populist agendas. Both share the profound distrust in elites and experts as their main drivers [45]. High levels of distrust and polarization are fertile areas for strengthening dissatisfaction against the elite [46].

Hypothesis 2 (H2). *Distrust in institutions is positively associated with political discontent (populism).*

Political ideology influences how policymakers address and solve healthcare issues [47]. Populist political parties know that vaccines are fertile ground for instilling doubt and gaining from polarized debates [48]. In pandemic and, mainly, post-pandemic scenarios, populists polarize pros and cons on vaccines, linking them with any other factionalizing feelings (anti-chemical, anti-science, anti-migration, anti-abortion, anti-government, etc.) [49]. Targeting the vaccine-hesitant population is very convenient for populists because they only need to convince a minority of citizens not to be vaccinated to achieve their destabilizing goals. New outbreaks will appear if the minimum herd immunity coverage is not reached, reinforcing a vicious circle of distrust in elites [23,33].

Hypothesis 3 (H3). *Political discontent (populism) is negatively associated with vaccine uptake.*

Hence, in this paper, considering political discontent as a proxy for political populism, we study how Populism mediates between Distrust and Vaccine Uptake. We expect that the higher the Distrust, the lower the Vaccine Uptake—total effect. As Figure 1 depicts, we hypothesized that those with a higher level of political dissatisfaction have lower vaccine uptake results—indirect effect. The total effect not explained by the populism mediation comprised the direct effect.

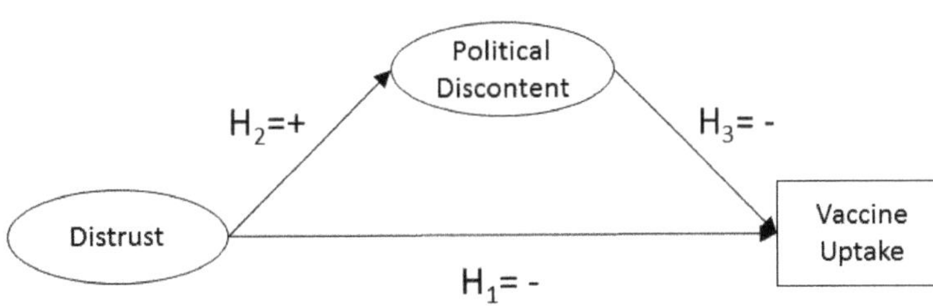

Figure 1. Conceptual model and hypotheses.

Finally, several studies also consider sociodemographic variables as moderators of vaccine uptake [12,50–52]. However, it is remarkable that they reach inconclusive or contradictory findings [53]. These could be explained by considering them as potential confounders of factors that determine vaccine uptake. Even though they could be related to vaccine uptake, they cannot explain its variation. They could help to target purposes, but the design of the planned intervention must rely on the other drivers that the model offers.

3. Materials and Methods

3.1. Sample

The data stemmed from the EUROBAROMETER survey 91.2 carried out between 15 and 29 March 2019 by the company Kantar Public, at the request of the European Commission [54]. The dataset was accessed through GESIS (Leibniz-Institute für Sozialwissenschaften, University of Cologne, Germany) at https://www.gesis.org/ (accessed on 16 October 2021). The EUROBAROMETER is part of wave 91.2 and covers the population of the respective nationalities of the European Union member states, residents in each of the member states, and aged 15 years and over. In these countries, the survey covers the national population of citizens of the respective nationalities and the population of citizens of the entire European Union member states that are resident in those countries and have a sufficient command of one of the respective national language(s) to answer the questionnaire. The basic sample design applied in all states is a multi-stage random one, totaling 27,524 respondents (see Table A1 in the Appendix A).

3.2. Measures

3.2.1. Model Measurement Constructs (Distrust)

The survey measured vaccine trust (Cronbach's Alpha = 0.77) using six items: " ... how much trust you have in certain media and institutions ... " Item 1. "The media", Item 2. "Political parties", Item 3. "Regional or local public authorities", Item 4. "The national government", Item 5. "The national parliament", Item 6. "The European Union". Respondents expressed their agreement with these statements on a two-item scale from 1 ("Totally agree") to 2 ("Totally disagree"). As the scale was reversed, we named the resulting latent variable as DISTRUST.

3.2.2. Mediator Variable (Populism)

The survey asked the interviewees three questions about political discontent (Cronbach's alpha = 0.63). The first one (Item 7), measured on a four-point scale from 1 ("Totally agree") to 4 ("Totally disagree"), was: "The interests of people like you are well taken into account by the political system in (OUR COUNTRY)". The second one (Item 8), measured on a four-point scale from 1 ("Totally agree") to 4 ("Totally disagree"), questioned "On the whole, are you very satisfied, fairly satisfied, not very satisfied, or not at all satisfied with the way democracy works in (OUR COUNTRY)?" The third one (Item 9), asked the participants "At the present time, would you say that, in general, things are going in the right direction or in the wrong direction, in (OUR COUNTRY?" We recoded this indicator in 1 ("Things are going in the right direction"), 2 ("Neither the one nor the other (SPONTANEOUS)), and 3 ("Things are going in the wrong direction"). As we commented in Section 2.2, political discontent and political populism are closely related concepts. Therefore, we use the first as a proxy for the latter.

3.2.3. Outcome Variable (Vaccine Uptake)

The main outcome was the vaccine uptake reported by participants. It took the value 1 ("Yes") if respondents answered affirmatively to either of the two survey questions "Have you had any vaccinations in the last five years?" and "Why have you not had any vaccination in the last five years? 1 You are still covered by vaccines you received earlier". For the rest, it took value 0 "No".

3.2.4. Confounders

We included the following covariates to explore their effects on vaccine uptake: age (15–24 years, 8.2%; 25–39 years, 19.8%; 40–54 years, 24.5%; 55 years and older, 47.5%), gender (man, 45.3%; woman, 54.7%), age upon leaving full education (no full-time education, 0.7%; up to 15 years, 14%; 16–19 years, 43.3%; 20 years and older, 34.7%; still studying, 6%; missing values 1.3%), marital status (unmarried, 16%; (re-)married/single with a partner, 64.8%; divorced or separated, 8.2%; widowed, 10.4%; missing values, 0.6%), Occupation (self-employed, 6.9%; managers, 10.8%; other white collars, 12.5%; manual workers, 21%; house persons, 4.7%; unemployed, 5.2%; retired, 33%; students, 6%), residential setting (rural area or village, 33.7%; small or medium-sized town, 37.5%; large town, 28.7%), problems paying bills (most of the time, 8.3%; from time to time, 23.4%; almost never/never, 66.8%), social class (the working class of society, 26.4%; the lower-middle class of society, 15.3%; the middle class of society, 47%; the upper-middle class of society, 7%; the higher class of society, 0.6%), views on political matters/left–right positioning (left, 24.5%; center, 34.5%; right, 21.7%; missing values, 19.3%), use of online social networks (every day or almost every day, 14.4%; two or three times a week, 4.3%; about once a week, 1.9%; less often, 10.4%; never, 44.7%; missing values, 19.9%), children living at home (none, 76%; one, 11.8%; two, 9.1%; three, 2.2%; four or more, 0.8%).

All these data were obtained from the baseline survey.

3.3. Statistical Analysis

Structural equation modeling (SEM) examined the hypothesized mediating effects using Mplus software version 8.7 (Muthén & Muthén, Los Angeles, CA, USA). All the variables considered in the measurement model were treated as categorical. In accordance, we used the weighted least-squares estimator with mean and variance adjustments (WLSMV). We applied the probit link because the model's dependent variable—vaccinated—was binary. The goodness of fit was assessed by computing the comparative fit index (CFI), Tucker–Lewis index (TLI), root mean square error of approximation (RMSEA), and standardized root mean residual (SRMR) [55]. The acceptable levels of the goodness-of-fit model parameters were CFI > 0.90, TLI > 0.90, RMSEA < 0.08, and SRMR < 0.08 [56]. Furthermore, to test the statistical significance of the mediating effects, we conducted bias-corrected bootstrap tests with 95% confidence intervals. We ran 20 different initial stage starts, and 10,000 bootstrap draws. The significance value was set at 0.05 in this study. The model also included all the potential confounders detailed previously.

4. Results

Figure 2 shows the final SEM model. This model was trimmed for the confounders that, in the first attempt, were not statistically significant in all the categories that each of them belonged to (gender, marital status, and residential setting). Fit statistics indicated that the SEM fitted the data well (χ^2 = 5369.989, df = 312, CFI = 0.964, TLI = 0.959 SRMR = 0.054, RMSEA (90% CI) = 0.025 (0.024, 0.025)), and all standardized path coefficients were significant, except for the direct effect of DISTRUST on VACCINE. The model explained 9.1% of the variance of the vaccine uptake.

Mediation analysis was conducted to examine the mediation role of POPULISM on the relationship between DISTRUST and VACCINE UPTAKE (see Table 1). The total effect of DISTRUST on VACCINE UPTAKE (see Table 2) was statistically significant (standardized path coefficient, $\beta = -0.115$; $p < 0.001$; 95% CI, −0.133–−0.098). The indirect effect between DISTRUST and VACCINE UPTAKE was also statistically significant (standardized path coefficient, indirect effect = −0.0.098; 95% CI, −0.133–−0.063). Two effects that were also statistically significant composed this indirect effect: the effect of DISTRUST on POPULISM (standardized path coefficient, $\beta = 0.800$; $p < 0.001$; 95% CI, 0.790–0.811) and the effect of POPULISM on VACCINE UPTAKE (standardized path coefficient, $\beta = -0.123$; $p < 0.001$; 95% CI, −0.165–−0.079). Therefore, hypotheses 2 and 3 hold. Finally, the direct effect of DISTRUST on VACCINE uptake was not statistically significant (standardized path coefficient, direct effect = −0.017; p = 0.432; 95% CI, −0.060–0.025). Hence, hypothesis 1 holds, and we conclude that Populism completely mediates the association between Distrust and Vaccine Uptake.

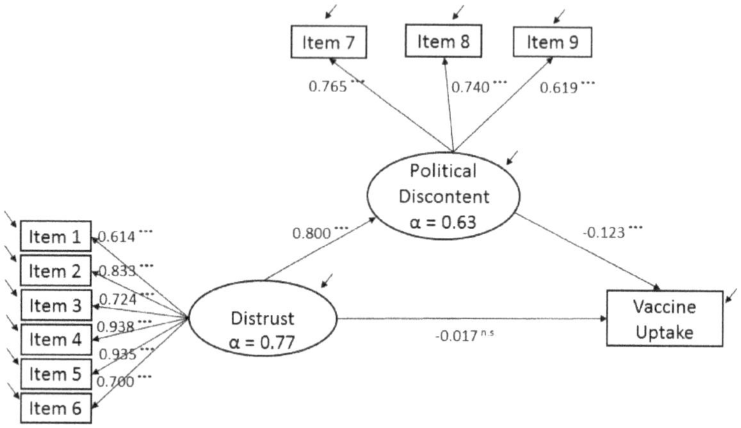

Figure 2. Structural Equation Model. Political populism mediation in the relationship between institutional distrust and vaccine uptake. Each latent variable has its associated Cronbach's alpha (α). All path loads from latent variables to items are in standardized terms. *** represents p-values significant at the 1% level of significance. $^{n.s.}$ means no statistically significant results.

Table 1. Direct, Indirect, and Total Effects of Distrust on Vaccine Uptake.

Paths	Unstandardized Path Coefficient, β Estimate (95% CI)	Standardized Path Coefficient, β Estimate (95% CI)	p
Direct Effect			
D → V	−0.029 (−0.102 0.043)	−0.017 (−0.060 0.025)	0.432
Indirect Effect			
D → P → V	−0.166 (-0.225 −0.107)	−0.098 (−0.133 −0.063)	<0.001
Total Effect			
D → V	−0.195 (−0.225 −0.165)	−0.115 (−0.133 −0.098)	<0.001

Abbreviations: CI, Confidence Interval; D, Distrust; P, Populism; V, Vaccine Uptake.

Table 2 shows how the different sociodemographic variables considered in our study affected vaccine uptake. Because these variables were categorical, we needed to transform them into dummy variables to perform the probit analysis. To facilitate the interpretation of the coefficients, we converted the probit coefficients into logit ones, following Muthén and Muthén [57] (p. 43). This was done by applying the formula $logit\hat{\beta} = probit\hat{\beta} * \sqrt{\pi^2/3}$ [58] (p. 234). Finally, we obtained the odds ratio by exponentiating the logit coefficients (e^{logit}).

Looking into the results depicted in Table 2, we see that odds ratios for vaccine uptake, adjusted for age, were lower for all the groups when compared to the youngest. Hence, participants between 25–39 years and 55 years and older had 13.8% (OR = 0.862, $p < 0.001$) lower odds than people between 15–24 years. Respondents between 40–54 had 16.4% lower odds than the reference group.

The second control variable, occupation, showed three categories that were not statistically significant: other white collars (OR = 1.011, p = 0.637), manual workers (OR = 0.998, p = 0.962), and house persons (OR = 0.977, p = 0.180). From the rest, there were three categories with higher odds (managers (OR = 1.071, $p < 0.05$), retired (OR = 1.065, $p < 0.05$), and students (OR = 0.083, $p < 0.05$)) and only the unemployed had lower odds for being vaccinated (OR = 0.940, $p < 0.001$).

Education was measured by answering the question at what age participants stopped full-time education. It was statistically significant for all the alternatives, except those consisting of people still studying (OR = 0.989, p = 0.511). The relationship between education and vaccine uptake was negative: higher education meant lower vaccination odds. Hence, when compared with respondents with no full-time education, participants that received education up to 15 years old had 4.1% higher odds to be jabbed (OR = 1.041, $p < 0.05$), those that stopped between 16 and 19 years old had 3.2% lower odds (OR = 0.968, $p < 0.05$), and participants with a higher education background had 16.6% lower odds to be vaccinated (OR = 0.844, $p < 0.001$).

Having children living at home represented higher odds to be vaccinated for one or two children, compared with families that had none (one (OR = 1.041, $p < 0.05$), two (OR = 1.033, $p < 0.05$)). However, the results for families with three or more children were not statistically significant (three (OR = 1.020, p = 0.172), four or more (OR = 0.993, p = 0.631)).

The economic situation of the interviewee also affected vaccine uptake. Those who declared problems with paying bills most of the time had 11.7% lower odds (0.883, $p < 0.001$). Furthermore, people that said that they had problems from time to time had 17.5% lower odds to be jabbed (OR = 0.825, $p < 0.001$) than people that said that they almost never/never had problems.

Social class was associated with vaccine uptake. Except for the higher social class that did not present statistically significant results (OR = 1.026, p = 0.084), we observe that the probability of being vaccinated was also higher as social class increased. Compared with the working class, the lower-middle class had 6.3% higher odds (OR = 1.063, $p < 0.01$), the middle class had 7.7% higher odds (OR = 1.077, $p < 0.001$), and the upper-middle class had 18.1% higher odds (OR = 1.181, $p < 0.001$) of being jabbed.

Political orientation was also related to vaccine uptake. The left-oriented participants were most likely to be vaccinated, with 11.9% higher odds than the center-oriented ones (OR = 1.119, $p < 0.001$). Results for right-oriented people were not statistically significant.

The use of online social networks did not shed any clear conclusion about its relationship with vaccine uptake. When compared to those who said they used online social networks every day or almost every day, three out of the five options available were not statistically significant (two or three times a week (OR = 0.029, p = 0.066), about once a week (OR = 1.002, p = 0.912), and two or three times a month (OR = 0.991, p = 0.572)). Participants who chose the less often (less than two or three times a week) option had 4.8% lower odds to be vaccinated than the reference group. The only clear insight we obtained was from comparing participants who never used online social networks with people who use them every day. The former had 10.5% greater odds of being vaccinated than the latter. Therefore, it depicted a clear difference between people who use or do not use online social networks. Still, there were no statistically significant differences among the different frequencies of use of online social networks, except for those who declared to use them less often than two or three times a week.

Table 2. Vaccine uptake confounders.

Variable	Categories	Probit	p	Logit	e^{logit}
Age	15–24 years	Ref.	Ref.	Ref.	Ref.
	25–39 years	−0.082	0.000	−0.148	0.862
	40–54 years	−0.099	0.000	−0.179	0.836
	55 years and older	−0.082	0.000	−0.148	0.862
Occupation	Self-employed	Ref.	Ref.	Ref.	Ref.
	Managers	0.038	0.001	0.069	1.071
	Other white collars	0.006	0.637	0.011	1.011
	Manual workers	−0.001	0.962	−0.002	0.998
	House persons	−0.013	0.180	−0.024	0.977
	Unemployed	−0.034	0.000	−0.062	0.940
	Retired	0.035	0.036	0.063	1.065
	Students	0.044	0.001	0.080	1.083

Table 2. *Cont.*

Variable	Categories	Probit	p	Logit	e^{logit}
Education	No full-time education	Ref.	Ref.	Ref.	Ref.
	Up to 15 years	0.039	0.000	0.071	1.073
	16–19	−0.018	0.045	−0.033	0.968
	20 years and older	−0.094	0.000	−0.170	0.844
	Still studying	−0.006	0.511	−0.011	0.989
Childs Living at Home	None	Ref.	Ref.	Ref.	Ref.
	One	0.022	0.007	0.040	1.041
	Two	0.018	0.037	0.033	1.033
	Three	0.011	0.172	0.020	1.020
	Four or more	−0.004	0.631	−0.007	0.993
Problems Paying Bills	Most of the time	−0.069	0.000	−0.125	0.883
	From time to time	−0.106	0.000	−0.192	0.825
	Almost never/never	Ref.	Ref.	Ref.	Ref.
Social Class	The working class	Ref.	Ref.	Ref.	Ref.
	The lower middle class	0.034	0.000	0.062	1.063
	The middle class	0.041	0.000	0.074	1.077
	The upper middle class	0.092	0.000	0.167	1.181
	The higher class	0.014	0.084	0.025	1.026
Political Left-Right	Left	0.062	0.000	0.112	1.119
	Center				
	Right	0.015	0.059	0.027	1.028
Use Online Social Network	Every day or almost every day	Ref.	Ref.	Ref.	Ref.
	Two or three times a week	0.016	0.066	0.029	1.029
	About once a week	0.001	0.912	0.002	1.002
	Two or three times a month	−0.005	0.572	−0.009	0.991
	Less often	−0.027	0.003	−0.049	0.952
	Never	0.055	0.000	0.100	1.105

Note: Dummy variables were created to perform the analysis. Ref. means the selected reference group. Logit coefficients were calculated from probit coefficients applying the formula $logit\hat{\beta} = probit\hat{\beta} * \sqrt{\pi^2/3}$. [58,59].

5. Discussion

This article explored the relationship between institutional distrust and vaccine uptake by recognizing the mediating role of political discontent (used as a proxy for measuring political populism). This research carried out SEM path analysis by using MPLUS 8.7. We found that institutional distrust was a significant predictor of vaccine uptake. Furthermore, the results also depicted that political populism fully mediated the relationship between institutional distrust and vaccine uptake. These outcomes corroborated the relationship observed by Kennedy [60]. Our research completes his work because we used data at the individual level, instead of macro data at the national level, for measuring populism. Additionally, we measured one of the main drivers of vaccine hesitancy [22], distrust of institutions, and its influence on vaccine uptake. Moreover, we went one step further, demonstrating that the effect of distrust on vaccine uptake was fully mediated by populism.

The consequences of our findings are clear: populist political parties could use vaccines as a battlefield because, when generating distrust in institutions, citizens with a higher level of political discontent had 11.5% lower odds of being vaccinated. It seems to be more than enough for reaching the destabilizing goals that populists pursue. Moreover, if the minimum herd immunity coverage is not achieved, new outbreaks will appear, reinforcing a vicious circle of distrust in elites [23,33]. These results are in line with several investigations that have studied the relationship between trust and vaccine uptake [25,26,61–64], while broadening and deepening the understanding of this link through the mediation role of political populism.

When analyzing the confounders, the results help predict whom populist political parties could target with their political marketing campaigns. The best profile for populists' purposes was that of people older than 25 years old, unemployed, that stopped their full-time education at 20 years old and older (highly educated), with problems for paying bills, that declared to belong to the working class, politically oriented to the center, and that use online social networks. From this profile, the economic variables (unemployed, problems paying bills, and belonging to the working class) arose as the more important ones for explaining not being vaccinated, in odds terms [65]. In a few words, in Europe, the disenchanted from the global economy are the optimal target for populist political campaigns.

In Europe, traditionally, populists have been categorized as "radical right" or "extreme right" [66]. On the other hand, some other populist leaders have been considered economically left-wing, oriented mainly in Central and Eastern Europe [67]. Our results showed that politically center-oriented European citizens have greater odds of being attracted by distrusting populists' proclaims to reject the vaccines. Hence, independently of the political orientation of the populist political party that tries to use distrust for campaigning, the main target will be the disenchanted and the politically center oriented.

The use of online social networks reduces the odds of being vaccinated compared to those who never use them. This result is congruent with several investigations [68,69] and shreds of evidence from the populist realpolitik [7]. Nevertheless, the frequency of use of these online social networks did not report any statistically significant difference. The communication media mix depends on the vaccine hesitancy segment that citizens belong to [70].

6. Conclusions

To reduce the adverse effects of these populist political strategies, it is necessary to reinforce citizens' institutional trust. Public health has used, and should continue doing so in the future, health education, health promotion, and social marketing, as effective tools for influencing behavior, in the fight against several communicable and non-communicable diseases [71–74]. As the evidence shows, compulsory measures to vaccinate hesitant people have never been the answer to the lack of confidence in vaccines [70,75–78]. Evidence indicates that social marketing has considerable value in voluntarily fostering vaccine acceptance [72,73,79]. These actions, necessarily, have to be accompanied by an improvement in the living standards of these citizens, harmed by the globalization process [80,81]. It seems not to be a lack of trust in the health system, in particular, but rather in the political and economic institutions that the populists are taking advantage of for instilling doubt and trying to gain advantage from polarized debates about vaccines [48].

7. Limitations

This study should be evaluated with its limitations. The clearest one is using the Eurobarometer's predefined items. Nevertheless, the benefit of the large-scale surveys, carried out by well-known public international organizations, is the high quality of the data obtained through a standardized sampling procedure. The authors intended to fill the gap that existed in the vaccine literature for testing the mediating role of political populism in the relationship between institutional distrust and vaccine uptake. For this purpose, Eurobarometer's data fit perfectly.

Our results showed that the institutional distrust with the mediating role of political populism partially explained vaccination uptake. However, this implies that other variables also sway an individual's decisions, since several circumstances finally influence vaccine uptake.

Author Contributions: Conceptualization, A.R.-R., M.R.-M. and M.V.R.-G.; methodology, A.R.-R., M.R.-M. and M.V.R.-G.; literature review, A.R.-R.; software, A.R.-R.; validation, A.R.-R.; formal analysis, A.R.-R.; investigation, A.R.-R.; data curation, A.R.-R.; writing the original draft, A.R.-R.; review and editing the manuscript, M.R.-M. and M.V.R.-G.; supervision M.R.-M. and M.V.R.-G. All authors have read and agreed to the published version of the manuscript.

Funding: This research received no external funding.

Institutional Review Board Statement: Not applicable.

Informed Consent Statement: Not applicable.

Data Availability Statement: Publicly available datasets were analyzed in this study. These data can be found through GESIS (University of Cologne, Germany) at https://www.gesis.org/en/eurobarometer-data-service/search-data-access/data-access (accessed on 16 October 2021).

Acknowledgments: We gratefully acknowledge the support of GESIS (University of Cologne, Germany) for providing access to the Eurobarometer dataset.

Conflicts of Interest: The authors declare no conflict of interest.

Appendix A

Table A1. Sample size by country, Total population older than 15 years (15+).

Country	Number of Interviews	Population 15+
Austria	1006	7,554,711
Belgium	1041	9,693,779
Bulgaria	1026	6,537,535
Croatia	1010	3,796,476
Czech Republic	1068	9,238,431
Denmark	1017	4,838,729
Estonia	1005	1,160,064
Finland	1000	4,747,810
France	1013	54,097,255
Germany	1507	70,160,634
Greece	1014	9,937,810
Hungary	1030	8,781,161
Ireland	1078	3,592,162
Italy	1021	52,334,536
Latvia	1012	1,707,082
Lithuania	1004	2,513,384
Luxemburg	512	457,127
Malta	497	364,171
Netherlands	1017	13,979,215
Poland	1011	33,444,171
Portugal	1013	8,480,126
Republic of Cyprus	505	741,308
Romania	1025	16,852,701
Slovakia	1020	4,586,024
Slovenia	1016	1,760,032
Spain	1014	39,445,245
Sweden	1021	7,998,763
United Kingdom	1021	52,651,777
TOTAL	27,524	431,452,219

Source: Eurobarometer 91.2. European Commission [54].

References

1. Velásquez, G. Entre la Ética, la Salud y la Economía. Available online: https://mondiplo.com/entre-la-etica-la-salud-y-la-economia (accessed on 14 September 2021).
2. da Fonseca, E.M.; Shadlen, K.C.; Bastos, F.I. The politics of COVID-19 vaccination in middle-income countries: Lessons from Brazil. *Soc. Sci. Med.* **2021**, *281*, 114093. [CrossRef] [PubMed]

3. Greer, S.L.; Bekker, M.; De Leeuw, E.; Wismar, M.; Helderman, J.K.; Ribeiro, S.; Stuckler, D. Policy, politics and public health. *Eur. J. Public Health* **2017**, *27*, 40–43. [CrossRef] [PubMed]
4. Speed, E.; Mannion, R. Populism and health policy: Three international case studies of right-wing populist policy frames. *Sociol. Health Illn.* **2020**, *42*, 1967–1981. [CrossRef] [PubMed]
5. Greer, S.L. Medicine, public health and the populist radical right. *J. R. Soc. Med.* **2017**, *110*, 305–308. [CrossRef] [PubMed]
6. Algan, Y.; Guriev, S.; Papaioannou, E.; Passari, E. The European Trust Crisis and the Rise of Populism. *Brook. Pap. Econ. Act.* **2017**, *78*, 309–382. [CrossRef]
7. Rinaldi, C.; Bekker, M.P.M. A scoping review of populist radical right parties' influence on welfare policy and its implications for population health in Europe. *Int. J. Health Policy Manag.* **2021**, *10*, 141–151. [CrossRef] [PubMed]
8. Lasco, G.; Curato, N. Medical populism. *Soc. Sci. Med.* **2019**, *221*, 1–8. [CrossRef] [PubMed]
9. Lasco, G. Challenging world leaders amid medical populism. *Lancet* **2020**, *396*, 1802–1803. [CrossRef]
10. Lasco, G. Medical populism and the COVID-19 pandemic. *Glob. Public Health* **2020**, *15*, 1417–1429. [CrossRef] [PubMed]
11. Gugushvili, A.; Koltai, J.; Stuckler, D.; McKee, M. Votes, populism, and pandemics. *Int. J. Public Health* **2020**, *65*, 721–722. [CrossRef]
12. Dubé, E.; Vivion, M.; MacDonald, N.E. Vaccine hesitancy, vaccine refusal and the anti-vaccine movement: Influence, impact and implications. *Expert Rev. Vaccines* **2015**, *14*, 99–117. [CrossRef] [PubMed]
13. McKee, M.; Gugushvili, A.; Koltai, J.; Stuckler, D. Are Populist Leaders Creating the Conditions for the Spread of COVID-19?; Comment on "A Scoping Review of Populist Radical Right Parties' Influence on Welfare Policy and its Implications for Population Health in Europe". *Int. J. Health Policy Manag.* **2021**, *10*, 511–515. [CrossRef] [PubMed]
14. Koltai, J.; Varchetta, F.M.; McKee, M.; Stuckler, D. Deaths of Despair and Brexit Votes: Cross-Local Authority Statistical Analysis in England and Wales. *Am. J. Public Health* **2020**, *110*, 401–406. [CrossRef] [PubMed]
15. Wang, J.L.; Keown, L.-A.; Patten, S.B.; Williams, J.A.; Currie, S.R.; Beck, C.A.; Maxwell, C.J.; El-Guebaly, N.A. A population-based study on ways of dealing with daily stress: Comparisons among individuals with mental disorders, with long-term general medical conditions and healthy people. *Soc. Psychiatry Psychiatr. Epidemiol.* **2009**, *44*, 666–674. [CrossRef] [PubMed]
16. Kelland, K.; Polityuk, P. Measles and Mistrust in Ukraine Weaken World's Defenses. Available online: https://www.reuters.com/article/us-health-measles-ukraine-insight-idUSKBN1XE15T (accessed on 26 February 2022).
17. Ghinai, I.; Willott, C.; Dadari, I.; Larson, H.J. Listening to the rumours: What the northern Nigeria polio vaccine boycott can tell us ten years on. *Glob. Public Health* **2013**, *8*, 1138–1150. [CrossRef] [PubMed]
18. Lasco, G.; Yu, V.G. Medical populism and the politics of dengue epidemics in the Global South. *Glob. Public Health* **2021**, *16*, 1–14. [CrossRef] [PubMed]
19. Abramowitz, S. Epidemics (Especially Ebola). *Annu. Rev. Anthropol.* **2017**, *46*, 421–445. [CrossRef]
20. Giuffrida, A. Italy's Five Star Movement Blamed for Surge in Measles Cases. Available online: https://www.theguardian.com/world/2017/mar/23/italys-five-star-movement-blamed-for-surge-in-measles-cases (accessed on 26 February 2022).
21. Bayerlein, M.; Boese, V.A.; Gates, S.; Kamin, K.; Murshed, S.M. Populism and COVID-19: How Populist Governments (Mis)Handle the Pandemic. *J. Polit. Inst. Polit. Econ.* **2021**, *2*, 389–428.
22. Larson, H.J.; Clarke, R.M.; Jarrett, C.; Eckersberger, E.; Levine, Z.; Schulz, W.S.; Paterson, P. Measuring trust in vaccination: A systematic review. *Hum. Vaccin. Immunother.* **2018**, *14*, 1599–1609. [CrossRef]
23. Brewer, N.T.; Chapman, G.B.; Rothman, A.J.; Leask, J.; Kempe, A. Increasing Vaccination: Putting Psychological Science Into Action. *Psychol. Sci. Public Interes.* **2017**, *18*, 149–207. [CrossRef]
24. Larson, H.J.; Schulz, W.S.; Tucker, J.D.; Smith, D.M.D. Measuring vaccine confidence: Introducing a global vaccine confidence index. *PLoS Curr.* **2015**, *7*, 1–36. [CrossRef] [PubMed]
25. Gilles, I.; Bangerter, A.; Clémence, A.; Green, E.G.T.; Krings, F.; Staerklé, C.; Wagner-Egger, P. Trust in medical organizations predicts pandemic (H1N1) 2009 vaccination behavior and perceived efficacy of protection measures in the Swiss public. *Eur. J. Epidemiol.* **2011**, *26*, 203–210. [CrossRef] [PubMed]
26. Casiday, R.; Cresswell, T.; Wilson, D.; Panter-Brick, C. A survey of UK parental attitudes to the MMR vaccine and trust in medical authority. *Vaccine* **2006**, *24*, 177–184. [CrossRef] [PubMed]
27. Hill, L.; Burrell, B.; Walls, T. Factors influencing women's decisions about having the pertussis-containing vaccine during pregnancy. *J. Prim. Health Care* **2018**, *10*, 62–67. [CrossRef] [PubMed]
28. Cooper, D.L.; Hernandez, N.D.; Rollins, L.; Akintobi, T.H.; McAllister, C. HPV vaccine awareness and the association of trust in cancer information from physicians among males. *Vaccine* **2017**, *35*, 2661–2667. [CrossRef] [PubMed]
29. Gilkey, M.B.; McRee, A.L.; Magnus, B.E.; Reiter, P.L.; Dempsey, A.F.; Brewer, N.T. Vaccination confidence and parental refusal/delay of early childhood vaccines. *PLoS ONE* **2016**, *11*, e0159087. [CrossRef] [PubMed]
30. Gilkey, M.B.; Reiter, P.L.; Magnus, B.E.; Mcree, A.-L.; Dempsey, A.F.; Brewer, N.T. Validation of the Vaccination Confidence Scale: A Brief Measure to Identify Parents at Risk for Refusing Adolescent Vaccines. *Acad. Pediatr.* **2016**, *16*, 42–49. [CrossRef]
31. National Vaccine Advisory Committee. Assessing the State of Vaccine Confidence in the United States: Recommendations from the National Vaccine Advisory Committee: Approved by the National Vaccine Advisory Committee on 9 June 2015 [corrected]. *Public Health Rep.* **2015**, *130*, 573–595. [CrossRef]
32. Recio-Román, A.; Recio-Menéndez, M.; Román-González, M.V. Vaccine Hesitancy and Political Populism. An Invariant Cross-European Perspective. *Int. J. Environ. Res. Public Health* **2021**, *18*, 12953. [CrossRef]

33. Oduwole, E.O.; Pienaar, E.D.; Mahomed, H.; Wiysonge, C.S. Current tools available for investigating vaccine hesitancy: A scoping review protocol. *BMJ Open* **2019**, *9*, e033245. [CrossRef]
34. MacDonald, N.E. Vaccine hesitancy: Definition, scope and determinants. *Vaccine* **2015**, *33*, 4161–4164. [CrossRef] [PubMed]
35. Lane, S.; MacDonald, N.E.; Marti, M.; Dumolard, L. Vaccine hesitancy around the globe: Analysis of three years of WHO/UNICEF Joint Reporting Form data-2015–2017. *Vaccine* **2018**, *36*, 3861–3867. [CrossRef] [PubMed]
36. Van Kessel, S. *Populist Parties in Europe: Agents of Discontent?/Stijn van Kessel*; Palgrave Macmillan: London, UK, 2015, ISBN 9781137414106.
37. Guiso, L.; Herrera, H.; Morelli, M.; Sonno, T. *Demand and Supply of Populism*; EIEF Working Papers Series; Einaudi Institute for Economics and Finance (EIEF): Rome, Italy, 2017.
38. Nowakowski, A. Do unhappy citizens vote for populism? *Eur. J. Polit. Econ.* **2021**, *68*, 101985. [CrossRef]
39. Elchardus, M.; Spruyt, B. Populism, Persistent Republicanism and Declinism: An Empirical Analysis of Populism as a Thin Ideology. *Gov. Oppos.* **2016**, *51*, 111–133. [CrossRef]
40. Laclau, E. *On Populist Reason*; Verso: New York, NY, USA, 2005, ISBN 9781859846413.
41. Berman, S. Populism is a Symptom Rather than a Cause: Democratic Disconnect, the Decline of the Center-Left, and the Rise of Populism in Western Europe. *Polity* **2019**, *51*, 654–667. [CrossRef]
42. Giebler, H.; Hirsch, M.; Schürmann, B.; Veit, S. Discontent with What? Linking Self-Centered and Society-Centered Discontent to Populist Party Support. *Polit. Stud.* **2020**, *69*, 900–920. [CrossRef]
43. Kitschelt, H. *Popular Dissatisfaction with Democracy: Populism and Party Systems BT-Democracies and the Populist Challenge*; Mény, Y., Surel, Y., Eds.; Palgrave Macmillan: London, UK, 2002; pp. 179–196. ISBN 978-1-4039-2007-2.
44. Voogd, R.; Dassonneville, R. Are the Supporters of Populist Parties Loyal Voters? Dissatisfaction and Stable Voting for Populist Parties. *Gov. Oppos.* **2020**, *55*, 349–370. [CrossRef]
45. Carvalho Bivar, G.C.; Santini Cesar de Aguilar, M.E.; Cavalcanti Santos, R.V.; Guabelto Cardoso, P.R. COVID-19, the anti-vaccine movement and immunization challenges in Brazil: A review. *Sci. Med.* **2021**, *31*, 33. [CrossRef]
46. Larson, H.J. *Stuck. How Vaccine Rumors Start—And Why They Don't Go Away*; Oxford University Press: New York, NY, USA, 2020.
47. Herwartz, H.; Theilen, B. Health Care and Ideology: A Reconsideration of Political Determinants of Public Healthcare Funding in the OECD. *Health Econ.* **2014**, *23*, 225–240. [CrossRef] [PubMed]
48. Holmberg, C.; Miller, J.H.; Blume, S.; Greenough, P. (Eds.) *The Politics of Vaccination. A Global History*; Manchester University Press: Manchester, UK, 2017.
49. Broniatowski, D.A.; Jamison, A.M.; Qi, S.; AlKulaib, L.; Chen, T.; Benton, A.; Quinn, S.C.; Dredze, M. Weaponized Health Communication: Twitter Bots and Russian Trolls Amplify the Vaccine Debate. *Am. J. Public Health* **2018**, *108*, 1378–1384. [CrossRef]
50. Deml, M.J.; Jafflin, K.; Merten, S.; Huber, B.; Buhl, A.; Frau, E.; Mettraux, V.; Sonderegger, J.; Kliem, P.; Cattalani, R.; et al. Determinants of vaccine hesitancy in Switzerland: Study protocol of a mixed-methods national research programme. *BMJ Open* **2019**, *9*, e032218. [CrossRef] [PubMed]
51. Klein, S.L.; Pekosz, A. Sex-based Biology and the Rational Design of Influenza Vaccination Strategies. *J. Infect. Dis.* **2014**, *209*, S114–S119. [CrossRef] [PubMed]
52. Yaqub, O.; Castle-Clarke, S.; Sevdalis, N.; Chataway, J. Attitudes to vaccination: A critical review. *Soc. Sci. Med.* **2014**, *112*, 1–11. [CrossRef] [PubMed]
53. Schmid, P.; Rauber, D.; Betsch, C.; Lidolt, G.; Denker, M.L. Barriers of Influenza Vaccination Intention and Behavior—A Systematic Review of Influenza Vaccine Hesitancy, 2005–2016. *PLoS ONE* **2017**, *12*, e0170550.
54. European Commission. *Eurobarometer 91.2, March 2019*; Gesis Data Archive: ZA7592, Data File Version 1.0.0; Kantar Public: Brussels, Belgium, 2019.
55. Hu, L.; Bentler, P.M. Cutoff criteria for fit indexes in covariance structure analysis: Conventional criteria versus new alternatives. *Struct. Equ. Model. A Multidiscip. J.* **1999**, *6*, 1–55. [CrossRef]
56. Marsh, H.W.; Hau, K.-T.; Wen, Z. In Search of Golden Rules: Comment on Hypothesis-Testing Approaches to Setting Cutoff Values for Fit Indexes and Dangers in Overgeneralizing Hu and Bentler's (1999) Findings. *Struct. Equ. Model. A Multidiscip. J.* **2004**, *11*, 320–341. [CrossRef]
57. Muthén, L.K.; Muthén, B.O. Regression Analysis, Exploratory Factor Analysis, Confirmatory Factor Analysis, and Structural Equation Modeling For Categorical, Censored, and Count Outcomes. Available online: http://www.statmodel.com/download/Topic2-v20[CompatibilityMode]1.pdf (accessed on 14 December 2021).
58. Muthén, B.O.; Muthén, L.K.; Asparouhov, T. *Regression and Mediation Analysis Using Mplus/Bengt O. Muthén, Linda K. Muthén, Tohomir 'Asparouhov*; Muthén & Muthén: Los Angeles, CA, USA, 2016, ISBN 9780982998311.
59. Agresti, A. *Categorical Data Analysis*, 3rd ed.; John Wiley & Sons: Hoboken, NJ, USA, 2013.
60. Kennedy, J. Populist politics and vaccine hesitancy in Western Europe: An analysis of national-level data. *Eur. J. Public Health* **2019**, *29*, 512–516. [CrossRef]
61. Lee, C.; Whetten, K.; Omer, S.; Pan, W.; Salmon, D. Hurdles to herd immunity: Distrust of government and vaccine refusal in the US, 2002–2003. *Vaccine* **2016**, *34*, 3972–3978. [CrossRef]
62. Das, J.; Das, S. Trust, learning, and vaccination: A case study of a North Indian village. *Soc. Sci. Med.* **2003**, *57*, 97–112. [CrossRef]

63. Manika, D.; Ball, J.G.; Stout, P.A. Factors associated with the persuasiveness of direct-to-consumer advertising on HPV vaccination among young women. *J. Health Commun.* **2014**, *19*, 1232–1247. [CrossRef]
64. Szilagyi, P.G.; Thomas, K.; Shah, M.D.; Vizueta, N.; Cui, Y.; Vangala, S.; Fox, C.; Kapteyn, A. The role of trust in the likelihood of receiving a COVID-19 vaccine: Results from a national survey. *Prev. Med.* **2021**, *153*, 106727. [CrossRef] [PubMed]
65. de Munter, A.C.; Klooster, T.M.S.-v.t.; van Lier, A.; Akkermans, R.; de Melker, H.E.; Ruijs, W.L.M. Determinants of HPV-vaccination uptake and subgroups with a lower uptake in the Netherlands. *BMC Public Health* **2021**, *21*, 1848. [CrossRef] [PubMed]
66. Norris, P. *Measuring Populism Worldwide*; Harvard Kennedy School-Faculty Research Working Paper Series; Harvard University: Boston, MA, USA, 2020.
67. Pirro, A.L.P.; Pirro, A.L.P. *The Populist Radical Right in Central and Eastern Europe Ideology, Impact, and Electoral Performance Conclusions*; ECPR Standing Grp Extremism & Democrac: London, UK, 2015; Volume 27, ISBN 978-1-315-73315-9.
68. Jarrett, C.; Wilson, R.; O'Leary, M.; Eckersberger, E.; Larson, H.J.; Eskola, J.; Liang, X.; Chaudhuri, M.; Dube, E.; Gellin, B.; et al. Strategies for addressing vaccine hesitancy—A systematic review. *Vaccine* **2015**, *33*, 4180–4190. [CrossRef] [PubMed]
69. Ortiz, R.R.; Smith, A.; Coyne-Beasley, T. A systematic literature review to examine the potential for social media to impact HPV vaccine uptake and awareness, knowledge, and attitudes about HPV and HPV vaccination. *Hum. Vaccin. Immunother.* **2019**, *15*, 1465–1475. [CrossRef] [PubMed]
70. Recio-Román, A.; Recio-Menéndez, M.; Román-González, M.V. Global Vaccine Hesitancy Segmentation: A Cross-European Approach. *Vaccines* **2021**, *9*, 617. [CrossRef] [PubMed]
71. European Centre for Disease Prevention and Control. *Social Marketing Guide for Public Health Programme Managers and Practitioners*; ECDC: Stockholm, Sweden, 2014, ISBN 9789291936052.
72. Opel, D.J.; Diekema, D.S.; Lee, N.R.; Marcuse, E.K. Social marketing as a strategy to increase immunization rates. *Arch. Pediatr. Adolesc. Med.* **2009**, *163*, 432–437. [CrossRef] [PubMed]
73. Nowak, G.J.; Gellin, B.G.; MacDonald, N.E.; Butler, R.; Eskola, J.; Liang, X.; Chaudhuri, M.; Dube, E.; Gellin, B.; Goldstein, S.; et al. Addressing vaccine hesitancy: The potential value of commercial and social marketing principles and practices. *Vaccine* **2015**, *33*, 4204–4211. [CrossRef]
74. Washington State Department of Health. *Social Marketing Recommendations for COVID-19 Vaccine*; Washington State Department of Health: Seattle, WA, USA, 2020.
75. Salmon, D.A.; Teret, S.P.; MacIntyre, C.R.; Salisbury, D.; Burgess, M.A.; Halsey, N.A. Compulsory vaccination and conscientious or philosophical exemptions: Past, present, and future. *Lancet* **2006**, *367*, 436–442. [CrossRef]
76. Salmon, D.A.; Dudley, M.Z.; Glanz, J.M.; Omer, S.B. Vaccine hesitancy Causes, consequences, and a call to action. *Vaccine* **2015**, *33*, D66–D71. [CrossRef]
77. Colgrove, J. The ethics and politics of compulsory HPV vaccination. *N. Engl. J. Med.* **2006**, *355*, 2389–2391. [CrossRef]
78. Brito, D.L.; Sheshinski, E.; Intriligator, M.D. Externalities and Compulsory Vaccinations. *J. Public Econ.* **1991**, *45*, 69–90. [CrossRef]
79. French, J.; Deshpande, S.; Evans, W.; Obregon, R. Key guidelines in developing a pre-emptive COVID-19 vaccination uptake promotion strategy. *Int. J. Environ. Res. Public Health* **2020**, *17*, 5893. [CrossRef] [PubMed]
80. Aupers, S. "Trust no one": Modernization, paranoia and conspiracy culture. *Eur. J. Commun.* **2012**, *27*, 22–34. [CrossRef]
81. Cata-Preta, B.D.; Wehrmeister, F.C.; Santos, T.M.; Barros, A.J.D.; Victora, C.G. Patterns in Wealth-related Inequalities in 86 Low- and Middle-Income Countries: Global Evidence on the Emergence of Vaccine Hesitancy. *Am. J. Prev. Med.* **2021**, *60*, S24–S33. [CrossRef]

healthcare

MDPI

Article

Competency and Related Factors in Preventing Emerging Infectious Diseases among Nurses in Long-Term Care Facilities in Taiwan

Po-Jen Kung [1,2] and Ching-Min Chen [2,3,4,*]

[1] Jianan Psychiatric Center, Ministry of Health and Welfare, Tainan City 717, Taiwan; t26084126@gs.ncku.edu.tw
[2] Department of Nursing, College of Medicine, National Cheng Kung University, Tainan City 701, Taiwan
[3] Institute of Gerontology, College of Medicine, National Cheng Kung University, Tainan City 701, Taiwan
[4] School of Nursing, Indiana University, Bloomington, IN 47408, USA
* Correspondence: chingmin@mail.ncku.edu.tw; Tel.: +886-6-235-3535 (ext. 5858)

Abstract: Emerging infectious diseases (EIDs) are a considerable threat to health, particularly in long-term care facilities (LTCFs), where residents are especially vulnerable. Nurses' competency in EID prevention is crucial to minimize the adverse effects of EIDs in LTCFs. This study investigated nurses' competency and related factors in EID prevention in LTCFs in Tainan, Taiwan. A cross-sectional design was employed, and nurses were recruited to complete an online survey examining the knowledge, attitude, and skills required to prevent EIDs in LTCFs. A total of 235 nurses completed the survey. The equivalent score index (SI) for knowledge regarding EID prevention was 68, indicating that the nurses did not have adequate knowledge regarding EID prevention. In contrast, the equivalent SI for the subscale of attitudes toward EID prevention was 78, indicating that the nurses exhibited moderately to highly positive attitudes toward EID prevention. However, they rated themselves as being highly skilled in EID prevention, corresponding to an equivalent SI of 91. Perceived supervisors' approval, marital status, attitudes toward EID prevention, EID prevention skills, knowledge regarding EIDs, and being in charge of infectious disease prevention were significant predictors of the nurses' competency. LTCF nurses, especially those working in nursing homes, should enhance their knowledge regarding EID prevention. These findings may help improve nurses' competency in preventing EIDs by encouraging the integration of practice strategies, education, research, and policy recommendations to eliminate EIDs in LTCFs.

Keywords: long-term care facilities; nurses; emerging infectious diseases; pandemic prevention

Citation: Kung, P.-J.; Chen, C.-M. Competency and Related Factors in Preventing Emerging Infectious Diseases among Nurses in Long-Term Care Facilities in Taiwan. *Healthcare* **2022**, *10*, 894. https://doi.org/10.3390/healthcare10050894

Academic Editors: Joachim G. Voss and Sandul Yasobant

Received: 3 April 2022
Accepted: 6 May 2022
Published: 12 May 2022

1. Introduction

Emerging infectious diseases (EIDs), as defined by the World Health Organization (WHO), are infectious diseases that are newly identified and were previously unknown and cause public health problems either locally or internationally [1]. In 2003, the Institute of Medicine outlined various factors that affect the spread of EIDs; these include microbial adaptation and change, changes in human demographics and behavior, international travel, and the breakdown of public health measures [2]. Increased modes of transportation and speed thereof have enhanced the probability of the sudden outbreak of acute viral respiratory infections. EIDs pose considerable challenges to the global health system and economies [3]. In particular, nurses working at the frontlines may experience substantial challenges.

In 2014, the WHO updated its guidelines for the prevention of epidemic- and pandemic-prone acute respiratory infections (ARIs). Because ARIs are the leading cause of morbidity and mortality from infectious disease worldwide, these guidelines call for preventing EIDs caused by infectious agents such as severe acute respiratory syndrome coronavirus (SARS-CoV) [4]. Coronavirus disease 2019 (COVID-19), the major recent EID, caused by

SARS-CoV-2 is an acute respiratory infection. The outbreak of COVID-19 was declared a pandemic by the WHO in March 2020, and as of 2022, confirmed COVID-19 cases and deaths are still high or increasing in many parts of the world. Because of insufficient knowledge regarding the disease at the beginning of the outbreak, most countries failed to introduce effective measures to curb the pandemic, and many frontline medical professionals were infected [5]. In October 2021, the International Council of Nurses (ICN) announced that more than 1.8 million medical professionals worldwide were infected with COVID-19 and that 6643 nurses had died from COVID-19 [6]. The ICN estimated that on average, nearly 10% of the confirmed cases in the world were medical workers, indicating that medical workers and their patients had a considerably high risk of infection than the general public [7].

Healthcare workers and residents of long-term care facilities have a higher risk of dying from COVID-19. Cluster infections in a medical institution can even result in the rapid service breakdown of surrounding medical facilities and thus affect the entire local medical system [8]. With the ongoing spread of COVID-19 worldwide, long-term care facilities in Taiwan are no exception. Confirmed COVID-19 infections and even deaths among the staff and residents of these facilities have been frequently reported [9].

In Taiwan, the 156th local COVID-19 case was the first long-term care facility nurse to be infected with COVID-19. Although the infection occurred during the peak of the pandemic worldwide, the nurse disregarded her symptoms, did not seek immediate medical attention, and continued to work until she received a diagnosis of COVID-19. This nurse did not have sufficient knowledge regarding the necessary measures to prevent infectious diseases and was reluctant to take precautions. In contrast, government agencies were more active in managing the case. The experience of this COVID-19 case indicated that once the professionals or residents of a long-term care facility are infected with an EID, it is likely to develop into a situation where the infection of one person can shut down the entire facility, thus multiplying the social costs of managing the outbreak [10].

Studies have suggested that the residents of long-term care facilities have an increased risk of infection because of their age, declining physical functions, and underlying diseases [11]. Moreover, because long-term care facility nurses work on the frontline to implement preventive measures, prolonged physical contact with residents is unavoidable. Therefore, their risk of infection is high [6]. These factors highlight the importance of determining the competency of long-term care facility nurses in EID prevention. In this study, competency in EID prevention was determined by considering three dimensions, namely knowledge, attitude, and skill [12,13]. In particular, competency in EID prevention involves participants' awareness of EIDs, attitude toward implementing EID preventive measures, and perceived skill level for implementing the preventive measures.

With rapid changes in the global environment and the accompanying crisis of EIDs, competency in EID prevention must evolve to reduce the damage caused by the rapid transmission of EIDs. This study investigated the competency of long-term care facility nurses in EID prevention. The aims of this study were as follows: (1) to develop a survey for examining the competency of long-term care facility nurses in EID prevention; (2) to describe the EID prevention competency of nurses in long-term care facilities; (3) to explore the degree of knowledge, attitudes, and skills of long-term care facility nurses regarding EID prevention; and (4) to identify critical factors affecting the EID prevention competency of long-term care facility nurses. The results of this study can help long-term care facilities in developing their in-service education and training courses for infectious disease prevention as well as assist health authorities in formulating relevant preventive measures.

2. Materials and Methods

2.1. Research Design

This study used a cross-sectional design with a self-developed questionnaire. Nurses from long-term care facilities in Tainan, Taiwan, were invited to participate in the study from May to July 2021, and data were collected through online questionnaires.

2.2. Participants

In this study, the workplace was adopted as the sampling unit. Registered nurses who could read and write Chinese, had hands-on long-term-care practice experience, and had an active nursing license in Tainan during the data collection period were included. Nurses who could not use the Internet to complete the questionnaire were excluded. Participants were selected using a cluster random sampling method. The list of facilities was archived in Excel software, and computer-generated random codes were used to ensure the representativeness of the sample.

2.3. Research Instruments

The self-developed "Competency of Nurses in Long-term Care Facilities in Emerging Infectious Diseases Prevention Scale, Chinese Version" was used as the research instrument in this study. This instrument includes three scales on knowledge, attitude, and skills. In the pilot study, the questionnaire responses of 61 nurses were evaluated. After deducting an invalid questionnaire (incomplete responses), we examined 60 valid questionnaires, of which 30 were from nurses employed in residential care homes and 30 from nurses employed in nursing homes. The instrument was reviewed by 10 experts from clinical practice, government, and academia in the fields of long-term care, infectious disease prevention, and instrument development; the content validity index (CVI) of the instrument was determined. The results revealed that the overall CVI for the personal attribute and professional background domains and the knowledge, attitude, and skills subscales was 0.98, 0.97, 0.96, and 0.97, respectively. The results of the reliability test indicated that the Cronbach's α value of the skills subscale was 0.94, indicating high internal consistency and above-average reliability. The Cronbach's α value of the attitude subscale was 0.79, indicating excellent internal consistency and satisfactory reliability. Finally, the overall Kuder–Richardson 20 (KR-20) of the knowledge subscale was 0.63, indicating acceptable reliability.

The 59 items included in the final test were structured as follows: 23 items in the skills subscale, 12 each in the attitude and knowledge subscales, and 12 in the personal attribute and professional background domains. Questions on knowledge regarding EID preventive measures, such as transmission-related precautions, were assigned a score of 1 for a correct response and 0 for an incorrect response. Responses for questions on attitudes toward EID prevention (e.g., willingness to work during an EID epidemic) were rated on a 4-point Likert scale, with 4, 3, 2, and 1 indicating strongly agree, agree, disagree, and strongly disagree, respectively; reverse questions were scored inversely. Responses for questions on EID prevention were rated on a 4-point Likert scale based on a participant's ability to perform a specific task (e.g., using appropriate personal protective equipment), with the scores of 4, 3, 2, and 1 indicating completely competent, mostly competent, mostly incompetent, and completely incompetent, respectively.

2.4. Data Collection Method and Process

The required sample size was estimated using G-Power version 3.1.9.3 software (Heinrich-Heine-Universität Düsseldorf, Düsseldorf, Germany) [14]. Given the effective response rate of the questionnaire in the pilot study and the intention to use the results of this study in an exploratory factor analysis to identify the underlying structure of numerous variables to provide information for questionnaire formulation and item simplification [15], we determined that a minimum of 230 participants was required for the study. Participants were recruited from residential care homes and nursing homes. After obtaining the relevant approval, we distributed questionnaire quick response code to nurses who agreed to participate in the survey. Data collection was performed until the required sample size was reached.

2.5. Research Ethics

A noninvasive survey was used in this study. To protect the rights and interests of the participants, we obtained approval from the Institutional Review Board of National Cheng

Kung University Hospital for the study protocol and informed consent all the participants who participated in the online survey; anonymity was guaranteed to the participants.

2.6. Data Processing and Analysis

The demographics of the long-term care facility nurses and the status quo of their competency in EID prevention are presented as descriptive statistics. Analysis of variance, Student's t test, and Pearson's correlation test were used to analyze the correlation between the personal attributes of the long-term care facility nurses and their performance in the three dimensions of knowledge, attitudes, and skills in terms of EID prevention. In addition, Pearson's correlation and path analysis were used to investigate the pairwise correlation among the three dimensions. Finally, multiple regression analysis was performed to identify the crucial predictors of the competency of the long-term care facility nurses in EID prevention.

3. Results

3.1. Demographics of Long-Term Care Facility Nurses

A total of 235 long-term care facility nurses provided valid responses (response rate = 97.1%) that were included in the analysis. Of these respondents, 104 (44.3%) worked in residential care homes and 131 (55.7%) worked in nursing homes, thus representing the proportion of the nursing workforce in long-term care facilities. The demographic factors of the long-term care facility nurses are listed in Table 1.

Table 1. Demographic characteristics of long-term care facility nurses (N = 235).

Variable	N	%	Mean (Standard Deviation)	Min	Max	Median
Long-term care facilities type						
Residential care homes	104	44.3				
Nursing homes	131	55.7				
Age			34.4 years (SD = 10)	20	65	33
Marital status						
Unmarried	122	51.9				
Married	102	43.4				
Divorced	11	4.7				
Working years (Nursing)			11.6 years (9.8)	0.3	42	10
Working years (LTC)			6.9 years (6.8)	0.3	35	4.4
Infectious disease care experience						
Yes	55	23.4				
No	180	76.6				
In-service education on infectious diseases						
Yes	93	39.6				
No	142	60.4				
In charge of infectious disease prevention						
Yes	36	15.3				
No	199	84.7				
Supervisor's perceived understanding [a]			3.1 (0.5)	1	4	3
Supervisor's perceived approval [a]			3.3 (0000.5)	2	4	3
Infectious disease prevention equipment						
Adequate	182	77.4				
Inadequate	53	22.6				

[a] "Supervisor's perceived understanding" and "Supervisor's perceived approval" were rated on a 4-point Likert scale, with scores of 4, 3, 2, and 1 indicating high understanding and agreement, moderate understanding and agreement, no understanding, and no understanding and no agreement, respectively. EID, emerging infectious diseases.

The results revealed that only 23.4% of the nurses in long-term care facilities had experienced an infectious disease outbreak and 39.6% of the nurses in long-term care facilities had received in-service education on infectious diseases. The majority (84.7%) of the participants were not responsible for infectious disease prevention in their facilities. The mean scores for supervisors' understanding and approval regarding infectious disease prevention in the facilities, as perceived by the nurses, was 3.1 (SD = 0.5) and 3.3 (SD = 0.5 4) out of 4, respectively. This finding indicated that the nurses perceived their supervisors to be moderately to highly competent in infectious disease prevention. The majority (77.4%) of the nurses felt that their facility was adequate in EID preparedness.

3.2. Competency of Long-Term Care Facility Nurses in EID Prevention

The average total score of the nurses in long-term care facilities for the knowledge of EID prevention subscale was 8.1 (out of 12; SD = 1.8). The average rate of providing correct responses to each question (correctness rate) was only 70%, and the score index (SI) was 68. Next, the six attributes of the knowledge subscale were analyzed. Although the average hit rate of each attribute ranged from 50% to 85%, the attributes "protective measures" and "relevant laws and policies" had the highest scores. By contrast, the attributes "basic knowledge regarding the disease" and "disease symptoms" had the lowest scores. The mean score of the "attitude toward EID prevention" subscale was 37.5 (with individual scores ranging from 26 to 48). The equivalent SI was 78, which was above average. Among the three attributes of the "attitudes toward EID prevention" subscale, the nurses' views on adherence to pandemic prevention policies and measures were the most positive (mean = 3.32), followed by those on willingness to participate in EID prevention (mean = 3.23) and awareness regarding EIDs (mean = 2.92). Finally, the mean score of the EID prevention skills subscale was 83.3 (with individual scores ranging from 59 to 92), the equivalent SI was 91. Table 2 summarizes the total scores of all the subscales.

Table 2. Analysis of questionnaire scores on the competency in EID prevention among long-term care facility nurses (N = 235).

Scale/Subscale	Items	Correctness Rate %	Mean (Standard Deviation)	Average Score [d]	Order
Knowledge scale of EID prevention [a]	**12**		8.1 (1.8)		
Basic knowledge regarding the disease	2	50.0	1.0 (0.8)	0.5	5
Pathogenic factors and transmission routes	2	63.6	1.3 (0.7)	0.65	4
Disease symptoms	2	47.7	1.0 (0.7)	0.5	6
Treatment	2	70.6	1.4 (0.6)	0.7	3
Protective measures	2	86.4	1.7 (0.5)	0.85	1
Relevant laws and policies	2	82.6	1.7 (0.5)	0.85	2
Attitudes scale toward EID prevention [b]	**12**		37.5 (4.9)	3.1	
Nurses' perception of EIDs	5		14.6 (2.6)	2.92	3
Willingness to work during EID epidemic	3		9.7 (1.5)	3.23	2
Feelings about compliance with epidemic prevention policies and preventive measures	4		13.3 (1.7)	3.32	1
EID prevention skills scale [c]	**23**		83.3 (7.8)	3.6	

[a] For questions on knowledge regarding EID prevention, a correct answer was assigned a score of 1 and an incorrect answer was assigned a score of 0. The higher the score was, the more accurate was the knowledge of the long-term care facility nurse regarding EID prevention, [b] The attitudes toward EID Prevention were scored on a 4-point Likert scale according to the participant's degree of agreement with the statement, with scores of 4, 3, 2, and 1 representing strongly agree, agree, disagree, and strongly disagree, respectively. Reverse questions were scored in a reverse order. The higher the score was, the more positive was the attitude of the long-term care facility nurse toward EID prevention, [c] The skills in EID prevention were scored on a 4-point Likert scale according to the participant's ability to complete a certain task, with scores of 4, 3, 2, and 1 representing totally competent, mostly competent, mostly incompetent, and totally incompetent, respectively. The higher the score was, the more skilled the long-term care facility nurse was at implementing EID prevention measures, [d] Average score = Average number/number of questions. EID, emerging infectious diseases.

3.3. Correlation between Demographics and Competency of Long-Term Care Facility Nurses

The type of long-term care facility nurses worked in was associated with large differences in the three dimensions of EID competence (knowledge: t = 2.3, p = 0.22; attitude:

$t = 1.7$, $p = 0.048$; skills: $t = 2.3$, $p = 0.022$). The results indicated that the nurses from residential care homes consistently scored higher than those from nursing homes on the knowledge, attitude, and skills dimensions of EID prevention. In addition, the facility type was the only factor affecting knowledge of EID prevention.

Significant variables related to attitudes toward EID prevention included whether the participants received supervision for infectious disease prevention ($t = 3.8$, $p = 0.006$), participants' perceived supervisors' understanding ($r = 0.3$, $p < 0.001$) and approval ($r = 0.4$, $p < 0.001$), and adequacy of infectious disease prevention equipment ($t = 1.7$, $p = 0.001$). The nurses who were involved in infectious disease prevention and those who believed that their facility equipment was adequate generally exhibited more favorable attitudes toward EID prevention. In addition, the belief that their supervisors understood the content of infectious disease prevention or approved the prevention activities they implemented significantly promoted the nurses' positive attitudes toward EID prevention.

Finally, the participant's age ($r = 0.2$, $p = 0.029$), marital status ($F = 11.8$, $p < 0.001$), years of nursing work experience ($r = 0.2$, $p = 0.001$), years of working in long-term care facilities ($r = 0.2$, $p = 0.001$), being in charge of infectious disease prevention ($t = 2.7$, $p = 0.002$), and perceived supervisor's understanding ($r = 0.3$, $p < 0.001$) and approval ($r = 0.3$, $p < 0.001$) were correlated with the skill dimension of EID prevention. Among these variables, age, years of nursing work experience, years of working in long-term care facilities, and perceived supervisors' understanding and approval were positively correlated with the participants' EID prevention skills. In addition, the nurses who believed that their facility's infection prevention equipment was adequate were more likely to implement EID prevention measures. Furthermore, the analysis of the participants' marital status performed using the Scheffé test indicated that the married and divorced nurses were more adept at EID prevention compared with their unmarried counterparts. The overall results of the analysis are presented in Table 3.

3.4. Pairwise Correlation of the Competency Dimensions of Long-Term Care FacilityNurses in EID Prevention

Significant correlations were observed among the different dimensions of the long-term care facility nurses' competence in EID prevention except for knowledge and skills ($r = 0.038$, $p = 0.557$). A positive correlation was noted between knowledge and attitude ($r = 0.174$, $p = 0.008$) and between attitude and skills ($r = 0.32$, $p < 0.001$).

On the basis of the results of correlation analysis, we performed path analysis to examine the causal relationship among the three dimensions of the nurses' competence in EID prevention and to confirm whether the attitude dimension exerted a mediating effect and whether knowledge regarding a mediator indirectly affected the skill related to a mediator. The knowledge dimension significantly affected the attitude dimension (Table 4). The effect of the attitude dimension on the skill dimension was significant; however, the effect of the knowledge dimension on the skill dimension was nonsignificant. Hence, as depicted in Figure 1, two of the three paths had a significant coefficient, indicating that attitudes must be first improved for knowledge to exert an effect on skills.

Table 3. Correlations among demographic attributes and EID prevention in long-term care facility nurses (N = 235).

Variable	N	Knowledge Mean (Standard Deviation)	Knowledge Test Statistic [a]	Knowledge p-Value	Attitudes Mean (Standard Deviation)	Attitudes Test Statistic [a]	Attitudes p-Value	Skills Mean (Standard Deviation)	Skills Test Statistic [a]	Skills p-Value
Long-term care facilitiestype	235		t = 2.3	0.022		t = 1.7	0.048		t = 2.3	0.022
Residential care homes	104	8.2 (1.6)			37.8 (5.3)			84.9 (7.2)		
Nursing homes	131	8.0 (2.0)			37.5 (4.6)			82.2 (8.0)		
Age	235		r = 0.0	0.926		r = −0.1	0.199		r = 0.2	0.029
Educational background			F = 1.2	0.324		F = 1.0	0.418		F = 1.1	0.361
Senior (High School)	10	7.7 (2.1)			36.7 (6.4)			82.9 (9.2)		
Associate degree	83	8.0 (1.7)			37.0 (5.2)			84.1 (7.5)		
Bachelor's degree	133	8.0 (1.9)			38.0 (5.0)			83.2 (7.1)		
Master's degree	9	9.1 (1.4)			39.1 (5.3)			79.5 (15.4)		
Marital status			F = 1.6	0.206		F = 1.7	0.178		F = 11.8	<0.001
Unmarried	122	7.9 (1.9)			38.2 (4.6)			81.3 (7.2)	Scheffe test	
Married	102	8.2 (1.7)			36.9 (4.9)			85.1 (7.9)	2,3 > 1	
Divorced	11	8.6 (2.1)			37.6 (7.2)			90.1 (4.4)		
Job title			F = 0.881	0.416		F = 2.94	0.054		F = 1.31	0.054
Manager	34	7.7 (2.0)			39.3 (4.3)			85.1 (9.2)		
Practice Nurses	193	8.1 (1.8)			37.2 (5.0)			83.0 (7.6)		
Other	8	7.9 (1.1)			39.1 (2.2)			85.1 (5.3)		
Working years (Nursing)			r = −0.0	0.904		r = −0.1	0.167		r = 0.2	0.001
Working years (LTC)			r = −0.1	0.080		r = −0.1	0.504		r = 0.2	0.001
Infectious disease care experience			t = −1.2	0.995		t = 0.2	0.074		t = −0.2	0.486
Yes	55	7.9 (1.9)			37.7 (5.4)			83.2 (7.6)		
No	180	8.1 (1.8)			37.6 (4.8)			83.4 (7.8)		
In-service education on infectious diseases			t = −1.2	0.058		t = 0.8	0.866		t = 2.1	0.066
Yes	93	7.9 (1.6)			37.9 (4.8)			84.7 (7.2)		
No	142	8.2 (2.0)			37.4 (5.0)			82.5 (8.1)		
In charge of infectious disease prevention			t = −1.6	0.977		t = 3.8	0.006		t = 2.7	0.002
Yes	36	7.6 (1.8)			39.8 (3.6)			85.9 (5.6)		
No	199	8.1 (1.8)			37.2 (5.0)			83.0 (8.0)		
Supervisor's perceived understanding			r = 0.0	0.702		r = 0.3	<0.001		r = 0.3	<0.001
Supervisor's perceived approval			r = −0.1	0.416		r = 0.4	<0.001		r = 0.3	<0.001
Infectious disease prevention equipment			t = 0.6	0.392		t = 1.7	0.001		t = 3.1	0.237
Adequate	182	8.1 (1.9)			37.8 (5.2)			84.2 (7.9)		
Inadequate	53	7.9 (1.6)			36.8 (3.3)			80.6 (6.8)		

[a] Test statistics: r refers to the Pearson's correlation coefficient, t refers to the t test, and F refers to one-way analysis of variance. EID, emerging infectious diseases.

Table 4. Path analysis for EID prevention knowledge, attitudes, and skills among nurses in long-term care facilities (N = 235).

Dimension	R	R^2	Standardized Regression Coefficients β	t	p-Value
"Knowledge dimension" vs. "Attitude dimension"	0.174	0.030	0.174	2.694	0.008
"Knowledge dimension" vs. "Skill dimension"	0.320	0.102	−0.018	0.279	0.780
"Attitude dimension" vs. "Skill dimension"	0.320	0.102	0.323	5.110	<0.001

EID, emerging infectious diseases.

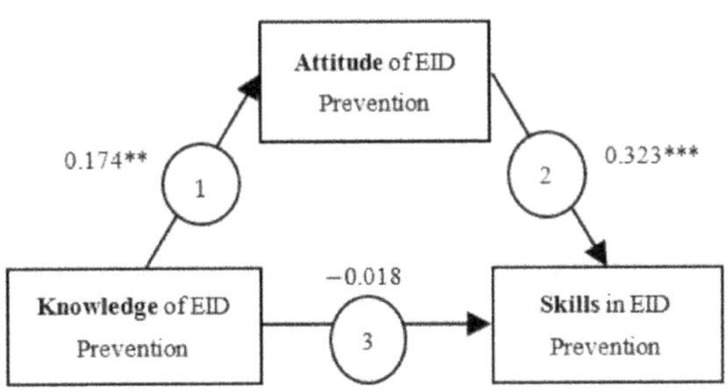

Figure 1. Path analysis diagram of the three dimensions of competency in emerging infectious disease (EID) prevention. ** $p < 0.01$; *** $p < 0.001$.

3.5. Significant Predictors of the Competency of Long-Term Care Facility Nurses in EID Prevention

To examine whether an independent variable (i.e., the personal attributes and professional background of the long-term care facility nurses and the three dimensions of their competence in EID prevention) would be a significant predictor of the dependent variables (i.e., the three dimensions of the nurses' competence in EID prevention), we performed a stepwise regression analysis. The results are summarized in Table 5. We observed that the attitude toward EID prevention was a significant predictor of the knowledge dimension because the attitude toward EID prevention explained 3% of the variance in the knowledge dimension ($\beta = 0.174$, $p < 0.01$). Similarly, significant predictors for the attitude dimension were perceived supervisors' approval ($\beta = 0.277$, $p < 0.001$), EID prevention skills ($\beta = 0.193$, $p < 0.01$), and being in charge of infectious disease prevention ($\beta = 0.125$, $p < 0.05$), which together explained 22.3% of the variance. Finally, significant predictors for the skills dimension were perceived supervisors' approval ($\beta = 0.197$, $p < 0.01$), marital status ($\beta = 0.307$, $p < 0.001$), and attitudes toward EID prevention ($\beta = 0.279$, $p < 0.001$), which together explained 24.8% of the variance.

Table 5. Critical factors affecting the EID prevention competency of nurses in long-term care facilities ($N = 235$).

Variables	Knowledge	Attitudes	Skills
	Standardized Regression Coefficients β	Standardized Regression Coefficients β	Standardized Regression Coefficients β
Supervisor's perceived approval	N/A	0.277 ***	0.197 **
Marital status	N/A	N/A	0.307 ***
Attitudes toward EIDs prevention	0.174 **	N/A	0.279 ***
EID prevention skills	N/A	0.202 **	N/A
Knowledge of EIDs	N/A	0.193 **	N/A
In charge of infectious disease prevention	N/A	0.125 *	−0.008
long-term care facilities type	−0.042	0.022	−0.096
Age	N/A	N/A	−0.120
Working years (Nursing)	N/A	N/A	0.012
Working years (LTC)	N/A	N/A	0.031
Supervisor's perceived understanding	N/A	0.029	0.105
Infectious disease prevention equipment in facilities	N/A	0.017	N/A
R^2	0.030	0.223	0.248
Adjusted R^2	0.026	0.210	0.238
t	2.694 **	2.083 *	4.500 ***

N/A not applicable; * $p < 0.05$; ** $p < 0.01$; *** $p < 0.001$. EID, emerging infectious diseases.

In summary, the aforementioned six variables were the primary predictors of the three main dimensions of the long-term care facility nurses' competence in EID prevention and explained 3–24.8% of the total variance. The participants who received approval from their supervisors to implement EID prevention measures, were married or divorced, had more knowledge regarding the disease, were more positive regarding EID prevention, were more confident in implementing EID prevention measures, and had experience in implementing infectious disease prevention measures at the facility were more competent in implementing EID prevention activities.

4. Discussion

4.1. Feasibility of the Research Instrument for Determining the Competency of Long-Term Care Facility Nurses in EID Prevention

Because of the unavailability of an effective research instrument to examine long-term care facility nurses' competency in EID prevention, we developed the instrument for this study. The Competency of Nurses in long-term care facilities in EID Prevention Scale, Chinese Version was well received by experts from clinical practice, government, and academia in terms of its accuracy and the appropriateness of its content. In addition, the comparison of reliability between the questionnaire used in the pilot study and the current questionnaire used in the formal study indicated acceptable-to-satisfactory internal consistency. The high internal consistency is probably due to the use of the stratified sampling method in this study, in which the samples were divided according to the type of institution. Such a research design reduced both sample variability and response instability, thus ensuring the credibility and stability of the research instrument when collecting data from the long-term care facility nurses.

The scale had a high CVI and internal consistency, confirming its value and potential for development. For future research, the instrument can be further developed through the inclusion of qualitative interviews, the Delphi method, confirmatory factors, and reliability testing to shorten the scale while maintaining or improving the high discriminatory power and accurate reflection of the constructs.

Because EIDs are constantly changing and their transmission paths are unpredictable, the knowledge dimension of the questionnaire should be continually updated. Situations that evolve over time and in different settings as well as knowledge derived from empirical bases imply that both the concepts and content of questions should be updated in real time.

4.2. Competency of Long-Term Care Facility Nurses in EID Prevention

The participants' inconsistent self-assessment on the three dimensions did not match distributions predicted using the knowledge-attitude-behavior model widely used in the field of health education. The model developed by Baranowski et al. [16] assumes that an individual's behavioral changes are affected by knowledge. The accumulation of knowledge by individuals changes their attitudes, thus promoting the adoption of appropriate behaviors. However, in our study, the results of path analysis indicated that knowledge alone cannot directly change skills unless the nurse has a positive attitude toward prevention and recognizes the importance of prevention skills. Therefore, nurses should not only learn regarding EIDs but also have a positive attitude while creating prevention plans. The research team recommends that nurses in long-term care facilities should make greater effort to acquire knowledge regarding preventing EIDs and that it is also important to promote their willingness through incentives. In addition, in the future, continuing education instructors should pay attention to the appropriateness of the course content [17] to increase participation rates and thus improve nurses' knowledge in certain areas [18].

Previous research indicated that supervisors can set an example of self-confidence and self-regulation through authentic leadership, therefore promoting the development of positive work attitudes in their subordinates, and that recognition by supervisors can positively affect subordinates' behavior [19,20]. This finding is in agreement with our observation that perceived supervisor approval was the most significant predictor of the three dimensions of the long-term care facility nurses' competence in EID prevention, accounting for 13.1% of the variance. The more the supervisor acknowledged the nurses' implementation of EID prevention measures, the better they were able to perform related tasks. Supervisors of long-term care facility nurses should acquire the right knowledge and skills for EID prevention to strengthen their recognition and promotion of the implementation of appropriate interventions. When long-term care facility supervisors clarified the meaning of EID prevention and promoted the understanding of staff regarding their respective roles, the nurses demonstrated higher work engagement and confidence, had more positive attitudes toward achieving work goals, and were more compliant with relevant regulations, thus effectively improving the quality of services provided by the facility. To enable nurses to realize the importance of EID prevention, they should be helped to acquire accurate and appropriate knowledge regarding EID prevention. In addition, the Regulation on Registration and Continuing Education of Medical Professionals requires nurses in Taiwan to complete 120 h of continuing education courses every 6 years. Therefore, measures to improve nurses' attitudes should be developed and used in continuing education courses on infection control in the future. Such courses can promote a deeper understanding of EID prevention among long-term care facility nurses and help them recognize the importance of EID prevention, which in turn, would help them develop the appropriate EID prevention skills. This finding is consistent with the results of studies conducted by Bartzokas and

Slade [21], Ben-Ari [22], and Berhe et al. [23] who reported that the dimensions of knowledge and skills can affect each other and that the appropriate knowledge can improve an individual's skills.

Compared with the mean score of public health nurses in EID prevention reported by Cai [24], which was 15.89 (SI = 63.5) for the knowledge dimension, 48.24 (SI = 68.9) for the attitude dimension, and 82.84 (SI = 75.3) for the ability dimension, the scores of the long-term care facility nurses in our study were considerably higher. This result suggests that nurses working in different settings, such as long-term care facilities or health centers, have different competencies in EID prevention. A comparison of the findings of this study with those reported by Cai indicated that nurses working in long-term care facilities were better able to perform their EID prevention tasks.

4.3. Limitations of Self-Report Questionnaires

The main disadvantage of using self-report questionnaires is the possibility of social desirability bias because respondents may not answer truthfully but in a socially acceptable manner. In addition, response bias, which refers to the tendency of an individual to answer in a certain manner regardless of the question, may be encountered. This study was conducted in Taiwan; thus, its results cannot be generalized to long-term care facilities in other countries.

The nurses were asked to voluntarily participate in this study, and those who participated might be significantly more motivated compared with those who refused. The personal characteristics of the participants in this study were significantly more positive than those of the refusers; this might have affected the results of the attitude construct. In addition, the accuracy of the results of the skills construct should be validated because the construct still depends on the effect of the presence of the actual cases of EIDs in the facility. If participants do not have experience managing EIDs, they may fill in responses based on hypothetical thinking. Thus, the overall scores on the attitudes and skills subscales may be overestimations and not accurately reflect the attitudes and skills of long-term care facility nurses regarding EIDs. However, the survey period coincided with the severe global outbreak of a specific infectious disease, COVID-19, which required nurses to acquire extensive knowledge regarding pandemic preparedness. The results of this study may be overstated due to the respondents' seeking to meet public expectations that healthcare workers should be trained in epidemic preparedness.

5. Conclusions

The Competence of Nurses in long-term care facilities in EID Prevention scale developed in this study confirmed its value and potential with a high CVI and internal consistency. For competence in EID prevention, nurses' knowledge was insufficient, but they showed moderate to very positive attitudes and were also confident that they had the necessary skills. An examination of the dimensions' degree in EID prevention indicated that the long-term care facility nurses who had knowledge regarding EIDs exhibited more positive attitudes toward EID prevention, properly implemented prevention measures, and developed appropriate EID management skills. In addition, perceived supervisor's approval, marital status, attitudes toward EIDs prevention, EID prevention skills, knowledge of EIDs, and being in charge of infectious disease prevention were significant predictors of the three dimensions of EID prevention. The results can serve as a reference for the development of continuing education programs for infectious disease prevention in long-term care facilities. A problem identified in this study is the difficulty in interpreting the long-term care facility nurses' perception regarding EID prevention. In the future, additional qualitative interviews should be conducted to understand participants' perceptions, to improve their acceptance of national or institutional policies in EID prevention.

Author Contributions: Conceptualization, P.-J.K.; Methodology, C.-M.C.; Software, P.-J.K.; Validation, C.-M.C.; Formal Analysis, P.-J.K.; Investigation, P.-J.K.; Writing—Original Draft Preparation, P.-J.K.;

Writing—Review & Editing, C.-M.C.; Supervision, C.-M.C.; Project Administration, C.-M.C. All authors have read and agreed to the published version of the manuscript.

Funding: This research received no specific grant from any funding agency in the public, commercial, or not-for-profit sectors.

Institutional Review Board Statement: The study was conducted according to the guidelines of the Declaration of Helsinki, and approved by the Institutional Review Board of National Cheng Kung University Hospital (protocol code: B-ER-110-036 and date of approval: March 2021).

Informed Consent Statement: Informed consent was obtained from all subjects involved in the study.

Data Availability Statement: Because the development of the instrument used in this study is ongoing and future contributions are expected, the data section is currently unavailable.

Acknowledgments: We are deeply grateful to frontline long-term care facility nurses for their commitment and enthusiasm to participate in this study despite the high risk of infection and for their dedication to long-term care and infectious disease prevention. We would also like to thank Li-Jung Elizabeth Ku (Department of Public Health, National Cheng Kung University) and Han-Siong Toh (Department of Intensive Care Medicine, Chi Mei Hospital) for an early review of this article and especially for their guidance on infectious disease control and statistical analysis.

Conflicts of Interest: The authors declare no conflict of interest.

References

1. WHO. Emerging Infectious Diseases. 1997. Available online: https://www.who.int/docstore/world-health-day/en/documents1997/whd01.pdf (accessed on 5 January 2022).
2. Institute of Medicine. *Microbial Threats to Health: Emergence, Detection, and Response*; The National Academies Press: Washington, DC, USA, 2003.
3. Jones, K.E.; Patel, N.G.; Levy, M.A.; Storeygard, A.; Balk, D.; Gittleman, J.L.; Daszak, P. Global trends in emerging infectious diseases. *Nature* **2018**, *451*, 990–993. [CrossRef] [PubMed]
4. WHO. Infection Prevention and Control of Epidemic-and Pandemic-Prone Acute Respiratory Infections in Health Care. 2014. Available online: https://apps.who.int/iris/bitstream/handle/10665/112656/9789241507134_eng.pdf?sequence=1&isAllowed=y (accessed on 7 January 2022).
5. Chen, W.; Huang, Y. To protect healthcare workers better, to save more lives. *Anesth. Analg.* **2020**, *131*, 97–101. [CrossRef] [PubMed]
6. International Council of Nurses. ICN Demands G20 Nations Take Action to Stop Nurses and Other Healthcare Workers Dying in the Pandemic, after WHO Confirms up to 180,000 Have Died Already. 2021. Available online: https://www.icn.ch/news/icn-demands-g20-nations-take-action-stop-nurses-and-other-healthcare-workers-dying-pandemic (accessed on 9 October 2021).
7. International Council of Nurses. International Council of Nurses COVID-19 Update. 2021. Available online: https://www.icn.ch/sites/default/files/inline-files/ICN%20COVID19%20update%20report%20FINAL.pdf (accessed on 1 July 2021).
8. Gandal, N.; Yonas, M.; Feldman, M.; Pauzner, A.; Tabbach, A.; Long-Term Care Facilities as a Risk Factor in Death from COVID-19. VoxEU & CEPR Coverage of the COVID-19 Global Pandemic. 2020. Available online: https://voxeu.org/article/long-term-care-facilities-risk-factor-death-covid-19 (accessed on 1 August 2020).
9. Central News Agency. COVID-19 Outbreak Has Been Detected in 85 Long-Term Care Facilities, and 48 Patients Have Been Diagnosed in a Nursing Home in Shilin District, Taipei City, Taiwan. 2021. Available online: https://www.cna.com.tw/news/ahel/202106210246.aspx (accessed on 21 June 2021).
10. Central News Agency. A Nurse Infected with COVID-19 Has Been in Contact with 95 People, Prompting Taoyuan City Government to Initiate Emergency Responses. 2020. Available online: https://www.cna.com.tw/news/ahel/202003220204.aspx (accessed on 23 March 2020).
11. Lin, P.; Lin, H.; Jiang, X.; Jian, R.; Chen, Y.; Xue, B. Analysis of the prevention and control strategies for tuberculosis in long-term care facilities in Taiwan. *Chin. J. Infect. Control* **2018**, *28*, 223–233. [CrossRef]
12. Cowan, D.T.; Norman, I.; Coopamah, V.P. Competence in nursing practice: A controversial concept–A focused review of literature. *Accid. Emerg. Nurs.* **2007**, *15*, 20–26. [CrossRef] [PubMed]
13. Spencer, L.M.; Spencer, S.M. *Competence at Work: Model for Superior Performance*; John Wiley & Sons: Hoboken, NJ, USA, 1993.
14. Kang, H. Sample size determination and power analysis using the G*Power software. *J. Educ. Eval. Health Prof.* **2021**, *18*, 17. [CrossRef] [PubMed]
15. Worthington, R.L.; Whittaker, T.A. Scale development research: A content analysis and recommendations for best practices. *Couns. Psychol.* **2006**, *34*, 806–838. [CrossRef]
16. Baranowski, T.; Cullen, K.W.; Nicklas, T.; Thompson, D.; Baranowski, J. Are current health behavioral change models helpful in guiding prevention of weight gain efforts? *Obes. Res.* **2003**, *11*, 23S–43S. [CrossRef] [PubMed]

17. Sibbald, S.; Jegatheeswaran, J.; Pocock, H.; Penney, G. A national survey of educational and training preferences and practices for public health nurses in Canada. *J. Contin. Educ. Nurs.* **2020**, *51*, 25–31. [CrossRef] [PubMed]
18. Rentala, S.; Thimmajja, S.G.; Bevoor, P.; Nanjegowda, R.B. Nurses' knowledge, attitude and practices on use of restraints at state mental health care setting: An impact of in-service education programme. *Investig. Educ. Enferm.* **2021**, *39*, e12. [CrossRef] [PubMed]
19. Chen, Y.; Shen, Q. Investigating the effect of the supervisor's approval and power distance tendency on the correlation between authentic leadership and service quality. *J. Hum. Resour. Manag.* **2015**, *15*, 1–25. [CrossRef]
20. Giallonardo, L.M.; Wong, C.A.; Iwasiw, C.L. Authentic leadership of preceptors: Predictor of new graduate nurses' work engagement and job satisfaction. *J. Nurs. Manag.* **2010**, *18*, 993–1003. [CrossRef]
21. Bartzokas, C.A.; Slade, P.D. Motivation to comply with infection control procedures. *J. Hosp. Infect.* **1991**, *18*, 508–514. [CrossRef]
22. Ben-Ari, A. Israeli professionals' knowledge and attitudes toward AIDS. *Soc. Work Health Care* **1996**, *22*, 35–52. [CrossRef] [PubMed]
23. Berhe, M.; Edmond, M.B.; Bearman, G.M.L. Practices and an assessment of health care workers perceptions of compliance with infection control knowledge of nosocomial infections. *Am. J. Infect. Control* **2005**, *33*, 55–57. [CrossRef] [PubMed]
24. Cai, Y. Discussions on Factors Related to the Knowledge, Attitude, and Skill of Public Health Nurses on the Prevention and Control of Emerging Infectious Disease. Master's Thesis, Institute of Clinical Nursing and Community Health Care, National Yang-Ming University, Taipei City, Taiwan, 2014.

International Journal of
Environmental Research and Public Health

MDPI

Article

Quality of Work Life and Work Process of Assistance Nurses

Denisse Parra-Giordano [1,*], Denisse Quijada Sánchez [1], Patricia Grau Mascayano [1] and Daniela Pinto-Galleguillos [2]

[1] Departamento de Enfermería, Universidad de Chile, Av. Independencia, Santiago 7760388, Chile; dquijada@uchile.cl (D.Q.S.); patricia.grau@uchile.cl (P.G.M.)
[2] Programa de Microbiología y Micología, Facultad de Medicina, Universidad de Chile, Av. Independencia, Santiago 7760388, Chile; dpintogalleguillos@gmail.com
* Correspondence: drparra@uchile.cl

Abstract: Background: The concept of Quality of Work Life (QWL) has been built multidimensionally through social reproduction; it is impacted by the perceptions of each individual and by the relationship between workers and the work environment. Objective: to analyze the Work Process and QWL of assisting nurses in public health. Methods: Research in a critical paradigm, descriptive, exploratory with a qualitative approach. The population corresponds to nurses who work in care work. Semi-structured guiding questions were applied and were analyzed with content analysis. Results: seven participants declared female; all Chilean; seven are young adults; six singles; only one has children, and one has a person dependent on her care; six are heads of household, and five receive help with housework. All have a nursing degree, five have a diploma, but none have a postgraduate. The work process has three subcategories: work object, instrument, organization, and work conditions; the QWL category has six subcategories: definition and perception of QWL, QWL potentiating factors, QWL exhausting factors, QWL improvement strategies, the emotional burden associated with QWL, and health problems. Conclusions: In this way, the lifestyle built by the assistance in the health area has repercussions on the quality of life and health in general.

Keywords: occupational health; quality of life; nurses; working conditions; work; primary health care

Citation: Parra-Giordano, D.; Quijada Sánchez, D.; Grau Mascayano, P.; Pinto-Galleguillos, D. Quality of Work Life and Work Process of Assistance Nurses. *Int. J. Environ. Res. Public Health* **2022**, *19*, 6415. https://doi.org/10.3390/ijerph19116415

Academic Editor: Guillermo A. Cañadas-De la Fuente

Received: 24 November 2021
Accepted: 8 January 2022
Published: 25 May 2022

Publisher's Note: MDPI stays neutral with regard to jurisdictional claims in published maps and institutional affiliations.

1. Introduction

Work is a central aspect of life, being a means to obtain social and economic benefits and position individuals in society, determining their acquisitive power [1].

The concept of Quality of Work Life (QWL) has been multidimensionally constructed through social reproduction, which determines their social insertion historically, considering the work performed by each person [2]. QWL is promoted by favorable working conditions [3], impacted by the perceptions and feelings of each individual [4], and by the relationship between workers and the work environment [5]. The QWL is also understood as the worker's satisfaction with their personal and work needs in the work process in a given position [6]. Must be valued and respected by the employer [4].

Nursing is the largest workforce in the health care system [5,7]. Therefore, QWL is essential for the nurse, recognized as the degree to which their personal needs are satisfied through quality care and organizational objectives [7,8]. However, many factors influence it [5]. Likewise, the nursing QWL plays a fundamental role in managing care [9], increases productivity, and reduces turnover and psychosocial impact [6,8].

Although it is thought that nurses, having the necessary knowledge and means, should provide an optimal QWL, different problems arise in their work development [10]. Likewise, globalization has brought changes in employment conditions and nursing work processes under the axis of capitalism, which has implied transformations in the work profile, and workers to adapt to the current economic model [11].

Nursing evolved from a trade to a professional career, with the work of Florence Nightingale being decisive in the formation of modern nursing. Under this model, nursing develops in five work processes: assistance, management, teaching, research, and political participation [11]. According to this classification, in Chile, assistance nurses work directly with people, providing care at different levels of care.

The work process has three elements: the work object where the activity is carried out; the instruments that are a set of tools between the worker and the object; the action that refers to work, its specific organization for a particular purpose and the conditions in which it is carried out [1]. Thus, for example, the healthcare nurse transforms the object (subject) using specific knowledge and own instruments.

The QWL of people is a historical and social result. However, on the other hand, the QWL of a group is determined by the time of life and work of everyone in society. Therefore, in terms of her work, each person develops a contradictory system of opposing forces of favorable and destructive processes that impact their Quality of Life (QoL) [11].

In this context, nurses' work situation is impacted by how health institutions are inserted into the labor market, influencing working conditions, explicitly nursing as a social practice. Regarding the working conditions of nurses, the Labor Code regulates the legal processes [12], and the Health Code [13] establishes the areas covered by article 113 "includes the management of care concerning promotion, maintenance, and restoration of health, prevention of diseases and injuries".

Professional burnout is a syndrome that has been the subject of many investigations, impacting their work and professional lives [14,15]. For example, direct care work is recognized as a source of occupational risk [14], even more so as nursing closest to the sick person [15]. Describing dissatisfaction with work, physical and emotional exhaustion [15], likewise, interference in family life.

The neoliberal economic model impacts the work of nursing; the consumer society encourages workers to have new houses, cars, and others. The National Research on Employment, Labor, Health, and Quality of Life of workers in Chile (2009–2010), refers that the worst evaluated aspects are the amount of money that enters the home and the level of debt [16]. In this way, healthcare nurses look for work sources outside the working day and in other institutions, taking time for family dedication and rest that impacts QWL.

Like any work process, care nursing generates favorable and destructive factors [14,15]. Therefore, the care nurse must know how working conditions affect the QoL and improve the quality of care delivered to the beneficiary population in the health network. Likewise, this knowledge will also promote health at work; these are direct contributions to the development of nursing in its practical and social context. Regarding the development of care, in Chile, a professional can develop in the three maintenance levels of the health network [17]. Furthermore, most studies are produced at the tertiary level, making it essential to carry out an approximation at the primary level.

Thus, because of the already known impact of the labor market on nursing professionals worldwide, it is necessary to broaden the knowledge of the nursing role that works in care in Chile. Therefore, this article aims to expand the lowdown on this topic, setting out the objective of analyzing the work process and the quality of work life referred to by public health care nurses.

2. Materials and Methods

Research in a critical paradigm, descriptive, exploratory with a qualitative approach.

Carried out in two Family Health Centers Primary level of care and a Type four Hospital of Santiago de Chile's Western Metropolitan Health Service. The population corresponds to nurses and nurses who work in care work. Inclusion criteria: workday 22 a 44 h (half or full workday), care exercise for at least six months in the workplace. Exclusion criteria: professionals on vacation or medical leave.

Instrument: According to the literature review, the researchers created the question guide for this research based on two previous categories, work process and quality of work life. Then, they applied the guiding questions to nurses with the same characteristics to adjust their relevance to the object of study. Thus, the researchers asked sociodemographic characterization questions and two semi-structured guiding questions: (1) What is your work process at the primary level in public health services? (2) What is your perception of the quality of working life at the primary level in public health services?

Data collection: The researchers contacted the head nurse of each institution to coordinate the interviews, inviting all nurses in each workplace to participate. According to time availability, individual interviews were agreed upon, developed by the researcher without a prior relationship with participants. After explaining and signing the informed consent, five interviews were conducted at the Primary Health Care (PHC) of care and three at the tertiary level until the object of study was saturated. The participants agreed to participate in the investigation (there were no refusals or desist from the interviews) in a room of each institution with total privacy. With 17 to 37 min, from April 2019 to December 2020. They were recorded and transcribed to guide the analysis.

Data analysis: The researchers analyzed the sociodemographic data with descriptive statistics (absolute and cumulative frequencies) and the interviews with content analysis methodology according to Bardin [18], considering the predefined and emerging categories. According to the analysis developed from the interviews, they obtained three subcategories from the previous work process categories: work object, instrument, organization, and work conditions; the quality of work life category is made up of five subcategories: definition and perception of QWL, QWL potentiating factors, exhausting factors of QWL, QWL improvement strategies and emotional burden associated with QWL. Likewise, the emerging category of Health problems emerges. The investigators identified each interview with the letter E, according to the consecutive number.

Aspects of rigor and ethics: the rigor criteria of the study, according to Guba [19], were applied.

3. Results

This research had eight participants (eight interviews). The sociodemographic characterization is in Table 1.

Table 1. Sociodemographic characterization ($n = 8$) Santiago, Chile (2019–2020).

Characteristics	Distribution in the Sample
Gender	
Female	7
Masculine	1
Age (average)	35 years old
Young adults	7
Average adult	1
Nationality	
Chilean	8
Marital status	
Single	1
Married	1
As a couple	6
Professional training	
Nursing degree (different universities)	8
Have a diploma	5
Have a postgraduate degree	0
Others	
Have children.	1
One person dependent on her care	1
Heads of household	6
Receive help with housework	5

3.1. Category 1. Work Process

The work process is built by the object, instruments, organization, and working conditions. Next, each subcategory is described with a summary result, and then add the individual respondents' statements to support it.

3.1.1. Subcategory 1.1—Work Object

The Work object is defined as gratification and pride for work, commitment, and vocation with the care of people.

> *"For my nursing, it is the maximum in human terms; everything is very important, very enriching. I feel that not all people can work in what I work and it gives me a certain pride to be a nurse."* E3

> *"For me, my goal is to give a good quality of care to the person."* E7

3.1.2. Subcategory 1.2—Work Instruments

The Work instruments are determined from the institution or be personal. *"What I need is a box first of all, because if not, I can't. Computer, I use my cell phone a lot; it's a great tool that helps me a lot because I'm connected to the mail all the time, which drives me. And schedules, notebook "*. E3

> *"The cell phone with the Internet, but sometimes I also walk with my notes."* E7

3.1.3. Subcategory 1.3—Organization and Division of Work

The organization and division work are identified: working hours, distribution of tasks, salary, environment, request for permits and perception of medical licenses, support for training and well-being, labor relations.

Six have a day shift, and two have a shift system; work seniority ranges from 1 to 23 years, with 12 to 1 years at the institution. Regarding the development of their work, three are sector nurses; two are in charge of the transversal program, one is in order of the shift, and two are clinical floor nurses. According to the commute to work, the minimum time is 15 min, and the maximum is 90 min, four use public transport, three own cars, and one owns a bicycle. Salaries also present a variability from $950 and $1650.

> *"The director chooses the positions. The director is the one who appoints you, and you are in charge of several tasks. Mostly, the unit boss manages the plan and my schedule. He is the one who sees your plans, blockades, your administrative hours, the hours that you see patients, etc."* E3

> *"In other words, I stay here, I go home, and I continue working on things that were pending. I have to review the files, and I have to see this other thing, but I never go on time ever."* E4

> *"I find work-relations good in general and, like in most places, there are always frictions within some people due to their personalities, I think, but in general, it is good. I don't know, but if I start to compare other places' stories, I find that the atmosphere here is good."* E5

> *"I have a fixed shift; my duties are defined in their protocol and everything."* E7

3.2. Category 2: Quality of Work Life—QWL

The QWL is formed based on the definition and perception, potentiating factors, exhausting factors, and emotional charge.

3.2.1. Subcategory 2.1—Definition and Perception of QWL

The QWL is defined and perceived as each person's expectation, feeling full at work and having personal time.

"Quality of life as the ideal that all the people who work should have, not being stressed, not worrying, not fighting, not arguing." E1

"Quality of life I believe that when one feels as good, as full in what one does, what he is doing. If he is with the individual part well, I think that is what it is, quality of life. I believe that it is not pure to work, but to have a little of everything, that is, to have time with the family, go out, have fun, for everything, and work too." E4

"I see work as very enriching for me, so for me, my quality of life at this time that has occurred at work is super good." E8

3.2.2. Subcategory 2.2—Potentiating Factors QWL

The potentiating factors QWL are a favorable work environment, having the necessary resources to develop work, closeness to the home, good relationship with colleagues, consideration in decision-making, and assessment at work.

"Yes, first of all, the work environment is favorable, I find it to be good, the conditions. I feel that this building is wonderful, everything is very clean. I have all the necessary resources to work well; I have nothing to complain about." E5

"I think that for me at this moment it has a positive influence, one that is close to work where I live, that I feel comfortable where I work, that my peers are cooperative and we all jump up to finish a shift well, that the boss takes into consideration what I think and encourages that, that one feels comfortable and valued in the place where he works, I think that is why I would not change my job." E8

3.2.3. Subcategory 2.3—Exhausting Factors (Negatively Affect) the QWL

The exhausting factors (negatively affect) the QWL are built by a long working day, the lack of resources that must be paid for personally, personal relationships, and the arrival of new professionals with a lack of preparation.

"External things, inputs could also be that they could facilitate our work" "then I have to pay for the supplies because no one was going to pay for it here, so they are things like that, as they should worry a little more about quality with that one works." E1

"I think personal relationships have a lot of weight, that is, relationships with your peers, with the heads, especially with the heads." E3

"Just like the colleagues too, suddenly they come very unprepared, I feel that there is not good training now, that's why I told you how the university is because I think that the colleagues, from other universities, do not come very well prepared; then it seems to me, that I think it is not favorable, there is no well-defined selection." E4

"I consider that my work is exhausting because it is twelve long hours of work." E8

3.2.4. Subcategory 2.4—QWL Improvement Strategies

The QWL improvement strategies are formed from activities to channel emotions, knowledge among team members, self-care activities; they can be from the company or personal.

"Do a workshop, go to an activity that helps us to channel our emotions a little." E1

"Being able to get to know each other more because one does not know each other here, he is known for the work we do, but one does not know either what problem the other colleague may be carrying." E2

"What happens is that some time ago we had self-care activities, we had healthy breaks, we had a person who came to do gymnastics, they gave us massages, things, as well as every so often, we had something that took us out of the work thing, but now like one or two years ago we have been without that." E4

3.2.5. Subcategory 2.5—The Emotional Burden Associated with QWL

The emotional burden associated with QWL is built from the development of the function of prioritizing care, receiving criticism from other professionals or relatives for lack of resources, and poor treatment of patients when things are not done personally.

> *"Or sometimes you can't cope with seeing all of them. Then you have to do a TRIAGE on who is worse, who comes later then maybe that is a burden as well as vital because it depends on you that the doctor sees that patient on the day Today, or why don't you see him first and not this one, then there are times when the patients are both super serious. You don't know who to prioritize. That is sometimes a bit harder."* E1

> *"I don't care if I don't have a box because I still come happy and I don't care, I solve it as I can, but for me, if I got on severely with my class, with all the nurses, even if I had a box and everything that they gave me, it would not be so, that is, it would be more difficult."* E3

> *"Some doctors or some relatives do not understand that we lack things to be able to do some things or follow-up, so I did not walk with my head one hundred percent as to be able to withstand so much pressure within everything. Because the family members are the same here, doctors treat people badly when things are not done their way."* E6

3.3. Category 3—Health Problems Associated with Work

It refers to health problems identified with an occupational cause by the interviewees. They are making up for difficulties falling asleep due to work problems, depression, anxiety disorder, workplace bullying, health problems associated with work stress.

> *"Sometimes it is a bit difficult for me to fall asleep, thinking about some work issues, as well as about a patient, how will the lady be so much that she was about to die, things like that you turn around or small things like tomorrow I have to do this, thinking about what I have to do tomorrow and what I did not do and what I have to do."* E1

> *"Yes, but no, feeling depressed, feeling bad, leading me to go to a psychologist or psychiatrist for a work issue or stress. I have not felt that way yet, and I am not too young for that, I think."* E2

> *"I was with a depression, a depression together with an anxiety disorder that was produced by an occupational disease, by a workplace harassment, I was 3 to 4 months on leave, with psychiatric treatment."* E3

> *"Yes, last year I had a TIA, an accident because I was very stressed that time; I kind of stressed a lot because besides I had a lot of trouble, I was on an emergency shift."* E4

> *"Yes, or of course, probably because of the stress as well."* E5

> *"We get quite stressed by the lack of supplies."* E6

4. Discussion

4.1. Sociodemographic and Labor Characteristics

As in the present research, in various studies on nursing care work the majority were women, Mexico 95.7% [20], Saudi Arabia 95% [21], China 94% [9], Malaysia 93% [22], Tehran Iran 90% [23], Kashan Iran 83% [24], Brasil 83% [25], Chile 83% [26], Irak 73% [4], Libano 60% [27]. In contrast, in Ethiopia, 51% were men [8]. Additionally, in most studies the participants have an average age of young adults (20 to 39 years) [4,5,8,9,20–22,24], Copiapó Chile [28]. Conversely, average age is 41 years [26]. Concerning marital status the marriage prevails in most studies [4,9,21,22,25,27,28], 68% had children [25], and 52% had responsibilities for the care of the elderly [9]. In other studies also the majority were graduates [4,21,23,27,28], but if they present diploma degree 96% [22], 87% had a higher degree [9].

4.2. Work Process

In other countries, different results are found in this research, where most of the workers are without a contract [4,20,26], only half had a full-time job, the most worked with a shift system [25–27], and they worked more than the contracted hours [8,25]. On the contrary to the present study, other research presents an average monthly income of CLP 500 [4], between CLP 1500 to CLP 3000 [26], more than CLP 1000 [28]. Complementing, most workers did not receive a risk allowance or certification compensation [8].

4.3. Definition and Perception of QWL

One study shows a high level of QoL, and the highest values are in managerial support and workload [28]; besides, the majority of nurses report being satisfied with the QWL in terms of the organizational culture [5]; and the well-being is higher in women [9]. Other research presents nursing QWL is mainly at a moderate level and needs improvement interventions [7,29], and the QWL is in the middle range [9]. On the contrary, more than half of the nurses reported a poor QWL [4,8]. This background implies a greater probability of leaving their job due to dissatisfaction with most of the components of the QWL (adequate and fair pay, safe and hygienic work environment, general atmosphere of work-life and social dependency of work-life) [4]. As evidenced in the present investigation one of the factors that influence QWL in the Nurse is stress [30]. Contact with death, patients and their families, conflicts with supervisors, and uncertainty about the therapeutic effect significantly increased pressure among participants [31]. Physical health has the best QoL and the lowest environmental field, mainly due to occupational stress [27].

Most PHC nurses are dissatisfied with work and family life factors, spend long hours, and are often exhausted after work [6]. In this way, nursing is perceived as strenuous work [31]. In Mexico, a study showed that dissatisfaction could be found in the QoL of the nursing professional in public health clinics in all dimensions. The dimensions with the most significant blow were inclusion in the workplace, personal development, and well-being achieved through work. The dimensions with the minor dissatisfaction were institutional support, free time management, job satisfaction, and job security [20]. In Chile, the perception of quality of care is acceptable, and the working environment conditions are evaluated as good except for the temperature [26].

4.4. QWL Potentiating Factors

As mentioned in the present research, organizational commitment negatively influences nurses' QWL and intention to change [22]. As mentioned in the narratives, managers can do self-care workshops or other strategies to improve the QWL by providing opportunities for growth and development of staff skills, providing conditions for greater employee engagement, promoting teamwork, and planning fair and equitable pay [23]. The nurses acknowledge that they have received cooperation from their respective departments, supporting their QWL [5]. The higher quality of professional life, the greater job satisfaction, presenting a mutual and strengthening relationship between the two [28]. QWL the highest scores were for job and professional satisfaction [9]. Some studies show that the QWL of nurses has significant positive associations with: education, marital status, work experience, night shifts, monthly per capita income, support from family members [5]; years of experience (1–3), number of night tasks (5–7 days), number of extraordinary tasks (3–4 days), work on days off, rest at the right time [7]; organizational commitment, positive work environment, and satisfaction of staff [23]. Likewise, the public image of a society, the nursing position, the department of work, educational level, availability of a safe place to rest, availability of drinking water, the factors of age, title, education, employment contract, sleep disorder, and nursing adverse events were associated with a good nursing QWL [8,9].

Regarding the position or training of assistance nurses, the QWL of the head nurse is three times better than that of the rest. Furthermore, the QWL of the nurses' undergraduate level is 2.3 times more than those who only have a diploma. It could influence the present investigation that there are no bosses or postgraduate degrees. In addition, the public image of a society, labor department, availability of a safe place to rest, and the availability of drinking water are associated with good QWL [4], and the socio-professional relationships [25] the latter as well as the present investigation.

4.5. Exhausting Factors of the QWL

As the nurses refer, nursing performance conditions are adverse, which may negatively impact their QWL and staff and their care. They felt helpless knowing the poorly performing care, expressing frustration and intention to change jobs and professions [32]. Complementing the stressing factors mentioned in this research in decreasing order, they are work overload, lack of supplies or poor quality of these, unsatisfactory salaries, number of nursing professionals inadequate to the demand, little clarity in functions, also mentioned as role ambiguity or multitasking, lack of security, lack of recognition, lack of opportunity for promotion, training and or updating, lack of benefits and rewards, lack of autonomy and participation, and poor organization [32]. Likewise, education, job title, workplace, a second nursing job, and age [27,28], time demand, frustration, effort levels, working rotating are significantly correlated with low QWL levels [24,27] are predictors of low QWL [24]. It is also essential to mention that the factors that cause dissatisfaction in nurses are inclusion in the workplace, personal development, and well-being achieved through work [20], communication difficulties, access to information to perform tasks, lack of support for professional development, lack of recognition, lousy work environment, and overload; besides, the last three were associated with low back pain [25]. The research participants mention occupational stress, a significant predictor of low QWL for nurses [9,27,31], while also influencing patient outcomes [31]. In addition, most studies affirm that the relationship between adverse working conditions and nursing health generates stress and job dissatisfaction. Body pain in the back, lower extremities, migraines, poor performance, discouragement, irritability, and depression [32]. In complement, a study in Bangladesh emerged seven barriers to the nurses working life: heavy workloads; lack of government accommodation and transportation; poor health; lack of support from nursing supervisors; lack of promotional opportunities; incomplete hospital policies and procedures; and lack of night shift and risk allowances [33]. For example, almost half of nurses wanted to quit their job in Iraq due to these conditions [4]. Therefore, improving QWL is essential to attracting and retaining employees, especially in healthcare [24].

4.6. QWL Improvement Strategies

As mentioned in the narratives of this article, in the first place, administrators must adopt effective strategies to propose favorable working conditions, consider work stressors, promote a better QWL in nursing workers, and optimize their work environments [4,8,27,33]. In addition, the use of preventive and efficient practices to manage stress seems essential [30], incorporating the levels of commitment to your organization [22], because the organization plays a critical role in determining the health risks associated with burnout syndrome [28].

As previously referred maintaining a healthy work-life is crucial for nurses to improve their QWL, increase retention, improve performance and productivity, promote safe nursing care [6], strengthen the educational level, and their awareness of community perceptions of nursing [8]. QWL improvement interventions include long-term care team talks, empowerment models, integration of focus groups and brainstorming roundtables, positive thinking training, stress inoculation programs, and participatory teamwork [29]; a stress inoculation program proved to be a cheap, safe, and effective way to improve the QWL of nurses [30].

The PHC research participants equally and other studies presents important pressure factors for nursing; besides rotation, they must consider developing improvement strategies in the QWL [6]. Interventions to improve the organizational climate will prevent job desertion by directly affecting the QWL; that is, a high QWL will retain the organization's employees [4]. Hospital managers can reform the environment, the programming, and the system according to the different factors that affect the QWL of the nurses, carry out the psychological evaluation, and the appropriate behavioral psychological intervention for the nurses to improve the QoL [9].

A greater understanding of the nursing work process and its relationship with nonspecific low back pain pointed out that changes must occur in the organization and working conditions to reduce the risks of nursing workers becoming ill [25]. In addition, it is necessary to pay more attention to the low QWL and its related factors, significantly the workload, to understand that a high QWL positively influences the quality of care [7,20,24,33].

4.7. The Emotional Burden Associated with QWL

Because of the multiple stressors that assistance nurses are faced with, as reported in this research, they report the highest frequency of stressful events related to their healthcare team workload [27]. So too, several variables can significantly influence QWL, age, marital status, and education, critical in developing programs to improve the quality of work-life of nursing [21]. Regarding psychosocial work conditions, the literature also refers that stress is one factor that has the most significant negative impact. However, it also mentions the type of contract that is not named a problem in this article [26]. Being one of the main concerns precisely the contractual one to guarantee job stability and continuity of labor rights [26]. Additionally, workload and dealing with death are the most common work sources for nurses, resulting in the highest frequency of occupational stressors [27,28].

4.8. Health Problems

While in Chile, almost half of the nursing professionals perceive their health condition as very good. The other half is as good [26], as in this investigation, nurses describe many problems and barriers that affect their working life, feel the little reward for their hard work, and their health suffers from their working conditions leading to a low QWL [33]. There is also a relationship between work organization and working conditions with low back pain, meaning moderate risks to occupational disease. Likewise, factors that cause job dissatisfaction, such as lack of recognition, lousy work environment, and overload, are associated with low back pain. In addition, those who say they are moody, fatigued, and overloaded have low back pain, which increases their low back pain. Regarding nutritional status, just over half are above the normal BMI, and less than half are normal weight [25]. The main limitation of this research is its conduct only from the public perspective (both primary care level and hospital level); the integration of private institutions for further research should be considered, complementing the current one. Likewise, having started the interviews at the primary level, only three interviews were conducted at the tertiary level of care.

5. Conclusions

The development of this study allowed us to fulfill the proposed objective.

The main results referred to the work process and QWL describe in six subcategories: definition and perception of QWL, QWL potentiating factors, QWL exhausting factors, QWL improvement strategies, the emotional burden associated with QWL (previous categories), and health problems (emergent category).

In this way, the lifestyle built by assistance in the health area affects the quality of work-life and health in general. Thus, the present study is an innovative contribution to the development of nursing by making visible how working conditions affect the QWL of healthcare nurses and unveiling the healthcare network's healthcare work process. Considering that nursing care work compromises the QoL of these professionals, the scarcity of studies on QWL in the nursing care network in Chile, it is expected that this study's contributions will be taken as input to deepen the subject.

Author Contributions: D.P.-G. (Denisse Parra-Giordano), D.Q.S., P.G.M. and D.P.-G. (Daniela Pinto-Galleguillos) have participated in the conceptualization, methodology, formal analysis, investigation, resources, data curation, writing—original draft preparation, writing—review and editing, funding acquisition, all authors. All authors have read and agreed to the published version of the manuscript.

Funding: Fondo de Investigación Departamento de Enfermería 0012017.

Institutional Review Board Statement: The study was conducted according to the guidelines of the Declaration of Helsinki, and approved by the Comité de Ética de Investigación en Seres Humanos de la Facultad de Medicina de la Universidad de Chile No. 148-2017 and by the Comité de Ética del SSMO.

Informed Consent Statement: Informed consent was obtained from all subjects involved in the study.

Data Availability Statement: Authors have available the recordings of the interviews and all the transcripts of each one of them just as they have the analysis in its entirety.

Acknowledgments: We thank each of the nurses participating in this research for opening their world of work, and those who wished to do so could not participate. In addition, to the respective headquarters that allowed the development of this.

Conflicts of Interest: The authors declare no conflict of interest.

References

1. Marx, K. El Capital. Crítica de la Economía Política. In *Libro Tercero: El proceso Global de la Producción Capitalista*; España, S., XXI, Ed.; Pedro Scaron: Madrid, Spain, 2017; 1117p.
2. Breilh, J. El Debate Determinantes-Determinación: Aportes Del Análisis Teórico, Epistemológico y Político. *Rev. Fac. Nac. Salud Pública* **2013**, *31*, 13–27.
3. Hipólito, M.C.V.; Masson, V.A.; Monteiro, M.I.; Gutierrez, G.L. Qualidade de vida no trabalho: Avaliação de estudos de intervenção. *Rev. Bras. Enferm.* **2017**, *70*, 189–197. [CrossRef]
4. Faraji, O.; Salehnejad, G.; Gahramani, S.; Valiee, S. The relation between nurses' quality of work life with intention to leave their job. *Nurs. Pract. Today* **2017**, *4*, 103–111.
5. Thakre, S.B.; Thakre, S.S.; Thakre, S.N. Quality of work life of nurses working at tertiary health care institution: A cross sectional study. *Int. J. Community Med. Public Health* **2017**, *4*, 1627–1636. [CrossRef]
6. Yunus, Y.M.; Idris, K.; Rahman, A.A.; Lai, H.I. The role of quality of nursing work life and turnover intention in primary healthcare services among registered nurses in Selangor. *Int. J. Acad. Res. Bus. Soc. Sci.* **2017**, *7*, 1201–1213. [CrossRef]
7. Hemanathan, R.; Sreelekha, P.P.; Golda, M. Quality of work life among nurses in a tertiary care hospital. *Health Care* **2017**, *5*, 1–8. [CrossRef]
8. Biresaw, H.; Boru, B.; Yimer, B. Quality of nursing work life and associated factors in Amhara Region Referral Hospitals, Northwest Ethiopia: A cross sectional study. *Int. J. Afr. Nurs. Sci.* **2020**, *13*, 100214. [CrossRef]
9. Wang, L.; Wang, X.; Liu, S.; Wang, B. Analysis and strategy research on quality of nursing work life. *Medicine (Baltimore)* **2020**, *99*, 1–5. [CrossRef] [PubMed]
10. Zavala, M.M.Q.; Klinj, T.P.; Carrillo, K.L.S. Calidad de vida en el trabajo del personal de enfermería de instituciones públicas de salud. *Rev. Lat. Am. Enferm.* **2016**, *24*, 1–8. [CrossRef]
11. Parra Giordano, D.; Felli, V.E.A. Work process of nursing professors. *Rev. Lat. Am. Enferm.* **2017**, *25*, 1–8. [CrossRef]
12. Ministerio de Salud Chile. *Código del Trabajo de la República de Chile: Artículo 211, Del Seguro Social Contra Riesgos de Accidentes del Trabajo y Enfermedades Profesionales*; Dirección del Trabajo: Santiago, Chile, 2013.
13. Ministerio de Salud Chile. *Código Sanitario de la República de Chile de 16 de Diciembre de 1997: Artículo 113, Reglamenta el Ejercicio Profesional de la Enfermera*; MINSAL: Santiago, Chile, 1997.
14. Ribeiro, R.P.; Martins, J.T.; Marziale, M.M.P.; do Carmo Cruz Robazzi, M.L. O adoecer pelo trabalho na enfermagem: Uma revisão integrativa. *Rev. Esc. Enferm. USP* **2012**, *46*, 495–504. [CrossRef]
15. Da Silva Hanzelmann, R.; Passos, J.P. Imagens e representações da enfermagem acerca do stress e sua influência na atividade laboral. *Rev. Esc. Enferm. USP* **2010**, *44*, 694–701. [CrossRef] [PubMed]
16. Gobierno de Chile; MINSAL. Primera Encuesta Nacional de Empleo, Trabajo, Salud y Calidad de Vida de los Trabajadores y Trabajadoras en Chile (ENETS 2009–2010). Available online: https://www.dt.gob.cl/portal/1629/articles-99630_recurso_1.pdf (accessed on 10 November 2021).
17. República de Chile; Ministerio de Salud. Subsecretaría de Redes Asistenciales. División de Gestión de la Red Asistencial. In *Modelo de Atención Integral de Salud*; Serie Cuadernos Modelo de Atención N°1; Ministerio de Salud: Santiago, Chile, 2005.
18. Bardin, L. *Análise de Conteúdo*; Edições 70: São Paulo, Spain, 2011; 280p.
19. Guba, E. Criterios de credibilidad en la investigación naturalista. In *La Enseñanza: Su Teoría y su Práctica. 6*; Sacristán, J.G., Gómez, A.P., Eds.; Ediciones AKAL: Madrid, Spain, 2008; pp. 148–165.

20. González-Cruz, N.L.; Peñarrieta-de Córdova, M.I.; Castañeda-Hidalgo, H.; Flores-Barrios, F.; Gutierrez-Gomez, T.; Caballero-Rico, F. Quality of work life in primary care of nursing professionals in public health clinics in Tampico, Mexico. *J. Hosp. Adm.* **2016**, *5*, 90. [CrossRef]
21. Albaqawi, H.M. Quality nursing work life among nurses in Hail Region, Kingdom of Saudi Arabia: Redefining the boundaries of work and life. *Adv. Soc. Sci. Res. J.* **2018**, *5*. [CrossRef]
22. Alzamel, L.G.I.; Abdullah, K.L.; Chong, M.C.; Chua, Y.P. The quality of work life and turnover intentions among Malaysian nurses: The mediating role of organizational commitment. *J. Egypt Public Health Assoc.* **2020**, *95*, 1–8. [CrossRef]
23. Hashempour, R.; Hosseinpour Ghahremanlou, H.; Etemadi, S.; Poursadeghiyan, M. The relationship between quality of work life and organizational commitment of Iranian emergency nurses. *Health Emerg. Disasters* **2018**, *4*, 49–54. [CrossRef]
24. Sadat, Z.; Aboutalebi, M.S.; Alavi, N.M. Quality of work life and its related factors: A survey of nurses. *Trauma Mon.* **2017**, *22*. [CrossRef]
25. Cargnin, Z.A.; Schneider, D.G.; de Oliveira Vargas, M.A.; Machado, R.R. Nonspecific low back pain and its relation to the nursing work process. *Rev. Lat. Am. Enferm.* **2019**, *27*, 1–10. [CrossRef]
26. Luengo, C.; Klijn, T.P.; Burgos, M. Calidad del cuidado del profesional de Enfermería y condiciones ambientales y psicosociales de trabajo. *Rev. Enferm. Trab.* **2016**, *6*, 117–125.
27. Anshasi, H.A.; Fawaz, M.; Alhalalmeh, S.; Ahmad, W.Q.; Tassi, A. Nurses' stressors and their quality of life: A study on nurses caring for older patients. *Nurs. Open* **2020**, *7*, 1698–1706. [CrossRef]
28. Salgado-Roa, J.A.; Lería-Dulčić, F.J. Burnout, satisfacción y calidad de vida laboral en funcionarios de la salud pública chilenos. *Univ. Salud* **2020**, *22*, 6–16. [CrossRef]
29. Viselita, F.; Handiyani, H.; Pujasari, H. Quality level of nursing work life and improvement interventions: Systematic review. *Enferm. Clin.* **2019**, *29*, 223–228. [CrossRef]
30. Safarzei, E.; Darban, F.; Mazloum, S. Effect of stress on the nurses' work life quality in psychiatric ward. *Iioab. J.* **2016**, *7*, 16–21.
31. Sarafis, P.; Rousaki, E.; Tsounis, A.; Malliarou, M.; Lahana, L.; Bamidis, P.; Niakas, D.; Papastavrou, E. The impact of occupational stress on nurses' caring behaviors and their health related quality of life. *BMC Nurs.* **2016**, *15*, 1–9. [CrossRef]
32. Luengo-Martínez, C.; Sanhueza, O. Condiciones de trabajo y su relación con la calidad del cuidado y salud del profesional de enfermería. *Med. Segur Trab.* **2016**, *62*, 368–380.
33. Akter, N.; Akter, M.K.; Turale, S. Barriers to quality of work life among Bangladeshi nurses: A qualitative study. *Int. Nurs. Rev.* **2019**, *66*, 396–403. [CrossRef] [PubMed]

International Journal of
Environmental Research and Public Health

MDPI

Article

How Do Health Teams Perceive International Migrant Users of Primary Care? †

Consuelo Cruz-Riveros [1,2,*], Alfonso Urzúa [1], Gustavo Macaya-Aguirre [3,‡] and Báltica Cabieses [4]

1 Escuela de Psicología, Universidad Católica del Norte, Antofagasta 1270709, Chile
2 Escuela de Enfermería, Facultad de Salud, Universidad Santo Tomás, Concepción 3460000, Chile
3 Facultad de Ciencias Sociales, Universidad Alberto Hurtado, Santiago 8320000, Chile
4 Facultad de Medicina Clínica Alemana, Universidad del Desarrollo, Santiago 7610658, Chile
* Correspondence: consuelocruzri@santotomas.cl

† This research is part of the doctoral thesis of the first author, under the framework of the project FONIS SA19I0066 ANID, Government of Chile.
‡ Estudiante de Doctorado en Sociología; Becario ANID-PFCHA/Doctorado Nacional/2020-Folio: 21200311.

Abstract: The following study aims to describe the perception of international migrants who use the primary level of care by health personnel and to explore how this perception can affect the care process in the commune of Antofagasta, north of Chile. *Methodology:* The methodology was qualitative using a phenomenological descriptive design, through which the discourses of the health personnel of three primary health care centers (n = 14) were explored. *Results:* The participants presented two thematic categories. The first one related to experiences during delivery of care to migrants and included perceptions and beliefs, factors associated with using services, and reasons for consultation. The second category related to stereotypes towards migrants, including prejudices, beliefs about their lives and reasons for migration. *Conclusions:* The therapeutic relationship with migrants in primary care depends on the health care personnel's acceptability of this population, hence, allowing the delivery of care based on respect for their culture and rights.

Keywords: health personnel; transients and migrants; primary health care

Citation: Cruz-Riveros, C.; Urzúa, A.; Macaya-Aguirre, G.; Cabieses, B. How Do Health Teams Perceive International Migrant Users of Primary Care? *Int. J. Environ. Res. Public Health* **2022**, *19*, 9940. https://doi.org/10.3390/ijerph19169940

Academic Editor: Paul B. Tchounwou

Received: 8 July 2022
Accepted: 4 August 2022
Published: 12 August 2022

Publisher's Note: MDPI stays neutral with regard to jurisdictional claims in published maps and institutional affiliations.

1. Introduction

Migration is defined by the World Health Organization (WHO) as the movement of people to a different territory, regardless of its size or composition [1]. This movement can be explained by multiple causes such as educational, political or socioeconomical (poverty, inequality, and job insecurity), natural disasters, health-related issues and family needs. Moreover, deciding to migrate will sometimes be associated with a conjunction of several factors that trigger migration [1–3].

The context in which migration takes place is generally associated with complicated historical processes from the country of origin and sometimes the receiving country [4,5]. However, the migrant world population has been increasing since the 1990s [2,3]. There is a growing interest in its study as a social, political and economic factor of human and social development, and raising awareness on human rights is a cornerstone dimension to consider among people on the move [4,5]. Statistically, since 2020 the population of the Americas reached 7.2% of the global population, while in South America, it reached 2.5% of the total population [4–7]. In Chile, migrants represent 8.6% of the population; the countries with the greatest presence in Chile are Venezuela (30.7%), Peru (16.3%), Haiti (12.5%), Colombia (11.4%) and Bolivia (8.5%) [6,7]. Regarding territorial distribution, the three regions with the highest percentage of foreign residents are: Metropolitan, with 63.1% of foreigners residing in the country; Antofagasta, with 7.1%; and Valparaíso, with 6.4%. Antofagasta is one of the regions with a greater weight on the total regional population, with 13.6% [6–10]. For its part, the main migratory flow in the country is intra-regional and most movements in past years have come from sectors of the Colombian coast and Venezuela, characterized by a large majority of Afro-descendants [8].

The interest in promoting respect for human rights in past decades has reached the world's capacity to generate international human rights pacts that most countries in Latin America have supported. This in turn has promoted the development of policies that aim at guaranteeing respect for every migrant person and the delivery of basic social protection including health care in receiving countries. Such policies and strategies aim to articulate actions for the protection of people on the move that might be exposed to multiple human rights violations during the migration process or during settlement in the host country [2,3]. The most reported types of human rights violations among migrant communities in the region are discrimination, poor working conditions, overcrowded housing, lack of basic sanitation, violence, contaminated environments and health inequities [8–13].

The exposure to multiple social and economic risk factors by international migrants in receiving countries can generate short-, medium-, or long-term deterioration in their health status, which is why the WHO includes migration as a social determinant of health [14]. Among the strategic indicators disseminated by the WHO for this population is the right to health, which establishes a set of minimum and universal services required for the fulfillment of the maintenance or improvement of their health [15]. Such services must include availability of resources and action for gender inequities in health, address distinctions based on the stage of the life course and take into account their particular culture. It also considers the time and geographical distance for effective accessibility to care, and discrimination based on preconceived prejudices or stereotypes that can be observed in the healthcare system, including those reproduced by health teams [16–18].

Some of the practices recommended by experts and health authorities in Chile include language adaptation, consideration of intercultural approaches, and addressing the social determinants of health of the international migrant population [9,19]. The purpose of these standards of care is to respond to the person's own needs and improve human-rights-oriented and culturally pertinent care at the different levels of the health system [15,19–24]. The implementation of these standards is challenging and continuously developed at different areas and levels of the healthcare system. In the meantime, the literature reports factors that can act as facilitators or barriers to the use of health services by international migrants. Facilitators that come from the healthcare system are, for example, efforts to reduce gaps in access to care, including updates for available services and actions to increase migrant registration in the healthcare system [21–24]. On the other hand, there are a number of barriers to healthcare, such as a lack of resources and limited implementation of regulations and programs that promote sensitive care. These results, in some cases, in practices based on personal criteria in which health personnel beliefs, prejudices (positive or negative), and in some cases, xenophobia emerge [21–24]. One example of negative beliefs towards migration reported in the existing literature is related to the idea that the undocumented migrants are "illegal" and do not deserve access to healthcare [25]. This could reflect a lack of knowledge and critical reflection on the part of health personnel about who the undocumented migrant is and his/her specific risks and needs [24]. Another example is discrimination to some migrants who come from some specific countries of origin that are considered of "lower caste". This is due to stereotypes historically forged in popular imaginaries about the different migratory groups in the country, like people coming from Peru, Haiti and Bolivia. In addition, there is literature suggesting the undocumented migrant users are considered more demanding for healthcare than other communities [15,21,26,27].

In social psychology, prejudice is an attitude that has three components: (i) the cognitive component associated with beliefs and the positive or negative assessment of the "stereotypes" of an outgroup, (ii) the component related to feelings and emotions towards the outgroup and (iii) the component related to behavior that can be positive or negative towards the outgroup [28,29]. Stereotypes are produced by generalized evaluations of simplified mental images or ideas about characteristics and attributes of the people that make up a group, based on cultural beliefs, and even generating prejudices based on stereotypes [28]. Another of its characteristics is the generalized assessment of people who are defined as a member of such a prejudiced group or community, guiding their attitudes and behaviors as if they all were the same [28]. Prejudice can also manifest itself overtly or subtly [29]. The first refers to traditional prejudice, characterized by perceived threats to resources, resulting in open rejection and contact with the outgroup [29]. The second is based on the defense of traditional values and where the perception of the outgroup is one of disrespect and of receiving undeserved benefits [29]. In short, people who experience negative feelings toward international migrants may present a negative stereotype about them and possibly discriminatory acts [28,29].

Based on the foregoing, and considering that the behavior towards international migrants during health care may be based on the perception, beliefs or prejudices that health providers have about this population, the following question arises: What is the perception by health personnel of international migrants who use primary care in Chile? Could their perceptions about international migrants affect the healthcare delivery process? Therefore, the objective of this research was to describe the perception by health personnel of international migrants who use the primary level of care in Chile and to explore how this perception might affect the process of care. We considered the commune of Antofagasta, located in the north of Chile and with the second highest concentration of international migrants in the country, as the setting for this study. This borough was especially affected during the COVID-19 pandemic as thousands of migrants entered illegally by foot though the Atacama Desert in the border between Chile, Peru and Bolivia, and ended in transient camps in the city of Antofagasta and other cities close by [10].

2. Method

2.1. Design

The study's methodology was qualitative, as it aims at exploring and unveiling the phenomenon of interest in its natural environment, trying to make sense of such phenomena through the perspectives of the people that are a part of it. This methodology allows the construction of the knowledge and understanding of people's behavior, assuming that reality is multiple, dynamic and changing [30–32]. The type of investigation is descriptive phenomenological, through which we investigate the thematic contents of the discourses of health personnel from five primary health care centers in the commune of Antofagasta in the north of Chile.

2.2. Participants

The sampling strategy was intentional using the snowballing technique and continued until saturation of qualitative information was reached. A total of 14 people participated voluntarily (8 in individual interviews and 6 in a single focus group). The participants belonged to five different public primary health care centers in the commune of Antofagasta, Chile. Data collection was carried out from April to August 2021 in person at the centers. The inclusion selection criteria considered were: (i) over 18 years of age and (ii) have provided health services to international migrants in the past.

2.3. Data Collection

Data was collected through multiple individual interviews and one focus group (Table 1). Semi-structured scripts were developed for each of these qualitative methodologies in order to provide in-depth information about the perception of health personnel concerning providing care to international migrants at the primary level. Conducting in-depth interviews reduced potential distractions or the desirability of responses produced by pressure or threats from other participants, as can occur with focus groups [31]. It also secures that every participant has sufficient time to express all of his/her ideas and experiences, something that can be challenging in focus groups [30,32]. In this study, the focus group was considered a complementary strategy of data collection to individual interviews, allowing the research team to review the relevance and significance of categories that emerged in the interviews and exploring potential new ones during the group conversation. Both the interviews and the focus group were carried out in the workplace, guaranteeing COVID-19 preventive safety measures and a calm environment that ensured confidentiality of participants, yet allowing for a face-to-face interaction.

Table 1. Description of study participants.

Health Centers	Code	Profession	Gender	Age	Years of Experience
1	EP3	Matron	Female	28	Greater than 1 year *
1	EP4	Administrative	Female	56	30
1	EP7	Social worker	Female	28	2
2	EP1	Psychologist	Female	29	4
2	EP6	Nurse	Female	39	6
3	EP2	Psychologist	Female	36	5
4	EP5	Social worker	Female	31	6
4	EGF1	Nursing Technician	Female	33	9
4	EGF2	Physician	Female	25	2 months
4	EGF3	Matron	Male	28	2
4	EGF4	Nursing	Female	36	36
4	EGF5	Psychology	Female	28	6 months
4	EGF6	Dentist	Male	31	3 months
5	EP8	Technical reference	Female	Over 18 *	Greater than 1 year *

* They do not indicate the exact time.

The participants were selected using the snowball sampling technique, starting with health workers invited to participate in the study at the primary centers during recruitment. Those who accepted to participate became the seed participant who then recommended other health workers to participate. We chose this sampling technique due to the difficulty of accessing health personnel; they were not easy to contact directly. However, they felt more confident and comfortable when a colleague spoke to them for the first time. The participants of the interviews and the focus group were different, to ensure a wide range of points of view. Participation was voluntary; before obtaining their consent, participants were informed about the research and their rights as participants in this research.

Semi-structured scripts for interviews and the focus group included flexible questions based on study objectives and were intended to delve into the perception that healthcare teams expressed about "being an international migrant". The scripts were revised by academic experts before piloting, after which some minor adjustments were made, and data collection proceeded. Some of the questions used were: How has the experience of providing care to international migrants in primary care been? Are there any specific healthcare protocols for migrants that have been established in this health center? What actions have you implemented to promote or improve care towards migrants? Are there any stereotypes about migrants among health workers in this center? What are they? How could these stereotypes, in your opinion, affect healthcare delivery to this population? The interviews lasted for 40 to 60 min and were audio recorded, transcribed verbatim, and then thematically analyzed based on main pre-defined categories from the scripts, yet allowing for emerging categories to be captured and analyzed.

2.4. *Rigor*

Scientific rigor in qualitative research can be performed by several techniques. One is triangulation, a method in which various sources of narrative information are contrasted. In this study, we included the triangulation of types of participants. The triangulation of perspectives included those provided by health personnel, intercultural referents, and authorities from the primary care centers [33]. A second rigor technique, audit trial, in our study was developed though a second researcher who took notes during data collection and followed up the path of decisions used during the investigation, reaching similar conclusions in terms of data saturation [34]. A third element of scientific rigor is reflectivity, which is performed through an exhaustive revision of steps and decisions made by the research team, especially during the analysis and interpretation phase.

2.5. Ethical Considerations

This research had the approval of the ethics committee of Universidad del Desarrollo (protocol code 2019-094 and approval date 22 November 2019) and was governed by the principles of voluntariness, autonomy and confidentiality of participants as well as protection of participants and data. It included the signing of an informed consent before data collection.

2.6. Data Analysis

Once the transcripts of the interviews were fully available in a Word document, the thematic analysis was carried out as it has been developed in similar previous studies [32,34]. The thematic analysis included first the repeated reading of transcriptions to identify main categories and related themes. The broad categories were coded from the matrix through the construction of analysis categories assigned by the researchers, assigning them one or more codes related to their meaning and intention. After that general descriptive phase, a process called "decanting" was carried out, following the open coding, then the axial coding and to finish later with the selective coding [35,36]. After analysis of interviews was carried out, we conducted the same analysis process for the focus group and then both techniques were integrated into a single analysis matrix. QTY. 1. New NVivo version 1.5 software for MAC (Antofagasta, Chile) was used to code the interviews.

3. Results

The study participants' perceptions related to providing care to international migrants in primary level included two main categories: (i) beliefs about the migration process, factors associated with the use of health services and reasons for consultation; and (ii) stereotypes based on personal beliefs and, in some cases shared by more than one health team member, concerning international migrants. The presence of prejudices about international migrants and migration itself could represent positive or negative ideas that could intervene in the healthcare delivery process regarding the disposition towards the resolution of the health needs of international migrant patients.

(1) Experiences of health teams related to international migrants during health care delivery: beliefs about the migration process, factors associated with the use of health services and reasons for consultation.

The participants reported having had previous experiences of healthcare delivery towards international migrants in the primary center. One of the most frequent aspects of such experience was related to their social integration process and their living conditions, which in their perspective proved to be relevant to address their particular health needs. Thus, according to primary care health workers, the causes of migration might go beyond mere labor and individual issues and could be oriented towards a better quality of life for themselves and their families. Some of the triggering factors for migration mentioned by the study participants were the search for better education, housing, health, family reunification and access to health. According to the health workers, migrants also report as relevant causes for the decision to migrate those concerning sociopolitical problems faced by their countries of origin.

> *" . . . They came from Peru because they suffered from meningitis there and did not receive medical support, they did not have as much access . . . Their migration was mainly for access to health so that their son would receive better health . . . "* (EP1).

> *" . . . .. they are looking for a better quality of life, education, health and housing, they also come for family unification . . . . Venezuelans attribute it to the political-social issue . . . . the Bolivian or Peruvian population has never told me something like that, only for education, health or housing..."* (EP5).

"...In general, migrants, mostly women, heads of households and people like in the case of Colombia, Peru and Bolivia, relatively young people, 30 years old, right?... Venezuela is an overwhelmed case, so to speak..." (EP2).

"... Most of the cases of patients who are foreigners are single mothers, there are very few who are in a couple, because sometimes the husband is there taking care of the children, she comes, she does not know that she is pregnant..." (EP3).

Based on previous experiences providing primary care to international migrants at their centers, study participants were able to identify factors that positively and/or negatively influenced the quality of care they provided and the continuity of care. They highlighted the lack of knowledge, on both sides, about each other's worldviews and understandings of health-related processes. Health care workers for example perceived poor knowledge and training regarding intercultural health and knowing cultural aspects necessary for the adaptation of interventions to the needs of international migrant communities. Also, according to study participants, migrant populations were unaware of the Chilean health system, its characteristics and availability of services. This lack of knowledge was often associated with a lack of understanding of the information, which could sometimes be explained by their educational level or differences with the health system from the country of origin (for example, the lack of primary care in their home country). Another factor that participants identified was language, as the ability to handle other languages and intercultural adaptations of existing health-related information (pamphlets, posters, etc.). A fourth factor, sometimes derived from those mentioned above, was that beliefs and ignorance triggered staff mistreatment towards international migrants. Finally, study participants described structural and historical weaknesses of the primary centers such as long waiting lists, financial constraints and staff shortage. All of these were also affecting the opportunity of access to care among both migrants and locals.

"...health professionals, in general, are not very aware of the issue, we must understand that there is a significant cultural shock, they have different customs, even different idioms, which interfere with our communication, that is why there are to be super empathic with them ... " (EP3).

" ... A patient who was Bolivian, from the highlands, I assumed she was Aymara, and she came as with her papers ... the person who had done her papers did not explain anything to her, and there is a cultural issue there ... she did not speak Spanish well" (EP1).

"...there are many who are informed and who know how to access health care, but there are many who are not informed..." (EP6).

(2) Stereotypes towards migrants, often based on personal beliefs from healthcare teams.

According to study participants, the deficit of resources and the poor understanding of the problems that have triggered the massive arrival of international migrants to Antofagasta in the past two years of pandemic are crucial to comprehend the reality of these communities and their health-related needs. In this regard, study participants visualize a high demand of health care from international migrants in the city in general and in primary care. Some health workers even connect such "relatively higher" health demand among migrants as a possible cause for a reduction in the rate of delivery of care for the local population.

" ... Peru or Bolivia tends to be very inward, but clearly the violence is much greater .... to control boys and girls" (EGF2).

"Psychomotor development, I have had a lot of children lately ... I have had a lot of children with a lot of delayed psychomotor development, and it is because they do not come, and they are not interested in the child having these tests or those controls up to date" (EGF4).

" .... .It depends a lot on the nationality of the foreigner, I have had more of the vision of the Bolivian foreigner, he is a little more negligent with his health" ... "They wait until

the end, they come like this when the thing is not to prevent, but rather Now to cure, I think that in the dental issue it is like this the point to come to remove the tooth" (EGF5).

" . . . . It is a population that one as a Chilean does not fully understand . . . . That is why if I could define them, I would say not rare, because it is not the specific word, but special, another way of understanding health which is what brings us here. I would also perhaps define them as very demanding; they tend to be poly-consultants and a little impatient" (EGF6).

Regarding stereotypes, the participants recognize the existence of negative ideas against migrants in the general society, including xenophobia and machismo. Some arguments that could explain the existence of stereotypes, according to study participants, are related to generalized views of foreigners based on nationality and their use of services. For example, health workers reported the perception that some types of migrants, based on country of origin, are less prone to self-care including basic hygiene and negligence of their offspring. These ideas are deeply embedded in their conceptions related to some migrant communities such as those coming from Bolivia or Peru. Health workers perceived that these types of ideas have an effect on the ways health care is delivered to them at the primary level.

" . . . on a professional level . . . I remember that recently an official told me mmm . . . hey, all the migrants come to get pregnant . . . " " . . . the other day I heard a colleague say << . . . super abusive with their children>>, and I have Bolivian patients who are a seven like mom" (EP1).

" . . . Venezuelans still have a lot of tools because they have a lot of studies and like they are very easy, docile in terms of their personality, that's why it's like it's easy for them to find work . . . the Bolivian and Peruvian population emm . . . obviously their personality a lot Sometimes it's like more submissive . . . " (EP2).

" . . . To the people of Bolivia, Peru, you have to explain more slowly, you have to ask them more times . . . "do you understand me? "yes", "no?". " . . . With Xenophobia, with machismo, especially from employers, because being a woman is already difficult for this society, imagine being a woman and apart from being a migrant (EP3).

" . . . They are very grateful, I have never been touched by a migrant person who has not been satisfied or who has given them the same, they are never, never grateful" (EP4).

"...A Bolivian person costs us a little more because sometimes they don't understand very well what one asks, they are also much shyer, they don't consult as much, and Peruvians are also a bit like that..." (EP6).

"... It is often the case that professionals believe they have the moral property of judging the patient for having passed through a border crossing...". "...Bolivians, because they have a slightly humbler culture, are not very good at dealing with some things" (EP7).

4. Discussion

The study explores the perception of international migrants who use public primary care in the city of Antofagasta in the north of Chile by health personnel, and how such perceptions could affect their interactions with this population. According to the WHO, international migration is considered a social determinant of health, and the risks experienced during the move and at arrival might deteriorate the health status of international migrants [37]. Traditionally, healthcare systems all over the world require considering the context in which the individual is inserted and their personal life trajectory, worldview and health-related beliefs, thereby investigating protective and risk factors that might affect health outcomes in a given context [37–42]. Among the risk factors related to the poor health of international migrants reported are: the relevance of socioeconomic and material living conditions (overcrowding, basic sanitation), working conditions, lack of social support, and others [41]. According to Hernando, cited by Aninat and Vergara [41], some accumulated deficiencies in the migrant communities that affect their health are the product of factors such as ignorance of their rights or poor governmental aid. In addition, they include those associated with their life experiences at their countries of origin that can lead to poor health over their life course, such as limited vaccination schemes, poor social protection, disasters and economic crises. Therefore, it is possible to appreciate that the migration status by itself is not a risk factor, but rather the associated conditions are the ones that can trigger health problems [27]. International migrants' particular experiences and needs could be considered as a relevant aspect of the improvement of healthcare to protect the health of all.

This study reported that health personnel's perceptions about providing care to international migrants might present facilitating factors and barriers. According to our findings, many of these facilitators and barriers could be interpreted from the lens of ethical clinical practice and human rights. From the guidelines provided by the WHO, it is essential to consider the right to health approach in health care for international migrants, where the dimension of availability and accessibility are relevant, but it is the acceptability of culturally sensitive quality care that needs further attention and development. Such dimension of universal coverage establishes the need to respect differences in culture, language, gender, migration status and other aspects as an essential articulating axis between therapeutic relationships in primary care [15].

Barriers to effective healthcare among international migrants have been widely studied, involving individual aspects such as limited information about the healthcare system in the receiving country, fear of deportation, language, lack of health insurance and educational level. Our study and other similar ones in the international literature suggest the relevance of paying attention to unethical practices in healthcare delivery, such as dehumanized treatment, communication problems, violation of the right to care, discrimination and health services without cultural adaptation to specific diverse communities [24,26,41–43]. According to Liberona, the relationship between the health personnel and international migrant users could be intervened by these factors, reproducing scenarios of power asymmetry between both actors [21]. Health personnel have the power to grant or decline the possibility of health care to migrants (i.e., a violation of the right to health) and migrants could be underpowered due to poor understanding of the health system and how to navigate it to find solutions to their unique health needs [21]. From the healthcare system and the health teams' perspectives, it is necessary to recognize the current shortcomings for the development of the necessary skills to be open to actions that allow diverse cultural practices during care delivery [42]. Current practices use a homogenizing criterion that ignores the differences between international migrants, not considering their diversity in nationality, language, ethnicity, migration process, country of origin, migration status, family context, and the adaptation, integration or marginalization they have faced while residing in Chile [24].

In all, when thinking of power relations in healthcare settings, the literature suggests some relevant elements that seem to emerge in the therapeutic relationship between the healthcare teams and international migrants. Such elements might act as facilitators or barriers to access, as described by various authors worldwide [37–39]. The dynamics produced in these therapeutic contexts can be influenced by experiences and knowledge built throughout life by each of the parts involved, in which the systems of beliefs, traditions, language and cultural codes act as mediators or blockers in the perceptions of how the healthcare process is being developed [38]. According to Roter, relations must be based on the acknowledgment from all actors of the principle of mutual respect and horizontal communication [39]. A therapeutic relationship that ignores these principles often risks the emergence of negative outcomes like fear, discrimination and limited continuity of care among migrants [38].

The findings from this study indicate that staff willingness to provide care to international migrants might be mediated by personal knowledge, beliefs or voluntariness in daily practice. A factor that acts as a barrier to care would be the lack of existence of standardized practices or that these are not known to all staff in primary care and in the healthcare system in general. For Avaria, this creates a barrier to access the health system, which can lead to a poor recognition of migrants as subjects of right by health providers [42].

The dimension of stereotypes found in our study tended to represent more negative than positive aspects of the relationship between healthcare workers and migrant patients. We found that some generalizations associated with nationality were linked by health workers to the migrants' ability to follow instructions, self-care practices and others. These findings are consistent with previous studies on negative beliefs and prejudiced attitudes related to many migrants' perception of job loss, opportunities and low quality of health care due to unsensitive or poorly culturally pertinent care provided to them [42–44]. According to Pino's study, each health team member's vision can be biased when providing care in the therapeutic relationship and can affect the quality of care [45].

The perception of health personnel regarding the international migrant population can affect their relationship with the health system more broadly. For instance, undergraduate students in training can learn through modeling about negative stereotypes and prejudices against migrants that they could reproduce later in their professional life. In fact, some studies show that negative attitudes are associated with the year of study: the lower the course, the better the attitude towards migrants [43]. The international literature has indicated that such attitudes are embedded in beliefs that connect migrants with delinquency, the collapse of the health system, excessive alcohol consumption and increased health spending [46]. It is relevant to know the perception of health personnel about the international migrant population and how it can positively and negatively influence health practices. Therefore, it is imperative to promote strategies and actions that involve both professionals and students in training for acquiring knowledge and skills that delve into ethical aspects and interculturality in order to reduce negative attitudes and prejudices that act as barriers to health care for migrants.

This study has a number of limitations. First, the scope is restricted to the city of Antofagasta in the northern area of Chile. Second, it does not include migrants form all relevant countries of origin, yet over 70% of them are from countries within the region. In future research, it would be pertinent to expand the sample to the country's different regions, include the different types of health personnel (auxiliary, administrative and professional) and different levels of care (secondary, tertiary).

5. Conclusions

To achieve progress in health care, training and awareness on ethical principles of healthcare delivery in contexts of social and cultural diversity and practical intercultural competencies for healthcare teams is fundamental. For this, it is necessary to recognize structural and historical shortcomings in most health systems when it comes to ethical, human-rights-oriented and culturally sensitive care for international migrants. These structural limitations trigger the failure to respond in a timely and adequate manner to the needs of international migrant populations. As a result, most health workers tend to homogenize migrant communities as a single, unified culture. When this occurs, preconceived ideas and attitudes such as stereotypes and prejudices act as a powerful barrier to effective healthcare. Despite the health team's lack of financial support or knowledge, they reported the willingness and commitment to provide more effective and culturally pertinent care according to local possibilities and realities.

Author Contributions: Conceptualization, B.C. and A.U.; methodology, G.M.-A.; software, C.C.-R.; validation, G.M.-A., C.C.-R. and A.U.; formal analysis, C.C.-R.; investigation, C.C.-R. and A.U.; resources, C.C.-R. and A.U.; data curation, C.C.-R. and A.U.; writing—original draft preparation, C.C.-R.; writing—review and editing, C.C.-R., A.U. and B.C.; visualization, C.C.-R.; supervision, A.U.; project administration, B.C.; funding acquisition, C.C.-R. and A.U. All authors have read and agreed to the published version of the manuscript.

Funding: The project FONIS SAI190066 ANID, Government of Chile.

Institutional Review Board Statement: The study was conducted in accordance with the Declaration of Helsinki and approved by the Institutional Review Board (or Ethics Committee) of Universidad del Desarrollo (protocol code 2019-094 and date 22 November 2019 of approval).

Informed Consent Statement: Informed consent was obtained from all subjects involved in the study.

Conflicts of Interest: The authors declare no conflict of interest.

References

1. Organización Mundial de la Salud. Salud de los Migrantes Informe de la Secretaría. 2008. Available online: http://apps.who.int/iris/bitstream/handle/10665/26222/A61_12-sp.pdf;jsessionid=679CA276189D0558869210CEE4C95BED?sequence=1 (accessed on 5 October 2021).
2. Avaria, A.; Báltica, C.; Alexandra, O. *Salud y Migraciones: Relevancia, Consideraciones Generales y Desafíos Para el Chile de Hoy*; Autonomous University of Chile: Providencia, Chile, 2021.
3. Herrera, R. La perspectiva teórica en el estudio de las migraciones. *Sequence* **2006**, *76*, 165–168.
4. Global Migration Data Portal. Migration Data Portal. South America. 2021. Available online: https://www.migrationdataportal.org/es/international-data?i=stock_abs_&t=2020&m=1&rm49=19 (accessed on 3 November 2021).
5. Migration Data Portal. Data Migration Statistics. 2021. Available online: http://www.migrationdataportal.org/data (accessed on 3 November 2021).
6. El 74.5% de las Personas Extranjeras Que Viven en Chile se Concentra en 42 Comunas: Las Principales Son Santiago, Antofagasta e Independencia. Default. Available online: http://www.ine.cl/prensa/2020/06/15/el-74-5-de-las-personas-extranjeras-que-viven-en-chile-se-concentra-en-42-comunas-las-principales-son-santiago-antofagasta-e-independencia (accessed on 15 February 2022).
7. Miradas País Vol. 2: Migración y Campamentos en la Ciudad de Antofagasta. Default. Available online: http://www2.superacionpobreza.cl/wp-content/uploads/2019/06/02_MP_Migracio%CC%81n-y-campamentos-en-la-ciudad-de-Antofagasta.pdf (accessed on 15 February 2022).
8. Echeverri, B.; Margarita, M. Otredad Racializada en la Migración Forzada de Afrocolombianos a Antofagasta (Chile). *Nómadas* **2016**, *45*, 91–103. Available online: http://www.scielo.org.co/scielo.php?script=sci_abstract&pid=S0121-75502016000200007&lng=en&nrm=iso&tlng=es (accessed on 20 February 2022). [CrossRef]
9. Población Extranjera Residente en Chile llegó a 1.462.103 Personas en 2020, un 0.8% más que en 2019. Default. Available online: http://www.ine.cl/prensa/2021/07/29/poblaci%C3%B3n-extranjera-residente-en-chile-lleg%C3%B3-a-1.462.103-personas-en-2020-un-0-8-m%C3%A1s-que-en-2019 (accessed on 20 February 2022).
10. Instituto de Ciencias e Innovación en Medicina, ICIM, Facultad de Medicina Clínica Alemana, Universidad del, Desarrollo. Encuesta Sobre COVID-19 a Poblaciones Migrantes Internacionales en Chile. 2020. Available online: https://migrantes.mineduc.cl/wp-content/uploads/sites/88/2020/11/Reporte-descriptivo-ENCUESTA-MIGRANTES-Y-COVID19.pdf (accessed on 2 November 2021).
11. Organización Mundial de la Salud. Salud de los Refugiados y Migrantes. Available online: https://www.who.int/es/news-room/fact-sheets/detail/refugee-and-migrant-health (accessed on 26 June 2022).
12. Llambías, J. Las Enfermedad de los Sistemas de Salud. *Rev. Gerenc. Políticas Salud* **2015**, *14*, 203–206.
13. Migration Policy Institute. El Pensamiento Creativo Definiendo las Respuestas a la Migración en América Latina—Portal Sobre Migración en América Latina y el Caribe. Available online: https://www.migrationportal.org/es/insight/pensamiento-creativo-definiendo-respuestas-migracion-america-latina/ (accessed on 3 November 2021).
14. Ministerio de Salud. Orientaciones Para la Implementación del Modelo de Atención Integral de Salud Familiar y Comunitaria. 2012. Available online: https://www.minsal.cl/portal/url/item/e7b24eef3e5cb5d1e0400101650128e9.pdf (accessed on 3 November 2021).
15. Organización Mundial de la Salud. 61ª Asamblea Mundial de la Salud. Available online: https://apps.who.int/gb/ebwha/pdf_files/WHA61-REC1/A61_REC1-sp.pdf (accessed on 30 December 2021).
16. Concha, N.P.L. De La Alterisación a La Discriminación En Un Sistema Público De Salud En Crisis: Conflictos Interétnicos a Propósito De La Inmigración Sudamericana En Chile. *Rev. Cienc. Soc. (Cl)* **2012**, *28*, 19–38. Available online: https://www.redalyc.org/articulo.oa?id=70824554002 (accessed on 3 December 2021).
17. Graneheim, U.H.; Lundman, B. Qualitative Content Analysis in Nursing Research: Concepts, Procedures and Measures to Achieve Trustworthiness. *Nurse Educ. Today* **2004**, *24*, 105–112. Available online: https://linkinghub.elsevier.com/retrieve/pii/S0260691703001515 (accessed on 3 December 2021). [CrossRef] [PubMed]
18. El Derecho a la Salud: Folleto Informativo No. 31—ACNUDH. Available online: https://acnudh.org/el-derecho-a-la-salud-folleto-informativo-no-31/ (accessed on 13 December 2021).
19. Organización Mundial de la Salud (OMS). Estadísticas Sanitarias Mundiales 2017: Monitoreo de la Salud Para los ODS. 2017. Available online: https://www.who.int/gho/publications/world_health_statistics/2017/en/ (accessed on 2 October 2021).
20. Salud del Inmigrante. Ministerio de Salud—Gobierno de Chile. Available online: https://www.minsal.cl/salud-del-inmigrante/ (accessed on 2 November 2021).

21. Liberona Concha, N. Poder, Contrapoder y Relaciones de Complicidad Entre Inmigrantes Sudamericanos y Funcionarios del Sistema Público de Salud Chileno. *Si Somos Am.* **2015**, *15*, 15–40. Available online: http://www.scielo.cl/scielo.php?script=sci_arttext&pid=S0719-09482015000200002&lng=en&nrm=iso&tlng=en (accessed on 2 November 2021). [CrossRef]
22. Vega, C.V.Z.; Campos, M.C.G. Discriminación y Exclusión Hacia Migrantes en el Sistema de Salud Chileno. Una Revisión Sistematizada. *Salud Soc.* **2019**, *10*, 188–204. Available online: https://revistas.ucn.cl/index.php/saludysociedad/article/view/3262 (accessed on 2 November 2021). [CrossRef]
23. Jelin, E.; Zamberlin, A.G.N. "¿Servicio?, ¿Derecho?, ¿Amenaza? La llegada de Inmigrantes de Países Limítrofes a los Servicios Públicos de Salud", en Elizabeth Jelin, dir., Salud y Migración Regional. Ciudadanía, Discriminación y Comunicación Intercultural, Buenos Aires, Instituto de Desarrollo Económico y Social (IDES). 2006. Available online: https://publicaciones.ides.org.ar/sites/default/files/docs/2020/jelin-2006-saludymigracionregional.pdf (accessed on 2 November 2021).
24. Aizenberg, L.; Rodriguez, M.L.; Carbonetti, A. Percepciones de los Equipos de Salud en Torno a las Mujeres Migrantes Bolivianas y Peruanas en la Ciudad de Córdoba. Repositorio Institucional CONICET Digital. 2015. Available online: https://ri.conicet.gov.ar/handle/11336/59751 (accessed on 2 November 2021).
25. Astorga-Pinto, S.M.; Cabieses, B.; Calderon, A.C.; McIntyre, A.M. Percepciones Sobre Acceso y Uso de Servicios de Salud Mental por Parte de Inmigrantes en Chile, Desde la Perspectiva de Trabajadores, Autoridades e Inmigrantes. Revista del Instituto de Salud Pública de Chile. 2019. Available online: https://revista.ispch.gob.cl/index.php/RISP/article/view/49 (accessed on 2 November 2021).
26. Concha, N.L.; Mansilla, M.Á. Pacientes Ilegítimos: Acceso a la Salud de los Inmigrantes Indocumentados en Chile. *Salud Colect.* **2017**, *13*, 507–520. Available online: https://www.scielosp.org/article/scol/2017.v13n3/507-520/ (accessed on 2 November 2021). [CrossRef] [PubMed]
27. Urrutia-Arroyo, R.H. Educación Médica Intercultural: Desafíos de la Atención Médica en Contextos de Población Inmigrante. *Búsqueda* **2019**, *6*, 402. Available online: https://revistas.cecar.edu.co/index.php/Busqueda/article/view/402 (accessed on 2 November 2021). [CrossRef]
28. López, M.; Cuadrado, I. Estereotipos. In *Introducción en Psicología Social*; Gaviria, E., Cuadrado, I., López, M., Eds.; Sanz Y Torres: Madrid, Spain, 2019; pp. 306–329.
29. Cuadrado, I. Análisis psicosocial del prejuicio. In *Introducción en Psicología Social*; Gaviria, E., Cuadrado, I., López, M., Eds.; Sanz Y Torres: Madrid, Spain, 2019; pp. 332–382.
30. Acocella, I. The focus groups in social research: Advantages and disadvantages. *Qual. Quant.* **2012**, *46*, 1125–1136. [CrossRef]
31. Byers, P.Y.; Wilcox, J.R. Focus Groups: A Qualitative Opportunity for Researchers. *J. Bus. Commun.* **1991**, *28*, 63–78. Available online: https://journals.sagepub.com/doi/10.1177/002194369102800105 (accessed on 1 June 2022). [CrossRef]
32. Diseño de Investigación Cualitativa. 2013. Available online: https://es.scribd.com/book/446030237/Diseno-de-investigacion-cualitativa (accessed on 1 June 2022).
33. Cornejo Cancino, M.; Salas Guzmán, N. Rigor y Calidad Metodológicos: Un Reto a la Investigación Social Cualitativa. *Psicoperspect. Individuo Soc.* **2011**, *10*, 12–34. Available online: https://www.psicoperspectivas.cl/index.php/psicoperspectivas/article/view/144 (accessed on 2 June 2022). [CrossRef]
34. Noreña, A.L.; Alcaraz-Moreno, N.; Rojas, J.G.; Rebolledo-Malpica, D. Aplicabilidad de los Criterios de Rigor y Éticos en la Investigación Cualitativa. *Aquichan* **2012**, *12*, 263–274. Available online: http://www.scielo.org.co/scielo.php?script=sci_abstract&pid=S1657-59972012000300006&lng=en&nrm=iso&tlng=es (accessed on 2 June 2022). [CrossRef]
35. Braun, V.; Clarke, V. Using Thematic Analysis in Psychology. *Qual. Res. Psychol.* **2006**, *3*, 77–101. Available online: https://www.tandfonline.com/doi/abs/10.1191/1478088706qp063oa (accessed on 1 June 2022). [CrossRef]
36. Weil, J. *Research Design in Aging and Social Gerontology Quantitative, Qualitative, and Mixed Methods*; Taylor & Francis: New York, NY, USA, 2017.
37. Ministerio de Salud. Política de Salud de Migrantes Internacionales. 2018. Available online: https://www.minsal.cl/wp-content/uploads/2015/09/2018.01.22.POLITICA-DE-SALUD-DE-MIGRANTES.pdf (accessed on 9 January 2022).
38. Cabieses, B.; Libuy, M.; Dabanch, J. De la Creencia a la Evidencia Para la Acción Sanitaria en Chile. 2019. Available online: http://www.colegiomedico.cl/wp-content/uploads/2019/10/documentos-migrantes_final_compressed.pdf (accessed on 20 January 2022).
39. Roter, D. The Enduring and Evolving Nature of the Patient-Physician Relationship. *Patient Educ. Couns.* **2000**, *39*, 5–15. Available online: https://pubmed.ncbi.nlm.nih.gov/11013543/ (accessed on 9 November 2021). [CrossRef]
40. Migration Data Portal. Migración y Salud. Available online: https://www.migrationdataportal.org/es/themes/migracion-y-salud (accessed on 13 December 2021).
41. Aninat, I.; Vergara, R. *Inmigración en Chile. Una Mirada Multidimensional*; Centros de Estudios Públicos: Santiago, Chile, 2019; pp. 283–284.
42. Avaria, A. Interacciones y diferencias entre las experiencias de parto de mujeres migrantes en la atención de salud pública en Santiago de Chile. In *Salud y Migraciones: Relevancia, Consideraciones Generales y Desafíos Para el Chile de Hoy*; Avaria, A., Cabieses, B., Obach, A., Eds.; Ril Editores: Providencia, Chile, 2021; pp. 131–158.
43. Sánchez-Ojeda, M.A.; Navarro-Prado, S.; Martín-Salvador, A.; Luque-Vara, T.; Fernández-Gómez, E.; Plaza del Pino, F.J. Nursing Students' Attitudes towards Immigrants' Social Rights. *Int. J. Environ. Res. Public Health* **2020**, *17*, 8875. Available online: https://www.ncbi.nlm.nih.gov/pmc/articles/PMC7730376/ (accessed on 9 November 2021). [CrossRef] [PubMed]

44. Lin, M.-H.; Hsu, H.-C. Effects of a Cultural Competence Education Programme on Clinical Nurses: A Randomised Controlled Trial. *Nurse Educ. Today* **2020**, *88*, 104385. Available online: https://www.sciencedirect.com/science/article/pii/S0260691719314522 (accessed on 9 November 2021). [CrossRef] [PubMed]
45. Plaza del Pino, F.J. Prejudices of the Nurses towards the Immigrant Population: An Outlook from the South of Spain. *Enfermería Glob.* **2012**, *11*, 87–96. Available online: https://scielo.isciii.es/scielo.php?script=sci_abstract&pid=S1695-61412012000300006&lng=en&nrm=iso&tlng=en (accessed on 9 November 2021). [CrossRef]
46. Ugarte Gurrutxaga, M.I.; Sánchez-Ojeda, M.A.; Segura-Fragoso, A.; Cardoso, M.L.; Molina Gallego, B. Attitudes towards Immigration among Students in the First Year of a Nursing Degree at Universities in Coimbra, Toledo and Melilla. *Int. J. Environ. Res. Public Health* **2020**, *17*, 7977. Available online: https://www.ncbi.nlm.nih.gov/pmc/articles/PMC7662216/ (accessed on 9 November 2021). [CrossRef] [PubMed]

healthcare

MDPI

Article

Adolescents' Sexual and Reproductive Healthcare-Seeking Behaviour and Service Utilisation in Plateau State, Nigeria

Esther Awazzi Envuladu [1,2,*], Karlijn Massar [3] and John de Wit [2]

1 Department of Community Medicine, College of Health Sciences, University of Jos, Jos P.M.B 2084, Nigeria
2 Department of Interdisciplinary Social Science, Utrecht University, P.O. Box 80140, 3508 Utrecht, The Netherlands; j.dewit@uu.nl
3 Department of Work & Social Psychology, Maastricht University, P.O. Box 616, 6200 Maastricht, The Netherlands; karlijn.massar@maastrichtuniversity.nl
* Correspondence: esvula@gmail.com; Tel.: +234-8034517244

Abstract: The high rate of sexual and reproductive health (SRH) challenges among adolescents in Nigeria has been linked with the poor access to and utilisation of health facilities. This study explores the factors that influence the actual use and willingness to use SRH services among adolescents. Survey questionnaires were administered to 428 adolescents aged 18 to 19 years in six local government areas (LGAs) in Plateau State. The results showed that more than one-third of the participating adolescents were currently sexually active, slightly more than three-quarters (76.6%) had never visited health facilities for SRH issues, and more than half (56.0%) were not willing to visit a health facility if they ever had any SRH issues. The most frequent reason for the non-use of health care facilities for SRH issues by adolescents was a perceived lack of privacy and confidentiality (66.1%), followed by the perceived negative attitude of health care providers (68.2%). However, being sexually active was the only independent covariate of seeking SRH care from health facility (AOR = 005; CI = 0.01–0.49; $p = 0.011$), while awareness of HIV was a significant covariate of willingness to seek SRH care in a health facility in the future (AOR = 3.17, 95% CI = 1.50–6.70; $p = 0.002$). We concluded that the utilisation of SRH services and willingness to do so in the future was fairly limited among adolescents in this study. Therefore, there is a need to address the challenges of privacy and confidentiality and commencement of the health promotion of SRH for adolescents ahead of sexual initiation to alleviate the SRH challenges adolescents encounter when sexually active.

Keywords: adolescents; health-seeking behaviour; utilisation; sexual and reproductive health; Nigeria

Citation: Envuladu, E.A.; Massar, K.; de Wit, J. Adolescents' Sexual and Reproductive Healthcare-Seeking Behaviour and Service Utilisation in Plateau State, Nigeria. *Healthcare* **2022**, *10*, 301. https://doi.org/10.3390/healthcare10020301

Academic Editors: Joachim G. Voss and Sandul Yasobant

Received: 2 January 2022
Accepted: 1 February 2022
Published: 4 February 2022

1. Introduction

The high prevalence of sexually transmitted infections (STIs), HIV and unintended pregnancies among adolescents, referred to as teenage pregnancy, in sub-Saharan Africa, Nigeria inclusive, is associated with unprotected sexual activities and continues to be a great public health concern [1,2]. Condomless sex and a lack of contraceptive use among sexually active adolescents have been widely reported in many studies in Nigeria [3–5]. Among the adolescents who do report condom use during sex, many report incorrect and inconsistent use, which equally places them at risk of sexual and reproductive health (SRH) problems [6,7].

The high rate of unprotected sex among adolescents, especially those involved in risky sexual behaviour such as sex with multiple partners, has been associated with poor knowledge of the risk of exposure to SRH problems, such as STIs, HIV, and unintended pregnancy [8–10] and the lack of access to contraceptives among adolescents, as reported in many studies [11–13]. Importantly, however, some of the major reasons for low condom and contraceptive use are the lack of adolescent-centred sexual and reproductive healthcare services, and the unwillingness of adolescents to seek care in health facilities [10,14].

Health care facilities provide an important setting for adolescents to access accurate SRH preventive information, testing and treatment services. Unfortunately, adolescents' utilisation of these facilities has remained low due to fear of being stigmatised, negative attitudes of health care providers and a lack of age-appropriate and adolescent-centred services [15,16]. For example, Odo et al. [17] report that, for adolescents in Enugu State, SRH services were perceived as financially inaccessible and not adolescent-friendly. In many African countries, religion and social structures create certain norms around ASRH, which in turn create barriers for adolescents using these services [15]. Rather than seek health care in health facilities, some adolescents in Nigeria have reported seeking SRH care from unprofessional providers such as medicine vendors, traditional healers, and others self-medicate by purchasing drugs without prescription against the backdrop of antibiotic abuse and resistance [18–20].

Promoting the appropriate use of SRH care is viewed as one of the key strategies in addressing the SRH challenges that adolescents face. However, there are still gaps in understanding the factors influencing the SRH-seeking behaviour of adolescents and why adolescents do not seek care in health facilities. This study explores the SRH-seeking behaviour of adolescents, the factors influencing health-seeking behaviour, and the willingness of adolescents to seek SRH care in health facilities in the future. The findings from this study can inform interventions that will provide responsive adolescent health services in Nigeria.

2. Methods

2.1. Study Design and Setting

A cross-sectional survey was conducted among adolescents in six local government areas (LGAs) in Plateau State, located in the north–central region of Nigeria. These LGAs have both public and private health facilities that provide SRH services, which adolescents can access. All participants self-completed a questionnaire adapted from the WHO [21,22] and other studies, with slight modifications to contextualise the content to the Nigerian setting after pre-testing of the questionnaire. Information on socio-demographic characteristics, sexual activity, awareness of SRH issues, past health seeking for SRH issues, willingness to seek SRH care at health facilities in the future, and reasons not to seek SRH from health facilities were collected.

2.2. Study Participants and Recruitment

Sample size was calculated using the Cochran formula ($n_0 = Z^2pq/e^2$), where n is the minimum sample size, Z is the standard normal deviate which corresponds to a 95% confidence interval (1.96) and p is the proportion of adolescents seeking health care for SRH in health facilities. Here, we assumed it to be 50%, where q is the complementary probability ($1 - p$), and e is the 5% margin of error. The minimum sample size required was N = 384, but 428 adolescents participated in the study.

The inclusion of participants occurred in three stages. First, six LGAs were selected from seventeen LGAs by balloting. Next, eighteen wards (three from each of the six LGAs) were randomly selected. The research team then liaised with representatives of organised youth groups in each ward to identify households with adolescents aged 18 or 19 years old, mainly because they could give consent to participate in the study. Trained research assistants went from house to house to distribute the questionnaire and waited to retrieve the anonymous self-completed questionnaires from the adolescents, ensuring that the questionnaires were properly filled out for analysis.

2.3. Measures

Socio-demographic characteristics assessed included gender, age, marital status, schooling status (in or out of school), and highest level of educational qualification. Whether participants were sexually active or not was assessed by asking if they were currently having sex. Awareness of SRH issues, STIs and HIV were assessed by directly asking if they had heard of sexual and reproductive health, sexually transmitted infections and HIV, respectively (yes/no; don't know responses were recorded as no).

Health seeking for SRH was assessed by asking participants if they ever visited a health facility for SRH issues in the past (yes/no). Willingness to seek SRH care at a health facility was assessed by asking if they would be willing to visit a health facility in the future if they ever experienced any SRH issues (yes/no).

Reasons for non-utilisation of health facilities for SRH issues were assessed with an open-ended question. Responses were grouped into three themes: perceived lack of privacy and confidentiality, perceived cost of services and commodities, and negative attitude of health care providers.

2.4. Data Analysis

Data were analysed using the IBM Statistical Package for Social Sciences (SPSS), version 23 (IBM Corp, Armonk, NY, USA). The socio-demographic characteristics, sexual activities, awareness of STIs and HIV were analysed as frequencies, and the level of utilisation of health facilities and willingness to use health facilities, including the reasons for non-utilisation of health facilities, were also analysed as frequencies.

The covariates of use of health facilities and willingness to use the health facilities for SRH problems were analysed using univariate and multivariate logistic regression. Here, the predisposing variables were the socio-demographic characteristics (age, gender, schooling status (either currently in school or out of school), educational status, etc.), sexual activity and awareness of SRH, STIs and HIV.

2.5. Ethical Approval

The Jos University Teaching Hospital (JUTH) Research Ethics Committee granted approval for this study. Permission was also obtained from the LGA authorities and leaders at the ward levels. All participants provided written informed consent before the commencement of the study.

3. Results

The study participants included both males and females (51.9% and 48.1%, respectively). Slightly more than half (52.3%) were 18 years old (47.7% were 19 years old). Few of the adolescents (5.8%) were married; 41.1% were out of school and the majority (74.1%) had a secondary education (See Table 1).

More than one-third (38.0%) of the adolescents were sexually active. About half (53.0%) were aware of SRH issues, nearly three-quarters (73.0%) were aware of STIs and the majority (85.0%) were aware of HIV. Slightly more than three-quarters (76.6%) had never visited a health facility for SRH issues, and more than half (56.0%) were not willing to visit a health facility if they ever had any SRH issues (See Table 2).

The most frequent reason for adolescents' non-use of health care facilities for SRH issues was a perceived lack of privacy and confidentiality (66.1%), followed by a perceived negative attitude of health care providers (68.2%), and the cost of services and commodities (39.0%) (See Table 3).

Bivariate logistic regression analysis showed that age, marital status, schooling status, sexual activity, and awareness of SRH, STIs and HIV were significantly associated with the odds of seeking care for SRH in a health facility ($p < 0.05$). Specifically, younger adolescents had reduced odds of seeking care in health facilities; the odds of health-seeking for SRH were about 2.3 times higher in the married compared to the unmarried; out of school adolescents had reduced odds of health seeking for SRH; those not sexually active had less odds of seeking health care in health facilities; the odds of health seeking for SRH in health facilities among those aware of SRH, STIs and HIV were 1.6 times, 3.1 times and 4.3 times, respectively, compared to those who were not aware. However, after controlling for the effects of all independent variables using a multivariate logistic regression, only being sexually active was independently associated with having sought SRH care from a health facility (AOR = 005; CI = 0.01–0.49; $p = 0.011$) (See Table 4).

Table 1. Socio-demographic characteristics of adolescents.

Socio-Demographic Characteristics	Frequency	Percentage
Gender		
Male	222	51.9
Female	206	48.1
Age in years		
18	224	52.3
19	204	47.7
Marital status		
Married	25	5.8
Not married	403	94.2
Religion		
Christianity	357	83.4
Islam	71	16.6
Schooling status		
In school	252	58.9
Out of school	176	41.1
Educational status		
None/primary	50	11.7
Secondary	317	74.0
Tertiary	61	14.3

Table 2. Sexual activity, awareness of SRH issues, STI, HIV and health-seeking behaviour.

Variables	Frequency	Percentage
Currently sexually active		
Yes	163	38.1
No	265	61.9
Aware of SRH issues		
Yes	227	53
No	201	47
Aware of STI		
Yes	312	73
No	116	27
Aware of HIV		
Yes	363	85
No	65	15
Use health facility for SRH issues		
Yes	100	23.4
No	328	76.6
Willingness to use health facility if there was ever a problem		
Yes	188	43.9
No	240	56.1

Table 3. Reasons for non-utilisation of health facilities by adolescents (multiple responses).

Reasons	Frequency (n = 428)	Percentage
Lack of privacy and confidentiality	283	66.1
Cost of services and commodities	167	39.0
Attitude of health care providers	292	68.2

Table 4. Covariate of SRH care seeking in health facility (n = 428).

	Seeking Care for SRH in Health Facility							
	Yes	No	OR	95% CI	p	AOR	95% CI	p
Gender								
Male	49(22.1)	173(77.9)	0.86	0.55–1.35	0.512	0.83	0.50–1.39	0.488
Female	51(24.8)	155(75.2)						
Age (yrs)								
18	38(17.0)	186(83.0)	0.47	0.30–0.75	0.001	0.86	0.49–1.53	0.614
19	62(30.4)	142(69.6)						
Marital status								
Married	10(40.0)	15(60.0)	2.32	1.01–5.34	0.048	1.88	0.74–4.77	0.182
Not married	90(22.3)	313(77.7)						
Religion								
Christianity	89(24.9)	268(75.1)	1.81	0.91–3.60	0.090	1.33	0.61–2.94	0.474
Islam	11(15.5)	60(84.5)						
Schooling status								
In school	48(19.0)	204(81.0)	0.56	0.36–0.88	0.012	0.92	0.52–1.64	0.781
Out of school	52(29.5)	124(70.5)						
Educational status								
Non-formal	17(41.5)	24(58.5)	1.18	0.88–158	0.279	1.33	0.95–1.87	0.099
Primary	3(33.3)	6(66.7)						
Secondary	57(18.0)	260(82.0)						
Tertiary	23(37.7)	38(62.3)						
Sexual activity								
Yes	68(41.7)	95(58.3)	0.19	0.12–0.31	0.001	0.05	0.01–0.49	0.011 *
No	32(12.1)	233(87.9)						
Aware of SRH								
Yes	62(27.3)	165(72.7)	1.61	1.02–2.55	0.041	1.04	0.63–1.72	0.887
No	38(18.9)	163(81.1)						
Aware of STI								
Yes	87(27.9)	225(72.1)	3.06	1.64–5.74	0.001	2.10	0.98–4.48	0.056
No	13(11.2)	103(88.8)						
Aware of HIV								
Yes	95(26.2)	268(73.8)	4.25	1.66–10.91	0.003	2.36	0.78–7.16	0.130
No	5(7.7)	60(92.3)						

* Significant p-value.

Bivariate logistic regression analysis revealed that only awareness of HIV was significantly associated with willingness to seek healthcare in a health facility in the future. Adolescents who were aware of HIV had about three times more odds of future SRH health seeking in health facilities compared to those who were not aware of HIV (AOR = 2.76, 95% CI = 1.51–5.03). After adjusting for the effect of other independent variables, those with a higher educational status were significantly associated with a willingness to seek care in a health facility in the future (AOR = 1.34, p-value = 0.049). Additionally, adolescents who were aware of HIV had three times greater odds of willingness to seek SRH care in health facilities in the future (AOR = 3.17, 95% CI = 1.50–6.70; p = 0.002) (See Table 5)

Table 5. Covariate of willingness to seek care in health facility (n = 428).

	Willingness to Seek SRH Care in Health Facility							
	Yes	No	OR	95% CI	p	AOR	95% CI	p
Gender								
Male	96(43.2)	126(56.8)	0.94	0.64–1.38	0.768	0.95	0.64–1.42	0.814
Female	92(44.7)	114(55.3)						
Age (yrs)								
18	102(45.5)	122(54.5)	1.15	0.78–1.68	0.482	1.17	0.74–1.84	0.506
19	86(42.2)	118(57.8)						
Religion								
Christianity	162(45.4)	195(54.6)	1.44	0.85–2.43	0.176	1.32	0.75–2.32	0.337
Islam	26(36.6)	45(63.4)						
Schooling status								
In school	115(45.6)	137(54.4)	1.184	0.80–1.75	0.394	1.46	0.92–2.32	0.112
Out of school	73(41.5)	103(58.5)						
Educational status								
Non-formal	22(53.7)	19(46.3)	1.21	0.93–1.57	0.154	1.34	1.00–1.80	0.049 *
Primary	6(66.7)	3(33.3)						
Secondary	134(42.3)	183(57.7)						
Tertiary	26(42.6)	35(57.4)						
Sexual activity								
Yes	80(49.1)	83(50.9)	0.71	0.48–1.06	0.452	0.69	0.39–1.24	0.218
No	108(40.8)	157(59.2)						
Aware of SRH								
Yes	104(45.8)	123(54.2)	1.18	0.80–1.73	0.403	0.88	0.57–1.37	0.581
No	84(41.8)	117(58.2)						
Aware of STI								
Yes	145(46.5)	167(53.5)	1.47	0.95–2.28	0.082	0.92	0.52–1.63	0.768
No	43(37.1)	73(62.9)						
Aware of HIV								
Yes	172(47.4)	191(52.6)	2.76	1.51–5.03	0.001	3.17	1.50–6.70	0.002 *
No	16(24.6)	49(75.4)						

* Significant p-value.

4. Discussion

Most adolescents, irrespective of their socio-demographic background, engage in sexual behaviours that could expose them to sexual and reproductive health challenges, such as STIs/HIV infections and unwanted pregnancies [9]. In Nigeria, access to sexual and reproductive healthcare or the willingness to seek SRH care in health facilities when the need arises is a matter of concern as a result of the negative outcome when adolescents seek care from unqualified people, resulting in an increased burden of morbidity and mortality [16–18]. In light of these concerns, the current research aimed to understand if adolescents accessed SRH care, and what influenced such health-seeking behaviour. To this end, we administered a survey to adolescents in Plateau State, Nigeria, across gender, marital status, school status and educational level.

The results showed that more than one-third of the participating adolescents were currently sexually active, usually without any form of protection such as a condom. This is comparable with what was documented from a study among adolescents with similar characteristics, reporting a high sexual activity with the risk of exposure to negative outcomes such as unintended pregnancy, HIV and STIs [19].

Despite the risk of sexual activity and the relatively high (about three-quarters) level of awareness of SRH issues, although higher for HIV than for STIs, nearly three-quarters of participants had never visited a health facility for information or services on SRH, and more than half were not willing to visit a health facility in the future for any SRH issues. Similarly, some studies in Nigeria reported good knowledge of SRH among adolescents, albeit, mostly centred on HIV and less about other STIs [23,24]. However, as we also report in the current study, despite the substantial knowledge of HIV recorded among adolescents, this has not affected their health seeking, as many of those who needed SRH services such as condoms, contraceptives and treatment of STIs did not do so in health facilities but rather sought care from non-professionals [16,24].

The reasons provided by adolescents in this study for not utilising, or wanting to utilise, these services in the health facilities were mainly lack of privacy and confidentiality, the negative attitude of health care providers, the cost of services and commodities that they are unable to afford, and the non-availability of the services for adolescents. We have seen from previous studies and reviews of other studies that there is inadequate privacy and confidentiality provided for adolescents in health care settings [18]. Additionally, the SRH services provided in most health facilities were adult-centred without any consideration for adolescents [25,26].

The unwillingness of adolescents to utilise health facilities is of concern, as young people can benefit from information and help regarding SRH issues when needed. Our results indicate that only about half of the participating adolescents would seek care in health facilities when in need, indicating that they would either self-medicate by treating themselves when they experience SRH issues or would seek unprofessional care [27]. Sexual and reproductive health care is a specialised type of care requiring trained providers, which is why it is important that care is sought from trained health care providers [27,28].

We assessed the relationship between the socio-demographic characteristics of adolescents and their SRH care seeking, and found that younger adolescents, unmarried adolescents and adolescents who were out of school were less likely to seek SRH care in a health facility. However, the multivariate analysis showed that being sexually active was the only significant factor associated with care seeking in health facilities. This may indicate their risk consciousness and perhaps reflect that adolescents who are at an increased risk of SRH challenges are more likely to access the services that may benefit them.

Many of the respondents indicated an unwillingness to seek SRH care in the health facilities but those with a higher level of awareness of HIV indicated more willingness to seek care in health facilities. Some studies have supported these findings with results reporting a better utilisation of health facilities for SRH care among adolescents with knowledge of SRH compared to those with less knowledge [29–31], but whether this will be actualised is uncertain, considering the earlier reasons given for not seeking care in health facilities.

Given these challenges, overcoming the high rate of unintended pregnancy, STIs and HIV among adolescents will require interventions targeted towards addressing these problems in Plateau State and Nigeria. Therefore, we recommend a study to explore the perspective of health care providers on the provision of ASRH care services. The findings from both client and provider perspectives will strengthen informed decision making towards the most appropriate intervention to improve the utilisation of health facilities for SRH in Nigeria.

5. Limitations

Although the study may not be generalised to the whole of Nigeria, it can, however, be generalised to Plateau State considering the stepwise systematic approach in the sampling and selection of the respondents. These findings may not be different from what is obtainable in other parts of the country. On the other hand, while this study has tried to uncover the health-seeking behaviour and future willingness of adolescents to seek care in health facilities, the possibility of social-desirability bias in reporting health seeking in health facilities can not be ruled out, for the fear of being judged for seeking SRH care in the wrong places. This was, however, mediated by allowing respondents to privately fill out a self-administered questionnaire without interference.

6. Conclusions

In conclusion, this study shows a fairly limited utilisation and willingness of adolescents to seek SRH care in health facilities, mostly for the lack of privacy and confidentiality and the negative attitude of health care providers, suggesting an opportunity to promote SRH care and address the challenge of privacy and confidentiality for adolescents in health facilities. Being sexually active was a significant covariate of seeking care in health facilities, while education and awareness of HIV were significantly associated with a willingness to seek SRH care in health facilities in the future. Therefore, there is a need for healthcare workers to consider the possibility of SRH health promotion activities for adolescents in schools and communities, ahead of becoming sexually active, in order to mitigate the negative health-seeking from unprofessional practitioners when in need.

Author Contributions: Conceptualization, E.A.E. and J.d.W.; methodology, E.A.E., K.M. and J.d.W.; software, E.A.E.; validation, E.A.E., K.M. and J.d.W.; formal analysis, E.A.E.; investigation, E.A.E.; resources, E.A.E. and J.d.W.; data curation, E.A.E., K.M. and J.d.W.; writing—original draft preparation, E.A.E.; writing—review and editing, K.M. and J.d.W.; visualization, E.A.E., K.M. and J.d.W.; supervision, K.M. and J.d.W. All authors have read and agreed to the published version of the manuscript.

Funding: This research received no external funding.

Institutional Review Board Statement: The guidelines of the Declaration of Helsinki were duly followed in conducting this study and approved was obtained by the Institutional Health Research Ethical Committee of Jos University Teaching Hospital JUTH/DCS/ADM/127/XXVIII/1187 on the 2 October 2018.

Informed Consent Statement: Informed consent was obtained from participants before commencement of the study.

Data Availability Statement: The dataset(s) supporting the conclusions of this article is(are) included within the article.

Acknowledgments: We sincerely acknowledge all the research assistants who participated in the data collection. The authors sincerely thank the medical students of the University of Jos, Nigeria who participated in the data collection.

Conflicts of Interest: The authors declare no conflict of interest.

References

1. Houlihan, C.F.; Baisley, K.; Bravo, I.G.; Kapiga, S.; de Sanjosé, S.; Changalucha, J.; Ross, D.A.; Hayes, R.J.; Watson-Jones, D. Rapid acquisition of HPV around the time of sexual debut in adolescent girls in Tanzania. *Int. J. Epidemiol.* **2016**, *45*, 762–773. [CrossRef] [PubMed]
2. Animasahun, V.; Sholeye, O.; Oduwole, A. Promoting the sexual and reproductive health of adolescent females in Ijebu-Ode, southwest, Nigeria: A study of sexual risk-taking. *Int. J. Adolesc. Med. Health* **2016**, *29*, 20160021. [CrossRef] [PubMed]

3. Adedini, S.A.; Babalola, S.; Ibeawuchi, C.; Omotoso, O.; Akiode, A.; Odeku, M. Role of religious leaders in promoting contraceptive use in Nigeria: Evidence from the Nigerian urban reproductive health initiative. *Glob. Health: Sci. Pract.* **2018**, *6*, 500–514. [CrossRef] [PubMed]
4. Ajayi, A.I.; Ismail, K.O.; Akpan, W. Factors associated with consistent condom use: A cross-sectional survey of two Nigerian universities. *BMC Public Health* **2019**, *19*, 1207. [CrossRef]
5. Sunmola, A.M. Developing a scale for measuring the barriers to condom use in Nigeria. *Bull. World Health Organ.* **2001**, *79*, 926–932.
6. Melesse, D.Y.; Mutua, M.K.; Choudhury, A.; Wado, Y.D.; Faye, C.M.; Neal, S.; Boerma, T. Adolescent sexual and reproductive health in sub-Saharan Africa: Who is left behind? *BMJ Glob. Health* **2020**, *5*, e002231. [CrossRef]
7. Mbachu, C.O.; Agu, I.C.; Obayi, C.; Eze, I.; Ezuma, N.; Onwuiekwe, O. Beliefs and misconceptions about contraception and condom use among adolescents in southeast Nigeria. *Reprod. Health* **2021**, *18*, 7. [CrossRef]
8. Odufuye, Z.O.; Ajuwon, A. Risky Sexual Behaviour and Experience of Sexual Coercion Among University Students in Ibadan, Nigeria. *Afr. J. Biomed. Res.* **2020**, *23*, 9–13.
9. Paul, M.; Chalasani, S.; Light, B.; Knuttson, A.; Fatusi, A. *Contraception for Adolescents and Youth: Being Responsive to their Sexual and Reproductive Health Needs and Rights*; UNFPA: New York, NY, USA, 2019.
10. Onwubuariri1, M.I.; Kasso, T. Teenage Pregnancy: Prevalence, Pattern and Predisposing Factors in a Tertiary Hospital, Southern Nigeria. *Asian J. Med. Health* **2019**, *17*, 1–5. [CrossRef]
11. Sanchez, E.K.; Speizer, I.S.; Tolley, E.; Calhoun, L.M.; Barrington, C.; Olumide, A.O. Influences on seeking a contraceptive method among adolescent women in three cities in Nigeria. *Reprod. Health* **2020**, *17*, 167. [CrossRef]
12. Odeigah, L.; Rasaki, S.O.; Ajibola, A.F.; Hafsat, A.A.; Sule, A.G.; Musah, Y. High risk sexual behavior among adolescent senior secondary school students in Nigeria. *Afri. Health Sci.* **2019**, *19*, 1467–1477. [CrossRef] [PubMed]
13. Cortez, R.; Saadat, S.; Marinda, E.; Odutolu, O. Adolescent sexual and reproductive health in Nigeria (English). In *Health, Nutrition and Population Global Practice Knowledge Brief*; World Bank Group: Washington, DC, USA, 2015.
14. Gueye, A.; Speizer, S.I.; Corroon, M.; Okigbo, C.C. Belief in family Planning myths at the individual and community levels and modern contraceptive use in Urban Africa. *Int. Perspect. Sex Reprod. Health* **2015**, *41*, 191–199. [CrossRef] [PubMed]
15. Nmadu, A.G.; Mohammed, S.; Usman, N.O. Barriers to adolescents' access and utilisation of reproductive health services in a community in northwestern Nigeria: A qualitative exploratory study in primary care. *Afr. J. Prm. Health Care Fam. Med.* **2020**, *12*, a2307. [CrossRef]
16. Nmadu, A.G.; Mohamed, S.; Usman, N.O. Adolescents' utilization of reproductive health services in Kaduna, Nigeria: The role of stigma. *Vulnerable Child. Youth Stud.* **2020**, *15*, 246–256. [CrossRef]
17. Odo, A.N.; Samuel, E.S.; Nwagu, E.N.; Nnamani, P.O.; Atama, C.S. Sexual and reproductive health services (SRHS) for adolescents in Enugu state, Nigeria: A mixed methods approach. *BMC Health Serv. Res.* **2018**, *18*, 1–12. [CrossRef] [PubMed]
18. Ravindran, T.S.; Govender, V. Sexual and reproductive health services in universal health coverage: A review of recent evidence from low-and middle-income countries. *Sex. Reprod. Health Matters* **2020**, *28*, 1779632. [CrossRef]
19. Sommer, M.; Mmari, K. Addressing structural and environmental factors for adolescent sexual and reproductive health in low-and middle-income countries. *Am. J. Public Health* **2015**, *105*, 1973–1981. [CrossRef]
20. Newton-Levinson, A.; Leichliter, J.S.; Chandra-Mouli, V. Sexually transmitted infection services for adolescents and youth in low-and middle-income countries: Perceived and experienced barriers to accessing care. *J. Adolesc. Health* **2016**, *59*, 7–16. [CrossRef]
21. WHO. Making Health Services Adolescent Friendly. 2012. Available online: http://apps.who.int/iris/bitstream/handle/10665/75217/9789241503594_eng.pdf? (accessed on 14 August 2018).
22. WHO. *Quality Assessment Guidebook: A Guide to Assessing Health Services for Adolescent Clients*; World Health Organization: Geneva, Switzerland, 2009.
23. Akokuwebe, M.E.; Daini, B.; Falayi, E.O.; Oyebade, O. Knowledge and attitude of sexually transmitted diseases among adolescents in Ikeji-Arakeji, Osun State, in South-Western Nigeria. *Afr. J. Med. Med. Sci.* **2016**, *45*, 281–289.
24. Nwatu, C.; Young, E.; Ezeala-Adikaibe, B.; Okafor, C.; Onwuekwe, I. HIV and Sexually Transmitted Infections knowledge and practices: A survey of female secondary school students in Enugu, South East Nigeria. *J. Med. Res.* **2017**, *3*, 66–70. [CrossRef]
25. Olaleye, A.O.; Obiyan, M.O.; Folayan, M.O. Factors associated with sexual and reproductive health behaviour of street involved young people: Findings from a baseline survey in Southwest Nigeria. *Reprod. Health* **2020**, *17*, 94. [CrossRef] [PubMed]
26. Thongmixay, S.; Essink, D.R.; De Greeuw, T.; Vongxay, V.; Sychareun, V.; Broerse, J.E. Perceived barriers in accessing sexual and reproductive health services for youth in Lao People's Democratic Republic. *PLoS ONE* **2019**, *14*, e0218296. [CrossRef] [PubMed]
27. Kyilleh, J.M.; Tabong, P.T.; Konlaan, B.B. Adolescents' reproductive health knowledge, choices and factors affecting reproductive health choices: A qualitative study in the West Gonja District in Northern region, Ghana. *BMC Int. Health Hum. Rights* **2018**, *18*, 6. [CrossRef]
28. Okereke, C.I. Unmet reproductive health needs and health-seeking behaviour of adolescents in Owerri, Nigeria. *Afr. J. Reprod. Health* **2010**, *14*, 43–54. [PubMed]

29. Bankole, A.; Adewole, I.F.; Hussain, R.; Awolude, O.; Singh, S.; Akinyemi, J.O. The Incidence of Abortion in Nigeria. *Int. Perspect. Sex. Reprod. Health* **2015**, *41*, 170–181. [CrossRef] [PubMed]
30. Cheptum, J.; Gitonga, M.; Mutua, E.; Mukui, S.; Ndambuki, J.; Koima, W. Barriers to Access and Utilization of Maternal and Infant Health Services in Migori, Kenya. 2014. Available online: http://41.89.227.156:8080/xmlui/handle/123456789/635 (accessed on 12 September 2020).
31. Abebe, M.; Awoke, W. Utilization of youth reproductive health services and associated factors among high school students in Bahir Dar, Amhara regional state. *Ethiop. Open J. Epidemiol.* **2014**, *4*, 69–75. [CrossRef]

healthcare

Article

Socio-Economic and Demographic Factors Associated with Knowledge and Attitude of HIV/AIDS among Women Aged 15–49 Years Old in Indonesia

Feny Deya Virdausi [1], Ferry Efendi [1,*], Tiyas Kusumaningrum [1], Qorinah Estiningtyas Sakilah Adnani [2], Lisa McKenna [3], Kadar Ramadhan [4] and Ika Adelia Susanti [1]

1 Faculty of Nursing, Universitas Airlangga, Surabaya 60115, Indonesia
2 Faculty of Medicine, Universitas Padjadjaran, Bandung 45363, Indonesia
3 School of Nursing and Midwifery, La Trobe University, Melbourne 3086, Australia
4 Department of Midwifery, Poltekkes Kemenkes Palu, Palu 94145, Indonesia
* Correspondence: ferry-e@fkp.unair.ac.id

Abstract: Women's susceptibility to HIV/AIDS infection is related to socio-economic and demographic factors. This study sought to analyze socio-economic and demographic factors related to knowledge and attitude of HIV/AIDS among women aged 15–49 years old in Indonesia. We conducted a secondary data analysis using the 2017 Indonesian Demographic and Health Survey (IDHS). Among 49,627 women, our study analyzed 25,895 women aged 15–49 years familiar with HIV terminology. Multiple logistic regression was utilized to analyze associations between socio-economic and demographic factors with knowledge and attitudes toward HIV/AIDS. Women's age, education level, wealth quintile, residential area and region, access to information, owning cell phones and autonomy were significantly associated with positive knowledge and attitudes toward HIV/AIDS. These findings revealed that several demographical and social factors contribute to knowledge and attitudes toward HIV/AIDS among women aged 15–49 years in Indonesia.

Keywords: AIDS; attitude; demographic factors; demographic health; HIV; knowledge; socio-economic; survey; women

Citation: Virdausi, F.D.; Efendi, F.; Kusumaningrum, T.; Adnani, Q.E.S.; McKenna, L.; Ramadhan, K.; Susanti, I.A. Socio-Economic and Demographic Factors Associated with Knowledge and Attitude of HIV/AIDS among Women Aged 15–49 Years Old in Indonesia. *Healthcare* **2022**, *10*, 1545. https://doi.org/10.3390/healthcare10081545

Academic Editor: Christian Napoli

Received: 26 June 2022
Accepted: 11 August 2022
Published: 15 August 2022

1. Introduction

Human Immunodeficiency Virus/Acquired Immune Deficiency Syndrome (HIV/AIDS) is still a significant global burden [1,2]. Even though substantial efforts have been made to reduce the HIV/AIDS infection rate and its prevalence, in 2019, more than 35 million people were living with HIV/AIDS (PLWHA); the majority reside in Sub-Saharan Africa [1,3,4]. The Southeast Asia region ranks second globally, with many PLWHA. Data from the United Nations (UN) revealed that approximately 19 million people do not know their HIV/AIDS status [5]. The World Health Organization (WHO) stated that 78% of new infections are in the Pacific region. A total of 5.1 million people in the Asia and Pacific Region are infected with HIV, including approximately 1.80 million adult women and 1.60 million adult men. As many as 3.8 million are infected with HIV/AIDS in Southeast Asia [6]. In low and middle-income countries, the prevalence of HIV/AIDS among women is three times higher than for men [7].

In Indonesia, in 2019, the number of HIV/AIDS cases reported was 50,282 [8]. In Indonesia, women are estimated to be four times more likely to be infected than men. Women are considered a vulnerable group infected with HIV/AIDS due to reproductive and genital anatomical structures facilitating the transmission of HIV through sexual intercourse [9]. Women's vulnerability is formed by several factors, including socio-cultural, economic and biological factors. The interconnection between gender inequality, migration, barriers to accessing health services and low levels of education increase women's vulnerability to contracting HIV/AIDS. In addition, many women contract HIV/AIDS from their husbands/partners who have unsafe sexual behavior and use drugs [5].

Lack of knowledge may lead to negative attitudes towards PLWHA. It could contribute to insufficient practice for prevention, treatment, and the risk of transmission among the community. Knowledge about HIV/AIDS and its transmission can be mainly achieved by increasing acceptance towards PLWHA and making people more caring [10,11]. Several studies have demonstrated that people tend to have negative attitudes and report not buying vegetables from PLWHA-status sellers [12–14]. These PLWHA have physical, economic, social and psychological consequences as HIV-infected patients are reportedly rejected by healthcare services [14], experience poor quality treatment, are refused when applying for jobs due to HIV/AIDS status, and experience forced early resignation from their employment [12,13].

Knowledge and attitudes may affect behaviour toward HIV/AIDS [15]. Sufficient knowledge and positive attitudes concerning HIV/AIDS provide empirical evidence for policymakers and stakeholders with which to design and implement appropriate prevention mechanisms [16,17]. Previous studies in East Africa and Vietnam revealed that lack of knowledge among women can be attributed to the negative attitudes towards PLWHA [15,18]. Some previous studies concluded that good knowledge and a positive attitude are important indicators in the prevention of HIV transmission [19–21]. One study among women of childbearing age in South Sudan showed that women living in urban areas had better knowledge compared to women living in rural areas [22]. Several studies have been conducted concerning HIV/AIDS prevention [23,24], while scarce literature addresses socio-economic and demographic factors associated with knowledge and attitudes toward HIV/AIDS in Indonesia. Knowledge and attitudes concerning HIV/AIDS among Indonesian women remain critical concerns as some studies revealed insufficient knowledge and negative attitudes [25–27]. Further, recent studies regarding the knowledge and attitudes of HIV/AIDS in Indonesia reemphasized that behavioral issues remain a challenge [9,28].

This study can aid in establishing knowledge, provide a basis for further research in HIV/AIDS and assist the government in strengthening and modifying the program to approach the HIV/AIDS issue. Possessing good knowledge and a positive attitude in relation to HIV/AIDS is very important for avoiding HIV transmission and to end the discrimination among PLWHA. There is increasing concern that some women of reproductive age lack accurate and complete information on how to prevent HIV/AIDS transmission. In line with these concerns, the objective of our study was to assess socio-economic and demographic factors related to knowledge and attitudes toward HIV/AIDS among women aged 15–49 years in Indonesia.

2. Methods

2.1. Design and Data Source

We conducted a secondary data analysis utilizing the most recent data from the 2017 Indonesia Demographic Health and Survey (IDHS). This study was part of an international DHS program that ensured ethical standards, including confidentiality, anonymity, and informed consent. IDHS ethical clearance was obtained from the Inner City Fund (ICF) International (ethical approval number 45 CFR 46). For this study, permission to use the data was obtained from ICF International. Additionally, ethical approval was obtained before the survey was conducted, and all participants provided written informed consent. All participation in this study was voluntary and subjects were able to withdraw their participation at anytime from the study.

This study used women's questionnaire topics which included questions that assessed women's knowledge of HIV and other sexually transmitted infections, the sources of their knowledge about HIV, knowledge about ways to avoid contracting HIV, HIV testing, stigma and discrimination, and high-risk sexual behaviour [29]. A series of questions on questionnaires about HIV/AIDS was required to be answered by women related to the (DHS) standard. The Model Questionnaires of the DHS Program emphasize basic indicators and several modules [30]. The data quality issue is a serious concern and sustained attention from DHS implementers to improve the validity and reliability of questionnaire is evident [31]. Continual improvement of the methodology including the questions for each questionnaire is performed collaboratively among various stakeholders. The questionnaire is open and available to the public at the DHS website, which can be accessed using the following link: https://dhsprogram.com/pubs/pdf/DHSQ8/DHS8_Womans_QRE_EN_8Apr2022_DHSQ8.pdf (accessed on 9 April 2022).

There were sections on knowledge and attitudes toward HIV/AIDS in the questionnaires. Questions on knowledge of HIV/AIDS included reducing risk, and concerned aspects such as always using a condom during sexual intercourse, only having one partner, getting HIV through mosquito bites or by sharing food with PLWHA, that people who appear healthy can have HIV, can contract HIV through supernatural powers, getting HIV through unsterilized needles, and that HIV can be transmitted during pregnancy, childbirth and breastfeeding. Questions on attitudes toward HIV/AIDS included wanting to keep HIV infection in the family a secret, willingness to care for families with AIDS, whether children with HIV are allowed to go to school with children who are not HIV positive and whether they would buy vegetables from a seller who has HIV.

The cross-sectional study represented 1970 census blocks of urban and rural areas covering 49,250 households across 34 provinces in Indonesia. This survey was conducted in several steps, including a pretest (July–August 2016), training of field staff (July 2017), and fieldwork (24 July–30 September 2017). A two-stage stratified cluster sampling method was employed to recruit the respondents in this study. First, several census blocks were selected by performing systematic sampling of the proportional size. Second, 25 ordinary households were chosen from the list via systematic sampling. With these data, the inclusion criteria for our study were as follows: aged 15–49 years, those who were interviewed during the survey and participants who completed all of the questions including those on HIV/AIDS issues. We excluded women who did not answered and complete all of the questions of the survey. Women's weight was obtained and individual recording of data during the analysis was applied. Among 49,627 women, our study analyzed 25,895 women aged 15–49 years based on the inclusion criteria. This study was a representative of national study involving women over all provinces in Indonesia.

2.2. Variables

The dependent variables were knowledge and attitudes toward HIV/AIDS. In this study, knowledge on HIV/AIDS was categorized into the following two groups: poor and good, while attitudes on HIV/AIDS were categorized into positive and negative. Knowledge was categorized as poor if respondents only answered less than five correctly, and categorized as good if respondents answered ≥ 5 correctly. Attitudes were divided into positive if respondents answered $\geq$3 questions correctly and negative if they only answered 1–2 questions correctly. In this study, the independent variables related to socioeconomic and demographic factors, including age, education level, occupation, head of household, wealth quintile, area of residence, region of residence, access to information, mobile phone, autonomy, and women's attitudes against wife-beating. The women's age was divided into seven categories (15–19, 20–24, 25–29, 30–34, 35–39, 40–44, 45–49 years old). Women' education levels were grouped into no school, primary, secondary, and higher education. Women' employment status was divided into two categories of not working and working. The head of the household was divided into two categories of women and men. Wealth quintile was grouped into the following five categories: poorest, poorer, middle, richer, and richest, and was scored based on wealth criteria on the DHS report [32]. Place of residence was separated into rural and urban areas, while the provinces of Indonesia were defined as East, Middle and West. Access to information was categorized into never, less than once, and more than once per week. Mobile phones were divided into yes and no, while women's autonomy was grouped into high and low. Women's attitudes against wife-beating was divided into two categories of agree and disagree. All categories' variables were determined based on the DHS report that adjusted to the minimum sample to meet the statistical interpretation [33].

2.3. Statistical Analysis

Descriptive statistics were used to describe the characteristics of the respondents. We used the chi-square test to assess associations between socio-economic and demographic factors and knowledge and attitudes toward HIV/AIDS. A multiple logistic regression analysis was performed, which presented an Odds Ratio (OR) and a 95% Confidence Interval (CI) to measure the variables' associations. The statistical significance was identified if a *p*-value was under 0.05, which was considered for results to enter the multivariate analysis. All statistical analyses were carried out using Stata 16.

3. Results

3.1. Characteristics of the Respondents

Table 1 presents the distribution of knowledge and attitudes toward HIV/AIDS according to sociodemographic and demographic factors among women aged 15–49 years old in Indonesia. A total of 25,895 women who had complete HIV/AIDS data were included in the analysis, and 88.74% of women had a high level of knowledge, while 60.28% had negative attitudes toward PLWHA. Nearly one quarter (20.64%) were 35–39 years old. More than half (59.15%) of the respondents had received secondary education and were working (61.27%). Close to all of the respondents' husbands were heads of the household (93.08%), while one quarter (25.15%) belonged to the wealthiest families. More than half (54.41%) resided in urban areas, while more than three quarters (84.51%) of the respondents lived in the West of Indonesia. More than half reported never accessing the Internet (55.76%), newspaper (58.93%), and radio (58.64%). More than three-quarters of the respondents' accessed information more than once per week from television (88.10%), had a mobile phone (81.89%), had high autonomy (85.97%), and disagreed with wife-beating (82.49%). Further information about the respondents' characteristics is presented in Table 1.

Table 1. Characteristics of women aged 15–49 years in Indonesia.

Characteristics	N	%
Age (Years)		
15–19	443	1.71
20–24	2561	9.89
25–29	4372	16.88
30–34	5106	19.72
35–39	5345	20.64
40–44	4425	17.09
45–49	3643	14.07
Education level		
No school	112	0.43
Primary	6398	24.71
Secondary	15,316	59.15
Higher	4069	15.71
Occupation		
Not working	10,029	38.73
Working	15,866	61.27
Head of household		
Men	24,104	93.08
Women	1791	6.92

Table 1. *Cont.*

Characteristics	N	%
Wealth index		
Poorest	2982	11.52
Poorer	4685	18.09
Middle	5507	21.27
Richer	6209	23.98
Richest	6512	25.15
Resident		
Rural	11,806	45.59
Urban	14,089	54.41
Province		
West of Indonesia	21,884	84.51
Middle of Indonesia	3485	13.46
East of Indonesia	526	2.03
Access to Internet		
Never	14,439	55.76
<1 per week	648	2.50
≥1 per week	10,808	41.74
Access to television		
Never	515	1.99
<1 per week	2567	9.91
≥1 per week	22,813	88.10
Exposure to newspaper		
Never	15,259	58.93
<1 per week	7991	30.86
≥1 per week	2645	10.21
Access to radio		
Never	15,184	58.64
<1 per week	7035	27.17
≥1 per week	3676	14.20
Mobile phone		
No	4690	18.11
Yes	21,205	
Autonomy		
Low	3632	14.03
High	22,263	85.97
Women's attitudes towards wife-beating		
Agree	4535	17.51
Disagree	21,360	82.49
Knowledge toward HIV/AIDS		
Poor	2915	11.26
Good	22,980	88.74
Attitudes toward PLWHA		
Negative	15,610	60.28
Positive	10,285	39.72

HIV/AIDS: Human Immunodeficiency Virus/Acquired Immune Deficiency Syndrome. PLWHA: People Living with HIV/AIDS.

3.2. Bivariate Analysis

In the bivariate analysis, an age of 15–19 years, lack of formal education, belonging to the poorest index, living in rural and West Indonesia, having no access to media, having no mobile phone, low autonomy and agreeing with wife-beating were associated with knowledge toward HIV/AIDS (Table 2). Similarly, an age of 15–19 years, having no formal education, belonging to the poorest index, living in rural and the West of Indonesia, having no access to the Internet, newspaper, radio, having no mobile phone, and agreeing with wife-beating were associated with attitudes toward HIV/AIDS (Table 3). No significant association was detected between an age of 20–49 years, occupation, and head of household.

Table 2. Socioeconomic and demographic information and knowledge toward HIV/AIDS among women aged 15–49 years old in Indonesia.

Characteristics	Knowledge				χ^2
	Poor		Good		
	n (2915)	%	*n* (22,980)	%	
Age (years)					
15–19	82	18.55	360	81.45	39.01 ***
20–24	308	12.03	2253	87.97	
25–29	489	11.19	3883	88.81	
30–34	540	10.57	4566	89.43	
35–39	542	10.14	4803	89.86	
40–44	490	11.08	3935	88.92	
45–49	464	12.72	3180	87.28	
Education level					
No school	37	33.05	75	66.95	891.11 ***
Primary	1318	20.60	5080	79.40	
Secondary	1453	9.49	13,863	90.51	
Higher	107	2.63	3962	97.37	
Occupation					
Not working	1185	11.81	8844	88.19	4.70
Working	1730	10.90	14,136	89.10	
Head of household					
Men	2726	11.31	21,378	88.69	0.87
Women	189	10.56	1602	89.44	
Wealth index					
Poorest	596	19.98	2386	80.02	679.12 ***
Poorer	779	16.63	3906	83.37	
Middle	715	12.99	4792	87.01	
Richer	546	8.79	5663	91.21	
Richest	279	4.28	6233	95.72	
Resident					
Rural	1824	15.45	9983	84.55	353.28 ***
Urban	1091	7.74	12,997	92.26	
Province					
West of Indonesia	2382	10.89	19,502	89.11	18.00 ***
Middle of Indonesia	464	13.30	3022	86.70	
East of Indonesia	69	13.13	456	86.87	
Access to internet					
Never	2283	15.81	12,156	84.19	651.30 ***
<1 per week	76	11.66	573	88.34	
≥1 per week	556	5.15	10,251	94.85	
Access to television					
Never	83	16.08	432	83.92	15.81 **
<1 per week	320	12.46	2247	87.54	
≥1 per week	2512	11.01	20,301	88.99	

Table 2. *Cont.*

Characteristics	Knowledge				χ^2
	Poor		Good		
	n (2915)	%	*n* (22,980)	%	
Exposure to newspaper					
Never	2075	13.6	13,184	86.40	236.43 ***
<1 per week	732	9.16	7259	90.84	
≥1 per week	108	4.08	2537	95.92	
Access to radio					
Never	1937	12.76	13,247	87.24	83.40 ***
<1 per week	684	9.72	6351	90.28	
≥1 per week	294	7.99	3382	92.01	
Mobile phone					
No	918	19.58	3771	80.42	367.78 ***
Yes	1997	9.42	19,209	90.58	
Autonomy					
Low	508	13.97	3124	86.03	28.90 ***
High	2407	10.81	19,856	89.19	
Women's attitudes towards wife-beating					
Agree	631	13.90	3905	86.10	35.71 ***
Disagree	2284	10.69	19,075	89.31	

** $\chi^2 < 0.01$. *** $\chi^2 < 0.001$.

Table 3. Socioeconomic and demographic information and attitudes toward HIV/AIDS among women aged 15–49 years old in Indonesia.

Characteristics	Attitudes				χ^2
	Negative		Positive		
	n (15,610)	%	*n* (10,285)	%	
Age (years)					
15–19	274	62.00	168	38.00	59.36 ***
20–24	1614	63.01	948	36.99	
25–29	2585	59.13	1787	40.87	
30–34	2937	57.53	2168	42.47	
35–39	3132	58.59	2213	41.41	
40–44	2713	61.32	1712	38.68	
45–49	2355	64.62	1289	35.38	
Education level					
No school	87	77.48	25	22.52	294.53 ***
Primary	4326	67.62	2071	32.38	
Secondary	9136	59.65	6180	40.35	
Higher	2061	50.64	2009	49.36	
Occupation					
Not working	6112	60.95	3916	39.05	2.81
Working	9498	59.86	6369	40.14	
Head of household					
Men	14,514	60.21	9590	39.79	0.62
Women	1096	61.19	695	38.81	

Table 3. *Cont.*

Characteristics	Attitudes				χ^2
	Negative		Positive		
	n (15,610)	%	*n* (10,285)	%	
Wealth index					
Poorest	2110	70.76	872	29.24	256.14 ***
Poorer	2993	63.87	1693	36.13	
Middle	3371	61.22	2135	38.78	
Richer	3605	58.06	2604	41.94	
Richest	3531	54.22	2981	45.78	
Resident					
Rural	7579	64.19	4228	35.81	128.11 ***
Urban	8031	57.01	6057	42.99	
Province					
West of Indonesia	12,846	58.70	9039	41.30	140.80 ***
Middle of Indonesia	2423	69.53	1062	30.47	
East of Indonesia	341	64.92	184	35.08	
Access to internet					
Never	9413	65.19	5026	34.81	317.08 ***
<1 per week	396	61.13	252	38.87	
≥1 per week	5801	53.67	5007	46.33	
Access to television					
Never	311	60.32	204	39.68	0.07
<1 per week	1541	60.04	1026	39.96	
≥1 per week	13,758	60.31	9054	39.69	
Exposure to newspaper					
Never	9482	62.14	5777	37.86	84.35 ***
<1 per week	4738	59.29	3253	40.71	
≥1 per week	1390	52.56	1255	47.44	
Access to radio					
Never	9286	61.16	5898	38.84	28.74 ***
<1 per week	4259	60.55	2776	39.45	
≥1 per week	2065	56.17	1611	43.83	
Mobile phone					
No	3214	68.55	1475	31.45	151.14 ***
Yes	12,396	58.46	8810	41.54	
Autonomy					
Low	2207	60.76	1425	39.24	0.37
High	13,403	60.21	8860	39.79	
Women's attitudes towards wife-beating					
Agree	2909	64.15	1626	35.85	31.73 ***
Disagree	12,701	59.46	8659	40.54	

*** $\chi^2 < 0.001$.

3.3. Multiple Logistic Regression Analysis

The final multiple logistic regression models in Table 4 were adjusted for association across variables. People aged 45–49 years old were 181% more likely to have good knowledge of HIV/AIDS compared to women aged 15–19 [1.81(1.26–2.60)]. Women with higher education levels were 6 times more likely to have good knowledge compared to women who received no education at all [6.32(3.59–11.11)]. Women in the richest wealth index were 167% more likely to have good knowledge of HIV/AIDS compared to women with the poorest wealth index [1.67(1.32–2.10)]. Women who lived in urban areas and East of Indonesia Province were 137% [1.37(1.22–1.54)] and 128% [1.28(1.00–1.68)] more likely to have good knowledge compared to those in rural areas and the middle Indonesia Provinces, respectively. Women who accessed information from the internet ≥1 per week were 174% more likely to have good knowledge compared to women who never access the internet [1.74(1.50–2.03)]. Women who were exposed to a newspaper ≥1 per week were as much as 132% more likely to have good knowledge than those never exposed to newspaper [1.32(1.04–1.67)]. This study found that women who access the information through radio ≥1 per week have a 131% [1.31(1.11–1.56)] propensity to acquire good knowledge compared to women who never access radio. Women who access information through a mobile phone were 126% [(1.26 (1.12–1.44)] more likely to have good knowledge compared to those who do not access from a mobile phone. Women with high autonomy were 123% more likely to have good knowledge compared to those with low autonomy [1.23(1.05–1.44)].

Table 4. Multiple logistic regression analysis of socioeconomic and demographic and knowledge-attitudes toward HIV/AIDS among women aged 15–49 years old in Indonesia.

Variable	Good Knowledge			Positive Attitudes		
	OR	95% CI		OR	95% CI	
		Lower	Upper		Lower	Upper
Age (years)						
15–19	1.00			1.00		
20–24	1.40	0.97	2.01	0.87	0.65	1.16
25–29	1.47 *	1.04	2.09	1.00	0.75	1.33
30–34	1.77 **	1.25	2.51	1.11	0.84	1.46
35–39	2.12 ***	1.49	3.00	1.10	0.83	1.46
40–44	2.04 ***	1.44	2.90	1.02	0.77	1.36
45–49	1.81 **	1.26	2.60	0.90	0.68	1.20
Education level						
No school	1.00			1.00		
Primary	1.54	0.92	2.57	1.35	0.75	2.41
Secondary	2.86 ***	1.71	4.78	1.64	0.922	2.93
Higher	6.32 ***	3.59	11.11	2.05 *	1.14	3.68
Wealth index						
Poorest	1.00			1.00		
Poorer	0.98	0.83	1.16	1.21 **	1.06	1.38
Middle	1.08	0.91	1.28	1.23 **	1.08	1.40
Richer	1.29 **	1.07	1.56	1.26 **	1.10	1.44
Richest	1.67 ***	1.32	2.10	1.22 **	1.05	1.41
Resident						
Rural	1.00			1.00		
Urban	1.37 ***	1.22	1.54	1.11 *	1.03	1.21
Province						
West of Indonesia	1.27 ***	1.12	1.45	1.59 ***	1.46	1.73
Middle of Indonesia	1.00			1.00		
East of Indonesia	1.28 *	1.00	1.68	1.32 **	1.12	1.57
Access to Internet						
Never	1.00			1.00		
<1 per week	1.17	0.87	1.57	1.13	0.92	1.38
≥1 per week	1.74 ***	1.50	2.03	1.26 **	1.15	1.37
Access to television						
Never	1.00			1.00		
<1 per week	0.85	0.59	1.22	0.79	0.61	1.03
≥1 per week	0.98	0.70	1.37	0.78	0.62	1.00

Table 4. *Cont.*

Variable	Good Knowledge			Positive Attitudes		
	OR	95% CI		OR	95% CI	
		Lower	Upper		Lower	Upper
Exposure to newspaper						
Never	1.00			1.00		
<1 per week	1.07	0.95	1.20	1.02	0.94	1.11
≥1 per week	1.32 *	1.04	1.67	1.07	0.95	1.20
Access to radio						
Never	1.00			1.00		
<1 per week	1.10	0.97	1.24	0.96	0.89	1.05
≥1 per week	1.31 **	1.11	1.56	1.13 *	1.03	1.24
Mobile phone						
No	1.00			1.00		
Yes	1.26 ***	1.12	1.44	1.17 **	1.06	1.29
Autonomy						
Low	1.00			1.00		
High	1.23 **	1.05	1.44	0.99	0.89	1.09
Women's attitudes towards wife-beating						
Agree	1.00			1.00		
Disagree	1.08	0.95	1.22	1.10 *	1.00	1.19

* *p*-value < 0.05. ** *p*-value < 0.01. *** *p*-value < 0.001.

There was no association observed in terms of access to television, newspaper and autonomy with positive attitudes toward HIV/AIDS.

4. Discussion

In this study, we found socio-economic and demographic factors were associated with knowledge and attitudes of HIV/AIDS among women aged 15–49 years. Among the representative sample in this study, more than three quarters (88.74%) had a high level of knowledge, while more than half (60.28%) of women had negative attitudes toward PLWHA, revealing the tendencies of women in understanding information on HIV/AIDS. Even though the study population was significantly knowledgeable about HIV/AIDS, negative attitudes towards PLWHA showed that accepting PLWHA still requires reasonable efforts and resources. Our study highlights the need for public and/or specific group awareness about HIV/AIDS, as suggested in previous studies [34–36]. Negative attitudes toward PLWHA may lead to persistent discrimination and their persistent rejection by community members [37–39]. Our study indicated that a high level of knowledge about HIV/AIDS does not translate to more positive attitudes and revealed the critical social barrier for PLWHA in Indonesia.

Our findings revealed that women's age played a vital role in possessing a high level of knowledge, while age was not associated with attitudes toward HIV/AIDS. Consistent with previous studies [20,40,41], age was associated with the person's opportunity to gather additional and appropriate information considered necessary for daily life. Mature age can be attributed to greater exposure to sexual health education, such as training related to sexual health and HIV/AIDS. One explanation why age was not associated with attitudes might be because age is related to someone's experience during their lifetime, while attitude represents a complex processes within human perception that can change constantly depending on specific situations [42].

Our study confirmed the findings of previous studies indicating that higher education was associated with knowledge and attitudes toward HIV/AIDS among women of reproductive age [20,43,44]. This may be due to educational attainment acts which have made information more easily accessible and better promoted the reception of such knowledge [18]. Further, appropriate resources might foster better knowledge and attitudes toward PLWHA, which can assist in the problem of HIV/AIDS infection, treatment, and transmission [18,45,46].

Further, our study found that socio-economic and demographic factors, including residing in urban areas, living in the West of Indonesia, having access to mass media, and having mobile phones were associated with knowledge and attitudes on HIV/AIDS. These results are similar to previous studies conducted in other countries such as India, Bangladesh, and Pakistan [34,47,48]. Our findings indicate an urgent need to target women from urban areas and who are exposed to mass media through appropriate campaigns [49]. Related to the current context of infectious diseases, the easy availability and accessibility of health information online can improve patient knowledge and practice related to HIV/AIDS [50,51]. A similar study also found that most people have a good level of knowledge and understand of preventative actions related to infectious disease such as COVID-19 [52]. In the Indonesian setting, robust policies and strategic programs have utilized the ABCDE (Abstinence, Be faithful, Condom, Do not use drugs, Education) campaigns to reduce the risk of contracting HIV in the East of Indonesia. A series of efforts has been made through promotional activities, counselling, and voluntary testing and treatment; however, HIV/AIDS cases remain high in East of Indonesia, especially in the Papua region [8]. Practical policies supplemented with local insights may need to be tested at the provincial level to understand how to achieve a better outcome.

Moreover, our study revealed that those women who were well-educated and with a more affluent wealth index were more likely to show good knowledge and positive attitudes towards HIV/AIDS. This finding aligns with another study conducted in South Sudan where wealth quintiles had a significant relationship with comprehensive knowledge and positive attitudes towards people with HIV/AIDS [22]. The ability of women to actively empower themselves with knowledge on HIV/AIDS relates to the personal awareness and comprehensive understanding of women about HIV/AIDS. These findings are also consistent with other studies conducted in Ethiopia and Pakistan [47,52] which suggested that women's autonomy is vital to address the effect of HIV/AIDS on women's health. Further, our findings showed that women who disagreed with wife-beating were more likely to have positive attitudes towards HIV/AIDS [47,52,53].

This study has certain strengths that should be highlighted. Our paper is the first survey report on socio-economic and demographic factors associated with knowledge and attitudes of HIV/AIDS among women aged 15–49 years old in Indonesia using well-recommended global tools. All data utilized in the analysis were weighted to reflect the statistical interpretation with rigorous methodology and techniques. A significant limitation of our study related to the completeness of data available from the DHS website [33], which intended to capture demographic and health indicators in Indonesia. The limitation of this study was found to be the study design which was cross-sectional; therefore, we cannot infer the causality here. Due to the use of secondary data, we also had no control over the confounding factors and indicators. Despite these limitations, the findings are important for the formulation of more effective policies concerning knowledge and attitudes toward HIV/AIDS.

5. Conclusions

This study analyzed socio-economic and demographic factors associated with knowledge and attitudes toward HIV/AIDS among women aged 15–49 years old in Indonesia. In order to combat HIV/AIDS in Indonesia, issues of knowledge and attitudes toward HIV/AIDS still must be addressed. In general, women with a higher level of education, higher wealth status, living in an urban area, residing in West Indonesia and having access to the Internet, radio, and mobile phones had significantly better levels of knowledge and positive attitudes towards HIV/AIDS. Our findings indicate that HIV/AIDS knowledge and attitudes related to personal background, place, and mode of media contributed to a high level of knowledge and positive attitudes towards HIV/AIDS. Appropriate health education programs are recommended as the key to increasing the level of comprehensive knowledge and attitudes related to HIV/AIDS among women. A health education campaign should be launched based on sociodemographic considerations by working with the local governments and relevant stakeholders.

Author Contributions: Conceptualization: F.D.V., F.E., T.K., L.M., K.R. Methodology: F.D.V., F.E., T.K., Q.E.S.A., L.M., K.R. Formal analysis: F.D.V., F.E., T.K., L.M., K.R. Writing—Original draft preparation: F.D.V., F.E., T.K., Q.E.S.A., L.M., K.R., I.A.S. Writing—Review and editing: F.E., T.K., Q.E.S.A., L.M., K.R., I.A.S. Funding acquisition: F.E. Resources: F.E., T.K., Q.E.S.A., L.M., K.R. Supervision: F.E., T.K., Q.E.S.A., L.M., K.R. All authors have read and agreed to the published version of the manuscript.

Funding: This research received no external funding.

Institutional Review Board Statement: The study was conducted in accordance with the Declaration of Helsinki, and approved by the Institutional Review Board (or Ethics Committee) of ICF IRB (protocol code FWA00000845, 03/11/2015).

Data Availability Statement: Data are available from https://dhsprogram.com/data/available-datasets.cfm (accessed on 4 January 2022) by applying through the DHS program via the website. The authors had no special access privileges to these data.

Conflicts of Interest: The authors confirm no known conflict of interest associated with this publication.

References

1. Jahagirdar, D.; Walters, M.K.; Novotney, A.; Brewer, E.D.; Frank, T.D.; Carter, A.; Biehl, M.H.; Abbastabar, H.; Abhilash, E.S.; Abu-Gharbieh, E. Global, regional, and national sex-specific burden and control of the HIV epidemic, 1990–2019, for 204 countries and territories: The Global Burden of Diseases Study. *Lancet HIV* **2021**, *8*, e633–e651. [CrossRef]
2. Piot, P.; Karim, S.S.A.; Hecht, R.; Legido-Quigley, H.; Buse, K.; Stover, J.; Resch, S.; Ryckman, T.; Møgedal, S.; Dybul, M. Defeating AIDS—advancing global health. *Lancet* **2015**, *386*, 171–218. [CrossRef]
3. Workie, K.L.; Birhan, T.Y.; Angaw, D.A. Predictors of mortality rate among adult HIV-positive patients on antiretroviral therapy in Metema Hospital, Northwest Ethiopia: A retrospective follow-up study. *AIDS Res. Ther.* **2021**, *18*, 1–11. [CrossRef]
4. Marrazzo, J.M.; Del Rio, C.; Holtgrave, D.R.; Cohen, M.S.; Kalichman, S.C.; Mayer, K.H.; Montaner, J.S.G.; Wheeler, D.P.; Grant, R.M.; Grinsztejn, B. HIV prevention in clinical care settings: 2014 recommendations of the International Antiviral Society–USA Panel. *JAMA* **2014**, *312*, 390–409. [CrossRef] [PubMed]
5. UNAIDS Data. 2017. Available online: https://www.unaids.org/en/resources/documents/2017/2017_data_book (accessed on 4 April 2022).
6. UNAIDS. UNAIDS. UNAIDS Joint United Nations Programme on HIV/AIDS. In *UNAIDS*; UNAIDS: Geneva, Switzerland, 2020; pp. 1–248. Available online: http://www.unaids.org/sites/default/files/media_asset/20170720_Data_book_2017_en.pdf (accessed on 4 April 2022).
7. WHO. *Highly Prevalence of Women with HIV/AIDS than Men*; WHO: Geneva, Switzerland, 2018.
8. Kemenkes, R.I. *Profil Kesehatan Indonesia Tahun 2019*; Kementerian Kesehatan Republik Indonesia: Bandung City, Indonesia, 2020; ISBN 9786024169770.
9. Efendi, F.; Pratama, E.R.; Hadisuyatmana, S.; Indarwati, R.; Lindayani, L.; Bushy, A. HIV-related knowledge level among Indonesian women between 15 years and 49 years of age. *Afr. Health Sci.* **2020**, *20*, 83–90. [CrossRef] [PubMed]
10. Sudha, R.T.; Vijay, D.T.; Lakshmi, V. Awareness, attitudes, and beliefs of the general public towards HIV/AIDS in Hyderabad, a capital city from South India. *Indian J. Med. Sci.* **2005**, *59*, 307–316.
11. Pachuau, L.N.; Tannous, C.; Agho, K.E. Factors Associated with Knowledge, Attitudes, and Prevention towards HIV/AIDS among Adults 15–49 Years in Mizoram, North East India: A Cross-Sectional Study. *Int. J. Environ. Res. Public Health* **2022**, *19*, 440. [CrossRef]
12. Ehiri, J.E.; Anyanwu, E.C.; Donath, E.; Kanu, I.; Jolly, P.E. AIDS-related stigma in sub-Saharan Africa: Its contexts and potential intervention strategies. *AIDS Public Policy J.* **2005**, *20*, 25–39. [PubMed]
13. Dahlui, M.; Azahar, N.; Bulgiba, A.; Zaki, R.; Oche, O.M.; Adekunjo, F.O.; Chinna, K. HIV/AIDS related stigma and discrimination against PLWHA in Nigerian population. *PLoS ONE* **2015**, *10*, e0168280. [CrossRef] [PubMed]
14. Moussa, A.B.; Delabre, R.M.; Villes, V.; Elkhammas, M.; Bennani, A.; Ouarsas, L.; Filali, H.; Alami, K.; Karkouri, M.; Castro, D.R. Determinants and effects or consequences of internal HIV-related stigma among people living with HIV in Morocco. *BMC Public Health* **2021**, *21*, 163. [CrossRef] [PubMed]
15. Hoang, C.D.; Tran, B.X.; Pham, M.D.; Nguyen, L.H.; Do, H.N.; Vuong, Q.H.; Ho, M.T.; Dam, V.N.; Vuong, T.T.; Nguyen, H.H. HIV-and AIDS-related knowledge and attitude of residents in border regions of Vietnam. *Harm Reduct. J.* **2019**, *16*, 11. [CrossRef] [PubMed]

16. Alwafi, H.A.; Meer, A.M.T.; Shabkah, A.; Mehdawi, F.S.; El-Haddad, H.; Bahabri, N.; Almoallim, H. Knowledge and attitudes toward HIV/AIDS among the general population of Jeddah, Saudi Arabia. *J. Infect. Public Health* **2018**, *11*, 80–84. [CrossRef] [PubMed]
17. Do, H.N.; Nathan, N.; Van Nguyen, B.; Le, H.T.; Nguyen, H.Q.T.; Nguyen, A.T.; Nguyen, H.D.; Bui, T.P.; Vu, T.B.T.; Le, K.T. Sociodemographic inequalities in substance use among young people in Vietnam. *Child. Youth Serv. Rev.* **2018**, *94*, 644–649. [CrossRef]
18. Agegnehu, C.D.; Geremew, B.M.; Sisay, M.M.; Muchie, K.F.; Engida, Z.T.; Gudayu, T.W.; Weldetsadik, D.S.; Liyew, A.M. Determinants of comprehensive knowledge of HIV/AIDS among reproductive age (15–49 years) women in Ethiopia: Further analysis of 2016 Ethiopian demographic and health survey. *AIDS Res. Ther.* **2020**, *17*, 1–9. [CrossRef] [PubMed]
19. Estifanos, T.M.; Hui, C.; Tesfai, A.W.; Teklu, M.E.; Ghebrehiwet, M.A.; Embaye, K.S.; Andegiorgish, A.K. Predictors of HIV/AIDS comprehensive knowledge and acceptance attitude towards people living with HIV/AIDS among unmarried young females in Uganda: A cross-sectional study. *BMC Womens Health* **2021**, *21*, 37. [CrossRef] [PubMed]
20. Zarei, E.; Khabiri, R.; Tajvar, M.; Nosratnejad, S. Knowledge of and attitudes toward HIV/AIDS among Iranian women. *Epidemiol. Health* **2018**, *40*, 1–7. [CrossRef]
21. Varni, S.E.; Miller, C.T.; Solomon, S.E. Sexual behavior as a function of stigma and coping with stigma among people with HIV/AIDS in rural New England. *AIDS Behav.* **2012**, *16*, 2330–2339. [CrossRef] [PubMed]
22. Mude, W.; Oguoma, V.M.; Gesesew, H.A.; Ameyaw, E.K.; Njue, C.; Nyanhanda, T.; Adeleye, A.O.; Dune, T.; Kaambwa, B.; Mwanri, L. HIV/AIDS knowledge and attitudes assessment among women of child-bearing age in South Sudan: Findings from a Household Survey. *PLoS ONE* **2020**, *15*, e0243969. [CrossRef] [PubMed]
23. Psaros, C.; Milford, C.; Smit, J.A.; Greener, L.; Mosery, N.; Matthews, L.T.; Harrison, A.; Gordon, J.R.; Mimiaga, M.; Bangsberg, D.R. HIV prevention among young women in South Africa: Understanding multiple layers of risk. *Arch. Sex. Behav.* **2018**, *47*, 1969–1982. [CrossRef] [PubMed]
24. Poteat, T.; Wirtz, A.; Malik, M.; Cooney, E.; Cannon, C.; Hardy, W.D.; Arrington-Sanders, R.; Lujan, M.; Yamanis, T. A gap between willingness and uptake: Findings from mixed methods research on HIV prevention among black and Latina transgender women. *J. Acquir. Immune Defic. Syndr.* **2019**, *82*, 131. [CrossRef] [PubMed]
25. Octavianty, L.; Rahayu, A.; Rosadi, D.; Rahman, F. Pengetahuan, Sikap dan Pencegahan HIV/AIDS Pada Ibu Rumah Tangga. *KEMAS J. Kesehat. Masy.* **2015**, *11*, 53–58. [CrossRef]
26. Faridah, I. Pengetahuan dan Sikap Tentang HIV/AIDS dan Upaya Pencegahan HIV/AIDS. *J. Kesehat.* **2020**, *9*, 43–58.
27. Irawan, R. *Hubungan Antara Tingkat Pengetahuan Dan Sikap Siswa Sma Pangudi Luhur Kelas X Yogyakarta Tentang HIV/AIDS*; Universitas Islam Indonesia: Daerah Istimewa Yogyakarta, Indonesia, 2012.
28. Arifin, H.; Ibrahim, K.; Rahayuwati, L.; Herliani, Y.K.; Kurniawati, Y.; Pradipta, R.O.; Sari, G.M.; Ko, N.-Y.; Wiratama, B.S. HIV-related knowledge, information, and their contribution to stigmatization attitudes among females aged 15–24 years: Regional disparities in Indonesia. *BMC Public Health* **2022**, *22*, 637. [CrossRef]
29. DHS Program. DHS Model Questionnair, Demographic and Health Surveys. 2022. Available online: https://dhsprogram.com/Methodology/Survey-Types/DHS-Questionnaires.cfmDHS (accessed on 7 April 2022).
30. DHS. DHS Questionnaires, The DHS Program. 2022. Available online: https://www.dhsprogram.com/Methodology/Survey-Types/DHS-Questionnaires.cfm (accessed on 2 January 2022).
31. Allen, C.K.; Fleuret, J.; Ahmed, J. DHS Methodological Reports No. 30: Data Quality in Demographic and Health Surveys That Used Long and Short Questionnaires. In *The DHS Program*; ICF: Fairfax, VA, USA, 2020.
32. DHSProgram. Wealth Index Rockville, MD2016. 2014. Available online: https://dhsprogram.com/topics/wealth-index/ (accessed on 9 June 2021).
33. BKKBN; BPS; Kemenkes; ICF. *Indonesia Demographic and Health Survey 2017*; ICF: Fairfax, VA, USA, 2018.
34. Yaya, S.; Bishwajit, G.; Danhoundo, G.; Shah, V.; Ekholuenetale, M. Trends and determinants of HIV/AIDS knowledge among women in Bangladesh. *BMC Public Health* **2016**, *16*, 812. [CrossRef] [PubMed]
35. Dai, X.; Wang, H. Change in knowledge and attitude about HIV/AIDS in sub-Saharan Africa, 1990–2017: An analysis of national survey data. *Lancet Glob. Health* **2019**, *7*, S4. [CrossRef]
36. Yaya, S.; Ghose, B.; Udenigwe, O.; Shah, V.; Hudani, A.; Ekholuenetale, M. Knowledge and attitude of HIV/AIDS among women in Nigeria: A cross-sectional study. *Eur. J. Public Health* **2019**, *29*, 111–117. [CrossRef]
37. Grossman, C.I.; Stangl, A.L. Global action to reduce HIV stigma and discrimination. *J. Int. AIDS Soc.* **2013**, *16*, 18881. [CrossRef]
38. Dos Santos, M.M.L.; Kruger, P.; Mellors, S.E.; Wolvaardt, G.; Van Der Ryst, E. An exploratory survey measuring stigma and discrimination experienced by people living with HIV/AIDS in South Africa: The People Living with HIV Stigma Index. *BMC Public Health* **2014**, *14*, 80. [CrossRef]
39. Stangl, A.L.; Lloyd, J.K.; Brady, L.M.; Holland, C.E.; Baral, S. A systematic review of interventions to reduce HIV-related stigma and discrimination from 2002 to 2013: How far have we come? *J. Int. AIDS Soc.* **2013**, *16*, 18734. [CrossRef]
40. Abiodun, O.; Sotunsa, J.; Ani, F.; Jaiyesimi, E. Knowledge of HIV/AIDS and predictors of uptake of HIV counseling and testing among undergraduate students of a privately owned university in Nigeria. *BMC Res. Notes* **2014**, *7*, 639. [CrossRef]
41. Emlet, C.A.; Brennan, D.J.; Brennenstuhl, S.; Rueda, S.; Hart, T.A.; Rourke, S.B. The impact of HIV-related stigma on older and younger adults living with HIV disease: Does age matter? *AIDS Care* **2015**, *27*, 520–528. [CrossRef] [PubMed]

42. Auzenbergs, M.; Delpech, V.; Gold, D.; Kall, M.; Petretti, S.; Smithson, K.; Summersbey, E. Changing Perceptions: Talking about HIV and attitudes. In *Positive Voices*; Public Health England: London, UK, 2018.
43. Gebremedhin, S.A.; Wang, Y.; Tesfamariam, E.H. Predictors of HIV/AIDS knowledge and attitude among young women of Nigeria and Democratic Republic of Congo: Cross-sectional study. *J. AIDS Clin. Res.* **2017**, *8*, 677. [CrossRef]
44. Mumtaz, G.R.; Hilmi, N.; Majed, E.Z.; Abu-Raddad, L.J. Characterising HIV/AIDS knowledge and attitudes in the Middle East and North Africa: Systematic review and data synthesis. *Glob. Public Health* **2020**, *15*, 275–298. [CrossRef] [PubMed]
45. Bulali, R.E.; Kibusi, S.M.; Mpondo, B.C.T. Factors associated with hiv status disclosure and its effect on treatment adherence and quality of life among children 6–17 years on antiretroviral therapy in southern highlands zone, Tanzania: Unmatched case control study. *Int. J. Pediatr.* **2018**, *2018*, 1–10. [CrossRef] [PubMed]
46. Doat, A.-R.; Negarandeh, R.; Hasanpour, M. Disclosure of HIV status to children in Sub-Saharan Africa: A systematic review. *Medicina* **2019**, *55*, 433. [CrossRef]
47. Iqbal, S.; Maqsood, S.; Zafar, A.; Zakar, R.; Zakar, M.Z.; Fischer, F. Determinants of overall knowledge of and attitudes towards HIV/AIDS transmission among ever-married women in Pakistan: Evidence from the Demographic and Health Survey 2012–13. *BMC Public Health* **2019**, *19*, 793. [CrossRef]
48. Bhagavathula, A.S.; Clark, C.C.T.; Sharma, R.; Chhabra, M.; Vidyasagar, K.; Chattu, V.K. Knowledge and attitude towards HIV/AIDS in India: A systematic review and meta-analysis of 47 studies from 2010. *Health Promot. Perspect.* **2021**, *11*, 148–160. [CrossRef] [PubMed]
49. Kasymova, S. Awareness and knowledge about HIV/AIDS among women of reproductive age in Tajikistan. *AIDS Care* **2020**, *32*, 518–521. [CrossRef]
50. Estacio, E.V.; Whittle, R.; Protheroe, J. The digital divide: Examining socio-demographic factors associated with health literacy, access and use of internet to seek health information. *J. Health Psychol.* **2019**, *24*, 1668–1675. [CrossRef]
51. Iradukunda, P.G.; Pierre, G.; Muhozi, V.; Denhere, K.; Dzinamarira, T. Knowledge, attitude, and practice towards COVID-19 among people living with HIV/AIDS in Kigali, Rwanda. *J. Community Health* **2021**, *46*, 245–250. [CrossRef]
52. Gallè, F.; Sabella, E.A.; Roma, P.; Ferracuti, S.; Da Molin, G.; Diella, G.; Montagna, M.T.; Orsi, G.B.; Liguori, G.; Napoli, C. Knowledge and lifestyle behaviors related to COVID-19 pandemic in people over 65 years old from southern Italy. *Int. J. Environ. Res. Public Health* **2021**, *18*, 10872. [CrossRef] [PubMed]
53. Ahmed, M.; Seid, A. Does women's autonomy matter on attitude towards condom use in reducing risk for HIV infection among married women in Ethiopia? *HIV/AIDS* **2020**, *12*, 489. [CrossRef] [PubMed]

International Journal of
Environmental Research and Public Health

MDPI

Article

Decreased Physical Activity during Pregnancy Is Associated with Excessive Gestational Weight Gain

Jia-Jing Sun [1,2] and Li-Yin Chien [3,*]

1 School of Nursing, College of Medicine, National Taiwan University, Taipei 112304, Taiwan; c22881@gmail.com
2 Department of Nursing, Heping Fuyou Branch of Taipei City Hospital, Taipei 112304, Taiwan
3 Institute of Community Health Care, College of Nursing, National Yang Ming Chiao Tung University, Yang-Ming Campus, Taipei 112304, Taiwan
* Correspondence: lychien@nycu.edu.tw; Tel.: +886-2-28267142; Fax: +886-2-28238614

Abstract: The majority of pregnant women in Taiwan are not considered physically active. During pregnancy, many women decrease their physical activity levels when compared to pre-pregnancy. The purpose of this study was to examine the association between decreased physical activity from pre-pregnancy to pregnancy and excessive gestational weight gain (GWG). This study applied a prospective panel design. Recruitment was conducted at six medical facilities in Taiwan and lasted from August 2016 to April 2017. Physical activity levels were determined both before and during pregnancy using the International Physical Activity Questionnaire—Short Form, with data subsequently being transformed into METs-min/week. Excessive GWG was determined based on the body mass index (BMI) specific GWG range. We recruited 747 pregnant women in their second trimester and followed them through to one-month postpartum. About 40% of participants (41.2%) exhibited excessive GWG. Physical activity decreased from an average of 2261 (SD = 3999) to 1252 (SD = 2258) METs-min/week from pre-pregnancy to pregnancy ($p < 0.0001$). Controlling for age and pre-pregnancy BMI, a logistic regression model revealed that a decline in physical activity of > 4000 METs-min/week from pre-pregnancy to pregnancy was associated with an increased risk for excessive GWG (OR = 2.83, 95% CI: 1.27–4.43). A substantial decrease in physical activity from pre-pregnancy to pregnancy was a risk factor for excessive GWG. Although most women decreased their physical activity during pregnancy, only those pregnant women who were physically active pre-pregnancy could show the kind of large decrease that resulted in excessive GWG. Health professionals should continue to develop strategies for counteracting the problematic trend of decreasing PA during pregnancy among low-risk pregnant women.

Keywords: pregnancy; physical activity; gestational weight gain; obesity; maternal

Citation: Sun, J.-J.; Chien, L.-Y. Decreased Physical Activity during Pregnancy Is Associated with Excessive Gestational Weight Gain. *Int. J. Environ. Res. Public Health* **2021**, *18*, 12597. https://doi.org/10.3390/ijerph182312597

Academic Editors: Joachim G. Voss and Sandul Yasobant

Received: 4 November 2021
Accepted: 27 November 2021
Published: 29 November 2021

1. Introduction

Estimates have shown that there were approximately 38.9 million overweight pregnant women throughout the world in 2014, with 14.6 million falling into the category of obesity [1]. Although there is a lack of recent data on the global burden of overweightness and obesity among pregnant women, estimates suggest that 20% of women will be obese by 2025 [2]. In this context, maternal obesity has become an increasing area of concern [2]. Looking specifically at Taiwan, a national breastfeeding survey (2012–2016) showed that the proportions of women with overweightness and obesity pre-pregnancy were 10.6% and 5.9%, respectively [3]. This is a notable issue, as women who are overweight or obese at conception are known to have increased risk of excessive gestational weight gain (GWG) and poor pregnancy outcomes [4].

Evidence also suggests there is an association between excessive GWG and future overweightness/obesity in the offspring [5,6]. Further, mothers with excessive GWG are at higher risk for preterm birth, cesarean delivery [7], and postpartum weight retention [8]. In response to the obesity epidemic in the Unites States, the American Institute of Medicine (IOM) defined optimal ranges of total GWG for each category of the pre-pregnancy body-mass index (BMI), as follows: 12.5–18 kg for underweight, 11.5–16 kg for normal weight, 7–11.5 kg for overweight, and 5–9 kg for obese women [9]. Weight gains below and beyond the recommended amounts are termed inadequate and excessive GWG, respectively. About 20% and 48% of women in the United States experience inadequate and excessive GWG, respectively [10]. The IOM criteria for GWG based on local cut-off for BMI (18.5, 24, and 27 kg/m^2 for underweight, normal, overweight, and obese, respectively) are adopted by the Taiwan Health Promotion Administration [11]. A national survey of postpartum women in Taiwan reported that the proportion of women with inadequate and excessive GWG was 41.5% and 22.4%, respectively [12]. Most women actually gain amounts of weight that fall outside the recommendations.

A growing number of studies have examined the efficacy of physical activity (PA) interventions during pregnancy. In this regard, a Cochrane review found no evidence to recommend or discourage exercise during pregnancy in view of its effect on maternal and infant health outcomes [13]. Nonetheless, exercise is often advocated during pregnancy due to its overall health benefits, particularly in preventing chronic diseases and unhealthy weight gain. Furthermore, women with low-risk pregnancies should be able to engage in high-intensity exercise programs that include jogging and aerobic activities, which also help with weight management [14–17]. In short, research has demonstrated that exercise during pregnancy does not harm the fetus, but can provide benefits for both the mother and baby [14,16]. On the other hand, pregnant women with low PA may be two to three times more likely to experience excessive GWG [7].

The guidelines suggesting that healthy women who are not already highly active or engaging in vigorous activity should spend at least 150 min per week walking or participating in moderate-intensity aerobic activities, while women who already engage in vigorous aerobics or large amounts of activity can continue doing so during pregnancy [14–16]. On the other hand, certain aspects of traditional Chinese culture suggest that PA can "disturb the fetus" meaning it should be avoided to prevent miscarriage-like symptoms such as abdominal pain and/or vaginal bleeding [18]. One study found that the median active PA time decreased from 80 min/week (IQR = 0–240 min/week) during pre-pregnancy to 0 min/week (IQR = 0–60 min/week) during both mid- and late pregnancy, with results also showing low overall active PA levels during pregnancy and significant drops in active PA times between pre- and during pregnancy [19].

Previous studies have suggested that regular exercise during pregnancy can reduce GWG [20–22], while meta-analyses also concluded that engagement in structured moderate physical exercise programs during pregnancy decreases the risk of gestational diabetes mellitus and diminishes maternal weight gain [21,23]. Nonetheless, a few studies have found that PA (or exercise) was not significantly associated with weight gain during pregnancy [24–26]. There was generally a lack of consideration of PA level before pregnancy and the drop in PA level during pregnancy. The literature thus offers no clear or consistent associations between PA and excessive GWG during pregnancy, especially in observational studies. While this may partially be due to the generally high prevalence of low PA during pregnancy, we are therefore not aware of any studies showing that reduced PA during pregnancy is directly associated with GWG. Based on the above and beginning with the hypothesis that excessive GWG is related to decreased PA during pregnancy, this study examined the crude and adjusted associations between decreased PA from pre-pregnancy to pregnancy and excessive GWG.

2. Methods

2.1. Design

This study applied a prospective panel design in which women were recruited during their second trimester of pregnancy (gestational weeks 14–27). All participants were evaluated during their second and third trimesters and at one-month postpartum using structured questionnaires.

2.2. Participants and Setting

Participants were recruited from four hospitals and two clinics in Taipei, Taiwan, and the study lasted from August 2016 to April 2017. Ethical approval for this study was obtained from 4 institutional review boards (Far Eastern Memorial Hospital: 105073-F; Taiwan Adventist Hospital: 105-E−03; Taipei City Hospital: TEHIRB−10505103; Buddhist Tzu Chi General Hospital—Taipei Branch: 05-M01–005). This included adult pregnant women who were receiving prenatal care at their respective locations of recruitment. None had pre-existing conditions or experienced complications during early pregnancy (e.g., habitual abortion, diabetes, high blood pressure, and hyperthyroidism). All pregnancies were considered stable. Participants were required to communicate in Mandarin Chinese. After receiving explanations of the study's purpose, those who agreed to participate signed consent forms and provided research personnel with their contact details, including email addresses, phone numbers, and postal addresses. A total of 985 women met the inclusion criteria, with 800 of those agreeing to participate in this study. Finally, the analysis included 747 women with complete records (successfully followed throughout 1 month postpartum), including information on PA levels and weight. While some were excluded due to missing information (n = 53), they did not significantly differ from those with complete information (n = 747) in regard to age, education level, work status, and number of pregnancies.

2.3. Sample Size Considerations

In the logistic regression model, when the event probability was set at 0.35, the odds ratio was 1.85, and the two-tailed alpha was 0.05, the required sample size to yield a power of 0.80 was 528, based on the sample size calculation using G-Power [27]. Consequently, we considered that the sample size of the study was adequate.

2.4. Measures

Study variables included sociodemographic factors (age, work status, education level, and marital status), PA levels, pre-pregnancy BMI, GWG, and parity. Sociodemographic factors, parity, BMI, and pre-pregnancy PA were collected during the second trimester of pregnancy, while PA levels during pregnancy were collected during both the second and third trimesters of pregnancy.

Physical activity levels were determined using the Taiwanese version of the International Physical Activity Questionnaire—Short Form (IPAQ-SF) [28]. This instrument was used to collect self-reported data on the frequency and duration of walking, moderate-intensity, and vigorous-intensity PA over the preceding seven-day period. A previous study reported that the total PA recorded by IPAQ-SF was acceptably reliable across three times (on days 1, 8, and 11) with an intra-class correlation coefficient (ICC) of 0.79 among Chinese adults in Hong Kong [29]. There were no significant differences in average PA between IPAQ-SF and PA-log, demonstrating acceptable concurrent validity. IPAQ-SF had good test–retest reliability in measuring time spent in moderate PA, vigorous PA, and moderate and vigorous PA (ICC ranged from 0.81–0.84) among pregnant women. However, concurrent validity between IPAQ-SF and an objective PA measure, SenseWear Armband, in measuring time spent in moderate PA, vigorous PA, and moderate and vigorous PA was low to fair (correlation coefficient 0.08–0.39). The low to fair concurrent validity between IPAQ-SF and objective measures were in line with other self-reported PA questionnaires [30].

We followed IPAQ guidelines stating that only 10 or more min of activity should be counted [31]. We then multiplied the metabolic equivalent values for the specific types of PA (e.g., walking = 3.3, moderate activity = 4, vigorous activity = 8) based on the number of min of the activity completed over one week to yield the METs-min/week measurements [32]. A previous study showed that moderate to vigorous PA did not differ between participants in their second and third trimesters of pregnancy [19]. Following this, we used the average METs-min during the second and third trimesters of pregnancy to represent PA levels during pregnancy. The Spearman correlation coefficient of total PA between the second and third trimester was 0.28 ($p < 0.001$) in this study. Pre-pregnancy PA was enquired in the second trimester and the participants were asked to answer their ordinary PA in a typical week before conception based on their recall.

Maternal weight was obtained from each participant's Mother's Handbook or hospital records, while pre-pregnancy BMI was calculated in kg/m^2 based on maternal pre-pregnancy weight and height in the medical records. We categorized pre-pregnancy BMI using the Taiwanese cutoffs of 18.5, 24, and 27 kg/m^2 for underweight, overweight, and obesity, respectively [11]. Total GWG was calculated by subtracting the pre-pregnancy weight from the weight at delivery, then categorized as excessive or non-excessive if above or below/within the BMI-specific weight gain ranges established by the Institute of Medicine, respectively [33].

2.5. Data Analysis

Statistical analyses were conducted using SPSS for Windows Version 24.0 (IBM Corp, Armonk, NY, USA). Participant characteristics were presented using frequencies and percentages for categorical variables, while means and standard deviations (SDs) were used for continuous variables. The crude associations between excessive GWG and PA or other characteristics were examined using the t-test or chi-squared test. The IPAQ group defined 601–4000 METs-min/week as moderate PA and >4000 METs-min/week as high PA [34]. Given those, PA and decline in PA was divided into <600, 600–4000, and >4000 METs-min/week in the analysis. The logistic regression model was used to examine the net association between PA and excessive GWG. We first fit the logistic regression model by entering all variables, then dropped the least significant variable from the model one at a time. This was repeated until all variables in the model were statistically significant, which was determined based on 2-sided p values < 0.05. Adjusted odds ratios (aOR) and 95% confidence intervals (95% CIs) were computed for the logistic model results.

3. Results

3.1. Characteristics of the Participants

Table 1 shows the characteristics of the 747 analyzed study participants. The mean age was 33.1 ± 4.4 years (ranging from 20 to 44). As shown, more than 70% (73.2%) had university-level educations or higher, and the majority were married (97.2%). More than half were primiparous (55%). More than one-fifth were overweight or obese before pregnancy (12.6% overweight and 8.4% obese).

Table 1. Participant Characteristics by Excessive Gestational Weight Gain (n = 747).

Sample Characteristics		Total n (%) N = 747	Excessive Gestational Weight Gain: No n (%) n = 439	Excessive Gestational Weight Gain: Yes n (%) n = 308	p-Value
Age (years)					0.255
	20–29	146 (19.5)	80 (18.2)	66 (21.4)	
	30–39	562 (75.2)	332 (75.6)	230 (74.7)	
	≥40	39 (5.2)	27 (6.2)	12 (3.9)	
Education					0.672
	High school or less	126 (16.9)	71 (16.2)	55 (17.9)	
	College/Vocational school	74 (9.9)	45 (10.3)	29 (9.4)	
	University	435 (58.2)	252 (57.4)	183 (59.4)	
	Postgraduate	112 (15.0)	71 (16.2)	41 (13.3)	

Table 1. *Cont.*

Sample Characteristics	Total *n* (%) N = 747	Excessive Gestational Weight Gain: No *n* (%) *n* = 439	Excessive Gestational Weight Gain: Yes *n* (%) *n* = 308	*p*-Value
Work status				0.492
Employed	552 (73.9)	325 (74)	227 (73.7)	
Unemployed	195 (26.1)	114 (26.0)	81 (26.3)	
Currently married				0.523
Yes	726 (97.2)	427 (97.3)	299 (97.1)	
No	21 (2.8)	12 (2.7)	9 (2.9)	
BMI (kg/m^2)				<0.0001
<18.5 (underweight)	110 (14.7)	93 (21.2)	17 (5.5)	
18.5–24.9 (normal)	480 (64.3)	303(69.0)	177 (57.5)	
25–26.9 (overweight)	94 (12.6)	23 (5.2)	71 (23.1)	
≥27 (obese)	63 (8.4)	20 (4.6)	43 (14.0)	
Number of pregnancies				0.08
1	411 (55.0)	227 (51.7)	184 (59.7)	
2	282 (37.8)	176 (40.1)	106 (34.4)	
≥3	54 (7.2)	36 (8.2)	18 (5.8)	
PA before pregnancy (METs-min/week)				0.005 **
0	152 (20.3)	99 (22.6)	53 (17.2)	
1–600	153 (20.5)	94 (21.4)	59 (19.2)	
601–4000	327 (43.8)	195 (44.4)	132 (42.9)	
>4000	115 (15.4)	51 (11.6)	64 (20.8)	
Declines in PA during pregnancy than before (METs-min/week)				
No decline	306 (40.9)	190 (43.3)	116 (37.7)	0.008 *
1–600	160 (21.4)	94 (21.4)	66 (21.4)	
601–4000	223 (29.9)	133 (30.3)	90 (29.2)	
>4000	58 (7.8)	22 (5.0)	36 (11.7)	

Abbreviations: BMI = body mass index; SD = standard deviation; PA = physical activity. *p*-values were calculated using the chi-squared test or *t*-test * $p < 0.05$, ** $p < 0.01$.

3.2. Physical Activity Levels before and during Pregnancy

Before pregnancy, 43.8% and 15.4% of participants had PA levels of 601–4000 and >4000 METs-min, respectively. About 60% revealed declines in PA levels during pregnancy when compared to pre-pregnancy levels; declines in PA (METs) were measured at 21.4%, 29.9%, and 7.8% for decreases of 1–600, 601–4000, and >4000 METs-min, respectively (Table 1).

Table 2 shows the proportions of participants who met the common recommended PA guidelines before and during pregnancy. Mean PA levels decreased from 2261 ± 3999 before pregnancy to 1252 ± 2258 METs-min/week during pregnancy ($p < 0.001$). The proportion of women who reported ≥600 METs-min/week PA decreased from 59.3% before pregnancy to 44.8% during pregnancy ($p < 0.001$). In terms of the type of PA, the decline among the proportion meeting vigorous PA ≥75 min/week was more than that of those meeting moderate PA ≥150 min/week (21.6% to 4.6% for vigorous; 20.9% to 10.8% for moderate; both $p < 0.001$). Walking is the most common type of PA among pregnant women in Taiwan, and is also the type recommended by the Mother's Handbook; the decline in walking ≥150 min/week appeared to be less pronounced (44.0% to 40.2%, $p < 0.001$).

Table 2. Physical Activity Before and During Pregnancy ($N = 747$).

Physical Activity	Pre-Pregnancy		During Pregnancy	
	n (%)	Mean METs (SD)	n (%)	Mean MET (SD)
Total physical activity		2261 (3999)		1252 (2258)
Vigorous (≥75min/wk)				
No	586 (78.4)	1618 (2985)	713 (95.4)	1150 (2071)
Yes	161 (21.6)	4603 (5913)	34 (4.6)	1625 (2815)
Moderate (≥150min/wk)				
No	591 (79.1)	1448 (2448)	666 (89.2)	947 (1702)
Yes	156 (20.9)	5340 (6488)	81 (10.8)	2408 (3438)
Walking (≥150min/wk)				
No	418 (56.0)	857 (2535)	447 (59.8)	690 (1504)
Yes	329 (44.0)	4045 (4743)	300 (40.2)	1967 (2794)
≥ 600METs-min/wk				
No	304 (40.7)	170 (201)	412 (55.2)	438 (679)
Yes	443 (59.3)	3696 (4679)	335 (44.8)	1811 (2743)

The comparisons of PA level at pre-pregnancy to pregnancy were performed using the chi-squared test or Student's t-test. All p were < 0.001 except for the mean METs between pre- and pregnancy at "Walking (≥150 min/wk) No," where $p = 0.03$. Abbreviations: METs = METs-min/week; min = min; wk = week.

The mean PA level was compared before and during pregnancy stratified by whether PA guidelines were met (Table 2). The mean METs-min/week appeared to be higher pre-pregnancy compared to during pregnancy (all $p < 0.001$) except for one. For those whose PA was <600 METs-min/week, their mean METs increased from 170 (before pregnancy) to 438 METs-min/week (during pregnancy; $p = 0.03$).

Declines in PA levels during pregnancy differed significantly by pre-pregnancy PA level (Table 3). Participants with higher pre-pregnancy PA levels showed greater declines during pregnancy than those with lower PA levels. For each pre-pregnancy PA level, about half of participants experienced substantial decreases during pregnancy when compared to their pre-pregnancy levels (50.4%, 54.4%, and 47.7% of those with >4000, 601–4000, and 1–600 METs-min before pregnancy had decreases of >4000, 601–4000, and 1–600 METs-min during pregnancy, respectively). For participants who were totally inactive before pregnancy (METs = 0), PA levels actually increased during pregnancy, although this was <600 METs-min/week.

Table 3. Declines in Physical Activity from Pre-pregnancy to Pregnancy Based on Pre-Pregnancy Levels ($n = 747$).

Decline in Physical Activity during Pregnancy	Physical Activity Before Pregnancy [a]				
	0 n (%)	1–600 n (%)	601–4000 n (%)	≥4000 n (%)	Total
No decline	152 (100)	80 (52.3)	61 (19.6)	10 (8.7)	306 (41)
1–600	0	73 (47.7)	85 (26)	2 (1.7)	160 (21.4)
601–4000	0	0	178 (54.4)	45 (39.1)	223 (29.9)
>4000	0	0	0	58 (50.4)	58 (7.8)
Total	152 (20.3)	153 (20.5)	327 (43.8)	115 (15.4)	747

p-values obtained via Fisher's exact test for frequency comparisons. $p < 0.0001$. [a] METs-min/week.

3.3. Crude Analysis of Factors Associated with Excessive GWG

In this study, 41.2% ($n = 308$) of participants experienced excessive GWG. Table 1 shows the crude associations between participant characteristics and excessive GWG. Of the study variables, pre-pregnancy BMI, pre-pregnancy PA levels, and declined PA during pregnancy were significantly related to excessive GWG. Participants with excessive GWG were significantly more likely to be overweight (23.1% versus 5.2%) and obese (14% versus 4.6%) before pregnancy. Those with excessive GWG showed both a higher mean pre-pregnancy PA level (2881 ± 4868 versus 1826 ± 3188 METs-min, $p = 0.001$) and greater mean decline in PA during pregnancy (1326 ± 3142 versus 785 ± 2657, $p = 0.014$). Using categorized PA levels, 20.8% of participants with excessive GWG were found to have pre-pregnancy PA levels >4000 METS-min, compared to 11.6% of those without excessive

GWG. About 11.7% of participants with excessive GWG showed declines >4000 METs-min during pregnancy, compared to 5% of those without excessive GWG. Other variables were not significantly related to excessive GWG.

3.4. Multivariate Logistic Regression Model on Factors Associated with Excessive GWG

Table 4 shows the multivariate regression results. Since pre-pregnancy PA was highly related to declined PA during pregnancy, we decided to use declined PA during pregnancy in the modeling. Further, older age was associated with a decreased odds for excessive GWG. Compared to participants who were younger than 30 years of age, those aged ≥40 and 30–39 were less likely to have excessive GWG (OR = 0.37, 95% CI: 0.16–0.86 for ≥ 40; OR = 0.66, 95% CI: 044–0.99 for 30–39). Pre-pregnancy BMI was positively associated with excessive GWG in that the OR for excessive GWG increased as body size increased from normal to overweight/obese comparing to participants who were underweight before pregnancy (ORs = 3.11, 17.29, and 12.71 for normal weight, overweight, and obesity, respectively). After adjusting for age and pre-pregnancy BMI, participants with PA declines >4000 METs-min during pregnancy were 2.38 (95% CI: 1.27–4.43) times more likely to have excessive GWG than those whose PA levels did not decline from pre-pregnancy to pregnancy. Other levels of decline (1–600, 601–4000 METS-min) were not significantly associated with excessive GWG (though OR estimates for these categories were 1.18, and 1.13, respectively).

Table 4. Logistic Regression Model for Factors Associated with Excessive Gestational Weight Gain ($n = 747$).

		OR [a]	95% CI	*p*-Value
Age (years)				
	20–29	1		
	30–39	0.66	(0.44–0.99)	0.045 *
	≥40	0.37	(0.16–0.86)	0.021 *
Pre-pregnancy BMI				
	Underweight	1		
	Normal	3.11	(1.78–5.41)	<0.0001 ***
	Overweight	17.29	(8.51–35.15)	<0.0001 ***
	Obese	12.71	(6.00–26.89)	<0.0001 ***
Declines in physical activity during pregnancy (METs)				
	No decline	1		
	1–600	1.18	(0.77–1.80)	0.441
	601–4000	1.13	(0.77–1.66)	0.519
	>4000	2.38	(1.27–4.43)	0.006 **

[a]. OR, odds ratio. ORs were adjusted for other variables in the model. Abbreviations: BMI = body mass index; CI = confidence interval; $p < 0.05$ *, $p < 0.01$ **, $p < 0.001$ ***.

4. Discussion

This study found that declines in PA levels >4000 METs-min/week from pre-pregnancy to pregnancy were positively associated with excessive GWG. While about 60% of participants decreased their PA levels during pregnancy, only those with high declines (>4000 METs-min/week) showed significant associations with excessive GWG. This finding may not be surprising, since GWG is influenced by many factors other than PA [35]; thus, only substantial declines in PA could retain statistical significance. Further, individuals with reduced levels of PA usually do not exhibit compensatory reductions in energy intake [36,37]. For that reason, a decrease in energy expenditure due to inactivity leads to a positive energy balance, thereby resulting in weight gain [38]. Contrary to previous observational studies, this study found that substantial declines in PA (rather than PA during pregnancy) was associated with excessive GWG. The lack of a significant association between PA and GWG demonstrated by previous observational studies may be due to the fact that PA levels are generally low among pregnant women [24,39]. The recommendations established by the ACOG, CDC, and ACSM assert that healthy women who engage in substantial amounts of PA can continue doing so during pregnancy unless there is a medical reason [16]. Based on the recommendations and our results, we suggest that low-risk pregnant women who are physically active before pregnancy should remain so during pregnancy in order to avoid excessive GWG.

There was a significant decline in the mean PA level from pre-pregnancy to pregnancy (2261 (SD 3999) to 1252 (SD 2258) METs-min/week, respectively). There were significant decreases in several types of PA during pregnancy, including vigorous PA, moderate-intensity PA, and even walking; based on proportions, however, declines were highest for vigorous (−17%), followed by moderate-intensity (−10.1%) and walking (−3.8%). These results are consistent with a previous study showing that, compared to pre-pregnancy levels, pregnant women experienced significant decreases in total PA levels during their second and third trimesters, including both vigorous and moderate-intensity activity types as well as walking [40]. Reasons for these declines may include self-identified physical limitations and restrictions, a lack of resources, decreased energy, and less time for exercise [41]. Further study is needed to examine reasons for decline in PA levels among pregnant women and to compare whether the reasons differed by their pre-pregnancy PA level and BMI group. Due to the overall benefits, pregnant women need exercise programs that are specifically designed around those barriers. In this regard, special attention should be given to help sustain pre-pregnancy PA levels, especially among women who were considered physically active prior to pregnancy.

Interestingly, we also found that about 40% of participants increased their PA levels during pregnancy, with those who were previously inactive being more likely to do so (pre-pregnancy 0 METs: 100%; ≦600 METs: 52.3% versus 601–4000 METs: 19.6%; >4000 METs: 8.7%; Table 3). Increased PA was mostly found in walking during the third trimester. A previous study found that participating women believed exercise helped them stay in shape and prepare for labor/delivery [42]. This study's results also suggest that the majority of women who are physically inactive before pregnancy may thus be motivated to increase their PA levels while pregnant. Since walking is widely accepted as a beneficial activity among pregnant women, this should be a good way to increase PA levels among women who were not physically active prior to pregnancy. A meta-analysis showed that exercise frequency of three times per week and exercise duration of 30 to 45 min each time can reduce maternal GWG for pregnant women [23]. However, what type and amount of exercise would most benefit pregnant women, or pregnant women with different BMIs or pre-pregnancy PA, remains to be explored by future studies.

More than 40% of this study's participants experienced excessive GWG, which supports previous findings [7]. This shows that emphasis should still be placed on appropriate weight gain during pregnancy. Further, more than 20% of participants were overweight/obese before pregnancy, which was also associated with excessive GWG. This also supports previous findings [4]. Health professionals should thus advise pregnant women on healthy GWG during pregnancy, with special attention given to those who are already overweight/obese.

In this study, a younger maternal age (<30 years) was associated with an increased risk of excessive GWG. The finding may be due to the fact that older women may be more concerned with appropriate GWG and smooth pregnancy experiences; as a result, they place greater emphasis on controlling weight gain during pregnancy. However, there is still controversy about whether this factor is generally associated with an increased or decreased risk for excessive GWG [43,44]. Regardless, the association between maternal age and excessive GWG requires additional research.

Limitations

The study women were from six clinics in a metropolitan area in northern Taiwan, posing concerns to the generalizability of the results. The study participants appeared to be older and more educated than the national data (mean age 32.12 and 58% with an educational level of university or higher in 2019 [45]). Although pre-pregnancy weights and heights were taken from medical records, pre-pregnancy weights were usually self-reported. As such, under- and over-reporting were possible issues. Physical activity was also self-reported; however, previous studies have supported the validity of the IPAQ-SF, which was used in this study [29]. Specifically, the IPAQ-SF enquires about PA during the preceding seven-day period; we averaged the two measures taken during the second and third trimesters to represent PA during pregnancy, since the two measures appeared to be similar. There was a lack of consideration of PA during the first trimester or of potential weekly differences in PA. Pre-pregnancy PA was self-reported in the second trimester and recall bias as well as the accuracy of the report may be a concern. Future studies should collect PA more often and include PA levels collected before pregnancy and during the first trimester in order to gain a more complete picture. In addition, an objective measure of PA such as an accelerometer could be used to further examine the validity of the IPAQ-SF and capture objective PA levels. A smaller effect may not be detected. We did not collect information on the total dietary calorie intake due to the complexity of the measure. Such unmeasured confounders could have influenced our results and should be considered in future studies.

5. Conclusions

A decrease in physical activity >4000 METs-min/week from pre-pregnancy to pregnancy was found to be a risk factor for excessive GWG. Women with substantial declines in PA from pre-pregnancy to pregnancy are usually those who were physically active prior to becoming pregnant. Health professionals should continue to develop strategies for counteracting the problematic trend of decreasing PA during pregnancy among low-risk pregnant women.

Author Contributions: L.-Y.C. designed and conceived the study. J.-J.S. and L.-Y.C. were involved in the data collection. J.-J.S. analyzed the data. J.-J.S. and L.-Y.C. interpreted the results and wrote the manuscript. All authors have read and agreed to the published version of the manuscript.

Funding: This work was supported by the Ministry of Science and Technology, Taiwan (MOST104-2314-B-010-029-MY3). The publication fee for this article was supported by the Ministry of Science and Technology (MOST108-2314-B-010-059-MY3).

Institutional Review Board Statement: This study was approved by institutional review boards at four hospitals (Far Eastern Memorial Hospital: 105073-F; Taiwan Adventist Hospital: 105-E-03; Taipei City Hospital: TEHIRB-10505103; Buddhist Tzu Chi General Hospital—Taipei Branch: 05-M01-005).

Informed Consent Statement: Informed consent was obtained from all subjects involved in the study.

Data Availability Statement: The datasets generated and/or analyzed during the current study are not publicly available due to confidentially reasons, but are available from the corresponding author on reasonable request.

Conflicts of Interest: The authors declare no conflict of interests.

References

1. Chen, C.; Xu, X.; Yan, Y. Estimated global overweight and obesity burden in pregnant women based on panel data model. *PLoS ONE* **2018**, *13*, e0202183. [CrossRef] [PubMed]
2. Poston, L.; Caleyachetty, R.; Cnattingius, S.; Corvalán, C.; Uauy, R.; Herring, S.; Gillman, M.W. Preconceptional and maternal obesity: Epidemiology and health consequences. *Lancet Diabetes Endocrinol.* **2016**, *4*, 1025–1036. [CrossRef]
3. Waits, A.; Guo, C.Y.; Chang, Y.S.; Chien, L.Y. Dose-response relationships between breastfeeding and postpartum weight retention differ by pre-pregnancy body-mass index in Taiwanese women. *Nutrients* **2020**, *12*, 1065. [CrossRef]
4. Liu, L.; Ma, Y.; Wang, N.; Lin, W.; Liu, Y.; Wen, D. Maternal body mass index and risk of neonatal adverse outcomes in China: A systematic review and meta-analysis. *BMC Pregnancy Childbirth* **2019**, *19*, 105. [CrossRef]
5. Lau, E.Y.; Liu, J.; Archer, E.; McDonald, S.M.; Liu, J. Maternal weight gain in pregnancy and risk of obesity among offspring: A systematic review. *J. Obes.* **2014**, *2014*, 524939. [CrossRef]
6. Ogden, C.L.; Carroll, M.D.; Flegal, K.M. High body mass index for age among US children and adolescents 2003–2006. *JAMA* **2008**, *299*, 2401–2405. [CrossRef]

7. Yong, H.Y.; Mohd Shariff, Z.; Koo, S.J.; Sa'ari, B.; Syurafak, N. Pre-pregnancy body mass index, height and physical activity are associated with rate of gestational weight gain among Malaysian mothers. *J. Obstet. Gynaecol. Res.* **2016**, *42*, 1094–1101. [CrossRef]
8. van der Wijden, C.L.; Steinbach, S.; van der Ploeg, H.P.; van Mechelen, W.; van Poppel, M.N. A longitudinal study on the relationship between eating style and gestational weight gain. *Appetite* **2014**, *83*, 304–308. [CrossRef] [PubMed]
9. Rasmussen, K.M.; Catalano, P.M.; Yaktine, A.L. New guidelines for weight gain during pregnancy: What obstetrician/gynecologists should know. *Curr. Opin. Obstet. Gynecol.* **2009**, *21*, 521. [CrossRef] [PubMed]
10. Weight Gain During Pregnancy. Atlanta at Centers for Disease Control and Prevention (US). Available online: https://www.cdc.gov/reproductivehealth/maternalinfanthealth/pregnancy-weight-gain.htm (accessed on 2 August 2020).
11. Body Mass Index by the Taiwan Health Promotion Administration. Available online: http://health99.hpa.gov.tw/OnlinkHealth/Onlink_BMI.aspx (accessed on 11 June 2020).
12. Waits, A.; Guo, C.Y.; Chien, L.Y. Inadequate gestational weight gain contributes to increasing rates of low birth weight in Taiwan: 2011–2016 nationwide surveys. *Taiwan J. Obstet. Gynecol.* **2021**, *60*, 857–862. [CrossRef]
13. Brown, J.; Ceysens, G.; Boulvain, M. Exercise for pregnant women with pre-existing diabetes for improving maternal and fetal outcomes. *Cochrane Database Syst. Rev.* **2017**, *12*, CD012696.
14. Physical Activity and Exercise During Pregnancy and the Postpartum Period by the American College of Obstetricians and Gynecologists. Available online: https://www.acog.org/clinical/clinical-guidance/committee-opinion/articles/2020/04/physical-activity-and-exercise-during-pregnancy-and-the-postpartum-period (accessed on 14 May 2021).
15. ACSM Health and Fitness Summit by the American College of Sports Medicine. Available online: http://forms.acsm.org/_frm/Summit2012/pdfs/72%20Mudd.pdf (accessed on 30 June 2021).
16. Healthy Pregnant or Postpartum Women by the Centers for Disease Control and Prevention (US). Available online: https://www.cdc.gov/physicalactivity/basics/pregnancy/index.htm (accessed on 17 September 2021).
17. Physical Activity Guidelines for Americans by the Disease Prevention and Health Promotion. Available online: https://health.gov/our-work/nutrition-physical-activity/physical-activity-guidelines/previous-guidelines/2008-physical-activity-guidelines (accessed on 5 November 2021).
18. Zhang, J.; Savitz, D.A. Exercise during pregnancy among US women. *Ann. Epidemiol.* **1996**, *6*, 53–59. [CrossRef]
19. Weng, S.S.; Lee, Y.H.; Chien, L.Y. Physical activity, sitting time and sleep duration before and during pregnancy and pregnancy outcomes: A prospective panel study. *J. Clin. Nurs.* **2020**, *29*, 3494–3505. [CrossRef] [PubMed]
20. Lamina, S.; Agbanusi, E. Effect of aerobic exercise training on maternal weight gain in pregnancy: A meta-analysis of randomized controlled trials. *Ethiop. J. Health Sci.* **2013**, *23*, 59–64. [PubMed]
21. Sanabria-Martínez, G.; García-Hermoso, A.; Poyatos-León, R.; Álvarez-Bueno, C.; Sánchez-López, M.; Martínez-Vizcaíno, V. Effectiveness of physical activity interventions on preventing gestational diabetes mellitus and excessive maternal weight gain: A meta-analysis. *BJOG* **2015**, *122*, 1167–1174. [CrossRef]
22. Streuling, I.; Beyerlein, A.; Rosenfeld, E.; Hofmann, H.; Schulz, T.; von Kries, R. Physical activity and gestational weight gain: A meta-analysis of intervention trials. *BJOG* **2011**, *118*, 278–284. [CrossRef]
23. Wang, J.; Wen, D.; Liu, X.; Liu, Y. Impact of exercise on maternal gestational weight gain: An updated meta-analysis of randomized controlled trials. *Medicine* **2019**, *98*, e16199. [CrossRef]
24. Chasan-Taber, L.; Silveira, M.; Lynch, K.E.; Pekow, P.; Solomon, C.G.; Markenson, G. Physical activity and gestational weight gain in Hispanic women. *Obesity* **2014**, *22*, 909–918. [CrossRef]
25. Han, S.; Middleton, P.; Crowther, C.A. Exercise for pregnant women for preventing gestational diabetes mellitus. *Cochrane Database Syst. Rev.* **2012**, *7*, CD009021. [CrossRef]
26. Kramer, M.S.; McDonald, S.W. Aerobic exercise for women during pregnancy. *Cochrane Database Syst. Rev.* **2006**, *3*, CD000180. [CrossRef]
27. Faul, F.; Erdfelder, E.; Lang, A.G.; Buchner, A. G* Power 3: A flexible statistical power analysis program for the social, behavioral, and biomedical sciences. *Behav. Res. Methods* **2007**, *39*, 175–191. [CrossRef]
28. International Physical Activity Questionnaire Short Form (IPAQ-SF) Taiwanese Version(in Chinese) by the Taiwan Health Promotion Administration. Available online: https://www.hpa.gov.tw/Pages/Detail.aspx?nodeid=876&pid=4900 (accessed on 1 November 2021).
29. Macfarlane, D.J.; Lee, C.C.; Ho, E.Y.; Chan, K.L.; Chan, D.T. Reliability and validity of the Chinese version of IPAQ. *J. Sci. Med. Sports* **2007**, *10*, 45–51. [CrossRef]
30. Sanda, B.; Vistad, I.; Haakstad, L.A.H.; Berntsen, S.; Sagedal, L.R.; Lohne-Seiler, H.; Torstveit, M.K. Reliability and concurrent validity of the International Physical Activity Questionnaire short form among pregnant women. *BMC Sports Sci. Med. Rehabil.* **2017**, *9*, 7. [CrossRef] [PubMed]
31. Fan, M.; Lyu, J.; He, P. Chinese guidelines for data processing and analysis concerning the International Physical Activity Questionnaire. *Zhonghua Liu Xing Bing Xue Za Zhi* **2014**, *35*, 961–964.
32. Lee, P.H.; Macfarlane, D.J.; Lam, T.H.; Stewart, S.M. Validity of the international physical activity questionnaire short form (IPAQ-SF): A systematic review. *Int. J. Behav. Nutr. Phys. Act.* **2011**, *8*, 115. [CrossRef] [PubMed]
33. Weight Gain during Pregnancy: Reexamining the Guidelines by the Institute of Medicine and National Research Council. Available online: https://www.cbsnews.com/htdocs/pdf/052809_pregnancy.pdf (accessed on 1 August 2021).

34. Guidelines for Data Processing and Analysis of the International Physical Activity Questionnaire (IPAQ) by the International Consensus Group. Available online: https://www.researchgate.net/file.PostFileLoader.html?id=5641f4c36143250eac8b45b7&assetKey=AS%3A294237418606593%401447163075131 (accessed on 2 August 2021).
35. Muktabhant, B.; Lawrie, T.A.; Lumbiganon, P.; Laopaiboon, M. Diet or exercise, or both, for preventing excessive weight gain in pregnancy. *Cochrane Database Syst. Rev.* **2015**, *15*, CD007145. [CrossRef]
36. Epstein, L.H.; Roemmich, J.N.; Paluch, R.A.; Raynor, H.A. Influence of changes in sedentary behavior on energy and macronutrient intake in youth. *Am. J. Clin. Nutr.* **2005**, *81*, 361–366. [CrossRef]
37. Stubbs, R.J.; Hughes, D.A.; Johnstone, A.M.; Horgan, G.W.; King, N.; Blundell, J.E. A decrease in physical activity affects appetite, energy, and nutrient balance in lean men feeding ad libitum. *Am. J. Clin. Nutr.* **2004**, *79*, 62–69. [CrossRef] [PubMed]
38. Ballor, D.L.; Keesey, R.E. A meta-analysis of the factors affecting exercise-induced changes in body mass, fat mass and fat-free mass in males and females. *Int. J. Obes.* **1991**, *15*, 717–726.
39. Kraschnewski, J.L.; Chuang, C.H.; Downs, D.S.; Weisman, C.S.; McCamant, E.L.; Baptiste-Roberts, K.; Zhu, J.; Kjerulff, K.H. Association of prenatal physical activity and gestational weight gain: Results from the first baby study. *Women's Health Issues* **2013**, *23*, e233–e238. [CrossRef]
40. Downs, D.S.; Chasan-Taber, L.; Evenson, K.R.; Leiferman, J.; Yeo, S. Physical activity and pregnancy: Past and present evidence and future recommendations. *Res. Q. Exerc. Sport* **2012**, *83*, 485–502. [CrossRef] [PubMed]
41. Marquez, D.X.; Bustamante, E.E.; Bock, B.C.; Markenson, G.; Tovar, A.; Chasan-Taber, L. Perspectives of Latina and non-Latina white women on barriers and facilitators to exercise in pregnancy. *Women Health* **2009**, *49*, 505–521. [CrossRef]
42. Lee, C.; Chiang, I.; Lin, S.; Lin, H.; Hsu, C. Physical activity pattern and related factors among women during pregnancy. *Formosan J. Med.* **2012**, *16*, 103–111.
43. Ebrahimi, F.; Shariff, Z.M.; Tabatabaei, S.Z.; Fathollahi, M.S.; Mun, C.Y.; Nazari, M. Relationship between sociodemographics, dietary intake, and physical activity with gestational weight gain among pregnant women in Rafsanjan City, Iran. *J. Health Popul. Nutr.* **2015**, *33*, 168–176. [PubMed]
44. Shulman, R.; Kottke, M. Impact of maternal knowledge of recommended weight gain in pregnancy on gestational weight gain. *Am. J. Obstet. Gynecol.* **2016**, *214*, e1–e754. [CrossRef] [PubMed]
45. Ministry of the Interior, Taiwan Statistical Report Year 2020 Week 20. Available online: https://www.moi.gov.tw/cp.aspx?n=11698https://www.moi.gov.tw/cp.aspx?n=11698 (accessed on 18 November 2021).

medicina

MDPI

Article

Incidence and Sociodemographic Correlates of Psychological Health Problems among Residents of the West Pomeranian Voivodeship during the COVID-19 Outbreak

Anna Maria Cybulska [1], Kamila Rachubińska [1,*], Małgorzata Starczewska [1], Labib Zair [2] and Mariusz Panczyk [3]

1 Department of Nursing, Faculty of Health Sciences, Pomeranian Medical University in Szczecin, Żołnierska 48, 71-210 Szczecin, Poland; anna.cybulska@pum.edu.pl (A.M.C.); malgorzata.starczewska@pum.edu.pl (M.S.)
2 Department of General Surgery and Transplantation, Pomeranian Medical University in Szczecin, Powstańców Wielkopolskich 72, 71-210 Szczecin, Poland; labib@poczta.onet.pl
3 Department of Education and Research in Health Sciences, Faculty of Health Science, Medical University of Warsaw, Litewska 14/16, 00-581 Warsaw, Poland; mariusz.panczyk@wum.edu.pl
* Correspondence: kamila.rachubinska@pum.edu.pl; Tel.: +48-721596764

Abstract: *Background and Objectives*: Psychological health problems have become an important topic of consideration for many scientists, because the epidemiology of these disorders is strongly influenced by stressful events such as the SARS-CoV-2 coronavirus pandemic. The aim of this study was to evaluate selected parameters of psychosocial functioning as well as socio-demographic correlates of depression, anxiety, sleep disorders and perceived stress among the residents of the West Pomeranian Voivodeship. *Materials and Methods*: An online questionnaire was completed by 323 participants, in whom the parameters of psychosocial functioning were assessed (symptoms of depression, anxiety, severity of sleep disorders and perceived stress). *Results*: The majority of the respondents (75.2%) scored high on the Perceived Stress Scale, and almost half of the respondents (47.1%) had sleep disorders. A total of 26% of the participants had no depressive symptoms. Age was significantly correlated with the severity of depressive symptoms and sleep disorders. There was a strong correlation between the severity of depression and anxiety (r = 0.76; $p < 0.0001$), a moderate correlation between depression and perceived stress (r = 0.47; $p < 0.0001$) and a strong correlation between depression and sleep disorders (r = 0.651; $p < 0.0001$). *Conclusions*: Age contributed to the severity of depressive symptoms and the occurrence of sleep disorders among the residents of the West Pomeranian Voivodeship during the SARS-CoV-2 pandemic. Some residents of the West Pomeranian Voivodeship showed moderate to severe depressive and anxiety symptoms, as well as high levels of stress and insomnia.

Keywords: health; COVID-19; SARS-CoV-2; depression; anxiety; stress; insomnia

Citation: Cybulska, A.M.; Rachubińska, K.; Starczewska, M.; Zair, L.; Panczyk, M. Incidence and Sociodemographic Correlates of Psychological Health Problems among Residents of the West Pomeranian Voivodeship during the COVID-19 Outbreak. *Medicina* **2022**, *58*, 196. https://doi.org/10.3390/medicina58020196

Academic Editors: Joachim G. Voss and Sandul Yasobant

Received: 24 November 2021
Accepted: 25 January 2022
Published: 27 January 2022

Publisher's Note: MDPI stays neutral with regard to jurisdictional claims in published maps and institutional affiliations.

1. Introduction

On 31 December 2019, a new coronavirus (COVID-19) disease emerged in Wuhan, Hubei Province, China, which was declared an international public health emergency by the World Health Organization (WHO) [1]. The scale of the pandemic gave rise to concern all over the world not only for the victims, but also for the psychological and socioeconomic consequences. Major changes that took place in the daily functioning of society contributed to increased psychological distress, including symptoms of depression, anxiety, stress, and sleep disorders [2]. The introduced restrictions, isolation, limits on civil liberties, and contact with an 'unknown enemy' against which there is no effective defense may have contributed to significant changes in the human psyche, including the development of generalized anxiety, depression, and anxiety symptoms.

There are individuals in society who are particularly vulnerable to stress and who cannot cope with a new and difficult situation. As a result of the restrictions imposed by the COVID-19 pandemic, many people may experience increased anxiety, loneliness or depression. In addition, all are forced to face new and serious challenges, such as financial difficulties. Moreover, the lack of opportunities or difficulties in developing effective methods of coping with stress, resulting, for example, from the lack of social support, may lead to emotional overload, including increased anxiety, sadness, and depressive symptoms. Most often, the conditions developed during a pandemic are an expression of temporary adaptation problems. However, in some people they may be a symptom of serious mental problems, requiring professional psychological care. Particularly prone to this stress are people who feel a real threat to their health or who have lost their jobs [3,4].

COVID-19 poses a threat to the physical health of both infected people and the general public. A Canadian survey demonstrated that 36% of the population was very concerned about the impact of COVID-19 on their health [5]. An online survey in China, based on the EuroQol-5D test assessing health-related quality of life, showed that 19% of the participants experienced physical pain or discomfort [6]. The COVID-19 pandemic, which has also severely affected the mental health of the public, may threaten the bodily integrity and autonomy of an individual, and subsequently result in comorbid psychiatric illnesses manifested by atypical symptoms, such as functional movement disorders [7,8].

Mental health is considered the most important condition for a good quality of life. Unfortunately, stressful events are strong adverse environmental factors that predispose people to mental disorders, especially depression [9]. During the COVID-19 pandemic, many people experienced negative emotional reactions; therefore, the National Health Commission issued guidelines to promote psychological crisis intervention targeted at patients, medical professionals, and civilians during the COVID-19 pandemic [10].

The aim of this study was to assess the severity of depression, anxiety, sleep disorders, and perceived stress depending on sociodemographic data, as well as to assess correlations between variables related to psychosocial functioning.

2. Materials and Methods

2.1. Settings and Design

The study adopted a cross-sectional survey design to assess the immediate psychological response of the residents of the West Pomeranian Voivodeship during the COVID-19 pandemic. An anonymous online questionnaire was used.

Due to the recommendations of the Polish government to minimize contact with other people, potential respondents were invited to take part in the survey electronically. The volunteers completed questionnaires in Polish via an online platform (https://docs.google.com/ accessed on 20 November 2021). The study received a positive opinion from the Bioethics Committee of the Pomeranian Medical University of Szczecin. The study was conducted in accordance with the principles contained in the Declaration of Helsinki. Participation in the study was voluntary and anonymous. The respondents were informed about the purpose of the study and the possibility of resignation and withdrawal of consent at each stage of the study.

The inclusion criteria for the study were: residency in the West Pomeranian Voivodeship; age over 18 years; and informed consent to participate in the study. The project was approved by the Bioethics Committee of the Pomeranian Medical University in Szczecin (KB-0012/25/04/2020/Z).

The size of the research sample was established on the basis of statistical data on the population of Szczecin and its vicinity aged 18–64 in 2020 [11]. The confidence level was set at 95%, the maximum error at 5%, and the estimated fraction size at 0.5. The total number of respondents who qualified for the study was 384. Finally, 323 respondents who correctly completed the questionnaires were included in the further analysis (Figure 1).

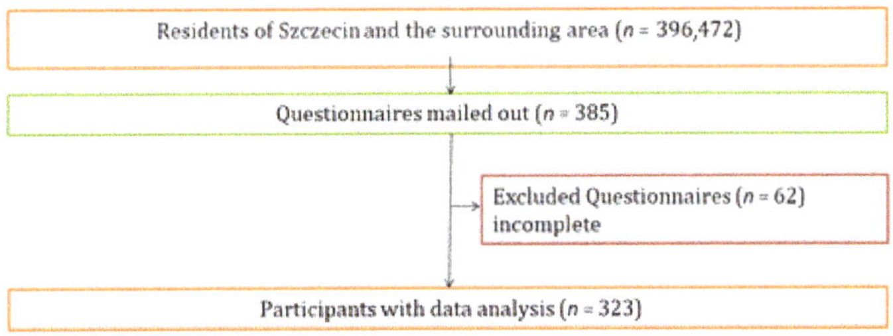

Figure 1. Flowchart of survey participation.

2.2. Research Instruments

The set of questionnaires was created after previous analysis of the literature on the impact of COVID-19 on the mental health of the population. The following standardized questionnaires were used:

Generalized Anxiety Disorder-7 (GAD-7): a screening tool used to determine feelings related to generalized anxiety disorder (GAD) [12].

Patient Health Questionnaire-9 (PHQ-9): a screening tool for depression, developed on the basis of the diagnostic criteria for depression included in the Diagnostic and Statistical Manual of Mental Disorders (DSM-IV) [13].

Athens Insomnia Scale (AIS): an eight-item scale that allows quantitative measurement of insomnia symptoms based on the ICD-10 criteria. The scale consists of eight statements regarding insomnia symptoms [14].

Perceived Stress Scale (PSS-10): an instrument used to assess the severity of stress related to the situation of the respondent in the last four weeks, in the context of subjective feelings and problems in personal life [15].

Demographic data (age, education, place of residence in the last 14 days, marital status, employment status, parental status, and household size), physical symptoms in the last 14 days (fever, chills, headache, muscle aches, cough, difficulty breathing, dizziness, sore throat, and persistent fever), history of exposure to COVID-19 (close contact with a person with confirmed COVID-19), and additional information required in relation to COVID-19 was collected using the authors' questionnaire.

2.3. Statistical Analysis

Descriptive statistics were calculated for sociodemographic characteristics, physical symptoms, contact history variables, and anxiety-related variables. The response rate was calculated based on the number of respondents per the total number of responses to the question. Analysis of quantitative variables (expressed as numbers) was performed by calculating the mean, standard deviation, median, quartiles, as well as minimum and maximum values. Student's t tests and ANOVA were used in this study.

All calculations were performed using STATISTICA TM 13.3 (TIBCO Software, Palo Alto, CA, USA). The level of statistical significance was set at $p < 0.05$.

3. Results

3.1. Characteristics of the Respondents

The study sample consisted of 323 individuals who correctly completed the questionnaires. The mean age was 35.4 years (SD = 10.9). The vast majority of the respondents were women: 79.3%; people in a formal relationship constituted 47.4%, those with higher education: 78.1%; and those living in a city with more than 100,000 inhabitants: 57% (Table 1).

Table 1. Sociodemographic variables.

Variables (N = 323)		n	%
Gender	Female	256	79.3
	Male	67	20.7
Marital status	Formal relationship	153	47.4
	Informal relationship	78	24.1
	Single/divorced/widowed	92	28.5
Education	Secondary	57	17.6
	post-secondary	14	4.3
	Higher (I)	99	30.7
	Higher (II)	141	43.7
	Higher (III)	12	3.7
Place of residence	village	67	20.7
	city with up to 10,000 people	16	5.0
	city with 10,000–100,000 people	56	17.3
	city with over 100,000 people	184	57.0
Children	No	160	49.5
	Yes	155	48.0
	Pregnancy	8	2.5

N, whole cohort size; n, number of; %, percent.

A total of 64.7% of the respondents had not been diagnosed with any chronic disease; 57.3% assessed their health as good; and 26.3% as very good. Only 9.6% of the subjects were in quarantine due to COVID-19, and 8.4% had a medical consultation in the past 14 days. Part of the participants (38.7%) had no contact with other people except for family members within four weeks of completing the survey questionnaire, whereas 31% had close contact and 20.4% had indirect contact with a person with confirmed COVID-19 infection.

Analysis was performed on depressive symptoms (according to the PHQ-9), anxiety (according to the GAD-7), sleep disorders (according to the AIS), and perceived stress (according to the PSS-10) among residents of the West Pomeranian Voivodeship during the SARS-CoV-2 pandemic.

For the Perceived Stress Scale, the mean score was 7.3 out of 10, and most of the respondents (75.2%) scored high. Mild anxiety was observed in 34.06%, moderate anxiety in 18.89%, and severe anxiety in 17.65% of the respondents. Almost half of the respondents (47.1%) suffered from sleep disorders. A total of 26% of the subjects had no depressive symptoms, while 28.79% showed mild, 23.53% moderate, 14.55% moderately severe, and 7.12% severe symptoms of depression (Tables 2 and 3).

Table 2. The psychosocial functioning (anxiety, depression, insomnia, stress) of the respondents.

	Severity Category (Points)					
Variables	**M**	**SD**	**Me**	**IQR/2**	**Min-Max**	**CV [%]**
AIS	7.56	4.51	7.0	3.5	0.0–24.0	59.6
GAD-7	15.34	5.95	14.0	4.5	7–28	38.8
PHQ-9	18.30	6.35	18.0	4.5	9–36	34.7
PSS-10	7.30	1.60	8.0	0.5	0.0–10.0	21.9

M—mean; SD—standard deviation; Me—median; IQR/2—interquartile range; Min—minimum; Max—maximum; CV—coefficient of variation; GAD-7—Generalized Anxiety Disorder-7; PHQ-9—Patient Health Questionnaire-9; AIS—Athens Insomnia Scale; PSS-10—Perceived Stress Scale.

Table 3. The psychosocial functioning (anxiety, depression, insomnia, stress) of the respondents.

	Severity Category		
	Variables (Points)	*n*	%
AIS	no insomnia disorder	171	52.9
	yes >8 points	152	47.1
GAD-7	no anxiety disorder (0–4 points)	95	29.41
	mild anxiety disorder (5–9 points)	110	34.06
	moderate anxiety disorder (10–14 points)	61	18.89
	severe anxiety disorder (15–21 points)	57	17.65
PHQ-9	no depression (0–4 points)	84	26.01
	mild depression (5–9 points)	93	28.79
	moderate depression (10–14 points)	76	23.53
	moderately severe depression (15–19 points)	47	14.55
	severe depression (20–27 points)	23	7.12
PSS-10	low stress (1–4 sten)	18	5.6
	medium stress (5–6 sten)	62	19.2
	high stress (7–10 sten)	243	75.2

GAD-7—Generalized Anxiety Disorder-7; PHQ-9—Patient Health Questionnaire-9; AIS—Athens Insomnia Scale; PSS-10—Perceived Stress Scale; *n*-number of, %-percent.

3.2. Analysis of the Relationship between Sociodemographic Variables (Age, Education, Place of Residence, Marital Status, Parental Status) and the Severity of Anxiety, Depression, Perceived Stress, and Insomnia among the Residents of the West Pomeranian Voivodeship during the SARS-CoV-2 Pandemic

Age was found to significantly correlate with the severity of depression and the presence of sleep disorders. There were no statistically significant correlations between age and the other scales (Table 4).

Table 4. Correlations between the respondents' age and their psychosocial functioning (anxiety, depression, insomnia, stress).

Psychosocial Functioning Parameters	**Pearson's r**	**t**	***p***
AIS	−0.11	−1.99	0.048
GAD-7	−0.06	−1.061	0.289
PHQ-9	−0.16	−2.907	0.004
PSS-10	0.01	0.155	0.877

GAD-7—Generalized Anxiety Disorder-7; PHQ-9—Patient Health Questionnaire-9; AIS—Athens Insomnia Scale; PSS-10—Perceived Stress Scale; t-Student's t-distribution, *p*—significance level.

Analysis of the data revealed statistically significant relationships between sex and the selected parameters of psychosocial functioning: depression, anxiety, and stress (Table 5).

Table 5. The psychosocial functioning (anxiety, depression, insomnia, and stress) of the respondents depending on their sex.

Variables	Women		Men		t	*p*
	M	SD	M	SD		
AIS	7.66	4.51	7.18	4.52	0.777	0.438
GAD-7	15.78	6.04	13.66	5.34	2.623	0.009
PHQ-9	18.71	6.38	16.75	6.00	2.270	0.024
PSS-10	7.40	1.49	6.90	1.92	2.328	0.021

M—mean; SD—standard deviation; t—Student's t-distribution, *p*—significance level; GAD-7—Generalized Anxiety Disorder-7; PHQ-9—Patient Health Questionnaire-9; AIS—Athens Insomnia Scale; PSS-10—Perceived Stress Scale.

Parental status was statistically significantly related to the severity of depression (PHQ-9). No other statistically significant correlations were observed between parental status and the other scales (Table 6).

Table 6. The psychosocial functioning (anxiety, depression, insomnia, stress) of the respondents depending on their parental status.

Variables	Children						F	*p* *
	Yes		No		Pregnancy			
	M	SD	M	SD	M	SD		
AIS	6.94	4.19	8.16	4.69	7.63	5.63	2.955	0.054
GAD-7	14.67	5.81	16.07	6.08	13.75	4.74	2.484	0.085
PHQ-9	17.14	5.98	19.53	6.54	16.25	5.09	6.201	0.002
PSS-10	7.30	1.68	7.31	1.52	7.00	1.51	0.141	0.868

M—mean; SD—standard deviation; F—the value of the test statistic; *p*—significance level; * one way ANOVA; GAD-7—Generalized Anxiety Disorder-7; PHQ-9—Patient Health Questionnaire-9; AIS—Athens Insomnia Scale; PSS-10—Perceived Stress Scale.

Analysis of the influence of other sociodemographic variables (education, place of residence, marital status) on levels of anxiety, depression, perceived stress, and insomnia among residents of the West Pomeranian Voivodeship during the SARS-CoV-2 pandemic did not reveal any statistically significant correlations (Supplementary material Tables S1–S3).

Analysis of the data demonstrated a strong, positive correlation between the severity of depression and the severity of anxiety ($r = 0.76$, $p < 0.001$) and the occurrence of sleep disorders ($r = 0.65$, $p < 0.001$), as well as a moderate positive correlation between depression and stress ($r = 0.45$, $p < 0.001$). Moreover, the level of anxiety strongly correlated with sleep disorders ($r = 0.53$, $p < 0.0001$) and the level of stress ($r = 0.50$ $p < 0.001$). The severity of stress showed a moderate correlation ($r = 0.32$, $p < 0.001$) with sleep disorders (Table 7).

Table 7. Correlations between the parameters of psychosocial functioning.

Variables		Pearson's r	t	*p*
GAD-7	AIS	0.53	11.24	<0.001
	PSS-10	0.50	10.236	<0.001
PHQ-9	GAD-7	0.76	21.14	<0.001
	AIS	0.65	15.35	<0.001
	PSS-10	0.45	8.919	<0.001
PSS-10	AIS	0.32	6.129	<0.001

GAD-7—Generalized Anxiety Disorder-7; PHQ-9—Patient Health Questionnaire-9; AIS—Athens Insomnia Scale; PSS-10—Perceived Stress Scale; *p*—significance level.

4. Discussion

The studies conducted so far among pandemic-affected populations clearly indicate its significant impact on their mental health [16]. There are many factors that predispose to mental illness [5,6]. The pandemic entails the need for quarantine and isolation, which are also among the risk factors with a psychological impact [4,7], as is worrying about the health of family, friends and acquaintances [17].

According to the pre-pandemic reports, symptoms of generalized anxiety disorder were found in about 9.6% of the Polish population, more often in women than in men [18]. On the other hand, Lubecka et al. [19] showed that the point criteria for anxiety disorders were met by 11.2% of the respondents, while a depressive episode was diagnosed in 14.4% [19].

The mental health of the general public is at greater risk compared to the situation before the outbreak [16,20]. Studies conducted during the previous SARS-CoV-1 epidemic showed that people who were directly affected (e.g., by quarantine) had psychiatric symptoms that lasted for several months after the epidemic ended [21], which may indicate that long-term SARS-CoV-2 consequences should also be expected. Our own study demonstrates anxiety of varying severity in the majority of the residents of the West Pomeranian Voivodeship. Similar results were obtained by Babicki et al. [8], who reported anxiety symptoms of different severity in about 75%, severe anxiety symptoms in 23%, and the features of generalized anxiety disorder in 44% of the respondents. Such a high percentage of positive results may be due to restrictions and the feeling of helplessness and powerlessness in the fight against the coronavirus. The possibility of direct interpersonal contact, which, according to specialists, is necessary to maintain a person's mental balance, was significantly limited [22,23]. Worldwide reports on the intensity of anxiety in populations severely affected by the COVID-19 pandemic, as in Poland, showed a significant increase in anxiety compared to the state before 2019. An analysis of a survey conducted with the use of the GAD-7 questionnaire among Chinese students showed that 25% of the respondents obtained a result indicating anxiety symptoms of varying severity [24]. A study of 1210 Chinese residents indicated the presence of anxiety symptoms in 36% of the subjects [25]. In addition, 51% of Iranians showed anxiety during the COVID-19 pandemic [26].

In our research, half of the respondents had moderate to severe depressive and anxiety symptoms, and 65% had moderate to severe anxiety symptoms. Our findings support the results obtained by Wang et al. [27] in their study based on the Impact of Event Scale-Revised (IES-R) and the Depression, Anxiety and Stress Scale (DASS-21), which confirmed a significant contribution of the COVID-19 epidemic to mental deterioration. Most of the respondents indicated a moderate or significant psychological impact of the epidemic and had major depressive symptoms. Among women, the impact of the epidemic on psychological functioning was more pronounced, as demonstrated by both the IES-R and the DASS-21 scales [27]. Another large population-based study conducted in China provided evidence that more than one-third (~35%) of the subjects experienced psychological distress ranging from mild to moderate (>29%) and severe (>5%) [28]. Verma et al. observed that the majority of the respondents in their study exhibited depressive and anxiety symptoms of varying severity [29]. Female sex, young age, higher education, student status, and having certain physical symptoms (muscle pain, dizziness, back pain) were significantly related to higher levels of stress, anxiety and depression [28,30,31]. Wang et al. also showed the negative impact of social media and massive amounts of information, as well as poor availability of personal protective equipment and accessibility to health care, on the level of psychological distress. Anxiety and depression are two different mental health disorders, and their biological development mechanisms are not identical [32].

As the data show, sex significantly differentiated the study group in terms of both anxiety and depressive symptoms. Women declared significantly more concerns about everyday life in the pandemic than men, and also showed significantly more depressive symptoms. However, due to large disparities between the studied groups of women and men, despite the use of appropriate tests, the observed differences should be approached with caution.

These results are consistent with those obtained by other authors, who also concluded that women are more likely to experience depression than men [33]. Furthermore, research conducted in Turkey during the pandemic indicates that women are more likely to suffer from depression than men [34]. A study conducted in China shows that women experience anxiety symptoms more often than men during a pandemic [30]. As shown by a study conducted in Poland at the beginning of May 2020, with a comparable number of women (49.7%) and men (50.3%), the incidence of both severe depressive symptoms and generalized anxiety is similar in women and in men [35]. Considering the above, and with some caution, due to the large disparities in the size of the studied groups of women and men, it can be concluded that women experience higher levels of anxiety and depressive symptoms during a pandemic.

In our study, almost half of the respondents developed sleep disorders. Roy et al. [36], based on their cross-sectional study conducted in India at the beginning of 2020, indicated that over 80% of the participants experienced preoccupation with COVID-19, and almost half felt panic about media reports.

Physical symptoms and poor self-rated health were significantly associated with a higher incidence of post-traumatic stress disorder and symptoms of stress, anxiety, and depression [37,38]. Both sleep problems [31] and suicidal thoughts [39] are serious mental health problems in the COVID-19 era. It can be hypothesized that deterioration in mental and physical health is significantly related to sleep problems and suicidal thoughts, which have become more common during the COVID-19 pandemic.

Ozamiz-Etxebarria et al. [40] found that women had more depressive, anxiety and stress-related symptoms than men, as measured by the DASS-21. The lowest severity of symptoms was recorded in the oldest age group (61 years and older). The authors suggest a link between this distribution of results and the additional stress experienced by young adults—mostly students—due to remote learning.

We found that age and parental status had an impact on the severity of depression, and age influenced the occurrence of sleep disorders. Research into the relationship between demographic characteristics and physical and mental health during the COVID-19 pandemic has revealed mixed results. One study provided evidence that aging people had a greater risk of physical pain or discomfort and depression or anxiety [14], while another research report revealed that young people were more likely to complain of mental health problems during the COVID-19 pandemic [18,23,31]. Moreover, several studies have confirmed that women are more likely to report poor mental health during the COVID-19 pandemic than men [18,23,25,32]. However, sex as a determinant of physical health during the COVID-19 pandemic has not been investigated. Further research is needed to determine if demographic factors are related to deterioration in physical and mental health during the COVID-19 pandemic.

The results of our research indicate a deterioration in the mental health of the residents of the West Pomeranian Voivodeship, but this problem affects people all over the world. A study conducted in China during the pandemic showed a significant decline in the well-being and mental health of the general population. A large population questionnaire-based study, performed using the Impact of Event Scale-Revised (IES-R) and the Depression, Anxiety and Stress Scale (DASS-21) demonstrated a significant contribution of the COVID-19 epidemic to psychological decline: 53.8% of the subjects reported a moderate or significant impact, 21.7% a mild impact, and only 24.5% experienced only a minimal psychological impact of the epidemic [27]. The results of the depression subscale of the DASS showed that 12.2% of the respondents experienced symptoms of moderate depression, and 4.3% had symptoms of severe depression. On the anxiety subscale, 7.5% of the subjects obtained results reflecting mild anxiety, 20.4%—moderate anxiety, and 8.4%—severe or very severe anxiety. According to the results of the stress subscale, 24.1% of the participants experienced mild stress, 5.5%—moderate stress, and 2.6%—severe stress.

An Italian study showed that sociodemographic variables explain about 30% of the variance in the results for anxiety, depression and stress [37]. This cross-sectional study used the DASS-21 and the Personality Inventory for DSM-5—Brief Form (PID-5-BF). For depressive symptoms, 17% of the subjects scored high and 15.4% scored very high; sociodemographic variables explained only about 9% of the variability in the results. Severe anxiety symptoms were declared by 7.2% of the respondents, and very severe by 12.6%. Young age, female sex, a family member with COVID-19, history of stressful events, and medical problems were associated with higher levels of anxiety. A total of 14.6% of the respondents declared a high level and 12.6%—a very high level of stress. Young age, female sex, the necessity of going to work (no possibility to work remotely), a history of stressful events and medical problems, and having a friend with a confirmed COVID-19 infection were associated with higher levels of stress. It can be assumed that most cases of elevated distress were related to adaptation difficulties and the trauma of the pandemic [36].

The analysis of the literature also confirms the results obtained. The groups of respondents in which high levels of anxiety, stress and depressive symptoms were observed, that is mainly young people, women, and people with offspring are described as those at higher risk of experiencing various types of mental health disorders as a consequence of the pandemic and the restrictions introduced in response to it [41–44].

5. Conclusions

- Our study demonstrated that during the pandemic, some residents of the West Pomeranian Voivodeship experienced moderate to severe depressive and anxiety symptoms, as well as sleep disorders and high levels of stress.
- During the COVID-19 pandemic, a negative impact on mental health was demonstrated in the study group of residents of the West Pomeranian Voivodeship, mainly including the risk of depression, anxiety or post-traumatic stress disorder. This was especially true for the elderly and people with parental status, as these respondents had experienced an increase in depression and a greater risk of sleep disorders.
- It has been shown that stress exposure is a risk factor for depressive symptoms and anxiety among the respondents; therefore, it is important to carefully monitor mental health during a pandemic so that preventative measures can be taken as early as possible.

6. Practical Recommendations

We divide recommendations by general lifestyle during the COVID-19 pandemic:

- Regular and sufficient sleep, regular and healthy meals, drinking sufficient fluids, and taking care of personal hygiene are essential not only for maintaining good physical health, but also for improving mental well-being.
- Taking up physical activity is not only essential for maintaining a healthy body, but it also helps to improve mood by lowering levels of stress hormones and stimulating the production of endorphins, and it has a beneficial effect on immune function.
- Using relaxation and stress reduction techniques (e.g., reading, writing, listening to music, meditation, autogenic training, and mindfulness exercises) can help you stay healthy and be aware of your emotions. When dealing with difficulties, talking openly about emotions with loved ones, asking for help, and feeling social support can be effective in reducing stress and anxiety.
- Enjoying interpersonal relationships: remember to meet regularly with your loved ones. Family time can include important conversations, party games or sports, eating meals and doing household chores together.
- Follow the WHO recommendations to stay up to date on pandemic and public health information by using credible news sources (e.g., watching reputable news programs once or twice a day) and limiting exposure to non-informed media. This can promote balanced and informed thinking about a pandemic.

Supplementary Materials: The following supporting information can be downloaded at: https://www.mdpi.com/article/10.3390/medicina58020196/s1. Table S1: The influence of education on the levels of anxiety, depression, perceived stress, and insomnia among the residents of the West Pomeranian Voivodeship during the SARS-CoV-2 pandemic. Table S2: The influence of place of residence on the levels of anxiety, depression, perceived stress, and insomnia among the residents of the West Pomeranian Voivodeship during the SARS-CoV-2 pandemic. Table S3: The influence of marital status on the levels of anxiety, depression, perceived stress, and insomnia among the residents of the West Pomeranian Voivodeship during the SARS-CoV-2 pandemic.

Author Contributions: Conceptualization, A.M.C. and K.R.; methodology, A.M.C. and K.R.; formal analysis, A.M.C., K.R. and M.S.; writing—original draft preparation, A.M.C.; writing—review and editing, K.R.; statistical analysis M.P.; supervision, M.S. and L.Z.; project administration, M.P. All authors have read and agreed to the published version of the manuscript.

Funding: This research received no external funding.

Institutional Review Board Statement: The study was carried out in accordance with the Declaration of Helsinki, and the protocol was approved by the Bioethical Commission of Pomeranian Medical University in Szczecin (approval number KB-0012/25/04/2020/Z). All subjects were informed about the study and all provided informed consent.

Informed Consent Statement: Informed consent was obtained from all subjects involved in the study.

Data Availability Statement: Data sharing not applicable.

Conflicts of Interest: The authors declare no conflict of interest.

References

1. Sohrabi, C.; Alsafi, Z.; O'Neill., N.; Khan., M.; Kerwan., A.; Al-Jabir, A.; Iosifidis, C.; Agha, R. World Health Organization declares global emergency: A review of the 2019 novel coronavirus (COVID-19). *Int. J. Surg.* **2020**, *76*, 71–76. [CrossRef] [PubMed]
2. Zhou, S.J.; Zhang, L.G.; Wang, L.L.; Guo, Z.C.; Wang, J.Q.; Chen, J.C.; Liu, M.; Chen, X.; Chen, J.X. Prevalence and socio-demographic correlates of psychological health problems in Chinese adolescents during the outbreak of COVID-19. *Eur. Child Adolesc. Psychiatry* **2020**, *29*, 749–758. [CrossRef] [PubMed]
3. Sekowski, M.; Gambin, M.; Hansen, K.; Holas, P.; Hyniewska, S.; Wyszomirska, J.; Pluta, A.; Sobańska, M.; Łojek, E. Risk of Developing Posttraumatic Stress Disorder in Severe COVID-19 Survivors, their Families and Frontline Healthcare Workers: What Should Mental Health Specialists Prepare For? *Front. Psychiatry* **2021**, *12*, 562899. [CrossRef] [PubMed]
4. Anderson, R.M.; Heesterbeek, H.; Klinkenberg, D.; Hollingsworth, T.D. How will country-based mitigation measures influence the course of the COVID-19 epidemic? *Lancet* **2020**, *395*, 931–934. [CrossRef]
5. Malhi, G.S.; Mann, J.J. Depression. *Lancet* **2018**, *392*, 2299–2312. [CrossRef]
6. Molarius, A.; Janson, S. Self-rated health, chronic diseases, and symptoms among middle-aged and elderly men and women. *J. Clin. Epidemiol.* **2002**, *55*, 364–370. [CrossRef]
7. Brooks, S.K. The psychological impact of quarantine and how to reduce it: Rapid review of the evidence. *Lancet* **2020**, *395*, 912–920. [CrossRef]
8. Babicki, M.; Mastalerz-Migas, A. Występowanie zaburzeń lękowych wśród Polaków w dobie pandemii COVID–19. *Psychiatr. Pol.* **2020**, *188*, 1–13.
9. Yang, L.; Zhao, Y.; Wang, Y.; Liu, L.; Zhang, X.; Li, B.; Cui, R. The effects of psychological stress on depression. *Curr. Neuropharmacol.* **2015**, *13*, 494–504. [CrossRef]
10. Soklaridis, S.; Lin, E.; Lalani, Y.; Rodak, T.; Sockalingam, S. Mental health interventions and supports during COVID- 19 and other medical pandemics: A rapid systematic review of the evidence. *Gen. Hosp. Psychiatry* **2020**, *66*, 133–146. [CrossRef]
11. Statistical Yearbook. *Zachodniopomorskie Voivodship 2020*; Statistical Office in Szczecin: Szczecin, Poland, 2020.
12. Spitzer, R.L.; Kroenke, K.; Williams, J.B.; Löwe, B. A brief measure for assessing generalized anxiety disorder. *Arch. Intern. Med.* **2006**, *166*, 1092–1097. [CrossRef] [PubMed]
13. Tomaszewski, K.; Zarychta, M.; Bieńkowska, A.; Chmurowicz, E.; Nowak, W.; Skalska, A. Walidacja polskiej wersji językowej Patient Health Questionnaire-9 w populacji hospitalizowanych osób starszych. *Psychiatr. Pol.* **2011**, *45*, 223–233. [PubMed]
14. Fornal-Pawłowska, M.; Wołyńczyk-Gmaj, D.; Szelenberger, W. Walidacja Ateńskiej Skali Bezsenności. *Psychiatr. Pol.* **2011**, *45*, 211–222. [PubMed]
15. Cohen, S.; Kamarck, T.; Mermelstein, R. *Skala Odczuwanego Stresu—PSS-10. W: Juczyński Z, Ogińska-Bulik N. Narzędzia do Pomiaru Stresu i Radzenia Sobie ze Stresem*; Pracownia Testów Psychologicznych PTP: Warszawa, Poland, 2009.
16. Fisher, A.; Roberts, A.; McKinlay, A.R.; Fancourt, D.; Burton, A. The impact of the COVID-19 pandemic on mental health and well-being of people living with a long-term physical health condition: A qualitative study. *BMC Public Health* **2021**, *21*, 1801. [CrossRef] [PubMed]

17. Vindegaard, N.; Benros, M.E. COVID-19 pandemic and mental health consequences: Systematic review of the current evidence. *Brain Behav. Immun.* **2020**, *89*, 531–542. [CrossRef] [PubMed]
18. Kiejna, A.; Piotrowski, P.; Adamowski, T.; Moskalewicz, J.; Wciórka, J.; Stokwiszewski, J.; Rabczenko, D.; Kessler, R.C. Epidemiology of mental disorders and access to mental health care. EZOP—Poland—research methodology. *Psychiatr. Pol.* **2015**, *49*, 15–27. [CrossRef]
19. Lubecka, B.; Lubecki, M.; Kasperczyk, J.; Jośko-Ochojska, J.; Pudlo, R. Risk Modifying Factors of Anxiety and Depressive Disorders, Using the Example of a Population Study in the Żywiec District. *Int. J. Environ. Res. Public Health* **2021**, *18*, 10248. [CrossRef]
20. Sonderskov, K.M.; Dinesen, P.T.; Santini, Z.I.; Ostergaard, S.D. The depressive state of Denmark during the COVID-19 pandemic. *Acta Neuropsychiatr.* **2020**, *132*, 226–228. [CrossRef]
21. Peng, E.Y.-C. Population-based post-crisis psychological distress: An example from the SARS outbreak in Taiwan. *J. Formos. Med. Assoc.* **2010**, *109*, 524–532. [CrossRef]
22. Xiao, C. A novel approach of consultation on 2019 novel coronavirus (COVID–19)-Related psychological and mental problems: Structured letter therapy. *Psychiatry Investig.* **2020**, *17*, 175–176. [CrossRef]
23. Kmietowicz, Z. Rules on isolation rooms for suspected COVID–19 cases in GP surgeries to be relaxed. *BMJ* **2020**, *368*, m707. [CrossRef] [PubMed]
24. Heerwegh, D. Mode differences between face-to-face and web surveys: An experimental investigation of data quality and social desirability effects. *Int. J. Public Opin. Res.* **2009**, *21*, 111–121. [CrossRef]
25. Burns, J.; Christensen, H.; Luscombe, G.; Mendoza, J.; Bresnan, A.; Blanchard, M.; Hickie, I. *Game on: Exploring the Impact of Technologies on Young Men's Mental Health and Wellbeing*; Findings from the First Young and Well National Survey; Young and Well Cooperative Research Centre: Melbourne, VIC, Australia, 2013.
26. Milton, A.C.; Ellis, L.A.; Davenport, T.A.; Burns, J.M.; Hickie, I.B. Comparison of Self-Reported Telephone Interviewing and Web-Based Survey Responses: Findings from the Second Australian Young and Well National Survey. *JMIR Ment. Health* **2017**, *4*, e37. [CrossRef] [PubMed]
27. Wang, C.; Pan, R.; Wan, X.; Tan, Y.; Xu, L.; Ho, C.S. Immediate psychological responses and associated factors during the initial stage of the 2019 coronavirus disease (COVID–19) epidemic among the general population in china. *Int. J. Environ. Res. Public Health* **2020**, *17*, 1729. [CrossRef]
28. Qiu, J.; Shen, B.; Zhao, M.; Wang, Z.; Xie, B.; Xu, Y. A nationwide survey of psychological distress among Chinese people in the COVID-19 epidemic: Implications and policy recommendations. *Gen. Psychiatry* **2020**, *b33*, e100213. [CrossRef]
29. Verma, S.; Mishra, A. Depression, anxiety, and stress and socio-demographic correlates among general Indian public during COVID-19. *Int. J. Soc. Psychiatry* **2020**, *66*, 756–762. [CrossRef]
30. Huang, Y.; Zhao, N. Generalized anxiety disorder, depressive symptoms and sleep quality during COVID-19 outbreak in China: A web-based cross-sectional survey. *Psychiatry Res.* **2020**, *288*, 112954. [CrossRef]
31. Li, S.; Wang, Y.; Xue, J.; Zhao, N.; Zhu, T. The impact of COVID-19 epidemic declaration on psychological consequences: A study on active Weibo users. *Int. J. Environ. Res. Public Health* **2020**, *17*, 2032. [CrossRef]
32. Wang, Y.; Di, Y.; Ye, J.; Wei, W. Study on the public psychological states and its related factors during the outbreak of coronavirus disease 2019 (COVID-19) in some regions of China. *Psychol. Health Med.* **2020**, *30*, 1e10. [CrossRef]
33. Jasik, K.; Jaślikowska, U.; Zbrojkiewicz, M.; Ślusarska, B.; Jasińska, M.; Grzegorczyk, M.; Nowicki, G.J. Czynniki związane z występowaniem depresji u osób dorosłych. Przegląd systematyczny literatury polskiej w latach 2009–2014. *J. Educ. Health Sport* **2016**, *6*, 297–318.
34. Firat, M.; Okanlı, A.; Kanbay, Y.; Utkan, M.; Demir Gökmen, B. The prevalence of pandemic anxiety, anxiety and depression during the COVID-19 pandemic in Turkey. *Psychiatry Clin. Psychopharmacol.* **2021**, *31*, 198–205. [CrossRef]
35. Gambin, M.; Sękowski, M.; Woźniak-Prus, M.; Cudo, A.; Hansen, K.; Gorfol, J.; Huflej-Łukasik, M.; Kmit, G.; Kubicka, K.; Łyś, A.E.; et al. *Uwarunkowania Objawów Depresji i Lęku Uogólnionego u Dorosłych Polaków w Trakcie Epidemii COVID-19—Raport z Pierwszej Fali Badania Podłużnego*; Uniwersytet Warszawski: Warsaw, Poland, 2020; pp. 1–27.
36. Roy, D.; Tripathy, S.; Kar, S.K.; Sharma, N.; Verma, S.K.; Kaushal, V. Study of knowledge, attitude, anxiety & perceived mental healthcare need in Indian population during COVID-19 pandemic. *Asian J. Psychiatry* **2020**, *51*, 102083.
37. Mazza, C.; Ricci, E.; Biondi, S.; Colasanti, M.; Ferracuti, S.; Napoli, C.; Roma, P. A Nationwide Survey of Psychological Distress among Italian People during the COVID-19 Pandemic: Immediate Psychological Responses and Associated Factors. *Int. J. Environ. Res. Public Health* **2020**, *2*, 3165. [CrossRef] [PubMed]
38. Douglas, P.K.; Douglas, D.B.; Harrigan, D.C.; Douglas, K.M. Preparing for pandemic influenza and its aftermath: Mental health issues considered. *Int. J. Emerg. Ment. Health* **2009**, *11*, 137–144.
39. Garza, K.; Jovanovic, T. Impact of Gender on Child and Adolescent PTSD. *Curr. Psychiatry Rep.* **2017**, *19*, 87. [CrossRef]
40. Ozamiz-Etxebarria, N.; Dosil-Santamaria, M.; Picaza-Gorrochategui, M.; Idoiaga-Mondragon, N. Stress, anxiety, and depression levels in the initial stage of the COVID-19 outbreak in a population sample in the northern Spain. *Cad. Saude Publica* **2020**, *36*, e00054020. [CrossRef]
41. Alkhamees, A.A.; Alrashed, S.A.; Alzunaydi, A.A.; Almohimeed, A.S.; Aljohani, M.S. The psychological impact of COVID-19 pandemic on the general population of Saudi Arabia. *Compr. Psychiatry* **2020**, *102*, 152192. [CrossRef]

42. Benke, C.; Autenrieth, L.K.; Asselmann, E.; Pane-Farre, C.A. Lockdown, quarantine measures, and social distancing: Associations with depression, anxiety and distress at the beginning of the COVID-19 pandemic among adults from Germany. *Psychiatry Res.* **2020**, *293*, 113462. [CrossRef]
43. Pedrosa, A.; Bitencourt, L.; Fróes, A.; Cazumbá, M.; Campos, R.; de Brito, S.; Simões e Silva, A. Emotional, Behavioral, and Psychological Impact of the COVID-19 Pandemic. *Front. Psychol.* **2020**, *11*, 566212. [CrossRef]
44. Smith, L.; Jacob, L.; Yakkundi, A.; McDermott, D.; Armstrong, N.; Barnett, Y.; López-Sánchez, G.; Martin, S.; Butler, L.; Tully, M. Correlates of symptoms of anxiety and depression and mental wellbeing associated with COVID-19: A cross-sectional study of UK-based respondents. *Psychiatry Res.* **2020**, *291*, 113138. [CrossRef]

International Journal of
Environmental Research and Public Health

MDPI

Article

Development of the Psychological Capital Scale for Male Nursing Students in Taiwan and Testing Its Measurement Invariance between Genders

Jiunnhorng Lou [1], Renhau Li [2] and Shuling Chen [3,*]

[1] Department of Nursing, Hsin Sheng College of Medical Care and Management, Taoyuan 325004, Taiwan; stujhl@gmail.com
[2] Department of Psychology, Chung-Shan Medical University, Taichung 40201, Taiwan; davidrhlee@yahoo.com.tw
[3] Department of Nursing, Hungkuang University, Taichung 433304, Taiwan
* Correspondence: slchen@hk.edu.tw; Tel.: +886-4-26318652 (ext. 3100)

Abstract: The aims of this study were to develop a psychological capital (PsyCap) scale for male nursing students and to compare the scores with those of female nursing students. Few past studies have focused on male nursing students to understand their PsyCap relative to female nursing students. We recruited 384 male nursing students in Taiwan to construct the PsyCap Scale with 16 items and four factors based on the relevant literature: hope, optimism, resiliency, and self-efficacy. The scale showed good model fit in confirmatory factor analysis with factor loadings from 0.62 to 0.78. Cronbach's alpha coefficients ranged from 0.75 to 0.83 for the four subscales and 0.91 for the total scale. We also conducted measurement invariance tests with data from 402 female nursing student volunteers in Taiwan. The invariance of factor loadings and intercepts of the established scale (i.e., with the same unit and origin between genders) indicated that the male nursing students had higher PsyCap in optimism and resiliency than the females. We developed a 16-item-scale to make administration rapid and convenient and applied advanced statistical methods for reliable and valid comparisons between sexes. The results may help the government to create education programmes or policies supporting male nursing students.

Keywords: male nursing students; psychological capital; hope; optimism; resiliency; self-efficacy; measurement invariance; brief scale

Citation: Lou, J.; Li, R.; Chen, S. Development of the Psychological Capital Scale for Male Nursing Students in Taiwan and Testing Its Measurement Invariance between Genders. *Int. J. Environ. Res. Public Health* **2022**, *19*, 3620. https://doi.org/10.3390/ijerph19063620

Academic Editor: Paul B. Tchounwou

Received: 18 February 2022
Accepted: 15 March 2022
Published: 18 March 2022

1. Introduction

Nursing has long been considered a profession predominately for women, and 'nursing knowledge' is equal to 'women's knowledge' from the perspective of traditional occupational and social culture. Therefore, the public image of nurses is tightly connected to that of good women and good mothers. As there are fewer studies, it is not known whether this perception of nursing decreases the psychological capital (PsyCap) of male nursing students and it therefore deserves further exploration.

PsyCap is an individual's positive psychological resource [1] that reflects a positive psychological state in their personal growth and development. It enables self-efficacy and characterises an individual's advantages, thus allowing them to realise their valuable potential [2]. Additionally, PsyCap encompasses invisible capital and positive energy, and it focuses on personal positive psychological development and strives to present personal good or positive facets, which enable one to overcome frustration and face hard times in life with a positive attitude [3]. Da et al. [4] argued that people with abounding PsyCap expect to have positive experiences at work, believe they are capable of achieving success, are unlikely to be influenced by setbacks, and are willing to help others. If students persist in their self-efficacy and resiliency, they are likely to earn good grades and have success in academic achievement [5,6]. Therefore, PsyCap emphasises positive psychological development, thus helping accumulate psychological resources [7]. PsyCap includes hope, optimism, resiliency, and self-efficacy [8,9]. Luthans, Youssef, and Avolio [10] described the four constructs as follows: hope—an approach to acquiring success with volition and effort; optimism—positive expectations about the future and attributions to the present; resiliency—coping well with adversity and negativity, and recovering quickly from setbacks to achieve success; and self-efficacy—the confidence to obtain success by making optimum efforts when facing challenging tasks. An et al. [11] thought that when someone has high PsyCap, they can offer more resources to organisational operations, maintain better relationships with colleagues, have optimistic perceptions and positive self-affirmation, and achieve positive performance.

PsyCap is a kind of psychological state with progressive development, thus significantly affecting nursing students' professional identification and nursing careers [12,13]. It can promote personal positive psychological development, help nursing students reach their present and future goals, and overcome obstacles to success [14]. Hence, PsyCap is viewed as an index to assess factors involving one's positive psychological development, such as success, learning satisfaction, well-being reinforcement, and achieving desirable goals [15]. Students with lower PsyCap had higher dropout rates [16]; however, nursing students with higher PsyCap would take different viewpoints towards learning stress and perform better in learning adjustment [17]. Eun and Mi-Ra [18] pointed out that PsyCap has a significant positive correlation with academic achievement. Terry et al. [19] also found that PsyCap helped nursing students in their study process by reinforcing their ability to overcome difficulties. However, Manoochehri et al. [20] found that gender has different relationships with PsyCap and spirituality. Pan et al. [21] found that PsyCap helped male nurses in the practice environment to develop their professional ability fully and increase their intent to engage in work. Some research has also found that male nursing students want people to refer to them as nurses rather than male nurses [22]. These studies imply that more research should be conducted to understand male nursing students in terms of variables, such as PsyCap, in comparison to female nurses.

In summary, PsyCap also has a positive influence on male nursing students' development of their nursing careers, professional performance, and role orientation. However, only a few studies have investigated the PsyCap of male nursing students relative to that of female nursing students; thus, more efficient education programmes for them cannot be developed. Whether the advantages of PsyCap for female nursing students are similar to those for male nursing students would need more research. In the present study, the PsyCap Scale for male nursing students was developed, and its differences relative to female nursing students were tested using advanced statistical methods.

2. Materials and Methods

The study was of an explanatory research design type, which employed a pragmatic methodology in terms of approach. It included a qualitative approach to literature review for writing a draft of the PsyCap Scale and for its scrutiny by experts, and a quantitative approach to data collection and statistical analysis using a cross-sectional survey method. The questionnaire included gender, age, general learning experiences, and a draft of the PsyCap Scale. The study was approved by the Institutional Review Board (IRB No. 202110-E101).

2.1. Procedures

In accordance with the definitions of PsyCap, a draft with 31 items was first developed by the authors, including seven items for hope, seven items for optimism, nine items for resiliency, and eight items for self-efficacy. After the draft of the scale was completed, five subject matter experts, including four nursing professionals and one psychological professional, were invited to participate. The purpose of the expert review was to test the content validity and construct the validity of the measurement tool and determine if the content adequacy, conceptual clarity, and question meaning were consistent in each subscale [23]. We deferred to their suggestions and reorganised the related item contents accordingly.

There were 1071 male nursing students studying in 18 nursing schools [24]. We utilised a purposive sampling design to recruit participants from each of the two nursing schools in the Northern, Central, and Southern areas of Taiwan. The follow-up procedure included a quantification administration of the male nursing students we recruited. The data were subjected to item selection by confirmatory factor analysis using LISREL 8.8 software, referring to Li [25], to obtain a formal version of the PsyCap Scale. To understand the status of PsyCap for male nursing students, we collected data from another questionnaire conducted on female nursing students for comparison. Measurement invariance tests were conducted to ensure meaningful comparisons between male and female nursing students on a common scale [26].

2.2. Participants

A total of 384 male nursing students from six nursing schools in Taiwan were recruited for this study. They were the main sample participants in the study, with their ages ranging from 18.1 to 23.5 years. The mean age of the sample was 21.00 years, and the standard deviation for age was 0.89. Of the 384 participants, 64.4% (247) had religious beliefs. We also recruited a sample of 402 female nursing students from a nursing school in Taiwan, with their ages ranging from 20.0 to 24.0 years. The mean age of the female nursing students was 20.61 years, with a standard deviation of 1.36. Of the 402 participants, 61.9% (249) had religious beliefs.

2.3. Instrument

To develop the PsyCap Scale for male nursing students, we referred to the existing literature [14,27–31] to obtain the connotations of the four subscales. Connotations for hope included a positive motivation state under which one orients to their goal to realize it; when the way to their goal is not available or is thwarted, they find another way, and never give up. Optimism was characterised by positive psychological characteristics that help individuals to cope with stress and adverse conditions. It is also a kind of working theory or style for attributing positive events and their persistence to the self, while attributing adverse events to external and situational factors. Resiliency was defined as the capability to bounce back or recover quickly from disadvantageous situations. It has important implications for promoting ability, such as obtaining positive energy and persistent belief, as well as the ability to overcome challenges, cope with stress, and endure plight to achieve success. Regarding self-efficacy, this was characterised as the belief in oneself that one can succeed when facing challenges and adversity. This belief stems from self-confidence in accomplishing a specific task.

Therefore, we created a 31-item draft encompassing the four dimensions. The draft of the scale was scored using a five-point Likert scale. Point 1 represented strongly disagree, 2 represented disagree, 3 represented no comment, 4 represented agree, and 5 represented strongly agree. Higher scores represented higher hope, optimism, resiliency, and self-efficacy; therefore, the higher the sum of all items, the higher the PsyCap. The content validity index was calculated according to the opinions and evaluations from the five experts, and it was 0.91.

2.4. Statistical Analyses

Structural equation modelling (SEM) was applied in the analyses. We randomly selected 60% (230) of the 384 male nursing students to test the four-factor model of the PsyCap Scale for confirmatory factor analysis. The measurement model of SEM was used to test the fit of the 31 items with the four factors. Li's [25] item selection strategies, mainly based on a modification index involving factor loadings or item error correlations, were considered in the test. In addition, items with factor loadings lower than 0.60 were eliminated. Once the final items were selected, the total male sample was used to confirm the four-factor model. The common model fit indices are listed [32,33], such as χ^2/df (the ratio of chi-square to degrees of freedom) < 5, comparative fit index (CFI) > 0.90, non-normed fit index (NNFI) > 0.90, adjusted goodness of fit index (AGFI) > 0.90, standardised root mean square residual (SRMR) < 0.06, and root mean square error of approximation (RMSEA) < 0.08.

In addition, to ensure that scores between male and female nursing students could be reliably compared, measurement invariance tests were conducted based on nested models. The steps included factor pattern invariance (configural invariance), factor loading invariance (metric invariance), and intercept invariance (scalar invariance) to ensure meaningful comparisons under a common origin and unit of scale. Measurement invariance tests were conducted mainly on the basis of differences in chi-square values ($\Delta\chi^2$) and degrees of freedom (Δdf) between the nested models. When $\Delta\chi^2$ was not significant, it indicated that constraining parameter estimates to be the same between genders was plausible because invariance had been built up. Once the measurement invariances were built up, the mean differences of the four factors could be acquired between genders.

3. Results

The four-factor model with 31 items was first tested using confirmatory factor analysis. The model fit indices showed $\chi^2 = 868.54$, $df = 428$, p-value < 0.001, $\chi^2/df = 2.03$, CFI = 0.98, NNFI = 0.98, AGFI = 0.85, SRMR = 0.045, and RMSEA = 0.052, indicating poor model fit. The factor loadings ranged from 0.59 to 0.78, with a mean factor loading of 0.67. The correlation coefficients among the four factors ranged from 0.75 to 0.92. The Cronbach's alpha reliability coefficients ranged from 0.85 to 0.89 for the four subscales and 0.95 for the total scale.

To promote the convenient use of the scale and increase the model fit to avoid validity shrinkage in other applied research, fewer and better items would be suitable. In the item selection process, eight items were eliminated because of high correlation between item errors, four items were eliminated because of loadings on non-principal factors, and three items were eliminated because of lower factor loadings. Finally, 16 items were selected based on the modification index of the SEM. The model fit indices for the model of the four factors with 16 items were $\chi^2 = 142.20$, $df = 98$, p-value = 0.02, $\chi^2/df = 1.45$, CFI = 0.99, NNFI = 0.99, AGFI = 0.94, SRMR = 0.035, and RMSEA = 0.034, indicating better model fit outcomes in general. The contents of the 16 items with four factors, their factor loadings, and reliability coefficients are presented in Table 1. It shows that the factor loadings ranged from 0.62 to 0.78, with a mean factor loading of 0.68, indicating better convergent validity. The Cronbach's alpha reliability coefficients were from 0.75 to 0.83 for the four subscales and 0.91 for the total scale, still indicating good internal consistency reliability. The correlation coefficients among the four factors ranged from 0.73 to 0.91. Although the correlation coefficients were a little high in general, the four-factor model passed the discrimination validity test compared with three-factor models by chi-squared difference tests (not shown in the tables).

Table 1. Factor loadings and reliability coefficients of the PsyCap Scale (N = 384).

Items	Factor Loading	Cronbach's Alpha
1. I have the power in my heart to support my learning in nursing.	0.76	
2. I struggle to reach the goal of being a nurse	0.78	
3. I think the nursing profession offers me a more promising future	0.75	
4. I would console myself and persist while facing plight in learning	0.68	0.83
5. I can face uncertainty with a positive attitude towards learning nursing	0.68	
6. I can face various difficulties with a positive attitude towards learning nursing	0.64	
7. I can actively search for solutions to problems in my nursing education	0.65	
8. I can maintain a positive belief in my prospects as a nurse in any situation	0.67	0.75
9. I can learn and grow from errors while facing problems	0.69	
10. I can find relevant persons (e.g., teacher, classmate, and senior schoolmate) to help solve problems	0.63	
11. I can face frustrations bravely during my nursing education	0.63	
12. I can recover rapidly from anger to a normal emotion while learning nursing	0.67	0.75
13. I am enthusiastic about learning nursing to realise my dream	0.69	
14. I dedicate myself to my future and goal	0.69	
15. I am confident to cope with accidents in my nursing education	0.70	
16. I believe that I can solve any problems related to learning nursing	0.62	0.77

Note: Hope includes items 1–4, Optimism includes items 5–8, Resiliency includes items 9–12, and Self-efficacy includes items 13–16. The Cronbach's alpha coefficient for all items was 0.91. The mean (standard deviation) for the Hope subscale is 14.27 (3.51), for the Optimism subscale is 14.53 (3.48), for the Resiliency subscale is 14.29 (3.52), for the Self-efficacy subscale is 13.54 (3.59), and for the PsyCap Scale is 56.63 (12.13).

Next, to avoid measurement errors interfering in male nursing students' PsyCap Scale scores for comparison with those of female nursing students, we conducted a series of measurement invariance tests (Table 2). The top panel of Table 2 shows that the models for both male and female nursing students passed tests involving configural invariance, metric invariance, and scalar invariance. Specifically, the good model fit indices of Model A, such as $\chi^2 = 351.03$, $df = 196$, p-value < 0.001, $\chi^2/df = 1.79$, CFI = 0.99, RMSEA = 0.045, and SRMR = 0.035 for male and 0.043 for female nursing students, indicated the same number of factors for both genders (configural invariance). Model B was compared to Model A with $\Delta\chi^2 = 9.74$ and $\Delta df = 12$, with a non-significant result ($p > 0.05$), indicating the same factor loadings between genders (metric invariance). Additionally, Model C was compared to Model B with $\Delta\chi^2 = 20.24$ and $\Delta df = 12$, also having a non-significant result ($p > 0.05$), indicating the same intercepts between genders (scalar invariance).

Table 2. Tests of measurement invariance in the PsyCap Scale between genders.

Models	Compared Model	χ^2 (df)	RMSEA	CFI	SRMR	$\Delta\chi^2$ (Δdf)
A. Configural invariance		351.03(196)	0.045	0.986	0.035/0.043	
B. Complete metric invariance	A	360.77(208)	0.043	0.986	0.037/0.049	9.74(12)
C. Complete scalar invariance	B	381.01(220)	0.043	0.985	0.037/0.049	20.24(12)
D. Complete invariance of error variances	C	528.11(236)	0.056	0.975	0.044/0.059	147.10(16) ***
E. Partial invariance of error variances	C	390.80(225)	0.043	0.985	0.038/0.051	9.79(5)
F. Complete invariance of factor variances	C	402.26(224)	0.045	0.984	0.083/0.085	21.25(4) ***
G. Partial invariance of factor variances	C	386.57(222)	0.043	0.985	0.056/0.061	5.56(2)
H. Complete invariance of factor covariances	G	406.30(228)	0.045	0.983	0.066/0.068	19.73(6) **
I. Partial invariance of factor covariances	G	389.89(225)	0.043	0.985	0.055/0.064	3.32(3)
J. Complete invariance of latent means	F	443.11(228)	0.049	0.980	0.082/0.084	40.85(4) ***
K. Partial invariance of latent means	F	406.47(226)	0.045	0.983	0.083/0.085	4.21(2)

** $p < 0.01$. *** $p < 0.001$.

After the three invariance tests involving the A, B, and C models were confirmed, the variances, covariances, and means of the four factors were compared between genders in the common unit (by metric invariance) and origin (by scalar invariance) of factors in the scale. The lower panel in Table 2, also called the structure invariance test, shows comparisons between genders in the variances, covariances, and means of the four factors, specifically when the same factor variances between genders were not met ($\Delta\chi^2 = 21.25$, $\Delta df = 4$, and $p < 0.001$). The partial factor variance invariance test indicated that two factors, hope and optimism, did not have the same factor variances between genders ($\Delta\chi^2 = 5.56$, $\Delta df = 2$, and $p > 0.05$). Although the same factor covariances between genders were not met ($\Delta\chi^2 = 19.73$, $\Delta df = 6$, and $p < 0.001$), the partial factor covariance invariance test showed that the three paired factor covariances (resiliency and self-efficacy, hope and optimism, and hope and self-efficacy) did not have the same factor covariances between genders ($\Delta\chi^2 = 3.32$, $\Delta df = 3$, and $p > 0.05$). Although the same factor means between genders were not met ($\Delta\chi^2 = 40.85$, $\Delta df = 4$, and $p < 0.001$), the partial factor mean invariance test showed that the two factors, optimism and resiliency, did not have the same factor means between genders ($\Delta\chi^2 = 4.21$, $\Delta df = 2$, and $p > 0.05$).

The estimated coefficients in the common metric completely standardised solution are presented in detail in Tables 3 and 4. Male nursing students had significantly higher optimism (2.27 vs. 2.15) and resiliency (2.28 vs. 2.17) factor means than female nursing students and significantly higher correlation coefficients between hope and optimism (0.92 vs. 0.74) and between hope and self-efficacy (0.89 vs. 0.76). The male nurses also had lower correlation coefficients between resiliency and self-efficacy (0.82 vs. 0.98) than the females.

Table 3. Invariant and non-invariant factor loadings, intercepts, error variances, and mean differences between genders.

Factors	Items	Factor Loadings	Intercepts	Error Variances	Latent Mean
Hope	h1	0.68	−0.11	0.46/0.62	2.49
	h2	0.69	−0.24	0.38/0.66	
	h3	0.65	0.13	0.43/0.70	
	h4	0.64	0.23	0.60	
Optimism	o5	0.61	0.05	0.52/0.77	2.27/2.15
	o6	0.59	0.21	0.65	
	o7	0.59	0.01	0.59/0.71	
	o8	0.63	−0.27	0.59	
Resiliency	r9	0.62	−0.13	0.50/0.71	2.28/2.17
	r10	0.60	0.14	0.65	
	r11	0.59	0.23	0.65	
	r12	0.59	−0.21	0.51/0.77	
Self-efficacy	e13	0.61	0.04	0.50/0.76	2.25
	e14	0.64	−0.22	0.48/0.70	
	e15	0.61	0.05	0.50/0.75	
	e16	0.58	0.13	0.58/0.74	

Note: All estimates are presented as a common metric and completely standardised solution. For factor loadings, intercepts, and error variances, non-invariant estimated coefficients are presented with a male/female pattern, and invariant estimated coefficients are presented with a single value.

Table 4. Interfactor correlation of the four factors of the PsyCap scale between genders.

Factors	Hope	Optimism	Resiliency	Self-Efficacy
Hope	1.22/0.79			
Optimism	0.92/0.74	1.13/0.88		
Resiliency	0.78	0.95	1.00	
Self-Efficacy	0.89/0.76	0.91	0.82/0.98	1.00

Note: All estimates are presented in a common metric completely standardised solution; hence, some values are higher than 1.00. Non-invariant estimated coefficients between genders are presented with a male/female pattern; invariant estimated coefficients are presented with a single value. Correlation with hope or optimism should be interpreted cautiously because of the non-invariance of variance in hope and optimism between genders.

4. Discussion

The PsyCap Scale was developed in this study with good reliability and validity. As shown in Table 4, the high correlation coefficients among the four factors showed that hope, optimism, resiliency, and self-efficacy had much variance overlapping, which reflected a common construct source, namely PsyCap. The study also implied that the definitions of the four constructs (factors) were similar, and they were included under the bigger construct, PsyCap. Nonetheless, although the high correlation coefficients among the four factors seemed to hinder discrimination between them at a glance, they met the test of discrimination validity between nested models with $\Delta\chi^2$. In fact, from the perspective of observed variables, the correlation coefficients among the four subscales were only from 0.58 to 0.69 for male nursing students and from 0.56 to 0.64 for female nursing students, and this was consistent with the general extent of correlation coefficients in most subscales summed for a total score for any scale.

The value of the measurement invariance test between genders lies in ensuring comparability of psychological scale scores between male and female nursing students. The invariance test of error that was not met (Model D) only hinders comparisons between individuals but not between groups in observed scores. Although invariances of factor loadings and intercepts between groups were met, they must be sufficient to guarantee between-group differences for factors (latent variables) and observed variables on a common scale because the expected value of measurement errors in group type was zero [33]. In addition, comparisons between genders in the means of latent variables also need to be based on the invariance of variances. Similar to the general t-test of differences in the group means of observed variables, equal variances must be assumed between groups in advance. Therefore, the test of invariance of the latent means was conducted based on Model F rather than Models C or E.

Some reports have found that male nursing students feel isolated and sidelined as they encounter more obstacles. They also report that male nurses experience more role stress and have more negative opinions than female nursing students [34–36]. However, no study has compared PsyCap between male and female nursing students. We found that male nursing students had higher PsyCap, including hope, optimism, resiliency, and self-efficacy, than female students on average. Statistically significant differences were observed in optimism and resilience. Hence, traditional occupations and social culture did not lower the PsyCap of male nursing students. It is worth noting that comparisons in latent means yield more reliable and valid outcomes because they are free of measurement errors. The results implied that male nursing students may have more potential for nursing care, despite facing more negative experiences and challenges, than female nursing students. However, there are many psychological variables and different skills related to nursing care that could be important for male nursing students to learn. Nonetheless, our research results should encourage more male nursing students to feel confident to persist in nursing. Nowadays, the shortage of nursing manpower is a challenge worldwide, and encouraging men involved in nursing would help to solve the problem [37]. In Taiwan, the growth rate of male nursing students has increased from 0.41% in 1985 to 11.68% in 2019, and over 1000 male students have majored in nursing in recent years [24]. It is believed that the present research results would benefit the government in developing relevant policies for career planning for male nursing students.

In addition, regardless of the perspectives of PsyCap as trait-like [14,38], having states [39–41], and requiring integration [30,42], they all agreed that PsyCap could be fostered and developed. Therefore, the design of different education programmes for male and female nursing students can refer to these results. For example, the results showing that male nursing students had higher correlation coefficients between hope and optimism and between hope and self-efficacy could be applied to training programmes. Interventions can be designed for male nursing students with low optimism or self-efficacy to promote their sense of hope to help increase their optimism and self-efficacy. Although the participants in this study were not sampled randomly, the sample size of male nursing students was large enough to be representative in Taiwan. Finally, the present results came from a non-experimental research design and would be difficult to execute in a causal-effect one; hence, more studies should be conducted to confirm them.

5. Conclusions

In this study, we developed the PsyCap Scale, which was shown to have good reliability and validity among male nursing students. In addition, because the scale is brief, including only 16 items, it can save time and is well-suited to the increasing use of online survey administration. Notably, based on advanced statistical methods and measurement invariance tests, we found that male nursing students had higher PsyCap levels of optimism and resiliency than female nursing students, and higher correlation coefficients between hope and optimism and between hope and self-efficacy. However, the male nurses had lower correlation coefficients between resiliency and self-efficacy than the female nurses. The results may be valuable in future research and training for male nursing students. In addition, the development of the PsyCap Scale can help male nursing students understand their potential and standing on hope, optimism, resiliency, and self-efficacy, and consequently, have enough confidence to face the many stressors in the learning stages, thus fostering ambition and devotion to their nursing profession.

Author Contributions: Conceptualization, J.L. and S.C.; methodology, J.L. and R.L.; software, J.L. and R.L.; validation, J.L., R.L. and S.C.; formal analysis, J.L. and R.L.; investigation, J.L. and R.L.; resources, J.L. and R.L.; data curation, J.L. and R.L.; writing—original draft preparation, J.L.; writing—review and editing, J.L., R.L. and S.C.; visualization, R.L.; supervision, J.L. and S.C.; project administration, J.L.; funding acquisition, J.L., R.L. and S.C. All authors have read and agreed to the published version of the manuscript.

Funding: This research received no external funding.

Institutional Review Board Statement: The study was conducted in accordance with the Declaration of Helsinki and approved by the Institutional Review Board (IRB No. 202110-E101).

Informed Consent Statement: Informed consent was obtained from all subjects involved in the study.

Data Availability Statement: The data presented in this study are available on request due to privacy restrictions.

Acknowledgments: The authors thank all participants for the completion of this study.

Conflicts of Interest: The authors declare no conflict of interest.

References

1. Seligman, M.E.P. Positive psychology, positive prevention, and positive therapy. In *Handbook of Positive Psychology*; Snyder, C.R., Lopez, S.J., Eds.; Oxford University Press: Oxford, UK, 2002; pp. 3–9.
2. Premchandran, R.; Pushpendra, P. The mediating impact of psychological capital on mentoring outcomes of trust in management and person-organisation fit-a conceptual model. *Int. J. Indian Cult. Bus. Manag.* **2017**, *14*, 326–346. [CrossRef]
3. Bakker, D.J.; Lyons, S.T.; Conlon, P.D. An exploration of the relationship between psychological capital and depression among first-year doctor of veterinary medicine students. *J. Vet. Med. Ed.* **2017**, *44*, 50–62. [CrossRef] [PubMed]
4. Da, S.; He, Y.; Zhang, X. Effectiveness of psychological capital intervention and its influence on work-related attitudes: Daily online self-learning method and randomised controlled trial design. *Int. J. Environ. Res. Public Health* **2020**, *17*, 8754. [CrossRef] [PubMed]
5. Huéscar Hernández, E.; Moreno-Murcia, J.A.; Cid, L.; Monteiro, D.; Rodrigues, F. Passion or perseverance? The effect of perceived autonomy support and grit on academic performance in college students. *Int. J. Environ. Res. Public Health* **2020**, *17*, 2143. [CrossRef]
6. Sagone, E.; De Caroli, M.E.; Falanga, R.; Indiana, M.L. Resilience and perceived self-efficacy in life skills from early to late adolescence. *Int. J. Adol. Youth* **2020**, *5*, 882–890. [CrossRef]
7. Park, N.; Peterson, C.; Szvarca, D.; Molen, R.J.V.; Kim, E.S.; Collon, K. Positive Psychology and physical health: Research and applications. *Am. J. Lifestyle Med.* **2016**, *10*, 200–206. [CrossRef] [PubMed]
8. Luthans, F. Positive organisational behaviour: Developing and managing psychological strengths. *Acad. Manag. Ex.* **2002**, *16*, 57–72. [CrossRef]

9. Ren, Z.; Zhang, X.; Li, X.; He, M.; Shi, H.; Zhao, H.; Zha, S.; Qiao, S.; Li, Y.; Pu, Y.; et al. Relationships of organisational justice, psychological capital and professional identity with job burnout among Chinese nurses: A cross-sectional study. *J. Clin. Nurs.* **2021**, *30*, 2912–2923. [CrossRef]
10. Luthans, F.; Youssef, C.M.; Avolio, B.J. *Psychological Capital: Developing the Human Competitive Edge*; Oxford University Press: New York, NY, USA, 2007. [CrossRef]
11. An, M.; Shin, E.S.; Choi, M.Y.; Lee, Y.; Hwang, Y.Y.; Kim, M. Positive psychological capital mediates the association between burnout and nursing performance outcomes among hospital nurses. *Int. J. Environ. Res. Public Health* **2020**, *17*, 5988. [CrossRef]
12. Hao, C.; Zhu, L.; Zhang, S.; Rong, S.; Zhang, Y.; Ye, J.; Yang, F. Serial-multiple mediation effect of professional identity, psychological capital (PsyCap), work-related stress, and work-related well-being among intensive care unit (ICU) nurses in China: A Cross-Sectional Questionnaire Survey. *Front. Psych.* **2020**, *11*, 3499. [CrossRef]
13. Woo, C.H.; Park, J.Y. Specialty satisfaction, positive psychological capital, and nursing professional values in nursing students: A cross-sectional survey. *Nurse Educ. Today* **2017**, *57*, 24–28. [CrossRef] [PubMed]
14. Luthans, F.; Youssef-Morgan, C.M. Psychological capital: An evidence-based positive approach. *Annu. Rev. Organ. Psychol. Organ. Behav.* **2017**, *4*, 339–366. [CrossRef]
15. Ho, H.C.; Chan, Y.C. Flourishing in the workplace: A one-year prospective study on the effects of perceived organisational support and psychological capital. *Int. J. Environ. Res. Public Health* **2022**, *19*, 922. [CrossRef] [PubMed]
16. Liang, L.; Xiao, Q.; Yang, Y. The psychological capital of left-behind university students: A description and intervention study from China. *Front. Psychol.* **2018**, *9*, 2438. [CrossRef] [PubMed]
17. Han, J.W.; Kang, K.I.; Joung, J. Enhancing happiness for nursing students through positive psychology activities: A mixed methods study. *Int. J. Environ. Res. Public Health* **2020**, *17*, 9274. [CrossRef]
18. Eun, J.; Mi-Ra, J. Effects of positive psychological capital, academic stress and academic achievement in nursing student on grit. *J. Digit. Converg.* **2018**, *16*, 309–317. [CrossRef]
19. Terry, D.; Peck, B.; Smith, A.; Nguyen, H. Occupational self-efficacy and psychological capital amongst nursing students: A cross sectional study understanding the malleable attributes for success. *Eur. J. Investig. Health Psychol. Educ.* **2020**, *10*, 159–172. [CrossRef]
20. Manoochehri, A.; Behroozi, N.; Yeylagh, M.S.; Maktabi, G. Testing and comparing the causal relationship between spirituality and social skills with adjustment and burnout mediated by psychological capital in male and female students. *Int. J. Adv. Appl. Sci.* **2018**, *5*, 112–118. [CrossRef]
21. Pan, X.; Mao, T.; Zhang, J.; Wang, J.; Su, P. Psychological capital mediates the association between nurses' practice environment and work engagement among Chinese male nurses. *Int. J. Nurs. Sci.* **2017**, *4*, 378–383. [CrossRef]
22. Ndou, N.P.; Moloko-Phiri, S.S. Four-year diploma male students' experiences in a profession traditionally perceived as a female domain at a selected public college of nursing in Limpopo South Africa. *Curationis* **2018**, *41*, a1932. [CrossRef]
23. Wyse, A.E.; Babcock, B. A comparison of subject matter experts' perceptions and job analysis surveys. *Pract. Assess. Res. Eval.* **2018**, *23*, 1–10. [CrossRef]
24. Open Data in Taiwan. Number of Students in Each Department of Universities. 2021. Available online: https://data.gov.tw/dataset/9622 (accessed on 25 June 2021).
25. Li, R.H. Reliability and validity of a shorter Chinese version for Ryff's psychological well-being scale. *Health Educ. J.* **2014**, *73*, 446–452. [CrossRef]
26. Hair, J.F.; Black, W.C.; Babin, B.J.; Anderson, R.E. *Multivariate Data Analysis*, 8th ed.; Cengage: Boston, MA, USA, 2018.
27. Dudasova, L.; Prochazka, J.; Vaculik, M.; Lorenz, T. Measuring psychological capital: Revision of the compound psychological capital scale (CPC-12). *PLoS ONE* **2021**, *16*, e0247114. [CrossRef] [PubMed]
28. Luthans, F.; Youssef, C.M. Human, social, and now positive psychological capital management: Investing in people for competitive advantage. *Organ. Dyn.* **2004**, *33*, 143–160. [CrossRef]
29. Luthans, F.; Avey, J.B.; Avolio, B.J.; Norman, S.M.; Combs, G.M. Psychological capital development: Toward a micro-intervention. *J. Organ. Behav.* **2006**, *27*, 387–393. [CrossRef]
30. Luthans, K.W.; Luthans, B.C.; Chaffin, T.D. Refining grit in Academic performance: The mediational role of psychological capital. *J. Manag. Educ.* **2019**, *43*, 35–61. [CrossRef]
31. Tan, C.; Tan, L.S. The role of optimism, self-esteem, academic self-efficacy and gender in high-ability students. *Asia-Pac. Educ. Res.* **2014**, *23*, 621–633. [CrossRef]
32. Li, R.H.; Kao, C.M.; Wu, Y.Y. Gender differences in psychological well-being: Tests of factorial invariance. *Qual. Life Res.* **2015**, *24*, 2577–2581. [CrossRef]
33. Little, T.D. *Longitudinal Structural Equation Modelling*; The Guilford Press: New York, NY, USA, 2013.
34. Abbas, S.; Zakar, R.; Fischer, F. Qualitative study of socio-cultural challenges in the nursing profession in Pakistan. *BMC Nurs.* **2020**, *19*, 20. [CrossRef]
35. Merry, L.; Vissandjée, B.; Verville-Provencher, K. Challenges, coping responses and supportive interventions for international and migrant students in academic nursing programs in major host countries: A scoping review with a gender lens. *BMC Nurs.* **2021**, *20*, 174. [CrossRef]
36. Stott, A. Exploring factors affecting attrition of male students from an undergraduate nursing course: A qualitative study. *Nurse Educ. Today* **2007**, *27*, 325–332. [CrossRef]

37. Cui, N.; Wang, R.; Song, F.; Jin, J. Experiences and perceptions of male nursing students in a single-sex class: A qualitative descriptive study. *Nurse Educ. Pract.* **2021**, *51*, 102996. [CrossRef] [PubMed]
38. Kyle Rudick, C.; Quiñones Valdivia, F.I.; Hudachek, L.; Specker, J.; Goodboy, A.K. A communication and instruction approach to embodied cultural and social capital at a public, 4-year university. *Commun. Ed.* **2019**, *68*, 438–459. [CrossRef]
39. Cavuş, M.F.; Gokçen, A. Psychological capital: Definition, components and effects. *Brit. J. Educ. Soc. Behav. Sci.* **2015**, *5*, 244–255. [CrossRef]
40. Slåtten, T.; Lien, G.; Evenstad, S.B.N.; Onshus, T. Supportive study climate and academic performance among university students: The role of psychological capital, positive emotions and study engagement. *Int. J. Qual. Serv. Sci.* **2021**, *13*, 585–600. [CrossRef]
41. Tomás, J.M.; Gutiérrez, M.; Georgieva, S.; Hernández, M. The effects of self-efficacy, hope, and engagement on the academic achievement of secondary education in the Dominican Republic. *Psychol. Sch.* **2020**, *57*, 191–203. [CrossRef]
42. Idris, A.M.; Manganaro, M. Relationships between psychological capital, job satisfaction, and organizational commitment in the Saudi oil and petrochemical industries. *J. Hum. Behav. Soc. Environ.* **2017**, *27*, 251–269. [CrossRef]

medicina

MDPI

Case Report

Successful Interventional Management of Life-Threatening Bleeding after Oocyte Retrieval: A Case Report and Review of the Literature

Hiroyuki Tokue *, Azusa Tokue and Yoshito Tsushima

Department of Diagnostic and Interventional Radiology, Gunma University Hospital, 3-39-22 Showa-Machi, Maebashi 371-8511, Gunma, Japan
* Correspondence: tokue@s2.dion.ne.jp; Tel.: +81-27-220-8401; Fax: +81-27-220-8409

Abstract: Life-threatening bleeding after oocyte retrieval is unusual. We report a case of massive vaginal bleeding requiring transcatheter arterial embolization (TAE) after transvaginal US-directed follicle aspiration for oocyte retrieval and provide a brief review of cases in which the pseudoaneurysm of the injured artery was managed with a TAE approach. A 40-year-old woman presented massive vaginal bleeding after transvaginal ultrasonography-directed follicle aspiration for oocyte retrieval. Contrast-enhanced computed tomography revealed active bleeding from the uterine ostium. Transcatheter arterial embolization was performed for a pseudoaneurysm of the right pudendal artery to manage the hemorrhage. Potentially life-threatening bleeding should be recognized as a rare complication after oocyte retrieval to promptly establish the diagnosis and preserve the uterus.

Keywords: oocyte retrieval; in vitro fertilization; pseudoaneurysm; hemorrhage; transcatheter arterial embolization

Citation: Tokue, H.; Tokue, A.; Tsushima, Y. Successful Interventional Management of Life-Threatening Bleeding after Oocyte Retrieval: A Case Report and Review of the Literature. *Medicina* **2022**, *58*, 1534. https://doi.org/10.3390/medicina58111534

Academic Editors: Joachim G. Voss, Sandul Yasobant and Udo Jeschke

Received: 24 September 2022
Accepted: 26 October 2022
Published: 27 October 2022

1. Introduction

In vitro fertilization (IVF) is a common treatment worldwide for people who cannot conceive naturally. IVF is generally very safe, and those undergoing IVF rarely experience any health or pregnancy-related problems associated with the procedure [1]. Transvaginal ultrasonography (US)-directed follicle aspiration is a standard procedure for oocyte retrieval for most IVF cases, and life-threatening bleeding after oocyte retrieval has been reported in 0.8% of IVF cases [1]. Potential risk factors for bleeding after oocyte retrieval include coagulation disorders, multiple punctures, and adhesion of the ovary to other organs [2–4].

Here, we report a case of massive vaginal bleeding requiring transcatheter arterial embolization (TAE) after transvaginal US-directed follicle aspiration for oocyte retrieval and review the relevant literature.

2. Case Presentation

A 40-year-old woman with a history of primary infertility for three years was transferred using emergency transportation from another hospital. She presented massive vaginal bleeding. Her vital signs were as follows: heart rate, 135 bpm; blood pressure, 80/65 mmHg; and respiratory rate, 25 breaths/min. The hemoglobin level was 6.1 g/dL. The patient became hemodynamically unstable and had hypotension. She had undergone transvaginal US-directed follicle aspiration to retrieve oocytes 6 h earlier at another hospital. This was her second attempt at oocyte retrieval.

The patient had no history of surgical intervention. Her left ovary with a chocolate cyst due to a history of endometriosis adhered to the uterus and was unsuitable for oocyte retrieval. Further, the right ovary was firmly fixed behind the middle uterine segment. Her physician assessed the difficulty in obtaining oocytes with conventional follicle aspiration through the vaginal fornix from the right ovary because the right ovary was malpositioned. In addition to conventional follicular aspiration through the vaginal fornix, transmyometrial oocyte retrieval was performed for the right ovary under US guidance using a 19-gauge aspiration needle. To perform transmyometrial puncture, an aspiration needle was inserted obliquely through the lower uterine segment to reach the right ovary. Color Doppler was used to check blood flow around the follicles and myometrium. Three oocytes were retrieved.

10 min after the procedure, Pulsatile vaginal bleeding and pain persisted after the procedure. Gauze packing did not stop the vaginal bleeding. She was transferred to our hospital using emergency transportation because she became hemodynamically unstable and developed hypotension with gauze packing alone.

Contrast-enhanced computed tomography (CT) on admission revealed active bleeding from the uterine ostium suggesting a ruptured pseudoaneurysm (Figure 1). TAE was performed after transfusion with two units of packed red blood cells. TAE was performed 60 min after arrival at our hospital. Aortography showed active bleeding from the branch of the right pudendal artery (Figure 2A). A 1.8-Fr microcatheter was introduced near the bleeding point (Figure 2B). After performing TAE using gelfoam, the patient became hemodynamically stable. TAE lasted 30 min. No adverse events related to the procedure or rebleeding were noted. The patient was discharged from our hospital five days after the TAE. Since then, she has been undergoing fertility treatment.

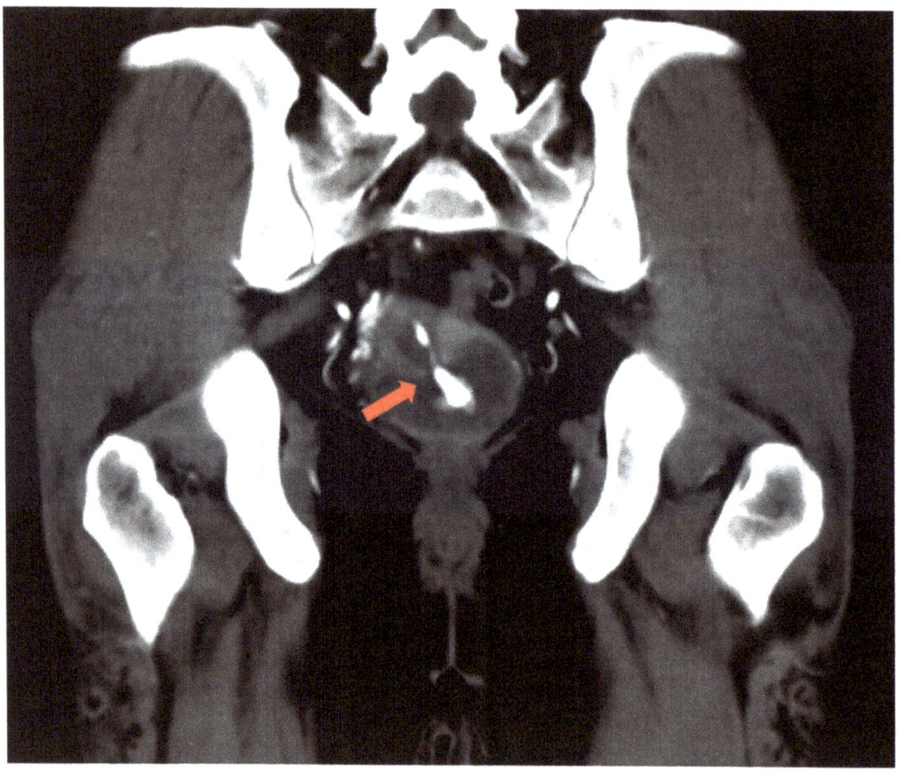

Figure 1. A case of a 40-year-old woman with massive vaginal bleeding. She underwent transvaginal US-directed follicle aspiration for oocyte retrieval 6 h earlier. Contrast-enhanced computed tomography (CT) on admission reveals active bleeding from the uterine ostium (arrow).

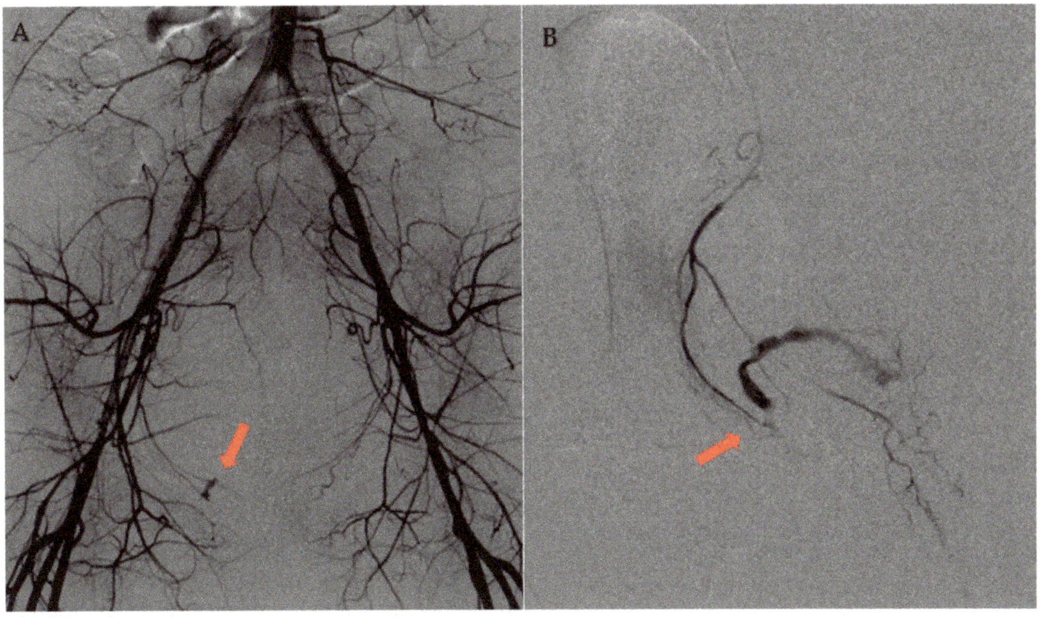

Figure 2. (**A**) Aortography showing active bleeding from the branch of the right pudendal artery (arrow). (**B**) A 1.8-Fr microcatheter is introduced near the bleeding point (arrow). TAE is performed using gelfoam.

IVF is an established treatment modality for infertility worldwide. In assisted reproduction, US-guided retrieval of oocytes through the vaginal fornix is now accepted as a safe and well-tolerated method involving a low overall complication rate [1]. Although bleeding is one of the complications of IVF resulting from US-guided transvaginal oocyte retrieval [2–6], it is generally insignificant and is often controllable with topical treatments, such as the application of pressure and/or topical hemostatic agents. Major vaginal hemorrhage due to vascular injury has been reported in 0.8% of IVF cases [1].

In our case, transmyometrial oocyte retrieval was performed in addition to conventional follicular aspiration through the vaginal fornix. This might have increased the risk of hemorrhage because vascular penetration with aspiration can cause myometrial trauma [7].

Very rare cases require TAE to stop bleeding associated with oocyte retrieval. We searched PubMed and Google Scholar to review the available literature (published until April 2022) on massive vaginal bleeding requiring TAE after transvaginal US-directed follicle aspiration for oocyte retrieval using the key terms "oocyte retrieval," and "arterial embolization". There were six cases (including our case) requiring TAE after transvaginal US-directed follicle aspiration for oocyte retrieval due to pseudoaneurysm (Table 1). Moreover, there were two cases (case No.2 and our case) punctured through the myometrium. The pseudoaneurysm was found immediately or seven days after oocyte retrieval in three of these cases [3,4] and, surprisingly, during pregnancy in the remaining three cases [2,5,6]. It might be speculated that increased blood flow to pelvic organs and hormonal changes during pregnancy would enlarge the pseudoaneurysm and make it visible. Therefore, in IVF pregnancy cases, the presence of pseudoaneurysms should be checked not only after oocyte retrieval but also during pregnancy.

Table 1. TAE cases after transvaginal US-directed follicle aspiration for oocyte retrieval due to the presence of pseudoaneurysm.

Case	Authors	Age of the Patient (Years)	Past Medical History	Symptoms	The Day Pseudoaneurysm Was Observed	Diagnosis of Pseudoaneurysm	The Injured Artery	The Embolic Material
1	Bozdag et al. [2]	22	Nothing	Nothing	29 weeks of gestation (33 weeks after OR)	US, MRI	Left inferior pudendal artery	NBCA
2	Takeda et al. [3]	34	Four miscarriages	Vaginal bleeding	7 days after OR	US	Right uterine artery	NBCA
3	Kart et al. [4]	40	Mild factor VIII deficiency	Pain, pale, hypotension	Same day of OR	US	Right and left uterine arteries	PVA
4	Pappin and Plant [5]	37	Not reported	Vaginal bleeding	12 weeks of gestation (6 years after OR)	US, MRI	Left internal iliac artery	Coils, thrombin
5a *	Mulkers et al. [6]	35	Laparoscopy	Pain	19 weeks and 2 days of gestation	US, MRI	Left uterine artery	Microsphere, gelfoam, coils
5b *		35	Laparoscopy	Pain, vaginal bleeding	30 weeks of gestation	US, MRI	Left uterine artery	Glue
6	The present case	40	Nothing	Pain, hypotension, vaginal bleeding	Same day of OR	CT	Right pudendal artery	Gelfoam

TAE, transcatheter arterial embolization; OR, oocyte retrieval; NBCA, N-butyl-2-cyanoacrylate; PVA: polyvinyl alcohol. * 5a and 5b are the same patients. Recanalization of the pseudoaneurysm required repeated TAE during pregnancy.

The management of pseudoaneurysms based on the fertility of the case may be controversial (Figure 3). TAE has some advantages. It is a safe, highly effective at stopping and preventing bleeding, minimally invasive technique that can be completed repeatedly. The disadvantage of TAE is the use of ionizing radiation, including the effect on fertility. However, the effects of exposure can be minimized by shortening the procedure time. Recanalization of a pseudoaneurysm requiring repeat TAE during pregnancy was noted in one of the six cases [6]. N-butyl-2-cyanoacrylate (NBCA) was used as the embolic material in three of the cases [2,3,6]. NBCA is a permanent liquid embolic material. None of them showed recurrence after TAE with NBCA, but subsequent gestation in women desiring future fertility has not been fully investigated. Gelfoam has a risk of pseudoaneurysm recanalization. However, we embolized the artery with a gelfoam considering future fertility. No reports of pregnancy and childbirth after the treatment of pseudoaneurysms after IVF are available. Further studies are required to determine the most appropriate embolic material.

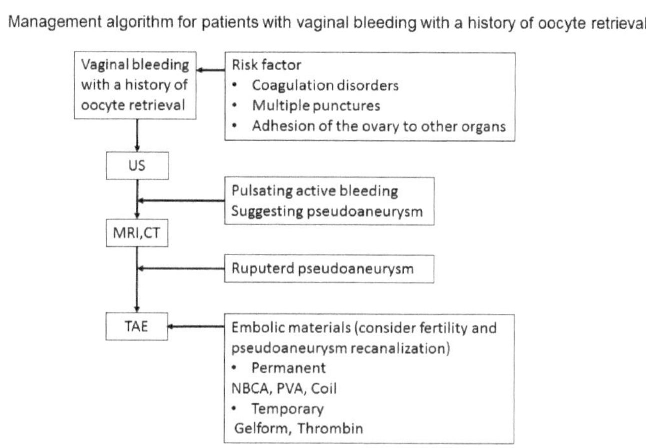

Figure 3. Management algorithm for patients with vaginal bleeding with a history of oocyte retrieval.

In conclusion, it is important to recognize pseudoaneurysm as a rare complication after IVF to achieve a prompt diagnosis and enact uterus-preserving management for this potentially life-threatening disorder. Both the fertility specialist and general obstetrician/gynecologist should be aware of this to ensure better counseling of their patients and effective treatment.

Author Contributions: Conceptualization, H.T., A.T. and Y.T.; Methodology, H.T.; Investigation, H.T.; Resources, H.T.; Data curation, H.T. and A.T.; Writing—original draft preparation, H.T.; Writing review and editing, H.T., A.T. and Y.T.; Visualization, H.T.; supervision, A.T. All authors have read and agreed to the published version of the manuscript.

Funding: This research received no external funding.

Institutional Review Board Statement: Not applicable.

Informed Consent Statement: Written informed consent was obtained from the patient for publication of this case report. A copy of the written consent is available for review by the Editor-in-Chief of this journal on request.

Data Availability Statement: The data presented in the present study are available on request from the correspondent author.

Conflicts of Interest: The authors declare no conflict of interest.

Abbreviations

IVF: in vitro fertilization; US: ultrasonographically; TAE: transcatheter arterial embolization; NBCA: N-butyl-2-cyanoacrylate.

References

1. Bennett, S.J.; Waterstone, J.J.; Cheng, W.C.; Parsons, J. Complications of transvaginal ultrasound-directed follicle aspiration: A review of 2670 consecutive procedures. *J Assist. Reprod. Genet.* **1993**, *10*, 72–77. [CrossRef] [PubMed]
2. Bozdag, G.; Basaran, A.; Cil, B.; Esinler, I.; Yarali, H. An oocyte pick-up procedure complicated with pseudoaneurysm of the internal iliac artery. *Fertil. Steril.* **2008**, *90*, 2004.e11–2004.e13. [CrossRef] [PubMed]
3. Takeda, A.; Koike, W.; Hayashi, S. Delayed hemorrhage as a result of ruptured uterine artery pseudoaneurysm after transmyometrial oocyte retrieval: Management by transcatheter arterial embolization using N-butyl-2-cyanoacrylate. *J. Obs. Gynaecol. Res.* **2017**, *43*, 1655–1659. [CrossRef] [PubMed]
4. Kart, C.; Guven, S.; Aran, T.; Dinc, H. Life-threatening intraabdominal bleeding after oocyte retrieval successfully managed with angiographic embolization. *Fertil. Steril.* **2011**, *96*, e99–e102. [CrossRef] [PubMed]
5. Pappin, C.; Plant, G. A pelvic pseudoaneurysm (a rare complication of oocyte retrieval for IVF) treated by arterial embolization. *Hum. Fertil. (Camb)* **2006**, *9*, 153–155. [CrossRef] [PubMed]
6. Mulkers, A.; Podevyn, K.; Dehaene, I. Recurrent uterine artery pseudo-aneurysm requiring repeat embolization during pregnancy—A case report. *Case Rep. Womens Health* **2020**, *29*, e00280. [CrossRef] [PubMed]
7. Wisanto, A.; Bollen, N.; Camus, M.; De Grauwe, E.; Devroey, P.; Van Steirteghem, A.C. Effect of transuterine puncture during transvaginal oocyte retrieval on the results of human in-vitro fertilization. *Hum. Reprod.* **1989**, *4*, 790–793. [CrossRef] [PubMed]

medicina

MDPI

Systematic Review

Effect of the Helping Babies Breathe Program on Newborn Outcomes: Systematic Review and Meta-Analysis

Sergio Agudelo-Pérez *, Annie Cifuentes-Serrano, Paula Ávila-Celis and Henry Oliveros

School of Medicine, Universidad de La Sabana, Campus Puente del Común, Km. 7, Autopista Norte de Bogotá, Chía 250001, Colombia

* Correspondence: sergioagpe@unisabana.edu.co; Tel.: +571-3105612142

Abstract: *Background and objectives:* In low- and middle-income countries, the leading cause of neonatal mortality is perinatal asphyxia. Training in neonatal resuscitation has been shown to decrease this cause of mortality. The program "Helping Babies Breathe" (HBB) is a program to teach basic neonatal resuscitation focused on countries and areas with limited economic resources. The aim of the study was to determine the effect of the implementation of the HBB program on newborn outcomes: mortality and morbidity. *Material and Methods:* A systematic review was carried out on observational studies and clinical trials that reported the effect of the implementation in low- and middle-income countries of the HBB program on neonatal mortality and morbidity. We carried out a meta-analysis of the extracted data. Random-effect models were used to evaluate heterogeneity, using the Cochrane Q and I2 tests, and stratified analyses were performed by age and type of outcome to determine the sources of heterogeneity. *Results:* Eleven studies were identified. The implementation of the program includes educational strategies focused on the training of doctors, nurses, midwives, and students of health professions. The poled results showed a decrease in overall mortality (OR 0.67; 95% CI 0.57, 0.80), intrapartum stillbirth mortality (OR 0.62; 95% CI 0.51, 0.75), and first-day mortality (OR 0.70; 95% IC 0.64, 0.77). High heterogeneity was found, which was partly explained by differences in the gestational age of the participants. *Conclusions:* The implementation of the program HBB in low- and medium-income countries has a significant impact on reducing early neonatal mortality.

Keywords: Helping Babies Breath Program; Basic Newborn Resuscitation; infant mortality; asphyxia neonatorum; critical care outcomes

Citation: Agudelo-Pérez, S.; Cifuentes-Serrano, A.; Ávila-Celis, P.; Oliveros, H. Effect of the Helping Babies Breathe Program on Newborn Outcomes: Systematic Review and Meta-Analysis. *Medicina* **2022**, *58*, 1567. https://doi.org/10.3390/medicina58111567

Academic Editor: Joachim G. Voss

Received: 23 September 2022
Accepted: 13 October 2022
Published: 31 October 2022

1. Introduction

The worldwide neonatal mortality rate is approximately 19 deaths per 1000 live births [1], of which 90% occur in low-income countries [2]. In this context, the Sustainable Development Goals (SDG) of the World Health Organization (WHO) proposed to end preventable deaths in newborns, reducing neonatal mortality to 12 per 1000 live births by 2030 [1]. During labor and birth, the highest mortality rate is concentrated at 73% of deaths in this period [3,4], mainly due to perinatal asphyxia [5].

On the other hand, the training of health personnel in neonatal resuscitation has been shown to be a strategy for reducing mortality and perinatal asphyxia [6,7]. Therefore, the WHO recommended the presence of a person skilled in neonatal resuscitation at all births [8]. So, implementing standardized programs in neonatal resuscitation training for personnel in charge of newborns during birth could reduce neonatal mortality [9].

Nevertheless, the current recommendations of the International Liaison Committee on Resuscitation (ILCOR) are aimed at high-income countries, which makes them difficult to implement in countries with the highest neonatal mortality rate [10]. Therefore, it is necessary to adapt the neonatal resuscitation recommendations to these countries [10]. The American Academy of Pediatrics (AAP), with the support of other agencies, has developed a modified neonatal resuscitation program called Helping Babies Breathe (HBB). It is an evidence-based educational program for low and middle-income countries and areas with limited economic resources, focused on the first minute of life or "golden minute", to teach respiratory support (Basic Neonatal Resuscitation) with a mask bag, thermoregulation, stimulation, evaluation, and early initiation of breastfeeding [11–13].

In some studies, it has been observed that the implementation of the program could influence the reduction of neonatal mortality [14,15], and the economic evaluation of the implementation of the program has been shown to be cost-effective in the prevention of neonatal mortality [16,17]. In this frame, it is important to recognize the importance of training health personnel and the implementation of basic neonatal resuscitation programs as a measure to deal with this problem. The objective of this study was to determine the effect of the implementation of the HBB program on newborn mortality and morbidity.

2. Materials and Methods

2.1. Literature Search Strategy

A systematic review using the PRISMA-2020 guideline for the identification, screening, and inclusion of studies was conducted. The protocol was registered in PROSPERO (International Prospective Register of Systematic Reviews) with the code CRD 42021264846.

The search was carried out from 1 to 30 June 2021 in the electronic databases Pubmed, EMBASE, LILACS (Literatura Latinoamericana y del Caribe en Ciencia de la Salud), Web of Science, and Cochrane Central Register of Controlled Trials. A manual search was also carried out on Google Scholar, the official website of the HBB program, the personal files of the researchers, and using the snowball method. The search was not restricted by language or year. When needed, additional information and clarified information from data published by individual trial authors were requested.

The search terms used included synonyms or thesauri from the MeSH (Medical Subjects Heading) web dictionaries: newborn, neonate, infant, Helping Babies Breathe, golden minute, neonatal resuscitation, and mortality. The following search strategy was used for Pubmed and was adapted for other electronic databases: ((helping [All Fields] AND ("infant" [MeSH Terms] OR "infant" [All Fields] OR "babies" [All Fields]) AND ("Breathe (Sheff)" [Journal] OR "breathe" [All Fields])) OR (golden [All Fields] AND minute [All Fields]) OR (("infant, newborn" [MeSH Terms] OR ("infant" [All Fields] AND "newborn" [All Fields]) OR "newborn infant" [All Fields] OR "neonatal" [All Fields]) AND ("resuscitation" [MeSH Terms] OR "resuscitation" [All Fields]))) AND mortality [All Fields].

2.2. Inclusion Criteria

1. The term newborn was considered as a gestational age of greater than or equal to 37 weeks of gestation and up to 30 days of life. The term preterm newborn was considered as a gestational age of fewer than 37 weeks and up to 30 days of life and/or 40 weeks of corrected age at term.
2. Studies, whose objective was to evaluate the effect of the implementation of the HBB program in private or public health institutions (hospitals or clinics), in low and middle-income countries or scenarios.
3. Reporting data on mortality and morbidity outcomes.
4. Clinical trials, quasi-experimental studies, and observational studies.

2.3. Exclusion Criteria

1. Literature reviews such as systematic, integrative, and/or narrative reviews; a summary of conferences and correspondence to the editor.
2. Poster presentations, conferences, and/or abstracts only.

2.4. Outcomes

The primary outcome was newborn mortality, defined as death in the period from birth to the first 28 days of life. The secondary outcomes were intrapartum mortality, defined as the birth of a viable fetus with a gestational age greater than 22 weeks or birth weight greater than 500 g, an Apgar score of 0 at minutes one and five, without signs of maceration, and presenting fetal heart sounds at the entrance and onset of labor; mortality in the first 24 h; early mortality, understood as the death of the newborn in the first 7 days of life, and late mortality, which was defined as death between 8 and 28 days of life. Morbidity outcomes were the effect on perinatal asphyxia, intraventricular hemorrhage, necrotizing enterocolitis, neonatal sepsis, bronchopulmonary dysplasia, and length of stay in the neonatal unit.

2.5. Screening and Inclusion of Studies

The initial search and selection of studies were carried out independently by two researchers (PA, AC). Initial results were compared, and discrepancies were resolved by consensus with a third researcher (SA). To define their final entry into the systematic review, the articles identified as relevant by screening were retrieved in full text for in-depth reading independently by the two researchers. Again, the discrepancies were resolved by consensus with a third investigator (SA).

2.6. Data Extraction and Synthesis

Information on the characteristics of the study was extracted in terms of bibliometric data (author, year, and country of publication) and data relevant to the study (type of health institution included and geographic area, study methods, characteristics of the included newborn cohort, methods of how the implementation of the program was carried out, educational strategy, and outcomes evaluated). This information was extracted independently by the reviewers. Differences were resolved through discussions and consensus. The assessment of the risk of bias in the observational studies was carried out with the Robins I checklist [18].

2.7. Statistical Analysis

Odds ratios (OR) with a 95% confidence interval (CI) were used as a measure of effect size. Random effects models were used to account for different sources of variation among studies. Heterogeneity was assessed using Q of Cochrane, which determined if the variability of the effects was greater than those expected by chance, and the I2 statistic test was used to rate the degree of heterogeneity as none <25%, low 25–49%, moderate 50–74%, and high ≥75%. If heterogeneity existed, subgroup analyses according to the quality and risk of bias of the studies were performed to determine its source. Report and publication bias was assessed by examining the degree of asymmetry in a funnel plot, and funnel plot symmetry was assessed with the Egger's test. STATA 14 software was used for analyses.

3. Results

3.1. Characteristics of Included Studies

A total of n = 6380 studies were identified. After deleting duplicates and initial screening, n = 22 studies were selected as potentially eligible. Finally, ten articles were chosen, and when performing the snowball strategy, one additional document was found. Therefore, for qualitative synthesis, eleven studies were included, while for meta-analysis, ten studies were included (Figure 1). The main causes of exclusion were another type of intervention, different outcomes, and types of study.

Regarding the study design, n = 8 were before and after studies, two were prospective cohort studies, and one was a clinical trial [19]. The implementation of the intervention was carried out in health institutions (private or public hospitals and rural or urban hospitals) and focused on the training of health personnel (nurses, doctors, and students) as well as midwives during vaginal births and cesarean sections.

The studies included a total of n = 412,741 infants, of which n = 106,317 were preterm newborns. However, not all studies report gestational age at birth. Additionally, it was observed that the implementation of HBB was carried out under different strategies and took different training times between the different cohorts. Finally, all studies were assessed overall, and subgroup mortality was given by intrapartum in the first 24 h, early, and late mortality. Regarding the morbidity reported in the included studies, only two studies [20,21] reported it, and it was in relation to the outcome of perinatal asphyxia (Table 1).

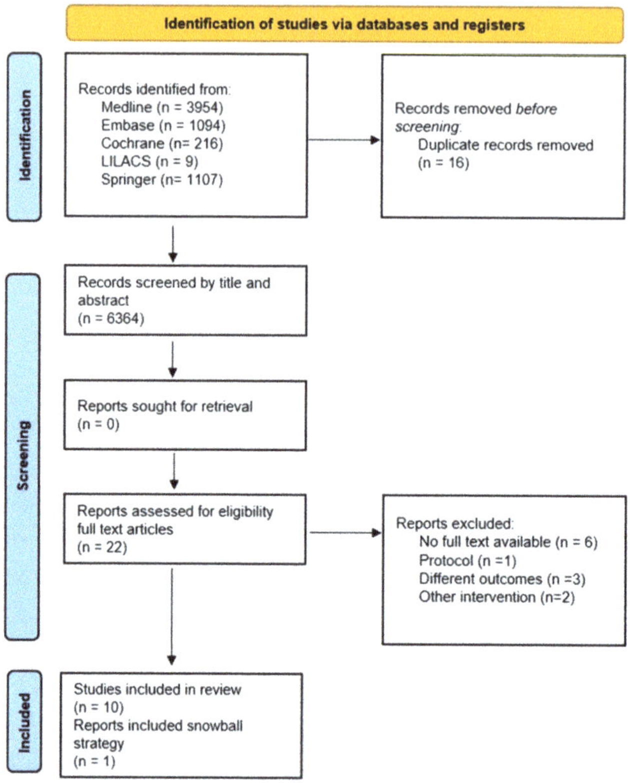

Figure 1. Study flowchart.

Table 1. Characteristics of the included studies.

Author, Year, Country	Design	Duration of Study	Sample and Place	Objective	Intervention-Implementation Strategy	Measured Outcomes
Msemo 2013 Tanzania [21]	Before and after	2 years	86.621 (8124 before and 78,500 after) 8 hospitals in Tanzania	To determine whether the implementation of HBB improves the basic skills of those attending deliveries, including the application of mask bag ventilation, and whether it reduces early neonatal mortality by 50% and death rate.	For 6 to 9 months: The principal investigator and trainers conducted a one-day training of healthcare providers at each hospital	Overall mortality, intrapartum mortality, 24 h mortality and asphyxia
Mduma 2015 Tanzania [22]	Before and after	2 years (2010–2012)	9807 (4894 before and 4812 after) 1 hospital in Tanzania	To assess whether frequent and brief HBB simulation training would affect clinical practice and reduce 24 h neonatal mortality.	Training in FBOS HBB simulation. One-day trainings for everyone who works in the delivery room. Monthly training sessions of 40 min duration. The practical sessions focused on the immediate basic care of stabilization and resuscitation intervention.	Overall mortality, intrapartum mortality, 24 h mortality

Table 1. *Cont.*

Author, Year, Country	Design	Duration of Study	Sample and Place	Objective	Intervention-Implementation Strategy	Measured Outcomes
Rule 2017 Kenya [20]	Before and after	21 months (1/2014–9/2015)	4117 (2106 before and 2011 after) 1 hospital in Bomet, Kenya	Describe a study that uses quality improvement. The hospital's Neonatal Task Force identified high rates of asphyxia at birth (BA) as a quality gap. With the implementation of HBB, they sought to reduce hospital BA rates by 50% over a six-month period.	An HBB coach joined the team for one year to train its members in the HBB methodology. Prior to initial training, reference practices in the delivery room were observed, staff members were interviewed, and task force members were trained as HBB teachers.	Asphyxia
Patel 2019 India [23]	Before and after	2 years (2011–2013)	78,948 (38,078 before and 40,870 after) 13 hospitals in Nagpur, India	To assess perinatal mortality at day 1 in facility deliveries before and after HBB implementation	HBB training of instructors who then trained birth attendants, introduction of a multifaceted follow-up program, and retraining of delivery attendants after six months. They were instructed to reanimate all non-macerated births, including those considered fresh stillbirths.	Overall mortality, intrapartum mortality, 24 h mortality
Innerdal 2019 Mali [24]	Before and after	3 years (2015–2018)	9769 (3125 before and 6644 after) 1 hospital in Mali and 13 district health centers.	Reduce neonatal mortality in Mali by introducing HBB.	The implementation of the first edition of HBB was 44 sessions, of 1 or 2 days. The evaluation of the training was carried out with a written test before and after the sessions. Then they trained in the second edition of HBB with a duration of 2 to 3 days and weekly repetition training was introduced.	Overall mortality, intrapartum mortality, 24 h mortality
KC et al., 2019 Nepal [19]	Randomized controlled trial	18 months (4/2017–10/2018)	89.014 (control 38.378, intervention 50,636) 12 public hospitals in Nepal	Phased implementation of a quality improvement package for neonatal resuscitation (HBB) in hospitals in Nepal	Implementation of a quality improvement package in neonatal resuscitation that includes facilitation strategies, training, weekly meetings, and information dissemination visits.	Intrapartum mortality, 24 h mortality, early mortality
KC et al., 2016 Nepal [25]	Prospective cohort study	14 months (7/2012–9/2013)	25,108 (control 9588, intervention 15,520) 1 tertiary hospital in Nepal	Improve adherence to the Helping Babies Breathe neonatal resuscitation protocol by using a quality improvement cycle	HBB protocol training, weekly review meetings, daily skills checks, use of self-assessment checklists, and refresher training.	Overall mortality, intrapartum mortality, 24 h mortality
Bellad et al., 2016 India y Kenia [26]	Before and after	24 months (1/2011–10/2013)	70,704 (before 35,595 and then 35,109) Belgaum: 33 centers Nagpur: 15 centers Kenya: 23 centers	To assess the impact of implementing a package of HBB interventions and monitoring in select health facilities representing a large proportion of births and perinatal mortality rate at sites in India and Kenya	Master trainer training and training of childbirth care teams. It included assessment of HBB knowledge and skills before and after training courses and updates 6 months later.	Overall mortality, intrapartum mortality, 24 h mortality, early mortality.
Wrammert J. et al., 2017 Nepal [27]	prospective cohort study	15 months (7/2012–9/2013)	24,665 (control 9390 and intervention 15,275) 1 tertiary hospital in Kathmandu	Describe the timing and causes of neonatal deaths in hospital before and after HBB training at a maternity health center in Nepal	Evaluation of the effect of HBB training on neonatal mortality rates	General mortality, 24 h mortality, early mortality, late mortality.

Table 1. *Cont.*

Author, Year, Country	Design	Duration of Study	Sample and Place	Objective	Intervention-Implementation Strategy	Measured Outcomes
Goudar et al., 2013 India [28]	Before and after	11 months (10/2009–09/2010)	9598 (before 4187 and then 5411) District hospitals in Karnataka, India, and urban hospitals in Belgaum	To assess the efficacy of HBB training in reducing stillbirths and neonatal mortality rate	Model of training and teaching and skills and practice, coaches were trained, including discussion, practice, and simulation. Training to trainers was continued and learning assessments were applied.	Overall mortality, intrapartum mortality, late mortality.
Arabi AME, et al., 2017 Sudan [29]	Before and after	24 months	4390 (before 1350 and after 4390) 6 rural medical centers in east Nile	Community-based intervention (village midwives) to assess the impact of HBB on neonatal mortality	Trainers at HBB instructed midwives, included simulator training kit and teaching materials, then weekly post-HBB follow-up	Intrapartum mortality, early mortality

3.2. *Assessment of Quality and Risk of Bias of the Studies*

The risk of bias in the studies was moderate to critical, especially in the domains of confusion, measurement of results, and selection bias. This was because the domain of confusion, population, and/or outcome was not well defined. Likewise, the measurement and selection of the results were not well reported (Table 2).

Table 2. Summary of Risk of Bias in Included Studies.

Article/Domain	Confusion	Participants Selection	Classification of Interventions	Deviations and Interventions	Lack of Data	Measurement of Results	Result Selection Reported	Global	Risk
Ashish KC 2016 [25]									Moderate
Bellad et al., 2016 [26]									Serious
Wrammert et al., 2017 [27]									Critical
Goudar et al., 2013 [28]									Serious
Ashish KC 2019 [19]									Moderate
Arabi AME, et al., 2017 [29]									Moderate
Msemo G, et al., 2013 [21]									Moderate
Patel A, et al., 2019 [23]									Moderate
Rule AL, et al., 2017 [20]									Serious
Innerdal M, et al., 2019 [24]									Serious
Mduma E, et al., 2015 [22]									Moderate

3.3. *Meta-Analysis Results*

The studies evaluated overall mortality and subgroups. The meta-analysis indicates that there is a reduction in the risk of overall death (OR 0.67; 95% CI 0.57, 0.8) Figure 2a, intrapartum stillbirth death (OR 0.62; 95% CI 0.51, 0.75) Figure 2b and first-day neonatal mortality (OR 0.57, 95% CI 0.41, 0.8) Figure 2c. Late mortality did not change with the intervention (Figure 2e).

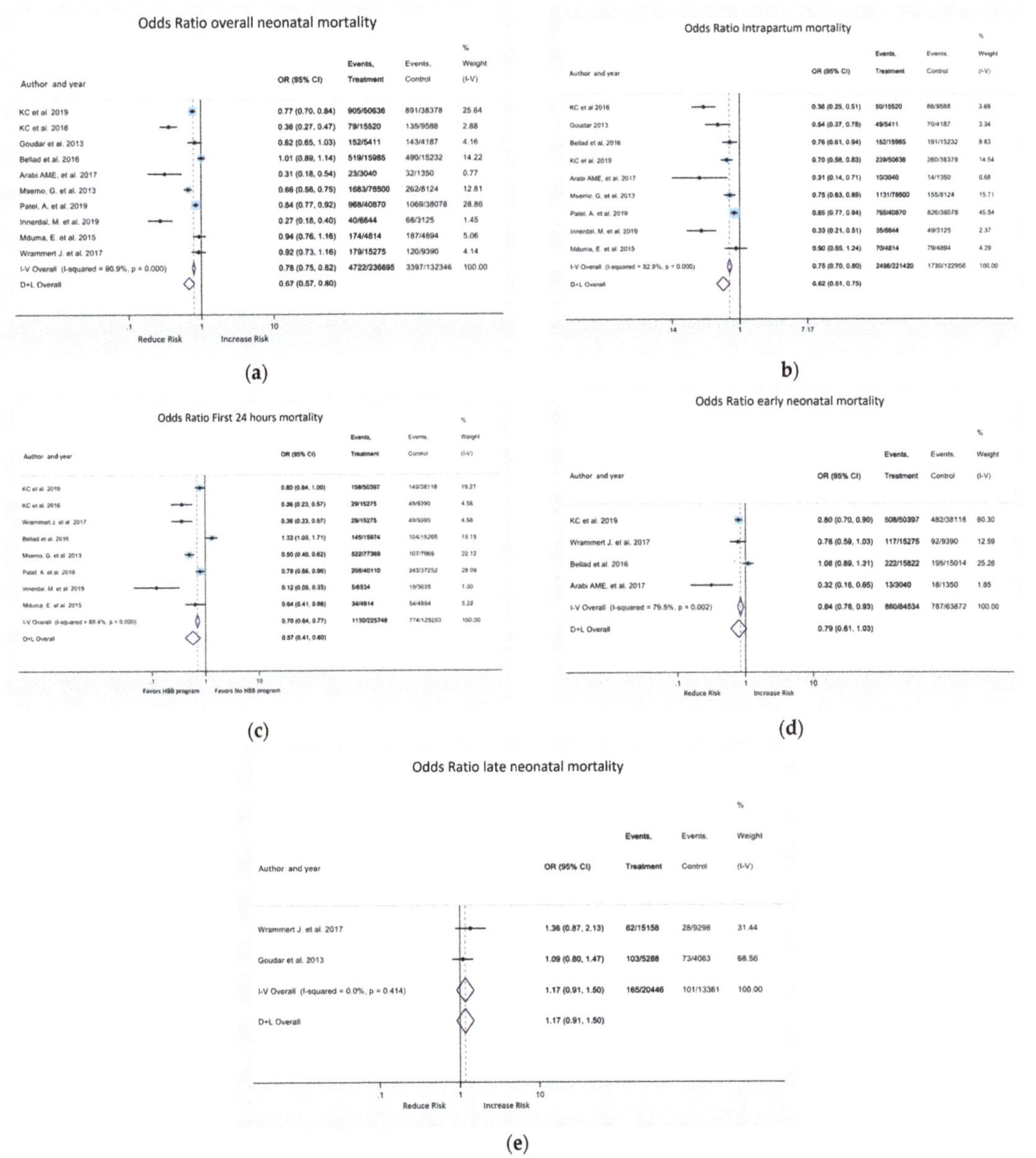

Figure 2. Forest plot for the effect of HBB program on neonatal mortality; (**a**) overall neonatal mortality; (**b**) intrapartum stillbirth mortality; (**c**) first-day neonatal mortality; (**d**) first week (early) neonatal mortality; (**e**) late neonatal mortality.

Regarding the morbidity outcome, only two studies [20,21] evaluated the effect on perinatal asphyxia. The meta-analysis of these studies shows a tendency to reduce this outcome with the implementation of the HBB program (OR 0.04; 95% CI 0.00, 0.98). However, heterogeneity is very high, and the confidence interval is wide (Figure 3). Rule et al. [20] showed a high decrease in the risk of asphyxia with the implementation of HBB, but this study has a high risk of bias, so we believe that the results were overestimated and are the cause of heterogeneity. Msemo et al. [21] was more accurate and had a low risk of bias.

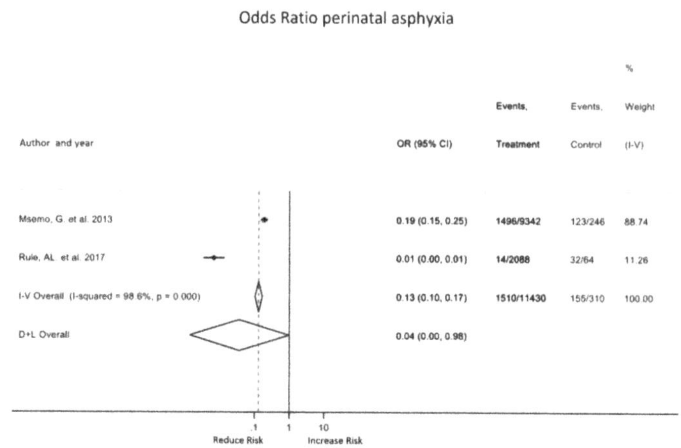

Figure 3. Forest plot for effect of HBB program on neonatal morbidity.

Of the overall mortality sensitivity analyses performed, six were at low risk of bias and four were at high risk of bias, finding that the quality of the studies does not affect the outcome (Figure 4). Finally, the funnel plot shows symmetry in most of the studies, ruling out publication bias in the studies (Figure 5).

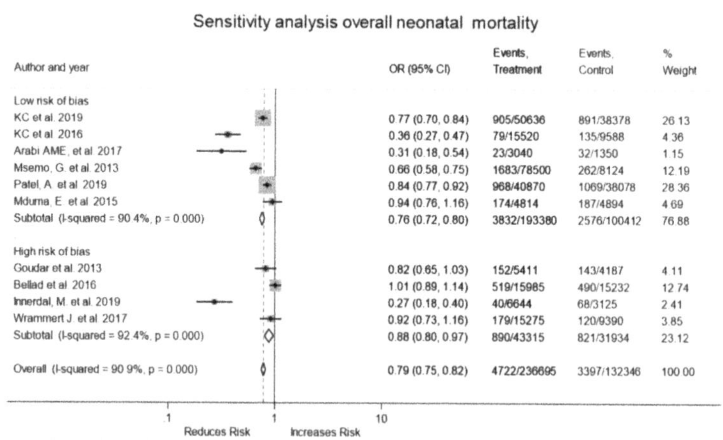

Figure 4. Forest plot for sensitivity analysis for overall neonatal mortality.

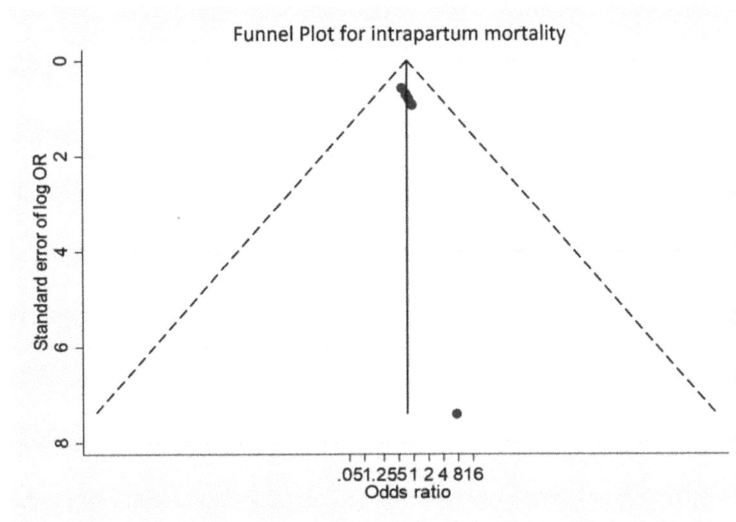

Figure 5. Funnel plot (asymmetry test).

4. Discussion

The systematic review and meta-analysis studied the effect of the implementation of the HBB program, in low- and middle-income countries, on neonatal mortality and morbidity. We found that the implementation of the program in the health institutions of these countries decreased neonatal mortality, especially intrapartum stillbirth, first-day neonatal mortality, and first-week neonatal mortality, with no observed effect on late neonatal mortality. On the other hand, the only morbidity outcome reported in the included studies was perinatal asphyxia, which showed a reduction in this outcome with the implementation of the HBB program.

These results are in line with those reported by other authors. For example, Morris [30], in a systematic review without meta-analysis, reports that the implementation of the HBB program seems to have benefits in reducing intrapartum neonatal mortality in the first week of life. Similarly, the meta-analysis of Versantvoor et al. [31] demonstrated that HBB impacts intrapartum stillbirth, and early neonatal mortality (first-day and first-week neonatal mortality), without effect on late mortality. Nevertheless, in the present study, we found and included a larger number of studies in the literature because we decided to include studies in low- and middle-income countries and studies that inform morbidity outcomes, while the study of Versantovoor assessed only the effects in low-income countries and mortality. Given that Colombia is classified as having middle economic income and part of the neonatal mortality occurs in this type of country, we wanted to expand the effect of the HHB program in middle-income countries.

Intrapartum and early neonatal deaths can explain 5 million neonatal deaths in the world, mainly in low-income countries. In the face of this challenge, the implementation of the HBB program at the country level could have a great effect on reducing neonatal mortality [32]. In addition, to achieve the potential of the program, an educational strategy for staff training is not enough: government efforts are required for an adequate implementation of the program [33]. In line with this, we propose, as observed in the qualitative review of these studies, that the effects on mortality reduction can be explained in part by the educational strategies and national implementation measures used at the country level that developed the studies for the implementation of the program. Therefore, The HBB program can then be proposed as a prevention strategy in newborn care and intervention that can contribute to achieving the millennium development goals, allowing a decrease in neonatal mortality in countries with a high incidence. Therefore, it is proposed to continue advancing in the integration of government and welfare actors for the actual implementation of the program in these countries and scenarios with limited economic resources.

Likewise, the effect of reducing mortality can be explained by the training of the personnel in charge of the newborn during birth, which offers the necessary skills to respond to intrapartum and birth complications, while late neonatal mortality may be associated with other causes unrelated to childbirth and/or late birth complications. Although the studies included in the meta-analysis show great heterogeneity in the trained personnel (doctors, nurses, midwives, and health profession students), it is also true that the evidence shows that the training of personnel in resuscitation is a strategy that decreases neonatal mortality [34]. Studies of the HBB program have shown that it has an impact on improving and retaining the skills and knowledge necessary for basic neonatal resuscitation [35]. It has a special effect on improving bag-mask ventilation and uses in the first minute, increasing the number of babies who receive it adequately when they need it [27,36]. This is relevant, given that about 95% of newborns manage to start breathing with adequate positive pressure bag-mask ventilation [37]. This strategy could not only impact the newborn child without vital signs (intrapartum stillbirth), but all newborns when it is applied in an appropriate way, decreasing the chance of dying in the first 24 h; this fact is important because the window of greatest mortality after a cardiorespiratory arrest or asphyxia occurs during the first 24 h.

Although heterogeneity was found in the type of staff trained in the program, it should also be recognized that the HBB strategy was implemented in health caregivers, midwives, doctors and nursing staff, including students and trainees in these areas; it focuses on all levels of health personnel, and the results obtained make the strategy attractive for obtaining necessary skills and access to all levels of training, in all the studies that meet the criteria.

On the other hand, the only morbidity outcome reported in these studies was perinatal asphyxia. It is important to note that there are no other types of pathologies recorded in the studies, such as length of stay in the neonatal intensive care unit, necrotizing enterocolitis, neonatal sepsis, bronchopulmonary dysplasia, intraventricular hemorrhage in the medium and long term in relation to neurodevelopment, so we suggest that future studies could take these outcomes into account.

Finally, although the effect on intrapartum and early mortality is important to meet the SDG, complementing the impact of combining it with other programs and/or neonatal support interventions such as when essential care for the newborn is recommended [38]. Therefore, we also propose evaluating the effect on early and late mortality in research studies with the establishment of programs in conjunction with others of interest in neonatal health, such as post-arrest stabilization and transport courses, such as STABLE®, Acute Care of at-Risk Newborns (ACoRN®) and with a properly established referral network allowing timely access to complex care to adequately continue post-arrest newborn care.

The study has some limitations. The first is the heterogeneity of the studies, which limits the validity of the results. We believe that heterogeneity is due to the lack of data in some studies, such as gestational age, educational strategy, and staff. Second, it is the low quality of the studies that limit the recommendations and extrapolation. The strengths of this study lie in the inclusion of recent literature with effects on low- and middle-income countries, where the highest neonatal mortality occurs, and in the evaluation of the impact on outcomes other than mortality that largely explain the burden of disease in neonates who survive birth complications and asphyxia; although only asphyxia is reported as an outcome, we believe that these data open new research opportunities that strengthen the HBB program. Finally, the methodology used for the systematic review and data extraction was its strength.

5. Conclusions

In conclusion, the HBB program is effective in reducing intrapartum stillbirth and early mortality (first day and first week). Given that the highest concentration of neonatal mortality occurs in this period and due to perinatal asphyxia, the HBB program has great potential to contribute to achieving the MDGs.

Author Contributions: Conceptualization S.A.-P., A.C.-S. and P.Á.-C.; methodology, S.A.-P., H.O., A.C.-S., and P.Á.-C.; formal analysis, A.C.-S., P.Á.-C. and H.O.; data curation, S.A.-P., A.C.-S., P.Á.-C. and H.O.; writing—original draft preparation, S.A.-P., A.C.-S., P.Á.-C. and H.O.; writing—review and editing, S.A.-P., A.C.-S. and P.Á.-C.; supervision, S.A.-P. and H.O.. All authors have read and agreed to the published version of the manuscript.

Funding: This research received no external funding.

Institutional Review Board Statement: Not applicable.

Conflicts of Interest: The authors declare no conflict of interest.

References

1. Objetivos y Metas de Desarrollo Sostenible—Desarrollo Sostenible. n.d. Available online: https://www.un.org/sustainabledevelopment/es/objetivos-de-desarrollo-sostenible/ (accessed on 18 September 2022).
2. Darmstadt, G.L.; A Bhutta, Z.; Cousens, S.; Adam, T.; Walker, N.; de Bernis, L. Evidence-based, cost-effective interventions: How many newborn babies can we save? *Lancet* **2005**, *365*, 977–988. [CrossRef]
3. Oestergaard, M.Z.; Inoue, M.; Yoshida, S.; Mahanani, W.R.; Gore, F.M.; Cousens, S.; Lawn, J.E.; Mathers, C.D.; on behalf of the United Nations Inter-agency Group for Child Mortality Estimation and the Child Health Epidemiology Reference Group. Neonatal Mortality Levels for 193 Countries in 2009 with Trends since 1990: A Systematic Analysis of Progress, Projections, and Priorities. *PLoS Med.* **2011**, *8*, e1001080. [CrossRef] [PubMed]
4. Lawn, J.E.; Blencowe, H.; Oza, S.; You, D.; Lee, A.C.; Waiswa, P.; Lalli, M.; Bhutta, Z.; Barros, A.J.D.; Christian, P.; et al. Every Newborn: Progress, priorities, and potential beyond survival. *Lancet* **2014**, *384*, 189–205. [CrossRef]
5. Liu, L.; Oza, S.; Hogan, D.; Chu, Y.; Perin, J.; Zhu, J.; Lawn, J.E.; Cousens, S.; Mathers, C.; Black, R.E. Global, regional, and national causes of under-5 mortality in 2000–15: An updated systematic analysis with implications for the Sustainable Development Goals. *Lancet* **2016**, *388*, 3027–3035. [CrossRef]
6. Baqui, A.H.; Arifeen, S.; Darmstadt, G.L.; Ahmed, S.; Williams, E.; Seraji, H.R.; Mannan, I.; Rahman, S.M.; Shah, R.; Saha, S.K.; et al. Effect of community-based newborn-care intervention package implemented through two service-delivery strategies in Sylhet district, Bangladesh: A cluster-randomised controlled trial. *Lancet* **2008**, *371*, 1936–1944. [CrossRef]
7. Opiyo, N.; English, M. In-service training for health professionals to improve care of the seriously ill newborn or child in low and middle-income countries (Review). *Cochrane Database Syst. Rev.* **2010**, *14*, CD007071. [CrossRef]
8. Ariff, S.; Lee, A.C.; Lawn, J.; Bhutta, Z.A. Global Burden, Epidemiologic Trends, and Prevention of Intrapartum-Related Deaths in Low-Resource Settings. *Clin. Perinatol.* **2016**, *43*, 593–608. [CrossRef]
9. Narayanan, I.; Rose, M.; Cordero, D.; Faillace, S.; Sanghvi, T. *The Components of Essential Newborn Care*; Basics Support for Institutionalizing Child Survival Project for the United States Agency for International Development: Arlington, VA, USA, 2004.
10. World Health Organization. *Guidelines on Basic Newborn Resuscitation*; World Health Organization: Geneva, Switzerland, 2012.
11. van Heerden, C. An introduction to Helping Babies Breathe: The "Golden Minute" is here for South African newborn babies. *Prof. Nurs. Today* **2012**, *16*, 6–7.
12. Steele, C. Helping Babies Breathe Around the World. *J. Obstet. Gynecol. Neonatal Nurs.* **2013**, *42*, 243–246. [CrossRef]
13. Helping Babies Survive. n.d. Available online: https://www.aap.org/en/aap-global/helping-babies-survive/ (accessed on 18 September 2022).
14. Carlo, W.A.; Goudar, S.S.; Pasha, O.; Chomba, E.; Wallander, J.L.; Biasini, F.J.; McClure, E.M.; Thorsten, V.; Chakraborty, H.; Wallace, D.; et al. Randomized Trial of Early Developmental Intervention on Outcomes in Children after Birth Asphyxia in Developing Countries. *J. Pediatr.* **2013**, *162*, 705–712.e3. [CrossRef]
15. Wallander, J.L.; Bann, C.; Chomba, E.; Goudar, S.S.; Pasha, O.; Biasini, F.J.; McClure, E.M.; Thorsten, V.; Wallace, D.; Carlo, W.A. Developmental trajectories of children with birth asphyxia through 36months of age in low/low–middle income countries. *Early Hum. Dev.* **2014**, *90*, 343–348. [CrossRef] [PubMed]
16. Wall, S.N.; Lee, A.C.C.; Niermeyer, S.; English, M.; Keenan, W.J.; Carlo, W.; Bhutta, Z.A.; Bang, A.; Narayanan, I.; Ariawan, I.; et al. Neonatal resuscitation in low-resource settings: What, who, and how to overcome challenges to scale up? *Int. J. Gynecol. Obstet.* **2009**, *107*, S47–S64. [CrossRef] [PubMed]
17. Chaudhury, S.; Arlington, L.; Brenan, S.; Kairuki, A.K.; Meda, A.R.; Isangula, K.G.; Mponzi, V.; Bishanga, D.; Thomas, E.; Msemo, G.; et al. Cost analysis of large-scale implementation of the 'Helping Babies Breathe' newborn resuscitation-training program in Tanzania. *BMC Health Serv. Res.* **2016**, *16*, 681. [CrossRef] [PubMed]

18. Jüni, P.; Loke, Y.; Pigott, T.; Ramsay, C.; Regidor, D.; Rothstein, H.; Sandhu, L.; Santaguida, P.L.; Schünemann, H.J.; Shea, B. Risk of bias in non-randomized studies of interventions (ROBINS-I): Detailed guidance. *Br. Med. J.* **2016**, *355*, i4919. [CrossRef]
19. Kc, A.; Ewald, U.; Basnet, O.; Gurung, A.; Pyakuryal, S.N.; Jha, B.K.; Bergström, A.; Eriksson, L.; Paudel, P.; Karki, S.; et al. Effect of a scaled-up neonatal resuscitation quality improvement package on intrapartum-related mortality in Nepal: A stepped-wedge cluster randomized controlled trial. *PLoS Med.* **2019**, *16*, e1002900. [CrossRef]
20. Rule, A.R.; Maina, E.; Cheruiyot, D.; Mueri, P.; Simmons, J.M.; Kamath-Rayne, B.D. Using quality improvement to decrease birth asphyxia rates after 'Helping Babies Breathe' training in Kenya. *Acta Paediatr.* **2017**, *106*, 1666–1673. [CrossRef]
21. Msemo, G.; Massawe, A.; Mmbando, D.; Rusibamayila, N.; Manji, K.; Kidanto, H.L.; Mwizamuholya, D.; Ringia, P.; Ersdal, H.L.; Perlman, J. Newborn Mortality and Fresh Stillbirth Rates in Tanzania After Helping Babies Breathe Training. *Pediatrics* **2013**, *131*, e353–e360. [CrossRef]
22. Mduma, E.; Ersdal, H.; Svensen, E.; Kidanto, H.; Auestad, B.; Perlman, J. Frequent brief on-site simulation training and reduction in 24-h neonatal mortality—An educational intervention study. *Resuscitation* **2015**, *93*, 1–7. [CrossRef]
23. Patel, A.; Bang, A.; Kurhe, K.; Bhargav, S.; Prakash, A.; Arramraj, S.; Hibberd, P.L. Comparison of perinatal outcomes in facilities before and after Global Network's Helping Babies Breathe Implementation Study in Nagpur, India. *BMC Pregnancy Childbirth* **2019**, *19*, 324. [CrossRef]
24. Innerdal, M.; Simaga, I.; Diall, H.; Eielsen, M.; Niermeyer, S.; Eielsen, O.; Saugstad, O.D. Reduction in Perinatal Mortality after Implementation of HBB Training at a District Hospital in Mali. *J. Trop. Pediatr.* **2020**, *66*, 315–321. [CrossRef]
25. Kc, A.; Wrammert, J.; Clark, R.B.; Ewald, U.; Vitrakoti, R.; Chaudhary, P.; Pun, A.; Raaijmakers, H.; Målqvist, M. Reducing Perinatal Mortality in Nepal Using Helping Babies Breathe. *Pediatrics* **2016**, *137*, e20150117. [CrossRef] [PubMed]
26. Bellad, R.M.; Bang, A.; Carlo, W.A.; McClure, E.; Meleth, S.; Goco, N.; Goudar, S.; Derman, R.; Hibberd, P.L.; Petal, A.; et al. A pre-post study of a multi-country scale up of resuscitation training of facility birth attendants: Does Helping Babies Breathe training save lives? *BMC Pregnancy Childbirth* **2016**, *16*, 222. [CrossRef] [PubMed]
27. Wrammert, J.; Kc, A.; Ewald, U.; Målqvist, M. Improved postnatal care is needed to maintain gains in neonatal survival after the implementation of the Helping Babies Breathe initiative. *Acta Paediatr.* **2017**, *106*, 1280–1285. [CrossRef] [PubMed]
28. Goudar, S.S.; Somannavar, M.S.; Clark, R.; Lockyer, J.M.; Revankar, A.P.; Fidler, H.M.; Sloan, N.L.; Niermeyer, S.; Keenan, W.J.; Singhal, N. Stillbirth and Newborn Mortality in India After Helping Babies Breathe Training. *Pediatrics* **2013**, *131*, e344–e352. [CrossRef] [PubMed]
29. Arabi, A.; Ibrahim, S.; Manar, A.; Abdalla, M.; Ahmed, S.; Dempsey, E.; Ryan, C. Perinatal outcomes following Helping Babies Breathe training and regular peer–peer skills practice among village midwives in Sudan. *Arch. Dis. Child.* **2018**, *103*, 24–27. [CrossRef] [PubMed]
30. Morris, S.M.; Fratt, E.M.; Rodriguez, J.; Ruman, A.; Wibecan, L.; Nelson, B.D. Implementation of the Helping Babies Breathe Training Program: A Systematic Review. *Pediatrics* **2020**, *146*, e20193938. [CrossRef]
31. Versantvoort, J.M.D.; Kleinhout, M.Y.; Ockhuijsen, H.D.L.; Bloemenkamp, K.; de Vries, W.B.; Hoogen, A.V.D. Helping Babies Breathe and its effects on intrapartum-related stillbirths and neonatal mortality in low-resource settings: A systematic review. *Arch. Dis. Child.* **2020**, *105*, 127–133. [CrossRef]
32. Travers, C.P.; Carlo, W.A. How to Save 1 Million Lives in a Year in Low- and Middle-Income Countries. *Neonatology* **2017**, *111*, 431–436. [CrossRef]
33. Hodgins, S. Helping Babies Breathe—Beyond Training. *Glob. Health Sci. Pract.* **2018**, *6*, 402–404. [CrossRef]
34. Dempsey, E.M.; Pammi, M.; Ryan, A.C.; Barrington, K.J. Standardised formal resuscitation training programmes for reducing mortality and morbidity in newborn infants. *Cochrane Database Syst. Rev.* **2015**, *2015*, CD009106. [CrossRef]
35. Dol, J.; Campbell-Yeo, M.; Murphy, G.T.; Aston, M.; McMillan, D.; Richardson, B. The impact of the Helping Babies Survive program on neonatal outcomes and health provider skills: A systematic review. *JBI Database Syst. Rev. Implement. Rep.* **2018**, *16*, 701–737. [CrossRef] [PubMed]
36. Budhathoki, S.S.; Gurung, R.; Ewald, U.; Thapa, J.; Kc, A. Does the Helping Babies Breathe Programme impact on neonatal resuscitation care practices? Results from systematic review and meta-analysis. *Acta Paediatr.* **2019**, *108*, 806–813. [CrossRef] [PubMed]
37. Aziz, K.; Lee, H.C.; Escobedo, M.B.; Hoover, A.V.; Kamath-Rayne, B.D.; Kapadia, V.S.; Magid, D.J.; Niermeyer, S.; Schmölzer, G.M.; Szyld, E.; et al. Part 5: Neonatal Resuscitation: 2020 American Heart Association Guidelines for Cardiopulmonary Resuscitation and Emergency Cardiovascular Care. *Circulation* **2020**, *142*, S524–S550. [CrossRef] [PubMed]
38. Niermeyer, S. Global gains after Helping Babies Breathe. *Acta Paediatr.* **2017**, *106*, 1550–1551. [CrossRef]

International Journal of
Environmental Research and Public Health

MDPI

Article

Scientometric Analysis of Global Scientific Literature on Aging in Place

Olugbenga Oladinrin [1], Kasun Gomis [1,*], Wadu Mesthrige Jayantha [2], Lovelin Obi [1] and Muhammad Qasim Rana [1]

1 School of Architecture and the Built Environment, Faculty of Science and Engineering, University of Wolverhampton, Wolverhampton WV1 1LY, UK; O.Oladinrin@wlv.ac.uk (O.O.); L.Obi@wlv.ac.uk (L.O.); m.q.rana@wlv.ac.uk (M.Q.R.)

2 School of Property, Construction and Project Management, College of Design and Social Context, RMIT University, Melbourne VIC 3000, Australia; wadu.jayantha@rmit.edu.au

* Correspondence: m.gomis2@wlv.ac.uk

Abstract: The amount of literature reporting "aging-in-place" studies has increased sharply in recent decades. However, the studies have taken a global view of the range and scope of the research that has taken place. This study presents a bibliometric analysis of the current status of the aging in place research themes published as scientific articles between 1970 and 2021, using the Web of Science database. VOSviewer software was employed to map and visualize the 1331 items of bibliographic data retrieved. The findings reveal a continuous growing trend in the publication of aging in place research. Most productive institutions derive from the USA. The International Journal of Environmental Research and Public Health is the most preferred Journal. The most popular research hotspots or areas include; older adults, aging, housing, dementia, long-term care, and technology, and their associations with the field of "aging in place" field were elucidated. This study offers several valuable insights to scholars, research institutions, and policymakers, enabling a better understanding of the developments in the aging in place research domain.

Keywords: aging in place; smart-home technologies; Gerontologist; VOSviewer

Citation: Oladinrin, O.; Gomis, K.; Jayantha, W.M.; Obi, L.; Rana, M.Q. Scientometric Analysis of Global Scientific Literature on Aging in Place. *Int. J. Environ. Res. Public Health* **2021**, *18*, 12468. https://doi.org/10.3390/ijerph182312468

Academic Editors: Joachim G. Voss and Sandul Yasobant

Received: 24 October 2021
Accepted: 24 November 2021
Published: 26 November 2021

1. Introduction

There is evidence of a rapid increase in population aging across the globe [1,2]. Countries across the world are confronted with significant challenges of an aging population. For instance, the USA [3], Great Britain [4], China [5], India [6], Japan, which was tagged a super-aging society [7], Australia [8], Hong Kong [9], and some regions in Europe [10] non-exclusively, are few examples of nations facing the challenges associated with population aging. According to United Nations estimates, it is projected that the global population over the age of 60 years will reach 1 billion by 2020 and almost 2 billion by 2050 [11]. Even though the numbers did not reach the anticipated projection in 2020, the aging population over 65 years remains critical at 727 million persons [12]. More so, it has been estimated that the annual net increase of those aged 65 years or older will continue to exceed 10 million people over the next decade [4]. Accordingly, 26 countries had over 2 million older people in 1990, but this extended to 31 nations by the year 2000 [13]. The United Nations has also projected that the number of people aged 80 or older is estimated to more than triple between 2017 and 2050, increasing from 137 million to 425 million globally [14]. All these projections imply increased demand for extra health care as older people experience more chronic conditions [15], aging-friendly homes [16], as well as pensions for older populations [17]. Population aging, therefore, is a significant concern for key stakeholders, governments, policymakers, and researchers across the globe.

This rapid increase in population aging necessitates a reevaluation of conventional economic, political, and social policies to mitigate the potential problems associated with population aging [18,19]. It has been established that scientific advance is central to the economic and cultural development of a country [20]. Hence, an objective evaluation of the quality of the scientific publications of researchers and research organizations is vital to recognize a country's present position and its potential for development in given domains [21,22]. As a component of science policy, it is necessary to track emerging research developments such as new fields and hotspots (i.e., areas of research concentration) worth special funding efforts or areas of growth and decline [23]. One of the approaches to forestalling the many challenges presented follows the recognition of the "aging in place" principle. Over the past few decades, concerned policymakers and elderly caregivers have advocated the conceptualization of aging in place as a realistic and valuable goal [24]. Golant [25] explores the current role of family support, housing, and care services in the private sector, government programmes, along with the promise of smart-home technology, creative planning, and long-term care strategies to ensure elderlies not only age in place but also age successfully in the right place. Consequently, aging in place has become an important area of interest in environmental gerontology and is the strong wish of both the elderly and their caregivers [24,26]. It is evident that not all older adults wish to age in place, especially those living in unsuitable or unsafe housing [27]. However, a recent study revealed that population aging already has, and will continue to have, significant consequences and effects in all areas of life; in the economic area, it is predicted that population aging would impact economic growth, employment, trade, labour markets, taxes and wealth and property transition from one generation to the next [28]. The concept of aging in place means that older people can age in a comfortable place and live in a familiar community with an emotional attachment to a long-term home. The term "place" refers to the home, community, or any physical space that people occupy and find significant. The larger part of older individuals needs to age-in-place, stay as independent, dynamic, and autonomous as long as possible, and live at domestic encompassed by family and companions [29,30]. The majority of older people aged 65 years and older are happier and more physically stable than earlier generations, indicating that older adults will live independently in the community later in the future [31]. Meanwhile, the aging of populations is expected to result in increased demand worldwide for long-term home care services [32]. Home-based care programs and age-friendly communities are some initiatives that reduce disability and promote aging in place [33,34]. However, aging in place operates in so many interacting ways that it requires proper policy and research attention [35].

Thus, aging in place has received, and is receiving, great attention from policymakers and scholars, with a surge in quantity and substance in the literature [24]. This surge may present a risk because of the difficulties in comprehending the existing state of the body of knowledge and the possibility of disregarding important questions and areas for research and practice improvement [36]. Avoiding this scientific risk requires a rigorous analysis of the domain. Up till now, this has not been sufficiently addressed. Past review studies on aging in place [24,37,38] (Graybill, McMeekin, & Wildman, 2014; Peek et al., 2014; Vasunilashorn, Steinman, Liebig, & Pynoos, 2012) have adopted a qualitative and narrative synthesis approach, based upon manual appraisals and by its nature subjective. Subjectivity is primarily conceptualized as how the investigation is affected by the researcher's viewpoints, values, social encounters, and perspective. Hence, using such a qualitative approach as a validity test remains subjective. The scientometric review is quantitative, objective, and more reliable [39]. Markoulli, Lee, Byington, and Felps [40] posited that qualitative, manual reviews could not be applied to a comprehensive overview of an intellectual structure. More so, as global research on aging in place deals with several diverse views and issues, most bibliographic studies have exclusively focused on specific and limited aspects of aging in place. For example, while some review studies [38,41] focused on using technology to assist aging in place, another study by Graybill et al. [37] focused on the cost-effectiveness of aging in place. Rowlands [42] posits that bibliometric analysis offers greater transparency and the prospect of innovation in an environment that has really become a little jaded.

As aging is a prevalent phenomenon, the question is, how has the development of the research literature on this topic fared over the year? More precisely, the following research questions are addressed: (1) Who are the geographic contributors to aging in place research, and how have contributions evolved over the past years? (2) Which countries and organizations attract the most citation activity and by whom? (3) What form do international collaborations take based on publication co-authorship relationships? (4) How have research fronts changed over time based on the prevalence and co-occurrence of author keywords? (5) What are the related and relevant sources for the publication of aging in place research? Thus, this study aims to provide a systematic overview and identify future aging in place research trends. Because of the vast increase in literature on aging in place, bibliometric methods were employed to provide a quantitative analysis of the output (measured by the number of publications) and impact (measured by the number of citations). Although there are ongoing discussions about the reliability of specific bibliometric indices, the importance of evaluating the productivity of scientific research through the analysis of the quality of the publication and the corresponding citation data cannot be undermined [43]. However, the shortcoming of bibliometric analysis is the risk of presenting figures for the sake of statistics, with little comprehension of what they mean [42]. The analysis helps to answer the questions on the development and characteristics of the field of aging in place. Furthermore, analysis enables the identification of the most productive and influential articles, authors, core journals, countries, and organizations, together with information about the extent of cooperation among them. The analysis also enables identification of the extent of globalization existing within the research domain, leading topics, and potential gaps [44]. The bibliometric analysis offers informative guidelines for journal editors, policymakers, and researchers by providing information on research trends, those productive authors, active institutions, and research hotspots. When making funding decisions and promoting the growth of research opportunities and weaknesses, policymakers focused on such bibliometric knowledge and assessments [45].

2. Methodology

The essence of the literature review study is to map and appraise the body of literature to identify potential research gaps and the frontiers of knowledge [46]. Structured literature reviews follow a systematic process including iterative cycles based on appropriate specified search keywords, followed by a bibliographic literature search, using an appropriate database, and a completing analysis [47]. Several researchers have used the bibliometric and scientometric review to evaluate the literature growth patterns, core journals, productive authors, influential institutions, contributing countries, research output performance, and research hotspots in a given field [48,49]. Bibliometric and scientometric analyses were employed in this study (see Figure 1). When conducting a literature review, Rowley and Slack [50] recommend a structured methodology for retrieving relevant resources, devising a mind map to organize the literature review, writing the review study, and developing the bibliography. A similar approach to bibliometric analysis by Sweileh et al. [51] was followed in this study.

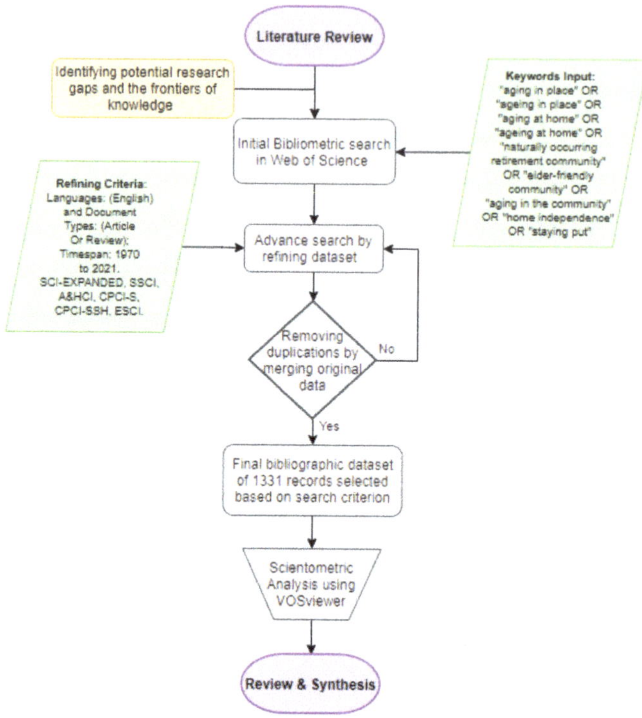

Figure 1. Methodology of the study.

2.1. Identification and Collection of Bibliographic Data

The Web of Science (Core Collection) was searched to collect bibliographic data used for the bibliometric analysis in this study because the Web of Science core collection contains comprehensive literature databases with high quality and influential articles [52]. Likewise, the Web of Science has been adjudged the most reliable scientific database [53], with the most reliable download function [54]. Moreover, the Web of Science core collection has advantages over other bibliographic databases such as Scopus. First, the citation matching algorithm in Scopus appears to need improvement when compared to Web of Science [55]. Second, duplicate articles in Scopus are a key source of data quality issues [56]. Hence, we chose to limit our search to the Web of Science only. A "topic" search was used based on search terms in the title, abstract and keywords, and keywords plus [57]. A wide range of terms representing the idea of aging in place identified by Vasunilashorn et al. [24] was used. The overall search string was as follows: TOPIC: ("aging in place" OR "ageing in place" OR "aging at home" OR "ageing at home" OR "naturally occurring retirement community" OR "elder-friendly community" OR "aging in the community" OR "home independence" OR "staying put"). Refined by: Languages: (English) and Document Types: (Article Or Review); Timespan: 1970 to 2021. SCI-EXPANDED, SSCI, A&HCI, CPCI-S, CPCI-SSH, ESCI. Due to the different language used between countries and cultures, as opined by Vasunilashorn et al. [24], the chosen search terms have restricted the inclusion of some publications by carefully removing unrelated research areas from the Web of Science before exporting the materials (e.g., agriculture and zoology). Only articles and reviews published in journals were involved as these are considered "certified knowledge" [58]. The knowledge contained in journals has already been subjected to a critical review and has succeeded in gaining approval from the research community; thus, enhancing the reliability of the analysis results. The search was conducted in September 2021, and 1331 records met the search criterion, becoming the bibliographic dataset. The data were downloaded as text files for analysis purposes. Web of Science searches are not sensitive to hyphenation [57]; thus, the search returned occurrences of duplications such as "ageing-in-place" and "aging in-place"; "older people" and "older adults". All the duplications were merged in the original bibliographic data files before the analysis was concluded.

2.2. Method of Analysis

Traditionally, bibliometric analyses have been categorized into two types; whether the analyses yield activity or relationship indicators [58]. Activity yielding indicators present data conveying the force of impact or strength of the influence of research efforts, while relationship indicators trace the links and interactions between different items, such as researchers, documents, and keywords. VOSviewer software (version 1.6.17) (Lens, Brisbane, Austrilia) was used to obtain these indicators using bibliographic data to build a network of co-authorship, co-occurrence, and co-citation analyses. VOSviewer was used to combine both activity yielding and relationship indicators analyses. The software was used to create knowledge maps of the identified productive authors, core journals, contributing countries and organizations, influential documents, and co-occurring keywords. VOSviewer is a freely available software program developed for constructing and viewing bibliometric maps. Unlike most computer programs (such as VantagePoint and CiteSpace) used for bibliometric mapping, VOSviewer is highly responsive to the graphical representation of bibliometric maps and useful for presenting large, easy-to-interpret, bibliometric maps [59]. VOSviewer has been used in analysing scientific outputs in different research fields, such as tourism and sustainability [60], ground-penetrating radar [61], and communication [62].

3. Results and Discussion

The 1331 published research articles were analysed, and the results were presented. Figure 2 reveals increased research in the aging in place domain. The figure shows an evident rise in the number of articles published on aging in place between 2010 and 2020, with the years 2019 (153 articles) and 2020 (192 articles) accounting for the most articles. Reasons for increased publications since 2010 was highlighted as a preference on maintaining the independence of older persons, emphasis of technology on non-institutional care, availability of grants in fostering aging in place, cost escalation of long-term institutional care, in addition to contemporary reforms and policies implemented [24,63]. The rapid decrease in publications for the years 2021 and 2022 is due to the incomplete bibliographic data records. This trend will probably continue to increase in the future research carried out. Hence, further analysis is required to gain more insights into the research direction in this domain.

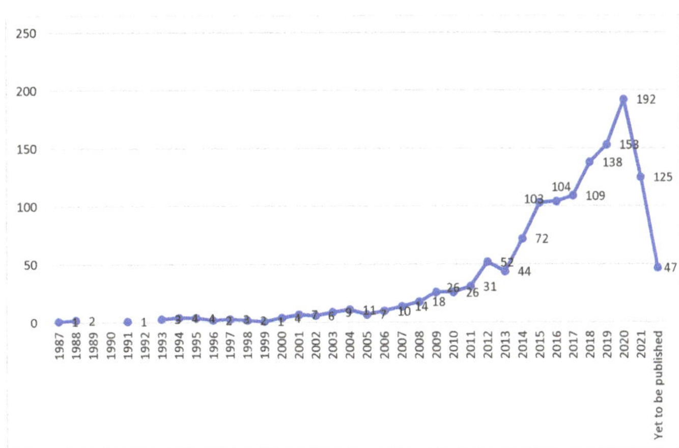

Figure 2. Number of publications from 1987 to 2021 in the Web of Science.

3.1. Co-Authorship Analysis

The "co-authorship" identification is one of the main options provided by the Create Map wizard in VOSviewer. Co-authorship network analysis includes reliable algorithms that can track almost every aspect of scientific collaboration [64]. Hosseini et al. [36] described co-authorship as a shorthand for scientific collaboration. Co-authorship network analysis helps evaluate the collaborative behaviour of researchers, organizations, and countries in novel ways by disclosing the collaborative structure and information about the centrality of network participants. The wide range of applications indicates the adaptability of the information retrieved using this technology and offers new avenues for research collaboration. It enables one to comprehend the research structure on specific issues, the growth of research networks through time, and the participation of a certain institution or nation in a specific network [65]. Given this, co-authorship analysis was used in this study to create maps of authors, organizations, and countries.

3.1.1. Authors

A total number of 3901 researchers participated in the 1331 bibliographic documents. However, in VOSviewer, the minimum number of documents for any author was set at five publications for clarity, which produced 40 authors meeting the threshold. This is to avoid the overlapping of many authors with fewer publications in the subsequent analysis of network visualization. The threshold was decided after several iterations, with five documents producing sufficient clarity. Moreover, articles with multiple authors were counted in full rather than proportionately to avoid confusion in their link strength. For each of the 40 authors, the corresponding number of citations and the total strength of their citation links with other authors were calculated as shown in Table 1. The total link strength attribute is used to evaluate the total strength of the co-authorship links of a given researcher with other researchers [66]. Szanton S.L. of the Johns Hopkins University in the United States produced the highest number of publications (18), joint with other authors and the highest total link strength (20). Thus, Rantz M.J. is the most influential author in aging in the place research domain. Rantz M.J. follows this with 15 submissions (link strength = 35) and Greenfield E.A. with 14 submissions (link strength = 13). Although the identity of this author showed as two different names, Rantz M.J. (nine articles) and Rantz M. (six articles), it was found that the two names were referring to the same author. All the influential authors are from the United States, indicating the extent of the research effort made those on aging in place. The findings seem like scholars in the United States have been at the forefront of concern about the global demographic shift, facilitating and championing the transition to ensure older people live comfortably in the places they desire. This could indicate that the US is a large country with an active aging society and high rates of funding for research.

Table 1. The top 10 most productive authors.

Author	Institution	Country	Total Publications	Citations	Total Link Strength
Szanton, S.I.	Johns Hopkins University	USA	18	405	20
Rantz, M.J.	University of Missouri-Columbia	USA	15	428	35
Greenfield, E.A.	State University of New Jersey	USA	14	243	13
Lehning, A.J.	University of Maryland	USA	12	233	14
Skubic, M.	University of Missouri-Columbia	USA	10	338	24
Gitlin, L.N.	Drexel University, Philadelphia	USA	10	308	18
Scharlach, A.E.	University of California	USA	10	161	16
Mihailidis, A.	University of Toronto	Canada	10	169	0
Iwarsson, S.	Lund University	Sweden	9	183	10
Park, S.	Washington University	USA	9	64	7

With such knowledge of the contemporary scientific collaboration networks, access to specialities, funds, expertise, and research productivity can be enhanced in this research domain [36]. Such knowledge is also crucial to broadening academic collaboration and communication by reducing isolation in research via the tracking of and connecting with investigators in various regions. Authors with minimum productivity of five documents were "visualized" using the VOSviewer technique. Figure 3 is a network visualization of highly productive authors based on the number of their publications. The map shows 40 circles, each representing one researcher with close circles indicating research collaborations between authors. These circles are clustered into ten, representing ten research communities. The lines in the map represent a link defining a connection between two scholars, indicating the number of co-authored publications. Through this collaborative practice, researchers build learning networks, promote different ways of thinking, and inspire solutions to research problems.

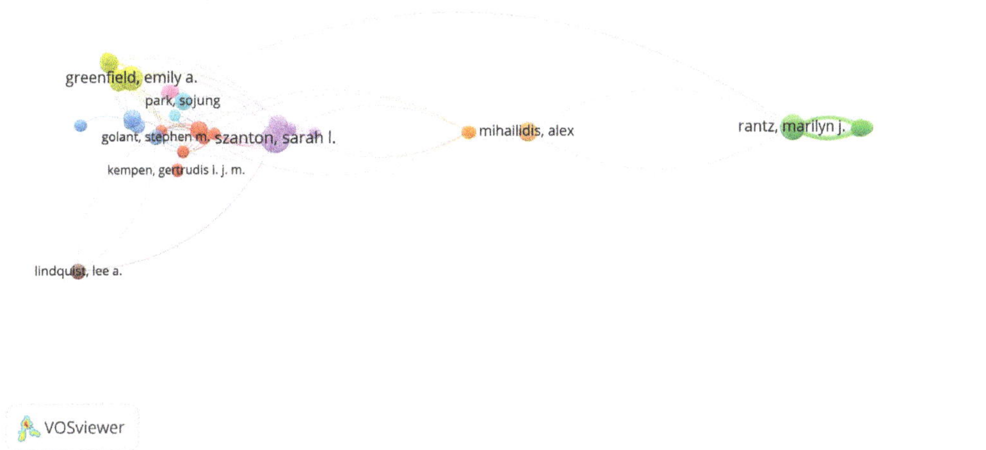

Figure 3. Network visualization of highly productive authors.

3.1.2. Organizations/Institutions

Many institutions from all over the world publish aging-in-place-related research papers. Table 2 presents the top ten institutions with the highest number of publications to identify the most productive ones. Out of 1304 organizations identified from the bibliographic data, only 121 meet the threshold of five publications. Table 2 shows the top-performing research institutions, their geographic locations, and the number of publications they contributed to aging-in-place research. The most active institutions in the field were in the USA. This corroborates the previous findings on productive authors in that the authors were from institutions in the US. The University of Missouri ranks first in terms of published articles related to aging in place, with 32 documents, followed by the University of Maryland and the University of Toronto with 25 publications each.

Table 2. The top 11 most productive institutions.

Institution	Location	Number of Publication	Citations
University of Missouri	USA	32	688
University of Toronto	Canada	25	573
University of Maryland	USA	25	509
Maastricht University	Netherland	21	251
Lund University	Sweden	20	352
Hong Kong Polytechnic University	Hong Kong	19	142
Washington University	USA	18	219
University of Michigan	USA	18	475
Karolinska Institute	Sweden	18	171
La Trobe University	Australia	18	235
University of Florida	USA	18	221

A network visualization map showing collaboration among those research institutions that have produced a productivity minimum of five documents is shown in Figure 4. The thickness of the lines connecting any two institutions indicates the strength of collaboration. Figure 4 demonstrates the operational closeness of the institutions in terms of collaboration and their ranking to serve as research centres. In performing aging-in-place studies, organizations from the United States, the United Kingdom, Europe, and Asia have succeeded in establishing collaborative relationships with each other.

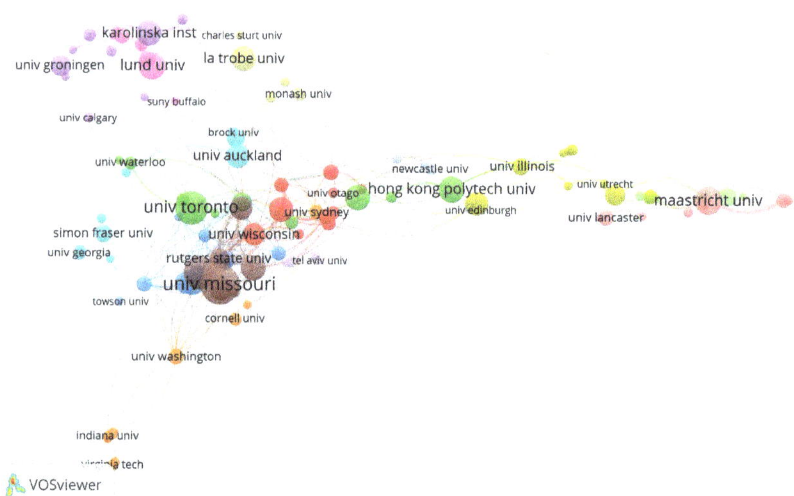

Figure 4. Network visualization of contributing organizations.

3.1.3. Countries

Fifty-five countries contributed to the publication of the retrieved documents, but only 30 met the threshold of five publications. The 10 most prolific countries are listed in Table 3. On the map of countries, the USA had the most significant number of publications (524), followed by Canada (139), the UK (127), Australia (110), and the Netherlands (92). Based on the analysis of English language publications, the findings show that the USA has moved further and faster in the aging in place research field than any other major research funding country. The result is not surprising because the USA has been leading the world in significant publication output. The finding also revealed that the significant contributions to research on aging in place derive from developed nations, whereas the research outputs from less developed nations are comparably low. This study does not identify the regional focus of the research carried out as it was beyond the scope of this study. The data does not identify that the research output of the developing countries is low compared to the developed countries, e.g., authors in developed countries could carry out research on developing countries (and vice versa). Nonetheless, the study identified an eminent lack of research from authors located in developing countries. Further reasons for this need to be researched with specific emphasis on regional focus.

Figure 5 illustrates the degree of collaboration among countries with a threshold of five documents each. The network includes 32 countries distributed over six different clusters, each country with a different colour. There are 134 links, which is an indication of good networking. The thickness of the link between any two countries indicates the strength of collaboration. The most substantial collaboration was between the following pairs of countries: USA–China (link strength = 15); USA–Canada and USA–South Korea (link strength = 14); England–Scotland (link strength = 12); USA–Australia (link strength = 11); USA–Sweden (link strength = 10). Hence, the high level of commitment of the country to aging in place has resulted in significant collaboration from other countries.

Table 3. The top 10 most participating countries.

Location	Number of Publication	Citations	Total Link Strength
USA	524	8508	117
Canada	139	2714	47
UK	127	2223	61
Australia	110	1306	56
The Netherlands	92	1423	53
China	85	687	57
Sweden	73	779	41
South Korea	37	159	27
New Zealand	34	1034	21
Taiwan	34	381	10

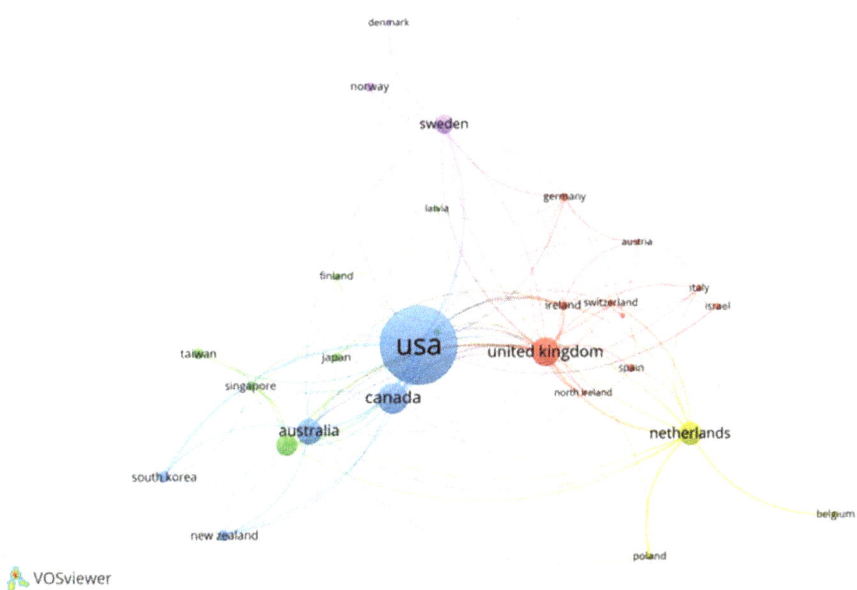

Figure 5. Network visualization of countries.

3.2. Co-Occurrence

Occurrences attributed in VOSviewer indicate the number of documents in which a specified keyword occurs [66]. Co-occurrence networks are graphs that show how frequently variables appear together. They are extensively used in text mining, where co-occurrence counts how frequently two words appear together at a sample site or how frequently two terms appear in a single document. A co-occurrence network allows us to investigate several pairs of co-occurring variables at the same time. Each variable is represented by a node or point in the construction of a co-occurrence network. The co-occurrence of two variables is represented by an edge, or connection, linking two nodes. Primary research focuses can be discovered by analysing the keywords found within the articles [52]. A keywords network provides a sound picture of a knowledge domain, enabling understanding of the topics covered and the interrelationship between various topics [67].

Keywords

VOSviewer technique was used to map the keywords, using author keywords rather than all keywords to achieve a reproducible and readable map [51,68]. With a threshold of 15 minimum occurrences, 37 keywords met the threshold out of a pool of 3045 keywords drawn from 1331 papers. After five attempted iterations, a minimum threshold of 15 produced a clear network visualization and was used for the analysis. The most popular keywords or research hotspots include: older adults, aging, housing, dementia, long-term care, and technology, in accordance with "aging in place". These keywords depict the main areas of current aging in place research. Obviously, the most popular keywords (i.e., aging in place) in Figure 6 occur because of their inclusion in the search keywords chosen for this study. The strength of the link connecting two keywords reflects the number of articles in which the keywords appear together, revealing the association of their respective research focuses [69].

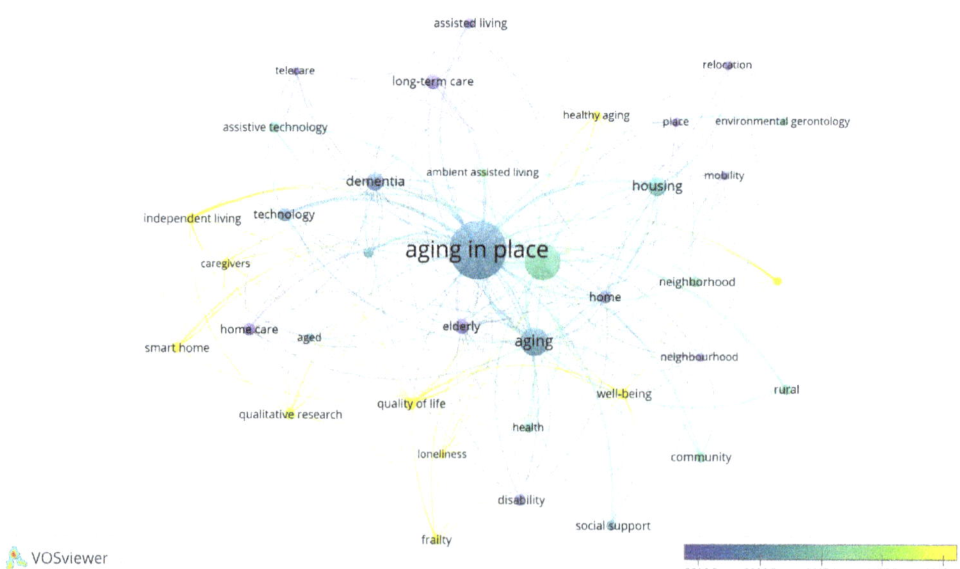

Figure 6. Overlay visualization of keywords.

The strongest links are among the following pairs of keywords: aging in place–older adults (link strength = 88); aging in place and aging (link strength = 30); aging in place–housing (link strength = 27); aging in place–dementia (link strength = 21); aging in place–

technology (link strength = 18); aging in place–independent living (link strength = 16). Therefore, older adults, aging, housing, dementia, technology, and independent living are the research hotspots on aging in place studies. This reveals multiple issues surrounding aging in place among diverse populations, thus creating various research directions for scholars in this field. Vasunilashorn et al. [24] put it that "third, aging in place is not a one-size-fits-all concept". VOSviewer commonly lists together keywords with the same colour. Overlay visualization was used to group the keywords according to their average year of occurrence, using VOSviewer selected years (2016–2018). The closer the colour to purple, the earlier the occurrence of the keywords, and the closer the colour to yellow, the more current or recent the keywords. It can be deduced that current research focuses on smart-homes, independent living, social care, frailty, quality of life, and healthy aging, as they all appear in yellow.

Older people will continue to live in their familiar surroundings for as long as they are able. To increase the age-friendliness of communities, housing activists and older citizens can address individual and community-wide challenges such as loneliness, dementia, long-term care, and disability. The growing population of older persons and their desire to age in place pose considerable healthcare and housing issues [70]. Previous studies on elderly housing primarily focused on senior housing, sheltered housing, nursing homes, and community dwellings. The global ageing issue emphasizes the gap between traditional housing and the fundamental level of housing necessary to allow individuals to dwell in their houses as their requirements evolve. Several studies have found that housing and neighbourhood surroundings influence the psychological well-being of the elderly [71]. Incorporating visitability and universal design elements into home development can increase the inventory of accessible houses available to older individuals and facilitate ageing in place [72]. The "neighbourhood" is another important factor in aging in place. As many older persons express a desire to age in place, it is critical to understand how neighbourhood change might help or hinder their capacity to do so [73]. As smart home automation technology advances, there is rising interest in its potential to enable older persons to age in place [74]. While the usage of smart technology in residential settings is increasing, research on how such technologies might give chances for safely and productively ageing in place by incorporating physical exercise into everyday routines and lowering sedentariness is limited [70].

3.3. Co-Citation Analysis

Co-citation analysis entails tracking pairs of publications that are referenced together in the source articles. The data gathered in the co-citation study were counts of the number of times two journal titles were jointly cited in later works. It is considered that the more two journals are referenced together, the more closely they are related. The co-citation analysis of sources enables the identification of the most cited and highly influential research documents and author journals responsible for aging in place studies. Academic journals play an important role in disseminating research findings [75]. Thus, it is critical to investigate the significant research outlets in the region when analysing the research trend. The goal is not to promote journals but to inform researchers about the best outlets and platforms for disseminating their research findings to have maximum impact in academia and industry.

Journals

Sources are referred to as journals in the VOSviewer platform. From the data analysis, it has been found that all the bibliographic references obtained from the Web of Science were included in 473 journals. Of these, only 24 meet the threshold of 10 publications. The minimum threshold was decided after five attempted iterations, with 10 producing a clear network visualization. As shown in Table 4, The International Journal of Environmental Research and Public Health is the topmost Journal with 45 articles, cited 372 times, with the highest total link strength of 82 (the link strength between two nodes denotes the frequency of co-occurrence of the journals being represented by the nodes), followed by Gerontologist, which published 43 articles, with a total link strength of 1956. Aging and Society (40 articles) and Journal of applied gerontology (32 articles) occupied the third and fourth positions, respectively. These journals have received the highest number of citations and total link strengths. These journals, therefore, have made significant contributions to aging in place studies. These findings help identify the core sets of journals, which publish the most in the field of aging in place. Researchers, practitioners, and librarians are informed of the journals they might prioritize in retrieving relevant sources, in publishing findings, and for inclusion in a library collection.

Table 4. The top 10 most productive journals.

Source Journal	Documents	Citations	Total Link Strength
International Journal of Environmental Research and Public Health	45	372	82
Gerontologist	43	1956	295
Ageing and Society	40	740	183
Journal of Applied Gerontology	32	313	78
Health and Social care in the community	30	289	45
Journal of Housing for the Elderly	29	145	86
BMC Geriatrics	27	298	42
Journal of Aging Studies	26	620	138
Research on Aging	17	392	69
Housing Studies	17	153	48

Figure 7 shows a network visualization map of co-citation analysis for journals with minimum citations of 150. With the largest circle size, Gerontologist received the highest number of citations (1992), with the highest number of links with other journals (total link strength = 27,884), indicating that this journal was co-cited within most other journals. Journals in the same cluster with the same colour are commonly co-cited. In essence, Gerontologist has the highest number of co-cited articles in aging in place related studies, and it also belongs to the broadest network.

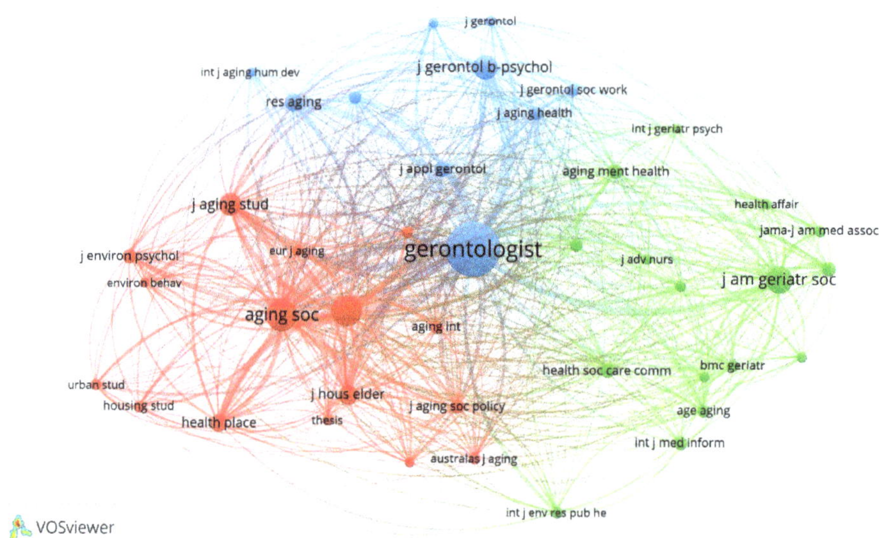

Figure 7. Network visualization of journal co-citations.

4. Conclusions

This study aimed at presenting a bibliometric analysis of the current status of the aging in place research themes. A global view of the publications produced in the research field of aging in place between 1970 and 2021 is presented in this paper. A total of 1331 original and review articles, published in 473 different peer-reviewed journals by a total of 3901 authors, were identified. The study focused on the Web of Science since it was deemed the most reliable and influential database for bibliometric research. The keywords selected for the bibliometric study was identified by the prominent research themes under aging in place.

The concept of aging in place was not common during the 1970s and 1980s, hence, the low number of publications. However, there has been a significant increase in publications from the 1990s upwards, with the most significant number of publications in recent years, in line with Vasunilashorn et al. [24]. The United States was the most productive in terms of the number of articles published in the English language. The International Journal of Environmental Research and Public Health is the journal that has published more articles in this area. Based on co-occurrence analysis, the research hotspots identified during the study include: older adults, aging, housing, dementia, long-term care, and technology, and their association with aging in place field. Moreover, the latest hotspots were identified, which may signify future research directions. A wide range of indicators was used in the study, including co-authorship, co-citation, and co-occurrence analyses, presented informatively from different perspectives so that interested readers can apply the results according to their interests and priorities. However, the findings should be cautiously interpreted to avoid misunderstanding in guiding future research.

The study can be viewed as the first step towards an objective analysis of the literature existing in the aging in place research field. The study identified housing, dementia, long-term care, and technology as emerging research focuses within the subject area. Noticeable contributions from the authors listed were prominent in underpinning future research focuses in the subject area. As bibliometric analysis is not static, for instance, concepts may gain or lose attention over time as more publications are released, relationships between authors, documents, and countries can be altered, and new research directions may emerge. Therefore, similar studies should be performed in the future to keep tracks of changes in the field. Nonetheless, the data analysed offer useful insights for guiding interested researchers and prioritizing future research efforts in aging in place studies. The analysis offers several insights that may aid aging in place researchers, educational institutions, and policymakers in their perception of the development of the field. Thus, this study has successfully achieved the primary objectives in recognizing the current context and future research trends in improving aging in place subject area.

The study further identified the degree of international collaborations and identified that most of the collaborations were carried out with the USA. Very limited collaborations were identified within Asian and Asian-pacific regions with the European regions. However, the study does not underpin the research carried out from developed and developing regions as the regional focus was not the scope of this study. Further research might be beneficial if more collaborations were carried out to identify the research emphasis from regional focus and weigh in the prominence of collaboration between Asian/Asian-pacific and European regions. Future research may also make data sources, such as Scopus, because Web of Science is not all-encompassing, and some critical articles might have been omitted. More so, the findings should be interpreted in line with the definition of aging in place given in this study. It is difficult to relate if all the included papers have anything to do with aging in place—some papers might be using the term as a buzzword in the title/abstract, while the inclusion of some papers published in languages other than the English language could alter the results.

Author Contributions: Conceptualization, O.O.; methodology, O.O. and K.G.; software, O.O. and K.G.; validation, O.O, K.G, W.M.J. and L.O.; formal analysis, O.O. and K.G.; data curation, O.O. and K.G.; writing—original draft preparation, O.O.; writing—review and editing, O.O., K.G., M.Q.R. and L.O.; visualization, K.G.; supervision, W.M.J., M.Q.R. and O.O. All authors have read and agreed to the published version of the manuscript.

Funding: No funding was available.

Institutional Review Board Statement: Not Applicable.

Informed Consent Statement: Not Applicable.

Data Availability Statement: Not Applicable.

Conflicts of Interest: The authors declare that they have no conflict of interest.

References

1. Gruber, J.; Wise, D. *Social Security and Retirement Around the World: Micro-Estimates*; Chicago University Press: Chicago, IL, USA, 2004.
2. He, W.; Goodkind, D.; Kowal, P.R. *An Aging World: 2015*; United States Census Bureau: Washington, DC, USA, 2016.
3. Ortman, J.M.; Velkoff, V.A.; Hogan, H. *An Aging Nation: The Older Population in The United States*; United States Census Bureau, Economics and Statistics Administration: Washington, DC, USA, 2014.
4. Powell, J.L. The power of global aging. *Ageing Int.* **2010**, *35*, 1–14. [CrossRef]
5. Feng, W.; Mason, A. Population Aging in China: Challenges, Opportunities, and Institutions. In *Population in China at the Beginning of the 21st Century*; Oxford University Press: Oxford, UK, 2007; pp. 177–196.
6. Rajan, S.I.; Sarma, P.S.; Mishra, U.J.J.; Mishra, U.S. Demography of Indian aging, 2001–2051. *J. Aging Soc. Policy* **2003**, *15*, 11–30. [CrossRef]
7. Muramatsu, N.; Akiyama, H.J.T.G. Japan: Super-aging society preparing for the future. *Gerontologist* **2011**, *51*, 425–432. [CrossRef]
8. Cubit, K.A.; Meyer, C. Aging in Australia. *Gerontologist* **2011**, *51*, 583–589. [CrossRef]
9. Cheng, S.-T.; Lum, T.; Lam, L.C.; Fung, H.H. Hong Kong: Embracing a fast aging society with limited welfare. *Gerontologist* **2013**, *53*, 527–533. [CrossRef]
10. Jakovljevic, M.; Laaser, U.J.S. Population aging from 1950 to 2010 in seventeen transitional countries in the wider region of South Eastern Europe. *South East. Eur. J. Public Health* **2015**, *3*. [CrossRef]
11. Bloom, D.E.; Canning, D.; Fink, G. Implications of population ageing for economic growth. *Oxf. Rev. Econ. Policy* **2010**, *26*, 583–612. [CrossRef]
12. United Nations, Department of Economic and Social Affairs. Population Division. In *World Population Ageing 2020 Highlights: Living Arrangements of Older Persons (ST/ESA/SER.A/451)*; United Nations: New York, NY, USA, 2020.
13. Powell, J.L.; Cook, I.G. *New Perspectives on China and Aging*; Nova Science: New York, NY, USA, 2007.
14. United Nations, Department of Economic Affairs. *Population Division World Population Ageing 2017*; United Nations: New York, NY, USA, 2017.
15. Ploeg, J.; Matthew-Maich, N.; Fraser, K.; Dufour, S.; McAiney, C.; Kaasalainen, S.; Emili, A. Managing multiple chronic conditions in the community: A Canadian qualitative study of the experiences of older adults, family caregivers and healthcare providers. *BMC Geriatr.* **2017**, *17*, 40. [CrossRef] [PubMed]
16. Scharlach, A. Creating aging-friendly communities in the United States. *Ageing Int.* **2012**, *37*, 25–38. [CrossRef]
17. Bloom, D.E.; Chatterji, S.; Kowal, P.; Lloyd-Sherlock, P.; McKee, M.; Rechel, B.; Smith, J.P. Macroeconomic implications of population ageing and selected policy responses. *Lancet* **2015**, *385*, 649–657. [CrossRef]
18. Banister, J.; Bloom, D.E.; Rosenberg, L. Population Aging and Economic Growth in China. In *The Chinese Economy*; Springer: Berlin/Heidelberg, Germany, 2012; pp. 114–149.
19. Weinberger, M.B. Population Aging: A Global Overview. In *Global Health and Global Aging*; Robinson, W.N.M., Clarence, E., Pearson, L.N., Eds.; Jossey-Bass: San Francisco, CA, USA, 2007; pp. 15–30.
20. Matcharashvili, T.; Tsveraidze, Z.; Sborshchikovi, A.; Matcharashvili, T. The importance of bibliometric indicators for the analysis of research performance in Georgia. *TRAMES A J. Humanit. Soc. Sci.* **2014**, *18*, 345–356. [CrossRef]
21. Allik, J. Quality of Estonian science estimated through bibliometric indicators (1997–2007). *Proc. Est. Acad. Sci. USA* **2008**, *57*, 255–265. [CrossRef]
22. Moed, H.F. *Citation Analysis in Research Evaluation*; Springer Science & Business Media: Berlin/Heidelberg, Germany, 2006; Volume 9.
23. Leydesdorff, L.; Cozzens, S.; Van den Besselaar, P. Tracking areas of strategic importance using scientometric journal mappings. *Res. Policy* **1994**, *23*, 217–229. [CrossRef]
24. Vasunilashorn, S.; Steinman, B.A.; Liebig, P.S.; Pynoos, J. Aging in place: Evolution of a research topic whose time has come. *J. Aging Res.* **2012**, *2012*, 120952. [CrossRef]
25. Golant, S.M. *Aging in the Right Place*; Health Professions Press: Baltimore, MD, USA, 2015.

26. Gitlin, L.N. Conducting research on home environments: Lessons learned and new directions. *Gerontologist* **2003**, *43*, 628–637. [CrossRef] [PubMed]
27. Golant, S.M. Commentary: Irrational Exuberance for the Aging in Place of Vulnerable Low-Income Older Homeowners. *J. Aging Soc. Policy* **2008**, *20*, 379–397. [CrossRef] [PubMed]
28. Mamun, S.A.K.; Rahman, M.M.; Khanam, R. The relation between an ageing population and economic growth in Bangladesh: Evidence from an endogenous growth model. *Econ. Anal. Policy* **2020**, *66*, 14–25, in press. Available online: https://www-sciencedirect-com.ezproxy.wlv.ac.uk/science/article/pii/S0313592619302528?via%3Dihub (accessed on 5 September 2021). [CrossRef]
29. AARP (American Association of Retired People). Aging in Place: A state Survey of Livability Policies and Practices. 2011. Available online: http://www.ncsl.org/documents/transportation/Aging-in-Place-brief.pdf (accessed on 22 February 2020).
30. Rantz, M.J.; Karen, D.; Myra, A.; Aud, R.A.; Johnson, D.O.; Rose, P. Tiger place: A new future of older adults. *J. Nurs. Care Qual.* **2005**, *20*, 1–4. [CrossRef] [PubMed]
31. Iecovich, E. Aging in place: From theory to practice. *Anthropol. Noteb.* **2014**, *20*, 21–33.
32. Amilon, A.; Ladenburg, J.; Siren, A.; Østergaard, S.V. Willingness to pay for long-term home care services: Evidence from a stated preferences analysis. *J. Econ. Ageing* **2020**, *17*, 100238. [CrossRef]
33. Szanton, S.L.; Leff, B.; Wolff, J.L.; Roberts, L.; Gitlin, L.N. Home-based care program reduces disability and promotes aging in place. *Health Aff.* **2016**, *35*, 1558–1563. [CrossRef]
34. Greenfield, E.A.; Oberlink, M.; Scharlach, A.E.; Neal, M.B.; Stafford, P.B. Age-friendly community initiatives: Conceptual issues and key questions. *Gerontologist* **2015**, *55*, 191–198. [CrossRef] [PubMed]
35. Wiles, J.L.; Leibing, A.; Guberman, N.; Reeve, J.; Allen, R.E.S. The meaning of "aging in place" to older people. *Gerontologist* **2012**, *52*, 357–366. [CrossRef] [PubMed]
36. Hosseini, M.R.; Martek, I.; Zavadskas, E.K.; Aibinu, A.A.; Arashpour, M.; Chileshe, N. Critical evaluation of off-site construction research: A Scientometric analysis. *Autom. Constr.* **2018**, *87*, 235–247. [CrossRef]
37. Graybill, E.M.; McMeekin, P.; Wildman, J. Can aging in place be cost effective? A systematic review. *PLoS ONE* **2014**, *9*, e102705.
38. Peek, S.T.; Wouters, E.J.; Van Hoof, J.; Luijkx, K.G.; Boeije, H.R.; Vrijhoef, H.J. Factors influencing acceptance of technology for aging in place: A systematic review. *Int. J. Med. Inform.* **2014**, *83*, 235–248. [CrossRef]
39. Yu, D.; Liao, H.J.; Systems, F. Visualization and quantitative research on intuitionistic fuzzy studies. *J. Intell. Fuzzy Syst.* **2016**, *30*, 3653–3663. [CrossRef]
40. Markoulli, M.P.; Lee, C.I.; Byington, E.; Felps, W.A. Mapping Human Resource Management: Reviewing the field and charting future directions. *J. Hum. Resour. Manag. Rev.* **2017**, *27*, 367–396. [CrossRef]
41. Connelly, K.; Mokhtari, M.; Falk, T.H. Approaches to understanding the impact of technologies for aging in place: A mini-review. *Gerontologist* **2014**, *60*, 282–288. [CrossRef] [PubMed]
42. Rowlands, I. What are we measuring? Refocusing on some fundamentals in the age of desktop bibliometrics. *FEMS Microbiol. Lett.* **2018**, *365*, fny059. [CrossRef]
43. Abramo, G.; D'Angelo, C.A. Evaluating research: From informed peer review to bibliometrics. *Scientometrics* **2011**, *87*, 499–514. [CrossRef]
44. Van Nunen, K.; Li, J.; Reniers, G.; Ponnet, K. Bibliometric analysis of safety culture research. *Saf. Sci.* **2018**, *108*, 248–258. [CrossRef]
45. Smith, K.; Marinova, D. Use of bibliometric modelling for policy making. *Math. Comput. Simul.* **2005**, *69*, 177–187. [CrossRef]
46. Tranfield, D.; Denyer, D.; Smart, P. Towards a methodology for developing evidence-informed management knowledge by means of systematic review. *Br. J. Manag.* **2003**, *14*, 207–222. [CrossRef]
47. Saunders, M.; Lewis, P.; Thornhill, A. *Research Methods for Business Students*, 5th ed.; Pearson: Harlow, UK, 2009.
48. Gandia, R.; Antonialli, F.; Cavazza, B.; Neto, A.; Lima, D.; Sugano, J.; Nicolai, I.; Zambalde, A. Autonomous Vehicles: Scientometric and Bibliometric Review. *Transp. Rev.* **2018**, *39*, 9–28. [CrossRef]
49. Thanuskodi, S. Journal of Social Sciences: A bibliometric study. *J. Soc. Sci.* **2010**, *24*, 77–80. [CrossRef]
50. Rowley, J.; Slack, F. Conducting a literature review. *Manag. Res. News* **2004**, *27*, 31–39. [CrossRef]
51. Sweileh, W.M.; Al-Jabi, S.W.; AbuTaha, A.S.; Sa'ed, H.Z.; Anayah, F.M.; Sawalha, A.F. Bibliometric analysis of worldwide scientific literature in mobile-health: 2006–2016. *BMC Med. Inform. Decis. Mak.* **2017**, *17*, 72. [CrossRef]
52. Cui, Y.; Liu, Y.; Mou, J. Bibliometric analysis of organizational culture using CiteSpace. *S. Afr. J. Econ. Manag. Sci.* **2018**, *21*, 1–12.
53. Şenel, E.; Demir, E. Bibliometric and scientometric analysis of the articles published in the Journal of religion and health between 1975 and 2016. *J. Relig. Health* **2018**, *57*, 1473–1482. [CrossRef] [PubMed]
54. Chen, C.; Song, I.-Y.; Yuan, X.; Zhang, J. The thematic and citation landscape of data and knowledge engineering (1985–2007). *Data Knowl. Eng.* **2008**, *67*, 234–259. [CrossRef]
55. Valderrama-Zurián, J.C.; Aguilar-Moya, R.; Melero-Fuentes, D.; Aleixandre-Benavent, R. A systematic analysis of duplicate records in Scopus. *J. Informetr.* **2015**, *9*, 570–576. [CrossRef]
56. van Eck, N.J ; Waltman, L. Accuracy of citation data in Web of Science and Scopus. *arXiv* **2019**, arXiv:1906.07011.
57. Nettle, D.; Frankenhuis, W.E. The evolution of life history theory: Bibliometric analysis of an interdisciplinary research area. *BioRxiv* **2019**, *286*, 510826. [CrossRef] [PubMed]

58. Ramos-Rodríguez, A.R.; Ruíz-Navarro, J. Changes in the intellectual structure of strategic management research: A bibliometric study of the Strategic Management Journal, 1980–2000. *Strateg. Manag. J.* **2004**, *25*, 981–1004. [CrossRef]
59. van Eck, N.; Waltman, L. Software survey: VOSviewer, a computer program for bibliometric mapping. *Scientometrics* **2009**, *84*, 523–538. [CrossRef] [PubMed]
60. Garrigos-Simon, F.J.; Narangajavana-Kaosiri, Y.; Lengua-Lengua, I. Tourism and sustainability: A bibliometric and visualization analysis. *Sustainability* **2018**, *10*, 1976. [CrossRef]
61. Gizzi, F.T.; Leucci, G. Global research patterns on ground penetrating radar (GPR). *Surv. Geophys.* **2018**, *39*, 1039–1068. [CrossRef]
62. Goerlandt, F.; Li, J.; Reniers, G. The landscape of risk communication research: A scientometric analysis. *Int. J. Environ. Res. Public Health* **2020**, *17*, 3255. [CrossRef]
63. Wagner, A. Aging in Place with Age-Related Cognitive Changes: The Impact of Caregiving Support and Finances. *Societies* **2021**, *11*, 31. [CrossRef]
64. Glänzel, W.; Schubert, A. Analyzing scientific networks through co-authorship. In *Handbook of Quantitative Science and Technology Research*; Springer: Berlin/Heidelberg, Germany, 2004; pp. 257–276.
65. e Fonseca, B.D.P.F.; Sampaio, R.B.; de Araújo Fonseca, M.V.; Zicker, F. Co-authorship network analysis in health research: Method and potential use. *Health Res. Policy Syst.* **2016**, *14*, 1–10. [CrossRef]
66. van Eck, N.J.; Waltman, L. *VOSviewer Manual*; Univeristeit Leiden: Leiden, The Netherlands, 2013; Volume 1.
67. Van Eck, N.J.; Waltman, L. Visualizing bibliometric networks. In *Measuring Scholarly Impact*; Springer: Berlin/Heidelberg, Germany, 2014; pp. 285–320.
68. Darko, A.; Chan, A.P.; Huo, X.; Owusu-Manu, D.-G. A scientometric analysis and visualization of global green building research. *Build. Environ.* **2019**, *149*, 501–511. [CrossRef]
69. van Eck, N.J.; Waltman, L. *VosViewer Manual: Manual for VosViewer Version 1.6.5*; CWTS: Leiden, The Netherlands, 2016.
70. Tural, E.; Lu, D.; Austin Cole, D. Safely and Actively Aging in Place: Older Adults' Attitudes and Intentions Toward Smart Home Technologies. *Gerontol. Geriatr. Med.* **2021**, *7*, 23337214211017340. [CrossRef] [PubMed]
71. Demirkan, H. Housing for the aging population. *Eur. Rev. Aging Phys. Act.* **2007**, *4*, 33–38. [CrossRef]
72. Pynoos, J.; Caraviello, R.; Cicero, C. Lifelong housing: The anchor in aging-friendly communities. *Generations* **2009**, *33*, 26–32.
73. Versey, H.S.; Murad, S.; Willems, P.; Sanni, M. Beyond housing: Perceptions of indirect displacement, displacement risk, and aging precarity as challenges to aging in place in gentrifying cities. *Int. J. Environ. Res. Public Health* **2019**, *16*, 4633. [CrossRef] [PubMed]
74. Arthanat, S.; Chang, H.; Wilcox, J. Determinants of information communication and smart home automation technology adoption for aging-in-place. *J. Enabling Technol.* **2020**, *14*, 73–86. [CrossRef]
75. Wuni, I.; Shen, G.; Osei-Kyei, R. Scientometric Review Of Global Research Trends On Green Buildings In Construction Journals From 1992 To 2018. *Energy Build.* **2019**, *190*, 69–85. [CrossRef]

healthcare MDPI

Article

Illness Perceptions and Self-Management among People with Chronic Lung Disease and Healthcare Professionals: A Mixed-Method Study Identifying the Local Context

Xiaoyue Song [1,2,*], Cynthia Hallensleben [1,2], Bo Li [3], Weihong Zhang [4], Zongliang Jiang [4], Hongxia Shen [1,2], Robbert J. J. Gobbens [5,6,7], Niels H. Chavannes [1,2] and Anke Versluis [1,2]

1 Department of Public Health and Primary Care (PHEG), Leiden University Medical Center, 2300 RC Leiden, The Netherlands
2 National eHealth Living Lab (NeLL), 2300 RC Leiden, The Netherlands
3 Faculty of Nursing and Health, Henan University, Kaifeng 475000, China
4 Faculty of Nursing and Health, Zhengzhou University, Zhengzhou 450001, China
5 Faculty of Health, Sports and Social Work, Inholland University of Applied Sciences, 1081 HV Amsterdam, The Netherlands
6 Zonnehuisgroep Amstelland, 1186 AA Amstelveen, The Netherlands
7 Department Family Medicine and Population Health, Faculty of Medicine and Health Sciences, University of Antwerp, 2610 Antwerp, Belgium
* Correspondence: x.song@lumc.nl; Tel.: +31-644211324; Fax: +31-715268259

Abstract: Self-management interventions (SMIs) may fail if they misalign with the local context. To optimize the implementation of SMIs in Chinese people with chronic lung disease (CLD), the local context was identified in Chinese primary care (PC) and secondary care (SC). A mixed-method study using semi-structured interviews and quantitative surveys was conducted on people with CLD and healthcare professionals (HCPs). The qualitative data was collected until data saturation was reached, and participants were invited to complete the survey after the interview. The qualitative data—analyzed with the framework approach—was triangulated with the quantitative data. A total of 52 participants completed the interviews, and 48 also finished the survey. Four themes were identified; (a) illness perceptions (e.g., patients had poor CLD knowledge and SM, inadequate resources lead to suboptimal disease control in PC); (b) self-management skills (e.g., most patients delayed exacerbation recognition and action, and some were admitted at the crisis point); (c) factors influencing self-management skills (e.g., (in)adequate disease knowledge and medical expenditure affordability); and (d) needs for self-management (e.g., increased disease knowledge, individualized self-management plan, eHealth, (healthcare insurance) policy support). Identified themes were dependent on each other and should be leveraged when implementing SMIs. Ultimately, such SMIs can optimize patient health outcomes.

Keywords: illness perception; self-management; chronic lung diseases; local context; mixed-method study; patients; healthcare professional; primary care; secondary care; nursing

Citation: Song, X.; Hallensleben, C.; Li, B.; Zhang, W.; Jiang, Z.; Shen, H.; Gobbens, R.J.J.; Chavannes, N.H.; Versluis, A. Illness Perceptions and Self-Management among People with Chronic Lung Disease and Healthcare Professionals: A Mixed-Method Study Identifying the Local Context. *Healthcare* **2022**, *10*, 1657. https://doi.org/10.3390/healthcare10091657

Academic Editors: Joachim G. Voss and Sandul Yasobant

Received: 24 June 2022
Accepted: 25 August 2022
Published: 30 August 2022

1. Introduction

There is a high prevalence of CLDs in low- and middle-income countries, such as China [1,2]. Specifically, more than one-fourth of CLD patients are in China; over 144 million Chinese people are affected by CLDs [1,2]. The high disease burden for CLD (mainly chronic obstructive pulmonary disease [COPD] and asthma) is due to ineffective intervention [3,4].

There is evidence that (blended) self-management interventions (SMIs) could significantly improve patients' quality of life and reduce emergency department visits [5]. Self-management (SM) is defined as an individual's ability to manage symptoms, treatment, physical and psychosocial consequences, and lifestyle changes inherent to life with a chronic illness [6]. In China, CLD SM is suboptimal [2,3,7]. Specifically, people with CLD in China take late action resulting in exacerbations, which indicates the need for effective SMIs [8]. Exacerbations are defined as sustained worsening of a patient's condition beyond normal day-to-day variations that are acute in onset, which may also require a change in medication with or without hospitalization [7].

Implementing effective SMIs in China may help to reduce the disease burden in people with CLD [5,9]. Many factors need to be considered when implementing SMI; the critical factor is the compatibility between SMI and the local context [10,11]. Local context is defined as the set of characteristics and circumstances surrounding the implementation effort, such as the local beliefs, local health behaviours, and socioeconomic aspects [12]. Identifying the local context, e.g., local illness perceptions and experience with and needs for SM, is essential to facilitate the alignment between SMI implementation and local context [10,11].

Illness perceptions involve the illness's identity, causes, consequences, length (timeline), and whether it can be cured or controlled [13,14]. Determining what illness symptoms are present can help identify how patients cope with or self-manage the disease [15]. This study aims to gain insight into two SM skills, i.e., exacerbation recognition and action. Both skills are essential because they help to reduce recovery time and decrease disease burden [9].

The current study aims to map the local context of CLD in China. People with CLD and healthcare professionals (HCPs) in Chinese primary care (PC) and secondary care (SC) will be included. HCPs are included because of their essential role in helping patients manage their diseases. Since patients and HCPs may hold different views in PC and SC, this study will be conducted in both settings. Altogether, we aimed to identify the local context, including illness perceptions, experience with, and needs for SM in people with CLD and HCPs in Chinese PC and SC.

2. Materials and Methods

2.1. Design

A mixed-method study involving semi-structured interviews and a survey was used [16].

2.2. Settings and Participants

The study was conducted in people with CLD and HCPs working with CLD—from November 2019 to May 2020—in PC and SC in Zhengzhou and Kaifeng. The inclusion criteria of patients were: (1) $\geq$18 years old, (2) diagnosed with CLD or repeated persistent cough lasting longer than eight weeks in the past two years [17], and (3) fluency in spoken and written Chinese. People with mental disabilities, as diagnosed by the physician, were excluded. HCPs were included when they worked in PC or the respiratory department of SC. Recruitment of participants was carried out through random and purposive techniques [18].

2.3. Measurements and Outcomes

2.3.1. Qualitative Interview

An interview topic list focused on illness perceptions towards CLD, experience with, and the needs for SM. Two vignettes—one focusing on COPD and one on asthma—introduced CLD to patients and HCPs. Both vignettes were checked by the CLD nurse specialist (CH) to ensure their validity and feasibility before being used. Interviews lasted between 45 and 70 min. The interview topic list can be found in Supplementary Materials.

2.3.2. Quantitative Survey

In patients, demographic and clinical characteristics were collected: age, gender, years with disease or symptoms, and the exacerbation frequency in the last year. Illness perceptions were measured with the 8-item Brief Illness Perceptions Questionnaire (BIPQ) [19].

The BIPQ helps identify patients' opinions on their disease: identification (symptoms experienced), illness coherence (understanding of disease), consequences, emotional responses, illness concern, timeline, and personal and treatment control. Each item is scored from 0–10, with higher scores indicating a more threatening view of the illness [19]. Items on personal control, treatment control, and emotional response were reverse scored. The total score on the BIPQ ranged from 0 to 80. The items and their implications can be found in Table 1. The BIPQ has good internal reliability and has been used with various illness groups [19]; the Chinese version of BIPQ has acceptable test-retest reliability, with a Cronbach's alpha of 0.54 to 0.76 [20]. Participants had to select the three most important causes of their illness from 18 possible causes. Next, there were questions on smoking behaviours used in other studies [21,22]. Ex-smokers were asked about the number of years they had smoked. Current smokers were asked the following eight questions: the number of years they smoked, the number of cigarettes smoked daily, type of smoking products, opinion on smoking damage, history of trying to stop smoking, the longest period managed to stop smoking, and interests and confidence to stop smoking.

Table 1. Interpretation of the Brief Illness Perception Questionnaire.

Items	A Higher Score Implies:
Consequences	Greater perceived influence of the illness
Timeline	A stronger belief in a chronic time course
Personal control	Greater perceived personal control
Treatment control	Greater perceived control of the treatment
Identity	Greater experience of severe symptoms as a result of the illness
Concern	Greater feelings of concern about illness
Coherence	A better understanding of the illness
Emotion	A stronger emotional response to the illness

For HCPs, the demographic characteristics included gender and years of work. An adjusted version of the BIPQ was used to identify HCPs' perception of the patients' disease with the mentioned eight illness representations [19]. Next, HCPs had to select the three most important causes of illness from the exact 18 causes shown to patients. Furthermore, HCPs' perceptions of CLD guideline recommendations and confidence in implementing guideline recommendations were assessed [23]. Respondents were asked to indicate their level of agreement using a five-point scale (frequency ranged from 'never' to 'always'; confidence ranged from 'not at all confident' to 'extremely confident'). The quantitative questionnaires for patients and HCP can be found in Supplementary Materials.

2.4. Data Collection

Before the interview, the researcher (XYS) provided detailed study information and asked for written consent. After obtaining the written consent from the participants, the researcher (XYS) used the topic list to guide the interview. Interviews were audiotaped, and notes were made if necessary. Then, participants were asked to complete the quantitative surveys. The data were collected at the healthcare settings or the participant's home.

2.5. Data Analysis

The framework approach [24] guided the qualitative analysis. Two researchers (XYS, ZLJ) transcribed and read all the interviews. In the first three transcripts, codes were made in the margin of the transcripts. Next, the two researchers discussed and agreed on 52 codes to apply in subsequent transcripts. Codes were defined and grouped into categories to form a working analytical framework. Emerging codes from subsequent interviews continuously improved the framework. The categories and codes were applied to index the interviews. A separate sheet, with one row (per interview) and one column (per code), was used for each category. The codes and the quotations (i.e., sentences indexed with the codes) from each interview were summarized for each category. Researchers systematically identified themes based on the study. Atlas. Ti 7.5 software and Excel were used to store and manage the qualitative data.

Quantitative data were entered by the researchers (XYS and ZLJ) and analyzed using the IBM SPSS software package version 23.0. Descriptive analyses (e.g., mean, standard deviation [SD], *N*, percentages) were used to summarize the quantitative data (e.g., demographic, clinical characteristics, BIPQ data). The mean BIPQ score was compared between groups using an independent *t*-test (i.e., patients from PC versus SC settings, HCPs from PC versus SC settings, and all patients versus all HCPs). All statistical tests were two-sided, with the significance at $p \leq 0.05$.

2.6. Validity and Reliability

XYS conducted the first interview, and three researchers checked the transcripts (CH, AV and RG) to ensure sufficient interview quality. Furthermore, two interviewed HCPs read their transcript to ascertain that the interviewer represented their perspectives accurately. These two participants did not suggest any changes. The self-developed questions, including smoking behaviors, perceptions of guideline recommendations, and confidence in implementing guideline recommendations, were based on the previously applied questionnaire with proven feasibility and acceptability.

Two Chinese researchers independently coded all interview transcripts (XYS and ZLJ). The Chinese researcher (XYS) translated the initial English analytical framework and checked it by the XYS and English-speaking researchers (CH and AV) to ensure validity. In the quantitative data analysis, two researchers independently entered the data into the SPSS software (XYS and ZLJ) to ensure data consistency after checking.

3. Results

3.1. Descriptive Statistics

A total of 27 patients and 25 HCPs participated in the interviews; 25 patients and 23 HCPs completed the quantitative survey. Reasons for not completing the survey were: having a health check-up or treatment (patients) and having an emergency meeting or insufficient time (HCPs). Detailed descriptive statistics on patients and HCPs are in Tables 2 and 3.

Table 2. Descriptive statistics of patients and healthcare professionals (HCPs).

Data about Patients	*N*	Data about HCPs	*N*
Location		Location	
Primary care	14	Primary care	13
Secondary care	11	Secondary care	10
Disease diagnosis		Gender	
COPD	18	Male	4
Emphysema	3	Female	19
Asthma	2	Years of working experience	
Chronic bronchitis	2	<5	2
Age (years) (mean ± SD)	69.60 ± 13.07	5–10	19
Years with disease		≥10	2
<5	5		
5–10	7		
≥10	13		
Number of exacerbations in the last year			
0	2		
1	10		
≥2	13		
Smoking status			
Current smokers	5		
Ex-smokers	16		
Never smoked	4		
Mean years of smoking			
Current smokers	33.75 ± 14.24		
Ex-smokers	48.80 ± 13.07		

COPD: chronic obstructive pulmonary disease; SD: standard deviation.

Table 3. Descriptive statistics of patients and healthcare professionals (HCPs).

Data about Patients	*N*
Current smokers' cigarette situation	
Mean daily smoking (cigarettes)	9.40 ± 3.78
Duration of quitting smoking (months)	
<6	2
6–12	3
≥12	0
Frequency of quitting smoking	
<2	1
≥2	4
Interest in quitting smoking	
Not at all	1
A little	1
Somewhat	2
Much	0
Very much	1

COPD: chronic obstructive pulmonary disease; SD: standard deviation.

3.2. *Theme 1: Illness Perception*

The qualitative data on illness perceptions were categorized using subthemes; see headings below. The quantitative data on illness perceptions is shown in Table 4.

Table 4. Comparison of Brief Illness Perception Questionnaire scores between patients and healthcare professionals (mean ± SD).

Domains	Patients (n = 25)			HCPs (n = 23)		
	PC (n = 14)	SC (n = 11)	Total (n = 25)	PC (n = 10)	SC (n = 13)	Total (n = 23)
Consequences	5.21 ± 0.80	5.91 ± 0.94	5.52 ± 0.92	5.90 ± 0.74 *b	4.46 ± 0.97	5.09 ± 1.12
Timeline	8.07 ± 2.53	9.18 ± 0.40	8.56 ± 1.96	9.40 ± 0.52	9.08 ± 0.49	9.22 ± 0.52
Personal control	5.29 ± 0.61	5.45 ± 0.69	5.36 ± 0.64	4.10 ± 0.88 *b	3.38 ± 0.51	3.70 ± 0.76 **c
Treatment control	6.71 ± 1.07	7.36 ± 1.21	7.00 ± 1.15	2.60 ± 0.52	3.08 ± 0.64	2.87 ± 0.63 **c
Coherence	6.64 ± 0.84	7.19 ± 0.75	6.88 ± 0.83	5.30 ± 1.42 *b	6.39 ± 1.04	5.91 ± 1.31 **c
Concern	7.27 ± 1.10	7.36 ± 0.93	7.32 ± 0.99	5.60 ± 1.17 **b	2.92 ± 0.28	4.09 ± 1.56 **c
Identity	6.27 ± 0.79	5.79 ± 0.80	6.00 ± 0.82	5.60 ± 0.52	5.77 ± 0.73	5.70 ± 0.63
Emotional response	7.45 ± 0.69	8.21 ± 0.80 *a	7.88 ± 0.83	4.54 ± 1.51 *b	3.30 ± 0.48	4.00 ± 1.31 **c
Total score	53.29 ± 3.99	56.09 ± 3.05	54.42 ± 3.81	41.80 ± 2.57 *b	39.62 ± 1.39	40.57 ± 2.23 **c

Notes: *a: significantly different compared with patients in PC, $p < 0.05$; *b: significantly different compared with HCPs in SC, $p < 0.05$; **b: significantly different compared with HCPs in SC, $p < 0.001$; **c: significantly different compared with patients, $p < 0.001$. Abbreviations: SD = standard deviation; HCP = healthcare professional; PC = primary care; SC = secondary care.

3.2.1. Theme 1a: Coherence and Identification

Most patients in PC and all patients in SC reported that the last exacerbation was a difficult time for them. That is because they suffered physical and psychosocial function deterioration. Yet two patients in PC felt the last exacerbation was not a problem because they experienced regular exacerbations during the winters. Patients in different healthcare settings described different symptoms, i.e., patients in PC experienced coughing, wheezing, and chest tightness while those in SC underwent dyspnea (Table 5, Q1).

Table 5. Themes presented from patients and healthcare professionals (HCPs) of illness perceptions and self-management (SM) skills with quotes.

Data From Patient			Data from Healthcare Professionals	
Quotes	**Category**	**Theme**	**Category**	**Quotes**
Q1: "It felt like a plastic bag on my face, and I could not breathe in the oxygen at that moment." (Patient 15, SC).	Illness coherence	1a. Illness coherence and identification	Illness coherence	Q2: "It is easy to diagnose it from my experience." (HCP1, PC) Q3: "We always recommend that patients have a spirometry test." (HCP 14, SC)
Q4: "Eating fried sunflower triggered my episode." (Patient 2, PC) Q5: "When I moved the goods, I was out of breath and fainted." (Patient 15, SC)	Illness disease	1b. perceived causes	Disease cause	Q6: "Air pollution is the most important reason." (HCP 23, SC)
Q7: "I used to participate in square dancing." (Patient 4, PC) Q8: "When I cough in public, people cover their mouths with their hands and go away from me. Their actions depress me." (Patient 19, SC) Q9: "I can't work now. I am like a burden to my family." (Patient 16, SC)	Reduced social interaction	1c. perceived consequences and emotional response	Physical limitation Decreased lung function Indifference on patient complains	Q10: "Patients work less after the exacerbation due to decreased physical function." (HCP1, PC) Q11: "A new exacerbation accounts for the decreased lung function." (HCP10, PC) Q12: "I do not have time to explore patients' feelings." (HCP6, SC)
Q13: "No episodes disturb my daily life. I am just as healthy as those who do not have COPD or other chronic diseases." (Patient 17, SC)	Asymptomatic equal to cured	1d. curable possibility and perceived duration	Incurable and chronic	Q14: "Chronic lung disease will accompany the patients for a lifetime." (HCP6, PC) Q15: "It could not be cured." (HCP16, SC)
Q16: "I cannot manage the disease by myself." (Patient 7, PC)	Poor self-management	1e. identified disease control	Poor patient self-management	Q18: "SM is helpful to control the disease, but few patients can make it due to limited disease knowledge." (HCP17, SC)

Table 5. *Cont.*

Data From Patient			Data from Healthcare Professionals	
Quotes	**Category**	**Theme**	**Category**	**Quotes**
Q17: "Doctors are the professionals. I do what they asked me to do." (Patient 20, SC)	Passive role with doctors		Guideline use in practice	Q19: "Patients' symptoms were more complicated than described in the guidelines." (HCP19, SC) Q20: "Few of us know the guidelines." (HCP9, PC)
Q21: "Well, when I had the early symptoms, I thought I had a cold." (Patient 8, PC)	Late exacerbation recognition	2. identified SM skills	Patient delayed action	Q25: "Some patients do not visit us until their family members force them." (HCP10, PC) Q26: "Patients did not contact us until they reached a crisis point leading to hospitalization."
Q23: "If my symptoms worsen, I will ask my daughter to contact my doctor immediately." (Patient 13, PC) Q24: "Early action can reduce the risk of being sent to the hospital." (Patient 14, PC)	Early exacerbation action		Patient prompt action	Q27: "He sends a message or dials a voice call to me via Wechat when he feels uncomfortable." (HCP16, SC)

Q: quotes; SC: secondary care; PC: primary care.

After reading vignettes on COPD and asthma, patients and HCPs identified the diseases differently (see Figure 1). Moreover, HCPs in PC diagnosed diseases by their working experience and those in SC using spirometry equipment (Table 5, Q2, Q3).

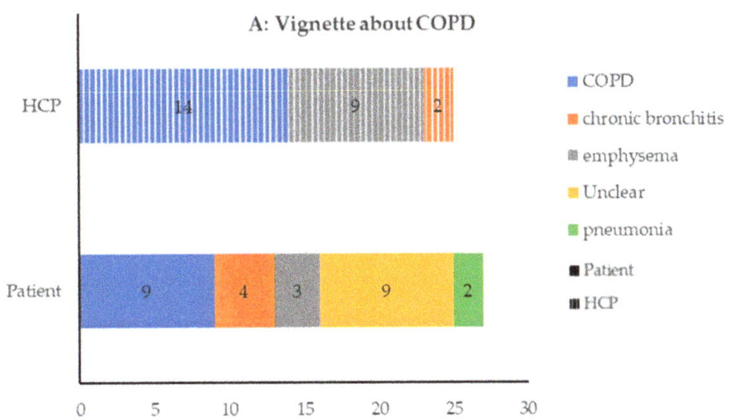

Figure 1. *Cont.*

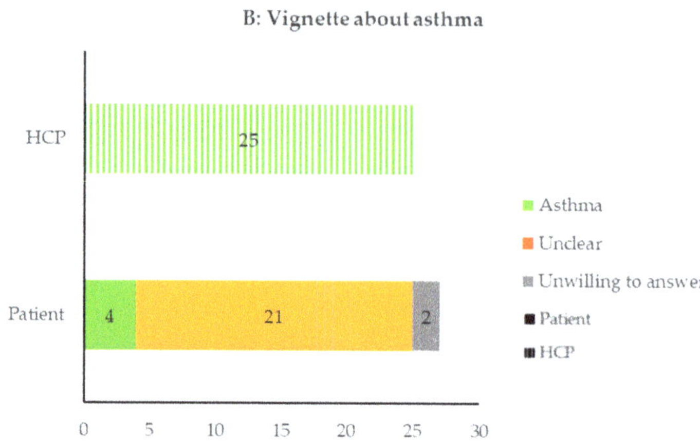

Figure 1. Identification of the chronic obstructive pulmonary disease (COPD) and asthma vignette from patients and healthcare professionals (HCPs).

3.2.2. Theme1b: Perceived Causes

When patients discussed the disease's cause, most attributed it to age, air pollution, and smoking. Because the Chinese term 'cause' can also mean 'to provoke', food and physical activity were mentioned as cause/triggers (Table 5, Q4, Q5). HCPs noted that the air pollution, age, smoking and seasonal changes from fall to winter contributed to the exacerbations (Table 5, Q6). Quantitative data showed that patients and HCPs perceived air pollution, smoking, and age as the prevailing disease causes, and patients additionally perceived weather as the disease cause. The distribution of the perceived causes are in Supplementary Materials.

Some participants identified the vignette as chronic lung disease without specific names; some patients reported that it was not their obligation to recognize a disease name unfamiliar to them.

3.2.3. Theme 1c: Perceived Consequences and Emotional Response

Patients mentioned that the exacerbations gradually deteriorated health-related quality of life. Some 15 patients' physical function was affected by the symptoms, and 5 of them experienced a negative impact on their sleep quality. The lack of a restful night's sleep and the morning battle of coughing and mucus expulsion left patients feeling exhausted, and the symptoms affected their mood the following day. Two patients said their daily life was limited. A total of 23 patients experienced reduced social interaction (Table 5, Q7, Q8). The misunderstanding from other people, for example, that the symptoms are contagious, pushed the patients away from social activities. Patients also frequently felt guilty due to their productivity losses (Table 5, Q9).

HCPs reported that physical limitation and decreased lung function were significant consequences of the diseases (Table 5, Q10, Q11). Moreover, most HCPs mentioned not paying enough attention to patient complaints (Table 5, Q12).

3.2.4. Theme 1d: Curable Possibility and Perceived Duration

A total of 20 patients believed that the disease was incurable and chronic after being informed by their HCPs, while 7 patients in SC stated that their disease was curable and acute, and they were cured when asymptomatic (Table 5, Q13). All HCPs highlighted that CLD was incurable and chronic (Table 5, Q14, Q15).

3.2.5. Theme1e: Identified Disease Control

Patients believed they were powerless to control the disease, while HCPs were sufficiently professional to help them manage it (Table 5, Q16, Q17). Therefore, they commonly perceived that they would SM the disease well when following medical advice. HCPs admitted that SM was helpful in managing diseases, but their patients showed poor SM (Table 5, Q18). Additionally, HCPs in PC mentioned that limited CLD medications were available in their settings. Moreover, all HCPs were encouraged to adopt the CLD guidelines in practice. Despite broad familiarity with the guidelines in SC, knowledge about guidelines in PC was suboptimal. In addition, HCPs did not always adhere to CLD guidelines for different reasons (Table 5, Q19, Q20). Moreover, most HCPs in PC sometimes or never applied the guideline recommendations, while those in SC always or often used the recommendations (see Figure 2).

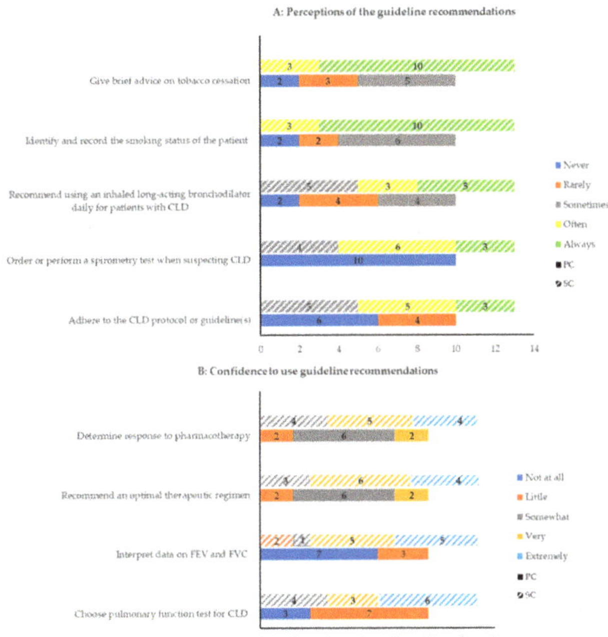

Figure 2. Perceptions of and confidence in using the guideline recommendations in practice by healthcare professionals (HCPs) in primary care (PC) and secondary care (SC).

3.3. Theme 2: Identified SM Skills

Most patients struggled to use SM skills, i.e., exacerbation recognition and action, while some patients recognized and took action on exacerbations early (Table 5, Q21–24). The distribution of identified SM skills in patients between PC and SC can be found in Supplementary Materials. Most HCPs noted that patients postponed exacerbation actions, yet two HCPs from PC observed that some patients went to them early (Table 5, Q25–27).

3.4. Theme 3: Factors Influencing SM Skills

Three generic factors were identified to influence exacerbation recognition and actions, including disease knowledge, former experience with exacerbations, and family support. Moreover, one specific factor influencing the ability to recognize the exacerbations was identified (i.e., perceived illness severity), and three specific factors influencing the performance of SM skills were identified (i.e., self-empowerment, Chinese herb, and medical expenditure affordability). These factors—with the facilitating and barrier aspects—were dependent on each other; details on how these factors influence SM skills can be found in Table 6, Q28–41.

Table 6. The theme presents factors influencing self-management (SM) skills with quotes.

Themes & Category	Explanation	Quotes
	Generic factors influencing SM skills	
Disease knowledge	Sufficient knowledge facilitated patients to develop SM skills, while insufficient knowledge was the barrier.	Q28: "I know nothing about the disease or the episode so that I could do nothing about it." (Patient 2, PC) Q29: "My knowledge of the disease helps a lot." (Patient 13, PC)
Former experience with exacerbations	Realizing the importance of early detection and prompt action from past experiences were the facilitators. Habituation to the disease from the former experience was the barrier.	Q30: "After my previous painful experience in the hospital, I realized that attention to the different symptoms (exacerbation) and visiting doctors early was essential." (Patient 15, SC) Q31: " . . . However, I frequently did nothing about the worsening symptoms because I learned to live with it." (Patient 16, SC)
	Specific factors influencing the exacerbation recognition	
Family support	Helpful family support was the facilitator. In contrast, insufficient family support when patients were at home was the barrier.	Q32: "My daughters sent me to the hospital and covered the diagnosis cost. Their actions are warm and helpful." (Patient 14, PC) Q33: "Family members regarded patients as well-functioned labor and expected them to do higher intensity household chores than the patient could endure. Such patients went on with the housework with all exacerbations." (HCP 23, SC)
Perceived illness severity	Perceiving the exacerbation as usual was a barrier. The perception that the exacerbation was a hazardous event facilitated recognizing exacerbations early.	Q34: "I must pay attention to my disease carefully. Otherwise, I will be published by the worsened exacerbations." (Patient 23, SC) Q35: "Some patients would not think breathlessness or coughing was a problem unless these symptoms disturb their eating and drinking." (HCP 23, SC)
Self-empowerment	High self-empowerment facilitated the patients' act on the exacerbations and vice versa.	Q36: "For the early symptoms, I can control them myself effectively. I will contact my daughter for the ambulance for symptoms out of my control." (Patient 13, PC) Q37: "I always try to avoid the medicine or the doctors, even if I know my symptoms get worse." (Patient 14, PC)
Chinese herb	Patients perceived the Chinese herb as facilitators, while HCPs perceived patients should take these medications with their suggestions.	Q38: "Chinese herb relieved aggravation." (Patient 4, PC) Q39: "Patients take the Chinese herbs by themselves without informing us. To make sure the medicine works well, they should ask our advice before taking unprescribed Chinese medicine from us." (Patient 5, PC)
Medical ex-penditure af-fordability	The higher medical expenditure affordability, the more likely the patient is to see a doctor early.	Q40: "Visiting the doctors means paying money, which is the last thing I want to do." (Patient 4, PC) Q41: "My retirement pension and medical insurance can cover all the medical costs. When I am uncomfortable, I just visit the doctors." (Patient 12, PC)

Q: quotes; PC: primary care; HCP: healthcare professional; SC: secondary care.

3.5. Theme 4: Needs for SM

The needs for SM addressed the expected facilitators, e.g., increased disease knowledge and the strategy to support the SM, e.g., eHealth use and individualized SM plan. The other details on the needs for SM are included in Table 7, Q42–51.

Table 7. The theme presents needs for self-management (SM) with quotes.

Categories	Explanation	Quotes
Increased disease knowledge		Q42: "The doctor told me I was diagnosed with COPD and left . . . I expected to know more about this disease." (Patient 15, SC)
		Q43: "With more information on disease and medications, patients will be more familiar with the seriousness of their condition, manage risk factors and change behavior, and then take action to meet their own needs for disease management." (HCP 23, SC)
Individualized SM plan		Q44: "I need one intervention to help me recognize the episode early and act on it early." (Patient 10, PC)
Nurse specialist		Q45: "A nurse specialist experienced in dealing with patients will be helpful to deliver SM information." (HCP 17, SC)
eHealth use		Q46: "eHealth will help us deliver SM information to patients, e.g., Wechat." (HCP 21, SC)
		Q47: "If we could remotely monitor patients' diseases, we could provide more care to more patients." (HCP 21, SC)
Sufficient family support		Q48: "When I forgot to take medicine, my family members remaindered me about it immediately. Family support can help me a lot." (Patient 10, PC)
Policy support		Q49: "With the economic policy support from the government, we will have more resources to provide SM." (HCP 2, PC)
		Q50: "If public medical insurance can cover more medical costs, more patients will choose to visit the doctors earlier." (HCP 22, SC)

Q: quotes; PC: primary care; HCP: healthcare professional; SC: secondary care.

4. Discussion

This mixed-method study identified the local context of people with CLD and HCPs in Chinese PC and SC. Four themes were identified, namely, (a) illness perceptions; (b) identified SM skills; (c) factors influencing SM skills; and (d) needs for SM. These themes were dependent on each other and should be addressed when implementing SMIs.

Most patients could not identify the CLD correctly; this finding was evidenced by a previous study showing that patients had limited disease knowledge [25]. Moreover, the disease decreased patients' physical and psychosocial functioning. Most patients believed the disease was chronic, yet a few believed it would not be long-term, possibly due to their limited understanding. Age, air pollution, and smoke were the leading disease causes in interviews, and the survey identified the weather as an additional cause. The weather was mentioned as the temperature variability can trigger exacerbations [26].

Compared with those in PC, patients in SC showed a more severe emotional response to the illness. This finding is not surprising because patients in SC suffer more severe exacerbations, which leads to more negative emotions [27]. Notably, no difference was found in total illness perception scores from patients between PC and SC, which could be due to the chronic nature of CLD. Most patients in this study had CLD for more than five years and went to PC and SC for mild and severe exacerbations; therefore, patients with long-term CLD may hold similar illness perceptions. Interestingly, no other existing studies have compared illness perceptions—in people with CLD—between PC and SC.

Most patients delayed exacerbation recognition and actions. It is likely that these patients had difficulties with exacerbation recognition and had limited knowledge of potential actions they could undertake. A few patients, mainly in PC, showed early exacerbation recognition and action. Their early response to the disease was because they applied their disease knowledge and former experience to identify the exacerbation and take prompt action. Early presenters were mostly from PC because of the accessibility, e.g., the location was closer to the patient's home, and the treatment cost was lower [28]. The identified illness perceptions among people with CLD were in line with the previous study [25].

Most HCPs correctly identified the CLD. HCPs agreed that CLD was chronic and could affect physical and psychosocial functioning. This finding complies with one previous study [29]. HCPs agreed that patients showed poor SM skills.

In general, HCPs in PC—compared with HCPs in SC—held a more threatening view of the CLD. The difference was possibly related to the healthcare service setup in China. HCPs in SC are better equipped with medical skills and more patient experience, contributing to their positive attitudes [30]. Compared with patients, HCPs held a less threatening view of CLD. It could be explained that HCPs had more disease knowledge after their medical training, which led to a better understanding of how to control CLD.

Unlike patients diagnosed with a spirometry test in SC, CLD was diagnosed based on disease history and clinical symptoms in PC due to the lack of test facilities. All HCPs (strongly) agreed with but did not adhere to the guideline recommendations for different reasons; namely, HCPs in SC considered the symptoms of people with CLD more complicated than described in the guidelines, while in PC, there was limited guideline knowledge. The lack of confidence in disease treatment in PC could be explained by a lack of spirometry tests and lower professional knowledge [31].

Many generic factors were found to influence patient SM. The first factor was disease knowledge. Patients who had more disease knowledge showed a higher SM ability. The second was the former experience with exacerbations. Some patients showed prompt action due to unwillingness to suffer the adverse outcomes of the delayed exacerbation action. Nevertheless, with the former exacerbation experience, some patients took late SM actions. That is possibly because they were used to living with the symptoms, making it difficult to recognize the exacerbation and take prompt action. The third was family support; it helped patients self-manage exacerbations, yet family members expected them to do housework beyond their physical ability. A lack of disease knowledge among family members is a potential explanation [32].

One specific factor influencing exacerbation recognition was identified as the perceived illness severity. Different factors were found to influence SM actions on exacerbation. The first was patient self-empowerment. The second was Chinese herbs. Patients used such herbs to reduce the exacerbations, while HCPs perceived patients should take these herbs with their suggestions. The finding on the Chinese herbs was not reported in other studies. The worry from HCPs was likely because patients taking the Chinese herbs without professional guidance may decrease the SM on exacerbations. The third was the medical expenditure affordability; the higher affordability, the earlier action on the exacerbations. The identified third factor aligns with the other study [33].

The needs for SM reflected the strategies to improve SM and expected facilitators to optimize patient SM. Both patients and HCPs expressed the need for increased disease knowledge, which was the facilitator for the SM. Moreover, public healthcare insurance was needed to cover medical expenditures for the CLD. In addition, the need for an individualized SM plan, eHealth use, and independent CLD specialist reflected effective strategies to deliver SMIs easily accessible and not restricted to certain places and times. The identified needs correspond with the previous study [25]. Notably, the HCPs further pointed out that obtaining (healthcare insurance) policy support from the government was necessary. Such a finding is not surprising as optimal SMIs have been more easily adopted with support from the government in China [34].

Several limitations need to be addressed. First, less detailed information could be obtained from participants because, during the study, there was a coronavirus outbreak in China. Some participants did not elaborate much on their SM experiences because they feared the risk of becoming infected if they talked to the interviewer for too long. Second, four participants did not participate in the survey. The missing quantitative data may underpower the triangulation. Third, the small sample size in the quantitative survey may be underpowered to triangulate the qualitative data, which may negatively impact this study's validity. Therefore, the results should be interpreted cautiously due to the mentioned limitations.

5. Conclusions

This study presented a comprehensive view of the local context—on the identified illness perceptions and experience with and needs for SM—in China. The identified findings addressed the importance of increasing disease knowledge, developing the strategies to deliver the SMI, and gaining (healthcare insurance) policy support during the SMI implementation. Ultimately, such SMIs can help to improve patient health outcomes and reduce the disease burden. Furthermore, this study provided that the local context should be emphasized and leveraged to ensure the SMI meets local needs. A large-scale quantitative study is needed to support the findings.

Supplementary Materials: The following supporting information can be downloaded at: https://docs.google.com/document/d/1xTNHwDBpKL-2UqEbAChCQT1x2_zrDawY/edit?usp=sharing&ouid=101850677973450774094&rtpof=true&sd=true (accessed on 2 July 2022) and https://docs.google.com/document/d/1VWqIeXd4bCI2eoJUVZKSWYEzbP_S0VD25GDg1Syy8PE/edit?usp=sharing (accessed on 2 July 2022).

Author Contributions: Conceptualization, X.S., H.S. and C.H.; methodology, X.S., A.V. and C.H.; software, X.S.; validation, A.V., C.H. and R.J.J.G.; formal analysis, X.S. and Z.J.; investigation, X.S. and Z.J.; resources, B.L. and W.Z.; data curation, X.S. and Z.J.; writing—original draft preparation, X.S.; writing—review and editing, A.V., C.H. and R.J.J.G.; visualization, A.V., C.H. and R.J.J.G.; supervision, A.V., C.H., R.J.J.G. and N.H.C.; project administration, N.H.C. All authors have read and agreed to the published version of the manuscript.

Funding: This research received funding from China Scholarship Council (201807040051).

Institutional Review Board Statement: The study was conducted according to the guidelines of the Declaration of Helsinki, and approved by the Ethics Committee of the University of Henan University (HUSOM-2019-112, 11 March 2019).

Informed Consent Statement: Informed consent was obtained from all subjects involved in the study.

Data Availability Statement: The datasets generated and analyzed during the current study are available from the corresponding author on reasonable request.

Conflicts of Interest: The authors declare no conflict of interest.

References

1. Huang, K.W.; Yang, T.; Xu, J.Y.; Yang, L.; Zhao, J.P.; Zhang, X.Y.; Bai, C.X.; Kang, J.; Ran, P.X.; Shen, H.H.; et al. Prevalence, risk factors, and management of asthma in China: A national cross-sectional study. *Lancet* **2019**, *394*, 407–418. [CrossRef]
2. Wang, C.; Xu, J.Y.; Yang, L.; Xu, Y.J.; Zhang, X.Y.; Bai, C.X.; Kang, J.; Ran, P.X.; Shen, H.H.; Wen, F.Q.; et al. Prevalence and risk factors of chronic obstructive pulmonary disease in China (the China Pulmonary Health CPH study): A national cross-sectional study. *Lancet* **2018**, *391*, 1706–1717. [CrossRef]
3. Wang, G.; Wang, F.; Gibson, P.G.; Guo, M.; Zhang, W.J.; Gao, P.; Zhang, H.P.; Harvey, E.S.; Li, H.; Zhang, J. Severe and uncontrolled asthma in China: A cross-sectional survey from the Australasian Severe Asthma Network. *J. Thorac. Dis. Dis.* **2017**, *9*, 1333–1344. [CrossRef] [PubMed]
4. Zhu, B.F.; Wang, Y.F.; Ming, J.; Chen, W.; Zhang, L.Y. Disease burden of COPD in China: A systematic review. *Int. J. Chronic Obstr. Pulm. Dis.* **2018**, *13*, 1353–1364. [CrossRef] [PubMed]

5. Song, X.Y.; Hallensleben, C.; Zhang, W.H.; Jiang, Z.L.; Shen, H.X.; Gobbens, R.J.J.; Van der Kleij, R.; Chavannes, N.H.; Versluis, A. Blended Self-Management Interventions to Reduce Disease Burden in Patients With Chronic Obstructive Pulmonary Disease and Asthma: Systematic Review and Meta-analysis. *J. Med. Internet Res.* **2021**, *23*, e24602. [CrossRef]
6. Lorig, K.R.; Holman, H.R. Self-management education: History, definition, outcomes, and mechanisms. *Ann. Behav. Med.* **2003**, *26*, 1–7. [CrossRef] [PubMed]
7. Pavord, I.D.; Jones, P.W.; Burgel, P.R.; Rabe, K.F. Exacerbations of COPD. *Int. J. Chronic Obstr. Pulm. Dis.* **2016**, *11*, 21–30. (In English) [CrossRef]
8. Lin, J.T.; Xing, B.; Tang, H.P.; Yang, L.; Yuan, Y.D.; Gu, Y.H.; Chen, P.; Liu, X.J.; Zhang, J.; Liu, H.G.; et al. Hospitalization Due to Asthma Exacerbation: A China Asthma Research Network (CARN) Retrospective Study in 29 Provinces Across Mainland China. *Allergy Asthma Immunol. Res.* **2020**, *12*, 485–495. [CrossRef]
9. Hallensleben, C.; Meijer, E.; Biewenga, J.; Kievits-Smeets, R.M.M.; Veltman, M.; Song, X.; van Boven, J.F.M.; Chavannes, N.H. Reducing Delay through edUcation on eXacerbations (REDUX) in patients with COPD: A pilot study. *Clin. eHealth* **2020**, *3*, 63–68. [CrossRef]
10. Brakema, E.A.; van der Kleij, R.; Poot, C.C.; Le An, P.; Anastasaki, M.; Crone, M.R.; Hong, L.; Kirenga, B.; Lionis, C.; Mademilov, M.; et al. Mapping low-resource contexts to prepare for lung health interventions in four countries (FRESH AIR): A mixed-method study. *Lancet Glob. Health* **2022**, *10*, E57–E70. [CrossRef]
11. Wong, S.S.L.; Abdullah, N.; Abdullah, A.; Liew, S.M.; Ching, S.M.; Khoo, E.M.; Jiwa, M.; Chia, Y.C. Unmet needs of patients with chronic obstructive pulmonary disease (COPD): A qualitative study on patients and doctors. *BMC Fam. Pract.* **2014**, *15*, 67. [CrossRef]
12. Daivadanam, M.; Ingram, M.; Sidney Annerstedt, K.; Parker, G.; Bobrow, K.; Dolovich, L.; Gould, G.; Riddell, M.; Vedanthan, R.; Webster, J.; et al. The role of context in implementation research for non-communicable diseases: Answering the 'how-to' dilemma. *PLoS ONE* **2019**, *14*, e0214454. (In English) [CrossRef] [PubMed]
13. Rivera, E.; Corte, C.; Steffen, A.; DeVon, H.A.; Collins, E.G.; McCabe, P.J. Illness Representation and Self-Care Ability in Older Adults with Chronic Disease. *Geriatrics* **2018**, *3*, 45. (In English) [CrossRef] [PubMed]
14. Leventhal, H.M.D.; Meyer, D.; Nerenz, D. The common sense representation of illness danger. *Med. Psychol.* **1980**, *2*, 7–30.
15. Achstetter, L.I.; Schultz, K.; Faller, H.; Schuler, M. Leventhal's common-sense model and asthma control: Do illness representations predict success of an asthma rehabilitation? *J. Health Psychol.* **2019**, *24*, 327–336. (In English) [CrossRef] [PubMed]
16. Sandelowski, M. Combining qualitative and quantitative sampling, data collection, and analysis techniques in mixed-method studies. *Res. Nurs. Health* **2000**, *23*, 246–255. (In English) [CrossRef]
17. Koo, H.K.; Park, S.W.; Park, J.W.; Choi, H.S.; Kim, T.H.; Yoon, H.K.; Yoo, K.H.; Jung, K.S.; Kim, D.K. Chronic cough as a novel phenotype of chronic obstructive pulmonary disease. *Int. J. Chronic Obstr. Pulm. Dis.* **2018**, *13*, 1793–1801. [CrossRef]
18. Fusch, P.I.; Ness, L.R. Are We There Yet? Data Saturation in Qualitative Research. *Qual. Rep.* **2015**, *20*, 1408–1416. [CrossRef]
19. Broadbent, E.; Petrie, K.J.; Main, J.; Weinman, J. The Brief Illness Perception Questionnaire. *J. Psychosom. Res.* **2006**, *60*, 631–637. [CrossRef]
20. Lin, Y.; Chiu, K.; Wang, T.J. Reliability and validity of the Chinese version of the brief illness perception questionnaire for patients with coronary heart disease. *J. Orient. Inst. Technol.* **2011**, *2*, 145–155.
21. Meijer, E.; Gebhardt, W.A.; Dijkstra, A.; Willemsen, M.C.; Van Laar, C. Quitting smoking: The importance of non-smoker identity in predicting smoking behaviour and responses to a smoking ban. *Psychol. Health* **2015**, *30*, 1387–1409. [CrossRef] [PubMed]
22. Meijer, E.; Van den Putte, B.; Gebhardt, W.A.; Van Laar, C.; Bakk, Z.; Dijkstra, A.; Fong, G.T.; West, R.; Willemsen, M.C. A longitudinal study into the reciprocal effects of identities and smoking behaviour: Findings from the. ITC Netherlands Survey. *Soc. Sci. Med.* **2018**, *200*, 249–257. [CrossRef] [PubMed]
23. Salinas, G.D.; Williamson, J.C.; Kalhan, R.; Thomashow, B.; Scheckermann, J.L.; Walsh, J.; Abdolrasulnia, M.; Foster, J.A. Barriers to adherence to chronic obstructive pulmonary disease guidelines by primary care physicians. *Int. J. Chronic Obstr. Pulm. Dis.* **2011**, *6*, 171–179. [CrossRef]
24. Gale, N.K.; Heath, G.; Cameron, E.; Rashid, S.; Redwood, S. Using the framework method for the analysis of qualitative data in multi-disciplinary health research. *BMC Med. Res. Methodol.* **2013**, *13*, 117. [CrossRef] [PubMed]
25. Yang, H.; Wang, H.J.; Du, L.Y.; Wang, Y.; Wang, X.J.; Zhang, R.M. Disease knowledge and self-management behavior of COPD patients in China. *Medicine* **2019**, *98*, e14460. [CrossRef]
26. Zhan, Z.Y.; Tian, Q.; Chen, T.T.; Ye, Y.S.; Lin, Q.X.; Han, D.; Ou, C.Q. Temperature Variability and Hospital Admissions for Chronic Obstructive Pulmonary Disease: Analysis of Attributable Disease Burden and Vulnerable Subpopulation. *Int. J. Chronic Obstr. Pulm. Dis.* **2020**, *15*, 2225–2235. [CrossRef]
27. Mathieson, A.; Grande, G.; Luker, K. Strategies, facilitators and barriers to implementation of evidence-based practice in community nursing: A systematic mixed-studies review and qualitative synthesis. *Prim. Health Care Res. Dev.* **2019**, *20*, e6. (In English) [CrossRef]
28. Wang, J.; Feng, Z.C.; Dong, Z.X.; Li, W.P.; Chen, C.Y.; Gu, Z.C.; Wei, A.H.; Feng, D. Does Having a Usual Primary Care Provider Reduce Polypharmacy Behaviors of Patients With Chronic Disease? A Retrospective Study in Hubei Province, China. *Front. Pharmacol.* **2022**, *12*, 802097. [CrossRef]

29. Soriano, J.B.; Kendrick, P.J.; Paulson, K.R.; Gupta, V.; Vos, T.; GBD Chronic Respiratory Disease Collaborators. Prevalence and attributable health burden of chronic respiratory diseases, 1990–2017: A systematic analysis for the Global Burden of Disease Study 2017. *Lancet Respir. Med.* **2020**, *8*, 585–596. [CrossRef]
30. Liu, Y.; Zhong, L.; Yuan, S.; van de Klundert, J. Why patients prefer high-level healthcare facilities: A qualitative study using focus groups in rural and urban China. *BMJ Glob. Health* **2018**, *3*, e000854. (In English) [CrossRef]
31. Hurst, J.R.; Buist, A.S.; Gaga, M.; Gianella, G.E.; Kirenga, B.; Khoo, E.M.; Mendes, R.G.; Mohan, A.; Mortimer, K.; Rylance, S.; et al. Challenges in the Implementation of Chronic Obstructive Pulmonary Disease Guidelines in Low- and Middle-Income Countries An Official American Thoracic Society Workshop Report. *Ann. Am. Thorac. Soc.* **2021**, *18*, 1269–1277. [CrossRef] [PubMed]
32. Sigurgeirsdottir, J.; Halldorsdottir, S.; Arnardottir, R.H.; Gudmundsson, G.; Bjornsson, E.H. Frustrated Caring: Family Members' Experience of Motivating COPD Patients Towards Self-Management. *Int. J. Chronic Obstr. Pulm. Dis.* **2020**, *15*, 2953–2965. [CrossRef] [PubMed]
33. Singh, S.; Surani, S.; McGuinness, S.; Eudicone, J.; Gilbert, I.; Subramanian, S. Current practice patterns, challenges, and educational needs of asthma care providers in the United States. *J. Asthma* **2021**, *58*, 1118–1127. [CrossRef] [PubMed]
34. Li, P.; Duan, Z.; Zhang, Z.; He, Y.; Li, W.; Jin, W. Impacts of government supervision on hospitalization costs for inpatients with COPD: An interrupted time series study. *Medicine* **2020**, *99*, e18977. (In English) [CrossRef] [PubMed]

medicina

MDPI

Article

Cervical Cancer Mortality in Romania: Trends, Regional and Rural–Urban Inequalities, and Policy Implications

Florentina Furtunescu [1,†], Roxana Elena Bohiltea [2,*,†], Adrian Neacsu [2,3], Corina Grigoriu [2,4], Corina Silvia Pop [5,6], Nicolae Bacalbasa [2], Ionita Ducu [4], Ana-Maria Iordache [7,*] and Radu Virgil Costea [8,9]

1. Department of Public Health and Management, Faculty of Medicine, "Carol Davila" University of Medicine and Pharmacy Bucharest, 050463 Bucharest, Romania; florentina.furtunescu@umfcd.ro
2. Department of Obstetrics and Gynecology, "Carol Davila" University of Medicine and Pharmacy Bucharest, 020021 Bucharest, Romania; adrianneacsu2006@yahoo.com (A.N.); corigri@gmail.com (C.G.); nicolae_bacalbasa@yahoo.ro or nicolaebacalbasa@gmail.com (N.B.)
3. Department of Obstetrics and Gynecology, "Sfantul Ioan" Emergency Clinical Hospital, 042122 Bucharest, Romania
4. Department of Obstetrics and Gynecology, University Emergency Hospital Bucharest, 050098 Bucharest, Romania; ionitaducu@gmail.com
5. Department of Internal Medicine and Gastroenterology, "Carol Davila" University of Medicine and Pharmacy Bucharest, 020021 Bucharest, Romania; cora.pop@gmail.com
6. Department of Internal Medicine and Gastroenterology, University Emergency Hospital Bucharest, 050098 Bucharest, Romania
7. Optospintronics Department, National Institute for Research and Development in Optoelectronics-INOE 2000, 409 Atomistilor, 077125 Magurele, Romania
8. Department of Surgery, "Carol Davila" University of Medicine and Pharmacy Bucharest, 020021 Bucharest, Romania; rcostea2000@yahoo.com
9. Department of Surgery, University Emergency Hospital Bucharest, 050098 Bucharest, Romania

* Correspondence: r.bohiltea@yahoo.com (R.E.B.); ana.iordache@yahoo.com (A.-M.I.)

† The authors contributed equally and should be regarded as the first author.

Citation: Furtunescu, F.; Bohiltea, R.E.; Neacsu, A.; Grigoriu, C.; Pop, C.S.; Bacalbasa, N.; Ducu, I.; Iordache, A.-M.; Costea, R.V. Cervical Cancer Mortality in Romania: Trends, Regional and Rural–Urban Inequalities, and Policy Implications. *Medicina* **2022**, *58*, 18. https://doi.org/10.3390/medicina58010018

Academic Editor: Jimmy T. Efird

Received: 31 October 2021
Accepted: 19 December 2021
Published: 23 December 2021

Abstract: *Background and Objectives:* Despite being largely preventable, cervical cancer mortality still remains an important public health problem globally, in Europe, and in Romania. The European Union member states are urged to implement systematic, population-based screenings for cervical cancer, but the programs developed by the countries remain very heterogeneous. This study aimed to investigate the differences in cervix cancer mortality between Romania and EU and within Romania over the last two decades and to reveal the major sources of inequalities and the policy implications. *Materials and Methods:* We analyzed the number of deaths and the mortality rates by cervical cancer, standardized using the direct method, over two decades (2001–2016 for the EU, and 2001–2019 for the national and sub-national analyses). Trends, mortality reduction over the years, and mortality differences at the beginning and end of the time interval have been calculated for the EU and Romania, at national and sub-national levels (rural–urban and regions). *Results:* Our results revealed differences in cervical cancer mortality between Romania and EU and within Romania (among regions and rural–urban areas). These differences used to be very high in the past and are still persisting. *Conclusions:* The country should revisit its national cervical cancer screening program, which has been implemented for many years, but with a very limited participation rate. Due to the similar problems existing in Central-Eastern Europe, targeted support from the EU for the members from this geographical area could contribute to the minimization of differences in cervical cancer mortality among the EU members.

Keywords: cervical cancer deaths; age-standardized mortality; cervical cancer screening; cervical cancer mortality

1. Introduction

Cervical cancer mortality is largely preventable, through vaccination against Human Papiloma Virus (HPV), citology- or HPV-based cancer screening, treatment of precancerous lesions, and improved access to diagnosis and treatment of the invasive cancers [1–3]. Despite this potential of preventability, cervix cancer still remains an important public health problem globally, with an estimate of 569,847 new cases and 311,365 deaths per year in 2018 [4]. From around 52% of cases, 60% of the deaths occur in low- and middle-income counties due to failure in implementing population-based preventive programs [4–6]. In Europe, cervix cancer is responsible for an estimate of 58,169 new cases, with 25,989 just in 2020 [7].

In the European Union (EU), a Recommendation of the Council since 2003 urges the member states to implement systematic, population-based cancer screenings for breast, cervix, and colon cancer [8]. In the case of cervical cancer, conventional cytology for cancer precursors with Papanicolau staining, validated liquid-based cytology, primary testing for oncogenic HPV with validated assays, and implementation of HPV vaccination programs have been recommended [9–11]. The last assessment of this recommendation revealed that 22 (out of 28) member states had implemented national or sub-national cervix cancer screening programs, ensuring an average coverage of 59.2% women aged 30–59 years, a participation rate of 50.7%, and an examination coverage of 29.8% [12]. Additionally, the screening programs developed by the countries were marked by wide heterogeneity, which made it difficult to compare the quality of the assurance measures, the monitoring and evaluation strategies, or the cost-effectiveness [12–14]. Still, cervix cancer was responsible for 9744 deaths in 2016 (last available year), with wide disparities in mortality rates still persisting among the countries (e.g., ten times variations between Italy and Romania, from 0.71 to 8.04 deaths per 10,000 women, standardized rates) and within the country itself [15].

Beyond the high number of deaths, cervical cancer has multiple effects on the health status, by affecting the quality of life, sexual health, and, due to its predilection in young women, by threatening fertility [16,17]. Even in the case of successful treatment of the precancerous lesions and preservation of fertility, it induces a risk of preterm birth [18–20].

Our study aimed to investigate the differences in cervical cancer mortality between Romania and the EU and within Romania over the last two decades and to reveal the major sources of inequalities and the policy implications for better control of this public health problem in the future.

2. Materials and Methods

We followed the differences in cervical cancer mortality from two perspectives—differences between Romania and EU and differences within the country itself, by regions, and rural–urban areas. We used the number of deaths and the mortality rates by cervical cancer—Code C53 upon the International Classification of Disease Revision 10 (ICD-10), which is currently in use in the country [21]. The time interval for the analysis was 2001–2016, for the comparison to EU average (2016 being the last available year for the EU average) and 2001–2019 for the national data.

The geographic area: for EU, we used the EU 27 data (the United Kingdom excluded). For Romania, we used data disaggregated by rural–urban area and by NUT 2 region (Nomenclature of territorial units for statistics for basic regions). Romania is the eighth largest EU country by surface and the sixth country by population (22.1 million citizens registered, among which 19.3 million inhabitants reside in the country) [22]. Currently, 46% of the total population lives in rural areas, this being the highest proportion of rural population among all the EU member states [23]. The country is divided into 42 counties and 8 regions NUTS 2: North-East (NE), South-East (SE), South (S), South-West (SW), West, North-West (NW), Center (C), and Bucharest–Ilfov (BI), last one being the most developed and including the capital city (Figure 1).

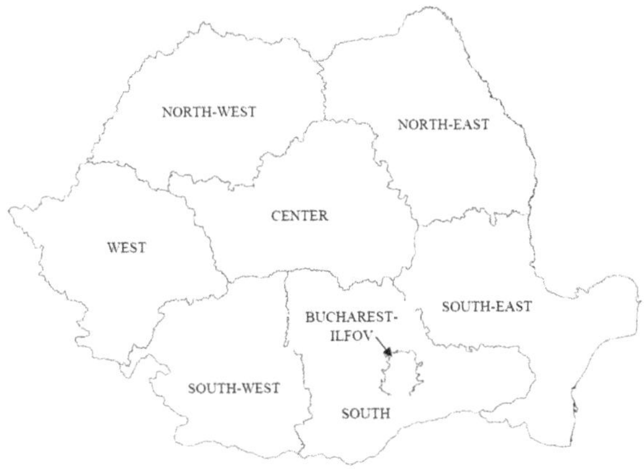

Figure 1. Romania—the geographic map by regions.

Deaths analysis: The deaths have been analyzed as annual number and percentage change in 2016/2019, compared to the baseline (2001).

Mortality rates analysis: For the comparison of Romania versus EU, we used the standardized mortality rates extracted from Eurostat [15]. For the further sub-national analysis, we have standardized the national and sub-national data using the direct method (standard population) [24]. We used the following data: (i) the number of deaths by cervical cancer, disaggregated by five years' age groups, region, and rural–urban areas [25]; (ii) the female population by five-year age-groups, per country, per region, and per rural–urban population [22]. Our standard population was represented by a national female population calculated for each five-year age group as the arithmetic mean of corresponding age group female population for years 2001, 2010, and 2019 (first, last, and middle year of the study interval).

We followed the trends in standardized mortality rate (SMR), mortality reduction (MR), and mortality difference (MD).

The mortality reduction (MR)

The mortality reduction has been calculated in EU, per country, and for the sub-national levels in the last year of the time interval, compared to the starting year. For the EU and country levels, we used the formula:

$$MR_A(\%) = (SMR_{A,2001} - SMR_{A,2016})/SMR_{A,2001} \quad (1)$$

where:

- $MR_A(\%)$ is the mortality reduction in area A, in 2016 compared to 2001, expressed as percentage;
- Area A is either Romania or EU;
- SMR_A is the standardized mortality rate in geographical area A.

For the subnational levels, we calculated MRs for urban national, rural national, regionals, urban regionals, and rural regionals SMRs, by using the following formula:

$$MR_B(\%) = (SMR_{B,2001} - SMR_{B,2019})/SMR_{RO,2001} \quad (2)$$

where:

- $MR_B(\%)$ is the mortality reduction in area B, in 2019, expressed as percentage from the national SMR for year 2001;
- Area B could be urban national, rural national, regional, or urban/rural regional level;
- SMR_B is the standardized mortality rate in geographical area B, for the corresponding year (2001 or 2019);

- $SMR_{RO,2001}$ is the standardized mortality rate in Romania, in 2001. We have chosen to express all the reductions as proportion from the national rate, for a unique baseline, which is the national model.

The mortality difference (MD)

It has been calculated as annual difference between Romania and EU SMRs or between national and sub-national levels. We explored the differences at the beginning and, respectively, the end of the time interval (2001 and 2016 for Romania and EU, and 2001 and 2019 within the country) by using the formulas:

$$MD_{RO,\ EU,i}(\%) = (SMR_{RO,\ year\ i} - SMR_{EU,i})/SMR_{EU,i} \quad (3)$$

where:

- $MD_{A,EU,i}$ is the mortality difference between Romania and EU in year i, expressed as percentage;
- Year i is either 2001 or 2016;
- $SMR_{RO,i}$ is the standardized mortality rate in Romania, for the year i;
- $SMR_{EU,i}$ is the standardized mortality rate in EU, for the year i.

$$MD_{B,j}(\%) = (SMR_{B,j} - SMR_{RO,j})/SMR_{RO,j} \quad (4)$$

where:

- $MD_{B,j}$ is the mortality difference between area B and Romania in year j, expressed as percentage.
- Area B could be any subnational area, like urban national, rural national, or region.
- Year j is either 2001 or 2019.
- $SMR_{B,j}$ is the standardized mortality rate in geographical area B for the corresponding year j.
- $SMR_{RO,j}$ is the standardized mortality rate in Romania, in year j, as it resulted from the national standardization.

$$RU\ MD_{C,j}(\%) = (SMR_{R,C,j} - SMR_{U,C,j})/SMR_{RO,j} \quad (5)$$

where:

- $RU\ MD_{C,j}$ is the rural–urban mortality difference in region C in year j, expressed as percentage of the national SMR.
- Area C could be any of the eight regions of the country.
- Year j could be 2001 or 2019.
- $SMR_{R,C,j}$ is the rural standardized mortality rate in region C for the corresponding year j.
- $SMR_{U,C,j}$ is the urban standardized mortality rate in region C for the corresponding year j.
- $SMR_{RO,j}$ is the standardized mortality rate in Romania, in year j, as it resulted from the national standardization.

The MRs were expressed as old–recent value, and the MDs were expressed as subnational–national values. Thus, due to the decline over the years, all the MRs are positive, and the subnational areas with rates below the national have negative MDs, which is a favorable situation.

Ranking: In the subnational analysis per region, we ranked the regions from 1 to 8, where 1 = most favorable and 8 = least favorable. If two regions had the same position, they received the same ranking.

Chi-square test was used for comparing the changes in number of deaths, with a significance level of 95%.

3. Results

3.1. Differences between Romania and the EU

3.1.1. Number of Deaths

In 2001, 10,570 deaths due to cervical cancer were registered in the EU, out of which 1763 (17%) were reported for Romania [15]. At that time, Romania had the third-highest number of deaths among the EU members, after Poland and Germany, and the three countries together accounted for 51% of EU deaths. In 2016, the annual number of deaths had decreased by 8% and 10% in the EU and Romania, respectively, compared to baseline (2001). In Germany and Poland, reductions of 11% and 13%, respectively, were revealed. Despite this reduction in deaths in Romania, the country still accounted for 15% of the EU cervix cancer deaths in 2016.

3.1.2. Mortality Rates

Both Romania and the EU have shown decreasing trends in cervix cancer mortality during the study interval, but the rates for Romania were constantly much higher compared to the EU. In 2002, Romania had the highest cervix cancer mortality in the EU, and the mortality difference compared to EU was enormous (276%, meaning 18.8 versus 4.8 deaths per 100,000 women in Romania and EU, respectively; the year 2001 was not available for EU). The second-highest SMR was found in Lithuania, followed by Poland (16.4 and 10.9 deaths/100,000 women).

In 2016, the mortality reduction reached 58% and 56% for the EU and Romania, respectively, compared to 2002. However, the mortality difference remained unchanged (277%). Lithuania and Poland have shown a 61% and 59% reduction in mortality over the years, and the ranking among the EU members did not change.

3.2. Differences within Romania

3.2.1. Number of Deaths

In 2019, Romania reported 1539 deaths, meaning a 13% decline compared to 2001. (A 10% decline was already reported for 2016.) In 2001, 51% came from rural areas, and this percentage changed significantly, to 46%, in 2019 ($p = 0.013$) (Table 1). A more important decline of deaths over the years was registered in rural areas (20% compared to 5% in urban areas).

Table 1. Deaths by cervix cancer in Romania, 2001 and 2019, national and subnational distribution and percentage change.

Sub-National Area	2001			2019			*p*-Value *	% Change in 2019
	Number	%	Rank	Number	%	Rank		
National	1763	100%	NA	1539	100%	NA	NA	13%
Urban	870	49%	NA	825	54%	NA	0.015	5%
Rural	893	51%	NA	714	46%	NA		20%
Regions								
North-East	316	18%	1	235	15%	2	0.041	26%
South-East	237	13%	3	224	15%	2	0.358	5%
South	246	14%	2	265	17%	1	0.009	−8%
South-West	228	13%	3	156	10%	5	0.012	32%
West	182	10%	4	165	11%	4	0.709	9%
North-West	243	14%	2	203	13%	3	0.619	16%
Center	184	10%	4	154	10%	5	0.684	16%
Bucharest–Ilfov	127	7%	5	137	9%	6	0.072	−8%

* Chi-square test; NA-not available

In 2001, the NE region was the biggest contributor to the total deaths, followed closely by S and NW, and the lowest contributor was the BI region. In 2019, S became the highest contributor to the total deaths, followed by NE and SE. BI remained the lowest contributor, despite an 8% increase in the number of deaths. The S region is the only one (except BI) with an increase in the number of deaths in 2019 (8%). If the situation of Bucharest was caused by an increase in population, due to the fact that this is the most developed region of the country, the S region probably had other determinants for this increase. In fact, significant changes in contribution to the total deaths occurred in only three regions: S (increase) and NE and SE (decrease) (Table 1). Overall, Romania, for the study interval (2001–2019), reported 32,558 cumulated deaths due to cervix cancer, out of which 47% occurred in the rural areas. Additionally, 61% of these deaths were registered in adult women (aged 0–64 years) (Table 2).

Table 2. Cumulated deaths by age groups and rural–urban areas, 2001–2019.

Age Group	Urban		Rural		National	
	No.	%	No.	%	No.	%
0–44 years	2251	13%	2318	15%	4569	14%
45–64 years	8771	51%	6577	42%	15,348	47%
65+ years	6022	35%	6619	43%	12,641	39%
Total	17,044	100%	15,514	100%	32,558	100%
% of national deaths	53%		47%		100%	

3.2.2. Trends in Cervix Cancer Mortality

The standardized mortality rate at the national level revealed a decreasing trend during the study period, but it was constantly higher in rural areas (Figure 2). The declining trend was seen at different extents in all the regions, but with the same pattern of higher mortality in the rural population (Figure 3).

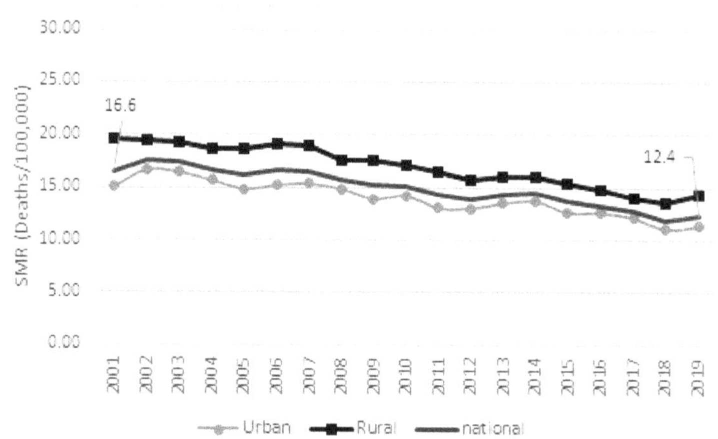

Figure 2. Trends in cervix cancer mortality, overall and by rural–urban areas, Romania, 2001–2019 (standardized mortality rates).

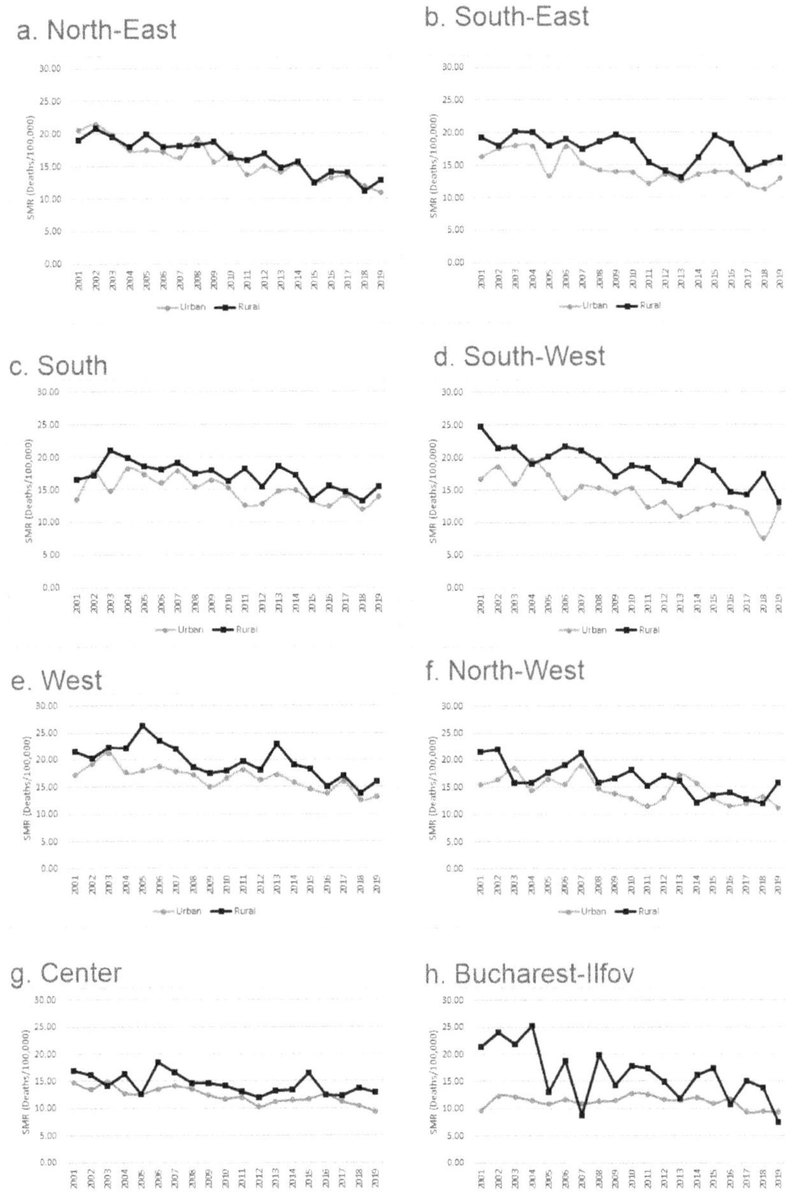

Figure 3. Regional trend in cervix cancer mortality by rural–urban areas, Romania, 2001–2019 (standardized mortality rates).

3.2.3. Mortality Reduction over the Two Decades

Overall, the mortality reduction reached 25% in 2019 compared to 2001 for the national rate and 22% and 32% for the urban and rural rates, respectively (Table 3). In the regions, the most important reduction was found for the SW and NE, reaching 44% and 43% decline compared to baseline, but important reductions also occurred in NW, C, and W (Table 3).

More limited progress was found in the SE (18%) and Bucharest (8%); meanwhile, in the S region, the situation remained almost unchanged compared to 2001 (Table 3).

Table 3. Mortality reduction over decades—national, regional, and urban–rural.

Type	National	NE	SE	S	SW	W	NW	C	BI
National	25%	43%	19%	2%	44%	27%	33%	28%	8%
Urban	22%	58%	20%	−2%	27%	25%	26%	32%	3%
Rural	32%	37%	20%	7%	71%	33%	35%	24%	84%

The analysis of rural and urban models of mortality by regions revealed a remarkable progress in improving the rural models of mortality in BI and SW regions, with an 84% and 71% reduction in rural mortality. To a moderate extent, this improvement also occurred in the NE, NW, and W (MR of 37%, 35%, and 33% in rural). The most modest improvement in rural mortality was noticed in the S (only 7%) (Table 3). The urban models have shown a marked progress in NE (58% MR) and a moderate one in the C, NW, and W (32%, 26%, and 25%, respectively); meanwhile, the MR was modest in BI (3%) and negative in the S (−2%) (Table 3). Overall, in five regions, the MR was more marked for rural (BI, SW, NW, W, and S); in the other two, it was more marked for urban areas (NE and C), and in the SE, the urban and rural improvements were similar.

3.2.4. Past and Current Differences in Mortality

In 2001, the most detrimental regional MDs were seen in the SW, NE, and W (19%, 14%, and 12% difference compared to the national model) and most favorable in BI, the S, and C (−37%, −11%, and −9%, respectively) (Table 4). The highest RU-MDs were seen in BI, the SW, and NW (40%, 49%, and 37%, respectively) and the lowest ones in the NE and C (−9% and 13%, respectively, the N being the only region in which rural mortality is lower than the urban one) (Table 4). At the national level, the RU MD reached 27%.

Table 4. Mortality difference by region and urban–rural areas.

	2001				2019			
Region	**Regional MD**	**Rank**	**RU MD per Region**	**Rank**	**Regional MD**	**Rank**	**RU MD per Region**	**Rank**
North-East	14%	7	−9%	1	−5%	3	16%	4
South-East	3%	4	18%	4	12%	6	25%	6
South	−11%	2	18%	3	17%	7	12%	3
South-West	19%	8	49%	7	0%	4	7%	2
West	12%	6	26%	5	14%	8	23%	5
North-West	11%	5	37%	6	5%	5	37%	8
Center	−9%	3	13%	2	−15%	2	28%	7
Bucharest–Ilfov	−37%	1	70%	8	−26%	1	−15%	1

In 2019, the W, S, and SE regions showed the highest MDs, and BI and C were in the best positions. Regarding the RU MD per region, it was most marked in the NW, C, and SE (37%, 28%, and 25%, respectively), and the lowest in BI and the SW (Table 4). For the national level, the RU MD reached 24%

4. Discussion

Our research revealed important differences in cervical cancer mortality between Romania and the EU and within Romania. These differences were very high in the past and, despite a 13% reduction in deaths and 25% reduction in mortality over the two decades, they are still persisting. At the EU level, Romania is keeping the first position in mortality rate and shows a huge difference compared to the EU's rate. Within the country, the rural population continues to remain more disadvantaged. Despite a higher reduction in rural mortality, compared to the urban one, the rural–urban mortality gap still achieved 24% of the national rate in 2019.

The analysis per region also reflects the different rhythms of progress in mortality reduction, persisting gaps compared to the national level, and, in some cases, major gaps between rural and urban populations. For example, the SW, NE, and W had the highest deviations compared to the national model in 2001, but meanwhile, the SW and NE succeeded to achieve good progress (44% and 43% MR), while the W region reached only a moderate one (27% MR). The poorest transformation was seen in the S region, which started with a favorable MD compared to the national model, but it achieved a very limited gain only in rural mortality. Another particular situation is related to the NW region, which has a very important tradition in implementing cervical cancer screening programs [12]. Despite this wide experience, the progress in the region was moderate, with a 33% mortality reduction over the two decades, a persistent mortality difference of 5% compared to the national model, and a constant rural–urban difference of 37% in favor of urban. The BI region had from far the most privileged situation in 2001 (37% mortality difference compared to the national model), but with the widest rural–urban gap in the country (70%). This gap has been corrected over the years, but it is uncertain if correction occurred due to mechanisms for improving access to services for the rural population or to the socio-economic particularities of the region. This region includes Bucharest (the capital city) and the county of Ilfov, with approximately one-fifth of the Bucharest population. The city of Bucharest is geographically surrounded by Ilfov, and the only rural population of the region (9%) belongs to the county of Ilfov. During the last two decades, the people mobility between Bucharest and Ilfov increased substantially, on the background of the economic development. This mobility could explain the yearly variation of mortality line in the rural population of Ilfov.

Our results underline the persisting barriers of access to preventive and curative services for the rural population, despite the fact that the legislative framework guarantees equitable access to services for all citizens. The health system in Romania is social-insurance-based, the health insurance is compulsory, and the system is defined to ensure universal access to primary care and referral-based specialized care [26]. For equity reasons, many vulnerable categories of people are insured without payment of financial contribution [26]. More than this, certain national health programs complement the package of services provided by health insurance, among which the oncology program (ensuring free access to cytostatic treatment for all oncologic patients, including the case of cervical cancer) and the cervix cancer screening program (ensuring free access to pap-smear screening for all insured and non-insured women) [27]. These programs, and in particular the cervix cancer screening, are, in theory, accessible for all, but the participation remains weak (5% achievement of the annual target for cervix cancer screening in 2018) [28]. In general, cancer diagnostic and treatment are available and fully covered by the insurance package (clinical procedures) and the national health program (cytostatic), being available for insured and non-insured women. The access to services is based on a referral from the family doctor or direct, in case of emergency (through the emergency department). Once diagnosed, there is direct access to all specialized services (surgical treatment, cytostatic, and/or radiotherapy).

On the contrary, the preventive services are fewer, less accessible, and partially or not covered by either the health insurance or the national programs, despite consistent efforts to develop them over the years. For example, the first attempt to introduce a free HPV vaccination was made in 2008, as a state-financed program targeting young girls (10–11 years old), but that program failed with only 2.5% of the eligible population being vaccinated due to the huge hesitancy of the parents [29]. Following this failure, the program has been changed, with the free vaccine provided based on request for girls aged 11 to 18 years, but the demand remains very limited. Boys and women older than 18 years of age were and are not targeted by the free vaccination program. For these categories of people, the vaccine was available in pharmacies, prescription-based, and with full out-of-pocket payment. In these circumstances, the HPV vaccination uptake remained very limited. Complementary, HPV testing is available in the country at full price (not included in the package of services covered by health insurance). This testing has been provided for free in some projects and revealed a high-risk HPV prevalence of 18% among women 18 to 70 years old [30]. Regarding early diagnosis, colposcopy is available in most outpatient specialized clinics and hospitals and covered by insurance in some circumstances, but the providers are located usually in cities, and women from rural or deprived areas have limited access due to geographic, information, and, sometimes, financial barriers [26]. No audit mechanisms have been implemented in relation to cervical cancer prevention services.

A major question is what actions should be taken to improve cervical cancer control in the future. There is obviously a prioritization of cervical cancer screening in the country. The national screening program has been introduced for many years, despite its failure in ensuring a population-based screening and appropriate participation [28]. Evidence for good practice models is available in the country and could serve as a basis for revisiting and improving the existing implementation of the national program [31–37]. Certain interventions are being planned, such as a project for the integration of primary HPV screening into the national cervical cancer screening program [36]. This project is planned to be implemented in two phases: a training and planning phase, which is in ongoing implementation, and the screening itself, which is planned to be implemented in the North-West, Center, South, and North-East, having at least 170,000 screened beneficiaries per region [38].

Our results provide the appropriate framework for understanding the evolution of cervical cancer mortality over decades, the differences within regions, and the rural–urban gaps. As a consequence, the national program should be remodeled, by focusing on the rural population and, in particular, in the West, South, and South-West regions, which still kept a major difference in mortality compared to the national level. Another essential premise for the national program is to ensure the population-based character of the screening, which is in line with the European guidelines, and with the Romanian law, which guarantees universal access to preventive services for all the citizens [9–11,14,26]. Despite being reported as a population-based program, due to the modest participation rate, the programs should be analyzed in their main stages, and more feasible remedial mechanisms should be identified.

Another important aspect is the active character of the program, with individual invitations through the screening registry or database (which does not exist in Romania), a fixed appointment date included in the invitation, and a continuum of services for positive cases [12]. Last but not least, dedicated human and financial resources and procedures and clear quality-assurance mechanisms should be analyzed and implemented [12].

Of course, the situation of Romania is not singular, despite its huge gap in cervical cancer mortality compared to the EU. Evidence suggests that cervical cancer mortality rates are higher in Central-Eastern Europe, and the access to organized screening programs is more detrimental compared to the rest of the continent [12,39–41]. All these facts are against the evidence that women attending organized screening programs versus non-attenders could benefit from a 41% to 92% reduction in cervix cancer mortality, according to a recent systematic review [42]. These facts could be considered at the EU level for building more accessible opportunities and exchanges related to cervical cancer screening as a feasible way to decrease the gaps in mortality among the EU member states.

5. Conclusions

In conclusion, cervical cancer represents an important public health problem in Romania, despite its declining number of deaths and mortality rate, over the last two decades. Important differences are persisting between Romania and the EU and within the country, on the background of the failure in organizing a population-based national screening program. The country should use the existing opportunities to improve its screening program in the upcoming years. Due to the similar problems existing in Central-Eastern Europe, targeted support from the EU for the members from this geographical area could contribute to the minimization of differences in cervical cancer mortality among the EU members.

Author Contributions: Conceptualization, F.F., R.E.B., C.G. and C.S.P.; methodology, F.F., R.E.B. and C.S.P.; validation F.F.; formal analysis, F.F., R.E.B. and C.S.P.; investigation, F.F., R.E.B., C.G. and C.S.P.; resources, A.N. and R.V.C.; writing—original draft preparation, F.F., R.E.B., C.G. and C.S.P.; writing—review and editing, A.N. and R.V.C.; visualization, N.B., I.D. and A.-M.I., supervision, A.N., N.B. and R.V.C. All authors have read and agreed to the published version of the manuscript.

Funding: This research received no external funding.

Institutional Review Board Statement: Not required due to the statistical analysis nature of the study.

Informed Consent Statement: Not applicable.

Data Availability Statement: The datasets used and analyzed during the current study are available from Eurostat and the National Institute of Statistics, Bucharest, Romania, on reasonable request.

Conflicts of Interest: The authors declare no conflict of interest.

References

1. World Health Organization. *Global Strategy to Accelerate the Elimination of Cervical Cancer as a Public Health Problem*; WHO: Geneva, Switzerland, 2020; Available online: https://www.who.int/publications/i/item/9789240014107 (accessed on 21 March 2021).
2. Brisson, M.; Drolet, M. Global elimination of cervical cancer as a public health problem. *Lancet Oncol.* **2019**, *20*, 319–321. [CrossRef]
3. Simms, K.T.; Steinberg, J.; Caruana, M.; Smith, M.A.; Lew, J.B.; Soerjomataram, I.; Castle, P.E.; Bray, F.; Canfell, K. Impact of scaled up human papillomavirus vaccination and cervical screening and the potential for global elimination of cervical cancer in 181 countries, 2020–2099: A modelling study. *Lancet Oncol.* **2019**, *20*, 394–407. [CrossRef]
4. Arbyn, M.; Weiderpass, E.; Bruni, L.; de Sanjose, S.; Saraiya, M.; Ferlay, J.; Bray, F. Estimates of incidence and mortality of cervical cancer in 2018: A worldwide analysis. *Lancet Glob. Health* **2019**, *8*, e191–e203. [CrossRef]
5. World Health Organization. *Comprehensive Cervical Cancer Prevention and Control—A Healthier Future for Girls and Women*; WHO Guidance Note; WHO: Geneva, Switzerland, 2013.
6. Gaffney, D.K.; Hashibe, M.; Kepka, D.; Maurer KA and Werner, T.L. Too many women are dying from cervix cancer: Problems and solutions. *Gynecol. Oncol.* **2018**, *151*, 547–554. [CrossRef] [PubMed]
7. World Health Organization and International Agency for Research on Cancer. Global Cancer Observatory. Cancer Today. Available online: https://gco.iarc.fr/ (accessed on 21 March 2021).
8. European Council. Council recommendation of 2 December 2003 on cancer screening (2003/878/EC). *Off. J. Eur. Union* **2003**, *327*, 34–38.
9. Arbyn, M.; Anttila, A.; Jordan, J.; Ronco, G.; Schenck, U.; Segnan, N.; Wiener, H.G.; Herbert, A.; Daniel, J.; von Karsa, L. *European Guidelines for Quality Assurance in Cervical Cancer Screening*, 2nd ed.; Office for Official Publications of the European Communities: Luxembourg, 2008.
10. Arbyn, M.; Anttila, A.; Jordan, J.; Ronco, G.; Schenck, U.; Segnan, N.; Wiener, H.; Herbert, A.; von Karsa, L. European guidelines for quality assurance in cervical cancer screening. Second edition—Summary document. *Ann. Oncol.* **2010**, *21*, 448–458. [CrossRef]
11. von Karsa, L.; Arbyn, M.; De Vuyst, H.; Dillner, J.; Dillner, L.; Franceschi, S.; Patnick, J.; Ronco, G.; Segnan, N.; Suonio, E. European guidelines for quality assurance in cervical cancer screening. Summary of the supplements on HPV screening and vaccination. *Papillomavirus Res.* **2015**, *1*, 22–31. [CrossRef]
12. Ponti, A.; Anttila, A.; Ronco, G.; Senore, C. Cancer Screening in the European Union. In *Report on the implementation of Council Recommendation on Cancer Screening*; European Commission: Brussels, Belgium, 2017.
13. Furtunescu, F.; Bohiltea, R.E.; Voinea, S.; Neacsu, A.; Pop, C.S. Breast cancer mortality gaps in Romanian women compared to EU after ten years of accession—Is breast cancer screening a priority for action in Romania? *Exp. Ther. Med.* **2021**, *21*, 268–273. [CrossRef] [PubMed]
14. Elfström, K.M.; Arnheim-Dahlström, L.; von Karsa, L.; Dillner, J. Cervical cancer screening in Europe: Quality assurance and organisation of programmes. *Eur. J Cancer* **2015**, *51*, 950–968. [CrossRef]
15. European Commission. Eurostat. Population and Social Condition. Available online: https://ec.europa.eu/eurostat (accessed on 21 March 2021).
16. Bentivegna, E.; Gouy, S.; Maulard, A.; Chargari, C.; Leary, A.; Morice, P. Oncological outcomes after fertility-sparing surgery for cervical cancer: A systematic review. *Lancet Oncol.* **2016**, *17*, e240–e253. [CrossRef]
17. Maltaris, T.; Seufert, R.; Fischl, F.; Schaffrath, M.; Pollow, K.; Koelbl, H.; Dittrich, R. The effect of cancer treatment on female fertility and strategies for preserving fertility. *EJOGRB* **2013**, *130*, 148–155. [CrossRef]

18. Bohîlțea, R.E.; Turcan, G.; Cîrstoiu, M.M.; Ionescu, C.; Nemescu, D.; Turcan, N.; Vladareanu, R. Clinical Implementation of Ultrasound Gynecological Examination Report (software REGU) Based on International Consensuses of Tumor Study Groups. Filodiritto Editore-Proceedings. In Proceedings of the 5th Romanian Congress Of The Romanian Society of Ultrasound in Obstetrics and Gynecology, Targu-Mures, Romania, 20–22 April 2017; pp. 99–104.
19. Bohîlțea, R.; Furtunescu, F.; Turcan, N.; Navolan, D.; Ducu, I.; Cîrstoiu, M. Prematurity and Intrauterine Growth Restriction: Comparative Analysis of Incidence and Short Term Complication. Proceedings of SOGR 2018. In Proceedings of the 17th National Congress of The Romanian Society of Obstetrics and Gynecology, Iasi, Romania, 20–22 September 2018; pp. 708–712.
20. Turcan, N.; Bohiltea, R.E.; Ionita-Radu, F.; Furtunescu, F.; Navolan, D.; Berceanu, C.; Nemescu, D.; Cirstoiu, M.M. Unfavorable influence of prematurity on the neonatal prognostic of small for gestational age fetuses. *Exp. Ther. Med.* **2020**, *20*, 2415–2422. [CrossRef]
21. World Health Organization. *ICD-10: International Statistical Classification of Diseases and Related Health Problems: Tenth Revision*, 2nd ed.; World Health Organization: Geneva, Switzerland, 2004. Available online: https://apps.who.int/iris/handle/10665/42980 (accessed on 21 March 2021).
22. National Institute of Statistics. Tempo On-Line Database. Available online: http://statistici.insse.ro:8077/tempo-online/#/pages/tables/insse-table (accessed on 21 March 2021).
23. World Bank Indicators. Proportion of Rural Population. Available online: https://data.worldbank.org/indicator/SP.RUR.TOTL.ZS?view=chart (accessed on 21 March 2021).
24. Naing, N.N. Easy way to learn standardization: Direct and indirect methods. *Malays. J. Med. Sci.* **2000**, *7*, 10–15.
25. National Institute of Public Health. Number of Deaths by Cause, Age-Group and Sub-Region. Available online: https://insp.gov.ro/contact/ (accessed on 21 March 2021).
26. Law regarding the Reform in Health No. 95/2006, with the Subsequent Amendments. 2006. Available online: http://legislatie.just.ro/Public/DetaliiDocument/71139 (accessed on 21 March 2021).
27. Government Decision no 155/2017 regarding the NATIONAL Health Programs with the Subsequent Ammendments. 2017. Available online: http://legislatie.just.ro/Public/DetaliiDocument/187856 (accessed on 21 March 2021).
28. Romania, Ministry of Health. Annual Activity Report. 2018. Available online: http://www.ms.ro/wp-content/uploads/2019/05/Raport-de-activitate-MS-2018-2.pdf (accessed on 12 February 2021).
29. Craciun, C.; Baban, A. "Who will take the blame?": Understanding the reasons why Romanian mothers decline HPV vaccination for their daughters. *Vaccine* **2012**, *30*, 6789–6793. [CrossRef] [PubMed]
30. Ilisiu, M.B.; Hashim, D.; Andreassen, T.; Støer, N.C.; Nicula, F.; Weiderpass, E. HPV Testing for Cervical Cancer in Romania: High-Risk HPV Prevalence among Ethnic Subpopulations and Regions. *Ann. Glob. Health* **2019**, *85*, 89. [CrossRef] [PubMed]
31. Nicula, F.A.; Anttila, A.; Neamtiu, L.; Žakelj, M.P.; Tachezy, R.; Chil, A.; Grce, M.; Kesić, V. Challenges in starting organised screening programmes for cervical cancer in the new member states of the European Union. *Eur. J. Cancer* **2009**, *45*, 2679–2684. [CrossRef] [PubMed]
32. Badea, M.; Baroş, A.; Bohîlţea, R.E.; Julea, I.E.; Furtunescu, F.L.; Istrate-Ofiţeru, A.M.; Iovan, L.; Cîrstoiu, M.M.; Burcin, M.R.; Turcan, N.; et al. Modern interdisciplinary monitoring of cervical cancer risk. *Rom. J. Morphol. Embryol.* **2019**, *60*, 469–478.
33. Boda, D.; Docea, A.O.; Calina, D.; Ilie, M.A.; Caruntu, C.; Zurac, S.; Neagu, M.; Constantin, C.; Branisteanu, D.E.; Voiculescu, V.; et al. Human papilloma virus: Apprehending the link with carcinogenesis and unveiling new research avenues. *Int. J. Oncol.* **2018**, *52*, 637–655. [CrossRef]
34. Ionescu, C.A.; Matei, A.; Navolan, D.; Dimitriu, M.; Bohâltea, R.; Neacsu, A.; Ilinca, C.; Ples, L. Correlation of ultrasound features and the Risk of Ovarian Malignancy Algorithm score for different histopathological subtypes of benign adnexal masses. *Medicine* **2018**, *97*, e11762. [CrossRef]
35. Bohiltea, R.E.; Zugravu, C.A.; Neacsu, A.; Navolan, D.; Berceanu, C.; Nemescu, D.; Bodean, O.; Turcan, N.; Baros, A.; Cirstoiu, M.M. The prevalence of Vitamin D deficiency and its obstetrical effects. A prospective study on Romanian patients. *Rev. Chim.* **2019**, *70*, 1228–1233. [CrossRef]
36. Iorga, L.; Marcu, R.D.; Diaconu, C.C.; Stanescu, A.M.A.; Pantea Stoian, A.; Mischianu, D.L.D.; Surcel, M.; Bungau, S.; Constantin, T.; Boda, D.; et al. Penile carcinoma and HPV infection (Review). *Exp. Ther. Med.* **2020**, *20*, 91–96. [CrossRef]
37. Todor, R.D.; Bratucu, G.; Moga, M.A.; Candrea, A.N.; Marceanu, L.G.; Anastasiu, C.V. Challenges in the Prevention of Cervical Cancer in Romania. *Int. J. Environ. Res. Public Health* **2021**, *18*, 1721. [CrossRef] [PubMed]
38. Ministry of European Funds. Guideline for Applicants "Be Responsible for Your Health. Regional Programs for Prevention, Early Diagnosis and Treatment for Cervix Cancer". Available online: http://mfe.gov.ro/pocu-apelul-fii-responsabila-de-sanatatea-ta-programe-regionale-de-preventie-depistare-precoce-diagnostic-si-tratament-precoce-al-cancerului-de-col-uterin-etapa-ii/ (accessed on 21 March 2021).
39. Kesic, V. Prevention of cervical cancer in Central and Eastern Europe and Central Asia: A challenge for the future. *Vaccine* **2013**, *31*, vii–ix. [CrossRef] [PubMed]
40. Altobelli, E.; Lattanzi, A. Cervical carcinoma in the European Union: An update on disease burden, screening program state of activation, and coverage as of March 2014. *Int. J. Gynecol. Cancer* **2015**, *25*, 474–483. [CrossRef]

41. Wojtyla, C.; Janik-Koncewicz, K.; La Vecchia, C. Cervical cancer mortality in young adult European women. *Eur. J. Cancer* **2020**, *126*, 56–64. [CrossRef] [PubMed]
42. Jansen, E.E.L.; Zielonke, N.; Gini, A.; Anttila, A.; Segnan, N.; Vokó, Z.; Ivanuš, U.; McKee, M.; de Koning, H.J.; de Kok, I.M.C.M. EU-TOPIA consortium: Effect of organised cervical cancer screening on cervical cancer mortality in Europe: A systematic review. *Eur. J. Cancer* **2020**, *127*, 207–223. [CrossRef]

healthcare MDPI

Article

Comparison of Metabolites and Gut Microbes between Patients with Parkinson's Disease and Healthy Individuals—A Pilot Clinical Observational Study (STROBE Compliant)

Cheol-Hyun Kim [1,2], Jeeyoun Jung [3], Young-ung Lee [1,2], Kwang-ho Kim [1,2], Sunny Kang [1,2], Geon-hui Kang [2,4], Hongmin Chu [1], Se-Young Kim [2] and Sangkwan Lee [1,2,4,*]

1 Department of Internal Medicine and Neuroscience, College of Korean Medicine, Wonkwang University, Iksan 54538, Korea; lambroskch@gmail.com (C.-H.K.); www8744@naver.com (Y.-u.L.); bzkimkh@naver.com (K.-h.K.); rkdsunny@gmail.com (S.K.); hongminchu2@gmail.com (H.C.)
2 Stroke Korean Medicine Research Center, Wonkwang University, Iksan 54538, Korea; sya0474@naver.com (G.-h.K.); kimse0@hanmail.net (S.-Y.K.)
3 KM Science Research Division, Korea Institute of Oriental Medicine, Daejeon 34054, Korea; jjy0918@kiom.re.kr
4 Hanbang Cardio-Renal Syndrome Research Center, College of Oriental Medicine, Wonkwang University, Iksan 54538, Korea
* Correspondence: sklee@wku.ac.kr; Tel.: +82-10-2632-0119

Abstract: Introduction: Even if levodopa, dopamine agonists, and others are used for patients with Parkinson's disease, the effect is not sustained, and side effects such as motor fluctuation and dyskinesia are more likely to appear as the dose increases. Thus, new approaches for managing Parkinson's disease are needed. This study aimed to compare the metabolites and gut microbes between patients with Parkinson's disease and healthy individuals. Methods: This was an observational study with a case-control design. Metabolite and gut microbial analyses were performed using blood and stool samples collected from the subjects. Results: Among the metabolites, the acetate, citrate, methionine, and trimethylamine levels were significantly different between the two groups. In the gut microbes, abundance of *Bacteroidetes*, *Prevotella*, *Phascolarctobacterium*, *Pseudoflavonifractor*, *Eisenbergiella*, and *Gemella* were also significantly different between the two groups. Discussion: Metabolites are the products of gut microbes. Therefore, when the gut microbes change, the metabolites change accordingly. Metabolites and gut microbes that were significantly different between the two groups were mostly those involved in lipid and glucose metabolism. Our data may be helpful for the development of new drugs targeting metabolites and gut microbes through large-scale studies in the future.

Keywords: gut microbes; metabolites; Parkinson's disease

Citation: Kim, C.-H.; Jung, J.; Lee, Y.-u.; Kim, K.-h.; Kang, S.; Kang, G.-h.; Chu, H.; Kim, S.-Y.; Lee, S. Comparison of Metabolites and Gut Microbes between Patients with Parkinson's Disease and Healthy Individuals—A Pilot Clinical Observational Study (STROBE Compliant). *Healthcare* **2022**, *10*, 302. https://doi.org/10.3390/healthcare10020302

Academic Editor: Markus Rauchenzauner

Received: 14 December 2021
Accepted: 3 February 2022
Published: 4 February 2022

1. Introduction

Parkinson's disease (PD) is the second most common neurodegenerative disease worldwide [1]. One percent of the population aged >60 years have PD, and its prevalence continues to increase [2]. Although PD has such a high prevalence and gradually worsens the quality of life of PD patients, there is still no clear treatment [3,4]. Even if levodopa, dopamine agonists, and others are used, the effect is not sustained, and side effects, such as motor fluctuation and dyskinesia are more likely to appear as the dose increases [5]. Several studies have reported candidates for neuroprotective agents such as vitamin D, beta-carotene, and bee venom that have the potential to replace conventional treatments, but the evidence is still lacking [6,7]. Therefore, new approaches to PD are needed.

Gut microbes and metabolites are currently in the spotlight as targets for new therapeutic approaches to PD [8]. There are hundreds of trillions of gut microbes in the human body, and they have a significant impact on normal physiology by producing metabolites [9,10]. Thus, imbalances in gut microbes and metabolites could be associated with neurologic disorders including PD [9]. In support of this hypothesis, Mertsalmi et al. reported that the use of certain antibiotics could increase the risk of PD by altering the gut microbes [11]. Houser and Tansey suggested in their study that the pathogenesis of PD originates from the gut [12]. Initial inflammation in the gut triggers changes in gut microbes, leading to changes in metabolites related to inflammation, which induces neuroinflammation by increasing the blood–brain barrier permeability, ultimately inducing neurodegeneration [12]. In addition, Sun et al. reported that gut microbial dysbiosis is observed in PD patients, and that microbial metabolites and products contribute to the PD pathology [13]. Considering these studies, drugs targeting gut microbes or metabolites could become new therapeutic candidates for PD.

The purpose of this study was to compare the differences in gut microbes and metabolites between patients with PD and healthy individuals to contribute to the existing research data to select a new therapeutic drug for PD in the future. Although the number of subjects was small, we report our findings because we obtained significant results.

2. Materials and Methods

Study Design

This research work was an observational study with a case-control design.

3. Subjects

3.1. Sample Size Calculation

Our investigation is a pilot study, and we could not find previous data indicating the sample size needed to yield significant results. For the pilot study, a sample size of 20–40 participants was suggested by Kieser and Wassmer [14]. The healthy control (HC) and PD groups were recruited through posters in communities and hospitals from December 2018. The HC group was recruited by matching the age and sex of the PD group.

3.2. Inclusion and Exclusion Criteria for the PD Group

The inclusion criteria were as follows: those diagnosed with PD and taking PD-related drugs who agreed to participate in this study and voluntarily signed the informed consent form and those who consumed traditional Korean dishes such as rice and kimchi.

The exclusion criteria were as follows: those diagnosed with diseases that may affect the results of this study such as diabetes mellitus (DM) and autoimmune diseases; those taking antibiotics or probiotics; those who regularly drank alcohol and smoked; those unable to collect blood or stool; and those judged to be unsuitable to participate in this study by medical staff.

3.3. Inclusion and Exclusion Criteria for the HC Group

The inclusion criteria were as follows: those who had no underlying disease and were not taking any drugs who agreed to participate in this study and voluntarily signed the informed consent form. Those who were judged to be unsuitable to participate in this study by medical staff were excluded from the study.

4. Variables

The variables were metabolites analyzed from the collected blood specimens and the gut microbes analyzed from the collected stool specimens.

4.1. Metabolite Analysis

4.1.1. Blood Collection Method

After collecting 5 mL of blood using the injection needle provided in the blood collection kit, the blood was divided into 3.0 and 2.0 mL samples and packed in serum separate tube and nonautologous-pooled human plasm containers, respectively. Then, the serum and plasma were separated.

4.1.2. Metabolite Analysis Method

The total of 250 μL of serum was mixed with 500 μL saline solution (10% D_2O for lock signal, NaCl 0.9%, 500 mM sodium phosphate buffer in D_2O containing TSP (Trimethylsilylpropanoic acid) 0.05% for chemical shift calibration, and concentration reference, pH 7.0). Then, samples were centrifuged at 12,000× *g* for 10 min, and 600 μL aliquots of the supernatant were transferred into 5-mm NMR tubes for analysis. Analysis was performed using the ASCEND 800 MHz, AVANCE III HD Bruker spectrometer equipped with a 5 mm CPTIC 1H-13C/15N/DZ-GRD Z1194227/0011 cryogenic probe. The Carr–Purcell–Meiboom–Gill (CPMG) spin-echo pulse sequence (RD−90°-(τ-180°-τ) n-ACQ) was used as the nuclear magnetic resonance (NMR) sequence (CPMG condition: total T2 relaxation time of 60, 4 K data point, 128 scans, four dummy scans, delay time of eight seconds). 1D data obtained through the NMR analysis were subjected to baseline correction using the Chenomx program. Then, Binning was performed in units of 0.05 ppm, and spectral alignment was performed using the COW algorithm in MATLAB. Data organized by MATLAB were subjected to multivariate analysis with SIMCA −P++.

For the quality control, TSP was used as an internal standard. We referenced the TSP peak to correct for chemical shifts and quantify metabolites.

4.1.3. Metabolite Pattern Analysis

To examine the difference in the metabolic pattern between the PD and HC groups, the 1H NMR spectrum was normalized to the total area and then orthogonal partial least-squares discriminant analysis (OPLS-DA) proceeded by UV scale.

4.2. Gut Microbe Analysis

4.2.1. Meal Adjustment Guide

The subjects were instructed not to drink alcohol or to eat excessively fatty foods the day before stool collection.

4.2.2. Stool Collection and Specimen Delivery

Stool (4 mg) was sealed in a kit for stool collection. The outside of the kit was labeled, so that the subjects' specimens could be distinguished. The specimens were then frozen at a temperature of −20 °C and delivered to the analytical laboratory.

4.2.3. Gut Microbe Analysis

A library was created to enable Illumina sequencing by creating a hybrid primer that selectively amplified the V3–V4 region from the 16S rRNA gene, which is the standard for identifying bacteria, and an adaptor sequence recognized by the Illumina sequencer. The complete sequencing library mixture was sequenced by 300 bp paired-end sequencing according to Illumina's MisSeq platform guide. After trimming the sequenced data, the quantitative insights into the microbial ecology (QIIME) pipeline was used to identify the bacteria. Greengenes was used as a library for bacterial identification. Analysis was conducted with a total of 20 samples that passed quality control. Alpha diversity, which compares the diversity distribution of gut microbes, was compared, and principal coordinate analysis (PCoA) was performed using the Bray–Curtis distance for pattern analysis.

5. Statistical Analysis

The data collected from the subjects were coded and analyzed using SPSS for Windows (ver. 20.0) statistical program. To check the normality of the data, the Shapiro–Wilk test was used for continuous variables. An independent t-test or Mann–Whitney U test was used to compare the levels of blood metabolites and gut microbes in the stool between the PD and HC groups. To control confounding factors, independent *t*-tests or Mann–Whitney U test were used for both groups of the sex and age. p values < 0.05 was considered as statistically significant.

6. Results

6.1. Subject Characteristics

From December 2019 to March 2020, 10 PD patients and 10 healthy individuals were recruited, and the characteristics of the subjects are presented in Table 1. The demographic characteristics including the sex and age did not show a significant difference between the two groups.

Table 1. Demographic characteristics and medical history of the enrolled subjects.

Classification		PD Group	HC Group	Total
Total		10	10	20
Sex (number)	Male	5	4	9
	Female	5	6	11
Age (years)	Minimum	50	51	50
	Maximum	74	68	74
	Average	66.6	58.7	62.65
Disease duration (years)	Minimum	0.17	-	0.17
	Maximum	12	-	12
	Average	5.02	-	5.02

PD, Parkinson's disease; HC, healthy control.

6.2. Metabolite Analysis

PCA ($R^2X = 0.629$, $Q^2 = 0.187$, Figure 1) and OPLS-DA ($R^2Y = 0.605$, $Q^2 = 0.37$, Figure 2) showed a clear differentiation of metabolites between the PD and HC groups. The established model was considered reliable according to the cross-validation with a 100-permutation test (Figure 3). Green R^2- and blue Q^2-values to the left were lower than the original points to the right, and the regression line of the Q^2-points intersected the vertical axis below zero ($R^2 = 0.278$, and $Q^2 = -0.220$). The corresponding regression coefficients for the included metabolites, ordered according to their variable importance in the OPLS-DA model, are shown Figure 4. Among the metabolites analyzed, the levels of acetate, citrate, methionine, and trimethylamine were significantly different between the two groups ($p < 0.05$). Acetate and citrate levels were significantly higher, and methionine and trimethylamine levels were significantly lower in the PD group than in the HC group (Figure 5).

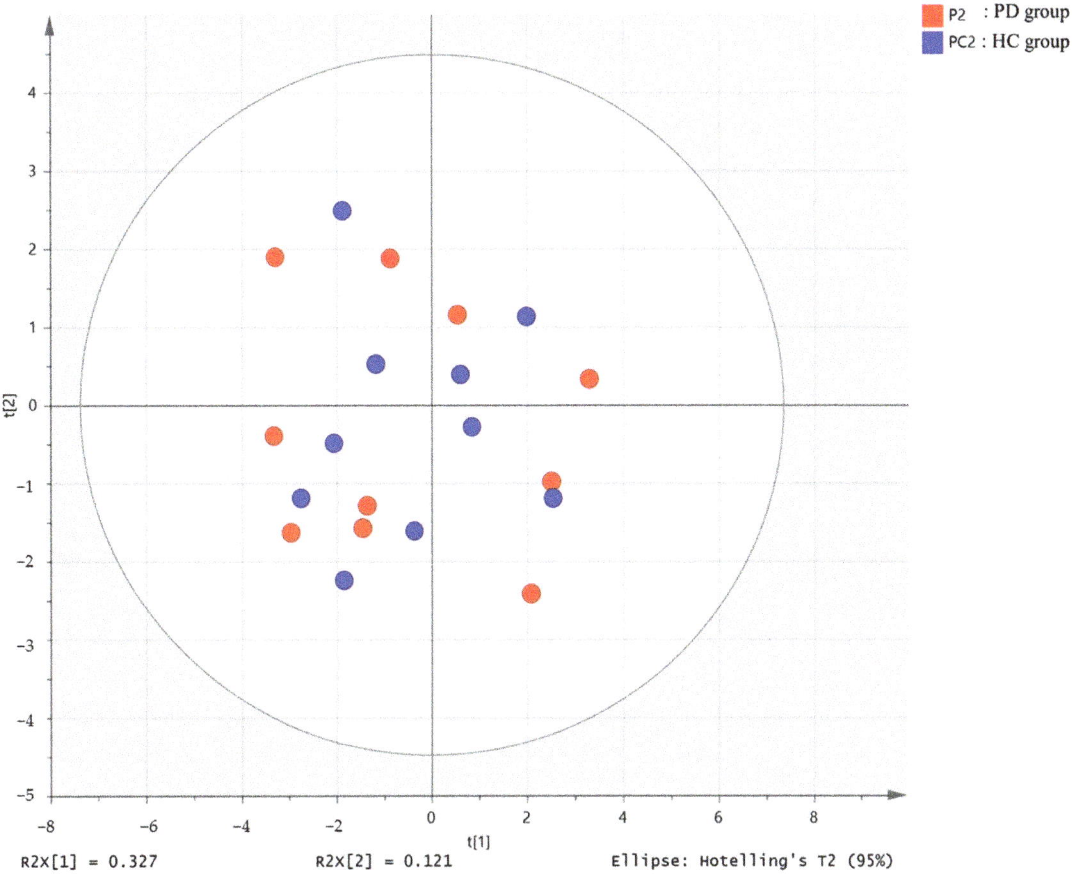

Figure 1. PCA score plot derived from the 1H-NMR spectra of serum from the Parkinson's disease (PD) patient group (n = 10) and healthy control (HC) group (n = 10). PD, Parkinson's disease; HC: healthy control.

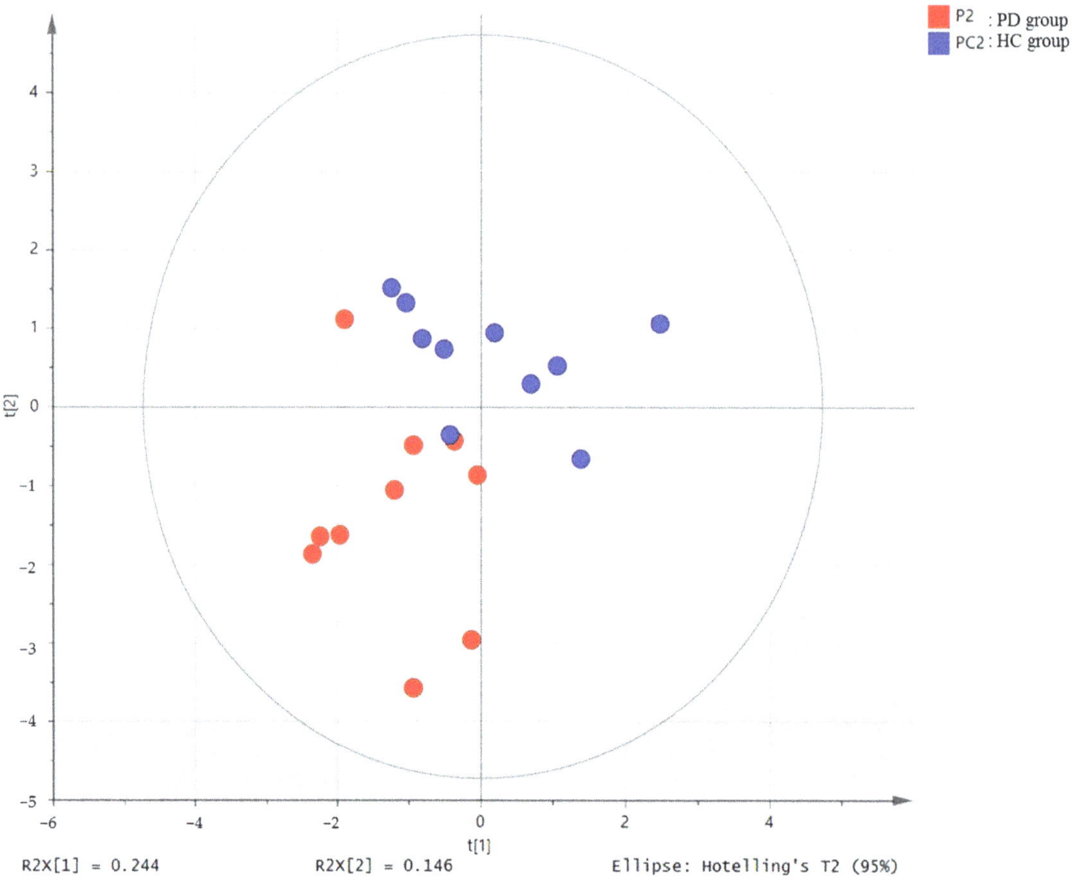

Figure 2. OPLS-DA score plot derived from the 1H-NMR spectra of serum from PD (n = 10) and HC groups (n = 10). OPLS-DA, orthogonal partial least-squares discriminant analysis; PD, Parkinson's disease; HC: healthy control: NMR, nuclear magnetic resonance.

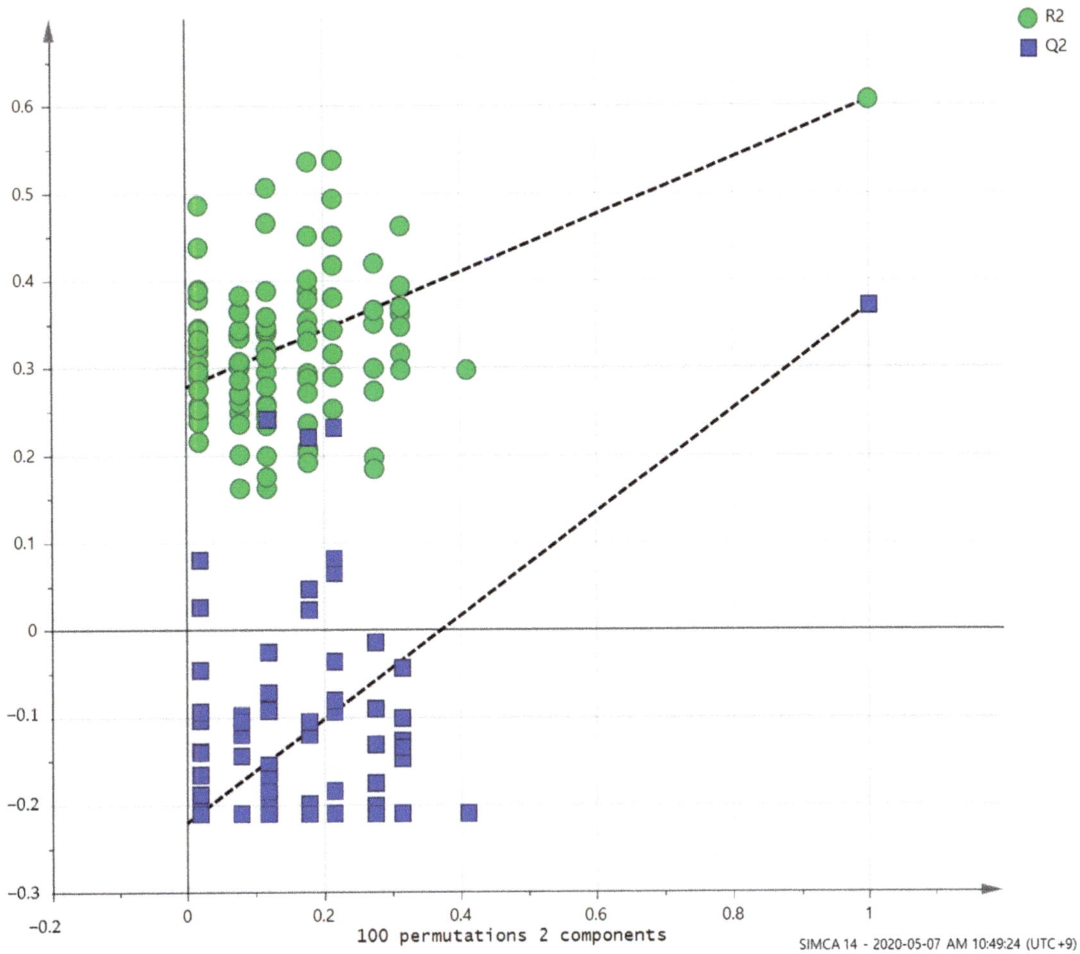

Figure 3. Validation of the OPLS model using the 100-permutation test.

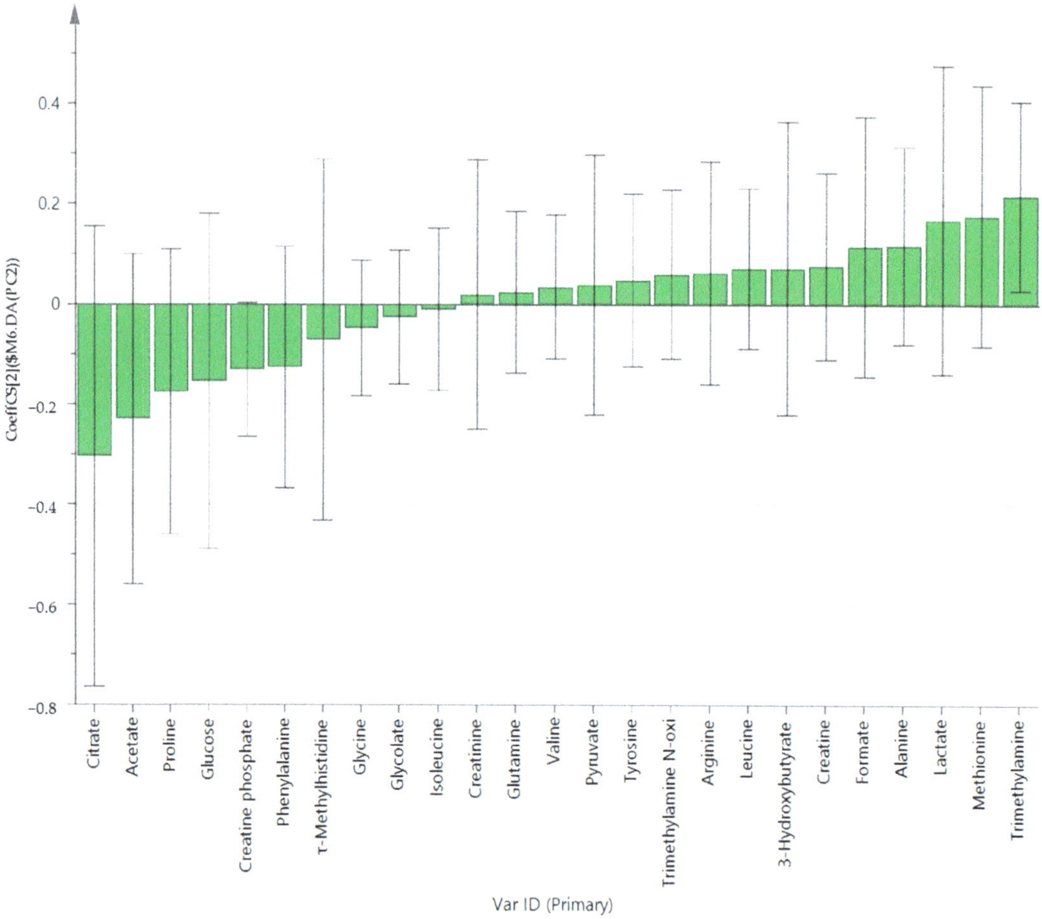

Figure 4. OPLS-DA coefficient plot of all metabolites in Parkinson's disease patients.

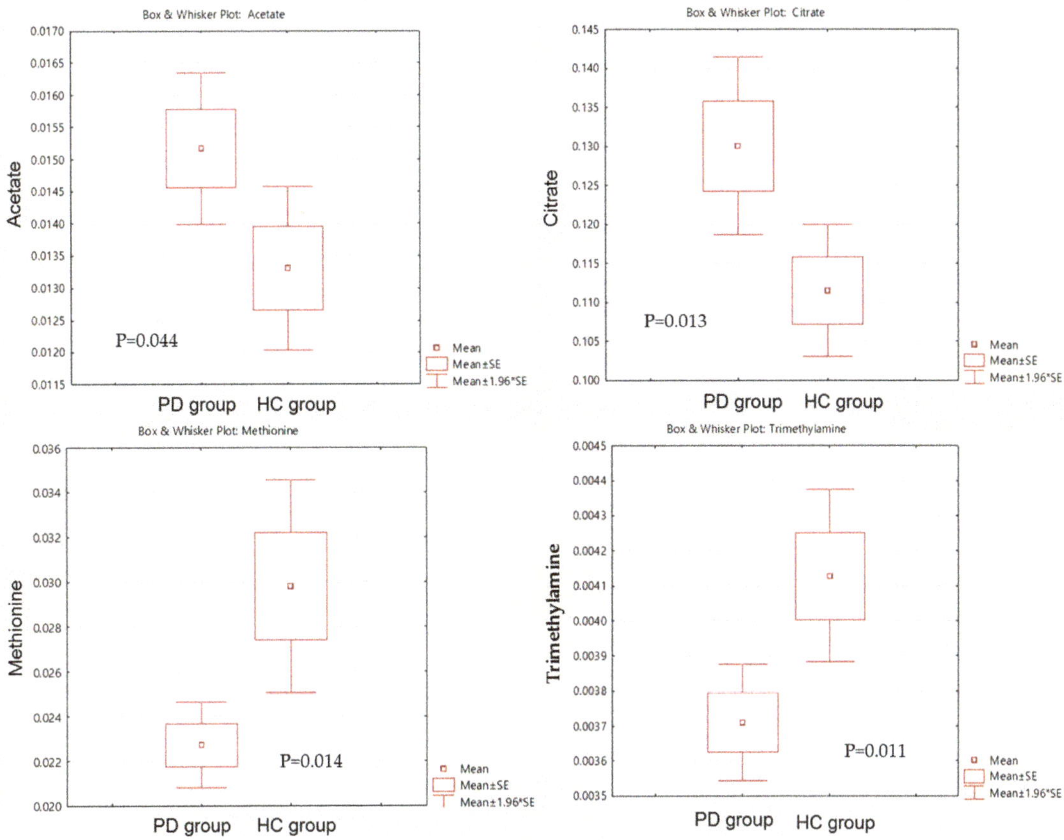

Figure 5. Box and whisker plot of acetate, citrate, methionine, and trimethylamine in the Parkinson's disease (PD) group and healthy control (HC) group. PD, Parkinson's disease; HC: healthy control.

6.3. Gut Microbe Analysis

Comparison of the alpha diversity between the two groups revealed that the PD group had significantly lower Chao1 levels, which indicates the diversity of gut microbes in this group compared to the HC group ($p = 0.036$).

Comparison of the results of the PCoA based on the Bray–Curtis distance showed that the two groups had different gut microbial patterns, but the patterns were not clear (Figure 6).

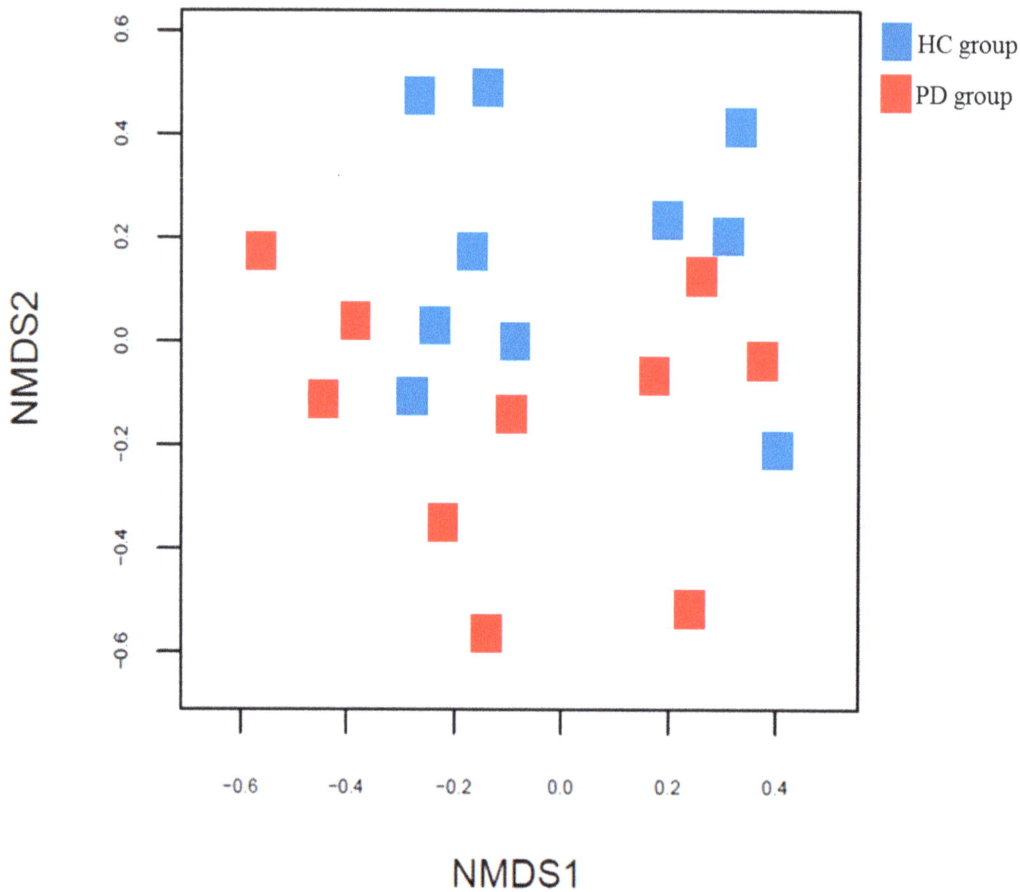

Figure 6. PCoA plots based on Bray–Curtis distances between the PPD and HC groups. PCoA, principal coordinate analysis (PCoA); Parkinson's disease; HC: healthy control.

In the distribution of gut microbe composition, *Bacteroidetes* in the phylum level showed a significant difference between the two groups. *Prevotella*, *Phascolarctobacterium*, *Pseudoflavonifractor*, *Eisenbergiella*, and *Gemella* at the genus level were also significantly different between the two groups (Table 2). Gut microbe composition at the phylum and genus levels of the PD and HC groups are shown in Figures 7 and 8, respectively.

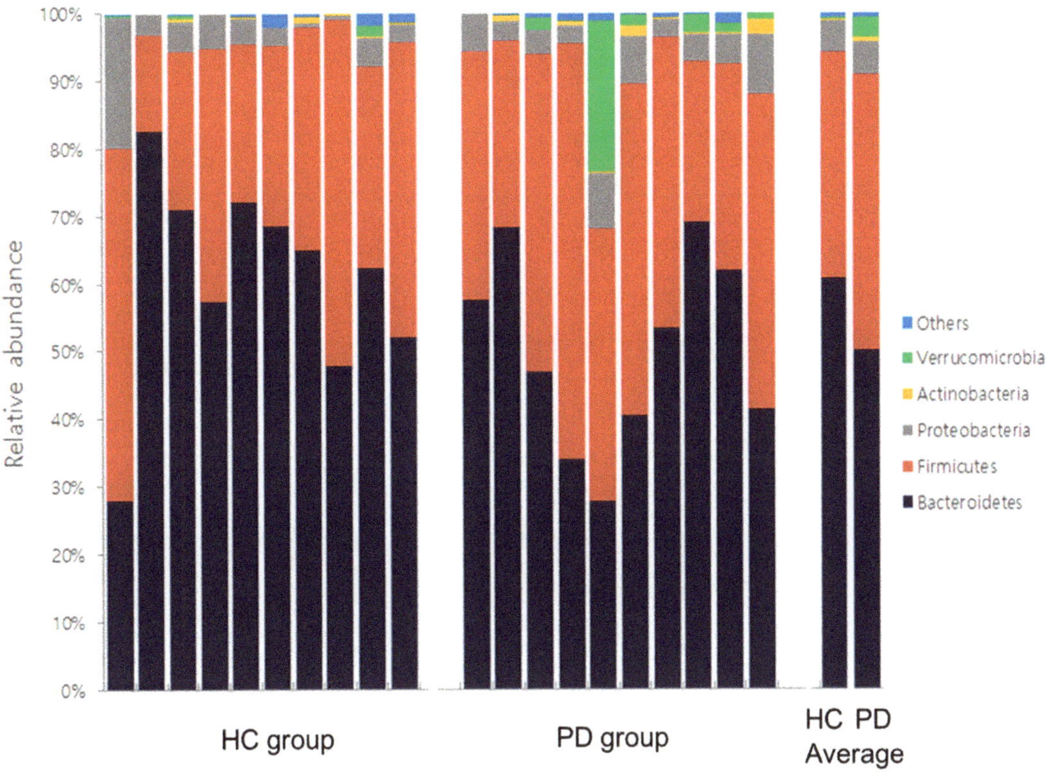

Figure 7. Gut microbe composition at the phylum levels of the HC and PD groups. HC: healthy control; PD: Parkinson's disease.

Table 2. Gut microbes that were significantly different between the PD and HC groups in this study.

Classification		Gut Microbes	PD Group vs. HC Group	
			↑/↓ §	Significance ($p < 0.05$)
Stool	Phylum level	*Bacteroidetes*	↓	0.012
	Genus level	*Prevotella*	↓	0.030
		Phascolarctobacterium	↓	0.047
		Pseudoflavonifractor	↓	0.037
		Eisenbergiella	↑	0.037
		Gemella	↓	0.014

PD, Parkinson's disease; HC, healthy control. § Arrows (↑ and ↓) indicate a decrease or an increase in the microorganism levels in patients with PD compared with healthy individuals.

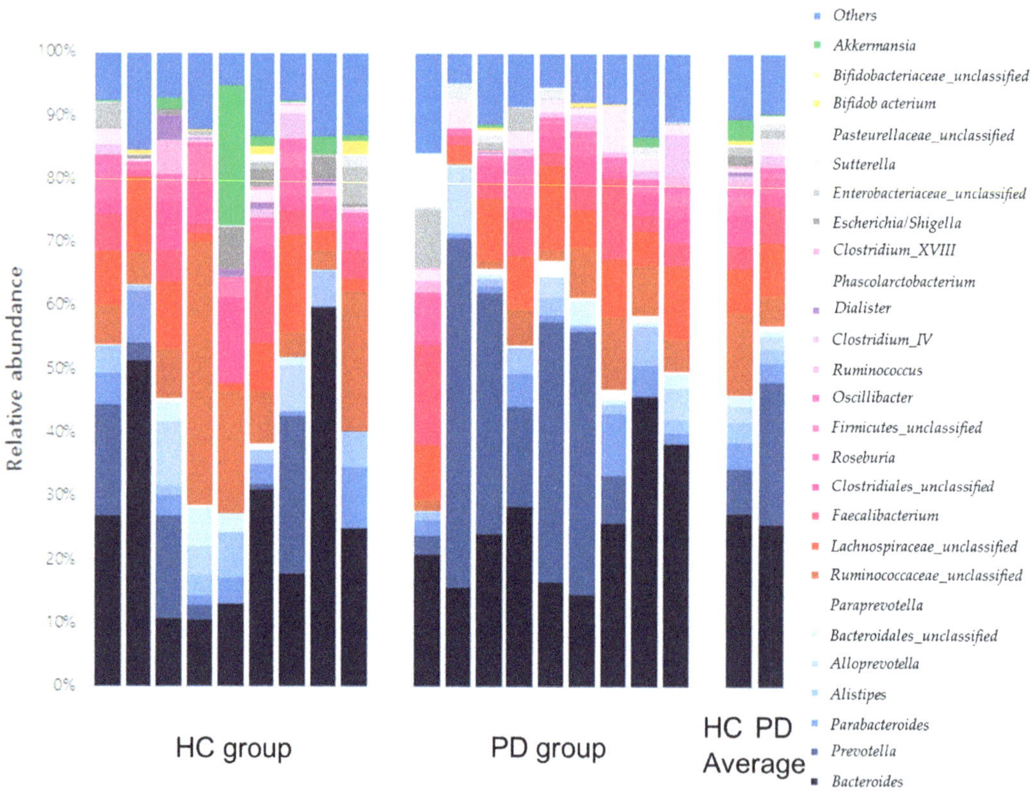

Figure 8. Gut microbe composition at the genus levels of the HC and PD groups. HC: healthy control; PD: Parkinson's disease.

7. Discussion

We performed metabolite and gut microbial analyses in 10 PD patients and 10 healthy individuals and compared their results. Among the metabolites, the acetate, citrate, methionine, and trimethylamine levels were significantly different between the two groups. In the gut microbes, the abundance of *Bacteroidetes*, *Prevotella*, *Phascolarctobacterium*, *Pseudoflavonifractor*, *Eisenbergiella*, and *Gemella* were also significantly different.

In this study, both acetate and citrate levels were higher in the PD group than in the HC group. Beynen et al. reported that acetate drastically increased the cellular level of citrate, which explains the results of this study [15].

Acetate enhances de novo lipid synthesis by activating lipogenic genes. That is, acetate is an immediate metabolic precursor and plays a role in inducing fatty acid synthesis [16]. Potashkin et al. reported that plasma oxidized LDL, a major contributor in atherosclerotic plaque formation in patients with PD, was high, which is in line with the results of this study, showing that PD patients had high acetate levels [17].

Citrate is an intermediate of the Kreb's cycle. Pyruvate is an end metabolite of glycolysis, which is converted into acetyl-coA by an enzyme called pyruvate dehydrogenase (PDH) and enters the Kreb's cycle. Citrate plays a role in regulating the activity of PDH [18]. In a 2019 study, it was reported that PD patients showed poor regulation of glucose metabolism in the substantia nigra pars compacta dopamine neurons [17]. Considering that citrate affects the Kreb's cycle, a representative pathway of glucose metabolism, the results of this study are consistent with the 2019 study [17].

Methionine and trimethylamine levels were significantly lower in the PD group than in the HC group, which is also consistent with the results of previous studies. Glaser et al. reported that the accumulation of α-synuclein in dopaminergic neurons of the substantia nigra is a crucial step in the pathogenesis of PD, and methionine oxidation inhibits the accumulation of α-synuclein [19]. Andreasson et al. reported that the development of polyneuropathy in patients with PD was associated with disorders of methionine cycle metabolism [20].

According to previous studies, it was reported that trimethylamine N-oxide (TMAO) was associated with the severity and progression of motor symptoms in PD, and PD patients have a significantly lower TMAO level than healthy individuals [21]. In this study, TMAO was not significantly different between the two groups, but the trimethylamine levels were found to be significantly lower in the PD group. Considering that TMAO is produced by the oxidation of trimethylamine, the results of this study cannot be said to be contrary to the existing results [21].

Among the gut microbes, *Bacteroidetes*, which was significantly different between the two groups, are known to produce favorable metabolites such as short-chain fatty acids (SCFAs) that reduce inflammation (e.g., allergic inflammation) [22]. In addition, Aho et al. reported that patients with PD had different gut microbes, SCFAs, and inflammation from those of healthy individuals, which is consistent with the results of this study [23].

Prevotella produces hydrogen sulfide (H_2S), which is a gasotransmitter that is closely related to neuroprotection as well as PD [8]. According to Kessel et al.'s gut microbe studies, the abundance of *Prevotella* showed a significant decrease in four out of 13 PD patients, and this study also showed a significant difference in *Prevotella* between the PD group and the HS group [8].

Phascolarctobacterium produces SCFAs and is known to be associated with the development of non-alcoholic fatty liver disease (NAFLD) [24]. Vural et al. reported that the prevalence of NAFLD in the PD group was significantly different from that of the HC group, consistent with *Phascolarctobacterium*, which showed a significant difference between the two groups in our study [25].

Pseudoflavonifractor is a gut microbe associated with energy metabolism and insulin sensitivity, which can exacerbate metabolic disorders in diabetic patients [26]. Hassan et al. reported that DM and PD are associated and have common mechanisms such as hyperglycemia, inflammation, and oxidative stress. Therefore, anti-diabetic drugs may have a beneficial effect on PD [27]. In our study, *Pseudoflavonifractor* showed a significant difference between the two groups, which is consistent with previous studies [26,27].

Eisenbergiella has been reported to be associated with major depressive disorder [28]. The significant difference in the abundance of *Eisenbergiella* between the two groups in our study may explain the reason why many PD patients experience depression [29]. This also means that drugs targeting *Eisenbergiella* can be used instead of antidepressants with various side effects.

Gemella has been reported as a gut microbe associated with Alzheimer's disease [30]. Considering that cognitive impairment is common in PD, a significant difference in *Gemella* between the two groups in our study is an acceptable result [31].

When synthesizing the previous studies above-mentioned, metabolites and gut microbes that were significantly different between the PD and HS groups in our study may be mainly related to lipid and glucose metabolism as well as inflammation (Table 3). Potashkin et al. also reported that PD patients exhibit abnormalities in lipid and glucose metabolism [17].

Table 3. Summary of metabolites and gut microbes that were significantly different between the PD and HC groups in this study.

Classification		Function
Metabolites	Acetate	Acetate is involved in lipid metabolism. It enhances de novo lipid synthesis by activating lipogenic genes [16].
	Citrate	Citrate is involved in glucose metabolism. As an intermediate of the Kreb's cycle, it regulates the activity of PDH, an enzyme that converts pyruvate to acetyl-coA [18].
	Methionine	Methionine is involved in the accumulation of α-synuclein. The accumulation of α-synuclein in the dopaminergic neurons of substantia nigra is a crucial step in the pathogenesis of PD [19].
	Trimethylamine	Trimethylamine is oxidized to produce TMAO. TMAO is related to the severity and the progression of motor symptoms of PD [21].
Gut microbes	*Bacteroidetes*	*Bacteroidetes* produces favorable metabolites such as SCFAs that reduce inflammation [22].
	Prevotella	*Prevotella* produces H_2S, which is a gasotransmitter closely related to neuroprotection [8].
	Phascolarctobacterium	*Phascolarctobacterium* has beneficial effects by producing SCFAs. It is known to be associated with the occurrence of NAFLD [24].
	Pseudoflavonifractor	*Pseudoflavonifractor* is associated with energy metabolism and insulin sensitivity [26].
	Eisenbergiella	*Eisenbergiella* is reported to be associated with major depressive disorder [28].
	Gemella	*Gemella* is reported to be associated with Alzheimer's disease [30].

H_2S: hydrogen sulfide; NAFLD, nonalcoholic fatty liver disease; PDH, pyruvate dehydrogenase; SCFAs, short-chain fatty acids; TMAO, trimethylamine N-oxide; PD, Parkinson's disease; HC, health control.

Sebastiaan et al. said that metabolites are the products of gut microbes [8]. Gibiino et al. reported that acetate production soon changes according to the change in *Firmicutes/Bacteroidetes* proportion [32]. This explains why metabolism involving metabolites and gut microbes, which showed significant differences between the two groups, were similar in our study. Additionally, this suggests that drugs that control gut microbes can also control metabolites and can have a positive effect in relieving symptoms in PD patients through a different route than the existing dopamine drugs. In another study supporting this hypothesis, Meng-Fei et al. reported that microbe-targeted interventions such as antibiotics, herbal medicine, probiotics, and fecal microbe transplantation could favorably affect PD [13].

Therefore, considering the results of this study and existing studies, an integrated approach is needed in the development of therapeutic drugs for PD because not only the brain but also the gut and diseases such as DM, hyperlipidemia, and PD must be considered. In addition, herbal medicine, probiotics, fecal microbe transplantation, and herbal medicines should be considered when selecting candidates for therapeutic drugs.

The limitations of this study are as follows. First, as the present work is a pilot study, the number of subjects analyzed is small; thus, they are insufficient to reflect the characteristics of all patients with PD. However, the reliability of the results is not expected to be low, since significant results were derived from our study despite the small number of patients, and are consistent with the existing research results. Second, this study did not compare the differences based on the subjects' detailed diet, the type of PD-related drugs they were taking, or their sex. However, it was the same in the broad framework of traditional Korean dishes and PD-related drugs such as levodopa and dopamine agonists. In addition, the male-to-female ratio between the two groups did not differ much. As a result, the importance of the findings of this study cannot be dismissed. Third, this study did not evaluate the potential correlations between the metabolites and gut microbes that showed a significant difference between the two groups. However, it was confirmed that they were commonly related to lipid and glucose metabolism and inflammation. Fourth, we could not suggest the names of gut microbes at the species level that showed a significant difference between the two groups. However, we were able to confirm the lack of gut microbe diversity at the species level in the PD group through an alpha diversity analysis, which evaluates the diversity of gut microbes at the species level.

In conclusion, to the best of our knowledge, most of the existing studies have only analyzed either the metabolites or gut microbes. However, in this study, both metabolites and gut microbes were collected from the same subjects, measured, and compared, and our data confirmed that the metabolites and gut microbes that were significantly different between the PD and HS groups were mostly related to lipid and glucose metabolism. If significant differences are confirmed through large-scale studies comparing gut microbes and metabolites before and after various treatments such as herbal or Western medicine, diet, and feces transplantation, the results will be helpful in the development of new therapeutic drugs for PD.

Author Contributions: Writing—original draft preparation, C.-H.K.; writing—review and editing, J.J.; visualization, Y.-u.L.; resources, K.-h.K.; software, S.K.; data curation, G.-h.K.; formal analysis, H.C. and S.-Y.K.; supervison, project administration, and funding acquisition, S.L. All authors have read and agreed to the published version of the manuscript.

Funding: This research and the APC was funded by the Integrative Medicine Research Project through Wonkwang University Jangheung Integrative Medical Hospital, funded by the Ministry of Health & Welfare, Republic of Korea (No. 1465029684) and the National Research Foundation of Korea grant funded by the Korean Government (MSIP) (No. 2017R1A5A2015805).

Institutional Review Board Statement: This study obtained ethical approval from the institutional review board (IRB) of Wonkwang University Korean Medicine Hospital in Gwangju (WKUGH) (WKIRB2017-20, 23 January 2018) and was registered in the Clinical Research Information Service (CRIS) of the Korea National Institute of Health, Republic of Korea (KCT0003482).

Informed Consent Statement: Informed consent was obtained from all subjects involved in the study. Written informed consent has been obtained from the subjects to publish this paper.

Data Availability Statement: The data in this study are available from the corresponding author, S.L., upon reasonable request.

Acknowledgments: This study was supported by the Integrative Medicine Research Project through Wonkwang University Jangheung Integrative Medical Hospital, funded by the Ministry of Health & Welfare, Republic of Korea (No. 1465029684) and the National Research Foundation of Korea grant funded by the Korean Government (MSIP) (No. 2017R1A5A2015805).

Conflicts of Interest: The authors declare no conflict of interest.

Abbreviations

CRIS = Clinical Research Information Service, DM = diabetes mellitus, H_2S = hydrogen sulfide, HC = healthy control, NAFLD = non-alcoholic fatty liver disease, NMN = nuclear magnetic resonance, OPLS-DA = orthogonal partial least-squares discriminant analysis, PCoA = principal coordinate analysis, PD = Parkinson's disease, PDH = pyruvate dehydrogenase, SCFAs = short-chain fatty acids, TMAO = trimethylamine N-oxide, WKUGH = Wonkwang University Korean Medicine Hospital in Gwangju.

References

1. Pringsheim, T.; Jette, N.; Frolkis, A.; Steeves, T.D. The prevalence of Parkinson's disease: A systematic review and meta-analysis. *Mov. Disord.* **2014**, *29*, 1583–1590. [CrossRef] [PubMed]
2. Tysnes, O.B.; Storstein, A. Epidemiology of Parkinson's disease. *J. Neural Transm.* **2017**, *124*, 901–905. [CrossRef] [PubMed]
3. Emrani, S.; McGuirk, A.; Xiao, W. Prognosis and Diagnosis of Parkinson's Disease Using Multi-Task Learning. In Proceedings of the 23rd ACM SIGKDD International Conference on Knowledge Discovery and Data Mining, Halifax, NS, Canada, 13–17 August 2017; Association for Computing Machinery (ACM): New York, NY, USA, 2017; pp. 1457–1466.

4. Cho, S.Y.; Lee, Y.E.; Doo, K.H.; Lee, J.H.; Jung, W.S.; Moon, S.K.; Park, J.M.; Ko, C.N.; Kim, H.; Rhee, H.Y.; et al. Efficacy of combined treatment with acupuncture and bee venom acupuncture as an adjunctive treatment for Parkinson's disease. *J. Altern. Complement. Med.* **2018**, *24*, 25–32. [CrossRef] [PubMed]
5. Jameson, J.L. *Harrison's Principles of Internal Medicine*; McGraw-Hill Education: New York, NY, USA, 2018.
6. Seidl, S.E.; Potashkin, J.A. The Promise of Neuroprotective Agents in Parkinson's Disease. *Front. Neurol.* **2011**, *2*, 68. [CrossRef]
7. Awad, K.; Abushouk, A.I.; Abdelkarim, A.; Mohammed, M.; Negida, A.; Shalash, A. Bee venom for the treatment of Parkinson's disease: How far is it possible? *Biomed. Pharmacother.* **2017**, *91*, 295–302. [CrossRef]
8. Van Kessel, S.P.; El Aidy, S. Bacterial metabolites mirror altered gut microbiota composition in patients with Parkinson's disease. *J. Parkinsons Dis.* **2019**, *9*, S359–S370. [CrossRef]
9. Wargo, J.A. Modulating gut microbes. *Science* **2020**, *369*, 1302–1303. [CrossRef]
10. Franzosa, E.A.; Sirota-Madi, A.; Avila-Pacheco, J.; Fornelos, N.; Haiser, H.J.; Reinker, S.; Vatanen, T.; Hall, A.B.; Mallick, H.; McIver, L.J.; et al. Gut microbiome structure and metabolic activity in inflammatory bowel disease. *Nat. Microbiol.* **2018**, *4*, 293–305. [CrossRef]
11. Mertsalmi, T.H.; Pekkonen, E.; Scheperjans, F. Antibiotic Exposure and Risk of Parkinson's Disease in Finland: A Nationwide Case-Control Study. *Mov. Disord.* **2019**, *35*, 431–442. [CrossRef]
12. Houser, M.; Tansey, M.G. The gut-brain axis: Is intestinal inflammation a silent driver of Parkinson's disease pathogenesis? *NPJ Park. Dis.* **2017**, *3*, 3. [CrossRef]
13. Sun, M.-F.; Shen, Y.-Q. Dysbiosis of gut microbiota and microbial metabolites in Parkinson's Disease. *Ageing Res. Rev.* **2018**, *45*, 53–61. [CrossRef] [PubMed]
14. Kieser, M.; Wassmer, G. On the use of the upper confidence limit for the variance from a pilot sample for sample size determination. *Biom. J.* **1996**, *38*, 941–949. [CrossRef]
15. Beynen, A.C.; Buechler, K.F.; Van der Molen, A.J.; Geelen, M.J. The effects of lactate and acetate on fatty acid and cholesterol biosynthesis by isolated rat hepatocytes. *Int. J. Biochem.* **1982**, *14*, 165–169. [CrossRef]
16. Gao, X.; Lin, S.-H.; Ren, F.; Li, J.-T.; Chen, J.-J.; Yao, C.-B.; Yang, H.-B.; Jiang, S.-X.; Yan, G.-Q.; Wang, D.; et al. Acetate functions as an epigenetic metabolite to promote lipid synthesis under hypoxia. *Nat. Commun.* **2016**, *7*, 11960. [CrossRef]
17. Potashkin, J.; Huang, X.; Becker, C.; Chen, H.; Foltynie, T.; Marras, C. Understanding the Links Between Cardiovascular Disease and Parkinson's Disease. *Mov. Disord.* **2020**, *35*, 55–74. [CrossRef]
18. Ahmed, S.S.; Santosh, W.; Kumar, S.; Christlet, H.T.T. Metabolic profiling of Parkinson's disease: Evidence of biomarker from gene expression analysis and rapid neural network detection. *J. Biomed. Sci.* **2009**, *16*, 63. [CrossRef] [PubMed]
19. Glaser, C.B.; Yamin, G.; Uversky, V.N.; Fink, A.L. Methionine oxidation, α-synuclein and Parkinson's disease. *Biochim. Biophys. Acta Proteins Proteom.* **2005**, *1703*, 157–169. [CrossRef]
20. Andréasson, M.; Brodin, L.; Laffita-Mesa, J.M.; Svenningsson, P. Correlations Between Methionine Cycle Metabolism, COMT Genotype, and Polyneuropathy in L-Dopa Treated Parkinson's Disease: A Preliminary Cross-Sectional Study. *J. Park. Dis.* **2017**, *7*, 619–628. [CrossRef]
21. Chung, S.J.; Rim, J.H.; Ji, D.; Lee, S.; Yoo, H.S.; Jung, J.H.; Baik, K.; Choi, Y.; Ye, B.S.; Sohn, Y.H.; et al. The gut microbiota-derived metabolite trimethylamine N-oxide as a biomarker in early Par-kinson's disease. *Nutrition* **2020**, *83*, 111090. [CrossRef]
22. Trompette, A.; Gollwitzer, E.S.; Yadava, K.; Sichelstiel, A.K.; Sprenger, N.; Ngom-Bru, C.; Blanchard, C.; Junt, T.; Nicod, L.P.; Harris, N.L.; et al. Gut microbiota metabolism of dietary fiber influences allergic airway disease and hematopoiesis. *Nat. Med.* **2014**, *20*, 159–166. [CrossRef]
23. Aho, V.T.E.; Houser, M.C.; Pereira, P.A.B.; Chang, J.; Rudi, K.; Paulin, L.; Hertzberg, V.; Auvinen, P.; Tansey, M.G.; Scheperjans, F. Relationships of gut microbiota, short-chain fatty acids, inflammation, and the gut barrier in Parkinson's disease. *Mol. Neurodegener.* **2021**, *16*, 1–14. [CrossRef] [PubMed]
24. Sobhonslidsuk, A.; Chanprasertyothin, S.; Pongrujikorn, T.; Kaewduang, P.; Promson, K.; Petraksa, S.; Ongphiphadhanakul, B. The association of gut microbiota with nonalcoholic steato-hepatitis in Thais. *BioMed Res. Int.* **2018**, *2018*, 9340316. [CrossRef] [PubMed]
25. Vural, S.; Ayvaz, M.A.; Kesicioğlu, T.; Turfan, S.; Ayraler, A. Prevalence of Non Alcoholic Fatty Liver Disease in patients with Parkinson Disease. *Anatol. J. Fam. Med.* **2019**, *2*, 38–40. [CrossRef]
26. Wang, Y.; Ouyang, M.; Gao, X.; Wang, S.; Fu, C.; Zeng, J.; He, X. *Phocea*, *Pseudoflavonifractor* and *Lactobacillus intestinalis*: Three Potential Biomarkers of Gut Microbiota That Affect Progression and Complications of Obesity-Induced Type 2 Diabetes Mellitus. *Diabetes Metab. Syndr. Obes. Targets Ther.* **2020**, *13*, 835–850. [CrossRef]
27. Hassan, A.; Kandel, R.S.; Mishra, R.; Gautam, J.; Alaref, A.; Jahan, N. Diabetes Mellitus and Parkinson's Disease: Shared Pathophysiological Links and Possible Therapeutic Implications. *Cureus* **2020**, *12*, e9853. [CrossRef] [PubMed]
28. Fontana, A.; Manchia, M.; Panebianco, C.; Paribello, P.; Arzedi, C.; Cossu, E.; Garzilli, M.; Montis, M.A.; Mura, A.; Pisanu, C.; et al. Exploring the Role of Gut Microbiota in Major Depressive Disorder and in Treatment Resistance to Antidepressants. *Biomedicines* **2020**, *8*, 311. [CrossRef]
29. Marsh, L. Depression and Parkinson's Disease: Current Knowledge. *Curr. Neurol. Neurosci. Rep.* **2013**, *13*, 1–9. [CrossRef]
30. Vogt, N.M.; Kerby, R.L.; Dill-McFarland, K.A.; Harding, S.J.; Merluzzi, A.P.; Johnson, S.C.; Carlsson, C.M.; Asthana, S.; Zetterberg, H.; Blennow, K.; et al. Gut microbiome alterations in Alzheimer's disease. *Sci. Rep.* **2017**, *7*, 1–11. [CrossRef]

31. Goetz, C.G.; Emre, M.; Dubois, B. Parkinson's disease dementia: Definitions, guidelines, and research perspectives in diagnosis. *Ann. Neurol. Off. J. Am. Neurol. Assoc. Child Neurol. Soc.* **2008**, *64* (Suppl. 2), S81–S92. [CrossRef]
32. Gibiino, G.; Lopetuso, L.R.; Scaldaferri, F.; Rizzatti, G.; Binda, C.; Gasbarrini, A. Exploring Bacteroidetes: Metabolic key points and immunological tricks of our gut commensals. *Dig. Liver Dis.* **2018**, *50*, 635–639. [CrossRef]

International Journal of
Environmental Research and Public Health

MDPI

Article

Risk of Glaucoma Associated with Components of Metabolic Disease in Taiwan: A Nationwide Population-Based Study

Ya-Wen Chang [1,†], Fung-Chang Sung [2,3,4,†], Ya-Ling Tzeng [1], Chih-Hsin Mou [3], Peng-Tai Tien [5], Cheng-Wen Su [6] and Yu-Kuei Teng [1,*]

1 School of Nursing, China Medical University, Taichung 406040, Taiwan; yawen172@mail.cmu.edu.tw (Y.-W.C.); tyaling@mail.cmu.edu.tw (Y.-L.T.)
2 Department of Health Services Administration, China Medical University, Taichung 406040, Taiwan; fcsung1008@yahoo.com
3 Management Office for Health Data, China Medical University Hospital, Taichung 404332, Taiwan; b8507006@gmail.com
4 Department of Food Nutrition and Health Biotechnology, Asia University, Taichung 41354, Taiwan
5 Department of Ophthalmology, China Medical University Hospital, Taichung 404332, Taiwan; miketien913@gmail.com
6 Department of Ophthalmology, Asia University Hospital, Taichung 41354, Taiwan; fashiongo0405@gmail.com
* Correspondence: tengyk@mail.cmu.edu.tw
† These authors contributed equally to this work.

Abstract: Purpose: This retrospective cohort study was conducted to determine the glaucoma risk associated with metabolic disease (MetD) using insurance claims data of Taiwan. Methods: From the database, we identified patients with newly diagnosed hypertension, diabetes and/or hyperlipidemia from the years 2000 to 2002 as the MetD cohort (N = 42,036) and an age-gender-diagnosis-date matched control cohort without MetD with a two-fold sample size than that of the MetD cohort. Both cohorts were followed until the development of glaucoma, death, or withdrawal, until 31 December 2013. The incidence of glaucoma, and the Cox method estimated hazard ratio (HR) of glaucoma were calculated. Results showed that the incidence of glaucoma was two-fold higher in the MetD cohort than in the controls (1.99 versus 0.99 per 1000 person-years), with an adjusted HR of 1.66 (95% CI: 1.50–1.85). The glaucoma incidence was higher in patients with diabetes than those with hypertension and hyperlipidemia (2.38 versus 1.95 and 1.72 per 1000 person-years, respectively). The incidence increased to 5.67 per 1000 person-years in patients with all three comorbidities, with an aHR of 4.95 (95% CI: 2.35–10.40). We also found higher incidence rates of primary open-angle glaucoma and primary angle-closure glaucoma with aHRs of 2.03 and 1.44, respectively. It was concluded that glaucoma risk increased with the number of MetD. Health providers need to monitor patients with MetD to prevent glaucoma.

Keywords: glaucoma; metabolic disease; diabetes mellitus; hypertension; hyperlipidaemia

Citation: Chang, Y.-W.; Sung, F.-C.; Tzeng, Y.-L.; Mou, C.-H.; Tien, P.-T.; Su, C.-W.; Teng, Y.-K. Risk of Glaucoma Associated with Components of Metabolic Disease in Taiwan: A Nationwide Population-Based Study. *Int. J. Environ. Res. Public Health* **2022**, *19*, 305. https://doi.org/10.3390/ijerph19010305

Academic Editor: Paul B. Tchounwou

Received: 7 October 2021
Accepted: 23 December 2021
Published: 28 December 2021

1. Introduction

Glaucoma is the second leading cause of irreversible blindness worldwide [1]. Vision loss from glaucoma not only causes significant negative effects on health-related quality of life, but also exerts an increasing economic burden for both patients and society as the disease progresses [2–4]. The lifetime indirect costs due to reduced productivity and reduced employment has been estimated to range from USD $5 billion to USD $7 billion [5]. A 3.54% global prevalence of glaucoma has been reported among individuals aged between 40–80 years. The number of individuals with glaucoma worldwide was estimated to be 76.0 million in 2020 and is estimated to increase to 111.8 million by 2040 [5]. Glaucoma is classified into two main subtypes: primary open-angle glaucoma (POAG) and primary angle-closure glaucoma (PACG) [2]. A systematic review and meta-analysis study indicated the estimated pooled global prevalence of POAG to be 3.05% and that of PACG to be 0.50%. As the prevalence of PACG has been the highest in Asians, particular emphasis was made on the development of methods to identify and treat PACG in Asia [6]. POAG is a singular and most common subtype of glaucoma with an open angle, normal-appearing anterior chamber, and the presence of glaucomatous optic disc change and/or visual field defects [2,7]. The mechanism of PACG involves pupillary block and anterior lens movement, leading to angle crowding and, consequently, intraocular pressure [8]. The risks of POAG and PACG are associated with demographic variables such as gender; age; individual socioeconomic status; and comorbidities such as hypertension, hyperglycaemia, and dyslipidaemia [8,9].

Metabolic diseases (MetD) have become a worldwide public health concern because a cluster of conditions may occur together, including key components of hypertension, hyperglycaemia, and dyslipidaemia with low serum high-density lipoprotein and visceral obesity [10,11]. A recent meta-analysis based on 27 studies with 45,811 participants reported that MetD could affect near 24% of type 1 diabetes patients [12]. Studies have also linked MetD with age-related cataract [13], age-related macular degeneration (AMD) [10], obstructive sleep apnea (OSA) [14], nonalcoholic fatty liver disease [15], depression, anxiety [16,17], and hypothyroidism [18]. Nevertheless, particular attention should be paid to the association between MetD and related eye diseases to prevent blindness.

Studies have indicated that hypertension [7,19] and diabetes mellitus [3] were important risk factors for the development and progression of glaucoma [20,21]. By contrast, a Korean cross-sectional study using survey data found that individuals with obesity had a lower prevalence of POAG than the nonobese population did [22]. The consistency of the association between MetD and glaucoma is thus unclear. Furthermore, a meta-analysis with 15 observation studies found that patients with glaucoma are at a high risk of central retinal vein occlusion (CRVO) with an odds ratio of 6.21 [13]. A case-control analysis using insurance data in Taiwan found the PACG cases had significant relationships with cataract and MetD [23]. Therefore, coexistence of cataract with glaucoma reflects that both eye disorders may share similar risk factors.

Studies have shown components of MetD are associated with POAG [20,22] or PACG [23]. However, to the best of our knowledge, no study has used population-based longitudinal data to explore the association between MetD and the risk of developing glaucoma (both PACG and POAG). Therefore, we used claims data from the National Health Insurance (NHI) of Taiwan to perform a retrospective cohort study to explore the development of glaucoma in individuals with and without diagnosed components of MetD.

2. Study Population and Methods

2.1. Data Source

The present population-based retrospective cohort study retrieved data from the Longitudinal Health Insurance Database (LHID) 2000, which is one of the databases of Taiwan's NHI Research Database (NHIRD) of all NHI beneficiaries, covering over 99% of Taiwan's population. LHID 2000 was created for research purposes by systematically and randomly selecting one million individuals from all populations registered in 2000 to represent the entire population. This database included information on demographic status of the beneficiaries and claims data for medical services provided to them from 1996 to 2013. The disease diagnoses were encoded in accordance with the International Classification of Diseases, Ninth Revision, Clinical Modification (ICD-9-CM). To protect personal privacy, the patients' personal identifications were encrypted from data released from National Health Research Institutes. Therefore, patient consent is not required to access the NHIRD. A large volume of research has been published based on the NHIRD in peer-reviewed international journals. This study was approved by the Ethical Research Committee at China Medical University and Hospital (CMUH104-REC2-115[CR-2]).

2.2. Study Cohorts Selection

Figure 1 shows the process of identifying patients for the retrospective cohort study. We used the diagnostic codes of the ICD-9-CM to identify individuals with any of the three major types of MetD including diabetes (ICD-9-CM 250), hypertension (ICD-9-CM 401–405), and hyperlipidaemia (ICD-9-CM 272) for the potential study cohort of MetD. Patients with glaucoma was identified at the baseline and those with missing information regarding gender or age were excluded. Patients who were newly diagnosed as having any of the three types of MetD between 2000 and 2002 (N = 42,036) were included as the study cohort of MetD. The first date of diagnosis of MetD was defined as the index date. For each patient with any MetD, two controls free of any MetD were randomly selected from the LHID2000, frequency-matched by sex, age (in 5-year age bands) and index year as controls of the non-MetD cohort (N = 84,072). Both cohorts were tracked from baseline until the development of glaucoma, loss to follow-up, withdrawal from NHI, or 31 December 2013 to examine the risk of glaucoma.

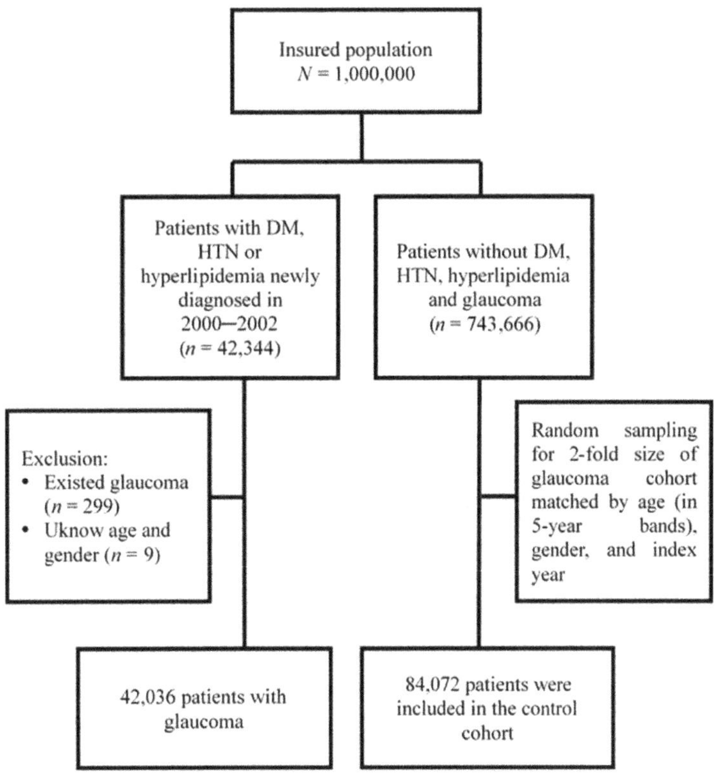

Figure 1. Flow chart of the study population selection.

2.3. Comorbidities and Drugs

Comorbidities that were considered as potential covariates in the inference of the association between MetD and glaucoma included hypothyroidism, OSA, depression, anxiety, headaches, liver diseases, peptic ulcers, cataract, central retinal vein occlusion (CRVO), and age-related macular degeneration (AMD).

Studies have indicated that some medications commonly used in patients may affect both PACG and POAG, including adrenergic drugs, anticholinergics, cholinergics, and sulfa-based medications [24,25]. We also included these drugs in one category as a covariate to evaluate the associated glaucoma risk.

2.4. Statistical Analysis

SAS software version 9.1 (SAS Institute, Cary, NC, USA) was used for the data analyses. We compared the distributions of sociodemographic characteristics and baseline comorbidities between cohorts with and without MetD. Medications that might associate with the development of glaucoma were also compared between the two groups. The Chi-square test and Student's t test were used to examine the categorical and continuous data, respectively.

The Kaplan–Meier method was used to calculate and plot the cumulative incidences of glaucoma for both cohorts and the log-rank test was used for comparison. We pooled data of both cohorts to calculate incidence rates of glaucoma (per 1000 person-years) for both cohorts and by sociodemographic status, comorbidity and the use of medication. The hazard ratio (HR) of glaucoma with a 95% confidence interval (CI) was calculated using the Cox proportional hazards regression analysis. The adjusted hazard ratio (aHR) was estimated using the multivariable regression analysis, after controlling for variables significant in measuring the crude HR. We also assessed the incidence rate and HRs of glaucoma associated with individual component and multi-components of MetD. Data analysis further estimated the incidence rate and HRs of PACG and POAG. All analyses were performed with a significance level using $\alpha = 0.05$.

3. Results

3.1. Basic Characteristics of Study Cohorts

With a mean age of near 51 years, both cohorts were similar in distributions of sex and age consisting of 54.3% men and 45.7% women, with 59.9% individuals aged 40–64 years old. Near 59% of persons had mean monthly incomes of less than NT$ 20,000 (58.8%). The MetD cohort had significantly higher comorbidities of obesity, hypothyroidism, OSA, depression, headaches, liver diseases, peptic ulcers, cataracts, AMD, and more users of glaucoma associated drug than the controls did ($p < 0.05$) (Table 1). However, prevalence rates of obesity, hypothyroidism, OSA, anxiety, CRVO were less than one percent.

With minimum and maximum follow-up times of 0.003 and near 14.0 years, respectively, the mean follow-up was longer in the MetD cohort than in the control cohort (11.4 (SD 2.97) versus 7.88 (SD 4.62) years). The numbers of study population at risk reduced to 23752 persons and in the MetD cohort and 21,885 persons in the control cohort. Figure 2 shows that the cumulative incidence of glaucoma was 1.5% greater in the MetD cohort than in the controls over the follow-up period ($p < 0.001$).

Table 1. Comparison of demographic characteristics, comorbidities and drug may induce glaucoma between cohorts with and without any metabolic disease (diabetes, hypertension, hyperlipidaemia).

Characteristic	With Metabolic Disease $N = 42{,}036$	Without Metabolic Disease $N = 84{,}072$	p Value
	n (%)	n (%)	
Obesity			<0.0001
No	41,762 (99.3)	84,028 (99.95)	
Yes	274 (0.65)	44 (0.05)	
Age, year			0.99
<40	8846 (21.0)	17,692 (21.0)	
40–64	25,194 (59.9)	50,388 (59.9)	
65+	7996 (19.0)	15,992 (19.0)	
Mean(SD)	51.4(14.6)	51.2(14.6)	0.20
Gender			0.99
Female	19,217 (45.7)	38,434 (45.7)	
Male	22,819 (54.3)	45,638 (54.3)	

Table 1. *Cont.*

Characteristic	With Metabolic Disease *N* = 42,036	Without Metabolic Disease *N* = 84,072	*p* Value
Monthly income, NTD			0.006
<20,000	24,712 (58.8)	49,579 (59.0)	
20,000–40,000	11,990 (28.5)	24,333 (28.9)	
>40,000	5334 (12.7)	10,160 (12.1)	
Comorbidity			
Hypothyroidism	99 (0.24)	86 (0.10)	<0.0001
OSA	55 (0.13)	30 (0.04)	<0.0001
Depression	1027 (2.44)	1013 (1.20)	<0.0001
Anxiety	49 (0.12)	45 (0.05)	0.0001
Headaches	5670 (13.5)	5843 (6.95)	<0.0001
Liver diseases	9338 (22.2)	7308 (8.69)	<0.0001
Peptic ulcers	12,085 (28.8)	16,543 (19.7)	<0.0001
Cataract	3828 (9.11)	5936 (7.06)	<0.0001
CRVO	9 (0.02)	4 (0.05)	0.014
AMD	473 (1.13)	562 (0.67)	<0.0001
Glaucomas-associated drug	22,356 (53.2)	33,349 (39.7)	<0.0001

NDT: New Taiwan Dollar; OSA: obstructive sleep apnea; CRVO: central retinal vein occlusion; AMD: age-related macular degeneration.

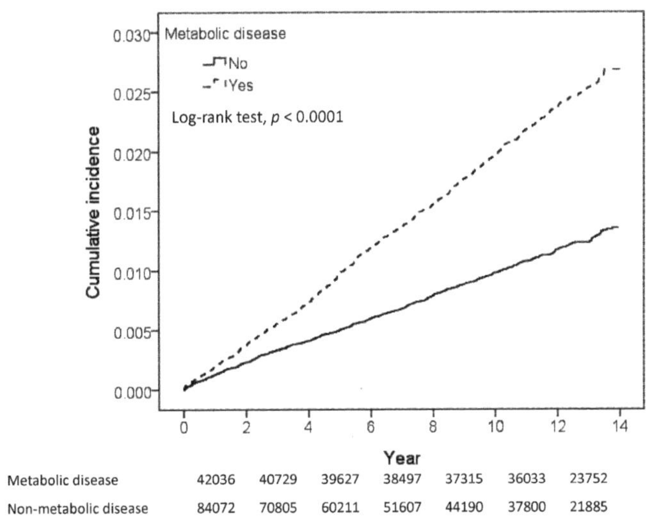

Figure 2. Kaplan-Meier method estimated cumulative incidence of glaucoma.

3.2. *Association between Metabolic Disease and Glaucoma*

Table 2 presents factors associated with the risk of development of glaucoma. The incidence rate of glaucoma was two-fold greater in the MetD cohort than in the control cohort (1.99 versus 0.99 per 1000 person-years) with an aHR of 1.66 (95% CI: 1.50–1.85) ($p < 0.0001$). The incidence of glaucoma was higher in women than in men with an aHR of 1.13 (95% CI = 1.03–1.25). Glaucoma incidence increased with age. Compared with the incidence of patients less than 40 years old, the incidence in those aged 40–64 years was near three-fold higher and that in the older patients was six-fold higher (0.47, 1.48 and 2.82 per 1000 person-years, respectively). Among comorbidities, AMD had the strongest association with the risk of glaucoma (aHR = 2.11; 95% CI: 1.59–2.80), followed by cataract (HR = 1.90, 95% CI = 1.66–2.19) and peptic ulcer (aHR = 1.13; 95% CI: 1.01–1.26). Moreover, the study results indicated that some drugs might have an association with developing glaucoma, but not significantly so (aHR = 1.10; 95% CI = 0.99–1.22).

Table 2. Incidence and hazard ratio of glaucoma by metabolic disease, demographic status, comorbidity and drugs may induce glaucoma in pooled study population.

Variables	Glaucoma *n*	Person-Years	Rate	Crude HR (95% CI)	*p*	Adjusted HR (95% CI)	*p*
Metabolic disease							
No	659	662,371	0.99	Ref.		Ref.	
Yes	951	478,927	1.99	2.00 (1.81–2.21)	<0.0001	1.66 (1.50–1.85)	<0.0001
Obesity							
No	1606	1,137,703	1.41	Ref.			
Yes	4	3595	1.11	0.78 (0.29–2.09)	0.6270		
Age (year)							
<40	136	290,859	0.47	Ref.		Ref.	
40–64	1025	691,465	1.48	3.19 (2.67–3.82)	<0.0001	2.83 (2.36–3.38)	<0.0001
65+	449	158,975	2.82	6.16 (5.08–7.47)	<0.0001	3.72 (3.03–4.58)	<0.0001
Gender							
Female	822	522,015	1.57	1.24 (1.12–1.36)	<0.0001	1.13 (1.03–1.25)	0.0142
Male	788	619,283	1.27	Ref.		Ref.	
Monthly income, NTD							
<20,000	926	656,740	1.41	1.04 (0.89–1.21)	0.6418		
20,000–40,000	479	333,856	1.43	1.06 (0.90–1.24)	0.5206		
>40,000	205	150,702	1.36	Ref.			
Comobidity							
Hypothyroidism							
No	1607	1,139,616	1.41	Ref.			
Yes	3	1682	1.78	1.26 (0.41–3.92)	0.6860		
OSA							
No	1608	1,140,454	1.41	Ref.			
Yes	2	844	2.37	1.68 (0.42–6.70)	0.4658		
Depression							
No	1570	1,123,495	1.40	Ref.		Ref.	
Yes	40	17,803	2.25	1.61 (1.17–2.20)	0.0031	1.21 (0.88–1.66)	0.2501
Anxiety							
No	1609	1,140,420	1.41	Ref.			
Yes	1	878	1.14	0.81 (0.11–5.73)	0.8295		
Headaches							
No	1437	1,036,655	1.39	Ref.		Ref.	
Yes	173	104,643	1.65	1.19 (1.02–1.39)	0.0300	0.92 (0.78–1.09)	0.3309
Liver diseases							
No	1339	987,052	1.36	Ref.		Ref.	
Yes	271	154,246	1.76	1.29 (1.13–1.47)	0.0001	1.12 (0.97–1.28)	0.1132
Peptic ulcers							
No	1120	893,273	1.25	Ref.		Ref.	
Yes	490	248,025	1.98	1.58 (1.42–1.75)	<0.0001	1.13 (1.01–1.26)	0.0401
Cataract							
No	1260	1,070,736	1.18	Ref.		Ref.	
Yes	350	70,562	4.96	4.24 (3.76–4.77)	<0.0001	1.90 (1.66–2.19)	<0.0001
CRVO							
No	1610	1,141,191	1.41	Ref.			
Yes	0	108	0.00	NA			
AMD							
No	1557	1,132,905	1.37	Ref.		Ref.	
Yes	53	8393	6.31	4.60 (3.50–6.05)	<0.0001	2.11 (1.59–2.80)	<0.0001
Glaucomas associated drug							
No	787	649,874	1.21	Ref.		Ref.	
Yes	823	491,424	1.67	1.38 (1.25–1.52)	<0.0001	1.10 (0.99–1.22)	0.0810

Rate, per 1000 person-years. OSA: obstructive sleep apnea; CRVO: central retinal vein occlusion; AMD: age-related macular degeneration. Adjusted HRs were measured by multivariate analysis using variables significant in measuring the crude HR.

Among the three types of MetD, individuals with diabetes mellitus had a stronger association with glaucoma than those with other two diseases, with an aHR of 2.14 (95% CI = 1.80–2.55) compared to controls (Table 3). The glaucoma incidence increased with the number of MetD, to 5.67 per 1000 person-years for those with all three diseases with an aHR of 4.95 (95% CI: 2.35–10.4; $p < 0.001$). Among patients having two diseases, the glaucoma incidence was greater in those with diabetes mellitus and hypertension than in those with diabetes mellitus and hyperlipidemia, and those with hypertension and hyperlipidemia (3.77 versus 2.70 and 1.48 per 1000 person-years).

Table 3. Incidence and hazard ratio of glaucoma among patients with one or more components of metabolic disease.

Variables	*N*	Glaucoma No.	Person-Years	Rate	Adjusted HR (95% CI)	*p*
None	84,072	659	662,371	0.99	Ref.	
Only Hypertension	21,863	478	244,949	1.95	1.48 (1.31–1.67)	<0.0001
Only Diabetes	6365	163	68,391	2.38	2.14 (1.80–2.55)	<0.0001
Only Hyperlipidemia	11,490	239	138,752	1.72	1.79 (1.54–2.09)	<0.0001
Diabetes + Hypertension	439	17	4510	3.77	2.87 (1.78–4.66)	<0.0001
Diabetes + Hyperlipidemia	1094	35	12,979	2.70	2.63 (1.87–3.69)	<0.0001
Hypertension + Hyperlipidemia	680	12	8110	1.48	1.33 (0.75–2.36)	0.3275
Diabetes + Hypertension + Hyperlipidemia	105	7	1235	5.67	4.95 (2.35–10.4)	<0.0001

Rate, per 1000 person-years; Adjusted HRs were measured after controlling for age, gender, depression, peptic ulcers, cataract, and age-related macular degeneration.

Table 4 shows that the incidence of glaucoma was slightly higher for POAG than for PACG, with aHRs of 2.03 (CI = 1.75–2.36) and 1.70 (CI = 1.53–1.88), respectively, compared with controls.

Table 4. Incidence rates of open angle glaucoma and Closure angle glaucoma and metabolism disease cohort to control cohort adjusted hazard ratios.

	Patients with One or More Metabolic Disease			Controls				
Outcome	Glaucoma (*n*)	Person-Years	Rate	Glaucoma (*n*)	Person-Years	Rate	Adjusted HR (95% CI)	*p*
Overall	951	478,927	1.99	659	662,371	0.99	1.66 (1.50–1.85)	<0.0001
Open angle glaucoma	487	478,927	1.02	292	662,371	0.44	2.03 (1.75–2.36)	<0.0001
Closure angle glaucoma	464	478,927	0.97	367	662,371	0.55	1.44 (1.25–1.66)	<0.0001

Rate, per 1000 person-years; Adjusted HRs were estimated after controlling for age, gender, depression, peptic ulcers, cataract, and age-related macular degeneration.

4. Discussion

Through this retrospective cohort study, we found that the incidence of glaucoma (both PACG and POAG) was higher in patients with MetD, which confirms a significant association between MetD and glaucoma. This finding is consistent with findings in previous studies and supports the hypothesis that patients with MetD are at a higher risk of glaucoma than those without MetD are [20]. The global prevalence of POAG was 3.05% and that of PACG was 0.5%. However, the study by Tham et al. indicated that the prevalence of PACG was the highest in the Asian population (2014). Asian patients constitute 76.7% of PACG cases and 53.4% of POAG cases worldwide. Asia may contribute approximately 60% of the glaucoma cases in the world and will still contain the greatest number of patients with POAG and PACG in 2040 [6]. This finding provides evidence of the importance of identifying POAG and PACG for Asian populations.

In our study, we observed that women were more likely than men to develop glaucoma. According to Healthy Vision 2010, women have a higher risk of visual impairment from glaucoma, particularly from PACG [26,27]. The most likely reason for the increased risk of glaucoma for women is that the life expectancy of women is approximately 6 years longer than that of men. Other reasons, such as differences in the propensity to seek medical care or gender inequality in access to medical care, may also contribute to this difference [26,28]. Some biological explanations for this difference have been speculated. First, closed glaucoma in women could be due to the shorter eyes and shallower anterior chamber in women, resulting in limited space at the corner of the eye and impaired outflow of aqueous humor [28]. Secondly, age-related decline in female sex hormones may increase the risk of developing glaucoma. However, insufficient evidence exists regarding the use of hormone replacement therapy to prevent glaucoma [9,28]. Hence, clinicians should pay attention to the development of glaucoma in female patients with MetD.

This study shows that the incidence of glaucoma among the age groups seems to be linear, and is the highest in older patients. Studies have concluded that age is a crucial factor related to the development of glaucoma and that the risk of developing glaucoma increases exponentially with age [27,29]. In addition, women and older individuals with a higher risk of developing MetD also have a higher risk of developing glaucoma [30,31].

Studies have reported that some drugs might be associated with the development of glaucoma [6,25,32]. For example, alpha-adrenergic agonists are found in a variety of drugs, including mydriatics, which ophthalmologists and optometrists usually use in phenylephrine eye drops to dilate the pupils for routine fundus examinations [6,32]. Mydriatics may cause closure of the iridocorneal angle and pupillary block, inducing PACG via two mechanisms [25]. Our study examined whether the development of glaucoma is associated with the use of adrenergic drugs, anticholinergics, cholinergics, and sulpha-based medications. We failed to observe a significant relationship. However, understanding the risk factors associated with glaucoma will help health providers determine which patients would benefit from screening for monitoring of the disease.

4.1. Components of Metabolic Disease and Glaucoma

Through this study, we demonstrated the association between MetD and glaucoma. The findings revealed that patients with three types of MetD concurrently, namely diabetes mellitus, hypertension, and hyperlipidaemia are at the highest risk (aHR = 4.95) of developing glaucoma. Individuals with both diabetes mellitus and hypertension also had a higher risk (aHR = 2.87) of developing glaucoma than those with a single MetD did. In addition, we analyzed the relationship between a single MetD and glaucoma. The results indicated that diabetes mellitus was independently associated with a higher risk of the development of glaucoma (HR: 2.14). A longitudinal study demonstrated that diabetes mellitus and hypertension, independently or in combination, were associated with an increased risk of developing POAG [20]. The results of a meta-analysis showed that diabetes mellitus was associated with a significantly increased risk of glaucoma, and the risk of glaucoma increased by 5% each year after the diagnosis of diabetes mellitus [2]. Several possible mechanisms have been inferred as underlying the association between diabetes mellitus and the increased risk of diabetic retinopathy and glaucoma. Diabetes mellitus is associated with abnormalities of lipid metabolism that may promote cellular apoptosis and increase oxidative stress—the same mechanism by which retinal ganglion cell loss occurs in glaucoma [33,34]. A previous study reported that the prevalence of retinopathy in patients with diabetes mellitus ranged 17%–29% in 5 years, and it increased to 78%–100% after 15 years [31]. Moreover, vascular dysregulation [35] of protein kinase C [36] also plays a contributory role in both diabetic eye disease and glaucoma.

Evidence revealed that hyperlipidaemia is significantly associated with an increased risk of glaucoma. In our study, hyperlipidaemia was an independent risk factor (HR: 1.79) for glaucoma, which was similar to the findings of another meta-analysis study [37]. However, a longitudinal study indicated that hyperlipidaemia alone was associated with a slightly reduced (5%) risk of POAG [20]. One possible explanation may be that excessive blood lipid levels increase scleral venous pressure and blood viscosity, resulting in a decrease in outflow facilities [37]. Recently, genetic predisposition has been indicated as another important factor associated with hyperlipidaemia and glaucoma. The ATP binding cassette subfamily A member 1 (ABCA1) may mediate lipid export and nascent high density lipoprotein (HDL) biogenesis [38], and caveolin 1 (CAV1) has been proven to be involved in lipid metabolism and its regulation [39]. These genes might be useful to detect the potential risk of glaucoma. In addition, hypertension was an independent risk factor (HR: 1.48) for glaucoma in our study. This result is similar to that of Langman et al.'s study. The common pathogenesis of ciliary and renal tubular epithelium can explain the co-occurrence of glaucoma and systemic hypertension [40].

The findings of the present study showed that MetD had a significant association with hypothyroidism, OSA, depression, headaches, liver diseases, peptic ulcers, cataract,

CRVO, and AMD, consistent with the results of another study in Taiwan [23]. However, the study investigated the role of comorbidities for patients with PACG but not with POAG. A previous study also indicated that thyroid functions (hypothyroidism) affect MetD parameters including triglycerides, HDL cholesterol, plasma glucose, and blood pressure [18]. Glaucoma has a long latency period, in which glaucomatous optic nerve damage continues but remains asymptomatic until later stages. Adherence to regular ophthalmological examinations should be emphasized in patients with MetD, especially among those with multiple diseases [21].

MetD has long been considered a risk factor for glaucoma [20,21,41]. However, no study has used a population-based follow-up design to explore the risk of developing glaucoma (both PACG and POAG) in patients with MetD and to evaluate the combined effects of the three types of MetD. The present study fills this gap and reveals that the risk of glaucoma is associated with MetD independently and jointly. Moreover, glaucoma is one of the most prevalent eye diseases in older adults, and the onset of MetD is usually in middle age [6]. Taken together, these data suggest that the components of MetD contribute to glaucoma development and that the joint effect of several components in middle-aged or older adults might worsen the glaucoma.

4.2. Strengths and Limitations

The major strengths of this research are as follows. First, we analyzed the relationship between MetD and the risk of developing glaucoma of two subtypes (POAG and PACG) and found the risk was greater for the subtype of POAG than that of PACG. Second, the study cohorts were matched by age, gender, and index year to exclude potential confounding effects of these variables. Third, the large sample size and long follow-up period increased the validity of the study. Fourth, patients were diagnosed as having MetD and glaucoma by physicians rather than based on patient self-reports. The accuracy of diagnosis is increased.

However, the study also has some limitations. First, information on laboratory and anthropometric measurements is not available in the claims data. We were unable to use measurements of body mass index, waist circumference, blood pressure, blood sugar, triglycerides, and high-density lipoprotein (HDL) to define the MetD cohort for this study. We therefore used the healthcare providers' diagnoses of hypertension, hyperglycaemia and dyslipidaemia available in the claims data to select the study cohorts. Secondly, information regarding the potential confounding effects of family history and personal lifestyle (including physical activity and smoking history) could not be obtained owing to database limitations. Third, patients with MetD and glaucoma were identified based on the physician's diagnosis rather than through the research assignment.

Further research is underway to validate the role of glaucoma-related obesity among patients with MetD in the development of glaucoma. Additionally, control of other characteristics related to the development of glaucoma, such as alcohol consumption, smoking, waist circumference, body mass index, and physical activity, must be considered.

5. Conclusions

The results of our study showed that the risk of developing glaucoma increased with MetD components. Patients with MetD were at a higher risk for POAG than for PACG compared with patients without MetD. As glaucoma is usually relatively asymptomatic, we recommend that primary care physicians provide appropriate screening for the risk of glaucoma and counsel patients with MetD. It is particularly important to detect glaucoma at an early stage in older patients with diabetes and provide treatment for blindness prevention.

Author Contributions: All authors designed the study; C.-H.M. performed the statistical analyses and generated figures and tables; Y.-W.C., Y.-K.T. and F.-C.S. wrote the manuscript draft; F.-C.S. and Y.-L.T. provided intellectual input and corrected the manuscript; Y.-K.T., Y.-L.T. and F.-C.S. were responsible for the editing and review of the manuscript; P.-T.T. and C.-W.S. proved the validity or accuracy of medicine data; all authors participated in the revision; Y.-K.T. supervised this study. All authors have read and agreed to the published version of the manuscript.

Funding: This study is supported in part by Taiwan Ministry of Health and Welfare Clinical Trial Center (MOHW109-TDU-B-212-114004), MOST Clinical Trial Consortium for Stroke (MOST 109-2321-B-039-002), China Medical University (DMR-105-109). and Tseng-Lien Lin Foundation, Taichung, Taiwan.

Institutional Review Board Statement: The Research Ethics Committee at China Medical University and Hospital approved this study (CMUH104-REC2-115-CR5). All personal identification were encrypted by the NHIA regulation to protect privacy.

Data Availability Statement: We are not allowed to duplicate the database used in this study. Requests for data can be sent as a formal proposal to the NHIRD (http://nhird.nhri.org.tw, accessed on 30 July 2021).

Acknowledgments: We are grateful to Health Data Science Center, China Medical University Hospital for providing administrative, technical and funding support, and to Ministry of Health and Welfare and Environmental Protection Administration for providing data.

Conflicts of Interest: The authors declare no conflict of interest.

References

1. Causes of blindness and vision impairment in 2020 and trends over 30 years, and prevalence of avoidable blindness in relation to VISION 2020: The Right to Sight: An analysis for the Global Burden of Disease Study. *Lancet Glob. Health* **2021**, *9*, e144–e160. [CrossRef]
2. Casson, R.J.; Chidlow, G.; Wood, J.P.; Crowston, J.G.; Goldberg, I. Definition of glaucoma: Clinical and experimental concepts. *Clin. Exp. Ophthalmol.* **2012**, *40*, 341–349. [CrossRef] [PubMed]
3. Zhao, D.; Cho, J.; Kim, M.H.; Friedman, D.S.; Guallar, E. Diabetes, fasting glucose, and the risk of glaucoma: A meta-analysis. *Ophthalmology* **2015**, *122*, 72–78. [CrossRef]
4. Agrawal, A.; Singh, A.; Mittal, S.K. Glaucoma in Asia- An epidemiological perspective. *Nepal. J. Ophthalmol.* **2017**, *9*, 208–211. [CrossRef]
5. Varma, R.; Lee, P.P.; Goldberg, I.; Kotak, S. An assessment of the health and economic burdens of glaucoma. *Am. J. Ophthalmol.* **2011**, *152*, 515–522. [CrossRef]
6. Tham, Y.C.; Li, X.; Wong, T.Y.; Quigley, H.A.; Aung, T.; Cheng, C.Y. Global prevalence of glaucoma and projections of glaucoma burden through 2040: A systematic review and meta-analysis. *Ophthalmology* **2014**, *121*, 2081–2090. [CrossRef]
7. Bae, H.W.; Lee, N.; Lee, H.S.; Hong, S.; Seong, G.J.; Kim, C.Y. Systemic hypertension as a risk factor for open-angle glaucoma: A meta-analysis of population-based studies. *PLoS ONE* **2014**, *9*, e108226. [CrossRef]
8. Gupta, D.; Chen, P.P. Glaucoma. *Am. Fam. Physician* **2016**, *93*, 668–674.
9. Wright, C.; Tawfik, M.A.; Waisbourd, M.; Katz, L.J. Primary angle-closure glaucoma: An update. *Acta Ophthalmol.* **2016**, *94*, 217–225. [CrossRef] [PubMed]
10. Poh, S.; Mohamed Abdul, R.B.; Lamoureux, E.L.; Wong, T.Y.; Sabanayagam, C. Metabolic syndrome and eye diseases. *Diabetes Res. Clin. Pr.* **2016**, *113*, 86–100. [CrossRef]
11. Alberti, K.G.; Zimmet, P.; Shaw, J. The metabolic syndrome–a new worldwide definition. *Lancet* **2005**, *366*, 1059–1062. [CrossRef]
12. Belete, R.; Ataro, Z.; Abdu, A.; Sheleme, M. Global prevalence of metabolic syndrome among patients with type I diabetes mellitus: A systematic review and meta-analysis. *Diabetol. Metab. Syndr.* **2021**, *13*, 25. [CrossRef] [PubMed]
13. Yin, X.; Li, J.; Zhang, B.; Lu, P. Association of glaucoma with risk of retinal vein occlusion: A meta-analysis. *Acta Ophthalmol.* **2019**, *97*, 652–659. [CrossRef] [PubMed]
14. Wu, W.T.; Tsai, S.S.; Shih, T.S.; Lin, M.H.; Chou, T.C.; Ting, H.; Wu, T.N.; Liou, S.H. The Association between Obstructive Sleep Apnea and Metabolic Markers and Lipid Profiles. *PLoS ONE* **2015**, *10*, e0130279. [CrossRef] [PubMed]
15. Kim, D.; Touros, A.; Kim, W.R. Nonalcoholic Fatty Liver Disease and Metabolic Syndrome. *Clin. Liver Dis.* **2018**, *22*, 133–140. [CrossRef]
16. Skilton, M.R.; Moulin, P.; Terra, J.L.; Bonnet, F. Associations between anxiety, depression, and the metabolic syndrome. *Biol. Psychiatry* **2007**, *62*, 1251–1257. [CrossRef] [PubMed]
17. Tang, F.; Wang, G.; Lian, Y. Association between anxiety and metabolic syndrome: A systematic review and meta-analysis of epidemiological studies. *Psychoneuroendocrinology* **2017**, *77*, 112–121. [CrossRef]
18. Uzunlulu, M.; Yorulmaz, E.; Oguz, A. Prevalence of subclinical hypothyroidism in patients with metabolic syndrome. *Endocr. J.* **2007**, *54*, 71–76. [CrossRef]
19. Zhao, D.; Cho, J.; Kim, M.H.; Guallar, E. The association of blood pressure and primary open-angle glaucoma: A meta-analysis. *Am. J. Ophthalmol.* **2014**, *158*, 615–627.e9. [CrossRef]
20. Newman-Casey, P.A.; Talwar, N.; Nan, B.; Musch, D.C.; Stein, J.D. The relationship between components of metabolic syndrome and open-angle glaucoma. *Ophthalmology* **2011**, *118*, 1318–1326. [CrossRef]
21. Rasoulinejad, S.A.; Kasiri, A.; Montazeri, M.; Rashidi, N.; Montazeri, M.; Montazeri, M.; Hedayati, H. The association between primary open angle glaucoma and clustered components of metabolic syndrome. *Open Ophthalmol. J.* **2015**, *9*, 149. [CrossRef]

22. Kim, H.A.; Han, K.; Lee, Y.A.; Choi, J.A.; Park, Y.M. Differential Association of Metabolic Risk Factors with Open Angle Glaucoma according to Obesity in a Korean Population. *Sci. Rep.* **2016**, *6*, 38283. [CrossRef] [PubMed]
23. Chen, H.Y.; Lin, C.L. Comparison of medical comorbidity between patients with primary angle-closure glaucoma and a control cohort: A population-based study from Taiwan. *BMJ Open* **2019**, *9*, e024209. [CrossRef] [PubMed]
24. Ah-Kee, E.Y.; Egong, E.; Shafi, A.; Lim, L.T.; Yim, J.L. A review of drug-induced acute angle closure glaucoma for non-ophthalmologists. *Qatar Med. J.* **2015**, *2015*, 6. [CrossRef]
25. Yang, M.C.; Lin, K.Y. Drug-induced Acute Angle-closure Glaucoma: A Review. *J. Curr. Glaucoma Pract.* **2019**, *13*, 104–109. [CrossRef] [PubMed]
26. Vajaranant, T.S.; Nayak, S.; Wilensky, J.T.; Joslin, C.E. Gender and glaucoma: What we know and what we need to know. *Curr. Opin. Ophthalmol.* **2010**, *21*, 91–99. [CrossRef] [PubMed]
27. Cho, H.K.; Kee, C. Population-based glaucoma prevalence studies in Asians. *Surv Ophthalmol.* **2014**, *59*, 434–447. [CrossRef]
28. Zetterberg, M. Age-related eye disease and gender. *Maturitas* **2016**, *83*, 19–26. [CrossRef]
29. Cook, C.; Foster, P. Epidemiology of glaucoma: What's new? *Can. J. Ophthalmol. J. Can. D'ophtalmol.* **2012**, *47*, 223–226. [CrossRef]
30. Mabry, R.M.; Reeves, M.M.; Eakin, E.G.; Owen, N. Gender differences in prevalence of the metabolic syndrome in Gulf Cooperation Council Countries: A systematic review. *Diabet. Med. A J. Br. Diabet. Assoc.* **2010**, *27*, 593–597. [CrossRef]
31. Ford, E.S.; Giles, W.H.; Dietz, W.H. Prevalence of the metabolic syndrome among US adults: Findings from the third National Health and Nutrition Examination Survey. *JAMA* **2002**, *287*, 356–359. [CrossRef]
32. Kuo, C.Y.; Ko, Y.C.; Kuang, T.M.; Chou, P.; Chiou, S.H.; Liu, C.J. Prevalence of glaucoma in the elderly population in Taiwan: The Shihpai Eye Study. *J. Chin. Med. Assoc. JCMA* **2020**, *83*, 880–884. [CrossRef]
33. Wong, V.H.; Bui, B.V.; Vingrys, A.J. Clinical and experimental links between diabetes and glaucoma. *Clin. Exp. Optom.* **2011**, *94*, 4–23. [CrossRef]
34. Song, B.J.; Aiello, L.P.; Pasquale, L.R. Presence and Risk Factors for Glaucoma in Patients with Diabetes. *Curr Diab. Rep.* **2016**, *16*, 124. [CrossRef] [PubMed]
35. Husain, S.; Abdul, Y.; Singh, S.; Ahmad, A.; Husain, M. Regulation of nitric oxide production by δ-opioid receptors during glaucomatous injury. *PLoS ONE* **2014**, *9*, e110397. [CrossRef]
36. Alexander, J.P.; Acott, T.S. Involvement of protein kinase C in TNFalpha regulation of trabecular matrix metalloproteinases and TIMPs. *Investig. Ophthalmol. Vis. Sci.* **2001**, *42*, 2831–2838.
37. Wang, S.; Bao, X. Hyperlipidemia, Blood Lipid Level, and the Risk of Glaucoma: A Meta-Analysis. *Investig. Ophthalmol. Vis. Sci.* **2019**, *60*, 1028–1043. [CrossRef]
38. Qian, H.; Zhao, X.; Cao, P.; Lei, J.; Yan, N.; Gong, X. Structure of the Human Lipid Exporter ABCA1. *Cell* **2017**, *169*, 1228–1239.e10. [CrossRef] [PubMed]
39. Li, M.; Chen, D.; Huang, H.; Wang, J.; Wan, X.; Xu, C.; Li, C.; Ma, H.; Yu, C.; Li, Y. Caveolin1 protects against diet induced hepatic lipid accumulation in mice. *PLoS ONE* **2017**, *12*, e0178748. [CrossRef]
40. Langman, M.J.; Lancashire, R.J.; Cheng, K.K.; Stewart, P.M. Systemic hypertension and glaucoma: Mechanisms in common and co-occurrence. *Br. J. Ophthalmol.* **2005**, *89*, 960–963. [CrossRef]
41. Jung, Y.; Han, K.; Park, H.Y.L.; Lee, S.H.; Park, C.K. Metabolic Health, Obesity, and the Risk of Developing Open-Angle Glaucoma: Metabolically Healthy Obese Patients versus Metabolically Unhealthy but Normal Weight Patients. *Diabetes Metab. J.* **2010**, *44*, 415–425. [CrossRef] [PubMed]

International Journal of
Environmental Research and Public Health

MDPI

Review

Oral Health Status among Migrants from Middle- and Low-Income Countries to Europe: A Systematic Review

Dorina Lauritano [1,*,†], Giulia Moreo [2,†], Francesco Carinci [1], Vincenzo Campanella [3], Fedora Della Vella [4] and Massimo Petruzzi [4]

[1] Department of Translational Medicine and for Romagna, University of Ferrara, 44121 Ferrara, Italy; crc@unife.it
[2] Dental and Maxillo-Facial Surgery Unit, IRCCS Ca' Granda Ospedale Maggiore Policlinico di Milano, 20122 Milan, Italy; giulia.moreo@unimi.it
[3] Department of Clinical Science and Translational Medicine, University of Rome "Tor Vergata", 00113 Rome, Italy; vincenzo.campanella@uniroma2.it
[4] Interdisciplinary Department of Medicine, University of Bari, 70121 Bari, Italy; dellavellaf@gmail.com (F.D.V.); massimo.petruzzi@uniba.it (M.P.)
* Correspondence: dorina.lauritano@unife.it; Tel.: +39-335-679-0163
† These authors contribute equally to this work.

Citation: Lauritano, D.; Moreo, G.; Carinci, F.; Campanella, V.; Della Vella, F.; Petruzzi, M. Oral Health Status among Migrants from Middle- and Low-Income Countries to Europe: A Systematic Review. *Int. J. Environ. Res. Public Health* **2021**, *18*, 12203. https://doi.org/10.3390/ijerph182212203

Academic Editors: Joachim G. Voss, Sandul Yasobant and Paul B. Tchounwou

Received: 23 September 2021
Accepted: 17 November 2021
Published: 20 November 2021

Abstract: Introduction. Economic inequality, political instability and globalization have contributed to the constant growth of the migration phenomenon in recent years. In particular, a total of 4.2 million people migrated to Europe during 2019 and most of them settled in Germany, France and Italy. Objectives. The objective of this study was to conduct a systematic review of studies analyzing the oral health condition among migrants from middle- and low-income countries to Europe and assessing the eventual association between their sociodemographic and socioeconomic characteristics and oral health status. Materials and Methods. A systematic review was conducted in PubMed, Cochrane Library, Scopus and Science Direct databases. After titles, abstracts and full-text examination, only 27 articles were selected on the basis of inclusion criteria and consequently included for quality assessments and data extraction. Results. Most of the studies reported a higher prevalence of caries experience, a poorer periodontal health and more difficulties in accessing dentalcare services among migrant groups compared with the non-migrant population. Inequalities were mostly associated with ethnic background, economic condition and social grade. Conclusion. Our review demonstrates the lack of dental health among migrants, underlining that their cultural beliefs and their social and economic living conditions could influence their oral health.

Keywords: oral health; migrants; oral health inequalities; migration to Europe; socioeconomic status

1. Introduction

According to the 2017 International Migration Report, the number of international migrants reached 220 million in 2010 and 258 million in 2017, showing a continuous growth in recent years [1]. Migrants represent 3.5% of the world's population (updated to 2019) and India has the highest number of individuals living abroad [2]. Europe, Asia and Northern America host two thirds of international migrants, mainly originating from middle- and low-income countries [3,4]. In particular, a total of 4.2 million people immigrated to one of the European Union (EU) Member States during 2019 (30% of who comes from non-EU countries). In the same year, the largest total number of immigrants was reported by Germany, followed by Spain, France and Italy [5]. The reasons that prompt people to move are known: economic inequality, political instability, increased globalization [6], and it has been demonstrated that immigration status is one of the main determinant in health disparities [7–9]. Several factors contribute to defining migrants as vulnerable subjects: health risks before, during and after migration, different disease pro-file from that of the population of the receiving countries and barriers in accessing health care services in hosting nations [10]. Difficulties in understanding the spoken language, different cultural habits, employment problems, low socio-economic position and lack of medical insurance are conditions that may affect migrants' general health, including their oral health status [11–14]. The risk of a poorer oral health among migrants compared to the host population has been demonstrated in the literature [15,16], even though information about this topic remains contradictory. Studies from Germany and Spain, included in the systematic review by Pabbla et al. [17], reported higher dental caries experience (DMFT Index) in migrants adolescents compared to the host population, but, on the contrary, re-searchers performed in United Kingdom (UK), Denmark and Sweden showed a lower DMFT Index among non-native subjects compared to the native population. Al-merich-Silla et al. demonstrated that immigration status and social class were significantly associated with higher caries level in immigrant children compared to Spanish children of the Valencia region [18]. DMFT score was also analyzed in migrant children attending schools in Heidelberg areas of disadvantaged socioeconomic status and reported to be significantly higher compared to non-migrants [19]. The cross-sectional study by Brzoska et al. [20] associated the scarce use of regular dental checkups by immigrants in Germany (36% lower chance than non-migrants) with their lower socio-economic status (SES), poor social support and lack of regular health insurance. Hagenfeld et al. [21] compared two migrants groups coming from Turkey and the Soviet Union with the German native population, recording a higher prevalence of maximal periodontal pocket depth above 5 mm and a lower use of dentalcare services in migrants. Therefore, migrants' poor oral health and difficulties in accessing dental care are related to their sociodemographic and socioeconomic characteristics: low income, education level, language barriers, religious affiliation and cultural habits belonging to the country of origin [15,22]. Dental treatments in hosting countries are often perceived as more expensive compared to those in home countries [23,24]. Oral health knowledge and beliefs are generally poor among migrants, as demonstrated by Skeie et al.: South Asian and Muslim populations in Norway give no importance to oral hygiene practices and believed that deciduous teeth are not important for the oral health of their children [25].

Quality of life could be affected by poor oral health, since it may interfere with everyday activities, such as eating and talking and it may increase the risk of developing chronic diseases: periodontal microorganisms can contribute to the onset of diabetes or cardiovascular diseases and protracted oral pain can lead to nutrition problems [26–29].

For all these reasons, intervention strategies aimed at improving the oral health condition of migrants population are required [30,31].

The objectives of our systematic review were the following:

1. What are the oral health conditions among migrants from middle- and low-income countries to Europe?
2. Considering the sociodemographic (ethnic background) and socioeconomic characteristics (income, social grade, professional status) of migrants, is there an association between these variables and migrants oral health status?

Clinical Question (PICO)

- P: A sample of migrants from middle- and low-income countries to Europe
- I: Analysis of the oral health condition, oral health habits, attitude towards oral health and use of dentalcare services
- C: Association between oral health condition, oral health habits, attitude to-wards oral health and use of dentalcare services and sociodemographic/socioeconomic characteristics
- O: Presence of dental caries, periodontal status, need for dental treatment, self-reported oral health, oral health habits, oral hygiene practices, impact of the oral health on life quality

2. Materials and Methods

2.1. Protocol and Registration

Methods and inclusion criteria were selected following the PRISMA statement [32], since it provides a suitable protocol for systematic reviews.

2.2. Eligibility Criteria

Inclusion and Exclusion criteria

All the items concerning the oral health status in a population of migrants from middle and low-income countries to Europe were selected and included in our research. Pa-per selection was based on the following inclusion criteria:

- o The selected population sample had to include subjects identified as migrants
- o Studies which assessed the social fragility of the migrants' selected subjects, by analyzing their socioeconomic characteristics (education level/professional status/money income/social class) or by identifying them as refugees or asylum seekers
- o Articles which reported quantitative or qualitative data about the oral health status of the migrants included participants
- o Papers written in English

Reviews and case reports were not selected and studies published before 2010 were excluded from our review, in order to collect the most recent data available in the literature.

2.2.1. Electronic Search

The databases of PubMed, Cochraine Library, Science Direct and Scopus were used to conduct electronic research, selecting relevant articles (published from 2010 to date) concerning the oral health status of migrants from middle- and low-income countries to Europe. Only articles written in the English language were considered, but no restrictions were imposed with regard to the age range of the participants and to the oral health evaluation methodology. Both items with or without non-immigrant (native) population control group were included. The keywords, with the Boolean term "AND", used for the electronic search in each database were "oral health status", "migrants", "oral health inequalities", and "migration to Europe".

2.2.2. Study Selection and Data Collection Process

Eligible articles were selected following the inclusion and exclusion criteria mentioned above by two independent reviewers, who analyzed the titles, abstracts and full text of all the articles that were found during the electronic search. Disagreements between reviewers were resolved by consensus. Data collection was performed by one researcher, who extracted from each article the following information: (a) design of the study (cross-sectional, prospective/retrospective longitudinal), (b) European country in which the study was conducted (Finland, Germany, Greece, Italy, Netherlands, Norway, Spain, Sweden and UK), (c) participants' sociodemographic characteristics (age, gender, country of origin, religious affiliation, place of residence), (d) participants' socioeconomic status (education level, social class, marital status, monthly net income, professional status), (e) methodology used for the oral health evaluation (clinical indices/parameters, self-reported questionnaires or oral interviews); (f) quantitative/qualitative data about the oral health condition of the included subjects (dental caries, periodontal status, oral health habits, oral hygiene practices, impact of the oral health on life quality) were also extracted and used as outcome measures (means and percentages). Furthermore, the researcher collected information regarding the (g) association between the oral health parameters and the sociodemographic (ethnic background) and socioeconomic (income, social grade, professional status) characteristics of the migrant population sample, reporting them as descriptive outcomes.

3. Results

3.1. Critical Appraisal

The JBI Critical Appraisal Tool [33] was used in order to evaluate the methodological quality of the included items (Tables 1–4) and to determine the risk of bias in their design, conduct and analysis. The JBI for case-control studies judges each study based on nine items: (1) target population, (2) participants selection methods, (3) sample size, (4) description of study subjects and setting, (5) response rate of participants, (6) diagnostic methods, (7) standardized and reliable way of measurements, (8) statistical analysis, (9) management of the participants' response rate. Cohort studies are investigated by the same tool based on 11 items: (1) population recruitment, (2,3) exposure, (4,5) confounding factors, (6,7) outcome, (8,9,10) follow-up, (11) statistical analysis. Authors indicate for each item "yes", "no", "unclear", "not applicable" and finally giving an overall appraisal.

Table 1. JBI for cross-sectional studies: population sample and study setting.

Studies	Was the Sample Appropriate to Address the Target Population?	Were Study Participants Sampled in an Appropriate Way?	Was the Sample Size Adequate?	Were the Study Subjects and Setting Described in Detail?
Aarabi et al. [34]	YES	YES	YES	YES
Agudelo-Suárez et al. 2019 [35]	YES	YES	YES	YES
Al-Haboubi et al. [36]	YES	YES	YES	YES
Aarora et al. 2019 [37]	YES	YES	YES	YES
Delgado-Angulo et al. 2018 [38]	YES	YES	YES	YES
Dujister et al. 2014 [39]	YES	YES	YES	YES
Erdsiek et al. 2011 [40]	YES	YES	YES	YES
Ferrazzano et al. 2019 [41]	YES	YES	YES	YES
Gatou et al. 2011 [42]	YES	YES	YES	YES
Goetz et al. 2018 [43]	YES	YES	NO	NO
Høyvik et al. 2019 [44]	YES	YES	YES	YES
Jacobsson et al. 2011 [45]	YES	YES	YES	YES
Marcenes et al. 2013 [46]	YES	YES	YES	YES
Mattila et al. 2016 [47]	YES	YES	NO	YES
Mustafa et al. 2020 [48]	YES	YES	YES	YES
Portero de la Cruz et al. 2020 [49]	YES	YES	YES	YES
Riatto et al. 2018 [50]	YES	YES	YES	YES
Rouxel et al. 2017 [51]	YES	YES	YES	YES
Solyman et al. 2018 [52]	YES	YES	YES	YES
Van der Tas et al. 2017 [53]	YES	YES	YES	YES
Van Meljeen-van Lunteren et al. 2019 [54]	YES	YES	YES	YES
Wigen et al. 2010 [55]	YES	YES	YES	YES

Table 2. JBI for cross-sectional studies: diagnosis, data analysis, response rate.

Studies	Was the Data Analysis Conducted with Sufficient Coverage of the Identified Sample?	Were Valid Methods Used for the Identification of the Condition?	Was the Condition Measured in a Standard, Reliable Way for all Participants?	Was There Appropriate Statistical Analysis?	Was the Response Rate Adequate, and If Not, Was the Low Response Rate Managed Appropriately?
Aarabi et al. [34]	YES	YES	YES	YES	NO
Agudelo-Suárez et al. 2019 [35]	YES	YES	YES	YES	YES
Al-Haboubi et al. [36]	YES	YES	YES	YES	NO
Aarora et al. 2019 [37]	YES	YES	YES	YES	NO
Delgado-Angulo et al. 2018 [38]	YES	YES	YES	YES	NO
Dujister et al. 2014 [39]	YES	YES	YES	YES	NO
Erdsiek et al. 2011 [40]	YES	YES	YES	YES	NO
Ferrazzano et al. 2019 [41]	YES	YES	YES	YES	NO
Gatou et al. 2011 [42]	YES	YES	YES	YES	NO
Goetz et al. 2018 [43]	YES	YES	YES	NO	YES
Høyvik et al. 2019 [44]	YES	YES	YES	YES	NO
Jacobsson et al. 2011 [45]	YES	YES	YES	YES	NO
Marcenes et al. 2013 [46]	YES	YES	YES	YES	NO
Mattila et al. 2016 [47]	YES	YES	YES	NO	NO
Mustafa et al. 2020 [48]	YES	YES	YES	NO	NO
Portero de la Cruz et al. 2020 [49]	YES	YES	YES	YES	NO
Riatto et al. 2018 [50]	YES	YES	YES	YES	NO
Rouxel et al. 2017 [51]	YES	YES	YES	YES	NO
Solyman et al. 2018 [52]	YES	YES	YES	YES	NO
Van der Tas et al. 2017 [53]	YES	YES	YES	YES	NO
Van Meljeen-van Lunteren et al. 2019 [54]	YES	YES	YES	YES	NO
Wigen et al. 2010 [55]	YES	YES	YES	YES	NO

Table 3. JBI for cohort studies: population, exposure, confounding factors.

Studies	Were the Two Groups Similar and Recruited from the Same Population?	Were the Exposures Measured Similarly to Assign People to Both Exposed and Unexposed Groups?	Was the Exposure Measured in a Valid and Reliable Way?	Were Confounding Factors Identified?	Were Strategies to Deal with Confounding Factors Stated?
Freiberg et al. 2020 [56]	NOT APPLICABLE	YES	YES	NO	NO
Julihn et al. 2010 [57]	YES	YES	YES	NO	NO
Julihn et al. 2021 [58]	YES	YES	YES	NO	NO

Most of the cross-sectional studies included an appropriate sample to address the target population, sampled participants in an appropriate way, choose an adequate sample size and described subjects and settings in detail [34–42,44–46,48–55]. Only two articles [43,47] did not select an adequate sample size and one research [43] did not describe subjects in detail. None of the included items indicated the response rate, except for two articles [35,43]. Only three of the selected research papers did not provide appropriate statistical analysis [43,47,48], while all the studies used standardized and reliable methodologies for condition identification and measurement.

Table 4. JBI for cohort studies: outcome, follow-up, statistical analysis.

Studies	Were the Participants Free of the Outcome at the Start of the Study?	Were the Outcomes Measured in a Valid and Reliable Way?	Was the Follow-Up Time Reported and Sufficient to Be Long Enough for Outcomes to Occur?	Was Follow-Up Complete, and If Not, Were the Reasons to Loss to Follow-Up Described and Explored?	Were Strategies to Address Incomplete Follow-Up Utilized	Was Appropriate Statistical Analysis Used?
Freiberg et al. 2020 [56]	YES	YES	NOT APPLICABLE	NO	NO	YES
Julihn et al. 2010 [57]	YES	YES	YES	YES	NOT APPLICABLE	YES
Julihn et al. 2021 [58]	YES	YES	YES	YES	NOT APPLICABLE	YES

The exposure measurements were similar for both exposed and unexposed group and statistical analysis was appropriate in all the included cohort studies [56–58], but confounding factors were not identified in any of these articles.

3.2. Study Selection and Characteristics

During the electronic search on PubMed, Cochrane Library, Scopus and Science Direct databases, a total of 681 articles were found. After duplication removal, 646 items were identified and consequently subjected to titles, abstracts and full-texts examination. Only 25 items (22 cross-sectional, 1 prospective longitudinal and 2 retrospective longitudinal) were selected on the basis of inclusion criteria and included for quality assessment and data extraction: 184 studies were not selected based on the publication date (prior to 2010), 72 citations were not included after analyzing titles, 391 after reading abstracts and full-texts (absence of sociodemographic/socioeconomic status assessment, non-representative sample size, quantitative/qualitative data about oral health not re-ported) and 1 study was excluded because it was written in German language. The flow chart of publication assessment is showed in Figure 1.

The list of the included studies is presented in Tables 5–7. For each item, several information were reported: author, publication date, country in which the research was conducted, study design, number and age range of the included mi-grants (MI) subjects, investigation method used for sociodemographic (SDS) and socioeconomic status (SES) assessment, clinical and qualitative oral health parameters evaluated, statistical test used to establish the association between the oral health and the SDS/SES of the selected subjects (Table 8).

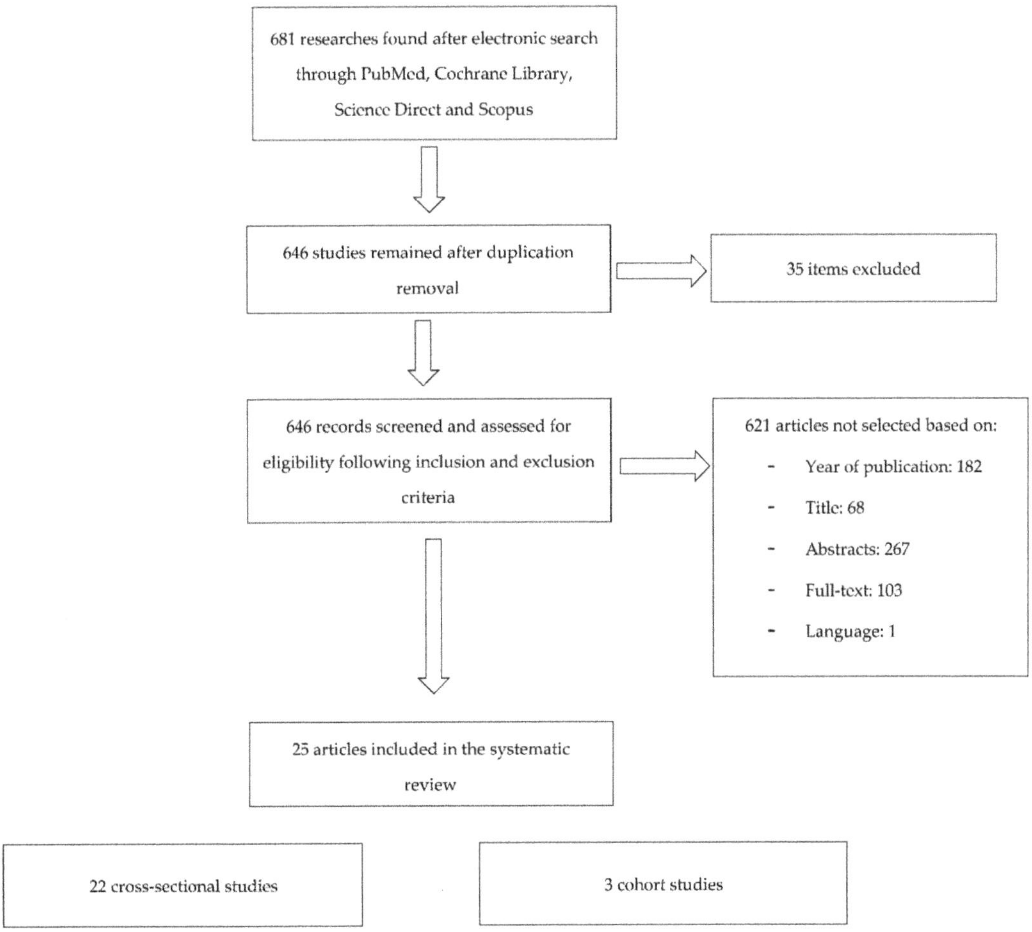

Figure 1. Flow chart of publication assessment.

Table 5. List of included studies: design, aim, number of MI and NMI, age range, migrants assessed characteristics.

Study	Design and Aim	Number of MI	Number of NMI	Age Range	MI Assessed Characteristics
Aarabi et al. 2018 (Hamburg, Germany) [34]	Cross-sectional	61	51	≥60	Sociodemographic status *: age, gender, religious affiliation, family status, country of origin Socioeconomic status **: education, professional status, monthly net income
Agudelo-Suárez et al. 2019 (Spain) [35]	Cross-sectional analysis from a prospective cohort study	300	101	12–17 ≥18	Sociodemographic status *: age, gender, country of origin Socioeconomic status **: education, marital status, social class (manual, non-manual)
Al Haboubi et al. 2013 (London, UK) [36]	Cross-sectional	229	466	≥16	Sociodemographic status *: age, gender, country of origin Socioeconomic status **: social grade
Arora et al. 2019 (England, Wales, Northern Ireland) [37]	Cross-sectional	624	10,435	≥16	Sociodemographic status *: age, gender, country of origin Socioeconomic status **: household tenure, education level, number of household members
Delgado-Angulo et al. 2018 (East London, UK) [38]	Cross-sectional	1036	874	16–65	Sociodemographic status *: age, gender, country of origin SEP: education, professional status
Dujister et al. 2015 (Netherlands) [39]	Cross-sectional	57	35	5 and 6	Sociodemographic status *: children age, children gender, country of origin Socioeconomic status **: parents' education level, family income, relationship status
Erdsiek et al. 2017 (Germany) [40]	Cross-sectional	3404	18,337	≥18	Sociodemographic status *: age, gender Socioeconomic status **: type of health insurance, measurement and categorization of Lampert et al. [59] → education level, occupational status, net equivalent income

Table 5. *Cont.*

Study	Design and Aim	Number of MI	Number of NMI	Age Range	MI Assessed Characteristics
Ferrazzano et al. 2019 (Naples, Italy) [41]	Cross-sectional	183	370	12–14	Sociodemographic status *: country of origin and other not specified Socioeconomic status **: family's annual income
Freiberg et al. 2020 (Halle, Germany) [56]	Retrospective longitudinal	475 asylum seekers	/	No age range	Sociodemographic status *: age, gender, country of origin
Gatou et al. 2011 (Greece) [42]	Cross-sectional	739	4377	5–12	Sociodemographic status *: age, gender, place of residence Socioeconomic status **: area-based income
Goetz et al. 2018 (Schleswig-Holstein, Germany) [43]	Cross-sectional	102 refugees in reception centers/collective living quarters	/	16–64	Sociodemographic status *: age, gender, country of origin
Høyvik et al. 2019 (Norway) [44]	Cross-sectional	132 refugees/asylum seekers	/	>18	Sociodemographic status *: age, gender, country of origin Socioeconomic status **: education level
Jacobsson et al. 2011 (Jönköping, Sweden) [45]	Cross-sectional	154	585	3/5/10/15	Sociodemographic status *: age, gender, country of origin Socioeconomic status **: education level
Julihn et al. 2010 (Sweden) [57]	Retrospective longitudinal	1378	14,160	13 and 19 (6 years of follow-up)	Sociodemographic status *: age, gender, country of origin Socioeconomic status **: parents' marital status, parents' education level, social welfare allowance, family income
Julihn et al. 2021 (Sweden) [58]	Prospective longitudinal	10,180	44,491	3 and 7 (4 years of follow-up)	Sociodemographic status *: age, gender, country of origin Socioeconomic status **: parents' marital status, parents' education level, social welfare allowance, family income

Table 5. *Cont.*

Study	Design and Aim	Number of MI	Number of NMI	Age Range	MI Assessed Characteristics
Marcenes et al. 2013 (Tower Hamlets, Hackney and Newham, London, England) [46]	Cross-sectional	89% of 2434 included subjects	10,94% of 2434 included subjects	3–4	Sociodemographic status *: age, gender, country of origin
Mattila et al. 2016 (Finland) [47]	Cross-sectional	9 asylum seekers 29 migrants studying at the Oulu Adult Education Centre and PASK-Adult Education Centre	/	17–53	Sociodemographic status *: age, gender, country of origin Socioeconomic status **: education level
Mustafa et al. 2020 (Norway) [48]	Cross-sectional	466	/	Mothers and fathers of 0–6 months old children	Sociodemographic status *: parental age, country of origin Socioeconomic status **: parents' education level, employment status
Portero de la Cruz et al. 2020 (Spain) [49]	Cross-sectional	253	4315	3–14	Sociodemographic status *: age, gender, country of origin Socioeconomic status **: type of household social class, size of town of residence
Riatto et al. 2018 (Melilla, Spain) [50]	Cross-sectional	156 Syrian refgees children living at the Center for Temporary Stay of MI	/	5–13	Sociodemographic status *: age, gender, religious affiliation country of origin
Rouxel et al. 2017 (England, Wales and Northern Ireland) [51]	Cross-sectional	1460	7081	5/8/12/15	Sociodemographic status *: age, gender, output area classification, country of origin Socioeconomic status **: index of Multiple Deprivation (IMD), analysis of children's school (deprived or not deprived school, eligibility for free school meals)

Table 5. *Cont.*

Study	Design and Aim	Number of MI	Number of NMI	Age Range	MI Assessed Characteristics
Solyman et al. 2018 (Berlin, Germany) [52]	Cross-sectional	386 refugees living in reception centers/shelters/private practices	/	18–60	Sociodemographic status *: age, gender, country of origin Socioeconomic status **: education level
Van der Tas et al. 2017 (Netherlands) [53]	Cross-sectional	1618	3446	6	Sociodemographic status *: age, gender, country of origin Socioeconomic status **: parental education level, parental employment status, net household income, single parenting teenage pregnancy
Van Meljeen-van Lunteren et al. 2019 (Rotterdam, Netherlands) [54]	Cross-sectional	611	2510	9	Sociodemographic status *: age, gender, country of origin Socioeconomic status **: maternal education level, household income, generational status
Wigen et al. 2010 (Norway) [55]	Cross-sectional	70	453	5	Sociodemographic status *: parents' age/gender, country of origin Socioeconomic status **: parents' education level

MI = migrants; NMI = non migrants; SEP = socio-economic position. * Sociodemographic characteristics: age/gender/religious affiliation/country of origin. ** Socioeconomic characteristics: education level/social class/marital status/net income/professional status.

Table 6. MI and NMI country of birth, quantitative oral health indicators (QnOHI) and data collection of the included studies.

Study	MI Country of Birth	NMI Country of Birth	QnOHI	Data Collection
Aarabi et al. 2018 [34]	36: Europe 25: Africa/Asia/America	51: Germany	• DMFT according to Barmes [60]	Clinical oral examination
Agudelo-Suárez et al. 2019 [35]	126: Ecuador 122: Colombia 52: Morocco	101: Spain	/	/
Al Haboubi et al. 2013 [36]	193: Africa/Caribbean/Other 36: India/Bangladesh/Pakistan/Other	466: British/Irish/Other	/	/
Arora et al. 2017 [37]	272: India 165: Pakistan or Bangladesh 187: Black	10.435: White British	• Presence of natural teeth • Presence of filled teeth • Presence of denture	ADHS 2009 Model [61]
Delgado-Angulo et al. 2018 [38]	1036: Africa/Caribbean/Pakistan/India/Bangladesh/Asia	874: UK	• DMFT	Clinical oral examination following UK ADHS protocol 1998 [62]
Dujister et al. 2015 [39]	31: Morocco 26: Turkey	35: Netherlands	• DMFT	Records from the pediatric dental center in the Haque (Netherlands): data were collected performing clinical oral examination
Erdsiek et al. 2017 [40]	3404: MI	18337: Germany	/	/
Ferrazzano et al. 2019 [41]	183: Eastern Europe/Asia/Africa/Turkey/South and Central America	370: Italy	• DMFT	Clinical oral examination
Freiberg et al. 2020 [56]	187: Syria 46: Afghanistan 38: Iran 29: Somalia 21: Guinea-Bissau 21: Russia 18: Eritrea 14: India 14: Kosovo 11: Benin 76: unknown/others	/	/	/

Table 6. *Cont.*

Study	MI Country of Birth	NMI Country of Birth	QnOHI	Data Collection
Gatou et al. 2011 [42]	739: MI	4377: Greece	• dmft • UTN • DI-S	Clinical oral examination
Goetz et al. 2018 [43]	25: Afghanistan 19: Iraq 15: Syria 14: Eritrea 11: Yemen 7: Armenia 5: Somalia 4: Iran 2: Chechnya	/	• DMFT	Clinical oral examination
Høyvik et al. 2019 [44]	45: Middle East (Syria/Iran/Iraq/Afghanistan) 87: Africa (Eritrea/Somalia/Sudan/Nigeria)	/	• DT	Clinical oral examination by Singh et al. [63]
Jacobsson et al. 2011 [45]	154: Asia/Africa/South America/North America/Scandinavia/European countries	585: Sweden	• Number of teeth • dfs/DFS • GI • PLI	Clinical and radiographic examination
Julihn et al. 2010 [57]	140: Western Europe 315: Eastern Europe 595: Asia 143: Africa 185: South America	14160: Sweden	• DMFSa	Data were provided by Public Dental Health Service, private practicioners and the Department of Dental Medicine, Division of Pediatric Dentistry at Karolinska Institutet
Julihn et al. 2021 [58]	2363: Africa/India 7351: Eastern Europe/South America/China/Asia/Vietnam/Oceania 872: Western Europe/South Europe/North America/Korea	44491: Sweden	• Presence of caries into dentin	Clinical and radiographic examination

Table 6. *Cont.*

Study	MI Country of Birth	NMI Country of Birth	QnOHI	Data Collection
Marcenes et al. 2013 [46]	1.94%: White Eastern Europe 2.74%: White other 15.6%: Black Africa 7.30%: Black Other 7%: India 30.11%: Bangladesh 6.36%: Pakistan 5.14%: Asian Other 4.04%: Middle East	10.94%: White British	• dmft • Number of teeth with untreated caries into dentin • % of children with one or more tooth with untreated caries into dentin • % of children with caries experience	Clinical oral examination
Mattila et al. 2016 [47]	9 asylum, seekers: Asia 12 MI: Asia 7 MI: Africa 10 MI: Europe	/	/	/
Mustafa et al. 2020 [48]	32: Afghanistan 17: Azerbai-jan/Bangladesh/Pakistan 4: Bosnia and Herzegovina 1: Dominican Republic 18: Philippines 2: Belarus 23: India 2: Indonesia 15: China 2: Kosovo 34: Lithuania 3: Moldova 2: Nepal 12: Romania 7: Russia 10: Srijlanka 1: Taiwan 10: South America 130: Africa	/	/	/
Portero de la Cruz et al. 2020 [49]	253: MI (nationality not specified)	4315: Spanish	/	/

Table 6. *Cont.*

Study	MI Country of Birth	NMI Country of Birth	QnOHI	Data Collection
Riatto et al. 2018 [50]	100: Arabian ethnicity 56: Caucasian ethnicity	/	• DMFT	Clinical oral examination
Rouxel et al. 2017 [51]	335: Black African and Caribbean 431: Pakistan/Bangladesh 142: India 552: Other White/Mixed White	7081: Britain/Ireland	• DFT • Presence of plaque • Gingivitis	Children's Dental Health Survey (CDHS) 2013
Solyman et al. 2018 [52]	239: Syria 147: Iraq	/	• DMFT • Dental trauma • Dean's Index (enamel fluorosis) • Need of treatmentPresence of plaque • Presence of calculus	Clinical oral examination
Van der Tas et al. 2017 [53]	1618: Non-Western	3446: Netherlands	• dmft	Clinical oral examination
Van Meljeen-van Lunteren et al. 2019 [54]	Mothers' country of birth: 143: Indonesia 104: Morocco 195: Suriname 169: Turkey	Mothers' country of birth: 2110: Netherlands	/	/
Wigen et al. 2010 [55]	Parents' country of birth 70: Turkey/Asia/Africa/South America/Central America/Eastern Europe	Parents' country of birth 453: Netherlands	• dmft	Clinical oral examination

ADHS 2009 = Adult Dental Health Survey 2009; API: Approximal Plaque Index; dfs = dcayed filled proximal teeth surfaces in primary dentition; DFS = Decayed Filled proximal teeth surfaces in permanent dentition; DFT = Decayed Filled permanent Teeth; DT = Decayed permanent Teeth; DI-S = Simplified Debris Index; DMFT= decayed (D), missing (M), filled (F) permanent teeth; dmft= decayed (d), missing (m), filled (f) primary teeth; DMFM = decayed, missing, filled first permanent molars; DMFSa = decayed, missing, filled surfaces approxymal; ECC = early childhood caries: GI = gingival indices; N = number; NICE = National Institute for Health and Clinical Excellence: PBI = Papillary Bleeding Index; PI = Plaque Index; PLI = Plaque indices grades 2 and 3 (Silness and Loe 1964); pufa index = pulpal involvement, ulceration, fistula and abscess in severe decayed primary teeth; UTN = Unmet Treatment Needs.

Table 7. Qualitative oral health indicators and data collection of the included studies.

Study	MI Country of Birth	NMI Country of Birth
Aarabi et al. 2018 [34]	• Use of dental care services/barriers • Oral hygiene behavior	Face to face interview: 18 questions corresponding to the German Oral Health Sruvey (DMS) IV (Micheelis and Schiffner 2006)
Agudelo-Suárez et al. 2019 [35]	• OHRQoL • Self-perceived dental caries/gingival bleeding/use of oral health services	OHIP-14 instrument [64]: 14 questions on impact of oral condition on people's quality of life
Al Haboubi et al. 2013 [36]	• Use of dental care services (NICE guidelines)	Home interview with a structured questionnaire
Arora et al. 2017 [37]	• Use of dental care services • Self-reported oral health	ADHS 2009 model [61]
Dujister et al. 2015 [39]	• Parents' dental health efficacy • Dental health-related Locus of control (Loc)	Validate questionnaire by Pine et al.
Erdsiek et al. 2017 [40]	• Use of dental check-ups in the 12c months prior to the interview (dichotomous variable)	Secondary analysis from the cross-sectional telephone survey "German Health Update 2010" by Robert Koch Institute [65]
Freiberg et al. 2020 [56]	• Dental healthcare utilization	Handwritten medical reports at Dental Department at Martin-Luther-University Halle-Wittenberg (Halle, Germany) from 1 January 2015 to 31 December 2015
Goetz et al. 2018 [43]	• Year of last dental visit • Regular visits to a dentist during childhood • Daily dental hygiene/access to dental hygiene products • Oral pain	Questionnaire
Høyvik et al. 2019 [44]	• Self-perceived oral health • Dental habits • OIDP	Oral questions for self-perceived oral health/utilization of dental services Opened questions about dental habits Questionnaire for OIDP with 8 questions

Table 7. *Cont.*

Study	MI Country of Birth	NMI Country of Birth
Mattila et al. 2016 [47]	• Oral health and use of dental care services • Oral health related habits • Dental fear	Interview of 30 min with closed and opened questions
Mustafa et al. 2020 [48]	• Parental oral health behaviors Following the Aizen's Theory of Planned Behavior (TPB) [66]; • Intention to brush child's teeth twice a day • Subjective norms towards child's toothbrushing twice a day • Perceived behavioral control Based on health belief model [67]: • Indulgence	Face to face interview of 15–20 min
Portero de la Cruz et al. 2020 [49]	• Use of dental services • Dental problems	Spanish National Health Survey 2017 [68]
Solyman et al. 2018 [52]	• Knowledge of toothbrushing and flossing • Attitude towards oral health practices of oral hygiene	Questionnaire proposed by WHO consisting of 11 opened questions [69]
Van Meljeen-van Lunteren et al. 2019 [54]	• OHRQoL	COHIP-ortho/COHIP-11
Wigen et al. 2010 [55]	• Parents' oral health behavior • Parents' attitude to oral health	Questionnaire

COHIP-11/ortho = Child Oral Health Impact Profile; OHRQoL = Oral Health Related Quality of Life; OIDP = oral impact on daily performance.

Table 8. Assessment of sociodemographic/socioeconomic status (SDS/SES), association between SDS/SES and quantitative/qualitative oral health indicators (QnOHI/QlOHI).

Study	Assessment of SDS	NMI Country of Birth	Association between SDS/SES and QnOHI of MI	Association between SDS/SES and QlOHI of MI
Aarabi et al. 2018 [34]	Non specified: face to face interview	Non specified: face to face interview	Logistic regression adjusted for gender, age, monthly net income, education: OR (95% CI) were reported	Logistic regression adjusted for gender, age, monthly net income, education: Coefficient (95% CI) were reported
Agudelo-Suárez et al. 2019 [35]	Structured questionnaire [70]	Based on: Social class classification → Spanish National Classification of Occupations 2011 using neo-Weberian and neo-Marxist approaches (Domingo-Salvany et al. 2013 [71])	/	Multivariate logistic regression analyses: association between SDS/SES and OHIP-4 dimension: - Unadjusted (crude OR) 1. Unadjusted OR by age, education, marital status, social class 2. Adjusted OR for oral health variables
Al Haboubi et al. 2013 [36]	Home interview with a structured questionnaire	Home interview with a structured questionnaire	/	Poisson regression models with robust variance: PR (95% CI) were reported
Arora et al. 2017 [37]	ADHS 2009 model [61]	ADHS 2009 model [61]	Logistic regression models adjusted for age, sex, education level, housing tenure, area socioeconomic deprivation quintile, area of residence	Logistic regression models adjusted for age, sex, education level, housing tenure, area socioeconomic deprivation quintile, area of residence
Delgado-Angulo et al. 2018 [38]	Supervised questionnaire	Supervised questionnaire: Education and the National Statistics Socio-Economic Classification (NS-SEC) were used for SEP indicators	Negative binomial regression adjusted for ethnicity, SEP, sex, age	/
Dujister et al. 2015 [39]	Self-report validate questionnaire	Self-report validate questionnaire	/	Logistic regression analysis: association of parental and family-related variables with the dental condition

Table 8. *Cont.*

Study	Assessment of SDS	NMI Country of Birth	Association between SDS/SES and QnOHI of MI	Association between SDS/SES and QlOHI of MI
Erdsiek et al. 2017 [40]	Secondary analysis from the cross-sectional telephone survey "German Health Update 2010" by Robert Koch Institute [65]	Secondary analysis from the cross-sectional telephone survey "German Health Update 2010" by Robert Koch Institute [65]	/	Multiple logistic regression models adjusted for age, gender, socioeconomic status, type of insurance
Ferrazzano et al. 2019 [41]	Questionnaire	ISEE certification for family's annual income	One-way ANOVA test: association between DMFT and mothers' education level	/
Freiberg et al. 2020 [56]	Handwritten medical reports at Dental Department at Martin-Luther—University Halle-Wittenberg (Halle, Germany) from 1 January 2015 to 31 December 2015	Handwritten medical reports at Dental Department at Martin-Luther—University Halle-Wittenberg (Halle, Germany) from 1 January 2015 to 31 December 2015	/	/
Gatou et al. 2011 [42]	Schools' archives	Ministry of Economy and Finance, based on the household's income statements of 2006	Binary logistic regression for caries prevalence adjusted for age, gender, ethnic background, residence area, area-based income: OR (95% CI) were reportedOrdinal logistic regression for DMFT/dmft adjusted for age, gender, ethnic background, residence area, area-based income: OR (95% CI) were reported	/
Goetz et al. 2018 [43]	Questionnaire	/	/	/
Høyvik et al. 2019 [44]	Not specified	Not specified	Multiple linear regression for OIDP adjusted for age, gender, education level	Multiple linear regression for DMFT/DT adjusted for age, gender, education level

Table 8. *Cont.*

Study	Assessment of SDS	NMI Country of Birth	Association between SDS/SES and QnOHI of MI	Association between SDS/SES and QIOHI of MI
Jacobsson et al. 2011 [45]	Not specified	Not specified	Logistic regression for dental caries adjusted for age, gender, parents' education level: OR (95% CI) were reported	/
Julihn et al. 2010 [57]	Swedish National Registers	Education National Register (for parents' education level) Total Enumeration Income Register for social-welfare allowance family income	Bivariate logistic regression analysis for DMFD adjusted for age, gender, parents' country of birth, parents' marital status, parents' education level, social welfare allowance income. OR (95% CI) were reported	/
Julihn et al. 2021 [58]	Swedish National Board of Health and Welfare and by Statistics Sweden (SCB) registries	Swedish National Board of Health and Welfare and by Statistics Sweden (SCB) registries	Binary logistic regression for deft adjusted by gender, maternal age, number of children, household income level: OR (95% CI) were reported	/
Marcenes et al. 2013 [46]	School records	/	Poisson regression model for dmft/percentage of children with caries, experience adjusted by gender, borough, ethnic group: OR (95% CI) were reported	/
Mattila et al. 2016 [47]	Oral interview	Oral interview	/	/
Mustafa et al. 2020 [48]	Oral interview	Oral interview	/	/
Portero de la Cruz et al. 2020 [49]	Spanish National Health Survey 2017 [68]	Spanish National Health Survey 2017 [68]	/	Nagelkerke's R^2 for use of dental services adjusted by age, gender, size of town residence, type of household, social class: OR (95% CI) were reported
Riatto et al. 2018 [50]	Oral questionnaire proposed by the WHO [72]	/	Pearson correlation between oral health and children's age	/

Table 8. *Cont.*

Study	Assessment of SDS	NMI Country of Birth	Association between SDS/SES and QnOHI of MI	Association between SDS/SES and QlOHI of MI
Roxel et al. 2017 [51]	School records	School records	Negative binomial regression model for dmft/DMFT adjusted by socioeconomic position PR (CI 95%) were reported Probit regression models for gingivitis plaque, periodontal health adjusted for socioeconomic position: PR (CI 95%) were reported	/
Solyman et al. 2018 [52]	Not specified	Not specified	Negative binomial regression model for DMFT adjusted for age, gender, education level, country for origin: Regression coefficient (standard error) was reported Ordered logistic regression for presence for plaque/presence of calculus adjusted for age, gender, education level, country of origin: OR (95% CI) were reported Multilevel mixed-effect generalized linear model for plaque/presence of calculus adjusted for age, gender, education level, country of origin: Regression coefficient (standard error) was reported	Multivariate linear regression for dental knowledge/attitude and practice adjusted for gender, age, education level, country of origin: Regression coefficient (standard error) was reported
Van der Tas et al. 2017 [53]	Questionnaire [73]	Questionnaire [73]	Multinomial logistic regression model for dmft unadjusted for parents' education level/employment status, household income, single parenting, teenage pregnancy: OR (95% CI) were reported	/
Van Meljeen-van Lunteren et al. 2019 [54]	Questionnaire [73]	Questionnaire [73]	/	Linear regression model for OHRQoL adjusted for age, gender, family income, education level,

Table 8. *Cont.*

Study	Assessment of SDS	NMI Country of Birth	Association between SDS/SES and QnOHI of MI	Association between SDS/SES and QlOHI of MI
Wigen et al. 2010 [55]	Questionnaire	Questionnaire	Bivariate logistic regression for dmft adjusted for parents' education level, stratified by parents' country of birth: OR (95% CI) were reported Multiple logistic regression (Nagelkerke R2) for dmft adjusted for parents' oral health behavior/attitude for oral health: OR (95% CI) were reported	/

CI = confidence interval.

Our review included in total 138,607 participants, of which 26,277 were MI and 112,330 were non-migrants (NMI). Country of origin of MI subjects were Africa, Asia, Central and South America and Eastern Europe. The following sociodemographic characteristics of each MI participant were reported: age, gender, religious affiliation and country of origin. Socioeconomic status was also investigated on the basis of education level, social class, marital status, monthly net income, and professional status.

The oral health condition of the selected sample was analyzed using different parameters. The main oral pathologies evaluated by performing clinical oral examination were:

(1) Dental caries
- Decayed Missing Filled Teeth Index/decayed missing filled teeth index (DMFT/dmft)
- Decayed Missing Filled first permanent molars (DMFM)
- Decayed Missing Filled Surfaces (DMFS)
- Early Childhood Caries (ECC)
- Number of teeth with untreated caries into dentine

(2) Periodontal status:
- Approximal Plaque Index (API)
- Debris Index Simplified (DI-S)
- Papillary Bleeding Index (PBI)
- Plaque Index (PI) by Silness and Loe (1964)
- Gingival status and bleeding on gentle probing (Loe and Silness 1963)
- Eichner's Index

(3) Others:
- Presence of natural teeth
- Presence of denture
- Unmet Treatment Needs (UTN)
- Presence of dental trauma
- Dean's Index for enamel fluorosis

Questionnaires, face to face interview and phone interviews were conducted in order to investigate self-reported oral health, use of dental care services, oral hygiene habits and oral health related quality of life (OHRQoL). Due to the heterogeneity of methodologies used for the oral health condition assessment, results were reported in descriptive way.

3.3. Results of Individual Studies

Quantitative data about the oral health of the MI population sample are reported in Tables 9 and 10. Results grouped by single country are presented in Tables 11–15. DMFT/dmft Index was the most used parameter to assess the presence of dental caries [34,35,38,41–44,46,50,52]. Periodontal health was evaluated using Approximal Plaque Index (API), Simplified Debris Index (DI-s), Papillar Bleeding Index (PBI), Plaque indices grades 2 and 3 (Silness and Loe 1964) (PLI) and Gingival indices grades 2 and 3 (gingival bleeding on gentle probing, Loe and Silness, 1963) [34,42,45,51,52].

Table 9. Dental caries in MI and NMI: dmft/DMFT, UTN, dsf/DFS, DMFSa. *Mean ±SD, Mean (CI 95%), %, Median (range).*

Study	Clinical Index	MI Mean ± SD; Mean (CI 95%); %; Median (Range)	NMI Mean ± SD; Mean (CI 95%); %; Median (Range)	*p* Value
Aarabi et al. 2018 [34]	DMFT	24.8 ± 3.9	23.4 ± 4.6	0.093
Ferrazzano et al. 2019 [41]	DMFT UTN	3.92 ± 2.92 86.3%	3.29 ± 3.21 68.4%	0.027
Gatou et al. 2011 [42]	dmft/DMFT	3.68 ± 0.13/1.14 ± 0.06	1.61 ± 0.04/0.61 ± 0.02	0.001
Goetz et al. 2018 [43]	DMFT	6.89 ± 5.5	/	/
Høyvik et al. 2019 [44]	DMFT	Middle East:10.7 ± 6.8 Africa: 5.7 ± 4.3	/	0.001
Jacobsson et al. 2011 [45]	Dfs/DFS	dfs/DFS in the different age group: 3 yo = 4.5 (1.8–7.1) 5 yo = 8.5 (4.7–12.3) 10 yo = 7.0 (4.8–9.2) 15 yo = 18.1 (13.2–23.0)	dfs/DFS in the different age group: 3 yo = 0.6 (0.3–1.0) 5 yo = 2.7 (1.4–3.9) 10 yo = 5.5 (4.8–6.2) 15 yo = 18.2 (15.1–21.2)	0.008 0.006 0.196 0.985
Julihn et al. 2010 [57]	DMFSa	DMFSa in the different age group (foreign-born adolescents with ≥1 foreign-born parents): 13 yo = 0.58 ± 1.34 19 yo = 2.77 ± 4.16	DMFSa in the different age group (adolescents with two Swedish-born parents): 13 yo = 0.24 ± 0.77 19 yo = 1.31 ± 2.68	/
	DMFSa increment > 0	DMFSa increment in foreign-born adolescents with ≥1 foreign-born parents: 53.9	DMFSa in adolescents with two Swedish-born parents: 34.7	
Julihn et al. 2021 [58]	Presence of caries into dentin	Children with: one or both parents foreign-born: 6.3% from high HDI: 7.2% from medium HDI: 16.7% from low HDI: 16.8%	Children with both parents born in Sweden: 3.0%	/

Table 9. *Cont.*

Study	Clinical Index	MI Mean ± SD; Mean (CI 95%); %; Median (Range)	NMI Mean ± SD; Mean (CI 95%); %; Median (Range)	*p* Value
Marcenes et al. 2013 [46]	dmft	Eastern European: 2.56 (1.12–3.99) Black African: 0.56 (0.26–0.87) Asian Indian: 0.84 (0.95, 1.56) Bangladeshi: 1.25 (0.94–1.83) Pakistani: 1.39 (0.24–1.07) Asian Other: 0.66 (0.04–1.10) Middle Eastern: 1.30 (0.34–2.24)	White British: 0.60 (0.29–0.92) (prevalence rate ratios (95% CI = 1))	0.001 0.85 0.30 0.01 0.004 0.85 0.09
	Number of teeth with untreated caries into dentine (dt)	Eastern European: 1.91 (0.75–3.09) Black African: 0.54 (0.23, 0.84) Asian Indian: 0.82 (0.53–1.12) Bangladeshi: 1.05 (0.80–1.29) Pakistani: 1.11 (0.83–1.40) Asian Other: 0.59 (0.20–0.99) Middle Eastern: 1.19 (0.22–2.17)	White British: 0.56 (0.25–0.87) (prevalence rate ratios (95% CI = 1))	0.006 0.89 0.28 0.04 0.03 0.91 0.12
Riatto et al. 2018 [50]	DMFT	Caucasian: 2.7 ± 3.6 Arabian: 3.5 ± 3.6	/	<0.05
Rouxel et al. 2018 [51]	DT (Decayed Teeth)	Indian: 2.83 ± 2.52 Pakistani: 3.04 ± 3.51 Bangladeshi: 2.52 ± 2.77 Black African: 0.81 ± 1.20 Black Caribbean:1.65 ± 1.52	White British & Irish: 1.48 ± 2.46	/
	FT (Filled Teeth)	Indian: 0.17 ± 0.39 Pakistani: 0.18 ± 0.55 Bangladeshi 0.20 ± 0.79 Black African:0.31 ± 0.96 Black Caribbean: 0.04 ± 0.21	White British & Irish: 0.09 ± 0.45	
Solyman et al. 2018 [52]	DMFT	6.38 ± 5.058	/	/

DFS = Decayed Filled Tooth Surfaces for Permanent Dentition; deft = decayed extracted filled primary teeth; dfs/DFS proximal = decayed filled tooth proximal surfaces; DMFSa = Decayed Missing Filled Surfaces approximal; DMFT = Decayed Missing Filled Permanent Teeth; dmft = decayed missing filled primary teeth; HDI = Human Development Index pufa index = pulpal involvement, ulceration, fistula and abscess in severly decayed primary teeth;; UTN = unment restorative treatment.

Table 10. Periodontal parameters in MI and NMI: API, PBI, DI-s. PLI, GI, presence of plaque and calculus on six sextants.

Study	Clinical Index	IM (Mean ± SD); Mean (CI 95%)	NIM (Mean ± SD); Mean (CI 95%)	*p* Value
Aarabi et al. 2018 [34]	API PBI	55.3 ± 32.3 46.3 ± 21.1	33.0 ± 28.2) 30.5 ± 4.5	0.002 0.016
Gatou et al. 2011 [42]	DI-s	0.94 ± 0.03	0.72 ± 0.01	0.001
Jacobsson et al. 2011 [45]	PLI	PI in the different age group: 3 yo = 13.5 (3.4–23.5) 5 yo = 13.6 (4.6–22.5) 10 yo = 53.1 (35.4–70.8) 15 yo = 31.8 (18.1–45.5)	PI in the different age group: 3 yo = 7.3 (4.2–10.3) 5 yo = 9.4 (6.7–12.0) 10 yo = 28.5 (22.3–34.7) 15 yo = 32.5 (25.8–39.2)	0.125 0.355 0.012 0.927
	GI	BoP in the different age group: 3 yo = 14.6 (7.9–21.2) 5 yo = 11.9 6.9–16.8 10 yo = 26.1 (20.2–32.0) 15 yo = 22.5 (14.7–30.4)	BoP in the different age group: 3 yo = 4.4 (3.5–5.3) 5 yo = 8.7 (6.9–19.5) 10 yo = 17.2 (14.5–20.0) 15 yo = 20.8 (16.9–24.7)	0.005 0.152 0.005 0.675
Rouxel et al. 2018 [51]	Gingivitis	Indian: 26.3% Pakistani: 25.1% Bangladeshi: 42.2% Black African: 11.9% Black Caribbean: 15.4%	White British & Irish: 23.3%	
	Plaque	Indian: 31.8% Pakistani: 50.8% Bangladeshi: 56.8% Black African: 25.4% Black Caribbean: 27.0%	White British & Irish: 32%	
Solyman et al. 2018 [52]	Presence of Plaque on six sextants	78.85%	/	/
	Presence of calculus on six sextants	29.86%	/	

API = Approximal Plaque Index; DI-S = Simplified Debris Index; GI = Gingival indices; MPS = Mucosal Plaque Index; PBI = Papillar Bleeding Index; PLI = Plaque indices grades 2 and 3 (Silness and Loe 1964).

Table 11. Dental caries in MI and NMI living in Germany.

Study	Clinical Index	MI Mean ± SD; Mean (CI 95%); %; Median (Range)	NMI Mean ± SD; Mean (CI 95%); %; Median (Range)	p Value
Aarabi et al. 2018 [34]	DMFT	24.8 ± 3.9	23.4 ± 4.6	0.093
Goetz et al. 2018 [43]	DMFT	6.89 ± 5.5	/	/
Solyman et al. 2018 [52]	DMFT	6.38 ± 5.058	/	/

DMFT = Decayed Missing Filled Permanent Teeth.

Table 12. Periodontal status in MI and NMI living in Germany.

Study	Clinical Index	IM (Mean ± SD); Mean (CI 95%)	NIM (Mean ± SD); Mean (CI 95%)	p Value
Aarabi et al. 2018 [34]	API	55.3 ± 32.3	33.0 ± 28.2)	0.002
	PBI	46.3 ± 21.1	30.5 ± 4.5	0.016
Solyman et al. 2018 [52]	Presence of Plaque on six sextants	78.85%	/	/
	Presence of calculus on six sextants	29.86%	/	

API = Approximal Plaque Index; PBI = Papillar Bleeding Index.

Table 13. Dental caries in MI and NMI living in United Kingdom.

Study	Clinical Index	MI Mean ± SD; Mean (CI 95%); %; Median (Range)	NMI Mean ± SD; Mean (CI 95%); %; Median (Range)	p Value
Marcenes et al. 2013 [46]	dmft	Eastern European: 2.56 (1.12–3.99) Black African: 0.56 (0.26–0.87) Asian Indian: 0.84 (0.95, 1.56) Bangladeshi: 1.25 (0.94–1.83) Pakistani: 1.39 (0.24–1.07) Asian Other: 0.66 (0.04–1.10) Middle Eastern: 1.30 (0.34–2.24)	White British: 0.60 (0.29–0.92) (prevalence rate ratios (95% CI = 1))	0.001 0.85 0.30 0.01 0.004 0.85 0.09
	Number of teeth with untreated caries into dentine (dt)	Eastern European: 1.91 (0.75–3.09) Black African: 0.54 (0.23, 0.84) Asian Indian: 0.82 (0.53–1.12) Bangladeshi: 1.05 (0.80–1.29) Pakistani: 1.11 (0.83–1.40) Asian Other: 0.59 (0.20–0.99) Middle Eastern: 1.19 (0.22–2.17)	White British: 0.56 (0.25–0.87) (prevalence rate ratios (95% CI = 1))	0.006 0.89 0.28 0.04 0.03 0.91 0.12

Table 13. *Cont.*

Study	Clinical Index	MI Mean ± SD; Mean (CI 95%); %; Median (Range)	NMI Mean ± SD; Mean (CI 95%); %; Median (Range)	*p* Value
Rouxel et al. 2018 [51]	DT (Decayed Teeth)	Indian: 2.83 ± 2.52 Pakistani: 3.04 ± 3.51 Bangladeshi: 2.52 ±2.77 Black African: 0.81 ± 1.20 Black Caribbean:1.65 ± 1.52	White British & Irish: 1.48 ± 2.46	/
	FT (Filled Teeth)	Indian: 0.17 ± 0.39 Pakistani: 0.18 ± 0.55 Bangladeshi 0.20 ± 0.79 Black African:0.31 ± 0.96 Black Caribbean: 0.04 ± 0.21	White British & Irish: 0.09 ± 0.45	

DMFT = Decayed Missing Filled Permanent Teeth; dmft = decayed missing filled primary teeth.

Table 14. Dental caries and periodontal status in MI and NMI living Spain, Italy and Greece.

Study	Clinical Index	MI Mean ± SD; Mean (CI 95%); %; Median (Range)	NMI Mean ± SD; Mean (CI 95%); %; Median (Range)	*p* Value
Ferrazzano et al. 2019 (Italy) [41]	DMFT	3.92 ± 2.92	3.29 ± 3.21	0.027
	UTN	86.3%	68.4%	
Riatto et al. 2018 (Spain) [50]	DMFT	Caucasian: 2.7 ± 3.6 Arabian: 3.5 ± 3.6	/	<0.05
Gatou et al. 2011 (Greece) [42]	dmft/DMFT	3.68 ± 0.13/1.14 ± 0.06	1.61 ± 0.04/0.61 ± 0.02	0.001
	DI-s	0.94 ± 0.03	0.72 ± 0.01	0.001

DI-S = Simplified Debris Index; DMFT = Decayed Missing Filled Permanent Teeth; dmft = decayed missing filled primary teeth; UTN = unment restorative treatment.

Table 15. Dental caries and periodontal status in MI and NMI living Norway and Sweden.

Study	Clinical Index	MI Mean ± SD; Mean (CI 95%); %; Median (Range)	NMI Mean ± SD; Mean (CI 95%); %; Median (Range)	*p* Value
Høyvik et al. 2019 (Norway) [44]	DMFT	Middle East:10.7 ± 6.8 Africa: 5.7 ± 4.3	/	0.001
Jacobsson et al. 2011 (Sweden) [45]	Dfs/DFS	dfs/DFS in the different age group: 3 yo = 4.5 (1.8–7.1) 5 yo = 8.5 (4.7–12.3) 10 yo = 7.0 (4.8–9.2) 15 yo = 18.1 (13.2–23.0)	dfs/DFS in the different age group: 3 yo = 0.6 (0.3–1.0) 5 yo = 2.7 (1.4–3.9) 10 yo = 5.5 (4.8–6.2) 15 yo = 18.2 (15.1–21.2)	0.008 0.006 0.196 0.985
	PLI	PLI in the different age group: 3 yo = 13.5 (3.4–23.5) 5 yo = 13.6 (4.6–22.5) 10 yo = 53.1 (35.4–70.8) 15 yo = 31.8 (18.1–45.5)	PLI in the different age group: 3 yo = 7.3 (4.2–10.3) 5 yo = 9.4 (6.7–12.0) 10 yo = 28.5 (22.3–34.7) 15 yo = 32.5 (25.8–39.2)	0.125 0.355 0.012 0.927
	GI	BoP in the different age group: 3 yo = 14.6 (7.9–21.2) 5 yo = 11.9 6.9–16.8 10 yo = 26.1 (20.2–32.0) 15 yo = 22.5 (14.7–30.4)	BoP in the different age group: 3 yo = 4.4 (3.5–5.3) 5 yo = 8.7 (6.9–19.5) 10 yo = 17.2 (14.5–20.0) 15 yo = 20.8 (16.9–24.7)	0.005 0.152 0.005 0.675
Julihn et al. 2010 (Sweden) [57]	DMFSa	DMFSa in the different age group (foreign-born adolescents with ≥1 foreign-born parents): 13 yo = 0.58 ± 1.34 19 yo = 2.77 ± 4.16	DMFSa in the different age group (adolescents with two Swedish-born parents): 13 yo = 0.24 ± 0.77 19 yo = 1.31 ± 2.68	/
	DMFSa increment > 0	DMFSa increment in foreign-born adolescents with ≥1 foreign-born parents: 53.9	DMFSa in adolescents with two Swedish-born parents: 34.7	
Julihn et al. 2021 (Sweden) [58]	Presence of caries into dentin	Children with: one or both parents foreign-born: 6.3% from high HDI: 7.2% from medium HDI: 16.7% from low HDI: 16.8%	Children with both parents born in Sweden: 3.0%	/

DFS = Decayed Filled Tooth Surfaces for Permanent Dentition; dfs/DFS proximal = decayed filled tooth proximal surfaces; DMFSa = Decayed Missing Filled Surfaces approximal; DMFT = Decayed Missing Filled Permanent Teeth; GI = Gingival indices; PLI = Plaque indices grades 2 and 3 (Silness and Loe 1964).

The DMFT of MI and NMI in the research by Aarabi et al. [34] were equal to 24.8 ± 3.9 and 23.4 ± 4.6, respectively (p value 0.093): the number of missing teeth (M) was similar in both groups, while the number of decayed teeth (D) was on average three times higher in MI subjects. After adjusting for gender, age, monthly net income and education, the number of decayed teeth in MI was higher than NMI. The higher values of API and PBI in MI group (API = 55.3 ± 32.3, p value 0.002; PBI = 46.3 ± 21.1, p value 0.016) demonstrate that the latter had a poorer oral hygiene compared with the native control group (API = 33.0 ± 28.2, p value 0.002; PBI = 30.5 ± 4.5, p value 0.016).

Delgado-Angulo et al. [38] associated the DMFT Index with ethnicity, nativity status and socio-economic position (SEP): Black and Asian MI had lower DMFT than White British and ethnic differences in DMFT remained significant after adjusting for SEP measures. Among MI, the higher the age of arrival and the longer the residence in the UK, the greater the DMFT (adjusted RR: 1.03 and 1.04 per additional year).

Marcenes et al. [46] highlighted that White European, Bangladeshi and Pakistani children had significantly higher dmft scores and number of untreated caries into dentine (mean dmft: 2.56, 1.25 and 1,39 respectively; mean dt: 1.91, 1.05, 1.11 respectively) than White British individuals (mean dmft: 0,60; mean dt: 0.56).

The number of decayed and filled teeth in MI children in the study by Ferrazzano et al. [41] were significantly higher (2.49 ± 1.98 and 0.56 ±1.10, p value < 0001) than those in NMI children (1.16 ± 1.35 and 0.38 ± 1.98, p value < 0001) also after adjusting for the educational level of the mothers. The unmet restorative treatment needs (UTN) in native children were lower compared to MI children (68.4% and 86.3% respectively).

Higher odds ratio of caries prevalence was found to be associated with higher age, immigrant background (OR = 2.65–4.40) and with living in lower income areas (OR = 1.34–1.72) in the article by Gatou et al. [42].

The mean DMFT of the 102 MI included by Goetz et al. [43] was equal to 6.89 ± 5.5 and only 13.7% of the refugees had a healthy dentition.

Høyvik et al. [44] registered a mean DMFT of 10.7 ± 6.8 in MI from the Middle East and of 5.7 ± 4.3 in African refugees. After adjusting for age, gender, origin and level of education, DMFT scores remained higher in Middle East subjects.

Jacobsson et al. [45] analyzed the oral health status of 154 MI and 585 native Swedish participants aged 3, 5, 10 and 15 years in 1993 and 2003: the Plaque indices (PLI) and the Gingival indices (GI) were higher in all age groups among MI group, compared to the NMI one, except the 15-year-olds. Both in 1993 and 2009, significantly less 3 and 5 year-olds in the MI group were caries-free compared with native subjects of the same age.

Julihn et al. (2010) [57] selected a cohort of 15538 adolescents aged 13 years (14,160 NMI, 1378 MI) and followed them until they were 19 years of age. The authors showed that MI adolescents with foreign-born parents had statistically significantly more caries compared to NMI adolescents with both parents born in Sweden. The same research recorded a higher DMFSa increment in MI adolescents with 1 or more parents born abroad (53.9) compared to NMI individuals with both Swedish parents (34.7). After adjusting for sociodemographic and socioeconomic confounders (age at migration, maternal/paternal birth region, maternal/paternal education level, marital status, family income, social welfare allowance), the study found out that subjects from Eastern Europe had a higher risk of developing approximal caries lesions during the follow-up period compared to NMI participants (OR = 1.44 (1.12–1.85)).

In 2021 Julihn et al. [58] followed a sample of 3 year-old children until they were 7 years of age, demonstrating that children with both NMI parents (born in Sweden) had a lower caries experience at 3 and 7 years of age (0.1 ± 0.6 and 0.5 ± 1.3 respectively) than children with MI parents. The risk of caries experience at age 7 years was adjusted for household income level and, with regards to the lowest income, OR (CI 95%) of children with both parents born in Sweden was equal to 1.49 (1.37–1.63), OR of children with parents from high-medium-low human development countries (according to Human Development Index, HDI) resulted to be 2.89 (1.64–5.09), 1.69 (1.31–2.17) and 1.90 (1.14–3.15) respectively.

The global DMFT was calculated to be higher in Arab individuals (3.5 ± 3.6) than in Caucasian migrants (2.7 ± 3.6) by Riatto et al. [50].

Rouxel et al. [51] highlighted the association between Decayed Teeth (DT) and ethnicity/socioeconomic position (SEP): the predicted rate for MI children from India and Pakistan (3.71 (1.08–6.34) and 2.85 (1.85–3.85) respectively) was about 2–2.5 times higher than those for White British/Irish children aged 5 (1.51 (1.30–1.77)).

Solyman et al. [52] analyzed the oral health of refugees from Syria and Iraq living in Germany (aged 18–60 years), reporting a mean DMFT = 6.38 ± 5.058 and demonstrating that DMFT score was significantly associated with age and with education level ((Regression Coefficient −0.019, p value 0.037). This study also reported that 79% of the selected participants had bacterial plaque in all six sextants and that 60% of them presented calculus in at least three sextants.

According to Wigen et al. [55], a 5-year-old children in Norway had a higher risk of developing caries into dentine if they had one or both parents of non-western origin (OR = 4.8) and one (OR = 2.1) or both parents (OR = 3.0) with low education.

Results about the use of dentalcare services by MI and NMI were contradictory: two thirds of the MI population included by Aarabi et al. [34] showed difficulties in accessing dental care because of costs and language barriers, presenting a poorer oral hygiene than NMI group; a greater dental services utilization (in United Kingdom) was observed by Al-Haboubi et al. [36] among Asian subjects compared to White and Black individuals. The same authors underlined that access to dental services decreased in lower social classes. On the contrary, Asian and Black participants of the article by Arora et al. [37] declared that they attended dental clinics only if they suffered symptoms (unlike White British people) and their oral hygiene practices, after adjusting for age, sex, education level, household tenure and other confounders, were poorer than the NMI population. Likewise, asylum seekers in Germany selected by Freiberg et al. [56] visited dentists only because of localized and non-localized pain. According to the research by Erdsiek et al. [40], MI adults presented lower socioeconomic status and lower utilization of dental check-ups than NMI individuals. A generally poor oral health was also recorded by Høyvik et al. [44] in refugees from Middle East and Africa to Norway, half of which had oral impacts on daily performances.

Mattila et al. [47] evaluated the utilization of dental care services among MI and asylum seekers in Finland and found that the latter (100%) were significantly less satisfied with access to dental treatment and the quality of treatment than MI (18%). In total, 48% and 11% of the MI and asylum seekers groups, respectively, were aware of caries prevention methods, and none of the asylum seekers knew how to prevent gingival bleeding, while 7% of the MI did.

MI and NMI children in Spain between 3 and 14 years old were compared by Portero de la Cruz et al. [49]: 51.78% and 35.43% of MI and NMI children did not use dental services for over a year respectively. According to socioeconomic and demographic variables, lower social classes and 3–6-year-olds were less likely to use regular dental check-ups.

Dental hygiene was practiced once per day by 44.1% of the refugees studied by Goetz et al. [43] and only 4.9% of them visited dental clinics twice per year during childhood.

Agudelo-Suárez et al. [35]. and Van Meljeren-van Lunteren et al. [56] assessed the OHRQoL of MI population in Spain and Netherlands, respectively. Surinamese and Turkish children showed significant lower OHRQoL than native Dutch children, after adjusting for age, gender of children, caries experience, family income and education level of the mother. On the contrary, the MI group in the Spanish study reported a general low impact of oral health on quality of life.

Mustafa et al. [48] investigated toothbrushing-related perceptions of parents living in Norway with MI background and found that 40% of parents have knowledge about caries as a common disease among children and that 80% of them are aware of the importance of toothbrushing in primary teeth. Moreover, it was demonstrated that oral attitudes were more favorable among MI who had lived in Norway for more than 6 years.

Dujister et al. [39] studied the association existing between parental and family-related factors and childhood dental caries in Moroccan, Turkish and Dutch children. Lower social class was significantly associated with more external locus of control (LoC), poorer parental oral hygiene practices and lower dental self-efficacy and, moreover, Moroccan and Turkish parents presented a more external LoC compared to native Dutch parents.

4. Discussion

Our review aimed to assess the oral health status, oral health habits and use of dentalcare services among migrant population from middle- and low-income countries to Europe. Data collected in our review highlighted, in general, a higher prevalence of dental caries [34,42,45,46,51,57,58] and a poorer periodontal condition [34,42,45,51] in MI population compared with NMI groups. The impact of inequalities in terms of socioeconomic status have been largely studied in literature [74]. The research conducted in Sweden in 2006 [75] hypothesized and demonstrated that the low socioeconomic status could limit access to dentalcare services, contributing to the social inequalities in oral health. Consequently, if socioeconomic position is linked to health status, it can be stated that inequalities in socioeconomic position could be associated to ethnic inequalities in health [76]. Borrel et al. (USA) [77] examined the relationship between individual and socioeconomic characteristics and periodontal disease and highlighted that low income and low education level were associated with severe periodontitis among Whites and African Americans.

The MI population studied by Aarabi et al. [34] (coming from East Europe, Africa, Asia and South America) had a lower socioeconomic status, a worse oral health and higher treatment needs compare to NMI individuals.

Similarly, 38% of the participants (White British/Irish, Black and Asian) included in the research by Al-Haboubi et al. [36] belonged to the lowest social grade (semi- and unskilled manual workers, state pensioners, casual or lowest-grade workers, unemployed with state benefits only): the authors assessed that dental services use decreased with decreasing social grade.

Erdsiek et al. [40] found a lower access to dentalcare services in Germany among MI, 53.8% and 17.8% of whom had a middle and low socioeconomic status respectively. Authors confirmed that having a higher socioeconomic status was associated with greater use of dental prevention.

The review by Scheppers et al. [78] investigated the potential barriers and factors that could interfere with the access to health services among ethnic minorities: low education, social and socioeconomic status, ethnic background, lack of financial resources and family/social support, cultural perception about symptoms, differences in health beliefs, language skills and unawareness of service availability.

For instance, Portero de la Cruz et al. [49] attributed the disparities in the utilization of dentalcare between MI and native Spanish group to the cultural differences regarding the way families seek dental health care and to the lack of information about health benefits.

Gatou et al. [42] estimated that children's ethnic background was the most strongly affecting risk factor for all the oral health parameters investigated in the study and reported that this relation became stronger when adjusted for independent variables, such as area-based income.

The higher caries prevalence proper of the MI group in the research by Ferrazzano et al. [41] was associated with language difficulties and inequalities in access to information and to health services.

Marcenes et al. [46] examined the inequalities in oral health between Whites, Blacks and Asians living in the most deprived boroughs in the Inner North East London: preschool children from Bangladesh and Pakistan presented a higher level of caries than White children (British, Eastern European), but, on the contrary, Indian children showed a lower level of caries than White children and Black individuals had similar dental health to Whites.

Data obtained in this research confirmed the information provided by other authors, underlining that African countries experience a lower caries level than the United Kingdom [79].

Our review included thirteen articles analyzing the oral heath in children/adolescents with age ranging from 0 to 19 years old [39,42,45,46,48–51,53–55,57,58]. Almost all the studies [39,42,45,46,49,51,54,55] recorded a better oral condition in native children of the control groups compared to the MI groups. Only Mustafa et al. [47] assessed a good knowledge about the importance of oral hygiene among MI parents, showing that they had on average favorable attitudes, subjective norms and strong perception of behavioral control in relation to child tooth brushing.

The oral hygiene practices and behaviors of parents has a direct influence on their children's oral health [80]. According to the socialization theory, family represents the primary socializing agent for children and, consequently, it is easy to explain why the latter adopt oral health-related habits [48]. Mothers and fathers with a foreign background are characterized by different cultures and tradition [45], migrating from their country of origin and facing several social and economic problems: this type of conditions may affect the general health of their children [78]. Julihn et al. [58] supported this theory, demonstrating that the social context of MI families from medium- and low-human development countries could be considered unfavorable for children's oral health. Furthermore, Al-Haj Ali et al. [81] determined the risk factors associated with the presence of ECC among preschool children in eastern Saudi Arabia: mother's occupation, carer's smoking status and feeding practices.

The data about the lack of good oral health among refugees included in five of the selected items [43,44,50,52] are in line with other studies published in literature, which reported a high prevalence of dental caries, periodontal diseases and poor oral hygiene [82–85]. Refugees left their country of origin because of fear of persecution and/or could not return because they were exposed to persecutory events; they migrate to other countries carrying around weighty problems, facing racism, homelessness, economic and language difficulties [86]. In such condition, since refugees have to face more pressing problems than oral health, they show a tendency to under-utilize dental services [87,88].

This review highlighted, in agreement with the literature, that oral health is one of the greatest unmet health needs of migrants [89]. Since oral health strongly influences quality of life, training and education programs about oral health prevention should be implemented [90], considering individuals' attitudes, capabilities, beliefs and cultural/ethnic background [91].

Strengths and Limitations of the Study

Our study not only provides an overview of the oral health conditions of migrants in Europe, but also analyzed the association between the prevalence of oral pathologies and risk factors of the target population. After performing a critical appraisal, we recorded that most of the selected papers presented a very high quality with regards to sample selection, reliability of measurement methodologies and statistical analysis. However, the included articles used different methods to determine oral health status and as a consequence, the results were presented in a descriptive way. In fact, due to this heterogeneity, it was not possible to provide an appropriate statistical analysis. Furthermore, the selected items conducted their research in different European countries, presenting different social security systems and social conditions. For this reason, we considered this systematic review as an initial analysis that should be followed by another study investigating the oral health status of migrants in a single host country or countries with similar social conditions.

5. Conclusions

This systematic review reported a poorer oral condition in MI subjects from middle- and low-income countries to Europe. Oral health parameters were analyzed in association with ethnicity and socioeconomic status: it was demonstrated that foreign background, low income and social grade could be considered as risk factors for having a worse dental health.

The creation of prevention programs becomes of primary concern, aiming at strengthening oral health knowledge and practices among the MI population.

Author Contributions: Conceptualization, D.L. and F.C.; methodology, G.M.; validation, V.C., investigation, G.M.; data curation, F.D.V.; writing—original draft preparation, D.L. and G.M.; writing—review and editing D.L. and G.M.; visualization, M.P.; supervision, F.C.; funding acquisition, F.C. All authors have read and agreed to the published version of the manuscript.

Funding: This research was funded by University of Ferrara, 44121 Ferrara, Italy; research grant 8/2021, titled "Dental caries prevention and screening among socially vulnerable subjects with difficult access to care".

Institutional Review Board Statement: Not applicable.

Informed Consent Statement: Informed consent was obtained from all subjects involved in the study.

Data Availability Statement: Not applicable.

Conflicts of Interest: The authors declare no conflict of interest.

References

1. United Nations, Department of Economic and Social Affairs. International Migration Report 2017: Highlights (ST/ESA/SER.A/403). 2017. Available online: https://www.un.org/en/development/desa/population/migration/publications/migrationreport/docs/MigrationReport2017_Highlights.pdf (accessed on 20 August 2021).
2. 2019 International Organization for Migration (IOM). World Migration Report. 2020. Available online: https://publications.iom.int/system/files/pdf/wmr_2020.pdf (accessed on 9 November 2020).
3. United Nations, Department of Economic and Social Affairs. International Migration Report 2015: Highlighlts. 2015. Available online: https://www.un.org/en/development/desa/population/migration/publications/migrationreport/docs/MigrationReport2015_Highlights.pdf (accessed on 21 August 2021).
4. Trost, M.; Wanke, E.M.; Ohlendorf, D.; Klingelhöfer, D.; Braun, M.; Bauer, J.; A Groneberg, D.; Quarcoo, D.; Brüggmann, D. Immigration: Analysis, trends and outlook on the global research activity. *J. Glob. Health* **2018**, *8*, 010414. [CrossRef]
5. Eurostat, Statistics Explained. Migration and Migrant Population Statistics. 2021. Available online: https://ec.europa.eu/eurostat/statistics-explained/index.php?title=Migration_and_migrant_population_statistics#Migration_flows:_Immigration_to_the_EU_from_non-member_countries_was_2.7_million_in_2019 (accessed on 4 September 2021).
6. Dao, T.H.; Docquier, F.; Maurel, M.; Schaus, P. Global migration in the twentieth and twenty-first centuries: The unstoppable force of demography. *Rev. World Econ.* **2021**, *157*, 417–449. [CrossRef]
7. Dragioti, E.; Tsamakis, K.; Larsson, B.; Gerdle, B. Predictive association between immigration status and chronic pain in the general population: Results from the SwePain cohort. *BMC Public Health* **2020**, *20*, 1462. [CrossRef] [PubMed]
8. Schenk, L. Migration and health—Developing an explanatory and analytical model for epidemiological studies. *Int. J. Public Health* **2007**, *52*, 87–96. [CrossRef] [PubMed]
9. Gotsens, M.; Malmusi, D.; Villarroel, N.; Vives-Cases, C.; Garcia-Subirats, I.; Hernando, C.; Borrell, C. Health inequality between immigrants and natives in Spain: The loss of the healthy immigrant effect in times of economic crisis. *Eur. J. Public Health* **2015**, *25*, 923–929. [CrossRef]
10. Norredam, M.; Nielsen, S.S.; Krasnik, A. Migrants' utilization of somatic healthcare services in Europe—A systematic review. *Eur. J. Public Health* **2009**, *20*, 555–563. [CrossRef]
11. Dahlan, R.; Ghazal, E.; Saltaji, H.; Salami, B.; Amin, M. Impact of social support on oral health among immigrants and ethnic minorities: A systematic review. *PLoS ONE* **2019**, *14*, e0218678. [CrossRef]
12. Borges, G.; Cherpitel, C.J.; Orozco, R.; Zemore, S.E.; Wallisch, L.; Medina-Mora, M.-E.; Breslau, J. Substance Use and Cumulative Exposure to American Society: Findings From Both Sides of the US-Mexico Border Region. *Am. J. Public Health* **2016**, *106*, 119–127. [CrossRef]
13. Documet, P.I.; Troyer, M.M.; Macia, L. Social Support, Health, and Health Care Access Among Latino Immigrant Men in an Emerging Community. *Health Educ. Behav.* **2019**, *46*, 137–145. [CrossRef]
14. Kowalski, C.; Loss, J.; Kölsch, F.; Janssen, C. Utilization of Prevention Services by Gender, Age, Socioeconomic Status, and Migration Status in Germany: An Overview and a Systematic Review. In *Health Care Utilization in Germany*; Springer: New York, NY, USA, 2013; pp. 293–320. [CrossRef]
15. Batra, M.; Gupta, S.; Erbas, B. Oral Health Beliefs, Attitudes, and Practices of South Asian Migrants: A Systematic Review. *Int. J. Environ. Res. Public Health* **2019**, *16*, 1952. [CrossRef]
16. Riggs, E.; Gussy, M.; Gibbs, L.; van Gemert, C.; Waters, E.; Kilpatrick, N. Hard to reach communities or hard to access services? Migrant mothers' experiences of dental services. *Aust. Dent. J.* **2014**, *59*, 201–207. [CrossRef]

17. Pabbla, A.; Duijster, D.; Grasveld, A.; Sekundo, C.; Agyemang, C.; van der Heijden, G. Oral Health Status, Oral Health Behaviours and Oral Health Care Utilisation Among Migrants Residing in Europe: A Systematic Review. *J. Immigr. Minor. Health* **2021**, *23*, 373–388. [CrossRef]
18. Almerich-Silla, J.M.; Montiel-Company, J.M. Influence of immigration and other factors on caries in 12- and 15-yr-old children. *Eur. J. Oral Sci.* **2007**, *115*, 378–383. [CrossRef] [PubMed]
19. Bissar, A.-R.; Oikonomou, C.; Koch, M.J.; Schulte, A.G. Dental health, received care, and treatment needs in 11- to 13-year-old children with immigrant background in Heidelberg, Germany. *Int. J. Paediatr. Dent.* **2007**, *17*, 364–370. [CrossRef]
20. Brzoska, P.; Erdsiek, F.; Waury, D. Enabling and Predisposing Factors for the Utilization of Preventive Dental Health Care in Migrants and Non-Migrants in Germany. *Front. Public Health* **2017**, *5*, 201. [CrossRef]
21. Hagenfeld, D.; Zimmermann, H.; Korb, K.; El-Sayed, N.; Fricke, J.; Greiser, K.H.; Kühnisch, J.; Linseisen, J.; Meisinger, C.; Schmitter, M.; et al. Periodontal Health and Use of Oral Health Services: A Comparison of Germans and Two Migrant Groups. *Int. J. Environ. Res. Public Health* **2019**, *16*, 3000. [CrossRef] [PubMed]
22. Zinah, E.; Al-Ibrahim, H.M. Oral health problems facing refugees in Europe: A scoping review. *BMC Public Health* **2021**, *21*, 1207. [CrossRef]
23. Croucher, R.; Sohanpal, R. Improving access to dental care in East London's ethnic minority groups: Community based, quali-tative study. *Community Dent. Health* **2006**, *23*, 95–100. [PubMed]
24. Newton, J.T.; Thorogood, N.; Bhavnani, V.; Pitt, J.; Gibbons, D.E.; Gelbier, S. Barriers to the Use of Dental Services by Individuals from Minority Ethnic Communities Living in the United Kingdom: Findings from Focus Groups. *Prim. Dent. Care* **2001**, *8*, 157–161. [CrossRef] [PubMed]
25. Skeie, M.S.; Riordan, P.J.; Klock, K.S.; Espelid, I. Parental risk attitudes and caries-related behaviours among immigrant and western native children in Oslo. *Community Dent. Oral Epidemiol.* **2006**, *34*, 103–113. [CrossRef]
26. Fisher, M.A.; Borgnakke, W.; Taylor, G.W. Periodontal disease as a risk marker in coronary heart disease and chronic kidney disease. *Curr. Opin. Nephrol. Hypertens.* **2010**, *19*, 519–526. [CrossRef] [PubMed]
27. Carramolino-Cuellar, E.; Tomas, I.; Jimenez-Soriano, Y. Relationship between the oral cavity and cardiovascular diseases and metabolic syndrome. *Med. Oral Patol. Oral Cir. Bucal* **2014**, *19*, e289–e294. [CrossRef] [PubMed]
28. Keboa, M.T.; Hiles, N.; Macdonald, M.E. The oral health of refugees and asylum seekers: A scoping review. *Glob. Health* **2016**, *12*, 59. [CrossRef]
29. Alrashdi, M.; Hameed, A.; Cervantes Mendez, M.J.; Farokhi, M. Education intervention with respect to the oral health knowledge, attitude, and behaviors of refugee families: A randomized clinical trial of effectiveness. *J. Public Health Dent.* **2021**, *81*, 90–99. [CrossRef]
30. Tiwari, T.; Albino, J. Acculturation and Pediatric Minority Oral Health Interventions. *Dent. Clin. N. Am.* **2017**, *61*, 549–563. [CrossRef]
31. Mouradian, W.E.; Huebener, C.E.; Ramos-Gomez, F.; Slavkin, H.C. Beyond access: The role of family and community in children's oral health. *J Dent. Educ.* **2007**, *71*, 619–631. [CrossRef]
32. Liberati, A.; Altman, D.G.; Tetzlaff, J.; Mulrow, C.; Gøtzsche, P.C.; Ioannidis, J.P.A.; Clarke, M.; Devereaux, P.; Kleijnen, J.; Moher, D. The PRISMA statement for reporting systematic reviews and meta-analyses of studies that evaluate health care interventions: Explanation and elaboration. *J. Clin. Epidemiol.* **2009**, *62*, e1–e34. [CrossRef] [PubMed]
33. Ma, L.-L.; Wang, X.; Yang, Z.-H.; Huang, D.; Weng, H.; Zeng, X.-T. Methodological quality (risk of bias) assessment tools for primary and secondary medical studies: What are they and which is better? *BMC* **2020**, *7*, 7. [CrossRef]
34. Aarabi, G.; Reissmann, D.R.; Seedorf, U.; Becher, H.; Heydecke, G.; Kofahl, C. Oral health and access to dental care—A comparison of elderly migrants and non-migrants in Germany. *Ethn. Health* **2017**, *23*, 703–717. [CrossRef]
35. Agudelo-Suárez, A.A.; Vivares-Builes, A.M.; Muñoz-Pino, N.; Martínez-Martínez, J.M.; Reid, A.; Ronda-Pérez, E. Oral Health-Related Quality of Life in Native and Immigrant Populations in the PELFI Study in Spain. *Int. J. Environ. Res. Public Health* **2019**, *16*, 1796. [CrossRef] [PubMed]
36. Al-Haboubi, M.; Klass, C.; Jones, K.; Bernabe, E.; Gallagher, J.E. Inequalities in the use of dental services among adults in inner South East London. *Eur. J. Oral Sci.* **2013**, *121*, 176–181. [CrossRef] [PubMed]
37. Arora, G.; Mackay, D.F.; Conway, D.I.; Pell, J.P. Ethnic differences in oral health and use of dental services: Cross-sectional study using the 2009 Adult Dental Health Survey. *BMC Oral Health* **2016**, *17*, 1. [CrossRef]
38. Delgado-Angulo, E.; Marcenes, W.; Harding, S.; Bernabé, E. Ethnicity, migration status and dental caries experience among adults in East London. *Community Dent. Oral Epidemiol.* **2018**, *46*. [CrossRef] [PubMed]
39. Duijster, D.; de Jong-Lenters, M.; de Ruiter, C.; Thijssen, J.; van Loveren, C.; Verrips, E.; Jong-Lenters, M. Parental and family-related influences on dental caries in children of Dutch, Moroccan and Turkish origin. *Community Dent. Oral Epidemiol.* **2014**, *43*, 152–162. [CrossRef]
40. Erdsiek, F.; Waury, D.; Brzoska, P. Oral health behaviour in migrant and non-migrant adults in Germany: The utilization of regular dental check-ups. *BMC Oral Health* **2017**, *17*, 84. [CrossRef] [PubMed]
41. Ferrazzano, G.; Cantile, T.; Sangianantoni, G.; Ingenito, A.; Rengo, S.; Alcidi, B.; Spagnuolo, G. Oral health status and Unmet Restorative Treatment Needs (UTN) in disadvantaged migrant and not migrant children in Italy. *Eur J. Paediatr. Dent.* **2019**, *20*, 10–14.

42. Gatou, T.; Kounari, H.K.; Mamai-Homata, E. Dental caries prevalence and treatment needs of 5- to 12-year-old children in relation to area-based income and immigrant background in Greece. *Int. Dent. J.* **2011**, *61*, 144–151. [CrossRef] [PubMed]
43. Goetz, K.; Winkelmann, W.; Steinhäuser, J. Assessment of oral health and cost of care for a group of refugees in Germany: A cross-sectional study. *BMC Oral Health* **2018**, *18*, 69. [CrossRef]
44. Høyvik, A.C.; Lie, B.; Grjibovski, A.M.; Willumsen, T. Oral Health Challenges in Refugees from the Middle East and Africa: A Comparative Study. *J. Immigr. Minor. Health* **2018**, *21*, 443–450. [CrossRef]
45. Jacobsson, B.; Koch, G.; Magnusson, T.; Hugoson, A. Oral health in young individuals with foreign and Swedish backgrounds—A ten-year perspective. *Eur. Arch. Paediatr. Dent.* **2011**, *12*, 151–158. [CrossRef]
46. Marcenes, W.; Muirhead, V.E.; Murray, S.; Redshaw, P.; Bennett, U.; Wright, D. Ethnic disparities in the oral health of three- to four-year-old children in East London. *Br. Dent. J.* **2013**, *215*, E4. [CrossRef] [PubMed]
47. Mattila, A.; Ghaderi, P.; Tervonen, L.; Niskanen, L.; Pesonen, P.; Anttonen, V.; Laitala, M.-L. Self-reported oral health and use of dental services among asylum seekers and immigrants in Finland-a pilot study. *Eur. J. Public Health* **2016**, *26*, 1006–1010. [CrossRef] [PubMed]
48. Mustafa, M.; Nasir, E.F.; Nordrehaug Åstrøm, A. Attitudes toward brushing children's teeth—A study among parents with immigrant status in Norway. *Int. J. Paediatr. Dent.* **2021**, *31*, 80–88. [CrossRef]
49. Portero de la Cruz, S.; Cebrino, J. Oral Health Problems and Utilization of Dental Services among Spanish and Immigrant Children and Adolescents. *Int. J. Environ. Res. Public Health* **2020**, *17*, 738. [CrossRef]
50. Riatto, S.G.; Montero, J.; Pérez, D.R.; Castaño-Séiquer, A.; Dib, A. Oral Health Status of Syrian Children in the Refugee Center of Melilla, Spain. *Int. J. Dent.* **2018**, *2018*, 2637508. [CrossRef] [PubMed]
51. Rouxel, P.; Chandola, T. Socioeconomic and ethnic inequalities in oral health among children and adolescents living in England, Wales and Northern Ireland. *Community Dent. Oral Epidemiol.* **2018**, *46*, 426–434. [CrossRef] [PubMed]
52. Solyman, M.; Schmidt-Westhausen, A.-M. Oral health status among newly arrived refugees in Germany: A cross-sectional study. *BMC Oral Health* **2018**, *18*, 132. [CrossRef]
53. Van der Tas, J.T.; Kragt, L.; Elfrink, M.E.; Bertens, L.C.; Jaddoe, V.W.; Moll, H.A.; Ongkosuwito, E.M.; Wolvius, E.B. Social inequalities and dental caries in six-year-old children from the Netherlands. *J. Dent.* **2017**, *62*, 18–24. [CrossRef]
54. Van Meijeren-van Lunteren, A.W.; Wolvius, E.B.; Raat, H.; Jaddoe, V.W.V.; Kragt, L. Ethnic background and children's oral health-related quality of life. *Qual. Life Res.* **2019**, *28*, 1783–1791. [CrossRef] [PubMed]
55. Wigen, T.I.; Wang, N.J. Caries and background factors in Norwegian and immigrant 5-year-old children. *Community Dent. Oral Epidemiol.* **2010**, *38*, 19–28. [CrossRef]
56. Freiberg, A.; Wienke, A.; Bauer, L.; Niedermaier, A.; Führer, A. Dental Care for Asylum-Seekers in Germany: A Retrospective Hospital-Based Study. *Int. J. Environ. Res. Public Health* **2020**, *17*, 2672. [CrossRef] [PubMed]
57. Julihn, A.; Ekbom, A.; Modéer, T. Migration background: A risk factor for caries development during adolescence. *Eur. J. Oral Sci.* **2010**, *118*, 618–625. [CrossRef] [PubMed]
58. Julihn, A.; Cunha Soares, F.; Hjern, A.; Dahllöf, G. Development level of the country of parental origin on dental caries in children of immigrant parents in Sweden. *Acta Paediatr.* **2021**, *110*, 2405–2414. [CrossRef]
59. Lampert, T.; Kroll, L.E.; Müters, S.; Stolzenberg, H. Messung des sozioökonomischen Status in der Studie 'Gesundheit in Deutsch-land aktuell' (GEDA) Measurement of the socioeconomic status within the German health update 2009 (GEDA). *Bundesgesundheitsbl. Gesundh. Gesundheitsschutz* **2013**, *56*, 131–143. [CrossRef] [PubMed]
60. Barmes, D.E. Indicators for oral health and their implications for developing countries. *Int. Dent. J.* **1983**, *33*, 60–66.
61. O'Sullivan, I.; Lader, D.; Beavan-Seymour, C.; Chenery, V.; Fuller, E.; Sadler, K. Foundation Report: Adult Dental Health Survey 2009 (Technical Information). 2011. Available online: http://www.hscic.gov.uk/pubs/dentalsurveyfullreport09 (accessed on 24 August 2021).
62. Kelly, M.; Steele, J.; Nuttall, N.; Bradnock, G.; Morris, J.; Nunn, J.; Pine, C.; Pitts, N.B.; Treasure, E.; White, D.; et al. *Adult Dental Health Survey: Oral Health in the United Kingdom*; The Stationary Office: London, UK, 2000.
63. Singh, H.K.; Scott, T.E.; Henshaw, M.M.; Cote, S.E.; Grodin, M.A.; Piwowarczyk, L.A. Oral Health Status of Refugee Torture Survivors Seeking Care in the United States. *Am. J. Public Health* **2008**, *98*, 2181–2182. [CrossRef]
64. Slade, G.D. Derivation and validation of a short-form oral health impact profile. *Community Dent. Oral Epidemiol.* **1997**, *25*, 284–290. [CrossRef]
65. Lange, C.; Jentsch, F.; Allen, J.; Hoebel, J.; Kratz, A.L.; Von Der Lippe, E.; Müters, S.; Schmich, P.; Thelen, J.; Wetzstein, M.; et al. Data Resource Profile: German Health Update (GEDA)—The health interview survey for adults in Germany. *Int. J. Epidemiol.* **2015**, *44*, 442–450. [CrossRef]
66. Ajzen, I. The theory of planned behaviour: Reactions and reflections. *Psychol. Health* **2011**, *26*, 1113–1127. [CrossRef]
67. Beale, D.; Manstead, A. Predicting Mothers' Intentions to Limit Frequency of Infants' Sugar Intake. *J. Appl. Soc. Psychol.* **1991**, *21*, 409–431. [CrossRef]
68. Encuesta Nacional de Salud de España. 2017. Available online: https://www.mscbs.gob.es/estadEstudios/estadisticas/encuestaNacional/encuesta2017.html (accessed on 24 August 2021).
69. World Health Organization. Annex 7, WHO Oral Health Questionnaire for Adults. 2013. Available online: https://www.who.int/oral_health/publications/pepannex7sohqbasicmethods.pdf?ua=1 (accessed on 28 August 2021).

70. Trabajo, Inmigracion y Salud en una Cohort de Población Inmigrante end España. Elena Ronda Pérez. 2016. Available online: https://web.ua.es/es/gi-saludpublica/trabajo-inmigracion-y-salud-en-una-cohorte-de-poblacion-inmigrante-en-espana.html (accessed on 30 August 2021).
71. Domingo-Salvany, A.; Bacigalupe, A.; Carrasco, J.M.; Espelt, A.; Ferrando, J.; Borrell, C. Proposals for social class classification based on the Spanish National Classification of Occupations 2011 using neo-Weberian and neo-Marxist approaches. *Gac. Sanit.* **2013**, *27*, 263–272. [CrossRef]
72. WHO. *Oral Health Surveys: Basic Methods*; World Health Organization: Geneva, Switzerland, 1997.
73. Kooijman, M.N.; Kruithof, C.J.; van Duijn, C.M.; Duijts, L.; Franco, O.; van Ijzendoorn, M.; de Jongste, J.C.; Klaver, C.; van Der Lugt, A.; MacKenbach, J.P.; et al. The Generation R Study: Design and cohort update 2017. *Eur. J. Epidemiol.* **2016**, *31*, 1243–1264. [CrossRef]
74. E Kunst, A.; Bos, V.; Lahelma, E.; Bartley, M.; Lissau, I.; Regidor, E.; Mielck, A.; Cardano, M.; Dalstra, J.A.; Geurts, J.J.; et al. Trends in socioeconomic inequalities in self-assessed health in 10 European countries. *Int. J. Epidemiol.* **2004**, *34*, 295–305. [CrossRef]
75. Wamala, S.; Merlo, J.; Boström, G. Inequity in access to dental care services explains current socioeconomic disparities in oral health: The Swedish National Surveys of Public Health 2004–2005. *J. Epidemiol. Community Health* **2006**, *60*, 1027–1033. [CrossRef] [PubMed]
76. Nazroo, J.Y. The Structuring of Ethnic Inequalities in Health: Economic Position, Racial Discrimination, and Racism. *Am. J. Public Health* **2003**, *93*, 277–284. [CrossRef] [PubMed]
77. Borrell, L.N.; Beck, J.D.; Heiss, G. Socioeconomic Disadvantage and Periodontal Disease: The Dental Atherosclerosis Risk in Communities Study. *Am. J. Public Health* **2006**, *96*, 332–339. [CrossRef]
78. Scheppers, E.F.; Van Dongen, E.; Dekker, J.; Geertzen, J. Potential barriers to the use of health services among ethnic minorities: A review. *Fam. Pr.* **2006**, *23*, 325–348. [CrossRef]
79. Petersen, P.E. The World Oral Health Report 2003: Continuous improvement of oral health in the 21st century—The approach of the WHO Global Oral Health Programme. *Community Dent. Oral Epidemiol.* **2003**, *31*, 3–24. [CrossRef] [PubMed]
80. Okada, M.; Kawamura, M.; Kaihara, Y.; Matsuzaki, Y.; Kuwahara, S.; Ishidori, H.; Miura, K. Influence of parents' oral health behaviour on oral health status of their school children: An exploratory study employing a causal modelling technique. *Int. J. Paediatr. Dent.* **2002**, *12*, 101–108. [CrossRef]
81. Al-Haj Ali, S.N.; Alsineedi, F.; Alsamari, N.; Alduhayan, G.; BaniHani, A.; Farah, R.I. Risk Factors of Early Childhood Caries Among Preschool Children in Eastern Saudi Arabia. *Sci. Prog.* **2021**, *104*, 368504211008308. [CrossRef]
82. Geltman, P.L.; Adams, J.H.; Cochran, J.; Doros, G.; Rybin, D.; Henshaw, M.; Barnes, L.L.; Paasche-Orlow, M. The Impact of Functional Health Literacy and Acculturation on the Oral Health Status of Somali Refugees Living in Massachusetts. *Am. J. Public Health* **2013**, *103*, 1516–1523. [CrossRef] [PubMed]
83. Cote, S.; Geltman, P.; Nunn, M.; Lituri, K.; Henshaw, M.; Garcia, R. Dental Caries of Refugee Children Compared with US Children. *Pediatrics* **2004**, *114*, e733–e740. [CrossRef]
84. Mariño, R.; Wright, F.; Minas, I. Oral Health Among Vietnamese Using a Community Health Centre in Richmond, Victoria. *Aust. Dent. J.* **2001**, *46*, 208–215. [CrossRef]
85. Angelillo, I.F.; Nobile, C.G.A.; Pavia, M. Oral health status and treatment needs in immigrants and refugees in Italy. *Eur. J. Epidemiol.* **1996**, *12*, 359–365. [CrossRef]
86. Fennell-Wells, A.V.L.; Yusuf, H. Child refugees and asylum seekers: Oral health and its place in the UK system. *Br. Dent. J.* **2020**, *228*, 44–49. [CrossRef]
87. Ghiabi, E.; Matthews, D.C.; Brillant, M.S. The Oral Health Status of Recent Immigrants and Refugees in Nova Scotia, Canada. *J. Immigr. Minor. Health* **2014**, *16*, 95–101. [CrossRef]
88. Davidson, N.; Skull, S.; Calache, H.; Murray, S.S.; Chalmers, J. Holes a plenty: Oral health status a major issue for newly arrived refugees in Australia. *Aust. Dent. J.* **2006**, *51*, 306–311. [CrossRef] [PubMed]
89. Ponce-Gonzalez, I.; Cheadle, A.; Aisenberg, G.; Cantrell, L.F. Improving oral health in migrant and underserved populations: Evaluation of an interactive, community-based oral health education program in Washington state. *BMC Oral Health* **2019**, *19*, 30. [CrossRef]
90. Nakre, P.D.; Harikiran, A.G. Effectiveness of oral health education programs: A systematic review. *J. Int. Soc. Prev. Community Dent.* **2013**, *3*, 103–115. [CrossRef] [PubMed]
91. Valdez, R.; Spinler, K.; Kofahl, C.; Seedorf, U.; Heydecke, G.; Reissmann, D.R.; Lieske, B.; Dingoyan, D.; Aarabi, G. Oral Health Literacy in Migrant and Ethnic Minority Populations: A Systematic Review. *J. Immigr. Minor. Health* **2021**, 1–20. [CrossRef] [PubMed]

International Journal of
Environmental Research and Public Health

MDPI

Article

Increased Anxiety and Depression Symptoms in Post-Acute Care Patients with Stroke during the COVID-19 Pandemic

Hsiang-Yun Chou [1,*], Yu-Chun Lo [2], Ya-Wen Tsai [1,*], Chia-Li Shih [1] and Chieh-Ting Yeh [3]

1 Department of Rehabilitation, An Nan Hospital, China Medical University, Tainan 709204, Taiwan; chiali771223@gmail.com
2 The Ph.D. Program for Neural Regenerative Medicine, College of Medical Science and Technology, Taipei Medical University, Taipei 11031, Taiwan; aricalo@tmu.edu.tw
3 Department of Nursing, An Nan Hospital, China Medical University, Tainan 709204, Taiwan; ritayeh0823@gmail.com
* Correspondence: chou3018@gmail.com (H.-Y.C.); T23895@mail.tmanh.org.tw (Y.-W.T.); Tel.: +886-6-355-3111 (ext. 3138) (H.-Y.C.)

Abstract: This study aimed to explore the quality and stability of post-acute care for patients with stroke, including their functional outcomes, mental health and medical care in Taiwan during the COVID-19 pandemic. In this retrospective case–control study—based on propensity score matching—we assessed 11 patients admitted during the pandemic period (in 2021) and 11 patients admitted during the non-pandemic period (in 2020). Functional outcomes, including the scores of the modified Rankin Scale, Barthel Index, EuroQoL-5 Dimension, Lawton–Brody instrumental activities of daily living, Berg Balance Scale, 5-metre walking speed and 6-min walking distance, were determined. Data on the length of acute care, length of post-acute care, destination after discharge and 14-days readmission were used to evaluate the quality of medical care. The Wilcoxon signed-rank test was used to compare functional performance before and after rehabilitation. The pandemic group showed no significant improvement in the scores of EuroQoL-5 Dimension, a self-reported health status assessment ($p = 0.13$), with the anxiety or depression dimension showing a negative effect ($r = 0.21$). Post-acute care programmes can efficiently improve the functional performance of patients with stroke during the COVID-19 pandemic in Taiwan. Mental health should therefore be simultaneously maintained while rehabilitating physical function.

Keywords: post-acute care; stroke; rehabilitation; functional outcome; mental health; anxiety; depression; COVID-19

Citation: Chou, H.-Y.; Lo, Y.-C.; Tsai, Y.-W.; Shih, C.-L.; Yeh, C.-T. Increased Anxiety and Depression Symptoms in Post-Acute Care Patients with Stroke during the COVID-19 Pandemic. *Int. J. Environ. Res. Public Health* **2022**, *19*, 162. https://doi.org/10.3390/ijerph19010162

Academic Editors: Joachim G. Voss, Sandul Yasobant and Marco Scarselli

Received: 9 November 2021
Accepted: 21 December 2021
Published: 24 December 2021

1. Introduction

Since 2019, the world has witnessed people struggle against COVID-19 daily. Taiwan, which has a population of 23.5 million, was able to successfully resist the COVID-19 outbreak throughout 2020 [1]. Unexpectedly, a COVID-19 outbreak occurred in Taiwan in May 2021. Based on the Taiwan Center for Disease Control's 'Pandemic Alert Standards and Response Measures', the government announced that Taiwan would be placed on third-level alert status starting 19 May 2021. The epidemic alert status is divided into levels 1, 2, 3 and 4, with higher levels corresponding to stricter control measures. From May 19, the government mandated the wearing of facial masks in public, cessation of gatherings involving more than 5 people indoors and 10 people outdoors and maintaining physical distance. To prevent excessive load on medical resources, non-essential medical activities, such as general health examinations, medical cosmetics and rehabilitation therapy, were discouraged. However, certain individuals, such as patients with stroke, still required urgent medical intervention and hospitalisation.

Stroke survivors usually experience severe functional loss, which reduces physical activity and social participation and increases socioeconomic burden [2,3]. In a recent review study, a decrease in emergency care for ischemic stroke was observed during the

COVID-19 outbreak, leading to an increase in disability and deaths, which will impose additional economic burdens on the healthcare system and society [4]. Timely inpatient rehabilitation can effectively reduce the mortality and disability rates and decrease subsequent socioeconomic burdens [5–7]. Therefore, physicians should actively engage in rehabilitation interventions following the stabilisation of the patient's medical condition after the acute phase. In 2014, the Taiwan National Health Insurance Administration launched its post-acute care cerebrovascular disease (PAC-CVD) programme [8], which emphasises high-intensity inpatient rehabilitation facilities (IRFs, 3–5 times daily) and a medical referral system for long-term care after discharge from community hospitals [8]. The PAC programme utilises per diem reimbursement, which differs from fee-for-service, to reduce daily expenditure [8]. A study showed that the length of stay (LOS) of PAC-CVD patients in Taiwan is slightly more than 1 month [9]. Despite the lack of recent data indicating whether patients with stroke have high COVID-19 infection rates, factors such as old age, obesity, smoking, hypertension, cardiovascular disease and diabetes have been strongly associated with increased infection rates in these patients [10–13]. Research has suggested that low levels of physical activity are associated with the risk of COVID-19, severe illness from COVID-19 and COVID-19-related death [14]. Therefore, motor function recovery may prevent COVID-19 and death.

Besides physical function, mental health requires attention. A recent study showed that people experienced substantial psychological impact in the form of stress, anxiety and depression during the COVID-19 outbreak [15]. The PAC programme significantly improves the motor function status, activities of daily living, quality of life, oral function and mental health of patients with stroke [8,16,17]. Since 2014, the PAC programme has never experienced an infectious disease outbreak. This study therefore aimed to investigate the quality and stability of the PAC-CVD programme in terms of improving functional outcomes and mental health status during the COVID-19 pandemic.

2. Materials and Methods

2.1. Study Design and Patients

The study population comprised all patients admitted with stroke to the PAC ward of a regional hospital that has expertly provided PAC service for >5 years. The patients were categorised into two groups: a non-pandemic group (admitted in 2020) and a pandemic group (admitted between mid-May to early August of 2021). The inclusion criteria of the PAC-CVD programme were as follows [16]: (1) admitted within 30 days after acute onset of cerebrovascular disease; (2) no deterioration in blood pressure, heart rate, body temperature and neurological condition for more than 72 h; (3) moderate-to-moderately-severe motor dysfunction, modified Rankin Scale (mRS) scores of 3–4 [18] and (4) basic cognition, learning ability and willingness. The covariates included patient demographics (age and sex), clinical attributes (stroke type, hypertension, coronary artery disease, diabetes mellitus, hyperlipidaemia and previous stroke), common risk factors (smoking and drinking) and pre-rehabilitation functional status. Ultimately, 11 patients in the pandemic group were compared with 11 patients in the non-pandemic group. All PAC patients completed the pre-rehabilitation and discharge-rehabilitation assessments. The study protocol was approved by the institutional review board of Taiwan Municipal An Nan Hospital-China Medical University (TMANH110-REC032). Before enrolment, all participants provided written informed consent.

2.2. Functional Status Instruments and Chart Review

The mRS, Barthel Index (BI), EuroQoL-5 Dimension (EQ-5D), Lawton–Brody instrumental activities of daily living (IADL), Berg Balance Scale (BBS), 5 m walking speed (5MWS) and 6-min walking distance (6MWD) were used to assess functional performance. mRS scores of 0, 1, 2, 3, 4, 5 and 6 correspond to no symptoms, no significant disability, slight disability, moderate disability, moderately severe disability, severe disability and death, respectively [19]. The BI scores indicate functional disability for activities of daily living, ranging from 0 (completely dependent) to 100 (independent) [20]. The EQ-5D, a self-reported health status assessment, comprises five dimensions corresponding to mobility, self-care, routine activities, pain or discomfort and anxiety or depression as part of a total health state, with higher scores indicating more severe or frequent problems [21]. The IADL, which comprises eight items corresponding to making phone calls, shopping, preparing food, housekeeping, laundering, taking pills, using transportation and managing finances, is used to evaluate how patients engage in activities of daily living [22]. The BBS, which comprises 14 items, is used to evaluate functional balance, with each item rated from 0 (poor balance) to 4 (good balance) [23]. The 5MWS assesses longitudinal changes in walking speed after stroke [24]. The 6MWD evaluates walking ability, with studies suggesting that accomplishing a distance of $\geq$205 m better defines community ambulation ability compared with walking speed [25].

The following patient data were obtained from medical records: age, sex, type of stroke, comorbidities (hypertension, coronary artery disease, diabetes mellitus and hyperlipidaemia), previous stroke, common risk factors (smoking and drinking), length of acute care, length of post-acute care, total score for each functional status measure before and after rehabilitation, readmission after 14 days and destination after discharge.

2.3. Public Health Policies for Rehabilitation

The patient and caregiver needed to have a negative polymerase chain reaction (PCR) test 3 days before being transferred to the regional hospital. Isolation equipment was worn, and an ambulance was used for transfers between hospitals to reduce the risk of exposure to infection. During hospitalisation, the patients were admitted to a ward dedicated to patients with stroke, accompanied by the same caregiver, and were instructed to avoid leaving the hospital arbitrarily. Family visits were limited to online video calls. Both the patients and caregivers were required to monitor their body temperature daily. Rehabilitation interventions were conducted in a separate room, with the equipment thoroughly disinfected after use. The stroke patient engaged in a highly intensive PAC programme, defined as a high frequency of rehabilitation (3–5 times daily), including physical therapy, occupational therapy, and speech therapy [8,26]. This significantly increased the period of contact with different healthcare workers. Healthcare workers were at high risk of infection during the COVID-19 pandemic, following WHO's recommendations for the frequent washing of soiled hands or the use of sanitizer for unsoiled hands to help reduce the spread of diseases [27]. The medical staff, including doctors, nurses, physical therapists, occupational therapists and speech therapists, were required to receive at least the first dose of the COVID-19 vaccine, report contact and cluster history and record their body temperature daily. Population-based measures, including the wearing of face masks, personal hygiene and appropriate physical distancing, were strictly implemented during rehabilitation [28].

2.4. Statistical Analysis

Statistical analysis was conducted using SPSS version 26.0 (IBM Corp., Armonk, NY, USA). Baseline clinical and descriptive statistics were utilised to depict the patients' demographics. To prevent non-comparability between the groups due to distortions in the estimation of the treatment effect, propensity score matching (PSM) was estimated using a multivariable logistic regression model adjusted for observed covariates, assigning one matched control for each patient admitted in 2020 according to the patient-level minimised systematic differences in baseline characteristics when comparing both groups [29–31]. The calliper matching method was used for PSM between the non-pandemic group and the pandemic group, and the match tolerance was set "0.2" for 1:1 matching. The independent samples t-test and Mann–Whitney U test were performed to determine whether significant differences existed between the groups, with data presented as means and standard deviations, proportions or medians. The Wilcoxon signed-rank test was used to compare functional performance before and after rehabilitation, with data presented as medians and interquartile ranges. Effect sizes (ES) were estimated to determine the magnitude of change in the functional outcome scores. A clinically meaningful effect was defined as an absolute value ES of ≥0.1, with an ES of ≥0.1, ≥0.3 and ≥0.5 indicating a small, moderate and large effect, respectively [32]. All tests were two-sided, and a *p*-value of <0.05 indicated statistical significance.

3. Results

Eighty-eight patients were admitted to the PAC programme at a regional hospital during the non-pandemic period of 2020, among whom three dropped out due to working medical conditions and another three requested withdrawal due to personal reasons. Therefore, 82 patients completed the programme and all evaluations during the non-pandemic period. During the pandemic period in 2021, when Taiwan entered the third-level alert status, 12 patients were admitted to the PAC programme. One patient dropped out due to the family's request. Ultimately, 11 patients completed the programme and all evaluations during the pandemic period. Before performing PSM, the non-pandemic group (n = 82) was significantly older than the pandemic group (n = 11) ($p < 0.05$). No significant differences in the male:female ratio, clinical attributes, common risk factors and pre-rehabilitation functional status were observed between the groups. After performing PSM, the non-pandemic (n = 11) and pandemic groups (n = 11) had no significant difference in age, sex, clinical attributes, common risk factors and pre-rehabilitation functional status scores (Table 1).

Table 1. Patients' characteristics before and after propensity score matching (PSM).

	Before Propensity Score Matching						After Propensity Score Matching					
Variables	**Pandemic Group (n = 11)**		**Non-Pandemic Group (n = 82)**		**SMD**	***p***	**Pandemic Group (n = 11)**		**Non-Pandemic Group (n = 11)**		**SMD**	***p***
Demographics	**Mean (SD) or *n* (%)**						**Mean (SD) or *n* (%)**					
Age, years	53.64 (15.85)		63.44 (14.65)		0.642	0.04 *	53.64 (15.85)		52.91 (17.71)		0.043	0.92
Sex Female	2 (18.2%)		26 (31.7)		0.320	0.33	2 (18.2%)		2 (18.2%)		0	1.0
Male	9 (81.8%)		56 (68.3%)				9 (81.8%)		9 (81.8%)			
Clinical Attributes												
Stroke Type					0.120	0.71					0	1.0
Ischemic	9 (81.8%)		63 (76.8%)				9 (81.8%)		9 (81.8%)			
Hemorrhagic	2 (18.2%)		19 (23.2%)				2 (18.2%)		2 (18.2%)			
Hypertension	10 (90.9%)		78 (95.1%)		0.152	0.57	10 (90.9%)		10 (90.9%)		0	1.0
Coronary Artery Disease	3 (27.3%)		20 (24.4%)		0.067	0.84	3 (27.3%)		3 (27.3%)		0	1.0
Diabetes Mellitus	2 (18.2%)		29 (35.4%)		0.382	0.22	2 (18.2%)		1 (9.1%)		0.252	0.56
Hyperlipidemia	6 (54.5%)		35 (42.7%)		0.235	0.46	6 (54.5%)		6 (54.5%)		0	1.0
Previous Stroke	3 (27.3%)		17 (21.5%)		0.137	0.63	3 (27.3%)		2 (18.2%)		0.206	0.63
Common Risk Factors												
Smoking	6 (54.5%)		16 (19.5%)		0.753	0.05	6 (54.5%)		6 (54.5%)		0	1.0
Drinking	3 (27.3%)		12 (14.6%)		0.289	0.29	3 (27.3%)		3 (27.3%)		0	1.0
Pre-rehabilitation Functional Status												
	Mean (SD)	Median (IQR)	Mean (SD)	Median (IQR)	SMD	*p*	Mean (SD)	Median (IQR)	Mean (SD)	Median (IQR)	SMD	*p*
mRS	3.55 (0.52)	4 (3–4)	3.65 (0.48)	4 (3–4)	0.20	0.52	3.55 (0.52)	4 (3–4)	3.64 (0.51)	4 (3–4)	0.175	0.67
BI	50.91 (15.12)	50 (40–65)	48 (20.58)	50 (35–61)	0.132	0.66	50.91 (15.12)	50 (40–65)	50 (18.17)	55 (40–60)	0.054	0.95
EQ-5D	8.82 (1.25)	8 (8–10)	8.95 (1.45)	8 (8–10)	0.096	0.77	8.82 (1.25)	8 (8–10)	8.64 (1.03)	8 (8–9)	0.157	0.85
IADL	1.09 (1.04)	1 (0–2)	1.24 (1.19)	1 (0–2)	0.134	0.69	1.09 (1.04)	1 (0–2)	1.36 (1.03)	2 (0–2)	0.261	0.51
BBS	22.73 (16.13)	20 (5–36)	18.04 (14.49)	11.5 (6–30.25)	0.306	0.32	22.73 (16.13)	20 (5–36)	22.45 (13.71)	23 (9–38)	0.019	0.95

SD: standard deviation; mRS: modified Rankin Scale; BI: Barthel Index; EQ-5D: EuroQoL-5 Dimension; IADL: Lawton–Brody instrumental activities of daily living; BBS: Berg Balance Scale; SMD: standardized mean difference. Values are expressed as mean (SD), median and interquartile range (IQR), or n %. * Statistically significant ($p < 0.05$).

After PAC intervention, the non-pandemic group showed significant improvements in all functional status measures (admission versus before discharge), including mRS, BI, EQ-5D, IADL, BBS, 5MWS and 6MWD. The pandemic group showed significant improvements in most measures of functional status after PAC intervention, including mRS, BI, IADL, BBS, 5MWS and 6MWD. EQ-5D scores were not significantly different in the pandemic group ($p = 0.13$) (Table 2).

Table 2. Total score for each functional status measure before and after the PAC program in both groups.

Measures	Pandemic Group ($n = 11$)			Non-Pandemic Group ($n = 11$)		
	Before PAC	After PAC	p	Before PAC	After PAC	p
mRS	4 (3–4)	3 (2–4)	0.02 *	4 (3–4)	2 (2–3)	0.01 *
BI	50 (40–65)	80 (60–100)	<0.01 *	55 (40–60)	85 (70–95)	<0.01 *
EQ-5D	8 (8–10)	8 (6–9)	0.13	8 (8–9)	7 (5–8)	<0.01 *
IADL	1 (0–2)	4 (0–5)	0.02 *	2 (0–2)	3 (2–4)	<0.01 *
BBS	20 (5–36)	52 (30–56)	<0.01 *	23 (9–38)	44 (27–50)	<0.01 *
5MWS	0 (0–0.21)	0.56 (0.13–1.22)	<0.01 *	0 (0–0)	0.42 (0–0.48)	0.01 *
6MWD	0 (0–100)	130 (40–416)	<0.01 *	0 (0–0)	150 (0–230)	0.01 *

PAC: post-acute care; mRS: modified Rankin Scale; BI: Barthel Index; EQ-5D: EuroQoL-5 Dimension; IADL: Lawton–Brody instrumental activities of daily living; BBS: Berg Balance Scale; 5MWS: 5-m walking speed; 6MWD: 6-min walking distance. Values are expressed as median and interquartile range (IQR), i.e., 4 (3–4) means the median is 4 and the interquartile range is from 3 to 4. * Statistically significant ($p < 0.05$).

The magnitude of change in the functional outcome scores was expressed in ES. In the non-pandemic group, BBS and BI had the largest training effect (ES: 0.63, large effect), whereas mRS (ES: 0.53, large effect) had the smallest training effect. In the pandemic group, BBS (ES: 0.63, large effect) had the largest training effect, whereas EQ-5D (ES: 0.32, moderate effect) had the smallest training effect. The largest difference between both groups was in EQ-5D (ES1-ES2: 0.23; ES1 and ES2 indicate the change in functional outcomes in the pandemic and non-pandemic groups, respectively), whereas the smallest difference between the groups was in BBS (ES1-ES2: 0). No significant difference in mRS, BI, IADL, BBS, 5MWS and 6WMD was observed between the groups (Table 3).

Table 3. Differences in effect size (ES) in each functional status measure before and after the PAC program: comparison between different groups.

Measures	Pandemic Group ($n = 11$)			Non-Pandemic Group ($n = 11$)			
	Before PAC	After PAC	ES1	Before PAC	After PAC	ES2	ES1-ES
mRS	4 (3–4)	3 (2–4)	−0.50	4 (3–4)	2 (2–3)	−0.53	0.03
BI	50 (40–65)	80 (60–100)	0.57	55 (40–60)	85 (70–95)	0.63	−0.06
EQ-5D	8 (8–10)	8 (6–9)	−0.32	8 (8–9)	7 (5–8)	−0.55	0.23
IADL	1 (0–2)	4 (0–5)	0.52	2 (0–2)	3 (2–4)	0.61	−0.09
BBS	20 (5–36)	52 (30–56)	0.63	23 (9–38)	44 (27–50)	0.63	0
5MWS	0 (0–0.21)	0.56 (0.13–1.22)	0.57	0 (0–0)	0.42 (0–0.48)	0.54	0.03
6MWD	0 (0–100)	130 (40–416)	0.57	0 (0–0)	150 (0–230)	0.54	0.03

PAC: post-acute care; mRS: modified Rankin Scale; BI: Barthel Index; EQ-5D: EuroQoL-5 Dimension; IADL: Lawton–Brody instrumental activities of daily living; BBS: Berg Balance Scale; 5MWS: 5-m walking speed; 6MWD: 6-min walking distance; ES, effect size. Values are expressed as median and interquartile range (IQR), i.e., 4 (3–4) means the median is 4 and the interquartile range is from 3 to 4. ES1 and ES2 indicate the change in functional outcome in pandemic and non-pandemic groups, respectively. ES1-ES2 indicates the difference between both two groups.

The five dimensions (mobility, self-care, usual activities, pain or discomfort and anxiety or depression) of the EQ-5D manifest the patients' self-reported mental health status. The pandemic group showed no significant difference in the five dimensions of patient self-expression after PAC intervention, with the self-care dimension having the largest absolute ES value (ES:0.4, moderate effect) and mobility, pain or discomfort and anxiety or depression having the smallest absolute ES value (ES:0.21, small effect; anxiety or depression showed a negative real number). In the non-pandemic group, significant differences in three dimensions (mobility, $p < 0.01$; self-care, $p = 0.04$; usual activities, $p < 0.01$) were observed after PAC intervention, with mobility and usual activities having the largest absolute ES value (ES: 0.56, large effect) and pain or discomfort having the smallest absolute ES value (ES: 0.21, small effect). The largest difference between the groups was in the anxiety or depression dimension (ES1-ES2: 0.51), whereas the smallest difference was in the pain or discomfort dimension (ES1-ES2: 0) (Table 4).

Table 4. The five dimensions in EQ-5D before and after PAC program: comparison between different groups.

Dimensions	Pandemic Group (n = 11)				Non-Pandemic Group (n = 11)				
	Before PAC	After PAC	p	ES1	Before PAC	After PAC	p	ES2	ES1-ES
Mobility	2 (2–2)	2 (1–2)	0.32	−0.21	2 (2–2)	1 (1–2)	<0.01 *	−0.53	0.35
Self-Care	2 (2–2)	2 (1–2)	0.06	−0.40	2 (2–2)	2 (1–2)	0.04 *	−0.43	0.03
Usual Activities	2 (2–3)	2 (2–3)	0.08	−0.37	2 (2–3)	2 (1–2)	<0.01 *	−0.56	0.19
Pain or Discomfort	1 (1–1)	1 (1–1)	0.32	−0.21	1 (1–1)	1 (1–1)	0.32	−0.21	0
Anxiety or Depression	1 (1–1)	1 (1–1)	0.32	0.21	1 (1–1)	1 (1–1)	0.16	−0.30	0.51

PAC: post-acute care; EQ-5D: EuroQoL-5 Dimension; ES, effect size. ES1 means the change in functional outcome in the pandemic group; ES2 means the change in functional outcome in the non-pandemic group. ES1-ES2 indicates the difference between the two groups. Values are expressed as median and interquartile range (IQR), i.e., 4 (3–4) means the median is 4 and the interquartile range is from 3 to 4. * Statistically significant ($p < 0.05$).

The quality of medical care, which was assessed using acute care LOS, PAC LOS, destination after discharge, readmission after 14 days and 6MWD $\geq$ 205 m, did not significantly differ between the groups (Table 5).

Table 5. Quality of medical care in both groups.

		Pandemic Group (n = 11)	Non-Pandemic Group (n = 11)	p
Acute Care LOS, day		16.09 (6.49)	15.36 (4.34)	0.76
PAC LOS, day		32.73 (10.97)	36.64 (12.40)	0.44
Destination after Discharge				1
Household		10 (91%)	10 (91%)	
Nursing Home		1 (9%)	1 (9%)	
Readmission in 14 days	Yes	0 (0%)	0 (0%)	1
6MWD $\geq$ 205		4 (36%)	3 (27%)	0.66

LOS: length of stay; PAC: post-acute care; 6MWD: 6-min walking distance. Values are expressed as mean (SD) or n %.

4. Discussion

This study explored the quality and stability of post-acute care for patients with stroke, including their functional outcomes, mental health and medical care, in Taiwan during the COVID-19 pandemic. The present study was the first to assess the mental health of PAC patients using the self-reported EQ-5D during the COVID-19 pandemic. The pandemic group showed no significant improvement in EQ-5D scores, and EQ-5D scores had the largest difference between the pandemic and non-pandemic groups. The PAC-CVD programme serves as a transitional phase between discharge from medical institutions and returning home or enrolment in long-term care systems [33]. This programme aims to reduce the disability and medical costs of patients with stroke and promote the rehabilitation of their functional ability. Most previous studies focused on the functional recovery of patients with stroke while ignoring their mental health [26,34]. Further analysis of the five dimensions of EQ-5D showed that anxiety or depression tended to be more severe during the pandemic. Estimates have shown that approximately 20% to 25% of patients develop anxiety disorders after stroke [35], which affects their quality of life [36]. A depressed or dysphoric mood affects approximately 30% of stroke survivors [37], reducing the motivation for rehabilitation and promoting poorer functional outcomes or even increased risk for suicide [38,39]. In a recent study, although depression did not significantly worsen, higher rates of anxiety were observed in patients with stroke during the COVID-19 pandemic [40]. After reviewing our patients' medical records, we found that the 11 patients were not diagnosed with post-stroke depression during the pandemic. However, those who experienced stroke during the COVID-19 pandemic may have exhibited some degree of anxiety or depressive symptoms, especially the younger patients. The mean age of the patients included in our study was 53 years, which was significantly younger than that in previous studies [9,26]. This difference may be attributed to the following reasons: as the risk for more severe COVID-19-associated outcomes increases with age, most patients aged ≥65 years chose to return home or preferred home-based rehabilitation instead of inpatient rehabilitation [13]. Telerehabilitation could potentially be taught and practiced at home during the COVID-19 pandemic via cell phones and Skype, or even be combined with modern technology, including virtual reality (VR) and robotic assistance [41,42]. Considering that rehabilitation is less effective in those aged ≥65 years than in those aged <65 years, patients and their families had a relatively negative perception of rehabilitation during the pandemic and showed reduced willingness to undergo the PAC programme [17]. Young and middle-aged patients were considered to have a longer lifespan, to be more productive, to be the source of household income and to have greater motivation for participating in rehabilitation [17]; the medical staff perceived younger patients with stroké who engaged in high-intensity rehabilitation to have good recovery benefits and actively persuaded them to undergo the PAC programme. COVID-19 has led to serious losses in many economies around the world, especially among low-income populations, causing a sharp rise in unemployment and poverty rates [43]. Besides physical anxiety, younger patients who were the source of household income perceived the COVID-19-related panic [15] and the lower household income caused by physical disabilities or the pandemic as stressors [44]. On the contrary, the different level of financial assets was associated with disability in stroke patients. Lower household income reflected a higher level of disability and increased the gap in participation and activities [45]. In addition to the huge financial burden of the long-term care of stroke, the burden of caregivers was intensive, especially the family caregiver during the COVID-19 pandemic [46]. The Taiwan government adopted strict social distancing measures and prevented excessive load on medical resources during the COVID-19 pandemic, resulting in the suspension of certain medical services such as rehabilitation centres. In addition to the provision of essential daily care, the family caregiver also assumed the additional role of a rehabilitation therapist at home, which caused not only physical but psychological burdens [46].

The PAC programme mainly emphasises physical function recovery and psychological intervention. Although it can improve mental health, psychological problems were only revealed during the outbreak. During the pandemic, the public experienced anxiety, stress, fear, uncertainty and insecurity [47], indicating the need for more psychological support among patients with stroke, who are considered a vulnerable population. Thus, the PAC phase helps in the early recognition of psychological problems and the provision of timely interventions. This may be attributed to the clinical staff's adjustment of the patient-personalised plan, assessment of mental health status and treatment of patients during this transitional phase, which would prepare them for their return to society. The clinical staff may even extend their service until after discharge from the hospital, following up patients during outpatient rehabilitation or through telephone.

This study revealed that during the outbreak, PAC-CVD patients showed no significant difference in functional recovery improvement compared with those included in previous studies under common conditions. No significant improvement was observed in the self-reported dimensions of mobility, self-care and usual activities during the outbreak. Evidence has shown that depressive syndrome is associated with lower general health perception and that physical functional disability affects the quality of life [48]. The lower general health perception may impede improvements in medical condition and the recovery of motor function. Thus, this programme is robust and effective in rehabilitating functional abilities among post-stroke patients during infectious disease outbreaks; psychological problems promote a vicious circle between physical and mental health. This suggests the importance of monitoring mental health status and preventing negative psychological consequences.

Case managers in institutions should be involved in the referral process. During this COVID-19 wave, they play an important role, including preparation before transfer, confirming negative PCR tests 3 days before admission and contacting the institution to which the patient is to be transferred before discharge. We found no significant difference in acute LOS between both groups. Besides medical treatment for acute stroke at the medical centre, including the preparation of the PAC programme for referral to the regional hospital, the acute LOS could indicate the timeliness and continuity of the PAC programme during the pandemic. The similar PAC LOS in both groups under the per diem reimbursement system suggests no increase in economy with efficient functional recovery during the pandemic. None of the patients were hospitalised within 14 days, and most returned home after discharge from the regional hospital. Previous studies determined the destination of the patients after discharge, which is important for our research considering the young age of our cohort. Nearly 30% of these young patients demonstrated a 6MWD $\geq$ 205 m after high-intensity rehabilitative interventions, which could indicate their ability for community ambulation [25].

This article was drafted during the period wherein Taiwan had been downgraded to second-level alert, which may have decreased the level of mental stress among the patients with stroke. Future research should focus on changes in psychological conditions to provide more substantial guidance for medical institutions. Fighting a pandemic is akin to running a marathon—one must never lower their guard. The end of the pandemic cannot be predicted. However, all individuals should adjust to the changes, even patients with stroke.

This study has some limitations. First, the sample size was small and was obtained from a single centre, which was one of the institutions in southern Taiwan with the greatest number of PAC cases. Notably, the hospitalisation period coincided with the small-scale cluster infection of COVID-19 in this district. Adopting a strict medical isolation public health policy in the case of limited medical capacity and maintaining the quality of the PAC-CVD programme are challenging. This study was expected to raise the awareness of the physical and psychological health of stroke patients during the COVID-19 pandemic, although the small sample size may not represent a macro-level analysis. Second, this was a retrospective study that reviewed medical records, observed phenomena and made clinical recommendations. Third, only PAC-CVD cases were enrolled due to the medical load reduction policy.

5. Conclusions

This study highlighted the quality and stability of the PAC-CVD programme for patients with stroke in medical care and improving functional outcomes. The PAC-CVD programme focuses on the recovery of the motor function of stroke patients, but COVID-19 has increased people's health awareness and psychological pressure. While restoring the motor function of the patients, attention should also be paid to their mental health and the provision of psychological support. This study also raised awareness of the huge burden on the economy and rehabilitation care for stroke patients during the COVID-19 pandemic. In addition to verifying the efficiency and stability of the PAC-CVD programme during the pandemic, this study could serve as a reference for framing public health policies for rehabilitation institutions.

Author Contributions: Conceptualization, H.-Y.C. and Y.-W.T.; methodology, H.-Y.C.; formal analysis, H.-Y.C. and C.-L.S.; resources, C.-T.Y.; data curation, H.-Y.C.; writing—original draft preparation,

H.-Y.C. and Y.-W.T.; writing—review and editing, H.-Y.C., Y.-W.T. and Y.-C.L.; supervision, Y.-W.T. All authors have read and agreed to the published version of the manuscript.

Funding: The research funding was provided by An Nan Hospital, China Medical University, Tainan, Taiwan (Funding Number: ANHRF108-14).

Institutional Review Board Statement: The study was conducted according to the guidelines of the Declaration of Helsinki, and approved by the Research Ethics Committee of Tainan Municipal An-Nan Hospital, China Medical University, Tainan, Taiwan (protocol code: TMANH110-REC032, 8 October 2021).

Informed Consent Statement: Patient consent was waived due to a retrospective study of medical records in this research.

Data Availability Statement: The data presented in this study are available on request from the corresponding author.

Acknowledgments: We appreciate the participants of the PAC programme, which provides valuable clinical information to clinical therapists for planning rehabilitation programmes.

Conflicts of Interest: The authors declare no conflict of interest.

References

1. Cheng, H.Y.; Chueh, Y.N.; Chen, C.M.; Jian, S.W.; Lai, S.K.; Liu, D.P. Taiwan's COVID-19 response: Timely case detection and quarantine, January to June 2020. *J. Formos. Med. Assoc.* **2021**, *120*, 1400–1404. [CrossRef]
2. Sturm, J.W.; Dewey, H.M.; Donnan, G.A.; Macdonell, R.A.; McNeil, J.J.; Thrift, A.G. Handicap after stroke: How does it relate to disability, perception of recovery, and stroke Subtype? The north North East Melbourne Stroke Incidence Study (NEMESIS). *Stroke* **2002**, *33*, 762–768. [CrossRef]
3. Mukherjee, D.; Patil, C.G. Epidemiology and the global burden of stroke. *World Neurosurg.* **2011**, *76*, S85–S90. [CrossRef]
4. Hernández, K.; Paredes, D.; Lenz, R. A Scoping Review of Consequences of Untreated Stroke: Economic Bur den Due to COVID-19? *Value Health* **2021**, *24*, S218. [CrossRef]
5. Kalra, L.; Langhorne, P. Facilitating recovery: Evidence for organized stroke care. *J. Rehabil. Med.* **2007**, *39*, 97–102. [CrossRef]
6. Lin, I.H.; Tsai, H.T.; Wang, C.Y.; Hsu, C.Y.; Liou, T.H.; Lin, Y.N. Effectiveness and superiority of rehabilitative treatments in enhancing motor recovery within 6 months poststroke: A systemic review. *Arch. Phys. Med. Rehabil.* **2019**, *100*, 366–378. [CrossRef]
7. Liao, W.L.; Chang, C.W.; Sung, P.Y.; Hsu, W.N.; Lai, M.W.; Tsai, S.W. The Berg balance scale at admission can predict community ambulation at discharge in patients with stroke. *Medicina* **2021**, *57*, 556. [CrossRef]
8. Wang, C.Y.; Chen, Y.R.; Hong, J.P.; Chan, C.C.; Chang, L.C.; Shi, H.Y. Rehabilitative post-acute care for stroke patients delivered by per-diem payment system in different hospitalization paths: A Taiwan pilot study. *Int. J. Qual. Health Care* **2017**, *29*, 779–784. [CrossRef]
9. Chiu, C.C.; Wang, J.J.; Hung, C.M.; Lin, H.F.; Hsien, H.H.; Hung, K.W.; Chiu, H.C.; Jennifer Yeh, S.C.; Shi, H.Y. Impact of multidisciplinary stroke post-acute care on cost and functional status: A prospective study based on propensity score matching. *Brain Sci.* **2021**, *11*, 161. [CrossRef]
10. Lee, S.W.; Yang, J.M.; Yoo, I.K.; Moon, S.Y.; Ha, E.K.; Yeniova, A.Ö.; Cho, J.Y.; Kim, M.S.; Shin, J.I.; Yon, D.K. Proton pump inhibitors and the risk of severe COVID-19: A post-hoc analysis from the Korean nationwide cohort. *Gut* **2021**, *70*, 2013–2015. [CrossRef]
11. Lee, S.W.; Yang, J.M.; Moon, S.Y.; Yoo, I.K.; Ha, E.K.; Kim, S.Y.; Park, U.M.; Choi, S.; Lee, S.H.; Ahn, Y.M.; et al. Association between mental illness and COVID-19 susceptibility and clinical outcomes in South Korea: A nationwide cohort study. *Lancet Psychiatry* **2020**, *7*, 1025–1031. [CrossRef]
12. Mehra, M.R.; Desai, S.S.; Kuy, S.; Henry, T.D.; Patel, A.N. Retraction: Cardiovascular disease, drug therapy, and mortality in COVID-19. *N. Engl. J. Med.* **2020**, *382*, 2582. [CrossRef]
13. CDC COVID-19 Response Team. Preliminary estimates of the prevalence of selected underlying health conditions among patients with coronavirus disease 2019—United States, February 12–March 28, 2020. *MMWR Morb. Mortal. Wkly. Rep.* **2020**, *69*, 382–386. [CrossRef] [PubMed]
14. Lee, S.W.; Lee, J.; Moon, S.Y.; Jin, H.Y.; Yang, J.M.; Ogino, S.; Song, M.; Hong, S.H.; Abou Ghayda, R.; Kronbichler, A.; et al. Physical activity and the risk of SARS-CoV-2 infection, severe COVID-19 illness and COVID-19 related mortality in South Korea: A nationwide cohort study. *Br. J. Sports Med.* **2021**, 1–13. [CrossRef] [PubMed]
15. Wang, C.; Pan, R.; Wan, X.; Tan, Y.; Xu, L.; Ho, C.S.; Ho, R.C. Immediate psychological responses and associated factors during the initial stage of the 2019 coronavirus disease (COVID-19) epidemic among the general population in China. *Int. J. Environ. Res. Public Health* **2020**, *17*, 1729. [CrossRef]
16. Hsieh, C.Y.; Tsao, W.C.; Lin, R.T.; Chao, A.C. Three years of the nationwide post-acute stroke care program in Taiwan. *J. Chin. Med. Assoc.* **2018**, *81*, 87–88. [CrossRef] [PubMed]

17. Wang, C.Y.; Miyoshi, S.; Chen, C.H.; Lee, K.C.; Chang, L.C.; Chung, J.H.; Shi, H.Y. Walking ability and functional status after post-acute care for stroke rehabilitation in different age groups: A prospective study based on propensity score matching. *Aging* **2020**, *12*, 10704–10714. [CrossRef] [PubMed]
18. Broderick, J.P.; Adeoye, O.; Elm, J. Evolution of the Modified Rankin Scale and its use in future stroke trials. *Stroke* **2017**, *48*, 2007–2012. [CrossRef]
19. Banks, J.L.; Marotta, C.A. Outcomes validity and reliability of the modified Rankin scale: Implications for stroke clinical trials: A literature review and synthesis. *Stroke* **2007**, *38*, 1091–1096. [CrossRef] [PubMed]
20. Wolfe, C.D.; Taub, N.A.; Woodrow, E.J.; Burney, P.G. Assessment of scales of disability and handicap for stroke patients. *Stroke* **1991**, *22*, 1242–1244. [CrossRef]
21. Rabin, R.; de Charro, F. EQ-5D: A measure of health status from the EuroQol Group. *Ann. Med.* **2001**, *33*, 337–343. [CrossRef]
22. Lawton, M.P.; Brody, E.M. Assessment of older people: Self-maintaining and instrumental activities of daily living. *Gerontologist* **1969**, *9*, 179–186. [CrossRef] [PubMed]
23. Chou, C.Y.; Chien, C.W.; Hsueh, I.P.; Sheu, C.F.; Wang, C.H.; Hsieh, C.L. Developing a short form of the Berg Balance Scale for people with stroke. *Phys. Ther.* **2006**, *86*, 195–204. [CrossRef] [PubMed]
24. Salbach, N.M.; Mayo, N.E.; Higgins, J.; Ahmed, S.; Finch, L.E.; Richards, C.L. Responsiveness and predictability of gait speed and other disability measures in acute stroke. *Arch. Phys. Med. Rehabil.* **2001**, *82*, 1204–1212. [CrossRef] [PubMed]
25. Fulk, G.D.; He, Y.; Boyne, P.; Dunning, K. Predicting home and community walking activity poststroke. *Stroke* **2017**, *48*, 406–411. [CrossRef]
26. Chien, S.H.; Sung, P.Y.; Liao, W.L.; Tsai, S.W. A functional recovery profile for patients with stroke following post-acute rehabilitation care in Taiwan. *J. Formos. Med. Assoc.* **2020**, *119*, 254–259. [CrossRef]
27. Keni, R.; Alexander, A.; Nayak, P.G.; Mudgal, J.; Nandakumar, K. COVID-19: Emergence, spread, possible treatments, and global burden. *Front. Public Health* **2020**, *8*, 216. [CrossRef]
28. Summers, J.; Cheng, H.Y.; Lin, H.H.; Barnard, L.T.; Kvalsvig, A.; Wilson, N.; Baker, M.G. Potential lessons from the Taiwan and New Zealand health responses to the COVID-19 pandemic. *Lancet Reg Health West. Pac.* **2020**, *4*, 100044. [CrossRef]
29. D'Agostino, R.B., Jr. Propensity score methods for bias reduction in the comparison of a treatment to a non-randomized control group. *Stat. Med.* **1998**, *17*, 2265–2281. [CrossRef]
30. Rosenbaum, P.R.; Rubin, D.B. The central role of the propensity score in observational studies for causal effects. *Biometrika* **1983**, *70*, 41–55. [CrossRef]
31. Wang, C.Y.; Hsien, H.H.; Hung, K.W.; Lin, H.F.; Chiou, H.Y.; Yeh, S.J.; Yeh, Y.J.; Shi, H.Y. Multidiscipline stroke post-acute care transfer system: Propensity-score-based comparison of functional status. *J. Clin. Med.* **2019**, *8*, 1233. [CrossRef] [PubMed]
32. Cohen, J. *Statistical Power Analysis for the Behavioral Sciences*; Routledge: Oxford, UK, 1988.
33. Lai, C.L.; Tsai, M.M.; Luo, J.Y.; Liao, W.C.; Hsu, P.S.; Chen, H.Y. Post-acute care for stroke—A retrospective cohort study in Taiwan. *Patient Prefer. Adherence* **2017**, *11*, 1309–1315. [CrossRef] [PubMed]
34. Huang, H.C.; Tsai, J.Y.; Liu, T.C.; Sheng, W.Y.; Lin, T.C.; Lin, C.W.; Lee, I.H.; Chung, C.P. Functional recovery of stroke patients with postacute care: A retrospective study in a northern medical center. *J. Chin. Med. Assoc.* **2019**, *82*, 424–427. [CrossRef] [PubMed]
35. Campbell Burton, C.A.; Murray, J.; Holmes, J.; Astin, F.; Greenwood, D.; Knapp, P. Frequency of anxiety after stroke: A systematic review and meta-analysis of observational studies. *Int. J. Stroke* **2013**, *8*, 545–559. [CrossRef]
36. Polikandrioti, M.; Goudevenos, J.; Michalis, L.K.; Koutelekos, J.; Kyristi, H.; Tzialas, D.; Elisaf, M. Factors associated with depression and anxiety of hospitalized patients with heart failure. *Hellenic J. Cardiol.* **2015**, *56*, 26–35.
37. Ayerbe, L.; Ayis, S.; Wolfe, C.D.; Rudd, A.G. Natural history, predictors and outcomes of depression after stroke: Systematic review and meta-analysis. *Br. J. Psychiatry* **2013**, *202*, 14–21. [CrossRef]
38. Subramanian, S.K.; Chilingaryan, G.; Sveistrup, H.; Levin, M.F. Depressive symptoms influence use of feedback for motor learning and recovery in chronic stroke. *Restor. Neurol. Neurosci.* **2015**, *33*, 727–740. [CrossRef]
39. Eriksson, M.; Glader, E.L.; Norrving, B.; Asplund, K. Poststroke suicide attempts and completed suicides: A socioeconomic and nationwide perspective. *Neurology* **2015**, *84*, 1732–1738. [CrossRef]
40. Ahmed, Z.M.; Khalil, M.F.; Kohail, A.M.; Eldesouky, I.F.; Elkady, A.; Shuaib, A. The prevalence and predictors of post-stroke depression and anxiety during COVID-19 pandemic. *J. Stroke Cerebrovasc. Dis.* **2020**, *29*, 105315. [CrossRef]
41. Knepley, K.D.; Mao, J.Z.; Wieczorek, P.; Okoye, F.O.; Jain, A.P.; Harel, N.Y. Impact of telerehabilitation for stroke-related deficits. *Telemed. e-Health* **2021**, *27*, 239–246. [CrossRef]
42. Marotta, N.; Demeco, A.; Moggio, L.; Ammendolia, A. Why is telerehabilitation necessary? A pre-post COVID-19 comparative study of ICF activity and participation. *J. Enabling Technol.* **2021**, *15*, 117–121. [CrossRef]
43. Martin, A.; Markhvida, M.; Hallegatte, S.; Walsh, B. Socio-economic impacts of COVID-19 on household consumption and poverty. *Econ. Disasters Clim. Change* **2020**, *4*, 453–479. [CrossRef] [PubMed]
44. Ciciurkaite, G.; Marquez-Velarde, G.; Brown, R.L. Stressors associated with the COVID-19 pandemic, disability, and mental health: Considerations from the Intermountain West. *Stress Health* **2021**, 1–14. [CrossRef] [PubMed]
45. Marotta, N.; Ammendolia, A.; Marinaro, C.; Demeco, A.; Moggio, L.; Costantino, C. International Classification of Functioning, Disability and Health (ICF) and correlation between disability and finance assets in chronic stroke patients. *Acta Bio Med. Atenei Parm.* **2020**, *91*, e2020064.

46. Lee, J.J.; Tsang, W.N.; Yang, S.C.; Kwok, J.Y.Y.; Lou, V.W.; Lau, K.K. Qualitative study of Chinese stroke caregivers' caregiving experience during the COVID-19 pandemic. *Stroke* **2021**, *52*, 1407–1414. [CrossRef]
47. Zakeri, M.A.; Maazallahi, M.; Ehsani, V.; Dehghan, M. Iranian psychosocial status during and after COVID-19 outbreak mandatory quarantine: A cross-sectional study. *J. Commun. Psychol.* **2021**, *49*, 2506–2516. [CrossRef]
48. Yoon, S.; Kim, H.Y.; Kim, S.R. A prediction model of health-related quality of life in young adult patients with stroke. *J. Clin. Nurs.* **2021**, *30*, 2023–2035. [CrossRef]

International Journal of
Environmental Research and Public Health

MDPI

Protocol

Construction of Progress Prediction Model of Urinary Incontinence in Elderly Women: Protocol for a Multi-Center, Prospective Cohort Study

Di Zhang [1,2,3,†], Lei Gao [1,2,3,†], Yuanyuan Jia [1,2,3], Shiyan Wang [1,2,3], Haibo Wang [4], Xiuli Sun [1,2,3,*] and Jianliu Wang [1,2,3]

1 Department of Obstetrics and Gynecology, Peking University People's Hospital, No. 11, Xi-Zhi-Men South Street, Xi Cheng District, Beijing 100044, China; 1911110388@bjmu.edu.cn (D.Z.); 1911110389@bjmu.edu.cn (L.G.); jiayuan@bjmu.edu.cn (Y.J.); 0062043910@bjmu.edu.cn (S.W.); wangjianliu@pkuph.edu.cn (J.W.)
2 The Key Laboratory of Female Pelvic Floor Disorders, Beijing 100044, China
3 Research Center of Female Pelvic Floor Disorders, Peking University, Beijing 100044, China
4 Clinical Research Institute, Peking University, Beijing 100191, China; wanghb_pucri@bjmu.edu.cn
* Correspondence: sunxiuli@pkuph.edu.cn
† These authors contributed equally to this work.

Abstract: Background: Urinary incontinence (UI) is a common health problem and seriously affects quality of life. Many women lack understanding of UI or are too ashamed to seek medical advice early, leading to a low treatment rate. The aim of this study is to establish an effective UI progress prediction model for elderly women with UI for earlier detection and better treatment. Methods: This study is conducted as a prospective, multi-center, cohort study, and recruits 800 women aged ≥60 with mild or moderate UI in China. Participants are divided into three groups: stress urinary incontinence group (SUI), urgency urinary incontinence group (UUI), and mixed urinary incontinence group (MUI). This study will investigate the general conditions of patients, after complete relevant pelvic floor function assessment, as well as after follow up at 6 months, 12 months, and 18 months by telephone. The primary endpoint is UI disease progress. Single factor and multi-factor Cox regression model analyses are undertaken to evaluate the associated risk factors affecting the progress of UI to establish a progress prediction model for elderly women. Discussion: This study will provide more predictive information for elderly women with UI, and new clinical references for the intervention and the treatment of UI for medical staff.

Keywords: elderly women with UI; disease progress; prediction model

Citation: Zhang, D.; Gao, L.; Jia, Y.; Wang, S.; Wang, H.; Sun, X.; Wang, J. Construction of Progress Prediction Model of Urinary Incontinence in Elderly Women: Protocol for a Multi-Center, Prospective Cohort Study. *Int. J. Environ. Res. Public Health* **2022**, *19*, 734. https://doi.org/10.3390/ijerph19020734

Academic Editors: Joachim G. Voss and Sandul Yasobant

Received: 19 November 2021
Accepted: 5 January 2022
Published: 10 January 2022

1. Background

Urinary incontinence (UI) is defined as an abnormal urinary control condition in which urine flows out of the urethral opening involuntarily [1]. It is common lower urinary tract symptom in women and one of the most frequently reported diseases associated with pelvic organ prolapse in adult women. UI can occur in all age groups, whereas it is more commonly seen in middle-aged and elderly patients. The globally reported UI prevalence in women ranges from 25% to 45% and increases year by year [2], and the prevalence of UI among adult women over 60 years old has been reported to be up to 38% [3]. Similarly, the reported UI prevalence in Chinese adult women differs from 8.7% to 69.8%, while that in older Chinese women reaches 16.9% to 61.6% [4]. UI is etiologically and pathophysiologically categorized for three types, as follows: stress urinary incontinence (SUI), urgency urinary incontinence (UUI), and mixed urinary incontinence (MUI) [5]. SUI is the most common type, accounting for 50% of all UI cases [6,7], and is defined as involuntary urinary leakage when physical exertion from coughing, sneezing, or laughing causes pressure to the bladder. Inadequate support of the urethra by the pelvic floor muscles and deficiency of the urethral intrinsic sphincter are the recognized essential mechanisms for UI. The reported UI-associated factors include patient age, body mass index (BMI), genetic factors, smoking, race, constipation, pregnancy and multiple childbirths, previous pelvic floor operations (e.g., hysterectomy), and hormone deficiency or menopause, all of which cause pelvic floor muscle weakness [3,8,9]. UUI prevalence has been reported in many studies to be between 1% to 7% [6,7], which is much lower than UI. UUI generally refers to an overactive bladder caused involuntary urinary leakage with urgency, which is usually caused by involuntary contractions of the bladder wall detrusor muscle. UUI may be triggered by simple daily phenomena and activities such as the sound of tap water, exposure to low temperatures, or drinking cold drinks, and has several congenital causes including myogenic, neurogenic, and urethral symptoms [3,8,10]. MUI is a mixture of symptoms of SUI and UUI, with a reported incidence of 7.5% to 25%, secondary to SUI [6,7]. Its etiology is also a combination of factors causing SUI and UUI [11,12].

UI in women is a huge global health problem. Besides affecting women's quality of life by limiting social activities, productivity, and social and sexual behaviors, it also has significant impacts on medical costs and even increases financial burden on women and society [4,13]. In addition, regarding the psychological impact of UI on women, numerous research works claim that it creates a long-term period of mental suffering, such as depression or anxiety [14–16]. However, some scholars have found, through study of female athletes, that UI does not cause depression and anxiety. Such conclusions are most possibly related to the study subjects, namely female athletes, who have an acknowledged relationship between UI and sport, with most suffering mild UI, as well as having a stronger sense of happiness because of their sport, thus UI might not impact their psychological mode [17].

UI as a common public health issue, is a worldwide problem that has not been indicated to most women, and thus not enough attention has been paid to its early diagnosis and treatment. The impacts of mild and moderate to severe UI on quality of life are greatly different. Although mild UI has little impact on quality of life, as it becomes more severe, it will not only worsen quality of life, but will also bring heavy financial burden to the family and society. Therefore, it is important to use early interventions to upgrade patients' quality of life and reduce the financial burden related to this disease by detecting any risk factors from patients with mild UI, so as to prevent their mild UI from progressing to moderate or severe.

The common interventions for the prevention of UI include lifestyle intervention, pelvic floor muscle training, biofeedback therapy, and electrical stimulation therapy, etc. However, all these interventions lack standard and systematic evaluations of their preventive effectiveness [18,19].

With the increasing popularity of big data technology, using machine learning to measure the situation and to predict the development of diseases closely related to human health has globally become a hot research topic and application field recently. At present, there is a precedent of using clinical diagnostic software based on large-scale epidemiological data analysis to predict the incidence of diseases in the world. A well-known prognostic model is the Framingham risk score, which predicts the risk of cardiovascular disease in 10 years [20]. Current studies on UI are all disease pathogenesis models, and there are no reports on UI development or the application of any prediction model or software for UI progress in elderly women.

The aims of this study are to systematically investigate the disease progress related factors for elderly women with UI, so as to establish a UI progress prediction model and to improve science-based interventions and preventive measures for UIs [19,21].

2. Materials and Methods

2.1. Study Design and Setting

The study is conducted as a prospective multicenter study to collect epidemiological factors for the analysis of the impacts of physical activity, chronic diseases, pregnancy and delivery, genetic characteristics, pelvic floor function assessment (e.g., pelvic floor muscle strength, pelvic floor ultrasound, pelvic floor electrophysiology, and morphology index), and other factors in elderly women. Data analysis will be conducted by means of bioinformatics and mathematical modeling objectives to investigate the influence of UI progress and prognosis related factors, and to construct a prediction model of UI progress in elderly women. This study is carried out by Peking University People's Hospital in Beijing, in cooperation with Wuhan University People's Hospital in Wuhan, China. A total of 800 patients will be recruited, 400 from Beijing and 400 from Wuhan. Four district-level hospitals in Beijing are involved as the sub-centers in Beijing, namely Tongzhou District Maternal and Child Health Care Hospital, Fengtai District Maternal and Child Health Care Hospital, Fangshan District Maternal and Child Health Care Hospital, and Changping District Maternal and Child Health Care Hospital. Two district-level hospitals in Wuhan are involved as the sub-centers in Wuhan, namely Wuhan Qingshan District Maternal and Child Health Hospital and Wuhan East Lake New Technology Development Zone Fozu Mountain Community Health Service Center. Each sub-center will select communities within the district that are targeted to recruit elderly female patients who are ≥60 years of age with mild to moderate UI by distributing a research subject leaflet. Eligible women need to sign informed consent before being enrolled in the cohorts. Figure 1 illustrates the flow diagram of the study for all subjects.

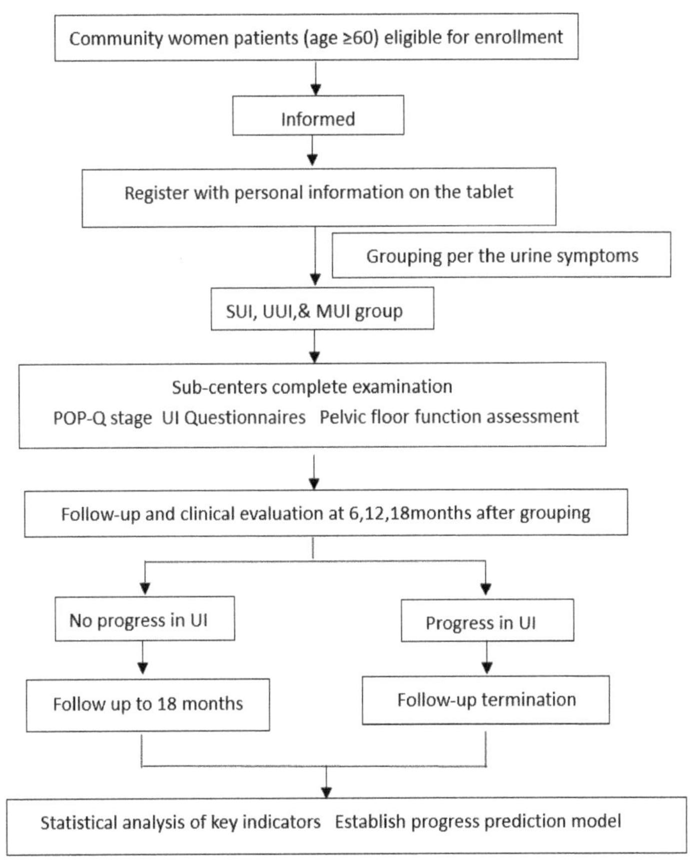

Figure 1. Study flow chart.

2.2. Participants

The project is approached by phone calls to women ≥60 years of age (the elderly women) and were recently diagnosed with mild or moderate UI. A primary screening survey is conducted during the approach by asking the women three simple questions by investigators: whether they have urine leakage, what is the urine leakage frequency, and what accompanying symptoms they have. Women who are primarily screened to have potential mild and moderate UI will be invited for further examination at the hospitals, where the preliminary examination will be conducted by trained doctors while recording the detailed patient's history.

2.2.1. Inclusion Criteria

Participants will be enrolled if they are: (1) ≥60 years of age; (2) educated enough to complete the questionnaires; (3) able to move freely to attend a hospital examination; (4) previously diagnosed as mild and moderate UI, including SUI, UUI, and MUI; (5) suffering urine leakage during occasional coughing, exertion, sneezing, fast walking, and other abdominal pressure; or (6) suffering frequent and urgent urination with urinary leakage and nocturia.

2.2.2. Exclusion Criteria

Patients will be excluded from the study if they were diagnosed as having: (1) severe pelvic organ prolapse, (2) serious cardiovascular and cerebrovascular diseases or other life-threatening diseases, (3) malignant tumor threatening patients life, (4) urogenital tract fistula, (5) previous history of anti-UI surgery and medication for UI, (6) no self-care ability and unable to complete the follow-up, and (7) severe UI and chronic urinary retention.

2.3. Randomization and Blinding

In this study, patients will be recruited using convenient sampling without randomization. All investigators, other than those conducting recruitments, will be masked in our study.

2.4. Informed Consent

All patients will sign the consent forms (two copies) after being fully informed about this study in detail and any questions they had were answered. One copy will be handed over to the patients, while another copy will be stored at the sub-center for unified management.

2.5. Intervention

This is an observational prospective cohort study with no intervention to the enrolled patients.

2.6. Initial Screening, Assessment, and Follow-Up

After informed consent, participants will be arranged in the hospital in batches. The patients will be received by a team that consists of physicians specialized in the pelvic floor and nurses. All investigators of the team are comparatively fixed and need to be trained by a principal investigator from Peking University People's Hospital on the research protocol, the inclusive and exclusive criteria, and the questionnaire interviewing. Roleplay on questionnaire interviewing was conducted to have each of the team members interview a provider's female family member who had no idea about the study, under the supervision of the principal investigator, to confirm that the question was raised using publicly understandable terms and to avoid inducive wording. Questionnaires to the participants will be completed via interview in a doctor's office at the clinic, which will be specially resettled for allowing participants to be interviewed under a comfortable circumstance so as to avoid answer bias from patient nervousness.

Every participant will be given a unique study ID. Participants' demographic information, including age, marital status, education level, occupation, BMI, living habits, menstruation, marriage, childbirths, sex life status, and chronic diseases, ect, were collected confidentially. Participants will be primarily grouped according to the questionnaire interview at the enrollment visit by the investigators. Included in the questionnaires are relevant questions regarding inclusive criteria for three types of UI, which were designed according to the UI classification of the International Continence Society [1]. Participants will be included in the SUI group if question 5 is satisfied, in the UUI group if question 6 is satisfied, or in MUI if question 5 and 6 are both satisfied. All the communication between providers and participants during the questionnaire interview will be monitored by the PI and will be fully recorded for quality control analysis.

For grouping the participants, we will grade the disease situation for each of the participants grouped in each of the groups according to the symptoms using the Ingelman-Sundberg Indexing method and International Continence Society standards [1]. Grading criteria are listed in the following form (Table 1): Participants will be excluded if they are graded to have severe UI.

Table 1. Diagnosis criteria for subtypes of UI.

UI Types	Grade	Criteria
SUI grading	Mild	UI appears when coughing or sneezing without the need for a urinal pad
	Moderate	UI appears when running, jumping, or fast walking, and a urinal pad is needed
	Severe	UI appears when changing body position or resting at bed
UUI grading		According to OABSS indicators Question 3 (urgency) has a score of 2 or more, and the total score is 3 or more)
	Mild	$3 \leq$ score ≤ 5
	Moderate	$6 \leq$ score ≤ 11
	Severe	Score ≥ 12
MUI grading		According to the grade of SUI and UUI related symptoms, highest grading to be matched

UI: urinary incontinence; SUI: stress urinary incontinence; UUI: urgency urinary incontinence; MUI: mixed urinary incontinence; OABSS: overactive bladder symptom score.

After collecting the above-mentioned data, all participants will completed a gynecological examination, one-hour urinal pad test, pelvic floor electrophysiological examination, uroflowmetry, pelvic floor ultrasound, and morphological examination (Table 2). All the examinations will be conducted by the teams, using the same model instruments to avoid data biases, and data will be recorded on tablets connected to the database. The items to be inspected are as follows:

(1) **Gynecological examination** includes uterus, vagina and appendages inspections; pressure inductive testing; bladder neck elevation testing; hand Oxford muscle strength classification testing; pelvic organ prolapse quantification (POP-Q); and one-hour urinal pad testing.
(2) **UI questionnaires** concerning International Consultation on Incontinence Questionnaire-Short Form (ICIQ-SF) for investigation of UI frequency, degree, and its impacts on quality of life via 0–21 scoring to represent the severity of the UI [22]; OABSS questionnaire for assessment of the symptoms of the participants whose bladders are overactive and the severities of their urinary frequency, nocturia, urinary urgency, and urinary incontinence via scoring 0–15 to indicate the lowest to highest severity [23,24]; and Urogenital Distress Inventory-6(UDI-6) for evaluation of the lower urinary tract dysfunction via scoring 0–24 to present the severity of the urinary incontinence [25,26].
(3) **Pelvic floor electrophysiological examination** on an instrument to collect data regarding indicators such as the maximum vaginal dynamic pressure, the vaginal resting pressure, the strength grades of type I and type II muscle, and the fatigue of type I and type II muscle fibers.

(4) **Uroflowmetry** on the maximum and average rate of urine flow, urination time, and the urine flow curve.
(5) **Pelvic floor ultrasound examination** performed by two attending doctors who have rich clinical experience of pelvic floor ultrasound for the residual urine, detrusor muscle thickness, bladder neck movement, urethral rotation angle, bladder posterior angle, the shape of the internal urethra opening, the distance from the lowest point of the bladder to the posterior lower edge of the pubic symphysis, levator ani muscle trauma, and levator ani hiatus area in the Valsalva status.
(6) **Morphological examination** a study reported that the pelvis architecture was closely related to UI in women, especially pelvic inlet and pelvic outlet diameters as risk factors for UI [27], therefore, we include pelvic floor morphology into the study, which mainly includes the inclination angle of the sacrum and the anterior superior iliac spine, and the pelvic tendency.

Table 2. Participant baseline screening, assessment, and follow-up schedule.

Characteristics	Baseline			Follow-Up (6 Months, 12 Months, 18 Months)		
	SUI	UUI	MUI	SUI	UUI	MUI
Age (≥60)	•	•	•			
Race	•	•	•			
Marital status	•	•	•			
Educational level	•	•	•			
Mainly physical labor	•	•	•			
BMI	•	•	•			
Parity	•	•	•			
Manner of delivery	•	•	•			
UI during pregnancy	•	•	•			
UI after childbirth	•	•	•			
Menopause	•	•	•			
Sex life	•	•	•			
Drink preference	•	•	•			
24-h Volume of liquid intake (mL)	•	•	•			
Smoking	•	•	•			
Comorbidities	•	•	•			
Chronic cough						
Asthma						
Diabetes						
Constipation						
Pelvic inflammatory disease	•	•	•			
Depression	•	•	•			
Urinary tract infection (last 4 weeks)	•	•	•			
History of gynecological surgery	•	•	•			
Family history of UI	•	•	•			
UI duration (year)	•	•	•	•	•	•
Frequency of urine leakage (time/month)	•	•	•	•	•	•
Symptoms accompaning urine leakage	•	•	•	•	•	•
Using urine pads (per/month)	▲	▲	▲	▲	▲	▲
Impact on life	•	•	•	•	•	•
POP-Q	•	•	•			
Hand test Oxford muscle strength grading	•	•	•			
One-hour urine pad test (g)	•	•	•			
Severity of UI	•	•	•	•	•	•
Mild						

Table 2. *Cont.*

Characteristics	Baseline			Follow-Up (6 Months, 12 Months, 18 Months)		
	SUI	UUI	MUI	SUI	UUI	MUI
Moderate						
Severe						
Pelvic floor electrophysiology examination	•	•	•			
Uroflowmetry	•	•	•			
Pelvic floor ultrasound	•	•	•			
Morphological examination	•	•	•			
ICIQ-SF score	•	•	•	•	•	•
OABSS score	•	•	•	•	•	•
UDI-6 score	•	•	•	•	•	•
UI progress				▲	▲	▲

•: Indicates mandatory items; ▲: Investigator will decide whether to perform the test according to clinical signs or clinical evaluation. UI: urinary incontinence; SUI: stress urinary incontinence; UUI: urgency urinary incontinence; MUI: mixed urinary incontinence; OABSS: overactive bladder symptom score; POP-Q: pelvic organ prolapse quantification; ICIQ-SF: International Consultation on Incontinence Questionnaire-short form; UDI-6: Urogenital Distress Inventory-6; BMI: body mass index.

Enrollment and participant grouping will be completed after all of the above procedures. Participant follow-up will be conducted for 6 months, 12 months, and 18 months from enrollment by investigators who were trained for each follow-up question. The follow-ups will be conducted by telephone to learn UI progress by inquiring participants' symptoms in terms of the history of urinary incontinence, the frequency of urine leakage, the urinary syndrome, the usage of urinal pad, and conscious impact on life, and using a manner of questionnaires (ICIQ-SF, OABSS, and UDI- 6) (Table 2). Patients whose situation could not be confirmed as progressive or who struggle to express their symptoms will be requested to return back to the hospital for follow-up. Follow-up will be terminated for participants whose UI symptoms have aggravated upgrading. Rehabilitation guidance will be provided to participants in the termination of follow-up. Follow-up will be continued for participants with no symptom aggravation for no more than three calls in a period of no longer than 18 months.

2.7. Study Endpoint

As there are no internationally accepted criteria for UI progress, we set up a series of criteria for referring literature, using the Ingelman-Sundberg Indexing method and International Continence Society [1] to judge UI progress in our study. The primary endpoint: UI progress will be judged if any of the following criteria are satisfied: For the SUI group, (1) urinary leakage inducive causes a change from coughing and sneezing to running, jumping and fast walking, or from running, jumping and fast walking to postural changes and rest at bed; (2) urinal pad usage changes from unneeded to needed; or (3) the baseline ICIQ-SF score is heightened for $\geq$4 [28]. For the UUI group, (1) OABSS score upgrades compared with the baseline, or (2) urinal pad usage changes from unneeded to needed. Progress will be confirmed for the MUI group if participants satisfy any of the progressive criteria for the SUI and UUI groups.

2.8. Data Management

All information from the study will be input into the computerized database developed by the Guangzhou Huibo Information Technology Co., Ltd. (Guangdong, China), under the study ID and together with the grouping data. Simultaneous double inputs by two independent providers will be adopted in order to match the two copies of the datasets so as to figure out any possible data error latterly. Data inputs will be managed by an experienced statistic professor.

2.9. Sample Size Consideration

According to one risk factor in the prediction model, 10 to 15 positive events (UI progress) are be required. It is preliminarily estimated that there are about 10 meaningful risk factors, so 100–150 cases need to be included in the study to get enough statistical power. In consideration of this, 15–20% of the patients were lost in follow-ups [6,9], and the number of participants in the training and validation groups are at a ratio of 2:1, at least 188–282 participants in total are required in order to have statistical power. As more than the anticipated number of targeted women expressed their willing for participation, we planned to recruit 800 participants at most in order to get greater power for the study.

2.10. Statistical Analysis and Progress Prediction Model Construction

Data analysis will be done using SAS® 9.3 software (software installation point authorization number: 11202165).

We set up a prediction model based on the Cox regression model. According to univariate Cox regression analysis, risk factors with a p value < 0.05 will be selected to enter the model predictive factors, and then the forward method will be used to carry out multi-factor Cox regression analysis to build the prediction model of the UI disease progress, predicting the risk of UI disease progress. The subjects will be randomly divided into training and validation cohorts according to the ratio of 2:1. The discriminative ability of the prediction model will be analyzed through the area under the ROC curve, and the accuracy of the model will be evaluated by the Hosmer–Lemeshow decile chi-square test. The calibration of the ten models will be assessed with the predicted versus observed probability plots, and the discrimination of the models will be assessed with the prognostic separation D-statistic (D-statistic). The bootstrap method will be used to further internally verify the discriminative ability and accuracy of the model. External validation uses different hospitals for spatial validation to evaluate the extrapolation of the model. Moreover, 100 bootstrap random samplings will be performed to generate 100 bootstrap test sets. For each test set, the area under the ROC curve method and Hosmer–Lemeshow deciles will be used in the square test to objectively evaluate the stability and variation range of the model's discriminative ability and accuracy.

3. Discussion

UI is one of the chronic diseases that seriously affects middle-aged and elderly women in their quality of life. More and more women are suffering from UI. However, due to a lack of knowledge or willingness to seek medical treatment, many women, especially the elderly, develop moderate to severe UI before they visit a doctor for treatment. It has been recognized by the medical society that early detection is of great significance for the treatment of UI. Although a lot of risk factors are reported to be associated with UI, only some of these factors have been identified to reduce UI incidence and prevalence through their mitigation, which includes constipation, parity, gynecological diseases, or cardiovascular diseases [4,8]. UI prevalence and the likely associated factors have been widely reported by researchers from many countries. However, few studies have really focused on UI progress criteria and the factors that can potentially reverse UI, even slightly.

There are several studies on UI curation nowadays. A study by Zhishun Liu [19], a randomized controlled trial (RCT), showed that a greater than 50% decrease in terms of urinary leakage amount in SUI patients was achieved by treatment with electroacupuncture involving the lumbosacral region. A similar study by Renly Lim [28] on the curation of SUI reported a four-point ICIQ-SF score reduction in women with nonsurgical treatments for UI, which showed the minimum clinically important difference (MCID) with the baselines. A clinical study conducted by Liliana Giraldo-Rodríguez [9] on the epidemiology, progress, and predictive factors of UI in community-dwelling Mexican adults aged ≥ 50 indicated that depression and falls could decrease the incidence of UI, but they did not come up with criteria for UI curation or progress because of some limitations. In referring to the above studies, based on criteria for SUI disease curation, we thought backwards about one criterion of disease progress. We define "≥4 points of ICIQ-SF score increase" as one of the progress criteria for SUI progress, as it is more objective and convenient than the calculation of urine leakage or the frequency of urine leakage. The other criteria of SUI progress mainly adopt the Ingelman-Sundberg Indexing method. The criteria of UUI progress are defined by our team in consideration of the questionnaire of OABSS's severity study on the UUI.

To date, there has been no published powerful clinical research on criteria for UI progress, suggesting that there is evidenced agreement on the risk-factors that can predict UI progress among the medical society. Meanwhile, there has been no research on disease progress models up to now, and the research on UI progress model is more meaningful for quality of life. Our work in this collaborative study aims to investigate the indicators most valuable for the prediction of UI development and progress through comparing the baseline and follow-up data for the same indicators, and, based on those data, by single factor and multi-factor Cox regression model analysis, we will try to develop a primary UI progress predication model for the world, which we believe will significantly contribute to the worldwide studies in this research area.

As screening for high-risk factors is mainly based on previous literature, many disease incidence prediction models are mainly based on questionnaires and basic gynecological examinations. The advantages of our study are that it includes morphology and ultrasound, electrophysiological examination, and other indicators that have rarely been performed. Those newly included indicators may provide early warning for UI progress and evidence for the early intervention and treatment of UI.

The UI predictive model will be developed to be an app compatible with mobile devices. When patients with symptoms of urine leakage enter relevant information and data via this app, the model system will automatically analyze their disease conditions to predict the potentiality of UI progress. It will serve to warm both the patients and the clinicians, remind the patients to seek medical treatments, and provide the clinicians evidence for preventive interventions. We believe that it could play an important role in alleviating the symptoms of urine leakage and promoting the recovery of UI.

The purpose for us recruiting patients from Beijing, a city in northern China, and Wuhan, a city in mid-southern China, is to ensure that the indicators and criteria could be determined from the analysis of the data from patients representing the northern and southern areas. If we succeed in the primary development of a predictive model for UI progress, the primary model should be applied in a large-scale study to demonstrate its effectiveness or to provide evidence for further modification.

Our study has some limits. Firstly, UI progress has not been clearly defined worldwide. The criteria for UI progress are defined by our team in referring a large amount of literature and the international recognized diagnostic criteria for UI and the questionnaire of ICIQ-SF and OABSS 's study on UI. These criteria have been demonstrated to have certain clinical significance, but the relevant criteria for each of the indicators still need to be further discussed and explored in a large clinical sample research. Secondly, we design a convenient follow-up procedure via phone calls to reduce the drop-off rate. To avoid any possible information bias via phone calls, we trained the investigators before having them conduct the follow-ups, and will request patients who could not be diagnosed with progress to return to the hospital for follow-up confirmation. Thirdly, the progress years of UI are not clearly defined in the literature. Our study will project following the participants for up to 18 months, which is fine to observe UI progress, but is still not long enough to give powerful answers. We hope we can contribute towards a large-scale study in UI progress prediction through long-term follow-ups.

4. Conclusions

To the best of our knowledge, this is the first study to investigate the progress prediction model of associated risk factors for UI disease progress in elderly women. This study may provide more prediction information for elderly female UI patients and improve their quality of life. Information from this study could also be used to guide medical attention and to properly shape interventions for UI for older adults. The information regarding the problem of early diagnosis, treatment, and improvement of long-term prognosis among UI women is particularly useful, as there are few such studies in this UI progress area.

Author Contributions: Conceptualization, X.S.; methodology, X.S., D.Z. and L.G.; software, H.W.; writing—original draft preparation, D.Z.; writing—review and editing, D.Z., L.G., Y.J. and S.W.; supervision and visualization, X.S. and J.W.; funding acquisition, Y.J. All authors have read and agreed to the published version of the manuscript.

Funding: This work is supported by the National Key Technology R&D Program of China (grant number: 2018YFC2002204).

Institutional Review Board Statement: This study protocol was approved by the Ethic Committee of Peking University People's Hospital (ethic file number: 2020PHB054-01).

Informed Consent Statement: Informed consent was obtained from all subjects involved in the study.

Data Availability Statement: Not applicable.

Acknowledgments: Appreciation to all participants in this study and all researchers in the recruitment hospitals for their contributions.

Conflicts of Interest: All authors declare that they have no competing interest.

Abbreviations

UI: urinary incontinence; SUI: stress urinary incontinence; UUI: urgency urinary incontinence; MUI: mixed urinary incontinence; POP-Q: pelvic organ prolapse quantification; ICIQ-SF: International Consultation on Incontinence Questionnaire-short form; OABSS: overactive bladder symptom score; UDI-6: Urogenital Distress Inventory-6; BMI: body mass index; RCT: Randomized Controlled Trial; MCID: minimum clinically important difference.

References

1. Haylen, B.T.; de Ridder, D.; Freeman, R.M.; Swith, S.E.; Berghmans, B.; Lee, J.; Schaer, G.N. An International Urogynecological Association (IUGA)/International Continence Society (ICS) joint report on the terminology for female pelvic floor dysfunction. *Int. Urogynecol. J.* **2010**, *21*, 5–26. [CrossRef]
2. Keller, K.D.; La Rosa, V.L.; Cerentini, T.M.; de Souza, C.M.; Costa, F.L.; da Rosa, P.V.; da Silva Klahr, P.; de Almeida Pereira, E.; da Rosa, L.H.T. Quality of Life and Urinary Incontinence Symptoms in Women Undergoing Bariatric Surgery: A Combined Case-Cohort Study. *Female Pelvic Med. Reconstr. Surg.* **2020**, *26*, e62–e67. [CrossRef]
3. Lukacz, E.S.; Santiago-Lastra, Y.; Albo, M.E.; Brubaker, L. Urinary Incontinence in Women: A Review. *Jama* **2017**, *318*, 1592–1604. [CrossRef] [PubMed]
4. Xue, K.; Palmer, M.H.; Zhou, F. Prevalence and associated factors of urinary incontinence in women living in China: A literature review. *BMC Urol.* **2020**, *20*, 159. [CrossRef]
5. Toye, F.; Barker, K.L. A meta-ethnography to understand the experience of living with urinary incontinence: "Is it just part and parcel of life?". *BMC Urol.* **2020**, *20*, 1. [CrossRef] [PubMed]
6. Hagen, S.; McClurg, D.; Bugge, C.; Hay-Smith, J.; Dean, S.G.; Elders, A.; Glazener, C.; Abdel-Fattah, M.; Agur, W.I.; Booth, J.; et al. Effectiveness and cost-effectiveness of basic versus biofeedback-mediated intensive pelvic floor muscle training for female stress or mixed urinary incontinence: Protocol for the OPAL randomised trial. *BMJ Open* **2019**, *9*, e024153. [CrossRef]
7. Abrams, P.; Andersson, K.E.; Apostolidis, A.; Birder, L.; Bliss, D.; Brubaker, L.; Cardozo, L.; Castro-Diaz, D.; O'Connell, P.R.; Cottenden, A.; et al. Recommendations of the International Scientific Committee: Evaluation and Treatment of Urinary Incontinence, Pelvic Organ Prolapse and Faecal Incontinence. In Proceedings of the 6th International Consultation on Incontinence, Tokyo, Japan, 12–14 September 2016; Volume 37, pp. 2271–2272.
8. Xu, C.; Chen, M.; Fu, J.; Meng, Y.; Qin, S.; Luo, Y. Urinary incontinence status and risk factors in women aged 50–70 years: A cross-sectional study in Hunan, China. *Int. Urogynecol. J.* **2021**, *32*, 95–102. [CrossRef]
9. Giraldo-Rodríguez, L.; Agudelo-Botero, M.; Mino-León, D.; Álvarez-Cisneros, T. Epidemiology, progression, and predictive factors of urinary incontinence in older community-dwelling Mexican adults: Longitudinal data from the Mexican Health and Aging Study. *Neurourol. Urodyn.* **2019**, *38*, 1932–1943. [CrossRef] [PubMed]
10. Yoshioka, T.; Kamitani, T.; Omae, K.; Shimizu, S.; Fukuhara, S.; Yamamoto, Y. Urgency urinary incontinence, loss of independence, and increased mortality in older adults: A cohort study. *PLoS ONE* **2021**, *16*, e0245724. [CrossRef]

11. Edwall, L.; Carlström, K.; Jonasson, A.F. Different estrogen sensitivity of urogenital tissue from women with and without stress urinary incontinence. *Neurourol. Urodyn.* **2009**, *28*, 516–520. [CrossRef]
12. Melville, J.L.; Fan, M.Y.; Rau, H.; Nygaard, I.E.; Katon, W.J. Major depression and urinary incontinence in women: Temporal associations in an epidemiologic sample. *Am. J. Obstet. Gynecol.* **2009**, *201*, 490.e1–490.e7. [CrossRef]
13. Gyhagen, M.; Åkervall, S.; Molin, M.; Milsom, I. The effect of childbirth on urinary incontinence: A matched cohort study in women aged 40–64 years. *Am. J. Obstet. Gynecol.* **2019**, *221*, 322.e1–322.e17. [CrossRef] [PubMed]
14. Liu, Y.J.; Wu, W.Y.; Hsiao, S.M.; Ting, S.W.H.; Hsu, H.P.; Huang, C.M. Efficacy of pelvic floor training with surface electromyography feedback for female stress urinary incontinence. *Int. J. Nurs. Pract.* **2018**, *24*, e12698. [CrossRef] [PubMed]
15. Vikström, N.H.; Wasteson, E.; Lindam, A.; Samuelsson, E. Anxiety and depression in women with urinary incontinence using E-health. *Int. Urogynecol. J.* **2021**, *32*, 103–109. [CrossRef] [PubMed]
16. Cheng, S.; Lin, D.; Hu, T.; Cao, L.; Liao, H.; Mou, X.; Zhang, Q.; Liu, J.; Wu, T. Association of urinary incontinence and depression or anxiety: A meta-analysis. *J. Int. Med. Res.* **2020**, *48*, 300060520931348. [CrossRef]
17. Velázquez-Saornil, J.; Méndez-Sánchez, E.; Gómez-Sánchez, S.; Sánchez-Milá, Z.; Cortés-Llorente, E.; Martín-Jiménez, A.; Sánchez-Jiménez, E.; Campón-Chekroun, A. Observational Study on the Prevalence of Urinary Incontinence in Female Athletes. *Int. J. Environ. Res. Public Health* **2021**, *18*, 5591. [CrossRef] [PubMed]
18. Radzimińska, A.; Weber-Rajek, M.; Strączyńska, A.; Podhorecka, M.; Kozakiewicz, M.; Kędziora-Kornatowska, K.; Goch, A. The impact of pelvic floor muscle training on the myostatin concentration and severity of urinary incontinence in elderly women with stress urinary incontinence—A pilot study. *Clin. Interv. Aging* **2018**, *13*, 1893–1898. [CrossRef] [PubMed]
19. Liu, Z.; Liu, Y.; Xu, H.; He, L.; Chen, Y.; Fu, L.; Li, N.; Lu, Y.; Su, T.; Sun, J.; et al. Effect of Electroacupuncture on Urinary Leakage among Women with Stress Urinary Incontinence: A Randomized Clinical Trial. *JAMA* **2017**, *317*, 2493–2501. [CrossRef]
20. D'Agostino, R.B.; Grundy, S.; Sullivan, L.M.; Wilson, P.; CHD Risk Prediction Group. Validation of the Framingham coronary heart disease prediction scores: Results of a multiple ethnic groups investigation. *JAMA* **2001**, *286*, 180–187. [CrossRef]
21. Wyman, J.F.; Harkins, S.W.; Choi, S.C.; Taylor, J.R.; Fantl, J.A. Psychosocial impact of urinary incontinence in women. *Obstet. Gynecol.* **1987**, *70*, 378–381. [PubMed]
22. Tadeu, J.; Maman, N. Validation of the "International Consultation on Incontinence Questionnaire—Short Form" (ICIQ-SF) for Portuguese. *Rev. Saúde Pública* **2004**, *38*, 438–444.
23. Homma, Y.; Yoshida, M.; Seki, N.; Yokoyama, O.; Kakizaki, H.; Gotoh, M.; Yamanishi, T.; Yamaguchi, O.; Takeda, M.; Nishizawa, O. Symptom assessment tool for overactive bladder syndrome—Overactive bladder symptom score. *Urology* **2006**, *68*, 318–323. [CrossRef] [PubMed]
24. Homma, Y. Re: Validation of the overactive bladder symptom score: J. G. Blaivas, G. Panagopoulos, J.P. Weiss and C. Somaroo J Urol 2007; 178: 543–547. *J. Urol.* **2008**, *179*, 791. [CrossRef] [PubMed]
25. Phé, V.; Zimmern, P.; Chartier-Kastler, E. Outcome measures for stress urinary incontinence treatment: Can we minimally agree? *World J. Urol.* **2015**, *33*, 1221–1234. [CrossRef]
26. Hwang, U.J.; Lee, M.S.; Jung, S.H.; Ahn, S.H.; Kwon, O.Y. Which pelvic floor muscle functions are associated with improved subjective and objective symptoms after 8 weeks of surface electrical stimulation in women with stress urinary incontinence? *Eur. J. Obstet. Gynecol. Reprod. Biol.* **2020**, *247*, 16–21. [CrossRef] [PubMed]
27. Stav, K.; Alcalay, M.; Peleg, S.; Lindner, A.; Gayer, G.; Hershkovitz, I. Pelvis architecture and urinary incontinence in women. *Eur. Urol.* **2007**, *52*, 239–244. [CrossRef]
28. Lim, R.; Liong, M.L.; Lim, K.K.; Leong, W.S.; Yuen, K.H. The Minimum Clinically Important Difference of the International Consultation on Incontinence Questionnaires (ICIQ-UI SF and ICIQ-LUTSqol). *Urology* **2019**, *133*, 91–95. [CrossRef]

healthcare

MDPI

Article

Study on Associating Emotions in Verbal Reactions to Facial Expressions in Dementia

SungHo Hwang [1], JiWon Hwang [2] and HyeonCheol Jeong [1,*]

[1] College of Nursing, Sahmyook University, Seoul 01795, Korea; sungho@xxhwangxx.net
[2] College of Nursing, Kyungdong University, Wonju 24695, Korea; chiwon0909@kduniv.ac.kr
* Correspondence: love2hc@syu.ac.kr; Tel.: +82-10-8858-5679

Abstract: The purpose of this study was to provide basic data on cognitive therapy and to improve social support programs for the elderly with dementia by identifying the difficulties they experienced in emotional communication by identifying how they recognized emotions in verbal reactions to facial expressions using Ekman's photographs of facial expressions and comparing their responses with the general elderly population. There were 141 participants in this study. Data collection was conducted from 3 April 2019 to 30 June 2019 in Seoul, in the Gyeonggi-do and Gangwon-do provinces of South Korea. This study performed descriptive research in which subjects made participative decisions with their guardian through recruitment. The tools used in this study included a general characteristic questionnaire and the Ekman 6 facial expressions photographs tool, which underwent intensive validity studies. The collected data were analyzed using the R version 3.5.1 statistic computing platform. The ability of the elderly with dementia to associate verbal expressions with facial expressions differed from that of the general elderly population. The rates of correct associations of verbal expressions to facial expressions were similar across dementia grades. There was a significant difference in the proportion of correct associations between positive and negative emotions in the elderly with dementia compared to the general elderly population. In the elderly with dementia, pictures showing fear, anger, and disgust had higher wrong rates of incorrect answers than correct answers. The average score of elderly with dementia in associating verbal expressions with six facial expressions was 2.69, which was even lower when they were asked to associate verbal expressions with pictures showing facial expressions of anger or disgust. This study shows that elderly persons with dementia have difficulties identifying two negative emotions (anger, disgust) and find it much easier to identify a positive emotion of happiness represented by a smiling face. Since the ability of the elderly with dementia to interpret verbal expressions to facial expressions was different from that of the general elderly population, careful attention and consideration are needed to support and communicate emotions to the elderly with dementia.

Keywords: elderly with dementia; emotion of verbal expression; emotion of facial expression

Citation: Hwang, S.; Hwang, J.; Jeong, H. Study on Associating Emotions in Verbal Reactions to Facial Expressions in Dementia. *Healthcare* **2022**, *10*, 1022. https://doi.org/10.3390/healthcare10061022

Academic Editors: Joachim G. Voss and Sandul Yasobant

Received: 21 March 2022
Accepted: 5 May 2022
Published: 1 June 2022

1. Introduction

1.1. Need for Study

According to a report from the World Health Organization (WHO), about 50 million people have dementia. All dementia patients and their family members live with physical, psychological, and social burdens. WHO also points out that around 1.1% of the global GDP (gross domestic product) in 2015 was spent on serious social problems [1–4]. According to a report by the Korean Dementia Observatory 2018, there are 705,473 estimated dementia patients, which corresponds to one out of ten of people who are 65 years old and above. The costs of dementia management in South Korea are estimated to make up 0.8% of the GDP, which is about 14.6 billion [5]. Dementia is recognized as a national problem as well as a family problem. Elderly with dementia experience difficulties in communicating their feelings with other people as compared to the normal elderly due to emotion recognition disorder which comes from the change in cognition due to dementia [6–12]. Difficulties that occur in relation to empathy and the ability to exchange and understand shared emotions in interpersonal relationships comes from their inability to properly understand others' emotional states [13–17]. In particular, it is necessary to understand the deficit in emotion recognition in the elderly with dementia.

Verbal expression refers to the communication of one's beliefs or opinions through speech or in writing [18–21], and emotions refer to conscious mental reactions such as anger or fear, subjectively experienced as strong feelings usually directed toward a specific object which are typically accompanied by physiological and behavioral changes in the body [22]. While there are several different emotions, Ekman has identified six basic emotions corresponding to facial expressions, including anger, disgust, fear, happiness, sadness, and surprise [23–26]. Since these facial expressions may be associated with these six emotions, Ekman came up with six facial expression photos which have proven to be valid and have been widely used for studies on emotion recognition. The Ekman facial expressions photos have also been proven to be valid and reliable for Korean people [23–26]. Although the recognition of emotions such as disgust and fear is somewhat low, Ekman facial expressions are evaluated as useful emotional stimuli in neuroscience studies on emotions, and are utilized as diagnostic tools applicable to the Korean population. Neuropsychological assessment using facial expression stimuli is simple. After an assessor shows the subject photo slides of the facial expressions, the subject selects a word printed on paper which best describes the facial expressions, and these results are scored and used as a diagnostic tool [27–31]. In the elderly with dementia, wherein cognitive disorder is a major symptom, the association between verbal expressions and facial expressions should be understood. In order to understand why it is difficult for the elderly with dementia to communicate, this study aims to demonstrate the ability of the elderly with dementia to associate emotions in verbal expressions with facial expressions using the Ekman facial expression photo tools and comparing their ability to that of the general elderly population. Definitions of dementia have not mentioned emotion recognition definitively. Hence, studies were needed to conduct on emotion recognition of the elderly who experienced dementia and to seek for alternatives to overcome the difficulty of emotion recognition in dementia elderly. This study contributes to the early detection of dementia through the evaluation of recognizing and associating the emotions in verbal expressions to facial expressions [32–36].

1.2. Purposes of Study

This study aimed to understand the ability of elderly with dementia to recognize and associate emotions in verbal expressions with facial expressions as compared to the general elderly, and the detailed purposes were as follows. We (1) considered the general characteristics of the elderly with dementia compared to the general elderly population who participated in this study, (2) compared the rate of correct recognition of emotions in the facial expressions of people with dementia with that of general elderly population, (3) compared the rate of correct recognition of emotions in the facial expressions of the elderly with dementia with that of general elderly population, (4) compared the rates of correct recognition of emotions in the facial expressions across different grades of dementia in the elderly, (5) compared the rates of correct recognition of emotions in facial expressions which were positive or negative, (6) determined the degrees of recognition of emotions in facial expressions, and (7) compared the degrees of recognition for facial expressions to the subjects' scores in associating verbal expressions with facial expressions.

2. Methods of Study

2.1. Design of Study

This was an explorative research study conducted to understand the inability of the elderly with dementia to recognize and associate emotions in verbal expressions with facial expressions, specifically in those who had features such as memory disorder, aphasia, apraxia, and agnosia.

2.2. Subjects of Study

The subjects included patients who were diagnosed with dementia residing in Seoul City, and the Gyeonggi-do province, Gangwon-do provinces. They participated voluntarily after they, along with their guardian, made participative decisions and signed the consent form which followed ethical principles. The sample size was calculated to a total 143 participants with an effect size of 0.3, significance level of 0.05, and power of 0.8 for setting contingency table for chi-square test between the elderly with and without dementia using G*Power 3.0.10 (Heinrich Heine University, Düsseldorf, Germany). In this study, 72 elderly people with dementia and 69 elderly people as control in which subjects who were analyzed for this study were 141 totally. We followed the same method in recruiting the control sample from the general elderly population. The inclusion criteria for each group were as follows: (1) an elderly person with dementia is a person diagnosed with long-term care dementia grades of 3–6 according to the Act on Long-Term Care Insurance for the Aged, while a (2) general elderly person is a person who does not fall under the long-term care grades according to the Act on Long-Term Care Insurance for the Aged.

2.3. Ethical Consideration

Consent to participate in the study was included in the questionnaire. The questionnaire could be completed within 30 min (or about 10 min for the general elderly population), considering the participant's fatigue while answering the questionnaire. We provide the subjects with a small gift for their participation in the questionnaire. Furthermore, we explained that they could stop answering the questionnaire at any time, with no disadvantage on their part. This study was conducted after receiving approval from the institutional research ethics committee in S university.

2.4. Data Collection and Analysis Procedure

The study was conducted from 3 April 2019 to 30 June 2019. Questionnaires for the elderly with dementia were collected from centers for dementia in Seoul, Gyeonggi-do, Gangwon-do. For the general elderly group, questionnaires were collected from community welfare centers in Seoul, Gyeonggi-do province, upon approval of the chief of the center. All in all, we collected 72 questionnaires from the group of elderly with, and 69 questionnaires from the general elderly group.

We progressed data collection with care workers who cared their recipients assisted. As for the procedure, we showed six photo slides displaying the Ekman facial expressions to the subjects, and we had the subject select one word printed on paper which best described the facial expression. We confirmed the association between verbal and facial expressions, identified correct answers, and the subjects' scores were used to find cut-off values and compared among the six expressions from contingency table.

2.5. Study Instruments and Data Analysis Methods

Instruments used in this study included a questionnaire which asked about personal identification and general characteristics, as well as photos of the most intense facial expressions for each emotion taken from Ekman's facial expression photos. The data collected in this study were analyzed using R version 3.5.1 statistical computing platform. The following methods of analysis were used [37]: (1) General characteristics of dementia and general elderly groups underwent frequency and percentage calculation and a χ^2 test; (2) the percentage of correct associations of verbal expressions with facial expressions was calculated, and these were subjected to a χ^2 test; (3) the ratio of correct associations of verbal with facial expressions was calculated; (4) correct answers across dementia grades were compared using percentages and average percentages; (5) correct answers between positive and negative emotions were expressed using percentages and underwent a χ^2 test for frequency; (6) scores of associating verbal expressions with facial expressions were subjected to *t*-test and receiver operating characteristic (ROC) analysis; and (7) logistic regressions between each correct answer and the six correct answer scores was performed, displaying the results as odds ratios.

2.6. Limitation of Study

Long-term care grades as dementia in South Korea were 1 to 6. Grades 1 and 2 were approximately severe dementia with any physical impairment. Grades 3 and 4 were approximately moderate dementia with any physical impairment. Grades 5 or 6 were mild dementia [38]. From exclusion criteria which excluded one who could not understand the study procedure, elderly dementia patients in long-term care with grades 1 and 2, or those who had severe or moderate degrees of mental and physical impairment, were excluded from the study and did not answer the questionnaire.

3. Results of Study

3.1. Characteristics of Study Participants

There were 141 participants in the study, with 72 elderly dementia patients and 69 in the general elderly group. With regards to sex, the elderly dementia group had 45 females (62.5%) and 27 males (37.5%). The general elderly group had 52 females (75.3%) and 17 males (24.6%). There was no significant difference in the sex between the elderly dementia group and the general elderly group ($\chi^2 = 2.14$, $p = 0.142$). As for age, there were 41 patients aged 80 or above in the elderly dementia group (56.9%), while there were 41 patients aged 70 and above in the general elderly group (59.4%). There was no significant difference in the ages between groups ($\chi^2 = 3.14$, $p = 0.075$). Long-term care grades of dementia in South Korea were 1 to 6. Grades 1 and 2 were approximately severe dementia with any physical impairment. Grades 3 and 4 were approximately moderate dementia, and grades 5 or 6 were mild dementia. In this study, 21 patients were classified as grades 5–6 (mild) (29.1%) and 51 were classified as grades 3–4 (moderate) (70.8%). Among all the participants, most had an income of less than 1,000,000 won (Table 1).

3.2. Correct Associations between Verbal Expressions and Facial Expressions

In totally, 11 (15.2%) of the 72 elderly dementia patients and 10 (14.4%) of the 69 general elderly participants gave the correct answers for the facial expression of fear. As for the anger expression, 33 (45.8%) of 72 elderly dementia patients and 52 (75.3%) of 69 general elderly participants correctly answered. For the sad expression, 41 (49.4%) of 72 elderly dementia patients and 51 (73.9%) general elderly participants gave the correct answer. For the happy expression, 52 (72.2%) elderly patients with dementia and 67 (97.1%) general elderly participants gave the correct answer. For the disgusted expression, 23 (31.9%) elderly dementia patients and 47 (66.6%) general elderly participants gave the correct answer. Lastly, 37 (51.3%) of 72 in the elderly dementia group and 62 (89.8%) of 69 in the general elderly group gave the correct answer for the surprised facial expression (Table 2).

The facial expression that had the highest number of correct answers was happiness (72.2%), while the facial expression with the least number of correct answers was fear (15.2%) in elderly dementia patients. Some of them were unable to answer as well. The facial expressions wherein the number of wrong answers exceeded that of correct answers included fear (81.7%), anger (51.5%), and disgust (65.0%) (Table 3).

Among the general elderly group, the facial expression that had the most correct answers was happiness (97.1%), while fear had the lowest number of correct answers (14.4%). The rates of wrong answers were 75.3% for fear, 15.9% for disgust, and 14.4% for anger (Table 4).

Table 1. Characteristics of subjects (n = 141).

Category	Subcategory	Elderly Dementia Patients (n = 72) n(%)	General Elderly Group (n = 69) n(%)	χ^2	p
Sex	Female	45 (62.5)	52 (75.3)	2.14	0.142
	Male	27 (37.5)	17 (24.6)		
Age	70 s	31 (43.0)	41 (59.4)	3.14	0.075
	80 s	41 (56.9)	28 (40.5)		
Long term care grade	6	9 (12.5)	NA	NA	NA
	5	12 (16.6)			
	4	23 (31.9)			
	3	28 (38.8)			
Educational degree [39]	≤Elementary	26 (36.1)	22 (31.8)	6.46	0.010
	≥Middle	19 (26.3)	47 (68.1)		
	Missingvalues	27 (37.5)	0 (0.0)		
Income (thousand won)	<100	58 (80.5)	53 (76.8)	0.45	0.498
	≥100	12 (16.6)	16 (23.1)		
	Missing value	2 (2.7)	0 (0.0)		

Table 2. Correct associations between verbal expressions to facial expressions (n = 141).

Expression Type	Elderly Dementia Patients (n = 72) % (n)	General Elderly Group (n = 69) % (n)	χ^2	p
Fear	15.2 (11)	14.4 (10)	0.04	0.827
Anger	45.8 (33)	75.3 (52)	4.24	0.039
Sad	59.4 (41)	73.9 (51)	1.08	0.297
Happy	72.2 (52)	97.1 (67)	1.89	0.169
Disgust	31.9 (23)	66.6 (46)	7.66	0.005
Surprise	51.3 (37)	89.8 (62)	6.31	0.011

3.3. Ratio of Correct Associations between Verbal and Facial Expressions

The ratios of correct associations between verbal expressions and facial expressions may be seen in (Table 5). All the ratios were less than one, except for fear.

3.4. Correct Associations between Verbal Expressions to Facial Expressions across Dementia Grades

The rate of correct associations between verbal expressions and facial expressions across dementia grades may be seen in Table 6. Grade 6 had a rate of 35.1% and grade 5 had a rate of 47.2% (mild grade dementia), whereas grade 4 had a rate of 50.7% and grade 3 had a rate of 44.0% (moderate grade dementia).

Table 3. Correct associations between verbal expressions and facial expressions in elderly dementia patients (n = 72).

Verbal Expressions	Facial Expressions Fear % (n)	Anger % (n)	Sad % (n)	Happy % (n)	Disgust % (n)	Surprise % (n)
Fear	15.2 (11)	9.7 (7)	12.5 (9)	2.7 (2)	13.8 (10)	8.3 (6)
Anger	9.7 (7)	45.8 (33)	2.7 (2)	2.7 (2)	22.2 (16)	6.9 (5)
Sad	6.9 (5)	11.1 (8)	59.4 (41)	4.1 (3)	11.1 (8)	6.9 (5)
Happy	5.5 (4)	4.1 (3)	4.1 (3)	72.2 (52)	2.7 (2)	4.1 (3)
Disgust	12.5 (9)	11.1 (8)	8.3 (6)	8.3 (6)	31.9 (23)	5.5 (4)
Surprise	41.6 (30)	9.7 (7)	2.7 (2)	2.7 (2)	9.7 (7)	51.3 (37)
Not answered	5.5 (4)	5.5 (4)	9.7 (7)	4.1 (3)	5.5 (4)	13.8 (10)

Table 4. Correct associations between verbal expressions and facial expressions in the general elderly group (n = 69).

Verbal Expressions	Facial Expressions Fear % (n)	Anger % (n)	Sad % (n)	Happy % (n)	Disgust % (n)	Surprise % (n)
Fear	14.4 (10)	5.7 (4)	4.3 (3)	0.0 (0)	2.8 (2)	2.8 (2)
Anger	0.0 (0)	75.3 (52)	4.3 (3)	0.0 (0)	15.9 (11)	2.8 (2)
Sad	8.6 (6)	7.2 (5)	73.9 (51)	2.8 (2)	8.6 (6)	0.0 (0)
Happy	0.0 (0)	2.8 (2)	1.4 (1)	97.1 (67)	4.3 (3)	2.8 (2)
Disgust	1.4 (1)	5.7 (4)	14.4 (10)	0.0 (0)	66.6 (46)	1.4 (1)
Surprise	75.3 (52)	2.8 (2)	1.4 (1)	0.0 (0)	1.4 (1)	89.8 (62)

Table 5. Ratio of correct associations between verbal and facial expressions.

Verbal Expressions	Fear % (n)	Anger % (n)	Sad % (n)	Happy % (n)	Disgust % (n)	Surprise % (n)
Fear	1.05					
Anger		0.60				
Sad			0.80			
Happy				0.74		
Disgust					0.47	
Surprise						0.57

Table 6. Correct associations between verbal expressions to facial expressions across dementia grades (n = 72).

Severity	Dementia Grades	Verbal Expressions to Facial Expressions Fear % (n)	Anger % (n)	Sad % (n)	Happy % (n)	Disgust % (n)	Surprise % (n)	M ± SD
Moderate	3 (n = 28)	17.8 (5)	50.0 (14)	60.7 (17)	64.2 (18)	28.5 (8)	42.8 (12)	44.0
	4 (n = 23)	17.3 (4)	43.4 (10)	52.1 (12)	78.2 (18)	39.1 (9)	73.9 (17)	50.7
Mild	5 (n = 12)	16.6 (2)	33.3 (4)	58.3 (7)	91.6 (11)	25.0 (3)	58.3 (7)	47.2
	6 (n = 9)	0.0 (0)	55.5 (5)	55.5 (5)	55.5 (5)	33.3 (3)	11.1 (1)	35.1

3.5. Correct Associations between Verbal Expressions and Facial Expressions between Positive and Negative Emotions

Fear, anger, sadness, and disgust are considered negative emotions, while happiness and surprise are considered positive emotions. We determined the difference in the rate of correct answers between positive and negative emotions in dementia patients and the general elderly group. In the elderly dementia group, the average percentage of correct answers for positive emotions was 61.7%, while this was 38.0% for negative emotions. In the general elderly group, the average percentage of correct answers for positive emotions was 93.4%, while for negative emotions, it was 57.5% (Table 7).

Table 7. Correct associations between verbal expressions and facial expressions between positive and negative emotions (n = 141).

Emotion Type		Dementia (n = 72)		General (n = 69)		
		%	M ± SD	%	M ± SD	χ^2 (p)
Positive	Happy	72.2	61.7	97.1	93.4	7.33 (0.006)
	Surprise	51.3		89.8		
Negative	Fear	15.2	38.0	14.4	57.5	9.74 (0.001)
	Anger	45.8		75.3		
	Sad	59.4		73.9		
	Disgust	31.9		66.6		

3.6. Scores of Correct Associations between Verbal Expressions and Facial Expressions between Elderly Dementia Patients and the General Elderly Group

The scores of correct associations between verbal expressions and facial expressions ranged from 0 to 6 points. For the elderly dementia patients, the average score was 2.69 points out of a total of 6 points. For the general elderly group, the average score was 4.14 points. The cut-off value between these two groups was 3.5 points (Table 8).

Table 8. ROC for scores of correct associations between verbal expressions and facial expressions between elderly dementia patients and the general elderly group.

Cutoff	Sensitivity	Specificity	Positive Predictability	Negative Predictability	AUC
5.5	0.95	0.11	0.27	0.46	0.74
4.5	0.83	0.46	0.27	0.38	
3.5	0.68	0.72	0.31	0.27	
2.5	0.41	0.92	0.39	0.14	
1.5	0.29	0.94	0.43	0.16	
0.5	0.12	0.97	0.48	0.18	

AUC: Area under the curve.

3.7. Logistic Regressions of Each Correct Answer versus Correct Answer Scores on All Six Items

Logistic regression analysis for each correct association (0 to 1) between verbal expressions and facial expressions versus the correct answer scores for all six items (0 to 6) was performed. This was done to understand the impact of answering correctly on one item on the total score.

The odds ratio of associating verbal expressions with facial expressions of fear was 2.75 (1.59~5.86) in elderly dementia patients, and this was 6.53 (2.30~26.55) in the general elderly group (Table 9). The even–odd of the association between verbal expressions and facial expressions was 5.22 in elderly dementia patients, while this was 5.80 in the general elderly group (Table 9). The average correct answer scores of 2.69 in elderly dementia patients and 4.14 in the general elderly group did not reach the even–odd (comparison in Table 10) (Figure 1).

Table 9. Logistic regressions of each correct answer versus correct answer scores on all six items.

Division			Estimate	SE	z	*p*	EO	OR	(95% CI)
Dementia elderly patients									
Fear	Score	Intercept	−5.28	1.34	−3.91	<0.001	5.22	2.75	(1.57, 5.68)
		Degree	1.01	0.31	3.19	0.001			
Anger	Score	Intercept	−5.38	1.38	−3.89	<0.001	2.95	6.20	(3.00, 18.58)
		Degree	1.82	0.44	4.05	<0.001			
Sadness	Score	Intercept	−2.85	0.76	−3.74	<0.001	2.29	3.46	(2.13, 6.51)
		Degree	1.24	0.28	4.43	<0.001			
Happiness	Score	Intercept	−1.78	0.63	−2.80	0.005	1.34	3.77	(2.19, 7.68)
		Degree	1.32	0.31	4.22	<0.001			
Disgust	Score	Intercept	−4.23	0.99	−4.24	<0.001	3.84	3.02	(1.88, 5.65)
		Degree	1.10	0.27	4.00	<0.001			
Surprise	Score	Intercept	−2.61	0.69	−3.75	<0.001	2.63	2.71	(1.79, 4.58)
		Degree	0.99	0.23	4.25	<0.001			
General elderly group									
Fear	Score	Intercept	−10.85	3.21	−3.37	<0.001	5.80	6.53	(2.30, 26.55)
		Degree	1.87	0.61	3.05	0.002			
Anger	Score	Intercept	−5.13	1.70	−3.01	0.002	3.10	5.23	(2.41, 14.98)
		Degree	1.65	0.45	3.60	<0.001			
Sadness	Score	Intercept	−5.78	1.79	−3.21	0.001	3.22	6.02	(2.67, 18.13)
		Degree	1.79	0.48	3.71	<0.001			
Happiness	Score	Intercept	−20.22	14915	−0.001	0.999	0.49	NA	(NA, NA)
		Degree	40.70	19153	0.002	0.998			
Disgust	Score	Intercept	−9.40	2.44	−3.84	<0.001	3.65	13.14	(4.59, 58.44)
		Degree	2.57	0.63	4.07	<0.001			
Surprise	Score	Intercept	−2.95	1.63	−1.80	0.071	2.00	4.35	(1.96, 15.44)
		Degree	1.47	0.49	2.96	0.003			

SE: Standard error, EO: Even odd, OR: Odds ratio, CI: Confidence interval.

Table 10. Scores between verbal expressions to facial expressions between dementia elderly patients and the general elderly group (n = 141).

Dementia Elderly Patients (n = 72) M ± SD	General Elderly Group (n = 69) M ± SD	t	*p*
2.69 ± 1.70	4.14 ± 1.34	5.63	<0.001

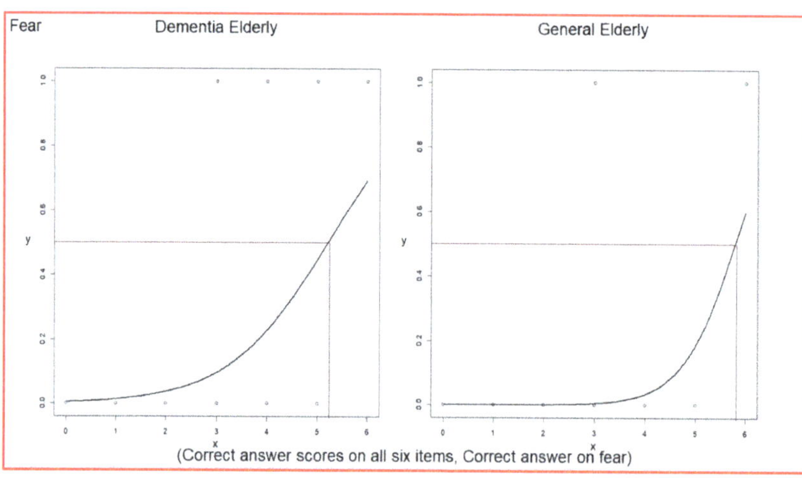

Figure 1. Logistic regressions of each correct answer versus correct answer scores on fear.

The odds ratio of associating verbal expressions with facial expressions of anger was 6.20 (3.00~18.58) in elderly dementia patients and 5.23 (2.41~14.98) in the general elderly group (Table 9). The even–odd of associating verbal expressions with facial expressions of anger was 2.95 in elderly dementia patients and 3.10 in the general elderly group (Table 9). The average score of correct answers was 2.69 in elderly dementia patients, which was lower than the even odd 2.95. Otherwise, the average correct answer score of 4.14 in the general elderly group was higher than the even odd 3.10 (comparison in Table 10) (Figure 2).

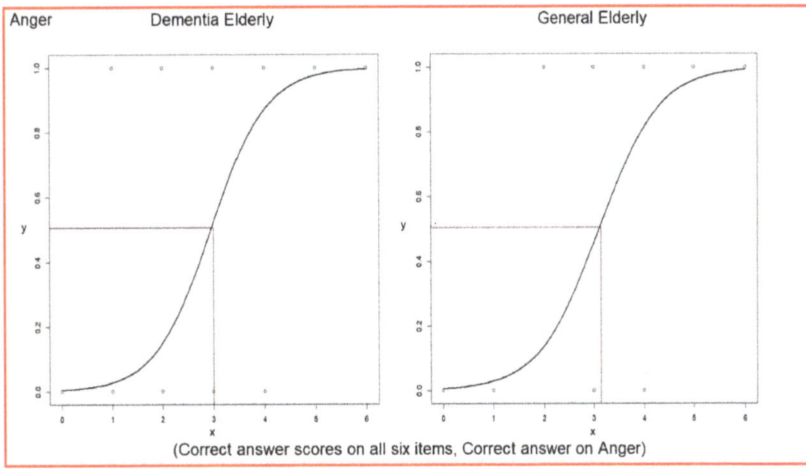

Figure 2. Logistic regressions of each correct answer versus correct answer scores on anger.

The odds ratio of associating verbal expressions with facial expressions of sadness was 3.46 (2.13~6.51) in elderly dementia patients, and was 6.02 (2.67~18.13) in the general elderly group (Table 9). The even–odd of associating verbal expressions with facial expressions of sadness was 2.29 in elderly dementia patients and 3.22 in the general elderly group (Table 9). The average score of correct answers was 2.69 in elderly dementia patients, which was higher than the even–odd 2.29. Furthermore, the average score of correct answers was 4.14 in the general elderly group, which was higher than the even–odd 3.22 (comparison in Table 10) (Figure 3).

The odds ratio of associating verbal expressions with facial expressions of happiness was 3.77 (2.19~7.68) in elderly dementia patients; otherwise, in general elderly, this was not significant (Table 9). The even–odd of associating verbal expressions with facial expressions of happiness was 1.34 in elderly dementia patients and was 0.496 in the general elderly group (Table 9). The average score of correct answers was 2.69 in elderly dementia patients, which was higher than the even–°odd 1.34. Furthermore, the average score of correct answers was 4.14 in the general elderly group, which was higher than the even–odd 0.496 (comparison in Table 10) (Figure 4).

The odds ratio of associating verbal expressions with facial expressions of disgust was 3.02 (1.88~5.65) in the elderly with dementia and was 13.14 (4.59~58.44) in the general elderly (Table 9). The even–odd of associating verbal expressions with facial expressions of disgust was 3.84 in elderly dementia patients and 3.65 in the general elderly group (Table 9). The average score of correct answers was 2.69 in elderly dementia patients, which was lower than the even–odd 3.84. Otherwise, the average score of correct answers was 4.14 in the general elderly group, which was higher than the even–odd 3.65 (comparison in Table 10) (Figure 5).

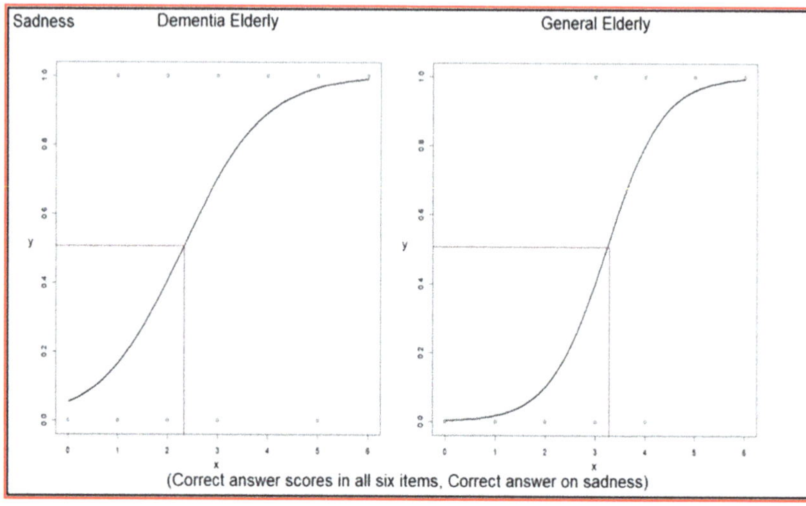

Figure 3. Logistic regressions of each correct answer versus correct answer scores on sadness.

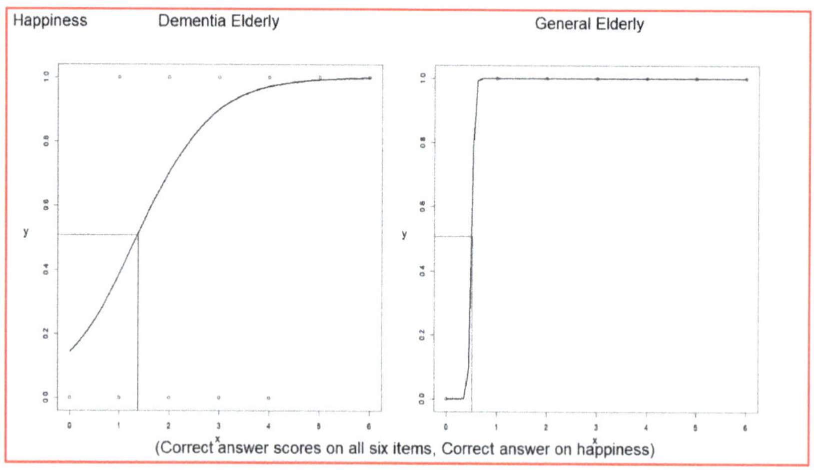

Figure 4. Logistic regressions of each correct answer versus correct answer scores on happiness.

Lastly, the odds ratio of associating verbal expressions with facial expressions of surprise was 2.71 (1.79~4.58) in elderly dementia patients and was 4.35 (1.96~15.44) in the general elderly group (Table 9). The even–odd of associating verbal expressions with facial expressions of surprise was 2.63 in elderly dementia patients and 2.00 in the general elderly group (Table 9). The average score of correct answers was 2.69 in elderly dementia patients, which was higher than the even–odd 2.63. Furthermore, the average score of correct answers was 4.14 in the general elderly group, which was higher than the even–odd 2.00 (comparison in Table 10) (Figure 6).

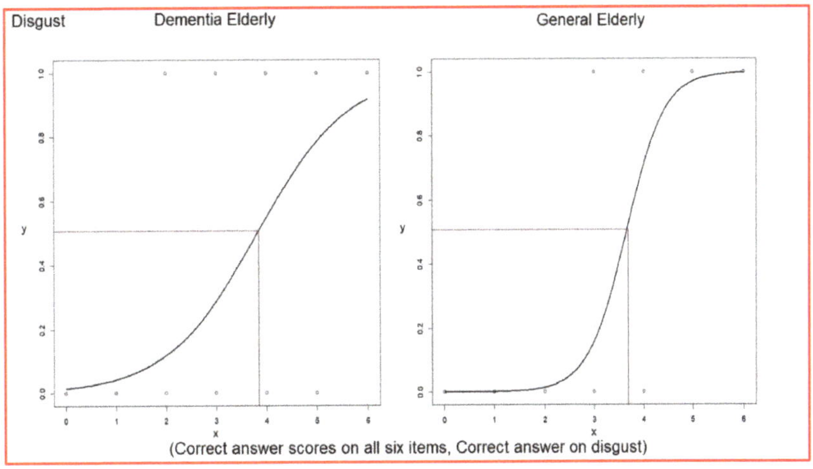

Figure 5. Logistic regressions of each correct answer versus correct answer scores on disgust.

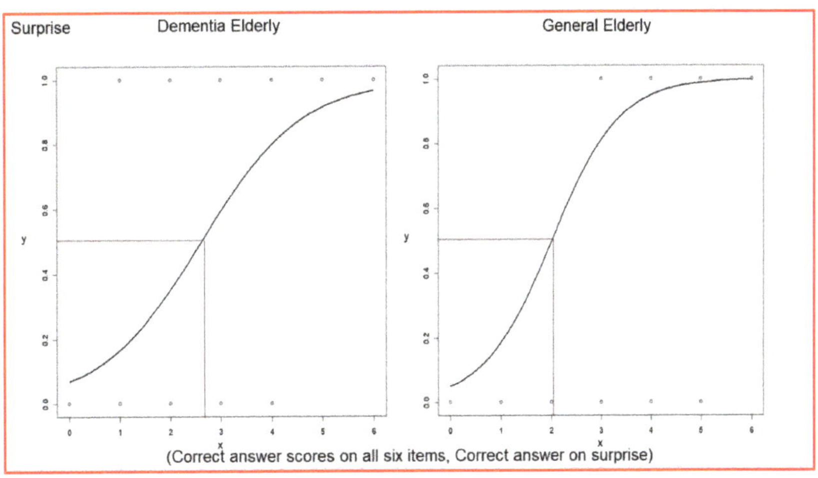

Figure 6. Logistic regressions of each correct answer versus correct answer scores on surprise.

4. Discussion

The study used six photos of facial expressions representing different emotions. We determined that the most intense pictures from the six different sets of emotions could be utilized as meaningful instruments.

In this study, subjects chose verbal expression on each of six face pictures. We identified the difference between dementia patients and control in the above condition [40]. Furthermore, the identification of the face pictures caused the difference between the two groups in the average scores on the even–odds.

The rates of correct answers of the elderly dementia patients were ranked as follows, from highest to lowest: happiness (72.2%), sadness (59.4%), surprise (51.3%), anger (45.8%), disgust (31.9%), and fear (15.2%). We suggest that further studies are necessary to explain the ranks of the rates of correct associations of verbal expressions with facial expressions.

There was no clearly observed trend with regard to the rate of correct associations of verbal expressions with facial expressions among grades of dementia. However, there was a clear difference in the correct associations of verbal expressions with facial expressions between dementia patients and the general elderly group. Further studies are necessary to explain why there was a significant difference in the rate of correct answers between the dementia patients and the general elderly group, but insignificant across grades.

In both the dementia patients and the general elderly group, the highest rate of correct answers occurred for the emotion of happiness. This implies that elderly dementia patients and the general elderly group recognize smiling faces and also understand the emotion of happiness. Therefore, it is important for nurses and caregivers to communicate with and support the patients by smiling.

In elderly dementia papers, the facial expressions that elicited the most wrong answers were fear, anger, and disgust. Of these, the facial expressions of anger and disgust scored higher than other facial expressions in terms of their even–odds. The even–odd of anger was 2.95 points while that of disgust was 3.84 points, which were both higher than the average score of 2.69 points. Further studies are necessary to determine if portraits of anger and disgust may be used in simple screening tests for the recognition of facial expression.

5. Conclusions and Recommendations

This study shows that elderly persons with dementia have difficulties identifying two negative emotions (anger, disgust) and have much easier identifying a positive emotion of happiness represented by smiling face.

The use of two facial expressions (anger, disgust) as a simple screening test for the recognition of facial expression in dementia patients might be considered in clinical uses and are needed for further studies and more interest of emotion recognition in dementia patients nationally and internationally.

Although the elderly with dementia experienced confusion in recognizing emotions in portraits, their recognition of happiness (smiling face) was high. These imply that elderly with dementia can understand the emotion of happiness and simultaneously recognize smiling faces. Therefore, it may be important for nurses and caregivers to communicate and support their elderly dementia patients by smiling at them.

As a result, our study showed that the ability of elderly dementia patients to recognize and associate emotions in verbal expressions with facial expressions is different from that of the general elderly population. Therefore, more careful attention is needed in communicating with and supporting the emotions of the elderly with dementia, and it is necessary to understand the relative and intrinsic difficulties in communicating the emotions which elderly dementia patients experience [41].

Author Contributions: Conceptualization: S.H., J.H. and H.J., Data curation: S.H. and J.H., Formal analysis: S.H., Investigation: all authors, Methodology: all authors, Resources: all authors, Software: S.H., Supervision: H.J., Validation: all authors, Visualization: S.H., Writing—original draft: S.H., Writing—review and editing: all authors, Approval of final manuscript: all authors. All authors have read and agreed to the published version of the manuscript.

Funding: This research had no external funding.

Institutional Review Board Statement: This study has been approved by the Institutional Review Board of the Sahmyook University (IRB No: 2019011HR).

Informed Consent Statement: Informed consent was obtained from all subjects involved in the study.

Data Availability Statement: Informed consent was obtained from all subjects involved in the study.

Acknowledgments: This paper was supported by the Research Fund of Sahmyook University in 2022. The authors thank all the authors and participants of articles.

Conflicts of Interest: The authors declare no conflict of interest.

References

1. WHO. Dementia. 2019. Available online: https://www.who.int/news-room/fact-sheets/detail/dementia (accessed on 15 January 2019).
2. Cobb, S. Presidential Address 1976. Social Support as a Moderator of Life Stress. *Psychosom. Med.* **1976**, *38*, 300–314. [CrossRef]
3. Gauthier, S.; Cummings, J.; Ballard, C.; Brodaty, H.; Grossberg, G.; Robert, P.; Lyketsos, C. Management of behavioral problems in Alzheimer's disease. *Int. Psychogeriatr.* **2010**, *22*, 346–372. [CrossRef]
4. Howorth, P.; Saper, J. The dimensions of insight in people with dementia. *Aging Ment. Health* **2003**, *7*, 113–122. [CrossRef]
5. National Institute of Dementia. Korean Dementia Observatory 2018. 2019. Available online: https://ansim.nid.or.kr/pds_view.aspx?page=&BID=194 (accessed on 15 January 2019).
6. Alzheimer's Society. Dementia 2013: The Hidden Voice of Loneliness. 2018. Available online: https://www.alzheimers.org.uk/site/default/files/migrate/downloads/dementia_2013_the_hidden_voice_of_loneliness.pdf (accessed on 15 January 2019).
7. Yanguas, J.; Pinazo-Henandis, S.; Tarazona-Samtabalbina, F.J. The complexity of loneliness. *Acta Biomed.* **2018**, *89*, 302–314. [CrossRef]
8. Hughes, M.E.; Waite, L.J.; Hawkley, L.C.; Cacioppo, J.T. A Short Scale for Measuring Loneliness in Large Surveys: Results from Two Population-Based Studies. *Res. Aging* **2004**, *26*, 655–672. [CrossRef]
9. Marano, H.E. The Dangers of Loneliness. Available online: https://www.psychologytoday.com/us/articles/200307/the-dangers-loneliness (accessed on 15 August 2003).
10. Hawkey, L.C.; Cacioppo, J.T. Loneliness Matters: A Theoretical and Empirical Review of Consequences and Mechanisms. *Ann. Behav. Med.* **2010**, *40*, 218–227. [CrossRef]
11. Russell, D.W. UCLA Loneliness Scale (Version 3): Reliability, Validity, and Factor Structure. *J. Pers. Assess.* **1996**, *66*, 20–40. [CrossRef]
12. Vanhalst, J.; Gibb, B.E.; Prinstein, M.J. Lonely adolescents exhibit heightened sensitivity for facial cues of emotion. *Cogn. Emot.* **2017**, *31*, 377–383. [CrossRef]
13. Rodríguez, T.M.; Galán, A.S.; Flores, R.R.; Jordán, M.T.; Montes, J.B. Behavior and Emotion in Dementia. *IntechOpen* **2016**. [CrossRef]
14. Virtanen, M.; Singh-Manoux, A.; Batty, G.; Ebmeier, K.; Jokela, M.; Harmer, C.; Kivimaki, M. The level of cognitive function and recognition of emotions in older adults. *Br. J. Psychiatry* **2017**, *206*, 509–516. [CrossRef]
15. Weiss, E.M.; Kohler, C.G.; Vonbank, J.; Stadelmann, E.; Kemmler, G.; Hinterhuber, H.; Marksteiner, J. Impairment in emotion recognition abilities in patients with mild cognitive impairment, early and moderate Alzheimer disease compared with healthy comparison subjects. *Am. J. Geriatr. Psychiatry* **2008**, *16*, 974–980. [CrossRef] [PubMed]
16. Guzmán-Véles, E.; Feinstein, J.S.; Tranel, D. Feelings without Memory in Alzheimer Disease. *Cogn. Behav. Neurol.* **2014**, *27*, 117–129. [CrossRef] [PubMed]
17. McLellan, T.; Johnston, L.; Dalrymple-Alford, J.; Porter, R. The recognition of facial expressions of emotion in Alzheimer's disease: A review of findings. *Acta Neuropsychiatr.* **2008**, *20*, 236–250. [CrossRef] [PubMed]
18. Vocabulary.com. Facial Expression. In Vocabulary.com Dictionary. Available online: https://www.vocabulary.com/dictionary/facial%20expression (accessed on 15 January 2019).
19. Vocabulary.com. Verbal Expression. In Vocabulary.com Dictionary. Available online: https://www.vocabulary.com/dictionary/verbal%20expression (accessed on 15 January 2019).
20. Coving, M.V.; Omelish, C.L. Take-Oriented Versus Competitive Learning Structures; Motivational and Performance Consequences. *J. Educ. Psychol.* **1984**, *76*, 1038. [CrossRef]
21. Olmwake, L. A study of sense of humor: Its relation to sex, age and personal characteristics. *J. Appl. Psychol.* **1937**, *21*, 688–704. [CrossRef]
22. Merriam-Webster. Emotion. In Merriam-Webster.com Dictionary. Available online: https://www.merriam-webster.com/dictionary/emotion (accessed on 15 January 2019).
23. Ekman, P.; Friesen, W.V.; Ellsworth, P. *Emotion in the Human Face: Guidelines for Research and an Integration of Findings*; Elsevier: Amsterdam, The Netherlands, 1972. [CrossRef]
24. Park, J.I.; Kang, J.I.; Cho, H.S.; Lee, E.; An, S.K. Reliability and Validity of Ekman's Pictures of Facial Affect for Koreans. *Mood Emot* **2010**, *8*, 145–151.
25. Lavenu, I.; Pasquier, F. Perception of Emotion on Faces in Frontotemporal Dementia and Alzheimer's Disease: A Longitudinal Study. *Dement. Geriatr. Cogn. Disord.* **2005**, *19*, 37–41. [CrossRef]
26. Park, S.; Kim, T.; Shin, S.A.; Kim, Y.K.; Sohn, B.K.; Park, H.-J.; Youn, J.-H.; Lee, J.-Y. Behavioral and Neuroimaging Evidence for Facial Emotion Recognition in Elderly Korean Adults with Mild Cognitive Impairment, Alzheimer's Disease, and Frontotemporal Dementia. *Front. Aging Neurosci.* **2017**, *30*, 389. [CrossRef]
27. Carr, A.R.; Ashla, M.M.; Jimenez, E.E.; Mendez, M.F. Screening for Emotional Expression in Frontotemporal Dementia: A Pilot Study. *Hindawi Behav. Neurol.* **2018**, *2018*, 8187457. [CrossRef]
28. Choe, J.; Youn, J.; Park, J.H.; Park, I.; Jeong, J.; Lee, W.; Lee, S.; Park, Y.; Jhoo, J.; Lee, D.; et al. The Severe Cognitive Impairment Rating Scale-an instrument for the assessment of cognition in moderate to severe dementia patients. *Dement. Geriatr. Cogn. Disord.* **2008**, *25*, 321–328. [CrossRef]

29. Diehl-Schmid, J.; Pohl, C.; Ruprecht, C.; Wagenpfeil, S.; Foerstl, H.; Kurz, A. The Ekman 60 Faces Test as a diagnostic instrument in frontotemporal dementia. *Arch. Clin. Neuropsychol.* **2007**, *22*, 459–464. [CrossRef] [PubMed]
30. Kohler, C.G.; Anselmo-Gallagher, G.; Bilker, W.; Karlawish, J.; Gur, R.E.; Clark, C.M. Emotion-discrimination deficits in mild Alzheimer disease. *Am. J. Geriatr. Psychiatry* **2005**, *13*, 926–933. [CrossRef] [PubMed]
31. Nagaratnam, N.; Nagaratnam, K.; Mara, D.O. Intersecting pentagon copying and clock drawing test in mild and moderate Alzheimer's disease. *J. Clin. Gerontol. Geriatr.* **2014**, *5*, 47–52. [CrossRef]
32. Douglas, S.; James, I.; Ballard, C. Non-pharmacological intervention in dementia. *Adv. Psychiatry Treat.* **2004**, *10*, 171–179. [CrossRef]
33. Inouye, S.K.; Studenski, S.; Tinetti, M.E.; Kuchel, G.A. Geriatric Syndromes: Clinical, research and policy implications of a core geriatric concept. *J. Am. Geriatr. Soc.* **2007**, *55*, 780–791. [CrossRef] [PubMed]
34. Lee, S.W. Technology trends of sensing the life pattern of elders and anomaly detection. *Commun. KIISE* **2011**, *29*, 83–92. (In Korean)
35. Jayawardena, C.; Kuo, I.H.; Unger, U.; Igic, A.; Wong, R.; Watson, C.I.; Stafford, R.Q.; Broadbent, E.; Tiwari, P.; Warren, J.; et al. Deployment of a service robot to help older people. In Proceedings of the IEEE/RSJ International Conference on Intelligent Robots and Systems, Taipei, Taiwan, 18–22 October 2010; IEEE: Taipei, Taiwan, 2010; Volume 2010, pp. 5990–5995. [CrossRef]
36. Stafford, R.Q.; Broadbent, E.; Jayawardena, C.; Unger, U.; Kuo, I.H.; Igic, A.; Wong, R.; Kerse, N.; Watson, C.; MacDonald, B.A. Improved robot attitudes and emotions at a retirement home after meeting a robot. In Proceedings of the 19th IEEE International Symposium on Robot and Human Interactive Communication, Viareggio, Italy, 13–15 September 2010; IEEE: Viareggio, Italy, 2010; pp. 82–87. [CrossRef]
37. Grove, S.K.; Gray, J.R.; Burns, N. *Understanding Nursing Research*, 6th ed.; Elsevier: Amsterdam, The Netherlands, 2015; pp. 248–280.
38. Perneczky, R.; Wagenpfeil, S.; Komossa, K.; Grimmer, T.; Diehl, J.; Kurz, A. Mapping scores onto stages: Mini-mental state examination and clinical dementia rating. *Am. J. Geriatr. Psychiatry* **2006**, *14*, 139–144. [CrossRef]
39. Sharp, E.S.; Gatz, M. The Relationship between Education and Dementia an Updated Systematic Review. *Alzheimer. Dis. Assoc. Disord.* **2011**, *25*, 289–304. [CrossRef]
40. Zandi, T.; Cooper, M.; Garrison, L. Facial Recognition: A Cognitive Study of Elderly Dementia Patients and Normal Older Adults. *Int. Psychogeriatr.* **1992**, *4*, 215–221. [CrossRef]
41. Touhy, T.A.; Jett, K. Ebersole & Hess. In *Toward Healthy Aging: Human Needs and Nursing Response*, 8th ed.; Elsevier: St. Louis, MO, USA, 2012; Chapter 18; pp. 338–364.

International Journal of
Environmental Research and Public Health

MDPI

Article

Impact of Internet Use on Mental Health among Elderly Individuals: A Difference-in-Differences Study Based on 2016–2018 CFPS Data

Huan Zhang, Hongyang Wang, Huiyu Yan and Xiaoyu Wang *

School of Social Development and Public Policy, Beijing Normal University, Beijing 100875, China; zhanghuan@bnu.edu.cn (H.Z.); wanghongyang0115@163.com (H.W.); 18866852982@163.com (H.Y.)
* Correspondence: wangxiaoyu9301@163.com

Abstract: The number of elderly Internet users has increased significantly in the past few years. However, the impact of Internet use on mental health remains unclear. In this study, we performed a difference-in-differences analysis using data from the 2016 and 2018 waves of the China Family Panel Studies (CFPS) to evaluate the impact of Internet usage on mental health among elderly individuals. A total of 5031 validated respondents were included to explore the relationship between Internet use and reduced levels of depression as well as improved life satisfaction among elderly individuals. The results showed that Internet use significantly reduced depression levels. Unexpectedly, Internet use was not found to improve life satisfaction. Moreover, discontinuing Internet use was not significantly associated with improvements in depression or life satisfaction. More research is needed to fully elucidate the relationship between Internet use and depression levels, as well as life satisfaction among elderly individuals.

Keywords: elderly; Internet; life satisfaction; depression level; difference-in-differences method

Citation: Zhang, H.; Wang, H.; Yan, H.; Wang, X. Impact of Internet Use on Mental Health among Elderly Individuals: A Difference-in-Differences Study Based on 2016–2018 CFPS Data. *Int. J. Environ. Res. Public Health* **2022**, *19*, 101. https://doi.org/10.3390/ijerph19010101

Academic Editor: Marta Tremolada

Received: 26 October 2021
Accepted: 22 December 2021
Published: 23 December 2021

1. Introduction

In the information age, the rapid spread of Internet technologies has strongly impacted all aspects of people's lives, and new technologies such as online social networking, travel reservations, and mobile payments have brought great convenience to the daily lives of elderly individuals. According to "The 47th China Statistical Report on Internet Development", issued by the China Internet Network Information Center, the proportion of "Elderly Internet users" reached approximately 260 million, as of December 2020, accounting for 18.4% of the total population. This percentage will continue to increase. Due to the use of the Internet, seniors can complete many tasks without leaving the home. As elderly individuals continually age, and their mobility becomes restricted, the Internet could be a convenient way to meet the diverse needs of seniors, and could be especially beneficial to seniors who prefer to remain in one place [1–3]. Considering the availability of home-based community care services, elderly people could use the Internet to establish connections with the outside world, integrate into society and increase their social participation. Furthermore, elderly individuals can also benefit from the diagnosis, treatment, and monitoring of diseases through telemedicine [4]. However, elderly individuals may also encounter numerous embarrassing and difficult situations because of the digital divide [5]. They develop negative emotions such as feeling disconnected from society and feeling useless as they grow older [6]. Occasionally, seniors may experience undesirable events such as Internet rumours and Internet scams, which diminish the experience of older Internet users [7]. Due to the rapid development of Internet technology, the subjective feelings and emotional reflections of older people need to be focused on.

Previous studies have shown that several factors affect the use of the Internet by elderly individuals. The first factor is the characteristics of elderly individuals themselves. Elderly men are more inclined to use the Internet than elderly women [8]. With declining vision and hearing, it is more difficult for elderly individuals to use the Internet [9], thus hindering their enthusiasm for the Internet and online participation in their daily lives [10]. Additionally, the more educated the elderly are, the more increasingly likely they are to use the Internet [11]. Seniors who have no physical pain prefer using the Internet than those with chronic illnesses or disabilities [5]. The second important factor is income level: higher-income older individuals are freer to use the Internet [12]. The third factor is the living area. In terms of place of residence, elderly individuals living in main urban areas appear to be more prone to using the Internet [13]. The last factor is social support: elderly people who have more friends prefer to use the Internet. The state's financial support and the development of communication technology infrastructure also affect the use of the Internet by the elderly [14].

Research has shown that diverse factors affect the mental health of elderly individuals. It is commonly believed that age, sex, and physical health status may affect people's mental health [15–17]. Additionally, the majority of seniors choose to live at home rather than in a nursing home; therefore, the community environment plays an increasingly important role in improving the mental health of elderly individuals [18,19].

Previous studies have identified a wide array of indicators between Internet usage and the mental health of elderly individuals. Several researchers believe that the Internet has a beneficial effect on social relationships, through providing convenient and effective means for communication among elderly individuals [20]. For example, Internet use could improve life satisfaction [21–24], enhance well-being [25–27], and reduce loneliness [28], as well as the depressive symptoms of elderly individuals [29–33]. In contrast, other studies found that Internet use may play negative roles in elderly people's lives. These studies insist that increased time spent online erodes elderly people's social interactions. Internet use leads to a reduction in social participation, a narrowing of social circles, and a weakening of the sense of community belonging and networks of friends [34,35]. For example, the digital divide brings distress and tension to elderly individuals [36,37]. Additionally, another view is that the impact of Internet use on mental health among elderly individuals cannot be generalized, because the research is inconsistent in terms of life satisfaction, depression, and loneliness. Shapira et al. [21] studied elderly people who received training in Internet use in day centres or nursing homes, and found significant improvements in the sense of mastery, depressive symptoms, and loneliness among the interventionists, but no significant results in terms of quality of life. Choi et al. [38] searched through the literature published in peer-reviewed journals and found no effects of Internet use noted in reducing depression in elderly individuals. Forsman et al. [39] conducted a systematic review of articles published in international databases, and found that 42 of 101 measures related to psychological perceptions were not significant, including quality of life, depression, functional independence, and loneliness. These results are interpreted with caution and explored with specific concern to the different age stages of Internet use and Internet content among elderly individuals.

In this paper, we investigate why there are inconsistent findings on the effects of Internet use on the mental health of elderly individuals, and what the influencing factors are. According to current studies, most results are based on data from a certain year, but ignore the causal and time effects. This study attempts to advance the literature by exploring the causal effect of Internet usage on the mental health of elderly individuals. Our research focuses on two main questions. We ask, does Internet use improve mental health among elderly individuals compared with those who do not use the Internet? Moreover, does withdrawing from Internet use diminish the mental health of elderly people compared with elderly people who use the Internet consistently? We used the difference-in-differences method to verify the impacts of Internet use or disuse on the mental health of elderly people over time. The paper is divided as follows: Section 2 presents the data, the main variables, and models of the influencing factors of Internet usage; Section 3 presents the verified stability of the research results; Sections 4 and 5 provide a brief discussion and concluding remarks.

2. Materials and Methods

2.1. Samples and Data Sources

The data were derived from the China Family Panel Studies (CFPS) (Data access link: http://www.isss.pku.edu.cn/cfps/ (accessed on 4 May 2018)), a social survey sponsored by the Institute of Social Science Survey (ISSS) of Peking University. The baseline survey was officially launched in 2010, and all family members and their future blood/adopted children, as genetic members of the CFPS, are also permanently tracked. The survey aims to track and collect data at three levels—individuals, families, and communities—to reflect the changes in China's economy, society, population, development of education, and individual health. The CFPS sample covers 25 provinces, municipalities, and autonomous regions, with a target sample size of 16,000 households, and includes all household members in the sample. This survey has been ethically reviewed, and provides real and reliable data for academic research and national and social policy decisions. In 2016, it began to include a survey of Internet usage.

In this study, we chose whether elderly individuals used the Internet as the independent variable based on the theory of Use and Disuse. Lamarck first proposed this theory to explain the evolutionary principles of human organs. It involved two principles: the first principle considered that the behaviour and habits of organisms cause changes in the organism and its parts, and the second principle considered that evolution is influenced by life, territory, and environment [40]. According to the theory of Use and Disuse, elderly individuals maintain the best control of their lives by actively interacting with their environment. The concept of "evolution in usage" implies that elderly people actively participate and integrate into society, use the Internet to enrich their daily communication, strengthen connections with children and friends and live a better life in their later years.

The dependent variables were selected concerning the meaning of mental health. The World Federation of Mental Health defines mental health into four categories: first, regulating the body, intelligence, and mood; second, adapting to the environment and maintaining humility in interpersonal relationships; third, having a sense of happiness; and fourth, giving full attention to one's ability to work, and living an efficient life. As reported by the guidelines for assessing the mental health of elderly individuals in China, mental health is usually measured by the following dimensions: cognitive efficacy, emotional experience, self-awareness, interpersonal interaction, and adaptability. A positive mental health state is reflected as life satisfaction, whereas a negative mental health state is manifested as loneliness and depression. Combining the items from the CFPS database, we measured the mental health of elderly individuals in terms of two dimensions: depressive status and life satisfaction. We applied the difference-in-differences model and data from the 2016 and 2018 waves of the China Family Panel Studies (CFPS), compared the changes of the two groups of elderly people (elderly individuals who began to use the Internet and elderly individuals who discontinued internet use) at two time points, and analysed the pure effect of Internet use on the mental health of elderly individuals. The following hypotheses were proposed for this study:

Hypothesis 1 (H1). *Elderly individuals who did not use the Internet in 2016 but used it in 2018 were less depressed than those who did not use it in both 2016 and 2018.*

Hypothesis 2 (H2). *Elderly individuals who did not use the Internet in 2016 but used it in 2018 had higher life satisfaction than those who did not use it in both 2016 and 2018.*

Hypothesis 3 (H3). *Elderly individuals who used the Internet in 2016 but no longer used it in 2018 had higher levels of depression than elderly individuals who used it in both 2016 and 2018.*

Hypothesis 4 (H4). *Elderly individuals who used the Internet in 2016 but no longer used the Internet in 2018 had lower life satisfaction than elderly individuals who used the Internet in both 2016 and 2018.*

The research subjects of this article were elderly individuals 60 years and older [41]. To track changes in the mental health of elderly individuals, dropouts and new entrants were excluded. The overall comparison of the basic conditions of elderly individuals in the sample in 2016 and 2018 is shown in Table 1.

Table 1. Characters of study subjects.

	2016		2018	
	Mean or %	**SD**	**Mean or %**	**SD**
Age	69.36	7.54	68.23	6.36
Female	51.90		49.74	
Education				
Low	76.03		70.56	
Middle	21.79		27.09	
High	2.18		2.35	
Health status				
Very healthy	15.24		17.08	
Relatively healthy	29.8		35.82	
Generally healthy	23.29		17.10	
Unhealthy	31.67		30.00	
Life satisfaction	3.85	1.06	4.24	0.93
Depression level	−0.26	4.67	−0.15	4.54
Use of Internet	0.06		0.12	
N	5031		5031	

Statistics from the 2016 and 2018 samples show that elderly individuals were between the ages of 68 and 70, with a male to female ratio close to 1:1. In terms of health status, the smallest percentage of seniors rated themselves as very healthy, while the percentage of seniors who rated themselves as unhealthy was over 30%. Compared to 2016, the mean value of respondents' life satisfaction in 2018 increased by 0.39, the mean depression level score increased by 0.1, and the percentage of elderly individuals who used the Internet increased by 6%.

2.2. Model Construction

In this paper, the endogeneity problem caused by the problem of self-selection bias and omitted variables is addressed by using the difference-in-differences (DiD) method. The method was first proposed by Heckman [42] for assessing public policy effects. As a quasi-experimental analysis method, the approach is often used to track the resulting changes caused by the change in the policy effect over time. It is based on the counterfactual framework to explore the changes of the dependent variables in the two states of policy that occur, or not. The difference between the core observed variables before and after implementation is calculated by dividing different economic individuals who are subjected to the policy shock, and those who are not, into a treatment group and a control group. The pure effect of the policy is obtained by eliminating the fixed effect and the influence of common time trends among different economic individuals. Compared with other experimental designs, the DiD method can solve the problem of missing variables that do not change with time and avoid the effects of external factors and selection deviation. Given these advantages, the method is commonly used for the quantitative evaluation of the effects of the implementation of a particular public policy or project, and is widely used in the field of econometrics, as well as in the field of sociology.

In this study, elderly individuals were divided into groups A and B. In group A, the experimental group was those who used the Internet in 2018 but did not use the Internet in 2016: they were named the Internet usage access group. The control group was those who did not use the Internet in either year: they were named the Internet unused group. The experimental group in group B is elderly individuals who used the Internet in 2016, but quit using it in 2018, they were named the Internet usage exit group. The control group was seniors who were using the Internet in both 2016 and 2018: they were named the Internet usage persistence group. On the one hand, the effect of Internet use on the mental health of elderly individuals was analysed by comparing the change in individuals between 2018 (using the Internet) and 2016 (not using the Internet). On the other hand, the effect of stopping Internet use on the mental health status of elderly individuals was analysed by comparing the change in individuals between 2018 (stopped using the Internet) and 2016 (used the Internet). Other factors that may have an impact on individuals' mental health status, including age, sex, education, and health status, were also controlled to further mitigate the bias of the results caused by omitted variables. In addition, the DiD estimation was needed to ensure that elderly individuals surveyed at both time points were in the same cohort, so the IDs in the questionnaire were used to exclude elderly individuals who were new to the CFPS survey, and those who dropped out in 2018. The DiD model was set as follows:

$$Y_{it} = \beta_0 + \beta_1 \text{Treatment} + \beta_2 \text{Time} + \beta_3 \text{Treatment} \cdot \text{Time} + \varepsilon_{it}$$

where β_0 indicates the control group, which is a constant term; β_1 indicates the gap of the elderly people's mental health itself; Treatment indicates whether or not to use the Internet, and takes the value of 1 for using the Internet and 0 for not using the Internet; β_2 indicates the time effect; Time indicates the time of elderly individuals using the Internet, and takes the value of 0 before using the Internet and 1 after using the Internet; β_3 represents the pure effect of change in the mental health of elderly individuals after removing the time effect and the disparity in elderly individuals themselves; and ε_{it} indicates the error term.

In the study, demographic variables such as sex and age, Internet use, depression level, and life satisfaction of elderly individuals were first described to obtain a basic picture of the data. Second, the DiD method was used to determine the causal relationship between the use of the Internet and changes in the mental health of elderly individuals from 2016 to 2018. Furthermore, the pure effect of Internet use on the mental health of elderly individuals was evaluated based on the difference in the change.

2.3. Variables and Operationalization

2.3.1. Use of the Internet

Both the 2016 questionnaire and the 2018 questionnaire in CFPS asked the following questions: "Do you use mobile devices, such as cell phones, tablets, to surf the Internet?" and "Do you use a computer to surf the Internet?" Respondents answered "yes" or "no", and those who used a computer, the cell phone, or a tablet to surf the Internet were defined as using the Internet and assigned a value of 1; those who did not use the Internet were assigned a value of 0.

2.3.2. Mental Health Status

The dependent variable in this study was the mental health of elderly individuals, and two scores, life satisfaction of elderly individuals and depression level of elderly individuals, were used as measures for the pure effect of Internet use on the mental health of elderly individuals. The subjective attitude module of the CFPS covered the measurement of life satisfaction. The measure of life satisfaction was divided into five levels, representing the degree of satisfaction with one's life, and was rated on a scale of 1 to 5. Depression level was measured using the CES-D scale short version of the CFPS questionnaire, which included 8 questions (6 measures of negative mood and 2 measures of positive mood) with 4 response options, namely, 0 = none, 1 = occasionally, 2 = often, and 3 = most of the time. Respondents' depression scores were calculated by summing together the scores from each question; the items "I feel happy" and "I live happily" were taken as the measure of positive emotion, and the negative values were taken and added together when calculating the scores. Higher scores indicated higher levels of depression.

2.3.3. Control Variables

Since the age, sex, education, and health status of elderly individuals are endogenous to a considerable degree, affecting both their mental health and their Internet use, they were used as control variables. The variables were defined as follows: the sex of the respondent was taken as 1 for males and 0 for females. Age referred to the difference between the year the respondent was born and the year when the respondent was interviewed. Education referred to the highest education level of the respondent at the time of graduation, including the lower level of education such as illiterate/semiliterate, elementary/junior high school, moderate level of education such as high school/junior high school/technical school/vocational high school, and higher education level such as college, bachelor's degree, master's degree, doctorate: in order, the values were taken as 1–8 points. Health status referred to the respondents' perception of their health, which was divided into 5 levels, with the lowest value being 1, meaning "very healthy", and the highest value being 5, meaning "unhealthy".

3. Results

3.1. Descriptive Analysis

Excluding dropouts and new entrants from the follow-up survey, a total of 5031 individuals were included in the sample for this study. First, descriptive analyses were performed on the percentage of Internet use, life satisfaction, and depression level of the sample in 2016 and 2018. Subsequently, differences in control and outcome variables were compared based on reported sample sizes for the Internet usage access group, the Internet unused group, the Internet usage exit group, and the Internet usage persistence group.

3.1.1. Sample Status

Table 2 reports the basic information on Internet use among elderly individuals in the sample in 2016 and 2018. In terms of age, the largest proportion of seniors aged 60–69 used the Internet, while none of the seniors aged 90 or older used the Internet. In terms of sex, the percentage of Internet use among elderly individuals was higher among men than women. In terms of education, the largest proportion of elderly people with a medium level of education used the Internet. In terms of health status, relatively healthy seniors tended to use the Internet more. The characteristics of seniors using the Internet in 2018 were similar to those in 2016, but the number of Internet users increased.

In terms of life satisfaction, elderly people aged 90 and above had the highest average scores of life satisfaction in 2016. In 2018, elderly individuals aged 80–89 had the highest life satisfaction. Older men had lower levels of satisfaction than women. Again, in terms of the self-rated health of elderly individuals, when elderly individuals were in extremely good health, they had the highest life satisfaction scores; when elderly individuals were in extremely bad health, they had the lowest life satisfaction scores in comparison.

In terms of depression level, the younger the age group in 2016, the higher the depression levels of the sample group. The lowest depression level was of the sample group aged 90 years and above. In 2018, elderly individuals aged 80–89 had the highest depression levels, and the sample group with the lowest depression levels was the same as that in 2016. Older men had lower levels of depression than women. When analysed in terms of education level, older Chinese individuals with high education levels had lower depression scores than those with low education levels. From the perspective of the health level analysis, the mean value of depression levels was the highest for unhealthy elderly people, and the mean value of very healthy elderly people was the lowest for depression.

Table 2. Results of the descriptive analysis on variables.

	2016							2018						
	% Of Internet Use	Life Satisfaction			Depression Level			% Of Internet Use	Life Satisfaction			Depression Level		
		Mean	SD	Mean Diff	Mean	SD	Mean Diff		Mean	SD	Mean Diff	Mean	SD	Mean Diff
Age														
60–69	5.49	3.80	1.07	0.222 ***	−0.54	4.51	0.005	8.49	4.21	0.94	0.108 ***	−0.16	4.44	0.053
70–79	1.11	4.00	0.99	−0.184 ***	−0.44	4.68	−0.130	2.62	4.30	0.89	−0.078 ***	−0.13	4.79	−0.020
80–89	0.12	4.15	0.90	−0.289 ***	−1.10	4.56	0.581 *	0.34	4.39	0.86	−0.152 ***	0.03	4.73	−0.175
90 and above	0.00	4.22	0.67	−0.355	−1.89	6.07	1.352	0.00	4.19	0.66	0.061	−0.75	5.35	0.613
Gender														
Male	4.27	3.83	1.03	0.072 **	−1.17	4.34	1.297 ***	7.10	4.22	0.93	0.064 **	−0.79	4.35	1.344 ***
Female	2.44	3.90	1.07	−0.072 **	0.13	4.70	−1.297 ***	4.35	4.28	0.91	−0.064 **	0.55	4.71	−1.344 ***
Education														
Low	1.37	3.89	1.07	−0.084 **	−0.12	4.68	1.402 ***	3.52	4.29	0.93	−0.151 ***	0.30	4.74	−1.615 ***
Medium	4.17	3.79	0.99	0.100 ***	−1.60	4.02	1.402 ***	6.66	4.13	0.89	0.157 ***	−1.23	3.90	1.442 ***
High	1.17	3.96	0.92	−0.091	−2.66	3.60	2.171 ***	1.27	4.22	0.85	0.025	−2.31	3.41	2.223 ***
Health status														
Very healthy	0.76	4.25	0.91	−0.462 ***	−2.46	3.61	1.651 ***	1.49	4.51	0.79	−0.319 ***	−2.04	3.81	2.281 ***
Relatively healthy	3.30	3.91	0.97	−0.065 **	−1.66	3.83	1.651 ***	5.57	4.27	0.86	−0.032	−1.16	3.86	1.605 ***
Generally healthy	1.75	3.79	1.03	0.100 ***	−0.65	4.10	0.145	1.77	4.16	0.92	0.104 ***	−0.27	4.24	0.160
Unhealthy	0.91	3.63	1.17	0.319 ***	2.14	5.06	−3.667 ***	2.62	4.13	1.02	0.177 ***	2.22	4.96	−3.372 ***
Sample size	5031							5031						

Note: *** $p < 0.01$, ** $p < 0.05$, * $p < 0.1$.

3.1.2. Comparison of Chi-Square Values of Different Subgroups

The study showed that 297 elderly people were in the Internet usage access group, and 4396 elderly people were in the Internet unused group. Additionally, 59 belonged to the Internet usage exit group, and 279 elderly people were in the Internet usage persistence group. Combining control variables and outcome variables, the samples of the four different groups were compared for significance with differences. The results are shown in Table 3.

Table 3. Comparison of the cardinal values of the four sample groups.

	Test Statistic a, b	
	Depression Level	Life Satisfaction
χ^2	150.609	26.975
df	3	3
Asymptotic Significance	0.00	0.00

Note: a: Kruskal–Wallis test; b: Grouping Variable.

Table 3 compares the chi-square values of the four groups of samples. The chi-squared value of depression level was 150.609, the chi-squared value of life satisfaction was 26.975, the degree of freedom was 3, and the asymptotic significance was 0.00 < 0.01. Therefore, the distribution of the depression level and life satisfaction of elderly individuals in the sample was different in the four different subgroups.

3.2. DiD Estimation

3.2.1. Model Estimation

To explore the impact of Internet use on the mental health of elderly individuals, we constructed four DiD models. After controlling for the age, sex, education, and health status of the sample, the DiD estimates were conducted for elderly individuals in the sample. The results are shown in Table 4.

Table 4. Results of the DiD estimation (Group A).

Group A	Depression Level	Life Satisfaction
Internet Usage Access Group (ref. Internet Unused Group)	−0.4374 *	−0.0359
	(−1.69)	(−0.61)
Age	−0.7143	1.1410 ***
	(−1.34)	(9.40)
Gender	−0.7039 ***	−0.0866 ***
	(−7.65)	(−4.14)
Health status	1.2463 ***	−0.1433
	(34.37)	(−17.38)
Education	−0.5624	−0.0319
	(−12.27)	(−3.06)
R-squared	0.1467	0.0760
N	4693	4693

Note: *** $p < 0.01$, * $p < 0.1$.

We can see that Internet use in Panel A had a significant effect on the level of depression among elderly individuals when compared with the Internet unused group. The coefficient of the interaction term of the DiD model was −0.4374, with a significance value of 10%, which indicates that Internet use had a negative leading effect on the depression level of the sample population. Elderly individuals who used the Internet reduced their depression level by 0.4374 points, compared with those who did not use the Internet. Compared with the Internet unused group in Group A, the effect of Internet use on the life satisfaction of elderly individuals had a coefficient of −0.0359 for the interaction term of the DiD model, but it is not significant. This indicates that Internet use does not affect the life satisfaction of elderly individuals.

Table 5 shows the effect of continued Internet use on life satisfaction and the depression levels of elderly individuals, compared with discontinued Internet use.

Table 5. Results of the DiD estimation (group B).

Group B	Depression Level	Life Satisfaction
Internet usage exit group (ref. Internet usage persistence group)	0.2717	−0.0210
	(0.98)	(−0.16)
Age	1.1390	1.0835 **
	(0.62)	(2.016)
Gender	−0.2407	−0.0987
	(−0.90)	(−1.36)
Health status	1.0687 ***	−0.2137 ***
	(7.94)	(−5.85)
Education	−0.3786 ***	0.0183
	(−3.53)	(0.63)
R-squared	0.1071	0.0859
N	338	338

Note: *** $p < 0.01$, ** $p < 0.05$.

As seen in Table 5, the coefficient of the interaction term of the DiD model for the effect of Internet usage exit group on the level of depression in elderly individuals, compared with the Internet usage persistence group, was 0.2717, which was not significant. The coefficient of the interaction term of the DiD model for life satisfaction was −0.0210, which was also not significant, indicating that discontinuing Internet use did not affect the depression level or life satisfaction of the elderly individuals.

We then examined whether the results on life satisfaction were confounded by the control variables. The four control variables were brought into the model for validation, and were significant when controlling sex and health, but no longer significant when age and education were added. This suggests that the correlation between Internet use and life satisfaction was driven to some extent by sex and health. We analysed the model by adding seven questions (the corresponding items in the questionnaire are QQ1011-QQ1017) that measured the activities of daily living of the elderly individuals from the CFPS database, and found that the results were still not significant.

3.2.2. Placebo Effect Test

In the DiD analysis, it is important to consider the impact of other random factors on mental health after Internet use by the elderly. The placebo effect test plays an important role in the model estimation, which could improve the robustness of the estimation results. The core idea is to fictionalize the processing team or estimate the time for fictitious policies. If the interaction term of DiD still changes significantly under the two treatments, this indicates that the conclusion drawn may have been affected by other factors, and some unconsidered bias. Thus, if a fictitious treatment group that had not been continuing to use the Internet, or a fictitious time when older adults began using the Internet still had a significant effect on their mental health, this would suggest that random factors were at work. If the results are not statistically significant, then the study results are robust.

Since only the Internet use of elderly individuals in the access group had a significant effect on the level of depression in the DiD estimates in this paper, only a placebo effect on the elderly people's Internet usage group was tested. We tested this by fictionalizing the amount of time elderly individuals spent using the Internet. In this study, the time cut-off point for whether elderly individuals used the Internet was 2018, and we advanced the time by one year to 2017. If there was still a significant effect of Internet use on elderly people's levels of depression, then this would indicate that the reduction in elderly people's depression levels was not solely due to Internet use, and therefore the results could not demonstrate the pure effect of the Internet on elderly individuals. Conversely, it indicated that elderly people's level of depression was not influenced by other factors, and that the reduction was due to Internet use.

Table 6 reports the results of the placebo effect test. As shown in Panel A, the interaction term of the DiD model was not significant in regression with the level of depression of elderly individuals, and the placebo effect test passed, indicating that the decrease in depression levels in elderly individuals was due to the use of the Internet.

Table 6. Results of Placebo effect test.

Group A	Depression Level
Internet Usage Access Group (ref. Internet Unused Group) DID_be	−0.1865
	(−0.73)
Age	−0.2146
	(−0.41)
Gender	−0.7107 ***
	(−7.71)
Health status	1.2450 ***
	(34.29)
Education	−0.5628
	(−12.27)
R-squared	0.144
N	4693

Note: *** $p < 0.01$.

4. Discussion

The main objective of this study was to use the DiD method to explore the effects of Internet use on the mental health of elderly Chinese people over time. Using CFPS data from 2016 and 2018, our study showed that elderly individuals who are younger, male, more educated, and in better health, are more likely to use the Internet. Using the DiD model, our study found that Internet use had a significant alleviating effect on the depression levels of elderly individuals, which is consistent with previous research [29–33,43], and confirms the theoretical view of "Use and Disuse". Unexpectedly, there was no significant relationship between Internet use and life satisfaction. This corresponds to previous studies in which the impact of Internet use on the mental health of elderly individuals cannot be generalized [21,38,39]. Moreover, a recent study from the Netherlands also found that ICT use in older age groups 65 years and older appears to be less likely to have an impact on their psychological adjustment (loneliness, life satisfaction, depression) [44]. Collectively, these results suggest that the impact of Internet use on the mental health of elderly people needs to be explored in the context of different mental health dimensions.

Additionally, the impact of Internet use on the mental health of elderly individuals is subject to a complex series of factors. The first is urban–rural difference. For example, the Internet affected the mental health and physical health of urban elderly people, and only affected physical health for rural elderly people [45]. The second is income difference: Internet use is effective in reducing mental health problems among low-income older people, while the effect is not significant for older people with higher income levels [46]. The third is the influence of Internet access preferences. Typically, elderly people spend more time online for recreational and leisure activities [47]. If they only use the Internet to search for information, the psychological situation of older people does not significantly change [19]. The fourth factor is the influence of the properties of the Internet itself: poor web usability and barriers to Internet use among older adults can lead to a lack of knowledge and confidence, fear of science and technology, and a distrust of social media or websites, reducing the overall experience [48]. If the functional aspects of the website design are very elaborate, elderly people will access healthier information and self-manage psychological states such as "low mood", "stress" and "anxiety" [49]. The fifth is external stimulus. External motivators, such as social connections, could increase motivation and self-efficacy to use the internet among elderly people [50]. It is evident from the above study that the relationship aspect of the impact of Internet use and the mental health of elderly individuals needs to be continuously and deeply explored. Nearly all elderly people have the mentality of not giving in to old age, and aim to prove their worth throughout their later years. According to the theory of Use and Disuse proposed by Lamarck, the use of the Internet can enhance the social participation of elderly individuals and help them rediscover their value while enabling them to communicate with the outside world and access resources and daily needs. Therefore, researchers may need to consider the impact that these factors might have on the mental health of elderly individuals in terms of their Internet use. In addition, it is also important to further explore the direction of the relationship among the effects of these influential factors.

This study enriches the literature on the effects of Internet use on the subjective well-being of elderly individuals. Additionally, the study enables academia to notice different findings on the impact of Internet use on the mental health of elderly individuals. Currently, the trend of an ageing society in China is becoming increasingly serious, and despite the tradition of preferring community-based home care for elderly individuals, there is an increasing trend of residential separation between children and parents. Based on the concept of age friendliness and the initial intention of caring for elderly individuals, this research on the impact of Internet use on the psychological health of elderly individuals is in line with the expectations of society. Almost every elderly person has a mindset of defying old age, hoping to connect with the outside world through media means and spending their old age in a fulfilling and pleasant way. Therefore, this research also has important practical significance.

Admittedly, there are some limitations to the study. First, the mental health of elderly individuals is influenced by multiple factors. Although we used four control variables (age, sex, education, and health), it is difficult to exclude possible confounding by other factors because of the high number of missing values and the fact that many macrolevel socioeconomic indicators are not addressed. Furthermore, elderly individuals in the sample span a large age range, and the lower and higher age groups have different levels of Internet acceptance and awareness, but we did not discuss them specifically in our analysis. Second, Internet use is a long-term behaviour. The CFPS only began to investigate Internet use in 2016, so the impact of Internet use on the mental health of elderly individuals was not as pronounced as expected. Third, we explored the impact of the Internet on the mental health of elderly individuals only in terms of whether they use the Internet, but not in terms of specific functions. These limitations may have confounded the study results to some extent. Attention needs to be paid to these issues in future research, by selecting a database with a large sample size and a long duration to further validate the relationship between Internet use and mental health in elderly individuals.

5. Conclusions

Internet use significantly reduces depression levels in elderly individuals. However, Internet use appears not to be associated with improved life satisfaction. Moreover, discontinuing Internet use had no significant effect on either depression levels or life satisfaction in elderly individuals. This study adds new empirical evidence to the research on the relationship between Internet use and the mental health of elderly individuals. Studies focusing on the effects of withdrawal from Internet use versus continued Internet use behaviour on the mental health of elderly individuals remain limited. Therefore, further research is needed to explore the relationship between persistent internet usage and the mental health of elderly individuals. Additionally, the results of studies on the effects of Internet use on the mental health of elderly individuals are still debated extensively. Our study encourages scholars to pay attention to inconsistent findings and analyses that lead to different results.

Author Contributions: H.Z. conceived the study design, conducted the statistical analyses, and prepared the manuscript. H.W., H.Y. prepared the manuscript. X.W. provided advice on writing the article, supervised all aspects of its implementation, and reviewed the manuscript. All authors have read and agreed to the published version of the manuscript.

Funding: This research was funded by Decision making the consulting project of the Beijing Social Science Foundation(21JCC101) and the 70th batch of general programs of the China Postdoctoral Science Foundation (2021M700461).

Institutional Review Board Statement: The data for this study came from the China Family Panel Studies (CFPS). CFPS was reviewed and approved by the Institute of Social Science Survey (ISSS) of Peking University.

Informed Consent Statement: All participants in the survey were asked to provide written informed consent.

Data Availability Statement: The data were released to the researchers without access to any personal data. Data access link: http://www.isss.pku.edu.cn/cfps/ (accessed on 4 May 2018).

Conflicts of Interest: The authors declare no potential conflict of interest with respect to the research, authorship, and/or publication of this article.

References

1. Sereny, M.D.; Gu, D. Living Arrangement concordance and its association with self-rated health among institutionalized and community-residing older adults in China. *J. Cross-Cult. Gerontol.* **2011**, *26*, 239–259. [CrossRef]
2. Henderson, E.; Caplan, G. Home sweet home? Community care for older people in Australia. *J. Am. Med. Dir. Assoc.* **2008**, *9*, 88–94. [CrossRef]
3. Ma, D.; Yuan, H. Neighborhood environment, Internet use and mental distress among older adults: The case of Shanghai, China. *Int. J. Environ. Res. Public Health* **2021**, *18*, 3616. [CrossRef] [PubMed]
4. Doica, I.P.; Florescu, D.N.; Oancea, C.N.; Turcu-Stiolica, A.; Subtirelu, M.S.; Dumitra, G.; Rogoveanu, I.; Gheonea, D.I.; Ungureanu, B.S. Telemedicine Chronic Viral Hepatitis C Treatment during the Lockdown Period in Romania: A Pilot Study. *Int. J. Environ. Res. Public Health* **2021**, *18*, 3694. [CrossRef] [PubMed]
5. Duplaga, M. The association between Internet use and health-related outcomes in older adults and the elderly: A cross-sectional study. *BMC Med. Inform. Decis. Mak.* **2021**, *21*, 150. [CrossRef]
6. van der Wardt, V.; Bandelow, S.; Hogervorst, E. The relationship between cognitive abilities, well-being and use of new technologies in older people. *Gerontechnology* **2012**, *10*, 187–207. [CrossRef]
7. Tripathi, K.; Robertson, S.; Cooper, C. A brief report on older people's experience of cybercrime victimization in Mumbai, India. *J. Elder Abus. Negl.* **2019**, *31*, 437–447. [CrossRef]
8. Vaportzis, E.; Clausen, M.G.; Gow, A.J. Older adults perceptions of technology and barriers to interacting with tablet Computers: A Focus Group Study. *Front. Psychol.* **2017**, *8*, 1687. [CrossRef]
9. Gitlow, L. Technology use by older adults and barriers to using technology. *Phys. Occup. Ther. Geriatr.* **2014**, *32*, 271–280. [CrossRef]
10. Ang, S.; Chen, T.Y. Going online to stay connected: Online social participation buffers the relationship between pain and depression. *J. Gerontol. Ser. B* **2019**, *74*, 1020–1031. [CrossRef] [PubMed]
11. Berner, J.; Rennemark, M.; Jogréus, C.; Anderberg, P.; Sköldunger, A.; Wahlberg, M.; Elmståhl, S.; Berglund, J. Factors influencing Internet usage in older adults (65 years and above) living in rural and urban Sweden. *Health Inform. J.* **2015**, *21*, 237–249. [CrossRef] [PubMed]
12. Hargittai, E.; Piper, A.M.; Morris, M.R. From internet access to internet skills: Digital inequality among older adults. *Univers. Access Inf. Soc.* **2018**, *18*, 881–890. [CrossRef]
13. Hanson, V.L. Influencing technology adoption by older adults. *Interact. Comput.* **2010**, *22*, 502–509. [CrossRef]
14. König, R.; Seifert, A.; Doh, M. Internet use among older Europeans: An analysis based on SHARE data. *Univ. Access Inf. Soc.* **2018**, *17*, 621–633. [CrossRef]
15. Sözeri-Varma, G. Depression in the elderly: Clinical features and risk factors. *Aging Dis.* **2012**, *3*, 465–471.
16. Kiely, K.M.; Brady, B.; Byles, J. Gender, Mental health and ageing. *Maturitas* **2019**, *129*, 76–84. [CrossRef]
17. Suwanmanee, S.; Nanthamongkolchai, S.; Munsawaengsub, C.; Taechaboonsermsak, P. Factors influencing the mental health of the elderly in Songkhla, Thailand. *J. Med. Assoc. Thail. Chotmaihet Thangphaet* **2012**, *95*, S8–S15.
18. Li, L.W.; Liu, J.; Zhang, Z.; Xu, H. Late-life depression in rural China: Do village infrastructure and availability of community resources matter? *Int. J. Geriatr. Psychiatry* **2015**, *30*, 729–736. [CrossRef]
19. Wang, Y.; Chen, Y.C.; Shen, H.W.; Morrow-Howell, N. Neighborhood and depressive symptoms: A comparison of rural and urban Chinese older adults. *Gerontologist* **2018**, *58*, 68–78. [CrossRef]
20. Pénard, T.; Poussing, N. Internet use and social capital: The strength of virtual ties. *J. Econ. Issues* **2010**, *3*, 569–595. [CrossRef]

21. Shapira, N.; Barak, A.; Gal, I. Promoting well-being in older adults through Internet training and use. *Aging Ment. Health* **2007**, *11*, 477–484. [CrossRef] [PubMed]
22. Cotten, S.R.; Anderson, W.A.; Mc Cullough, B.M. The impact of Internet use on loneliness and contact with others among older adults. A cross-sectional analysis. *J. Med. Internet Res.* **2013**, *15*, e39. [CrossRef]
23. Heo, J.; Chun, S.; Lee, S.; Lee, K.H.; Kim, J. Internet use and well-being in older adults. *Cyberpsychol. Behav. Soc. Netw.* **2015**, *18*, 268–272. [CrossRef] [PubMed]
24. Sims, T.; Reed, A.E.; Carr, D.C. Information and communication technology use is associated with well-being in older adults. *J. Gerontol. Psychol. Sci.* **2017**, *72*, 761–770. [CrossRef]
25. Quintana, D.; Cervantes, A.; Sáez, Y.; Isasi, P. Internet use and psychological well-being at advanced age. Evidence from the British Longitudinal Study of Ageing. *Int. J. Environ. Res. Public Health* **2018**, *15*, 480. [CrossRef]
26. Haase, A.Q.; Mo, G.Y.; Wellman, B. Connected seniors: How older adults in East York exchange social support online and offline. *Inf. Commun. Soc.* **2017**, *20*, 967–983. [CrossRef]
27. Neves, B.B.; Franz, R.L.; Munteanu, C.; Baecker, R. Adoption and feasibility of a communication app to enhance social connectedness amongst frail institutionalized oldest old: An embedded case study. *Inf. Commun. Soc.* **2018**, *21*, 1681–1699. [CrossRef]
28. Wang, Y.; Zhang, H.; Feng, T.; Wang, H.Y. Does internet use affect levels of depression among older adults in China? A propensity score matching approach. *BMC Public Health* **2019**, *19*, 1474. [CrossRef] [PubMed]
29. Choi, N.G.; DiNitto, D.M. Internet use among older adults. Relationships with health needs, psychological capital, and social capital. *J. Med. Internet Res.* **2013**, *15*, e97. [CrossRef]
30. Cotten, S.R.; Ford, G.; Ford, S.; Hale, T.M. Internet use and depression among retired older adults in the United States. A longitudinal analysis. *J. Gerontol. Ser. B Psychol. Sci. Soci. Sci.* **2014**, *69*, 763–771. [CrossRef] [PubMed]
31. Chopik, W.J. Benefits of social technology use among older adults are mediated through reduced loneliness. *Cyberpsychol. Behav. Soc. Netw.* **2016**, *19*, 551–556. [CrossRef]
32. Xiang, X.L.; Wu, S.Y.; Ashley, Z.; Kathryn, N.; Tomasino, R.A.; Joseph, A.H. Internet-delivered cognitive behavioral therapies for late-life depressive symptoms: A systematic review and meta-analysis. *Aging Ment. Health* **2020**, *24*, 1196–1206. [CrossRef]
33. Lee, M.A.; Ferraro, K.F.; Kim, G. Digital technology use and depressive symptoms among older adults in Korea: Beneficial for those who have fewer social interactions? *Aging Ment. Health* **2020**, *11*, 1–9. [CrossRef] [PubMed]
34. Gilleard, C.; Hyde, M.; Higgs, P. Community and communication in the third age: The impact of Internet and cell phone use on attachment to place in later life in England. *J. Gerontol. Ser. B Psychol. Sci. Soc. Sci.* **2007**, *62*, S276–S283. [CrossRef]
35. Hage, E.; Wortmann, H.; Offenbeek, M.V.; Boonstra, A. The dual impact of online communication on older adults' social connectivity. *Inf. Technol. People* **2016**, *29*, 31–50. [CrossRef]
36. Blažič, B.J.; Blažič, A.J. Overcoming the digital divide with a modern approach to learning digital skills for the elderly adults. *Educ. Inf. Technol.* **2020**, *25*, 259–279. [CrossRef]
37. Nimrod, G. Technostress: Measuring a new threat to well-being in later life. *Aging Ment. Health* **2018**, *22*, 1086–1093. [CrossRef] [PubMed]
38. Choi, M.; Kong, S.; Jung, D. Computer and internet interventions for loneliness and depression in older adults: A meta-analysis. *Healthc. Inf. Res.* **2012**, *18*, 191–198. [CrossRef]
39. Forsman, A.K.; Nordmyr, J. Psychosocial Links between Internet Use and Mental Health in Later Life: A Systematic Review of Quantitative and Qualitative Evidence. *J. Appl. Gerontol.* **2017**, *36*, 1471–1518. [CrossRef] [PubMed]
40. Lamarck, J.B. *Zoological Philosophy: An Exposition with Regard to the Natural History of Animals*; The University of Chicago Press: Chicago, IL, USA, 1984; ISBN 0226468097.
41. Zheng, X.D.; Fang, X.M. The Social Pension Scheme and the Subjective Well-being of the Elderly in Rural China. *J. Financ. Econ.* **2018**, *44*, 80–94.
42. Heckman, J.J. Sample selection bias as a specification error. *Econom. J. Econom. Soc.* **1979**, *47*, 153–161. [CrossRef]
43. Mu, A.; Deng, Z.; Wu, X.; Zhou, L. Does digital technology reduce health disparity? Investigating difference of depression stemming from socioeconomic status among Chinese older adults. *BMC Geriatr.* **2021**, *21*, 264. [CrossRef] [PubMed]
44. Schwaba, T.; Bleidorn, W. Log on and prosper? Little evidence for codevelopment between psychological adjustment and technology use in older adulthood. *J. Gerontol. B Psychol. Sci. Soc. Sci.* **2021**, *76*, 67–77. [CrossRef]
45. Wang, L.X. The influence mechanism of Internet use on the physical and mental health of the elderly–an empirical analysis based on CGSS 2013 data. *Mod. Econ. Res.* **2018**, *4*, 101–108. (In Chinese)
46. Hao, Y. Internet use and mental health problems among older people in Shanghai, China: The moderating roles of chronic diseases and household income. *Aging Ment. Health* **2021**, *25*, 657–663. [CrossRef]
47. Gallistl, V.; Nimrod, G. Media-Based Leisure and Wellbeing: A study of older Internet users. *Leis. Stud.* **2020**, *39*, 251–265. [CrossRef]
48. Moult, A.; Burroughs, H.; Kingstone, T.; Chew-Graham, C.A. How older adults self-manage distress-does the internet have a role? A qualitative study. *BMC Fam. Pract.* **2018**, *19*, 185. [CrossRef]
49. Haase, K.R.; Sattar, S.; Holtslander, L.; Thomas, R. The role of Internet cancer information for older adults with cancer: Perspectives of older adults and healthcare professionals. *Int. J. Older People Nurs.* **2020**, *15*, e12303. [CrossRef]
50. Leone, C.; Lim, J.S.L.; Stern, A.; Charles, J.; Black, S.; Baecker, R. Communication technology adoption among older adult veterans: The interplay of social and cognitive factors. *Aging Ment. Health* **2018**, *22*, 1666–1677. [CrossRef] [PubMed]

International Journal of
Environmental Research and Public Health

MDPI

Article

The Relationship between Korean Parents' Smartphone Addiction and That of Their Children: The Mediating Effects of Children's Depression and Social Withdrawal

Shin-Il Lim [1] and Sookyung Jeong [2,*]

[1] Department of Educational Psychology, College of Nursing, Jesus University, Jeonju 54989, Korea; imsi@jesus.ac.kr
[2] Department of Nursing, College of Medicine, Wonkwang University, Iksan 54538, Korea
* Correspondence: sookyung7424@wku.ac.kr; Tel.: +82-63-850-6015

Abstract: With the number of smartphone users growing around the world, children are using smartphones from an increasingly early age. Consequently, a significant number of children are being exposed to the risk of smartphone addiction, which is emerging as a serious social problem. Smartphone addiction can negatively impact children's physical, cognitive, and social development. Previous studies have demonstrated that parental smartphone addiction influences that of their children. Therefore, this study explores the relationship between parental smartphone addiction and children's smartphone addiction and the mediating effects of children's depression and social withdrawal. Data are drawn from National Youth Policy Institute's 2018 Korean Children and Youth Panel Survey. Respondents comprise 2011 fourth-grade elementary school students and their parents. Data were analyzed using SPSS version 21.0 and AMOS 21.0 software. Results show that the relationship between parental smartphone addiction and that of their children has a significantly positive mediating effect on children's social withdrawal, but no such effect on children's depression and there were no serial effects of children's depression and social withdrawal. Consequently, educational programs that control parents' smartphone usage, improve the parent–child relationship, and engender social sensitivity should be developed to reduce and prevent smartphone addiction among children.

Keywords: smartphone addiction; parent–child relationship; parenting style; depression; social withdrawal

Citation: Lim, S.-I.; Jeong, S. The Relationship between Korean Parents' Smartphone Addiction and That of Their Children: The Mediating Effects of Children's Depression and Social Withdrawal. *Int. J. Environ. Res. Public Health* **2022**, *19*, 5593. https://doi.org/10.3390/ijerph19095593

Academic Editors: Joachim G. Voss and Sandul Yasobant

Received: 2 April 2022
Accepted: 30 April 2022
Published: 5 May 2022

1. Introduction

The global number of smartphone users is increasing, with smartphone usage steadily growing among children. Compared to other screening devices, including televisions, smartphones are frequently used for educational purposes among young children [1], such as reading books and watching educational programs. Consequently, the majority of children are being exposed to smartphones at an early age. Indeed, 38.7% of Argentine children between the ages of two and four can use mobile screens without help from their parents [2], while some 46% of American children are believed to have begun using smartphones below the age of two [3]. Research indicates that Korean children typically start using smartphones at 4.6 years old [4]. According to the Korean Statistical Information Service [5], 96.7% of South Korean children aged 10–19 use smartphones, with 27.3% classified as high-risk for smartphone addiction [6].

Kang and Park (2012) defined smartphone addiction as a disorder in which everyday life is affected due to nervous anxiety caused by excessive immersion in smartphones [7]. Lin et al. (2014) identified four main factors: compulsive behavior, tolerance, withdrawal, and functional impairment [8]. Previous studies proved that smartphone addiction in children is connected to their mental health, including depression [9], emotion and quality of life [10], self-esteem, parents' smartphone addiction [11–14], and parental attitude [15]. Taking these into account, we can infer that it can negatively impact their life; thus, necessitating various interventions [16]. Several studies have shown that parents are strong influencing factors on children's smartphone addiction [8–11]. Among these factors, parental smartphone addiction has the most profound impact on children. According to family systems theory, each family member can be a subsystem within the family and members influence each other [17]. Considering this, the influence of parental smartphone addiction on their children needs to be explored further.

Research has confirmed the mediating effect of children's depression on the relationship between parental and children's smartphone addiction. More specifically, scholars have observed a serial mediating effect: parental smartphone addiction influences parenting style [18] or parental rejection [19], which affects children's depression and causes children's smartphone addiction. Parents with a smartphone addiction spend their time mostly chatting or using social networking services. Thus, they cannot attentively care for their children [20]. Moreover, it was found that they showed negative parenting styles including rejection and neglect as compared to parents who did not have a smartphone addiction [21]. As negative parenting style is known to weaken the relationship between parents and children and challenges stable bonding between the parties, it leads to the development of depression in children [22]. Consequently, failing to establish a stable relationship with their parents, children immerse themselves in a virtual relationship through smartphones [23,24]. Based on existing literature, we can expect the mediating effect of depression among parental smartphone addiction and their children's smartphone addiction.

Social sensitivity is defined as "attention, prominence, and emotions involved in processing information about social assessment and social status" [25]. A previous study suggests that it is an important phenomenon in peer interaction among children [26], as it represents the ability to admit mistakes, accept others as they are, make others feel good, and be a flexible thinker. Although research has yet to confirm whether parental smartphone addiction affects children's social withdrawal, parental "technoference" has been shown to influence Chinese adolescents' smartphone addiction, with social sensitivity having a mediating effect on the relationship between the variables [27]. The term "technoference" was coined in reference to the daily disruption of interpersonal interaction or time spent together caused by digital and mobile technology [28]. Similarly, people with smartphone addiction have characteristics such as they do not communicate with others or interact with their family and friends due to overuse of smartphones [7]. Technoference and smartphone addiction point to the problem of interruption in interpersonal interaction due to overuse of smartphones, although interference includes a broader spectrum of electronic devices including wearables, tablets, and other mobile devices. Accordingly, the term infers smartphone addiction. Several other studies have demonstrated that social withdrawal and smartphone addiction are closely linked [29,30].

Despite the rapid increase in children's smartphone addiction, few studies have explored how parental smartphone addiction affects that of their children. Moreover, although there are individual studies that indicate that parental smartphone addiction affects depression among children and causes social withdrawal, which further leads to smartphone addiction in children, there are a few studies that systematically verify this relationship. In addressing these gaps, this study analyzes the effect of parental smartphone addiction on children's smartphone addiction among fourth-grade elementary schoolchildren, and discerns the mediating effect of children's social withdrawal and depression in this regard.

2. Research Questions

This study examines the mediating effects of children's depression and social withdrawal in the relationship between parental and children's smartphone addictions (Figure 1). More specifically, this study evaluates first the direct effect of parental smartphone addiction on children's smartphone addiction. Second, it confirmed the mediating effects of children's depression and their social withdrawal. Finally, we tested the serial mediating effects of parental smartphone addiction, children's depression, children's social withdrawal, and children's smartphone addiction. In doing so, this study seeks to answer the following three research questions:

1. Is the structural model suitable for parental smartphone addiction, children's depression, social withdrawal, and smartphone addiction?
2. What kind of direct effects are at play in the relationship between parental smartphone addiction, children's social withdrawal, depression, and smartphone addiction?
3. Do children's depression and social withdrawal mediate the relationship between parental smartphone addiction and children's smartphone addiction?

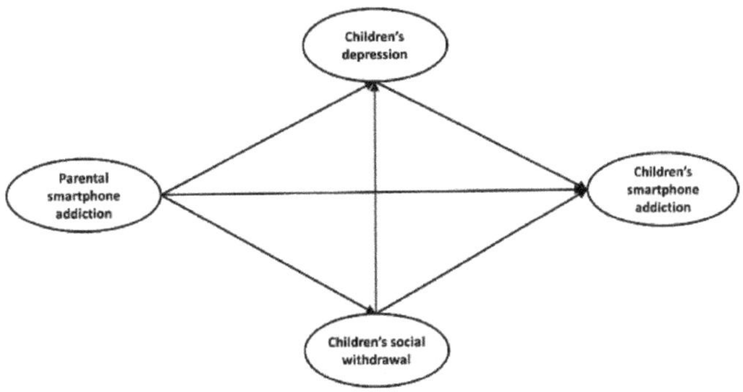

Figure 1. Hypothesized research model.

3. Methodology

3.1. Study Participants

This study used data collected through the first wave of the Korean Children and Youth Panel Survey 2018 (hereinafter, KCYPS 2018) [31], a longitudinal study conducted by the National Youth Policy Institute. For sampling, a multi-stage stratified cluster sampling was used to construct the original sample using four steps. In the first step, 17 cities and provinces in South Korea, 6040 schools nationwide, and 471,566 students were identified as the population. In the second step, stratified sampling was used, which can provide population representativeness with a small sample size. In the third step, sample allocation was proportionally distributed based on the number of students to 17 cities and provinces, assuming an average of about 70% effective responses. In the fourth and final step, the surveyed schools were selected using probability proportional to size sampling (PPS sampling).

To achieve the aims of this study, we selected only fourth-grade elementary school students for two reasons. First, although missing values occur over time due to the characteristics of the panel data, there are almost no missing values in the first year, thereby ensuring that it is representative of the characteristics of the population. Second, as the fourth grade of elementary school is the middle grade between the lower and upper grades, they represent the characteristics of elementary school students well.

More specifically, this study selected 2607 fourth-grade elementary school students (1313 males and 1294 females) from the panel survey. As this study examines the influences of the variables related to children and their parents' smartphone addiction, the sample was narrowed to a total of 2011 students (968 males and 1054 females) who owned smartphones and whose parents or primary caregivers owned smartphones. Accordingly, this study comprises a total of 4022 participants, namely, 2011 students and 2011 parents.

3.2. *Measurements*

3.2.1. Parental Smartphone Addiction

This study used the smartphone addiction proneness scale for adults developed by [32] Kim et al. This scale comprises 15 items: five items related to disturbance in daily life (e.g., "excessive use of smartphones reduces work ability"), two items related to seeking virtual worlds (e.g., "When I can't use my smartphone, I feel like I've lost the whole world"), four items related to smartphone withdrawal symptoms (e.g., "Without a smartphone, I feel restless and anxious"), and four items related to tolerance regarding overusing smartphones (e.g., "It is a habit to spend a lot of time on a smartphone"). Items are measured on a four-point Likert scale, ranging from 1 ("not at all") to 4 ("strongly agree"). The higher the score, the higher the addiction to smartphones. The reliability of the original scale as measured by Cronbach's alpha was 0.814, while the scale of this study has a reliability of 0.801.

3.2.2. Children's Smartphone Addiction

This study uses the smartphone addiction proneness scale developed by Kim et al. [21] to evaluate children's smartphone addiction. As in the parental smartphone addiction scale above, this scale comprises five subdomains: five items related to disturbance in daily life, two items related to seeking virtual worlds, four items related to smartphone withdrawal symptoms, and four items regarding tolerance about smartphone usage. However, the scales differ in respect to the items pertaining to disturbance in daily life, with the children's scale containing items such as "School grades drop due to excessive use of smartphones." The higher the score, the higher the addiction to smartphones. The reliability of Yoon's study (2021) as measured by Cronbach's alpha was 0.875 [18], and this scale has a reliability of 0.824.

3.2.3. Children's Depression

To examine children's depression related to smartphone addiction, this study surveyed a total of 10 items by modifying and supplementing the existing items related to the KCYPS [31]. Items (e.g., "I have no energy") were measured on a four-point Likert scale ranging from 1 ("not at all") to 4 ("strongly agree"). Higher scores are indicative of depression. The reliability of original scale as measured by Cronbach's alpha was 0.923, whereas the scale of this study scale has a reliability of 0.893.

3.2.4. Children's Social Withdrawal

This study used a modified and supplemented version of Kim and Kim's [33] scale to evaluate children's social withdrawal. The scale comprises a total of five items, including "It is awkward to have a lot of people around me." Items are measured according to a four-point Likert scale, ranging from 1 (not at all) to 4 (strongly agree). A higher score means a higher degree of social withdrawal. The reliability of original scale as measured by Cronbach's alpha was 0.940, while scale of this study scale has a reliability of 0.857.

3.3. *Data Analysis*

Data were analyzed using SPSS Version 21.0 (IBM Corp., New York, NY, USA) and AMOS 21.0 software (IBM Corp., New York, NY, USA). Following basic statistical analysis and confirming the normal distribution of the data, Confirmatory Factor Analysis (CFA) was performed to verify the fit of the measurement model. In accordance with this study's theoretical framework, a model was established based on the relationship between potential variables, and the fit was verified through chi-square (χ^2), Comparative Fit Index (CFI), Tucker Lewis Index (TLI), and Root Mean Square Error of Approximation (RMSEA) analyses. As χ^2 is sensitive to the number of samples, CFI and TLI were analyzed based on a value of 0.90 or higher and RMSEA was analyzed based on a value of 0.80 or less [34]. Finally, to examine the mediating effect on the relationship between elementary school student and parental smartphone addictions, children's depression, children's social withdrawal, and children's smartphone addiction, bootstrap sampling was performed

2000 times using the Panton variable, confirming a significance level of 5% using a 95% confidence interval.

4. Results

4.1. Descriptive Results

Table 1 presents the mean, standard deviation, minimum, maximum, skew, and kurtosis of the variables analyzed in this study. Descriptive statistics of the variables indicate that the mean and standard deviation ranged from 1.547 to 2.048 (0.423 to 0.738). The minimum value of all variables was 1, and the maximum value was 3.76–4.0. Additionally, as for psychometric purposes, skewness and kurtosis values between −2 and +2 are acceptable [35,36]. The significance probability (P) of the Kolmogorov–Smirnov Z-value was higher than 0.05 [37]. Synthetically, the assumption of normality was satisfied.

Table 1. Statistics of variables (n = 2011).

	Mean	SD	Min	Max	Kolmogorov–Smirnov Z(P)	Skew	Kurtosis
Parental smartphone addiction	1.7365	0.4235	1.0000	3.7625	0.6404(0.776)	0.4639	0.2336
Children's depression	1.5473	0.5383	1.0000	4.0000	0.9728(0.230)	1.1204	1.2136
Children's social withdrawal	2.0489	0.7389	1.0000	4.0000	0.5119(0.878)	0.2825	−0.6415
Children's smartphone addiction	1.7756	0.4955	1.0000	4.0000	0.6303(0.807)	0.6877	0.5308

4.2. Validation of the Fitness for the Measurement Model

The fitness index of the measurement model in this study was χ^2 (DF) = 1476.5848 (224), p-value = 0.0000, CFI = 0.9348, TLI = 0.9263, and RMSEA = 0.0527; therefore, the model is suitable. The equality of each variable was confirmed by verifying convergent validity and discriminant validity. Convergent validity is verified if the standard estimate is 0.50 or more, Average Variance Extracted (AVE) is 0.5 or more, and composite reliability (CR) is 0.70 or more [38]. Table 2 presents the result of convergent validity. In respect to the standardized regression weights of each observed variable (β), parental smartphone addiction was 0.6079–0.7690, children's depression was 0.5362–0.7871, children's social withdrawal was 0.6269–0.8201, and children's smartphone addiction was 0.7214–0.7693. All the variables were significant at $p < 0.001$.

Table 2. Analysis of convergent validity.

	Unstandardized Coefficients (B)	Standardized Coefficients (β)	Standard Error	t	AVE	CR
PSA→tolerance	1.0000	0.7690 *				
PSA→withdrawal	0.9091	0.7498 *	0.0312	29.2783	0.5086	0.8048
PSA→virtual world	0.8264	0.7128 *	0.0293	28.2954		
PSA→disturbance	0.7249	0.6079 *	0.0296	24.5779		
CD→CD1	1.0000	0.6877 *				
CD→CD2	1.1068	0.7871 *	0.0351	31.9411		
CD→CD3	1.0805	0.6244 *	0.0429	25.8182		
CD→CD4	0.8582	0.6804 *	0.0312	27.9794		
CD→CD5	0.8871	0.5362 *	0.0403	22.3583	0.5711	0.8982
CD→CD6	1.0289	0.6488 *	0.0385	26.7732		
CD→CD7	0.9967	0.7174 *	0.0346	29.3795		
CD→CD8	0.8575	0.7043 *	0.0304	28.8818		
CD→CD9	0.8325	0.6664 *	0.0304	27.4462		
CD→CD10	1.0112	0.7742 *	0.0324	31.4737		

Table 2. *Cont.*

	Unstandardized Coefficients (B)	Standardized Coefficients (β)	Standard Error	t	AVE	CR
CSW→CSW1	1.0000	0.7073 *				
CSW→CSW2	1.1109	0.8201 *	0.0345	32.8343		
CSW→CSW3	0.9864	0.7367 *	0.0333	30.0393	0.5502	0.8587
CSW→CSW4	1.1352	0.7981 *	0.0357	32.1941		
CSW→CSW5	0.8497	0.6269 *	0.0332	25.8332		
CSA→disturbance	1.0000	0.7324 *				
CSA→SVW	0.9477	0.7214 *	0.0333	28.7590	0.5467	0.8281
CSA→withdrawal	0.9881	0.7693 *	0.0334	30.2454		
CSA→tolerance	1.1673	0.7322 *	0.0400	29.1237		

Notes: * $p < 0.001$. PSA = parental smartphone addiction; tolerance = tolerance about using smartphones; SVW = seeking virtual world; disturbance = disturbance in daily life; CD = children's depression; CSW = children's social withdrawal; CSA = children's smartphone addiction.

Convergent validity was confirmed through AVE values, with all latent variables found to be over 0.50 and CR values over 0.70. As discriminant validity indicates the difference between each latent variable, it can be verified by comparing AVE and the square of the correlation between construct concepts [38]. Table 3 shows the correlations between construct concepts based on CFA.

Table 3. Relationship between construct concepts, convergent validity, and multicollinearity.

		PSA	CD	CSW	CSA
	PSA	1.0000			
	CD	0.1053 *	1.0000		
	CSW	0.0647 *	0.5138 *	1.0000	
	CSA	0.1440 *	0.2977 *	0.2696 *	1.0000
convergent validity	AVE	0.5086	0.5711	0.5502	0.5467
	composite reliability	0.8048	0.8982	0.8587	0.8281
multicollinearity	tolerance	0.9750	0.7061	0.7211	0.8804
	VIF	1.0257	1.4161	1.3868	1.1358

Notes: * $p < 0.001$. PSA = parental smartphone addiction; CD = children's depression; CSW = children's social withdrawal; CSA = children's smartphone addiction; VIF = variance inflation factor.

4.3. Verification of Research Model

The structural equation model analysis was conducted to examine the structural causal relationships between parental smartphone addiction, children's depression, children's social withdrawal, and children's smartphone addiction. Figure 2 presents the research model.

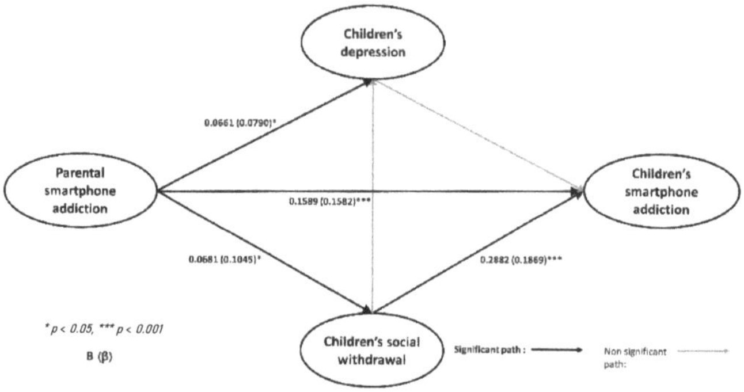

Figure 2. Path coefficients for the research model.

This study used the maximum likelihood method as the parameter estimation method. Table 3 presents the multicollinearity of parental smartphone addiction, children's depression, children's social withdrawal, and children's smartphone addiction. As the tolerance was 0.7061–0.9750, which is close to 1, the VIF was 1.0257–1.4161, and all variables were below 10, multicollinearity was satisfied. The fitness of the research model was χ^2 (DF) = 1476.5848 (224), *p*-value = 0.0000, CFI = 0.9348, TLI = 0.9263, and RMSEA = 0. Therefore, the model is suitable. As this model is an equivalent to the measurement model in the previous section, it shows the same goodness of fit.

Table 4 presents the pathways of the research model. Based on Figure 2 and Table 4, the significant pathways of the research model and each pathway coefficient are as follows. First, parental smartphone addiction had a significant positive effect on children's depression ($\beta = 0.0661$, $p < 0.05$), children's social withdrawal ($\beta = 0.0681$, $p < 0.05$), and children's smartphone addiction ($\beta = 0.1589$, $p < 0.001$). Second, children's depression did not have a significant impact on children's social withdrawal and children's smartphone addiction. Third, children's social withdrawal had a significant positive effect on children's smartphone addiction ($\beta = 0.2882$, $p < 0.001$).

Table 4. Pathways of the research model.

Pathway of Variables	Standardized Coefficients (β)	Unstandardized Coefficients (B)	Standard Error	CR
PSA→CD	0.0661 *	0.0790	0.0311	2.5385
PSA→CSW	0.0681 *	0.1045	0.0409	2.5551
PSA→CSA	0.1589 ***	0.1582	0.0265	5.9677
CD→CSW	0.0071	0.0091	0.0324	0.2829
CD→CSA	−0.0184	−0.0153	0.0207	−0.7436
CSW→CSA	0.2882 ***	0.1869	0.0174	10.7268

Notes: * $p < 0.05$, *** $p < 0.001$. PSA = parental smartphone addiction; CD = children's depression; CSW = children's social withdrawal; CSA = children's smartphone addiction.

Based on the results presented in Table 4, the mediating effect of children's social withdrawal in the relationship of parental smartphone addiction and children's smartphone addiction was examined using bootstrapping. As Table 5 shows, children's social withdrawal had a significantly positive mediating effect (0.0204, $p < 0.001$) in the relationship between parental smartphone addiction and children's smartphone addiction.

Table 5. Verification of indirect effects.

Pathway of Variables	Indirect Effect	95% Confidence Interval
Parental smartphone addiction → children's social withdrawal → children's smartphone addiction	0.0204 *	0.0058–0.0364

Note: * $p < 0.001$.

5. Discussion

In the growing IT industry, smartphones have become a must-have item and an essential good in everyday life [39]. Consequently, regardless of age, most people own smartphones, resulting in an increasingly large number of people with a smartphone addiction. Previous studies have identified and verified the risk factors associated with children's smartphone addiction, including the length of time of smartphone use, parental styles, and parental smartphone addiction. According to Lin et al. [40] and Sözbilir and Dursun [41], the length of time children spend using smartphones is closely related to smartphone addiction. As smartphone usage increases, so does the likelihood of smartphone addiction. Such children can retain this addiction in adulthood, making it important to control and guide children's smartphone usage.

Parents are believed to play a vital role in reducing children's smartphone addiction. For example, children's smartphone addiction has been found to decline with higher levels of parental risk perception about mobile devices and restrictive mediation [42]. Meanwhile, negative parenting style [43] and parental neglect [44] have been found to exacerbate children's smartphone addiction. Additionally, several studies have demonstrated that parents' smartphone addiction influences that of their children [45–47]. The results of these studies align with our findings. Smartphone addiction in adults has also been linked to a tendency to isolate and seldom engage in conversation with their family [48], as well as a lack of self-control [49]. Consequently, if parents are addicted to smartphones, they are able to control neither their own nor their children's smartphone usage. Therefore, parents' smartphone addiction should be considered as a risk factor of children's smartphone addiction, suggesting the need for intervention programs that educate parents and children together.

In this study, the mediating effect of social withdrawal revealed the path through which parental smartphone addiction leads to children's smartphone addiction (Figure 2). Examining the same context, Liu et al. [27] similarly found that parental technoference is related to their children's smartphone addiction, with social sensitivity having a mediating effect. Social withdrawal refers to various responses including nervousness and withdrawal when encountering unfamiliar persons or environment, and difficulties in forming and maintaining good relationships with people, which lead to emotional and social maladaptation [50,51]. Previous studies have established the negative effects of social withdrawal in childhood. Significantly, social withdrawal lasts for a long time, leading to social anxiety, social phobias, and depression [51], as well as difficulties in peer relationships [52]. More specifically, adults with smartphone addiction tend to be less interested and neglectful in caring for their children, leading to issues in the parent–child relationship [53,54]. Consequently, given the importance of the parental role, children whose parents are addicted to their smartphones may be left alone more frequently and experience difficulties in social development. Furthermore, even though there is limited empirical evidence to suggest the optimal amount of time for children to be exposed to screens and efficacious parenting behaviors related to limiting children's screen time, research indicates that positive parent–child relationships and effective family communication serve to reduce children's problematic smartphone use [55] and social withdrawal [56]. In sum, the parent–child relationship plays a key role in preventing children's social withdrawal and smartphone addiction. However, this study did not evaluate the parent–child relationship and parenting behavior as mediating effects. Therefore, further research must test how parenting behavior, parent–child relationship, and social withdrawal influence the relationship between parental smartphone addiction and their children's smartphone addiction.

This study explored the structural relationship between parental smartphone addiction, children's depression, and children's smartphone addiction. Results show that children's depression does not play a mediating role in the relationship between parental smartphone addiction and their children's addiction. This finding contradicts those of other studies [18,57]. These studies clarified serial mediating effects of parenting style and children's depression and the relationship between parental smartphone addiction and their children's smartphone addiction. The higher the level of smartphone addiction, the higher the negative parenting behaviors such as overprotection, rejection, and neglect. Whereas, the lower the level of smartphone addiction, the higher the positive parenting behaviors such as encouragement and warmth [58]. Parents with a smartphone addiction tend to have a negative parenting style, since they do not have much time to care for their children due to their smartphone addiction [48,49]. Nonetheless, negative parenting behaviors worsen the parent–child relationship, which is linked to their children's depression [59,60]. As the children were unable to have a stable relationship with their parent, they tend to immerse themselves in the virtual world to form relationships with others, which consequently leads to smartphone addiction [23]. However, there are some studies that suggest that smartphone addiction can be a predicting factor of depression as people with higher smartphone addiction showed higher depression scores [61]. Consequently, considering bidirectionality among two variables, further research needs to confirm the direction of the correlation for children.

This study has several limitations. First, this study used children's self-reporting data, which means that there is a possibility that data do not correctly reflect respondents' attitudes. Additionally, as respondents were fourth-grade elementary students, data are not representative of all Korean children. Therefore, further research covering various age cohorts is necessary. Second, the results of this study cannot be generalized to middle and high school students because they may be less influenced by their parents. Accordingly, a follow-up study is needed to determine how the results of this study differ from those pertaining to middle and high school students. Third, as this study utilized secondary data of a panel survey, the influence of variables not included in the analysis cannot be excluded. This needs to be taken into account when interpreting the results of this study. To address this limitation, further study including more variables that influence smartphone addiction in adults and children is necessary. Additionally, since this study used panel data, we cannot include hours of parental smartphone usage for examining parental smartphone addiction symptoms. Therefore, further research needs to include a quantitative description of parental smartphone usage to evaluate parents' own perceptions about smartphone overuse.

6. Conclusions

This study demonstrates that parental smartphone addiction can influence children's smartphone addiction, with children's social withdrawal found to have a mediating effect on the relationship between parental and children's smartphone addiction.

This study can contribute to understanding of the influence of parental smartphone addiction on their children. In this study, we found that it is important to control not only children's smartphone usage but also that of their parents. Therefore, it is necessary to develop educational programs that control both parents' and their children's smartphone usage in school and community centers. Additionally, this study verified that parental smartphone addiction increased children's social withdrawal, which led to their smartphone addiction. However, as previous studies proved that parental behaviors or parenting styles and children's social withdrawal had serial mediating effects on the relationship between parents' and children's smartphone addiction, further studies must be conducted to better understand the systematic relationships among these variables. Additionally, individual/group counseling and education to improve the parent–child relationship and social sensitivity should be conducted and implicated. As children with smartphone addiction are more likely to develop depression within a few years, we recommend conducting a follow up cohort study on this group.

Author Contributions: Conceptualization, methodology, formal analysis, data curation, S.-I.L.; Methodology, writing—original draft preparation, writing—review and editing, funding acquisition, S.J. All authors have read and agreed to the published version of the manuscript.

Funding: This research was funded by the Wonkwang University Research Fund in 2021.

Institutional Review Board Statement: The study was conducted in accordance with the Declaration of Helsinki and approved by the Institutional Review Board of Wonkwang University (protocol code WKIRB-202203-SB-015 and 15 March 2022).

Informed Consent Statement: Informed consent was obtained from all subjects involved in the study.

Data Availability Statement: The following are available online at https://www.nypi.re.kr/archive/mps/program/examinDataCode/dataDwloadAgreeView?menuId=MENU00226 (accessed on 2 February 2022).

Conflicts of Interest: The authors declare no conflict of interest.

References

1. Christakis, D.A. Interactive media use at younger than the age of 2 years: Time to rethink the American Academy of Pediatrics guideline? *JAMA Pediatrics* **2014**, *168*, 399–400. [CrossRef] [PubMed]
2. Waisman, I.; Hidalgo, E.; Rossi, M.L. Screen use among young children iMan a city of Argentina. *Arch. Argent. Pediatr.* **2018**, *116*, e186–e195. [PubMed]
3. Rideout, V. The Commonsense Census: Media Use by Kids Age Zero to Eight. 2017. Available online: https://www.commonsensemedia.org/research/the-common-sense-census-media-use-by-kids-age-zero-toeight-2017 (accessed on 26 March 2022).
4. Lee, M.; Park, S. Factors associated with smartphone overdependency in preschool children. *Child Health Nurs. Res.* **2018**, *24*, 383–392. [CrossRef]
5. Korean Statistical Information Service. Smartphone High-Risk Group 2016–2020. Available online: https://kosis.kr/statHtml/statHtml.do?orgId=127&tblId=DT_120019N_2016_001&vw_cd=MT_ZTITLE&list_id=110_12019_2016&seqNo=&lang_mode=ko&language=kor&obj_var_id=&itm_id=&conn_path=MT_ZTITLE (accessed on 16 March 2022).
6. Korea Information Society Development Institute. Smartphone ownership by age. 2021. Available online: https://stat.kisdi.re.kr/statHtml/statHtml.do?orgId=405&tblId=DT_405001_I002&vw_cd=undefined&list_id=undefined&scrId=&seqNo=&language=ko&obj_var_id=undefined&itm_id=undefined&conn_path=I2&path= (accessed on 16 March 2022).
7. Kang, H.; Park, C. Development and validation of the smartphone addiction inventory. *Korean J. Psychol. Gen.* **2012**, *31*, 563–580.
8. Lin, Y.H.; Chang, L.R.; Lee, Y.H.; Tseng, H.W.; Kuo, T.B.; Chen, S.H. Development and validation of the Smartphone Addiction Inventory (SPAI). *PLoS ONE* **2014**, *9*, e98312. [CrossRef] [PubMed]
9. Chiang, J.T.; Chang, F.C.; Lee, K.W.; Hsu, S.Y. Transitions in smartphone addiction proneness among children: The effect of gender and use patterns. *PLoS ONE* **2019**, *14*, e0217235. [CrossRef]
10. Lee, S.Y.; Lee, H.K.; Choi, J.S.; Bang, S.Y.; Park, M.H.; Jung, K.I.; Kweon, Y.S. The Matthew effect in recovery from smartphone addiction in a 6-month longitudinal study of children and adolescents. *Int. J. Environ. Res. Public Health* **2020**, *17*, 4751. [CrossRef]
11. Noh, C.R.; Kim, S.Y. The effects of parenting attitudes on adolescents' smartphone dependency: The mediating effects of adolescents' depression and aggression. *Stud. Korean Youth* **2016**, *27*, 87–114. [CrossRef]
12. Cho, Y. Mediating effects of online-based leisure between parenting attitudes and children's smartphone dependency. *Korean J. Child Stud.* **2021**, *42*, 695–706. [CrossRef]
13. Ching, K.H.; Tak, L.M. The structural model in parenting style, attachment style, self-regulation, and self-esteem for smartphone addiction. *IAFOR J. Psychol. Behav. Sci.* **2017**, *3*, 85–103.
14. Oh, S.; Kim, J. Relationship between parents' smartphone dependency and adolescents' smartphone dependency: The double-mediation of negative parenting attitude and academic helplessness. *Korean J. Youth Stud.* **2021**, *28*, 201–229. [CrossRef]
15. Fischer-Grote, L.; Kothgassner, O.D.; Felnhofer, A. Risk factors for problematic smartphone use in children and adolescents: A review of existing literature. *Neuropsychiatrie* **2019**, *33*, 179–190. [CrossRef] [PubMed]
16. Jeon, Y.; Nam, T. The influence of smartphone dependency on juvenile delinquency. *J. Digit. Converg.* **2020**, *18*, 139–151. [CrossRef]
17. Van Velsor, P.R.; Cox, D.L. Use of the collaborative drawing technique in school counseling practicum: An illustration of family systems. *Couns. Educ. Superv.* **2000**, *40*, 141–152. [CrossRef]
18. Yoon, S.; Lee, M.; Lee, J.; Hong, S. The Effects of Parent's Smartphone Dependency on Child's Smartphone Dependency: Serial Mediating Effects of Parenting, Child's Depression and Aggression. *Korean J. Child Stud.* **2021**, *42*, 707–720. [CrossRef]
19. Mun, I.B.; Lee, S. How does parental smartphone addiction affect adolescent smartphone addiction? Testing the mediating roles of parental rejection and adolescent depression. *Cyberpsychol. Behav. Soc. Netw.* **2021**, *24*, 399–406. [CrossRef]
20. Kim, J.H.; Ahn, G.Y.R. The effects of parents' rearing attitudes as perceived by middle school students for school adjustment: Self-regulation as a mediating variable. *Korean J. Health Psychol.* **2013**, *18*, 823–836. [CrossRef]
21. Lee, J.Y.; Jang, S.Y. The intermediary effect of ego-resilience in the relationship between a mother's parenting behaviors and smartphone addiction. *Korean J. Child Educ. Care* **2014**, *14*, 61–79.
22. Milevsky, A.; Schlechter, M.; Netter, S.; Keehn, D. Maternal and paternal parenting styles in adolescents: Associations with self-esteem, depression and life-satisfaction. *J. Child Fam. Stud.* **2007**, *16*, 39–47. [CrossRef]
23. Kang, B.G.; Shin, H.J. Risk and Protective Factors Affecting Mobile Phone Addiction in Adolescence: With a Special Focus on the Comparison by gender. *Korean J. Youth Stud.* **2014**, *21*, 213–241.
24. Ryu, K.H.; Hong, H.Y. The Relationship between Overt, Covert Narcissism and Smart Phone Addiction of Middle School Students: The Mediating Effects of Aggression. *Korean J. Youth Stud.* **2014**, *21*, 213–241.
25. Somerville, L.H. The teenage brain: Sensitivity to social evaluation. *Curr. Dir. Psychol. Sci.* **2013**, *22*, 121–127. [CrossRef] [PubMed]
26. Blakemore, S.J.; Mills, K.L. Is adolescence a sensitive period for sociocultural processing? *Annu. Rev. Psychol.* **2014**, *65*, 187–207. [CrossRef] [PubMed]
27. Liu, Q.; Wu, J.; Zhou, Z.; Wang, W. Parental technoference and smartphone addiction in Chinese adolescents: The mediating role of social sensitivity and loneliness. *Child. Youth Serv. Rev.* **2020**, *118*, 105434. [CrossRef]
28. McDaniel, B.T.; Coyne, S.M. "Technoference": The interference of technology in couple relationships and implications for women's personal and relational well-being. *Psychol. Pop. Media Cult.* **2016**, *5*, 85. [CrossRef]
29. Park, Y.S.; Yoo, J.Y. The effect of rejective parenting attitudes on smartphone dependence: Focusing on mediating effects of social withdrawal. *J. Welf. Correct.* **2022**, *76*, 121–145. [CrossRef]

30. Sohn, S.Y. Impact of social withdrawal and school environment on adolescents' smartphone dependency: The mediating effect of self-esteem and depression. *J. Digit. Converg.* **2021**, *19*, 577–586. [CrossRef]
31. NYPI Youth and Children Data Archive. Korean Children and Youth Panel Survey (Overview). Available online: https://www.nypi.re.kr/archive/board?menuId=MENU00329 (accessed on 28 March 2022).
32. Kim, D.I.; Chung, Y.J.; Lee, J.Y.; Kim, M.C.; Lee, Y.H.; Kang, E.B.; Keum, C.M.; Nam, J. Development of smartphone addiction proneness scale for adults: Self-report. *Korean J. Couns.* **2012**, *13*, 629–644.
33. Kim, S.H.; Kim, K.Y. Development of behavior problem scale for children and adolescence. *Korean Home Manag. Assoc.* **1998**, *16*, 155–166. [CrossRef]
34. Hu, L.T.; Bentler, P.M. Cutoff criteria for fit indexes in covariance structure analysis: Conventional criteria versus new alternatives. *Struct. Equ. Modeling: A Multidiscip. J.* **1999**, *6*, 1–55. [CrossRef]
35. George, D.; Mallery, M. *SPSS for Windows Step by Step: A Simple Guide and Reference, 17.0 Update*, 10th ed.; Pearson: Boston, MA, USA, 2010.
36. Khan, A.F. Assessment of Midlife Career Stress on Indian Managers. Ph.D. Thesis, Aligarh Muslim University, Aligarh, India, 2015.
37. Chakravarti, I.M.; Laha, R.G.; Roy, J. *Handbook of Methods of Applied Statistics*; Wiley: New York, NY, USA, 1967.
38. Noh, K. *A Well-Known and Well-Written Paper Statistical Analysis SPSS & AMOS 21*; Hanbit Academy Publisher: Seoul, Korea, 2014.
39. Barnes, S.J.; Pressey, A.D.; Scornavacca, E. Mobile ubiquity: Understanding the relationship between cognitive absorption, smartphone addiction, and social network services. *Comput. Hum. Behav.* **2019**, *90*, 246–258. [CrossRef]
40. Lin, Y.H.; Lin, Y.C.; Lee, Y.H.; Lin, P.H.; Lin, S.H.; Chang, L.R.; Tseng, H.-W.; Yen, L.-Y.; Yang, C.H.C.; Kuo, T.B.J. Time distortion associated with smartphone addiction: Identifying smartphone addiction via a mobile application (App). *J. Psychiatr. Res.* **2015**, *65*, 139–145. [CrossRef] [PubMed]
41. Sözbilir, F.; Dursun, M.K. Does social media usage threaten future human resources by causing smartphone addiction? A study on students aged 9–12. *Turk. J. Addict.* **2018**, *5*, 185–203. [CrossRef]
42. Chang, F.C.; Chiu, C.H.; Chen, P.H.; Chiang, J.T.; Miao, N.F.; Chuang, H.Y.; Liu, S. Children's use of mobile devices, smartphone addiction, and parental mediation in Taiwan. *Comput. Hum. Behav.* **2019**, *93*, 25–32. [CrossRef]
43. Lian, L.; You, X.; Huang, J.; Yang, R. Who overuses smartphones? Roles of virtues and parenting style in smartphone addiction among Chinese college students. *Comput. Hum. Behav.* **2016**, *65*, 92–99. [CrossRef]
44. Sun, J.; Liu, Q.; Yu, S. Child neglect, psychological abuse and smartphone addiction among Chinese adolescents: The roles of emotional intelligence and coping style. *Comput Human Behav.* **2019**, *90*, 74–83. [CrossRef]
45. Son, H.G.; Cho, H.J.; Jeong, K.H. The effects of Korean parents' smartphone addiction on Korean children's smartphone addiction: Moderating effects of children's gender and age. *Int. J. Environ. Res. Public Health* **2021**, *18*, 6685. [CrossRef]
46. Jeong, J.S.; Lee, H.K. A study on factors affecting smartphone addiction in children and adolescents: Focusing on the comparison between 4th-grade elementary school students and 1st-grade middle school students. *J. Youth Welf.* **2020**, *22*, 211–241.
47. Park, J.; Hyun, E.J. Analysis on the structural relationships of young children's smartphone overdependence, young children's aggression, mothers' parenting stress, and mothers' smartphone addiction tendency. *J. Child. Lit. Educ.* **2018**, *19*, 219–248.
48. Li, L.; Lin, T.T. Over-connected? A qualitative exploration of smartphone addiction among working adults in China. *BMC Psychiatry* **2019**, *19*, 1–10. [CrossRef]
49. Lee, H.; Kim, J.W.; Choi, T.Y. Risk factors for smartphone addiction in Korean adolescents: Smartphone use patterns. *J. Korean Med. Sci.* **2017**, *32*, 1674–1679. [CrossRef] [PubMed]
50. Rubin, K.H.; Burgess, K.B. Social withdrawal and anxiety. In *The Development Psychopathology of Anxiety*; Vasey, M.W., Dadds, M.R., Eds.; Oxford University Press: Oxford, UK, 2001; pp. 407–434.
51. Rubin, K.H.; Coplan, R.J.; Bowker, J.C. Social withdrawal in childhood. *Annu. Rev. Psychol.* **2009**, *60*, 141–171. [CrossRef] [PubMed]
52. Gazelle, H.; Ladd, G.W. Anxious solitude and peer exclusion: A diathesis-stress model of internalizing trajectories in childhood. *Child Dev.* **2003**, *74*, 257–278. [CrossRef] [PubMed]
53. Kildare, C.A.; Middlemiss, W. Impact of parents mobile device use on parent-child interaction: A literature review. *Comput. Hum. Behav.* **2017**, *75*, 579–593. [CrossRef]
54. Radesky, J.S.; Kistin, C.J.; Zuckerman, B.; Nitzberg, K.; Gross, J.; Kaplan-Sanoff, M.; Augustyn, M.; Silverstein, M. Patterns of mobile device use by caregivers and children during meals in fast-food restaurants. *Pediatrics* **2014**, *133*, e843–e849. [CrossRef]
55. Ting, C.H.; Chen, Y.Y. Smartphone addiction. In *Adolescent Addiction*, 2nd ed.; Essau, C.A., Delfabbro, P.H., Eds.; Academic Press: Cambridge, MA, USA, 2020; pp. 215–240.
56. Chang, C.; Yang, H. The effects of parental neglect on middle school students' mobile phone dependency: Mediating roles of self-esteem and social withdrawal. *Soc. Sci. Res. Rev.* **2015**, *31*, 133–156. [CrossRef]
57. Cho, S.H.; Cho, A.N. The relationship between parents' smartphone dependence and adolescent's smartphone dependence: The mediating effects of negative parenting attitude and adolescent's depression. *J. Learn. -Cent. Curric. Instr.* **2021**, *21*, 369–379. [CrossRef]
58. Lee, M.R.; Park, S.J. The Structural Relationship Among Parents' Compulsory, Autonomy Support, Smartphone Overdependence and Problem Behaviors by School Level. *Stud. Korean Youth* **2020**, *27*, 169–191. [CrossRef]
59. Jung, J. An analysis on the casual model between parent-child' negative interaction and adolescent' aggression: Focusing on sex differences. *Stud. Korean Youth* **2014**, *25*, 237–263. [CrossRef]

60. Park, E.; Park, K. The Mediating Effects of Depression and Aggression on the Relationship between Perceived Parental Rearing Attitudes and Smart Phone Addiction—A Focus on Gender Differences. *Korean J. Play. Ther.* **2014**, *17*, 209–224.
61. Kwon, Y.S.; Paek, K.S. The influence of smartphone addiction on depression and communication competence among college students. *Indian J. Sci. Technol.* **2016**, *9*, 1–8. [CrossRef]

healthcare

MDPI

Article

Effect of Home-Based Tele-Pilates Intervention on Pregnant Women: A Pilot Study

Ah-Hyun Hyun, Joon-Yong Cho and Jung-Hoon Koo *

Department of Exercise Biochemistry and Exercise, Korea National Sport University, Seoul 05541, Korea; knupe838@knsu.ac.kr (A.-H.H.); chojy86@knsu.ac.kr (J.-Y.C.)
* Correspondence: mt634@knsu.ac.kr

Abstract: Pilates is effective for training the core muscles and stabilizing the hip joints, which provides relief from pelvic pain and low back pain during pregnancy. However, there are no specific guidelines on appropriate physical exercises for pregnant women due to the current pandemic. We aimed to apply the exercise standard proposed by the American College of Obstetricians and Gynecologists to home-based tele-Pilates exercise (HTPE), to determine its effect on the physical and mental health of pregnant women. We randomly divided the subjects into the following two groups who completed 8 weeks of HTPE (50 min/day, 2 days/week): (a) Pilates exercise (PE, $n = 7$) and (B) non-Pilates exercise (CON, $n = 7$). HTPE was performed by adjusting the program every 3 weeks, based on pain and physical fitness levels. We measured body composition, muscles of the hip joint, pelvic tilt, Oswestry Disability Index (ODI), and Pittsburgh Sleep Quality Index (PSQI), before and after HTPE. Following HTPE, while the percentage of body fat and body mass index had significantly decreased, the body fat mass did not change in the PE group ($p < 0.05$). The PE group showed an increase in strength of the left and right hip flexion and hip abduction, compared to the CON group ($p < 0.01$). The ODI and PSQI were significantly decreased in the PE group ($p < 0.05$). Therefore, the 8-week HTPE program is an effective exercise for pregnant woman that reduces body fat metabolism and strengthens muscles of the hip joint, thus alleviating pregnancy-induced low back pain and insomnia.

Keywords: COVID-19; pregnancy; physical exercise; hip flexion; hip abduction; pelvic tilt

Citation: Hyun, A.-H.; Cho, J.-Y.; Koo, J.-H. Effect of Home-Based Tele-Pilates Intervention on Pregnant Women: A Pilot Study. *Healthcare* **2022**, *10*, 125. https://doi.org/10.3390/healthcare10010125

Academic Editor: Masafumi Koshiyama

Received: 13 December 2021
Accepted: 6 January 2022
Published: 8 January 2022

1. Introduction

Coronavirus disease 2019 (COVID-19), a viral respiratory disease, has caused social, economic, and cultural disruption across the world. COVID-19 is highly contagious and causes fatal damage to elderly people with underlying conditions [1]. Pregnant women are classified as another high-risk group and are predicted to be exposed to great danger during the COVID-19 pandemic [2,3]. This can be attributed to the high incidences of miscarriage, premature birth, immature fetal growth, kidney failure, and vascular disease during the 2003 SARS outbreak. Although some studies have reported on the susceptibility of pregnant women to pneumonia and respiratory infections during the current pandemic [4], there are limited studies on COVID-19 and pregnant women. Thus, it is difficult to establish obstetric prevention guidelines.

During pregnancy, women undergo major changes in their body mechanics, physiology, and psychology. It is characterized by severe anterior pelvic tilt and lumbar curve changes due to fetal growth and an increased abdominal size [5,6]. The later stages are characterized by tension in the hip flexors and lumbar muscles, and weakening of the abdominal and hip joint muscles. These eventually lead to pelvic pain, thus resulting in body instability and low back pain [7,8]. In addition to the stress caused by the aforementioned physical changes, the psychological anxiety among pregnant women regarding the COVID-19 pandemic can further increase their stress. Increased anxiety and stress in potential mothers can cause side effects such as nausea, vomiting, loss of weight, and depression.

These, in turn, can induce diabetes, hypertension, and obesity [9]. A previous study has reported a two-fold increase in anxiety disorders in pregnant women after COVID-19. This has been attributed to stress caused by hospital visits for obstetric exanimations, fetal infections during childbirth, and social isolation due to quarantine [10]. Furthermore, a study analyzed the Pittsburgh Sleep Quality Index (PSQI) in 166 pregnant women during the COVID-19 pandemic and reported that 88% of the pregnant women experienced difficulty in sleeping [10]. This necessitates a therapeutic approach to alleviate their high stress and anxiety about COVID-19.

The American College of Obstetricians and Gynecologists (ACOG) recommends non-physical therapies, such as meditation, breathing, music, and reading, and physical activities, such as yoga, swimming, and walking for at least 150 min weekly to maintain the health of the fetus [11]. Physical activity during pregnancy effectively enhances the physical fitness of the mother and relieves pain. Moreover, it facilitates short contractions during childbirth, rapid postpartum recovery, and diet [12]. However, the participation of pregnant women in physical activity has sharply declined due to pandemic-mediated environmental limitations. Nevertheless, considering the impact of physical exercise on improving anxiety and sleep disorders in pregnant women, an alternative program to increase their daily physical activity in the current environment should be initiated [13]. Pregnant women who performed voluntary exercise after COVID-19 were shown to have a lower index of depressive disorder than the control group with a sedentary lifestyle. Moreover, the insomnia severity index was alleviated in the group that performed yoga [14]. Therefore, physical activity can partially alleviate the psychological instability in pregnant women in the context of COVID-19. However, the mechanism underlying psychological stability is unclear. Moreover, there is insufficient research on the mechanism of relieving low back pain in pregnant women (muscles of the hip joint and pelvic tilt) and related pain indicators. The aforementioned women performed voluntary exercise independently during COVID-19. Hence, there is a lack of motivation for exercise and corrective feedback on the exercise method and programs, compared to face-to-face exercise. This necessitates the need for an exercise program that not only improves the muscles of the hip joint in pregnant women but also provides detailed feedback on exercise in the context of COVID-19.

Pilates not only improves basic physical strength through a combination of aerobic and anaerobic exercise, but also stabilizes the hip joint by strengthening the deep muscles close to the spine. This, in turn, alleviates physical discomfort, such as low back pain and pelvic pain [15]. Previous studies have reported on increased physical strength and hip joint muscle strength in pregnant women who participated in Pilates, and a significant decrease in visual analog scale scores (a measure of back pain) [16,17]. However, it has been difficult for pregnant women to participate in exercise due to the closure of sports facilities and the recommendations to stay at home during the COVID-19 pandemic. This calls for a program that can solve environmental constraints while maintaining the beneficial effects of Pilates.

Following COVID-19, non-face-to-face remote systems have been widely used in industrial, educational, and cultural aspects through the web service of IT platforms. The culture of non-contact consumption has dramatically increased the home-training population, where people participate in online workouts at home. However, the abuse of unverified information and content can impair exercise-related judgments. Participation in physical activity without proper knowledge of the precautions can lead to serious injuries [18]. Pain and severity in pregnant women vary according to the number of weeks of pregnancy. This necessitates a program that considers the posture to protect weakened joints, breathing for childbirth, prevention of falls, contraindications, and a two-way communication method that provides real-time education. Non-face-to-face remote exercise is generally limited to programs used to prevent muscle loss in the elderly [19,20], for rehabilitation in sports medicine [21,22], and in patients with other diseases [23,24]. Therefore, the participation of physically inactive pregnant women in home-based tele-pilates exercise (HTPE) will enable them to overcome COVID-19-associated environmental constraints and control pelvic floor muscle depression and pain. We aimed to verify whether 8 weeks of HTPE partially improves the pelvic tilt and muscles of the hip joint, low back pain, and insomnia during pregnancy in the COVID-19 context. The identification of HTPE-associated positive factors will present a new paradigm of exercise suitable for pregnant women who voluntarily practice social distancing due to limitations in the activity radius and changes in body shape in the post-COVID-19 era.

2. Materials

2.1. Subject

We selected the subjects from among the women registered at the 'C' Cultural Center in Bundang, Gyeonggi-do, Korea, who completely understood the purpose of the study and offered their voluntary participation and consent. The selected subjects included pregnant women under the age of 45 years, at 20–24 weeks of single-fetus pregnancy. Moreover, they did not receive medications and did not participate in home-training. This study was a cluster randomized controlled experiment. We used a lottery method for randomization, and all subjects chose a mini ball marked with 1 or 2. A total of 18 subjects were classified into the control group (CON, $n = 9$) and the exercise group (PE, $n = 9$). We excluded four subjects ($n = 2$ per group) who expressed discomfort while participating in the exercise and dropped out (CON ($n = 7$), 34.14 ± 3.82 years, 63.57 ± 3.57 kg, 37.72 ± 3.82% body fat; PE ($n = 7$), 31.71 ± 3.03 years, 67.44 ± 5.18 kg, 38.85 ± 5.53% body fat). A comparison of the reference values between the groups was performed by obtaining Cohen's r values. Following approval from the Korean National Sports University (1263-202103-HR-002-01), we requested the subjects to fill out a written consent form and all procedures performed herein conformed to the principles outlined in the Declaration of Helsinki.

2.2. HTPE Program

The HTPE program consisted of warm-up, main, and cool-down exercises, and was conducted for 50 min/day, twice a week, for a total of 8 weeks according to the ACOG (Figure 1). A 20 s break was allotted between the exercises. Moreover, the exercise intensity was maintained at a 10–13 rating of perceived exertion (RPE) by the ACOG (50–60% of the maximum heart rate) and Borg's scale. We gradually increased the exercise intensity every 3 weeks, based on the subject's physical fitness level and pain status. Table 1 summarizes the HTPE program. We restricted the number of participants to <10 to help the instructor observe the movement and pain level of all subjects by reflecting on the characteristics of non-face-to-face exercise. Their incorrect postures were corrected and the RPE was monitored to maintain an appropriate intensity. Furthermore, the subjects were able to maximize the mutual exercise effect by adjusting the distance from the instructor by using a television or a tablet in their respective spaces, receiving feedback on their posture, and real-time conversations on the degree of discomfort, before and after the movement.

2.3. Body Composition

The subjects maintained a fasting state and removed metal accessories before their height and body measurement using a DS-103M automatic height meter (Jenix Co., Seoul, Korea) and a InBody H20B body composition analyzer (Biospace Co., Seoul, Korea), respectively. Both hands and feet were disinfected before the measurement. They were directed to stand on the platform and hold the handles with the electrodes in each hand. During the test, both arms were kept slightly open to prevent contact with the torso. Moreover, talking was prohibited and they were requested to maintain comfortable breathing. The measurement factors included body weight (BW, kg), body fat mass (BFM, kg), skeletal muscle mass (SMM, kg), body mass index (BMI, kg/m^2), percentage of body fat (PBF, %), and fat free mass (FFM, kg).

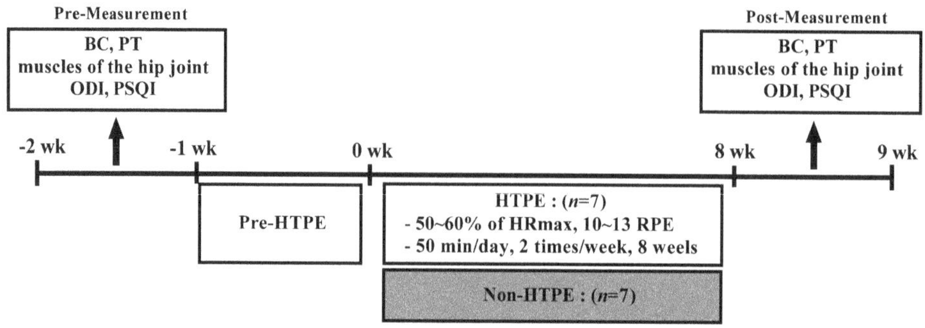

Figure 1. Experimental design. BC: body composition, PT: pelvic tilt, ODI: Oswestry Disability Index, PSQI: Pittsburgh Sleep Quality Index, HTPE: home-based tele-pilates exercise, HRmax: maximal heart rate, RPE: rating of perceived exertion.

Table 1. HTPE program.

Modes	Contents	Time (min)	Reps, Set, and Rest	RPE
Warm-up	Low-impact stretching and Breathing	10		10
Main exercise	Level 1: 1–3 week Arm circle, Cat cow, Bridge, Clam, Half-spine rotation, Leg circles, Half-squat Level 2: 4–6 week Donkey kick, Hip hinge, Leg side up, Half-saw, Half-lunges, Kneeing push-up Level 3: 7–8 week Half-lunge twist, Side lateral raise, Squat, Low-impact down dog, Deep breathing	30	12–15 reps × 3 set 10 s rest between sets	11–13
Cool-down	Total body stretching	10		10

2.4. Pelvic Tilt

A posturemeter (Spomedic healthcare, Seoul, Korea) was used to measure the pelvic tilt, such as the coronal plane tilt (CPT) and sagittal plane tilt (SPT) [25]. After standing upright, the subjects lowered their arms comfortably and stared straight ahead. The examiner marked the anterior superior iliac spine in the front and posterior superior iliac spine at the back of the pelvis with stickers. The posturemeter was placed on the marked anterior iliac spine to measure the CPT tilt. In contrast, the SPT was measured by applying a posturemeter on the marked poles on the anterior and posterior iliac spines in the sagittal plane. The posturemeter protractor was set to 0 degrees before the measurement, and the average of two measurements was noted and recorded.

2.5. Muscles of the Hip Joint

Muscles of the hip joint that are involved in right hip flexion (RHF), right hip abduction (RHA), left hip flexion (LHF), and left hip abduction (LHA) were measured using a manual muscle strength meter (HOGGAN PROOF Preferred, HOGGAN HEALTH, Salt Lake City, UT, USA). An isometric muscle test was used for the measurement and conducted using the active straight leg-raising method with the subject in a supine position [26]. The subjects practiced once, and the measurement was performed twice. The examiner measured the maximum muscle strength range at which the subjects did not feel pain with their trunk fixed. The muscle strength was measured by fixing a manual muscle strength meter on the right ankle and requesting the subjects to raise their foot to the ceiling to the maximum extent possible. This enabled the measurement of the RHF and LHF. For measuring the RHA and LHA, the examiner fixed the manual muscle strength tester to the upper ankle while the subjects were laid on their side with the head comfortably placed on one arm, and the knees bent to fold in both feet. They were then asked to lift the upper foot towards the ceiling on the side of the hip joint to measure the muscle strength. All measurements were repeated twice, and the average value was used for the analysis. A 30 s break was allotted for each muscle group. The unit of the instrument was 1 lb with a ±1% margin of error.

2.6. ODI Test

The Oswestry Disability Index (ODI) test is a questionnaire developed to measure the level of symptoms in patients with lower back pain. Furthermore, it enables the verification of pain-associated degree of dysfunction. The evaluation items consist of 10 questions on pain management, personal management, walking, standing, sitting, sleep, and social life, and each question is evaluated on a scale of 0–5. The scores for each item are added to obtain the total score, which is then divided by 50 and multiplied by 100 to obtain a percentage. Values in the range of 0–20%, 21–40%, 41–60%, 61–80%, and 81–100% indicate minimal disability, moderate disability, severe disability, paralyzed, and patients who must be bed-bound, respectively [27]. The test was scored twice before and after the experiment, and the total score was recorded.

2.7. PSQI Test

We used the PSQI developed and modified to evaluate sleep quality [28]. PSQI is a self-reported questionnaire that measures sleep quality and sleep disturbances over the past month. It includes 18 items and seven primary factors, namely sleep quality, sleep delay, sleep duration, habitual sleep efficiency, sleep disability, sleep medication use, and daytime dysfunction. The scale is evaluated based on a total score, and each item is scored from 0 to 3. The total score is obtained by summing the scores of the aforementioned seven factors. The total score ranges from 0 to 21. Higher the total score, the lower the sleep quality is. A total score ≤ 5 indicates sound sleep. In contrast, a score ≥ 8 indicates a sleep problem. While the reliability of the PSQI tool has been measured to obtain a Cronbach's alpha of 0.85, we obtained a Cronbach's alpha of 0.81 [29].

2.8. Statistical Analyses

We analyzed the differences in the body composition, pelvic tilt and muscles of the hip joint, ODI, and PSQI before and after HTPE using SPSS 22.0. The result of the normality test revealed unsatisfactory normal distribution. Therefore, statistical analyses were conducted using a non-parametric test method. The difference between the groups was analyzed using the Mann–Whitney U test, based on the average difference obtained through the change-score analysis. The difference between the pre- and post-test status within the groups was analyzed using the Wilcoxon signed-rank test. All statistical values are presented as median (interquartile range), and the level of significance for was set to $p < 0.05$.

3. Results

3.1. Effect of HTPE on the Body Composition

There was no statistically significant difference in the pre- and post-body composition between the groups (Table 2). All body composition factors of the CON group increased significantly post-HTPE (BW: $p = 0.018$, SMM: $p = 0.028$, TFM: $p = 0.018$, PBF: $p = 0.018$, BMI: $p = 0.018$, and FFM: $p = 0.018$). While PBF and BMI had significantly decreased (PBF: $p = 0.043$ and BMI: $p = 0.018$), other factors had significantly increased (BW: $p = 0.018$, SMM: $p = 0.018$, and FFM: $p = 0.018$); no significant difference was observed in the BFM in the PE group.

3.2. Effect of HTPE on Muscles of the Hip Joint

The muscle strength in the hip joint, and the RHF, RHA, LHF, and LHA of all muscles were significantly increased in the PE group, compared to the CON group (RHF: $p = 0.001$,

RHA: $p = 0.001$, LHF: $p = 0.001$, and LHA: $p = 0.001$, Table 3). Moreover, all muscles in the PE group showed a significant increase after HTPE (RHF: $p = 0.180$, RHA: $p = 0.180$, LHF: $p = 0.180$, and LHA: $p = 0.180$). Although a decreasing trend in all muscles was observed in the CON group, the difference was not significant.

Table 2. Body composition.

	CON (n = 7)		PE (n = 7)		Diff (Post-Pre)	
	Pre	**Post**	**Pre**	**Post**	p	**Cohen's d**
BW (kg)	64.50 (8.70)	69.90 (8.90) *	69.10 (13.00)	72.50 (16.20) *	0.456	0.337
SMM (kg)	27.70 (9.00)	28.20 (10.70) *	23.40 (8.70)	29.50 (8.10) *	0.805	0.228
BFM (kg)	23.70 (12.10)	24.90 (10.90) *	25.10 (8.00)	29.50 (8.10)	0.259	0.706
PBF (%))	39.30 (14.20)	40.40 (9.80) *	37.90 (11.10)	37.70 (14.60) *	0.209	0.768
BMI (kg/m^2)	23.50 (1.60)	25.50 (2.10) *	25.30 (5.10)	26.90 (4.80) *	0.383	0.706
FFM (kg)	39.70 (10.40)	39.90 (8.80) *	40.60 (13.60)	44.50 (18.20) *	0.128	0.861

Values are presented as median (interquartile range) (n = 7 per group). Main time effect: * $p < 0.05$, pre- versus post-HTPE period in the within groups. CON: non-pilates exercise, PE: pilates exercise, BW: body weight, SMM: skeletal muscle mass, BFM: body fat mass, PBF: percentage of body fat, BMI: body mass index, FFM: fat free mass.

Table 3. Muscle strength in the hip joint.

	CON (n = 7)		PE (n = 7)		Difference (Post-Pre)	
	Pre	**Post**	**Pre**	**Post**	p	**Cohen's d**
RHF (lbs) ##	3.80 (2.40)	3.60 (2.30)	4.30 (2.20)	6.40 (3.80) *	0.001	2.939
RHA (lbs) ##	3.50 (0.80)	3.20 (0.70)	5.00 (3.60)	7.10 (1.70) *	0.001	6.958
LHF (lbs) ##	3.60 (1.20)	3.40 (1.00)	4.80 (3.00)	6.80 (2.90) *	0.001	4.482
LHA (lbs) ##	3.30 (0.80)	3.20 (1.40)	4.30 (1.50)	7.00 (1.80) *	0.001	6.889

Values are presented as median (interquartile range) (n = 7 per group). ## $p < 0.01$ change (post–pre) between groups. Main time effect: * $p < 0.05$, pre- versus post-HTPE period within groups. CON: non-pilates exercise, PE: pilates exercise. RHF: right hip flexion, RHA: right hip abduction, LHF: left hip flexion, LHA: left hip abduction.

3.3. Effect of HTPE on the Pelvic Tilt

There was no substantial difference in the amount of change in the pelvic tilt such as CPT and SPT between the groups (Table 4). Moreover, there was no statistically significant difference in the CPT in the PE group, though we observed an increase in the SPT (SPT: $p = 0.017$). However, the CON group revealed increased inclination in both the CPT and SPT (CPT: $p = 0.038$ and SPT: $p = 0.017$).

Table 4. Pelvic tilt.

	CON (n = 7)		PE (n = 7)		Diff (Post-Pre)	
	Pre	**Post**	**Pre**	**Post**	p	**Cohen's d**
CPT (°)	2.00 (0.00)	3.00 (2.00) *	2.00 (1.00)	2.00 (2.00)	0.259	0.681
SPT (°)	22.00 (8.00)	28.00 (5.00) *	24.00 (18.00)	28.00 (12.00) *	0.456	0.774

Values are presented as median (interquartile range) (n = 7 per group). Main time effect: * $p < 0.05$, pre- versus post-HTPE period in the within groups. CON: non-pilates exercise, PE: Pilates exercise, CPT: coronal plane tilt, SPT: sagittal plane tilt.

3.4. Effect of HTPE on the ODI and PSQI

Changes in the ODI and PSQI were significantly decreased in the PE group, compared to the CON group (ODI: $p = 0.001$ and PSQI: $p = 0.001$, Figure 2). Following HTPE, we observed a significant decrease in the ODI and PSQI in the PE group (ODI: $p = 0.028$ and PSQI: $p = 0.161$). There was no significant difference in the ODI in the CON group; however, the PSQI was increased ($p = 0.017$).

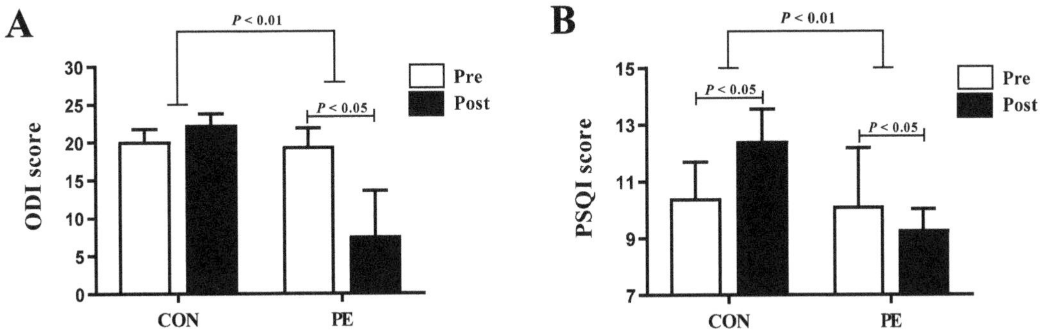

Figure 2. HTPE reduced ODI and PSQI score in Korean pregnant woman. (**A**) ODI score and (**B**) PSQI score (n = 7 per group). Error bars represent mean ± SD. CON: non-pilates exercise, PE: Pilates exercise, ODI: Oswestry Disability Index, PSQI: Pittsburgh Sleep Quality Index.

4. Discussion

Researchers have recently emphasized the importance of exercise for pregnant women. This can be attributed to the impact of regular exercise on reducing anxiety and stress during pregnancy. Moreover, it exerts anti-inflammatory and antiviral effects [30]. Various methods have been proposed to overcome the limitations of physical activity during pregnancy in the midst of the COVID-19 pandemic [31]. Non-face-to-face online alternative programs are used in some areas of rehabilitation. Nonetheless, there is little evidence regarding their effectiveness in pregnant women. Therefore, we determined the positive effect of HTPE on various physiological changes, such as the body composition, pelvic tilt, and muscles of the hip joint during pregnancy, and the resulting low back pain and insomnia.

Following HTPE, there was no statistically significant difference in body composition changes among pregnant women. This phenomenon is commonly caused by increased insulin and lipid hormones during pregnancy. Our results were similar to those of previous studies that reported weight gain in pregnant women [32]. Weight gain during pregnancy is inevitable. However, excessive weight gain causes complications such as hypertension, diabetes, and hyperlipidemia, thus necessitating proper diet control and exercise [33,34]. Pilates is reportedly effective at controlling body weight and body fat in pregnant women and facilitates childbirth by increasing the skeletal muscle mass [35]. Thus, we aimed to confirm whether HTPE triggered changes in body fat metabolism. There was no significant difference in the BFM in the PE group. The PBF and BMI had decreased after HTPE, thus indicating that HTPE suppressed the increase in body fat mass during pregnancy. This may be attributed to the ACOG-based intensity of HTPE that is sufficient to reduce the fat mass. Our results were similar to those of previous studies that have reported loss in body fat after Pilates exercise. In addition, resistance movements, such as the contraction and relaxation of skeletal muscles, along with a Pilates-induced reduction in body fat increase the SMM and muscle strength [35]. Accordingly, an HTPE-mediated increase in the SMM would likely occur. However, SMM was significantly increased in both groups post-HTPE. This might be associated with a partial increase in skeletal muscle, a factor of body composition, due to increased body weight during pregnancy. Thus, we failed to interpret our results as an HTPE-mediated increase in SMM. However, we observed a significant increase in the muscle strength of the hip joint in the PE group, compared to the CON group. This was consistent with the findings in previous studies that mentioned that Pilates exercise strengthens the pelvic muscles with core exercise [36]. Therefore, HTPE is considered an effective form of exercise that can reduce the elevated body fat metabolism during pregnancy and strengthen the muscles of the hip joint.

The anterior tilt of the hip joint increases during the later stages of pregnancy, thus, collapsing the pelvic inclination, and causing back pain with spinal deformity [37,38]. The CPT and SPT significantly increased in the CON group, which was consistent with the findings of previous studies that have reported on pelvic tilt deformity in pregnant women [39,40]. However, there was no significant difference in the CPT in the PE group. Hence, HTPE possibly alleviated the pelvic tilt during pregnancy. Our findings were consistent with those of previous studies that reported on pelvic tilt relief through Pilates exercise [41]. In contrast, changes in anterior and posterior pelvic tilt in the SPT increased with the gestation period in both groups. This was consistent with the finding of a study that mentioned that hip flexors become shortened during pregnancy and the lumbar curve becomes severe, which results in falls due to body imbalance. In addition, loss of balance is usually observed in late pregnancy [42]. In our study, although the difference was not statistically significant, the amount of change in the SPT tended to decrease in the PE group, compared to the CON group. Therefore, HTPE is considered an effective exercise method that can partially alleviate pelvic imbalance during pregnancy. However, the mechanism underlying the control of pelvic imbalance is unclear. This may be related to the strengthening of hip joint muscles by HTPE. Interestingly, we confirmed an increase in the muscle strength of the hip joint following HTPE. Thus, HTPE supposedly improves pelvic tilt imbalance by strengthening the muscles around the pelvis during pregnancy.

Most pregnant women suffer from insomnia during pregnancy due to back pain. The post-ODI and PSQI scores increased in the CON group compared with before. An increase in stress can have a negative effect on the mother and child. Thus, an appropriate treatment is required to relieve low back pain. Considering the impact of HTPE on increasing pelvic strength and improving the pelvic tilt, our study findings may facilitate relieving low back pain and related insomnia during pregnancy. The ODI and PSQI scores significantly decreased in the PE group post-HTPE. Therefore, Pilates strengthens the core muscles, thus stabilizing the radius and alleviating low back pain and insomnia during pregnancy [43,44]. In other words, HTPE alleviates low back pain and insomnia during pregnancy. This can be attributed to the strengthening of the hip joint muscles and relieving the pelvic tilt imbalance. Therefore, HTPE is an effective exercise method that can partially alleviate low back pain and sleep disturbances that occur during pregnancy. The effects of exercise on pregnant women in this study point toward the benefits of an online learning platform for sports [45]. This is attributable to the development of applications that facilitate real-time interactions. In the future, subjects should be able to use epidemiological and physiological data to practice through online training using artificial intelligence such as Metabus.

The limitations of our study include our inability to mobilize larger subjects due to its design that required pregnant women. Moreover, some mothers were unable to participate in the exercise due to personal circumstances that arose during pregnancy. In addition, we could not recruit a large number of participants to provide individual communication about the exercise and accurate feedback through video. This can be attributed to the non-face-to-face exercise program. Consequently, we could not generalize the results. This would enable the management of larger subjects in the future. Hence, it is necessary to use remote technology to develop an exercise program specialized for pregnant women. In addition, it is considered necessary to further study whether this non-face-to-face exercise program can be applied to postpartum women who may be vulnerable to depression as well as during pregnancy.

5. Conclusions

Eight weeks of HTPE resulted in a limited increase in body fat and increased the pelvic strength, thereby reducing the pelvic tilt caused by pregnancy. In addition, HTPE reduced back pain and relieved sleep disturbances resulting from pregnancy. Therefore, HTPE may be considered an effective exercise for enhancing the physical and mental changes that occur in pregnant women, similar to face-to-face Pilates exercise. Furthermore, HTPE will likely serve as a suitable remote technology exercise program that can alleviate the anxiety and physical discomfort experienced by pregnant women in future pandemics.

Author Contributions: Original draft; A.-H.H. and J.-H.K., Project administration; A.-H.H., Data curation; A.-H.H., Visualization; J.-Y.C., Methodology; J.-H.K., Writing; A.-H.H., Review & Editing; J.-Y.C. and J.-H.K., Supervision; J.-H.K. All authors have read and agreed to the published version of the manuscript.

Funding: This study did not receive any funding.

Institutional Review Board Statement: The study was conducted according to the guidelines of the Declaration of Helsinki, and approved by the Institutional Review Board (This study was approved by the institutional review board at Korea National Sports University (1263-202103-HR-002-01).

Informed Consent Statement: Informed consent was obtained from all subjects involved in the study.

Data Availability Statement: The datasets used and analyzed during the current study are available from the corresponding author on reasonable request.

Conflicts of Interest: The authors declare no conflict of interest.

References

1. Mappa, I.; Distefano, F.A.; Rizzo, G. Effects of coronavirus 19 pandemic on maternal anxiety during pregnancy: A prospectic observational study. *J. Perinat. Med.* **2020**, *48*, 545–550. [CrossRef] [PubMed]
2. Ayaz, R.; Hocaoğlu, M.; Günay, T.; Yardımcı, O.D.; Turgut, A.; Karateke, A. Anxiety and depression symptoms in the same pregnant women before and during the COVID-19 pandemic. *J. Perinat. Med.* **2020**, *48*, 965–970. [CrossRef] [PubMed]
3. Silva-Jose, C.; Sánchez-Polán, M.; Diaz-Blanco, Á.; Coterón, J.; Barakat, R.; Refoyo, I. Effectiveness of a Virtual Exercise Program During COVID-19 Confinement on Blood Pressure Control in Healthy Pregnant Women. *Front. Physiol.* **2021**, *12*, 279. [CrossRef]
4. Marbán-Castro, E.; Pons-Duran, C.; García-Otero, L.; Chen, H.; Herrera, L.B.; Gil, M.d.M.; Goncé, A.; Ferriols-Pérez, E.; Rodríguez, M.Á.; Toro, P.; et al. Acceptability of Clinical Trials on COVID-19 during Pregnancy among Pregnant Women and Healthcare Providers: A Qualitative Study. *Int. J. Environ. Res. Public Health* **2021**, *18*, 10717. [CrossRef]
5. Long, G.; Haoning, M.; Ping, Y.; Mingsheng, T. Asymmetry in Paraspinal Muscles as a Predictor of the Development of Pregnancy-Related Low Back and Pelvic Pain: A Prospective Study. *Res. Sq.* **2021**. [CrossRef]
6. Morino, S.; Ishihara, M.; Umezaki, F.; Hatanaka, H.; Yamashita, M.; Kawabe, R.; Aoyama, T. The effects of pelvic belt use on pelvic alignment during and after pregnancy: A prospective longitudinal cohort study. *BMC Pregnancy Childbirth* **2019**, *19*, 305. [CrossRef] [PubMed]
7. Signe, N.; Nina, K.; Siv, M.; Kjell, Å.; Hilde, S. Impact of job adjustment, pain location and exercise on sick leave due to lumbopelvic pain in pregnancy: A longitudinal study. *Scand. J. Prim. Health Care* **2019**, *37*, 218–226.
8. Chen, H.; D'Onofrio, G.; Hameed, F. Role of Exercise Treatment of Low Back Pain in Pregnancy. *Curr. Phys. Med. Rehabil. Rep.* **2020**, *8*, 322–328. [CrossRef]
9. Pascual-Morena, C.; Cavero-Redondo, I.; Álvarez-Bueno, C.; Lucerón-Lucas-Torres, M.; Sanabria-Martínez, G.; Poyatos-León, R.; Rodríguez-Martín, B.; Martínez-Vizcaíno, V. Exercise versus Metformin to Improve Pregnancy Outcomes among Overweight Pregnant Women: A Systematic Review and Network Meta-Analysis. *J. Clin. Med.* **2021**, *10*, 3490. [CrossRef]
10. Sultan, A.; Burcu, A.; Ayseren, C.; Ebru, G.; Sule, G. The Effects of COVID-19 Pandemic on Pregnant Women: Perceived Stress, Social Support and Sleep Quality. *Yonago Acta Med.* **2020**, *63*, 360–367.
11. ACOG. Practice Advisory: Novel Coronavirus 2019 (COVID-19). 2020. American College of Obstetricians and Gynecologists. 2019. Available online: https://www.acog.org/Clinical-Guidance-and-Publications/Practice-Advisories/Practice-Advisory-Novel-Coronavirus (accessed on 12 December 2021).
12. Mazzarino, M.; Kerr, D.; Morris, M. pilates program design and health benefits for pregnant women: A practitioners' survey. *J Bodyw. Mov. Ther.* **2018**, *22*, 411–417. [CrossRef]
13. Rodrigo, S.; Leonardo, A.; Deivison, S. Effects of the practice of Pilates in pregnancy: A literature review. *Rev. Saúde Física Ment.* **2019**, *7*, 30–44.
14. Nadholta, P.; Bali, P.; Singh, A.; Anand, A. Potential benefits of Yoga in pregnancy-related complications during the COVID-19 pandemic and implications for working women. *Work* **2020**, *67*, 269–279. [CrossRef] [PubMed]
15. Rahul, T.; Pravin, K. The effects of selected Pilates exercise on the body composition of obese people. *J. Crit. Rev.* **2020**, *7*, 3374–3381.
16. Rodríguez-Díaz, L.; Ruiz-Frutos, C.; Vázquez-Lara, J.M.; Ramírez-Rodrigo, J.; Villaverde-Gutiérrez, C.; Torres-Luque, G. Effectiveness of a physical activity programme based on the Pilates method in pregnancy and labour. *Enferm. Clín.* **2017**, *27*, 271–277. [CrossRef]
17. Fairbank, J.; Couper, J.C.; Davies, J.B.; O'Brien, J.P. The Oswestry Low Back Pain Disability Questionnaire. *Physiotherapy* **1980**, *66*, 271–273.

18. DiPietro, L.; Al-Ansari, S.S.; Biddle, S.J.; Borodulin, K.; Bull, F.C.; Buman, M.P.; Cardon, G.; Carty, C.; Chaput, J.P.; Chastin, S.; et al. Advancing the global physical activity agenda: Recommendations for future research by the 2020 WHO physical activity and sedentary behavior guidelines development group. *Int. J. Behav. Nutr. Phys. Act.* **2020**, *17*, 1–11. [CrossRef]
19. Alessandro, G.; Gian, P.; Fabio, V.; Mara, P.; Palmira, B.; Laura, C.; Amerigo, G. Feasibility and cost-effectiveness of a multidisciplinary home-telehealth intervention programme to reduce falls among elderly discharged from hospital: Study protocol for a randomized controlled trial. *BMC Geriatr.* **2016**, *16*, 209.
20. Hong, J.; Kim, J.; Kim, S.; Kong, H. Effects of home-based tele-exercise on sarcopenia among community-dwelling elderly adults: Body composition and functional fitness. *Exp. Gerontol.* **2017**, *87 Pt A*, 33–39. [CrossRef]
21. James, H.; Mohanraj, T.; Hui, Y.; Dori, P.; Tracy, T.; Emily, R.; Tapan, M. Rationale and design of the tele-exercise and multiple sclerosis (TEAMS) study: A comparative effectiveness trial between a clinic- and home-based telerehabilitation intervention for adults with multiple sclerosis (MS) living in the deep south. *Contemp. Clin. Trials* **2018**, *71*, 186–193.
22. Mohanraj, T.; James, H.; George, J.; Jereme, W.; Tapan, M.; Byron, L. TEAMS (Tele-Exercise and Multiple Sclerosis), a Tailored Telerehabilitation mHealth App: Participant-Centered Development and Usability Study. *JMIR Mhealth Uhealth* **2018**, *6*, e1018.
23. Jen, J.; Dan, M.; Fadia, H.; Anna, S.; Eliezer, N.; Shlomit, R. Tele-Exercise as a Promising Tool to Promote Exercise in Children With Cystic Fibrosis. *Front Public Health* **2018**, *6*, 269.
24. Jorge, C.; Jorge, P.; Serafín, D.; José Carlos, C.; Manuel, G.; Jorge, R.; Laura, M.; Sabina, B.; María, M.; Angelina, P.; et al. Cost-Effectiveness of "Tele-Square Step Exercise" for Falls Prevention in Fibromyalgia Patients: A Study Protocol. *Int. J. Environ. Res. Public Health* **2020**, *17*, 695.
25. Park, D.S.; Jung, S.H. Effects of hamstring self-stretches on pelvic mobility in persons with low back pain. *Phys. Ther. Rehabil. Sci.* **2020**, *9*, 140–148. [CrossRef]
26. Back, C.; Joo, J.; Kim, Y. Association between muscular strengths and gait characteristics of elderly people aged 65 to 74 and 75 and above. *J. Korea Acad. -Ind. Coop. Soc.* **2020**, *2*, 415–422.
27. Lee, S.; Nam, S. Effects of Active Release Technique on Pain, Oswestry Disability Index and Pelvic Asymmetry in Chronic Low Back Pain Patients. *Korean Soc. Phys. Med.* **2020**, *15*, 133–141. [CrossRef]
28. Kim, K.; Cho, Y.; Bae, J. Quality of sleep and quality of life measured monthly in pregnant women in South Korea. *Sleep Breathin.* **2020**, *24*, 1219–1222. [CrossRef]
29. Suran, G.; Wenmei, S.; Chang, L.; Siwei, W. Structural Validity of the Pittsburgh Sleep Quality Index in Chinese Undergraduate Students. *Front. Psychol.* **2016**, *3*. [CrossRef]
30. Birsner, M.; Bannerman, C. Physical activity and exercise during pregnancy and the postpartum period: ACOG committee opinion, number 804. *Obs. Gynecol.* **2020**, *135*, 178–188.
31. Evangelou, C.; Sakkas, G.K.; Hadjicharalambous, M.; Aphamis, G.; Petrou, P.; Giannaki, C.D. The effect of a three month, low-load- high-repetitions group-based exercise program versus pilates on physical fitness and body composition in inactive women. *J. Bodyw. Mov. Ther.* **2021**, *26*, 18–23. [CrossRef]
32. Sonmezer, E.; Özköslü, M.; Yosmaoğlu, H. The effects of clinical pilates exercises on functional disability, pain, quality of life and lumbopelvic stabilization in pregnant women with low back pain: A randomized controlled study. *J. Back Musculoskelet. Rehabil.* **2021**, *34*, 69–76. [CrossRef] [PubMed]
33. Kharitonova, L.; Papysheva, O.; Kotaish, G. The role of dyslipidemia in pregnant women with diabetes mellitus in the genesis of comorbid conditions in children. *Exp. Clin. Gastroenterol.* **2020**, *1*, 66–75. [CrossRef]
34. Semra, Ç.; Cuma, E.; Murat, Ş.; Nedim, Ç.; Alaeddin, A. The Effects of Pilates and Aerobic Exercise on Blood Pressure, Heart Rates, and Blood Serum Lipids in Sedentary Females. *J. Educ. Train. Stud.* **2019**, *7*, 2324–8068.
35. Hyun, H.; Jeon, J. Effect of Mat Pilates on Body Fluid Composition, Pelvic Stabilization, and Muscle Damage during Pregnancy. *Appl. Sci.* **2020**, *10*, 9111. [CrossRef]
36. Baek, S. The Effect of 12weeks Pilates Mat Exercise on Body Composition and Lipid Metabolism in Obese Middle-aged Women. *DAEHAN Soc. Ind. Manag.* **2020**, *18*, 108–117.
37. Hu, X.; Ma, M.; Zhao, X.; Sun, W.; Liu, Y.; Zheng, Z.; Xu, L. Effects of exercise therapy for pregnancy-related low back pain and pelvic pain: A protocol for systematic review and meta-analysis. *Medicine* **2020**, *99*, 17318. [CrossRef] [PubMed]
38. Lene, C.; Nina, K. Trunk, pelvic and hip kinematics during the Stork test in pregnant women with pelvic girdle pain, asymptomatic pregnant and non-pregnant women. *Clin. Biomech.* **2020**, *80*, 105168.
39. Saori, M.; Mika, I.; Fumiko, U.; Hiroko, H.; Mamoru, Y.; Tomoki, A. Pelvic alignment changes during the perinatal period. *PLoS ONE* **2019**, *10*, e0223776. [CrossRef]
40. Kulkarni, M.; Saini, S.; Palekar, T.; Hamdulay, N. Effects of pilates on core muscle strength and endurance in post 6 months delivered women. *Proteus J.* **2020**, *11*, 0889–6348.
41. Sakamoto, A.; Nakagawa, H.; Nakagawa, H.; Gamada, K. Effects of exercises with a pelvic realignment device on low-back and pelvic girdle pain after childbirth: A randomized control study. *J. Rehabil. Med.* **2018**, *50*, 914–919. [CrossRef]
42. Bogaert, J.; Stack, M.; Partington, S.; Marceca, J.; Tremback-Ball, A. The effects of stabilization exercise on low back pain and pelvic girdle pain in pregnant women. *Ann. Phys. Rehabil. Med.* **2018**, *61*, 157–158. [CrossRef]
43. Pascoal, G.; Stuge Mota, P.; Hilde, G.; Bø, K. Therapeutic Exercise Regarding Musculoskeletal Health of the Pregnant Exerciser and Athlete. In *Exercise and Sporting Activity During Pregnancy*; Springer Science and Business Media LLC: Berlin, Germany, 2019; pp. 309–326.

44. Buysse, D.; Reynolds, C.; Monk, T.; Berman, S.; Kupfer, D. The Pittsburgh sleep quality index: A new instrument for psychiatric practice and research. *Psychiatry Res.* **1989**, *28*, 193–213. [CrossRef]
45. Picerno, P.; Pecori, R.; Raviolo, P.; Ducange, P. Smartphones and Exergame Controllers as BYOD Solutions for the e-tivities of an Online Sport and Exercise Sciences University Program. In *Higher Education Learning Methodologies and Technologies Online*; Burgos, D., Ed.; HELMeTO 2019. Communications in Computer and Information Science; Springer: Cham, Switzerland, 2019; Volume 1091. [CrossRef]

International Journal of
Environmental Research and Public Health

MDPI

Article

Utilization of Postnatal Care Services among Thai Women during the COVID-19 Pandemic: Results of a Web-Based Survey

Yin Min Aye [1], Soo Jung Kim [2], Wichukorn Suriyawongpaisal [1], Seo Ah Hong [1,*] and Yan-Shing Chang [3]

1 ASEAN Institute for Health Development, Mahidol University, Nakhon Pathom 73170, Thailand; smurfyinmin123@gmail.com (Y.M.A.); wichukorn.sur@mahidol.ac.th (W.S.)
2 Department of Health Sciences, Hamburg University of Applied Sciences, 20099 Hamburg, Germany; skim615@gmail.com
3 Florence Nightingale Faculty of Nursing, Midwifery & Palliative Care, King's College London, London SE1 8WA, UK; yan-shing.chang@kcl.ac.uk
* Correspondence: seoah.hon@mahidol.ac.th; Tel.: +66-2441-9040

Abstract: The postnatal period is an underserved aspect of maternity care, potentially worsened by the COVID-19 pandemic. This study aims to identify postnatal care (PNC) use by health personnel within the 42 days of childbirth among postpartum mothers in Thailand. This web-based, cross-sectional study was conducted from July to October 2021 (n = 840). Multiple binary and ordinal logistic regressions were conducted to predict three outcome variables (≥2 times, ≥3 times, or level of PNC use). Women who received PNC were in low numbers (≥2: 30.7% and (≥3: 12.9%), while 54.4% of women reported no barriers to access PNC, and 31.9% reported barriers, including worries over COVID-19 infection, followed by movement restrictions imposed by the government (11.7%) and the closure of healthcare centers (10%). Women working in a self-employed capacity, living in urban areas, and undergoing a Caesarean section with no/less worry about COVID-19 infection were more likely to utilize postnatal care (≥2 or number of PNC). This study provides timely information, revealing that a relatively low percentage of postpartum women received PNC, particularly among the socially deprived group. Since the fear of COVID infection is listed as a major barrier, the provision of PNC services, including a telehealth program should be considered.

Keywords: postnatal care service; women; barriers; Thailand; COVID-19

Citation: Aye, Y.M.; Kim, S.J.; Suriyawongpaisal, W.; Hong, S.A.; Chang, Y.-S. Utilization of Postnatal Care Services among Thai Women during the COVID-19 Pandemic: Results of a Web-Based Survey. *Int. J. Environ. Res. Public Health* **2022**, *19*, 6536. https://doi.org/10.3390/ijerph19116536

Academic Editor: Paul B. Tchounwou

Received: 27 April 2022
Accepted: 25 May 2022
Published: 27 May 2022

1. Introduction

According to the World Health Organization, the postnatal period is defined as beginning immediately after the birth of the baby and extending for up to six weeks (42 days) after birth [1]. The postnatal period is a critical window of opportunity for lifesaving intervention delivery for both the mother and newborn. Since most maternal and infant deaths occur during this period [2], the service provision of maternity care at this time, known as postnatal care (PNC), is considered essential for the mother and her newborn baby in the first 42 days of life [3]. Appropriate PNC can help in preventing maternal and child morbidity and mortality, particularly in low- and middle-income countries (LMICs) [4,5]. Nevertheless, this essential service is neglected, with more emphasis placed on antenatal and intrapartum care [6]. Moreover, the coronavirus disease (COVID-19), emerging from the Hubei Province in the People's Republic of China in December 2019 and subsequently spreading throughout the world, has resulted in alterations to healthcare structures and processes, such as reduced maternity service provision, including PNC [7–12]. However, to our knowledge, only a few studies have examined the PNC uptake using a quantitative approach during the pandemic in Ethiopia [13], Bangladesh [14], and the UK [15].

In Thailand, since the first COVID-19 case was reported on 13 January 2020 [16], a series of public health and social measures, such as wearing masks, an evening curfew, lockdown measures, social distancing, and travel restrictions were implemented under the direct leadership of the Prime Minister [16]. Thailand was considered to be the only middle-income country nominated in the global top 10 of pandemic preparedness according to the Global Health Security Health Index [17]. Despite the successful control of COVID-19 in 2020, resurgent outbreaks caused by the Alpha and Delta variants (third and fourth waves) from April to December 2021 and the Omicron variant (fifth wave) occurring since December 2021 have hit the entire country, accounting for more than 4,046,953 cases and 27,006 deaths as of 18 April 2022 [18]. A shortage of medical equipment and supplies was reported in many hospitals due to the exponential rise in cases.

With 99.1% of births assisted by skilled health personnel, the maternal mortality ratio (MMR) in Thailand (24.6 per 100,000 live births in 2015) is much lower than the sustainable development goal (SDG) of 70 per 100,000 live births [19]. However, it is still considerably higher than the national target (15 per 100,000 live births), with significant regional variations [19]. Similar to antenatal care (ANC), PNC can be freely accessed from public hospitals through benefit packages under universal health coverage (UHC) [20]. Three postnatal contacts are recommended in three different time periods [21]. The PNC coverage was underutilized in Thailand even before the COVID-19 pandemic [21] and may have been further neglected during the pandemic. The lack of information has led to an investigation of PNC use and its barriers to access during the COVID-19 pandemic.

Many studies have reported that the fear of COVID-19 infection hindered the uptake of maternity care services [9–11]. Good COVID-19 knowledge and attitude improve the overall practice of preventative measures aimed at reducing the burden of the disease. COVID-19-related knowledge, attitude, and practice (KAP) may affect the utilization of PNC. Despite some studies reporting COVID-19-related KAP among pregnant women [22–24], to the best of our knowledge, there is still no published study on COVID-19-related KAP and its association with PNC use among postpartum women.

This study aims to assess the prevalence of PNC checkups, barriers to assessing PNC, and its associated factors among postpartum mothers during the COVID-19 pandemic. The findings will contribute to and assist in planning future services for women and their partners and tailoring the care to meet women's expectations and needs as the COVID-19 pandemic continues and beyond. The findings of this study will support health professionals and policymakers by providing timely information for better utilization of postnatal maternity services to improve maternal health, leading to SDG achievement.

2. Materials and Methods

2.1. Study Design and Subjects

This is a web-based, cross-sectional study involving a total of 840 postpartum mothers in Thailand, conducted from 12 July to 28 October 2021. Data collection was performed using an online Google Form. Postpartum women aged 18–49 years old, up to six months after childbirth, with the ability to access an online survey and literate in the Thai language, completed the survey. A total of 919 women completed the survey. Those who were not living in Thailand during the survey period or did not otherwise meet the inclusion criteria were excluded. The number of respondents eligible to participate in the survey according to the inclusion criteria was 840, all of whom were included in the analysis.

Since the local government applied social distancing measures to prevent the spread of COVID-19, convenience sampling was used to recruit postpartum women. The study was advertised to midwifery and obstetric groups, and groups for mothers who were encouraged to share the study with their friends and family members, as well as online through email and social media such as Line or Facebook. Women were sent a survey link together with an online consent form, which provided information on the study aims, procedure, its voluntary nature, and confidentiality. The study was conducted according to the guidelines of the Declaration of Helsinki and approved by the Mahidol University

Ethical Committee (No:2021/03-042). Mothers were informed that their participation was voluntary, and if they wanted to participate, they would need to mark the appropriate box indicating their consent, and this was then collected upon completion of the questionnaire.

2.2. Variable Measures

The outcome variable, postnatal case use, was obtained by asking the question, "How many times have you received postnatal care from health personnel within 42 days of childbirth?" (response options: 1 = Never, 2 = Once, 3 = Twice, 4 = Three times, and 5 = Four times or higher). In Thailand, PNC programs involve the examination of both the mother and child. Previously, two PNC visits were recommended [25,26]. Currently, postnatal health checks on mothers and newborns are scheduled at three time points: (1) within seven days following the day of birth, (2) between 8 and 15 days after the day of birth, and (3) between 16 and 42 days after the day of birth [21]. Thus, two binary outcome variables were coded into two categories ($\geq$2 vs. <2 times and $\geq$3 vs. <3 times). In addition, to assess a single-unit increase in PNC visits, an ordinal scale was employed (never, 1, 2, 3, or $\geq$4 visits) as an outcome variable.

The independent variables included sociodemographic factors (mother's age, education, marital status, working status, region, residence, intended pregnancy, number of children, birth interval, mode of delivery, preterm delivery, low birth weight, and health problems during delivery and postpartum), COVID-19-related factors (family income during the COVID-19 pandemic, food insecurity changes due to COVID-19, worried about becoming infected with COVID-19, diagnosed as COVID-19 positive, ever taken a COVID-19 vaccine), and COVID-19-related KAP. The variable "family income changes during the COVID-19" was obtained by asking the open-ended question, "Currently, how much estimated income did you and/or your family earn per month during the COVID-19 in 2020 and 2021?"; the responses were categorized into three equal tertiles (low, middle, and high). The variable "food insecurity" was created from the combination of two questions—"Did you ever run out of food before the end of the month or cut down on the amount you eat to feed others in 2019 before COVID?" and "Did you ever run out of food before the end of the month or cut down on the amount you eat to feed others during COVID in 2020 and 2021?"—and then coded into three categories (still insecure over time, secure to insecure, insecure to secure/still secure over time). The variable "worried about becoming infected with COVID-19" was gained from the question "How worried/fearful are you about becoming (re)infected by the coronavirus?" Five options were provided (not at all worried, a little worried, moderately worried, very worried, and extremely worried) and then coded into three categories (not at all worried/a little worried, moderately worried, very worried/extremely worried). The variable "ever diagnosed as COVID-19 positive" was acquired from the question "Have you ever been diagnosed as COVID-19 positive?" (yes and no responses) and coded into two categories (yes, no). The variable "ever taken a COVID-19 vaccine" was attained from the question "Have you taken a COVID-19 vaccine? (response options: yes, no, and do not know)" and then coded into two categories (yes, no/do not know).

For the variable "COVID-19 knowledge", there were questions with response options of true, false, and do not know. One point was recorded for a correct answer, with total scores ranging from 0 to 9. Attitude toward the severity and prevention of COVID-19 was assessed with seven questions, and the responses were recorded on a five-point Likert scale ("strongly disagree" to "strongly agree"), with total scores varying from 7 to 35. The practice of COVID-19 precautions was measured with six questions, and the responses were recorded on a Likert scale ranging from 1 to 4 ("never" to "always") with total scores ranging from 6 to 24. Good knowledge, a positive attitude, and adequate practices were based on the higher score of each variable. The three variables were coded into three equal tertiles (low, moderate, or high).

2.3. Statistical Analyses

Statistical Package for Social Science (SPSS) version 21 (IBM Corp., Armonk, NY, USA) was used to perform the statistical analyses. The frequency and percentage of sociodemographic factors, barriers to accessing maternity care since the COVID-19 pandemic, and COVID-19-related factors, including tertiles of COVID-19 KAP and number of PNC checkups within 42 days, were used for descriptive analysis. Two binary dependent variables ($\geq$2 vs. <2 times and $\geq$3 vs. <3 times) and an ordinal scale variable (never, 1, 2, 3, and $\geq$4) were employed in the analyses. For bivariate analyses, chi-square tests or Fisher's exact tests were performed to assess the level of association between independent and dependent variables. Variables with a p-value < 0.1 in the bivariate analyses were selected for binary and ordinal logistic analysis as appropriate. Multiple logistic regression was carried out to estimate the adjusted odds ratio (AOR), with a 95% confidence interval (CI), to explore the factors associated with PNC use. A p-value < 0.05 was considered as significant.

3. Results

3.1. Percentage of Postnatal Care Uptake and Barriers to Accessing Postnatal Care Services

From a total of 840 postpartum women, the percentage of women who utilized PNC was low ($\geq$2 times 30.7% and $\geq$3 times 12.9%), while those receiving at least one PNC checkup was 70.7% (one time 40%, twice 17.9%, three times 5.1%, and 7.7% four times or more) (Figure 1).

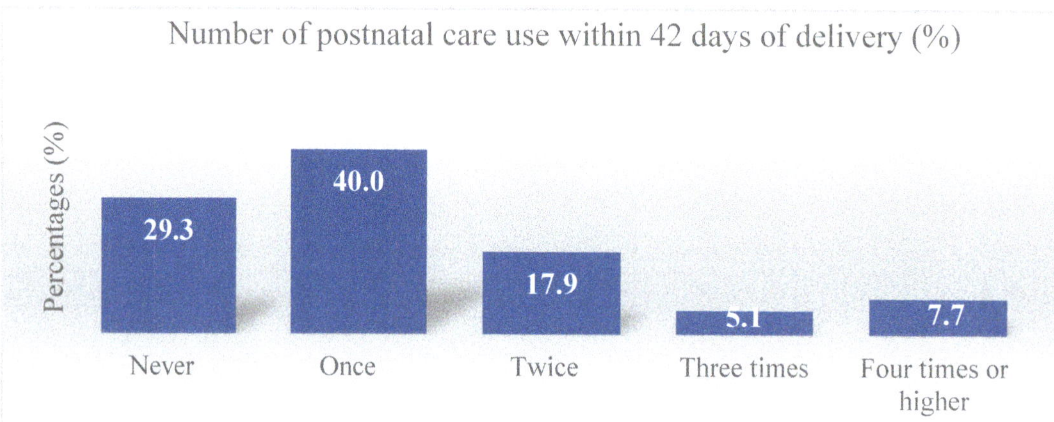

Figure 1. Percentage distribution of postnatal care use among postpartum women aged 18–49 years old at up to six months postpartum in Thailand during the COVID-19 pandemic.

As evident in Figure 2, although the majority of postpartum women (54.4%) reported having no barriers to accessing maternity care during the COVID-19 pandemic, some barriers were reported, such as being worried about becoming infected with COVID-19 (31.9%), government movement restrictions (11.7%), closure of healthcare centers (10%), healthcare centers that—although open—could not provide timely care (9.2%), lack of transportation (8.6%), lack of money to spend on medical costs (7.5%), and "family members hindered me from going out" (8.1%) during the pandemic.

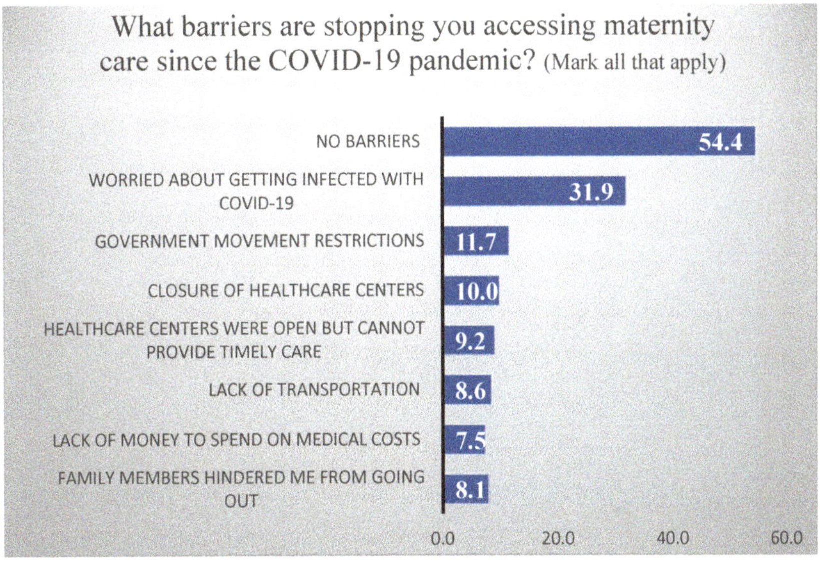

Figure 2. Percentage of barriers stopping the accessibility of postpartum women to maternity care during the COVID-19 pandemic. (Mark all that apply.)

3.2. General Characteristics of the Study Subjects

As presented in Tables 1 and 2, the majority of participants were married (90.4%) and intended the pregnancy (83.9%). More than 50% of women were 29 years old and younger, had a secondary school and lower education level, resided in rural areas, and gave birth naturally. About 40% of women reported being extremely worried about becoming infected with COVID-19. While half of the mothers had food security during the COVID-19 pandemic, 49.5% reported food insecurity (28.1% continuous food insecurity and 21.4% experiencing food insecurity during COVID-19). Furthermore, 17% of mothers reported having been diagnosed as COVID-19 positive, while 55.8% had received at least one dose of a COVID-19 vaccine.

3.3. Bivariate Associations between Independent Factors and Postnatal Care Uptake

According to the bivariate analysis, independent factors such as the mother's education, working status, residence, mode of delivery, family income during the COVID-19 pandemic, worries about COVID-19 infection, ever taken a COVID-19 vaccine, and COVID-19-related knowledge were significantly associated with the PNC uptake ($\geq$twice and the number of uptakes) ($p < 0.05$), while urban residence, health problems during delivery, COVID-19-related knowledge, and attitude were associated with PNC visits ($\geq$3 times) ($p < 0.05$).

Table 1. Bivariate association between sociodemographic factors and postnatal care use.

	Total		Number of Postnatal Care Uptakes											
			<2	≥2		<3	≥3		Never	1	2	3	≥4	
	n	(%)	%	%	*p*-Value	%	%	*p*-Value	%	%	%	%	%	*p*-Value
Total number	840	(100)	69.3	30.7		87.1	12.9		29.3	40.0	17.9	5.1	7.7	
Mother's age (years)														
18–29	489	(58.2)	60.3	53.5	0.0645	58.6	55.6	0.5484	62.2	58.9	52.0	51.2	58.5	0.2940
30–49	351	(41.8)	39.7	46.5		41.4	44.4		37.8	41.1	48.0	48.8	41.5	
Education of mother (secondary school or lower)	458	(54.5)	58.4	45.7	0.0007	55.1	50.9	0.4212	57.3	59.2	42.0	39.6	58.5	0.0015
Marital status (married)	759	(90.4)	89.7	91.9	0.3257	90.2	91.7	0.6214	91.5	88.4	92.0	93.0	90.8	0.6160
Working status														
Waged/employed	252	(30.0)	29.9	30.2	0.0028	29.8	31.5	0.1086	28.1	31.3	29.3	27.9	33.9	0.0791
Self-employed/family business	105	(12.5)	10.0	18.2		11.7	17.6		9.8	10.1	18.7	23.3	13.9	
On maternity leave	171	(20.4)	20.1	20.9		19.9	23.1		22.8	18.2	19.3	20.9	24.6	
Housewife/unemployed	312	(37.1)	40.0	30.6		38.5	27.8		39.4	40.5	32.7	27.9	27.7	
Region														
Central (incl. Bangkok)	308	(36.7)	34.9	40.7	0.1280	36.5	38.0	0.5515	35.0	34.8	42.7	41.9	35.4	0.0685
North/Northeast	105	(12.5)	13.8	9.7		13.0	9.3		9.4	17.0	10.0	4.7	12.3	
South	427	(50.8)	51.4	49.6		50.5	52.8		55.7	48.2	47.3	53.5	52.3	
Residence (urban)	382	(45.5)	42.4	52.3	0.0079	43.6	58.3	0.0040	45.5	40.2	48.0	65.1	53.9	0.0128
Intended pregnancy (yes)	705	(83.9)	83.5	84.9	0.6158	83.6	86.1	0.5082	85.8	81.9	84.0	86.1	86.2	0.7204
Number of children (one child)	495	(58.9)	59.6	57.4	0.5400	58.3	63.0	0.9906	61.8	58.0	53.3	69.8	58.5	0.2898
Birth interval														
No sibling	436	(51.9)	52.6	50.4	0.3113	51.9	51.9	0.1330	52.4	52.7	49.3	58.1	47.7	0.3010
Less than three years	102	(12.1)	11.0	14.7		11.3	17.6		13.0	9.5	12.7	20.9	15.4	
Three years or higher	302	(36.0)	36.4	34.9		36.7	30.6		34.6	37.8	38.0	20.9	36.9	
Delivery mode (Caesarean section)	351	(41.8)	37.1	52.3	<0.0001	41.0	47.2	0.2198	35.4	38.4	56.0	32.6	56.9	<0.0001
Preterm delivery (less than 37 weeks)	173	(20.6)	21.3	19.0	0.4443	20.8	19.4	0.7514	24.8	18.8	18.7	16.3	21.5	0.3769
Low birth weight (<2.5 kg)	81	(9.6)	9.8	9.3	0.8238	9.6	10.2	0.8379	10.6	9.2	8.7	4.65	13.85	0.5543
Health problems during delivery (yes)	98	(11.7)	10.5	14.3	0.1079	10.8	17.6	0.0399	12.2	9.2	12.0	14.0	20.0	0.1572
Health problems during postpartum (yes)	73	(8.7)	8.8	8.5	0.9109	8.7	8.3	0.8878	11.0	7.1	8.7	7.0	9.2	0.5890

Table 2. Bivariate association between COVID-19-related factors and postnatal care use.

	Total		Number of Postnatal Care Uptakes											
			<2	≥2		<3	≥3		Never	1	2	3	≥4	
	n	(%)	(%)	(%)	*p*-Value	(%)	(%)	*p*-Value	(%)	(%)	(%)	(%)	(%)	*p*-Value
COVID-19-related factors														
Family income during the COVID-19 pandemic														
1st tertile (low)	278	(33.3)	34.8	29.8	0.0200	34.3	26.2	0.1200	41.1	30.2	32.4	23.8	27.7	0.0171
2nd tertile	309	(37.0)	38.4	33.7		37.0	36.4		32.9	42.4	31.8	33.3	38.5	
3rd tertile (high)	249	(29.8)	26.9	36.5		28.7	37.4		26.0	27.5	35.8	42.9	33.9	
Food insecurity before and during COVID-19														
No change (insecure–insecure)	236	(28.1)	29.2	25.6	0.2720	28.8	23.1	0.3624	29.3	29.2	27.3	20.9	24.6	0.8660
Worse (secure–insecure)	180	(21.4)	22.2	19.8		21.6	20.4		23.2	21.4	19.3	18.6	21.5	
Better or no change (secure–secure)	424	(50.5)	48.6	54.7		49.6	56.5		47.6	49.4	53.3	60.5	53.9	
Worried about COVID-19 infection														
A little worried/Not at all	299	(35.6)	34.2	38.8	0.0070	34.4	43.5	0.1452	28.5	38.4	35.3	48.8	40.0	0.0077
Moderately worried	199	(23.7)	21.6	28.3		23.8	23.1		24.8	19.4	32.0	18.6	26.2	
Very worried/Extremely worried	342	(40.7)	44.2	32.9		41.8	33.3		46.8	42.3	32.7	32.6	33.9	
Ever diagnosed as COVID-19 positive (yes)	143	(17.0)	47.0	18.2	0.5401	17.1	16.7	0.9158	18.7	14.9	19.3	11.6	20.0	0.4869
Ever taken a COVID-19 vaccine (yes)	469	(55.8)	52.9	62.4	0.0107	54.8	63.0	0.1100	50.0	55.1	62.0	74.4	55.4	0.0188
COVID-19-related KAP														
COVID-19-related knowledge														
1st tertile (low)	321	(38.2)	40.9	32.2	0.0270	39.1	32.4	0.0060	43.5	39.0	32.0	23.3	38.5	0.0117
2nd tertile	166	(19.8)	19.9	19.4		20.9	12.0		17.1	22.0	24.7	14.0	10.8	
3rd tertile (high)	353	(42.0)	39.2	48.4		40.0	55.6		39.4	39.0	43.3	62.8	50.8	
COVID-19-related attitude														
1st tertile (low)	236	(28.1)	28.4	27.5	0.3710	29.4	19.4	0.0281	28.9	28.0	33.3	16.3	21.5	0.1881
2nd tertile	364	(43.3)	44.5	40.7		43.4	42.6		46.8	42.9	39.3	41.9	43.1	
3rd tertile (high)	240	(28.6)	27.1	31.8		27.2	38.0		24.4	29.2	27.3	41.9	35.4	
COVID-19-related practice														
1st tertile (low)	275	(32.7)	35.2	27.1	0.0590	33.3	28.7	0.5590	37.4	33.6	26.0	32.6	26.2	0.4095
2nd tertile	279	(33.2)	31.4	37.2		32.7	37.0		32.1	31.0	37.3	37.2	36.9	
3rd tertile (high)	286	(34.0)	33.3	35.7		34.0	34.3		30.5	35.4	36.7	30.2	36.9	

3.4. Multivariate Association with Postnatal Care Uptake

As shown in Table 3, women who were self-employed or involved in a family-based business (AOR = 1.96, 95% CI = 1.20–3.20) had an urban residence (AOR = 1.45, 95% CI = 1.06–2.00), Cesarean section (AOR = 1.86, 95% CI = 1.34–2.57), and worried about COVID-19 infection (AOR = 1.66, 95% CI = 1.15–2.39 for no/a little worried and AOR = 1.64, 95% CI = 1.10–2.45 for moderately worried vs. very/extremely worried) were more likely to utilize PNC (≥twice). Regarding PNC visits (≥3 times), urban residence (AOR = 1.69; 95% CI = 1.12–2.57) and a COVID-19-related attitude (AOR = 1.90, 95% CI = 1.07–3.39) were associated with the uptake of these.

Table 3. Multivariate binary and ordinal logistic regression analyses of associations between selected factors and postnatal care use.

	Binary (≥2)		Binary (≥3)		Ordinal	
	AOR	(95% CI)	AOR	(95% CI)	AOR	(95% CI)
Maternal age (18–29 vs. 30–49 years)	1.00	(0.71–1.40)				
Education of mother (secondary school or lower)	0.81	(0.56–1.16)			0.98	(0.73–1.32)
Working status						
Waged/employed vs. unemployed	1.01	(0.67–1.52)			1.06	(0.76–1.47)
Self-employed/family business vs. unemployed	1.96	(1.20–3.20)			1.58	(1.04–2.39)
On maternity leave vs. unemployed	0.88	(0.55–1.41)			0.83	(0.57–1.21)
Region						
North/Northeast vs. Central					1.09	(0.82–1.47)
South vs. Central					1.02	(0.68–1.53)
Health problems during delivery (yes vs. no)			1.67	(0.95–2.92)		
Residence (urban vs. rural)	1.45	(1.06–2.00)	1.69	(1.12–2.57)	1.21	(0.93–1.58)
Delivery mode (Caesarean section vs. vaginal)	1.86	(1.34–2.57)			1.59	(1.22–2.08)
COVID-19-related factors						
Family income during the COVID-19 pandemic						
Middle vs. Low	0.85	(0.57–1.25)			1.20	(0.87–1.64)
High vs. low	1.08	(0.70–1.69)			1.30	(0.89–1.90)
Worried about COVID-19 infection						
Not at all/A little vs. very/extremely worried	1.66	(1.15–2.39)			1.74	(1.30–2.33)
Moderately vs. very/extremely worried	1.64	(1.10–2.45)			1.32	(0.96–1.83)
Ever taken a COVID-19 vaccine (yes vs. no)	0.79	(0.56–1.10)			0.80	(0.61–1.04)
COVID-19-related KAP						
COVID-19-related knowledge						
Middle vs. Low	1.29	(0.83–2.01)	0.63	(0.32–1.23)	1.42	(1.00–2.01)
High vs. low	1.23	(0.85–1.78)	1.42	(0.89–2.25)	1.30	(0.97–1.75)
COVID-19-related attitude						
Middle vs. Low			1.35	(0.77–2.34)		
High vs. low			1.90	(1.07–3.39)		
COVID-19-related practice						
Middle vs. Low	1.30	(0.88–1.93)				
High vs. low	1.20	(0.81–1.78)				

Ordinal logistic analysis similarly showed that a single-unit increase in the number of PNC visits was associated with women who were self-employed or involved in a family-based business (AOR = 1.58, 95% CI = 1.04–2.40), had a Caesarean section (AOR = 1.57, 95% CI = 1.20–2.05), and worried about COVID-19 infection (AOR = 1.70, 95% CI = 1.26–2.28 for no/a little worried vs. very/extremely worried).

4. Discussion

A recent study from Ethiopia reported that early PNC checkups decreased by 9.3% in the period from March to October 2020 (the first eight months of the pandemic) compared with the period from July 2019 to February 2020 [13]. Thailand still lacks nationally representative data in relation to PNC health checkups [21]. Before the pandemic, the prevalence of married women aged 15–49 years whose last living child was aged 2–11 months and who had received two postpartum checkups was 56.8% in 2020 [27] and 65.5% in 2009 [28]. Meanwhile, Thailand's multiple indicator cluster survey (MICS) from 2015–2016 revealed that the national prevalence of PNC checkups among women aged 15–49 years with a live birth in the last two years was 22% (≥2 times) and 3% (≥3 times) [21]. Our study reveals a relatively higher percentage of PNC checkups (30.7% for ≥2 times and 12.8% for ≥3 times). On the other hand, the percentage of postpartum women who had never had a PNC checkup (29.3%) was also higher in our study than that according to the national estimate in 2015–2016 (18.2%) [21]. Although one should be cautious when interpreting the results due to the use of non-random sampling in this study, the higher percentage of women who had never used PNC in our study may be associated with COVID-19. Further studies are needed to identify the impact of COVID-19 on PNC uptake among Thai women using a nationally representative sample. Meanwhile, the discrepancy between our estimates and the national estimates regarding access to PNC checkups may be partly explained by the impact of COVID-19 mitigation measures, such as lockdowns and travel bans, and the consequent financial loss of household income during the pandemic, which may have prevented some women from utilizing healthcare services including PNC [17]. In Thailand, there are three health schemes: UHC, social security, and civil servant medical benefits, depending on which the baby's parent is applying for. Despite there being no cost involved in accessing essential services in the public sector, some conditions, such as delivery in a private facility, or the need for extra services, such as a special room, meals, and additional drugs or treatment, may involve additional costs. Thus, financial difficulties may hinder postnatal mothers from accessing essential maternity services, resulting in socioeconomic inequality [12]. In this study, we also identified government movement restrictions (11.7%), lack of transportation (8.6%), and lack of money to spend on medical costs (7.5%) as barriers to the accessibility of PNC checkups during the pandemic. The results of the bivariate analyses in this study indicate that those with high incomes during the COVID-19 pandemic were more likely to have PNC, despite the multivariate analyses showing no significance in this respect. In Thailand, women accounted for approximately 91% of manufacturing jobs losses and 58% of jobs overall when the COVID-19 impact on the labor market was at its height during the second quarter of 2020 [29]. Socially deprived women such as employees in the informal sector, those residing in conflict-affected areas and rural communities, migrants, and minor ethnic groups, tend to suffer the most from limited movement and income reduction. Many women in the informal economy, such as market vendors, agriculture, massage therapists, domestic workers, and caregivers, face a reduction in income and unemployment and have been left with limited eligibility for social security schemes and stimulus packages by the government [30]. The findings of this study also indicated that self-employed women or those involved in a family-based business made greater use of postpartum service. The use of healthcare services depends on the ability to pay opportunity costs (time and money), as well as direct financial costs (such as medical fees, medical supplies, and transportation costs). Self-employed mothers or those involved in a family-based business are more likely to be able to pay both costs compared with housewives/unemployed or waged/employed.

During the pandemic, some hospitals faced challenges in managing COVID-19 and protecting their health workers. Modified arrangements had to be made to allow patients access to healthcare facilities [31]. Since urban health systems in Thailand are dominated by hospital-oriented care, private clinics, and hospitals [32], women with no economic problems might seek services from private hospitals during temporary health services disruption at public hospitals during the pandemic. One study reported a lack of access to maternity care in public facilities during the pandemic, with some women attempting to seek maternity services at expensive private clinics or hospitals, which are unaffordable for the poor [33]. Although it was reported that the effect of urban–rural residence in PNC utilization was generally moderate in all Asian countries compared with sub-Saharan [34], our study revealed that those living in urban areas utilized PNC more often. People living in rural areas tend to face more obstacles in trying to access health service providers, such as longer travel distances and lack of transportation. On the other hand, those living in urban areas have more choice of healthcare providers (public hospitals and private clinics) and have easier access to the healthcare provider of their choice. Thus, it may be associated with higher PNC use in urban areas in this study.

Meanwhile, Caesarean section delivery is positively associated with higher utilization of PNC in this study. This may be partly explained by women's understanding that the content of postpartum service is different according to the method of delivery [20]. For example, women undergoing a Caesarean section need to take extra precautions after delivery since it takes about six weeks to recover. Thus, despite worries over COVID-19 infection, they need to go to health centers for their doctors to inspect the incision site and check the progress of recovery. Therefore, those undergoing a Caesarean section may adhere to the PNC schedule for the follow-up examination of the incision rather than participate in other postpartum examinations [26].

This study demonstrated that a third of mothers reported a fear of becoming infected with COVID-19 to be a barrier to accessing maternity care services (31.9%), and this is supported by a Thai survey [35]. Mass media mostly focuses on the casualties and adverse effects of COVID-19 on society, inducing additional stress, fear, and worry [17]. In our study, the odds of utilizing the maternal health service were found to be higher among mothers who did not fear COVID-19 infection. A study from central Ethiopia supports these findings, revealing that women who did not fear COVID-19 infection were about three times more likely to utilize maternal health services during the pandemic in comparison to those who feared infection [36]. Several studies reported that the fear of becoming infected in hospitals was the reason for lower PNC use [9–11,37–39].

This study showed that although the significance disappeared in the multiple logistic regression model, COVID-19-related knowledge was positively associated with PNC uptake in bivariate analyses. However, the COVID-19-related attitude remained significantly associated with PNC ($\geq$3 times) in the multivariate model. Training on COVID-19 prevention and the provision of related information may help to enhance positive attitudes and practices toward avoiding COVID-19 infection. A study in central Ethiopia reports that mothers who practiced COVID-19 preventative measures were 5.8 times more likely to use maternal healthcare services, including postnatal care, compared with those who did not [36]. Efforts should be made to improve COVID-19-related KAP through health education among postnatal women.

This study has some limitations. Since it is a web-based, cross-sectional study, the causal relationship between independent variables and outcome cannot be established. In addition, some women residing in rural areas were illiterate and did not have a phone/computer, internet access, or a sufficient level of digital literacy to participate in this study. Furthermore, with the use of convenience sampling, women participated voluntarily in this study, and those who did not participate may have had different experiences. Therefore, caution should be applied when interpreting the results. Although this study has some limitations, it can aid the understanding of maternity service utilization by postpartum mothers in Thailand. Due to the limited information available on PNC uptake, particularly during COVID-19, the findings of this study provide timely information on PNC in Thailand, which is underutilized by mothers and health professionals, and policymakers are urged to pay special attention to this area. In particular, efforts need to be made to ensure socially deprived women living in rural areas experiencing economic problems are protected during COVID-19 and any future pandemic. While healthcare was traditionally delivered face to face during the pre-COVID-19 era, the spread of COVID-19 has accelerated the growth of new approaches to healthcare provision, such as the telehealth program, including virtual consultations or video conferencing, with the utilization of updated technologies and applications during the pandemic [40,41]. Even during the COVID-19 pandemic, face-to-face contact with health personnel was still possible through the practice of social distancing, although telephone contact tended to be the most popular form of communication. Thus, a new approach to healthcare provision, such as the telehealth program, with the utilization of updated technologies and applications, should be considered to provide maternity care services during the pandemic and beyond. A recent study revealed that the shift to telehealth during the COVID-19 pandemic generally improved patient satisfaction and reduced racial disparity, although not ideal for new patient visits or those with serious health conditions [41]. For future research, a qualitative study is recommended to provide an in-depth understanding of postnatal service utilization during the pandemic.

5. Conclusions

This study provides timely information, revealing that a third of participants reported never using postnatal care, and only about 13% of postpartum women accessed postnatal care three times or more during the COVID-19 pandemic. Socially deprived women made far less use of postnatal care. Since the fear of becoming infected with COVID-19 was found to be a major barrier to women's accessibility to PNC checkups during the pandemic, the provision of postnatal care services, including the telehealth program, should be urgently considered, especially for the socially disadvantaged.

Author Contributions: Conceptualization, S.A.H.; methodology, S.A.H. and Y.-S.C.; data curation, S.A.H. and W.S.; writing—original draft preparation, Y.M.A. and S.A.H.; writing—review and editing, Y.-S.C., S.J.K. and W.S.; project administration, W.S.; funding acquisition, S.A.H. All authors have read and agreed to the published version of the manuscript.

Funding: This research project is supported by Mahidol University.

Institutional Review Board Statement: This study was conducted according to the guidelines of the Declaration of Helsinki and approved by the Mahidol University Ethical Committee (No:2021/03-042).

Informed Consent Statement: Informed consent was obtained from all subjects involved in the study.

Data Availability Statement: The data underlying this study cannot be made publicly available, since approval was not obtained from study participants to make their data openly available.

Acknowledgments: The authors would like to thank the postpartum mothers who participated in this study.

Conflicts of Interest: The authors declare no conflict of interest.

References

1. World Health Organization; United Nations Children's Fund; World Bank Group. *Nurturing Care for Early Childhood Development: A Framework for Helping Children Survive and Thrive to Transform Health and Human Potential*; World Health Organization: Geneva, Switzerland, 2018.
2. Ronsmans, C.; Lancet Maternal Survival Series Steering Group. Maternal mortality: Who, when, where, and why. *Lancet* **2006**, *368*, 1189–1200. [CrossRef]
3. Wudineh, K.G.; Nigusie, A.A.; Gesese, S.S.; Tesu, A.A.; Beyene, F.Y. Postnatal care service utilization and associated factors among women who gave birth in Debretabour town, Northwest Ethiopia: A community-based cross-sectional study. *BioMec Cent. Pregnancy Childbirth* **2018**, *18*, 508.
4. Countdown Coverage Writing Group; Countdown to 2015 Core Group; Daelmans, B.; Dwivedi, A.; Fauveau, V.; Lawn, J.E.; Mason, E.; Newby, H.; Shankar, A.; Starrs, A.; et al. Countdown to 2015 for maternal, newborn, and child survival: The 2008 report on tracking coverage of interventions. *Lancet* **2008**, *371*, 1247–1258.
5. Countdown to 2030 Collaboration. Countdown to 2030: Tracking progress towards universal coverage for reproductive, maternal, newborn, and child health. *Lancet* **2018**, *391*, 1538–1548. [CrossRef]
6. Sacks, E.; Langlois, E.V. Postnatal care: Increasing coverage, equity, and quality. *Lancet Glob. Health* **2016**, *4*, e442–e443. [CrossRef]
7. Roberton, T.; Carter, E.D.; Chou, V.B.; Stegmuller, A.R.; Jackson, B.D.; Tam, Y.; Sawadogo-Lewis, T.; Walker, N. Early estimates of the indirect effects of the COVID-19 pandemic on maternal and child mortality in low-income and middle-income countries: A modelling study. *Lancet Glob. Health* **2020**, *8*, e901–e908. [CrossRef]
8. Townsend, R.; Chmielewska, B.; Barratt, I.; Kalafat, E.; van der Meulen, J.; Gurol-Urganci, I.; O'Brien, P.; Morris, E.; Draycott, T.; Thangaratinam, S.; et al. Global changes in maternity care provision during the COVID-19 pandemic: A systematic review and meta-analysis. *eClinicalMedicine* **2021**, *37*, 100947. [CrossRef]

9. Cameron, E.S.; Ramos, H.; Aston, M.; Kuri, M.; Jackson, L. "COVID affected us all:" the birth and postnatal health experiences of resettled Syrian refugee women during COVID-19 in Canada. *BioMed Cent.* **2021**, *18*, 256.
10. Ombere, S.O. Access to maternal health services during the COVID-19 pandemic: Experiences of indigent mothers and health care providers in Kilifi County, Kenya. *Front. Sociol.* **2021**, *6*, 613042. [CrossRef]
11. Oluoch-Aridi, J.; Chelagat, T.; Nyikuri, M.M.; Onyango, J.; Guzman, D.; Makanga, C.; Miller-Graff, L.; Dowd, R. COVID-19 effect on access to maternal health services in Kenya. *Front. Glob. Womens Health* **2020**, *1*, 599267. [CrossRef]
12. Irvine, I.C.; Chisnall, G.; Vindrola-Padros, C. The Impact of Maternity Service Restrictions Related to COVID-19 on Women's Experiences of Giving Birth in England during the Pandemic: A Qualitative Study and Policy Review. *Res. Square* **2022**. [CrossRef]
13. Gebreegziabher, S.B.; Marrye, S.S.; Kumssa, T.H.; Merga, K.H.; Feleke, A.K.; Dare, D.J.; Hallstrom, I.K.; Yimer, S.A.; Shargie, M.B. Assessment of maternal and child health care services performance in the context of COVID-19 pandemic in Addis Ababa, Ethiopia: Evidence from routine service data. *Reprod. Health* **2022**, *19*, 42. [CrossRef] [PubMed]
14. Mhajabin, S.; Hossain, A.T.; Nusrat, N.; Jabeen, S.; Ameen, S.; Banik, G.; Tahsina, T.; Ahmed, A.; Rahman, Q.S.; Gurley, E.S.; et al. Indirect effects of the early phase of the COVID-19 pandemic on the coverage of essential maternal and newborn health services in a rural subdistrict in Bangladesh: Results from a cross-sectional household survey. *Br. Med. J.* **2022**, *12*, e056951. [CrossRef]
15. Jardine, J.; Relph, S.; Magee, L.A.; von Dadelszen, P.; Morris, E.; Ross-Davie, M.; Draycott, T.; Khalil, A. Maternity services in the UK during the coronavirus disease 2019 pandemic: A national survey of modifications to standard care. *BJOG* **2021**, *128*, 880–889. [CrossRef] [PubMed]
16. World Health Organization. *How a Strong Health System Fights a Pandemic*; World Health Organization: Geneva, Switzerland, 2020.
17. Oxford Policy Management. *Social Impact Assessment of COVID-19 in Thailand*; Oxford Policy Management: Oxford, UK, 2020.
18. Thailand: Overview. Johns Hopkins University & Medicine. Available online: https://coronavirus.jhu.edu/region/thailand (accessed on 20 March 2022).
19. Kanchanachitra, C.; Kanchanachitra, M.; Apipornchaisakul, K. *Thai Health 2017: Empowering Vulnerable Populations Creating an Inclusive Society*; Institute for Population and Social Research, Mahidol University: Nakhon Pathom, Thailand, 2017.
20. Topothai, C.; Chaweewan, T. *Maternal and Child Health: Benefit Package under the Thai Universal Health Coverage*; Department of Health, Ministry of Public Health: Nonthaburi, Thailand, 2018.
21. National Statistical Office; United Nations Children's Fund. *Thailand Multiple Indicator Cluster Survey 2015–2016*; NSO and UNICEF: Bangkok, Thailand, 2016.
22. Lee, R.W.K.; Loy, S.L.; Yang, L.; Chan, J.K.Y.; Tan, L.K. Attitudes and precaution practices towards COVID-19 among pregnant women in Singapore: A cross-sectional survey. *BMC Pregnancy Childbirth* **2020**, *20*, 675. [CrossRef]
23. Ayele, A.D.; Mihretie, G.N.; Belay, H.G.; Teffera, A.G.; Kassa, B.G.; Amsalu, B.T. Knowledge and Practice to Prevent against Corona Virus Disease (COVID-19) and Its Associated Factors among Pregnant Women in Debre Tabor Town Northwest Ethiopia: A Community Based Cross-Sectional Study. *BMC Pregnancy Childbirth.* **2021**, *21*, 397. [CrossRef]
24. Anikwe, C.C.; Ogah, C.O.; Anikwe, I.H.; Okorochukwu, B.C.; Ikeoha, C.C. Coronavirus disease 2019: Knowledge, attitude, and practice of pregnant women in a tertiary hospital in Abakaliki, southeast Nigeria. *Int. J. Gynecol. Obstet.* **2020**, *151*, 197–202. [CrossRef]
25. Bureau of Health Service System Development. *Manual of Primary Health Care Unit Standard Evaluation and Quality Assurance*; Department of Health Service Support, Ministry of Public Health: Nonthaburi, Thailand, 2003.
26. Pothisiri, W. *Postpartum Care in Thailand: Experience, Practice and Policy*; Department of Social Policy, The London School of Economics and Political Science: London, UK, 2010.
27. Ministry of Public Health; World Health Organization. *Thailand Reproductive Health Profile*; Department of Health, Ministry of Public Health: Nonthaburi, Thailand; Regional Office for Southeast Asia: New Delhi, India; The World Health Organization: Geneva, Switzerland, 2003.
28. National Statistical Office. The Reproductive Health Survey 2009. National Statistical Office, Bangkok. 2010. Available online: http://www.nso.go.th/sites/2014en/Survey/social/health/reproductive/2009/6.%20Full%20Report.pdf (accessed on 20 March 2022).
29. The Pandemic Has Pushed Women Out of Work. These Policies Can Help. Available online: https://blogs.adb.org/blog/pandemic-has-pushed-women-out-work-these-policies-can-help (accessed on 10 March 2022).
30. Against the Odds: Stories from Women in Thailand during COVID-19. Available online: https://asiapacific.unwomen.org/en/news-and-events/stories/2020/06/against-the-odds-stories-from-women-in-thailand-during-covid19 (accessed on 15 February 2022).
31. Thailand Launches "New Normal" Healthcare System to Build Back Better after COVID-19. Available online: https://www.who.int/thailand/news/feature-stories/detail/thailand-launches-new-normal-healthcare-system-to-build-back-better-after-covid-19 (accessed on 10 February 2022).
32. Jongudomsuk, P.; Srithamrongsawat, S.; Patcharanarumol, W.; Limwattananon, S.; Pannarunothai, S.; Vapatanavong, P.; Sawaengdee, K.; Fahamnuaypol, P. *The Kingdom of Thailand Health System Review*; WHO Regional Office for the Western Pacific: Manila, Philippines, 2015.
33. Sahoo, K.C.; Negi, S.; Patel, K.; Mishra, B.K.; Palo, S.K.; Pati, S. Challenges in Maternal and Child Health Services Delivery and Access during Pandemics or Public Health Disasters in Low-and Middle-Income Countries: A Systematic Review. *Healthcare* **2021**, *9*, 828. [CrossRef]
34. Fort, A.L.; Kothari, M.T. *Postpartum Care. Levels and Determinants in Developing Countries, MEASURE DHS (Demographic and Health Surveys)*; Macro International: Calverton, MD, USA, 2006.

35. Impact of COVID-19 on Thailand's Households—Insights from a Rapid Phone Survey. Available online: https://blogs.worldbank.org/eastasiapacific/impact-covid-19-thailands-households-insights-rapid-phone-survey (accessed on 7 March 2022).
36. Temesgen, K.; Wakgari, N.; Debelo, B.T.; Tafa, B.; Alemu, G.; Wondimu, F.; Gudisa, T.; Gishile, T.; Daba, G.; Bulto, G.A.; et al. Maternal health care services utilization amidst the COVID-19 pandemic in West Shoa zone, Central Ethiopia. *PLoS ONE* **2021**, *16*, e0249214. [CrossRef]
37. Banke-Thomas, A.; Semaan, A.; Amongin, D.; Babah, O.; Dioubate, N.; Kikula, A.; Nakubulwa, S.; Ogein, O.; Adroma, M.; Anzo Adiga, W.; et al. A mixed-methods study of maternal health care utilisation in six referral hospitals in four sub-Saharan African countries before and during the COVID-19 pandemic. *BMJ Glob. Health* **2022**, *7*, e008064. [CrossRef]
38. Balogun, M.; Banke-Thomas, A.; Sekoni, A.; Boateng, G.O.; Yesufu, V.; Wright, O.; Ubani, O.; Abayomi, A.; Afolabi, B.B.; Ogunsola, F. Challenges in access and satisfaction with reproductive, maternal, newborn and child health services in Nigeria during the COVID-19 pandemic: A cross-sectional survey. *PLoS ONE* **2021**, *16*, e0251382. [CrossRef] [PubMed]
39. Pant, S.; Koirala, S.; Subedi, M. Access to maternal health services during COVID-19. *Eur. J. Med. Sci.* **2020**, *2*, 46–50. [CrossRef]
40. Bar-Zeev, S.; Breen-Kamkong, C. *COVID-19 Technical Brief Package for Maternity Services Part 1: Delivery of Facility Based Maternity Services-Interim Guidance*; UNFPA: New York, NY, USA, 2020.
41. Bilimoria, K.Y.Z.T.; Durst, D.A.; Merkow, R.P.; Sama, P.R.; Bahaveolos, S.A.; Chrisman, H.B. Comparison of Patient Experience with Telehealth vs. In-Person Visits before and during the COVID-19 Pandemic. *Jt. Comm. J. Qual. Patient Saf.* **2021**, *47*, 533–536. [CrossRef] [PubMed]

International Journal of
Environmental Research and Public Health

MDPI

Review

European Educational Programmes in Health Emergency and Disaster Management: An Integrative Review

Juana Perpiñá-Galvañ [1,2], Rocío Juliá-Sanchis [1,2,*], Érika Olmos-Castelló [1], Salvador Mollá-Pérez [1] and Ángela Sanjuan-Quiles [1]

[1] Department of Nursing, University of Alicante, 03690 Alicante, Spain; juana.perpina@ua.es (J.P.-G.); eolcas@alumni.uv.es (É.O.-C.); salva.molla@ua.es (S.M.-P.); angela.sanjuan@ua.es (Á.S.-Q.)
[2] Alicante Institute for Health and Biomedical Research (ISABIAL), 03690 Alicante, Spain
* Correspondence: rjulia@ua.es

Abstract: There is a need for trained health professionals who can swiftly respond to disasters occurring worldwide. Little is known about whether the currently available programmes in disaster management are in line with the recommendations of expert researchers. Our objective was to qualitatively review the characteristics of European educational programmes in health emergency and disaster management and to provide guidance to help improve their curricula. We carried out an integrative review to extract the main characteristics of the 2020/21 programmes available. We identified 34 programmes, the majority located in Spain, the UK or France. The primary qualification types awarded were master's degrees, half of them lasting one year, and the most common teaching method was in person. Almost all of the programmes used a virtual university classroom, a third offered multidisciplinary disaster management content and teachers, and half of them employed situational simulations. The quality of European educational programmes in health emergency and disaster management has improved, especially in terms of using more practical and interactive teaching methodologies and in the inclusion of relevant topics such as communication, psychological approaches and evaluation of the interventions. However, generally, the educational programmes in disaster management have not yet incorporated the skills related to the intercultural and interprofessional awareness aspects.

Keywords: educational programme; emergencies; European; disasters

Citation: Perpiñá-Galvañ, J.; Juliá-Sanchis, R.; Olmos-Castelló, É.; Mollá-Pérez, S.; Sanjuan-Quiles, Á. European Educational Programmes in Health Emergency and Disaster Management: An Integrative Review. *Int. J. Environ. Res. Public Health* **2021**, *18*, 11455. https://doi.org/10.3390/ijerph182111455

Academic Editors: Joachim G. Voss and Sandul Yasobant

Received: 21 September 2021
Accepted: 29 October 2021
Published: 30 October 2021

1. Introduction

In recent years, emergencies such as natural disasters (earthquakes, tsunamis, floods or fires), the outbreak of the SARS-CoV-2 pandemic, intercontinental travel of migrant and refugee populations, and other human-made disasters (armed conflicts, terrorist attacks, or nuclear or chemical technological failures) have had a worldwide effect [1,2]. Situations are considered disasters when the event exceeds the capacity of a country or community to cope with it, thus generating material, economic, environmental or human losses (between one thousand and one million) [3], and seriously disrupting the functioning of the affected society [4]. Regardless of the disaster trigger, the result is often a cascade of human suffering in the form of large-scale displacements, food shortages, disease outbreaks, violations of people's rights and dignity, and even deaths [5]. Thus, at a global level, different disaster risk-reduction strategies have been implemented to increase nations' and communities' resilience to disasters and to reduce losses in human lives and in social, economic and environmental assets [3].

With the agreement of the 2015–2030 Sendai Framework for Disaster Risk Reduction, measures were established for the three dimensions of disaster risk (exposure to hazards, vulnerability and capacity, and hazard characteristics) to help prevent new risks, reduce risks and increase the resilience of communities or regions [6,7]. In addition, Marco Sendai highlighted improvement in the training of health and non-health responders as a key element in effective disaster responses [7]. Intervention teams often feel insufficiently prepared to act because they believe that their level of knowledge and technical skills are inadequate, and their psychological or organisational preparation is poor [5,8]. In addition, they believe that they have a diffuse leadership and an ambiguous distribution of roles [9] during disasters. All of this tends to lead to misunderstandings and organisational chaos, especially in terms of the command–control–communication triad [10] between the involved parties (firefighters, state security forces, architects, engineers or other healthcare professionals). This has significant negative implications for the effectiveness of interventions, responses to the complex demands of disasters and the health outcomes of the affected population [11,12]. Thus, we believe that training in disaster management should be improved [10,13,14].

A European multidisciplinary team of experts collaborated to develop a standardised curriculum for international crises management, hereby referred to as DITAC (Disaster Training Curriculum), funded by the European Union in 2014 [15]. The DITAC Project developed a holistic and standardised training plan aimed at all potential disaster responders and managers. Researchers started by reviewing 140 educational programmes in disaster management (EPDM) to search for commonalities between them. Thus, they proposed that the minimum characteristics of an EPDM were that it should be skills-based, practical and multidisciplinary, and competent to help resolve disaster scenarios. Subsequently, these researchers proposed a new programme for integrated operational, tactical and strategic training at every level of disaster coordination, communication and cooperation [16], not to re-educate professionals in their profession but, rather, to train them in disaster management with a greater intercultural and interinstitutional emphasis [10] based on the following themes: (1) the theory of intercultural cooperation, setting out the general principles of disasters, disaster cycles and their management, cultural factors, political considerations and European organisation models; (2) intercultural awareness, addressing the principles of public health, the main medical problems, search and rescue, security and protection, logistics, mental health care and psychological support, all based on an intercultural understanding; (3) interprofessional skills, especially communication skills in planning and management, leadership and decision making, information gathering and exchange, legal and ethical factors, non-governmental and voluntary organisations, risk and vulnerability analysis, recovery and reconstruction; (4) complex scenarios (holistic training) that would combine all of the above through simulations [10,15].

Without contradicting the global approach taken by the DITAC project, the 2015–30 Sendai Framework places human health at the centre of disaster management and considers the development of healthcare personnel in this area a vital issue [6]. However, since then, several publications have shown that the technical (knowledge) and methodological (know-how) skills of doctors and nurses remain insufficient in this field [9,13,16–20]. Despite the efforts made to standardise EPDMs over the last 7 years, we still do not know whether the European EPDMs aimed at health professionals have incorporated the evidence-based recommendations that standardised curricula should be developed to deal with the challenges posed by disasters. Based on recent literature reviews [21], we hypothesised that gaps in skills development in this area still persist in these workers. Thus, there is a need to renew European health professionals' understanding of EPDMs and to provide directions for their further development. Therefore, the purpose of this study was to qualitatively review the characteristics of European EPDMs and to provide guidance on ways their curricula could be improved.

2. Materials and Methods

Three researchers conducted a qualitative synthesis of the content regarding disaster management published on European university websites, by implementing an integrative review framework [22]. This review is presented in accordance with the ENTREQ presentation criteria [23]. The ENTREQ statement helps researchers to report the stages associated with the synthesis of qualitative health research: searching and selecting qualitative research, quality appraisal and methods for synthesising qualitative findings [23]. The review protocol was not pre-registered.

2.1. Study Selection

The inclusion criteria for the courses considered were (1) postgraduate EPDM; (2) aimed at medical or nursing professionals; (3) available during the 2020/21 academic year; (4) information (curricula and teaching guides) that could be cross-checked on the university website or upon request by email; (5) information expressed in English, French or Spanish; (6) course delivery by a public or private university; (7) conducted in one of the following European countries (Denmark, Sweden, Norway, Finland, Netherlands, Switzerland, Luxembourg, United Kingdom, Ireland, Portugal, Spain, Italy, France, Belgium, Germany, Hungry, Austria, Poland, Czech Republic, Romania, Bosnia, Bulgaria, Croatia, Greece, Cyprus, Malta, Slovenia, Slovakia, Estonia, Latvia or Lithuania); (8) award of a certificate recognised, at minimum, at the national level. Training programmes aimed at other professional profiles such as psychologists, social workers, pharmacists, engineers or architects were excluded.

2.2. Search Strategy

Public and private universities were listed by country. The search engines on the university websites were then used to identify potential EPDMs by entering the following keywords: 'disaster', 'catastrophes' or 'crisis intervention'. Additional records were identified through other sources (master's degree advertising or by searching a specific search engine https://www.masterstudies.com/ (accessed on 18 November 2020).

2.3. Data Extraction

The search was conducted between June 2020 and April 2021. A PRISMA flow diagram was used to document the output of our search results (Figure 1) [24].

A total of 294 programmes were identified by two independent reviewers. The full information of 37 curricula were thoroughly screened and assessed for eligibility. Any disagreements between the researchers were discussed with a third reviewer. We finally included 34 programmes. The outcomes were: country, university and programme title; qualification type (master's degree/postgraduate diploma or specialisation course); number of European Credit Transfer and Accumulation System (ECTS) credits awarded; programme duration; learning delivery modality (on-campus/online/blended); participation of teaching staff external to the university (yes/no) and their professional category; use of situational simulations (yes/no); use of information and communication technologies (ICTs; yes/no; which one); content included in the curricula; competencies acquired by the students.

2.4. Data Synthesis

Three of the researchers, who were all experienced female nurses with doctorate degrees working as assistant professors, conducted the data synthesis. They were guided by the principles of integrative analysis, which required them to order, encode, categorise and summarise the data. The overarching stages specified by Whittemore and Knafl [22], namely data reduction, data display and conclusion drawing, were followed. Qualitative analysis of the course curricula was conducted by content analysis to break down the data and group them into categories [25]. A descriptive analysis of the response frequencies was performed for each of the categorical items, and the mean and standard deviation were calculated ($\dot{x} \pm SD$) for the continuous variables. SPSS® statistical software (version 26.0) for Windows® (IBM Corp., Armonk, NY, USA) was used to analyse the data.

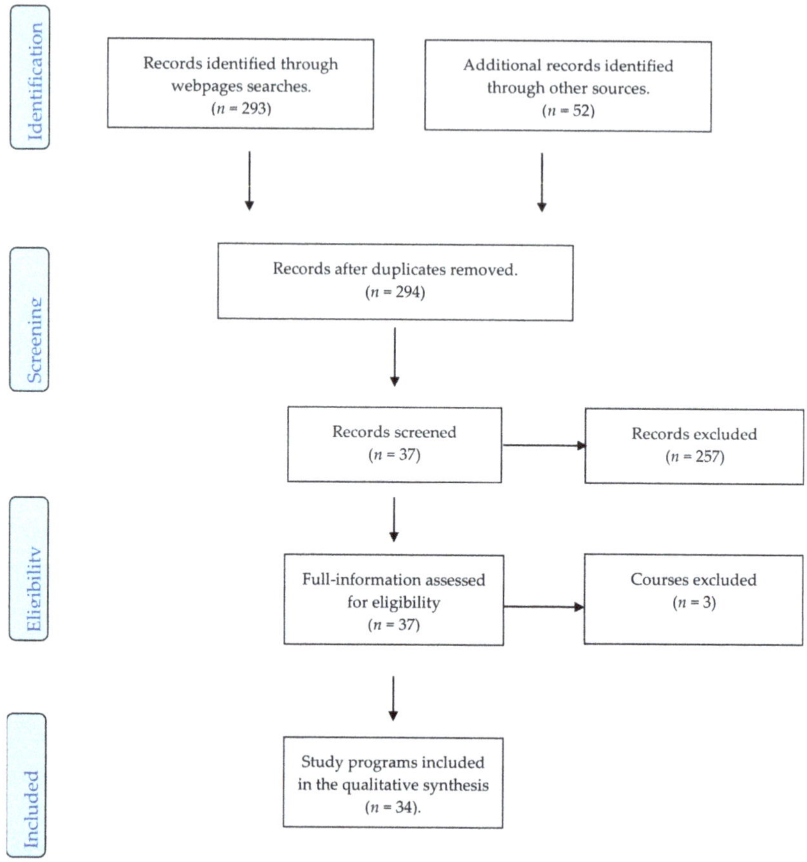

Figure 1. PRISMA flow diagram of the search process.

3. Results

As summarised in Table 1, we identified 34 EPDMs from Belgium [26], Denmark [27,28], France [29–33], Germany [34–36], Greece [37], Italy [38,39], Portugal [40,41], Spain [42–52], Switzerland [53] and the United Kingdom [54–59]; 17 countries examined did not offer any relevant programmes. A total of 69.7% (n = 23) of these EPDMs were master's degrees and 20.5% (n = 7) were specialisation courses. Some 89% of the programmes used the ECTS credit system, awarding a mean of 83.3 ECTS points (SD = 68.3; range 3–315 ECTS credits); however, no information on the academic credit system was available for 11% of the courses [31,32,35,56]. The programmes lasted from 2 weeks to 4 years, with those lasting one year being the most common (50%, n = 17). Only three EPDMs (8.8%) lasted less than 100 h [31,32,41].

Table 1. Characteristics of the educational programmes in disaster management assessed in this study.

Title	Country and University	Qualification Awarded, ECTS/Duration	Delivery Modality	Simulation Training Method	External Teaching Staff	ICTs
Risk and Disaster Management [26]	Belgium, University Sciences of Liège	Master's degree, 60 ECTS/1 year	On-campus	Unknown	Yes	Virtual classroom
Disaster Management [27]	Denmark, University of Borne	Master's degree, 60 ECTS/1 year	On-campus	Yes	No	Virtual classroom
Disaster Management [28]	Denmark, University of Copenhagen	Master's degree, 60 ECTS/1 year	On-campus	Yes	Unknown	No
Environment, Health, and Disaster Management [29]	France, University of Montreal	Postgraduate diploma, 30 ECTS/1 year	On-campus	No	No	Virtual classroom
Nursing in Disaster Situations [30]	France, University of Neith	Specialisation course, 20 ECTS/1 year	On-campus	Yes	No	No
Disaster Medicine and Exceptional Health Situations [31]	France, University of Rennes	Postgraduate diploma, ECTS unknown/96 h	On-campus	Unknown	No	Virtual classroom
Disaster Medicine [32]	France, University of Lorraine	Postgraduate diploma, ECTS unknown/96 h	On-campus	Unknown	Unknown	Virtual classroom
Disaster and Natural Risk Management [33]	France, University of Paul Valéry	Master's degree, 60 ECTS/1 year	On-campus	No	No	Virtual classroom
Disaster Management and Risk Governance [34]	Germany, University of Bonn	Master's degree, 120 ECTS/3 years	On-campus	Yes	Civil Protection	Virtual classroom
Emergency Management [35]	Germany, University of Hochschule	Master's degree, ECTS unknown/4 years	Blended	Yes	Unknown	Virtual classroom
Crisis and Emergency Management [36]	Germany, Carl Remigius Medical School	Master's degree, 90 ECTS/2 years	Blended	Yes	Unknown	Virtual classroom
World Health—Disaster Medicine [37]	Greece, University of Athens	Master's degree, 120 ECTS/2 years	On-campus	Unknown	EMs, academics, military, civil protection unit and healthcare organisations	Unknown
Crisis, Emergency, and Disaster Management [38]	Italy, University of Ciels	Master's degree, 120 ECTS/2 years	On-campus	Yes	No	Virtual classroom
European Disaster Medical Sciences [39]	Italy, University of Piemonte Orientale	Master's degree, 60 ECTS/1 year	On-campus/Online	No	WHO members, Doctors Without Borders NGO, European Society of EMs.	Virtual classroom

Table 1. *Cont.*

Title	Country and University	Qualification Awarded, ECTS/Duration	Delivery Modality	Simulation Training Method	External Teaching Staff	ICTs
Emergencies, Traumas, and Disasters [40]	Portugal, Santa Maria School of Health	Master's degree, 30 ECTS/1 year	Unknown	Unknown	Unknown	Virtual classroom
Emergency and Disaster Medicine [41]	Portugal, University of Nova	Specialisation course, 3 ECTS/2 weeks	On-campus	Unknown	Unknown	Unknown
Emergencies and Catastrophes [42]	Spain, University of Alicante	Master's degree, 60 ECTS/1 year	Blended	Yes	Yes	Virtual classroom
Study of Interventions in Emergencies, Disasters, and International Cooperation [43]	Spain, University of Camilo José Cela	Master's degree, 60 ECTS/1 year	Online	Yes	No	Virtual classroom
Disaster Management [44]	Spain, University CEU-Cardenal Herrera	Specialisation course, 16 ECTS/400 h	Online	Yes	No	Virtual classroom
Disaster Management [45]	Spain, Complutense University of Madrid	Master's degree, 90 ECTS/2 years	On-campus	Yes	Unknown	Virtual classroom
Security, Crisis and Emergency Management [46]	Spain, University of Rey Juan Carlos	Master's degree, 60 ECTS/1 year	On-campus	Yes	Unknown	Virtual classroom
Integrated Disaster Risk Management [47]	Spain, University of Rey Juan Carlos	Specialisation course, 30 ECTS/300 h	On-campus	Yes	Yes	Virtual classroom
Emergencies and Disasters [48]	Spain, University San Pablo CEU	Master's degree, 60 ECTS/1 year	On-campus	Yes	Yes	Virtual classroom
Emergencies and Disaster Analysis and Management [49]	Spain, University of Oviedo	Master's degree, 60 ECTS/1 year	On-campus	Unknown	Unknown	Virtual classroom
Emergency Health Care in Extreme Situations and Disasters [50]	Spain, Alcala Formation	Specialisation course, 20 ECTS/500 h	Online	No	No	Virtual classroom

Table 1. *Cont.*

Title	Country and University	Qualification Awarded, ECTS/Duration	Delivery Modality	Simulation Training Method	External Teaching Staff	ICTs
Integrated Care in Health Catastrophes [51]	Spain, Alcala Formation	Specialisation course, 8 ECTS/200 h	Online	No	No	Virtual classroom
Civil Strife, Disasters, and Catastrophes [52]	Spain, Escuela SAMU	Specialisation course, 29 ECTS/725 h	Blended	Unknown	Unknown	Unknown
Public Health Disaster Management [53]	Switzerland, James Lind Institute	Master's degree, 138 ECTS/2 years	Online	Unknown	Unknown	Virtual classroom
Disaster Management [54]	United Kingdom, University of Bournemouth	Master's degree, 180 ECTS/1–2 years	On-campus/Online	Unknown	Unknown	Spreadsheets and word processing
Disaster Management and Resilience [55]	United Kingdom, University of Coventry	Master's degree, 180 ECTS/1–3 years	On-campus/Online	Yes	Unknown	Virtual classroom
Risk, Crisis and Disaster Management [56]	United Kingdom, University of Leicester	Master's degree ECTS unknown/2 years	Online	No	Safety and Civil Protection Unit	Virtual classroom and Digital Library
Crisis and Disaster Management [57]	United Kingdom, University of Lincoln	Master's degree, 315 ECTS/1–2 years	On-campus	Yes	Civil Protection Unit	Virtual classroom
International Disaster Management [58]	United Kingdom, University of Manchester	Master's degree, 180 ECTS/1–2 years	On-campus	No	NGOs and civil organisations	Virtual classroom
Risk, Crisis and Resilience Management [59]	United Kingdom, University of Portsmouth	Master's degree, 180 ECTS/1–2 years	On-campus	Yes	Fire and Rescue Service and City Council	Spreadsheets and word processing

ICTs, information and communication technologies; ECTS, European Credit Transfer and Accumulation System; NGOs, non-governmental organisations; EMs, emergency medical staff.

The on-campus modality was used in 58.8% (n = 20) of cases; 17.6% (n = 6) were online and the remaining courses employed the blended modality. Virtual university classrooms were the most common ICT types used (87.9%, n = 29). Half of the programmes used situational simulations (n = 17), although no information on these was available for 27.3% of the programmes. Almost a third (n = 10) of the programmes used external multidisciplinary teachers such as health professionals, firefighters or civil protection members. The contribution of international organisations, such as the World Health Organization and non-governmental organisations including Doctors Without Borders and the Red Cross, in some programmes (the Piemonte Orientale programme) was of special note. Finally, despite the variability in the denominations of the different study programme subjects, there were ten main subcategories, each framed within the four phases described by Blanchard [60] for disaster management (Table 2). It should be noted that the information contained on the web pages of some EPDMs was scarce [30,32,33,37,50], while others were extensive and detailed [27,34].

Table 2. Categories and Subcategories of Disaster Management, framed within Blanchard's four phases of disaster management [60].

Categories	Subcategories
Phase 1. Preparedness	**Introduction to risks and disasters** [26–31,33–35,39,44,47,51,53,59]. These standard curricula subjects provided knowledge about disasters and their risks. They included the general concepts, characteristics of risks and population vulnerability analyses. **Typology of risks and disasters** [27–29,31,33,34,37,38,40,42,43,45,47,49,52–54,56]. The relevance varied among the programmes from 'curriculum subject' to 'topic'. These included classification of risk and disasters, risk estimation and the hazard–threat binomial. **Legal framework** [27–29,31,34,36,39,42,43,46,49] This included legal topics related to disaster and emergency management, the functions of governments and general and specific national and international regulations.
Phase 2. Response	**Disaster management and planning** [26–36,38–43,45–47,49,51,53–59] This included management stages, management strategies and techniques, leadership, management to reduce risk (security), logistics and medical management. **Communication management** [27,29,31,34,35,40,46,47,51,53,54] These curricula subjects explained how organisations, countries and people involved in a disaster communicate and stay updated at all times. **Intervention and evaluation** [27,30,34,38,40–47,49,54–58] This included specific knowledge about the professional response, its analysis and evaluation using different tools and feedback. **Epidemiology and biostatistics** [27,29,34,52,53,58] This standard curriculum subject provided knowledge for the collection, analysis and understanding of data. **Specific health training in disasters** [27,30–32,34,36,37,39–45,48,50–52] A standard curricula subject that provided general knowledge about prevalent pathologies according to the disaster type and that trained specific healthcare team skills.
Phase 3–4. Recovery and Mitigation	**Post-disaster response** [26,28,35,38,39,45,47,51,53,54,58,59] These standard curricula subjects included the impact of disasters on populations and communities, crisis intervention, emotional recovery and post-traumatic stress disorder.
Dissertation	Master's programmes included a final assignment that allowed the students to demonstrate the integration of the training contents and their skills/capabilities [26,27,33,34,42,43,45–50,53,56,58,59].

Almost half of the programs addressed general concepts related to disasters: (i) risks and characteristics, (ii) types of disasters, (iii) disaster management and planning, (iv) professional intervention and (v) specific health training. Approximately, one-third of the programs included the ethical and legal framework, as well as psychological support [35,38,39,47,51,53] and international cooperation [28,34,38,42,43,45,47,51,52,58].

Few programs addressed specific content on the response to terrorist attacks [38], the management of refugees and camps in disasters [28] or pandemics [29,53]. Only two programs contemplated the development of intercultural cooperation [36,56], and none referred to the development of interprofessional competencies. We did not find any pattern to the contents of the programmes, according to the different countries.

4. Discussion

This study provides a general overview and an updated database of the European EPDM courses directed towards healthcare professionals that were available in the 2020/21 academic year. We aimed to identify whether universities offering EPDMs have improved the quality of their curricula in recent years [61] by incorporating the proposed recommendations that holistic and standardised programmes should have developed [15]. According to our results, there were 34 EPDMs based in Europe that were aimed at healthcare professionals. This figure is far from the 140 found by the DITAC group [15] because these researchers included courses aimed at any participant type. However, when the DITAC results were broken down, they had indeed included a similar number of programmes aimed at healthcare professionals.

Over the last 7 years, the geographical distribution of these courses remained stable, although the number of countries offering this type of programme had decreased. In line with international recommendations [7,62], most of the EPDMs were master's degrees with an average duration of one year. Compared to the DITAC project, an increasing number of programmes used the ECTS credit system, although it is important to note that DITAC included professional courses undertaken in non-university settings (which did not use the ECTS system).

Although the most common learning modality was still in person, the COVID-19 pandemic had encouraged faculties to find new ways to improve student experiences and to ensure the safety of both students and staff. According to our results, the online modality increased from 11% to 18% in recent years. However, the blended modality was presented as the most useful and suitable teaching method for disaster management because it can combine both theory and practice as well as cooperative and individual work. Moreover, although still limited, thanks to the development of virtual teaching platforms, clinical simulations could be implemented without students having to attend every session in person [16,63]. These semi-presential courses allowed students to access course materials, online sessions and collaborative work rooms.

Computer-generated simulation (virtual reality or augmented reality) is a growing trend in the educational health context [64,65]. Virtual reality generates a three-dimensional image or environment that a person can interact with in a seemingly real or physical way using special electronic equipment, such as a helmet with a screen inside or gloves fitted with sensors. Augmented reality is an enhanced version of the real physical world that is achieved through digital visual elements, sound or other sensory stimuli delivered via technology. Moreover, the augmented reality technology superimposes a computer-generated image on a user's view of the real world, thus providing a composite view.

The computer-generated simulation could be incorporated into EPDMs to allow students to train for different scenarios by recreating situations and psychological states as if they were real [64]. Students could interact with different in-disaster or post-disaster environments without putting themselves or third parties in danger. For example, they could train their risk management of geological processes such as earthquakes, tsunamis or floods [65].

In line with expert recommendations, and following the aforementioned teaching methodologies, half of the identified programmes used clinical simulations [8,11]. Simulation is considered the most effective teaching–learning methodology currently available [63,66] for training complex scenarios (for example, triaging multiple victims or hospital situations in the field). This self-directed learning combines theory and practice, engages students and increases their levels of satisfaction and self-confidence [67–69]. However, as with all virtual reality systems, high-fidelity simulation has a huge economic cost because it requires the use of standardised mannequins or patients, software packages and specific training for instructors [64,69].

In another vein, we noted that the main subjects addressed in the EPDMs reviewed went beyond those defined by DITAC [15] (management, vulnerability analysis, logistics and transport, law and ethics, and protection and security). In addition to these topics, the

EPDMs considered the management of communications, interventions and evaluations, epidemiology and biostatistics, and post-disaster responses, and, in the case of master's degrees, also incorporated a dissertation. The end-of-course dissertation is a relevant way to develop future researchers' skills to solve clinical practice problems.

Although the 'response phase' [60] has been highlighted as a desirable part of the course content [10,70,71], the university websites reviewed contained insufficient data. For example, we extracted information from just one EPDM about how to address terrorist events, even though the academic literature suggests inadequate levels of preparedness among healthcare staff in this regard [8]. Recent terrorism events in Europe have shown the importance of being prepared, establishing community coalitions in advance to promote efficient and effective mobilization, and responding successfully to the mental and physical health needs of individuals affected by such disasters [72].

Similarly, the management of pandemics was named by just two EPDM. SARS-CoV-2 has been considered a pandemic since 11 March 2020. With almost 200 million confirmed global cases of COVID-19, more than 4 million resulting deaths and in excess of 3500 million vaccine doses administered, the pandemic still continues to spread [73]. Thus, in our opinion, this highlights the fact that specific subject areas related to significant emergencies such as terrorism or the management of pandemics must be included in EPDMs to train professionals to deal with the severe psychological and physical consequences of such acute emergency events. We suggest that EPDMs should be regularly updated to include diverse types of disasters and that these education programmes must be made consistent with the national plans and healthcare systems of different geographical regions [8].

Finally, it is important to mention the general structure of the revised training programmes. DITAC proposed a comprehensive programme split into two cycles: the first in an undergraduate setting, and the second in the context of a master's degree, each worth 30 ECTS credits. However, their intended purpose was not to train course members in their profession or area of specialisation (that is, instructing nurses in nursing or logisticians in logistics) but, rather, education in the specific elements of disaster management [10]. However, this proposal contradicts the general perception of doctors and nurses about their deficit in technical competence in the context of disaster management [16–20], a perception that arises from the lack of undergraduate degree training in subjects related to emergencies at most European universities.

We cannot aspire to create a revolution in the undergraduate teaching plans of potential disaster responders in the short to medium term. Thus, we think a more attainable goal would be the implementation of a first cycle worth 30 postgraduate ECTS for the acquisition of knowledge in order to train doctors and nurses.

This would then be complemented by a second cycle, also worth 30 ECTS, to improve their performance in terms of intercultural cooperation (how to work and behave in an international team), intercultural awareness (understanding professional skills in different intercultural contexts) and interprofessional skills (practical training with an interinstitutional approach, especially in communication skills and flexibility) [10].

Although our results indicate that the current EPDM course coverage of the topics from the first cycle is adequate, only two EPDMs seem to have, as of yet, incorporated the skills suggested for the second cycle. This deficit was also noted when considering that only one-third of the programmes incorporated non-university-based multidisciplinary teaching teams to facilitate closer descriptions of the realities of disasters [10,62,74], an aspect that should be generally improved by EPDM managers. As a summary, to provide guidance for updates or new potential programmes aimed at healthcare professionals, we have provided evidence-based suggestions in Figure 2.

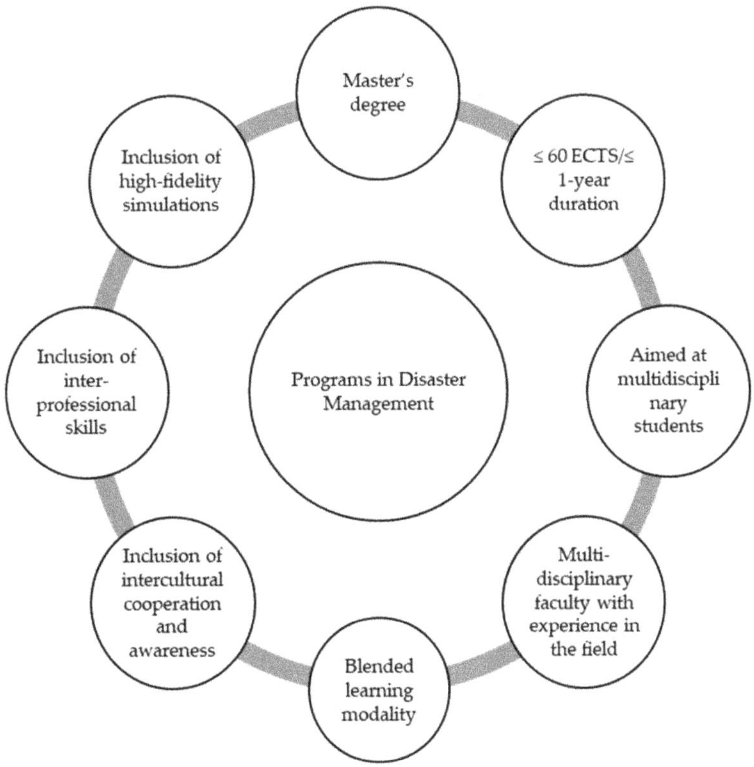

Figure 2. Suggestions to establish and improve the curriculums used in disaster management training.

Limitations

The first limitation of this current work was its inclusion criteria. The EPDM search was limited to university contexts only, even though this type of accreditation is obtained by other means in some regions of the world. However, the 2015–30 Sendai Framework placed human health at the centre of disaster management and considers the development of healthcare personnel in this area a vital issue [6]. This paper wanted to provide updated data on what EPDMs look like, and how they can be better reorganized to improve healthcare personnel competencies. Moreover, all of the authors are professors at a European university that teaches an EPDM course directed towards doctors and nurses.

Another possible limitation was the methodology we used to search for training programmes. Although we performed an in-depth search, some relevant training courses may have been missed. As Ingrassia et al. [63] identified, this is probably because there is no comprehensive database for training and educational initiatives for disaster management, either at the European or national level.

It is necessary to provide complete and detailed information on EPDMs on the web pages and use a standardized vocabulary based on the literature. It is also necessary that the extensive offer of EPDMs is compiled in a single institutional or collegial platform. Different European associations, organizations or institutions interested in disaster risk reduction or management could favour this compilation of training offers, such as the Emergency Response Coordination Centre (ERCC) for European Civil Protection and Humanitarian Aid Operations [75]. The Centre ensures the cooperation and coherence of European Union action at the interinstitutional level, focusing on coordination mechanisms with the European External Action Service, the Council and European Union Member States. It also acts as a permanently available contact point when the solidarity clause is invoked and provides emergency communications and monitoring tools through the Common Emergency Communication and Information System (CECIS), an alert and notification application to exchange information in real time. There are other non-European organizations with an interest in disaster risk reduction or management. For example, the Alliance of International Science Organizations on Disaster Risk Reduction (ANSO-DRR) is an international, non-profit and non-governmental scientific alliance bringing together academies of science, research organizations and universities that share a strong interest in disaster risk reduction in the regions along the land-based and maritime routes of the Belt and Road Initiative [7].

Nonetheless, this exploratory work did provide useful information that could be further expanded by consulting critical informants to obtain information that may not be otherwise readily obtainable and to identify new programme topics. Finally, the lack of similar studies in other regions meant that there were no benchmarks with which to compare our results or to monitor the evolution of this type of education globally over time. For future recommendations, similar studies should be conducted to enable the benchmarking of programmes.

5. Conclusions

This study presents an updated database of the EPDMs available at European universities in the 2020/21 academic year and provides educators and researchers in healthcare with an understanding of the current state of the training in health emergency and disaster management. EPDMs have improved the quality of their teaching methodologies by making them more practical and interactive, introducing relevant topics such as communication and the evaluation of interventions, and developing research skills through dissertations. However, the EPDMs have not yet incorporated the recommendation about intercultural and interprofessional awareness skills.

Author Contributions: Conceptualization, J.P.-G.; methodology, J.P.-G. and R.J.-S.; software, É.O.-C. and R.J.-S.; investigation, J.P.-G., É.O.-C. and R.J.-S.; resources, J.P.-G., É.O.-C. and R.J.-S.; data curation, Á.S.-Q.; writing—original draft preparation, J.P.-G., É.O.-C. and R.J.-S.; writing—review and editing, Á.S.-Q. and S.M.-P.; supervision, Á.S.-Q. All authors have read and agreed to the published version of the manuscript.

Funding: This research received no external funding.

Institutional Review Board Statement: Not applicable.

Informed Consent Statement: Not applicable.

Acknowledgments: Not applicable.

Conflicts of Interest: The authors declare no conflict of interest.

References

1. Gowing, J.R.; Walker, K.N.; Elmer, S.L.; Cummings, E.A. Disaster Preparedness among Health Professionals and Support Staff: What is Effective? An Integrative Literature Review. *Prehosp. Disaster Med.* **2017**, *32*, 321–328. [CrossRef] [PubMed]
2. Nunez-Villaveiran, T.; González-Castro, A.; Nevado-Losada, E.; García-de-Lorenzo, A.; Garro, P. All for One and One for All: Voluntary Physicians in the Intensive Medicine Units During the COVID-19 Outbreak in Spain. *Disaster Med. Public Health Prep.* **2020**, 1–7. [CrossRef] [PubMed]
3. Ball, D.J.; Ball-King, L. Safety management and public spaces: Restoring balance. *Risk Anal.* **2013**, *33*, 763–771. [CrossRef]
4. Powell, S.K.; Owen, M. Mass Casualties and Case Management. *Prof. Case Manag.* **2020**, *25*, 1–4. [CrossRef]
5. World Health Organization. *Building Back Better: Sustainable Mental Health Care after Emergencies*; WHO: Geneva, Switzerland, 2013.
6. UNDRR. Sendai Framework for Disaster Risk Reduction. Available online: https://www.unisdr.org/we/inform/publications/43291 (accessed on 21 July 2021).
7. Chan, E.Y.Y.; Wong, C.S.; Hung, K.K.C.; Kalonji, G.; Cui, P.; Zhou, G.; Shaw, R. Report of Alliance of International Science Organizations on Disaster Risk Reduction (ANSO-DRR) Conference 2020. *Int. J. Environ. Res. Public Health* **2020**, *17*, 8772. [CrossRef] [PubMed]
8. Said, N.B.; Chiang, V.C.L. The knowledge, skill competencies, and psychological preparedness of nurses for disasters: A systematic review. *Int. Emerg. Nurs.* **2020**, *48*, 100806. [CrossRef]

9. Setyawati, A.D.; Lu, Y.Y.; Liu, C.Y.; Liang, S.Y. Disaster Knowledge, Skills, and Preparedness among Nurses in Bengkulu, Indonesia: A Descriptive Correlational Survey Study. *J. Emerg. Nurs.* **2020**, *46*, 633–641. [CrossRef]
10. Khorram-Manesh, A.; Lupesco, O.; Friedl, T.; Arnim, G.; Kaptan, K.; Djalali, A.R.; Foletti, M.; Ingrasia, P.L.; Ashkenazi, M.; Arculeo, C.; et al. Education in Disaster Management: What Do We Offer and What Do We Need? Proposing a New Global Program. *Disaster Med. Public Health Prep.* **2016**, *10*, 854–873. [CrossRef]
11. Walsh, L.; Subbarao, I.; Gebbie, K.; Schor, K.W.; Lyznicki, J.; Strauss-Riggs, K.; Cooper, A.; Hsu, E.B.; King, R.V.; Mitas, J.A., 2nd; et al. Core competencies for disaster medicine and public health. *Disaster Med. Public Health Prep.* **2012**, *6*, 44–52. [CrossRef]
12. Pek, J.H.; Kang, H.M.; Anantharaman, V. Teaching Disaster Site Medical Support in Indonesia. *Disaster Med. Public Health Prep.* **2020**, *14*, 733–738. [CrossRef]
13. Camacho, N.A.; Hughes, A.; Burkle, F.M., Jr.; Ingrassia, P.L.; Ragazzoni, L.; Redmond, A.; Norton, I.; von Schreeb, J. Education and Training of Emergency Medical Teams: Recommendations for a Global Operational Learning Framework. *PLoS Curr.* **2016**, *8*. [CrossRef]
14. Mortelmans, L.J.; Lievers, J.; Dieltiens, G.; Sabbe, M.B. Are Belgian military students in medical sciences better educated in disaster medicine than their civilian colleagues? *J. R. Army Med. Corps* **2016**, *162*, 383–386. [CrossRef]
15. Ingrassia, P.L.; Foletti, M.; Djalali, A.; Scarone, P.; Ragazzoni, L.; Corte, F.D.; Kaptan, K.; Lupescu, O.; Arculeo, C.; von Arnim, G.; et al. Education and training initiatives for crisis management in the European Union: A web-based analysis of available programs. *Prehosp. Disaster Med.* **2014**, *29*, 115–126, Erratum in: *Prehosp. Disaster Med.* **2014**, *29*, 38. Khorrram-Manesh, Amir [corrected to Khorram-Manesh, Amir].. [CrossRef] [PubMed]
16. Khorram-Manesh, A.; Ashkenazi, M.; Djalali, A.; Ingrassia, P.L.; Friedl, T.; von Armin, G.; Lupesco, O.; Kaptan, K.; Arculeo, C.; Hreckovski, B.; et al. Education in Disaster Management and Emergencies: Defining a New European Course. *Disaster Med. Public Health Prep.* **2015**, *9*, 245–255. [CrossRef] [PubMed]
17. Labrague, L.J.; Hammad, K.; Gloe, D.S.; McEnroe-Petitte, D.M.; Fronda, D.C.; Obeidat, A.A.; Leocadio, M.C.; Cayaban, A.R.; Mirafuentes, E.C. Disaster preparedness among nurses: A systematic review of literature. *Int. Nurs. Rev.* **2018**, *65*, 41–53. [CrossRef]
18. Hung, K.K.C.; Mashino, S.; Chan, E.Y.Y.; MacDermot, M.K.; Balsari, S.; Ciottone, G.R.; Della Corte, F.; Dell'Aringa, M.F.; Egawa, S.; Evio, B.D.; et al. Health Workforce Development in Health Emergency and Disaster Risk Management: The Need for Evidence-Based Recommendations. *Int. J. Environ. Res. Public Health* **2021**, *18*, 3382. [CrossRef] [PubMed]
19. Fil, S.L.; Champion, J.D.; Christiansen, B. Perceptions of disaster management knowledge and skills among advanced practice registered nurses. *J. Am. Assoc. Nurse Pract.* **2020**, *33*, 514–520. [CrossRef] [PubMed]
20. Goniewicz, K.; Burkle, F.M.; Khorram-Manesh, A. The gap of knowledge and skill—One reason for unsuccessful management of mass casualty incidents and disasters. *Am. J. Emerg. Med.* **2020**, *10*, S0735-6757(20)30863-9. [CrossRef]
21. Loke, A.Y.; Guo, C.; Molassiotis, A. Development of disaster nursing education and training programs in the past 20 years (2000–2019): A systematic review. *Nurse Educ. Today* **2021**, *99*, 104809. [CrossRef] [PubMed]
22. Whittemore, R.; Knafl, K. The integrative review: Updated methodology. *J. Adv. Nurs.* **2005**, *52*, 546–553. [CrossRef] [PubMed]
23. Tong, A.; Flemming, K.; McInnes, E.; Oliver, S.; Craig, J. Enhancing transparency in reporting the synthesis of qualitative research: ENTREQ. *BMC Med. Res. Methodol.* **2012**, *12*, 181. [CrossRef]
24. Moher, D.; Liberati, A.; Tetzlaff, J.; Altman, D.G.; PRISMA Group. Preferred reporting items for systematic reviews and meta-analyses: The PRISMA statement. *PLoS Med.* **2009**, *6*, e1000097. [CrossRef] [PubMed]
25. Flick, U. *Introduction to Qualitative Research*, 2nd ed.; Ediciones Morata: Madrid, Spain, 2007.
26. University of Liège. 2021. Available online: https://www.programmes.uliege.be/cocoon/20192020/programmes/S3GRCA01_C.html/ (accessed on 2 July 2020).
27. University of Borne. Available online: https://www.ug.dk/uddannelser/masteruddannelser/samfundsvidenskabeligeuddannelser/master-i-katastrofehaandtering (accessed on 28 November 2020).
28. University of Copenhagen. Available online: https://www.ug.dk/uddannelser/masteruddannelser/samfundsvidenskabeligeuddannelser/master-i-katastrofehaandtering/ (accessed on 15 September 2020).
29. University of Montréal. Available online: https://admission.umontreal.ca/programmes/dess-en-environnement-sante-et-gestion-des-catastrophes/structure-du-programme/ (accessed on 15 July 2020).
30. University of Neith. Available online: http://unice.fr/faculte-de-medecine/fmc/DU/du-2017/17-soinsinfirmiers-cata.pdf (accessed on 15 July 2020).
31. University of Rennes. Available online: https://formations.univ-rennes1.fr/diplome-duniversite-medecine-de-catastrophe-et-des-situations-sanitaires-exceptionnelles-capacite (accessed on 11 October 2020).
32. University of Lorraine. Available online: https://formations.univ-lorraine.fr/fr/diplome-d-universite-du-diplome-inter-universitaire-diu/2657-diplome-universitaire-medecine-de-catastrophe.html (accessed on 11 November 2020).
33. University of Paul Valéry. Available online: https://cales-new.univ-montp3.fr/fr/index/offre-de-formation/master-lmd-XB/sciences-humaines-et-sociales-SHS/master-1-geographie-amenagement-environnement-et-developpement-program-fr_rne_0341089z_pr_1298298094452/parcours-gestion-des-catastrophes-et-des-risques-naturels-subprogram-parcours-gestion-des-catastrophes-et-des-risques-naturels.html (accessed on 28 October 2020).
34. University of Bonn. Available online: https://www.kavoma.de/ (accessed on 28 November 2020).

35. University of Hochschule. Available online: https://www.akkon-hochschule.de/management-in-der-gefahrenabwehr-b-sc-katastrophenmanagement.html (accessed on 28 November 2020).
36. Carl Remigius Medical School. Available online: https://www.carl-remigius.de/studium/notfallmanagement-krisenmanagement-master/ (accessed on 28 September 2020).
37. University of Athens. Available online: http://crisis.med.uoa.gr/ (accessed on 28 September 2020).
38. University of Ciels. Available online: https://www.ciels.it/indirizzo-in-gestione-delle-crisi-delle-emergenze-e-delle-catastrofi/ (accessed on 9 November 2020).
39. University of Piemonte Orientale. Available online: https://crimedim.uniupo.it/the-emdm/ (accessed on 15 November 2020).
40. Santa Maria School of Health. Available online: https://eduportugal.eu/opcoes-de-estudo/emergencia-trauma-e-catastrofe/ (accessed on 12 October 2020).
41. University of Nova. Available online: https://guia.unl.pt/pt/2020/fcm/program/9813/course/11132 (accessed on 12 October 2020).
42. University of Alicante. Available online: https://web.ua.es/es/masteres/emergencias-y-catastrofes/ (accessed on 11 July 2020).
43. University of Camilo José Cela. Available online: https://www.ucjc.edu/estudio/master-universitario-en-el-estudio-de-las-intervenciones-en-emergencias-catastrofes-y-cooperacion-internacional/ (accessed on 9 August 2020).
44. University of CEU-Cardenal Herrera. Available online: https://www.google.com/search?q=Espa%C3%B1a.+Universidad+CEU-Cardenal+Herrera.+Experto+Universitario+en+Gesti%C3%B3n+de+Cat%C3%A1strofes&oq=Espa%C3%B1a.+Universidad+CEU-Cardenal+Herrera.+Experto+Universitario+en+Gesti%C3%B3n+de+Cat%C3%A1strofes&aqs=chrome..69i57.167j0j7&sourceid=chrome&ie=UTF-8 (accessed on 22 August 2020).
45. University Complutense of Madrid. Available online: http://blogs.mat.ucm.es/mgd/ (accessed on 17 August 2020).
46. University of Rey Juan Carlos. Available online: https://www.urjc.es/estudios/master/818-gestion-de-seguridad-crisis-y-emergencias (accessed on 11 July 2020).
47. University of Rey Juan Carlos. University Clinic. Available online: https://www.clinicaurjc.es/formacion/expertos/experto-universitario-en-gestion-integral-de-riesgos-de-desastre/programa-experto-universitario-en-gestion-integral-de-riesgos-de-desastre/ (accessed on 10 July 2020).
48. University of San Pablo CEU. Available online: https://www.uspceu.com/oferta-formativa/posgrado/master-universitario-en-urgencias-emergencias-y-catastrofes (accessed on 23 July 2020).
49. University of Oviedo. Available online: http://www.uniovi.es/-/master-universitario-en-analisis-y-gestion-de-emergencia-y-desastre/ (accessed on 28 July 2020).
50. Alcalá Formation (a). Available online: https://www.formacionalcala.es/enfermeria/expertos-universitarios-online/experto-universitario-en-atencion-sanitaria-urgente-en-situaciones-extremas-y-catastrofes (accessed on 15 November 2020).
51. Alcalá Formation (b). Available online: https://www.formacionalcala.es/medicina/cursos-online/atencion-integral-en-catastrofes-sanitarias (accessed on 15 November 2020).
52. SAMU School. Available online: https://escuelasamu.com/catalogo/cursos-de-especializacion/experto-en-conflictos-civiles-desastres-y-catastrofes/ (accessed on 23 August 2020).
53. University James Lind (Switzerland). Available online: https://www.onlinestudies.com//Master-of-Public-Health-(MPH-%E2%80%93-Disaster-Management)/Switzerland/James-Lind-Institute-Switzerland/ (accessed on 13 October 2020).
54. University of Bournemouth. Available online: https://www.bournemouth.ac.uk/study/courses/msc-disaster-management-1 (accessed on 1 September 2020).
55. University of Coventry. Available online: https://www.coventry.ac.uk/course-structure/pg/2020-21/eec/disaster-management-msc/ (accessed on 20 September 2020).
56. University of Leicester. Available online: https://le.ac.uk/courses/risk-crisis-and-disaster-management-msc-dl/2020/ (accessed on 16 September 2020).
57. University of Lincoln. Available online: https://www.masterstudies.com/Master-in-Crisis-and-Disaster-Management/United-Kingdom/University-of-Lincoln/ (accessed on 8 September 2021).
58. University of Manchester. Available online: https://www.manchester.ac.uk/study/masters/courses/list/09910/msc-international-disaster-management/ (accessed on 10 September 2020).
59. University of Portsmouth. Available online: https://www.port.ac.uk/study/courses/msc-crisis-and-disaster-management/ (accessed on 23 September 2020).
60. Blanchard, W. Guide to Emergency Management and Related Terms, Definitions, Concepts, Acronyms, Organisations, Programs, Guidance, Executive Orders & Legislation: A Tutorial on Emergency Management, Broadly Defined, Past and Present. 2007. Available online: https://training.fema.gov/hiedu/docs/terms%20and%20definitions/terms%20and%20definitions.pdf (accessed on 21 May 2021).
61. Stabback, P. What Makes a Quality Curriculum? I.B.E./2016/WP/CD/02. 2016, pp. 1–41. Available online: https://unesdoc.unesco.org/ark:/48223/pf0000243975 (accessed on 15 June 2021).
62. Gallardo, A.R.; Djalali, A.; Foletti, M.; Ragazzoni, L.; Della Corte, F.; Lupescu, O.; Arculeo, C.; von Arnim, G.; Friedl, T.; Ashkenazi, M.; et al. Core Competencies in Disaster Management and Humanitarian Assistance: A Systematic Review. *Disaster Med. Public Health Prep.* **2015**, *9*, 430–439. [CrossRef] [PubMed]

63. Ingrassia, P.L.; Ragazzoni, L.; Tengattini, M.; Carenzo, L.; Della Corte, F. Nationwide program of education for undergraduates in the field of disaster medicine: Development of a core curriculum centered on blended learning and simulation tools. *Prehosp. Disaster Med.* **2014**, *29*, 508–515. [CrossRef]
64. Aymerich-Franch, L. Virtual reality as a tool for the study of psychological and social phenomena. *Orbis* **2012**, *24*, 102–115. Available online: www.revistaorbis.org.ve/ (accessed on 17 March 2021).
65. De Leo, G.; Ponder, M.; Molet, T.; Fato, M.; Thalmann, D.; Magnenat-Thalmann, N.; Bermano, F.; Beltrame, F. A virtual reality system for the training of volunteers involved in health emergency situations. *Cyberpsychol. Behav.* **2003**, *6*, 267–274. [CrossRef]
66. Kim, T.E.; Shankel, T.; Reibling, E.T.; Paik, J.; Wright, D.; Buckman, M.; Wild, K.; Ngo, E.; Hayatshahi, A.; Nguyen, L.H.; et al. Healthcare students interprofessional critical event/disaster response course. *Am. J. Disaster Med.* **2017**, *12*, 11–26. [CrossRef]
67. Warren, J.N.; Luctkar-Flude, M.; Godfrey, C.; Lukewich, J. A systematic review of the effectiveness of simulation-based education on satisfaction and learning outcomes in nurse practitioner programs. *Nurse Educ. Today* **2016**, *46*, 99–108. [CrossRef]
68. Calamassi, D.; Nannelli, T.; Guazzini, A.; Rasero, L.; Bambi, S. High Fidelity Simulation Experience in Emergency settings: Doctors and nurses satisfaction levels. *Acta Biomed.* **2016**, *87*, 38–50.
69. Baptista, R.C.; Martins, J.C.; Pereira, M.F.; Mazzo, A. Students' satisfaction with simulated clinical experiences: Validation of an assessment scale. *Rev. Lat. Am. Enfermagem* **2014**, *22*, 709–715. [CrossRef] [PubMed]
70. Djalali, A.; Della Corte, F.; Foletti, M.; Ragazzoni, L.; Gallardo, A.R.; Lupescu, O.; Arculeo, C.; von Arnim, G.; Friedl, T.; Ashkenazi, M.; et al. Art of disaster preparedness in European union: A survey on the health systems. *PLoS Curr.* **2014**, *6*. [CrossRef] [PubMed]
71. Ngo, J.; Schertzer, K.; Harter, P.; Smith-Coggins, R. Disaster Medicine: A Multi-Modality Curriculum Designed and Implemented for Emergency Medicine Residents. *Disaster Med. Public Health Prep.* **2016**, *10*, 611–614. [CrossRef] [PubMed]
72. Duan, L.; Zhu, G. Psychological interventions for people affected by the COVID-19 epidemic. *Lancet Psychiatry* **2020**, *7*, 300–302. [CrossRef]
73. World Health Organization. Available online: https://covid19.who.int (accessed on 23 July 2021).
74. Greene, C.; Williams, A.; Harris, P.; Travis, S.; Kim, S. Unfolding Case-Based Practicum Curriculum Infusing Crisis, Trauma, and Disaster Preparation. Couns. *Educ. Superv.* **2016**, *55*, 216–232. [CrossRef]
75. Emergency Response Coordination Centre (ERCC). European Civil Protection and Humanitarian Aid Operations. Available online: https://ec.europa.eu/echo/what/civil-protection/emergency-response-coordination-centre-ercc_en (accessed on 22 October 2021).

International Journal of
Environmental Research and Public Health

MDPI

Article

Can the School Fruit and Vegetable Scheme Be an Effective Strategy Leading to Positive Changes in Children's Eating Behaviours? Polish Evaluation Results

Katarzyna Wolnicka *, Anna Małgorzata Taraszewska and Joanna Jaczewska-Schuetz

National Institute of Public Health—National Institute of Hygiene—National Research Institute, Department of Nutrition Education, 24 Chocimska Street, 00–791 Warsaw, Poland; ataraszewska@pzh.gov.pl (A.M.T.); jschuetz@pzh.gov.pl (J.J.-S.)
* Correspondence: kwolnicka@pzh.gov.pl; Tel.: +48-22-5509638

Abstract: Background: The School Fruit and Vegetable Scheme (SFVS) was developed to form the habit of eating fruit and vegetables (F&V) among children. The survey aimed to identify both the strengths of the scheme and areas that required support and strengthening in the further implementation of school schemes. Methods: The study was conducted from 2012 to 2015 among students of randomly selected 85 primary schools that participated in the programme (intervention group) or did not participate therein (control group). The F&V consumption among the students was evaluated based on the 3 day food record method. Other behaviours were evaluated via frequency and preference questionnaires. Results: Over the three years of implementing SFVS, fruit consumption significantly increased by approximately 30 g/day, i.e., by 18%. In the control group, it increased only by approximately 4%. At the same time, no increase in vegetable consumption was observed. A number of other positive effects of SFVS were also found. These concerned students' nutritional attitudes and behaviours, such as a further increase in the children's knowledge on the health aspects of F&V consumption, the levels of their consumption and an increased preference for fruit in general. Conclusions: The results indicate that providing F&V in schools free of charge can be an effective strategy for enhancing F&V consumption among children, in particular by raising the awareness of the health importance of F&V consumption and gradually influencing children's eating habits, especially when it comes to the habit of fruit consumption. The issue of vegetable consumption is an area for intervention enhancement. There is also a need for further, in-depth analyses, taking into account the impact of potential confounding factors.

Keywords: nutrition; fruit; vegetable; children; school; intervention programme; education

Citation: Wolnicka, K.; Taraszewska, A.M.; Jaczewska-Schuetz, J. Can the School Fruit and Vegetable Scheme Be an Effective Strategy Leading to Positive Changes in Children's Eating Behaviours? Polish Evaluation Results. *Int. J. Environ. Res. Public Health* **2021**, *18*, 12331. https://doi.org/10.3390/ijerph182312331

Academic Editors: Joachim G. Voss and Sandul Yasobant

Received: 8 October 2021
Accepted: 20 November 2021
Published: 24 November 2021

1. Introduction

The School Fruit and Vegetable Scheme was developed as one of the European Commission's operations aimed at improving the health and nutrition of children. In Poland, the scheme was carried out from the 2009/2010 to the 2016/2017 school years and was funded from the budget of the EU Common Agricultural Policy. The main principles of the scheme were specified in the Polish National Implementation Strategy for the School Fruit and Vegetable Scheme developed for individual school years.

The School Fruit and Vegetable Scheme aimed to change children's dietary habits by increasing the consumption of fruit and vegetables in the daily diet at a stage when nutritional habits are shaped. Secondary goals concerned raising the social awareness of proper nutrition, especially when it comes to children, and promoting healthy dietary habits and knowledge on the origin of fruit and vegetables by various educational measures at schools. Schools were obliged to carry out at least two educational activities a year from a specified list of accompanying measures, such as organising thematic competitions and festivals, outings to farms, discussions, healthy food days, cooking classes, running a school newspaper, maintaining a school garden, or having a second breakfast together with tasting fruit and vegetables. The beneficiaries of the School Fruit and Vegetable Scheme in Poland in the evaluated years (2012–2016) were children in Year 1–3 of primary school (6–10 years old). The scheme was very popular—98% of the target group, i.e., more than 1.3 M of children from 11 thousand primary schools, participated in it. As part of the scheme, children received vegetables and fruit free of charge. Children were given fresh fruits (such as apples, pears, strawberries and blueberries), fresh vegetables (such as carrot, sweet pepper, radish, -kohlrabi and cherry tomatoes), as well as fruit, vegetable or mixed juices. The products were selected to include as many fresh fruit and vegetable and regional products of the highest diversity and quality as possible. Fruit, vegetables and juices given away as part of the scheme could not contain added fat, salt, sugar or sweeteners. Each child participating in the scheme received 2–3 portions of fruit and vegetables per week for a total of 20 weeks in a school year. Ready-to-eat portions of fruit and vegetables were prepared and delivered to schools by approved suppliers. The School Fruit and Vegetable Scheme was carried out as part of a cooperation between the sectors of agriculture, public health and education. An authority responsible for implementing the School Fruit and Vegetable Scheme in Poland was Agricultural Market Agency (now, National Support Centre for Agriculture).

The School Fruit and Vegetable Scheme was subject to a regular effectiveness assessment that was to determine whether and how it achieved the set goals. In Poland, the scientific evaluation of the scheme covered the 2011/2012–2015/2016 school years and was carried out by the experts from the Food and Nutrition Institute (now National Institute of Public Health–National Institute of Hygiene–National Research Institute). The aim of the evaluation was to identify the strengths of the scheme and areas requiring support and reinforcement for the further implementation of such school schemes.

From the 2017/2018 school year, the assumptions and goals of the School Fruit and Vegetable Scheme and the School Milk Scheme were combined in the School Scheme.

The results of studies on interventional and educational schemes conducted in the school environment and their effects on nutritional habits and diet quality (including fruit and vegetable consumption) indicate that these can be an effective tool for improving the implementation of nutritional recommendations [1–3]. This is confirmed by, for example, effectiveness assessment data concerning fruit and vegetable consumption promotion schemes combined with fruit and vegetables being supplied free of charge at German or Norwegian schools, where their short-term influence on increasing fruit and vegetable consumption or long-term positive influence on fruit consumption (but not vegetables) were demonstrated [2,4–7].

2. Material and Methods

The study was conducted from 2012 to 2016 at randomly selected 85 primary schools that participated or did not participate in the EU School Fruit and Vegetable Scheme among students in Years 1–3 (6–10 years old). The study also involved the children's parents/legal guardians.

The study was nationwide. It was conducted in five regions of Poland, representing the central, eastern, western, northern and southern areas of the country. Stratified sampling was used, with the school being the basic sampling unit. Before sampling, schools were stratified into urban and rural areas. The study was designed in a way as to make the student sample reflect the structure of population of students attending rural and urban schools in Poland.

At each school, the headmaster chose two classes to participate in a survey. If there was only one class in a school, the next school was chosen. The survey was carried out at primary schools that participated in the School Fruit and Vegetables Scheme (intervention group) and at primary schools that did not participate in the scheme (control group).

In terms of sociodemographic data such as gender of children participating in the study, parental education, net income per family member and number of children in the family, no statistical differences were found between the intervention and control groups. The evaluation study was conducted in the form of a panel study. The evaluation involved several stages from 2012 to 2016.

The study was approved by the Bioethics Committee operating at the Food and Nutrition Institute in Warsaw.

2.1. Material

The study involved students from randomly chosen schools who, in 2012, began their school education in Year 1 classes indicated by the headmaster. A total of 3385 students from 85 schools that participated or did not participate in the School Fruit and Vegetable Scheme were invited to take part in the study. The parents of 3113 students gave their informed consent to the participation in the study. In the first year of the study, 2798 students actually took part in it. The same students participated in the study in subsequent school years (study stages) until 2016. Throughout the study, the school sample size decreased, which was due to the joining of schools that, at the beginning of the evaluation, did not participate in the scheme. Nonparticipating schools that joined the scheme during the study did not take part in the further study stages. The student sample size also decreased, which was caused by both the decreasing number of schools included in the study and the absence of students on the survey day, their changed place of residence or a failure to fully complete the survey and the consumption diary. In the third year of the study, an informed consent to the participation in the study was given by the parents of 2631 students in total, with 2251 students actually taking part in the study (Table 1). The final survey return rate in the study amounted to 80.5%.

Table 1. Changes in the sample size of children taking part in the evaluation study in the years 2012–2015.

Year of Study	Total Number of Children Invited to the Study	Total Number of Children Taking Part in the Study	Number of Schools Participating in the Study		Number of Children Participating in the Study	
			Included in the Scheme	Not Included in the Scheme	Included in the Scheme	Not Included in the Scheme
2012	3385	2798	41	44	1518	1280
2013	3333	2773	41	44	1500	1273
2014	3003	2075	41	36	1269	806
2015	2631	2251	41	25	1463	788

2.2. Research Tool

A research tool for children and parents was an anonymous survey. In addition, children who took part in the study were measured and weighed by a school nurse.

The parent survey contained questions relating to sociological data, open-ended and multiple-choice questions relating to lifestyle, dietary habits with an emphasis on fruit and vegetable consumption, and knowledge on proper nutrition, as well as the child's fruit and vegetable consumption, dietary habits and lifestyle. The questionnaire included questions relating to the child's consumption of fresh fruit, vegetables, including salads, other raw vegetables (sliced or whole) and boiled vegetables.

The child survey contained questions related to the knowledge of proper nutrition, dietary habits with an emphasis on fruit and vegetable consumption, lifestyle and dietary preferences, including fruit and vegetables. Children's knowledge of proper nutrition was measured by an open-ended question "What should you do to live a healthy life?". Another question was measured by the item "How many portions of fruit and vegetables should you eat?" using a scale ranging from 1 to 7 where, 1 = "should not eat fruit and vegetables at all" and 7 = "5 or more portions per day", acknowledged as correct knowledge. Children's dietary preferences were measured by an open-ended question "What do you like to eat?".

Fruit consumption frequency was determined based on the question related to the fresh fruit consumption frequency. Vegetable consumption frequency was determined based on three questions by adding up the consumption frequency of vegetables in the form of salads, other raw vegetables (sliced or whole) and boiled vegetables (excluding potatoes).

In addition, the students' dietary habits were assessed using the 3 day food record method. The parents were required to fill in a 3 day food record with the child, where they included products, meals, beverages (along with their weights or home-based measures) consumed by their child during two school days and one weekend day. The parents were trained by the interviewer and additionally received written tips on how to fill in the food record correctly.

The consumption assessment and analysis were carried out using the DIETA 5.0 computer software (National Institute of Public Health-National Institute of Hygiene-National Research Institute, Warsaw, Poland)designed to assess individual and group diet as well as to plan and analyse consumption among tested populations against nutritional standards. It allows for calculating energy and nutritional value of diets as well as the consumption volume of products and dishes. It also ensures standardization of data input regarding products and dishes consumed (order and accuracy of determining the type and composition of dishes), dish recipes, serving size determination (choice of serving sizes suggested in the software), calculation method (identical reduction volumes) and results obtained (ingredient quantity and comparison to standards).

2.3. Course of Study

In accordance with the methodology, the study was conducted in two school groups: schools that participated in the scheme (intervention group) and schools that did not participate in the scheme (control group). The survey was conducted near the end of the school year (May/June). The first study stage was an exception, as it took place at the beginning of the school year (October), before the start of actions associated with the School Fruit and Vegetable Scheme.

2.4. Statistical Methods

The statistical analysis was conducted using the Statistica 10.0 software (StatSoft Inc., Tulsa, OK, USA 2011). When it comes to the analyses of key study variables, that is fruit and vegetable consumption frequency and consumption expressed in grams, tests of normality (Shapiro-Wilk test) were conducted. Because the distributions of the aforementioned variables significantly deviated from the normal distribution, nonparametric methods were used to verify the hypotheses. For comparisons between the two groups in an independent plan (comparisons between the intervention group and the control group), the Mann–Whitney U test was used; for comparisons in a dependent plan (comparisons between two study stages), the Wilcoxon signed-rank test was used. Basic parameters of descriptive statistics were also calculated: medians, arithmetic means and standard deviations. For comparing proportions in the groups, Pearson's chi-squared test was used, while for comparisons between measurements, the sign test was used, and numbers and proportions were given. When it comes to variables expressed on ordinal scales, a comparative analysis was additionally performed for means calculated for codes attributed to individual answers. Because this analysis only complemented the previously conducted chi-squared tests and its purpose was to discover potential tendencies to change attitudes, by way of exception, parametric Student's t-tests were used for independent variables (when comparing groups) and dependent variables (when comparing measurements). The significance level was set at $\alpha = 0.05$. Results were statistically significant when the calculated test probability was $p < 0.05$.

3. Results

3.1. Fruit and Vegetable Consumption by Children

After one year in the scheme, the amount of consumed fruit ($p < 0.0009$), vegetables ($p < 0.027$) and fruit and vegetables together ($p < 0.0003$) significantly increased among the children who were included in the intervention. The results related to fruit and vegetable consumption (on school and weekend days) are shown in Figures 1–3. At the same time, the control group recorded a lower amount of fruit consumed ($p < 0.043$), while the amount of vegetables did not significantly change. After one year in the scheme, the intervention group consumed 11% more fruit than the control group and 9% more fruit and vegetables together. Two years in the scheme, on school and weekend days, in the intervention group, the total fruit and vegetable consumption significantly increased by 9 g ($p = 0.004$), which was mainly due to increased fruit consumption ($p < 0.00001$ for fruit alone). In the control group, no statistically significant increase in the total fruit and vegetable consumption was recorded, but there was a statistically significant increase in fruit consumption ($p = 0.01$), although lower than in the intervention group. At the end of the second year of intervention, the total fruit and vegetable consumption in the intervention group was still higher—the difference was 21 g, which constitutes a 7% difference ($p = 0.0008$). On both school and weekend days, in the group included in the scheme, the consumption of fruit and vegetables together significantly rose (by 20.4 g; $p < 0.000$) after three years, which was due to the increased consumption of both fruit and vegetables. In the control group, there also was a statistically significant increase in the consumption of fruit and vegetables together, which was mainly associated with the increase in vegetable consumption. However, at the end of the third year of the intervention, in the group included in the scheme, the total fruit and vegetable consumption on school and weekend days together was still significantly higher than in the control group (which was attributed to higher fruit consumption in the intervention group than in the control group; 19.5 g difference, $p = 0.018$).

Throughout the three years of the School Fruit and Vegetable Scheme, fruit consumption increased by 30 g/day, i.e., 18%, while in the control group by 4%. Vegetable consumption remained at a similar level for the first two years of the scheme, while in the third year, it rose significantly in both groups (no statistically significant differences between the groups at the end of the scheme).

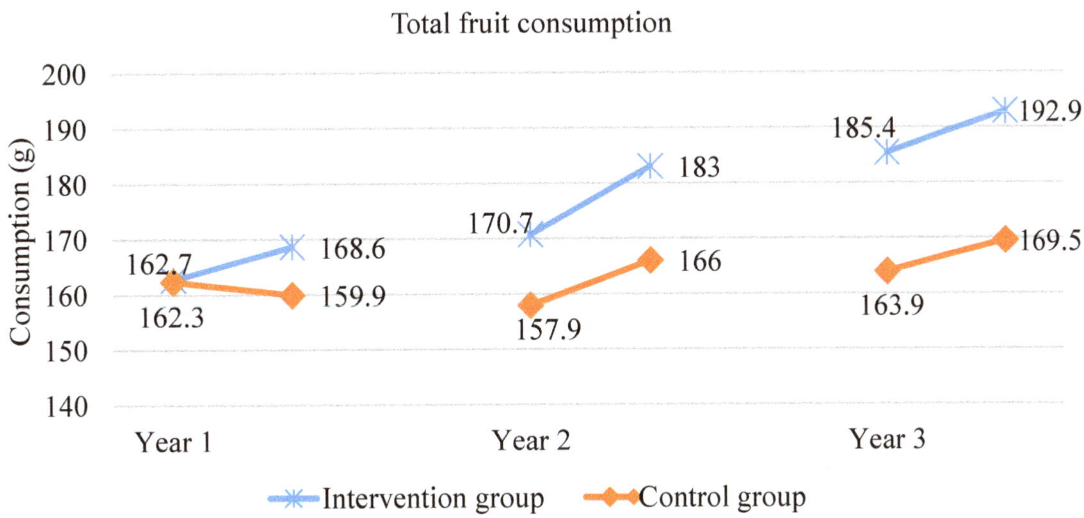

Figure 1. Fruit consumption (on both school and weekend days) during the three years of the study.

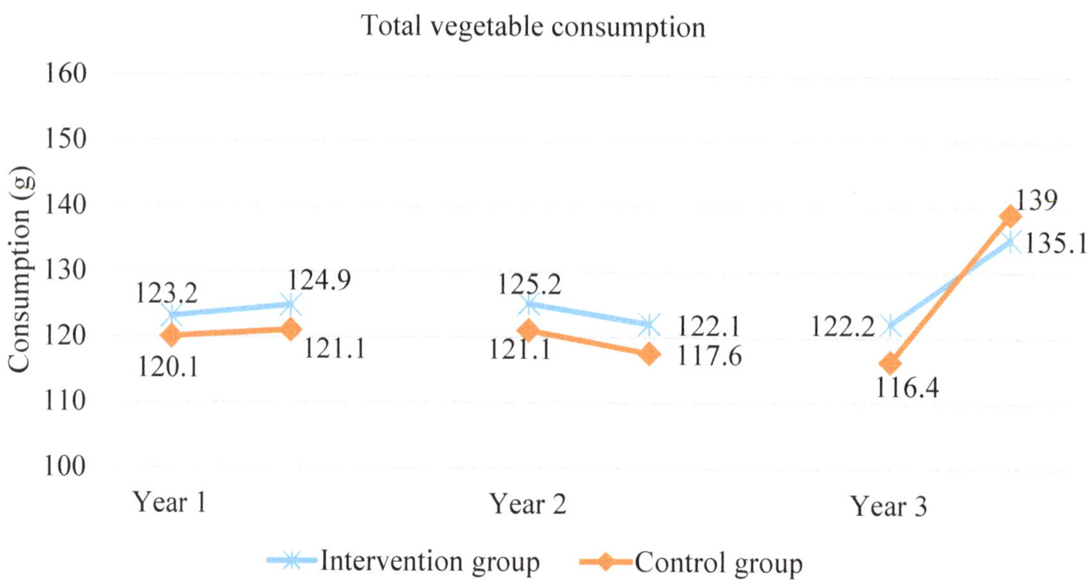

Figure 2. Vegetable consumption (on both school and weekend days) during the three years of the study.

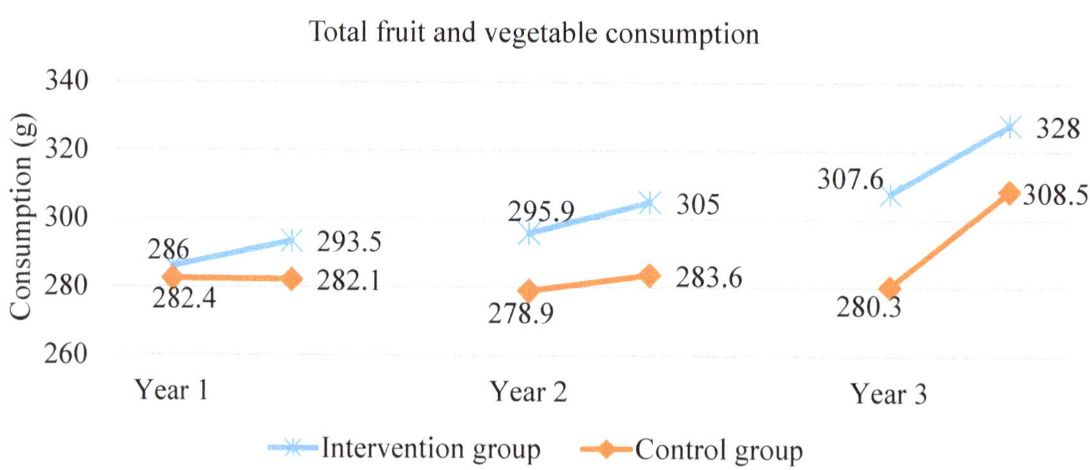

Figure 3. Total fruit and vegetable consumption (on both school and weekend days) during the three years of the study.

3.2. Children's Knowledge on Proper Nutrition

There was a significant rise in children's awareness in link between fruit and vegetable consumption and health in the first year of the scheme. After one year in the scheme, to the open-ended question "What should you do to live a healthy life?" in the intervention group, significantly more children answered "eat vegetables" and "eat fruit" but also "be more physically active" and "do not eat sweets". In the second year of the scheme, the children's awareness that eating fruit and vegetables is important for their health was maintained. In the intervention group, the proportion of children indicating "vegetable consumption" increased by 14.9%, while in the control group by 10.9%. At the end of the second year of the scheme, in the intervention group, children significantly more often answered "eat vegetables" compared to the control group children (70.3% vs. 57.8%, respectively, $p < 0.00001$). In addition, the link between fruit consumption and health was pointed by significantly more children in the intervention group—72.6% compared to 60.8% of children from the control group ($p < 0.000001$). In the third year of the study, in the intervention group, the percentage of children arguing that one needs to eat fruit and vegetables in order to be healthy did not significantly change relative to the previous year. In the control group, however, the number of children arguing that one needs to eat fruit and vegetables in order to be healthy increased to the level of the intervention group. At the end of the third year, the results achieved did not significantly differ between the intervention group and the control group. The data are shown in Figures 4 and 5. In both groups, after three years in the scheme, approximately three out of four children indicated that one needs to eat fruit and vegetables in order to be healthy. The level of knowledge on this matter in the control group matched the higher level of knowledge among the intervention group children achieved in the previous two years.

After the first year, there was a significant increase in the knowledge of the children participating in the scheme on the recommended daily portion of fruit and vegetables. In the second year of the scheme, the proportion of correct answers related to the recommended daily portion of fruit and vegetables increased again (by 7.3%, $p = 0.001$), while in the control group, this knowledge did not change. At the end of the second year of the study, the intervention group children answered correctly more often than the control group children—50.5% and 40.2% of correct answers, respectively ($p < 0.000$). After the third year of the scheme, in the intervention group, there was a further increase (by 9.5%) in the proportion of children having knowledge of the recommended vegetable and fruit portions. At the same time, a significant drop in the number of children correctly answering the question "How many portions of fruit and vegetables should you eat?" in the control group was observed. At the end of the third year of the scheme, significantly more children in the intervention group had correct knowledge on the recommended daily portion of fruit and vegetables (59.8% vs. 31.5%; $p < 0.000$). The data are shown in Figure 6.

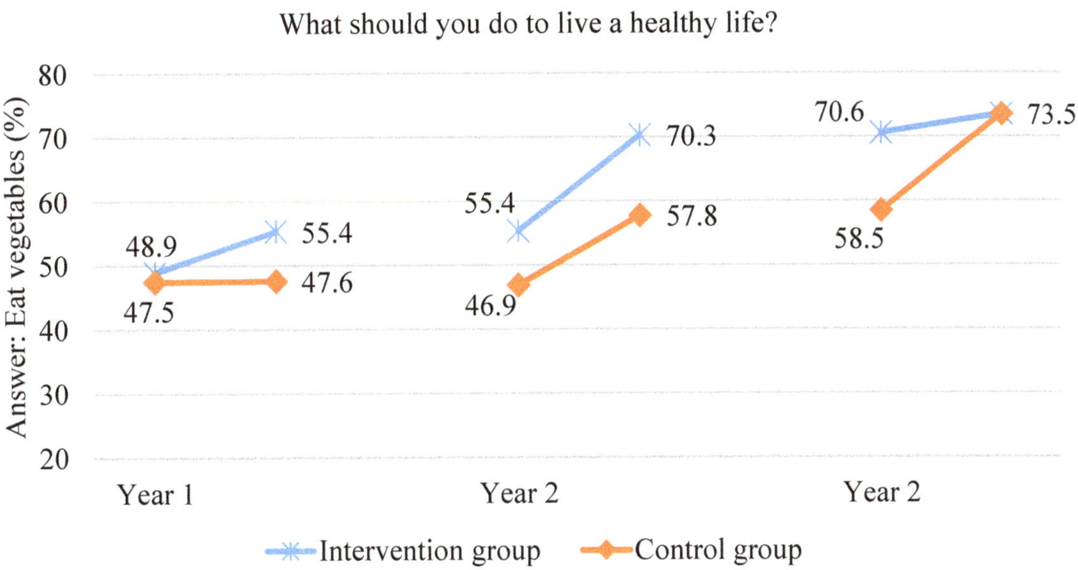

Figure 4. Proportion of children indicating vegetable consumption as a health-supporting behaviour during the three years of the study.

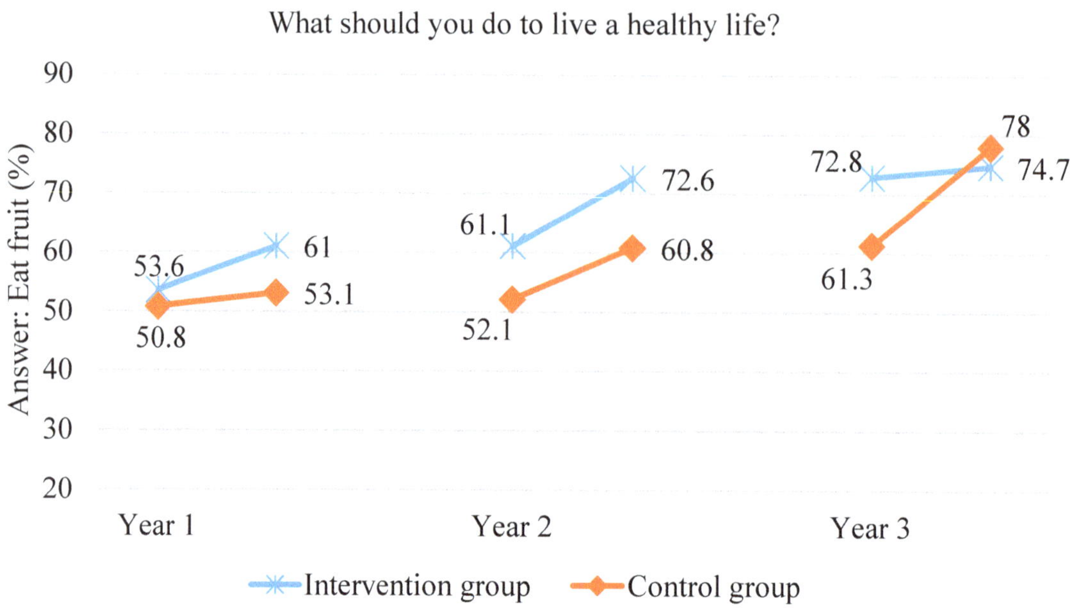

Figure 5. Proportion of children indicating fruit consumption as a health-supporting behaviour during the three years of the study.

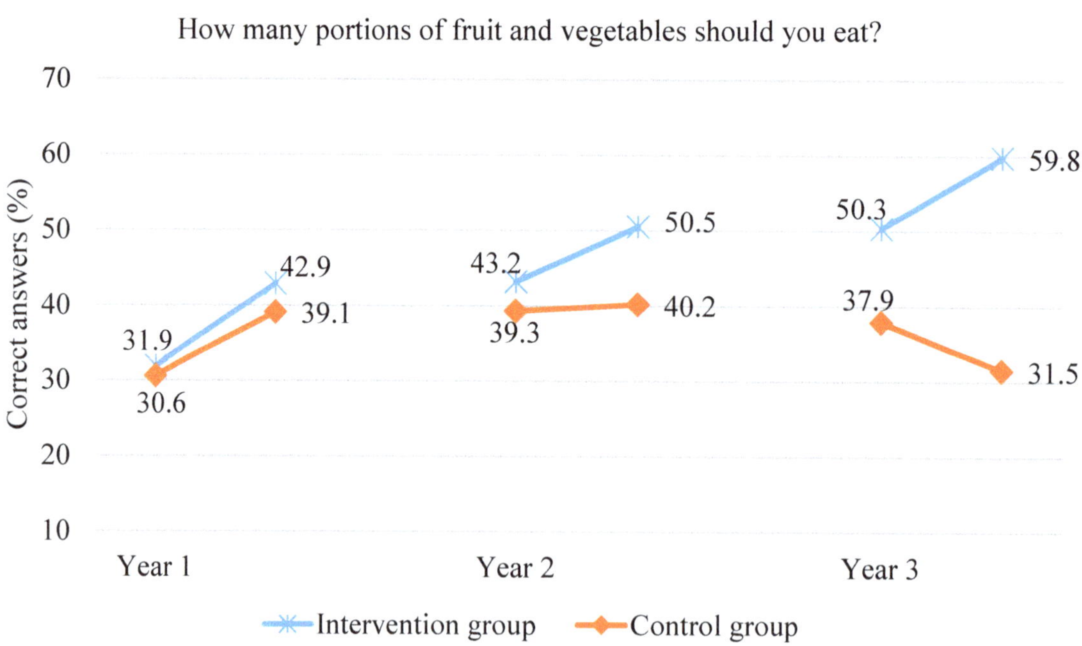

Figure 6. The proportion of children correctly answering the question "How many portions of fruit and vegetables should you eat?" during the three years of the study.

3.3. Children's Dietary Preferences

After one year in the scheme, to the question "What do you like to eat", "fruit" was the answer given more frequently in the intervention group than in the control group (30.1% vs. 23.3%; $p = 0.0001$). Only 15.5% of the students from the intervention group and 13.5% of the students from the control group indicated vegetables after one year in the scheme, but the differences were not significant. After two years in the scheme, children in the intervention group also answered "fruit" to the aforementioned question more often than in the control group (39.5% vs. 34.9%, respectively, $p = 0.03$). In both groups, fewer children indicated vegetables as products they liked, as opposed to fruit. After three years in the scheme, the number of children indicating vegetables as products they liked was significantly higher in the intervention group than in the control group (34.6% vs. 24.5%; $p < 0.000$). What is more, in the intervention group, the number of children who liked fruit was significantly higher (42.3% vs. 35.7%; $p = 0.007$). The data are shown in Figures 7 and 8.

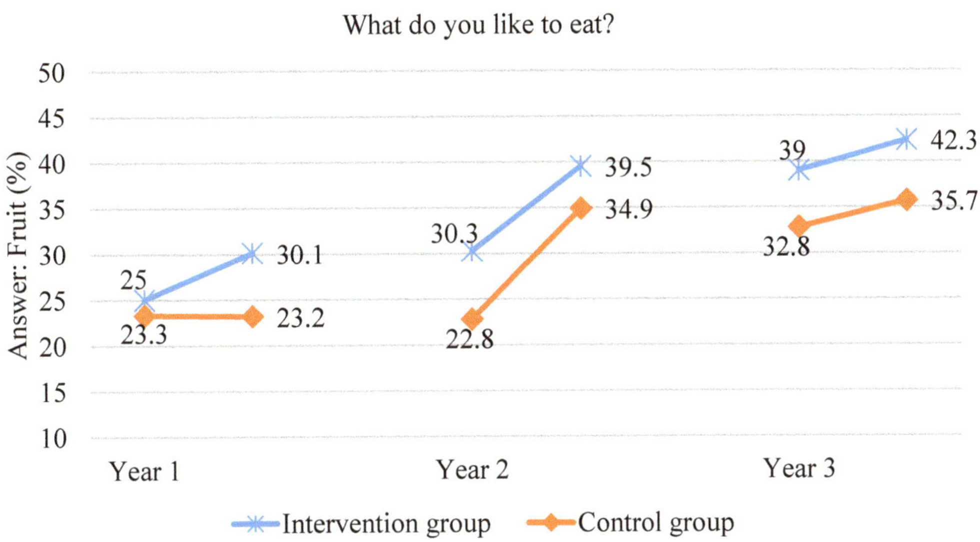

Figure 7. The proportion of children indicating fruit as products they like to eat during the three years of the study.

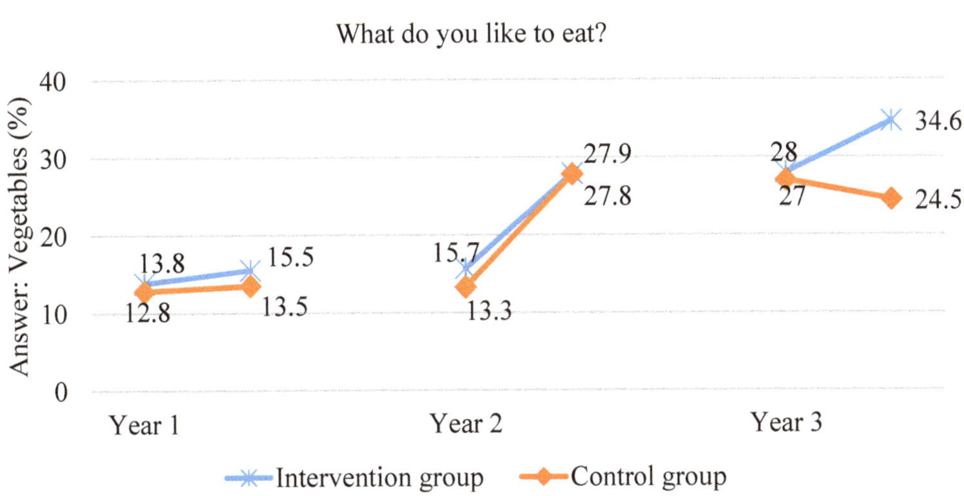

Figure 8. The proportion of children indicating vegetables as products they like to eat during the three years of the study.

4. Discussion

Health-supporting dietary habits developed in childhood translate into children's health and correlate with adult health, reducing the risk of numerous noninfectious diseases [8–10].

One of the important aspects of a health-supporting nutritional model is the regular consumption of fruit and vegetables. According to the recommendations by World Health Organisation (WHO), one should consume at least 400 g of fruit and vegetables with a frequency of at least five portions a day [11]. However, studies indicate that achieving this minimum is problematic. The results of the IDEFICS study suggest that only 8.8% children meet the recommendations on fruit and vegetable consumption [12]. Children aged 6–11 consume, on average, from two to three portions of fruit and vegetables per day, as suggested by studies carried out in Europe, Australia and the United States [13].

Studies indicate that the consumption of fruit and vegetables by children and adolescents in Poland is also unsatisfactory. According to the COSI study (2016), only 23.8% of 8 year-olds consumed vegetables every day, while 63.4% consumed them several times a week. When it comes to fruit, 35.7% children consumed them every day, while 59% children had fruit on several days in a week [14]. The HBSC study (2018) conducted among a group of adolescents aged 11–15 demonstrated that 38.2% of teenagers consumed fruit and 34.2% vegetables with recommended frequency. Daily fruit consumption became increasingly rarer with age in both sexes. The lowest proportion of adolescents consuming vegetables at least once a day was recorded for 13 year-olds, both boys and girls. Compared to the results of the HBSC study of 2014, the proportion of adolescents who had vegetables every day rose by 4.9%, while fruit rose by 4.4% [15,16]. Therefore, there is still a need to conduct various campaigns to popularise health-supporting habits, including an increase in fruit and vegetable consumption among children and adolescents. One of such campaigns was the EU educational and interventional School Fruit and Vegetable Scheme, implemented in Poland since 2009.

An extremely important aspect of conducting such schemes is their evaluation in order to assess the effectiveness of actions taken and determine areas that require corrections. The analysis of data from the evaluation of the Polish edition of the School Fruit and Vegetable Scheme indicated that, over the three years of the scheme, fruit consumption significantly increased by approximately 30 g per day, i.e., 18%. Although this amount is not significant, it indicates an upward trend in the consumption of food products, which are so crucial for the proper functioning of the young organism. At the same time, in the control group, it only rose by approximately 4%. Vegetable consumption remained at a similar level for the first two years of the scheme, while in the third year, it rose significantly in both groups (no statistically significant differences between the groups at the end of the scheme). The results showed positive effects of the scheme mostly on fruit consumption. Studies by other authors also confirmed a higher preference for fruit compared to vegetables [17]. The reason for this preference can be fruit's sweet flavour as opposed to vegetables. The literature's data indicate that the preference for sweet and salty flavours is the highest in the early childhood and decreases slightly with age [18,19].

Despite higher fruit consumption observed as a result of the scheme, the low total fruit and vegetable consumption as compared to the WHO recommendations is still a concern, as is the minimal effect of the scheme on vegetable consumption. The small effect of the School Fruit and Vegetable Scheme on vegetable consumption can be caused by the fact that, one portion of fruit and vegetables made available twice a week consisted of less vegetables (60 g) than fruit (100–150 g). Additionally, it needs to be noted that juices were distributed four times in 10 weeks.

Previous studies related to the effectiveness of schemes aimed at increasing fruit and vegetable consumption among children showed that it is easier to boost fruit consumption than vegetable consumption due to fruit's sweet flavour being better tolerated by children [4,20].

One of these studies assessed the effectiveness of the School Fruit and Vegetable Scheme and the influence of the frequency of providing fruit and vegetable portions on changing children's habits. Supplying fruit for three days, but also for two days, in a school week caused an increase in fruit and vegetable consumption among children. It was observed that children who attended an after-school club derived greater benefits from the supply of fruit to school, which the authors attributed to the fact that the fruit and vegetable that were left in the morning were given to children participating in an after-school club. Thus, students who spent a whole day at school had more opportunities to access fruit and vegetables. The authors conclude that the EU School Fruit and Vegetable Scheme is generally a useful tool aimed at increasing the consumption of fruit and vegetables by primary school students [21].

In the School Fruit and Vegetable Scheme, the practical aspect of free distribution of fruit and vegetables among children at school is important. The authors of a study evaluating the effectiveness of the *5 a day for KIDS* scheme concluded that 135 min educational classes at school did not seem to increase fruit and vegetable consumption among children. According to the researchers, the scheme's effectiveness can be improved, e.g., by increasing the involvement of parents and/or supplying free fruit/vegetables every day [22]. In another study, it was demonstrated that the School Fruit and Vegetable Scheme increased fruit and vegetable consumption in a group that received fruit free of charge. The effect was evident after three months of distribution. After seven months, the effect remained significant, although it decreased and returned to the baseline level in the second year, when the students were no longer included in the scheme. The scheme brought a short-term effect of increased fruit and vegetable consumption. The authors argue that further studies on the influence of factors that bring long-term effects of increased fruit and vegetable consumption among children are necessary [23].

A systematic review of 10 interventions increased fruit and vegetables intake in primary school children, resulting in a significant effect on fruit and vegetable consumption, ranging from 0.3 to 0.99 portions a day [24].

The School Fruit and Vegetable Scheme is also an educational scheme consisting of accompanying measures aimed at increasing children's and parents' knowledge, as well as reinforcing health-supporting behaviours among students included in the scheme.

As a result of the programme, there was an increase in children's awareness of the importance of eating fruit and vegetables for their health, an increase in knowledge about the recommended number of daily portions of fruit and vegetables and an increase in preference for this group of products.

It can be assumed that these positive observations relating to knowledge and preferences were affected by the educational measures conducted as part of the scheme. The School Fruit and Vegetable Scheme, which relied both on supplying fruit and vegetables and on conducting accompanying educational measures, constitutes good practice that contributes to increasing children's knowledge on healthy nutrition. Children who did not participate in the scheme showed poorer knowledge on the recommended number of fruit and vegetable portions and more rarely answered that they liked to eat vegetables. The evaluation results indicate that the children's knowledge and awareness of the health impact of fruit and vegetables and recommendations on their consumption systematically rose.

However, it needs to be noted that, after three years of participation in the scheme, only slightly more than half of the intervention group students were able to tell the correct recommended number of fruit and vegetable portions. This leads to the conclusion that information passed in the form of accompanying educational measures may be insufficient, incoherent or delivered in a manner that is not attractive enough. Accompanying measures as an integral part of the scheme should, then, be reinforced and continued at various levels of student's school education. Educational measures that accompany the School Fruit and Vegetable Scheme should, first and foremost, be supported by a package of unified and systematised educational materials to be used by the teachers of all the schools participating in the scheme, including lesson scenarios, teaching aids, both for working with the students and their parents, which would help the schools achieve set goals in an attractive and unified way.

It has been proven that the most effective educational programmes on correct nutrition and physical activity are based in the school environment. The school environment, including students, teachers and other school employees, as well as parents or even the local community, provides numerous opportunities to spread knowledge in the form of various measures and activities reinforcing health-supporting behaviours, including higher fruit and vegetable consumption. In light of the increasing issue of overweight and obesity among children and adolescents, it is necessary to organise health-promoting educational measures covering the entire school environment [6–8].

In accordance with expert recommendations, prevention schemes aimed at increasing the knowledge and shaping correct nutritional attitudes and habits require far-reaching measures. Single actions or interventions do not bring expected results and should be a part of long-term programmes [8,25].

A significant factor that affects children's fruit and vegetable consumption are parents' dietary habits. Numerous studies suggest that higher fruit and vegetable consumption among school-aged children depend on such familial factors as the parents' fruit and vegetable consumption, encouraging the child to eat fruit and vegetables, giving the child fruit and vegetables to school, the availability of fruit and vegetables at home and the parents' knowledge on the recommended fruit and vegetable intake. The results indicate the great importance of educational measures targeted at parents, which are needed to increase fruit and vegetable consumption among children [26–29]. Parents' dietary habits and their health-supporting behaviours play an extremely significant role in shaping the children's preferences for fruit and vegetables, which means that working with parents on an ongoing basis, with an emphasis on health-promoting education, should be an inherent part of the scheme's accompanying measures. Schools should have tools at their disposal for conducting systematised and planned educational measures targeted at parents. Working with parents gives the chance to create a unified educational environment and, as a result, a higher effectiveness of measures aimed at increasing fruit and vegetable consumption.

The choice of fruit and vegetables shared as part of the scheme should be diverse. Expanding the range of products offered to children at school and thus making it more attractive, provided that it spans for a longer period, might contribute to increasing the effectiveness of measures conducted.

Headmasters should enforce the quality of products delivered by suppliers because reduced quality, even if it affects only some product batches, may influence the food characteristics that children find important, such as sweetness, crispiness or juiciness, and constitute a critical point affecting the consumption among children and the scheme's effectiveness.

According to the authors, a strength of the study is that it compares changes not only between the different stages of the study (years) but also between the intervention and control groups. There were some limitations of the study. In the present study, all data were self-reported by parents with children and thereby may be limited by their comprehension and memory. Another limitation was that the sample size at the last year of the study was lower than planned for the control group, which was due to the joining of schools which, at the beginning of the evaluation, did not participate in the scheme. A limitation related to data analysis might be the fact that observed differences between study groups might not be due only to the intervention but also to the changes in individual or school-level characteristics. This is particularly important in case, as many schools were dropped from the control group in later years of the intervention. However, in terms of sociodemographic data such as gender of children participating in the study, parental education, net income per family member and the number of children in the family, no statistical differences were found between the intervention and control groups in every year/stage of survey. In addition, the analyses were conducted each year, between years, in the form of a panel study in the same group of children.

5. Conclusions

Supplying portions of fruit and vegetables free of charge at school can be an effective strategy leading to increased fruit and vegetable consumption among children. Participation in a scheme whereby fruit and vegetables are supplied along with conducting accompanying measures raises the awareness of the health importance of eating fruit and vegetables and the gradual effects on children's dietary habits, especially when it comes to the habit of eating fruit. The issue of vegetable consumption is an area for intervention enhancement. There is also the need for further, in-depth analyses, taking into account the impact of potential confounding factors.

Author Contributions: Conception, K.W. and A.M.T.; methodology, K.W.; data analysis and interpretation, K.W., A.M.T., J.J.-S.; writing—original draft preparation, K.W., A.M.T., J.J.-S.; writing—review and editing, K.W. and A.M.T.; visualization, K.W. and A.M.T.; supervision, K.W.; project coordination, K.W.; All authors have read and agreed to the published version of the manuscript.

Funding: This research was funded by Agricultural Market Agency (now National Support Centre for Agriculture) in Poland as framework agreement OWS/01/2012 and the article was produced as part of the assignment FE-1/2020 in National Institute of Public Health—National Institute of Hygiene—National Research Institute. And The APC was funded by National Institute of Public Health—National Institute of Hygiene—National Research Institute.

Institutional Review Board Statement: The study was conducted according to the guidelines of the Declaration of Helsinki, and approved by the Ethics Committee of National Food and Nutrition Institute (positive opinion, 02.10.2012).

Informed Consent Statement: Informed consent was obtained from all subjects involved in the study.

Conflicts of Interest: The authors declare no conflict of interest.

References

1. Fogarty, A.W.; Antoniak, M.; Venn, A.J.; Davies, L.; Goodwin, A.; Salfield, N.; Stocks, J.; Britton, J.; Lewis, S.A. Does participation in a population-based dietary intervention scheme have a lasting impact on fruit intake in young children? *Int. J. Epidemiol.* **2007**, *36*, 1080–1085. [CrossRef] [PubMed]
2. Methner, S.; Maschkowski, G.; Hartmann, M. The European School Fruit Scheme: Impact on children's fruit and vegetable consumption in North Rhine-Westphalia, Germany. *Public Health Nutr.* **2017**, *20*, 542–548. [CrossRef]
3. Stea, T.H.; Hovdenak, I.M.; Rønnestad, J.; Rennestraum, K.; Vik, F.N.; Klepp, K.I.; Bere, E. Effects of 1 y of free school fruit on intake of fruits, vegetables, and unhealthy snacks: 14 y later. *Am. J. Clin. Nutr.* **2018**, *108*, 1309–1315. [CrossRef]
4. Bere, E.; Hilsen, M.; Klepp, K.I. Effect of nationwide free school fruit scheme in Norway. *Br. J. Nutr.* **2010**, *104*, 589–594. [CrossRef] [PubMed]
5. Muckelbauer, R.; Libuda, L.; Clausen, K.; Reinehr, T.; Kersting, M. A simple dietary intervention in the school setting decreased incidence of overweight in children. *Obes. Facts* **2009**, *2*, 282–285. [CrossRef]
6. Sa, J.; Lock, K.E. Will European agricultural policy for school fruit and vegetables improve public heath? A review of school fruit and vegetable programmes. *J. Public Heath* **2008**, *18*, 558–568.
7. Silveira, J.; Taddei, J.; Guerra, P.; Nobre, M.R. The effect of participation in school-based nutrition education interventions on body mass index: A meta-analysis of randomized controlled community trials. *Prev. Med.* **2013**, *56*, 237–243. [CrossRef]
8. Weihrauch-Blüher, S.; Kromeyer-Hauschild, K.; Graf, C.; Widhalm, K.; Korsten-Reck, U.; Jödicke, B.; Markert, J.; Müller, M.J.; Moss, A.; Wabitsch, M.; et al. Current Guidelines for Obesity Prevention in Childhood and Adolescence. *Obes. Facts* **2018**, *11*, 263–276. [CrossRef]
9. Bowen, K.J.; Sullivan, V.K.; Kris-Etherton, P.M.; Petersen, K.S. Nutrition and Cardiovascular Disease—an Update. *Curr. Atheroscler. Rep.* **2018**, *20*, 8. [CrossRef] [PubMed]
10. Aune, D.; Giovannucci, E.; Boffetta, P.; Fadnes, L.T.; Keum, N.; Norat, T.; Greenwood, D.C.; Riboli, E.; Vatten, L.J.; Tonstad, S. Fruit and vegetable intake and the risk of cardiovascular disease, total cancer and all-cause mortality-a systematic review and dose-response meta-analysis of prospective studies. *Int. J. Epidemiol.* **2017**, *46*, 1029–1056. [CrossRef] [PubMed]
11. *WHO European Action Plan for Food and Nutrition 2007–2012*; WHO: Copenhagen, Denmark, 2008.
12. Kovacs, E.; Siani, A.; Kenn, K.; de Hadjigeorgiou, C.; Bourdeaudhuij, I.; Eiben, G.; Lissner, L.; Gwozdz, W.; Reisch, L.A.; Pala, V.; et al. IDEFICS consortium. Adherence to the obesity-related lifestyle intervention targets in the IDEFICS study. *Int. J. Obes.* **2014**, *38* (Suppl. S2), 144–151. [CrossRef]
13. Evans, G.W.; MacKenzie, L.; Jones-Rounds, M.L.; Belojevic, G.; Vermeylen, F. Family income and childhood obesity in eight European Cities: The mediating roles of neighborhood characteristics and physical activity. *Soc. Sci. Med.* **2012**, *75*, 477–481. [CrossRef]

14. Fijałkowska, A.; Oblacińska, A.; Stalmach, M. (red.). *Nadwaga i Otyłość u polskich 8-Latków w Świetle Uwarunkowań Biologicznych, Behawioralnych i Społecznych. Raport z Międzynarodowych Badań WHO European Childhood Obesity Surveillance Initiative (COSI)*; Instytut Matki i Dziecka: Warszawa, Poland, 2017; (polish version).
15. Mazur, J.; Małkowska-Szkutnik, A. (red). *Zdrowie Uczniów w 2018 roku na tle Nowego Modelu Badań HBSC*; Instytut Matki i Dziecka: Warszawa, Poland, 2018; (polish version).
16. Mazur, J. (red.). *Zdrowie i Zachowania Zdrowotne Młodzieży Szkolnej w Polsce na tle Wybranych Uwarunkowań Socjodemograficznych. Wyniki Badań HBSC 2014*; Instytut Matki i Dziecka: Warszawa, Poland, 2015; (polish version).
17. Brug, J.; Tak, N.I.; te Velde, S.J.; Bere, E.; de Bourdeaudhuij, I. Taste preferences, liking and other factors related to fruit and vegetable intakes among schoolchildren: Results from observational studies. *Br. J. Nutr.* **2008**, *99*, 7–14. [CrossRef] [PubMed]
18. Mennella, J.A.; Finkbeiner, S.; Lipchock, S.V.; Hwang, L.D.; Reed, D.R. Preferences for salty and sweet tastes are elevated and related to each other during childhood. *PLoS ONE* **2014**, *9*, e92201.
19. Mennella, J.A. Ontogeny of taste preferences: Basic biology and implications for health. *Am. J. Clin. Nutr.* **2014**, *99*, 704S–711S. [CrossRef] [PubMed]
20. Mennella, J.A.; Bobowski, N.K. The sweetness and bitterness of childhood: Insights from basic research on taste preferences. *Physiol. Behav.* **2015**, *152*, 502–507. [CrossRef] [PubMed]
21. Haß, J.; Lischetzke, T.; Hartmann, M. Does the distribution frequency matter? A subgroup specific analysis of the effectiveness of the EU School Fruit and Vegetable Scheme in Germany comparing twice and thrice weekly deliveries. *Public Health Nutr.* **2018**, *21*, 1375–1387. [CrossRef]
22. Mittmann, S.; Austel, A.; Ellrott, T. Behavioural effects of a short school-based fruit and vegetable promotion programme: 5-a-Day for kids. *Health Educ.* **2016**, *116*, 222–237. [CrossRef]
23. Ransley, J.K.; Greenwood, D.C.; Cade, J.E.; Blenkinsop, S.; Schagen, I.; Teeman, D.; Scott, E.; White, G.; Schagen, S. Does the school fruit and vegetable scheme improve children's diet? A non-randomised controlled trial. *J. Epidemiol. Community Health* **2007**, *61*, 699–703. [CrossRef]
24. Knai, C.; Pomerleau, J.; Lock, K.; McKee, M. Getting children to eat more fruit and vegetables: A systematic review. *Prev. Med.* **2006**, *42*, 85–95. [CrossRef] [PubMed]
25. Hoelscher, D.; Kirk, S.; Ritchie, L.; Cunningham-Sabo, L. Academy Positions Committee. Position of the Academy of Nutrition and Dietetics: Interventions for the prevention and treatment of pediatric overweight and obesity. *J. Acad. Nutr. Diet.* **2013**, *113*, 1375–1394. [CrossRef] [PubMed]
26. Wolnicka, K.; Taraszewska, A.; Jaczewska-Schuetz, J.; Jarosz, M. Factors within the family environment such as parents' dietary habits and fruit and vegetable availability have the greatest influence on fruit and vegetable consumption by Polish children. *Public Health Nutr.* **2015**, *18*, 2705–2711. [CrossRef] [PubMed]
27. Pearson, N.; Biddle, S.J.; Gorely, T. Family correlates of fruit and vegetable consumption in children and adolescents: A systematic review. *Public Health Nutr.* **2009**, *12*, 267–283. [CrossRef] [PubMed]
28. Wyse, R.; Campbell, E.; Nathan, N.; Wolfenden, L. Associations between characteristics of the home food environment and fruit and vegetable intake in preschool children: A cross-sectional study. *BMC Public Health* **2011**, *11*, 938–947. [CrossRef] [PubMed]
29. Rasmussen, M.; Krølner, R.; Klepp, K.I.; Lytle, L.; Brug, J.; Bere, E.; Due, P. Determinants of fruit and vegetable consumption among children and adolescents: A review of the literature. Part I: Quantitative studies. *Int. J. Behav. Nutr. Phys. Act.* **2006**, *11*, 22–40. [CrossRef] [PubMed]

International Journal of
Environmental Research and Public Health

MDPI

Article

Evaluation of Stress Levels of Trainee Cardiac Surgery Residents during Training Interventions Using Physiological Stress Parameters

George Awad [1], Robert Pohl [2,*], Sabine Darius [2], Beatrice Thielmann [2], Boris Kuzmin [1], Ingo Slottosch [1], Jens Wippermann [1], Hendrik Schmidt [3,4], Maximilian Philipp Scherner [1] and Irina Böckelmann [2]

1 Department of Cardiothoracic Surgery, Otto-von-Guericke University Magdeburg, Leipziger Strasse 44, 39120 Magdeburg, Germany; george.awad@med.ovgu.de (G.A.); boris.kuzmin@med.ovgu.de (B.K.); ingo.slottosch@med.ovgu.de (I.S.); Herzchirurgie@med.ovgu.de (J.W.); maximilian.scherner@med.ovgu.de (M.P.S.)

2 Department of Occupational Medicine, Otto-von-Guericke University Magdeburg, Leipziger Strasse 44, 39120 Magdeburg, Germany; sabine.darius@med.ovgu.de (S.D.); beatrice.thielmann@med.ovgu.de (B.T.); irina.boeckelmann@med.ovgu.de (I.B.)

3 Clinic for Cardiology and Diabetology, Magdeburg Clinic, Birkenallee 34, 39130 Magdeburg, Germany; kardiologie@klinikum-magdeburg.de

4 University Clinic for Internal Medicine III, Martin Luther University Halle-Wittenberg, Ernst-Grube-Straße 40, 06120 Halle, Germany

* Correspondence: robert.pohl@med.ovgu.de; Tel.: +49-391-67-25126

Citation: Awad, G.; Pohl, R.; Darius, S.; Thielmann, B.; Kuzmin, B.; Slottosch, I.; Wippermann, J.; Schmidt, H.; Scherner, M.P.; Böckelmann, I. Evaluation of Stress Levels of Trainee Cardiac Surgery Residents during Training Interventions Using Physiological Stress Parameters. *Int. J. Environ. Res. Public Health* **2021**, *18*, 11953. https://doi.org/10.3390/ijerph182211953

Academic Editors: Joachim G. Voss and Sandul Yasobant

Received: 22 September 2021
Accepted: 11 November 2021
Published: 14 November 2021

Abstract: Background: This study analysed the psychological and psycho-emotional stress in cardiac surgery. Using heart rate variability (HRV) analysis, it is possible to record intraoperative objective stress responses in surgeons. The aim of the study was to assess with the help of HRV parameters the postulated increased stress levels of cardiac surgeons in training compared to experienced senior cardiothoracic surgeons in exactly the same work situation in order to make qualification-differentiated statements about physiological stress during surgical interventions. Methods: During surgical teaching procedures, long-term ECG data (n = 15 each) for two operating residents and their assisting senior physicians were recorded. Time and frequency domain HRV parameters were analysed. Results: The time-related parasympathetic-dominated HRV parameters RMSSD (19.5 ms vs. 28.1 ms), NN50 (297.67 vs. 693.40), and cardiac interval mean RR (692.8 ms vs. 737.3 ms) indicate a higher stress level in the operating residents compared to the experienced surgeons. The higher stress index (11.61 vs. 8.86) confirms this. Conclusion: Compared to experienced surgeons, operating residents showed lower parasympathetic activity and higher stress levels during cardiac surgery training procedures.

Keywords: heart rate variability; stress responses in surgeons; senior surgeons; surgery residents

1. Introduction

Compared to other occupational groups, the medical profession in general is associated with specific psychosocial stresses [1], and surgical physicians are exposed to additional risks and hazards. As various studies have shown [2–4], it is mainly work-related psychological stress that characterises the everyday life of a surgeon. The hazards resulting from work-related stress can have different health effects on those affected [5,6]. Burnout in particular has been a frequent component of diverse research related to stress identification in surgeons or physicians due to the presence of numerous long-lasting stressors that lead to impairment in the area of mental and psychosomatic health [7]. Prevalence estimates for burnout among physicians in Germany vary from about 4–20% [8]. A major part of the daily work in cardiac surgery consists of performing and assisting in surgical procedures. In this field of activity, surgeons are exposed to specific stressors, which can have an impact not only on the psychological strain, but also on intraoperative performance in the form of complications [9].

Training scenarios are crucial for the cardiac surgery profession, and there is limited availability of surgical simulators similar to those used in pilot training [10]. Moreover, these are not systematically used in training; most learning experiences occur during the operation itself. In this scenario, the senior surgeon also has a special position, especially due to the fact that he or she must constantly monitor and consider several processes (is the physician in training performing the current part of the operation adequately? What are the potential dangers that need to be pointed out? Is it responsible to let the junior surgeon also perform the upcoming steps, or is it necessary to take over the operation?). The above-mentioned processes are repeated continuously throughout the course of the operation, which also results in an especially tense situation for the instructor. In addition, the senior surgeon has the ultimate legal and medical responsibility for the course of the operation and for the patient.

Therefore, the aim of the current study was to determine:

1. The extent to which stress levels affect heart rate variability (HRV) in trainee cardiac surgeons.
2. The difference in stress levels between junior surgeon trainees and senior surgeons during cardiac surgery teaching procedures.
3. Whether preventive and health-promoting measures can be derived from the resulting findings and conclusions can be drawn for clinical practice, for example, in terms of arranging the operating room schedule.
4. Which valuable findings regarding stress should be generated for occupational groups in the context of occupational medicine and science.

However, mental stress in the operating room is difficult to measure. A number of vegetative and objective stress parameters to measure work stress/work strain have already been established [11]. Due to increasingly smaller measurement instruments and lower costs [12], the analysis of HRV is considered a feasible objective non-invasive measurement method in occupational medicine/occupational sciences in order to make statements about the degree of stress in a wide range of occupational groups as well as about the quality of the regulation of the cardiovascular system. In a review by Thielmann and Böckelmann 2016 [11], various studies related to the psychological stress of surgeons were pointed out, and it was confirmed that the heart rate increases in stressed surgeons and the HRV parameters show lower expressions.

2. Study Design and Sample Description

In a cooperative study by the Department of Occupational Medicine at the Otto-von-Guericke University Magdeburg and the Clinic for Cardiac and Thoracic Surgery of the University Hospital Magdeburg, the objective stress of residents and senior physicians during surgical teaching procedures in aortocoronary bypass (ACB) operations was investigated over a period of 6 months. The positive vote of the ethics committee of the Otto-von-Guericke University Magdeburg under the registration number 2020/185/19 is available, and the ethical standards of the Declaration of Helsinki in its currently valid version were observed. The current study is concerned with the analysis of recorded intraoperative stress parameters in assistant and senior physicians in the same work situation. On the basis of the results, statements will be made on the objective stress by means of the collected HRV parameters. Thus, the differences in stress levels during surgical teaching interventions between operating residents and assisting senior physicians will be shown.

The analysed ACB procedures were all performed using a heart-lung machine in mild hypothermia and cardioplegic arrest. These were elective procedures in patients with stable coronary 3-vessel disease. The ACB procedures considered for this study were performed in the daytime schedule starting in the second position of the surgical schedule, that is, usually between 11 am and 2 pm. This had the advantage that the influence of circadian rhythm on the HRV of the subjects could be ignored [13].

The physicians in training operated under the assistance of the senior physician volunteers. Intraoperative times were documented by an external person using a pre-prepared surgical protocol. In each case, the time from the start of the heart-lung machine to complete weaning from cardiopulmonary bypass was analysed.

The maximum number of surgical trainee residents within the clinic who could be considered and used as surgeons for teaching procedures is limited to two. This is a result of the number of appropriate training cases from across the surgical spectrum and the necessary frequency of training surgeries to achieve learning success. The two residents volunteered to participate in this collaborative study as subjects. The residents had previously performed 10 and 15 ACB procedures, respectively, under supervision. Both subjects had been in residency training for cardiac surgery for 6 years [14]. Before and during their surgical training they were able to participate in various training activities to learn surgical skills, for example, suture training in animal experiments or on cadavers. The attending senior physicians were also regularly involved in surgical training in the role of instructors.

3. Methodology, Heart Rate Variability Analysis, and Sample Description

The two male residents (age group 30–35 years) and the five senior physicians (age group 35–55 years) were healthy individuals without any pre-existing diseases. None of them were on any medications. Body mass index (BMI) breaks down within the sample between normal weight (1 resident with a BMI of 21.7 and 2 senior physicians with a BMI of 24.7 and 24.9) and slightly overweight (1 resident with a BMI of 29.7 and one senior physician with 27.4). The residents were non-smokers and there was one smoker among the senior physicians.

The data from the 30 24-h ECG recordings (2 ECGs each for 15 operations) of both groups of subjects served as the basis for the subsequent HRV analysis. The ECG recordings were made using a 2-lead ECG device (model MT-101, Schiller AG, Switzerland). The quality criteria of the Task Force of the European Society of Cardiology and the North American Society of Pacing and Electrophysiology [15] and of the AWMF-s2k guideline [12] were considered. The 24-h ECG recordings of all subjects were performed in sections of equal length and analysed in equal segments of the same length (180 min in the same work situation).

The data series from the NN intervals recorded at a sampling frequency of 1000 Hz was transferred to the Medilog DARWIN software. Artifacts were first automatically verified and in a second step, checked for plausibility by trained medical personnel; if necessary, these were manually corrected. The data series of successive cardiointervals was exported to a text file (.txt format) for subsequent HRV analysis and then processed using the Kubios HRV Premium program (Kubios, Kuopio, Finland) [16,17].

The mathematically calculated HRV parameters in the time and frequency domain as well as non-linear methods belong to the informative stress indicators. For the current study, selected HRV parameters were chosen (Table 1), which according to the AWMF-s2k guideline [12] allow conclusions to be drawn about mental stress that has occurred.

This HRV combines a variety of mathematically calculated parameters that characterize the variance, rhythmicity, or complexity of a time series of successive cardiac actions, the so-called NN intervals [12]. In this context, HRV is based to a significant extent on the tone of the vagus nerve, which excites the atria of the heart and modulates the self-sustained sinus rhythm of the sinus or Keith flack node. Especially in body rest and recovery phases, parasympathetic activity predominates and in a chronic stress state, sympathetic activity dominates [18]. This interplay of the sympathetic and parasympathetic nervous system can be estimated in a more differentiated way by HRV analysis during different demands [12].

Table 1. Explanation of the HRV parameters used according to the AWMF-s2k guideline [12].

HRV Parameters	Explanation	Activity as Part of the Autonomic Nervous System
	Time domain parameters	
Mean HR [1/min]	Heart rate	Sympathetic and parasympathetic nervous system
Mean RR or NN [ms]	Distance between two R-pins or NN-intervals	No clear assignment
RMSSD [ms] (Root Mean Square of successive differences)	Square root of the mean of the sum of all squared differences between adjacent RR intervals	Parasympathetic nervous system
NN50	Number of consecutive RR intervals that differ from each other by more than 50 ms	Parasympathetic nervous system
	Frequency domain parameters	
FFT_LF_po [ms^2]	Power density spectrum in the frequency range from 0.04 to 0.15 Hz	Sympathetic and parasympathetic nervous system
FFT_HF_po [ms^2]	Power density spectrum in the frequency range from 0.15 to 0.40 Hz	Parasympathetic nervous system
FFT LF/HF	Measure of sympatho-vagal balance as quotient of LF and HF	Sympathetic and parasympathetic nervous system
	Stress, PNS, and SNS Index	
Stress Index	The stress index is the square root (to make the index normally distributed) of the Baevsky stress index, where values from 150–500 are claimed as the normal range (12.2–22.4 when the square root is applied)	Sympathetic nervous system
PNS index	Activity of the parasympathetic nervous system described by the mean values of RR, RMSSD, and SD 1(%)	Parasympathetic nervous system
SNS index	Sympathetic nervous system activity described by mean values of mean HR, stress index, and SD2 (%)	Sympathetic nervous system

The methods of HRV analysis or the HRV parameters obtained from them are divided into time, frequency, and nonlinear domains. In the analyses of the time domain, the NN intervals are mathematically evaluated with respect to their variance and reproduced in rhythm measures with a time dimension (usually ms) or in percentages. In the frequency domain, a power density spectrum is calculated from the stored RR series (NN intervals). In particular, the fast Fourier transform (FFT) and autoregression (AR) are the most widely used methods. In nonlinear analysis of HRV parameters, different methods are used to map the structure and complexity of heart rate time courses. These methods include the Lorenz plot or a trend-correcting fluctuation analysis [12].

In addition to the three main domain analyses, there is also the opportunity to gain an overview of the level of HRV parameters (divided into parasympathetic nervous system (PNS) tone and sympathetic nervous system (SNS) tone). In addition, it is possible to obtain a representation of the time periods in which subjects were in stress zones during a recording via the stress index [19].

Statistical Analysis

IBM SPSS Statistics 26 (IBM Corp., Armonk, NY, USA) was used for statistical analysis. The Kolmogorov–Smirnov test was used to test the interval-scaled data for normal distribution. Homogeneity of variances was checked using Levene's test. Depending on the equality of variances, the significance of the robust t test was determined. The level of significance was set to $p < 0.05$.

4. Results

Table 2 provides an overview of the time- and frequency-related HRV parameters used with the respective significance level (p). The mean values (mv) and the standard deviation (sd) of the HRV parameters of the residents were compared with those of the senior physicians.

Table 2. Comparison of selected time-related HRV parameters as well as parameters from FFT analysis during ACB interventions in the cannulation to decannulation phase between the operating residents (n = 15) and the assisting senior physicians (n = 15).

Parameter	Residents			Senior Physicians			p-Value
	mv		sd	mv		sd	
Mean RR [ms]	692.8	±	56.59	737.3	±	42.43	0.021
Mean HR [1/min]	87.2	±	7.34	81.6	±	4.85	0.022
RMSSD [ms]	19.5	±	6.42	28.1	±	9.69	0.008
NN50	297.67	±	379.03	693.40	±	479.68	0.018
FFT_LF_po [ms^2]	936.41	±	491.49	1658.90	±	893.40	0.012
FFT_HF_po [ms^2]	148.05	±	105.99	276.42	±	266.82	0.094
FFT_LF/HF	7.2	±	1.76	7.2	±	2.84	0.974

All time-related parameters differ from each other ($p < 0.05$). The mean HR outside the operating room showed the same range in both groups (residents: 76.8 [1/min] vs. 77.7 [1/min] senior physician). Thus, both groups started with similar HR. Based on the lower parameters of mean RR (692.8 ms vs. 737.3 ms), RMSSD (19.5 ms vs. 28.1 ms), NN50 (297.67 vs. 693.40), as well as pNN50 (2.61% vs. 6.96%), the group of operating residents showed a higher stress level than the assisting senior physicians. This can also be seen in the higher mean HR value of 87.2 vs. 81.6 beats/min. The power density spectrum in the LF range (ms^2) shows significantly higher values ($p = 0.012$) in the senior physicians (936.41 ms^2 vs. 1658.90 ms^2). The mean values of the LF/HF do not differ from each other ($p > 0.05$).

Table 3 contains the comparison of the stress HRV parameters of the examined groups.

Table 3. Comparison of the stress HRV parameters during ACB interventions in the cannulation to decannulation phase between the operating residents (n = 15) and the assisting senior physicians (n = 15).

Parameter	Residents			Senior Physicians			p-Value
	mv		sd	mv		sd	
PNS Index	−1.76	±	0.32	−1.32	±	0.45	0.004
SNS Index	1.84	±	0.62	1.01	±	0.56	0.001
Stress Index	11.61	±	2.17	8.68	±	1.61	0.000

All three of the listed parameters (Table 3) differ from each other in the two groups studied ($p < 0.05$). The activity of the parasympathetic part (parameter PNS-Index) was lower in the residents than in the senior physicians (−1.76 to −1.32). The activity of the sympathetic part, reflected in the SNS index, was higher in the residents (1.84) than in the senior physicians (1.01).

5. Discussion

Various studies have already used HRV to objectify stress in the medical profession. A systematic review on the workload of emergency physicians shows that the established parasympathetically mediated HRV parameters seem to be suitable parameters for objectifying stress [20]. Using HRV analysis, Mandegar and colleagues [21], for example, came to the conclusion that the type of surgery has an influence on the stress level of the surgeon. The stress level is higher in "off-pump" surgery (without heart-lung machine) than in "on-pump" coronary surgery (with heart-lung machine).

Demirtas [22] concluded, based on HRV analyses performed in surgical activities, that the assistance of a senior surgeon should be specifically included in studies related to psychological stress. The extent to which stress levels during surgical procedures are dependent on experience has hardly been investigated. While some studies make reference to this, there is potential for further surveys to elucidate differences between the stress levels of experienced and inexperienced physicians [23,24].

Performing operations in general is known to lead to a higher stress level [11]. In examining stress levels, our study focused on the comparison of residents in training and their senior facilitator. The collected physiological stress parameters of this study extend the existing research contributions on stress reactions in surgeons during surgical activities. Nevertheless, the results should not be generalized. On the one hand, the study presented here is a small sample, and on the other hand there is no control group or comparative HRV parameters from rest periods, for example. Moreover, in cardiac surgery, the use of a heart-lung machine and the ischemia time of the heart during coronary anastomoses are additional stressors due to the time factor, which is decisive in the course of the operation. Various factors that may have influenced the stress level of the surgeons could not be completely taken into account. These factors can lead to falsification of HRV values. These include workloads outside the operating room. The recording of sleep times and the consumption of beverages containing caffeine are based on the information provided by the subjects. Sleep-related impairments may be associated with clinical treatment failures in physicians [25]. Whether caffeine consumption can influence cardiovascular autonomic activity has not yet been adequately evaluated [26]. Nevertheless, caffeine should be avoided for half an hour before the measurement [12]. Within the study, there may be possible bias due to age as a confounding factor. The influence of age on HRV [27] and the occurring decline in cognitive and physical abilities should be considered in similar HRV analyses. One further aspect is that one of the analysed subjects is a smoker. Smoking is not a contraindication for HRV measurements [12]. Active smoking can affect heart rate and lead to a reduction in HRV [28,29]. However, as our proband was not a heavy smoker and smoking normally took place in the evening hours, we did not consider this as a significant influence on our HRV measurements.

The higher sympathetic activities of the residents confirm that young surgeons are exposed to a particularly high level of stress in the operating room. This is especially evident in our data when looking at the stress index and the defined stress zones of Tarvainen et al. [19] following the Baevski index. There, both values of the physician groups were in the normal range (7.1–12.2), but the residents nevertheless showed a higher sympathetic activity (11.61) than the senior physicians (8.68). In the RMSSD zones defined according to Tarvainen et al. [19], the assistant physicians with an RMSSD of 19.5 ms are in the lower zone (12–27 ms) and the senior physicians with 28.1 ms are in the normal zone (27–72 ms). In this respect, in comparison to the senior physicians, lower parasympathetic activity can be seen in the residents. During the survey, the senior physicians participating in the study were exposed to the challenge of providing adequate guidance to their younger colleagues, and at the same time bearing the responsibility for a complication-free surgical procedure. Nevertheless, the HRV parameters among assisting senior physicians showed less stress and more relaxation during coronary surgery teaching procedures.

Rieger et al. [23] analysed the intra-individual workload differences between surgeon and assistant using the objective physiological parameters of heart rate, respiratory rate, and skin temperature. Unlike the current study, in Rieger et al., the work of a primary surgeon did not lead to a higher workload; however, the setting of surgical training was not investigated. When analysing the stress levels of experienced and inexperienced surgeons during a cardiac surgery procedure, Kuhn et al. [24] concluded that surgical experience was not associated with reduced stress levels. However, this work was based on analysis of the heart rate and sympatho-vagal balance. In summary, the current work represents the first comprehensive study of stress within cardiac surgery training based on detailed statistical analysis of the HRV parameters shown.

Prichard et al. [30] studied HRV parameters in experienced and less experienced surgeons in a cross-over design with 50 thyroidectomies and 50 lobectomies each. There, the more inexperienced surgeons showed a higher stress level when operating than when assisting. Despite a lack of statistical significance, this was shown by lower RMSSD and pNN50 parameters as well as by a higher LF/HF ratio. This is in agreement with the results of the current study, where the parameters used to detect parasympathetic activity (RMSSD, NN50, and pNN50) also have lower expressions. For the remaining parameters from the time domain, both sympathetic and parasympathetic activity are discussed [18].

Taking into account the fact that many stressors in the daily work of residents also occur outside the operating room (including ward work, night and emergency duties, the degree of responsibility towards patients and superiors [31], and that the medical profession is characterized by above-average working hours), young physicians belong to a group that is at high risk of health problems.

Reference values and analysis possibilities of HRV were already mentioned in 1996 in the recommendations of the Task Force of the European Society of Cardiology and the North American Society of Pacing and Electrophysiology [15]. The results presented here can only be compared with these to a limited extent. The reference values published at that time were based on HRV analyses lying down and on 5 min time intervals. In addition, studies show that significant differences in the analysed HRV parameters exist when directly comparing old tape recorder systems (from the recommendations of the European Society of Cardiology and the North American Society of Pacing and Electrophysiology) vs. the newer hard disk recorders [32].

The professional group of physicians and especially the specialist discipline of surgeons should be the focus for early preventive approaches with regard to psychological stress in the future. Young physicians in particular should be considered as a potential target group for interventions and, if necessary, therapeutic measures. Resilience training can be used to learn methods and techniques to strengthen one's own resilience. Studies on the benefits of resilience programs among healthcare professionals (including physicians) suggest at least short-term benefits. After resilience training, they show a short-term increase in resilience and decrease in depression symptoms [33]. Prospective surgeons might benefit from structured training to increase their perceived stress resources or stress coping skills.

It must be taken into account that the acquisition of surgical skills creates high levels of stress for young surgeons. Nevertheless, early skill acquisition as well as stress adaptation strategies should be encouraged with the help of regular training programs (e.g., Skills Lab). It has been shown that (in laparoscopic procedures) there is indeed a correlation between skill improvements and stress reduction in novice surgeons. There is a correlation (in laparoscopic procedures) between skill improvement and stress reduction in trainee surgeons [34]. This indicates that repeated confrontation with a learning task can promote positive stress adaptations. The relationship between skill improvement and stress reduction in trainee surgeons has also been demonstrated [34]. Studies on the effects of stress management courses among physicians are scarce. However, surveys of students do show positive effects on physiological stress parameters [35,36]. There is still a need for research using HRV analysis to demonstrate the effects of different training programs on the stress levels of surgeons.

6. Conclusions

The present study analysed physiological stress responses during cardiac surgery training procedures using HRV analysis. Our study indicates that less experienced residents exhibit higher psychological stress levels than the more experienced supervising senior surgeons. Therefore, focus on well-designed training programs might lead to improved stress management and an enhanced learning progress. Further evaluation of stress response during cardiac surgery procedures is required.

Author Contributions: Conceptualization, R.P., G.A., I.B. and M.P.S.; Data curation, G.A., I.B. and M.P.S.; Formal analysis, R.P. and I.B.; Investigation, G.A., R.P. and I.B.; Methodology, R.P., G.A., I.B. and M.P.S.; Project administration, R.P., G.A., I.B. and M.P.S.; Resources, R.P., G.A., I.B. and M.P.S.; Software, R.P., G.A., I.B. and M.P.S.; Supervision, S.D., B.T., I.B. and M.P.S.; Validation, R.P., G.A., I.S. and M.P.S.; Visualization, B.T., B.K., J.W. and H.S.; Writing—original draft, R.P., G.A. and I.B.; Writing—review and editing, S.D., B.T., B.K., I.S., J.W., H.S. and M.P.S. All authors have read and agreed to the published version of the manuscript.

Funding: This research received no external funding.

Institutional Review Board Statement: The study was conducted according to the guidelines of the Declaration of Helsinki, and approved by the Institutional Review Board (or Ethics Committee) of the ethics committee of the Otto-von-Guericke University Magdeburg (protocol code 2020/185/19, 16 December 2019).

Informed Consent Statement: Informed consent was obtained from all subjects involved in the study.

Data Availability Statement: The data can be requested from the author team.

Conflicts of Interest: The authors declare no conflict of interest.

References

1. von Voltmer, E.; Kieschke, U.; Spahn, C. Arbeitsbezogenes Verhalten und Erleben bei Ärzten im dritten bis achten Berufsjahr. *Z. Psychosom. Med. Psychother.* **2007**, *53*, 244–257. [CrossRef] [PubMed]
2. von dem Knesebeck, O.; Klein, J.; Frie, K.G.; Blum, K.; Siegrist, J. Psychosocial stress among hospital doctors in surgical fields: Results of a nationwide survey in Germany. *Dtsch. Arztebl. Int.* **2010**, *107*, 248–253. [CrossRef]
3. Pereira, D.; Müller, P.; Elfering, A. Workflow interruptions, social stressors from supervisor(s) and attention failure in surgery personnel. *Ind. Health* **2015**, *53*, 427–433. [CrossRef]
4. Kern, M.; Buia, A.; Tonus, C.; Weigel, T.F.; Dittmar, R.; Hanisch, E.; Zapf, D. Psychische Belastungen, Ressourcen und Wohlbefinden von Chirurgen in Deutschland: Eine Querschnittsstudie. *Der Chirurg* **2019**, *90*, 576–584. [CrossRef] [PubMed]
5. Kivimäki, M.; Virtanen, M.; Vartia, M.; Elovainio, M.; Vahtera, J.; Keltikangas-Järvinen, L. Workplace bullying and the risk of cardiovascular disease and depression. *Occup. Environ. Med.* **2003**, *60*, 779–783. [CrossRef]

6. Huth, C.; Thorand, B.; Baumert, J.; Kruse, J.; Emeny, R.T.; Schneider, A.; Meisinger, C.; Ladwig, K.-H. Job strain as a risk factor for the onset of type 2 diabetes mellitus: Findings from the MONICA/KORA Augsburg cohort study. *Psychosom. Med.* **2014**, *76*, 562–568. [CrossRef]
7. Unrath, M. Psychische Gesundheit von Ärzten in Deutschland: Prävalenz psychischer Erkrankungen und Risikofaktoren. *Hessisches Ärzteblatt* **2012**, *2*, 86–90.
8. Beschoner, P.; Limbrecht-Ecklundt, K.; Jerg-Bretzke, L. Psychische Gesundheit von Ärzten: Burnout, Depression, Angst und Substanzgebrauch im Kontext des Arztberufes. *Nervenarzt* **2019**, *90*, 961–974. [CrossRef] [PubMed]
9. Anton, N.E.; Montero, P.N.; Howley, L.D.; Brown, C.; Stefanidis, D. What stress coping strategies are surgeons relying upon during surgery? *Am. J. Surg.* **2015**, *210*, 846–851. [CrossRef]
10. Brunner, S.; Kröplin, J.; Meyer, H.-J.; Schmitz-Rixen, T.; Fritz, T. Einsatz chirurgischer Simulatoren in der Weiterbildung—eine deutschlandweite Analyse. *Chirurg* **2021**, *92*, 1040–1049. [CrossRef] [PubMed]
11. Thielmann, B.; Boeckelmann, I. Herzfrequenzvariabilität als Beanspruchungsindikator für psychische Belastungen bei Chirurgen—ein Literaturüberblick. *Zentralblatt für Chirurgie* **2016**, *141*, 577–582. [CrossRef] [PubMed]
12. Sammito, S.; Thielmann, B.; Seibt, R.; Klussmann, A.; Weippert, M.; Böckelmann, I. Nutzung der Herzschlagfrequenz und der Herzfrequenzvariabilität in der Arbeitsmedizin und der Arbeitswissenschaft: Reg-Nr. 002-042. 2014. Available online: https://www.awmf.org/uploads/tx_szleitlinien/002-042l_S2k_Herzschlagfrequenz_Herzfrequenzvariabilit%C3%A4t_2014-07.pdf (accessed on 12 November 2021).
13. Sammito, S.; Sammito, W.; Böckelmann, I. The circadian rhythm of heart rate variability. *Biol. Rhythm. Res.* **2016**, *47*, 717–730. [CrossRef]
14. Bundesärztekammer. Bundesärztekammer. (Muster-)Weiterbildungsordnung. 2018. Available online: https://www.bundesaerztekammer.de/fileadmin/user_upload/downloads/pdf-Ordner/Weiterbildung/20210630_MWBO_2018.pdf (accessed on 1 November 2021).
15. Task Force of the European Society of Cardiology and the North American Society of Pacing and Electrophysiology. Heart rate variability: Standards of measurement, physiological interpretation and clinical use. *Circulation* **1996**, *93*, 1043–1065. [CrossRef]
16. Niskanen, J.-P.; Tarvainen, M.P.; Ranta-Aho, P.O.; Karjalainen, P.A. Software for advanced HRV analysis. *Comput. Methods Programs Biomed.* **2004**, *76*, 73–81. [CrossRef]
17. Tarvainen, M.P.; Niskanen, J.-P.; Lipponen, J.A.; Ranta-Aho, P.O.; Karjalainen, P.A. Kubios HRV-heart rate variability analysis software. *Comput. Methods Programs Biomed.* **2014**, *113*, 210–220. [CrossRef] [PubMed]
18. Sammito, S.; Böckelmann, I. Analyse der Herzfrequenzvariabilität. Mathematische Basis und praktische Anwendung. *Herz* **2015**, *40* (Suppl. 1), 76–84. [CrossRef]
19. Tarvainen, M.P.; Lipponen, J.A.; Niskanen, J.P.; Ranta-Aho, P.O. Kubios HRV (ver. 3.5) User's Guide: ©Kubios Oy. 2021. Available online: https://www.kubios.com/downloads/Kubios_HRV_Users_Guide.pdf (accessed on 12 November 2021).
20. Thielmann, B.; Pohl, R.; Böckelmann, I. Heart rate variability as a strain indicator for psychological stress for emergency physicians during work and alert intervention: A systematic review. *J. Occup. Med. Toxicol.* **2021**, *16*, 24. [CrossRef]
21. Mandegar, M.H.; Saidi, B.; Roshanali, F.; Alaeddini, F. A Comparison of Cardiac Surgeon's Stress Level During Off- Pump and On-Pump CABG by Cardiac Variability Indices, A Case-Report. *J. Clin. Exp. Cardiol* **2010**, *1*, 112. [CrossRef]
22. Demirtas, Y.; Tulmac, M.; Yavuzer, R.; Yalcin, R.; Ayhan, S.; Latifoglu, O.; Atabay, K. Plastic surgeon's life: Marvelous for mind, exhausting for body. *Plast. Reconstr. Surg.* **2004**, *114*, 923–931. [CrossRef]
23. Rieger, A.; Fenger, S.; Neubert, S.; Weippert, M.; Kreuzfeld, S.; Stoll, R. Psychophysical workload in the operating room: Primary surgeon versus assistant. *Surg. Endosc.* **2014**, *29*, 1990–1998. [CrossRef]
24. Kuhn, E.W.; Choi, Y.-H.; Schönherr, M.; Liakopoulos, O.J.; Rahmanian, P.B.; Choi, C.Y.-U.; Wittwer, T.; Wahlers, T. Intraoperative stress in cardiac surgery: Attendings versus residents. *J. Surg. Res.* **2013**, *182*, e43–e49. [CrossRef]
25. Trockel, M.T.; Menon, N.K.; Rowe, S.G.; Stewart, M.T.; Smith, R.; Lu, M.; Kim, P.K.; Quinn, M.A.; Lawrence, E.; Marchalik, D.; et al. Assessment of Physician Sleep and Wellness, Burnout, and Clinically Significant Medical Errors. *JAMA Netw. Open* **2020**, *3*, e2028111. [CrossRef] [PubMed]
26. De Oliveira, R.A.M.; Araújo, L.F.; de Figueiredo, R.C.; Goulart, A.C.; Schmidt, M.I.; Barreto, S.M.; Ribeiro, A.L.P. Coffee Consumption and Heart Rate Variability: The Brazilian Longitudinal Study of Adult Health (ELSA-Brasil) Cohort Study. *Nutrients* **2017**, *9*, 741. [CrossRef]
27. Garavaglia, L.; Gulich, D.; Defeo, M.M.; Thomas Mailland, J.; Irurzun, I.M. The effect of age on the heart rate variability of healthy subjects. *PLoS ONE* **2021**, *16*, e0255894. [CrossRef] [PubMed]
28. Cagirci, G.; Cay, S.; Karakurt, O.; Eryasar, N.; Kaya, V.; Canga, A.; Yesilay, A.B.; Kilic, H.; Topaloglu, S.; Aras, D.; et al. Influence of heavy cigarette smoking on heart rate variability and heart rate turbulence parameters. *Ann. Noninvasive Electrocardiol.* **2009**, *14*, 327–332. [CrossRef]
29. Dinas, P.C.; Koutedakis, Y.; Flouris, A.D. Effects of active and passive tobacco cigarette smoking on heart rate variability. *Int. J. Cardiol.* **2013**, *163*, 109–115. [CrossRef] [PubMed]
30. Prichard, R.S.; O'Neill, C.J.; Oucharek, J.J.; Holmes, C.Y.V.; Delbridge, L.W.; Sywak, M.S. A prospective study of heart rate variability in endocrine surgery: Surgical training increases consultant's mental strain. *J. Surg. Educ.* **2012**, *69*, 453–458. [CrossRef]
31. Bergner, T. Burn-out bei Ärzten: Lebensaufgabe statt Lebens-Aufgabe. Mindestens 20 Prozent der Ärzte leiden am Burn-out-Syndrom.Die Entwicklung emotionaler Kompetenz kann davor schützen. *Dtsch. Arztebl.* **2004**, *101*, 2232–2234.

32. Körber, T.; Ismer, B.; Knorre, G.H. von. Die klinische Bedeutung der Verwendung unterschiedlicher Rekordertechnologien für die Ergebnisse der Analyse der Herzfrequenzvariabilität aus dem Langzeit-EKG. *Herzschrittmacherther. Elektrophysiol.* **2000**, *11*, 110–116. [CrossRef]
33. Kunzler, A.M.; Helmreich, I.; Chmitorz, A.; König, J.; Binder, H.; Wessa, M.; Lieb, K. Psychological interventions to foster resilience in healthcare professionals. *Cochrane Database Syst. Rev.* **2020**, *7*, CD012527. [CrossRef]
34. Crewther, B.T.; Shetty, K.; Jarchi, D.; Selvadurai, S.; Cook, C.J.; Leff, D.R.; Darzi, A.; Yang, G.-Z. Skill acquisition and stress adaptations following laparoscopic surgery training and detraining in novice surgeons. *Surg. Endosc.* **2016**, *30*, 2961–2968. [CrossRef] [PubMed]
35. Thielmann, B.; Ackermann, E.; Frommer, J.; Böckelmann, I. Beurteilung eines Stressbewältigungskurses für Studierende. *Präv Gesundheitsf* **2010**, *5*, 282–288. [CrossRef]
36. Thielmann, B.; Schumann, X.; Ackermann, E.; Frommer, J.; Böckelmann, I. *Psychophysiologische Untersuchungen zu Studiumsbezogenen Belastungen bei Teilnehmern eines Stressbewältigungskurses für Studenten*; 49; Jahrestagung der Deutschen Gesellschaft für Arbeitsmedizin und Umweltmedizin e.V. (DGAUM): Aachen, Germany, 2009; pp. 439–440.

International Journal of
Environmental Research and Public Health

MDPI

Article

The Spirit of Adventure: A Driver of Attractiveness of the Hospitality Industry for Young People during a Pandemic Crisis

Adriana Burlea-Schiopoiu [1,*], Mara Del Baldo [2] and Samuel O. Idowu [3]

1 Department of Management, Marketing, Business Administration, University of Craiova, 200585 Craiova, Romania
2 Department of Economics, Society and Politics, University of Urbino Carlo Bo, 61029 Urbino, Italy; mara.delbaldo@uniurb.it
3 Guildhall School of Business and Law, London Metropolitan University, London EC2M 6SQ, UK; s.idowu@londonmet.ac.uk
* Correspondence: adriana.burlea@edu.ucv.ro; Tel.: +40-721-195-174

Abstract: The COVID-19 pandemic has strongly affected tourism and leisure activities worldwide, especially in the hospitality and tourism sectors. Within this context, this study aimed to evaluate the impact of the pandemic on the future attractiveness of the hospitality industry (HI) to young people. The conceptual model underpinning the empirical research proposes a direct relationship between job attractiveness and the spirit of youth adventure. Findings prove that young people are enthusiastic about working in the HI because they can easily practice their creative ideas. Communicating with other people and dealing with clients' complaints is challenging for them in the pandemic crisis created by COVID-19. The results are of interest to policymakers in terms of suggestions on how to transform the challenges into opportunities by using the constraints imposed by the pandemic crisis that have limited the socialisation between people, enhancing the creativity of young people, and motivating them to work in the HI. Moreover, our research provides managers and other decisionmakers with some motivational factors to increase the attractiveness of their companies to young people and suggestions helpful to scholars involved in HI research to cultivate resilience capabilities by giving them inherent skills.

Keywords: attractiveness; COVID-19; hospitality industry; job insecurity; perceptions; spirit of adventure; young people

Citation: Burlea-Schiopoiu, A.; Baldo, M.D.; Idowu, S.O. The Spirit of Adventure: A Driver of Attractiveness of the Hospitality Industry for Young People during a Pandemic Crisis. *Int. J. Environ. Res. Public Health* **2022**, *19*, 1913. https://doi.org/10.3390/ijerph19041913

Academic Editor: Joachim G. Voss

Received: 22 December 2021
Accepted: 7 February 2022
Published: 9 February 2022

1. Introduction

In late 2019, our world was besieged by an unprecedented pandemic that has caused severe devastation to people's lives, the global economy, the social and political environments globally [1]. It was reported that about 50 million people had lost their lives during that pandemic [2]. Governments of all nations are doing their utmost to support corporate bodies and individual citizens. While nation-states have begun reopening their economies, the surge in infections (i.e., the second and third waves) has raised calls for modified quarantine policies. However, the pandemic continues to plague all sectors of the global economy [3] and generate uncertainty.

The hospitality industry (HI) employs over 200 million people across the globe [4]; economically, it is a source of many jobs and supports livelihoods of millions of workers and their families. Moreover, it plays a crucial role in societalisation that the current pandemic has severely compromised, pointing out how extreme disruptive events affect the role of business in society [5].

Travel bans and border closure policies and restrictions have significantly disrupted tourism and leisure activities around the globe [6]. Strategies to flatten the COVID-19 curve (i.e., community lockdowns, social distancing, stay-at-home orders, travel and mobility restrictions) have resulted in many forced widespread requirements due to the risk of infection and death among the vulnerable community segments [7,8].

Consequently, these strategies significantly decreased the demand for hospitality businesses that were allowed to continue to operate [9].

The negative impacts of these actions have threatened the survival of many businesses, making employees redundant in large numbers. Top groups, such as Hilton and Marriot, have announced furloughs and Southwest Airlines asked its labour unions to accept pay cuts to avoid layoffs [10]. The World Travel and Tourism Council estimates that globally, somewhere between 98 to almost 200 million travel and tourism jobs are in jeopardy worldwide [11].

As a result of this extraordinary scenario, a growing number of researchers have turned attention to the implications for the future of tourism [12,13] and tourist destinations [14]. The behaviours of the HI operators are related to their critical concerns regarding the changes necessary to tackle the pandemic outbreaks and prepare for the next normality.

Taking into consideration the objective of our research to evaluate the impact of the pandemic crisis generated by COVID-19 on the future attractiveness of the hospitality industry (HI) to young people, we organized the paper as follows: Section 2 explores the literature on the HI in the COVID-19 scenario and introduces our hypotheses; Section 3 describes the methodology employed to present the theoretical model of the research, followed by data analysis and validation. The findings and the emerging issues are explored in Section 4. Section 5 closes the paper with our conclusions.

2. Theoretical Background and Hypotheses Development

In the recent years, several works have triggered an intense and ongoing debate on the HI in the face of the current global pandemic. A systemic review of the prior studies pointed out the most relevant topics and the methodologies used to investigate the impact of COVID-19 on the HI [15]. The studies mainly identified the implications relative to the recovery of the HI market demands, discussing the resumption of activities during and after the pandemic, the revenue losses, and the COVID-19 spread patterns in the HI, including event, cruise, hotel, and restaurant industries. The issues related to travel behaviours, preferences of customers, and social costs of the pandemic received less attention than several types of research that have deepened the understanding of implications of job losses and employment of hospitality workforce, safety, and health aspects.

2.1. The Impact of COVID-19 on the HI and the Disease-Related Discussion: The Issues of Vulnerability and Resilience

Most of the studies gravitate towards disease-related discussions [16–18]. The emerging research field of HI and infectious diseases addresses the key concerns, ways of coping, business model innovation [19], risk perceptions [20], crisis management in extreme contexts [21], and the changes undertaken by the HI [22]. The impact of COVID-19 on the HI mirrors what occurred during previous pandemics such as SARS and MERS [23] and other disasters like the 2004 Indian Ocean Tsunami [24].

The effects of similar past events have been carefully considered to help frame the historical context [25,26] and understand and predict the consequences of the measures to fight the COVID-19 pandemic.

Baum et al. [27] highlight the immediate impacts of the current pandemic on the hospitality workforce, offering a critical assessment of the effects on the global hospitality workforce at three levels: macro (global, policy, government), meso (organisational), and micro (employee). At the macro level, the structural features of the HI generate precarity and vulnerability for hospitality workers. At the meso/organisational level, those companies that assign great attention to human resource management continue to improve their "people first" approaches [28] despite the uncertainty and look for creative ways to generate revenues, thereby employing people and ensuring a future for the business. In this vein, Reynolds et al. [29] consider that the HI employees have a role in ensuring the entertaining atmosphere and positively contributing to customer experience [30].

HI workers' mood, motivation, and wellness have repercussions for providing service and health comprising physical, mental, and social well-being [31]. In this regard, prior studies on the tourism worker context have pointed out that long work hours and insufficient breaks are linked with reduced motivation and poorer customer service in the HI [32] and, more broadly, with increased turnover, especially in young hospitality and tourism employees [33]. In a similar vein, we claim that the young people who want to access the HI and work in this sector face many challenges due to the current pandemic. COVID-19 generated mobility restrictions at the microlevel that have negatively affected people's capacity to participate in hospitality and tourism activities [34].

A vulnerability assessment based on the perceptions of practitioners (including business leaders among cruise lines, hotels, travel agencies, and touristic attractions) investigated through questionnaires and interviews depicts a grim picture in the short term, marked by economic loss, recovery concerns, and uncertainty. However, the prior studies did not investigate youth perceptions and their expected behaviours concerning precarity and vulnerability of future employment opportunities and careers in the HI.

The theory of resilience [35] has also been widely adopted before the pandemic as a conceptual framework including different dimensions (i.e., personal, community, economic, organisational, and systems resilience) in the HI literature. At the personal level, self-efficacy has proven instrumental in supporting one's persistence in the face of aversive experiences and obstacles [36] affecting task effort, the level of goal difficulty chosen for performance, or expressed interest.

Adaptive capacity, flexibility, or fostering a culture which promotes innovation and self-efficacy, are critical factors in improving organisational resilience [37]. This capacity is strongly linked to the system's overall vulnerability to a particular disaster or crisis event [38]. An integrative framework based upon six forms of capital (cultural, economic, human, natural, physical, and social capital) has been suggested as an extension of the theory of resilience, specifically geared towards developing disaster resilience in the hotel sector [37].

2.2. COVID-19 and Safety Compliance in the HI

To face the socioeconomic impacts on employees and one's livelihood adjustments, hospitality operators and managers' choices are primarily manifested through how day-to-day activities are undertaken and coupled with increasing awareness of new health and safety protocols [39].

COVID-19 has engendered a set of other health and safety regulations and procedures (e.g., social distancing) that are critical to closely monitor employee safety because protecting employees from the infection not only demonstrates the organisation's responsibility to help contain the spread of the virus, but also determines the survival of the organisation during this crisis [40].

Organisations comply with the COVID-19 safety measures (requirements and protocols) to protect both employees and customers in response to this unprecedented health crisis and the consequent changes in working conditions [40]. Safety compliance refers to core safety tasks (including a set of behaviours that aim to meet an organisation's safety requirements, i.e., safety rules and procedures, as well as wearing personal protective equipment) individuals carry out to maintain workplace safety [41]. Increased awareness of health and safety risks underpins the intention of attaining safety goals motivation that drives deep compliance behaviour beyond personal protection and other organisation's members' safety and incorporates a sense of moral responsibility for external stakeholders (i.e., customers) as well as the public [40].

Safety leadership has gained momentum during the current global crisis. It has been argued that hotel safety leadership positively affects employee safety behaviour (compliance, participation, and adaptation) [42]. Therefore, management strategies should emphasise safety leadership and promote employees' safety behaviour from key aspects (i.e., safety coaching, care, motivation, and control), thus enhancing support of the organisation.

2.3. Employability and Job Insecurity in the HI

Job security is considered one of the essential parts of the quality of jobs. By contrast, job insecurity affects life and job satisfaction and commitment to the organisation [43,44].

Job insecurity refers to feeling concerned due to the perceived threat or uncertainty about the future of the job beyond the actual protection of the employee's rights [45,46]. Namely, subjective job insecurity—a personal concern about the future of the job—refers to the psychological dimension of job insecurity [47,48].

Prior studies have proved that perceptions of job insecurity depend on several causes and that the solutions adopted to cope with its negative effects depend on the following factors: type of the employment contract [46], self-rated job performance [44], as well as several employees' attributes and individual/personal resources [49], such as age [50], trust [51], and support [52].

Job insecurity is also affected by the perception of employability which expresses the subjective evaluation of an employee's ability to obtain a new job or maintain the existing one [53]. Çalıskan and Özkoç [54] empirically demonstrate that employees' perceptions of job insecurity are positively affected by frequency and impact of change and negatively by planning involved in change; the perception of employability moderates the relationships between the characteristics of organisational change and job insecurity. The perception of employability has gained momentum in recent years due to increased concerns about job insecurity.

In this vein, it has been considered an essential source in helping employees to deal with changeable organisation environment [55,56]. However, both perception of employability and job insecurity studies have not received adequate attention in the tourism and hospitality literature, instead being considered critical features for current and potential employees in light of the pandemic that undermines job stability, especially for young people. Therefore, we postulated the following hypothesis:

Hypothesis 1 (H1). *The COVID-19 pandemic is a negative factor that initiates change in the HI, directly influencing the spirit of youth adventures (NFC > SofA).*

2.4. Young People's Perceptions of Work and Career in the Hospitality Industry

Investigating young people's perceptions of work in the hospitality industry, Mooney [57] observed that although they form a high proportion of the hospitality workforce in many countries, young people are not adequately valued, and inequitable power relations persist in the HI. Their perceptions of work in the hospitality industry—as temporary and unpredictable rather than an aspirational career choice—are at the basis of high turnover. Therefore, it has been claimed that the HI should retain its youthful workers rather than wasting this finite human resource [58].

The results are consistent with previous research addressing four-year tourism management school students' who reported unfavourable or negative evaluations towards several dimensions of working in the HI [59,60]. Hoque and Ashif [61] explored the students' undergraduate tourism and hospitality perceptions in Bangladesh, and their results indicate that the students' perceptions of careers in the HI are unfavourable because some factors, such as a friendly working environment, a safe job, excellent promotion prospects, and an attractive starting salary are not important in the HI.

Tuzunkan [62] examined the perceptions and attitudes of undergraduate Korean tourism students. On the one hand, the findings showed that a tourism job is interesting, worth doing, needs fewer skills, people can use their ability and skills and get pleasure while working. On the other hand, some negative perceptions and prejudices about the tourist industry emerged.

Barron and Maxwell [63] pointed out that hospitality management students tended to have high ambitions for their future working careers when they began their studies. However, their ambitions changed after recognising the actual circumstances of the industry (negative working environments) and were disappointed with the HI when they had work experience. In addition, Khan and Krishanamurthy [64] revealed that factors like gender non-discrimination, promotion opportunities, and physical working conditions play a crucial role in motivating students, while other factors, such as the high risk of accidents, discourage the attitude towards choosing tourism as their future job and hence the tourism studies.

Knowledge, skills, and attitudes in specific areas (i.e., customer service, problem-solving, and leadership) are essential top competencies for hospitality managers and a priority concerning the educational process of a hospitality programme [65]. Interpersonal communication is a crucial skill for successful leaders in all organisations, including the service industry [66], while young people tend to be deficient in these skills when entering the business world [67].

Assuming the youth as a distinct workforce entity, Golubovskaya et al. [68] pointed out that hospitality jobs represent a critical developmental context for young people due to the misalignment with the workforce composition of the HI, the latter being dominated by young, often unexperienced workers. Therefore, they call for the need for recalibration and a pathway forward by paying greater attention to the development of talent and a more employee-focused and inclusive approach, allowing career jobs.

As a result of the literature review, we elaborated the following hypothesis:

Hypothesis 2 (H2). *The COVID-19 pandemic is a negative factor that initiates change in the HI and directly influences the attractiveness of jobs in this sector for young people (NFC > AofJ).*

2.5. Job Attractiveness and the Spirit of Adventure in the HI

The theory of planned behaviour (TPB) argues that individual behaviour is influenced by attitudes, subjective norms, and perceived self-control [69]. Researchers have commonly used this theory to explain human behaviour in various studies. In this vein, some scholars argue that it represents a basic theoretical valuable framework in explaining individual behaviour in a pandemic context [70].

Uncertainty and inadequate knowledge decrease the perceived risk, which leads to lower control over practicing physical distancing and increasing intention to travel during the pandemic. Moreover, this theoretical lens has been used to investigate travellers' destination choices of university students in China [70] and explain the consequences of COVID-19 for tourists' behaviours, perceived travel risk, animosity, and intention to travel. Edwards et al. [71] consider that the work environment influences the attractiveness of a job, and the employees' strategic renewal is positively affected by these factors and by demographic variables (i.e., age, gender, and educational level).

As per our knowledge, the studies aimed at evaluating the employment-generating capacity of the HI [72] did not deepen HI attractiveness concerning the youth. Young people's behaviours in the HI have not received adequate attention, thus calling for further research to address young people's perceptions and attitudes and contribute to filling this gap.

Kakoudakis et al. [73] investigated the socioeconomic benefits through job search behaviour, and their findings agree with those of Kanfer et al. [74] that the commitment to future employment is one of the main factors that can influence people when they choose a HI job. The self-determination theory and commitment offer interesting insights into what sustains human behaviour in work situations [75].

Based on the literature review, we suggested the following hypothesis:

Hypothesis 3 (H3). *The spirit of youth adventure developed for a job in the HI directly influences the attractiveness of jobs in this sector for young people (SofA > AofJ).*

The individual's inspiration for engaging in inherently interesting and enjoyable actions is nourished by the desire to satisfy the basic psychological needs mentioned above. When individuals evaluate certain activities as contributing to satisfying these needs, they are prone to continue performing those activities.

Self-motivation or autonomous motivation is essential for active engagement, involvement, and persistence in activities. As the highest form of autonomous motivation, intrinsic motivation is associated with autonomy and competence needs [76]. The need for relatedness—the desire to feel connected to others—is satisfied when people experience close relations (colleagues, clients, friends, and the family).

The workplace provides individuals with opportunities for social contacts and networks that contribute to satisfying this need. However, the contribution of work toward relatedness may depend on the nature of work that can facilitate or limit interactions with others [76]. Emotional intelligence has been found to positively influence performance in various fields, including business and the HI, where employees were proved to perceive emotional labour when performing their direct line of work [77].

We consider that all employees in the HI can be actors of adventure games, and we argue that the spirit of adventure can inspire young people to choose a job in the HI. Therefore, we wanted to fill the literature gap related to the spirit of adventure and explain the positive impacts of adventure on the attractiveness of a job in the HI for young people. Prior literature explored the adventure related to an activity and not to an invisible enemy like the COVID-19 virus.

Starting from the definition of adventure given by Muller and Cleaver [78], "relatively high levels of sensory stimulation, usually achieved by including physical challenging experiential components", we adapted it to a new framework generated by COVID-19. We defined the spirit of adventure of young people working in the HI as a challenge that motivates them to promote teamwork to deal with the complaints from clients and overcome the danger of COVID-19.

Based on the above literature analysis, we derived our hypotheses that are described as follows:

Hypothesis 4 (H4). *Evolution of the HI after the end of the COVID-19 period mediates the relationship between the spirit of youth adventure developed for a job in the HI and the attractiveness of jobs in this sector for young people (SofA > EHI > AofJ).*

Hypothesis 5 (H5). *The COVID-19 pandemic is a negative factor that moderates the relationship between the evolution of the HI after the end of the COVID-19 period and the attractiveness of jobs in this sector for young people (AofJ > NFC > EHI).*

Tourism researchers tend to approach the research problem from the perspectives of operators, the tourists' perspective, and the perspectives of the residents of the destinations' communities [79]. By contrast, little attention has been paid to the perspectives of future generations among the research streams that are gaining momentum (i.e., crisis and disaster management; safety management; tourism resilience).

To fill this gap, a conceptual model was formulated to illustrate the relationship between the attractiveness of jobs in the HI for young people, the evolution of the HI after the end of the COVID-19 period, the interaction between the people working in the HI in the COVID-19 pandemic scenario and the spirit of youth adventure (Figure 1).

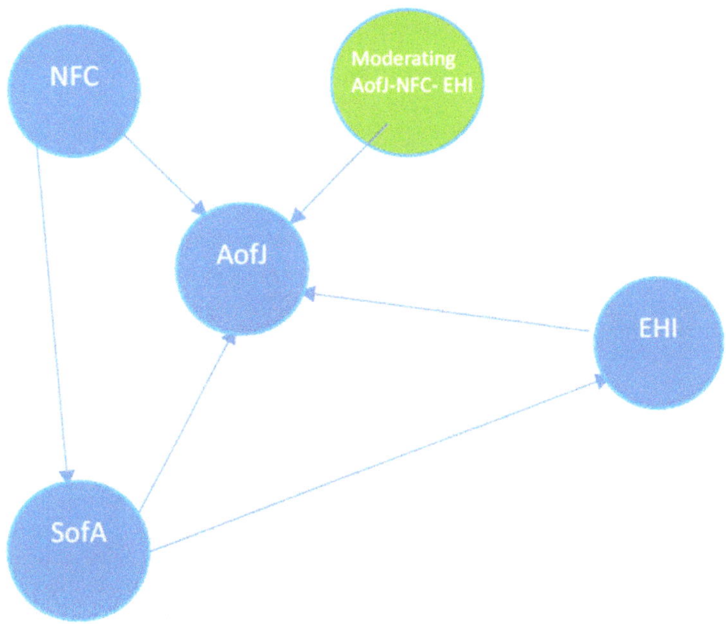

Figure 1. The theoretical model of the research. AofJ-the attractiveness of jobs in the hospitality industry for young people; EHI-evolution of the hospitality industry after the end of the COVID-19 period; NFC-the COVID-19 pandemic is a negative factor that initiates change in the hospitality industry; SofA-a job in the hospitality industry is motivated by the spirit of youth adventure.

3. Methodology

According to prior studies [34,61], the data used in our research were collected through quantitative survey-based research from 1 July to 31 October 2020.

The respondents were young Romanian people (121 employees from the HI, 75 students, and 112 unemployed people) who answered an online questionnaire. The questionnaire was pretested within a pilot study with a sample of 70 respondents over ten days.

We followed the example of Hair et al. [80] and the questionnaires with missing values were eliminated; at the end of the period, 308 valid questionnaires were obtained, of which 44.8% were answered by men, 55.2%—by women. Moreover, following Bagozzi and Yi [81], we checked the questionnaires for incomplete responses, and 25 responses were eliminated.

Concerning age, 211 respondents (68.5%) were 21–25 years old and 97 respondents (31.5%) were 26–30 years old. One of our research objectives was to validate the scale of measurement of the attractiveness of jobs in the HI for the youth during a crisis period. All the variables were measured using a five-point Likert scale from 1 (totally disagree) to 5 (totally agree). According to Chin et al. [82], we used the partial least squares structural equation modelling (PLS-SEM) approach to better explain the variance in the model's dependent variables. PLS-SEM was used to clearly estimate formatively specified constructs and measure the model parameters [83,84].

After a confirmatory factor analysis, the items with loadings under 0.70 were removed, and Table 1 presents the final 14 items of the four variables that had their reliability values (outer loading) above the recommended value of 0.70 [85].

Analysing Table 1, we observe that the highest outer loading value (0.899) is registered by the items of the variable related to the COVID-19 pandemic as a negative factor that initiates change in the HI.

Table 1. Outer Loading and Variance Inflation Factors (VIF).

Variables/Items	Outer Loadings	VIF
AofJ—the attractiveness of jobs in the hospitality industry for young people—adapted from Yeh [86], who adapted from Gursoy and Gavcar [87]		
AofJ1—If I take protective measures and respect them, a job in the HI seems very attractive to me and will influence the development of high and new competences	0.845	2.533
AofJ2—I like working in the hospitality industry because I consider that team decisions are encouraged	0.878	2.673
AofJ3—I want to work in the hospitality industry because I can communicate with other people	0.845	2.465
AofJ4—I like working in the hospitality industry because I consider that personal risk has a low negative impact on my activities	0.847	2.443
AofJ5—I feel enthusiastic about working in the hospitality industry because I can put into practice my creative ideas	0.861	2.732
EHI—evolution of the hospitality industry after the end of the COVID-19 period—own scale		
EHI1—I consider that greater attention will be paid to human resources	0.860	1.902
EHI2—The hospitality industry will be reorganized according to the rules of social distancing because these rules will be maintained for a long time	0.885	2.304
EHI3—Communications between customers and employees will take place mainly through electronic devices	0.897	2.328
NFC—the COVID-19 pandemic is a negative factor that initiates change in the hospitality industry—own scale		
NFC1—The COVID-19 pandemic has positively affected the hospitality industry in terms of development of more sustainable and smarter offers and solutions	0.831	2.155
NFC2—The COVID-19 pandemic changed the vision about planned deadlines in the hospitality industry	0.899	1.930
NFC3—The COVID-19 pandemic improved the external regulatory demands for the hospitality industry	0.898	2.460
SofA—a job in the hospitality industry is motivated by the spirit of youth adventure—own scale		
SofA1—As a possible employee in the hospitality industry, I consider that the COVID-19 virus is a challenge that I will overcome	0.788	1.626
SofA2—Teamwork becomes a challenge because it turns into a win–win–win gamble: I protect myself—I protect you—we protect clients	0.873	1.993
SofA3—To deal with complaints from clients is a challenge for me in a pandemic crisis such as this generated by COVID-19	0.883	1.801

An item of the variable related to the spirit of youth adventure (0.788) allows us to affirm that the COVID-19 pandemic differently influencing the perception of adventure by young people registers the lowest outer loading value. This pandemic crisis has improved the external regulatory demands for the HI (0.898) and influenced the development of high and new competences (0.845).

Please see the detailed analysis of the values of the outer loadings in Section 4.

In Table 1, variance inflation factor (VIF) values of latent variables fall between 1.626 and 2.732, which takes cognisance of those issues related to collinearity. We continued measuring the reliability of the internal scale through Cronbach's alpha, Dijkstra–Henseler statistics (rho_A), composite reliability (CR), and the average variance extracted (AVE) methods. The Cronbach's alpha value ranges from 0.809 to 1.000 and proves the constructs' consistency reliability [88].

The values of rho_A are above 0.7 (0.840 to 1.000) and are in consensus with the previous studies of Schuberth et al. [89] who showed that rho_A is a coefficient that requires values greater than 0.6. The composite reliability ranges between 0.833 and 0.936, and the CR is greater than 0.6 according to Bagozzi and Yi [81] or 0.7 according to [80]. All the five AVE values are above 0.50. Thus, we proved that the results are reliable, and the internal consistency and convergent validity are good. Moreover, we analysed the discriminant validity through the heterotrait–monotrait ratio (HTMT) and observed that HTMT values are not greater than 0.90 [90] and prove that the convergent validity is good.

We tested the structural model using R squared to measure the levels of the variables, and these values are moderate and range from 0.214 to 0.618. The structural model was also assessed using the standardized root-mean-square residual (SRMR), and the value of this indicator is 0.078; it does not surpass the threshold value of 0.10, confirming adequate goodness of model fit [91].

4. Findings and Discussions

A breakdown of the hypotheses testing is presented in Table 2.

Table 2. The breakdown of the hypotheses testing.

	Original Sample (O)	Sample Mean (M)	Standard Deviation (STDEV)	T-Statistics (|O/STDEV|)	*p*-Values	Hypotheses
SofA > EHI > AofJ	0.267	0.267	0.041	6.508	0.000	H1: supported
Moderating AofJ–NFC–EHI	0.430	0.426	0.064	6.762	0.000	H2: supported
SofA > AofJ	0.245	0.248	0.058	4.208	0.000	H3: supported
NFC > AofJ	−0.181	−0.181	0.061	2.984	0.003	H4: supported
NFC > SofA	0.462	0.463	0.046	10.030	0.000	H5: supported

The first hypothesis is validated (p = 0.000 and T-value = 6.508). It underlines the mediating role of the HI's evolution after the COVID-19 period between the spirit of youth adventure developed for a job in the HI and the attractiveness of jobs in this sector for young people (SofA > EHI > AofJ). Thus, when the evolution is positive, the spirit of adventure is emphasised, and the attractiveness of jobs in the HI increases.

The second hypothesis is validated, and it proves that the COVID-19 pandemic is a negative factor that moderates the relationship between the HI's evolution after the COVID-19 period and the attractiveness of jobs in this sector for young people (p = 0.002 and T-value = 6.762).

The third hypothesis shows that the spirit of youth adventure developed for a job in the HI directly influences the attractiveness of jobs in this sector for young people (p = 0.000 and T-value = 4.208), and it is validated.

The fourth hypothesis is also validated and shows that the COVID-19 pandemic is a negative factor that initiates change in this sector and has a psychological effect on young people and influences the attractiveness of jobs in this sector of activity (p = 0.003 and T-value = 2.984).

The fifth hypothesis proves that the COVID-19 pandemic is a negative factor that initiates change in the HI and the interactivity between people working in the HI in the COVID-19 pandemic scenario (p = 0.000 and T-value = 10.030), and it is validated. Table 3 shows path coefficient values and the specific indirect effects.

Table 3. Path coefficients and specific indirect effects.

	Original Sample (O)	Sample Mean (M)	Standard Deviation (STDEV)	T-Statistics (|O/STDEV|)	*p*-Values
Age > AofJ	0.041	0.041	0.032	1.279	0.201
Gender > AofJ	−0.046	−0.045	0.036	1.287	0.199
NFC > SofA > AofJ	0.113	0.114	0.026	4.379	0.000
NFC > SofA > EHI	0.271	0.272	0.032	8.325	0.000

Age ($p = 0.201$) and gender ($p = 0.199$) do not influence the attractiveness of jobs in the HI for young people. These findings prove gender equality and an equal opportunity for young people to have a job in the HI. It is obvious that the spirit of youth adventure mediates two relationships: first, between the changes initiated in the HI and the attractiveness of jobs in the HI ($p = 0.000$), and second, between the changes-initiated change in the HI and its evolution after the COVID-19 period ($p = 0.000$).

The work environment [72] influences the attractiveness of a job. Therefore, we oriented our research to young people with the potential to evaluate the attractiveness of a job in the HI from other perspectives and transform the challenges of the COVID-19 pandemic into opportunities, for example, the opportunity to turn teamwork into a win–win–win gamble: I protect myself—I protect you—we protect clients—and contribute to the development of high and new competences of the young people in this sector.

Most young people consider pandemics a challenge to overcome, and they will choose to work in the HI regardless of the risks. However, some young people do not like working under the pressure generated by the COVID-19 pandemic and consider that the risk of becoming infected with COVID-19 is a challenge for them as they measure their level of protection. Our findings are sustained by Rather's [92] research that concluded that perceived risk had a significant negative effect on Indian people during the COVID-19 crisis. These findings prove that young people will not avoid a job in the HI because it offers them the possibility of combining challenges with their adventure spirit.

Houge Mackenzie and Raymond [93] identified the key elements of adventure in New Zealand guide experiences related to determinants of people's psychological well-being, and one of them was preventing ill-being. Consequently, during a pandemic crisis, the spirit of adventure of young people is moderated by self-protection and self-health. Young people consider that only high quality of services will make the difference between HI companies, and they are very confident that a new vision and their adventure spirit will concur to the improvement of the quality of services in the HI [94].

Ntounis et al. [95] arrived at the conclusion that in England, the people working in the HI are affected by the lack of information about the lockdown's duration, and for this reason, when they return to a new normality, they will need additional ongoing assistance.

As a result, the pandemic crisis does not only negatively influence touristic service quality because it contributes to going ahead, thus soliciting the development of more sustainable and more thoughtful offers and solutions, changes the vision about planned deadlines in this sector, and highly improves the external regulatory demands for the HI [21]. Moreover, young people consider communication face-to-face with other people (i.e., colleagues and customers) as an opportunity to develop their competences and overcome the barriers raised by electronic devices. On the one hand, research on the HI and perceptions under extreme conditions has mainly investigated other categories' perceptions, such as operators' perceptions or a travellers' or residents' perception towards the existing and future tourism development [85].

We proved that the HI is fascinating for young people that could develop their competences and satisfy their spirit of adventure. Thus, the HI needs to rebuild and reimagine jobs amid the coronavirus crisis to reduce the level of COVID-19 exposure [96].

Finally, the findings point out that young people manifest a high spirit of adventure and want to work in the HI because the personal risk has a low negative impact on their activities, and if they take protective measures and respect them, a job in this sector seems very attractive to them.

Consequently, we consider that employment risk in the HI is associated with the spirit of adventure for young people. The spirit of adventure can be related to managing stress, and this strange relationship can be explained by this critical component of the HI represented by the COVID-19 pandemic. Paradoxically, these two factors can be transformed in motivation for young people if the hospitality environment offers them the image of well-being and unexplored adventures.

Our findings agree with the research of Skurvydas et al. [97] that recommended the future strategies be focused on product adjustment and transformation of business structures, seeking governmental guidance and policies in restoring market confidence in the HI.

5. Conclusions

The COVID-19 crisis poses considerable risks to education and employment [98]. Governments are forced to adjust plans to cover both public services (e.g., education) and economic sectors (e.g., tourism) to build back better for all generations. This objective will be attended by integrating a stronger focus on young people and future generations in government action and letting the youth and intergenerational considerations be mainstreamed in the governments' strategies for the economic response to COVID-19. These actions will include measures to help the youth develop their skills, gain professional experience, and contribute to acting as connective tissue in public institutions and decision-making processes [99].

The crisis caused by coronavirus disease 2019 has posed wide-ranging problems for all sectors of the global economy. It has changed the world forever in an unimaginable respect and has heavily influenced international travel and tourist demands and the HI is tackling one of the most severe operational, commercial, and financial crises. All market players in the touristic and hospitality value chain areas have been forced to either minimize or completely stop provision of their services, resulting in the sudden and total cutoff of their revenue streams. Consequently, jobs lost or made redundant in the sector might take a long time to resurface and fully recover from the adverse impacts of the pandemic.

Our research's originality consists of analyzing the relationship between the spirit, the adventure, and the attractiveness of jobs to young people in the HI. To the best of the authors' knowledge, this study presents the first empirical evidence on young people's attitudes and perceptions in this pandemic situation. Moreover, the significance of this study lies in the fact that its subject had not been addressed before from the perspective of the hospitality industry. It could be deciphered that the implications of our research are both theoretical and practical.

Theoretical implications. Due to the magnitude of the crisis and its devastating effects, previous conceptual and theoretical frameworks may prove inadequate or insufficient to understand its complex implications. Our research contributes to the tourism management literature by evaluating the impact of the pandemic on the future attractiveness of the HI to young people. Our theoretical research model underlines the importance of the spirit of youth adventure as a critical factor that generates new knowledge and develops young people's work-related skills and general understanding of the job environment in the sector. The results relate to the HI system's resilience from the socioeconomic perspective, affecting the macro-, meso-, and microlevels because of the impact on individuals, including the youth, businesses, communities, and nations [100].

Scientific discourse on the implications of the HI's COVID-19 pandemic crisis framework is emerging. In this context, Cohen [101] emphasized environmental and social—rather than merely economic—concerns. In this regard, the future agenda should include a charter for sustainable tourism after the COVID-19 pandemic [102] that incorporates the enforcement of social distancing and regulations, safety measures and tools, stakeholder mapping, and anticipates changes in tourist behavior, ensures connectivity, and strengthens relationships.

The HI's enthusiasm to return to normality is consistent with the youth's spirit and orientation towards sustainability since the outbreak has revealed many changes in the relationships between sustainability in terms of intergenerational justice in the work environment and the HI. However, our study has proved that most young people have a strong desire to communicate face-to-face and be physically active in their workplaces. For this reason, these people prefer to work in the HI even in a pandemic crisis because they apply the rule: I protect myself—I protect you—we protect clients. The other contribution consists of validating the scale for evaluating the attractiveness of a job in the HI in a period of crisis. The validation of the scale is an answer to the recommendations by Gössling et al. [103] that outlined the potential negative impact of the COVID-19 crisis, suggesting that one of the HI's main challenges is learning how to accelerate the transition to a sustainable future of the sector. Finally, we filled the gap in the HI literature related to the attractiveness of a job in the HI for young people during a period of crisis.

Practical implications. Our findings can ensure a better understanding of the managers and decisionmakers the HI to motivate young people to work in the sector that has been negatively impacted by this crisis. Young people consider that the HI will always be an opportunity for dreaming and keeping their souls young. Our study will be of interest to policymakers in terms of suggestions on how to transform challenges into opportunities by using the constraints imposed by a pandemic crisis that limits the socialisation between people, enhancing the creativity of young people working in the HI. The managers and decisionmakers in the HI should bear in mind that this current pandemic crisis is likely to reinforce this sector, and young people with a developed spirit of adventure represent a valuable workforce for their organizations because they are aware of clients' expectations. They would certainly be ready to promote proactive communications. Our findings provide a practical value for managers and other decisionmakers, some motivational factors that would increase the attractiveness of their companies to young people, and research suggestions helpful to scholars involved in educational projects addressed to students of hospitality management programs to cultivate resilience capabilities by giving them inherent skills and competencies [104]. Finally, our research can help the managers and decisionmakers, particularly from the less developed countries, face social, economic, and environmental challenges and increase their organizational performance by using the young people's spirit of adventure.

Regarding its limitations, we are aware that the findings from a study carried out in one European country are not likely to be wholly replicated elsewhere in the world. Therefore, we wanted to understand how these potential young corporate leaders perceive the impact of the pandemic on their future careers in the HI.

The future research will be oriented to improving the young people's relationship with their spirit of adventure and responsibility. The new normality comes with a new approach to the activity in the HI and new challenges for both employees and employers. In this new light, sustainability acquires a new dimension that is much more social and personalized according to the HI's particularities and spirit of adventure of the employees in the HI. The business model in the HI will be delineated by the pandemic crisis on the one hand and the new normality on the other.

Author Contributions: Conceptualization, A.B.-S., M.D.B. and S.O.I.; methodology, A.B.-S.; validation, A.B.-S., M.D.B. and S.O.I.; formal analysis, A.B.-S., M.D.B. and S.O.I.; investigation, A.B.-S., M.D.B. and S.O.I.; writing—original draft preparation, A.B.-S., M.D.B. and S.O.I.; writing—review and editing, A.B.-S., M.D.B. and S.O.I.; visualization, A.B.-S., M.D.B. and S.O.I.; supervision, A.B.-S., M.D.B. and S.O.I.; project administration, A.B.-S., M.D.B. and S.O.I. All authors have read and agreed to the published version of the manuscript.

Funding: This research received no external funding.

Institutional Review Board Statement: Not applicable.

Informed Consent Statement: Not applicable.

Data Availability Statement: The data presented in this study are available on request from the corresponding author.

Conflicts of Interest: The authors declare no conflict of interest.

References

1. OECD. OECD Interim Economic Assessment-Coronavirus: The World Economy at Risk. 2020. Available online: https://www.oecd.org/berlin/publikationen/Interim-Economic-Assessment-2-March-2020.pdf. (accessed on 9 October 2020).
2. World Health Organization (WHO). Coronavirus Disease (COVID-19) Pandemic. 2020. Available online: www.who.int/emergencies/diseases/novel-coronavirus-2019 (accessed on 12 January 2021).
3. World Economic Forum (WEF). The Global Risks Report. 2021. Available online: https://www3.weforum.org/docs/WEF_The_Global_Risks_Report_2021.pdf (accessed on 21 December 2021).
4. OECD. Enterprises and Employment in Tourism. OECD Tourism Statistics. 2022. Available online: https://doi.org/10.1787/065e083a-en (accessed on 21 December 2021).
5. Brammer, S.; Branicki, L.; Linnenluecke, M.K. Societalization, and the Future of Business in Society. *Acad. Manag. Perspect.* **2020**, *34*, 493–507. [CrossRef]
6. Wen, J.; Kozak, M.; Yang, S.; Liu, F. COVID-19: Potential effects on Chinese citizens' lifestyle and travel. *Tour. Rev.* **2020**, *76*, 74–87. [CrossRef]
7. Nicola, M.; Alsafi, Z.; Sohrabi, C.; Kerwan, A.; Al-Jabir, A.; Iosifidis, C.; Agha, M.; Agha, R. The socio-economic implications of the coronavirus and COVID-19 pandemic: A review. *Int. J. Surg.* **2020**, *78*, 185–193. [CrossRef]
8. Rivera, M.A. Hitting the reset button for hospitality research in times of crisis: COVID-19 and beyond. *Int. J. Hosp. Manag.* **2020**, *87*, 102528. [CrossRef]
9. Bartik, A.W.; Bertrand, M.; Cullen, Z.B.; Glaeser, E.L.; Luca, M.; Stanton, C.T. How are small businesses adjusting to COVID-19? Early evidence from a survey (No. w26989). *Natl. Bur. Econ. Res.* **2020**, 26989. Available online: https://www.nber.org/papers/w26989 (accessed on 21 December 2021).
10. Borden, T.; Akhtar, A.; Hadden, J.; Bose, D. The Coronavirus Outbreak Has Triggered Unprecedented Mass Layoffs and Furloughs. Here are Major Companies that have Announced They are Downsizing Their Workforces. 2020. Available online: https://www.businessinsider.com/coronavirus-layoffs-furloughs-hospitality-service-travel-unemployment-2020?r=US&IR=T. (accessed on 20 December 2021).
11. WTTC. Research Note: Travel & Tourism Recovery Scenarios 2020 and Economic Impact from COVID-19. 2020. Available online: https://wttc.org/Research/Economic-Impact/Recovery-Scenarios-2020-Economic-Impact-from-COVID-19. (accessed on 10 October 2020).
12. DeMicco, F.; Cetron, M.; Davies, O.; Guzman, J. COVID-19 Impact on the Future of Hospitality and Travel. *J. Hosp. Tour. Res.* **2021**, *45*, 911–914. [CrossRef]
13. Karabulut, G.; Bilgin, M.H.; Demir, E.; Doker, A.C. How pandemics affect tourism: International evidence. *Ann. Tour. Res.* **2020**, *84*, 102991. [CrossRef]
14. Prayag, G. 2020, Time for Reset? COVID-19 and Tourism Resilience. *Tour. Rev. Int.* **2020**, *24*, 179–184. [CrossRef]
15. Davahli, M.R.; Karwowski, W.; Sönmez, S.; Apostolopoulos, Y. The Hospitality Industry in the Face of the COVID-19 Pandemic: Current Topics and Research Methods. *Int. J. Environ. Res. Public Health* **2020**, *17*, 7366. [CrossRef]
16. Bloom, D.E.; Cadarette, D. Infectious disease threats in the 21st century: Strengthening the global response. *Front. Immunol.* **2019**, *10*, 549. [CrossRef]
17. Fauci, A.S.; Morens, D.M. The perpetual challenge of infectious diseases. *N. Engl. J. Med.* **2012**, *366*, 454–461. [CrossRef]
18. Hall, C.M. Biological invasion, biosecurity, tourism, and globalisation. In *Handbook of Globalisation and Tourism*; Dallen, J., Ed.; Edward Elgar Publishing: Cheltenham, UK, 2019; pp. 114–125.
19. Breier, M.; Kallmuenzer, A.; Clauss, T.; Gast, J.; Kraus, S.; Tiberius, V. The role of business model innovation in the hospitality industry during the COVID-19 crisis. *Int. J. Hosp. Manag.* **2021**, *92*, 102723. [CrossRef]
20. Godovykh, M.; Pizam, A.; Bahja, F. Antecedents and outcomes of health risk perceptions in tourism, following the COVID-19 pandemic. *Tour. Rev.* **2021**, *76*, 737–748. [CrossRef]
21. Baker, S.R.; Farrokhnia, R.A.; Meyer, S.; Pagel, M.; Yannelis, C. How Does Household Spending Respond to an Epidemic? Consumption during the COVID-19 Pandemic. 2020. Working Paper. Available online: https://www.nber.org/papers/w26949.pdf (accessed on 6 October 2021).
22. Aldao, C.; Blasco, D.; Poch Espallargas, M.; Palou Rubio, S. Modelling the crisis management and impacts of 21st century disruptive events in tourism: The case of the COVID-19 pandemic. *Tour. Rev.* **2021**, *76*, 929–941. [CrossRef]
23. Yang, H.-Y.; Chen, K.-H. A general equilibrium analysis of the economic impact of a tourism crisis: A case study of the SARS epidemic in Taiwan. *J. Pol. Res. Tour. Leis. Events* **2009**, *1*, 37–60. [CrossRef]
24. Henderson, J. Corporate social responsibility and tourism: Hotel companies in Phuket, Thailand, after the Indian Ocean tsunami. *Int. J. Hosp. Manag.* **2007**, *26*, 228–239. [CrossRef]

25. Baker, D.M.A. Tourism and the health effects of infectious diseases: Are there potential risks for tourists? *Int. J. Saf. Secur. Tour. Hosp.* **2015**, *1*, 1.
26. Hall, C.M. Crisis events in tourism: Subjects of crisis in tourism. *Curr. Issues Tour.* **2010**, *13*, 401–417. [CrossRef]
27. Baum, T.; Mooney, S.K.K.; Robinson, N.R.S.; Solnet, D. COVID-19's impact on the hospitality workforce–new crisis or amplification of the norm? *Int. J. Contemp. Hosp. Manag.* **2020**, *32*, 2813–2829. [CrossRef]
28. Solnet, J.D.; Ford, C.R.; Richard, N.S.; Robinson, R.N.S.; Ritchie, W.B.; Olsen, M. Modeling locational factors for tourism employment. *Ann. Tour. Res.* **2014**, *45*, 30–45. [CrossRef]
29. Reynolds, A.C.; Pabel, A.; Ferguson, S.A.; Naweed, A. Causes and consequences of sleep loss and fatigue: The worker perspective in the coral reef tourism industry. *Ann. Tour. Res.* **2021**, *88*, 103160. [CrossRef]
30. Baum, T.; Kralj, A.; Robinson, R.N.; Solnet, D.J. Tourism workforce research: A review, taxonomy and agenda. *Ann. Tour. Res.* **2016**, *60*, 1–22. [CrossRef]
31. Baum, T. Human resources in tourism: Still waiting for change?—A 2015 reprise. *Tour. Manag.* **2015**, *50*, 204–212. [CrossRef]
32. Poulston, J.M. Working conditions in hospitality: Employees' views of the dissatisfactory hygiene factors. *J. Qual. Assur. Hosp. Tour.* **2009**, *10*, 23–43. [CrossRef]
33. Rand, S.; Hermann, B.; Muheim, F.; Beck, J.; Holsboer-Trachsler, E. Sleep patterns, work, and strain among young students in hospitality and tourism. *Ind. Health* **2008**, *46*, 199–209.
34. Abraham, V.; Bremser, K.; Carreno, M.; Crowley-Cyr, L.; Moreno, M. Exploring the consequences of COVID-19 on tourist behaviors: Perceived travel risk, animosity and intentions to travel. *Tour. Res.* **2020**, *76*, 701–717. [CrossRef]
35. Pocinho, M.; Garcês, S.; de Jesus, S.N. Wellbeing and Resilience in Tourism: A Systematic Literature Review During COVID-19. *Font. Psychol.* **2022**, *12*, 6016. [CrossRef]
36. Bandura, A.; Adams, N.E. Analysis of self-efficacy theory of behavioural change. *Cognit. Ther. Res.* **1977**, *1*, 287–310. [CrossRef]
37. Brown, N.A.; Rovins, J.E.; Feldmann-Jensen, S.; Orchiston, C.; Johnston, D. Exploring disaster resilience within the hotel sector: A systematic review of literature. *Int. J. Disaster Risk Reduct.* **2017**, *22*, 362–370. [CrossRef]
38. Tsao, C.; Ni, C. Vulnerability, resilience, and the adaptive cycle in a crisis-prone tourism community. *Tour. Geogr.* **2016**, *18*, 80–105.
39. Kim, J.-H.; Ahn, S.; Lee, E. Effect of Power Message on Employee Response and Job Recruitment in the Hospitality Industry. *J. Hosp. Tour. Res.* **2021**. [CrossRef]
40. Hu, X.; Yan, H.; Casey, T.; Wu, C.H. Creating a safe haven during the crisis: How organizations can achieve deep compliance with COVID-19 safety measures in the hospitality industry. *Int. J. Hosp. Manag.* **2020**, *102662*, 1–25. [CrossRef]
41. Christian, M.S.; Bradley, J.C.; Wallace, J.C.; Burke, M.J. Workplace safety: A metaanalysis of the roles of person and situation factors. *J. App. Psychol.* **2009**, *94*, 1103. [CrossRef]
42. Zhang, J.; Xie, C.; Wang, J.; Morrison, A.M.; Coca-Stefaniak, J.A. Responding to a major global crisis: The effects of hotel safety leadership on employee safety behaviour during COVID-19. *Int. J. Contemp. Hosp. Manag.* **2020**, *32*, 3365–3389. [CrossRef]
43. McGinley, S.P.; Martinez, L. The Moderating Role of Career Progression on Job Mobility: A Study of Work–Life Conflict. *J. Hosp. Tour. Res.* **2018**, *42*, 1106–1129. [CrossRef]
44. Van Vuuren, T.; de Jong, J.P.; Smulders, P.G.W. The association between subjective job insecurity and job performance across different employment groups. Evidence from a representative sample from the Netherlands. *Car. Dev. Int.* **2020**, *25*, 229–246. [CrossRef]
45. De Witte, H.; Vander Elst, T.; De Cuyper, N. Job Insecurity, Health and Well-Being. In *Sustainable Working Lives. Aligning Perspectives on Health, Safety and Well-Being*; Vuori, J., Blonk, R., Price, R., Eds.; Springer: Dordrecht, The Netherlands, 2015. [CrossRef]
46. Sverke, M.; Hellgren, J. The nature of job insecurity: Understanding employment uncertainty on the brink of a new millennium. *App. Psychol.* **2002**, *51*, 23–42. [CrossRef]
47. Klandermans, B.; Van Vuuren, T. Job Insecurity: Introduction. *Eur. J. Work Organ. Psychol.* **2010**, *1*, 145–153. [CrossRef]
48. Hartley, J.; Jacobson, D.; Klandermans, B.; Van Vuuren, T. *Job Insecurity: Coping with Jobs at Risk*; Sage: London, UK, 1991.
49. Van den Heuvel, M.; Demerouti, E.; Bakker, A.B.; Schaufeli, W.B. Personal resources and work engagement in the face of change. In *Contemporary Occupational Health Psychology: Global Perspectives on Research and Practice*; Houdmont, J., Leka, S., Eds.; Wiley-Blackwell: Oxford, UK, 2010; pp. 124–150.
50. Lukeš, M.; Feldmann, M.; Vegetti, F. Work values and the value of work: Different implications for young adults' self-employment in Europe. *Ann. Am. Acad. Political Soc. Sci.* **2019**, *682*, 156–171. [CrossRef]
51. Ugboro, I.O. Influence of managerial trust on survivors' perceptions of job insecurity and organizational commitment in a post restructuring and downsizing environment. *J. Behav. App. Manag.* **2016**, *4*, 231–265.
52. Blackmore, C.; Kuntz, J.R. Antecedents of job insecurity in restructuring organisations: An empirical investigation. *N. Z. J. Psych* **2011**, *4*, 7–18.
53. Vanhercke, D.; De Cuyper, N.; Peeters, E.; De Witte, H. Defining perceived employability: A psychological approach. *Personn. Rev.* **2014**, *43*, 592–605. [CrossRef]
54. Çalıskan, N.; Gökhan Özkoç, A. Organizational change and job insecurity: The moderating role of employability. *Int. J. Contemp. Hosp. Manag.* **2020**, *32*, 971–3990. [CrossRef]
55. Arnold, A.; Staffelbach, B. Perceived post-restructuring job insecurity: The impact of employees' trust in one's employer and perceived employability. *German J. Hum. Res. Manag.* **2012**, *26*, 307–330. [CrossRef]

56. De Cuyper, N.; Mäkikangas, A.; Kinnunen, U.; Mauno, S.; De Witte, H. Cross-lagged associations between perceived external employability, job insecurity, and exhaustion: Testing gain and loss spirals according to the conservation of resources theory. *J. Organiz. Behav.* **2012**, *33*, 770–788. [CrossRef]
57. Mooney, S. Wasted youth in the hospitality industry: Older workers' perceptions and misperceptions about younger workers. *Hosp. Soc.* **2016**, *6*, 9–30. [CrossRef]
58. Alacovska, A.; Fieseler, C.; Wong, I.S. 'Thriving instead of surviving': A capability approach to geographical career transitions in the creative industries. *Hum. Rel.* **2021**, *74*, 751–780. [CrossRef]
59. Kusluvan, S.; Kusluvan, Z. Perceptions and attitudes of undergraduate tourism students towards working in the tourism industry in Turkey. *Tour. Manag.* **2000**, *21*, 251–269. [CrossRef]
60. Sigala, M. Rethinking of Tourism and Hospitality Education When Nothing Is Normal: Restart, Recover, or Rebuild. *J. Hosp. Tour. Res.* **2021**, *45*, 920–923. [CrossRef]
61. Hoque, M.A.; Ashif, A.S.M. Dream career in tourism and hospitality industry: Myth or reality? *Int. J. Tour. Policy* **2020**, *10*, 142–162. [CrossRef]
62. Tuzunkan, D. Inizio modulo Fine modulo Undergraduate tourism students' perceptions and attitudes towards tourism industry: The case of Daejeon, South Korea. *Geoj. Tour. Geosites* **2018**, *21*, 103–111.
63. Barron, P.; Maxwell, G. Hospitality management students' image of the hospitality industry. *Int. J. Hosp. Manag.* **1993**, *5*, v–viii. [CrossRef]
64. Khan, M.F.R.; Krishanamurthy, J. Future of Oman Tourism Perception of the Students in Tourism Studies. *Int. J. Tour. Hospit. Rev.* **2016**, *3*, 1–11. [CrossRef]
65. Cheung, C.; Law, R.; He, K. Essential hotel managerial competencies for graduate students. *J. Hosp. Tourism Educ.* **2010**, *22*, 25–32. [CrossRef]
66. English, D.E.; Manton, E.J.; Walker, J. Human resource perceptions of selected communication competencies. *Education* **2007**, *127*, 410–418.
67. Lolli, J.C. Interpersonal communication skills and the young hospitality leader: Are they prepared? *Int. J. Hosp. Manag.* **2013**, *32*, 295–298. [CrossRef]
68. Golubovskaya, M.; Robinson, R.N.S.; Solnet, D. The meaning of hospitality: Do employees understand? *J. Contemp. Hosp. Manag.* **2017**, *29*, 1282–1304. [CrossRef]
69. Ajzen, I. The theory of planned behaviour. *Organ. Behav. Human Decis. Proc.* **1991**, *25*, 179–211. [CrossRef]
70. Wang, L.; Weng Wong, P.P.; Zhang, Q. Travellers' destination choice among university students in China amid COVID-19: Extending the theory of planned behaviour. *Tour. Rev.* **2021**, *76*, 749–763. [CrossRef]
71. Edwards, J.R.; Cable, D.M.; Williamson, I.O.; Lambert, L.S.; Shipp, A.J. The phenomenology of fit: Linking the person and environment to the subjective experience of person-environment fit. *J. App. Psychol.* **2006**, *91*, 802–827. [CrossRef] [PubMed]
72. Koens, A.; Wood, R.C. An analysis of international employment levels in hospitality occupations using secondary statistics. *Int. J. Tour. Res.* **2017**, *19*, 496–504. [CrossRef]
73. Kakoudakis, K.; McCabe, S.; Story, V. Social tourism and self-efficacy Exploring links between tourism participation, job-seeking and unemployment. *Ann. Tour. Res.* **2017**, *65*, 108–121. [CrossRef]
74. Kanfer, R.; Wanberg, C.R.; Kantrowitz, T.M. Job search and employment: A personality-motivational analysis and meta-analytic review. *J. App. Psychol.* **2001**, *86*, 837–855. [CrossRef] [PubMed]
75. Deci, E.L.; Ryan, R.M. The 'what' and 'why' of goal pursuits: Human needs and the self-determination of behaviour. *Psychol. Inq.* **2000**, *11*, 227–268. [CrossRef]
76. Gagné, M.; Deci, E.L. Self-determination theory and work motivation. *J. Org. Beh.* **2005**, *6*, 331–362. [CrossRef]
77. Jacobs-Gray, N.P. Examining the Effects of Emotional Labor, Emotional and Spiritual Intelligence in Hospitality and Tourism Education. Ph.D. Thesis, Oklahoma State University, Stillwater, OK, USA, 2017. Available online: https://hdl.handle.net/11244/300058 (accessed on 21 December 2021).
78. Muller, T.E.; Cleaver, M. Targeting the CANZUS baby boomer explorer and adventurer segments. *J. Vacat. Mark.* **2000**, *6*, 154–169. [CrossRef]
79. Qiu, R.T.R.; Park, J.; Li, S.N.; Song, H. Social costs of tourism during the COVID-19 pandemic. *Ann. Tour.* **2020**, *84*, 102994. [CrossRef]
80. Hair, J.F.; Hult, G.T.M.; Ringle, C.; Sarstedt, M. *A Primer on Partial Least Squares Structural Equation Modeling (PLS-SEM)*, 2nd ed.; SAGE Publishing: Southend Oaks, CA, USA, 2017.
81. Bagozzi, R.P.; Yi, Y. On the evaluation of structural equation models. *J. Acad. Market. Sci.* **1988**, *16*, 74–94. [CrossRef]
82. Chin, W.W.; Cheah, J.-H.; Liu, Y.; Ting, H.; Lim, X.-J.; Cham, T.H. Demystifying the role of causal-predictive modeling using partial least squares structural equation modeling in information systems research. *Ind. Manag. Data Syst.* **2020**, *120*, 2161–2209. [CrossRef]
83. Hair, F.J., Jr.; Hult, M.G.T.; Ringle, M.C.; Sarstedt, M.; Danks, P.N.; Ray, S. *Partial Least Squares Structural Equation Modeling (PLS-SEM) Using R*; Springer: Berlin/Heidelberg, Germany, 2021.
84. Ringle, C.M.; Wende, S.; Becker, J.-M. SmartPLS3. 2015. Available online: https://www.smartpls.com (accessed on 21 December 2021).
85. Rasoolimanesh, S.M.; Roldán, J.L.; Jaafar, M.; Ramayah, T. Factors influencing residents' perceptions toward tourism development: Differences across rural and urban world heritage sites. *J. Travel Res.* **2017**, *56*, 760–775. [CrossRef]

86. Yeh, C.M. Tourism Involvement, Work Engagement and Job Satisfaction among Frontline Hotel Employees. *Ann. Tour. Res.* **2013**, *42*, 214–239. [CrossRef]
87. Gursoy, D.; Gavcar, E. International leisure tourists' involvement profile. *Ann. Tour. Res.* **2003**, *30*, 906–926. [CrossRef]
88. Nunnally, J.C.; Bernstein, I.H. *Psychometric*; McGraw-Hill Series in Psychology; McGraw-Hill: New York, NY, USA, 1994; Volume 3.
89. Schuberth, F.; Dijkstra, T.K.; Henseler, J. Partial least squares path modelling using ordinal categorical indicators. *Qual Quant* **2018**, *52*, 9–35. [CrossRef] [PubMed]
90. Henseler, J.; Ringle, C.M.; Sarstedt, M. A new criterion for assessing discriminant validity in variance-based structural equation modeling. *J. Acad. Mark. Sci.* **2015**, *43*, 115–135. [CrossRef]
91. Henseler, J.; Hubona, G.; Ray, P.A. Using PLS path modeling in new technology research: Updated guidelines. *Ind. Manag. Data Syst.* **2016**, *116*, 2–20. [CrossRef]
92. Rather, R.A. Monitoring the impacts of tourism-based social media, risk perception and fear on tourist's attitude and revisiting behaviour in the wake of COVID-19 pandemic. *Curr. Issues Tour.* **2021**, *24*, 3275–3283. [CrossRef]
93. Houge Mackenzie, S.; Raymond, E. A conceptual model of adventure tour guide well-being. *Ann. Tour. Res.* **2020**, *84*, 102977. [CrossRef]
94. Burlea-Schiopoiu, A.; Idowu, S.; Vertigas, S. (Eds.). *Corporate Social Responsibility in Times of Crisis: A Summary*; Springer: Berlin/Heidelberg, Germany, 2017.
95. Ntounis, N.; Parker, C.; Skinner, H.; Steadman, C.; Warnaby, G. Tourism and Hospitality industry resilience during the Covid-19 pandemic: Evidence from England. *Curr. Issues Tour* **2022**, *25*, 46–59. [CrossRef]
96. Stergiou, P.D.; Farmaki, A. Ability and willingness to work during COVID-19 pandemic: Perspectives of front-line hotel employees. *Int. J. Hosp. Manag.* **2021**, *93*, 102770. [CrossRef]
97. Skurvydas, A.; Lisinskiene, A.; Lochbaum, M.; Majauskiene, D.; Valanciene, D.; Dadeliene, R.; Fatkulina, N.; Sarkauskiene, A. Physical Activity, Stress, Depression, Emotional Intelligence, Logical Thinking, and Overall Health in a Large Lithuanian from October 2019 to June 2020: Age and Gender Differences Adult Sample. *Int. J. Environ. Res. Public Health.* **2021**, *18*, 12809. [CrossRef] [PubMed]
98. OECD 2020b. Youth and COVID-19: Response, Recovery and Resilience. Tackling Coronavirus (COVID-19) Contributing to a Global Effort. Available online: https://www.oecd.org/coronavirus/policy-responses/youth-and-covid-19-response-recovery-and-resilience-c40e61c6/ (accessed on 21 December 2021).
99. OECD 2020c. Global Report on Youth Empowerment and Intergenerational Justice. Available online: https://www.oecd.org/gov/youth-governance.htm (accessed on 21 December 2021).
100. Duan, J.; Xie, C.; Morrison, A.M. Tourism Crises and Impacts on Destinations: A Systematic Review of the Tourism and Hospitality Literature. *J. Hosp. Tour. Res.* **2021**. [CrossRef]
101. Cohen, M.J. Does the COVID-19 outbreak mark the onset of a sustainable consumption transition? *Sustain. Sci. Pract. Policy* **2020**, *16*, 1–3. [CrossRef]
102. Chang, C.L.; McAleer, M.; Ramos, V. A Charter for Sustainable Tourism after COVID-19. *Sustainability* **2020**, *12*, 3671. [CrossRef]
103. Gössling, S.; Scott, D.; Hall, C.M. Pandemics, tourism and global change: A rapid assessment of COVID-19. *J. Sustain. Tour.* **2020**, *29*, 1–20. [CrossRef]
104. Burlea-Schiopoiu, A.; Balan, D.A. Modelling the impact of corporate reputation on costumers' behavior. *Corp. Soc. Resp. Environ. Manag.* **2021**, *28*, 1142–1156. [CrossRef]

International Journal of
Environmental Research and Public Health

MDPI

Article

Development of Leisure Valuation Assessment Tool for the Elderly

Da Sol Park [1] and Hae Yean Park [2,*]

[1] Department of Occupational Therapy, Jeonju Kijeon College, Jeonju 54989, Korea; otdasol@gmail.com
[2] Department of Occupational Therapy, College of Software Digital Healthcare Convergence, Yonsei University, Wonju 26493, Korea
* Correspondence: haepark@yonsei.ac.kr

Abstract: This study aimed to develop a leisure valuation assessment tool to revitalize leisure activities for the elderly living in the community. The research method, literature review, and Delphi survey were conducted for the expert panel. Then, the leisure value and participatory leisure activity items were derived to form the assessment items. The two Delphi surveys revealed 38 leisure value assessment items and 41 participating leisure activity items. We attempted to verify the model suitability and validity of the leisure value assessment items through confirmatory factor analysis. The verification showed a good fit. Based on the intensive validity test result, AVE (average variance extracted) values were 66 for physical leisure activities, 65 for emotional leisure activities, and 65 for social leisure activities. The conceptual reliability was 0.96 for physical leisure activities, 0.95 for emotional leisure activities, and 0.96 for social leisure activities. Regarding the internal consistency for reliability verification, Cronbach's alpha values for physical leisure, emotional leisure, and social leisure activities were 0.909, 0.925, and 0.955, respectively. Hence, the items were highly interrelated and homogeneous tests that measured the same characteristics. The assessment tool can be used to identify useful information on the leisure activities of the elderly and to activate leisure activities for the elderly.

Keywords: assessment tool; leisure activities; model fit; occupational therapy; reliability; the elderly; validity; values

Citation: Park, D.S.; Park, H.Y. Development of Leisure Valuation Assessment Tool for the Elderly. *Int. J. Environ. Res. Public Health* **2022**, *19*, 6678. https://doi.org/10.3390/ijerph19116678

Academic Editors: Joachim G. Voss and Sandul Yasobant

Received: 26 April 2022
Accepted: 27 May 2022
Published: 30 May 2022

1. Introduction

Leisure refers to non-forced and internally motivated activities that involve free time other than mandatory participation in work, self-management, or sleep [1]. From a life cycle perspective, leisure activities play an important role at all ages; however, they have greater significance for the elderly. Leisure activities in old age are not simply concepts of rest, but activities to improve the quality of life in old age, which positively affects retirement life and helps to slow aging [2]. According to the 2019 National Leisure Activity Survey, leisure activity participation time in the 30s to beyond the 70s tends to increase with age; however, the number of leisure activities participated in is decreasing [3]. This means that the diversity of leisure activities for the elderly is decreasing and not being activated. To present leisure activities that meet the needs of the elderly, it is necessary to grasp the values pursued by them when participating in leisure activities. Value refers to the qualitative factors that the participant thinks are important and correct [4,5]. It is also defined as the fundamental attitude toward the world, including oneself, or the ideas therein [6]. Accordingly, leisure value—a perspective formed based on one's assessment of the significance and role of leisure in an environment including individuals—can be said to be an important qualitative factor when participating in leisure activities [7].

These leisure values were continuously evaluated in the past; they are clearly distinguishable from quantitative assessments, such as leisure activity participation time, frequency, and degree of performance in existing studies [8–11]. Studies related to leisure value assessment were conducted about 40 years ago. They include the Elder Version of

Leisure-Time Activity Enjoyment Scale Assessment Tool for Leisure Tendency of Elder Adults, Leisure Time Situation Scale, and Leisure Activity Party Scale [9,12,13].

However, the existing assessment tools related to leisure values have limitations. First, it is difficult to use these tools designed for evaluating specific leisure activities and has limited opportunity to present new leisure activities that meet the needs of the elderly. Second, since the participants of the assessment are diverse, such as foreigners, adults, and the disabled, it cannot be said to be an elderly-oriented assessment tool. Hence, there is a limit to its application to the elderly living in domestic communities.

Therefore, this study aimed to (1) develop a "leisure valuation assessment tool for the elderly" (LVAT-E) to revitalize leisure activities for the elderly living in the community and (2) verify the suitability, reliability, and validity of this model's assessment tool for the elderly living in the community.

2. Methods

This study was conducted in two stages. The first step was to collect preliminary items and organize the items of the LVAT-E through Delphi research. The second step was to develop assessment tools through model suitability, reliability, and validity verification (Figure 1). This study was approved by the Yonsei University Future Campus Bioethics Review Committee (1041849-202007-BM-089-03).

2.1. Composition of Assessment Items

To construct the assessment items, related prior studies were considered, and Delphi surveys were conducted on a group of experts in related occupations. Based on the derived results, leisure value assessment and participatory leisure activity items were included.

2.1.1. Literature Review and National Leisure Activity Survey

As this study was conducted in Korea, mainly journals that included relatively many Korean studies were searched for the literature review. We searched the databases of Pubmed, Google Scholar, and Riss, and the search terms were "Leisure" and "Assessment" or "Measure" or "Scale". The detailed criteria for selection and exclusion were as follows.

- Selection criteria
  (1) Research published in academic journals in the last 10 years (2011–2020);
  (2) Study written in Korean or English;
  (3) A study on the Quality Assessment Tool for Leisure Activities for the Elderly.
- Exclusion criteria
  (1) A study on the evaluation of specific leisure activities;
  (2) A paper that is impossible to read in full;
  (3) Research in the forms of meta-analyses, degree theses, books, and posters.

Classification Criteria for Leisure Activities for the Elderly

The same classification was used in this study based on the classification of elderly leisure activities into physical, emotional, and social leisure activities using elderly activity theory, continuous theory, and social exchange theory, which are related to elderly leisure [14,15] (Table 1).

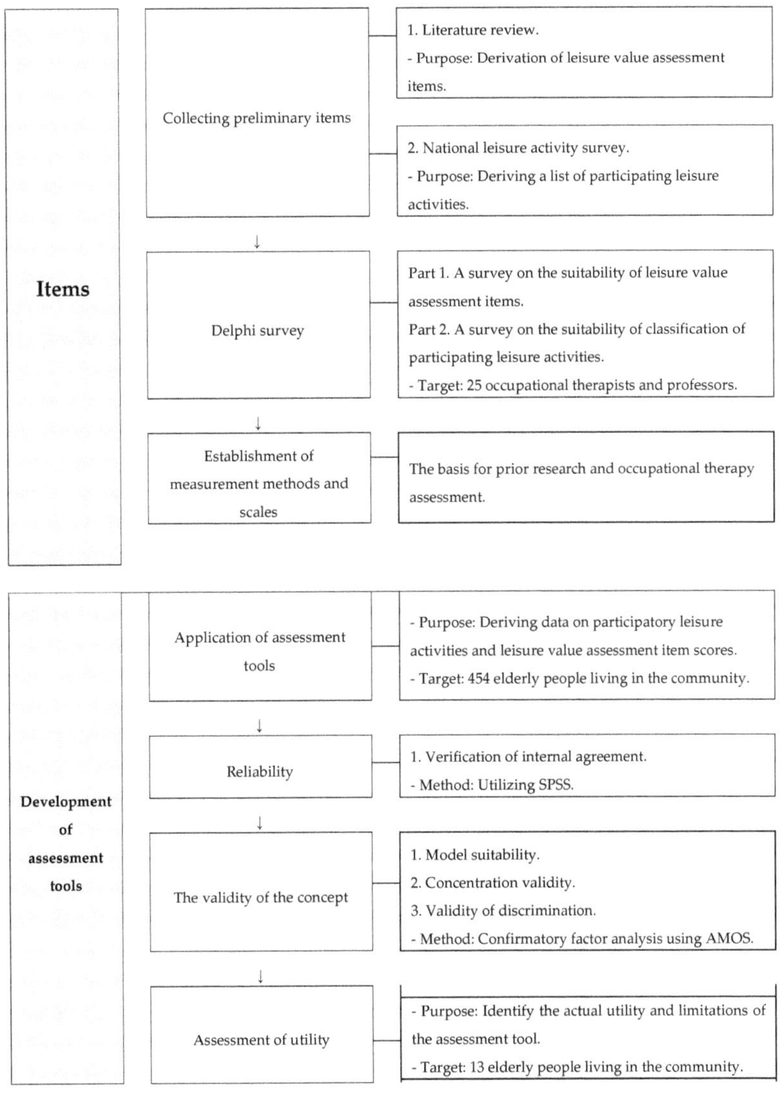

Figure 1. Research process and assessment tool development process.

Table 1. Classification and definition of leisure activities for the elderly.

Classification	Name of Leisure Activities
Physical leisure	Leisure activities that include indoor sports activities and outdoor sports activities and promote physical health.
Emotional leisure	Activities for emotional stability, hobbies for cultural and artistic entertainment, and activities including education through paid and free educational institutions to promote education.
Social leisure	Activities that include community activities or social activities that express roles and beliefs and wills as members of society through them, and activities that return various experiences of life to society.

2.1.2. Delphi Survey

A Delphi survey was conducted to construct the assessment items. The Delphi survey consisted of 25 people who had more than seven years of clinical and educational experience with the elderly and community occupational therapy or a master's degree in occupational therapy. Detailed information on the experts is presented in Table 2. The Delphi survey in this study was conducted twice via e-mail in August 2020. In this study, a modified Delphi technique using a structured questionnaire different from the first Delphi was used [16].

Table 2. General information of experts.

Career (Month/Year) [Clinical/Education/Research]			Educational Background	Job
3 m 7 y	6 y	6 y	Ph.D.	Professor
6 m 8 y	4 y	-	Ph.D.	Professor
5 y	15 y	-	Ph.D.	Professor
5 y	3 y	4 y	Ph.D.	Professor
4 y	-	6 m	Ph.D.	Occupational therapist
3 y	3 y	-	Ph.D.	Professor
-	-	11 m 4 y	Ph.D.	Researcher
6 m 7 y	-	-	Master's	Occupational therapist
4 y	2 y	3 y	Ph.D.	Professor
4 y	6 m	-	Ph.D.	Occupational therapist
1 y	-	6 m 3 y	Ph.D.	Professor
1 y	-	6 m 1 y	Master's	Occupational therapist
3 m 4 y	3 y	4 y	Master's	Professor
1 y	-	8 m 2 y	Ph.D.	Occupational therapist
6 m	-	2 m 2 y	Master's	Occupational therapist
1 y	-	8 m 2 y	Ph.D.	Occupational therapist
6 m 5 y	6 m 1 y	8 m 4 y	Ph.D.	Professor
7 y	4 y	-	Ph.D.	Professor
1 y	-	2 y	Master's	Occupational therapist
4 y	1 y	2 m 2 y	Ph.D.	Professor

Fitness was evaluated on a 4-point Likert scale (1 point: very inappropriate, 4 points: very appropriate). In the data analysis, the content validity ratio (CVR), average, standard deviation, stability, convergence, and consensus were analyzed for the responded content.

2.2. *Development of Assessment Tool*

2.2.1. Application of Assessment Tools

After the Delphi survey, an assessment tool was applied to 454 elderly (aged $\geq$ 60 years) living in the community from August to September 2020. The number of participants was calculated based on the findings of Mitchell (1993), which stated that a sample size of at least 10 times the number of observation variables was required. The selection criteria were as follows, and general information is shown in Table 3 [17]:

- A community resident aged 60 or older.
- A person who has not been diagnosed with dementia, cognitive impairment, etc., and who can understand the contents of the evaluation tool.

Table 3. General information of participants.

Classification		Mean (Standard Deviation)	N	%
Age	60~65	68.12 (3.28)	115	25.3
	66~70		242	53.3
	71~75		75	16.5
	76~80		22	4.8
Final academic background	University		302	66.5
	High school		128	28.2
	Middle school		18	4.0
	Elementary school		5	1.1
	No education		1	0.2
Housemate	Living alone		28	6.2
	Husband and wife		302	66.5
	A married child		20	4.4
	An unmarried child		90	79.8
	Other		14	3.1
Residential area	Big city		34	7.5
	Small- or medium-sized city		420	92.5
Subjective health conditions	Great health		11	2.4
	Good health		120	26.4
	Normal		230	48.5
	Unhealthy		96	21.1
	Very unhealthy		7	1.5

In principle, a tool is a self-checklist and involves offline implementation, but it was implemented in the form of an online survey through research companies due to environmental constraints caused by COVID-19. Online explanations and consent forms for the study subjects were presented, and only those who pressed the study consent button participated in the study. SPSS 25 was used for the statistical analysis, and descriptive statistics and one-way analysis of variance were used.

2.2.2. Reliability

Verification of Internal Consistency

In general, in the field of social science, the internal consistency is judged as "acceptable," "good," and "very good" when it is $\geq$0.6, $\geq$0.7, and $\geq$0.8, respectively [17].

2.2.3. Construct Validity

Confirmatory factor analysis using Analysis of Moment Structures (AMOS) was conducted to verify construct validity. Confirmatory factor analysis is useful for measuring construct validity because it can evaluate the overall fit of the model and measure the factor load between observations and latent variables. The construct validity verification procedure was performed in the following order: model suitability, convergent validity verification, and discriminant validity verification.

2.2.4. Assessment of Utility

The effectiveness of the assessment tool was evaluated by applying it to 13 elderly people living in the community. The criteria for selecting participants were as follows:

- A community resident aged 60 or older.
- A person who has not been diagnosed with dementia, cognitive impairment, etc., and who can understand the contents of the evaluation tool.

The utility test was evaluated on a 5-point Likert scale for item understanding, assessment method understanding, and appropriateness of writing time.

3. Results

3.1. Item Composition Result

3.1.1. Literature Review and National Leisure Activity Survey Results

Of the collected items, 39 were about leisure value and 45 about participating in leisure activities. They were derived by integrating similar concepts and deleting overlapping items (Tables 4 and 5).

Table 4. The 39 leisure value items found through the literature review [12].

Name of Assessment Tool	Concepts
The Leisure Time Satisfaction Scale (LTS)	- Activities with family - Activities with friends - Social support
Elderly version of Leisure-Time Activity Enjoyment Scale (LAES)	- Achieve an accomplishment - Affirmative change of the mind - Affirmative change of the body - Enjoyment - Pleasure - Socialization
The Leisure Assessment Inventory	- Adaptive behavior - Life satisfaction
Assessment Tool for Leisure Tendency of Older Adults	- Leisure lifestyle - Leisure motivation
Leisure Nostalgia Scale	- Group identity - Leisure experience - Personal identity - Socialization
The Leisure Boredom Scale	- Boredom
Physical Activity and Leisure Motivation Scale	- Affiliation - Appearance - Others' expectations - Enjoyment - Competition - Ego - Physical condition - Psychological condition
Global Leisure Meanings Scale (GLMS)	- Escaping pressure - Group harmony - Leisure friendship - Passing time - Self-development
Leisure Activity Participation Scale	- Activity with an attractive environment - Developmental - Entertaining - Esthetic - Exciting - Productive - Relaxing - Social

Table 5. The 45 participating in leisure activities items found through the National Leisure Activity Survey.

Classification of Leisure Activities (Physical/Emotional/Social)	Names of Leisure Activities
Physical leisure	- Participation in ball sports - (gateball, soccer, basketball, golf, tennis, badminton, bowling, etc.) - Swimming - Fitness - Aerobics - Stretching - Yoga and pilates - Fishing - Visit zoos, botanical gardens, and amusement parks - Walking and walking - Mountain climbing
Emotional leisure	- Exhibitions, performances, and movies - Watching sports events - Listening to music - Collection activities - Driving a car - Cooking - Taking care of pets - Singing - Taking a photo - Painting - Calligraphy - Playing musical instruments - Gardening - Napping - Watching TV - Listening to the radio - Using Internet media - Writing - Reading discussions - Reading newspapers and magazines - Acquiring language, skills, and certificates - Studying - Going on a trip
Social leisure	- Volunteer activity - Religious activities - Family and relatives - A peer group - Shopping/eating out - Go, chess, hwatu - Chatting, calling, and texting - Games and puzzles - A picnic - Going to a hot spring or a bathhouse - Participate in local festivals and feasts - Going to a senior citizen center

3.1.2. Delphi Survey Results

Following the analysis of the response values of two Delphi surveys, all items in parts 1 and 2 showed significant values of the minimum value with a CVR of $\geq$0.37, convergence of 0.5, agreement of $\geq$0.75, and stability of $\leq$0.8 (Table 6). Thirty-eight leisure value assessment items and forty-one leisure activities were assessed.

Table 6. Results of the 1st and 2nd Delphi surveys.

	Average	SD	Convergence	Agreements	Stability	CVR
1st Delphi part 1	3.72	0.46	0.48	0.72	0.20	0.78
2nd Delphi part 1	3.43	0.55	0.33	0.82	0.16	0.89
1st Delphi part 2	3.46	0.62	0.42	0.76	0.18	0.80
2nd Delphi part 2	3.55	0.51	0.27	0.86	0.15	0.93

3.2. Results of Developing Assessment Tools

3.2.1. Construct Validity Results

Model Fit Results

The model suitability results showed good suitability; however, the GFI was 0.825, which is slightly above the standard of 0.8 (Table 7).

Table 7. Model fit.

χ^2	df	CMIN/DF	RMSEA	SRMR	CFI	TLI	GFI
1416.182	479	2.957	0.066	0.0561	0.902	0.892	0.825

Convergence Validity Results

The AVE values and conceptual reliability values are shown in Table 8.

Table 8. Convergence validity results.

Sub-Item Classification	AVE	Conceptual Reliability
Physical leisure activity	0.67	0.96
Emotional leisure activity	0.65	0.95
Social leisure activity	0.65	0.96

Discriminant Validity Results

The discriminant validity analysis showed that the AVE of all the corresponding observation variables was larger than the square of the correlation coefficient (Table 9).

Table 9. Discriminant validity results.

Sub-Item Classification	Square Correlation Coefficient	AVE
Physical—emotional leisure	0.63	$\Phi^2 < 66$ (physical) $\Phi^2 < 64$ (emotional)
Emotional—social leisure	0.57	$\Phi^2 < 64$ (emotional) $\Phi^2 < 65$ (social)
Physical—social leisure	0.25	$\Phi^2 < 66$ (physical) $\Phi^2 < 65$ (social)

3.2.2. Reliability Results

Internal Consistency Results

The internal match analysis revealed that all three areas of the leisure activity sub-items had very high reliability (Table 10).

Table 10. Internal consistency results.

Sub-Item Classification	Crohnbach's Alpha Value
Physical leisure activity	0.909
Emotional leisure activity	0.925
Social leisure activity	0.955

3.2.3. The Results of the Utility Assessment

Based on the result of the utility assessment, it took 10–15 min per person to apply the assessment tool. The results are shown in Table 11.

Table 11. Discriminant validity results of utility assessment.

Sub-Item Classification	Very Positive	Positive	Usually	Negative	Very Negative
	N (%)	N (%)	N (%)	N (%)	N (%)
The level of understanding	6 (46.2)	6 (46.2)	1 (7.6)	0 (0)	0 (0)
Assessment method understanding	7 (53.8)	5 (38.5)	1 (7.6)	0 (0)	0 (0)
Appropriateness of writing time	5 (38.5)	6 (46.2)	1 (7.6)	1 (7.6)	0 (0)

4. Discussion

To revitalize the leisure activities of the elderly living in the community, this study attempted to develop an LVAT-E that can evaluate various leisure values that relate to the leisure activities of the elderly.

The leisure value assessment items of the developed assessment tool have the advantage of being an indicator of what factors the elderly consider important when participating in leisure activities and being able to closely explain the elderly's desire for leisure activities. This is partially consistent with the argument in foreign studies that participants' individual characteristics should be identified because they influence the leisure activities they participate in [18–20].

The participatory leisure activity items developed in this study have the advantage of being able to separately present "leisure activities they are currently participating in" and "leisure activities that they are not currently participating in but are willing to participate in the future." If the leisure value assessment items developed in this study and the participatory leisure activity items are used together, the needs of the elderly can be closely understood. Additionally, the participatory leisure activity items can provide practical help when planning leisure activities. Moreso, the LVAT-E can be seen in previous studies as an assessment tool that clearly supports the opinion that qualitative and quantitative factors should be evaluated together when evaluating leisure activities for the elderly [8–12].

The process used to develop the assessment tool in this study had some limitations. First, when applying the assessment tool, the age group was unevenly distributed. In addition, most of the subjects were highly educated. The participants' age and educational background are factors that influence their participation in leisure activities, and the frequency and type of participation change accordingly [3]. In future studies, reliability and validity should be verified by considering the age group and educational background of the sample.

Second, the assessment tool was applied in the form of an Internet-based survey due to the influence of COVID-19. Since the participants were aged 60 years or older, in future studies, it will be necessary to conduct offline self-checklists when applying assessment tools in consideration of the characteristics of the elderly.

Third, some previous studies used a measurement method and a method of improving the completeness of the assessment scale establishment of the expert advisory meeting when establishing the assessment tool scale. However, this study used a 5-point Likert scale based on previous studies without an expert advisory meeting. In future studies, expert opinions on leisure activities should be reflected in the process of establishing measurement methods and assessment scales.

Despite these limitations, the LVAT-E is not limited to the assessment of specific leisure activities. Additionally, it is possible to evaluate various values pursued by the subject when participating in leisure activities. Hence, the significance of this study is that it can help the subject to plan new leisure activities or suggest a direction in which the leisure activities they are currently participating in should be improved. In modern society, the time for the elderly to participate in leisure activities is increasing; however, the diversity of the leisure activities they participate in is decreasing. It is expected that the assessment tool developed in this study can be used to identify helpful information on the leisure activities of the elderly and to activate leisure activities.

5. Conclusions

This study aimed to develop an LVAT-E and verify the reliability and validity of revitalizing leisure activities for the elderly living in the community. The significance of this study is that it can help the elderly to plan new leisure activities or suggest directions in which the leisure activities they are currently participating in should be improved. The assessment tool developed in this study can be used to identify helpful information on the leisure activities of the elderly and to activate leisure activities.

Author Contributions: Conceptualization, D.S.P. and H.Y.P.; methodology, D.S.P.; formal analysis, D.S.P.; investigation, D.S.P.; writing—review and editing, D.S.P. and H.Y.P.; visualization, D.S.P.; supervision, H.Y.P.; project administration, H.Y.P.; funding acquisition, H.Y.P. All authors have read and agreed to the published version of the manuscript.

Funding: This work was supported by a National Research Foundation of Korea (NRF) grant funded by the Korean government (MSIT) (NRF-2020R1C1C1011374).

Institutional Review Board Statement: The study was approved by the Institutional Review Board of Yonsei University (YUWIRB-1041849-202007-BM-089-03).

Informed Consent Statement: Informed consent was obtained from all the participants involved in the study.

Data Availability Statement: The data that support the findings of this study are available on request from the corresponding author (H.Y.P.). The data are not publicly available owing to restrictions (e.g., they contain information that could compromise the privacy of the research participants).

Conflicts of Interest: The authors declare no conflict of interest.

References

1. American Occupational Therapy Association. Occupational therapy practice framework: Domain and process (3rd edition). *Am. J. Occup. Ther.* **2014**, *68* (Suppl. 1), S1–S48. [CrossRef]
2. Park, K.H.; Kim, D.K. Analyzing elderly's leisure to improve the quality of life in the era of 100 aging society in Korea: Series 1. Analyzing elderly's leisure repertoire. *J. Tour. Leis. Res.* **2013**, *25*, 85–104.
3. Ministry of Culture, Sports and Tourism. *2019 National Leisure Activity Survey*; Ministry of Culture, Sports and Tourism: Sejong, Korea, 2019.
4. Kielhofner, G. *Doing and Becoming: Occupational Model of Human Occupation: Theory and Application*; Lippincott Williams & Wilkins: Baltimore, MD, USA, 2008; p. 126.
5. Moyers, P.; Dale, L.M. The guide to occupational therapy practice. *Am. J. Occup. Ther.* **1999**, *53*, 247–322. [CrossRef] [PubMed]
6. National Institute of Korean Language. *Standard Korean dictionary*; Human Culture Arirang: Seoul, Korea, 2014.
7. Yeo, J.E. Exploring of the formation process for leisure values of university students. *J. Leis. Stud.* **2016**, *14*, 37–52.
8. Kim, J.S. The development of global leisure meaning scale for Korean immigrants. *J. Leis. Stud.* **2018**, *16*, 1–28.
9. Jeong, E.H.; Park, J.H. A systematic study on the leisure assessment tool for the elderly. *Korean J. Occup. Ther.* **2018**, *26*, 39–55. [CrossRef]
10. Auger, D. The diverse meanings of leisure. *Soc. Leis.* **2016**, *39*, 173–176.
11. Kelly, J.R.; Freysinger, V.J. *21st Century Leisure: Current Issues*; Allyn & Bacon: Boston, MA, USA, 2000.
12. Park, D.S.; Shin, G.I.; Lee, H.S.; Park, H.Y. Qualitative Assessment Tools of Leisure Activities for the Elderly: Convergence study. *J. Korea Converg. Soc.* **2020**, *11*, 433–440.
13. Hwang, S.H.; Seo, H.J. Relationships among leisure constraints, leisure constraints negotiation, and serious leisure. *Korean J. Sport Sci.* **2009**, *20*, 298–307. [CrossRef]
14. Park, E.H. Mediating Effects of Ego-Integrity on the Relationship between Leisure Activity of Elders and Successful Aging Focused Using Senior Welfare Center. Ph.D. Thesis, Seoul Christian University, Seoul, Korea, 2016.
15. Kim, Y.K. A Study on the Physical, Social, and Leisure-Welfare Factors in the Quality of Life for the Aged. Ph.D. Thesis, Seoul Christian University, Seoul, Korea, 2013.
16. Murry, J.W., Jr.; Hammons, J.O. Delphi: A versatile methodology for conducting qualitative research. *Rev. High. Educ.* **1995**, *18*, 423–436. [CrossRef]
17. Mitchell, R.J. Path analysis: Pollination. In *Design and Analysis of Ecological*; Chapman & Hall: New York, NY, USA, 1993; pp. 211–231.

18. Hills, P.; Argyle, M. Positive moods derived from leisure and their relationship to happiness and personality. *Personal. Individ. Differ.* **1998**, *25*, 523–535. [CrossRef]
19. Kraaykamp, G.; Van Eijck, K. Personality, media preferences, and cultural participation. *Personal. Individ. Differ.* **2005**, *38*, 1675–1688. [CrossRef]
20. Melamed, S.; Meir, E.I.; Samson, A. The benefits of personality-leisure congruence: Evidence and implications. *J. Leis. Res.* **1995**, *27*, 25–40. [CrossRef]

International Journal of
Environmental Research and Public Health

MDPI

Article

Development and Psychometric Testing of a Taiwanese Team Interactions and Team Creativity Instrument (TITC-T) for Nursing Students

Hsing-Yuan Liu [1,2], Su-Ching Sung [3], Chun-Yen Chao [4], Nai-Hung Chen [1], Hsiu-Fang Chen [1,2,*] and Sheau-Ming Wu [1,*]

1 Department of Nursing, Chang Gung University of Science and Technology, Taoyuan City 33303, Taiwan; hyliu@mail.cgust.edu.tw (H.-Y.L.); nhchen@mail.cgust.edu.tw (N.-H.C.)
2 Department of Nursing, Linkous Chang Gung Memorial Hospital, Taoyuan City 33305, Taiwan
3 Department of Gerontology and Health Care Management, Chang Gung University of Science and Technology, Taoyuan City 33303, Taiwan; scsung@mail.cgust.edu.tw
4 Department of Cosmetic Science, Chang Gung University of Science and Technology, Taoyuan City 33303, Taiwan; cychao@mail.cgust.edu.tw
* Correspondence: fang@mail.cgust.edu.tw (H.-F.C.); sheamwu@mail.cgust.edu.tw (S.-M.W.)

Citation: Liu, H.-Y.; Sung, S.-C.; Chao, C.-Y.; Chen, N.-H.; Chen, H.-F.; Wu, S.-M. Development and Psychometric Testing of a Taiwanese Team Interactions and Team Creativity Instrument (TITC-T) for Nursing Students. *Int. J. Environ. Res. Public Health* **2022**, *19*, 7958. https://doi.org/10.3390/ijerph19137958

Academic Editors: Joachim G. Voss, Sandul Yasobant and Paul B. Tchounwou

Received: 8 June 2022
Accepted: 27 June 2022
Published: 29 June 2022

Abstract: Background: How well team members work together can be affected by team interactions and creativity. There is no single instrument for measuring both variables in healthcare education settings in Taiwan. The purpose of this study is to develop an instrument to measure team interactions and team creativity for Taiwanese nursing students. Methods: A 34-item team interactions and team creativity self-report instrument was developed for nursing students in Taiwan (TITC-T). Items consisted of statements about how a participant perceived their team members' constructive controversy, helping behaviors, communication, and creativity. Nursing students (n = 275) were recruited from two campuses of a science and technology university to examine the psychometric properties of the TITC-T. The reliability and psychometric properties were evaluated. Results: The Cronbach's alpha was 0.98. The confirmatory factor analysis resulted in a one-dimensional factor structure that fit well with the model (Comparative Fit Index = 0.995, Tucker Lewis Index = 0.908, Root Mean Square Error of Approximation = 0.098). Conclusions: The TITC-T is a valid and reliable tool for evaluating team interactions and team creativity for students enrolled in nursing programs in Taiwan.

Keywords: team interaction; team creativity; scale development; nursing education; Taiwan

1. Introduction

Creativity and innovation in nursing enhances healthcare quality, reduces healthcare costs, and generates an environment structured to reduce work-related stressors and emotional exhaustion, which can reduce burnout for healthcare professionals [1]. Fostering creativity and innovation in nursing students can improve patient healthcare and outcomes [1]. Interdisciplinary collaboration among healthcare teams is also increasing, resulting in more comprehensive healthcare for the treatment of patients [2].

A systematic review on interprofessional education [3] argued that higher education must implement interdisciplinary learning opportunities. Students among different academic areas should be capable of communicating with a common language, thus affording them the opportunity to tackle more complex issues. The Word Health Organization (WHO) describes interdisciplinary education (IDE) as providing instruction from faculty with two or more professional backgrounds, which enables effective collaboration among students and improves healthcare outcomes [4]. Students involved in IDE programs not only learn relevant skills from multiple disciplines, but also learn how to communicate and collaborate. However, an understanding of interdisciplinary team interactions is critical for IDE to effectively improve student collaborations [5].

Studies have been implemented to improve training methods that can reduce barriers to and increase collaborations among team members [6,7]. However, evaluating whether team interactions and team creativity impact collaboration outcomes in nursing education have not been examined. Although many instruments have been developed to assess these variables on an individual-level, few are available for use in Taiwan that are specific for nursing education. Therefore, there is a need for the development of a valid self-report instrument for assessing team interactions and team creativity that is directed at students in nursing programs in Taiwan, especially students enrolled in IDE programs.

Boosting positive interactions and increasing creativity among team members is not only critical for the success of groups and organizations, but also a key solution to many modern challenges facing world economies, including healthcare teams [8,9]. Innovation among team members requires divergent thinking, which is more likely to occur in an atmosphere where each member feels free to express their ideas without boundaries, risks of judgment, or fear of ridicule from others [8,10]. Therefore, communication is a dominant process and an important component of team interactions that is critical to the success of healthcare teams [9,11].

Cragan et al. [12] defined four characteristics important for successful team interactions because they give the team purpose: problem solving, role playing, team building, and trust building. Constructive team interactions generate solutions to problems that have a higher level of acceptance among team members than solutions shaped by interactions that are passive or aggressive [11,13]. Team interactions, including collaboration and communication, can act as mediators between transformational leadership and performance [11,14,15].

Ilgen et al. [16] proposed that how team members interact (input) effects the product created (output). They suggested that a model of input-mediator-output-input (IMOI) could be used to understand the range of variables that are important mediators for team interactions. The IMOI model allows for a broadening of variables that can influence team interactions beyond communication and performance, described by Marlow et al. [17].

The IMOI model is the basis of several instruments developed to examine additional variables deemed important components of team interactions. Constructive controversy [18–20], involves open-minded discussions of incompatible views for the mutual benefit of all team members [21], and helping behaviors [20,22], consist of deliberate, straightforward efforts to assist another member of the team [23]. Assisting others has been shown to increase team interactions in general [24] and improve team creativity, which leads to the development of products that are more innovative [2,10]. Spontaneous communication [25,26] describes informal and unplanned exchanges with other members of the team outside the normal routine, which provides team members with a different perspective for problem solving [25,27]. Spontaneity helps individuals to take the initiative and be self-starting [28].

The most widely used instruments for team creativity were developed by Farh, Lee, and Farh [29], Oldham and Cummings [30] to assess team creativity for employees, and Leroy et al. [31], who assessed team creativity in the context of organizational behavior. These instruments measure collaborative behaviors, which is an important component of successful creative interdisciplinary teams and has been demonstrated to foster productivity among team members [27,30]. Instruments have also been developed to measure interaction behaviors, which can influence creativity and include constructive controversy, helping behaviors, and spontaneous communication [15,18,26]. These instruments have been adapted for studies on leadership behaviors, goal orientation, and cognitive dissonance [14,21,32].

Several qualities are important for team creativity. Effective team collaboration in an inter-professional setting has been shown to enhance patient safety and outcomes [33,34]. This requires cooperation, collaboration, and communication among members of interdisciplinary teams, and is an important component of healthcare [35]. Interactive behaviors can improve teamwork competency, which includes qualities labeled as constructive controversy, helping behavior, and spontaneous communication [36].

Creativity is considered as a collaborative behavior of successful interdisciplinary teams and has been demonstrated to foster productivity among team members [27,31]. Effective team collaboration in an inter-professional setting has been shown to enhance patient safety and outcomes [33,34]. This requires cooperation, collaboration, and communication among interdisciplinary team members, and is an important component of healthcare [35]. Interactive behaviors can improve teamwork competency, which includes qualities labeled as constructive controversy, helping behavior, and spontaneous communication [36]. Derdowski et al. [37] suggested the interactive behavior of constructive controversy can improve group performance and increase team creativity. Helping behaviors are positively related to creative innovation for healthcare teams [38]. McAlpine [39] demonstrated that spontaneous communication among team members can improve creativity by facilitating a better flow of information.

Many instruments have been developed or adapted as measures of team creativity [14,15,18,29–32]. However, these were not developed for use with nursing students in Taiwan or were administered to non-native English speakers without confirmation of the translation [14,21]. To our knowledge, there is no valid measurement instrument available for use in Taiwan that incorporates team interactions, team creativity, and competency in the healthcare setting of nursing. Therefore, because we considered it important that a self-report instrument reflects characteristics of nursing student teams, this study aimed to merge components of developed instruments for use with teams of nursing students, translate the new self-report scale into Taiwanese, and determine its validity and psychometric properties.

2. Materials and Methods

2.1. Research Design

This exploratory and cross-sectional study was performed in several steps to develop, translate, and validate an instrument to measure team interactions and team creativity for undergraduate nursing students in Taiwan.

2.2. Instrument Development

Although instruments for assessing team creativity and team interactions are available, they have not been developed for nursing students. Therefore, we merged relevant components from Chinese and English language scales to assess team creativity and interactions for nursing students in Taiwan. We translated all English language statements to Mandarin Chinese, the language spoken in Taiwan, using the forward translation/back translation procedure described by Brislin [40]. This translation process was used to maintain content equivalence of terminology describing team interactions in Taiwanese. English language statements were independently translated by two bilingual members of the research team who were fluent in both English and Taiwanese. An English language expert back translated the Taiwanese versions into English without any knowledge of the original English version and compared each statement to the original, to confirm semantic equivalence. The two bilingual translators confirmed the semantic equivalence of the original English statements and the back translated Mandarin Chinese statements, which indicated the final translation was satisfactory.

Team interactions assessed three components: constructive controversy [18–20], helping behaviors [15,20,22], and spontaneous communication [11,25,26]. The domains are measured with statements about how an individual feels about interactions among members of their team. Team creativity has been measured for information technology teams in China using a team creativity scale developed by Farh et al. for teams of employees [29], which was a modification developed by Oldham and Cummings to measure employee creativity [30]. The self-report instrument measures creative ideas, innovation, and performance and has good reliability, with a Cronbach's alpha of 0.85 [29]. Yang et al. [15] made further modifications to measure team creativity in a research and development setting in China, again with employees rather than students; this scale has a Cronbach's alpha of 0.95. We revised statements from the Mandarin Chinese language instruments of Farh et al. [29], Yang et al. [15], and Zhang et al. [32]. Some of the wording for the statements about team creativity was not relevant to nursing students and the challenges they would encounter as nurses. Therefore, we added statements about aspects of creativity from English language instruments that were more appropriate for an educational setting: creative performance [41] and innovation [42]. The English language statements from Shally et al. [41] and Scott and Bruce [42] were translated from English to Mandarin Chinese as described above.

We combined the items for interactions and creativity into a 34-item instrument, the Taiwanese Team Interactions and Team Creativity scale (TITC-T). A 5-point Likert scale from 1 (strongly disagree) to 5 (strongly agree) was used for the three subscales for team interactions (constructive controversy (4 items), helping behaviors (10 items) and spontaneous communication (10 items)) and 10 items for team creativity. Each item completes the statement "Members of my team ... " The 34 items are shown in Table 1. The score for the three domains of team interactions is the average of the sum of all item scores in each domain and the total score for team interactions is the average of the sum of the three domains; higher scores indicate a greater perception of team interactions. The total score for team creativity is the average of the sum for all 10 items; higher scores indicate greater team creativity. The final TITC-T scale was a 34-item self-report measurement instrument for team interactions (three dimensions) and team creativity for nursing students.

Table 1. Items for the Team Interactions and Team Creativity scale for nursing students in Taiwan (TITC-T).

Construct	Items
Team interactions	Members of my team ...
Constructive Controversy	1. Encourage me to share thoughts that differ from them. 2. Listen to diverse perspectives in a supportive manner. 3. Provide constructive feedback. 4. Respectful of conflicting thoughts and suggestions.
Helping behaviors	1. Collaborate effectively. 2. Work efficiently together to complete projects. 3. Patiently explain new concepts if someone does not understand. 4. Act as a negotiator if there are conflicting perspectives. 5. Willingly offer assistance when others need help. 6. Share the workload equally. 7. Offer encouragement if a product fails. 8. Provide constructive suggestions. 9. Do not hesitate to help others if a problem arises. 10. Know the team leader will support them.
Spontaneous Communication	1. Are open to exchanging different solutions to a problem. 2. Are open to discussing new ideas and skills. 3. Do not hesitate to ask others for information. 4. Readily share knowledge and skills with other members. 5. Are available anytime for me to share ideas. 6. Willing to exchange different methods. 7. Collaborate with others to stay on schedule. 8. Offer new methods for old problems. 9. Encourage discussion to clarify confusing ideas. 10. Encourage exchanging difficulties as well as successes.
Team creativity	1. Have ideas that are new. 2. Use new techniques to solve problems. 3. Are able to identify needed healthcare products. 4. Develop healthcare products that are novel. 5. Think "outside the box". 6. Are good at developing practical solutions. 7. Can revamp a design to improve it. 8. Think in ways that are imaginative. 9. Adds to knowledge and skills to the group. 10. Can identify a healthcare product that will be useful.

2.3. Participants

To test the scale, nursing students (n = 275) were recruited from capstone courses that were part of nursing programs on two campuses of a university of science and technology in northern Taiwan. Nursing students who enrolled in the course were included if they provided signed informed consent at the conclusion of the capstone course, indicating they were willing to participate in the study.

The Capstone Course

The capstone course is conducted over 18 weeks by instructors who are faculty members from the programs in nursing and design. The course emphasizes working collaboratively in teams to evaluate what healthcare products could improve patient care, and then designing a prototype of the product that has the potential for being patented. Teams are comprised not only of nursing students but also students from the school of design, although the design students are not participants in the study. Students receive a midterm grade based on a written exam. The final grade consists of a group presentation at the conclusion of the course, which is presented to faculty members by each team of students.

2.4. Data Collection and Analysis

Data from nursing students were collected at the end of the 18-week course between October 2017 and January 2018. Two structured questionnaires were distributed to students in coded packets by a faculty member who was not part of the research team. One questionnaire collected demographic data, including age and gender; the second questionnaire was the newly developed self-report TITC-T instrument, which collected data on nursing students' perceptions of team interactions and creativity for use in confirmatory factor analysis (CFA). Prior to analyzing the data, the faculty member checked each packet for a signed consent form. All packets contained signed consent forms, and thus, all 275 students were included in the analysis.

2.5. Statistical Analysis

We used SPSS version 20.0 (IBM, Chicago, IL, USA) for Windows to analyze demographics descriptive and inferential statistical analyses. Demographic and participant characteristics were analyzed via mean, standard deviation, percentage, and frequency. To explore the fit and confirm the structure of the TITC-T, we conducted CFA with structural equation modeling using AMOS 25 software (IBM, Chicago, IL, USA). All statistical tests were two-tailed, and the significance level was set to a standard of $\alpha < 0.05$.

2.6. Ethical Considerations

Before beginning the study, approval was obtained from the university's Institutional Review Board (IRB) (IRB201800212; IRB0C502). To maintain students' confidentiality, data were anonymized by coding the packets and questionnaires distributed to the nursing students.

3. Results

3.1. Participant Demographics and Mean Scale Scores

The mean age of participants was 21.4 years (SD = 0.93; range = 19 to 27 years) and 82.5% were female. The mean total scores for team interactions were 4.23 (SD = 0.48) and the three constructs were similar, as was the mean score for creativity (4.11, SD = 0.69) indicating moderately high levels of team interactions. Details of scores for each measure are shown in Table 2.

Table 2. Mean scores on the Team Interactions and Team Creativity scale for nursing students in Taiwan (TITC-T) (n = 275).

TITC-T Scores	Mean	SD
Team interactions total	4.23	0.48
Subscales		
Constructive controversy	4.00	0.62
Helping behaviors	4.09	0.71
Spontaneous communication	4.05	0.69
Team Creativity total	4.11	0.69

SD = standard deviation.

3.2. Confirmatory Factor Analysis

The four-factor model of the TITC-T was tested by CFA. Because the number of participants in our study exceeded 200, which can result in false positives when an χ^2 index is used, we included the chi-squared value/degree of freedom (χ^2/df) index [43]. In the analyzed sample (n = 275), indices of goodness of fit for CFA were as follows: χ^2/df = 4.213, the goodness of fit index (GFI) = 0.832, the adjusted goodness of fit index (AGFI) = 0.973, the normed fit index (NFI) = 0.985, the incremental fit index (IFI) = 0.995, the comparative fit index (CFI) = 0.995, the Tucker–Lewis index (TLI) = 0.908, and the root mean square error of approximation (RMSEA) = 0.098. These indices indicated a good fit with the data; χ^2/df = 4.213 suggested the model had an acceptable validity [44]. Thus, the model was considered appropriate.

An analysis of the TITC-T with CFA resulted in a four-factor model. Standardized factor loadings for all items of the four factors ranged from moderate to strong: 0.78 to 0.91 for the factor of constructive controversy; 0.68 to 0.88 for helping behaviors; 0.64 to 0.90 for the factor of spontaneous communication; and 0.77 to 0.89 for the fourth factor of team creativity. An examination of the factor loadings suggested that the TITC-T was strongly related to the constructs of constructive controversy, helping behaviors, spontaneous communication, and team creativity with item one (λ = 0.87) and item two (λ = 0.85) for constructive controversy, item three (λ = 0.97) and item four (λ = 0.90) for helping behaviors, item five (λ = 0.93) and six (λ = 0.85) for spontaneous communication, and item seven (λ = 0.84) and eight (λ = 0.90) for team creativity (Figure 1).

3.3. Internal Consistency Reliability

The reliability of the TITC-T, as determined by Cronbach's alpha, was 0.98. The Cronbach's alpha coefficients for the domains of constructive controversy, helping behaviors, spontaneous communication, and team creativity, were 0.90, 0.95, 0.94, and 0.95, respectively. The results indicated good internal consistency reliability for the TITC-T.

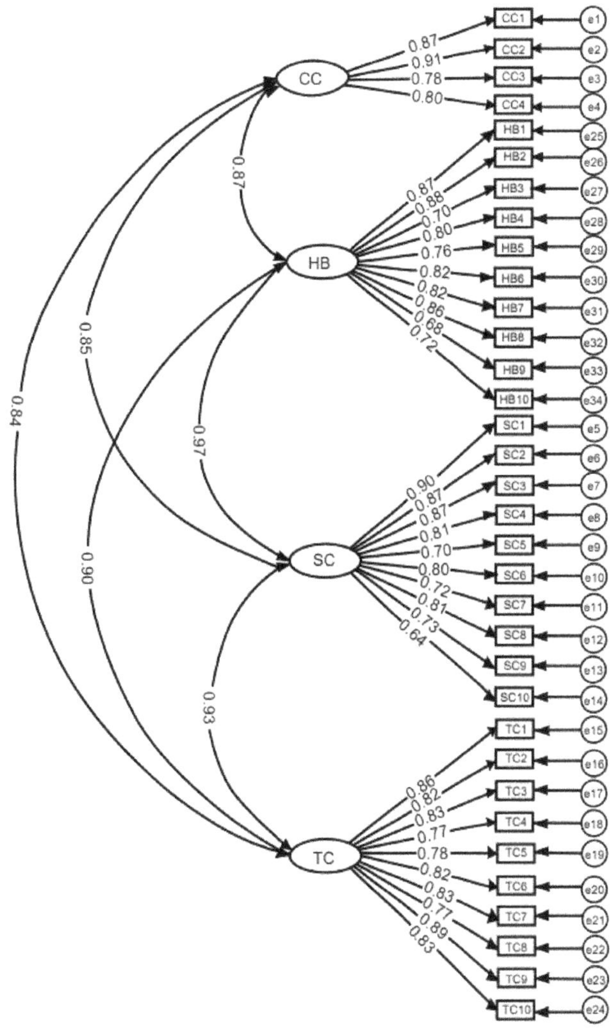

Figure 1. Confirmatory factor analysis of the Team Interactions and Team Creativity scale for Taiwanese nursing students (TITC-T) demonstrated a 4-factor model with standardized factor loadings: constructive controversy (CC), helping behaviors (HB), spontaneous communication (SC), and team creativity (TC). Note: Residual errors (e) indicated as follows: e1 to e4 for CC; e5 to e14 for SC; e15 to e24 for TC; e25 to e34 for HB; CC1 to CC4 denotes the questionnaire items for CC; HB1 to HB10 denotes the questionnaire items for HB; SC1 to SC10 denotes the questionnaire items for SC; and TC1 to TC10 denotes the questionnaire items for TC.

4. Discussion

Examining the role of interactions and creativity among team members in the context of collaboration in higher education in Taiwan, especially nursing education, can help one understand and broaden the discussion about interdisciplinary learning [1,3,13,45]. However, a reliable and valid instrument that measures interactions and creativity and specifically targets healthcare populations is not available in Taiwan. Therefore, we developed a measurement instrument for team interactions and team creativity, which was designed for use with Taiwanese nursing students. The psychometric properties of the

TITC-T were evaluated with CFA. The TITC-T had a strong internal consistency reliability, as demonstrated by the Cronbach's alpha for all domains and an acceptable construct validity as demonstrated by CFA, which confirmed the one-dimensional structure. The CFA also confirmed our proposed instrument's construct validity (χ^2/df = 4.213, RMSEA = 0.098, NFI = 0.985, CFI = 0.995, IFI = 0.995).

CFA is a theory-driven method; thus, CFA was used to determine if the proposed model identified from the TITC-T fit the data for nursing education. Previous research has established that constructive controversy, helping behaviors, and spontaneous communications influence team creativity and innovation. Our results are comparable to the instruments used in other studies [8,21,32] and have the same results. For instance, Bastian et al. [8] and Marlow et al. [17] showed that providing opportunities for communication and sharing among team members can increase supportive interactions and creativity. Xiang et al. [21] and Derdowski et al. [37] revealed that the interactive behavior of constructive controversy can improve individual and team performance and increase creativity. Therefore, there are correlations among constructive controversy, helping behaviors, spontaneous communication, and creativity. Team interaction and creativity require multiple domains to assess learning effectiveness. The TITC-T is an appropriate assessment tool.

Compared with some existing instruments that assess team interactions and team creativity targeting at the Chinese-speaking populations [14,21], the current study employed forwards- and backwards-translation as recommended by Brislin [40] for the translation of several items of the TTCT-T instrument, which can overcome obstacles of cultural or linguistic differences in the original text. Our study reported significant positive associations between scores for team interactions and team creativity. However, it remains unclear as to whether strong team interactions increased team creativity, vice versa, or both. Longitudinal studies are recommended to examine the direction of causality.

4.1. Limitations

This study had some limitations. The TITC-T is a self-report instrument, which assessed nursing students' perceived abilities and not their true abilities. Studies including participants' subjective assessments as well as measures that are objective, including the grade from the final team presentation and more objective assessments of creativity are recommended. Second, although our findings would be more compelling if we were able to demonstrate the superiority of the TITC-T scale with another similar measure of team interactions and team creativity, our instrument was developed specifically for nursing students in a novel teaching course, and no similar instrument is in use in Taiwan. Third, most of the nursing students in our study were female (83%). Although this is a reflection of the small percentage of male nurses in Taiwan, it may prevent generalization to other Chinese-speaking cultures with a more heterogeneous representation of nurses. Finally, the participants were recruited from one university, which may also prevent generalization of our findings to other areas of Taiwan.

4.2. Implications for Nursing Education

Assessing team interactions and team creativity among nursing students can improve IDE in undergraduate healthcare education programs consisting of interdisciplinary teams, which may improve team creativity [1,36]. The validation and reliability of the TITC-T suggest this could be a promising instrument for nurse educators who wish to have insight into measures of team interactions and team creativity for interdisciplinary nursing student teams in Taiwan and possibly other Asian nursing programs. The TITC-T could also help nurse educators gain an understanding of areas in team interactions that need improvement. Strategies that increase interactions could increase collaboration and team creativity during the development of patentable healthcare-related products.

5. Conclusions

This is the first study to develop and validate a self-report scale for measuring team interactions and creativity among nursing students in Taiwan. The results from the CFA and cross-validation conducted in this study indicated that the new TITC-T instrument is psychometrically sound, valid, and reliable. The short statements of the 34-item instrument make it easy to complete. The TITC-T can serve as an assessment tool to identify the strengths of nursing students' interactions and creativity when working and collaborating in interdisciplinary teams whose goal is to develop patentable healthcare products. In the future, we will promote the TITC-T to be tested and compared by other countries.

Author Contributions: Conceptualization, H.-Y.L. and H.-F.C.; Data curation, H.-Y.L., S.-C.S., C.-Y.C., N.-H.C., H.-F.C. and S.-M.W.; Formal analysis, H.-Y.L., S.-C.S., H.-F.C. and S.-M.W.; Funding acquisition, H.-Y.L.; Investigation, C.-Y.C., N.-H.C. and S.-M.W.; Methodology, H.-Y.L. and S.-C.S.; Project administration, H.-Y.L.; Resources, H.-F.C.; Software, N.-H.C.; Supervision, H.-Y.L.; Writing—original draft, H.-F.C.; Writing—review & editing, H.-Y.L., H.-F.C. and S.-M.W. All authors have read and agreed to the published version of the manuscript.

Funding: This study was funded by research grants from the Ministry of Science and Technology (MOST), Taiwan (MOST 107-2511-H-255-008 and 108-2511-H-255-007).

Institutional Review Board Statement: This study was approved by the Institutional Review Board of the Chang Gung Memorial Medical Foundation (IRB201800212; IRB0C502).

Informed Consent Statement: Informed consent was obtained from all subjects involved in the study.

Data Availability Statement: The data that support the findings of this study are available on request from the corresponding author, H.-F.C.

Acknowledgments: The authors wish to thank Ministry of Science and Technology Taiwan for their funding support. We sincerely thank of the participants and research assistants who participated in this study.

Conflicts of Interest: The author declares no conflict of interest.

References

1. Liu, H.Y.; Wang, I.T.; Huang, D.H.; Hsu, D.Y.; Han, H.M. Nurturing and Enhancing Creativity of Nursing Students in Taiwan: A Quasi-Experimental Study. *J. Creat. Behav.* **2019**, *54*, 799–814. [CrossRef]
2. Holmes, L.; Cresswell, K.; Williams, S.; Parsons, S.; Keane, A.; Wilson, C.; Islam, S.; Joseph, O.; Miah, J.; Robinson, E.; et al. Innovating Public Engagement and Patient Involvement through Strategic Collaboration and Practice. *Res. Involv. Engagem.* **2019**, *5*, 30. [CrossRef]
3. Goncalves, J.R.D.S.N.; Goncalves, R.N.; da Rosa, S.V.; Orsi, J.S.R.; Moyses, S.J.; Werneck, R.I. Impact of Interprofessional Education on the Teaching and Learning of Higher Education Students: A Systematic Review. *Nurse. Educ. Pract.* **2021**, *56*, 103212. [CrossRef]
4. World Health Organization. *Framework for Action on Interprofessional Education and Collaborative Practice*; No. WHO/HRH/HPN/10.3; World Health Organization: Geneva, Switzerland, 2010.
5. Yi, J.Y.; Lee, H.; Park, K. The Role of Academic-Practice Partnerships from Perspectives of Nursing Students: A Cross-Sectional Study. *Nurse Educ. Today* **2020**, *89*, 104419. [CrossRef]
6. Hannon, J.; Hocking, C.; Legge, K.; Lugg, A. Sustaining Interdisciplinary Education: Developing Boundary crossing Governance. *High. Educ. Res. Dev.* **2018**, *37*, 1424–1438. [CrossRef]
7. Kim, H.N. A Conceptual Framework for Interdisciplinary Education in Engineering and Nursing Health Informatics. *Nurse Educ. Today* **2019**, *74*, 91–93. [CrossRef]
8. Bastian, B.; Jetten, J.; Thai, H.A.; Steffens, N.K. Shared Adversity Increases Team Creativity through Fostering Supportive Interaction. *Front. Psychol.* **2018**, *9*, 2309.
9. Song, W.; Li, H.; Ding, N.; Zhao, W.; Shi, L.; Wen, D. Psychometrics Properties of the Team Interaction Scale and influencing Factors of Team Interaction of Tertiary Hospital Physicians in China: A Cross-Sectional Study. *BMJ Open* **2019**, *9*, e026162. [CrossRef]
10. Kremer, H.; Villamor, I.; Aguinis, H. Innovation Leadership: Best-Practice Recommendations for Promoting Employee Creativity, Voice, and Knowledge Sharing. *Bus. Horiz.* **2018**, *62*, 65–74. [CrossRef]
11. Yang, L.-R.; Wu, K.-S.; Wang, F.-K.; Chin, P.-C. Relationships among Project Manager's Leadership Style, Team Interaction and Project Performance in the Taiwanese Server Industry. *Qual. Quant.* **2010**, *46*, 207–219. [CrossRef]

12. Cragan, J.F.; Wright, D.W.; Kasch, C.R. *Communication in Small Groups: Theory, Process, and Skills*; Wadsworth Cengage Learning: Boston, MA, USA, 2009.
13. Newell, C.; Bain, A. *Team-Based Collaboration in Higher Education Learning and Teaching: A Review of the Literature*; Springer: Singapore, 2018.
14. Chen, S.-C. Paternalistic Leadership and Cabin Crews' Upward Safety Communication: The Motivation of Voice Behavior. *J. Air Transp. Manag.* **2017**, *62*, 44–53. [CrossRef]
15. Yang, Z.R.; Xie, Z.S.; Bao, G.M. The Mechanism of Teams' Swift Trust and Interaction Behavior on Team Creativity. *J. Fuzhou Univ. (Philos. Soc. Sci.)* **2010**, *6*, 31–34.
16. Ilgen, D.R.; Hollenbeck, J.R.; Johnson, M.; Jundt, D. Teams in Organizations: From Input-Process-Output Models to IMOI Models. *Annu. Rev. Psychol.* **2005**, *56*, 517–543.
17. Marlow, S.L.; Lacerenza, C.N.; Paoletti, J.; Burke, C.S.; Salas, E. Does Team Communication Represent a One-Size-Fits-All Approach? A Meta-Analysis of Team Communication and Performance. *Organ. Behav. Hum. Decis. Process.* **2018**, *144*, 145–170. [CrossRef]
18. Alper, S.; Tjosvold, D.; Law, K.S. Interdependence and Controversy in Group Decision Making: Antecedents to Effective Self-managing Teams. *Organ. Behav. Hum. Decis. Process.* **1998**, *74*, 33–52. [CrossRef]
19. Bond, M.H.; Ng, I.W.-C. The Depth of a Group's Personality Resources: Impacts on Group Process and Group Performance. *Asian J. Soc. Psychol.* **2004**, *7*, 285–300. [CrossRef]
20. LePine, J.A.; Van Dyne, L. Predicting Voice Behavior in Work Groups. *J. Appl. Psychol.* **1998**, *83*, 853–868.
21. Xiang, S.; Chen, G.; Liu, W.; Zhou, Q.; Xing, S. An Empirical Study of the Impact of Goal Orientation on Individual Ambidexterity–Moderating Roles of Goal Interdependence and Constructive Controversy. *Nankai Bus. Rev. Int.* **2019**, *10*, 465–484. [CrossRef]
22. Ng, K.Y.; Van Dyne, L. Antecedents and Performance Consequences of Helping Behavior in Work Groups: A Multilevel Analysis. *Group Organ. Manag.* **2005**, *30*, 514–540. [CrossRef]
23. Dalal, R.S.; Sheng, Z. When is Helping Behavior Unhelpful? A Conceptual Analysis and Research Agenda. *J. Vocat. Behav.* **2019**, *110*, 272–285. [CrossRef]
24. MacKenzie, S.B.; Podsakoff, N.P.; Podsakoff, P.M. Individual-and Organizational-Level Consequences of Organizational Citizenship Behaviors. In *The Oxford Handbook of Organizational Citizenship Behavior*; Podsakoff, P.M., MacKenzie, S.B., Podsakoff, N.P., Eds.; Oxford University Press: New York, NY, USA, 2018; pp. 105–145.
25. Frese, M.; Fay, D.; Hilburger, T.; Leng, K.; Tag, A. The Concept of Personal Initiative: Operationalization, Reliability and Validity in Two German Samples. *J. Occup. Organ. Psychol.* **1997**, *70*, 139–161. [CrossRef]
26. Tjosvold, D.; Andrews, I.R.; Struthers, J.T. Leadership Influence: Goal Interdependence and Power. *J. Soc. Psychol.* **1992**, *132*, 39–50. [CrossRef]
27. Furlan, A.; Galeazzo, A.; Paggiaro, A. Organizational and Perceived Learning in the Workplace: A Multilevel Perspective on Employees' Problem Solving. *Organ. Sci.* **2019**, *30*, 280–297. [CrossRef]
28. Parker, S.K.; Wang, Y.; Liao, J. When Is Proactivity Wise? A Review of Factors That Influence the Individual Outcomes of Proactive Behavior. *Annu. Rev. Organ. Psychol. Organ. Behav.* **2019**, *6*, 221–248. [CrossRef]
29. Farh, J.-L.; Lee, C.; Farh, C.I.C. Task Conflict and Team Creativity: A Question of How Much and When. *J. Appl. Psychol.* **2010**, *95*, 1173–1180. [CrossRef]
30. Oldham, G.R.; Cummings, A. Employee Creativity: Personal and Contextual Factors at Work. *Acad. Manag. J.* **1996**, *39*, 607–634.
31. Leroy, H.; Buengeler, C.; Veestraeten, M.; Shemla, M.; Hoever, I.L. Fostering Team Creativity through Team-Focused Inclusion: The Role of Leader Harvesting the Benefits of Diversity and Cultivating Value-In-Diversity Beliefs. *Group Organ. Manag.* **2021**, 1–42. [CrossRef]
32. Zhang, L.; Xia, Y.; Liu, B.; Han, L. Why Don't I Help You?—The Relationship between Role Stressors and Helping Behavior from a Cognitive Dissonance Perspective. *Front. Psychol.* **2018**, *8*, 2220. [CrossRef]
33. Brashers, V.; Haizlip, J.; Owen, J.A. The ASPIRE Model: Grounding the IPEC Core Competencies for Interprofessional Collaborative Practice within a Foundational Framework. *J. Interprof. Care* **2020**, *34*, 128–132. [CrossRef]
34. Interprofessional Education Collaborative (IPEC). *Core Competencies for Interprofessional Collaborative Practice: 2016 Update*; Interprofessional Education Collaborative: Washington, DC, USA, 2016.
35. Rosen, M.A.; DiazGranados, D.; Dietz, A.S.; Benishek, L.E.; Thompson, D.; Pronovost, P.J.; Weaver, S.J. Teamwork in Healthcare: Key Discoveries Enabling Safer, High-Quality Care. *Am. Psychol.* **2018**, *73*, 433–450. [CrossRef]
36. Liu, H.Y.; Wang, I.T.; Hsu, D.Y.; Huang, D.H.; Chen, N.H.; Han, C.Y.; Han, H.M. Conflict and Interactions on Interdisciplinary Nursing Student Teams: The Moderating Effects of Spontaneous Communication. *Nurse Educ. Today* **2020**, *94*, 104562. [CrossRef]
37. Derdowski, L.; Ogaard, T.; Marnburg, E.; Mathisen, G.E. Creative and Innovative Behaviours of Corporate Directors: An Elusive Role of Task-Related Conflicts. *J. Manag. Gov.* **2018**, *22*, 1045–1069. [CrossRef]
38. Moser, K.S.; Dawson, J.F.; West, M.A. Antecedents of Team Innovation in Health Care Teams. *Creat. Innov. Manag.* **2019**, *28*, 72–81. [CrossRef]
39. McAlpine, K.L. Flexible Work and The Effect of Informal Communication on Idea Generation and Innovation. *Acad. Manag. Proc.* **2018**, *2018*, 15092. [CrossRef]
40. Brislin, R.W. The Wording and Translation of Research Instrument. In *Field Methods in Cross-Cultural Research*; Lonner, W.J., Berry, J.W., Eds.; Sage Publications: Beverly Hills, CA, USA, 1986; pp. 137–146.

41. Shalley, C.E.; Gilson, L.L.; Blum, T.C. Interactive Effects of Growth Need Strength, Work Context, and Job Complexity on Self-Reported Creative Performance. *Acad. Manag. J.* **2009**, *52*, 489–505. [CrossRef]
42. Scott, S.G.; Bruce, R.A. Determinants of Innovation Behavior: A Path Model of Individual Innovation in the Workplace. *Acad. Manag. J.* **1994**, *37*, 580–607.
43. Joreskog, K.G. Analysis of Covariance Structures. In *Handbook of Multivariate Experimental Psychology*; Nesselroade, J.R., Cattell, R.A., Eds.; Plenum Press: New York, NY, USA, 1988; pp. 207–230.
44. Whittaker, T.A.; Schumacker, R.E. Review of a Beginner's Guide to Structural Equation Modeling. In *Structural Equation Modeling: A Multidisciplinary Journal*, 5th ed.; Routledge: New York, NY, USA, 2022; p. 400.
45. You, J.W. Investigating the Effects of Achievement Goals on Team Creativity and Team Achievement in Learning Communities at a South Korean University. *High. Educ.* **2021**, *81*, 367–383. [CrossRef]

healthcare

MDPI

Article

Validation of the Spanish Version of the Questionnaire on Environmental Awareness in Nursing (NEAT)

Olga María Luque-Alcaraz [1,2,3,*], Antonio Gomera [2], África Ruíz [4], Pilar Aparicio-Martinez [3,*] and Manuel Vaquero-Abellan [2,3]

[1] Neurosurgery Department, University Hospital Reina Sofia's, Andalusian Health Care System, 14004 Cordoba, Spain
[2] Service of Environmental Protection, Environmental Protection Office (SEPA), University of Córdoba, 14071 Cordoba, Spain; agomera@uco.es (A.G.); en1vaabm@uco.es (M.V.-A.)
[3] IMIBIC GC 12 Research Groups of Clinical-Epidemiological Research in Primary Care, Biomedical Program for Occupational Medicine, Occupational Epidemiology and Sustainability, Nursing, Pharmacology and Physiotherapy, Faculty of Medicine and Nursing of Cordoba, 14071 Cordoba, Spain
[4] Quantitative Methods for Economics and Business, Department of Applied Economics I. Sevilla University, 41004 Seville, Spain; africaruiz@us.es
* Correspondence: olgaluque33@gmail.com (O.M.L.-A.); n32apmap@uco.es (P.A.-M.)

Abstract: Environmental awareness of the ecological problems caused by this climate crisis and its impact on global health has been growing globally. Nurses are health care agents that usually hurt the environment and contribute to the unsustainability of the care system. Such behavior is perpetuated without the nurses' awareness and is even magnified by the current pandemic, jeopardizing the health systems and the Sustainable Development Goals. However, there is no Spanish version of any survey that measures the awareness of these agents, only the Nurses Environmental Awareness Tool (NEAT) is available. The current research presents a unique investigation based on a mixed method, using the Spanish version of the NEAT, also called NEAT-es. The results of the mixed analysis (N = 376), a cognitive interview, and descriptive analysis indicated perfect consistency (Cronbach's alpha > 0.80), better than the original. The survey validation achieved higher values and can be used to measure environmental awareness in Spain and Spanish-speaking countries.

Keywords: awareness; nursing; environmental health; climate change; sustainable development goals

Citation: Luque-Alcaraz, O.M.; Gomera, A.; Ruíz, Á.; Aparicio-Martinez, P.; Vaquero-Abellan, M. Validation of the Spanish Version of the Questionnaire on Environmental Awareness in Nursing (NEAT). *Healthcare* **2022**, *10*, 1420. https://doi.org/10.3390/healthcare10081420

Academic Editors: Joachim G. Voss and Sandul Yasobant

Received: 12 June 2022
Accepted: 26 July 2022
Published: 29 July 2022

1. Introduction

The health sector significantly impacts the environment, generating a considerable climate footprint and directly impacting the population's health. The global climate footprint from the health care sector represents more than 4.4% of net greenhouse gas (GHG) emissions since it is a great consumer of resources and energy [1].

In addition, the health sector is an excellent waste generator, and chemical products, such as single-use non-biodegradable plastic containers, increase the generation of microplastics [2,3]. Proper environmental awareness is the primary reason to avoid unsustainable health systems [4–6].

Theoretical Foundation: Nursing, Awareness, and Sustainability

Since the beginning of modern nursing, environmental awareness has become a relevant issue to address in nursing. Florence Nightingale listed five critical elements for an environment to be considered healthy: fresh air, sunlight, clean water, waste disposal, and hygiene, and indicated that the environment is an essential factor to help recover or maintain good health [7–9]. This idea continues and has grown, as indicated by one of the statements of the International Code of Nurses, "Nurses contribute to the population's health and work to achieve the Sustainable Development Goals" [10].

However, previous studies have shown how the health society, nurses, and other health professionals live in a paradox since they are both relevant agents in health and creators of significant amounts of waste and pollutants [8,11,12]. This paradox is known as environmental hyperopia among nurses [13,14]. Nurses take care of patients, but they do not seem to care so deeply about the environment surrounding them, even though all care has an intrinsic ecological impact [6,13,14]. Moreover, in case of further system pressure and life-threatening situations, such as the current pandemic, nurses continue to have a lack or little increase of environmental awareness. Additionally, nurses oversee administering and managing care as the health agents within the multidisciplinary team. It can significantly impact their patients' environment and health if they are unaware. At the same time, if they maintain sustainable behavior, they can reduce their climate footprint and environmental problems to achieve the Sustainable Development Goals (SDGs) set for the agency for the year 2030 [15–17]. Recent articles have indicated that high waste production continues [6,13,14,18,19]. It could explain such difficulties via the disequilibrium between environmental sustainability and sanitary activity and the possibility of measuring nursing perception regarding environmental awareness in any country and moment [20].

This environmental awareness can be defined as the system of experiences and knowledge that individuals actively apply to their relationship with the environment [21]. It is a multidimensional concept that embraces all associated understanding, beliefs, values, attitudes, and behavior related to the environment. Therefore, it is a primary stimulus in searching for ways to attain sustainability, the measurement of this awareness among nurses being highly important. As indicated by the International Council of Nurses [22], nursing as a profession is committed to reducing its role in GHG and, therefore, its environmental awareness [23]. In this sense, environmental awareness is increasing the responsibility [24] to achieve a balance (ecological sustainability) in the healthy environment around us [15,25,26], to ensure the well-being of current and future generations [8].

Despite the previous contradictions, nursing throughout this decade has been aligning with the SDGs and raising awareness and taking responsibility for environmental problems [27,28]. However, it is more essential than before to measure the environmental awareness of nurses to provide sustainable improvements in their daily care practice, as has been reflected by the waste and consumption during the COVID-19 pandemic [13]. In this sense, this need has been highlighted during the pandemic and the high waste production [27,28], highlighting the reasoning and importance behind creating the questionnaire focused on nurses' environmental awareness [29].

However, there is a reduced number of validated surveys focused on nurses' perceptions regarding environmental impact, climate change, and awareness. The available surveys have been created in the United States of America, and there are not available in different languages [30,31]. Precisely, among the available validated questionnaires, the Climate, Health, and Nursing Tool, or CHANT [30,32], measures nurses' perception of climate change and does not specifically evaluate environmental awareness. The same authors created other validated surveys measuring nurses' perceptions and behavior related to environmental awareness. This specific survey focused on environmental awareness in nursing is called Nurse's Environmental Awareness Tool (NEAT) questionnaire, which has three sub-scales (Nurse Awareness Scales: NAS; Nurse Professional Ecological Behaviors Scales: NPEB; Personal Ecological Behaviors Scales: PEB). The NEAT provides the necessary information to determine nurses' environmental awareness [31], which is key to adequate protocols and activities to reduce the GHG produced by the health system and waste from nursing activities [15–17]. The NEAT was created and validated in the United States to measure environmental awareness in nursing, but only for English speakers, leaving out Hispanic populations. In this sense, other studies authors have indicated the relevance of having translated validated surveys for the work of nurses [29,33].

Based on the need to measure nurses' environmental awareness and the lack of translated NEAT in other languages, the process for its validation in other languages is essential for several countries worldwide. Therefore, it is necessary to have a Spanish version of the NEAT that measures the environmental awareness of Spanish speakers since it is in the top four of the most spoken languages in the world [34]. Therefore, this study aims to develop and validate a Spanish version of the original English NEAT, guaranteeing conceptual, semantic, and contextual equivalence between both questionnaires. Additionally, the hypothesis, based on the consistency and validity of another survey, was that a validated Spanish version of the NEAT would be obtained.

2. Materials and Methods

2.1. Study Design

The research design was a qualitative and quantitative mixed method carried out. The qualitative part was carried out using cognitive interview (CI) techniques [35] to validate the content of the construct. In these semi-structured CIs, the participants were measured to ask about the level of understanding, completion, and presentation of the online format. Subsequently, the pre-test, which was included in the NEAT-es questionnaire of the pilot study, was intended to measure the face validity [36]. Three sections were included: a question that asked about the degree of difficulty in completing the questionnaire with a five-point Likert scale, where one = very difficult and five = very easy, one about the time to complete it; and an open question was included for participants to have comments in a text box, which focused on "Would you like to comment any further on the survey?"

Finally, a quantitative observational descriptive study was started to validate psychometry (reliability and factor analysis). The psychometric analysis was used, using the same criteria used by the original author [31,37], whose reliability was found through Cronbach's alpha analysis and factor analysis using the maximum likelihood method [38], assuming that these factors are correlated, oblique rotation (Promax) was used [39]. This same psychometric methodology was carried out in the preliminary pilot project, the pilot study, and the samples by validation for the study exploratory factor analysis (EFA) and the confirmatory factor analysis (CFA) (Figure 1).

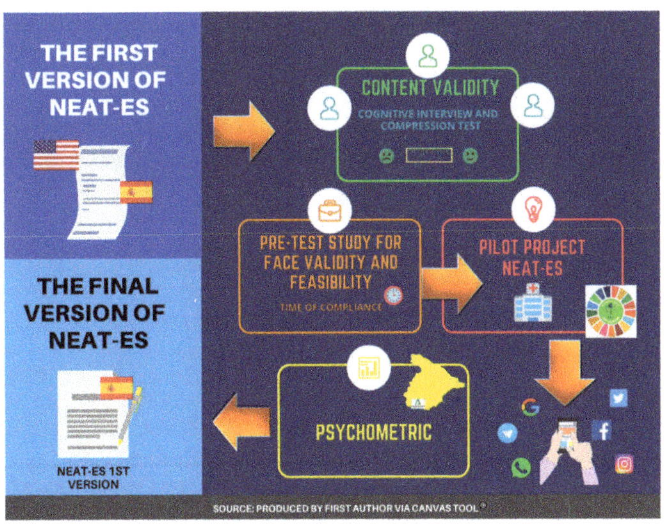

Figure 1. Study design and procedure followed for the validation.

2.2. Sample

All the nursing staff, from nursing assistant technicians, nursing registered nurses, and students of both categories working or studying in health systems, mainly public hospitals, from Andalusia were approached to participate. Nurses were included in the study regardless of their contractual relationship with the hospital (contract or permanent staff) or training status, such as postgraduate nurses or specialists. The study excluded nurses whose primary work was not related to nursing competencies.

The sampling was based on the population of nurses in Spain in 2019, estimated at 388,153 nurses. From this population, the sampling was carried out using the GRANMO Sample Size Calculator (Program of Research in Inflammatory and Cardiovascular Disorders, Institut Municipal d'Investigació Mèdica, Barcelona, Spain) and Epidat version 4.2 (Servicio de Epidemiología de la Dirección Xeral de Saúde Pública da Consellería de Sanidade, Xunta de Galicia, Spain) [40], with a confidence level of 95% and a margin of error of 5.05%. From this, we found that we needed 376 nurses. Therefore, a representative, random and homogeneous sample of the Spanish nursing population was carried out. Intentional sampling was conducted, with data collection from November 2019 to March 2021.

To evaluate the test–retest reliability, 40 nurses were randomly selected for the initial evaluation of the translated version in the pre-test phase. After the pre-test phase, 63 nurses evaluated the first version of the survey, randomly selected from 376 nurses. For the construct validity, the total sample was used for the final evaluation of the survey.

2.3. *Validation Process*

The validation process followed the DETAC protocol [41] and the recommendations of Sousa, V. D. and Rojjanasrirat, W. [42]. In this sense, the translation, adaptation, and validation process followed the methodology of Lauffer et al. (2013) [40] to prevent bias during the validation process.

2.3.1. Translation and Back Translation

In line with the methodological guidelines, two types of translation were implemented: direct, literal translation, and reverse translation. The direct translation was carried out by two bilingual translators who were experts in English to Spanish translations. The questionnaire was sent in an independent text, including sections to write the literal translation together with instructions about the aims of the study. After the translation into Spanish, the surveys were back translated to English and later evaluated by the experts. In this sense, two new translators, blind to the original questionnaire, one an English native from the United States of America and the other a nurse with a fluent command of Spanish, were separately sent the consensus version produced by the first translators. No contact was allowed between them, and they were unaware of the study's purpose and the original questionnaire in English. This synthesis was then sent to the author of the original questionnaire.

2.3.2. Participants of Cognitive Interview (CI)

The cognitive interview (CI) was done in a neutral room and at a table to get a fluid dialogue between the participants and the interviewer.

A multidisciplinary technical group of three environmental technicians and a nurse with expertise in sustainability or environmental education participated in the CI to validate the content of the survey after the translation and back translation version of the NEAT questionnaire. Environmental technicians mainly formed the multidisciplinary team since they formed the technical team for the verification.

This research team conducted the cross-analysis and discussion of the translation concerning the original version to check the reliability of the translation (direct and back translation). The process focused on the formulation of questions, on the one hand, using a 5-point Likert scale on item difficulty, scale of understanding the questionnaire, and difficulty of the test, and on the other, through open questions with cognitive interviews, as quality control. The multidisciplinary team recorded their opinions on the online form's understanding, completion, and presentation, obtaining its first version by consensus. In the back translation, no differences were found from the original.

However, the semantic, linguistic, concept, content, experimental, and cultural equivalence were analyzed by the research team formed by the panel of multidisciplinary experts. This team observed the need to adapt items A1 to A6 to the Spanish environment and context, as they contained data exclusively related to the United States of America. After extensive research, checking the existing literature, and consulting environmental experts, the items were contextualized for the Spanish territory regarding health, social health services, and others. The first consensus version of the questionnaire was obtained and denominated NEAT-es.v.1.

2.3.3. Participants in End-Users Group Analysis and Pre-Test

With this first version, the end-users group analysis was conducted on five participants of the total pilot sample formed by nursing personnel with university degrees (registered or graduate nurses), nursing care technicians (nursing assistants), and students who perform practical work in both categories (student nursing specialists). The characteristics of the sample were primarily women with more than 20 years of experience and nurses with a university degree who worked in a public hospital in the morning shift, and they were chosen at random before sending the questionnaires to the final total sample to measure the degree of difficulty and the time to complete the questionnaire, using a Likert scale. This focus group evaluated the NEAT-es.v.1., showing a consensus about the usability of the survey.

After the end-users group analysis, the sample was increased and a pre-test was carried out. This analysis was performed with 40 participants, 52.5% women and 47.5% men, with an average age of 44.53 ± 1.9. Only 27.5% had less than ten years of working experience. Additionally, 87% were nurses, 7.5% were nursing students, 5% were nursing care technicians, 62.5% worked in the hospital, 22.5% in primary care, and 15% in others. Although this study was not conclusive regarding the validation process, it was consistent. After this inconclusive data, the sample was expanded to a total of 63 participants, that is, a more significant number of the questionnaire items to obtain validity, carrying out a pilot analysis with this sample.

2.3.4. Participants of the Pilot Study and Final Sample

The sample for the pilot study consisted of 63 nurses (registered or graduate nurses), nursing care technicians (nursing assistants), students who perform practical work in both categories, and students as nursing specialists. All other categories were excluded. This pilot sample comprised 38.10% men and 61.90% women, most of whom were between 30 and 40 years old, and 40.03% had more than 20 years of work. In addition, 76.19% belonged to the capital's public health or surroundings (Table 1). With this sample (n = 63), the face validity was measured, and a Likert scale was performed on the difficulty of the test.

The final sample consisted of 376 participants with the same personnel characteristics as the pilot study. From this sample of 376, one-third was randomly taken for the export validation study. The exploratory factor analysis (EFA), based on two-thirds of the total participants, were selected patients (n = 251) and confirmatory factor analysis (CFA) with the selection of final participants (N = 376). The majority were women with more than 20 years of experience, nurses with a university degree, who worked in a public hospital, and whose sociodemographic characteristics are described in Table 1.

The sociodemographic data of both samples indicated homogeneity among the nurses and similar data regarding the years of experience and working in public centers. Such sociodemographic data are relevant factors that contribute to the validation of a survey, especially in environmental awareness [43], being similar to the NEAT validation process [31] and relevant since the term was introduced two decades ago [44].

Table 1. Sociodemographic characteristics of the pilot project and final sample.

	Pilot Project (N = 63)	Final Sample (N = 376)
Age	40.76 (13.78)	37.7 (0.62)
Gender		
Female	39 (61.9%)	275 (73.1%)
Male	24 (38.1%)	101 (26.9%)
Non-binary	0	0
Working experience (years in the field)		
More than 20 years	29 (46.0%)	142 (37.8%)
Between 11 and 20 years	9 (14.3%)	65 (17.3%)
Between 10 and 5 years	3 (4.8%)	51 (13.5%)
Less than 5 years	22 (34.9%)	118 (31.4%)
Occupation		
Nursing Assistant	4 (6.3%)	23 (6.1%)
Nursing of Assistant Student	1 (1.6%)	1 (0.3%)
Nurse with Certificate from University	41 (65.1%)	267 (71.0%)
Nursing Student to Obtain University Certificate	15 (23.8%)	72 (19.1%)
Nursing Specialist Students	2 (3.2%)	13 (3.5%)
Workplace		
Local Hospital	28 (44.4%)	139 (37.0%)
Local Primary Health Care	10 (16.0%)	68 (18.1%)
Regional Hospital	14 (22.2%)	124 (33.0%)
Regional Primary Health Care	2 (3.2%)	12 (3.2%)
Socio-Sanitary (i.e., hospice)	5 (7.9%)	14 (3.7%)
Others	4 (6.3%)	19 (5.0%)
Center Financial status		
Public	48 (76.2%)	330 (87.9%)
Private	8 (12.7%)	20 (5.2%)
In Collaboration with Public and Private entities	7 (11.1%)	26 (6.9%)
Work shift		
Only Morning	30 (47.6%)	185 (49.2%)
Only Afternoons	4 (6.3%)	18 (4.8%)
Only Nights	2 (3.2%)	11 (2.9%)
Rotating Shift (switch between other shifts)	24 (38.1%)	160 (42.6%)
Others	3 (4.8%)	2 (0.5%)

2.4. Nurse's Environmental Awareness Tool

First, to determine the current degree of ecological awareness among nurses, it was necessary to identify an adequate survey. Therefore, diverse databases (PubMed, Web of Science, Scopus, and others) were reviewed, and we identified only one survey in the BiblioPRO library (Biblio-Pro, 2021). However, we did not find a Spanish version of such a questionnaire. The validated questionnaire in English found to measure the environmental awareness of nursing personnel is called the Nurses Environmental Awareness Tool (NEAT) [31,37]. The NEAT questionnaire allows the measurement and evaluation of environmental awareness in nursing, as it consists of a series of ecological awareness scales specifically developed for nurses. The NEAT questionnaire is self-administered and is divided into three scales: "Nurse Awareness Scales" (NAS), "Nurse Professional Ecological Behaviors Scales" (NPEB), and "Personal Ecological Behaviors Scales" (PEB).

First, the (NAS) focuses on determining nurse awareness and it consists of 11 items. The items focus on statements related to two questions ("Have you heard of this information before?" and "How related to health impacts do you think this is?"), being answered on a five-point Likert scale, with one = never/not at all and five = definitely/a lot.

The second, the NPEB scale, measures the professional behavior of nurses to mitigate environmental effects and consists of nine items, presented as affirmations with two questions, ("How often do you do this behavior?" and "How easy or difficult is this behavior to do?"), being also answered using a five-point Likert scale. The third and final scale, the PEB based on ecological behavior, with 11 items and the same questions as the NPEB.

Permission was granted by the author of the original NEAT questionnaire to translate it into Spanish, now denominated as NEAT-es in all its different versions. For the validation, the NEAT-es questionnaire was distributed online through a subscription-based platform (Google), available via a link, and accessible by the participants in Spain. Additionally, the quick response (QR) code was created based on the link and located in hospitals and other centers across the country in person and online through direct messages via social media (such as Facebook, Twitter, or Instagram).

2.5. Data Analysis

2.5.1. Qualitative Study: Cognitive Interview

The cognitive interviews of the multidisciplinary group were collected in a field notebook and recorded. This interview contained a question about the five-point Likert scale, where one = very difficult and five = very easy, to verify the degree of difficulty and understanding of the items in the final questionnaire and an open question. This open question followed a transcription process using the ATLAS.ti version 9 software. The Microsoft Word 2019 software (Microsoft CLUF (EULA), Albuquerque, NM, United States) was used for the Likert scale. Then the prioritization process was followed to produce a single final version for each item. After the cognitive interviews, a triangulation process was carried out between techniques and researchers to add objectivity and validity to our research.

2.5.2. Pre-Test Study and Pilot Study

The pretest was included in the NEAT-es questionnaire of the pilot study. It was intended to measure the face validity in which three sections were included: a question with a five-point Likert scale, which asked for the degree of difficulty when completing the questionnaire, one on the time to complete it, and finally an open question was included for the participants to have comments in a text box.

2.5.3. Statistical Analysis: Descriptive and Psychometrics for Final Validation

Several methods were used for the final validation: reliability (internal consistency) was verified by Cronbach's alpha and was followed by two factorial analyzes that evaluated the factorial structure of 62 items (31 items with two responses each). On the one hand, an exploratory factor analysis (EFA) with 2/3 of the total sample of participants was selected, that is, a sample of n = 251 patients, and on the other a confirmatory factor analysis (CFA) with the sample of n = 376 participants. For the validity of the construct for the EFA and CFA was carried out using the Statistical Package for Social Science (SPSS) (IMB, Endicott, Nueva York, United States of America) for the CFA and R commander, using the R package [45], via the lavaan package (V.3.5.0), for the CFA with the same method used by the author of the original NEAT; that is, the maximum likelihood method was used for the extraction of the factors present an oblique rotation (Promax) was used [31,37]. Moreover, other statistical analyses used for the CFA of the validation were implemented such as the chi-square goodness of fit statistics, comparative fit index (CFI), goodness of fit index (GFI), Tucker–Lewis index (TLI), root mean squared error of approximation (RMSEA), and its respective *p*-value or the root mean square residuals (RMSR). Finally, convergent and discriminant validity were evaluated via the average variance extracted (AVE) and heterotrait monotrait ratio (HTMT). For such analyses, the R studio, PROGRAMA, and Programa2Salida were implemented by the researchers [45].

2.6. Ethical Considerations

The research will respect the principles of Bioethics of the Oviedo Convention, the Helsinki Declaration, and the current Spanish Data Protection Laws (5 December 2018). The participant's confidentiality is always acknowledged, and their data are dealt with anonymously. The study was approved by the Reginal Biomedical Research Ethics Coordinating Committee (No. 267, ref. 3605). Additionally, it is part of the doctoral thesis project called "The Nursing Responsibility in the Environmental Sustainability" of the Biomedicine doctoral program.

3. Results

3.1. Qualitative Study: Cognitive Interview

After asking the multidisciplinary team in the cognitive interviews about the level of understanding, completion, and presentation of the online format, four "easy" answers were obtained on the five-point Likert scale, where one = very difficult and five = very easy. A similar result was obtained for the open question, with only the comments about the excessive number of items, 62 in total (31 answers, with two solutions each). The mean time to complete the NEAT-es questionnaire was 8.7 (±1.9) minutes.

3.2. Pre-Test and Pilot Study

After obtaining the NEAT-es first version questionnaire, it was tested in a pre-test by five nursing professionals, who estimated their level of understanding and the suitability of the format (face validity), obtaining a score of 4 (easy) for each of the questions in the five-point Likert scale, indicating a good level of understanding when completing the questionnaire. In this case, the mean time to complete the NEAT-es questionnaire was 9.6 (±2.7) minutes, the same as the expert results and the original NEAT. In addition, the degree of difficulty of the NEAT-es-v.1 (the first version) was established. The questionnaire was included in the pilot of 63 participants. A score of 3.8 was obtained in "comprehension" on the five-point Likert scale, where one = very difficult and five = very easy.

A preliminary exploratory pilot study with n = 40 participants was carried out. Despite having high consistency (Cronbach's alpha = 0.909), we did not obtain good results in the factorial analysis (0.455–0.597), perhaps due to the high number of elements (62 items) and the small sample size (n = 40). When the sample was expanded to 63 participants, better internally consistent results were obtained (Cronbach's alpha) for each sub-scale with two questions: NAS-es = 0.832/0.889; NEPB-es = 0.805/0.703; PEB = 0.809/0.738. The factory analysis with results between 0.013 and 0.980, so it was decided to continue expanding the sample size due to the high consistency of the questionnaire.

3.3. Result Psychometric for Final Validation: Reliability and Exploratory Factor Analysis (EFA) and Confirmatory Factor Analysis (CFA)

Cronbach's alpha checked reliability (internal consistency) and a factor analysis assessed the factor structure of the 63 items. For reliability (internal consistency) of NEAT-es v.1. and the 62 items, Cronbach's alpha was estimated and the internal consistency was internally consistent (Cronbach's alpha for each sub-scale > 0.80). The questionnaire could follow a similar behavior regarding its metric equivalences to the original [31,37].

An exploratory study of EFA was carried out with n = 251 participants, and CFA with = 376 participants, for each of the three sub-scales, NAS-es, NPEB-es, and PEB-es with two questions for each item are collected in the following sections with their corresponding table.

3.3.1. NAS-es Scale: Reliability, EFA, and CFA

The internal consistency estimated by Cronbach's alpha for the two NAS-es questions was high in both EFA/CFA factorial analyses. When asked for awareness, it was 0.886/0.891, and when asked for health, it was 0.891/0.886. Both factor analyses, EFA and CFA of the NAS-es, show high significance since a p-value of 0.000 or a lower p-value is obtained, making it significant; in addition, there are no items below 0.4 or 0.3, as recommended by the author of the NEAT questionnaire, so the saturation of the items is adequate (Tables 2 and 3).

Table 2. Factor loadings and Cronbach's alphas for the Nurse Awareness Scale (NAS-es) of the questionary NEAT-es 1st version EFA (n = 251 participants).

NAS-es SCALE									
Validation EFA									
NAS-e		**Awareness**				**Health**			
Items		**Loadings**							
Factor		**Pattern**		**Structure**		**Pattern**		**Structure**	
		1	**2**	**1**	**2**	**1**	**2**	**1**	**2**
A1		−0.119	1.0	0.565	0.995	0.979	−0.176	0.869	0.431
A2		0.154	0.659	0.575	0.757	0.957	−0.128	0.877	0.466
A3		0.457	0.119	0.533	0.410	0.586	0.186	0.701	0.549
A4		0.614	0.008	0.619	0.400	0.368	0.396	0.614	0.625
A5		0.585	0.263	0.752	0.636	0.607	0.231	0.751	0.608
A6		0.263	0.149	0.653	0.505	0.351	0.386	0.590	0.603
A7		0.767	−0.002	0.766	0.487	0.210	0.537	0.543	0.667
A8		0.661	−0.010	0.655	0.412	0.028	0.602	0.401	0.619
A9		0.720	−0.071	0.675	0.389	0.008	0.688	0.436	0.693
A10		0.608	0.014	0.617	0.403	−0.036	0.832	0.480	0.809
A11		0.601	−0.024	0.585	0.359	−0.159	0.740	0.300	0.641
Kaiser–Meyer–Olkin measure of sampling adequacy		0.879				0.892			
Bartlett's Sphericity Test	**Statistic**	1217.385				1404.342			
	***p*-value**	<0.001				<0.001			
Cronbach's Alpha		0.886				0.891			

Table 3. Factor loadings and Cronbach's alphas for the Nurse Awareness Scale (NAS-es) of the questionary NEAT-es 1st version CFA (n = 376 participants).

NAS-es SCALE									
Validation CFA									
NAS-es		**Awareness**				**Health**			
Items		**Loadings**							
Factor		**Pattern**		**Structure**		**Pattern**		**Structure**	
		1	**2**	**1**	**2**	**1**	**2**	**1**	**2**
A1		0.979	−0.176	0.869	0.431	0.944	−0.155	0.853	0.401
A2		0.957	−0.128	0.877	0.466	0.940	−0.131	0.862	0.422
A3		0.586	0.186	0.701	0.549	0.621	0.134	0.699	0.499
A4		0.368	0.396	0.614	0.625	0.460	0.272	0.621	0.543
A5		0.607	0.231	0.751	0.608	0.648	0.187	0.757	0.568
A6		0.351	0.386	0.590	0.603	0.291	0.419	0.538	0.590
A7		0.210	0.537	0.543	0.667	0.163	0.535	0.478	0.631
A8		0.028	0.602	0.401	0.619	−0.013	0.638	0.363	0.631
A9		0.008	0.688	0.436	0.693	0.042	0.681	0.443	0.706
A10		−0.036	0.832	0.480	0.809	−0.016	0.774	0.440	0.765
A11		−0.159	0.740	0.300	0.641	−0.141	0.743	0.296	0.660
Comparative Fit Index (CFI)		0.98				0.98			
RMSEA	**Statistic**	0.049				0.068			
	***p*-value**	0.48				0.123			
Cronbach's Alpha		0.891				0.886			

The EFA indicated values on the limit in 1 point in the second pattern or factor in A1, so we analyzed the discrepancy in the CFA (Table 3), for which not only Tukey but other analyses were implemented. The RMSEA indicated great values, accepting the model with the adequation of the factors with values lower than 0.3. The chi-square fitness was 957.064 ($p < 0.001$), with a good TLI (0.973), AIC (935.565), BIC (9364.431), and SRMR (0.031) for awareness. For "Health", the two-factor model of the items indicated acceptable values since the chi-square fitness was 1025.294 ($p < 0.001$), with a good TLI (0.964), AIC (5481.647), BIC (5540.591), and SRMR (0.041). The factors graph represents the two factors obtained in the study, indicating the mode of the number of factors that must be chosen (Figure 2).

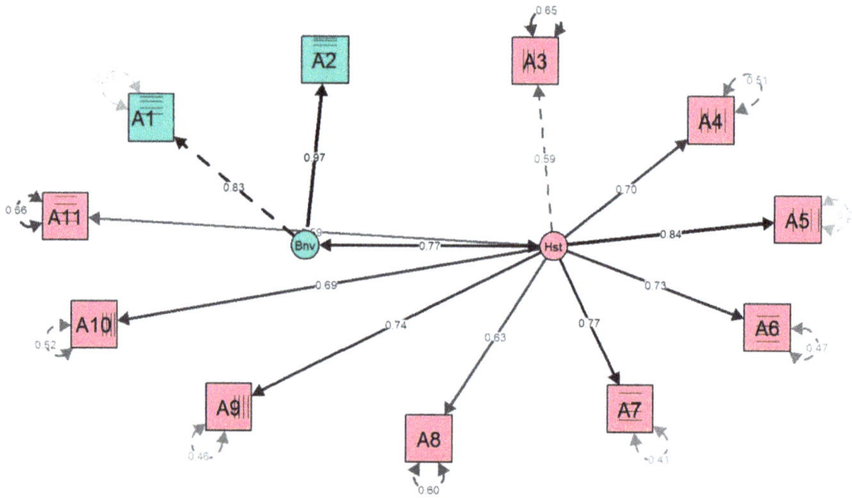

Figure 2. Factors graph of the NEAT-es NAS for the CFA. Note: A1, A2, A3, A4, A5, A6, A7, A8, A9, A10 and A11 correspond to the factors of the NAS-es scale of the NEAT-es.

Moreover, the reliability and validity were good for both sub-scales (AVE = 0.69; HTMT = 0.763; heterotrait correlation = 0.478).

3.3.2. NPEB-es Scale: Reliability and Exploratory and Confirmatory Factor Analysis

The internal consistency of the NPEB-es questionnaires was estimated using Cronbach's alpha. For each factor analyzed, AFE and CFA show high significance (p-value < 0.001), which makes it significant; in addition, even though values below 0.4 or 0.3 were found as recommended by the author, it was decided not to extract any factor to adapt it to the original, since the US version was already validated. From Tables 4 and 5, the consistency of each factor was determined, indicating an excellent and good internal consistency. Despite the difference between factors, Cronbach's alpha was higher than the range considered acceptable, being good and in some cases being close to excellent. Additionally, the results of sub-scale behavior and difficulty (Table 5) indicated an acceptable model for the items (chi-square fitness was 347.440 ($p < 0.001$), with a good TLI (0.973), AIC (6728.602), BIC (6779.582), and SRMR (0.039) for sub-scale behavior vs. chi-square fitness 563.581 ($p < 0.001$), TLI (0.93), AIC (9278.305), BIC (9344.972), and SRMR (0.044) for difficulty). The reliability and validity were good for both sub-scales (HTMT = 0.636 and heterotrait correlation = 0.278)

Table 4. Factor loadings and Cronbach's alphas for the Nurse Professional Ecological Behaviors Scales (NPEB-es) of the questionary NEAT-es 1st version EFA (n = 251 participants).

		NPEB-es SCALE									
		Validation EFA									
		Behavior				Difficulty					
Items		Loadings									
Factor		Pattern		Structure		Pattern			Structure		
		1	2	1	2	1	2	3	1	2	3
B1		0.113	0.408	0.338	0.471	0.109	0.445	0.052	0.297	0.502	0.258
B2		0.247	0.206	0.361	0.342	−0.045	10.0	−0.129	0.268	0.989	0.201
B3		−0.004	0.677	0.369	0.675	0.104	0.109	−0.234	0.022	0.068	−0.144
B4		−0.046	0.881	0.440	0.855	0.048	0.062	0.796	0.482	0.348	0.842
B5		0.552	0.226	0.677	0.530	0.449	0.027	0.258	0.592	0.276	0.499
B6		0.769	−0.075	0.728	0.349	0.722	−0.010	−0.200	0.615	0.184	0.169
B7		0.805	−0.004	0.803	0.439	0.837	−0.032	−0.088	0.780	0.241	0.333
B8		0.593	−0.007	0.589	0.320	0.665	0.060	−0.065	0.653	0.278	0.298
B9		0.350	0.055	0.380	0.248	0.458	0.023	0.146	0.542	0.238	0.390
Kaiser–Meyer–Olkin measure of sampling adequacy		0.826				0.774					
Bartlett's Sphericity Test	Statistic	600.988				481.724					
	p-value	<0.001				<0.001					
Cronbach's Alpha		0.799				0.730					

Table 5. Factor loadings and Cronbach's alphas for the Nurse Professional Ecological Behaviors Scales (NPEB-es) of the questionary NEAT-es 1st version CFA (n = 376 participants).

		NPEB-es SCALE							
		Validation CFA							
		Behavior				Difficulty			
Items		Loadings							
Factor		Pattern		Structure		Pattern		Structure	
		1	2	1	2	1	2	1	2
B1		0.131	0.350	0.300	0.413	0.074	0.580	0.328	0.612
B2		0.271	0.233	0.384	0.364	−0.009	0.776	0.331	0.772
B3		−0.085	0.639	0.224	0.598	−0.039	0.194	0.046	0.177
B4		0.021	0.809	0.412	0.820	0.370	0.194	0.455	0.356
B5		0.504	0.222	0.611	0.466	0.520	0.082	0.556	0.310
B6		0.797	−0.080	0.758	0.305	0.679	−0.067	0.649	0.231
B7		0.812	−0.054	0.785	0.338	0.830	−0.089	0.791	0.275
B8		0.594	0.006	0.597	0.293	0.682	−0.013	0.676	0.286
B9		0.388	0.059	0.417	0.246	0.484	0.051	0.507	0.264
Comparative Fit Index (CFI)		0.966				0.953			
RMSEA	Statistic	0.061				0.06			
	p-value	0.259				0.219			
Cronbach's Alpha		0.780				0.744			

3.3.3. PEB-es Scale: Reliability and Exploratory and Confirmatory Factor Analysis

Tables 6 and 7 focus on the reliability and confirmatory factor analysis of each factor for the Nurse Professional Ecological Behavior (PEB) and the Nurse Professional Behavior (PEB) difficulty scales EFA and the relatedness to health scale for 251 (Table 6) and the final sample of 376 participants (Table 7). Both tables showed how the items of each sub-scale (behavior and difficulty) were acceptable (over 0.5). Only in the case of C11 for the structure of the difficulty, was the obtained value low in both cases. Only in some cases, such as factor C11 in the behavior section (value = 0.029) (Table 7), do the data indicate lower relevance when compared to other factors, such as factor C3 (value = 0.690). Moreover, the results of the Barlett's sphericity test showed a high significance (p-value < 0.001), and the Cronbach's alphas were good for the sub-scale behavior (value = 0.831 in Table 6 and value = 0.825 in Table 7) and acceptable for the difficulty (value = 0.783 in Table 6 and value = 0.774 in Table 7). Additionally, the sub-scale behavior indicated regarding RMSEA is acceptable (0.066), with the p-value of the RMSEA adequate (0.06), matching acceptable values of chi-square fitness (1012.978, $p < 0.001$), TLI (0.925), AIC (11011.744), BIC (11094.266), and SRMR (0.043), being similar but lower for difficulty (RMSEA = 0.066, with p-value of RMSEA = 0.055). Finally, the reliability and validity were acceptable for both sub-scales (HTMT = 0.676 and heterotrait correlation = 0.321)

Table 6. Factor loadings and Cronbach's alphas for the Nurse Professional Ecological Behavior (PEB-es) of the questionary NEAT-es 1st version EFA (n = 251 participants).

		PEB-es SCALE											
		Validation EFA											
		Behavior						Difficulty					
Items		Loadings											
Factor		Pattern			Structure			Pattern			Structure		
		1	2	3	1	2	3	1	2	3	1	2	3
C1		−0.005	−0.037	1.0	0.413	0.364	0.999	0.077	0.122	0.487	0.351	0.272	0.547
C2		0.012	0.120	0.450	0.286	0.307	0.503	0.050	−0.037	0.879	0.400	0.184	0.892
C3		0.518	0.297	−0.007	0.709	0.633	0.337	0.702	−0.041	0.026	0.690	0.360	0.312
C4		0.368	0.430	0.021	0.658	0.679	0.352	0.708	−0.010	0.070	0.732	0.404	0.366
C5		0.274	0.090	0.050	0.355	0.289	0.205	0.321	0.081	0.019	0.375	0.266	0.172
C6		0.668	−0.001	−0.071	0.637	0.407	0.219	0.398	0.354	−0.079	0.565	0.561	0.167
C7		0.868	−0.125	0.052	0.809	0.463	0.380	−0.131	10.0	0.100	0.499	0.993	0.274
C8		0.767	−0.045	0.020	0.747	0.464	0.336	0.392	0.499	−0.118	0.623	0.694	0.156
C9		0.052	0.704	0.030	0.525	0.750	0.333	0.457	−0.030	0.108	0.485	0.251	0.293
C10		0.266	0.272	−0.050	0.423	0.427	0.174	0.311	0.118	0.008	0.381	0.295	0.165
C11		−0.129	0.823	0.029	0.421	0.751	0.301	0.079	0.067	0.019	0.125	0.115	0.067
Kaiser–Meyer–Olkin measure of sampling adequacy		0.861						0.811					
Bartlett's Sphericity Test	**Statistic**	913.469						671.674					
	***p*-value**	<0.001						<0.001					
Cronbach's Alpha		0.831						0.783					

The final version of the questionnaire in Spanish was obtained, known as "NEAT-es", or in its final version "NEAT-es.v.1." (Appendix A), based on the results of the final sample (Table 7) and the significance of the results presented through the tests (p-value < 0.001; Cronbach's alphas > 0.7), the low values of some items studied in the final analysis were not insignificant.

Table 7. Factor loadings and Cronbach's alphas for the Personal Ecological Behaviors Scales (PEB-es) of the questionary NEAT-es 1st version CFA (n = 376 participants).

	PEB-es SCALE									
	Validation CFA									
	Behavior				Difficulty					
Items	Loadings									
Factor	Pattern		Structure		Pattern			Structure		
	1	2	1	2	1	2	3	1	2	3
C1	0.191	0.324	0.405	0.450	0.021	−0.035	0.699	0.270	0.336	0.689
C2	0.115	0.273	0.295	0.349	−0.020	0.083	0.644	0.278	0.401	0.679
C3	0.363	0.401	0.628	0.641	−0.033	0.704	0.011	0.387	0.690	0.359
C4	0.194	0.587	0.581	0.714	0.025	0.718	0.020	0.457	0.743	0.398
C5	0.248	0.153	0.349	0.317	0.169	0.200	0.022	0.295	0.311	0.189
C6	0.550	0.102	0.617	0.465	0.367	0.361	−0.072	0.552	0.541	0.255
C7	0.878	−0.105	0.808	0.474	0.990	−0.148	0.068	0.928	0.471	0.374
C8	0.718	0.030	0.738	0.504	0.545	0.317	−0.081	0.701	0.597	0.292
C9	−0.013	0.752	0.483	0.744	0.000	0.374	0.236	0.312	0.495	0.428
C10	0.233	0.276	0.414	0.429	0.143	0.202	0.179	0.331	0.378	0.337
C11	−0.116	0.756	0.383	0.679	0.013	0.009	0.025	0.028	0.029	0.035
Comparative Fit Index (CFI)	0.943				0.94					
RMSEA **Statistic**	0.066				0.07					
RMSEA ***p*-value**	0.06				0.055					
Cronbach's Alpha	0.825				0.774					

4. Discussion

The current research has presented the Spanish validation of the NEAT through psychometric validation in Spanish, which has been described as a key tool for determining environmental awareness among nurses and therefore having a future positive effect on environmentally sustainable systems.

The results indicated that all the items were rated above good ranking, making it an excellent tool to measure Spanish nurses' awareness. Despite being unable to compare to other validated versions of the NEAT, these results are highly interesting since other validations have indicated that more than two items usually tend to have Cronbach's alphas under 0.7 in the score of patterns [33,46], which suggests that this validation provides a high-quality translated survey.

The preliminary descriptive stage indicated that internal consistency was also good, with a higher Cronbach's alpha (0.90) and the subsection was more relevant. However, the EFA of this preliminary analysis, being standardized that the factor loadings are between -1 and 1, identified values on the limit of 1 point, usually in pattern 2. These results can be explained by the obliquely rotated factorial solution, which indicated the association of two latent factors (patterns 1 and 2) that group all the variables, surpassing the factorial loads [47]. Despite the initial surpassing of the factorial loads, the confirmatory analysis showed factor loads between the standardized limits, confirmed in complementary studies that were represented only once (Figure 2), but also confirmed in all the analyses with the R commander.

Moreover, the consistency and validity of the NEAT-es have indicated similar results to the creators of the NEAT [30,32]. Although no previous study has validated NEAT in other languages, the creation and validation of the original NEAT indicated a high consistency in matching the current findings regarding the sub-scales [31,37]. The similarities between the original NEAT and NEAT-es could be interpreted as the result of a satisfactory validation of the Spanish version, in sync with the initial hypothesis.

These results are relevant since the previous analysis of English-speaking nurses indicated that they are conscious of their significant impact on their daily work and have skills to mitigate them [30,32] and their insufficient knowledge about the questionnaire topics. Nonetheless, such results could not be compared since the NEAT is unavailable in other languages. Still, the findings indicated that the NEAT-es questionnaire is a suitable tool to measure and correct environmental deficits in the daily care of nurses.

Additionally, the psychometrics data related to ecological awareness have highlighted the overlooked nurses' experiences regarding their competencies, mainly skills, knowledge, and aptitudes. Despite having present knowledge, the skills and application of such knowledge require further investment and application in actual conditions. These findings could be associated with the spread and pressure suffered during the pandemic, which contributes to the worsening of the health care systems and the health of the professionals [48]. Such a situation causes difficulty in carrying out sustainable procedures, worsening the nurses' sustainable awareness [49,50]. Therefore, environmental awareness and sustainability through the SDGs for nurses, having under consideration the multidisciplinary concept in health care systems [21], could be the most effective measure for community engagement and modification of unsustainable behaviors [24,37].

As with any research, the current study presents limitations. The limitation of the research is the approach taken for the validation of the survey. The methodology of pre-data collection strategy, including CI to analyze an instrument, is relatively recent, requiring additional reproduction with other instruments. The survey validation occurred partially during the beginning of the pandemic, with the instrument's validity linked to the cross-cultural approach.

Despite these limitations, the current NEAT-es has implications for the SDGs, policies, and nursing education via understanding the current view of nurses. Moreover, since there is much-needed improvement in education, environment, and nursing training [51], this survey can promote more research on environmental sustainability in health care [52–54]. It refers to the fact that it is a Spanish version adapted in the Spanish territory; however, it is possible that it can be used for other Spanish-speaking countries as translated.

5. Conclusions

A Spanish version of the NEAT questionnaire was obtained, which was the objective of this research, and was renamed the NEAT-es questionnaire, which has been validated using psychometric characteristics. This questionnaire could help measure Spanish nurses' environmental awareness and contribute to health teams' environmental awareness. The NEAT-es questionnaire was tested in a pilot project with a high completion rate and good compression results, obtaining the final version of the NEAT-es questionnaire with a four-point Likert scale (accessible). The Likert scale referred to the difficulties in the questionnaire and was distributed on the Google Forms platform.

The first version of NEAT-es has been developed and psychometrically tested and is ready for further use and study in Spanish or Spanish-speaking populations. There is no questionnaire to measure environmental awareness in nursing specifically in Spain, so it is interesting to obtain it to measure environmental awareness in Spain. Additionally, the questionnaire can be adapted to Spanish-speaking countries.

Author Contributions: Conceptualization, O.M.L.-A., A.G. and M.V.-A.; methodology, all. software, all. validation, all; formal analysis, Á.R., A.G. and O.M.L.-A.; investigation, all. resources, O.M.L.-A.; data curation, O.M.L.-A. and Á.R. writing—original draft preparation, O.M.L.-A.; writing—review and editing, all. visualization, O.M.L.-A. and P.A.-M.; supervision, M.V.-A. and A.G. All authors have read and agreed to the published version of the manuscript.

Funding: This project has partically funded the excellent official nursing school of Cordoba Spain, in 2020, through the XXV grant research award.

Institutional Review Board Statement: The data collection presented in this study was conducted according to the Declaration of Helsinki guidelines; all investigation details have been discussed and approved by the investigators, the team principal, and the team's staff.

Informed Consent Statement: Informed consent was obtained from all subjects involved in the study.

Data Availability Statement: The data presented in this study are available on request from the corresponding author. The data are not publicly available due to privacy restrictions.

Acknowledgments: The whole multidisciplinary team: E. Sheck, for providing the original NEAT questionnaire; the panel of environmental experts who made up the groups (environmental technicians from the Environmental Protection Service of the Cordoba University and Clara Luján from the Environmental Management Unit at the Reina Sofia Hospital, Córdoba); the translation team (A. Gregory, S. Amour, E. Delgado, I. Rodríguez Lopera, and L. Martínez), and all the nurses and nursing students who responded and took part in the pre-testing and pilot questionnaire, despite being in a pandemic.

Conflicts of Interest: The authors declare no conflict of interest.

Appendix A

The final version of the questionnaire in Spanish NEAT-es.

1.-NAS: Escala de conciencia del personal enfermero.			
Ítems	**Por favor. lea las afirmaciones y conteste: Responda con la escala de la derecha.**	**¿Ha oído hablar antes de esta información? Escala likert: 1.-No. nunca he oído hablar. 5.-Sí. definitivamente he oído hablar.**	**¿Cómo cree que esto impacta sobre la salud? Escala likert: 1.-Nunca 5.-Mucho**
A1	De acuerdo con el Ministerio de Energía. la atención sanitaria se sitúa como el cuarto mayor consumidor de la energía dentro del sector servicios.		
A2	Los hospitales y centros de salud usan un 2% del consumo energético total. lo que supone un 30% respecto el sector de los edificios.		
A3	La mayor parte de la energía consumida en España. incluida la del sector sanitario. se basa en fuentes no renovables.		
A4	Cerca del 80% de los españoles se desplaza en vehículo privado (coche o moto). La energía utilizada puede igualar o exceder la energía requerida para el funcionamiento de un edificio de oficinas (incluyendo un hospital).		

1.-NAS: Escala de conciencia del personal enfermero.			
Ítems	**Por favor. lea las afirmaciones y conteste: Responda con la escala de la derecha.**	**¿Ha oído hablar antes de esta información? Escala likert: 1.-No. nunca he oído hablar. 5.-Sí. definitivamente he oído hablar.**	**¿Cómo cree que esto impacta sobre la salud? Escala likert: 1.-Nunca 5.-Mucho**
A5	La energía utilizada en el transporte de productos médicos. alimentos y suministros representa una parte significativa de la energía total utilizada en la asistencia sanitaria.		
A6	Los hospitales españoles y centros de salud producen más de 700 toneladas de residuos al día.		
A7	Los productos químicos tóxicos usados en la asistencia sanitaria han contribuido a la acumulación de Mercurio. Dioxinas y Ftalatos en nuestro medio ambiente.		
A8	En las analíticas de sangre y orina. el personal enfermero puede mostrar niveles de algún agente químico tóxico.		
A9	Algunos plastificantes que ablandan los plásticos para facilitar su uso (por ejemplo en tubos para muestras sangre) son disruptores hormonales.		
A10	El Triclosán. una sustancia antibacteriana presente. por ejemplo jabones. está siendo objeto de estudio por su posible alteración hormonal.		
A11	La comida servida de manera convencional en hospitales puede contener restos de pesticidas y herbicidas.		
2.-NPEB: Escala de comportamientos ecológicos profesional del personal enfermero.			
Ítems	Por favor. lea las afirmaciones y conteste: Responda con la escala de la derecha.	¿Con qué frecuencia lo hace? Escala Likert: 1.-Nunca 5.-Siempre	¿Cómo de difícil o de fácil le resulta hacerlo? Escala Likert: 1.-Muy Difícil 5.-Siempre
B1	En el trabajo. apago las luces conscientemente cuando no están en uso.		
B2	En el trabajo. apago los monitores del ordenador cuando no están en uso.		

2.-NPEB: Escala de comportamientos ecológicos profesional del personal enfermero.			
B3	En el trabajo. reciclo.		
B4	En el trabajo. motivo a mis compañeros/as para reciclar.		
B5	Trabajo para reducir el uso de los agentes químicos tóxicos en el hospital (tales como el Mercurio. DEHP o Triclosán).		
B6	Hago búsquedas en la literatura o en la web sobre agentes químicos tóxicos utilizados en la asistencia sanitaria.		
B7	En el trabajo. informo a otros miembros del personal sobre agente químicos tóxicos.		
B8	En el trabajo. educo a los/as pacientes sobre riesgos de exposiciones ambientales tales como los productos químicos tóxicos o la contaminación.		
B9	En el trabajo. animo al servicio de hostelería a servir alimentos locales.		
3.-PEB: Escalas de comportamientos ecológicos personales			
Ítems	Por favor. lea las afirmaciones y conteste: Responda con la escala de la derecha.	Con qué frecuencia lo hace? Escala likert: 1.-Nunca 5.-Siempre	¿Cómo de difícil o de fácil le resulta hacerlo? Escala likert: 1.-Muy Difícil 5.-Siempre
C1	En casa. calculo cuántos kWh de electricidad consumo.		
C2	Periódicamente. realizo el mantenimiento de mis tuberías para comprobar las fugas de agua y hago las reparaciones necesarias.		
C3	En casa. compro productos reciclados.		
C4	En casa. tomo decisiones en las compras teniendo en cuenta evitar la producción de residuos.		
C5	En casa. no uso pesticidas ni herbicidas.		
C6	En casa. compro productos ecológicos.		
C7	En casa. evito el uso de productos de cuidado personal que contengan productos químicos.		

3.-PEB: Escalas de comportamientos ecológicos personales	
C8	En casa. uso productos de limpieza respetuosos con el medioambiente.
C9	Leo sobre temas relacionados con el medio ambiente y salud en los medios de comunicación.
C10	Soy voluntario/a en acciones para apoyar un medio ambiente saludable (participo en Asociaciones. Organizaciones No Gubernamentales (ONG). etc).
C11	Como enfermera/o. debato cuestiones sobre medio ambiente y salud con mis amistades y familiares.

References

1. Al Huraimel, K.; Alhosani, M.; Kunhabdulla, S.; Stietiya, M.H. SARS-CoV-2 in the Environment: Modes of Transmission, Early Detection and Potential Role of Pollutions. *Sci. Total Environ.* **2020**, *744*, 140946. [CrossRef] [PubMed]
2. Yuan, X.; Wang, X.; Sarkar, B.; Ok, Y.S. The COVID-19 Pandemic Necessitates a Shift to a Plastic Circular Economy. *Nat. Rev. Earth Environ.* **2021**, *2*, 659–660. [CrossRef] [PubMed]
3. Paavola, J. Health Impacts of Climate Change and Health and Social Inequalities in the UK. *Environ. Health* **2017**, *16*, 113. [CrossRef] [PubMed]
4. Harris, C.; Green, S.; Ramsey, W.; Allen, K.; King, R. Sustainability in Health Care by Allocating Resources Effectively (SHARE) 1: Introducing a Series of Papers Reporting an Investigation of Disinvestment in a Local Healthcare Setting. *BMC Health Serv. Res.* **2017**, *17*, 323. [CrossRef] [PubMed]
5. Persaud, D.D. Enhancing Learning, Innovation, Adaptation, and Sustainability in Health Care Organizations: The ELIAS Performance Management Framework. *Health Care Manag. (Frederick)* **2014**, *33*, 183–204. [CrossRef]
6. Álvarez-Nieto, C.; Richardson, J.; Navarro-Perán, M.Á.; Tutticci, N.; Huss, N.; Elf, M.; Anåker, A.; Aronsson, J.; Baid, H.; López-Medina, I.M. Nursing Students' Attitudes towards Climate Change and Sustainability: A Cross-Sectional Multisite Study. *Nurse Educ. Today* **2022**, *108*, 105185. [CrossRef]
7. Dossey, B.M.; Rosa, W.E.; Beck, D.-M. Nursing and the Sustainable Development Goals: From Nightingale to Now. *AJN Am. J. Nurs.* **2019**, *119*, 44–49. [CrossRef]
8. Kiang, K.M.; Behne, C. Delivering Environmental Sustainability in Healthcare for Future Generations: Time to Clean up Our Own Cubby House. *J. Paediatr. Child Health* **2021**, *57*, 1767–1774. [CrossRef]
9. Wyssusek, K.H.; Keys, M.T.; van Zundert, A.A.J. Operating Room Greening Initiatives–the Old, the New, and the Way Forward: A Narrative Review. *Waste Manag. Res.* **2019**, *37*, 3–19. [CrossRef]
10. International Council of Nurses International Council of Nurses Calls for Increased Nursing Leadership to Combat Effects of Climate Change on Health. Available online: https://www.icn.ch/system/files/2021-10/ICN_Code-of-Ethics_EN_Web_0.pdf (accessed on 21 April 2019).
11. Nhamo, L.; Ndlela, B. Nexus Planning as a Pathway towards Sustainable Environmental and Human Health Post COVID-19. *Environ. Res.* **2021**, *192*, 110376. [CrossRef]
12. Perez, H.L.R. Sostenibilidad ambiental de la práctica clínica, una nueva visión para enfermería. *Acc Cietna* **2020**, *7*, 116–125. [CrossRef]
13. Osingada, C.P.; Porta, C.M. Nursing and Sustainable Development Goals (SDGs) in a COVID-19 World: The State of the Science and a Call for Nursing to Lead. *Public Health Nurs.* **2020**, *37*, 799–805. [CrossRef] [PubMed]
14. Kitt-Lewis, E.; Adam, M.; Buckland, P.; Clark, D.; Hockenberry, K.; Jankura, D.; Knott, J. Creating a Generation of Sustainable Nurses: Sustainability Efforts in Nursing Education. *Nurs. Clin. N. Am.* **2020**, *55*, 1–10. [CrossRef] [PubMed]
15. Lilienfeld, E.; Nicholas, P.K.; Breakey, S.; Corless, I.B. Addressing Climate Change through a Nursing Lens within the Framework of the United Nations Sustainable Development Goals. *Nurs. Outlook* **2018**, *66*, 482–494. [CrossRef] [PubMed]
16. United Nations Open Working Group Proposal for Sustainable Development Goals. Available online: https://sustainabledevelopment.un.org/focussdgs.html (accessed on 12 April 2021).
17. Capolongo, S.; Bottero, M.C.; Lettieri, E.; Buffoli, M.; Bellagarda, A.; Birocchi, M.; Cavagliato, E.; Dervishaj, A.; di Noia, M.; Gherardi, G.; et al. Healthcare Sustainability Challenge. In *Improving Sustainability During Hospital Design and Operation: A*

Multidisciplinary Evaluation Tool; Capolongo, S., Bottero, M.C., Buffoli, M., Lettieri, E., Eds.; Springer International Publishing: Cham, Switzerland, 2015; pp. 1–9. ISBN 978-3-319-14036-0.
18. Sarkodie, S.A.; Owusu, P.A. Impact of COVID-19 Pandemic on Waste Management. *Environ. Dev. Sustain.* **2021**, *23*, 7951–7960. [CrossRef]
19. Baker, N.; Bromley-Dulfano, R.; Chan, J.; Gupta, A.; Herman, L.; Jain, N.; Taylor, A.L.; Lu, J.; Pannu, J.; Patel, L.; et al. COVID-19 Solutions Are Climate Solutions: Lessons from Reusable Gowns. *Front. Public Health* **2020**, *8*, 590275. [CrossRef]
20. Gök, N.D.; Firat Kiliç, H. Environmental Awareness and Sensitivity of Nursing Students. *Nurse Educ. Today* **2021**, *101*, 104882. [CrossRef]
21. Febles, M. *Sobre la Necesidad de la Formación de una Conciencia Ambiental*; Facultad de Psicología, Universidad de La Habana: Havana, Cuba, 2004.
22. International Council of Nurses. *The Icn Code of Ethics for Nurses*; International Council of Nurses: Geneva, Switzerland, 2021; p. 32.
23. Goodman, B. Developing the Concept of Sustainability in Nursing. *Nurs. Philos.* **2016**, *17*, 298–306. [CrossRef]
24. Leonard, A.; Power, N.; Mayet, S.; Coetzee, M.; North, N. Engaging Nurses in Research Awareness Using a New Style of Hospital Journal Club—A Descriptive Evaluation. *Nurse Educ. Today* **2022**, *108*, 105123. [CrossRef]
25. Workman, M.; Darch, G.; Dooley, K.; Lomax, G.; Maltby, J.; Pollitt, H. Climate Policy Decision Making in Contexts of Deep Uncertainty-from Optimisation to Robustness. *Environ. Sci. Policy* **2021**, *120*, 127–137. [CrossRef]
26. Schwerdtle, P.N.; Maxwell, J.; Horton, G.; Bonnamy, J. 12 Tips for Teaching Environmental Sustainability to Health Professionals. *Med. Teach.* **2020**, *42*, 150–155. [CrossRef] [PubMed]
27. Rosa, W.E.; Catton, H.; Davidson, P.M.; Hannaway, C.J.; Iro, E.; Klopper, H.C.; Madigan, E.A.; McConville, F.E.; Stilwell, B.; Kurth, A.E. Nurses and Midwives as Global Partners to Achieve the Sustainable Development Goals in the Anthropocene. *J. Nurs. Scholarsh.* **2021**, *53*, 552–560. [CrossRef] [PubMed]
28. Pollitt, P.; Sattler, B.; Butterfield, P.; Anderko, L.; Brody, C.; Mood, L.; Huffling, K.; Schenk, E.; Cook, K. Environmental Nursing: Leaders Reflect on the 50th Anniversary of Earth Day. *Public Health Nurs.* **2020**, *37*, 614–625. [CrossRef] [PubMed]
29. Orts-Cortés, M.I.; Moreno-Casbas, T.; Squires, A.; Fuentelsaz-Gallego, C.; Maciá-Soler, L.; González-María, E. Content Validity of the Spanish Version of the Practice Environment Scale of the Nursing Work Index. *Appl. Nurs. Res.* **2013**, *26*, e5–e9. [CrossRef] [PubMed]
30. Schenk, E.C.; Cook, C.; Demorest, S.; Burduli, E. CHANT: Climate, Health, and Nursing Tool: Item Development and Exploratory Factor Analysis. *Annu. Rev. Nurs. Res.* **2019**, *38*, 97–112. [CrossRef]
31. Schenk, E.; Butterfield, P.; Postma, J.; Barbosa-Leiker, C.; Corbett, C. Creating the Nurses' Environmental Awareness Tool (NEAT). *Workplace Health Saf.* **2015**, *63*, 381–391. [CrossRef]
32. Schenk, E.C.; Cook, C.; Demorest, S.; Burduli, E. Climate, Health, and Nursing Tool (CHANT): Initial Survey Results. *Public Health Nurs.* **2021**, *38*, 152–159. [CrossRef]
33. Fuentelsaz-Gallego, C.; Moreno-Casbas, M.T.; González-María, E. Validation of the Spanish Version of the Questionnaire Practice Environment Scale of the Nursing Work Index. *Int. J. Nurs. Stud.* **2013**, *50*, 274–280. [CrossRef]
34. García, O.; Lin, A. Extending Understandings of Bilingual and Multilingual Education. In *Bilingual and Multilingual Education. Encyclopedia of Language and Education*, 3rd ed.; García, O., Lin, A.M.Y., May, S., Eds.; Springer International Publishing: Cham, Switzerland; New York, NY, USA, 2017; pp. 1–20. ISBN 978-3-319-02257-4.
35. Wolcott, M.; Lobczowski, N. Using Cognitive Interviews and Think-Aloud Protocols to Understand Thought Processes. *Curr. Pharm. Teach. Learn.* **2020**, *13*, 181–188. [CrossRef]
36. Bolarinwa, O. Principles and Methods of Validity and Reliability Testing of Questionnaires Used in Social and Health Science Researches. *Niger. Postgrad. Med. J.* **2016**, *22*, 195–201. [CrossRef]
37. Schenk, E.; Corbett, C.; Barbosa-Leiker, C.; Postma, J.; Butterfield, P. Psychometric Properties of the Nurses' Environmental Awareness Tool. *J. Nurs. Meas.* **2016**, *24*, 55E–71E. [CrossRef]
38. Tucker, L.R.; Lewis, C. A Reliability Coefficient for Maximum Likelihood Factor Analysis. *Psychometrika* **1973**, *38*, 1–10. [CrossRef]
39. DeVellis, R.F.; Thorpe, C.T. *Scale Development: Theory and Applications*; Sage Publications: Newbury Park, CA, USA, 2021; ISBN 1-5443-7935-8.
40. Pérez, M.I.; Hervada Vidal, X.; Naveira-Barbeito, G.; Silva, L.C.; Fariñas, H.; Vázquez, E.; Bacallao, J.; Mujica, O. El Programa Epidat: Usos y Perspectivas. *Rev. Panam. Salud Publica-Pan Am. J. Public Health Rev. Panam Salud Publica* **2010**, *27*, 80–82. [CrossRef] [PubMed]
41. Lauffer, A.; Solé, L.; Bernstein, S.; Lopes, M.H.; Francisconi, C.F. Cómo Minimizar Errores al Realizar La Adaptación Transcultural y la Validación de los Cuestionarios Sobre Calidad de Vida: Aspectos Prácticos. *Rev. Gastroenterol. México* **2013**, *78*, 159–176. [CrossRef]
42. Sousa, V.; Rojjanasrirat, W. Translation, Adaptation and Validation of Instruments or Scales for Use in Cross-Cultural Health Care Research: A Clear and User-Friendly Guideline. *J. Eval. Clin. Pract.* **2011**, *17*, 268–274. [CrossRef]
43. Rowen, D.; Carlton, J.; Elliott, J. PROM Validation Using Paper-Based or Online Surveys: Data Collection Methods Affect the Sociodemographic and Health Profile of the Sample. *Value Health* **2019**, *22*, 845–850. [CrossRef]
44. Çabuk, B.; Karacaglu, C. Investigation of University Students' Environmental Sensitivity. *Ank. Univ. J. Fac. Educ. Sci.* **2003**, *36*, 189–198.
45. Fox, J. The R Commander: A Basic-Statistics Graphical User Interface to R. *J. Stat. Soft.* **2005**, *14*, 1–42. [CrossRef]

46. María Isabel, O.-C.; Moreno-Casbas, T.; Squires, A.; Fuentelsaz-Gallego, C.; Maciá-Soler, L.; González-María, E. Validation of a Spanish Version of the Practice Environment Scale of the Nursing Work Index in the Colombian Context. *Hisp. Health Care Int.* **2014**, *12*, 34–42.
47. López-Aguado, M.; Gutiérrez-Provecho, L. Cómo realizar e interpretar un análisis factorial exploratorio utilizando SPSS. *REIRE* **2019**, *12*, 1–14. [CrossRef]
48. Shakil, M.H.; Munim, Z.H.; Tasnia, M.; Sarowar, S. COVID-19 and the Environment: A Critical Review and Research Agenda. *Sci. Total Environ.* **2020**, *745*, 141022. [CrossRef] [PubMed]
49. Rosa, W.E.; Fitzgerald, M.; Davis, S.; Farley, J.E.; Khanyola, J.; Kwong, J.; Moreland, P.J.; Rogers, M.; Sibanda, B.; Turale, S. Leveraging Nurse Practitioner Capacities to Achieve Global Health for All: COVID-19 and Beyond. *Int. Nurs. Rev.* **2020**, *67*, 554–559. [CrossRef] [PubMed]
50. United Nations Educational, Scientific and Cultural Organization (UNESCO). Anthropocene: The Vital Challenges of a Scientific Debate. Available online: https://en.unesco.org/courier/2018-2/anthropocene-vital-challenges-scientific-debate (accessed on 20 October 2019).
51. Cruz, J.P.; Alshammari, F.; Felicilda-Reynaldo, R. Predictors of Saudi Nursing Students' Attitudes towards Environment and Sustainability in Health Care. *Int. Nurs. Rev.* **2018**, *65*, 408–416. [CrossRef] [PubMed]
52. González, A.G.; Sanz-Calcedo, J.; Salgado, D. A Quantitative Analysis of Final Energy Consumption in Hospitals in Spain. *Sustain. Cities Soc.* **2017**, *36*, 169–175. [CrossRef]
53. Fitriani, I.; Sangadji, S.; Kristiawan, S. Energy Efficiency Evaluation of Hospital Building Office. *J. Phys. Conf. Ser.* **2017**, *795*, 012067. [CrossRef]
54. Haines, A.; Dora, C. How the Low Carbon Economy Can Improve Health. *BMJ* **2012**, *344*, e1018. [CrossRef]

MDPI
St. Alban-Anlage 66
4052 Basel
Switzerland
www.mdpi.com

MDPI Books Editorial Office
E-mail: books@mdpi.com
www.mdpi.com/books

www.ingramcontent.com/pod-product-compliance
Lightning Source LLC
Chambersburg PA
CBHW061501220926
51850CB00004B/146
9783036595061